I0796564

THE HENDRICKSON DICTIONARY *of*

New Testament Words & Concepts

THE HENDRICKSON DICTIONARY *of*

New Testament Words & Concepts

Edited by JONATHAN G. KLINE

Based on the work of STEPHEN D. RENN

HENDRICKSON

The Hendrickson Dictionary of New Testament Words & Concepts

Hendrickson Publishers
3 Centennial Drive
Peabody, Massachusetts 01960
www.hendricksonpublishers.com

ISBN 979-8-4005-0249-1

Library of Congress Control Number: 2025932191

Printed in the United States of America

First Printing — July 2025

Contents

Preface

The material in this book derives from the *Expository Dictionary of Bible Words: Word Studies for Key English Bible Words Based on the Hebrew and Greek Texts*, which was prepared by Stephen D. Renn for Hendrickson Publishers and published in 2005.[1] Since its appearance two decades ago, the *Expository Dictionary* has remained a valuable reference tool for pastors, students, and lay teachers of Scripture who wish to learn about the meaning and usage of many of the Hebrew (and Aramaic) and Greek terms that underlie the English words found in translations of the Bible, as well as to understand how themes that run through both the Old and New Testaments find their fulfillment in the person and work of Jesus Christ.[2] The present book supplements and builds on Renn's work in the *Expository Dictionary* by reproducing the New Testament material from that volume and presenting it in a new framework. Whereas the *Expository Dictionary* is structured alphabetically by English key word (thus allowing readers to look up a particular English word in order to learn about the Hebrew and Greek words that can be translated by it and the relationships between these Hebrew and Greek words), in the present volume the articles on the Greek words are arranged according to thematic and contextual categories (and grouped, within these categories, under updated English headings).[3] These categories, which were developed by Jonathan G. Kline, senior editor at Hendrickson Publishers, bring together Greek terms that have similar meanings, that occur in related contexts in Scripture, or that belong to the same realm of life, society, or the like.[4] The categories should not be viewed as semantic domains in a scientific sense, as rigidly separated from one another, or as precise reflections of how the biblical authors might have mentally organized their world (something we cannot fully know); instead, they should be understood as pedagogically oriented "conceptual-contextual clusters" whose purpose is to provide a fresh entry point for students and teachers of Scripture to explore connections within the biblical text and to better understand the multiple, sometimes overlapping contexts to which the words and concepts of Scripture belong.[5] In this way, the present book follows the *Expository Dictionary*'s dictum that, when it comes to studying the original words of Scripture, "the precise meaning of any particular term is never determined just by its lexical definition or its etymology (i.e., by tracing the evolution of meaning throughout the linguistic history of a particular word). Rather, it is literary usage and context that determine the precise sense of any given term—a significant principle that underlies the compilation of this work" (p. vii). Indeed, the *Hendrickson Dictionary of New Testament Words & Concepts* follows this principle by providing readers with wide additional windows (thematic, conceptual, and contextual) through which they can look broadly and deeply into the riches of the Greek words of the New Testament.[6]

---

1. Stephen D. Renn, ed., *Expository Dictionary of Bible Words: Word Studies for Key English Bible Words Based on the Hebrew and Greek Texts* (Hendrickson, 2005).

2. In addition to its articles on Hebrew, Aramaic, and Greek words, the *Expository Dictionary* contains "Additional Notes" that trace motifs across the Testaments, emphasize the unity of the Testaments, and point to the culmination of the biblical story in the redemptive work of Jesus Christ.

3. Generally speaking, the articles themselves have been left as intact as possible (though they have been lightly edited to adapt them to their present context). The credit for the content of the articles, and for their fundamental organization into groups, belongs to Stephen Renn.

4. Within each category, the Greek articles continue to be listed under headings that reflect how the Greek words can be translated, as in the *Expository Dictionary*. Although in some cases these headings are identical to ones from the *Expository Dictionary*, in many cases they have been expanded or modified in order to more closely reflect the contextual meanings of the Greek words they comprise.

5. Because many Greek words can be translated in more than one way, there is some repetition across entries in this book, including sometimes within a given category. This repetition is intentional and is intended to help the reader better understand the different ways a given word is used.

6. For this reason, the present book is not at all a replacement for the *Expository Dictionary*, which provides readers with easy access to a wealth of information about the original Hebrew and Greek words of Scripture. Rather, the present book supplements the *Expository Dictionary* by providing readers with another entry point for delving into the riches specifically of the New Testament text.

In order to further facilitate the reader's ability to study the similarities and differences among related Greek words and concepts, this book contains a pair of indexes and a robust system of internal cross-references, of which there are two types: (1) A cross-reference that follows the discussion of a particular Greek word's meaning and usage points the reader to each English heading in this book under which *the same Greek word* appears. (2) A cross-reference that follows the header "SEE ALSO" points to *other Greek words* found in this book that are related in meaning to the present Greek word, that can be compared or contrasted with it, or that can be translated similarly in English. Together, the indexes and cross-references provide a number of roadmaps by which one can journey through the book's material, with the goal of continually discovering new connections and gaining fresh insights.

Hendrickson Publishers is pleased to present Stephen Renn's work afresh in this new format in the hopes that this *Dictionary of New Testament Words & Concepts*, alongside the *Expository Dictionary of Bible Words*, will enrich the study and ministry of a new generation of pastors, teachers, and students of the Bible.

Key to Greek Transliteration

α	***a***	*alpha*
β	***b***	*bēta*
γ	***g***	*gamma*
γ	***n***	*gamma* nasal (before γ, κ, ξ, χ)
δ	***d***	*delta*
ε	***e***	*epsilon*
ζ	***z***	*zēta*
η	***ē***	*ēta*
θ	***th***	*thēta*
ι	***i***	*iōta*
κ	***k***	*kappa*
λ	***l***	*lambda*
μ	***m***	*mu*
ν	***n***	*nu*
ξ	***x***	*xi*
ο	***o***	*omicron*
π	***p***	*pi*
ρ	***r***	*rho*
ῥ	***rh***	initial *rho*
σ, ς	***s***	*sigma*
τ	***t***	*tau*
υ	***y***	*upsilon* (not in diphthong)
υ	***u***	*upsilon* (in diphthongs: *au*, *eu*, *ēu*, *ou*, *ui*)
φ	***ph***	*phi*
χ	***ch***	*chi*
ψ	***ps***	*psi*
ω	***ō***	*ōmega*
῾	***h***	rough breathing (precedes initial vowel or diphthong)

Sample Entry

SIGHT

eidos εἶδος 1491

eidos is a noun expressing the sense of "appearance," "form" in most of its five occurrences. Only in 2 Cor 5:7 does ***eidos*** mean "sight." Here Paul declares that believers "walk by faith, not by sight," affirming that the exercise of one's physical and rational faculties of perception is not adequate for maintaining a vital relationship with God.

▸ **81.** Forms, Groups, Patterns, Order > FORM, SHAPE

SEE ALSO

▸ **21.** Die, Perish, Kill, Destroy > SPECTACLE
theōria

▸ **64.** Reveal, Explain, Hiddenness, Secrecy > VISION
horama, horasis, optasia

Each Greek word is presented in transliteration and Greek script, followed by the word's Strong's number.

A cross-reference following the discussion of a Greek word's meaning and usage points to another English heading (preceded by the name of the thematic category to which it belongs) under which *this same Greek word* appears.

A cross-reference following "SEE ALSO" points to *other Greek words* (preceded by the name of the English heading under which they fall and that heading's thematic category) that are related in meaning to the present Greek word, that can be compared or contrasted with it, or that can be translated similarly in English.

1. Celestial Realm, Earthly Realm

BRIGHTNESS, BRILLIANCE

lamprotēs λαμπρότης 2987

lamprotēs is a rare noun found only in Acts 26:13 denoting the "brightness" or "brilliance" of the sun.

SEE ALSO

▸ **8.** Light, Darkness, Visible, Invisible, Color > BRIGHT *lampros*

EARTH, LAND, GROUND, EARTHLY

gē γῆ 1093

gē appears in the NT nearly two hundred times, with the principal meanings "earth," "land," "ground."

gē refers to "land" in the sense of "country" in a number of places, indicating the land of Israel or Judah in Matt 2:6, 20ff.; John 3:22. See also Matt 27:45; 15:33; Luke 4:25; Acts 7:11ff.; 13:19; Heb 11:9. References to other "lands," including the tribal regions of Zebulun and Naphtali near Galilee, are noted in Matt 4:15. See also Matt 9:26; 10:15; 11:24; Heb 8:9; Jude 5 The meaning "land" in contrast to "sea" is indicated in Mark 4:1; 6:47, 53; Luke 5:24; John 6:21.

The "earth" as the sphere of God's punishment is indicated in Luke 21:23ff.; Rom 9:28; Rev 6:10; 7:1ff.; 8:7; 9:1ff.; 14:18ff.; 16:1ff.; and as the sphere of his authority in Rom 9:17; 1 Cor 10:26; Rev 5:13; 11:4.

The "earth" is also designated as the sphere of God's punishment of Satan (Rev 12:4ff.); and also the domain of the "unholy trinity" in Rev 13:3ff.

The "earth" as the place of Jesus' ministry is noted in John 12:32; 17:4.

gē also refers to the earth in the general sense of "the world" as a whole in Matt 5:5; 10:34; Luke 11:31; Acts 1:8.

God is designated as Lord of the earth in Matt 11:25; Luke 10:21; Acts 17:24; and as the creator of the earth in Acts 4:24; 14:15; Col 1:18; Heb 1:10; 2 Pet 3:5; Rev 14:7.

"Earth" is contrasted to "heaven" in Matt 5:18; 6:10; 16:19; 18:18; 24:35; 28:18; Mark 13:27ff.; Luke 2:14; 16:17; Eph 3:15; Jas 5:12.

References to the "new heavens and the new earth" are found in 2 Pet 3:13; Rev 21:1.

The term also denotes "ground" with reference to the surface of the earth in Matt 10:29; 13:5ff.; 25:25; Luke 24:5; John 8:6ff.; Acts 9:4. It refers to "soil" in Mark 4:8, 20ff.; Luke 8:8, 15; Jas 5:18. In particular, 1 Cor 15:47 refers to Adam as "the first man from the earth."

Eph 4:9 indicates the "lower parts of the earth," with probable reference to the realm of the dead.

epigeios ἐπίγειος 1919

epigeios is an adjectival form found in six places, meaning "earthly."

The meaning "earthly" in the sense of "belonging to the earth" indicates that which is wicked or sinful in Jas 3:15; Phil 3:19. "Earthly" matters in a neutral sense are noted in John 3:12. "Earthly, or terrestrial bodies," referring possibly to geological features such as mountains, oceans, and valleys, are noted in 1 Cor 15:40. The human body is described symbolically in 2 Cor 5:1 as an "earthly house."

oikoumenē οἰκουμένη 3625

oikoumenē refers to the "world" in the sense of the "(universally) inhabited earth" throughout the fifteen occurrences of the term.

The "world" as the arena of gospel preaching is noted in Matt 24:14; Rom 10:18.

General references to the "world" as the "universally inhabited earth" are found in Luke 2:1; 4:5; Acts 11:28; 17:6; 19:27; 24:5; Heb 1:6; Rev 3:10; 12:9; 16:14.

The "world" as the sphere of divine judgment is indicated in Luke 21:26; Acts 17:31.

▸ **1.** Celestial Realm, Earthly Realm > WORLD, WORLDLY

GULF

chasma χάσμα 5490

chasma is a rare noun found only in Luke 16:26, denoting the great "gulf" that was fixed between heaven and hell in the story Jesus told of Lazarus and the rich man.

HADES, HELL, GRAVE

hadēs ᾅδης 86

hadēs functions both as a name and as a noun derived from the significance of that name. Hades refers firstly to the god of the underworld in classical Greek mythology. This usage does not appear in the NT canon, but the noun derived from that name does. Hades, in the biblical context, also refers to the realm of the dead (i.e., "hell" or the "grave"). ***hadēs*** occurs ten times in the NT.

In some of these contexts, "hell" or "grave" denotes divine judgment. The terrible fate of Capernaum is one such example — this village is cast down to hell as a consequence of rejecting the Messiah (Matt 11:23; Luke 10:15). Similar punishment is handed out to the rich man in Luke 16:23. It is also the universal fate of the wicked in Rev 20:13f. Other texts, such as Matt 16:18, refer literally to the "gates of hell" being impotent before the infinitely greater power of Christ and his church, against which this power of death will never prevail. In a similar vein, Rev 1:18 refers to Christ's utter supremacy over the kingdom of death (see also Rev 6:8).

Finally, Acts 2:27, 31 refer to God's sovereign power over hell (or Hades) in that the Messiah, of whom David spoke, will never be abandoned by God to the grave, and his body will not suffer corruption. Such a reference is, of course, a prophetic reflection on the resurrection of Christ. Note: In 1 Cor 15:5, the best reading is "death" (***thanatos***) rather than "grave" (***hadēs***).

HEAVEN, SKY, HEAVENLY

ouranos οὐρανός 3772

ouranos occurs around three hundred times with the primary meaning "heaven(s)" in both a natural and spiritual sense. The natural connotation of the term conveys the idea of the expanse of the sky and everything in it (i.e., all celestial bodies), the universe. The spiritual sense of ***ouranos***, on the other hand, refers to the dwelling place of God and his heavenly court beyond the created order of things, in addition to a number of related meanings.

In reference to the created phenomenon of "the heavens" or "sky," ***ouranos*** is found in a number of contexts. General references to "sky" as the created order are found in Mark 4:32; Luke 12:56; Acts 4:24; Col 1:16; Heb 1:10; 11:12; Jas 5:18; 2 Pet 3:5; Rev 10:6. The dissolution of the heavens as evidence of the impending apocalyptic end of the universe is indicated in Jesus' discourse on the signs of the end of the age in Matt 24:29; Mark 13:25. See also 2 Pet 3:10, 12, and the spectacular imagery of Rev 6:13, 14; 8:10; 9:1; 20:11 in this regard. In a related context, the passing away of heaven and earth is also cited in Matt 24:35; Mark 13:31. See also Luke 16:17; 21:23. The establishment of a "new heavens and new earth" is mentioned in 2 Pet 3:13; Rev 21:1. Luke 4:25 refers to drought as the closing of the heavens. Mark 13:27 refers to the uttermost ends of the heavens and the earth. The term "heaven" is used as a synonym for "world" in Acts 2:5; 4:12; Col 1:23; Rev 5:13. The concept of heaven also denotes the rule or kingdom of God among humankind, as in the phrase "kingdom of heaven." General references to this phenomenon are found in Matt 5:19; 11:11; 19:14; 21:25; and the phrase is also found in the context of Jesus' parables (see Matt 8:11; 13:24, 31ff.; 18:23). Matt 13:11 refers to the mysteries of the kingdom of heaven. References to the authority of the kingdom of heaven are found in Matt 16:18; 18:18; and Matt 28:18 affirms that all power in heaven and earth is given to Jesus by his Father.

A number of contexts also speak about how to enter the kingdom of heaven and enjoy its profound benefits. There are a number of prerequisites for gaining entry into this kingdom — repentance (Matt 3:2; 4:17; 10:7); righteousness (Matt 5:20; 7:21); and obedience linked to faith (Matt 19:23). Possession of the kingdom is guaranteed to those who are "poor in spirit" and "persecuted because of righteousness" (Matt 5:3, 10). Rewards in the kingdom of heaven are spoken of in Matt 5:12; Luke 6:23; as are "treasures in heaven" in Matt 6:20; 19:21; Mark 10:21; Luke 12:33; 18:22.

"Heaven" is also alluded to as the domain of God, or his dwelling place. For example, in Luke 20:4, the question is asked whether John's baptism is from heaven, or from human beings. At the baptism of Jesus by John the Baptist, God's voice "from heaven" is heard confirming the identity and authority of Jesus as his Son (Matt 3:17; Mark 1:11; Luke 3:22). On the same occasion, the Spirit of God descends from heaven in the form of a dove (Matt 3:16; Mark 1:10; John 1:32). Other references to the divine voice from heaven are found in John 12:28; Acts 2:2; 2 Pet 1:18; Acts 11:9; Heb 12:25; Rev 14:2, 13; 18:4; 21:3. Jesus looks to his Father in heaven in an attitude of prayer in Matt 14:11; Mark 6:41; Luke 9:16; John 17:1. Phenomena related to heaven include "manna" or "bread from heaven" (Luke 15:7); "light from heaven" (Acts 9:3; 22:6); divine wrath from heaven (Rom 1:18); wonders in heaven (Acts 2:19; Rev 3:12; 4:1, 2; 10:1ff.; 12:1ff.; 13:6; 19:1, 11); an "open heaven" (John 1:51; Acts 10:11); signs from heaven (Luke 21:11); and "sin against heaven" (Luke 15:18ff.). Paul speaks of his visionary experience of the "third heaven" in 2 Cor 12:2, and of angels from heaven in Gal 1:8 (see also Rev 18:1; 20:1).

John 3:31; 6:38, 42 describe Christ's coming into the world as his coming from heaven. With reference to the conclusion of Jesus' earthly ministry, mention is made of him ascending, or being carried into, heaven (Luke 24:51; John 3:13; Eph 4:10; Heb 4:14). The return of Christ at the end of the age is frequently anticipated, when he will descend from heaven (1 Thess 1:10; 4:16; 2 Thess 1:7). Jesus' return is also depicted as the appearing of the Son of Man "in heaven" (Matt 24:30; 26:64; Mark 14:62).

God is described as "Lord of heaven" in Matt 11:25; Luke 10:21; Acts 17:24. This is also implied through reference to the "God of heaven" in Rev 11:3; 16:11, 17. God is referred to as "Father in heaven" in Matt 5:16, 45; 10:32; 16:17; 6:9; Mark 11:25; Luke 11:2.

ouranos also refers to the "heavenly throne," the heart of God's authority and majesty (Mark 16:19). Heb 9:23, 24 indicate that the real temple in heaven is represented by the earthly temple and its furniture, such as the ark of the covenant. See also Acts 7:49, where ***ouranos*** refers to heaven as the throne of God. In related contexts, heaven is the origin of the judgment of divine fire (Luke 9:54; 17:29); and the place where the names of God's people are written down (Luke 10:20; Heb 12:23). Finally, heaven is also the place from which Satan fell like lightning in Luke 10:18.

▸ **11.** Meteorology, Water > AIR

ouranios οὐράνιος 3770

This adjectival term occurs only six times and means "heavenly" or "coming from heaven."

ouranios refers to the "heavenly Father" in Matt 6:14, 26, 32; 15:13; the "heavenly host" in Luke 2:13; and a "heavenly vision" in Acts 26:19, where Paul makes his defense before Agrippa.

epouranios ἐπουράνιος 2032

epouranios is a synonym for ***ouranios*** (above) meaning "heavenly" in an adjectival sense about twenty times.

This term is found, for example, in Matt 18:35 with reference to the "heavenly Father." "Heavenly things" that concern ultimate spiritual realities are indicated in John 3:12; Phil 2:10. Heb 8:5 refers to the tabernacle as the shadow of true heavenly realities; and Heb 9:23 mentions the heavenly realities to which the earthly temple pointed. Stars and planets are described as heavenly or celestial bodies in 1 Cor 15:40. "Heavenly (i.e., post-resurrection) bodies" of human beings are contrasted with earthly human existence in 1 Cor 15:48, 49.

Eph 1:3, 20 refer to the "heavenly" realm of the supraterrestrial sphere in reference to the position granted to Christ; and Eph 2:6 refers to our position as believers with the Lord. Godly heavenly powers are mentioned in Eph 3:10 in contrast to the dark, evil powers of Eph 6:12. In a similar context, the heavenly kingdom of God is mentioned in 2 Tim 4:18; Heb 11:16; as is the heavenly Jerusalem in Heb 12:23. See also Heb 3:1; 6:4, which describe one's heavenly calling and gift, respectively.

ouranothen οὐρανόθεν 3771

This adverb is rare, found only twice in Acts 14:17; 26:13 and meaning "from heaven." The former reference indicates rain from heaven; the latter, light from heaven.

HELL

geenna γέεννα 1067

geenna is the Greek equivalent for the Hebrew *gê(ben)-hinnōm*, the Valley of Hinnom, which became the site of a rubbish dump for the city of Jerusalem, where all refuse was burned. The original Valley of Hinnom had been infamous as a place where Israelite kings sacrificed their children to the god Molech.

In the NT, ***geenna*** is translated "hell," a place reserved for the eternal fiery destruction of the wicked. Jesus refers to it as such in Matt 5:22, 29, 30; 10:28; 18:9; 23:15, 33; Mark 9:43ff.; Luke 12:5. See also Jas 3:6.

MOON

selēnē σελήνη 4582

selēnē occurs nine times and refers to the "moon" predominantly in the context of the cataclysmic changes to the cosmos that will take place at the consummation of history when Christ shall return in glory. Six of these texts refer to the darkening of the moon along with the destruction of the sun as one of the signs of cosmic dissolution at the end of the age (Matt 24:29; Mark 13:24; Luke 21:25; Acts 2:20; Rev 6:12; 8:12). A general reference to the light of the moon is found in 1 Cor 15:41. Rev 12:1 refers to the moon in an apocalyptic vision of the Christ child and his mother, who is described as having the moon under her feet. Rev 21:23 describes the illumination of the heavenly city as a supernatural one, not needing the light of the moon or the sun.

PARADISE

paradeisos παράδεισος 3857

The term ***paradeisos*** occurs only three times, all with reference to the heavenly realm, the dwelling place of God. Luke 23:43 contains Jesus' promise to the dying thief on the cross, that he would join him that very day in "paradise." 2 Cor 12:4 refers to Paul's supernatural transporting to "paradise" (synonymous with the "third heaven" in this context), where he heard words he could not describe or repeat. Rev 2:7 refers to heaven as the "paradise of God."

PIT, ABYSS, DEEP

abyssos ἄβυσσος 12

abyssos is a synonym for ***phrear*** (below), translated as "abyss," "bottomless pit," or "deep," and referring in each of the nine occurrences to the realm of the dead, the place of departed spirits (Luke 8:31; Rom 10:7; Rev 9:1ff.; 11:7; 17:8; 20:1, 3).

▸ **21.** Die, Perish, Kill, Destroy > GRAVE, TOMB

SEE ALSO

▸ **9.** Land, Geography, Topography > PIT, WELL
bothynos, phrear

SET

dynō δύνω 1416

dynō is a rare verb found only twice, referring to the "setting" sun in Mark 1:32; Luke 4:40.

SEE ALSO

▸ **51.** Knowledge, Wisdom, Remember, Forget > SET ONE'S MIND ON
phroneō

▸ **83.** Set, Put, Place, Prepare, Establish > SET
tithēmi, paratithēmi, peritithēmi, histēmi, keimai, prokeimai, epibibazō

STAR, MORNING STAR

astēr ἀστήρ 792

astēr is a noun meaning "star" in each of the nearly twenty-five occurrences of the term.

Literal references to stars as heavenly bodies include those in Matt 24:29; Mark 13:25; 1 Cor 15:41. In the book of Revelation, all such references occur in a visionary context (Rev 6:13; 8:10ff.; 9:1; 12:1, 4). One reference to a star is especially significant. In Matt 2:2ff., the star from the east is sighted over Bethlehem "announcing" the birth of the Christ child.

In metaphorical contexts, Jude 24 refers to false prophets, among other things, as "wandering stars." The "seven stars" held in the hand of the heavenly Christ symbolize the angels of the seven churches of Asia (Rev 1:16, 20; 2:1; 3:1). Rev 2:28; 22:16 refer to Christ as "the morning star."

astron ἄστρον 798

astron is a variant form of ***astēr*** (above) found in four places and meaning "star."

Luke 21:25; Acts 27:20; Heb 11:12 refer to stars as heavenly bodies. Acts 7:43 mentions a "star god" in reference to a pagan idol.

phōsphoros φωσφόρος 5459

phōsphoros is a rare noun found only in 2 Pet 1:19 with reference to "the morning star," symbolizing the person of Christ.

SUN

hēlios ἥλιος 2246

hēlios is a noun occurring thirty times, meaning "sun" throughout most of this usage. Literal references to the sun include those in Matt 5:45; Mark 1:32; Luke 4:40; Acts 13:11; 1 Cor 15:41; Eph 4:26; Rev 7:16; 21:23.

Repeating the OT apocalyptic theme of cosmic disintegration, the darkening of the sun is noted in Matt 24:29; Mark 13:24; Luke 23:45 (see also Luke 21:25); Acts 2:20; Rev 6:12.

hēlios is also utilized in metaphorical contexts. The righteous are said to "shine like the sun" (Matt 13:43); as is the face of Christ on the occasion of his transfiguration (Matt 17:2), and in heaven (Rev 1:16; 10:1). The woman in Rev 12:1, most likely at one level a symbolic depiction of Mary the mother of Christ, is described in John's vision as being "clothed with the sun."

WORLD, WORLDLY

kosmos κόσμος 2889

kosmos denotes "world" throughout the nearly two hundred occurrences of the term. There are a variety of connotations associated with this term.

The meaning "world," denoting the realm of humankind inhabited by various kingdoms and nations, is indicated in Matt 4:8; 13:38; 26:13; Mark 14:19; 16:15; Luke 12:30; Rom 1:8; 5:12; 1 Tim 1:15. In John 18:36, Christ explicitly declares, however, that his kingdom is not of this "world." The "world" is said to be illuminated by the true light of the gospel of Christ (Matt 5:14; John 1:9; 8:12; 9:5; 12:46).

In related contexts, ***kosmos*** also denotes the "world" as the universal community of humankind. This "world" is subject to divine judgment and wrath (Matt 18:7; John 3:19; 12:31; 16:8; Heb 11:7; 1 John 2:2); and is also alienated from God (John 14:27; 15:18ff.; 16:28, 33; 17:6, 11ff.; 1 Cor 1:20ff.; 3:19ff.; 5:10; Phil 2:15; Jas 1:27; 1 John 2:15ff.; 4:4ff.). Such a "world" is therefore identified as unbelieving and subject to divine condemnation (John 1:10, 29; 8:23; 1 Cor 11:32; 2 Pet 1:4; 2:5). John 14:17 affirms that the "world" is incapable of discerning spiritual truth, and it is also declared to be ruled by the devil (John 14:30; 16:11; Eph 2:2). In positive contexts, the "world" is granted saving grace and belief in Christ (John 17:21). It is also designated as the object of God's love (John 3:16ff.) and the salvation of Christ (John 4:42; 6:33; 12:47; 2 Cor 5:19; 1 John 4:14).

kosmos also refers to the "world" in terms of the universe at the point of creation (Matt 13:35; 24:21; Luke 11:50; John 17:5, 24; Acts 17:24; Rom 1:20; Eph 1:14; Heb 4:3; 9:26; 1 Pet 1:20; Rev 13:8, 17). Gal 4:3; Col 2:8, 20 refer to the "world" as identification with the universe in relation to its elemental spirits, an understanding embraced by the pagans. John 12:25 refers to "this world" in the sense of "this life," "this age."

In addition, ***kosmos*** denotes "world" in the figurative sense of the sum total of one's realized ambition for wealth, power, and prestige (Matt 16:26; Mark 8:36; Luke 9:25). The term is also used hyperbolically, referring to the "world" as a great number of people (John 12:19; 18:20).

aiōn αἰών 165

aiōn is a noun occurring about 130 times meaning "age" in the sense of "world" in about one-third of these contexts. It can also mean unending, everlasting duration, as in "forever," "ever more."

The designation "world" in the sense of "age," indicating the temporal duration of the created universe, is found in general contexts (e.g., Matt 12:32; Eph 1:21; 1 Tim 6:17; Heb 1:2; 11:3). 1 Cor 2:7 speaks of God's wisdom evident "before the world began." References to "the end of the age" as the time of judgment are found in Matt 13:39ff.; 24:3; 28:20; 1 Cor 10:11; Heb 9:26. This "age" is designated as evil in 2 Cor 4:4; Eph 6:12. See also John 9:32; Acts 15:18; Eph 3:9. General references to "the sons of this world (i.e., age)," implying hostility to God, are found in Luke 16:8; 20:34. See also Luke 16:8; 20:34; 1 Cor 1:20; 2:6ff.; 3:18; 2 Tim 4:10.

aiōn also refers to the future age (or world), to come, depicting eternal life with God (Mark 10:30; Luke 18:30; 20:35; Eph 2:7; Heb 6:5 [implied]).

▸ **3.** Periods of Time, Duration, Frequency, Speed > ETERNAL

▸ **3.** Periods of Time, Duration, Frequency, Speed > EVER, EVERLASTING, FOREVER

oikoumenē οἰκουμένη 3625

oikoumenē is a noun denoting "world" throughout the fifteen occurrences of the term.

For the most part, ***oikoumenē*** refers to "world" in the sense of the entire inhabited earth. It is depicted as the sphere for the proclamation of the gospel (Matt 24:14; Rom 10:18), and also as the sphere for divine judgment at the end of time (Acts 17:31). Other general references to the "world" in this sense are found in Luke 2:1; Acts 11:28; Heb 1:6; Rev 3:10; 12:9; 16:14. See also Luke 4:5; Acts 19:27.

oikoumenē is also used hyperbolically, designating the vast majority of the land of Palestine as "the world" (Acts 17:6; 24:5).

oikoumenē also denotes the world to come as the eternal age (Heb 2:5).

▸ **1.** Celestial Realm, Earthly Realm > EARTH, LAND, GROUND, EARTHLY

kosmikos κοσμικός 2886

kosmikos is a rare adjective denoting the sense of "worldly" in Titus 2:12 with reference to "worldly desires." In Heb 9:1 it refers to the "earthly" tabernacle.

2. Supernatural Beings/Forces, Spiritual Realm

ALMIGHTY

pantokratōr παντοκράτωρ 3841

The noun ***pantokratōr*** denotes the divine title "Lord (God) Almighty" throughout the ten occurrences of the term (2 Cor 6:18; Rev 1:8; 4:8; 11:17; 15:3; 16:7, 14; 19:6, 15; 21:22).

ANGEL, MESSENGER

angelos ἄγγελος 32

angelos is a common NT term occurring nearly 190 times with the predominant sense of "angel" (i.e., divine messenger).

Angels are mediators of divine revelation in relation to the birth of Christ in Matt 1:20ff.; 2:13ff.; Luke 1:28ff.; 2:9ff.; to the birth of John the Baptist in Luke 1:11ff. They also function this way in John's vision of the heavenly realms (Rev 1:1; 22:6; and in particular as divine messengers to the seven churches in Asia Minor [Rev 1:20; 2:1, 8, 12, 18; 3:1, 5, 7, 14]).

General references to angels include those in Matt 4:6; 18:10; 22:30; Luke 4:10; Rom 8:38; 1 Cor 6:3; Heb 1:4ff.; 13:2. Angels are depicted as instruments of divine judgment and redemption in a number of places (Matt 13:39ff.; 28:2ff.; Mark 13:25; Luke 16:22; John 1:51; Acts 5:19; 12:7ff.; Rev 7:1ff.; 8:2ff.; 9:1ff.; 12:7ff.; 14:6ff.; 15:1ff.; 16:1ff.; 17:1ff.; 20:1). Angelic beings form part of the entourage of Christ at his final appearing (Matt 16:27; Mark 8:38; Luke 9:26).

angelos is also translated "messenger" in certain contexts: Human messengers are indicated in Luke 7:24; Jas 2:25. Prophetic "messengers" who foreshadow the coming of the Messiah are found in Matt 11:10; Mark 1:2; Luke 7:27 (all quotations from Mal 3:1). "Messengers of Satan" are mentioned in 2 Cor 12:7. "Fallen angels" are indicated in Jude 6; Rev 12:7.

ANTICHRIST

antichristos ἀντίχριστος 500

The term ***antichristos*** occurs five times and denotes the archetypal enemy of Christ and his people, the embodiment of satanic opposition to Jesus Christ. The usage denotes not just one person, but rather the spirit of such a one indwelling all those who deny that Jesus is the incarnation of God in human form (1 John 2:18ff.; 4:3; 2 John 7).

APPARITION, GHOST

phantasma φάντασμα 5326

phantasma is a rare noun, found only twice, denoting an "apparition" or "ghost" in Matt 14:26; Mark 6:49.

ARCHANGEL

archangelos ἀρχάγγελος 743

archangelos is a rare noun occurring only twice with reference to the archangel in general in 1 Thess 4:16; and to Michael in particular in Jude 9.

CHERUBIM

cheroubim Χερουβίμ 5502

cheroubim is the Greek transcription of the Hebrew term *kerûbîm*, denoting these creatures as the guardians of the heavenly throne. It is found only in Heb 9:5.

CHRIST, MESSIAH

Christos Χριστός 5547

Christos is the dynamically equivalent Greek term for the Hebrew *māshîaḥ*, constituting the name and title of Christ. It is found over 550 times, often in connection with the name Jesus (e.g., Matt 1:1; Mark 1:1; John 17:3; Acts 2:38; Rom 1:1ff.; 1 Cor 9:1; Gal 1:1ff.; Eph 2:6ff.; Phil 2:5; Col 2:6ff.; 1 Tim 2:5; Titus 2:13; Phlm 3ff.; Heb 3:1; 2 Pet 3:18; 1 John 4:2ff.; Rev 1:1ff.; 22:21).

The designation "Christ" is also indicated, for example, in Matt 2:4; 26:68; Mark 9:11; John 4:25; Acts 2:36; Rom 5:6; 2 Cor 1:5; Gal 1:6ff.; Eph 1:10ff.; Phil 1:13ff.; Col 2:2ff.; 1 Tim 2:7; Heb 3:6; 1 Pet 3:16ff.; Rev 11:15; 20:4.

Elsewhere ***Christos*** occurs with the definite article, thus emphasizing the full significance of Christ's person as "the Messiah" (i.e., the Christ; Matt 16:16; Mark 8:29; Luke 9:20). Peter confesses that Jesus is indeed "the Christ"; as does Martha in John 11:27. Other occurrences include Matt 26:63; Luke 3:15; 22:67; John 1:20; 7:41; 20:31; 1 John 2:22; 5:1.

DEMON, DEMON-POSSESSED, DEMONIC

daimōn δαίμων 1142

daimōn is a noun denoting "demons" in all five of its occurrences. Matt 8:31; Mark 5:12 refer to the demons cast out of the Gadarene demoniac by Christ. Luke 8:29 records the impact of the demon on the man he possessed — driving him into the wilderness. Spirits of "demons" are said to perform miracles in Rev 16:14. Babylon is described as a haunt of "demons" in Rev 18:2.

daimonion δαιμόνιον 1140

daimonion is a derivative form of ***daimōn*** (above) with the consistent meaning of "demon" throughout the sixty occurrences of the term.

"Demons" are driven out by Christ in miracles of exorcism in Matt 7:22; 12:24ff.; Mark 1:34; 3:15; 7:26ff.; Luke 4:41; 11:14ff. Christ's disciples also drive them out in Mark

6:13; Luke 9:1; 10:17. See also Mark 9:38. References to people possessed by a "demon" or "demons" are found in Matt 11:18; Luke 4:33ff.; 8:27ff.; 9:42.

Christ is falsely accused of being demon-possessed in Luke 11:15, 18; John 7:20; 8:48ff.; 10:20. Rev 9:20 refers to pagans worshiping demons. 1 Cor 10:20ff. describes the sacrifices pagans offered to demons. 1 Tim 4:1 refers to the teaching of demons. Jas 2:19 notes that "demons" are said to believe in God.

daimonizomai δαιμονίζομαι 1139

daimonizomai is a verb with the consistent meaning "be possessed by a demon (or demons)" (Matt 4:24; 8:16ff.; 9:32; 12:22; 15:22; Mark 1:32; 5:15ff.; Luke 8:36; John 10:21).

▸ **2.** Supernatural Beings/Forces, Spiritual Realm > POSSESS, POSSESSION

daimoniōdēs δαιμονιώδης 1141

daimoniōdēs is a rare adjectival form, found only in Jas 3:13 and referring to worldly wisdom being "of the devil."

DEVIL

diabolos διάβολος 1228

diabolos is the sole term denoting "the devil" in the NT as the prince of demonic beings. This meaning is evident for most of the nearly forty occurrences of the term.

A number of references describe the forty-day temptation of Christ at the outset of his public ministry in the hands of the devil (Matt 4:5ff.; Luke 4:2ff.).

The devil is described as the archenemy of the people of God in Matt 13:39; Luke 8:12; Eph 4:27; 6:11; 2 Tim 2:26; Jas 4:7; 1 Pet 5:8; Rev 2:10; 12:9, 12. He is also described as "the father" of unbelievers in John 8:44; Acts 13:10. See also John 13:2; Eph 4:27.

The ultimate fate of the devil, as one tormented in the lake of eternal fire, is noted in Matt 25:41; Rev 20:10; and implied in 1 Tim 3:6; 1 John 3:8ff. See also Rev 20:2.

The devil is described as the great spiritual oppressor of humankind in Acts 10:38; Heb 2:14; Jude 9. General reference to "devil" is found in John 6:70. ***diabolos*** is also translated "slanderer" in 1 Tim 3:11; 2 Tim 3:3; Titus 2:3.

▸ **58.** Vices > ACCUSATION
▸ **58.** Vices > SLANDER, SLANDERER

DIVINATION

pythōn πύθων 4436

pythōn is a rare noun literally denoting the name "Python," referring to the dragon in Greek mythology that guarded the oracle at Delphi. In the NT it is found only in Acts 16:16, referring to the Philippian girl who had a "spirit of divination" (i.e., spirit of Python), which Paul subsequently cast out.

DIVINE

theios θεῖος 2304

theios is an adjective found three times denoting "divine" power in 2 Pet 1:3; and his "divine" nature in 2 Pet 1:4. See also Acts 17:29.

GOD

theos θεός 2316

theos is the one Greek term (occurring nearly 1,350 times) that functions as the broad dynamic equivalent for the Hebrew terms *'ělōhîm* and *YHWH*. The former denotes the general expression for God as Creator and omnipotent deity, the latter constitutes the covenant name "Lord," the divine suzerain, initiator of the intimate bond with his people Israel. While ***theos*** is not used with as many different titles as are the Hebrew names for God, ***theos*** does convey a number of significant nuances in a variety of contexts.

The designation "God" as the one true and living deity, without any other qualifying title or attribute, is indicated, for example, in Matt 1:23; 19:26; Mark 2:7; Luke 1:37; John 1:18; 3:16ff.; Acts 15:4ff.; Rom 1:18, 25ff.; 8:28; Gal 3:6; Eph 4:6; Col 1:15; 1 Tim 2:15; Heb 3:12; Jas 2:19; 1 Pet 2:17; 1 John 4:8ff.; Rev 19:1ff.

Specific references to God the Spirit are found in Matt 3:16; John 4:24; Rom 8:9; 15:19; 1 Cor 2:14; 2 Cor 3:3; Eph 4:30; 1 John 4:2.

The full title "the Lord your God" (as well as variations on the pronoun) suggests the link with the OT title of Yahweh the Lord (of the covenant) (e.g., Matt 4:7; Mark 12:29ff.; Luke 1:32; Acts 3:22; 7:37; Rev 4:8; 11:17). This perspective is reinforced in reference to the deity as the God of Abraham, Isaac, and Jacob (Acts 3:13; 5:30; 7:32; 22:14).

God is described as one who lives among his people in his "house" (i.e., the temple) in Matt 12:4; 21:12; Mark 2:26; Luke 6:4. In 2 Cor 10:16; Eph 2:22; Heb 10:21, the "dwelling place of God" refers symbolically to the spiritual community of the people of God. In particular, the heavenly temple of God is noted in Rev 11:1, 19; 21:3, 22. God as supreme ruler is indicated in the expression "kingdom of God," depicting him as the unparalleled monarch ruling over the dominion of human beings and the hearts of his people (e.g., Matt 12:28; Mark 1:14ff.; 4:26ff.; Luke 10:9ff.; John 3:3ff.; Acts 8:12; 1 Cor 4:20; Eph 5:5; Rev 12:10). This phenomenon is also evident in relation to Jesus' position of authority at "the right hand of God" in Mark 16:19; Acts 2:33; 7:56; Col 3:1; Heb 10:12; 12:2. God's throne designates his infinite power and authority in Rev 22:3.

The fatherhood of God is affirmed in relation to Jesus Christ, depicted as the "Son of God" in many places (e.g., Matt 14:33; 27:40ff.; Mark 1:1; 15:39; Luke 1:35; John 3:18; 19:7; Acts 9:20; Rom 1:4; Gal 2:20; Heb 4:14; 1 John 3:8; 5:10ff.). This is emphasized in particular in Jesus' cry from the cross "My God, why have you abandoned me?" (Matt 27:46; Mark 15:34). Explicit references to God as Father are found in John 8:42; Rom 1:7; 1 Cor 1:3; 2 Cor 1:3;

11:31; Gal 1:1ff.; Eph 1:3; Phil 2:9ff.; Col 1:3; Titus 1:4; Jas 1:27; Rev 2:18. God is also the consummate "lawgiver," the one who reveals his precepts to human beings (Matt 15:4; Mark 7:8).

The title "most high God" is found in Mark 5:7, emphasizing the unique, supreme status of God as a transcendent, omnipotent deity.

The phrase "the word of God" also confirms that God is the one who communicates with humankind (Mark 7:13; Luke 3:2; Acts 4:31; Heb 4:12; 13:7; 1 Pet 1:23; Rev 1:12). In particular, Christ is described as the incarnation of the Word of God in John 1:1, 12ff.; 10:35. In related contexts, God is said to have spoken by the mouth of his prophets (Acts 3:21). God is described as Creator in Mark 10:6ff.; 13:19; Acts 14:15; 17:24; Heb 11:3; Rev 3:14.

God is described as savior in Luke 1:47; Jude 25. God's role as universal judge is indicated in Heb 12:23; 13:4.

IMMANUEL

Emmanouēl Ἐμμανουήλ 1694

This term only occurs in Matt 1:23, where it refers to the infant Jesus as the direct fulfillment of the sign given to the prophet Isaiah (Isa 7:14).

JESUS

Iēsous Ἰησοῦς 2424

Iēsous is the Greek equivalent of the Hebrew term *yeshûʿāh*, which means "(God is) salvation." The name Jesus occurs almost one thousand times in the NT and refers almost exclusively to Christ, the Son of God. The angel of the Lord revealed this name directly to his mother Mary (Matt 1:21).

The name ***Iēsous Christos*** or "Jesus Christ" occurs around two hundred times and is found in a number of settings, such as in the genealogical listings of his Davidic ancestry (Matt 1:1); in significant events of his earthly life including his birth (Matt 1:18); and as a formal introduction to his person at the beginning of the majority of NT books outside the Gospels.

In other contexts, the name ***Iēsous Christos*** is associated with his person and work. For example, John 1:17 describes Jesus Christ as the source of grace and truth. See also Rom 5:15, 17, 21; 6:23; Gal 2:16; Phil 1:11. References to Jesus' divine authority and power are found in relation to forgiveness (Acts 2:38); and in association with his miracles (Acts 3:6; 4:10; 16:18). Rom 6:11 declares Jesus Christ to be the sole means of gaining a personal relationship with God. He is the Lord of the universe (Phil 3:20) and the Lord of glory (Jas 2:1). The goal of sanctification and its realization in the lives of believers are bound up with the person of Jesus Christ. He is also declared, for example, to be co-creator with God (1 Cor 8:6); the founder of our faith (1 Cor 3:11; Eph 2:20); the one who rose from the dead (2 Tim 2:8; 1 Pet 1:3; 3:21); our great high priest (1 Pet 2:5); the ruler of the heavenly kingdom (2 Pet 1:11); the full incarnation of God in human form (1 John 4:2; 2 John 7); the one whose blood cleanses his people from all their sin (1 John 1:7). The above list is by no means exhaustive.

Use of the name ***Iēsous*** by itself, especially in the Gospels, usually designates the activity and actions of our Lord during his earthly life. The name "Jesus" occurs approximately six hundred times in the four Gospels. Other NT occurrences of "Jesus" refer to aspects of his person and work. For example, Acts 1:11 affirms that the risen Jesus will return to earth in the same way he left to ascend into heaven. "Jesus" is the authoritative name under heaven before whom all people will one day bow (Phil 2:10). Jesus is declared to be the Savior of the world (Acts 13:23; 1 Thess 1:10); and a man attested by God with mighty works and signs (Acts 2:22; 10:38). He is also said to be the Christ (Acts 5:42; 17:33; 18:28); the crucified Christ (Acts 2:36); the risen Christ in heaven (Acts 7:55).

References to Jesus as Lord are found in Acts 19:13; 20:21; Rom 4:24; 1 Thess 4:1. Jesus is also identified as our high priest (Heb 4:14; 6:20); as the guarantor of a better covenant (Heb 7:22); as the mediator of the new covenant (Heb 12:24); and as the pioneer and perfecter of our faith (Heb 12:2). These references form an extensive, though not exhaustive, listing of the name of "Jesus" in the NT.

MAGIC, SORCERER, SOOTHSAYER

magos μάγος 3097

magos is found in six contexts meaning "wise man" or "sorcerer," indicating a scholarly class highly trained in astrology and other occult arts. In Matt 2:1, 7, 16, ***magos*** refers to the wise men who followed the star in the east leading to the birthplace of the infant Jesus in Bethlehem. Acts 13:6, 8 refer to the Jewish sorcerer, or magician, on the island of Cyprus.

▸ **2.** Supernatural Beings/Forces, Spiritual Realm > WISE MAN, SORCERER, MAGICIAN

pharmakos φάρμακος 5333

pharmakos occurs only in Rev 22:15, where it refers to sorcerers among a whole group of the wicked who are cast outside the heavenly kingdom.

manteuomai μαντεύομαι 3132

manteuomai is found only in Acts 16:16, where the term (in its participial form) refers to the slave girl possessed by an evil spirit that gave her powers of "fortune telling" or "soothsaying."

mageuō μαγεύω 3096

mageuō occurs only in Acts 8:9, where it refers to the occult skills of Simon, who "practiced magic arts."

PERSON, PRESENCE

prosōpon πρόσωπον 4383

prosōpon is a noun found in nearly eighty contexts with the primary sense of "face." However, it occasionally refers to "the face" of God, or the "person" of God (Matt 18:10; Luke 1:76; 1 Pet 3:12; Rev 6:16; 22:14). ***prosōpon*** also refers to "the presence" (i.e., the person) of God in several places (Acts 2:28; 3:19; 2 Thess 1:9).

- ▸ **16.** Body, Bodily Functions > FACE
- ▸ **85.** Movement, Position, State > BEFORE, IN THE PRESENCE OF

POSSESS, POSSESSION

daimonizomai δαιμονίζομαι 1139

The verb ***daimonizomai*** consistently refers to the state of "being possessed by a demon (or demons)." The term occurs thirteen times and on each occasion refers to persons so afflicted, who were subsequently cured by Jesus (Matt 4:24; 12:22; Mark 1:32; 5:15ff.; Luke 8:36; John 10:21).

- ▸ **2.** Supernatural Beings/Forces, Spiritual Realm > DEMON, DEMON-POSSESSED, DEMONIC

SEE ALSO

- ▸ **25.** Family, Marriage, Adoption, Inheritance > POSSESSIONS ***peripoiēsis***
- ▸ **30.** Money, Business, Wealth, Poverty > GOODS, PROPERTY, POSSESSIONS ***ktēma***

SATAN

Satanas Σατανᾶς 4567

Satanas is a proper noun used exclusively to refer to "Satan," the prince of demons. The term occurs nearly forty times in various contexts.

Satan is explicitly rebuked by Christ in Matt 4:10; Mark 8:33; Luke 4:8. His activity is also alluded to in the public ministry of Christ (Matt 12:26; Mark 3:23ff.; Luke 11:18); and is observed elsewhere as well (Acts 5:3; 1 Cor 5:5; 2 Cor 7:5; 1 Thess 2:18; 1 Tim 1:20). Luke 22:3; John 13:27 refer to Satan's entrapment of Judas Iscariot; and 1 Tim 5:5 refers to his entrapment of others.

Satan unsuccessfully seeks to tempt Christ to sin during his period of testing in the wilderness (Mark 1:13). In Luke 10:18, Christ says that he saw Satan fall like lightning from heaven. Deliverance from Satan's power is indicated in Acts 26:18; Rom 16:20. Rev 2:13 refers to Satan's throne. "Satan" is also mentioned as the alternate name for the devil in Rev 12:9; 20:2, 7.

There are metaphorical references to apostate members of a "synagogue of Satan" in Smyrna and Philadelphia in Rev 2:9; 3:9. See also Rev 2:24.

SPIRIT, SPIRITUAL, SPIRITUALLY

pneuma πνεῦμα 4151

pneuma is found in over 140 contexts. Its root meaning is "spirit," which refers to "the Spirit of God," or "the Holy Spirit," and "the Spirit of Christ," as well as the human spirit — all in a wide variety of contexts.

References to the Holy Spirit are numerous. He is designated as the supernatural agent of conception in the birth of Christ, with Mary as mother of the child (Matt 1:18ff.; Luke 1:35ff.). Luke 4:1 describes Jesus Christ as being full of the Holy Spirit.

In relation to the people of God, or true followers of Christ, believers are said to be baptized with the Holy Spirit (Matt 3:11; Mark 1:8; Luke 3:16). The Holy Spirit is given to the new covenant people of God in fulfillment of OT prophecy (Joel 2:28; John 20:23; Acts 1:8; 2:4, 17, 18, 33, 38; 4:31; 8:15ff.; 10:44). The Spirit is also given to believers as a seal, a guarantee of salvation (2 Cor 1:22; Eph 1:13). He illuminates divine truth in the believer (1 Cor 2:10ff.; Eph 3:5); gives divine guidance (Acts 8:29; 13:2); and is the source of godly "fruit" or virtues (Gal 5:22ff.). The Spirit comes upon and indwells the believer as noted in Luke 1:15, 67; Acts 6:3ff.; Rom 5:5; 8:2ff.; 1 Cor 3:16; Gal 3:2ff. The believer is described as the temple of the Holy Spirit in 1 Cor 6:19ff.; Eph 2:22. The Holy Spirit is also designated as the agent of regeneration or new birth (John 3:5ff.; 6:63); and as the agent of sanctification (Rom 15:16; Gal 5:16ff.).

The Holy Spirit is linked with the triune Godhead in Matt 28:19; Rom 1:4. He is also designated as the source of divine revelation through the prophets in 2 Pet 1:21.

References to the Spirit of God are less common, though the identity with the Holy Spirit is clearly established. He is declared to be the giver of spiritual gifts in 1 Cor 12:4ff. References to placing the Spirit of God on the messianic Servant are found in Matt 12:18; Luke 4:18 — an experience which Christ self-consciously claims as his own. God's unique nature is designated as that of a spirit in John 4:24; 2 Cor 3:17ff.

pneuma also refers to the "spirit" of human beings. It designates aspects of character, such as those who are "poor in spirit" (Matt 5:3). The term also indicates the human "spirit" as the heart of the human emotional rational faculty (Matt 26:41; Luke 1:47; 1 Cor 5:3ff.; Eph 4:23; 1 Pet 3:4). This is also predicated of Christ (Mark 2:8; Luke 2:40; John 11:33).

pneuma also means "life" referring to people (Matt 27:50; 1 Cor 5:5); and to the "life" of Christ, which he voluntarily surrendered (lit., "gave up his spirit") to God on the cross (Luke 23:46; John 19:30). The Spirit of Christ is equated with the Holy Spirit in Phil 1:19; 1 Pet 1:11.

pneuma also refers to the "spirit" of human beings in conjunction with their bodies and souls (Heb 4:12).

Evil spirits, or demons, are also denoted by ***pneuma*** (Matt 8:16; 12:43; Mark 1:23ff.; Luke 4:36; Acts 8:7; Eph 2:2; Rev 16:14). Angels are described as "ministering spirits" in Heb 1:14.

- ▸ **11.** Meteorology, Water > WIND
- ▸ **16.** Body, Bodily Functions > BREATH, BREATHE

pneumatikos πνευματικός 4152

pneumatikos is an adjective derived from ***pneuma*** (above) meaning "spiritual," referring to both the human and divine spirit.

In the sense of "being derived from God," ***pneumatikos*** is applied to gifts for God's people (Rom 1:11; 1 Cor 12:1; 14:1); truth (1 Cor 2:3); law (Rom 7:14); songs (Eph 5:19; Col 3:16); and understanding (Col 1:9).

In relation to the non-material world, the designation "spiritual" is applied to blessings (Rom 15:27; Eph 1:3); food (1 Cor 10:3); the post-resurrection bodies of believers (1 Cor 15:44); and sacrifices (1 Pet 2:5).

A "spiritual person" is a child of God (1 Cor 2:15; 3:1; 14:37; Gal 6:1); and Christ is the "spiritual Rock" (1 Cor 10:4). ***pneumatikos*** also refers to "spiritual forces of evil," as in the demonic spirit realm in Eph 6:12.

pneumatikōs πνευματικῶς 4153

pneumatikōs is an adverbial form found in only two places. In 1 Cor 2:14 it refers to those truths "spiritually" discerned only by the spiritual person through Christ. See also Rev 11:8.

WISE MAN, SORCERER, MAGICIAN

magos μάγος 3097

magos is a noun denoting "wise man" or "sorcerer." It is found in six places. Matt 2:1, 7, 16 refer to the wise men witnessing the birth of Christ. These were people skilled in the knowledge of natural phenomena, most likely astrologers. ***magos*** also refers to a "(pagan) magician" or "sorcerer" in Acts 13:6, 8.

- ▸ **2.** Supernatural Beings/Forces, Spiritual Realm > MAGIC, SORCERER, SOOTHSAYER

SEE ALSO

- ▸ **51.** Knowledge, Wisdom, Remember, Forget > WISDOM, WISE
sophia, sophos, phronimos, phronēsis

WONDER, MIRACLE, OMEN, SIGN

teras τέρας 5059

teras is a noun occurring in sixteen places and meaning "wonder," "miracle," "omen," "sign" throughout.

The meaning "wonder" in the sense of a supernatural phenomenon is indicated in Matt 24:24; Mark 13:22; 2 Thess 2:9, where false prophets perform such things in order to try and deceive the elect.

Elsewhere, "wonders" are said to be wrought by God as evidence of his power (John 4:48; Acts 7:36). In particular, these are "omens," constituting a prelude to the final day of judgment (Acts 2:19). "Wonders" were also performed by Christ as a vindication of his divine power and authority (Acts 2:22). Such "miracles" are also performed by the apostles and early Christian leaders as a testimony to their God-given, Spirit-empowered ministry, as inheritors of Christ's authority (Acts 2:43; 4:30; 5:12; 6:8; 14:3; 15:12; Rom 15:19; 2 Cor 12:12; Heb 2:4).

SEE ALSO

- ▸ **19.** Mind, Spirit, Emotions, Feelings, Desires > WONDER, MARVEL AT
thaumazō
- ▸ **88.** Qualities, Characteristics > WONDERFUL
thaumasios, thaumastos

3. Periods of Time, Duration, Frequency, Speed

DAILY

epiousios ἐπιούσιος 1967

epiousios is a rare adjectival form found only in Matt 6:11; Luke 11:3 referring to God supplying people with their "daily" bread, sufficient for their needs day by day.

ephēmeros ἐφήμερος 2184

ephēmeros is a rare synonym for ***epiousios*** (above) found only in Jas 2:15, with reference to one's "daily" food.

kathēmerinos καθημερινός 2522

kathēmerinos is another rare adjective denoting the "daily" distribution of food, found only in Acts 6:1.

DAWN, DAYBREAK

diaugazō διαυγάζω 1306

diaugazō is a rare verb denoting the "dawning" of a day, found only in 2 Pet 1:19.

epiphōskō ἐπιφώσκω 2020

epiphōskō is a rare synonym for ***diaugazō*** (above), also indicating the "dawning" of a new day, in Matt 28:1; Luke 23:54.

orthros ὄρθρος 3722

orthros is a noun denoting "daybreak," translated "early in the morning" or "at dawn" in Luke 4:21; John 8:2; Acts 5:21.

▸ **3.** Periods of Time, Duration, Frequency, Speed > MORNING

DAY, PERIOD, AGE, TIME

hēmera ἡμέρα 2250

hēmera is the most common term for "day" in the NT. It signifies "day" in both literal and metaphorical contexts with a variety of nuances.

The meaning "days," signifying a "period," "age," or "time," is indicated with regard to a regnal period in Matt 2:1; Luke 1:5; Acts 7:45; Rev 2:13. Jesus' "day," signifying the time of his coming to earth, is noted in John 8:56. The expression "these last days" refers to the period of Christ's incarnation in Heb 1:2. Reference to "the days" that will usher in the new covenant age is found in Heb 8:8. The designation "today" denotes the current new covenant age in Heb 3:13. The "day" of Israel's rebellion in the wilderness is noted in Heb 13:8. The "days" leading up to the period of final judgment are mentioned in Matt 9:15; Mark 2:20.

The meaning "day" as a literal twenty-four-hour period is indicated, for example, in Matt 4:2; Mark 4:35; Luke 2:44; 17:29; John 1:39; Acts 21:10ff.; Rev 14:11. The forty-day period of Christ's temptation in the wilderness is noted in Mark 1:13; Luke 4:2. The third day after Christ's death — the day of his resurrection — is noted in Matt 16:21; 27:64; Mark 9:31; Luke 9:22; Acts 10:40; 1 Cor 15:4. See also Matt 6:34.

The expression "on that day," as well as variations singular and plural, signifying the consummate time of God's judgment on the earth at the end of time (viz. the Day of the Lord) are found in a number of places. The phrase denotes a time when God will pass a final sentence on the wicked and vindicate the righteous who belong to him in Christ. The negative perspective of "judgment" is found, for example, in Matt 7:22; 24:19ff.; Mark 13:17ff.; Luke 10:12; 21:22ff.; Acts 2:20; Rom 2:5, 16; 1 Cor 1:8; 1 Thess 5:12ff.; 2 Thess 1:10; 2 Tim 1:12; 2 Pet 3:3ff.; 1 John 4:17; Rev 10:7. The positive aspect of "blessing" in relation to the day is indicated in Matt 26:29; Mark 14:25; Luke 6:23; John 16:23ff.; Acts 2:17ff.; 1 Cor 5:5; Eph 4:30; Phil 1:6ff.; Heb 10:25. Specific reference to the "last day" of divine judgment is found in John 6:39ff.; 12:48; 1 Pet 2:12.

In other contexts, various references are made to a specific "day" of major significance — for example, the Sabbath day in Luke 4:16; 13:16; 14:5; Acts 13:14; 16:13. In a related context, Heb 4:4ff. refers to the eschatological "day" of rest, symbolized by the land of Canaan, that anticipates the ultimate heavenly rest for the believer. The "day of unleavened bread" is indicated in Luke 22:7; Acts 20:6. See also Luke 23:54. The "Lord's Day" is noted in Rev 1:10. Acts 2:1; 20:16 refer to the "day of Pentecost." Other such references include Luke 1:80; Gal 4:10; 1 Pet 3:20; Rev 11:9ff.

▸ **15.** Gender, Reproduction, Youth, Aging > AGE, STATURE

ETERNAL

aiōn αἰών 165

aiōn is a noun found in nearly 130 places with the primary senses of "world," "ever," as in the expression "forever and ever." In two contexts, ***aiōn*** indicates the meaning "eternal." Eph 3:11 refers to the "eternal" purpose of God's redemptive plans that culminate in Christ. Then, 1 Tim 1:17 refers to God as the "eternal" king.

▸ **1.** Celestial Realm, Earthly Realm > WORLD, WORLDLY
▸ **3.** Periods of Time, Duration, Frequency, Speed > EVER, EVERLASTING, FOREVER

aiōnios αἰώνιος 166

aiōnios is an adjectival form derived from ***aiōn*** (above) with the principal meanings "eternal," "everlasting."

The meaning "eternal" in the sense of "unending" is found in relation to the judgment of hell fire in Matt 18:8; 25:41. "Eternal" destruction is indicated in 2 Thess 1:9; Heb 6:2; Jude 7.

In particular, "eternal" or "everlasting" life, the blissful state of unbroken fellowship with God in heaven, is noted in Matt 19:16, 29; Mark 10:17; Luke 10:25; 18:18; John 5:39; 6:27ff.; 12:25; Acts 13:46ff.; Rom 2:7; 5:21; 6:22; Gal 6:8; 1 Tim 6:12; Titus 3:7; 1 John 3:15; Jude 15.

Mark 3:29 refers to the "eternal" sin of blasphemy against the Holy Spirit. The sense of "eternal" here denotes a transgression of which there can be no forgiveness.

God is described as the source of "eternal" life in John 17:2; Rom 2:7; 1 John 2:25; 5:11ff. Christ is also designated as the source and giver of eternal life in John 3:15ff.; 4:14; 5:24; 6:40; 10:28; Rom 6:23; 1 Tim 1:16; Heb 5:9; 9:12; 1 John 1:2.

Other uses of ***aiōnios*** include references to the "eternal" weight of glory in 2 Cor 4:17. See also 2 Tim 2:10; 1 Pet 5:10. Unseen "eternal" things are noted in 2 Cor 4:18. "Eternal" comfort derived from God is indicated in 2 Thess 2:16. 1 Tim 6:16 refers to God's "eternal" dominion. The believer's "eternal" inheritance is noted in Heb 9:15; the "eternal" covenant in Heb 13:20; the "eternal" kingdom of God in 2 Pet 1:11; and the "eternal" gospel in Rev 14:6. ***aiōnios*** also denotes the Spirit of God as "eternal" in Heb 9:14.

aidios ἀΐδιος 126

aidios is a rare adjectival variant of ***aiōnios*** (above) denoting God's "eternal" power in Rom 1:20; and the "eternal" chains of confinement in Hades in Jude 6.

EVENING

hespera ἑσπέρα 2073

hespera is a noun found three times, denoting "evening" in the literal sense of the period after sunset (Luke 24:29; Acts 4:3; 28:23).

opsia ὀψία 3798

opsia is synonymous with ***hespera*** (above) and also denotes "evening" in its natural sense, in fifteen contexts (e.g., Matt 8:16; 14:15; 27:57; Mark 1:32; 4:35; John 6:16; 20:19).

opse ὀψέ 3796

opse is a rare variant of ***opsia*** (above) denoting "evening" in Mark 11:19; 13:35.

EVER, EVERLASTING, FOREVER

aiōn αἰών 165

aiōn is a noun with the primary meanings "world," "age," and "ever" throughout the nearly 130 occurrences of the term. The latter meaning is found primarily in the expressions "forever," "evermore," denoting the unending passage of time. The meaning "ever" is linked to "forever" in the sense of unending duration (Luke 1:33; Heb 1:8; 13:8; 2 John 2; Jude 13, 25; Rev 18:6; 14:11; 20:10).

In particular, the phenomenon of "living forever," in the context of eternal life, is indicated in John 6:51, 58.

In John 8:35, Christ the Son is said to continue "forever" (see also John 12:34; Rev 1:18). He is also declared as a priest "forever" in the order of Melchizedek in Heb 5:6; 6:20; 7:17ff. John 14:16 affirms that the Holy Spirit will remain with his people forever. The ascribing of blessing or glory to God "forever" is indicated in Rom 1:25; 9:5; 11:36; 2 Cor 11:31; Gal 1:5; Phil 4:20; 2 Tim 4:18; 1 Pet 4:11; 2 Pet 3:18; Rev 1:6; 5:13; 7:12 (see also Heb 13:21). The everlasting reign of Christ is indicated in Rev 11:15.

The phenomenon of the punishment of the wicked lasting "forever" is indicated in Rev 14:11; 15:7; 19:3; 20:10.

The contrasting negative meaning of "never" is indicated in John 4:14; 8:51ff.; 10:28; 11:26; 13:8.

▸ **1.** Celestial Realm, Earthly Realm > WORLD, WORLDLY
▸ **3.** Periods of Time, Duration, Frequency, Speed > ETERNAL

HASTE, HASTEN, HURRY, QUICKLY

spoudē σπουδή 4710

spoudē is a noun with several meanings including "earnestness," "diligence," and also "haste." The term occurs twelve times but only means "haste" on two occasions, both of which are literal (Mark 6:25; Luke 1:39). Both texts refer to hurried action.

▸ **46.** Wait, Hope, Be Vigilant, Pay Attention To > DILIGENCE, DILIGENT, DILIGENTLY

speudō σπεύδω 4692

speudō is the verbal root form of ***spoudē*** (above). The term occurs six times, and all but one translate "make haste" or "hurry" in the literal sense of quick action (Luke 2:16; 19:5, 6, Acts 20:16; 22:18). In 2 Pet 3:12, ***speudō*** refers to the "hastening of the Day of the Lord" as the result of an eager anticipation of the final consummation of God's plan of redemption.

tacheōs ταχέως 5030

tacheōs is an adverb occurring ten times, meaning "hastily," "quickly." In regard to quick or hurried action, the term is found in Luke 14:21; 16:6; John 11:31; 1 Cor 4:19. Concerning shortness of time, ***tacheōs*** occurs in Phil 2:19; 2:24; 2 Thess 2:2; 1 Tim 5:22; 2 Tim 4:9. Gal 1:6 refers to Paul's anguish over the Galatian congregation's rapid deserting of the Lord after their conversion experience.

HOUR

hōra ὥρα 5610

This term is fairly common in the NT, occurring around one hundred times. ***hōra*** means "hour" in a variety of contexts, referring both to literal periods of times as well as to specific occasions and moments of great import.

With the literal sense of sixty-minute intervals, ***hōra*** occurs in Matt 26:40; Mark 14:37; Luke 22:59; Acts 5:7; 19:30. In Rev 18:19, with reference to the destruction of Babylon in one hour, the term probably indicates symbolic time. ***hōra*** is also used to indicate the specific time of day (e.g., Matt 20:5ff.; Mark 6:35; Luke 12:39, 46; John 19:14; Acts 10:30; Rev 11:13). Occasionally, ***hōra*** is found in the expression "the same hour," meaning "immediately" (Matt 8:13; 9:22; Luke 2:38; Acts 16:18).

The most significant use of ***hōra*** is in contexts where it means a "time" or "period of time" that is of special import. The translation "hour" is retained in these texts — for example, the hour of Jesus' trial in Gethsemane (Mark

14:35); the hour of incense, in reference to worship (Luke 1:10); the hour of Jesus' earthly destiny in reference to his arrest and crucifixion (Luke 22:53; John 2:4; 7:30); the hour of Jesus' suffering (John 12:27; 13:1); the hour for the Son of Man to be glorified (John 12:23; 17:1); the last hour, in an eschatological sense (1 John 2:18; Rev 14:7, 15).

IMMORTAL, IMMORTALITY

eis tōn aiōna εἰς τὸν αἰῶνα 165

This phrase is found about thirty times and is translated "ever," "forever" (and "never" in negative contexts).

Regarding the concept "forever," Luke 1:55 refers to the perpetuity of the Abrahamic covenant. In John 6:51 there is the promise of eternal life for those who eat the "living bread" offered by Christ. John 8:35 refers to Christ's eternal existence as one who lives forever. Similarly, 2 Cor 9:9 affirms that God's righteousness lasts forever. Heb 1:8 refers to God's "everlasting" throne. Heb 5:6; 6:20; 7:17ff. mention Jesus Christ as a priest "forever" after the order of Melchizedek (Gen 14). 1 John 2:17 records the promise that he who does the will of God remains forever (see also 2 John 2).

The meaning "never" is also frequently used to describe the positive blessing of eternal life as a negative — that is, to never die, or never hunger or thirst (John 8:51, 52; 10:28; 11:26).

SEE ALSO

- ▸ **22.** Life, Renewal, Immortality > IMMORTAL, IMMORTALITY, IMPERISHABLE ***athanasia, aphtharsia, aphthartos***

MONTH

mēn μήν 3376

mēn is the only term for "month" in the NT, occurring eighteen times in all. In most of these occurrences ***mēn*** is used in a durative sense, referring to various lengths of time involving months (e.g., Luke 1:24, 56; 4:25; 7:20; Acts 18:11; 28:11; Gal 4:10; Rev 9:5ff.; 11:2; 13:5; 22:2). The majority of contexts in the book of Revelation indicate these periods of time as episodes of divine judgment and chastisement. The exception is Rev 22:2, which speaks of the tree of life in the heavenly city yielding its fruit each month for the healing of the nations. These periods of time mentioned in Revelation are likely to be non-literal.

In three places ***mēn*** refers to "month" as a point in time, or date. Luke 1:26 refers to the sixth month of Elizabeth's pregnancy (carrying her son, John) as the time of the angelic visitation to Mary, announcing that she would be the mother of the messianic king, the Son of God. See also Luke 1:36. Rev 9:15 designates a particular day, month, and year as the time for a savage punitive judgment on a third of humankind. The specific date is not mentioned, and once again a real, though non-literal, phenomenon is in view.

MORNING

prōi πρωΐ 4404

prōi is an adverbial form and occurs fourteen times meaning "(early) in the morning," in the natural temporal sense (e.g., Matt 16:3; 21:18; 27:1; Mark 1:35; 11:20; John 20:1; 21:4; Acts 28:23).

orthros ὄρθρος 3722

orthros is a synonym for ***prōi*** (above) and is likewise translated as an adverbial phrase "early in the morning" (Luke 24:1; John 8:2; Acts 5:21).

- ▸ **3.** Periods of Time, Duration, Frequency, Speed > DAWN, DAYBREAK

orthrizō ὀρθρίζω 3719

orthrizō is the verb from which ***orthros*** (above) is derived. It is found only in Luke 21:38, meaning "to come early in the morning."

prōinos πρωϊνός 4407

prōinos is an adjectival form related to the adverb ***prōi***, which has the sense of "in relation to the morning." It is used only in Rev 2:28 with reference to the "morning star," the promised reward from the ascended Christ in heaven to those who persevere in faithful obedience to Christ to the end.

NIGHT

nyx νύξ 3571

nyx is the standard NT term for "night." It occurs in approximately sixty contexts with both literal and metaphorical connotations.

The dominant usage of ***nyx*** indicates the sense of "night" (in contrast to "day") in literal contexts (e.g., Matt 2:14; 26:31ff.; Mark 4:27; 14:30; Luke 2:37; John 3:2; 21:3; Acts 5:19; 20:31; 1 Cor 11:31; 1 Thess 2:9; 1 Tim 5:6). See also Rev 8:12.

Occasionally, ***nyx*** refers metaphorically to the "night" as a period of moral darkness (John 9:4; 11:10; 13:10; Rom 13:12; 1 Thess 5:5).

Jesus' fasting in the desert for a period of "forty days and forty nights" just prior to his testing by the devil in Matt 4:2 may suggest a patterning along the lines of old covenant periods of trial and/or divine revelation, such as Israel's forty-year wandering in the desert and Moses' forty-day and forty-night audience with Yahweh on Mount Sinai. Another chronological expression, "three days and three nights," is used with respect to the sign of Jonah, referring to the time he spent in the belly of the great fish (Matt 12:40). This expression relates to the anticipation of Christ's approaching death and resurrection, a period identical with the duration of Jonah's "trial."

The expression "day and night" metaphorically conveys the idea of continuous, unending experience, applicable both to the joys of heaven and the agonies of eternal punishment (Rev 4:8; 7:15; 12:10; 14:11; 20:10). Rev 4:8; 7:15;

12:10; 14:11; 20:10 refer to the constancy of doing something "day and night." Rev 21:25; 22:5 indicate that there will be no night in heaven.

In two places ***nyx*** means "midnight" (Matt 25:6; Acts 27:27).

dianyktereuō διανυκτερεύω 1273

dianyktereuō is found only in Luke 6:12, referring to Jesus "spending the whole night" in prayer.

PRESENT

enistēmi ἐνίστημι 1764

enistēmi is a verb that is predominantly utilized as an adjective and a noun, as well as a verb with intransitive force. It occurs sixteen times.

The meaning "present" in the sense of the current age, period of time, or history is found in Rom 8:38; 1 Cor 3:22. The adjectival sense of "present" or "current" is indicated in 1 Cor 7:26 with reference to this "present distress" (i.e., persecution, troubled time). In Gal 1:4 ***enistēmi*** refers to this "present evil world"; and in Heb 9:9 to "this present time." 2 Thess 2:2 refers to the Day of the Lord "being at hand" (i.e., has come; is now present).

SEE ALSO

- ▸ **70.** Give, Take, Seize, Touch > PRESENT
  paristēmi, histēmi
- ▸ **85.** Movement, Position, State > BE PRESENT, COME
  pareimi, paraginomai, sympareimi

SPEND TIME

chronotribeō χρονοτριβέω 5551

chronotribeō is a rare verb found only in Acts 20:16 with reference to "spending" time.

SEE ALSO

- ▸ **30.** Money, Business, Wealth, Poverty > SPEND
  dapanaō, prosdapanaō
- ▸ **55.** Bondage, Captivity, Servitude > SPEND COMPLETELY, GIVE ONESELF
  ekdapanaō

SUDDENLY

exaiphnēs ἐξαίφνης 1810

exaiphnēs is used adverbially in five contexts denoting the sense of "suddenly" (Mark 13:36; Luke 2:13; 9:39; Acts 9:3; 22:6).

TIME

chronos χρόνος 5550

chronos is a noun occurring around fifty times meaning "time" throughout most of its usage, in the sense of "measured moments of duration," including assessment of time as either long or short.

General references to measured time include those in Acts 1:6, 21; 17:30; 1 Pet 4:2. ***chronos*** refers to "time" for giving birth (Luke 1:57); a moment of time (Luke 4:5); a "long time" (Matt 25:19; Luke 8:27; John 14:9; Acts 8:11; 27:9; Heb 4:7); and "short times" (John 12:35; Rev 20:3). See also Acts 20:8; 1 Cor 16:7.

chronos also refers to "times" fixed by God (Acts 1:7; 3:21), including the fulfillment of prophecy and promise (Acts 7:17; Gal 4:4), and the designation "last times" (Jude 18).

kairos καιρός 2540

kairos is a noun occurring nearly ninety times with the primary sense of "time" that is somewhat broader than that of ***chronos*** (above). ***kairos*** indicates "time" not only in the sense of "measured duration of moments" but also in the sense of "epoch," "age," or "era," which manifests purpose or fulfillment to a greater or lesser degree.

The meaning "time" in the sense of an age or era appointed by God in accordance with his redemptive purposes is evident in a number of contexts. General references include those in Acts 1:7; 7:20; Rom 3:26. The concept of "this time" or "this present age" is evident in Luke 18:30; Rom 8:18; 1 Cor 7:29; 2 Cor 6:2; Eph 5:16; Heb 9:9. The "time" of the fulfillment of divine judgment is noted in Mark 13:33; 1 Pet 4:17; Rev 1:3; 11:18; 22:10. Matt 16:3; Luke 12:56 refer to "the signs of the times" as indicators that this world age may be drawing to a close. The "last times" (i.e., prior to final judgment) are noted in 1 Tim 4:1; 1 Pet 1:5 (see also 2 Tim 3:1).

The "time" of the fulfillment of God's purpose and plan in relation to his Son, Jesus Christ, and his kingdom, is indicated in several places. Matt 26:18 refers to Jesus' claim that his "time is at hand" (i.e., his death and resurrection are drawing near). See also John 7:6ff. In relation to the coming kingdom of God, Mark 1:15 refers to John the Baptist's words, "The time has come." Luke 21:24 speaks of "the time of the Gentiles" (i.e., the full extent of their salvation). Rom 5:6; 1 Tim 2:6 affirm that Christ died "at the right time." Eph 1:10 mentions "the fullness of time" (i.e., the consummation of all of God's redemptive purposes).

TOMORROW

aurion αὔριον 839

aurion is an adverbial form found in fourteen places with the consistent meaning "tomorrow" (e.g., Matt 6:30ff.; Luke 10:35; Acts 23:15; Jas 4:13f.).

WEEK, WEEKS

sabbaton σάββατον 4521

sabbaton is a common term for "Sabbath" in the NT, occurring around seventy times. However, in several places ***sabbaton*** means "week," specifically referring to the first day of the week. See also Matt 28:1; Mark 16:2ff.; Luke 18:12; 24:1; John 20:19; Acts 20:7; 1 Cor 16:2.

▸ **40.** Holy Days, Feasts, Festivals > SABBATH

WINTER, SPEND THE WINTER

paracheimazō παραχειμάζω 3914

paracheimazō is a verb occurring four times meaning "to pass, spend the winter" (Acts 27:12; 28:11; 1 Cor 16:6; Titus 3:12). See also Acts 27:12.

SEE ALSO

▸ **11.** Meteorology, Water > WINTER, STORMY
cheimōn

YEAR

etos ἔτος 2094

etos occurs nearly fifty times and means "year" throughout.

The designation "years" with reference to specific periods of time is indicated in Matt 9:20; Mark 5:25; Luke 2:36ff.; John 2:20; 2 Cor 12:2; Gal 1:18; Heb 13:21. References to "years" as periods of indefinite duration are found in Luke 12:19; Acts 24:10; Rom 15:23.

"Years" as significant periods of time are noted in Acts 7:16; Gal 3:17 in relation to the four hundred years of Israel's captivity in Egypt. Acts 7:36ff.; Heb 3:9, 17 mention Israel's forty-year wandering in the wilderness.

etos also denotes a person's age in terms of "years" in Luke 2:42; 3:23; John 8:57; 1 Tim 5:9. Regnal years are also indicated in relation to the Roman emperor (Luke 3:1).

The expression "every year" (i.e., annually) is used to describe the celebration of ritual festivals in Luke 2:41.

etos is also used metaphorically in 2 Pet 3:8 to refer to a "thousand years" as the equivalent of "one day" in the sight of God. Rev 20:2ff. refers to the "thousand year" rule of Christ.

eniautos ἐνιαυτός 1763

eniautos is a noun found in fourteen places meaning "year" throughout.

General references to a "year" as a point in time, or date, are found in John 11:49ff.; 18:13. ***eniautos*** refers to a period of time in Acts 11:26; 18:11; Jas 4:13; 5:17; Rev 9:15, and also in the ritual context of the observance of festivals (Gal 4:10; Heb 9:7, 25; 10:1ff.).

The phrase "year of the Lord" is a figurative expression, akin to "the Day of the Lord" — a climactic event in the calendar of redemptive history signifying the coming of the Messiah (Luke 4:19).

perysi πέρυσι 4070

perysi is an adverb signifying "a year ago," found only twice, in 2 Cor 8:10; 9:2.

trietia τριετία 5148

trietia occurs once and denotes a period of "three years" (Acts 20:31).

dietia διετία 1333

dietia is a noun found only twice, in Acts 24:27; 28:30, denoting a period of "two years."

SEE ALSO

▸ **15.** Gender, Reproduction, Youth, Aging > YEAR
dietēs, hekatontaetēs

YESTERDAY

echthes ἐχθές 5504

echthes is an adverb meaning "yesterday" in all three occurrences of the term. In John 4:52; Acts 7:28, it is used literally. In Heb 13:8, ***echthes*** refers metaphorically to Christ's person being unchanged "yesterday, today, and forever."

4. Beginning, Continuing, Finishing, Postponing

BEGIN, BEGINNING

archomai ἄρχομαι 756

The verb ***archomai***, meaning "begin," occurs about eighty times.

The translation "begin," in the sense of "be the first to do something," is indicated in relation to Jesus' preaching activity in Matt 4:17; to his teaching the crowds in Matt 11:7; Mark 4:1; 12:1; Luke 7:24; 11:29; and to showing his disciples that he must die in Matt 16:21; Mark 10:32. See also Matt 12:1; Mark 11:15; Luke 3:23; John 13:5; Acts 1:1.

Other general uses of "begin" include Matt 14:30; 26:74; Mark 2:23; Luke 5:21; Acts 2:4; 18:26; 27:35. The expression "judgment begins at the house of God" is found in 1 Pet 4:17.

enarchomai ἐνάρχομαι 1728

enarchomai is a rare variant of ***archomai*** (above) with the meaning "begin" in Gal 3:3; Phil 1:6.

proenarchomai προενάρχομαι 4278

proenarchomai is another rare variant of ***archomai*** (above), with the sense of "make a beginning already, or before" (2 Cor 8:6, 10).

archē ἀρχή 746

The noun ***archē*** is found in about sixty contexts with the primary meaning "beginning," with a variety of nuances.

The translation "beginning," with reference to the creation of the world, is indicated for example in Matt 19:4, 8; Mark 10:6; 13:19; John 8:44; 2 Thess 2:13; Heb 1:10; 2 Pet 3:4. Specific reference to Christ's pre-existent state with God before creation as "the beginning" is indicated in John 1:1ff.; Col 1:18. In Rev 1:8; 21:6; 22:13 Christ is described as "the Alpha and the Omega" — the "beginning" and the "end." General, non-specific references to "beginning" include Luke 1:2; John 15:27; Acts 11:15; Heb 7:3; 1 John 2:7, 13ff.; 3:8ff.

The meaning "beginning" in the sense of "commencement" is used metaphorically to describe the beginnings of trials at the end time as birth pangs in Matt 24:8; Mark 13:8. References to the "commencement" or "beginning" of the gospel of Christ are found in Mark 1:1; Phil 4:15; 1 John 1:1.

▸ **35.** Clothing, Adornment, Textiles > CORNER

CEASE, STOP

pauō παύω 3973

pauō is a verb found fifteen times with the meaning "cease" in a variety of contexts.

General references to the action of "ceasing" or "stopping" are found in Acts 20:1; 1 Pet 4:1. ***pauō*** is also used in relation to the cessation of speaking in Luke 5:4. The miracle of Christ "putting an end" to a storm is recorded in Luke 8:24. 1 Cor 13:8 contains the promise that tongues "would cease." Luke 11:1 records that Jesus "finished" his praying. Eph 1:16; Col 1:9 both refer to Paul's practice of "never ceasing" to pray. Acts 5:42 notes that the apostles "never stopped" preaching the gospel. See also Acts 6:13; 20:31; Heb 10:2.

dialeipō διαλείπω 1257

dialeipō is a rare verb found only in Luke 7:45 referring to the actions of a woman who never "stopped" kissing Jesus' feet during a visit to a Pharisee's home.

kopazō κοπάζω 2869

kopazō is a rare verb found only in Matt 14:32; Mark 4:39; 6:51. It refers to the wind "ceasing" at the command of Christ.

adialeiptōs ἀδιαλείπτως 89

adialeiptōs is an adverb meaning "without ceasing," "constantly." It is used in the context of praying in Rom 1:9; 1 Thess 2:13; 5:17. See also 1 Thess 1:3.

CONTINUE, REMAIN

menō μένω 3306

menō is a verb found about 120 times with the predominant sense of "abide," "remain," along with several related nuances. One of these nuances is "continue," which overlaps in meaning with "remain" in a number of places.

John 8:31 contains Jesus' exhortation to his disciples to "continue" in his word, to maintain an attitude of respect with constant attention and obedience to it. In John 15:9 Jesus also exhorts his followers to "continue" to cultivate among themselves the love of God as manifested in his own person. Heb 13:1 contains the exhortation to "let brotherly love continue." Similar references to "continuing" in faith, love, and holiness are made in 1 Tim 2:15; 2 Tim 3:14. See also 1 John 2:19. Heb 7:24 refers to Christ "continuing" forever in his high priestly ministry.

▸ **4.** Beginning, Continuing, Finishing, Postponing > ENDURE, REMAIN
▸ **24.** Dwell, Live, Gather, Hospitality > ABIDE, STAY, REMAIN
▸ **24.** Dwell, Live, Gather, Hospitality > DWELL, DWELLING
▸ **85.** Movement, Position, State > REMAIN, STAY, ABIDE, DWELL

emmenō ἐμμένω 1696

emmenō is a rare variant form of ***menō*** (above) meaning "continue" in three places. The need for "continuing" in the faith is indicated in Acts 14:22, as is the importance of "continuing" to do everything as written in the book of the law in Gal 3:10. Israel's failure to "continue" to observe the law covenant is recorded in Heb 8:9.

epimenō ἐπιμένω 1961

epimenō is another variant of ***menō*** (above), meaning "continue," "remain," along with related nuances, in nineteen places.

The practice of "continuing" to ask questions is indicated in John 8:7. Continual knocking on the door is indicated in Acts 12:16. 1 Tim 4:16 contains an exhortation to "persevere" in living a godly life.

The meaning "continue" in the sense of "remain" is found in relation to: God's grace (Acts 13:43); God's kindness (Rom 11:22); a sinful condition (Rom 6:1). Col 1:23 contains a general reference to "continuing" in the faith.

▸ **24.** Dwell, Live, Gather, Hospitality > ABIDE, STAY, REMAIN

paramenō παραμένω 3887

paramenō is another rare synonym for the entries listed above, meaning "continue," "remain" in three places. This state of "continuing" in the priestly office is noted in Heb 7:23. The desirability of "continuing" in the law of liberty in the gospel, indicating the underlying sense of "perseverance," is noted in Jas 1:25.

▸ **24.** Dwell, Live, Gather, Hospitality > ABIDE, STAY, REMAIN

prosmenō προσμένω 4357

prosmenō is a verb found in seven places with the meaning "remain," "stay." In 1 Tim 5:5, however, the term describes Christian women who "continue" in prayer night and day.

proskartereō προσκαρτερέω 4342

The verb ***proskartereō*** has the underlying sense of "continue," along with various nuances, for most of its ten occurrences. It means "continue with," in the sense of "give attention to" or "devote oneself to," in reference to prayer (Acts 1:14; 2:42, 46; 6:4); and to the study of apostolic doctrine (Rom 12:12; Col 4:2).

DELAY, LINGER

okneō ὀκνέω 3635

okneō is a rare verb found only in Acts 9:38 with the negative sense of "not to delay."

chronizō χρονίζω 5549

chronizō is a verb found six places with the meaning "linger," "delay." It is used in the positive sense in Matt 24:48; 25:5; Luke 1:21; 12:45. Heb 10:37 refers to the Messiah as one "who will not delay" in his coming.

anabolē ἀναβολή 311

anabolē is a rare noun found only in Acts 25:17, where it refers to Festus, the Roman governor of Judea, taking "no delay" in establishing his tribunal to hear the defense of Paul.

END, BRING TO AN END

telos τέλος 5056

telos is a noun denoting an "end" for most of the nearly forty occurrences of the term in various contexts.

In a temporal sense, ***telos*** denotes the "end" of the age, the time when God will consummate his redemptive purposes for humankind that will include both the judgment of the wicked and the salvation of the righteous — all to take place when Christ returns for the last time (Matt 24:6, Mark 13:7; Luke 21:9; John 13:1; 1 Cor 1:8; 15:24; Heb 3:14; 6:11; 1 Pet 4:7; Rev 2:26; 21:6; 22:13). The kingdom of God and Christ is described as a kingdom "without end" in Luke 1:33.

In more mundane contexts, ***telos*** refers to "end" as the termination or completion of a particular circumstance or event (Matt 26:58). More significantly, 2 Cor 3:13 refers to the "end" of the radiance (i.e., its fading) on Moses' face on Mount Sinai, a phenomenon that the Israelites were prevented from seeing. See also Heb 7:3.

The meaning "end" in the sense of "destruction" is used in relation to Satan and his kingdom in Mark 3:26; 2 Cor 11:15; Phil 3:19; 1 Pet 4:17. See also Heb 6:8.

"End" in the sense of "consequence" is indicated in Rom 6:21 in relation to eternal death as the result of sin, and in relation to eternal life as the result of faith and sanctification in Rom 6:22; 1 Pet 1:9.

telos also refers to Christ as the "end" or "fulfillment" of the law in Rom 10:4.

synteleō συντελέω 4931

synteleō is a variant form of ***telos*** (above) found seven times and meaning "bring to an end," "finish," or "complete." Matt 7:28 refers to Jesus "completing" his discourse to the multitude. The "accomplishment" of Jesus' miracles is indicated in Mark 13:4. The "ending" of the days of Christ's temptation by the devil is noted in Luke 4:2, 13. See also Acts 21:27.

▸ **4.** Beginning, Continuing, Finishing, Postponing > FINISH, COMPLETE, FULFILL, BRING TO AN END, COME TO AN END

▸ **84.** Do, Make, Accomplish, Occur > CARRY OUT, COMPLETE, FULFILL, ACCOMPLISH

synteleia συντέλεια 4930

synteleia is a noun derived from ***synteleō*** (above) found six times and meaning "end" in the sense of "consummation." All references denote the "end" of the world, anticipating the climax of divine judgment, embracing both eternal destruction and life in glory (Matt 13:39ff.; 24:3; 28:20; Heb 9:26).

SEE ALSO

▸ **6.** Location, Position, Direction, Extension > END, TIP
peras, akron

ENDURE, REMAIN

menō μένω 3306

menō is a common verb found in 120 places with the primary meanings "remain," "abide," "dwell." The sense of "endure" or "last" is also evident in 1 Pet 1:25 in relation to the word of God enduring forever.

▸ **4.** Beginning, Continuing, Finishing, Postponing > CONTINUE, REMAIN
▸ **24.** Dwell, Live, Gather, Hospitality > ABIDE, STAY, REMAIN
▸ **24.** Dwell, Live, Gather, Hospitality > DWELL, DWELLING
▸ **85.** Movement, Position, State > REMAIN, STAY, ABIDE, DWELL

SEE ALSO

▸ **49.** Allow, Accept, Approve, Refuse > ENDURE
tropophoreō

▸ **60.** Virtues > ENDURE, BEAR, FORBEAR
hypomenō

FINISH, COMPLETE, FULFILL, BRING TO AN END, COME TO AN END

teleō τελέω 5055

teleō is a verb found twenty-six times with the primary senses of "finish," "fulfill," as well as related nuances.

The meaning "finish" implies "complete (a task)" in Matt 11:1; 13:53; 19:1; 26:1; 2 Tim 4:7; Rev 11:7.

There is an overlap in meaning with "fulfill" in a number of places, where ***teleō*** is translated "finish" in the sense of "accomplish." The contexts here all relate to "completing" or "accomplishing" God's redemptive purposes through Christ's death on the cross (Luke 12:50; 18:31; 22:37; John 19:28, 30).

The meaning "finish" also connotes the sense of "come to an end" in Rev 15:8; 20:3ff.

▸ **30.** Money, Business, Wealth, Poverty > PAY, RENDER
▸ **84.** Do, Make, Accomplish, Occur > CARRY OUT, COMPLETE, FULFILL, ACCOMPLISH

teleioō τελειόω 5048

teleioō is a verb roughly synonymous with ***teleō*** (above) meaning "perfect," "make perfect" in most of its nearly twenty-five occurrences.

Several occurrences of the term also denote the act of "finishing." Luke 2:43 refers to a feast "coming to an end," "finishing." In addition, ***teleioō*** means "finish" in the sense of "accomplish," in relation to the redemptive work of Jesus Christ in John 5:36; 17:4; 19:28. Similarly, John 4:34 records Christ's intention to "finish" or "accomplish" the work of his Father. Acts 20:24 refers to Paul "finishing" the course of his ministry.

▸ **61.** Integrity, Innocence, Piety > PERFECT, PERFECTION, COMPLETE
▸ **84.** Do, Make, Accomplish, Occur > CARRY OUT, COMPLETE, FULFILL, ACCOMPLISH

ekteleō ἐκτελέω 1615

ekteleō is a rare verb found only twice in Luke 14:29, 30, meaning "finish," "complete" in the context of building a tower.

synteleō συντελέω 4931

synteleō is a verb found seven times with the primary meaning "finish" in the sense of "bring (a task) to an end" in Matt 7:28; Luke 4:13. The simple sense of "finish," "come to an end" is indicated in Luke 4:2; Acts 21:27.

▸ **4.** Beginning, Continuing, Finishing, Postponing > END, BRING TO AN END
▸ **84.** Do, Make, Accomplish, Occur > CARRY OUT, COMPLETE, FULFILL, ACCOMPLISH

dianyō διανύω 1274

dianyō is a rare verb found only in Acts 21:7, describing Luke's "completing" or "finishing" a sea voyage.

plēthō πλήθω 4130

plēthō is a verb occurring nearly thirty times, with the dominant sense of "fill." However, in Luke 1:23 it means "finish" or "come to an end," in reference to the completion of Zechariah's priestly duties.

▸ **7.** Quantity, Amount, Number, Size, Measure > FILL, FILL UP, FULFILL, BE FULL, BE FILLED

FOUNDATION

katabolē καταβολή 2602

katabolē means "foundation" and is found exclusively in the expression "foundation of the world."

For the most part, the contexts of this expression all relate to the "beginning of creation" as the starting point for God's redemptive purposes and revelation that would ultimately culminate in the person of Christ (Matt 13:35; 25:34; John 17:24; Heb 4:3; 9:26; 1 Pet 1:20; Rev 17:8). In particular, Eph 1:4 refers to God having chosen his people from "before the foundation or creation of the world." Similarly, Rev 13:8 mentions the Lamb's book of life inscribed with the names of the elect, again "before the foundation of the world." See also Luke 11:50.

▸ **15.** Gender, Reproduction, Youth, Aging > CONCEIVE

SEE ALSO

▸ **33.** Architecture > FOUNDATION, LAY A FOUNDATION
themelios, themelioō

5. Old, New, First, Last

DECAY, WEAR OUT, GROW OBSELETE

palaioō παλαιόω 3822

palaioō is a verb found in four places with the meaning "grow old," "wear out." The term is used in relation to clothes and bags (or purses) in Luke 12:33; Heb 1:11. In Heb 8:13 ***palaioō*** refers metaphorically to the old covenant "becoming obsolete."

▸ **5.** Old, New, First, Last > OLD

SEE ALSO

▸ **21.** Die, Perish, Kill, Destroy > DECAY
diaphtheirō

FORMER, PREVIOUS

prōtos πρῶτος 4413

prōtos is a common adjective found over one hundred times with the predominant sense of "first," as well as several related nuances, throughout. In one context ***prōtos*** denotes "the former things" as having passed away, signifying the end of the earthly age (Rev 21:4).

▸ **7.** Quantity, Amount, Number, Size, Measure > FIRST
▸ **31.** Kingdom, Empire, Rule, Military, Warfare > CHIEF

proteros πρότερος 4387

proteros is a comparative adjectival form meaning "former" in three places. Eph 4:22 refers to the "former" (i.e., previous) way of life of the Ephesians. The sense of "previous" is also evident in the phrase "former days" in Heb 10:32. 1 Pet 1:14 refers to the passions of one's "former" ignorance.

LAST

eschatos ἔσχατος 2078

eschatos is an adjectival form occurring around fifty times, with the predominant meaning "last" in both a temporal and spatial sense, as well as referring to that of lowest status.

In the sense of "last," indicating the final element in a significant series, personal or impersonal, ***eschatos*** is found in a number of places. Matt 5:26; Luke 12:59 record, for example, the "last penny" of a debt. 1 Cor 15:52 refers to the "last trumpet" as the prelude to the return of Jesus Christ at the end of the age. And, in 1 Cor 15:26, Paul declares that the "last enemy" to be destroyed is death. With reference to people, ***eschatos*** is found in 1 Cor 15:8, referring to Paul as "the last of the apostles." The term also refers to Christ, who is described in 1 Cor 15:45 as "the last Adam." Finally, in this particular sense, ***eschatos*** occurs in Rev 1:11, 17; 2:8; 22:13, where the risen Christ refers to himself as "the first and the last." Other mundane references to "last" in this sense are found in Matt 20:8ff.; John 7:37; 8:9.

eschatos also indicates the meaning "last" in the sense of a final stage in a process. For example, in Matt 12:45, Jesus declares that if a man, having had demons removed from his person, does not have that spiritual void replaced by the Spirit of God (by implication), then his "last state" will be worse than the first. See also Matt 27:64; 2 Pet 2:20. Then, in Rev 15:1; 21:9, the "last seven" angelic plagues of judgment against the earth are declared to be the completion of God's wrath against the wickedness of humankind.

Perhaps the most significant use of ***eschatos*** in this sense is found in the expression "the last day," indicating the final stage of divine judgment against humankind (John 6:39ff.; 11:24; 12:48). Similarly, the phrase "in the last days" refers to the final period of human history before the consummation, resulting in eternal blessing for the righteous and condemnation for the wicked (Acts 2:17; 2 Tim 3:1; Heb 1:2; Jas 5:3; 1 Pet 1:5, 20; 2 Pet 3:3; 1 John 2:18; Jude 18).

eschatos also means "last" in the sense of rank, or status. Commonly, reference is made to the reversal of status in the sight of God with the declaration, "the first shall be last, and the last shall be first" (Matt 19:30; Luke 11:26).

NEW, NEWNESS

kainos καινός 2537

kainos is an adjectival form occurring in about forty contexts with the exclusive meaning "new" in both mundane and highly significant contexts.

kainos indicates the meaning "new" primarily in the sense of "fresh." With regard to material substances and objects, the term refers to new wine and wineskins (Mark 2:22; Matt 9:17; Luke 5:38); a new tomb (Matt 27:60; John 19:41); and a fresh patch of material used to cover a tear in an old wineskin (Mark 2:21; Luke 5:36). See also Matt 13:52. New tongues, or languages, are indicated in Mark 1:6, 17.

The remaining uses of ***kainos*** are found in passages of distinctive theological significance, especially in relation to the "new" phenomena associated with the coming of the new covenant age as embodied in the person and work of Christ. The wine of the Passover feast as celebrated by Jesus with his disciples on the evening prior to his crucifixion is declared to represent the blood of the "new covenant," which Jesus is soon to inaugurate (Luke 22:20; 1 Cor 11:25). Paul refers to believers as "ministers of the new covenant" in 2 Cor 3:6. The new covenant itself, as a fulfillment of the old, is indicated in Heb 8:8, 13; 9:15. Associated with this centrally important phenomenon is the affirmation of the believer's "new creation" in Christ in 2 Cor 5:17; Gal 6:15. The emergence of the "new man," Christ Jesus, who has brought together Jew and Gentile in peace, is indicated in Eph 2:15. The anticipated fulfillment of "the new heavens and new earth" is noted in 2 Pet 3:13; Rev 21:1. The emergence of the "new Jerusalem" coming down out of heaven is described in Rev 3:12; 21:2. Rev 21:5 refers to making "all things new."

Elsewhere, the "new song" in worship of God and the Lamb is mentioned in Rev 5:9; 14:3. The "new name" promised to believers is indicated in Rev 2:17. The "new nature" of the believer is affirmed in Eph 4:24.

Jesus issues his "new command" to love one another in John 13:34. This command is referred to elsewhere in 1 John 2:7, 8; 2 John 5.

kainos is also translated "new" in the sense of "different" in Mark 1:27; Acts 17:19, where it refers to "new doctrine."

The term is also used adverbially in Matt 26:29; Mark 14:25, where it is translated "anew," with the sense of "once more" or "again."

kainotēs καινότης 2538

kainotēs is the noun from which ***kainos*** (above) is derived. The term occurs only twice, in Rom 6:4; 7:6. In both contexts, ***kainotēs*** refers to the new quality of life granted to the believer as the consequence of coming to faith in Christ. Rom 7:6 speaks of the "newness" of life; and Rom 7:6 refers to the "new life" of the Spirit.

neos νέος 3501

neos is an adjective found in approximately twenty places meaning "new," "young(er)." The former meaning occurs in about half of these contexts. The term is occasionally used in a nominal sense.

The meaning "new" in the sense of "fresh" is applied to wine in Matt 9:17; Mark 2:22; Luke 5:37ff.; and to the covenant in Heb 12:24, where Jesus is depicted as the mediator of a new covenant.

In metaphorical contexts, ***neos*** refers to the believer's desired spiritual condition in 1 Cor 5:7, where he is likened to a "new" batch of dough, uncontaminated by the leaven (or yeast) of sinfulness. Col 3:10 refers to one's "new nature" in Christ. Here the term "nature" is included in the term ***neos*** itself (there is no accompanying noun in the text).

▸ **15.** Gender, Reproduction, Youth, Aging > YOUNG, YOUNGER, YOUNGEST

prosphatos πρόσφατος 4372

prosphatos is an adjective that occurs only once, in Heb 10:20, referring to the "new" and living way opened up by Christ to peace with God through his sacrifice on the cross.

SEE ALSO

▸ **35.** Clothing, Adornment, Textiles > NEW, UNSHRUNK *agnaphos*

▸ **40.** Holy Days, Feasts, Festivals > NEW MOON *neomēnia*

OLD

palaios παλαιός 3820

palaios is an adjective found nineteen times in all, with the consistent meaning "old," in the sense of "worn (out)," "aged," "former."

The meaning "worn (out)" is applied to "old" articles of clothing in Matt 9:11; Mark 2:21; Luke 5:36. The description "old" in the sense of "aged" is applied to wine bottles (Matt 9:17; Mark 2:22; Luke 5:37); to wine (Luke 5:39); and also to personal valuables (Matt 13:52).

The phrase "old man" in Rom 6:6; Eph 4:22; Col 3:9 refers to one's former sinful nature prior to conversion, as does the description "old leaven" in 1 Cor 5:7, 8. The "old covenant" is referred to in 2 Cor 3:14 with this nuance of "former," as is the "old commandment" in 1 John 2:7.

palaioō παλαιόω 3822

palaioō is the verb from which the adjective ***palaios*** (above) is derived. ***palaioō*** means "to grow old" and is found in only three places. In Luke 12:33 it refers to money bags "growing old." Heb 1:11 refers to the heavens and the earth "growing old," or moving to a state of decay. And in Heb 8:13, the writer refers to the old covenant "growing old," or becoming obsolete, giving way to the emergence of the new covenant age.

▸ **5.** Old, New, First, Last > DECAY, WEAR OUT, GROW OBSELETE

gēraskō γηράσκω 1095

gēraskō is a verb synonymous with ***palaioō*** (above) and means "grow old." ***gēraskō*** is also rare, occurring only twice. In John 21:18 it refers to a man being old; and in Heb 8:13 the term indicates the process whereby the old covenant is "growing old" and is ready to disappear.

SEE ALSO

▸ **15.** Gender, Reproduction, Youth, Aging > OLD *presbytēs, gēras, gerōn*

OLD, ANCIENT, FORMER

archaios ἀρχαῖος 744

archaios is an adjective found in twelve contexts meaning "old," "ancient." It also has the adverbial sense of "from old" or "long ago."

The adverbial sense of ***archaios*** is found in Matt 5:21; 27:33 with reference to people from former times, "of old." It is used similarly in Acts 15:7, 21 with reference to "days of old."

As an adjective, ***archaios*** is found in Luke 9:8, 19 with reference to "old prophets" in the sense of "former prophets." Mnason of Cyprus is literally described in Acts 21:16 as an "old disciple," yet the term here indicates that he was an "early disciple," or one of the first group. The "old" or "ancient world" is noted in 2 Pet 2:5 in connection with the generation of Noah's day that was destroyed by the great flood. The "ancient serpent," indicating the guise of Satan, is mentioned in Rev 12:9; 20:2. In 2 Cor 5:17, Paul affirms that the "old has passed away . . . ," indicating that the former era of the old covenant has gone forever, and that in its place the new has come, inaugurated through the person and work of Christ.

SEE ALSO

▸ **15.** Gender, Reproduction, Youth, Aging > OLD *presbytēs, gēras, gerōn*

6. Location, Position, Direction, Extension

BROAD, BREADTH, WIDE, WIDTH

eurychōros εὐρύχωρος 2149

eurychōros is a rare adjective denoting "broad" or "wide," used metaphorically in Matt 7:13 to describe the way to eternal destruction.

platynō πλατύνω 4115

platynō is a verb found three times with the meaning "to enlarge," "widen," or "make wide." In Matt 23:5 the term describes the phylacteries worn by the religious leaders of the Jews. It is used symbolically in 2 Cor 6:11ff. in a plea to "widen" one's heart, or cultivate a generous spirit.

platos πλάτος 4114

platos is a noun denoting "breadth," "width." It is used in Eph 3:18 to depict the extent of God's love. In Rev 20:9; 21:16 it describes the dimensions of the heavenly city of Jerusalem.

CORNER, CORNERSTONE

gōnia γωνία 1137

gōnia is a noun denoting a "corner" in a variety of contexts. The "corner" of a street is noted in Matt 6:5.

The "chief cornerstone" of a building, referring metaphorically to the Messiah, is indicated in Matt 21:42; Mark 12:10; Luke 20:17; Acts 4:11; 1 Pet 2:7.

The phrase "things done in a corner," in Acts 26:26, indicates secrecy.

The expression "four corners of the earth," denoting universal extent, is recorded in Rev 7:1; 20:8.

SEE ALSO

▸ **35.** Clothing, Adornment, Textiles > CORNER
archē

DEEP, DEPTH

bathos βάθος 899

bathos is a noun found in nine contexts, with an adjectival as well as a nominal force.

The term denotes "deep water" in a literal sense in Luke 5:4. "Deep" (i.e., extreme) poverty is indicated in 2 Cor 8:2.

Metaphorically, ***bathos*** refers in Rom 8:39 to the unlimited "depth" of the protection offered to believers by the love of God. Similarly, the term denotes the immeasurable "depth" of God's love in Eph 3:18, and the "depth" of his wisdom in Rom 11:33. The incomprehensible "deep things" of God are indicated in 1 Cor 2:10; and by contrast the "deep secrets" of Satan are noted in Rev 2:24.

bathys βαθύς 901

bathys is an adjectival form found only three times, denoting a "deep" well in John 4:11; and a "deep" sleep in Acts 20:9.

bathynō βαθύνω 900

bathynō is a rare verb found only in Luke 6:48, meaning "dig deep" in relation to the foundation of a house.

pelagos πέλαγος 3989

pelagos is a rare noun denoting the "depth" of the sea in Matt 18:6.

SEE ALSO

▸ **21.** Die, Perish, Kill, Destroy > GRAVE, TOMB
abyssos

DOWN

katō κάτω 2736

katō is an adverbial form meaning "down" in about half of its eleven occurrences. In vain, Satan commands Christ to "throw himself down" from the pinnacle of the temple in Matt 4:6; Luke 4:9. John 8:6 describes Jesus "stooping down" to write in the dust. The act of "falling down" is noted in Acts 20:9.

EAST

anatolē ἀνατολή 395

anatolē is a noun denoting the direction "east" throughout most of its ten occurrences.

Matt 2:1 refers to the "east" as the direction from which the wise men had come in order to pay homage to the infant Jesus. The star which had been the initial indicator of the birth of Christ to the magi was first seen by them in "the east" (Matt 2:2, 9). Other references to the east include Matt 8:11; 24:27; Luke 13:29; Rev 7:2; 16:12; 21:13.

END, TIP

peras πέρας 4009

peras is a noun found in four places, three of which indicate the meaning "end" as part of the expression "the uttermost ends of the earth" (Matt 12:42; Luke 11:31; Rom 10:18).

akron ἄκρον 206

akron is a noun found in four places meaning "end," "tip," or "point."

In two places, the term refers to the remote corners of the earth, or "the ends" of the earth (Matt 24:31; Mark 13:27). Luke 16:24 refers to the "tip" of a finger; and Heb 11:21 to the "end" of a staff.

SEE ALSO

▸ **4.** Beginning, Continuing, Finishing, Postponing > END, BRING TO AN END
telos, synteleō, synteleia

FAR, DISTANT

makros μακρός 3117

makros is a rare adjective meaning "far" in the sense of "distant" countries in Luke 15:13; 19:12.

▸ **6.** Location, Position, Direction, Extension > LONG, LENGTH, FAR

makran μακράν 3112

makran is an adverb meaning "far," "far off," "far away."

The meaning "far off" in the sense of "some distance away" is indicated in Matt 8:30.

The state of "not being far" from the kingdom of heaven is noted in Mark 12:34 in reference to one's spiritual proximity to peace with God. The contrary sense of being "far away" from God is indicated in several places, each of them affirming that such people would be brought near to Yahweh through faith and repentance (Acts 2:39; Eph 2:13, 17). God is described as "not being far away" from his people in Acts 17:27.

The sense of "far away" in a physical, literal sense is indicated in Luke 7:6; 15:20; John 21:8; Acts 22:21.

HIGH, HEIGHT

hypsos ὕψος 5311

hypsos occurs six times and refers to "height" or "high" as both a measurement and the exalted position of rank, in relation to God and human beings.

The phrase "on high," indicating a heavenly origin, is found in Luke 1:78 concerning a visitation of God. In Luke 24:49, Jesus promises the gift of the Holy Spirit as a divine endowment after the risen Christ ascends into heaven and returns to his Father. Concerning the ascension of our Lord, Eph 4:8 refers to Jesus ascending "on high" and taking captivity captive — a probable reference to Christ's destruction of his spiritual enemies through his atoning death on the cross.

In Paul's prayer for the Ephesians, he attempts to describe the character of Christ's love and asks that they may know the height of that love along with its other "dimensions" (Eph 3:18).

Rev 21:16 describes the height of the wall of the heavenly city. In Jas 1:9, the writer refers to an "exalted" standing of social privilege.

hypsōma ὕψωμα 5313

This term is also rare, found only twice. On both occasions it means "height" or "elevation" in a metaphorical sense. Rom 8:39 indicates that which can never separate one from the love of Christ — "neither height nor depth nor anything else in all of creation." 2 Cor 10:5 speaks of every "high thing," in the sense of arrogance or pride, that opposes the knowledge of God.

hypsēlos ὑψηλός 5308

hypsēlos is an adjective indicating that which is "high," "lofty" in a literal sense. It is also used metaphorically to describe people and things as "exalted" in the sense of an eminent rank or position. The term occurs eleven times.

The literal sense of "high" in relation to a mountain is found in several places (Matt 4:8; 17:1; Mark 9:2; Luke 4:5; Rev 21:10). Rev 21:12 also refers to the high wall of the heavenly city of Jerusalem.

The designation "highly esteemed" (i.e., among people) is found in Luke 16:15, in a negative context of judgment against human pride. Similarly, Rom 12:16 contains the injunction not to be proud, or haughty.

In relation to God, ***hypsēlos*** refers to his "high (i.e., uplifted) arm" in Acts 13:7. This is a reference to divine power with respect to God's action in delivering his people from their Egyptian bondage.

hypsistos ὕψιστος 5310

hypsistos is a superlative adjectival form, referring literally to the "highest" places or regions and also to the rank of God as "most high" or "highest." The word is found thirteen times.

As a title for God, ***hypsistos*** occurs in Mark 5:7; Luke 1:32, 33, 76; 6:35; 8:28; Acts 7:48; 16:17; Heb 7:1.

The term also designates heaven as the "highest (of all regions)" (Matt 21:9; Mark 11:10; Luke 2:14; 19:38). These texts all express praise to God through the person of Christ.

LEFT, LEFT HAND, LEFT SIDE

aristeros ἀριστερός 710

aristeros is an adjective found in only three places, all referring to the direction "left." Matt 6:3 refers metaphorically to the attitude of giving with pure motive, "not letting your left hand know what your right hand is doing." Luke 23:33 indicates placing two criminals next to Christ on the hill of Golgotha, one on his right and one on his left. 2 Cor 6:7 refers metaphorically to God's weapons of righteousness in both one's left and right hands.

euōnymos εὐώνυμος 2176

euōnymos is synonymous with ***aristeros*** (above) and occurs ten times.

Matt 20:21, 23; Mark 10:37, 40 describe being seated on the right and left of Jesus' throne in heaven. The placement of thieves on the left side of Jesus at his crucifixion is indicated in Matt 27:38; Mark 15:27. See also Acts 21:3; Rev 10:2. Significantly, placing "goats" on the "left-hand side" of Christ in Matt 25:33, 41 indicates that they (i.e., the wicked) are destined for judgment.

LONG, LENGTH, FAR

makros μακρός 3117

makros is an adjectival form that is translated "long," "far." The term occurs five times and means "long" in three of these places, all referring to the "long" self-righteous prayers of the Pharisees (Matt 23:14; Mark 12:40; Luke 20:47).

▸ **6.** Location, Position, Direction, Extension >
FAR, DISTANT

mēkos μῆκος 3372

mēkos is a noun that occurs only three times, meaning "length." Eph 3:18 refers metaphorically to the immeasurable "length, breadth, and height" of the love of Christ. In Rev 21:16, ***mēkos*** (twice) refers to the length of the heavenly city of Jerusalem.

NORTH

borras βορρᾶς 1005

borras is found only twice in the NT, referring once to the "north" as one of the directions from which people from all over the world will come to participate in the consummate feast of the kingdom of God at the end of the age (Luke 13:29). Rev 21:13 refers to the three gates situated on the north wall of the heavenly city of Jerusalem.

RIGHT, RIGHT HAND, RIGHT SIDE

dexios δεξιός 1188

dexios is the only term in the NT expressing the direction or position "right." It is adjectival in form, though it is also used as a noun, usually referring to the "right hand." ***dexios*** occurs around fifty times and is used both literally and metaphorically.

Literal, mundane references to "right" in relation to parts of the body are found in Matt 5:9, 30; 6:3; 27:29, 38; Luke 6:6; Acts 3:7. See also John 21:6; Luke 1:11.

More frequently, and with greater significance, ***dexios*** refers to the "right hand" as a position of honor and authority. It refers to human beings (Matt 20:21ff.; 22:44; 25:33ff.; Mark 10:37, 40; 12:36), as well as to the "right hand" of Christ himself and that of God as the supreme position of divine honor and authority (Matt 26:64; Mark 14:62; Luke 20:42; 22:69; Acts 2:25ff.; 7:55ff.; Rom 8:3; Eph 1:20; Col 3:1; Heb 1:3, 13; 10:12; 12:2; 1 Pet 3:22). The "right hand" of Christ in heaven is mentioned as part of the opening vision in Revelation (Rev 1:16ff.). See also Rev 2:1; 5:1; 10:2.

Rev 13:16 refers to the mark of the beast placed on the "right hand" and forehead of all who worship him.

In two places, ***dexios*** refers to the "right side." In Mark 16:5 it refers to the tomb of Christ, and in Luke 1:11 to the altar in the temple.

SEE ALSO

▸ **16.** Body, Bodily Functions > SIDE
pleura

WEST

dysmē δυσμή 1424

dysmē is a noun referring to the region of the west in a number of different contexts. It is found five times.

The expression "from east to west" indicates origins from all over the world (Matt 8:11; Luke 13:29). The region of the sunset is noted in Matt 24:27. A general reference to the west is found in Luke 12:54. The western gates of the heavenly city are indicated in Rev 21:13.

7. Quantity, Amount, Number, Size, Measure

ABOUND, INCREASE, EXCEED, OVERFLOW, ABUNDANCE

perisseuō περισσεύω 4052

perisseuō is a verb found in approximately forty places with the primary meaning "abound," as well as several related nuances.

"Abound," with the underlying sense of "increase in magnitude," is indicated with respect to God's glory in Rom 3:7; to God's grace in Rom 5:15; to thanksgiving to God in 2 Cor 4:15; Col 2:7; to the hope of salvation in Rom 15:13 and love in Phil 1:9; 1 Thess 3:12. The meaning "increase in number" is evident in Acts 16:5. The meaning "exceed" with the sense of "going beyond a fixed measure" is found in relation to Pharisaic righteousness in Matt 5:20. See also 2 Cor 3:9.

perisseuō also expresses the meaning "have abundance" (i.e., have a great deal). It occurs in Matt 13:12; 25:29 in relation to spiritual knowledge, and also in regard to material wealth in Matt 12:44; Luke 12:15; 21:4.

The meaning "excel," "achieve a high standard" is indicated in relation to the work of the Lord in 1 Cor 15:58, and to faith and love in 2 Cor 8:7.

- ▸ **7.** Quantity, Amount, Number, Size, Measure > EXCEED, EXCEEDINGLY
- ▸ **7.** Quantity, Amount, Number, Size, Measure > INCREASE, GROW
- ▸ **23.** Food, Drink, Cooking > SPARE
- ▸ **85.** Movement, Position, State > REMAIN, STAY, ABIDE, DWELL

perisseia περισσεία 4050

perisseia is a noun derived from ***perisseuō*** (above) found in four places and indicating an "abundance" of grace (Rom 5:17); joy (2 Cor 8:2); and wickedness (Jas 1:21). ***perisseia*** is used adverbially in 2 Cor 10:15, with the sense of "greatly."

perisseuma περίσσευμα 4051

perisseuma is a synonym for ***perisseia*** (above). It is found in five places, indicating the "abundance" of the heart in Matt 12:34; Luke 6:45. In 2 Cor 8:14 the term refers to "abundance," denoting material wealth. Mark 8:8 refers to bread that is "left over."

hyperperisseuō ὑπερπερισσεύω 5248

hyperperisseuō is a rare variant form of ***perisseuō*** (above) with the meaning "abound, exceed beyond all measure." The word expresses this sense in Rom 5:20 in relation to the grace of God. In 2 Cor 7:4 the term denotes "being filled (i.e., to overflowing)" with comfort.

perissos περισσός 4053

perissos is an adjectival form with the underlying adverbial sense of "more abundantly" (i.e., to a high degree, to the greatest extent). It is translated variously throughout the ten contexts in which it is found.

The meaning "more abundantly" is applied to the gaining of life through the person and work of Christ in John 10:10. In Eph 3:20 ***perissos*** refers to God's infinite capacity to act in ways that far exceed the limits of our imaginations.

Elsewhere ***perissos*** is translated "utterly," with reference to people's astonishment in Mark 6:51; "vehemently," in relation to the expression of anger in Mark 14:31; "very earnestly," in connection with prayer in 1 Thess 3:10; "very highly," with regard to the expression of esteem in 1 Thess 5:13. See also Matt 5:37, 47; Rom 3:1; 2 Cor 9:1.

- ▸ **72.** Need, Gain, Loss, Advantage, Seek, Find > ADVANTAGE, PROFIT

perissoteron περισσότερον 4054 4056

perissoteron is an adverbial comparative form with the sense of "more abundantly," "all the more," "far more," with related nuances. It is found in nearly twenty contexts (Mark 7:36; 15:14; 1 Cor 15:10; 2 Cor 2:4; 7:13ff.; 11:23; 12:15; Gal 1:14; 1 Thess 2:17; Heb 7:15; 13:19).

perissōs περισσῶς 4057

perissōs is an adverbial form derived from ***perissos*** (above) with the meaning "greatly," "exceedingly," "all the more" in all three of its occurrences (Matt 27:23; Mark 10:26; Acts 26:11).

hyperperissōs ὑπερπερισσῶς 5249

hyperperissōs is a rare adverbial variant of ***perissōs*** (above) with the meaning "exceedingly" or "beyond measure." It is found only in Mark 7:37, where it refers to people's astonishment at the miraculous cures Christ performed.

- ▸ **7.** Quantity, Amount, Number, Size, Measure > MEASURE, QUANTITY, STANDARD, CRITERION

pleonazō πλεονάζω 4121

pleonazō is a verb synonymous with ***perisseuō*** (above) with the meanings "abound," "increase" evident throughout its ten occurrences.

The phenomenon of "increasing" or "abounding" grace is indicated in Rom 5:20; 6:1; 2 Cor 4:15; as is the proliferation of sin in Rom 5:20. Reference to Christian virtues (i.e., "fruit") "increasing" in the life of the believer is made in Phil 4:17; 2 Pet 1:8, and to love in particular in 1 Thess 3:12; 2 Thess 1:3. See also 2 Cor 8:15.

- ▸ **7.** Quantity, Amount, Number, Size, Measure > INCREASE, GROW

hyperpleonazō ὑπερπλεονάζω 5250

hyperpleonazō is a rare variant form of ***pleonazō*** (above) found only in 1 Tim 1:14, with the meaning "overflow" (i.e., be exceedingly abundant).

plēthynō πληθύνω 4129

plēthynō is another synonym for the entries above. It is found in twelve places, with the consistent meanings of "multiply," "abound," or "increase."

The "increase" or "proliferation" of wickedness is indicated in Matt 24:12.

References to the growth or increase of the early church due to new converts are found in Acts 6:1, 7; 7:17; 9:31. Acts 12:24 refers to the "growth" or "spread" of God's word.

Heb 6:14 mentions the Abrahamic covenant promise in which God pledges to "multiply" the descendants of the patriarch.

The invoking of God's grace and peace, "multiplied" in the life of the believer, is noted in 1 Pet 1:2; 2 Pet 1:2; Jude 2. See also 2 Cor 9:10.

hyperbolē ὑπερβολή 5236

hyperbolē is a noun found in eight places variously translated as "abundance" or "exceeding(ly)."

The adverbial meaning "exceedingly" refers to the phenomenon of increased sin in Rom 7:13; to the experience of persecution in 2 Cor 1:8; Gal 1:13; to the anticipation of eternal glory in 2 Cor 4:17.

hyperbolē is also translated "more excellent" when it describes the way of salvation in 1 Cor 12:31. See also 2 Cor 4:7.

2 Cor 12:7 makes reference to the "abundance" of revelations given to the apostle Paul.

▸ **7.** Quantity, Amount, Number, Size, Measure > EXCEED, EXCEEDINGLY

plousiōs πλουσίως 4146

plousiōs is an adverbial form with the meaning "richly," "abundantly" evident in all four of its occurrences. Each reference indicates the granting of salvation by God as something rich and abundant (see 1 Tim 6:17; Titus 3:6; 2 Pet 1:11). In particular, Col 3:16 makes reference to the word of God dwelling "richly" in the life of the believer.

ADD, INCREASE

epitithēmi ἐπιτίθημι 2007

The verb ***epitithēmi*** is found in about fifty places with the predominant sense of "lay," "put," plus several related nuances. In Rev 22:18 the term is twice translated "add," referring to the warning "not to add" anything to the prophetic words of the book of Revelation, and also to the inevitable punishments that God would "add" to any who would do such a thing.

▸ **83.** Set, Put, Place, Prepare, Establish > PUT, PLACE, LAY

prostithēmi προστίθημι 4369

prostithēmi is a verb found in eighteen places, in several different contexts, with the meanings "add," "increase."

The term is predicated of God in Matt 6:33; Luke 12:31 where Christ declares that God will "add" material blessings to those who make the kingdom of God first priority in their lives. Elsewhere, both implicitly and explicitly, God is declared to be responsible for "adding" new converts to the fledgling Christian church (Acts 2:41, 47; 5:14; 11:24).

In non-personal contexts, Matt 6:27; Luke 12:25 affirm the impossibility of anyone "adding" to his or her own life span. Paul explains in Gal 3:19 that the law "was added" by God because of transgressions. Luke 3:20 describes the action of "adding" an extra transgression to one's list of sins. In Luke 17:5, the disciples appeal to Christ to "increase their faith."

▸ **7.** Quantity, Amount, Number, Size, Measure > INCREASE, GROW

prosanatithēmi προσανατίθημι 4323

prosanatithēmi is a rare variant form of ***prostithēmi*** (above) found in Gal 2:6, with reference to the rivals of the apostle Paul who, he declares, "added nothing" to his message.

epidiatassomai ἐπιδιατάσσομαι 1928

epidiatassomai is a rare verb found only in Gal 3:15, where the declaration is made that no one "adds" to a human covenant.

epichorēgeō ἐπιχορηγέω 2023

epichorēgeō is a verb found in five contexts with the sense of "furnish," "supply" in most of these. 2 Pet 1:5 contains the exhortation to "add" virtue to one's faith.

ALL, EACH, EVERY, WHOLE

pas πᾶς 3956

pas is an adjectival particle occurring over one thousand times, denoting "all," "each," "every" in relation to people and all sorts of non-personal phenomena (e.g., Matt 2:3ff.; Mark 4:11ff.; Luke 1:63ff.; John 3:15ff.; Acts 1:18ff.; 2:5; Rom 1:16; 3:2; 9:5ff.; 1 Cor 2:15; 2 Cor 8:7; Gal 3:8ff.; Eph 1:3; Phil 1:3ff.; Col 1:6ff.; 1 Thess 5:14ff.; 1 Tim 2:1ff.; 2 Tim 3:16; Heb 1:2ff.; Jas 3:7; 1 Pet 1:24; 1 John 1:7ff.; Rev 6:14; 13:7ff.).

hapas ἅπας 537

hapas is a variant adjectival form of ***pas*** (above) occurring around forty times with the primary meanings "all," "all things."

The word means "all," in a general descriptive sense, in Matt 24:39; Mark 16:5; Luke 4:6; 7:16; Acts 2:4, 44; 13:29; Jas 3:2.

The designation "all things" or "everything" is found in Matt 6:32; 28:11; Luke 2:39; Acts 2:44; 4:32; 10:8.

holos ὅλος 3650

holos is another synonym for the entries listed above, an adjective denoting "all," "whole" throughout the more than one hundred occurrences of the term (see, e.g., Matt 1:22; 4:23f.; 20:6; Mark 6:55; 12:30ff.; Luke 8:43; 13:21; Acts 2:2; 13:49; Rom 16:23; Gal 5:3; Jas 3:2ff.; Rev 13:3).

DECREASE, MAKE LOW

elattoō ἐλαττόω 1642

elattoō is a rare verb found in three places with the meaning "decrease" in relation to John the Baptist's declaration that the Christ must "increase" (i.e., become greater) and he must "decrease." In Heb 2:7, 9 the term refers to human beings, whom God "has made a little lower" than the angels.

DOUBLE, DOUBLE-MINDED

diplous διπλοῦς 1362

diplous is an adjective meaning "double" in 1 Tim 5:17, referring to elders worthy of "double honor." Rev 18:6 refers to the divine sentence passed on Babylon, who will receive "double repayment" for her sins.

diploō διπλόω 1363

diploō is a verb signifying "to double," "to repay or render twofold" (Rev 18:6).

dipsychos δίψυχος 1374

dipsychos is a rare adjective referring to those who are "double-minded," signifying emotional and spiritual immaturity (Jas 1:8; 4:8).

▸ **47.** Show, Persuade, Confidence, Doubt > UNCERTAIN, DOUBLE-MINDED

EIGHT, EIGHTEEN, EIGHTH

oktō ὀκτώ 3638

oktō is a term denoting the cardinal number "eight" (or "eighteen," when accompanied by *deka*, "ten," in the phrase *deka kai oktō*, lit., "ten and eight") in nine places. Reference to the first eight-day period of an infant boy's life leading to his ritual circumcision is noted in Luke 2:21. A period of eight days is indicated in Luke 9:28; John 20:26. 1 Pet 3:20 refers to the eight members of Noah's family saved from the flood. Luke 13:4 mentions the "eighteen" people killed in the collapse of the Tower of Siloam. See also Luke 13:11, 18; John 5:5; Acts 9:33.

ogdoos ὄγδοος 3590

ogdoos is the term for the ordinal number "eighth" in five places. The "eighth" day in relation to the ritual of circumcision is noted in Luke 1:59; Acts 7:8. See also 2 Pet 2:5; Rev 17:11; 21:20.

oktaēmeros ὀκταήμερος 3637

oktaēmeros is a rare adjectival form of ***ogdoos*** (above) found only in Phil 3:5, with reference to Paul's claim to Jewish orthodoxy in respect of his being circumcised on the "eighth" day.

EMPTY, EMPTY-HANDED

kenoō κενόω 2758

kenoō is a verb found in five places with the underlying metaphorical sense of "to render null and void," "be in vain." In several places ***kenoō*** is translated "to empty" with these symbolic meanings.

Rom 4:14 affirms that if eternal life were ever to be gained through obedience to the law, faith would be rendered "null and void," or "emptied" of its effect and importance. Similarly, 1 Cor 1:17 claims that the cross of Christ would run the risk of "being emptied of its power," should the preaching of the gospel ever be grounded in human wisdom, and be received accordingly by its hearers as mere folly. Of particular significance is the statement in Phil 2:7 that Christ "emptied himself" by taking the form of a man and becoming a servant of humankind in accordance with God's purposes.

This "emptying" centers on the willingness of Christ to voluntarily put aside his status as a heavenly, divine figure and to assume a full human identity so that he might accomplish God's redemptive purpose in gaining salvation for humankind. See also 1 Cor 9:15; 2 Cor 9:3, which mention the futility of boasting, "to render it void."

▸ **53.** Value, Worth > VAIN, MAKE VAIN, MAKE VOID

kenos κενός 2756

kenos is an adjectival form derived from ***kenoō*** (above) found eighteen times with the primary sense of "vain," "futile." In several places, however, ***kenos*** also means "empty-handed," or lacking in property and/or wealth (Mark 12:3; Luke 1:53; 20:10, 11).

▸ **53.** Value, Worth > VAIN, MAKE VAIN, MAKE VOID

EXCEED, EXCEEDINGLY

perisseuō περισσεύω 4052

perisseuō is a verb found nearly forty times with the principal meaning "abound," as well as related nuances.

The meaning "exceed" in the sense of "be greater than" is indicated in Matt 5:20, referring to the need for a person's righteousness to "exceed" that of the Pharisees.

▸ **7.** Quantity, Amount, Number, Size, Measure > ABOUND, INCREASE, EXCEED, OVERFLOW, ABUNDANCE

▸ **7.** Quantity, Amount, Number, Size, Measure > INCREASE, GROW

▸ **23.** Food, Drink, Cooking > SPARE

▸ **85.** Movement, Position, State > REMAIN, STAY, ABIDE, DWELL

hyperbolē ὑπερβολή 5236

hyperbolē is found in eight places, with an adjectival and adverbial sense as well as a nominal one.

The meaning "exceedingly" or "beyond measure" is used in relation to the divine commandment that provoked a sinful response in the apostle Paul (Rom 7:13). Gal 1:13 refers to Saul persecuting the early Christians "violently," or with excessive force. 2 Cor 1:8 refers to the "exceedingly" great force of the apostle's affliction. 2 Cor 4:7 refers to the "all-surpassing" power of God; and 2 Cor 4:17 to the glory of God that "far outweighs" everything else.

hyperbolē is translated nominally in 2 Cor 12:7 with reference to "the abundance" of revelations given to the apostle Paul.

▸ **7.** Quantity, Amount, Number, Size, Measure > ABOUND, INCREASE, EXCEED, OVERFLOW, ABUNDANCE

SEE ALSO

▸ **52.** Status, Identity, Reputation, Honor, Shame > EXCEL, EXCELLENT
kratistos, prōteuō, philoprōteuō

▸ **53.** Value, Worth > EXCEL, EXCELLENT
hyperballō, diaphoros

FEW, LITTLE, SMALL

oligos ὀλίγος 3641

oligos is an adjective meaning "few," "little," "small" for most of its nearly forty occurrences.

The meaning "few," denoting "a small number," is used in relation to people in Matt 7:14; 22:14; Luke 13:23 in the context of the comparatively small number who find true salvation and peace with God. In particular, Noah and his family are described as the "few" who were saved from the great flood in 1 Pet 3:20. Other general references include Matt 9:37; Mark 6:5; Rev 3:4.

"Few" is used in a non-personal way in Matt 15:34; Mark 8:7; Luke 10:2; 12:48; Acts 17:4; Rev 2:14, 20.

▸ **7.** Quantity, Amount, Number, Size, Measure > LITTLE, SMALL, LEAST, FEW

FILL, FILL UP, FULFILL, BE FULL, BE FILLED

plēroō πληρόω 4137

plēroō is a common verb found in nearly one hundred places with the principal meaning "fulfill." Other meanings of ***plēroō*** include "fill," "be full."

Christ tells the Pharisees to "fill up" the measure of the sins of their forefathers — an exhortation to maintain their hypocritical stance and thereby bring upon themselves the wrath of God (Matt 23:32).

The state of "being filled" with wisdom is predicated of Christ in Luke 2:40; being "filled" with emotion in John 16:6; Acts 13:52; Rom 15:13; 2 Tim 1:4; being "filled with the fullness" of God's Spirit in Eph 3:19; 5:18; and being "filled" with righteousness in Phil 1:11. Metaphorical reference to the "filling" of a valley is indicated in Luke 3:5. The "filling" of Ananias' heart with Satan is noted in Acts 5:3.

plēroō also means "be full" in several places. Matt 13:48 refers to a net "full" of fish. John 15:11; 16:24; 1 John 1:4; 2 John 12 all contain the wish that people's joy "may be made complete" (lit., "full").

See also John 12:3; Acts 2:2; 5:28; Rom 1:29; 15:14; 2 Cor 7:4; Eph 4:10; Col 1:9.

▸ **84.** Do, Make, Accomplish, Occur > CARRY OUT, COMPLETE, FULFILL, ACCOMPLISH

anaplēroō ἀναπληρόω 378

anaplēroō is a variant form of ***plēroō*** (above) found in six places and meaning "fulfill," "fill up" in three of these.

In 1 Thess 2:16 Paul declares that his Jewish detractors "fill up" their sins by hindering his efforts to evangelize the Gentiles.

▸ **84.** Do, Make, Accomplish, Occur > CARRY OUT, COMPLETE, FULFILL, ACCOMPLISH

symplēroō συμπληρόω 4845

symplēroō is another rare variant of ***plēroō*** (above) and refers to boats "filling up" with water in Luke 8:23.

empimplēmi ἐμπίπλημι 1705

empimplēmi is a verb meaning "fill," "be full" in most of its six occurrences.

Luke 1:53 refers to God "filling" the hungry with good things. Other references to people being "full" with food are found in Luke 6:25; John 6:12. Acts 14:17 refers metaphorically to God "satisfying" or "filling" people's hearts with food and gladness.

chortazō χορτάζω 5526

chortazō is a verb found in sixteen places with the consistent senses of "satisfy," "fill," "be full," in both a literal and metaphorical sense.

Matt 5:6; Luke 6:21; 9:17 affirm that those who earnestly desire righteousness "shall be satisfied."

The physical state of "being filled" with food is noted in Matt 14:20; Mark 6:42; John 6:26; Phil 4:12; Jas 2:16. Other references to "feeding" people include those in Matt 15:33; Mark 8:4; Luke 16:21. Birds "gorged" with flesh are described in Rev 19:21.

gemizō γεμίζω 1072

gemizō is a verb with the consistent sense of "fill," "fill up" in each of its six occurrences.

Reference to boats "filling" with water is found in Mark 4:37. A sponge was "filled" with vinegar before it was offered to Christ on the cross is noted in Mark 15:36. "Filling" a house with people is indicated in Luke 14:23. "Filling" baskets with leftover food after Jesus' miraculous feeding of the multitude is recorded in John 6:13. See also John 2:7.

In visionary contexts, ***gemizō*** denotes "filling" a censer with fire from the heavenly altar in Rev 8:5; and "filling" the temple with smoke in Rev 15:8.

mestoō μεστόω 3325

mestoō is a rare verb found only in Acts 2:13, referring to the false claim that the apostles "were full" of new wine, as observers mistook their Spirit-filled state for drunkenness.

plēthō πλήθω 4130

plēthō is a verb found nearly thirty times with the primary meaning "to fill."

"Filling" a sponge with vinegar and offering it to Christ on the cross to ease his pain is described in Matt 27:48; John 19:29. "Filling" boats with fish is indicated in Luke 5:7.

The state of "being filled" with the Spirit is indicated in Luke 1:15, 41, 67; Acts 2:4; 4:8, 31; 9:17; 13:9.

plēthō is also used metaphorically to mean "to be filled" with anger (Luke 4:28; 6:11); with awe (Luke 5:26; Acts 3:10); with jealousy (Acts 5:17; 13:45). Acts 19:29 refers to a city "filled" with confusion.

▸ **4.** Beginning, Continuing, Finishing, Postponing > FINISH, COMPLETE, FULFILL, BRING TO AN END, COME TO AN END

plērēs πλήρης 4134

plērēs is an adjective with the consistent meaning "full," "filled up" throughout its seventeen occurrences.

The literal sense of "full" is indicated in relation to baskets of food scraps in Matt 14:20; 15:37; Mark 6:43; 8:19; and to the ripe ear of grain in Mark 4:28. A diseased man is described as "full" of leprosy in Luke 5:12.

Luke 4:1 refers to Jesus being "full" of the Holy Spirit prior to his temptation in the wilderness. Christ is also described as being "full" of grace and truth in John 1:14.

Believers are depicted as "full" of the Holy Spirit in Acts 6:3ff.; 7:55; 11:24. Other contexts refer to people being "full" of a particular quality. Dorcas is described as a woman "full of good works" (Acts 9:36); Elymas the sorcerer as one "full of deceit" (Acts 13:10); a crowd as "full of wrath" (Acts 19:28). See also 2 John 8.

mestos μεστός 3324

mestos is an adjective found eight times with the consistent meaning "full," in both personal and impersonal contexts.

A bowl "full" of vinegar is noted in John 19:29; a net "full" of fish in John 21:11.

People "full" of hypocrisy are indicated in Matt 23:28; those "full" of envy in Rom 1:29; and those "full" of adultery in 2 Pet 2:14. The human tongue is designated as "full" of evil in Jas 3:8. Conversely, divine wisdom is said to be "full" of mercy; and the Roman believers are said to be "full" of goodness.

gemō γέμω 1073

gemō is a verb found in eleven places with the consistent meaning "to be full."

Christ condemns the Pharisees for "being full" of greed and wickedness in Matt 23:25; Luke 11:39. In a similar context, the Pharisees are likened to whitewashed tombs in Matt 23:27. The mouth of the wicked is said to "be full" of cursing and bitterness in Rom 3:14.

Elsewhere, ***gemō*** is found in the figurative context of the book of Revelation. The heavenly creatures surrounding the throne of God are described as "being full of eyes," both front and back, in Rev 4:6, 8. Rev 5:8 refers to bowls "full of incense" held by the twenty-four elders surrounding the throne. See also Rev 15:7; 17:3ff.; 21:9.

FIRST

prōtos πρῶτος 4413

prōtos is the standard adjectival form in the NT denoting the sense of "first" for most of the hundred or so occurrences of the term.

The designation "first" in the context of a sequence is indicated in Matt 10:2; Mark 12:20; John 8:7; 1 Cor 15:45ff.; Phil 1:5. In particular the "first" (i.e., old) covenant is discussed in Heb 8:7ff.; 9:15ff.; Rev 2:4ff.; 20:5ff.; 21:1, 19.

The meaning "first" in the sense of a "former" state is noted in Matt 12:45; 27:64; Luke 11:26. The temporal sense of "former" is evident in Matt 21:31; Acts 1:1.

The state of being "first" in the sense of "most important" is noted in the paradoxical truth affirming that "the first shall be last, and the last first" in Matt 19:30; Mark 9:35; Luke 13:30. See also Matt 20:27; Acts 16:12. Matt 22:38; Mark 12:28ff. refer to the "first" (i.e., the chief) commandment as the requirement to love God with all one's heart. See also Acts 25:2.

The heavenly Christ is described in Rev 1:17 as "the first and the last," signifying his omnipotent authority (see also Rev 2:8; 22:13).

▸ **5.** Old, New, First, Last > FORMER, PREVIOUS

▸ **31.** Kingdom, Empire, Rule, Military, Warfare > CHIEF

mia μία 3391

mia denotes the cardinal sense of "one" for most of its nearly eighty occurrences. Several contexts, however, indicate the sense of "first."

The meaning "first" in relation to a time sequence is indicated in Matt 28:1; Mark 16:2; Luke 24:1; John 20:1, 19; Acts 20:7; 1 Cor 16:2, all with reference to the "first" day of the week.

FOUR, FORTY

tessares τέσσαρες 5064

tessares is an adjectival form denoting the number "four" in about forty places.

The expression "four winds" denotes the full extent of the world in a geographic sense (Matt 24:31; Mark 13:27).

Mundane usage is indicated, for example, in Matt 13:27; Luke 2:37; John 11:17; Acts 10:11; 27:29.

The usage of the term in the book of Revelation is entirely symbolic. The number "four" suggests completeness or entirety — for example, the "four living creatures" surrounding the throne of God indicate a complete symbolic protection (Rev 4:6ff.; 5:6ff.; 6:1ff.; 7:11; 14:3; 15:7; 19:4). The "four winds" symbolically denote the universal extent of divine judgment in Rev 7:1.

The number 144,000 symbolically indicates the entirety of God's people in Rev 7:4; 14:13. Rev 9:13ff. mentions the "four angels" set aside as instruments of divine judgment against wicked humankind. See also Rev 20:8.

tessarakonta τεσσαράκοντα 5062

tessarakonta denotes "forty" in approximately twenty places.

The significant reference to Jesus' forty-day period of temptation in the desert is found in Matt 4:2; Mark 1:13; Luke 4:2. Other notable symbolic references to the number forty are found in Rev 7:4; 14:1ff., in relation to the metaphor of the 144,000 constituting the elect of God. See also Rev 11:2; 13:5; 21:17. References to Israel's forty-year wandering in the wilderness are found in Acts 7:36, 42; Heb 3:9, 17.

Other mundane references to the number forty include those in John 2:20; Acts 1:3; 4:22; 23:13, 21; 2 Cor 11:24.

FULLNESS, FULFILLMENT

plērōma πλήρωμα 4138

plērōma is a noun meaning "fullness," "fulfillment" in most of its seventeen occurrences.

The sense of "fullness" indicates that which contains a full measure, something abundant and ample, or vast. The term is used in relation to God's grace (John 1:16); to the blessing of Christ (Rom 15:29); to God's universal possession (1 Cor 10:26ff.); to the fullness of his presence (Eph 1:23); and to the fullness of his being (Eph 3:19; Col 1:19). In particular, the "fullness" of Christ's person and authority is indicated in Eph 4:13. The "fullness" of God's divine nature is said to dwell in Christ in Col 2:9. The "fullness" of Christ's blessing in relation to the gift of salvation is noted in Rom 15:29.

A significant use of ***plērōma*** is found in Rom 11:12, 25, where it is translated "fullness" in relation to the Gentiles. It signifies the full extent of their conversion from paganism to faith in Christ in accordance with his redemptive purposes, and constitutes a catalyst for God's intent to redeem "all Israel." In the broader context of NT teaching on the end times, the "fullness of the Gentiles" signals the ushering in of the climactic new heavens and the new earth.

Love is said to be the "fulfillment" of the law in Gal 4:4.

There is another use of ***plērōma*** in Gal 4:4; Eph 1:10 — texts containing the phrase the "fullness of time." In these contexts, "fullness" denotes "fulfillment," referring to the completion of God's redemptive purposes founded on the person of Christ.

▸ **84.** Do, Make, Accomplish, Occur >
CARRY OUT, COMPLETE, FULFILL, ACCOMPLISH

GREAT, ABUNDANT, SUPREME, LOUD, LARGE

megas μέγας 3173

megas is the predominant adjectival term signifying "great" in the NT, with a variety of nuances in a number of contexts. ***megas*** occurs nearly two hundred times.

The designation "great" in the sense of "abundant" is noted in relation to joy (Matt 2:10; Luke 2:10; Acts 15:3); to the "light" of salvation (Matt 4:16a); and to faith (Matt 15:28).

The meaning "great" in relation to a position of "supreme importance," "honor," or "standing" is evident in connection with the kingdom of God (Matt 5:19; 20:26); and the law commandments (Matt 22:36ff.). "Greatness" in the sight of God is indicated in Luke 1:15, 32. General references to "great men" include that in Mark 10:42. God is described as the "great" king in Matt 5:35. Conversely, Acts 19:27ff. refers to the Greek goddess Diana. Jesus Christ is designated as our "great God and Savior" (Titus 2:13) and as our "great high priest" (Heb 4:14). Rev 17:5 refers to the symbolic incarnation of evil, "Babylon the Great" (see also Rev 18:10ff.).

megas indicates physical enormity in Matt 8:24; Mark 4:37; Luke 21:11; Rev 6:12. Rev 20:1 refers to God's "great white throne."

The meaning "great" in the qualitative sense of "supreme," "to a large extent," is indicated with reference to the destruction of a house (Luke 6:49); to persecution and distress (Luke 21:23; Acts 8:1); to the Day of the Lord (Acts 2:20; Jude 6; Rev 6:17); to the power of God (Acts 4:33; 8:10); to signs and miracles (Acts 6:8; 8:13; Rev 13:13); and to fear (Rev 11:11).

megas also signifies "great" in the sense of "loud" in Matt 24:31; Mark 1:26; 5:7; Luke 4:33; 17:15; John 11:43; Acts 7:57; Rev 1:10; 10:3.

polys πολύς 4183

polys is another common adjectival form found over 350 times, denoting the primary senses of "many," "much." The term also means "great" in about sixty places, with a variety of nuances.

The meaning "great" in the sense of "loud" is indicated in relation to mourning in Matt 2:18.

polys means "great" in the sense of "numerically large" in Matt 4:25; Mark 3:7ff.; Acts 11:21; Rev 19:6. "Abundant" is the sense attached to "great" in Matt 5:12 in relation to one's reward in heaven.

The sense of "supreme," implying that which is best, is found in the designation "great glory" (Matt 24:30); in relation to "violence" (Acts 24:7); and to God's love (Eph 2:4). Acts 22:28 uses ***polys*** to emphasize quantity, or size.

▸ **7.** Quantity, Amount, Number, Size, Measure >
MANY, MUCH

megethos μέγεθος 3174

megethos is a rare noun denoting the "greatness" of God's power in Eph 1:19.

HALF

hēmisys ἥμισυς 2255

This word refers to the product of that which is equally divided into two, whether of physical matter or time. ***hēmisys*** is rare, occurring only five times.

Mark 6:23 refers to half of the kingdom belonging to King Herod. Luke 19:8 indicates Zacchaeus' offer to give away half of his wealth to the poor. Three references in the book of Revelation (11:9, 11; 12:14) recall the prophetic formula in Dan 12:7 (the first two indirectly, the latter specifically). Rev 11:9, 11 refer to the symbolic period of three and a half days. In Rev 11:9, this time refers to the period during which the bodies of the two witnesses are exposed; and after which the Spirit of God resurrects them. Rev

12:14 rehearses the precise formula of Dan 12:7, referring to "a time, times and half a time" during which the visionary woman is protected by God from the serpent. One can only assume that this eschatological, apocalyptic formula shares the same point of reference in both the OT and NT, indicating that God's timing in bringing about the completion of his redemptive work will be perfect and precise.

HUNDRED, HUNDREDFOLD, HUNDRED TIMES

hekaton ἑκατόν 1540

This Greek numeral refers to the number "one hundred" as well as the concept of "hundred times," indicating abundant increase. ***hekaton*** occurs seventeen times.

In regard to substantial increase, the expression "hundredfold," or hundred times, is found in the parable of the sower, where Christ refers to the powerful spread of God's word in the world, symbolized by the abundant crop sown in the fertile soil of spiritually receptive hearts (Matt 13:8, 23; Mark 4:8, 20). In reference to number of animals, ***hekaton*** is found in Matt 18:12; Luke 15:4; John 2:11. Similarly, with reference to people, the term occurs in Mark 6:40; Acts 1:15; Rev 7:4; 14:13. In Matt 18:28 ***hekaton*** refers to money, and in Rev 21:17 to the wall of the heavenly Jerusalem.

hekatontaplasiōn ἑκατονταπλασίων 1542

This numerical adjective occurs only three times (Matt 19:29; Mark 10:30; Luke 8:8), all of which indicate the concept of a "hundred times" as a measure of abundant increase.

INCREASE, GROW

auxanō αὐξάνω 837

auxanō is a verb occurring around twenty times with the primary meanings "grow" and "increase." ***auxanō*** refers to growth or increase in the size of plants, or population, and the metaphorical sense of spiritual growth in believers.

In reference to natural phenomena, ***auxanō*** indicates the physical growth of plants in Mark 4:8 in relation to the good seed which fell on fertile ground in the parable of the sower. Acts 7:17 refers to the increase of the Israelite population in Israel prior to their enslavement.

Other occurrences of ***auxanō*** refer to increase in status or importance. In John 3:30, John the Baptist defers to the person of Christ. The increase of God's word as it spreads throughout Jerusalem and Judea is recorded in Acts 6:7; 12:24. The increase in spiritual growth and knowledge of God, all of which is accomplished by God, is indicated in 1 Cor 3:6, 7; 2 Cor 9:10; Col 1:10. Increase in faith is mentioned in 2 Cor 10:15 in relation to the Corinthian congregation.

▸ **85.** Movement, Position, State > GROW, INCREASE

perisseuō περισσεύω 4052

perisseuō is normally translated "abound," "be in abundance," and occurs around forty times. However, in Acts 16:5 the term explicitly refers to the increase in the number of believers in the Galatian region.

▸ **7.** Quantity, Amount, Number, Size, Measure > ABOUND, INCREASE, EXCEED, OVERFLOW, ABUNDANCE
▸ **7.** Quantity, Amount, Number, Size, Measure > EXCEED, EXCEEDINGLY
▸ **23.** Food, Drink, Cooking > SPARE
▸ **85.** Movement, Position, State > REMAIN, STAY, ABIDE, DWELL

prokoptō προκόπτω 4298

prokoptō is found on six occasions meaning "advance," "promote," and "increase." The latter meaning occurs in two contexts. Luke 2:52 refers to Jesus increasing in wisdom and stature and in favor with God and human beings. 2 Tim 2:16 contains a warning against godless chatter, which will lead to an increase in ungodliness.

prostithēmi προστίθημι 4369

prostithēmi is found in eighteen places with the primary sense of "add." In Luke 17:5, however, the term is translated "increase," as the apostles ask the Lord to increase their faith.

▸ **7.** Quantity, Amount, Number, Size, Measure > ADD, INCREASE

pleonazō πλεονάζω 4121

This term is synonymous with ***perisseuō*** (above) and occurs ten times. ***pleonazō*** is translated "abound" in most cases, but the underlying meaning is that of "increase."

The increasing influence of both sin and grace is referred to in Rom 5:20. Rom 6:4 contains the question that indicates profound misunderstanding of the gospel: "Shall we sin that grace may abound (i.e., increase)?" The abundant increase of grace in the life of the Corinthian church is mentioned in 2 Cor 4:15. Increase in godliness is indicated in Phil 4:17, as is increase in love in 1 Thess 3:12; 2 Thess 1:3.

▸ **7.** Quantity, Amount, Number, Size, Measure > ABOUND, INCREASE, EXCEED, OVERFLOW, ABUNDANCE

endynamoō ἐνδυναμόω 1743

endynamoō occurs eight times with the principal meaning "be strong" or "endow with strength." In Acts 9:22 it indicates the sense of increasing in strength, denoting this as characteristic of Saul, the zealous Pharisee, in his persecution of Christians.

INSIGNIFICANT, UNIMPORTANT, MEAN

asēmos ἄσημος 767

asēmos is found only in Acts 21:39 with reference to Tarsus as "a not insignificant city" (or "no mean city") — a city of considerable significance.

LITTLE, SMALL, LEAST, FEW

mikros μικρός 3398

mikros is an adjectival form found in thirty places, with the primary senses of "small," "little," and associated nuances, with reference to size, time, and quantity.

References to "little" in term of smallness of stature are found in Matt 10:42; 18:6ff.; Mark 9:42; and Luke 17:2, in relation to children. Luke 19:3 refers to Zacchaeus' short stature. Tiny seeds are mentioned in Matt 13:32; Mark 4:31. "Little" in the sense of "powerless" is indicated in Luke 12:32.

The meaning "least," in terms of rank or importance, is indicated in general terms in Acts 8:10; Heb 8:11; Rev 11:18; 19:5, 18. Concerning the kingdom of God, Jesus declares that the "least" in that kingdom is greater than John the Baptist (Matt 11:11; Luke 7:28). Then, there is the paradoxical statement of Christ that the one who considers himself "least" among his brethren is in fact the greatest (Luke 9:18).

"Little" in relation to quantity is the sense expressed in 1 Cor 5:6; Gal 5:9, concerning the harmful effect of even a little leaven, symbolizing the presence of a sinful attitude.

The phrase "a little longer," with reference to time, is found in John 7:33; 12:35; Rev 6:11. In Rev 20:3, there is the declaration that Satan will be set free from his bondage "for a short time," prior to his final doom.

▸ **53.** Value, Worth > LEAST

mikron μικρόν 3397

mikron is an adjectival variant of ***mikros*** (above) with essentially the same meanings ("small," "little"), with reference to quantity, time, and distance.

Referring to distance, ***mikron*** is translated "a little farther" in Matt 26:39; Mark 14:35. In regard to quantity, 2 Cor 11:1 refers to a "little foolishness." Concerning time, the phrase "a little while" is indicated in Matt 26:73; Mark 14:70; Heb 10:37; and in John's Gospel the occurrences of ***mikron*** all refer to the "little while" that will take effect before the return of Christ.

oligos ὀλίγος 3641

oligos is an adjective synonymous with the preceding entries. It likewise indicates "small," "little" in regard to quantity, size, and time. ***oligos*** occurs around forty times.

The sense of "few" (in number) is found in Matt 7:14; Luke 13:23, with reference to those who have been saved. 1 Pet 3:20 refers to Noah and his family as the few who had been rescued from the flood. Jesus notes in Matt 9:37 that only a few laborers are available for the harvest of souls. The expression "many are called but few are chosen" is found in Matt 22:14. See also Matt 15:34; 6:5; Mark 8:7.

With regard to "little" in the sense of quantity, ***oligos*** occurs in Matt 25:21ff., referring to the fact that he who is faithful in "little" will be entrusted with greater things. Luke 7:47 declares that he who is forgiven little, loves little. See also 1 Tim 5:23. A "little distance" is mentioned in Mark 1:19; Luke 5:3.

The phrase a "little while" is found in several contexts (Mark 6:31; Acts 26:28; Heb 12:10). Jas 4:14 utilizes it in regard to the brevity of life. Peter mentions the same in regard to suffering in 1 Pet 5:10. And Rev 12:12 mentions the fact that the devil's time is short.

▸ **7.** Quantity, Amount, Number, Size, Measure > FEW, LITTLE, SMALL

elachistos ἐλάχιστος 1646

elachistos is a superlative adjectival term (from *elachys*, meaning "short") that means "least," "very little." It refers to size and importance and occurs in about ten contexts.

Concerning that which is "least" in size, ***elachistos*** is used in a general away in Luke 12:26. In Luke 16:10; 19:7, the principle is expounded that he who is faithful in little will be faithful over much. The town of Bethlehem is described as being "by no means least" among the rulers of Judah (from the prophecy in Mic 5:2). Jas 3:4 refers to a rudder that is "very small."

elachistos also refers to that which is least in importance. Matt 5:19 refers to the least important commandment. The least of Jesus' "brothers" is referred to in Matt 25:40, 45. The most trivial of legal cases is mentioned in 1 Cor 6:2, and Paul describes himself as the least of the apostles in 1 Cor 15:9.

▸ **53.** Value, Worth > LEAST

brachys βραχύς 1024

brachys is an adjective that means "little" in several different senses. ***brachys*** occurs seven times, and in three of these contexts it expresses the sense of "a little while" (Luke 22:58; Acts 5:34; Heb 2:7, 9). John 6:7 refers to a little amount of bread. Acts 27:28 uses the term in a spatial sense with the phrase "a little farther." ***brachys*** is also translated "briefly" in Heb 13:22.

MAGNIFY, ENLARGE

megalynō μεγαλύνω 3170

megalynō is a verb occurring eight times meaning "magnify," "enlarge."

Matt 23:5 refers to priests "enlarging" their phylacteries. There are a number of references to the Lord being praised or "magnified" (Luke 1:46; Acts 10:46; 19:17; Phil 1:20). ***megalynō*** also refers to faith "increasing" in the life of believers in 2 Cor 10:15. Acts 5:13 refers to the apostles being "held in high honor."

In the one context where God is the subject of ***megalynō***, Luke 1:58 declares that God "had shown great mercy" to Elizabeth, the mother of John the Baptist. The noun "mercy" is unqualified, thus the sense of ***megalynō*** here is "to manifest, or show greatness."

MANY, MUCH

polys πολύς 4183

polys occurs around 350 times with the three predominant senses of "many," "much," "great."

The quantitative sense of "many" accounts for the bulk of the usage of ***polys***. General references to great numbers of people are common (e.g., Matt 8:1; 20:8; Mark 2:2; 10:31; Luke 1:1; 21:8). In particular, mention is made of many people who come to faith in Christ — John's Gospel and the book of Acts emphasize this phenomenon (John 2:12; 8:30; 10:42; Acts 9:42; 11:21; 13:43; 17:12; 19:18). See also John 4:39ff.; Heb 2:10 in this regard. Mark 14:24 also records Jesus' words at the Last Supper, affirming that his blood would be shed for the forgiveness of many.

The designation "many" is also applied to Pharisees (Matt 3:7); prophets, both true and false (Matt 13:17; Matt 24:11; Luke 10:24; 1 John 4:1; 2 John 7); the wicked (Matt 7:13, 22); all manner of sick people, including the demon-possessed, who were healed by Jesus (Matt 8:16; 12:15; Mark 4:27; 7:21; John 5:3), as well as those healed by the apostles (Acts 8:7); the enemies of the gospel (1 Cor 16:9); widows (Luke 4:25); angels (Rev 5:11); and those who are born again (Rom 8:29). "Many nations" are also indicated in Rom 4:17, 18 in reference to the fulfillment of the Abrahamic covenant.

polys is used in non-personal contexts with this sense to refer to "many" animals (Matt 8:30; 10:31; Luke 12:17); numerous parables (Mark 5:9); possessions (Mark 10:22); demons cast out by Jesus (Luke 8:30); gods (1 Cor 8:5); sins (Luke 7:47; Rom 5:16); and members (or parts) of the body (Rom 12:4; 1 Cor 12:14). Nondescript reference to "many things" is found in Mark 8:31; Luke 10:41; John 8:26; 21:25; Jas 3:2. John 20:30 refers to the many signs, or miracles, performed by Jesus during his earthly ministry; Acts 2:43; 5:12 refer to the same phenomena during the apostolic ministry.

With reference to the person and work of Christ, ***polys*** indicates his many good works (John 10:32); the many heavenly mansions he is preparing for his people (John 14:7); and the many crowns placed on his head in his role as the heavenly conqueror of the armies of Satan and his followers (Rev 19:12). The metaphorical reference to "the sound of many waters" (Rev 1:5; 14:2; 19:6) indicates the supreme authority of the voice of the heavenly Christ.

In a handful of contexts, ***polys*** refers to "many" in a temporal sense — for example, "many days" (Luke 15:13; John 2:12; Acts 1:5; 16:18); "many years" (Rom 15:23).

With the sense of "much," ***polys*** likewise reflects a quantitative sense in most of its usage. Various phenomena are indicated: soil (Matt 13:5; Mark 4:5); water for baptism (John 3:23); grass (John 6:10); money or wealth (Matt 26:9; Luke 12:19; Acts 16:16); wine (1 Tim 3:8; Titus 2:3); and fruit (John 12:24). Nontangible usage includes references to "much murmuring" about the activities of Jesus (John 7:12); tribulation (Acts 14:22; 1 Thess 1:6; 1 Tim 6:10; 2 Tim 4:14); fear and trembling (1 Cor 2:3); patience (2 Cor 6:4); and fruit in the spiritual sense of evidence of godly virtue through one's relationship with Christ (John 15:5). Luke 12:48 contains the principle "to whom much is given, much is required," indicating the importance of being a good steward of all that God gives, to equip one for kingdom ministry.

In several places, ***polys*** is used in an adverbial sense to indicate a degree of enhancement — "much more," "all the more." For example, Rom 5:10, 15 refer to the powerful impact of salvation fulfilled in Christ. See also Matt 6:30; Luke 18:39. In Phil 1:23, Paul declares that to be with Christ is "far better."

▸ **7.** Quantity, Amount, Number, Size, Measure > GREAT, ABUNDANT, SUPREME, LOUD, LARGE

MEASURE, QUANTITY, STANDARD, CRITERION

metron μέτρον 3358

metron has very little reference in the NT to literal or physical dimension. Rather, the term is translated "measure," with the sense of "criterion," or "standard," and also "quantity" in a metaphorical or spiritual sense.

metron indicates the sense of "criterion," or "standard," in Matt 7:2; Mark 4:24; Luke 6:38. All these texts speak of the principle of just judgment whereby the "measure" (i.e., standard) someone applies to others will be used against that person on the day of judgment.

metron means "measure" in various contexts, with the underlying non-literal sense of quantity. Matt 23:32 refers to Jesus' caustic exhortation to the hypocritical Pharisees to "fill up the measure of the sin" of their forefathers. Luke 6:38 refers to the "measure" of one's spiritual reward. The provision of the Spirit "not by measure" (i.e., without limit) is mentioned in John 3:34. "Measure," in the sense of "portion," is indicated in Rom 12:3 with reference to the believer's faith; and in Eph 4:17 with reference to God's grace made possible by the work of Christ. See also 2 Cor 10:13. Eph 4:13 speaks of the "measure of fullness" in metaphorical reference to the maximum spiritual impact of the spirit of Christ in the life of the believer.

There is one reference to the linear measure of a cubit in Rev 21:7.

hyperperissōs ὑπερπερισσῶς 5249
ametros ἄμετρος 280

These two terms are both adverbs meaning "beyond measure" or "limitless." ***hyperperissōs*** occurs only in Mark 7:37, with reference to "astonishment beyond measure." ***ametros*** refers in 2 Cor 10:13, 15 to unlimited boasting, which Paul denies ever having done.

▸ **7.** Quantity, Amount, Number, Size, Measure > ABOUND, INCREASE, EXCEED, OVERFLOW, ABUNDANCE

metreō μετρέω 3354

metreō is the verb form from which the noun ***metron*** (above) is derived. ***metreō*** means "to measure," with the underlying sense of "to judge by," "rule," or "standard," as well as having the physical sense of spatial measurement.

The sense of judging by a criterion or standard is indicated in Matt 7:2; Mark 4:24; Luke 6:38, all of which refer to the principle of judgment, whereby the standard one uses is the standard one receives. 2 Cor 10:12 speaks of measuring or comparing oneself with others in a vain, self-centered way.

Rev 11:1f. contains the divine instruction to the apostle John to measure the temple of God and the altar in a visionary experience. In Rev 21:15ff., the interpreting angel sets out to measure the heavenly city of Jerusalem.

SEE ALSO

▸ **23.** Food, Drink, Cooking > MEASURE
choinix

MILE

milion μίλιον 3400

milion is the sole term for "mile" in the NT, occurring only in Matt 5:41.

NUMBER

arithmos ἀριθμός 706

arithmos is the only noun meaning "number" in the NT. It occurs eighteen times exclusively with this sense.

The meaning "number" is found predominantly in literal contexts. It refers to the twelve disciples (Luke 22:3); to the people of Israel (Rom 9:27); and to the crowd whom Jesus miraculously fed from a meager source of food (John 6:10). In the book of Acts, ***arithmos*** refers to the number of those who believed in Christ after hearing the preaching of the apostles (Acts 4:4; 6:7; 11:21); and also to the increase in the size of the NT church (Acts 16:5).

arithmos is also used symbolically in the book of Revelation to indicate the number of the earth beast, given to all his followers (Rev 13:17, 18; 15:2); the number of Israel's enemies arrayed against them (Rev 20:8); and the number of the elect, the 144,000 chosen by God as his people (Rev 7:4). In addition, Rev 5:11 refers to the countless numbers of angels surrounding the throne of God in heaven.

arithmeō ἀριθμέω 705

arithmeō is the verb corresponding to the term ***arithmos*** (above). ***arithmeō*** is found in only three places, meaning "to number." Mark 10:30; Luke 12:7 refer to divine providential care and knowledge, and the hairs of our head being all numbered by God. Rev 7:9 describes the huge multitude of saints in heaven of whom it is said, "no one could number."

katarithmeō καταριθμέω 2674

The verb ***katarithmeō*** is found only in Acts 1:17, where it refers to the traitor Judas as one who was originally "numbered" among the twelve apostles of Christ.

SEE ALSO

▸ **52.** Status, Identity, Reputation, Honor, Shame > NUMBER
logizomai

ONE

heis εἷς 1520

heis is the most common term for "one" in the NT, designating both the numeral itself and the numerical adjectival sense. It is also used as a pronoun. ***heis*** is found in around 340 places.

In relation to the meaning "one" in a numerical adjectival sense, examples of a general usage are found in Matt 6:27; 12:11; Mark 15:6; Luke 15:10. Other particular instances include references to "one jot of the law" in Matt 5:18. Matters of import are often prefaced by the phrase "one thing . . ." (Matt 21:24; Mark 10:21; Luke 10:42; John 9:25; Phil 3:13; 2 Pet 3:8). ***heis*** is also translated "certain" in Matt 8:19; Mark 14:51 as a general designation for particular individuals.

heis is also used in theologically significant contexts. Eph 4:5 refers to "one Lord" and to "one faith." ***heis*** describes Christ as "one teacher" (Matt 23:8); "one master" (Matt 23:10); and "one shepherd" (John 10:16). God himself is also indicated in expressions such as "one Father" (Matt 23:9; John 8:44); "one lawgiver" (Jas 4:12); and "one God" (1 Tim 2:5; Jas 2:19). The Holy Spirit is likewise indicated in the phrase "one spirit" in 1 Cor 12:13; Eph 2:18; 4:4 (see also 1 Cor 6:17). Elsewhere, references to "one man" in John 11:50; 18:14; 2 Cor 5:14; Rom 5:12, 16 all point to the unique person and redemptive work of Jesus Christ. Rom 5:16 refers to the "one sin" that entered the world and brought death to all human beings. The expression "one body" is a metaphorical reference to the communion of all believers, found in Rom 12:4ff.; 1 Cor 12:12, 20; Eph 2:16; 4:4; Col 3:15 (see also 1 Cor 6:16). Similarly, the expression "one mind" is found in Phil 2:2.

As a pronoun, ***heis*** is likewise translated "one" in numerous contexts. Examples of a general usage are found in Matt 5:29; 6:24; Mark 5:22; 9:42; Luke 11:46; John 6:70. ***heis*** refers to "one of the prophets" (Matt 16:14; Mark 6:15); "one of the scribes" (Mark 12:28); "one of the twelve (disciples)" (Mark 14:43; John 6:71); "one of the four beasts" (Rev 6:1); and "one of the seven angels" (Rev 21:9).

Paul refers to all believers being "one in Christ," reflecting a universal spiritual communion with the Savior (Gal 3:28). The expressions "I and my Father are one" (John 10:30) and "the Lord our God is one" (Mark 12:29, 32; Rom 3:30; 1 Cor 8:4, 6; Gal 3:20) reflect both an adjectival and a pronominal sense of ***heis***. Similarly, in John 17:11, 21ff., the people of God are described as "one." Several texts declare that there is only "one" who is good, namely God himself (Matt 19:17; Mark 10:18; Luke 18:19).

heis has the negative sense of "none," or "no one," in Acts 4:32; 1 Cor 6:5. Rom 3:10 affirms that there are "none" righteous before God. Similarly, ***heis*** is used negatively in John 1:3 to mean "nothing" in the context of divine creation, described as a cooperative venture between God the Father and his Son, the "Word," without whom "nothing was made."

The meaning "every one" or "each one" is evident in Eph 5:33; Col 4:6; 1 Thess 2:11.

OVERFLOW, RUN OVER

hyperekchynnō ὑπερεκχύννω 5240

hyperekchynnō occurs only in Luke 6:38 meaning "to run over," referring generally to the "overflowing" of a measured portion (e.g., of grain).

SEE ALSO

- ▸ **29.** Boats, Fishing, Maritime Activity > RUN UNDER, RUN AGROUND ***hypotrechō, epikellō***
- ▸ **85.** Movement, Position, State > RUN ***trechō, episyntrechō, syntrechō, peritrechō, protrechō***
- ▸ **86.** Movement Toward or Away From > RUN, RUN TOWARD, RUN DOWN ***prostrechō, eistrechō, katatrechō, hormaō***

SECOND

deuteros δεύτερος 1208

deuteros is a numerical adjective meaning "second" and is found in nearly fifty contexts.

The number "second" is indicated in a variety of contexts. There are references to time, or occasion, in Matt 26:42. More commonly, ***deuteros*** indicates "second" in a group, or series — the second of the Ten Commandments (Matt 22:39; Mark 12:31); the "second" death (Rev 2:11; 20:6, 14; 21:8); and the "second" seal of judgment (Rev 6:3). Heb 8:7 speaks of the new covenant as the "second" covenant. See also Heb 9:3, 7.

SEVEN, SEVENTH, SEVENTY

hepta ἑπτά 2033

hepta is the only term in the NT for the cardinal number seven, occurring around ninety times.

Literal, mundane usage includes that in Matt 12:45; Mark 8:5ff.; Luke 11:26; Acts 6:3; Rev 1:4, 11.

Significant figurative uses of the number "seven" include Jesus' expression "seventy times seven," referring symbolically to the unlimited capacity of one's forgiving attitude to those who wrong us (Matt 18:22).

The remaining symbolic uses of "seven" are found exclusively in the book of Revelation. Rev 1:12ff. refers to the seven golden lampstands that represent the seven churches of Asia. In the same context, reference to the "seven stars" in Rev 1:16, 20; 2:1; 3:1 is equated with the angels of the seven churches of Asia. Cycles of judgment also revolve around the number seven — ***hepta*** refers to seven seals (Rev 5:1, 5); seven trumpets (Rev 8:2); seven bowls (Rev 16:1; 17:1; 21:9); and "seven angels" of judgment (Rev 15:1, 6ff.). See also Rev 10:3, 4; 11:13; 12:3; 13:1; 17:3.

hebdomos ἕβδομος 1442

hebdomos is an adjectival form designating the ordinal number "seventh," occurring nine times.

It is used literally in John 1:14 and symbolically in Rev 21:20.

In significant contexts, ***hebdomos*** refers to the "seventh" day (Heb 4:4); the "seventh" seal of judgment (Rev 8:1); and the "seventh" angel of judgment (Rev 10:7; 11:15; 16:17).

hebdomēkontakis ἑβδομηκοντάκις 1441

This is an adverbial form, indicating the numeral "seventy" in Christ's expression "seventy times seven," which refers symbolically to the limitless number of times he expected his followers to forgive those who had wronged them (Matt 18:22).

hebdomēkonta ἑβδομήκοντα 1440

hebdomēkonta is a noun occurring five times, referring to the number "seventy" (Luke 10:1, 17; Acts 23:23). See also Acts 7:14; 27:37.

SHORTEN, FALL SHORT

hystereō ὑστερέω 5302

hystereō is a verb with the primary sense of "lack," "fail," "want." Rom 3:23 describes the state of all humankind, who "have fallen short" of God's standard.

koloboō κολοβόω 2856

koloboō is a verb found four times with reference to the phenomenon of "shortening" the days of tribulation prior to the return of Christ for the sake of the elect (Matt 24:22; Mark 13:20).

8. Light, Darkness, Visible, Invisible, Color

APPEARANCE

eidea εἰδέα 2397

eidea is a rare noun found only in Matt 28:3, denoting the dazzling "appearance" of the angel who appeared at the tomb from which Christ had risen from the dead.

SEE ALSO

- ▸ **16.** Body, Bodily Functions > FACE
  prosōpon, opsis, stoma

BLACK

melas μέλας 3189

melas is an adjective describing the color "black" in Matt 5:36 (human hair); Rev 6:12 (darkening of the sun); and Rev 6:5 (one of the four "apocalyptic" horses of John's vision).

- ▸ **36.** Reading, Writing > INK

BRIGHT

lampros λαμπρός 2986

lampros is an adjective denoting that which is "bright" or "splendid" in most of its nine occurrences. The explicit sense of "bright" in relation to the brilliance of angelic clothing is evident in Acts 10:30; and in relation to one of the titles for the heavenly Christ — the "bright and morning star" (Rev 22:16).

- ▸ **8.** Light, Darkness, Visible, Invisible, Color > CLEAR
- ▸ **8.** Light, Darkness, Visible, Invisible, Color > WHITE, WHITEN, WHITEWASH

SEE ALSO

- ▸ **1.** Celestial Realm, Earthly Realm > BRIGHTNESS, BRILLIANCE
  lamprotēs

CLEAR

krystallizō κρυσταλλίζω 2929

krystallizō is a rare verb meaning "to be as clear as crystal," denoting a high degree of brilliance and transparency. It is found only in Rev 21:11.

lampros λαμπρός 2986

lampros is an adjective meaning "bright" in most of its nine occurrences. However, in Rev 22:1 the river of the water of life is described as "clear" as crystal.

- ▸ **8.** Light, Darkness, Visible, Invisible, Color > BRIGHT
- ▸ **8.** Light, Darkness, Visible, Invisible, Color > WHITE, WHITEN, WHITEWASH

DARK, DARKNESS, DARKEN

skotizō σκοτίζω 4654

skotizō is a verb meaning "to darken," "cover with darkness" in both literal and metaphorical contexts. References to the sun "being darkened" as one of the signs of the impending final day of judgment are found in Matt 24:29; Mark 13:24; Luke 23:45; Rev 8:12; 9:2. Metaphorical usage is indicated in contexts where the eyes, hearts, and minds of unbelievers "are darkened," preventing them from discerning spiritual truth.

skotia σκοτία 4653

skotia is a noun derived from ***skotizō*** (above) occurring sixteen times and denoting "darkness" in both literal and metaphorical contexts.

References to the "darkness" of night include Matt 10:27; Luke 12:3; John 6:17; 20:1. More commonly, ***skotia*** indicates a moral "darkness" that grips the hearts and minds of unbelievers — their natural state of spiritual hostility against and enmity with God (John 1:5; 8:12; 12:35, 46; 1 John 2:9, 11). 1 John 1:5 affirms that there is no such trace of darkness in God; and 1 John 2:8 notes that the age of spiritual "darkness" is passing away and the light of salvation is already shining.

skoteinos σκοτεινός 4652

skoteinos is an adjectival term denoting the "darkness" of spiritual blindness or moral perverseness, found only in Matt 6:23; Luke 11:34, 36.

skotos σκότος 4655

Found over thirty times, ***skotos*** is the most common noun denoting "darkness" in the NT. Since this term is predominantly used in a metaphorical sense, its significance is profound where it refers to literal darkness.

The "darkness" of spiritual blindness, preventing people from understanding the truth of the gospel, is noted in Matt 4:16; Luke 1:79; Acts 26:18; Rom 2:19; 2 Cor 4:6; 1 Thess 5:4.

The "darkness" of moral evil in one's heart is indicated in Matt 6:23; Luke 11:35; John 3:19; Rom 13:12; 1 Cor 4:5; Eph 5:11; 1 John 1:6.

The phrase "outer darkness" symbolically designates the realm of everlasting punishment in Matt 8:12; 22:13; 25:30.

The "darkness" that fell on the earth during the crucifixion of Christ immediately prior to his death signifies the judgment of God coming upon his Son, whereby he suffers the divine wrath as a consequence of bearing the sin of the world (Matt 27:45; Mark 15:33; Luke 23:44).

Reference to the "power of darkness" indicates satanic influence in relation to those who had come to arrest Jesus (Luke 22:53). See also 2 Pet 2:17; Jude 13.

The phenomenon of the sun "turning black" (i.e., into darkness) to indicate the imminent arrival of the final Day of the Lord judgment is noted in Acts 2:20. The "darkness" of physical blindness is indicated in Acts 13:11.

The realm of moral "darkness" of satanic origin is indicated in 2 Cor 6:14; Eph 5:8; 6:12; Col 1:13; 1 Thess 5:5. 1 Pet 2:9 refers to God's people being "called out of darkness" into the light.

The "darkness" of the theophanic cloud containing the presence of God at Sinai is mentioned in Heb 12:18.

auchmēros αὐχμηρός 850

auchmēros is a rare adjective, referring literally to a "dark" place in 2 Pet 1:19.

zophos ζόφος 2217

zophos is a noun found in four places denoting the "darkness" of the realm of eternal punishment to which the enemies of God are consigned (2 Pet 2:4, 17; Jude 6, 13).

gnophos γνόφος 1105

gnophos is a rare noun found only in Heb 12:18, denoting the "darkness" or "blackness" of the theophanic cloud at Mount Sinai (Heb 12:18).

DAZZLING

astraptō ἀστράπτω 797

astraptō is a rare verb denoting the "dazzling" of lightning in Luke 17:24; and the "dazzling" appearance of angelic apparel in Luke 24:4.

exastraptō ἐξαστράπτω 1823

exastraptō is a verb found only in Luke 9:29 referring to the glistening clothing of Christ that "became dazzling white" during his transfiguration on the mountain.

INVISIBLE

aoratos ἀόρατος 517

This adjectival form occurs five times and is translated "invisible" in each case. 1 Tim 1:17; Heb 11:27 refer to the invisible God. Rom 1:20 declares that the invisible aspects or qualities of God's being have been made plain through creation. Concerning the person of Christ, Col 1:15, 16 indicate that he is the revealed image of the invisible God, and in him all things visible and invisible were created by God through and for him.

LAMP, TORCH

lampas λαμπάς 2985

lampas occurs in nine contexts and means "lamp," "torch," in both a literal and metaphorical sense.

Torches for lighting one's way at night are indicated in Matt 25:1ff.; John 18:3; Acts 20:8.

lampas refers metaphorically in Rev 4:5 to fiery lamps illuminating the throne of God in heaven. In Rev 8:10, ***lampas*** refers to a star falling from heaven, blazing like a torch.

lychnos λύχνος 3088

lychnos is a synonym for ***lampas*** (above). It occurs in fourteen places and is likewise translated "lamp."

Mundane usage is indicated in Matt 5:15; Mark 4:21; Luke 8:16; 11:33, 36; 12:35; 15:8. See also Rev 18:23; 22:5.

In metaphorical contexts, ***lychnos*** refers first of all to the eye as the "lamp of the body" in Matt 6:22; Luke 11:34. Scripture is depicted as a guiding "lamp" in 2 Pet 1:19. In Rev 21:23, the Lamb of God is described as the "lamp" of the heavenly city. John 5:35 depicts John the Baptist as a "shining lamp."

LIGHT, GIVE LIGHT, ILLUMINATE

phōs φῶς 5457

phōs is a noun found approximately seventy times, with the consistent meaning "light." It indicates physical light from natural sources, as well as supernatural light revealed from heaven. In addition, ***phōs*** conveys a distinctive metaphorical sense of "light," associated both with the person of God and the abstract phenomena of moral and spiritual truth.

phōs means "light" in a mundane sense (Matt 10:16; Luke 12:3; Eph 5:13) where daylight is mentioned. Firelight is indicated in Mark 14:54; and lamplight in Luke 8:16; Acts 16:29; Rev 18:23.

phōs refers to the supernatural light of Christ's transfiguration (Matt 17:2); to heavenly light at Saul's conversion (Acts 9:3; 22:6ff.); to angelic light (Acts 12:7); and to the light of the heavenly city (Rev 21:24; 22:5).

phōs is also used in metaphorical contexts relating to light and the person of God. First of all, reference is made to the light of God's salvation for the Gentiles, anticipating the coming of the Messiah (Matt 4:16; Luke 2:32; Acts 13:47; 26:18). Divine light is depicted as the source of eternal life, represented supremely by Jesus (John 1:4ff.; 3:19ff.; 11:10; 12:35ff.; 2 Cor 4:6; 1 Pet 2:9; 1 John 2:8ff.). In this connection, Jesus is described as "the light of the world." 1 Tim 6:16; Jas 1:17; 1 John 1:5, 7 refer to the light of God, indicating the essence of his being (i.e., as unapproachable).

Metaphorical usage of ***phōs*** also extends to the human sphere. The believer's "armor of light" is indicated in Rom 13:12. The people of God are described as "children of light" in Eph 5:8; 1 Thess 5:5 (see also John 5:35; Col 1:12). In related contexts, God's people are depicted as the "light of the world" in Matt 5:14; Rom 2:19. In more general contexts, "light" is the equivalent of moral uprightness, or godliness (Matt 5:16; 6:23; Luke 11:35; 2 Cor 6:14).

phōteinos φωτεινός 5460

phōteinos is an adjective signifying "full of light," "bright." It occurs four times. Three of these occurrences are found in Matt 6:22; Luke 11:34, 36, where the body is said to be "full of light" if the eyes are sound. Matt 17:5 refers to the bright cloud overshadowing Christ and his disciples on the mountain of his transfiguration.

phengos φέγγος 5338

phengos is a noun, found only three times, meaning "light." In Matt 24:29; Mark 13:24 it refers to moonlight; and in Luke 11:33 to the light of a lamp.

haptō ἅπτω 681

haptō conveys the meaning "to light a lamp or fire." It occurs only four times (Luke 8:16; 11:33; 15:8; 22:55).

phōtizō φωτίζω 5461

phōtizō is a verb occurring around ten times, meaning "give, shed light," "enlighten," "illuminate," in both literal and metaphorical contexts.

The literal meaning "give, shed light" is found in Luke 11:36 with reference to a lamp, and in Rev 21:23 with reference to the effect of the glory of God in the heavenly city. See also Rev 22:5.

With symbolic reference to illuminating people's hearts and minds with the "light" of revealed truth, ***phōtizō*** occurs in John 1:9; 1 Cor 4:5; Eph 1:18; 2 Tim 1:10; Heb 6:4; 10:32.

phōtismos φωτισμός 5462

phōtismos is the noun derived from ***phōtizō*** (above). It occurs only in 2 Cor 4:4, 6, referring to the "light of the knowledge of the gospel," denied to the unbelieving Jews but given to all true believers.

epiphauskō ἐπιφαύσκω 2017

epiphauskō occurs only in Eph 5:14, referring to the action of the risen Christ in giving the "light" of new life to all those who died in him and awoke from death.

phōstēr φωστήρ 5458

phōstēr is a noun meaning "light" in the sense of the radiance emanating from the glory of God. It occurs only twice: once in Phil 2:15, where it refers to believers who shine as lights in the world (i.e., radiating God's glory in their lives); and once in Rev 21:11, referring to the heavenly city of Jerusalem, radiating light from the glorious presence of God within her walls.

SCARLET

kokkinos κόκκινος 2847

kokkinos occurs six times, always with reference to the color "scarlet."

The Roman soldiers place a scarlet robe on Christ prior to his crucifixion in mockery of his claims to be king of the Jews (Matt 27:28).

Heb 9:19 refers to scarlet thread as a component of the offering of consecration for covenant renewal.

Rev 17:3, 4 mention the scarlet beast in the symbolic description of Babylon, portrayed as a demonic "queen," an idolatrous "prostitute," the epitome of blasphemy against God. Rev 18:12, 16 refer to scarlet material as merchandise.

SHADOW, SHADE

skia σκιά 4639

skia means "shadow" or "shade" in all seven of its occurrences.

The literal "shade" or shelter of a tree is indicated in Mark 4:32, and the shadow of a man in Acts 5:15.

Metaphorical reference to the "shadow" of sin and death from which people have been delivered is noted in Matt 4:16; Luke 1:79. Elsewhere, the "shadows" of old covenant realities anticipate the coming of Christ, who fulfills those realities (Col 2:17). Examples of the "shadow" phenomenon are found in relation to the tabernacle (Heb 8:5) and to the law (Heb 10:1).

aposkiasma ἀποσκίασμα 644

aposkiasma is a rare noun found only in Jas 1:17, referring metaphorically to a "shadow" as evidence of change in a person. This is then deemed impossible for God, who never changes.

SEE ALSO

▸ **34.** Craftsmanship, Artisanship, Furniture, Implements > OVERSHADOW
kataskiazō

SHINE

lampō λάμπω 2989

lampō is a verb found nine times meaning "shine," "give light."

lampō refers to light "shining" (Matt 5:15); to the metaphorical "light" of one's life (Matt 5:16); to the "shining" of Moses' face (Matt 17:2); to the "light" of God's glory in one's heart (2 Cor 4:6); and to angelic light (Acts 12:7).

eklampō ἐκλάμπω 1584

eklampō is a variant form of ***lampō*** (above) found only in Matt 13:43 and referring to the righteous who "shine" like the sun.

perilampō περιλάμπω 4034

Another variant of ***lampō*** (above), ***perilampō*** is found only twice, expressing the sense of "shine around" or "shine round about" in relation to divine glory (Luke 2:9; Acts 26:13).

phainō φαίνω 5316

phainō is a verb occurring about thirty times, meaning "appear," "shine" in most of these contexts.

The phenomenon of "shining" is evident in natural contexts referring to lightning (Matt 24:27), light (John 1:5; 2 Pet 1:19; Rev 8:12), the sun (Rev 1:16), and the moon (Rev 21:23).

phainō indicates the metaphorical sense of "shining light" in relation to John the Baptist (John 5:35) and believers (Phil 2:15). The "light" of new life in Christ is indicated in 1 John 2:8.

▸ **64.** Reveal, Explain, Hiddenness, Secrecy > APPEAR, APPEARING, APPARENT

periastraptō περιαστράπτω 4015

periastraptō is a verb found three times, identical in meaning to ***perilampō*** (above). It refers to the glory of God in Acts 9:3; 12:6.

VISIBLE

horatos ὁρατός 3707

horatos is a rare adjectival form denoting that which is "visible" (i.e., open to view) in creation, fashioned through the divine power of God in Christ (Col 1:16).

WHITE, WHITEN, WHITEWASH

leukos λευκός 3022

leukos is an adjective meaning "white," as a color and also with the sense of a "brilliant radiance."

General references to "white" are found in Matt 5:36; Mark 9:3. In John 4:35, fields are declared to be "white for harvest," referring to people ready to receive the news of the gospel. ***leukos*** also refers to the "white throne" of judgment occupied by God (Rev 20:11); to the "white horse," bearing Christ the King of kings (Rev 19:11, 14); to another "white horse" symbolizing military conquest (Rev 6:2); and to the "white cloud" bearing the Son of Man coming into heaven to receive his kingdom (Rev 14:14). A number of texts refer to the "white linen garments" of the saints in heaven, signifying their purity (Rev 3:4, 5; 4:4; 6:11; 7:9, 13). See also Rev 2:17.

Elsewhere, ***leukos*** means "white" denoting a brilliant, dazzling radiance. It refers, for example, to the appearance of Christ the King in heaven (Rev 1:14), to the appearance of Christ's garments during his transfiguration (Matt 17:2; Luke 9:29), and to angelic clothing (Matt 28:3; Mark 16:5; John 20:12; Acts 1:10).

leukainō λευκαίνω 3021

leukainō is a rare verb meaning "to make white," "whiten." It refers literally to clothes in Mark 9:3, and metaphorically to the clothes of the saints in heaven, "made white" (i.e., "purified") in the blood of the Lamb (Rev 7:14).

lampros λαμπρός 2986

lampros is an adjective occurring nine times with the underlying sense of that which is "bright" or "clean." Occasionally it refers to brightness of appearance in the sense of "dazzling white" (Acts 10:30). It refers to angelic apparel (Rev 15:6), and to the clothing of the saints in heaven (Rev 19:8).

▸ **8.** Light, Darkness, Visible, Invisible, Color > BRIGHT
▸ **8.** Light, Darkness, Visible, Invisible, Color > CLEAR

koniaō κονιάω 2867

koniaō is a rare verb referring to the process of "whitewashing," or covering with lime to impart a white color to something dirty. It refers metaphorically to hypocritical leaders of the people who are likened to "whitewashed tombs" (Matt 23:27; Acts 23:3).

9. Land, Geography, Topography

CAVE, DEN

spēlaion σπήλαιον 4693

spēlaion is a noun found six times with the dual senses of "cave," "den." References to "caves" are literal, whereas Matt 21:13; Mark 11:17; Luke 19:46 all mention Christ's denunciation of those who had desecrated the Jerusalem temple, making it a "den of thieves."

COUNTRY, LAND

agros ἀγρός 68

The noun ***agros*** means "field" throughout its nearly forty occurrences.

The sense of "country" (i.e., "countryside") is indicated in Mark 5:14; 15:21; Luke 8:34; 23:26.

▸ **28.** Agriculture, Viticulture, Animal Husbandry > FIELD, FIELD OF GRAIN, CORNFIELD

patris πατρίς 3968

patris is a noun found in eight places with the meaning "country," "homeland." References to one's own "homeland" or "country" are found in Matt 13:54, 57; Mark 6:1, 4; Luke 4:23ff.; John 4:44. Heb 11:14 refers to people seeking a "homeland," a metaphor for the search after one's "eternal home."

chōra χώρα 5561

chōra is a noun denoting "country" in the sense of "region," "countryside," "native land" for most of the nearly thirty occurrences of the term. References to "country" denoting "native, or foreign land" are found in Matt 2:12; Mark 1:5; Luke 15:13; 19:12; Acts 10:39 (Judea); 12:20.

The meaning "region" is indicated in Matt 4:16; 8:28; Luke 3:1; 8:26; John 11:54; Acts 8:1; 13:49; and "countryside" is noted in Mark 5:10; Luke 21:21.

▸ **9.** Land, Geography, Topography > REGION
▸ **28.** Agriculture, Viticulture, Animal Husbandry > FIELD, FIELD OF GRAIN, CORNFIELD

perichōros περίχωρος 4066

perichōros is a variant form of ***chōra*** (above) denoting "surrounding countryside," "surrounding region" throughout its ten occurrences (Matt 3:5; 14:35; Mark 1:28; 6:55; Luke 3:3; 4:14, 37; 7:17; 8:37; Acts 14:6).

▸ **9.** Land, Geography, Topography > REGION

oreinos ὀρεινός 3714

oreinos is a rare adjective found only in Luke 1:39, 65 denoting the "hill country" of Judea.

apodēmeō ἀποδημέω 589

apodēmeō is a verb found in six places with the meaning "travel to a far country" in most of these contexts (Matt 21:33; Mark 12:1; Luke 15:13; 20:9).

▸ **85.** Movement, Position, State > TRAVEL, TRAVELER
▸ **86.** Movement Toward or Away From > JOURNEY

EARTHQUAKE

seismos σεισμός 4578

seismos is a noun denoting an "earthquake" in most of the fourteen occurrences of the term.

Literal references to "earthquakes" as recorded historical phenomena are found in several places, all of which depict these events as divine indicators of a particularly significant point in time. They took place, for example, at the death of Christ in Matt 27:54; and at the moment of his rising from the dead in Matt 28:2. Acts 16:26 records that an earthquake shook the foundation of the prison holding the apostle Peter, thus allowing him to escape.

Elsewhere, earthquakes are depicted as future indicators of divine judgment, one of the signs that will characterize the last days before the return of Christ (Matt 24:7; Mark 13:8; Luke 21:11). In the book of Revelation, earthquakes are depicted as one of the catastrophic manifestations of divine wrath poured out against wicked humankind (Rev 6:12; 8:5; 11:13; 16:18). See also Rev 11:19.

GROUND

edaphos ἔδαφος 1475

edaphos is a rare noun found only in Acts 22:7, referring to Saul falling to the "ground" when confronted by the heavenly Christ.

chamai χαμαί 5476

chamai is a rare adverbial form found only twice, meaning "on/to the ground" in a directional sense (John 9:6; 18:6).

SEE ALSO

▸ **21.** Die, Perish, Kill, Destroy > THROW TO THE GROUND ***edaphizō***
▸ **83.** Set, Put, Place, Prepare, Establish > ESTABLISH, FIX, GROUND, STRENGTHEN ***themelioō***

HOLE, LAIR

phōleos φωλεός 5454

phōleos is a rare term, occurring only twice. Matt 8:20; Luke 9:58 refer to a fox's hole, or lair.

ISLAND

nēsos νῆσος 3520

nēsos occurs nine times and consistently indicates the meaning "island." Various islands are mentioned in conjunction with Paul's missionary journey (Acts 13:6; 27:26; 28:1, 7, 9, 11). The apostle John's banishment to the island of Patmos is indicated in Rev 1:9. In the context of apocalyptic divine judgment against a sinful world, Rev 6:14; 16:20 refer to every island on earth being removed from its place.

nēsion νησίον 3519

nēsion is a diminutive of ***nēsos*** (above) occurring only once, in Acts 27:16, and indicating a "small island."

MOUNTAIN, MOUNT

oros ὄρος 3735

oros is the only term for "mount," "mountain" in the NT. It occurs around sixty times.

The natural sense of "mountain" as a geological or geographic location is indicated, for example, in Matt 17:20; Mark 5:5; Luke 21:21; 1 Cor 13:2. Mountain locations are often mentioned in association with Jesus' ministry (Matt 5:1; 14:23; 15:29; Mark 3:13; John 6:3); and in particular, the Mount of Olives (e.g., Matt 21:1; Mark 11:1; Luke 19:29; John 8:1). Jesus sometimes withdrew to mountain areas to pray (Mark 6:46; Luke 6:12; 9:28). The temple mount was also the location for one of the temptations of Christ initiated by Satan (Matt 4:5; Luke 4:8).

Occasionally, specific mountain areas are given a particular significance in the NT. Matt 17:1; Mark 9:2; 2 Pet 1:18 refer to the so-called Mount of Transfiguration, where Jesus provided a glimpse of his essential heavenly glory to his disciples Peter, James, and John. John 4:20, 21 refer indirectly to Mount Gerizim as the central shrine of Samaritan worship. ***oros*** refers in several places to Mount Sinai — as the place where God spoke to Moses in the burning bush (Acts 7:30); as the place where God revealed to Moses the pattern of the tabernacle to be built as the focal point for Israelite worship (Heb 8:5); and as the allegorical representation of the old covenant (Gal 4:24, 25). Heb 12:18 refers to the historical Mount Sinai in contrast to "Mount Zion" in Heb 12:22, the symbolic designation of the heavenly Jerusalem to which all believers have now come. Similarly, Rev 14:1; 21:10 indicate "Mount Zion" as symbolic of the heavenly dwelling place of Christ and his people.

In the apocalyptic imagery of the book of Revelation, the dissolution of the cosmos on the great Day of the Lord includes the destruction of mountains (Rev 6:14ff.; 8:8; 16:20). See also Rev 17:9.

PATH

tribos τρίβος 5147

tribos is found in only three places, all with reference to the quotation from Isa 40:3, citing the prophetic command to prepare for the coming of Yahweh by making straight his "paths." In these contexts, "paths" refers metaphorically to the removal of all obstacles to the coming of the Messiah (Matt 3:3; Mark 1:3; Luke 3:4).

trochia τροχιά 5163

trochia is found only in Heb 12:13, meaning "paths" and referring metaphorically to a godly lifestyle.

PIT, WELL

bothynos βόθυνος 999

bothynos is found only three times. It refers to a "pit" as a trap, dug presumably to capture wild animals, but which may also cause injury to the unwary passerby — whether animal (Matt 12:11) or human (Matt 15:14; Luke 6:39).

phrear φρέαρ 5421

phrear occurs in five contexts, referring to a literal "pit" in Luke 14:5; and to a "well" for drinking in John 4:11, 12. In Rev 9:1, 2 ***phrear*** refers to the bottomless "pit" of Hades (or the underworld), the place of fiery judgment for the wicked.

SEE ALSO

▸ **1.** Celestial Realm, Earthly Realm > PIT, ABYSS, DEEP ***abyssos***

PLACE

topos τόπος 5117

topos is a noun meaning "place" in the large majority of the ninety or so contexts in which it is found. There are a number of varying nuances and contexts connected with this term.

There are a number of references to "place" as a general designation for a geographic location, or position. ***topos*** commonly refers to desert or arid "places" (Matt 12:43; 14:13ff.; Mark 1:35; Luke 4:42; 1 Cor 1:2; Rev 6:11). Other references to places that are named include Golgotha (Matt 27:33); Armageddon (Rev 16:16); and Canaan (Heb 11:8). The "place" of Jesus' burial is indicated in Matt 28:6; Mark 16:6; Luke 23:33. Other non-specific references include those in Matt 14:35; Luke 4:17; John 6:10; Acts 4:31.

topos also refers to the holy "place" of the temple in Matt 24:15; Acts 6:13, 14; 21:28; and to the holy "place" (i.e., ground) where Moses stood when confronted by Yahweh at the site of the burning bush in the desert of Sinai (Acts 7:33).

Finally, ***topos*** refers to "place" as a heavenly destiny prepared by Jesus for his followers (John 14:2ff.), and to heaven itself (Rev 12:8). Conversely, Acts 1:25 speaks of the "place" to which Judas had gone, implying the realm of everlasting judgment.

▸ **24.** Dwell, Live, Gather, Hospitality > ROOM

chōrion χωρίον 5564

chōrion is a noun that means "field" or "piece of land" in most of the ten occurrences in which it is found. However, in two contexts it is translated "place" with reference to the garden of Gethsemane (Matt 26:36; Mark 14:32).

▸ **28.** Agriculture, Viticulture, Animal Husbandry > FIELD, FIELD OF GRAIN, CORNFIELD

PLAIN

pedinos πεδινός 3977

pedinos is found only in Luke 6:17 with reference to a "plain" or "area of level ground" on which Jesus stood as he ministered to the crowd through miraculous healing and teaching.

QUAKE

seiō σείω 4579

The primary meaning of ***seiō*** is to "shake" or "tremble." It occurs only five times, and in Matt 27:51 it refers to the shaking of the earth at the precise moment of Christ's death on the cross — an undoubted reference to an earthquake.

▸ **85.** Movement, Position, State > SHAKE

REGION

perichōros περίχωρος 4066

perichōros is found eleven times and means "region (or countryside)" or "surrounding region." It is used exclusively in regard to literal geographic areas in and around the land of Israel (Matt 3:5; 14:35; Mark 1:28; 6:55; Luke 3:3; 4:14, 37; 7:17; 8:37 [twice]; Acts 14:6).

▸ **9.** Land, Geography, Topography > COUNTRY, LAND

chōra χώρα 5561

chōra occurs nearly thirty times, meaning "country" in most of these contexts. ***chōra*** can also mean "region," with an occasional ambiguity between these two meanings.

References to a geographic region include those in Luke 3:1; John 11:54; Acts 8:1; 13:49; 16:6. Ambiguous references to "region" or "country" are found in Matt 8:28; Mark 5:1; Luke 8:26.

There is one metaphorical reference to "region" in Matt 4:16, where ***chōra*** indicates a "region of death," referring to the realm of spiritual darkness.

▸ **9.** Land, Geography, Topography > COUNTRY, LAND
▸ **28.** Agriculture, Viticulture, Animal Husbandry > FIELD, FIELD OF GRAIN, CORNFIELD

klima κλίμα 2824

klima is a noun found only three times, referring to geographic regions (Rom 15:23; 2 Cor 11:10; Gal 1:21).

RIVER

potamos ποταμός 4215

potamos is a noun found in sixteen places meaning "river," "flood," or "stream" in each of these contexts. General references to "river(s)" are found in Acts 16:13; 2 Cor 11:26; Mark 1:5.

potamos is used metaphorically in John 7:38, where "rivers" of living water refer to the blessing of eternal peace and satisfaction. Rivers are also mentioned in the apocalyptic visions of Rev 8:10; 9:14; 12:15ff.; 16:4. The "river" of the water of life is noted in Rev 22:1, 2.

▸ **11.** Meteorology, Water > FLOOD

SEA

thalassa θάλασσα 2281

thalassa means "sea" in the approximately ninety occurrences of the term. General references to the sea are found in Matt 8:27; 18:6; Mark 4:41; Luke 17:6; Acts 27:38; Rom 9:27; Heb 11:2; Jude 13; Rev 5:13; 7:1ff.; 10:2ff.; 18:17ff. The "seas" as created by God are mentioned in Acts 14:15. Rev 21:1 contains a vision of the disappearance of the sea in the new heavens and the new earth. The Re(e)d Sea is indicated in Acts 7:36; 1 Cor 10:1, 2; Heb 11:29.

A metaphorical reference to a "sea of glass" is found in Rev 4:6.

SHORE, SEASHORE

aigialos αἰγιαλός 123

aigialos is a noun found six times with reference to "shore," "seashore" (Matt 13:2, 48; John 21:4; Acts 21:5; 27:39, 40).

cheilos χεῖλος 5491

cheilos is a term meaning "lip" in most of its six occurrences. In Heb 11:12, ***cheilos*** refers to the "seashore."

▸ **16.** Body, Bodily Functions > LIP

VALLEY

pharanx φάραγξ 5327

pharanx is a noun found only Luke 3:5 meaning "valley," citing the text of Isa 40:4: "every valley shall be raised up." This NT text affirms that the birth of Christ is a direct fulfillment of the Isaianic prophecy anticipating the coming of the messianic king.

WAY, PATH, ROAD

hodos ὁδός 3598

hodos is a noun occurring around one hundred times with the primary meaning "way" in the literal sense of "road," "route," "journey" and the figurative sense of "way of life," "lifestyle."

Literal references to a "road" or "(well-traveled) path" include those in Matt 21:8; Mark 10:32; Luke 18:35; Acts 8:26. ***hodos*** refers to a "journey" (Matt 10:10; Mark 6:8; Luke 2:44; 11:6; Acts 1:12); a "path" or "route" (Matt 2:12; Mark 4:4; Luke 8:5, 12); and "access" to the temple sanctuary (Heb 9:8; 10:20).

Figurative usage of ***hodos*** is more common. The meaning "path" or "way," for instance, refers to Christ's claim that he is "the way," affirming that the road to eternal life lies exclusively with him (John 14:6). In contrast, Matt 7:14

indicates that there is a "broad way" to destruction. Acts 16:17 refers to "the way of salvation," indicating access to eternal life and peace with God. Similarly, Luke 1:79; Rom 3:17 refer to "the way of peace," implying a state of full reconciliation with God. The phrase "way of righteousness" in Matt 21:32; 2 Pet 2:21 refers to a righteous lifestyle. General references to people's "ways," both good and bad, are found in 1 Cor 4:17; 12:31; Jas 1:8; 2 Pet 2:15; Jude 11.

The figurative "way of the Lord," as a prepared "route" for the coming of the Messiah, is indicated in Matt 3:3; 11:10; Mark 1:2ff.; John 1:23 — all quotations derived from Isa 40:3. Other general references to "the ways of God," denoting his methods of interacting with his people, include those in Rom 11:33; Heb 3:10. His own "righteous paths" are noted in Acts 13:10. In particular, "the way of God," as the divinely prescribed conduct for those who wish to follow him, is noted in Matt 22:16; Mark 12:14; Luke 1:76; Acts 18:25ff.

Acts 9:2; 19:23; 22:4 describe early Christian disciples as "followers of the way."

▸ **86.** Movement Toward or Away From > JOURNEY

WILDERNESS, DESERT

erēmia ἐρημία 2047

erēmia is a noun found four times denoting a "wilderness" or "desert" throughout (Matt 15:33; Mark 8:4; 2 Cor 11:26; Heb 11:38).

erēmos ἔρημος 2048

erēmos is an adjectival form used primarily in the nominal sense of "wilderness," "desert" throughout the fifty occurrences of the term.

John the Baptist's preaching in the "wilderness," preparing for the coming of Christ, is indicated in Matt 3:1ff.; 11:7; Mark 1:3, 4; Luke 3:2ff.; 7:24; John 1:23. Jesus' temptation by the devil in the "wilderness" is recorded in Matt 4:1; Mark 1:12ff.

General references to "wilderness" include Matt 14:13; 24:26; Mark 6:31ff.; Luke 5:16; 15:4; John 11:54; Acts 21:38; Rev 12:6, 14; 17:3.

John 3:14 refers to Moses lifting up the serpent in the "wilderness" — the serpent that provided the catalyst for divine healing. References to Israel's wandering in the "wilderness" between Egypt and Canaan are found in John 6:31, 49; Acts 7:30ff.; 13:18; 1 Cor 10:5; Heb 3:8, 17, emphasizing the divine actions of both blessing and judgment.

10. Earth, Dust, Rocks, Minerals, Metals, Stones

AMETHYST

amethystos ἀμέθυστος 271

amethystos is a rare noun found only in Rev 21:20 denoting an "amethyst," a rare gemstone and one of the twelve foundation stones of the wall surrounding the heavenly Jerusalem.

BERYL

bēryllos βήρυλλος 969

bēryllos is a rare noun found only in Rev 21:20, denoting a "beryl" as the key component of the eighth gate of the heavenly city of Jerusalem.

BRONZE, BRASS

chalkos χαλκός 5475

chalkos is a noun found in five contexts denoting the metal "bronze," "brass" in various forms such as "money" in Matt 10:9; Mark 6:8; 12:41; a "gong" (i.e., musical instrument) in 1 Cor 13:1; and the metal itself in Rev 18:12.

- ▸ **30.** Money, Business, Wealth, Poverty > MONEY

chalkeos χάλκεος 5470

chalkeos is a rare adjective meaning "brazen," or "made of brass," referring to idols and found only in Rev 9:20.

chalkion χαλκίον 5473

chalkion is a rare noun denoting a "bronze vessel, utensil" found only in Mark 7:4.

- ▸ **34.** Craftsmanship, Artisanship, Furniture, Implements > VESSEL, ARTICLE, UTENSIL, BASKET, FLASK

chalkolibanon χαλκολίβανον 5474

Here is another rare noun denoting "burnished, polished bronze." It is used metaphorically in Rev 1:15; 2:18 as a means of describing the glistening feet of the heavenly Christ in John's apocalyptic vision.

CLAY

pēlos πηλός 4081

pēlos denotes "clay" in six places, referring to the mixture of dirt and spittle that Jesus applied to the eyes of a blind man, which led to the restoration of his sight in John 9:6ff. Rom 9:21 refers to the potter's "clay."

CUT

latomeō λατομέω 2998

latomeō is a rare verb found only twice, indicating the action of "cutting a tomb from the rock" (Matt 27:60; Mark 15:46).

laxeutos λαξευτός 2991

laxeutos is a rare adjective denoting a tomb that had been "cut from the rock" or "cut out of stone."

SEE ALSO

- ▸ **21.** Die, Perish, Kill, Destroy > CUT TO PIECES
  dichotomeō
- ▸ **28.** Agriculture, Viticulture, Animal Husbandry > BREAK OFF, CUT, CUT OFF
  koptō
- ▸ **76.** Force, Harm, Oppress > CUT, CUT OFF
  katakoptō, aphaireō
- ▸ **78.** Act Upon, Push, Pull, Break, Cut > CUT OFF, CUT DOWN
  apokoptō, ekkoptō

DUST

chous, choos χοῦς, χόος 5522

chous is a rare noun found only twice, referring literally to "dust" in Mark 6:11. Rev 18:19 refers to throwing dust over one's head as a sign of mourning.

koniortos κονιορτός 2868

koniortos is a synonym for ***chous*** (above) denoting "dust" in the expression "to shake the dust off one's feet" as a symbolic gesture of rejection, curse, and denial for most of the five occurrences of the term (Matt 10:14; Luke 9:5; 10:11; Acts 13:51). See also Acts 22:23.

EARTHEN, EARTHY

ostrakinos ὀστράκινος 3749

ostrakinos is a rare adjective found only twice. In 2 Tim 2:20 it refers to household vessels "made of earth (or clay)." In 2 Cor 4:7 it refers metaphorically to the believer's human frailty as "earthen vessels," the fragile "containers" that enjoy the treasure, the blessings of the gospel.

choikos χοϊκός 5517

choikos is a rare adjective found three times referring to the original man created by God as a man "of the earth" (1 Cor 15:47ff.).

EMERALD

smaragdos σμάραγδος 4665

smaragdos is a rare noun found only in Rev 21, referring to the "emerald" that is one of the precious stones adorning one of the twelve gates of the heavenly city — each gate representing one of the twelve tribes of Israel.

smaragdinos σμαράγδινος 4664

smaragdinos is a rare adjectival form derived from ***smaragdos*** (above) found only in Rev 4:3, where it relates the likeness of the rainbow encircling the throne of God to an "emerald," the semi-translucent precious stone of a light green hue.

GOLD, GOLDEN

chrysos χρυσός 5557

chrysos denotes the precious metal "gold" throughout its approximately twenty occurrences (Matt 2:11; 10:9; 23:16ff.; Acts 3:6; 17:29; 1 Cor 3:12; 1 Tim 2:9; Heb 9:4; Jas 5:3; 1 Pet 1:7ff.; Rev 9:7; 17:4; 18:12ff.; 21:18ff.).

chryseos χρύσεος 5552

chryseos is the adjectival form derived from ***chrysos*** (above) and has the consistent meaning "golden," "of gold" throughout the eighteen occurrences of the term.

Literal references are found in 2 Tim 2:20; Heb 9:4.

The remaining usage of ***chryseos*** is metaphorical, found exclusively in the book of Revelation. The "golden" lampstand of the heavenly temple scene is noted in Rev 1:12, 20; 2:1; the "golden" altar in Rev 8:3; 9:13. The "golden" belt wrapped around the heavenly Christ is indicated in Rev 1:13, also worn by angels in Rev 15:6. Crowns of "gold" worn by the elders surrounding the throne of God are depicted in Rev 4:4 (see also Rev 14:14). "Golden" bowls full of incense, depicting the outpouring of God's wrath, are noted in Rev 15:7. See also Rev 17:4; 21:15.

IRON

sidērous σιδηροῦς 4603

sidērous is an adjectival term that signifies "made of iron" or "iron." It occurs five times. Acts 12:10 refers literally to an "iron gate." Rev 2:27; 12:5; 19:15 refer to the "rod of iron" as a symbol of divine power and authority. Rev 9:9 mentions the "iron breastplates" of the visionary locusts, symbolizing the ravages of a divinely initiated plague against a godless humanity.

sidēros σίδηρος 4604

sidēros occurs only in Rev 18:12, referring to implements of iron owned by merchants.

kaustēriazō καυστηριάζω 2743

kaustēriazō signifies "to sear with a hot iron" and is found only in 1 Tim 4:2, where it is used metaphorically to refer to hardened liars whose consciences have been seared by their deceit.

JASPER

iaspis ἴασπις 2393

iaspis occurs four times, and only in the book of Revelation. Rev 4:3 likens the appearance of the divine figure on the heavenly throne to jasper; while Rev 21:11, 18, 19 liken the appearance of the heavenly city of Jerusalem to that of jasper and other preciousmetals and stones.

MARBLE

marmaros μάρμαρος 3139

marmaros occurs only in Rev 18:12, referring to "marble" as part of the inventory of the merchandise belonging to the nations of the world who traded with the city of Babylon, now earmarked for total destruction.

PEARL

margaritēs μαργαρίτης 3135

margaritēs is a term referring to "pearls" in each of the nine contexts in which it is found. Matt 7:6; 13:45ff.; 1 Tim 2:9; Rev 18:12 refer literally to precious ornaments. In Rev 17:4; 18:16; 21:21, "pearls" are indicated in the apocalyptic visions of the apostle John.

ROCK

petra πέτρα 4073

petra is the principal term for "rock" in the NT, found in sixteen contexts.

General references to rocks are found in Matt 7:24ff.; Mark 15:46; Luke 6:48; Rev 6:15, 16.

In significant theological contexts, ***petra*** is used, for example, as the name "Rock." Christ takes this title in Matt 16:18, thereby affirming his divine nature as the foundation of the new covenant church. Christ is also described as the "rock of offense" to unbelievers in Rom 9:33; 1 Pet 2:8 — citing the same title used for Yahweh in Isa 8:14, and indicating the same fate for unbelievers. ***petra*** also refers to Christ as the "Rock" in 1 Cor 10:4, where Paul identifies Christ as that same "rock" that provided water for Israel in the wilderness.

trachys τραχύς 5138

This noun is found in only two places, referring to the rocky shoreline where the ship in which Paul was sailing en route to Rome was wrecked (Acts 27:29). In Luke 3:5, ***trachys*** refers to "rough ways (or roads)," indicating a rocky, stony surface.

SAND

ammos ἄμμος 285

ammos is a noun found in only four places, meaning "sand" or "sandy ground." The literal sense is found in Matt 7:26. Rom 9:27; Heb 11:12 refer to the enormous number of Israelite people as "sand on the shore." Rev 20:8 uses the same metaphor.

SILVER

argyros ἄργυρος 696

argyros is a noun occurring five times, all with reference to "silver."

"Silver" as money is indicated in Matt 10:9; Rev 18:12. As a valuable metal, it is noted in 1 Cor 3:12; Jas 5:3. Acts 17:29 refers to silver as a component of an idol statue.

argyrion ἀργύριον 694

argyrion is a synonym for ***argyros*** (above) occurring twenty times. References to "money" are found in Matt 25:18, 27; 28:12ff.; Mark 14:11; Luke 9:3; 22:5; Acts 7:16; 8:20. "Pieces of silver" are noted in Matt 26:15; 27:3ff.; Acts 19:19. General references to silver are found in Acts 3:6; 20:33; 1 Pet 1:18.

argyrous ἀργυροῦς 693

argyrous is an adjectival form derived from ***argyros*** (above) meaning "made of silver." It refers to idols in Acts 19:24; Rev 9:20; and to silver containers in 2 Tim 2:20.

SEE ALSO

▸ **34.** Craftsmanship, Artisanship, Furniture, Implements > SILVERSMITH
argyrokopos

STONE

lithos λίθος 3037

lithos is a noun meaning "stone" throughout its sixty occurrences. It is used both literally and metaphorically. Literal references to "stones" include those in Matt 3:9; 27:60ff.; Mark 13:2; 2 Cor 3:7. Precious stones are indicated in 1 Cor 3:12; Rev 4:3; 21:11.

As its Hebrew dynamic equivalent*'eben* is used metaphorically to refer to Yahweh, so ***lithos*** is used symbolically to refer to Christ. Following upon the OT usage, there are several references to the "stone" rejected by the builders becoming the chief cornerstone (Matt 21:42; Mark 12:10; Luke 20:17; 1 Pet 2:4ff. — an identification self-consciously adopted by Christ). Christ is also identified with the "stumbling stone," upon which those who refuse to accept him as the Messiah will "stumble" (Rom 9:32, 33; 1 Pet 2:8).

In 1 Pet 2:5, believers are described metaphorically as "living stones" forming part of Christ's body.

lithinos λίθινος 3035

lithinos is an adjective meaning "made of stone" in John 2:6; 2 Cor 3:3; Rev 9:20.

psēphos ψῆφος 5586

psēphos is a noun denoting a "small smooth stone" (or pebble), referring metaphorically to the "stone" in Rev 2:17 (twice) on which the new name of Christ will be written.

petrōdēs πετρώδης 4075

petrōdēs is an adjective referring to "stony" ground in Matt 13:5, 20; Mark 4:5, 16.

SEE ALSO

▸ **21.** Die, Perish, Kill, Destroy > STONE
lithazō, lithoboleō

11. Meteorology, Water

AIR

aēr ἀήρ 109

aēr is a noun denoting "air" in each of the seven contexts in which it is found. Most of these refer to the atmosphere (Acts 22:23; 1 Cor 9:26; 14:9; 1 Thess 4:17; Rev 9:2; 16:17). In Eph 2:2, the term refers to the satanic "prince of the power of the air." The term "air" denotes the atmospheric region between earth and heaven as the domain of Satan.

ouranos οὐρανός 3772

ouranos is a common noun denoting "heaven" as the dwelling place of God throughout most of the nearly three hundred occurrences of the term. In several places, however, ***ouranos*** also denotes "air," or the atmosphere above the earth, the domain of birds (Matt 6:26; 8:20; 13:32; Mark 4:4, 32; Luke 8:5; 9:58; 13:19; Acts 10:12; 11:6).

▸ **1.** Celestial Realm, Earthly Realm > HEAVEN, SKY, HEAVENLY

BLOW

pneō πνέω 4154

pneō is a verb found seven times that refers to the "blowing" of the wind (Matt 7:25, 27; Luke 12:55; John 3:8; 6:18; Acts 27:40; Rev 7:1).

hypopneō ὑποπνέω 5285

hypopneō is a rare variant of ***pneō*** (above) found only in Acts 27:13 and referring to the "gentle blowing" of the wind.

CLOUD

nephos νέφος 3509

nephos is a rare noun, used only in Heb 12:1 in a metaphorical reference to the "cloud" of heavenly witnesses that surrounds all believers as a means of their spiritual encouragement to godliness.

nephelē νεφέλη 3507

The noun ***nephelē*** denotes a "cloud" throughout the nearly thirty occurrences of the term.

Literal reference to a "cloud" is found in Luke 12:54. Then, a "cloud" is said to take the risen Christ out of the sight of his disciples and up into heaven in Acts 1:9.

In other places ***nephelē*** denotes the theophanic "cloud" of God's presence. From this cloud God commends his son as the one with whom he is well pleased in Matt 17:5; Mark 9:7; Luke 9:35. Christ is depicted coming at the end of the age in the "clouds" of heaven (Matt 24:30; 26:64; Mark 13:26; 14:62; Luke 21:27; 1 Thess 4:17; Rev 1:7). Reference to the cloud that enveloped Christ and his three disciples on the Mount of Transfiguration is found in Luke 9:34. 1 Cor 10:1ff. mentions the "cloud," the presence of Yahweh, leading the people of Israel through the desert. Rev 14:14ff. refers to the cloud "throne" on which the heavenly Son of Man figure sits.

Other metaphorical uses of ***nephelē*** include those in 2 Pet 2:17; Jude 12; Rev 10:1; 11:12.

DRY, WATERLESS

anydros ἄνυδρος 504

anydros is an adjective denoting the state of being "dry," "without water" in four places. "Dry" or "waterless" places are noted in Matt 12:43; Luke 11:24. "Waterless" springs are mentioned in 2 Pet 2:17; clouds "without water" are indicated in Jude 12.

▸ **11.** Meteorology, Water > WATER

SEE ALSO

▸ **88.** Qualities, Characteristics > DRY, DRY UP, WITHER, WITHERED
xēros, xērainō

FLOOD

kataklysmos κατακλυσμός 2627

kataklysmos is a noun found in four contexts denoting the divine judgment of the universal "flood" in the days of Noah (Matt 24:38f.; Luke 17:27; 2 Pet 2:5).

plēmmyra πλήμμυρα 4132

plēmmyra is a rare noun denoting a literal "flood" in Luke 6:48.

potamos ποταμός 4215

potamos is a noun occurring sixteen times with the predominant sense of "river." However, on four occasions it denotes a "flood," brought about by torrential rain (Matt 7:25, 27; Mark 6:48, 49).

▸ **9.** Land, Geography, Topography > RIVER

FOAM

epaphrizō ἐπαφρίζω 1890

epaphrizō is a rare noun found only in Jude 13, referring to false teachers depicted metaphorically as "casting up the foam" of their own shame.

SEE ALSO

▸ **20.** Illness, Disease, Health, Healing > FOAM
aphrizō

HAIL

chalaza χάλαζα 5464

This is a rare term in the NT, occurring only three times. It is found only in the book of Revelation, and each occurrence refers solely to sending hail as an expression of divine wrath. In Rev 8:7, hail forms part of the "first trumpet" judgment. In Rev 11:19, it constitutes an element of the "seventh trumpet" judgment, a climactic Day of the Lord phenomenon issuing from the heavenly throne room. It is also found in Rev 16:21 as part of the "seventh bowl" judgment (see also Rev 11:19).

LIGHTNING

astrapē ἀστραπή 796

astrapē is a noun that occurs eleven times with the sense of "lightning," "flash of lightning," in all but one of these contexts.

Matt 24:27; Luke 17:24 refer to lightning in general terms. ***astrapē*** also likens the appearance of Christ's divine glory to lightning (Matt 28:3). In Matt 10:18, Jesus declares that he saw Satan fall like lightning from heaven. In two places in the book of Revelation, ***astrapē*** refers to flashes of lightning as part of a vision of the heavenly throne room of God, the source of divine judgment (Rev 4:5; 11:19). In addition, the Apocalypse of John records the occurrence of lightning as an accompaniment to God's punishment of the wicked on earth (Rev 8:5; 16:18).

MIST

achlys ἀχλύς 887

achlys is found only in Acts 13:11, where it refers to "mist" in a metaphorical sense, indicating the temporary blindness experienced by the apostle Paul after his conversion.

RAGE

klydōn κλύδων 2830

klydōn is found in only two contexts. In Luke 8:24 it refers to the "raging" of the stormy waters of the Sea of Galilee. In Jas 1:6 ***klydōn*** is translated "wave," but the context indicates that it is a wave driven by stormy seas.

- ▸ **11.** Meteorology, Water > WAVE

SEE ALSO

- ▸ **19.** Mind, Spirit, Emotions, Feelings, Desires > RAGE
  phruassō

RAIN

brechō βρέχω 1026

brechō is a verb found eight times, meaning "to rain," "send rain" in a literal sense in Matt 5:45; Jas 5:17; Rev 11:6. It also refers to Yahweh causing fire and sulfur to "rain down" upon Sodom and Gomorrah.

- ▸ **11.** Meteorology, Water > SEND RAIN
- ▸ **80.** Related to Liquids > WASH, BATHE, WASHING, WETTING

brochē βροχή 1028

brochē is a noun derived from ***brechō*** (above) found in only two places and referring to the "rain" that flooded the earth during the days of Noah (Matt 7:25, 27).

hyetos ὑετός 5205

hyetos is a synonym for ***brochē*** (above) that indicates literal "rain" on six occasions (Acts 14:17; 28:2; Heb 6:7; Jas 5:7, 18; Rev 11:6).

RAINBOW

iris ἶρις 2463

iris is a term found only twice, referring to a "rainbow" surrounding the throne of God (Rev 4:3) and encircling the head of a mighty angel (Rev 10:1).

ROAR

ēcheō ἠχέω 2278

This verb is found in two places. Luke 21:25 refers to the "roaring" of the sea; and 1 Cor 13:1 describes an undefined "noisy" gong.

SEE ALSO

- ▸ **14.** Animals > ROAR
  mykaomai, ōryomai

SALT, SALT WATER

halykos ἁλυκός 252

halykos is an adjectival form found only in Jas 3:12, where it refers to "salt" water.

SEE ALSO

- ▸ **23.** Food, Drink, Cooking > SALT
  halas, halizō, analos

SEND RAIN

brechō βρέχω 1026

brechō is a verb found in seven contexts with the primary meanings "to rain" or "wash." In Matt 5:45 it refers to God "sending rain."

- ▸ **11.** Meteorology, Water > RAIN
- ▸ **80.** Related to Liquids > WASH, BATHE, WASHING, WETTING

SEE ALSO

- ▸ **63.** Speak, Tell, Declare, Call > SEND FOR
  metapempō
- ▸ **79.** Throw, Send, Drive, Mix, Remove > SEND, SEND AWAY, SEND OUT
  apostellō, exapostellō, synapostellō, pempō, anapempō, sympempō, ekballō, apolyō

STORM

lailaps λαῖλαψ 2978

lailaps is a term found only three times, meaning "windstorm" in Mark 4:27; Luke 8:23; 2 Pet 2:17.

THUNDER

brontē βροντή 1027

brontē is a noun meaning "thunder" in each of its twelve occurrences.

References to "thunder" as a natural phenomenon are found in the context of divine revelation that includes judgment (Rev 4:5; 11:19; 14:2; 16:18), all of which refer to thunder emanating from the throne of God in heaven. See also John 12:28; Rev 6:1; 8:5; 19:6.

In Mark 3:17, ***brontē*** is used metaphorically as a nickname for a volatile personality in relation to two of Jesus' disciples, James and John, who are described here as "sons of thunder." Rev 10:3ff. refers to "seven thunders," described as elements of divine judgment against a wayward humanity.

WATER

hydōr ὕδωρ 5204

hydōr is a noun occurring about eighty times with the consistent meaning "water."

hydōr refers generally to "water" (Matt 8:32; Mark 9:41; Luke 7:44; John 2:7ff.; 1 Pet 3:20; Rev 1:15; 16:4ff.). 2 Pet 3:6 refers to "flood waters," and 2 Pet 3:5 to created bodies of water.

Water is used for baptism (Matt 3:11, 16; Mark 1:8ff.; Luke 3:16; John 1:26ff.; Acts 1:5; 8:36ff.; 11:16), and for ceremonial ritual (Heb 9:19).

hydōr is used symbolically in several very significant texts. In John 3:5, Christ refers to the importance of being "born of water," indicating a cleansing from sin through personal confession. See also Eph 5:26; Heb 10:22. In John 4:10ff.; 7:38, Christ identifies himself as the source of "living water," symbolizing the gift of eternal life and peace with God. Rev 21:6 refers to the "fountain (or river) of the water of life" in heaven (Rev 21:6; 22:1, 17).

anydros ἄνυδρος 504

anydros is an adjective denoting the quality of "waterless" or "dry" (Matt 12:43; Luke 11:24; 2 Pet 2:17; Jude 12).

▸ **11.** Meteorology, Water > DRY, WATERLESS

SEE ALSO

▸ **23.** Food, Drink, Cooking > WATER
hydria, hydropoteō

WAVE

kyma κῦμα 2949

kyma is a noun occurring five times. It refers to "waves of the sea" in Matt 8:24; 14:24; Mark 4:37; Acts 27:41. In Jude 13, the use is symbolic, depicting the harm done by false prophets and teachers in the church.

salos σάλος 4535

salos is a rare noun denoting "waves" of the sea in Luke 21:25.

klydōn κλύδων 2830

klydōn is a rare term denoting "raging, storm-tossed waves" in Luke 8:24; Jas 1:6.

▸ **11.** Meteorology, Water > RAGE

WELL, SPRING, FOUNTAIN

pēgē πηγή 4077

pēgē is a noun found twelve times meaning "fountain," "well," "spring" throughout, both in a literal and metaphorical sense.

A pathological menstrual hemorrhage is described in relation to a woman's illness as a "flow" (lit., "fountain of blood") in Mark 5:29.

Literal references to a "well" or "spring" are found in John 4:6; Jas 3:11ff.; Rev 8:10; 14:7; 16:4.

Elsewhere, ***pēgē*** is used metaphorically to denote a "spring of water" that symbolizes the spiritual life force emanating from Christ that will guarantee its possessor an unbroken relationship with God throughout eternity (John 4:14). The heavenly consummation of the "springs of living water" is found in Rev 7:17; 21:6. Both texts indicate that these "springs" constitute the visionary symbolic source of eternal life.

WIND

anemos ἄνεμος 417

anemos is a noun occurring around thirty times denoting "wind" throughout.

"Wind," as a natural phenomenon, is noted in Matt 7:25ff.; 8:26ff.; Mark 4:37ff.; Luke 7:24; 8:23ff.; Acts 27:4ff.; Rev 6:13; Jude 12.

anemos is also used metaphorically, denoting the "four winds" of the compass (Matt 24:31; Rev 7:1).

notos νότος 3558

notos is a noun found in seven places meaning "south," "south wind." The latter sense is indicated in Luke 12:55; Acts 27:13; 28:13.

pneuma πνεῦμα 4151

pneuma is a noun occurring over 140 times with the predominant sense of "spirit." In John 3:8, however, ***pneuma*** denotes the "wind" in a general sense.

▸ **2.** Supernatural Beings/Forces, Spiritual Realm > SPIRIT, SPIRITUAL, SPIRITUALLY
▸ **16.** Body, Bodily Functions > BREATH, BREATHE

pnoē πνοή 4157

pnoē is a rare noun denoting "wind" in Acts 2:2, where it refers to the supernatural phenomenon of a visitation of the Holy Spirit.

▸ **16.** Body, Bodily Functions > BREATH, BREATHE

anemizō ἀνεμίζω 416

anemizō is a rare verb found only in Jas 1:6, referring to "being driven by the wind."

WINTER, STORMY

cheimōn χειμών 5494

cheimōn is a noun that occurs six times, denoting "winter" in four instances (Matt 24:20; Mark 13:18; John 10:22; 2 Tim 4:21) and "stormy weather" twice (Matt 16:3; Acts 27:20).

SEE ALSO

▸ **3.** Periods of Time, Duration, Frequency, Speed > WINTER, SPEND THE WINTER
paracheimazō

12. Fire, Heat, Smoke, Burning

ASH

spodos σποδός 4700

The noun ***spodos*** is found in three contexts. It refers to "ashes" sprinkled on sackcloth and one's body as a symbolic expression of anguish and grief in Matt 11:21; Luke 10:13. In Heb 9:13 the term denotes the "ashes" of a heifer sprinkled on ceremonially unclean people as a means of purifying them.

tephroō τεφρόω 5077

tephroō is a rare verb with the meaning "to reduce to ashes" (i.e., by fire) found only in 2 Pet 2:6 in relation to the destruction of the cities of Sodom and Gomorrah.

BURN, BURNING, LIGHT, SET ON FIRE

kaiō καίω 2545

The verb ***kaiō*** means to "burn," "light a fire." It is used both literally and metaphorically in twelve contexts. Matt 5:15 refers to "lighting" a candle. Luke 12:35 refers to lamps "burning."

Elsewhere, ***kaiō*** is used in a metaphorical sense. There are numerous "burning" phenomena in the apocalyptic visions of John, including torches before the divine throne (Rev 4:5), a star (Rev 8:10), a mountain (Rev 8:8), and the lake of "burning" sulfur (Rev 19:20; 21:8). Heb 12:18 describes the mountain "blazing" with fire (Mount Sinai), which symbolizes the divine presence. "Burning" is an indication of divine judgment in John 15:6 (see also 1 Cor 13:3). The "burning" of one's heart, indicating an awareness of a strong, inner perception, is indicated in Luke 24:32.

katakaiō κατακαίω 2618

katakaiō is a variant form of ***kaiō*** (above) found in twelve places with the meaning "burn up," "consume by fire."

Acts 19:19 describes the destruction of magic books by fire; and Heb 13:11 refers to the "burning" of the sin offering.

In metaphorical contexts, ***katakaiō*** indicates the consuming fire of divine judgment against the wicked (Matt 3:12; 13:30, 40; Luke 3:17; 2 Pet 3:10; Rev 8:7; 17:16; 18:8). It also constitutes the symbolic means of testing the believer's life work (1 Cor 3:15).

ekkaiō ἐκκαίω 1572

ekkaiō is a rare variant of ***kaiō*** (above) found only in Rom 1:27 and referring to the perverse passion of men "burning with lust" for one another.

pyroō πυρόω 4448

pyroō is a verb with the meaning "burn," "set on fire" in both literal and metaphorical contexts. It occurs six times.

Literal references to the process of refinement, to "purification by fire" are found in Rev 1:15; 3:18. Metaphorically, ***pyroō*** signifies to "burn" with lust or passion in 1 Cor 7:9. The vision of the cosmic elements "on fire," as a sign of the apocalyptic end of the world, is recorded in 2 Pet 3:12. Eph 6:16 refers to the "flaming" arrows (or darts) of the devil.

▸ **12.** Fire, Heat, Smoke, Burning > REFINE

kausis καῦσις 2740

kausis is a rare noun found only in Heb 6:8 with the literal meaning "burning," signifying the end of the earth. It is translated "to be burned."

pyrōsis πύρωσις 4451

pyrōsis is a noun denoting a "burning," "fiery ordeal or trial." The latter meaning is noted in 1 Pet 4:12; the former in relation to the fiery destruction of the city of Babylon, personified as a whore (Rev 18:9, 18).

▸ **75.** Suffering, Distress, Sadness > TRIAL

thymiaō θυμιάω 2370

thymiaō is a rare noun with the meaning to "burn incense" found only in Luke 1:9.

▸ **41.** Sacrifice, Offering, Worship, Praise > INCENSE

phlogizō φλογίζω 5394

phlogizō is a rare verb meaning "to set on fire" found only in Jas 3:6.

COAL, CHARCOAL

anthrax ἄνθραξ 440

anthrax is a rare noun used metaphorically to refer to the experience of guilt. It is found only in Rom 12:20, where it denotes "burning coals" heaped on the head of one's enemies in response to love being shown to them.

anthrakia ἀνθρακιά 439

anthrakia is a noun found only in John 18:18; 21:9, denoting a "charcoal fire" in both instances.

DISSOLVE, MELT

lyō λύω 3089

lyō is a verb found approximately forty times in all, with the predominant meanings "release" or "loose(n)."

In a couple of places, however, ***lyō*** is also translated "melt" or "dissolve." In 2 Pet 3:10ff. it refers to the apocalyptic destruction of the cosmos through a fiery heat.

▸ **21.** Die, Perish, Kill, Destroy > DESTROY, DESTROYER, DESTRUCTION
▸ **55.** Bondage, Captivity, Servitude > RELEASE
▸ **78.** Act Upon, Push, Pull, Break, Cut > BREAK

EXTINGUISH, QUENCH, UNQUENCHABLE

sbennymi σβέννυμι 4570

sbennymi is a verb occurring eight times meaning "quench" or "extinguish," mostly in metaphorical contexts.

Matt 25:8 refers literally to lamps being extinguished, or going out.

The remaining usage of ***sbennymi*** is symbolic. Matt 12:20 alludes to the gentle rule of the Servant of Yahweh, who "will not quench a smoldering wick." ***sbennymi*** refers to the unquenchable fire of the wicked in hell (Mark 9:44ff.); to the shield of faith "quenching" the fiery arrows (or darts) of the devil (Eph 6:16); and to believers "quenching" raging fire (Heb 11:34). 1 Thess 5:19 enjoins the believer not to "quench" the spirit of God.

asbestos ἄσβεστος 762

asbestos is an adjective meaning "unquenchable" in all four occurrences of the term. In each case it refers to the fire of divine judgment (Matt 3:12; Mark 9:43, 45; Luke 3:17).

FIRE, FIERY

pyr πῦρ 4442

pyr is virtually the sole term for "fire" in the NT, and it is found over seventy times.

References to literal "fire" are found in Matt 3:10; Mark 9:22; Luke 22:55; Acts 28:5; Jas 3:5. In addition, "fire" as the vehicle for a divine theophany is noted in Acts 7:30 in relation to the "burning bush" in the Sinai wilderness where God had appeared to Moses. See also Heb 12:18. "Fire" in the metaphorical context of divine revelation is indicated in Matt 3:11; Luke 3:16, with reference to baptism in the Holy Spirit; and in Acts 2:3 in relation to speaking in tongues as a consequence of baptism in the Holy Spirit. The phenomenon of "fire" as a sign accompanying the end of time is noted in Acts 2:19.

More commonly, "fire" is indicated symbolically as the instrument of divine wrath (Matt 3:12; 25:41; Mark 9:43ff.; Luke 3:17; John 15:6; Heb 10:27; 2 Pet 3:7; Jude 7; Rev 14:10; 16:8; 19:20; 20:9ff.; 21:8); and of divine judgment (1 Cor 3:13ff.; 1 Pet 1:7; Rev 3:18). God himself is described as a "consuming fire" of judgment (Heb 12:29); and "fire" is associated with the essential being of God (Rev 1:14; 10:1), and of Christ (Rev 19:12; 2:18). Other metaphorical references to "fire" include Heb 1:7; Jas 3:6; 5:3; Rev 8:5ff.; 9:17ff.; 17:16.

pyrinos πύρινος 4447

pyrinos is a rare adjective found only in Rev 9:17, describing the visionary breastplates of demonic creatures as "fiery."

FLAME

phlox φλόξ 5395

phlox denotes "flame(s)" in each of its seven occurrences. Acts 7:30 refers to a literal "flame" in relation to the theophanic fire from which God revealed himself to Moses.

The sense of "flame" in the context of divine judgment is recorded in Luke 16:24. Elsewhere, the expression "flame(s) of fire" refers to one visionary aspect of God and Christ in theophanic revelation (Rev 1:14; 2:18; 19:12). Similarly, Heb 1:7 describes the servants of God as "flames of fire," probably denoting heavenly creatures alongside angelic beings.

FURNACE

kaminos κάμινος 2575

kaminos is a noun found four times denoting a metaphorical "furnace" of fire. It refers to a "fiery furnace" of eternal torment in Matt 13:42, 50; Rev 9:2. In Rev 1:15, the feet of the heavenly Christ are likened to those refined in a furnace.

HEAT

kausōn καύσων 2742

This noun is rare, occurring only three times with the sense of the "burning heat" of the day (Matt 20:12; Luke 12:25; Jas 1:12).

kauma καῦμα 2738

kauma is also rare, occurring only twice with the literal sense of "heat of the day" in Rev 7:16 and the "scorching heat" of divine judgment in Rev 16:9.

thermē θέρμη 2329

This term is found only in Acts 28:3, referring to the scorching heat of fire.

HOT

zestos ζεστός 2200

zestos is a rare adjective, found only three times in Rev 3:15, 16 with reference to the Laodicean congregation's lack of fervor or zeal in the practice of their Christian faith. Their condemnation by the risen Christ rests on the fact that they are "lukewarm" in their commitment to him — "neither cold nor hot."

MELT

tēkō τήκω 5080

tēkō is found only in 2 Pet 3:12, where it refers to the cosmic dissolution brought about by the ultimate judgment of the Day of the Lord. The text refers to the elements melting with fire.

REFINE

pyroō πυρόω 4448

pyroō is a verb found six times, meaning "burn" in four of these contexts, with both literal and metaphorical force.

In two places, ***pyroō*** refers to metals "refined by fire" (Rev 3:15 [bronze]; 3:18 [gold]).

▸ **12.** Fire, Heat, Smoke, Burning > BURN, BURNING, LIGHT, SET ON FIRE

SCORCH

kaumatizō καυματίζω 2739

kaumatizō is a verb found in four places, meaning "scorch" in the sense of "burn with intense heat."

Reference is made in Matt 13:6; Mark 4:6 to plants "scorched" or "withered" by the sun. Rev 16:8, 9 refers to "scorching" the wicked — an indication of their fiery torment.

SMOKE

kapnos καπνός 2586

The noun ***kapnos*** means "smoke" and is found thirteen times.

Acts 2:19 contains a general reference to "smoke." Elsewhere, ***kapnos*** is found exclusively in the book of Revelation, referring to the smoke of incense in the temple (Rev 8:4); smoke from the bottomless pit of destruction (Rev 9:2ff.); smoke pouring from the mouth of demonic creatures (Rev 9:17ff.); smoke issuing from the fiery destruction of the demonic "beasts" and the "Babylonian whore" (Rev 14:11; 18:9, 18; 19:3); and smoke filling the temple in connection with a divine theophany (Rev 15:8).

SULFUR, BRIMSTONE

theion θεῖον 2303

theion denotes "brimstone" or "burning sulfur." It refers to the discharge of molten lava and sulfurous gases associated with volcanic eruption, and it is used primarily in the context of divine judgment against the wicked.

Yahweh literally hurls "burning sulfur" against the cities of Sodom and Gomorrah in response to their flagrant sexual perversity (Luke 17:29, citing Gen 19:24).

The remaining usage of ***theion*** is metaphorical. In Rev 9:17ff. an emission of "burning sulfur" comes from the mouths of demonic horse-like creatures, symbolizing their capacity to hand out pain and destruction to humankind. Then, the hand of God hurls "burning sulfur" against the wicked in Rev 14:10. The ultimate fate of the wicked is to be cast into the lake of "burning sulfur" described in Rev 19:20; 20:10; 21:8.

theiōdēs θειώδης 2306

theiōdēs is a rare adjective, found only in Rev 9:17 and meaning "of brimstone" or "of sulfur" in relation to the color of the demonic horses.

13. Plants, Trees, Flora

BRANCH

klados κλάδος 2798

klados is a noun found eleven times and translated "branch" throughout.

Literal references to "branches" include Matt 13:32; 21:8; Mark 4:32; 13:28; Luke 13:19.

klados also signifies "branches" in a symbolic sense referring to the people of Israel in Rom 11:16ff.

klēma κλῆμα 2814

klēma is a noun found in four places, all of which use the term metaphorically to denote true followers of Christ as "branches" who derive their life from him, the vine (John 15:2, 4ff.).

stoibas στοιβάς 4746

stoibas is a rare noun occurring only in Mark 11:8 denoting a "branch" or "leafy limb."

baion βάϊον 902

baion is another rare noun found only in John 12:13 referring to "branches" of a palm tree.

BUSH

batos βάτος 942

batos is a noun denoting a "bush" in Mark 12:26; Luke 6:44; Luke 20:37; Acts 7:30, 35.

FIG TREE

sykē συκῆ 4808

sykē is a term denoting a literal "fig tree" in each of the sixteen contexts in which it is found (Matt 21:19ff.; 24:32; Mark 11:13ff.; 13:28; Luke 13:6ff.; John 1:48ff.; Jas 3:12; Rev 6:13).

FLOWER

anthos ἄνθος 438

anthos is the sole term for "flower" in the NT, found only four times (Jas 1:10f.; 1 Pet 1:24 [twice]).

FRANKINCENSE

libanos λίβανος 3030

libanos refers to "frankincense" and occurs rarely in the NT. In Matt 2:11 frankincense is one of the three gifts brought by the magi to the infant Jesus, along with gold and myrrh. In Rev 18:13, this fragrant perfume is found among the list of wares traded by the nations of the world with Babylon.

GARDEN

kēpos κῆπος 2779

kēpos is a noun found in five contexts. It denotes a "garden" in a general sense in Luke 13:19. John 18:1, 26; 19:41 refer to the garden of Gethsemane where Jesus was betrayed and arrested.

GRASS

chortos χόρτος 5528

chortos is a noun denoting "grass" throughout most of its fifteen occurrences (Matt 6:30; 14:19; Mark 6:39; Luke 12:28; John 6:10; Jas 1:10ff.; 1 Pet 1:24; Rev 8:7; 9:4).

HERB, SHRUB, VEGETABLE

lachanon λάχανον 3001

lachanon occurs four times and refers to "herbs" or "shrubs" (Matt 13:32; Mark 4:32; Luke 11:42; Rom 14:2).

botanē βοτάνη 1008

botanē is found only in Heb 6:7, where it refers to green herbs or vegetation.

LEAF

phyllon φύλλον 5444

phyllon is the sole NT term for "leaf" and is found on five occasions. Matt 21:19; 24:32; Mark 11:13; 13:28 refer literally and metaphorically to the leaves of a fig tree, illustrating Israel's spiritual vitality, or lack thereof. In Rev 22:2, ***phyllon*** refers to the leaves of the tree of life, located in the heavenly Jerusalem — leaves designated for the healing of the nations.

LILY

krinon κρίνον 2918

krinon is found only twice in the NT, both times in connection with Jesus' description of God's care for his creation, "Consider the lilies of the field . . ." (Matt 6:28; Luke 12:27).

MUSTARD

sinapi σίναπι 4615

sinapi is a noun referring to a "mustard seed." It is found in only five contexts, three of which liken the kingdom of God to a mustard seed (Matt 13:31; Mark 4:31; Luke 13:19). Like the "mustard seed," a tiny seed from which grows a large tree, so the kingdom of God grows to enormous proportions from the smallest beginnings. In Matt 17:20; Luke 17:6, the point is made that genuine faith need only be as large as a mustard seed in order to be fully effective.

▸ **28.** Agriculture, Viticulture, Animal Husbandry > SEED, SOW

MYRRH

smyrna σμύρνα 4666

smyrna refers to "myrrh" in only two places. Matt 2:11 lists it is one of the gifts, along with gold and frankincense, brought by the oriental magi to the Christ child. In John 19:39, myrrh is indicated in combination with bitter aloes as an embalming product intended for the body of Christ.

SEE ALSO

▸ **20.** Illness, Disease, Health, Healing > MYRRH
smyrnizō

OLIVE, OLIVE TREE

agrielaios ἀγριέλαιος 65

agrielaios is found only in Rom 11:17, 24 with reference to a "wild olive tree."

▸ **28.** Agriculture, Viticulture, Animal Husbandry > WILD

kallielaios καλλιέλαιος 2565

kallielaios occurs only in Rom 11:24 and signifies a "cultivated olive tree," as opposed to the wild variety.

elaia ἐλαία 1636

elaia is a noun referring primarily to the "olive" as a fruit, incorporated in the title "Mount of Olives." The term is found in Matt 21:1; 24:3; Mark 11:1; 13:3; 14:26; Luke 19:29, 37; 21:37; John 8:1. A literal "olive tree" is indicated in Rom 11:17, 24; and a metaphorical usage is found in Rev 11:4, where the "two witnesses" as anointed servants of God are symbolically described as "two olive trees." Only in Jas 3:12 does ***elaia*** refer to "olives" as a fruit.

elaiōn ἐλαιών 1638

elaiōn occurs only in Acts 1:12, where it is translated "Olivet." The term refers to an olive plantation and is an alternative title to the "Mount of Olives."

PALM TREE

phoinix φοῖνιξ 5404

phoinix is found only twice, with the literal sense of "palm tree" in each case (John 12:13; Rev 7:9).

PLANT

phyteia φυτεία 5451

phyteia is found only in Matt 15:13, referring metaphorically to genuine children of God, whom Jesus refers to as viable plants that will remain in the ground and not be "pulled up" for judgment.

phyteuō φυτεύω 5452

phyteuō is a verb referring to "planting" in each of the twelve contexts in which it occurs. The usage is both literal and symbolic and is predicated of both God and human beings. Literal references to "planting" vineyards and trees are found in Matt 21:33; Mark 12:1; Luke 13:6; 17:6, 28; 20:9.

In 1 Cor 3:6ff.; 9:7, ***phyteuō*** indicates the spiritual ministry of "planting," undertaken by apostolic preachers who, in proclaiming the gospel, "sowed the seed" of potential followers of Christ. Matt 15:13 refers to the divine action of "planting" true children of God.

REED

kalamos κάλαμος 2563

kalamos is a noun occurring twelve times with the underlying meaning "reed" in a variety of contexts.

There is reference first of all to the "reed" as a plant (Matt 11:7; 12:20; Luke 7:24). ***kalamos*** also refers to a "stick" or "staff" in Matt 27:29ff., 48; Mark 15:19. 3 John 13 refers to a "pen" (lit., a "writing reed"). Rev 11:1; 21:15, 16 speak of a "measuring rod" (or "measuring reed").

▸ **36.** Reading, Writing > PEN

ROOT

rhiza ῥίζα 4491

rhiza is found in seventeen contexts and means "root" in both a literal and metaphorical sense.

Literal references to "roots" of plants include those in Matt 3:10; 13:6; Mark 4:6; 11:20; Luke 3:9.

As with the Hebrew term *shōresh*, ***rhiza*** manifests a varied figurative usage. Rom 11:16ff., for example, refers to the "root" of the Israelite people as a remnant. The expression "root of Jesse" is mentioned in Rom 15:12 (see Isa 11:10); and the phrase "root of David" in Rev 5:5; 22:16. Both expressions refer to the messianic line of promise through the tribe of Judah and allude to the messianic promises of the OT that utilize the same terminology. ***rhiza*** is also found in the expression "root of bitterness," indicating a deep-seated attitude of resentment in Heb 12:15 (see Deut 29:18). 1 Tim 6:10 refers to the love of money as the "root of all evil." ***rhiza*** is also used negatively in Matt 13:21; Mark 4:17; Luke 8:13, referring to people who have "no root," or no permanent, enduring faith or trust in God and his word.

ROOTED

rhizoō ῥιζόω 4492

rhizoō indicates the phenomenon of "being rooted, or grounded" in the love of Christ (Eph 3:17), as well as in Christ himself (Col 2:7).

SEE ALSO

▸ **28.** Agriculture, Viticulture, Animal Husbandry > UPROOT
ekrizoō

SEED, KERNEL, GRAIN

kokkos κόκκος 2848

kokkos is a noun denoting "grain" in all seven occurrences of the term. It refers to a "grain" of mustard seed in Matt 13:31; 17:20; Mark 4:31; Luke 13:19; 17:6. John 12:24 refers to a "kernel" of wheat, and 1 Cor 15:37 to a "grain" of an indeterminate kind.

SPROUT, SHOOT FORTH, SPRING UP

proballō προβάλλω 4261

proballō is a verb meaning "to shoot forth" in relation to plants in Luke 21:30.

blastanō βλαστάνω 985

blastanō is a verb found in four places indicating the "sprouting" or "springing up" of vegetation in Matt 13:26; Mark 4:27. Heb 9:4 refers to the "budding" of Aaron's staff. See also Jas 5:18.

phyō φύω 5453

phyō is a verb found in only three places. In Luke 8:6ff. it refers to vegetation "sprouting" or "springing up." The term is used metaphorically in Heb 12:15, warning believers against allowing the root of bitterness to "spring up" within them.

SYCAMORE TREE

sykomorea συκομορέα 4809

sykomorea is found only in Luke 19:4, with reference to a "sycamore tree."

TENDER

hapalos ἁπαλός 527

hapalos is an adjective found only in Matt 24:32; Mark 13:28, referring to a "tender" branch that is ready to bud.

SEE ALSO

▸ **60.** Virtues > TENDERHEARTED
eusplanchnos

THORN, BRIAR

skolops σκόλοψ 4647

skolops is a term found only in 2 Cor 12:7, referring metaphorically to Paul's "thorn in the flesh" — an unidentified source of pain and anguish given to him by God, after an extraordinary vision of heavenly realities.

akantha ἄκανθα 173

akantha is a noun found in fourteen contexts, meaning "thorns" or "briars" throughout (Matt 7:16; 13:7ff.; Mark 4:7; Luke 6:44; John 19:2; Heb 6:8).

akanthinos ἀκάνθινος 174

akanthinos is found only in Mark 15:17, referring to the "crown of thorns" placed on the head of Christ prior to his crucifixion.

TREE

dendron δένδρον 1186

dendron is a term referring to "tree" throughout all twenty-five occurrences.

General references to trees include those in Matt 13:32; 21:8; Mark 8:24; Luke 13:19. Trees are also mentioned in the book of Revelation, but these are always found in symbolic contexts (Rev 7:1, 3; 8:7; 9:4).

A number of metaphorical contexts refer to a person as a "tree," whose true moral character is revealed to God, who stands ready to "chop down" any that bear "bad fruit" (Matt 3:10; 12:33; Luke 3:9; 6:43ff.).

xylon ξύλον 3586

xylon is a noun found in nearly twenty places, meaning "tree" in exclusively metaphorical contexts. The literal sense of ***xylon*** indicates various products made from wood, such as "clubs," "containers."

One figurative sense of ***xylon*** refers to the "tree" as an instrument of execution — a gibbet, or cross. It is used in relation to Christ's death, as one "who hung on a tree" (Acts 5:30; 10:39; 13:29; Gal 3:13; 1 Pet 2:24). In addition, the "tree of life" is depicted in the vision of the heavenly city in Rev 22:3, 14. See also Rev 2:7.

WOODEN

xylinos ξύλινος 3585

xylinos is a rare adjective meaning "wooden" or "made of wood." It refers in 2 Tim 2:20 to wooden utensils, and in Rev 9:20 to wooden idols.

14. Animals

BEAR

arkos ἄρκος 715

arkos is a rare term found only in Rev 13:2 with symbolic reference to a "bear" — part of the makeup of the satanic beast that came up out of the sea.

BEAST, LIVING CREATURE, ANIMAL

zōon ζῷον 2226

The noun ***zōon*** occurs about twenty times with the senses of "beast," "living creature."

The term denotes animals that have been slaughtered for sacrifice in Heb 13:11. Then, in 2 Pet 2:12; Jude 10, ***zōon*** refers metaphorically to false teachers as "irrational beasts." Most commonly, ***zōon*** refers to the "living creatures" (four in all) that guard the throne of God in Revelation. These "living creatures" are most likely cherubim, as illustrated in the visions of the prophet Ezekiel (Ezek 1; 10). They are found in Rev 4:6ff.; 5:6ff.; 6:1ff.; 7:11; 14:3; 15:7; 19:4.

thērion θηρίον 2342

The noun ***thērion*** occurs about fifty times with the consistent meaning "beast," in both literal and metaphorical contexts.

General references to "wild beast(s)" or "beasts of prey" include Mark 1:13; Acts 10:12; 11:6; Heb 12:20; Jas 3:7; Rev 6:8. In Acts 28:4ff., ***thērion*** specifically denotes a "viper."

The term is also used metaphorically as a term of abuse against the citizens of Crete, described as "beasts" in Titus 1:12. Elsewhere, ***thērion*** denotes the satanic "beast" sent to effect judgment on wicked humankind in Rev 11:7. It also denotes the satanic "beasts" from sea and earth, members of the so-called "unholy trinity" who mimic the person and role of Christ and the Holy Spirit respectively (Rev 13:1ff.; 14:9ff.; 15:2; 16:2, 10, 13; 19:10; 20:4, 10). Similarly, ***thērion*** makes reference to the dragon, the great satanic opponent set against God the Father, as a "beast" with seven heads and ten horns (Rev 17:7ff.).

▸ **14.** Animals > WILD

ktēnos κτῆνος 2934

The noun ***ktēnos*** occurs four times denoting "beast(s)" in the senses of "cattle" (Rev 18:13); "animals" in general in 1 Cor 15:39; "horses" in Acts 23:24; and "donkey" in Luke 10:34.

tetrapous τετράπους 5074

tetrapous is a term denoting "beast" or "animal," emphasizing their characteristic of having four feet. It is found in only three places (Acts 10:12; 11:6; Rom 1:23).

sphagion σφάγιον 4968

sphagion is a rare noun, found only in Acts 7:42 denoting a "beast" marked out for ritual sacrifice or slaughter.

thēriomacheō θηριομαχέω 2341

thēriomacheō is a rare verb found only in 1 Cor 15:32 with the meaning "to fight against wild beasts."

▸ **77.** Resist, Oppose, Fight, Rebel > FIGHT

BIRD

peteinon πετεινόν 4071

peteinon is a noun denoting "bird" in a general sense in fifteen contexts (e.g., Matt 6:20; Mark 4:4; Luke 8:5; 9:58; Acts 10:12; Rom 1:23; Jas 3:7; 1 Cor 15:39).

orneon ὄρνεον 3732

orneon is a noun found in three places denoting "birds" (Rev 18:2; 19:17, 21).

BULL, OX, COW

tauros ταῦρος 5022

tauros is a rare noun denoting "bull" or "ox." A bull slaughtered for food is indicated in Matt 22:4. Slaughter in a general ritual context is noted in Acts 14:13. The "blood of bulls" in a sacrificial sense is indicated in Heb 9:13; 10:4.

bous βοῦς 1016

bous means "ox" or "cow" in eight contexts, referring to oxen as beasts of burden (Luke 13:15; 14:5, 19; 1 Cor 9:9 [twice]; 1 Tim 5:18), and as animals suitable for temple sacrifice (John 2:14f.).

CATTLE

thremma θρέμμα 2353

thremma is a rare noun denoting "cattle" in a general sense, found only in John 4:12.

COLT

pōlos πῶλος 4454

pōlos is a noun found twelve times, denoting a "colt" (i.e., the young of a horse or donkey) throughout (Matt 21:2ff.; Mark 11:2ff.; Luke 19:30ff.; John 12:15).

DOG

kyōn κύων 2965

kyōn is a term translated "dog" in each of the five occurrences of the term. Literal references to "dogs" are found in Matt 7:6; Luke 16:21; 2 Pet 2:22. The term is also used metaphorically in Phil 3:2; Rev 22:15, describing people who are ceremonially impure as "dogs." It also has the underlying sense of "moral perversity."

kynarion κυνάριον 2952

kynarion is a diminutive form of ***kyōn*** (above) referring to "dogs" in the literal sense in each of the four occurrences of the term (Matt 15:26f.; Mark 7:27f.).

DONKEY, ASS

onos ὄνος 3688

onos is a noun denoting a "donkey" or "ass" in all six occurrences of the term (Matt 21:2, 5, 7; Luke 13:15; 14:5; John 12:15).

hypozygion ὑποζύγιον 5268

hypozygion is a rare synonym for ***onos***, denoting a "donkey" or "ass" in Matt 21:5; 2 Pet 2:16.

DOVE, TURTLEDOVE, PIGEON

peristera περιστερά 4058

peristera is a noun found ten times with the meaning "dove."

Literal references to "doves" include Matt 10:16; 21:12; Mark 11:15; John 2:14, 16. The term also refers symbolically to the form of a dove that settled upon Christ after his baptism at the outset of his public ministry, indicating his Father's personal stamp of approval (Matt 3:16; Mark 1:10; Luke 3:22; John 1:32).

In Luke 2:24 ***peristera*** refers to "pigeons."

trygōn τρυγών 5167

trygōn is a rare noun denoting "turtledove" in Luke 2:24.

nossos νοσσός 3502

nossos is a rare noun denoting "young pigeons" only in Luke 2:24.

SEE ALSO

▸ **15.** Gender, Reproduction, Youth, Aging > YOUNG, YOUNGER, YOUNGEST
neaniskos, neos, neanias, elassōn

DRAGON

drakōn δράκων 1404

drakōn is a noun found thirteen times denoting a "dragon." The term has exclusive metaphorical reference to the devil in his most potent guise, and is found only in the book of Revelation (Rev 12:3ff.; 13:2ff.; 16:13; 20:2).

EAGLE

aetos ἀετός 105

aetos refers to "eagles" as birds of prey in Matt 24:28; Luke 17:37. Rev 4:7; 12:14 refer to "eagles" in the visions of the apostle John.

FISH

ichthys ἰχθύς 2486

ichthys denotes "fish" throughout its twenty occurrences, all of them literal (Matt 7:10; 17:27; Mark 6:38ff.; Luke 11:11; John 21:6ff.; 1 Cor 15:39).

ichthydion ἰχθύδιον 2485

ichthydion is a rare diminutive form of ***ichthys*** (above) denoting "small, little fish" in Matt 15:34; Mark 8:7.

opsarion ὀψάριον 3795

opsarion is a rare synonym for ***ichthys***, denoting "fish" in five contexts (John 6:9ff.; 21:9ff.).

SEE ALSO

▸ **29.** Boats, Fishing, Maritime Activity > FISH, FISHERMAN
halieus, halieuō

FLOCK

poimnē ποίμνη 4167

poimnē is a noun found in only four places, denoting a "flock" of herd animals such as sheep or goats in Luke 2:8; 1 Cor 9:7. The term refers metaphorically to God's people as his "flock" in Matt 26:31; John 10:16.

poimnion ποίμνιον 4168

poimnion is a diminutive form of ***poimnē*** (above). It designates a "flock" in the sense of the people of God in general terms in Luke 12:32. It is also found in Acts 20:28ff.; 1 Pet 5:2ff., denoting Christian congregations as "the flock" of God under pastoral care.

FOX

alōpēx ἀλώπηξ 258

alōpēx is a rare noun found only three times, referring to literal "foxes" in Matt 8:20; Luke 9:58. In Luke 13:32 Jesus refers to Herod the tetrarch (i.e., Antipas) as a "fox," indicating that he is a crafty, deceitful, and dangerous man.

GOAT

eriphos ἔριφος 2056

eriphos is a rare noun found only three times, denoting "goats" in general in Luke 15:29; and a "kid goat" in Matt 25:32, 33.

tragos τράγος 5131

tragos is a rare noun found only in Heb 9:12 referring to the sacrificial blood of "goats."

HEIFER

damalis δάμαλις 1151

damalis occurs only once, in Heb 9:13, referring to the ritual offering of a heifer.

HEN

ornis ὄρνις 3733

ornis is a rare term, referring to a "hen" only in Matt 23:37; Luke 13:34.

HERD

agelē ἀγέλη 34

agelē refers exclusively to a "herd" (of pigs), and is found eight times (Matt 8:30ff.; Mark 5:11, 13; Luke 8:32, 33).

HORN

keras κέρας 2768

keras occurs eleven times and is translated "horn" on each occasion in a variety of contexts, with all but one occurring in the book of Revelation.

The messianic "horn of salvation" is depicted in Luke 1:69. In the apocalyptic vision of John, ***keras*** refers to the "horns of the lamb" (i.e., Jesus Christ) (Rev 5:6); and the horns of the golden altar (Rev 9:13). In two central visions of this book, horns refer figuratively to the satanic forces of evil and darkness — in reference to the "unholy trinity" of the dragon, sea beast, and earth beast (Rev 12:3; 13:1 [twice], 11). See also Rev 17:3, 7. Horns are also mentioned in connection with the ten kings associated with the destruction of Babylon, the "great harlot" (Rev 17:12, 16).

HORSE

hippos ἵππος 2462

hippos means "horse" and occurs sixteen times.

hippos is used generally in Jas 3:3; Rev 14:20; 18:13. In the remaining usage, entirely in the book of Revelation, ***hippos*** designates the visionary horses of the apocalypse in a number of contexts. Rev 6:2ff., for example, refers to the horses and their riders, symbolizing divine judgment. Rev 9:7, 9, 17 refer to the demonic horses of fiery plague judgment. Rev 19:18 affirms that the horses of the conquered armies of the antichrist will be destroyed. Rev 19:11, 21 describe the messianic King of kings riding on the white horse, symbolizing God's victorious army conquering the forces of evil. There is also a retinue of white horses following the white rider in Rev 19:14.

LAMB

arēn ἀρήν 704

arēn occurs only in Luke 10:3, where it is used metaphorically. Here Jesus sends out the disciples "like lambs in the midst of wolves."

amnos ἀμνός 286

amnos is a rare term for "lamb," occurring four times. In John 1:29, 36 it is used by John the Baptist in reference to Jesus Christ as the "Lamb of God," who takes away the sin of the world. In Acts 8:32 the Ethiopian eunuch reads Isa 53, which speaks of the Messiah's docile submission to his tormentors — "as a lamb before its shearers is silent." 1 Pet 1:19 speaks of the efficacy of the blood of Christ as that "of a spotless lamb."

arnion ἀρνίον 721

arnion is a diminutive form of ***arēn*** (above) occurring around thirty times and meaning "lamb." ***arnion*** refers exclusively to Christ as the Lamb who is King (i.e., the risen king in heaven) in the book of Revelation (Rev 5:6ff.; 7:9ff.; 12:11; 13:8ff.; 14:1ff.; 19:7ff.; 21:14, 22ff.; 22:1ff.).

The exception to this usage is found in John 2:15, where Jesus instructs Peter to look after his disciples, saying "feed my lambs."

LEOPARD

pardalis πάρδαλις 3917

pardalis is found only in Rev 13:2, referring to the leopard-like beast that emerged from the sea. This is the satanic beast that served as a counterfeit to the true Messiah.

LION

leōn λέων 3023

leōn is the only term for "lion" in the NT and is found in nine contexts.

leōn is used metaphorically in 2 Tim 4:17 to indicate the narrowness of Paul's escape from the attacks of his enemies, when he testifies that he was "delivered from the lion's mouth." Heb 11:33 refers to the exploits of the old covenant heroes of faith who, among other things, "stopped the mouths of lions."

The book of Revelation contains various metaphorical references to lions — as part of the physiognomy of the cherubim (Rev 4:7); demonic creatures inflicting torment on human beings (Rev 9:8, 17); the satanic sea beast (Rev 13:2). The voice of the angel of the Lord in Rev 10:3 is also described as "like the roar of a lion."

Two other significant uses of ***leōn*** remain. One occurs in 1 Pet 5:8, where Satan is described as a "roaring lion" seeking his prey among humankind. The other is in Rev 5:5, where the risen Christ is described as the "lion of the tribe of Judah," recalling the prophetic designation of that tribe in Gen 49:9.

LOCUST

akris ἀκρίς 200

akris is the only term for "locusts" in the NT, occurring four times. Twice it refers literally to locusts as part of John the Baptist's diet (Matt 3:4; Mark 1:6). Rev 9:3, 7 refer symbolically to the demonic creatures, released from the abyss of hell, who had the appearance of huge, grotesque locusts.

MEAT, FLESH

kreas κρέας 2907

kreas is a rare noun denoting the "meat," "flesh" of sacrificial animals in Rom 14:21; 1 Cor 8:13.

SEE ALSO

▸ **16.** Body, Bodily Functions > FLESH
sarx

▸ **57.** Evil, Wickedness, Sin > FLESHLY, CARNAL, WORLDLY
sarkikos

MOTH

sēs σής 4597

sēs is found only three times in the NT, referring to "moth" in a metaphorical sense on each occasion. Matt 6:19, 20; Luke 12:33 refer to the corruptibility and transitory nature of human possessions. Jesus exhorts his hearers to build up heavenly wealth that cannot be subject to the process of rot and decay brought on by moth infestation, or loss through theft.

sētobrōtos σητόβρωτος 4598

sētobrōtos is found only in Jas 5:2, meaning "moth-eaten" in relation to one's clothes.

NEST

kataskēnoō κατασκηνόω 2681

kataskēnoō occurs only twice in the NT, referring on both occasions to Jesus' claim that unlike the birds "who make nests," he has nowhere permanent to live (Matt 8:20; Luke 9:58).

▸ **24.** Dwell, Live, Gather, Hospitality > LODGE, LODGING

PIG, SWINE

choiros χοῖρος 5519

choiros denotes "swine," "pigs," in all fourteen of its occurrences (Matt 7:6; 8:3ff.; Mark 5:11ff.; Luke 8:32ff.; 15:15f.).

RAVEN

korax κόραξ 2876

korax is found only in Luke 12:24, referring to "ravens" as an illustration in Christ's exhortation to his hearers not to worry about the necessities of life, which will be provided by God.

ROAR

mykaomai μυκάομαι 3455

mykaomai is a verb found only in Rev 10:3, referring to the loud voice of an angel, which is likened to the "roaring" of a lion.

ōryomai ὠρύομαι 5612

ōryomai is a verb found only in 1 Pet 5:8 as a simile, referring to the devil prowling around like a "roaring" lion.

SEE ALSO

▸ **11.** Meteorology, Water > ROAR
ēcheō

SCORPION

skorpios σκορπίος 4651

skorpios refers to "scorpions" in all five occurrences of the term. Literal references to the animal are found in Luke 10:19; 11:12. Metaphorical references occur in Rev 9:3, 5, 10, where an aspect of divine punishment on the wicked is likened to the sting of a scorpion.

SERPENT

ophis ὄφις 3789

ophis is a noun found fourteen times, meaning "serpent."

Literal references to these reptiles are found in Matt 7:10ff.; Mark 16:18; Luke 10:19; 11:11; 1 Cor 10:9. See also John 3:14 with reference to the bronze serpent of Num 21:8. 2 Cor 11:3; Rev 12:9ff.; 20:2 refer to the serpent in the garden of Eden, the embodiment of satanic deceit, who beguiled Eve.

Matt 23:33 refers metaphorically to "serpents" in relation to the hypocritical cunning and self-righteousness of the Pharisees. Rev 9:19 refers to "serpents" as visionary creatures from hell, unleashed on godless humanity.

SHEEP

probaton πρόβατον 4263

probaton is a noun occurring forty times with the primary meaning "sheep," though it may also indicate any kind of small herd animal or cattle.

Mundane usage of the term is found in Matt 12:11ff.; Luke 15:4ff. Ritual references to "sheep" are indicated in John 2:14ff.

General metaphorical references to "sheep" include those in Matt 7:15; 10:16; Mark 6:34; Rom 8:36; 1 Pet 2:15. There are specific metaphorical references to the "house of Israel" as "sheep" in a number of contexts. ***probaton*** alludes, for example, to Israel as God's "sheep," the object of his affection (Matt 26:31; John 10:2ff.; Heb 13:20); and to Israel as "lost sheep" (Matt 10:6; 15:24). The redeemed people from among the nations are referred to as "sheep" on the day of judgment (Matt 25:32ff.). God's people under one's pastoral care are also described as "sheep" in John 21:16ff. The designation "sheep" in the context of ritual sacrifice also refers to Christ (Acts 8:32).

SEE ALSO

▸ **33.** Architecture > GATE
probatikos

TAIL

oura οὐρά 3769

oura is a noun found five times, referring metaphorically to the "tails" of hellish beasts depicted in the book of Revelation — to scorpions (Rev 9:10); serpents (Rev 9:19); and a dragon, i.e., Satan (Rev 12:4).

VIPER

echidna ἔχιδνα 2191

echidna is a noun denoting a "viper" in five contexts. Acts 28:3 refers literally to a "viper" that attacked Paul on the island of Malta. The remaining usage is figurative, with John the Baptist denouncing the hypocritical spiritual leaders of Israel as a "brood of vipers" in Matt 3:7; Luke 3:7. Jesus makes a similar denunciation in Matt 12:34; 23:33.

WILD

thērion θηρίον 2342

thērion is a noun with the general sense of "beast" throughout its nearly fifty occurrences. In several places it refers explicitly to "wild beasts" (Mark 1:13; Acts 10:12; 11:6).

▸ **14.** Animals > BEAST, LIVING CREATURE, ANIMAL

SEE ALSO

▸ **28.** Agriculture, Viticulture, Animal Husbandry > WILD
agrios, agrielaios

WING

pteryx πτέρυξ 4420

pteryx is a noun meaning "wings" in several different contexts. It occurs five times, each in a figurative context.

Matt 23:37; Luke 13:34 refer to the "wings" of a hen, figuratively indicating a protective, nurturing mother. Rev 4:8; 9:9 refer to the "wings" of demonic creatures that wreak havoc on humankind. In Rev 12:4, ***pteryx*** denotes the "wings" of an eagle, symbolically indicating the vehicle of divine deliverance.

WOOL

erion ἔριον 2053

erion is a rare noun referring to "wool" in Heb 9:19; Rev 1:4.

WORM

skōlēx σκώληξ 4663

skōlēx is a rare noun denoting "the worm" that feeds upon dead bodies (Mark 9:44ff.).

skōlēkobrōtos σκωληκόβρωτος 4662

skōlēkobrōtos is a rare adjective meaning "eaten by worms," referring in Acts 12:23 to the grisly death suffered by King Herod.

15. Gender, Reproduction, Youth, Aging

AGE, STATURE

hēlikia ἡλικία 2244

The noun ***hēlikia*** is found eight times in all, with the meanings "stature," "age." The latter sense is indicated in John 9:21ff. with reference to "being of age" (i.e., adult maturity). In Heb 11:11, the term refers to "the age" of a woman in relation to her childbearing capacity.

hēmera ἡμέρα 2250

The noun ***hēmera*** means "day(s)" throughout its usage (approximately forty times). In Luke 2:36, the prophetess Anna is described as being of a "great age" (lit., "a woman of many days").

▸ **3.** Periods of Time, Duration, Frequency, Speed > DAY, PERIOD, AGE, TIME

BARREN

steira στεῖρα 4723

steira is an adjectival form found in five contexts meaning "barren." In four of these places, the term denotes women who have not been able to conceive and bear children (Luke 1:7, 36; 23:29; Gal 4:27).

BEGET, GIVE BIRTH, BE BORN

gennaō γεννάω 1080

gennaō is a verb occurring about one hundred times with the primary meanings "beget," "give birth to."

This term is commonly employed in genealogical listings referring to the origin of successive generations, especially in relation to the earthly lineage of Jesus Christ (Matt 1:1ff.). See also Acts 7:8, 20, 29.

The general sense of "to be born" is indicated in relation to Christ in Matt 2:1ff.; Luke 1:35; John 18:37. Other general references include Matt 19:12; Mark 14:21; Luke 1:57; Acts 22:3; Gal 4:23; Heb 11:23.

The metaphorical sense of "to be born illegitimately" (i.e., as the result of an immoral liaison) is indicated in John 8:41. Elsewhere, the phrase "bear children for slavery" is a symbolic reference to Israel's condition under the bondage of the old covenant (Gal 4:24, 29). John 9:23 refers to "being born in sin." The expression "to become one's spiritual father" is found in connection with Paul's relationship to his converts in 1 Cor 4:15; Phlm 10.

The most significant metaphorical usage of ***gennaō*** is found in the expression "to be born again," which indicates a new spiritual sensitivity to the movement of the Spirit of God, producing saving faith in Christ and leading to membership in the kingdom of God (John 1:13; 3:3ff.). The expression "to be born of God" indicates a similar reality (1 John 2:29; 3:9; 4:7; 5:4, 18). In addition, "being born of God" describes the process by which Christ the Son came to have a filial relationship with God the Father, indicated by the statement: "You are my son, today I have begotten you" (Acts 13:33; Heb 1:5; 5:5).

The state of "being born blind" in a literal, physical sense is noted in John 9:2, 19ff.

apokyeō ἀποκυέω 616

apokyeō is a rare verb found only twice with the symbolic meaning "to bring forth" in relation to the process by which sin ultimately results in death in Jas 1:15. Positively, Jas 1:18 refers to the action of the divine will whereby God "has brought us forth" by the word of truth — he has constituted his people as his children through faith and trust in him.

tiktō τίκτω 5088

The verb ***tiktō*** occurs about twenty times with the underlying sense of "to bring forth," referring literally to the begetting of children and the cultivation of plants. It also has a metaphorical usage.

Literal references to "giving birth" to children include the birth of Jesus the Messiah (Matt 1:21ff.; 2:2; Luke 1:31, 57; 2:6ff.; Heb 11:11 [see also Gal 4:27]). Heb 6:7 refers to the "bringing forth" of plants.

tiktō is used metaphorically in Jas 1:15 to indicate that desire "gives birth" to sin. And in Rev 12:2ff. there is a symbolic reference to the birth of Christ.

teknogoneō τεκνογονέω 5041

teknogoneō is a rare verb with the meaning "to bear children," found only in 1 Tim 5:14.

SEE ALSO

▸ **25.** Family, Marriage, Adoption, Inheritance > CHILD
teknon, pais, paidion, nēpios, teknotropheō

▸ **27.** Community, Partnership, Unity, Discord > CHILDREN
teknion

BIRTH

genesis γένεσις 1083

genesis is a rare noun occurring twice and denoting the "birth" of Christ in Matt 1:18; Luke 1:14.

▸ **25.** Family, Marriage, Adoption, Inheritance > GENEALOGY

ektrōma ἔκτρωμα 1626

ektrōma is a rare noun found only in 1 Cor 15:8 referring metaphorically to the atypical origin of Paul's apostolic authority as one who had an "untimely birth."

SEE ALSO

▸ **22.** Life, Renewal, Immortality > BE BORN AGAIN
anagennaō

CHILD, INFANT, BABE

brephos βρέφος 1025

brephos is a noun found in eight contexts with the meanings "babe" (baby); "infant"; "(young) child."

In Luke 1:41ff., ***brephos*** refers to the baby in Elizabeth's womb — John the Baptist, the forerunner of Christ. In Luke 2:12ff., the term refers to the newborn "infant" Jesus. Elsewhere, Luke 18:15; Acts 7:19; 1 Pet 2:2 refer to "newborn infants." 2 Tim 3:15 refers to one's "(early) childhood."

nēpios νήπιος 3516

nēpios is a synonym for ***brephos*** (above) again denoting "babe," "infant," "little child" throughout the fourteen occurrences of the term.

nēpios denotes "little children" in general (Rom 2:20; Gal 4:1ff.).

More commonly, ***nēpios*** is used metaphorically to indicate "little children," "infants" as suitable recipients of divine revelation — those who have a childlike devotion to, and trust in, God (Matt 11:25; Luke 10:21). See also Matt 21:16. The expression "babes in Christ" denotes immature believers in 1 Cor 3:1; Eph 4:14; Heb 5:13. The simile "like/as a child" is found in 1 Cor 13:11.

▸ **25.** Family, Marriage, Adoption, Inheritance > CHILD

gennētos γεννητός 1084

gennētos is a rare adjective denoting "that which is born of woman" (i.e., children) (Matt 11:11; Luke 7:28).

artigennētos ἀρτιγέννητος 738

artigennētos is a rare adjectival variant of ***gennētos*** (above) found only in 1 Pet 2:2 and denoting "newborn" babies.

SEE ALSO

▸ **22.** Life, Renewal, Immortality > BE BORN AGAIN
anagennaō

CHILD, OFFSPRING

paidarion παιδάριον 3808

paidarion is a rare term denoting "child," "children" in Matt 11:16; John 6:9.

nepiazō νηπιάζω 3515

nepiazō is a rare verb with the meaning to "be, act like a child" found only in 1 Cor 14:20, in relation to spiritual maturity.

enkyos ἔγκυος 1471

enkyos is a rare adjective indicating the state of pregnancy — "expecting a child" — found only in Luke 2:5 and referring to Mary, the mother of Jesus.

genos γένος 1085

genos refers to the combined number of individuals of the same nature or kind. It occurs in around twenty contexts, meaning "kind," "family," "race" (or nationality), and "offspring."

With the sense of "children" or "descendants," ***genos*** refers in Acts 17:28, 29 to believers as the "offspring of God." In Rev 22:16, the risen Christ refers to himself as the "offspring of David."

▸ **81.** Forms, Groups, Patterns, Order > KIND

CHILDLESS

ateknos ἄτεκνος 815

ateknos is an adjective found in three places with reference to the state of being "without children," "childless" (Luke 20:28ff.).

SEE ALSO

▸ **25.** Family, Marriage, Adoption, Inheritance > CHILD
teknon, pais, paidion, nēpios, teknotropheō

▸ **27.** Community, Partnership, Unity, Discord > CHILDREN
teknion

CONCEIVE

syllambanō συλλαμβάνω 4815

syllambanō is a verb found sixteen times with the meaning "conceive" in about one-third of these contexts.

References to Elizabeth conceiving John the Baptist are noted in Luke 1:24, 36; and to Mary miraculously conceiving Jesus by the mysterious operation of the Holy Spirit in Luke 1:31; 2:21.

▸ **62.** Care For, Protect, Guard, Watch > HELP, HELPER

▸ **70.** Give, Take, Seize, Touch >
APPREHEND, SEIZE, CAPTURE, ARREST

katabolē καταβολή 2602

katabolē is a noun with the primary meaning "foundation" in reference to the foundation of the world. However, in Heb 11:11 this term refers to Sarah's capacity to "conceive," as granted to her by God in fulfillment of his promise to her husband Abraham, leading to the birth of their son Isaac.

▸ **4.** Beginning, Continuing, Finishing, Postponing >
FOUNDATION

ELDER, OLDER, OLD MAN

presbyteros πρεσβύτερος 4245

presbyteros is the predominant term for "elder" in the NT, found nearly seventy times.

The term refers primarily to the "elders" as one section of the civil and ritual leadership of first-century Judean society, comprising also the priests, scribes, and Pharisees (e.g., Matt 15:2; 26:47ff.; 27:1ff.; Mark 7:3ff.; 11:27; 14:43ff.; Luke 7:3; 22:52; Acts 4:15ff.; 6:12; 25:15).

presbyteros also refers to the "elder" brother in the parable of the prodigal son (Luke 15:25). See also John 8:9.

The term also denotes "old men" in Acts 2:17; 1 Tim 5:1. See also 1 Tim 5:2 and the "elders" of the local church in

Acts 11:30; 15:2ff.; 1 Tim 5:17ff.; Titus 1:5; Jas 5:14; 1 Pet 5:1ff.; 2 John 1; 3 John 1. The heavenly "elders" that surround the throne of God and Christ are indicated in Rev 4:4, 10; 5:5ff.; 7:11ff.; 11:16; 14:3; 19:4.

▸ **15.** Gender, Reproduction, Youth, Aging > WOMAN

SEE ALSO

▸ **38.** Covenant, Law, Rites, Roles > ELDER
sympresbyteros, presbyterion

EUNUCH

eunouchos εὐνοῦχος 2135

eunouchos is a noun denoting a "eunuch" in all eight occurrences of the term. The word refers generally to people who are sterile in a sexual sense in Matt 19:12 and have chosen to remain celibate in their service of the kingdom of God. In Acts 8:27ff. the term refers to the Ethiopian "eunuch" — a high official in the royal court of that country. Men such as this were incapable of fathering children, and so a likely position for this Ethiopian official was as head of the royal harem.

eunouchizō εὐνουχίζω 2134

eunouchizō is a rare verb found only in Matt 19:12, meaning "to make a eunuch" in both passive and reflexive senses. The sense indicated is that of "castrate," "remove a man's manhood."

FEMALE

thēlys θῆλυς 2338

thēlys is an adjectival form found in five places used nominally to denote a "woman" or "female."

The designation "female," referring to God's creative work in bringing the woman Eve into the world, is noted in Matt 19:4; Mark 10:6. In Gal 3:28 Paul affirms, among other things, that there is neither male nor "female" in Christ Jesus — there is a complete equality of status. In Rom 1:26, 27, ***thēlys*** denotes "women" in the generalized context of those leading immoral, sexually promiscuous lifestyles, which brings down the wrath of God.

▸ **15.** Gender, Reproduction, Youth, Aging > WOMAN

FIRSTBORN

prōtotokos πρωτότοκος 4416

prōtotokos is an adjective found nine times with the meaning "firstborn" in both a literal and figurative sense.

References to Jesus as Mary's "firstborn" son are found in Matt 1:25; Luke 2:7; Heb 1:6. Heb 11:28 refers to the "firstborn" of Egyptian families destroyed by the avenging angel, a divine judgment precipitating the exodus of the Israelite captives.

In metaphorical contexts, the meaning "firstborn" signifies the person of Jesus Christ, who is described as the "firstborn" of creation in Col 1:15, the initial representative of a regenerate communion of believers who would continue throughout eternity. Col 1:18; Rev 1:5 refer to Christ as the "firstborn" from the dead, the prime example of the resurrected members of his body, the church. Rom 8:29 designates Christ as the "firstborn" among many, and Heb 12:23 makes reference to the "firstborn" enrolled in heaven, speaking of the saints.

SEE ALSO

▸ **22.** Life, Renewal, Immortality > BE BORN AGAIN
anagennaō

GIRL, MAID, MAIDEN

paidion παιδίον 3813

paidion is a diminutive form of ***pais*** denoting a "(young) child" in most of its nearly fifty occurrences. However, in Mark 5:39ff. ***paidion*** denotes the "young girl" brought back to life by Jesus.

▸ **25.** Family, Marriage, Adoption, Inheritance > CHILD

korasion κοράσιον 2877

korasion is found in eight places and consistently refers to a "girl" or "maiden" in generalized contexts. Matt 9:24, 25; Mark 5:41, 42 refer to Jairus' daughter, whom Jesus brought back to life, as a "young girl." Similarly, ***korasion*** refers to the daughter of Herodias as a "young girl" (Matt 14:11; Mark 6:22, 28).

MAN, MALE

arsēn ἄρσην 730

arsēn is an adjectival term, occurring nine times and meaning "male" on each occasion. It is used predominantly, however, as a noun.

Matt 19:4; Mark 10:6 refer to God fashioning the human species as male and female from the beginning of creation. Luke 2:23 refers to firstborn male children as holy to the Lord.

Rom 1:27 (twice) alludes to males (i.e., men) committing shameless acts with one another that bring down the wrath of God upon them. Gal 3:28 declares that no distinction in status is made between male and female, since all believers are one in Christ. Rev 12:5, 13 refer to the male child borne by the woman who is pursued in vain by the dragon who seeks to destroy the child. The context clearly suggests that the male child is the infant Christ child; the woman is his mother Mary; and the dragon is Satan himself.

anthrōpos ἄνθρωπος 444

anthrōpos is the most common term for "man" in the NT and has a broad spectrum of senses alongside the primary meaning "man." ***anthrōpos*** occurs about five hundred times.

The meaning "man" or "men" in the sense of "humankind" is indicated in Matt 4:4; Mark 2:27; Luke 2:14, 52; John 1:4; 5:41; Acts 4:12; 17:26; Gal 1:11; 1 Thess 2:15; 2 Pet 1:21. Specifically, ***anthrōpos*** refers to the "wickedness of men" (Rom 1:18); to "the wisdom of man" (1 Cor

2:5); and to the destruction of "one-third of humankind" (Rev 9:15).

The title "Son of man" is a title adopted by Christ, borrowed from the designation given to the prophet Ezekiel (and also occasionally to Daniel), signifying our Lord's genuine incarnation and identification with humankind. This usage accounts for approximately one-fifth of the total occurrences of ***anthrōpos*** (Matt 8:20; 9:6; 24:27; Mark 2:10; 13:34; Luke 5:24; John 1:51; 5:27; Rev 1:13; 14:14 [implied]).

"Men," in the general sense of "people," is the meaning indicated, for example, in Matt 4:19; 6:1; Mark 1:13; Luke 5:10; 6:22; John 4:28; Acts 4:13; Rom 12:18; 1 Cor 4:9; 2 Cor 5:11; Heb 9:27.

In a number of contexts, ***anthrōpos*** is translated "men" with the underlying sense of ordinary human beings, or those who are mortal (Acts 14:15; Rom 2:9; Gal 1:1; Heb 1:1; 7:8). Phil 2:7 describes Jesus as one made "in the likeness of men," emphasizing the genuineness of his humanity. Col 2:8 refers to "human traditions" (i.e., the traditions of men). Rev 13:18 refers to the number 666 as "man's number."

anthrōpos also means "one," "someone," with the underlying sense of "man" or "person" — an unspecified individual, not necessarily or exclusively male (Matt 7:9; Mark 7:11; Luke 15:4; John 1:9; John 3:27; Acts 4:17; Rom 10:5; 2 Cor 3:2; Gal 3:12; 1 Tim 6:16; Jas 1:19). Note, in particular, Paul's exhortation in 1 Cor 11:28, "let a man examine himself" prior to taking part in the Lord's Supper. John 3:4 also illustrates this usage with regard to Nicodemus' question of Jesus: "How can a man be born again?" In Rom 3:28, Paul teaches that "one is justified by faith."

The translation "man," "men" may also refer to specific individuals in various contexts. For example, the Roman centurion declares to Jesus in Matt 8:9; Luke 7:8 that he is "a man under authority." At Jesus' trial the Roman procurator, Pontius Pilate, parades him before the crowd and declares: "Behold the man!" Rom 5:12 draws a contrast between Adam and Christ by affirming that just as sin entered the world through "one man" (i.e., Adam), so also did righteousness emerge through the ministry of "one man" (i.e., Jesus Christ). A similar truth is expressed in Rom 2:15; 1 Cor 15:21, 45. "The man of lawlessness," the final incarnation of a satanic personage prior to the return of Christ, is referred to in 2 Thess 2:3. See also Mark 1:23; 5:2; John 1:6; Acts 4:9; 2 Tim 3:17.

In the Pauline correspondence, ***anthrōpos*** also refers variously to "man" in the sense of the innermost self, or the old self (e.g., Rom 6:6; 7:22; Eph 3:16). The "old man," or the old, corrupt sinful nature prior to conversion, is mentioned in 2 Cor 4:16; Eph 4:22; Col 3:9. Such a nature is cast off when the "new nature" replaces it. This "new man" is fashioned in believers by the ministry of the Holy Spirit (Eph 2:15; 4:24).

anēr ἀνήρ 435

anēr means "man" in the sense of "male" in various contexts, and it is also commonly translated "husband." ***anēr*** occurs around two hundred times.

References to a "husband" in narrative contexts are found in the Gospels and Acts (Matt 1:16; Mark 10:2; Luke 1:34; John 4:16ff.; Acts 5:9, 10). Instruction regarding the appropriate godly conduct of a husband towards his wife is indicated in Rom 7:2, 3; 1 Cor 7:2ff.; 11:3; 14:35; Eph 5:22ff.; Col 3:18, 19; 1 Pet 3:1, 5, 7). See also 1 Tim 3:2; 5:9; Titus 1:6; 2:5. In 2 Cor 11:2; Eph 5:22ff.; Rev 21:2, ***anēr*** is used metaphorically in relation to Christ's role as the "husband" of his "bride," the church.

anēr also refers to "man" in the general sense of "person," as in Matt 7:24, 26, which refers to the wise and foolish man in Christ's parable. No specific individual is in view. Likewise, in Rom 4:8, Paul affirms the blessed state of the man whose sin will not be counted against him.

The meaning "man," "men," in the sense of "male individual(s)" or "group of men" is found in Matt 12:41; Mark 6:20, 44; Luke 1:27; 8:41; Acts 1:10ff.; 8:2, 12; Rom 11:4; 1 Cor 11:3ff.; 13:11; 1 Tim 2:8; Jas 1:8.

anēr also means "man" in the sense of "mankind," as in relating to the human species, or "humankind" (John 1:13). In addition, this term conveys the concept of "manhood," the quality of being a man (Eph 4:3).

▸ **25.** Family, Marriage, Adoption, Inheritance > HUSBAND

▸ **27.** Community, Partnership, Unity, Discord > FELLOW

NURSE

trophos τροφός 5162

trophos occurs only in 1 Thess 2:7 with reference to a "nurse" taking care of her children.

OLD

presbytēs πρεσβύτης 4246

presbytēs is a noun derived from ***presbyteros***, meaning "old man." It is found in only three places (Luke 1:18; Titus 2:2; Phlm 9).

gēras γῆρας 1094

gēras is a noun found only in Luke 1:36, referring to the "old age" of Elizabeth, mother of John the Baptist.

gerōn γέρων 1088

gerōn is a rare adjectival form, occurring only in John 3:4 with reference to a man being "old" in the context of the question Nicodemus asked Jesus, "How can a man be born when he is old?"

SEE ALSO

▸ **5.** Old, New, First, Last > OLD, ANCIENT, FORMER
archaios, palaios, palaioō, gēraskō

ONLY CHILD

monogenēs μονογενής 3439

monogenēs is translated "only child" (son or daughter), in relation both to ordinary people and to Christ as the "only begotten" Son of God. ***monogenēs*** is found nine times.

Luke 7:12 refers to the deceased son of a widow from the town of Nain as her "only son." Jairus, a ruler of the synagogue, is recorded as having an "only daughter" in Luke 8:42, whom Jesus raised from the dead. In Luke 9:38, a man whose "only son" is under the control of a demon begs Jesus to heal him.

The remaining uses of ***monogenēs*** refer to Christ as the "only begotten" Son of God, indicating that the birth of the Messiah-Redeemer was by natural human procreation, but supernatural or divine in its conception (John 1:14, 18, 36; 3:16, 18; Heb 11:17; 1 John 4:9). The fact that Jesus Christ is the "only begotten" Son of the Father constitutes one of the unique features of the Christian faith, emphasizing the unparalleled distinctiveness of God being found in the form of a man in order to bring about salvation for humankind.

PREGNANT

gastēr γαστήρ 1064

gastēr is a noun denoting a woman who is pregnant (1 Thess 5:3).

▸ **16.** Body, Bodily Functions > BELLY, STOMACH, WOMB, HEART

REST

epiloipos ἐπίλοιπος 1954

epiloipos occurs only once, in 1 Pet 4:2, where it refers to "the rest" (i.e., the remainder) of one's life.

SEE ALSO

▸ **85.** Movement, Position, State > REMAIN, STAY, ABIDE, DWELL
menō, perisseuō, perileipō, diamenō, apoleipō, loipos

UNMARRIED

parthenos παρθένος 3933

parthenos is a noun denoting a "virgin" throughout the fourteen occurrences of the term. In Acts 21:9 ***parthenos*** expresses the precise nuance of "unmarried daughters" (of Philip the evangelist).

▸ **15.** Gender, Reproduction, Youth, Aging > VIRGIN

agamos ἄγαμος 22

agamos is an adjective referring to "unmarried" or "single women" four times in 1 Cor 7:8ff., 32ff.

▸ **25.** Family, Marriage, Adoption, Inheritance > UNMARRIED

SEE ALSO

▸ **18.** Strength, Weakness, Capability > WEAK-WILLED
gunaikarion

VIRGIN

parthenos παρθένος 3933

parthenos refers to women without sexual experience of a man, as well as (rarely) to men who are likewise designated "virgin." ***parthenos*** occurs fourteen times.

Literal references to women as "virgins" include those in Matt 25:1, 7, 11; Acts 21:9; 1 Cor 7:25ff. In particular, Matt 1:23 refers to the Isaianic prophecy of the "virgin," who will give birth to the Messiah. In Luke 1:27, Mary the betrothed bride of Joseph is identified as a "virgin," and is clearly viewed by the NT as the one who fulfills the OT prophecy from Isa 7:14. In 1 Cor 7:25, Paul refers to "the unmarried" as a collective designation, presumably, for women and men who are chaste.

In 2 Cor 11:12, Paul refers figuratively to the community of believers as a "pure (i.e., virgin) bride" betrothed to Christ, "her husband." Rev 14:4 refers to saints in heaven as those who have not defiled themselves with women, who are "pure" or "chaste." This reference is probably symbolic, using "chastity" as a symbol for separation from a pagan world system, and not sexual purity, for clearly this group contains both men and women.

▸ **15.** Gender, Reproduction, Youth, Aging > UNMARRIED

WOMAN

gynē γυνή 1135

gynē, a noun occurring over two hundred times, is translated "woman," "wife." ***gynē*** always refers to a woman, either married or unmarried, and there is overlap between the two senses.

The general meaning "woman" is indicated in a number of contexts (e.g., Matt 5:28; 9:20ff.; 11:11; Mark 7:25; Luke 7:37ff.; 8:2ff.; Acts 1:14; 8:12; Rev 14:4. Specific individuals are referred to in John 4:7ff.; 8:3; Acts 16:14. "Woman" is used as a term of address in John 2:4, when Jesus speaks to his mother.

Legislation involving a "married woman" or "wife" is found in Rom 7:2; 1 Cor 7:1ff. A woman's role or function in the context of worship is set out in 1 Cor 11:3ff.; 14:34ff. 1 Tim 2:9ff. describes the demeanor required of godly women.

gynē is also used metaphorically to denote a "woman" in John's vision, symbolizing Mary, the mother of Christ (Rev 12:1ff.). See also Rev 2:20. In addition, Rev 17:3ff. describes an evil woman — again in a visionary context — depicting the city of Babylon as a "prostitute," the embodiment of idolatrous blasphemy.

thēlys θῆλυς 2338

thēlys is an adjectival form, used nominally on five occasions to refer to a "woman" or "female." The designation "female" in conjunction with "male" (i.e., human beings created by God, equal in status as divine image-bearers), is found in Matt 19:4; Mark 10:6.

General references to "women" are found in Rom 1:26, 27; Gal 3:28.

▸ **15.** Gender, Reproduction, Youth, Aging > FEMALE

presbyteros πρεσβύτερος 4245

presbyteros is an adjective with the predominant nominal sense of "elder." The adjectival meaning "older" is rare and is used only once in the feminine form, referring to "older women" in 1 Tim 5:2.

▸ **15.** Gender, Reproduction, Youth, Aging > ELDER, OLDER, OLD MAN

presbytis πρεσβῦτις 4247

presbytis is a rare feminine noun found only in Titus 2:3, denoting "old women."

SEE ALSO

▸ **18.** Strength, Weakness, Capability > WEAK-WILLED ***gunaikarion***

WOMB

mētra μήτρα 3388

mētra is a rare noun referring to a woman's "womb" (Rom 4:19), and to the womb of both women and female animals (Luke 2:23).

SEE ALSO

▸ **16.** Body, Bodily Functions > BELLY, STOMACH, WOMB, HEART ***gastēr***

YEAR

dietēs διετής 1332

dietēs is a rare adjectival form found only in Matt 2:16, meaning "two years old."

hekatontaetēs ἑκατονταετής 1541

hekatontaetēs is a rare adjective signifying "one hundred years old," found only in Rom 4:19.

SEE ALSO

▸ **3.** Periods of Time, Duration, Frequency, Speed > YEAR ***etos, eniautos, perysi, trietia, dietia***

YOUNG, YOUNGER, YOUNGEST

neaniskos νεανίσκος 3495

neaniskos is a noun meaning "young man," "youth" throughout its ten occurrences (Matt 19:20ff.; Mark 14:51; 16:5; Luke 7:14; Acts 5:10; 1 John 2:13ff.). Acts 2:7 refers to "young men" as a class of people distinct from those who are "old."

neos νέος 3501

neos is an adjectival form found in approximately twenty places meaning "new," "young," as well as related senses.

The designation "young" is applied to men (Acts 5:6; 1 Tim 5:1), and to women (Titus 2:4). The comparative "younger" is predicated of women (1 Tim 5:2, 11ff.); of a son (Luke 15:12ff.); of men (Titus 2:6); and in general terms (1 Pet 5:5). The meaning "youngest" is evident in Luke 22:26. See also John 21:18.

▸ **5.** Old, New, First, Last > NEW, NEWNESS

neanias νεανίας 3494

neanias is a noun indicating a "young man" (Acts 7:58; 20:9; 23:17ff.).

elassōn ἐλάσσων 1640

elassōn is a comparative adjective denoting "less" in three of its four occurrences. In Rom 9:12, however, ***elassōn*** refers to Esau, the elder brother who will serve Jacob, the "younger."

SEE ALSO

▸ **14.** Animals > DOVE, TURTLEDOVE, PIGEON ***nossos***

YOUTH, YOUTHFUL

neotēs νεότης 3503

neotēs is a noun occurring five times, indicating one's "youth" or "early years" in Matt 19:20; Mark 10:20; Luke 18:21; Acts 26:4; 1 Tim 4:12.

neōterikos νεωτερικός 3512

neōterikos is a rare adjective meaning "youthful" in reference to the passions of one's early years (2 Tim 2:22).

16. Body, Bodily Functions

ARM

ankalē ἀγκάλη 43

ankalē is a rare noun denoting "the arms" of Simeon, who held the infant Jesus on the occasion of the child's consecration in the temple (Luke 2:28).

brachiōn βραχίων 1023

brachiōn is a noun found in only three places denoting metaphorically the "arm" of God in each case, indicating his mighty power (Luke 1:51; John 12:38; Acts 13:17).

enankalizomai ἐναγκαλίζομαι 1723

enankalizomai is a verb occurring four times with reference to Jesus "taking little children into his arms" in order to bless them (Mark 9:36; 10:16).

BACK

nōtos νῶτος 3577

nōtos is a rare noun found only in Rom 11:10 with reference to people "bending their backs."

SEE ALSO

▸ **36.** Reading, Writing > BACK
opisthen

BELLY, STOMACH, WOMB, HEART

koilia κοιλία 2836

koilia occurs about twenty times and means "womb" or "belly" (or stomach) in most of the occurrences. ***koilia*** also refers metaphorically to the "heart" as the seat of human emotions.

Matt 12:40 refers to the "belly" of a great fish, citing the story of Jonah. The term is also used metaphorically, indicating the "belly" as the seat of human emotions (though it is best translated "heart"; see John 7:38). Elsewhere ***koilia*** refers to the "stomach" (Matt 15:17; Mark 7:19; Luke 15:16; 1 Cor 6:13; Rev 10:9f.). In Rom 16:18; Phil 3:19 ***koilia*** implies the sense of "gluttony."

References to a woman's (or a mother's) womb are found in Matt 19:12; Luke 1:15, 41ff.; 23:29; John 3:4; Acts 3:2; 14:8; Gal 1:15.

gastēr γαστήρ 1064

gastēr is a noun found in nine places denoting the condition of pregnancy, or "being with child," and in Luke 1:31 it specifically refers to Mary's womb, which will carry the messianic child. Elsewhere, ***gastēr*** denotes "bellies" in reference to gluttony (Titus 1:12).

▸ **15.** Gender, Reproduction, Youth, Aging > PREGNANT

SEE ALSO

▸ **15.** Gender, Reproduction, Youth, Aging > WOMB
mētra

BLOOD

haima αἷμα 129

The noun ***haima*** occurs around one hundred times, denoting "blood" in various contexts.

The phrase "flesh and blood" is a metaphorical expression referring to "humanity" in generalized contexts (Matt 16:17; John 1:13; 1 Cor 15:50; Gal 1:16; Eph 6:12; Heb 2:14).

General references to "blood" in a literal, physiological sense include Mark 5:25; Luke 8:43ff.; John 19:34. In particular, Acts 15:20, 29; 21:25 rehearse the old covenant law forbidding the consumption of blood. The "shedding of blood," denoting murder and killing, is indicated in general contexts in Matt 27:4ff.; Luke 13:1; Acts 2:19; 20:26; Rom 3:15; Rev 19:2. In particular, the slaughter of the Hebrew prophets is described thus (Matt 23:30ff.; Luke 11:50ff.; Acts 5:28); as is the suffering of martyrs who likewise had their blood shed (Heb 12:4; Rev 6:10; 17:6; 18:24). In addition, the "shedding of blood" takes place in the context of "divine judgment" (Rev 8:7ff.; 14:20; 16:3ff.).

Undoubtedly the most theologically significant usage of ***haima*** occurs in contexts where the "blood of Christ" is the dominant motif. Christ's "blood" of the new covenant is symbolized by the Passover cup, given new significance just prior to his own death (Matt 26:28; Mark 14:24; Luke 22:20; 1 Cor 10:16; 11:25ff.). Elsewhere, Christ is said to purchase the salvation of his people with his own "blood" — through his atoning self-sacrifice on the cross (Acts 20:28; Rom 3:25; 5:9; Eph 1:7; 2:13; Col 1:14, 20; Heb 9:12ff.; 10:19, 29; 1 Pet 1:2, 19; 1 John 1:7; Rev 1:5; 5:9; 12:11; 19:13). The "blood" of the old covenant sacrifice is deemed ultimately ineffective. For it is the blood of Christ that secures forgiveness of sins and lasting peace with God (Heb 9:13ff.; 10:4ff.). General references to the sacrificial blood of the old covenant are found in Heb 11:28; 13:11.

The metaphorical expression "to drink the blood of Christ" denotes the dedication of one's life to follow him and obey his teaching (John 6:53ff.).

References to "the moon turning to blood" reflect a cosmic catastrophe, the dissolution of the celestial bodies, heralding the end of time (Acts 2:20; Rev 6:12).

SEE ALSO

▸ **20.** Illness, Disease, Health, Healing > HEMMORHAGE, FLOW OF BLOOD
haimorroeō

▸ **38.** Covenant, Law, Rites, Roles > BLOOD
haimatekchysia

BODY, BODILY

sōma σῶμα 4983

sōma is a noun found in approximately 150 contexts meaning "body," with a variety of nuances and several different contexts.

General references to the human body include Matt 5:29ff.; 6:22ff.; 26:12; Mark 5:29; Luke 11:34ff.; 12:22ff.; Rom 1:24; 4:19; 1 Cor 5:3; 9:27; 12:22ff.; 2 Cor 5:6ff.; Gal 6:17; Col 2:23; Jas 2:26; Jude 9. The term "body" can also indicate the whole person, or being (Rom 12:1; 1 Cor 6:13ff.; Eph 5:28; Heb 10:22). A reference to animal carcasses is found in Heb 13:11.

The other significant literal sense of ***sōma*** is that of "(human) corpse," used in general contexts such as John 19:31; Matt 14:12. "Bodies" undergoing the miracle of resurrection are indicated in Matt 27:52; Acts 9:40; 1 Cor 15:35ff. In particular, references to the "body" of Christ removed from the cross are found in Matt 27:58ff.; Mark 15:43ff.; Luke 23:52ff.; John 19:38ff.

Other uses of ***sōma*** are metaphorical. For example, the "body of Christ" is represented by the bread of the Passover meal, a "body" about to be broken to the cross (Matt 26:26; Mark 14:22; Luke 22:19; 1 Cor 10:16; 11:24ff.). The phrase "body of Christ" also functions as a summary expression for Christ's atoning sacrifice (Rom 7:4; Eph 2:16; Col 1:22; Heb 10:5, 10; 1 Pet 2:24); and as a metaphor for the whole community of God's people (1 Cor 12:27; Eph 4:4, 12ff.; 5:30; Col 2:19). John 2:21 refers to the "body of Christ" as a temple. And, finally, the expression is equated with the church in Eph 1:23; 5:23.

Elsewhere, the term "body" symbolizes the totality of the people of God in Rom 12:4ff.; 1 Cor 10:17. And the expression "sinful body" symbolizes the finite, fallen aspect of the nature of humankind in Rom 6:6; 7:24; 8:10ff.; Phil 3:21; Col 2:11.

sōmatikos — σωματικός 4984

sōmatikos is a rare adjective found only twice, meaning "bodily" in the sense of relating or pertaining to a bodily form. Luke 3:22 describes the Holy Spirit descending on Jesus in the "bodily" form of a dove. 1 Tim 4:8 refers to "bodily" exercise.

sōmatikōs — σωματικῶς 4985

sōmatikōs is an adverb, related to ***sōmatikos*** (above), found only in Col 2:9, with reference to the fullness of the Godhead dwelling "bodily" in Christ.

syssōmos — σύσσωμος 4954

syssōmos is an adjectival form found only in Eph 3:6 affirming that Gentile believers are members "of the same body" (i.e., of Christ, the church).

chrōs — χρώς 5559

chrōs is a rare noun denoting the "surface of one's body" in Acts 19:12.

SEE ALSO

▸ **21.** Die, Perish, Kill, Destroy > CORPSE, DEAD BODY
ptōma

BONE

osteon — ὀστέον 3747

osteon is a noun found in five places with the meaning "bone."

The "bones" of corpses are noted in Matt 23:27; and also in Heb 11:22 in the context of burial. Elsewhere, "bones" in the literal, physiological sense are indicated in Luke 24:39; John 19:36. The term is also used metaphorically in the sense of "body" in Eph 5:30.

BOSOM, LAP, BREAST, CHEST

kolpos — κόλπος 2859

The noun ***kolpos*** primarily denotes that part of the human body between the arms. The translation "bosom" is somewhat archaic. The translations "lap" or "breast" are more contemporary, as noted in Luke 6:38; 16:22ff.; John 13:23. The term is used metaphorically in John 1:18 to denote the "lap" of the Father.

stēthos — στῆθος 4738

stēthos is a noun signifying the "breast" or "chest" in a general sense. It is found in five contexts. The phrase "beating one's breast" as a sign of mourning is indicated in Luke 18:13; 23:48. References to "breast" in a general sense are found in John 13:25; 21:20; Rev 15:6.

mastos — μαστός 3149

mastos is a noun found in three places denoting a woman's "breasts" in the context of nursing one's children (Luke 11:27; 23:29). Rev 1:13 refers to the "breast" (or "chest") of the heavenly Christ in the apocalyptic vision of the apostle John.

BREATH, BREATHE

pnoē — πνοή 4157

pnoē is a rare noun denoting the "breath" of life that God gives to all creatures (Acts 17:25). It denotes "wind" in Acts 2:2.

▸ **11.** Meteorology, Water > WIND

pneuma — πνεῦμα 4151

pneuma is a common noun denoting "spirit," referring to both human beings and God. However, in Rev 11:11; 13:15 the term indicates the "breath" of life imparted by God to those who are both dead and inanimate.

▸ **2.** Supernatural Beings/Forces, Spiritual Realm > SPIRIT, SPIRITUAL, SPIRITUALLY
▸ **11.** Meteorology, Water > WIND

empneō — ἐμπνέω 1709

empneō is a rare verb translated "breathe out" in the metaphorical sense of "voicing a desire" to destroy all Christian disciples of the early church. It is found in Acts 9:1 in relation to Saul the Pharisee's dire threats against the followers of Christ.

emphysaō ἐμφυσάω 1720

emphysaō is a rare verb found only in John 20:22 in relation to Christ "breathing on" his disciples so that they might receive the Holy Spirit.

CRY, CRY OUT, SHOUT

kraugē κραυγή 2906

kraugē is a noun denoting a "sharp cry," "shout(ing)" in each of the six contexts in which it is found. A "cry" of surprise is indicated in Matt 25:6; a "cry" of support for the innocence of the apostle Paul is noted in Acts 23:9. "Shouting" in the context of unrestrained brawling occurs in a list of vices in Eph 4:31. Heb 5:7 refers to the "loud cries" of Christ offered to God in prayer during times of trial in his ministry on earth. The saints in heaven are described as being free from the "crying" of anguish and pain in Rev 21:4.

kraugazō κραυγάζω 2905

kraugazō is a verb found seven times meaning "cry out" or "cry aloud" in each case (Matt 12:19; 15:22; John 11:43; 18:40; 19:6, 15; Acts 22:23).

boē βοή 995

boē is a rare noun denoting a "cry" of protest in the face of injustice found only in Jas 5:4.

boaō βοάω 994

The verb ***boaō*** means "cry out" throughout its eleven occurrences in a variety of contexts.

General references to "crying out" are found in Acts 17:6; 21:34. "Crying out" in the context of a proclamation is evident in Mark 1:3; Luke 3:4; John 1:23. Gal 4:27 refers to "crying out" in joy. Jesus' "cry" of anguish on the cross is noted on Mark 15:34. The distressed "cries" of the elect in prayer to God are found in Luke 18. There is a "pleading" with Christ for a miraculous healing from blindness in Luke 18:38. Acts 8:7 contains a "cry" of terror from evil spirits cast out by the power of Christ from people whom they had previously oppressed.

anaboaō ἀναβοάω 310

anaboaō is a rare variant of ***boaō*** (above) found in only three places and meaning "cry out" in Matt 27:46 in relation to Jesus' cry of anguish on the cross as he experiences the rejection of his Father. In Luke 9:38 a father cries out to Jesus to exorcise the evil spirit from his son.

epiboaō ἐπιβοάω 1916

epiboaō is another rare variant of ***boaō*** (above). It denotes the "shouting" of a crowd in Acts 25:24.

krazō κράζω 2896

krazō means "cry," "cry out" throughout the nearly sixty occurrences of the term in various contexts.

Evil spirits "cry out" in fear of Christ in Matt 8:29; Mark 1:26; Luke 4:41 (see also Acts 16:17). People afflicted with sickness or disability "cry out," seeking healing from Christ in Matt 9:27; 20:30ff.; Mark 9:24; 10:47; Luke 18:39. "Calling out" in prayer to God is indicated in Rom 8:15; Gal 4:26. In Rev 6:10 the saints "beseech" God for revenge on their enemies. In contrast, Matt 21:9; Mark 11:9; John 12:13; Rev 7:10 record "crying out" in praise of God. Jesus' "cry" at the point of his death is recorded in Matt 27:50. In Mark 15:13, the Jerusalem crowd "cries out" demanding the death of Jesus.

General references to "crying out" include Matt 15:23; Mark 5:5; John 1:5; Acts 7:57; Rev 18:18. See also Matt 14:26ff.; Acts 19:28; Rev 12:2. A metaphorical reference to stones "crying out" is indicated in Luke 19:40.

anakrazō ἀνακράζω 349

anakrazō is a variant form of ***krazō*** (above) meaning "cry out" in each of its five occurrences. The cry of anguish from those possessed by evil spirits is noted in Mark 1:23; Luke 4:23. In Luke 8:28 the cry comes from the demon itself, struck with terror at the prospect of being confronted by Christ. A cry of fear is recorded in Mark 6:49. Luke 23:18 records the crowd's "clamoring shout" demanding that Pilate release Barabbas, the revolutionary, instead of Jesus.

epiphōneō ἐπιφωνέω 2019

epiphōneō is a rare variant form meaning "cry, shout out" in relation to a crowd (Luke 23:21; Acts 12:22; 22:24).

▸ **63.** Speak, Tell, Declare, Call > SHOUT

EAR

ous οὖς 3775

The noun ***ous*** is found nearly forty times meaning "ear," used in both literal and metaphorical contexts.

Literal references to the human "ear" include Matt 11:15; Mark 4:9; 7:33; Luke 1:44; 4:21; 8:8; 22:50; Acts 7:57; 11:22; 1 Cor 2:9; Rev 2:7ff.; 3:6ff.; 13:9. A symbolic reference to the human ear is found in 1 Cor 12:16. The term ***ous*** also refers to a person's "ear," indicating spiritual perception or understanding. Lack of such understanding is indicated in Matt 13:15; Mark 8:18; Acts 28:27; Rom 11:8. In particular, Acts 7:51 refers to the "uncircumcised ears" of people who offer resistance to the prompting of the Holy Spirit. Conversely, the capacity for such discernment is noted in Matt 13:16.

ous also refers anthropomorphically to the "ears" of the Lord of Hosts, who becomes aware of human injustice in Jas 5:4. The "ears" of the Lord are also declared to be open to the prayers of the righteous in 1 Pet 3:12.

ōtion ὠτίον 5621

ōtion is a rare diminutive form of ***ous*** (above) found only in Matt 26:51; Mark 14:47; Luke 22:51; John 18:10, 26. It refers exclusively to the "ear" of the high priest's servant cut off by the sword of the apostle Peter.

akoē ἀκοή 189

akoē is a noun occurring around twenty times with the primary sense of "hearing" and the associated senses of "fame," "report," "audience." In Mark 7:35; Acts 17:20, the term refers literally to the human ear. In 2 Tim 4:3 the term refers metaphorically to "itching ears," denoting an indiscriminate curiosity for strange doctrine.

- ▸ **17.** Senses, Actions, Abilities, Disabilities > HEAR, HEARING, LISTEN
- ▸ **52.** Status, Identity, Reputation, Honor, Shame > FAME
- ▸ **63.** Speak, Tell, Declare, Call > REPORT, FAME
- ▸ **63.** Speak, Tell, Declare, Call > RUMOR

EYE

ophthalmos ὀφθαλμός 3788

ophthalmos is the predominant term for "eye" in the NT. It is used both literally and metaphorically and is found in approximately one hundred contexts.

References to the "eye(s)" in the literal, physiological sense are found in Matt 5:29; 13:15ff.; Mark 8:18; Luke 2:30; 24:31; John 4:35; 11:37ff.; Acts 9:8; 26:18, 27; 1 Cor 12:16ff.; Gal 3:1; 4:15; Heb 4:13; 1 John 1:1; Rev 1:7; 3:18; 21:4.

The expression "before one's eyes" indicates the sense of "from one's heart or mind" as a response to something observed, like the fear of God (Rom 3:18).

Metaphorical references to the "eye(s)" as an instrument of spiritual perception are evident in Rom 11:8, 10; 1 Cor 2:9; Eph 1:18; 1 John 2:11. "Eyes full of adultery" are noted in 2 Pet 2:14. The vice of the "lust of the eyes" is noted in 1 John 2:16. The phrase "twinkling of an eye," indicating the briefest moment of time, is found in 1 Cor 15:52.

Anthropomorphic references to the "eyes of the Lord" are found in 1 Pet 3:12; and in the visionary context of John's revelation in Rev 1:14; 2:18; 5:6; 19:12. See also Rev 4:6ff.

omma ὄμμα 3659

omma is a rare term denoting a "human eye," found only in Mark 8:23.

SEE ALSO

- ▸ **17.** Senses, Actions, Abilities, Disabilities > ONE-EYED
  monophthalmos
- ▸ **34.** Craftsmanship, Artisanship, Furniture, Implements > EYE
  trymalia, trypēma

FACE

prosōpon πρόσωπον 4383

prosōpon is a noun occurring nearly eighty times with underlying reference to the front of the human head, translated for the most part "face," "countenance."

Literal references to the human face include those in Matt 6:16; 17:6; Mark 14:65; Luke 5:12; 17:6; Acts 20:25; 1 Cor 14:25; 2 Cor 11:20; Jas 1:23; Rev 4:7; 7:11; 9:7. The expression "face to face," indicating a personal confrontation, is found in Acts 25:16; 1 Thess 3:10; 2 Cor 10:1; Gal 2:11, in a human setting. It is also found in the context of a human being in the presence of the Lord in 1 Cor 13:12 (see also 2 Cor 3:18).

Occasionally the term is used as a synonym for one's person, translated as the personal pronoun "you" in Matt 11:10; Mark 1:2; Luke 7:27, and as "him" in Luke 10:1.

The metaphorical sense of "appearance" is indicated with reference to the "sky" in Matt 16:3; Luke 12:56.

The transfigured "face" of Christ on the mountain before his disciples Peter, James, and John is described in Matt 17:2; Luke 9:29; as is the "face" of Stephen, the first Christian martyr, at the point of his death in Acts 6:15. Reference to Moses' "face" is found in 2 Cor 3:7. Other references to the "face" of Christ include 2 Cor 4:6; Rev 10:1.

The "face" (i.e., surface) of the earth is referred to in Luke 21:35; Acts 17:26; Rev 20:11.

Anthropomorphic references to the "face" of God are found in Matt 18:10; 1 Pet 3:12; Rev 6:16; 22:14. Similarly, the expression "before the face of the Lord" is often simply translated "before the Lord" (e.g., Luke 1:76). Acts 23:19; 2 Thess 1:9; Heb 9:24 mention the Lord's "presence."

The expression "set one's face," denoting a determined intention, is noted in relation to Christ in Luke 9:51ff.

prosōpon also denotes a person's "presence" in Acts 2:28; 3:13.

- ▸ **2.** Supernatural Beings/Forces, Spiritual Realm > PERSON, PRESENCE
- ▸ **85.** Movement, Position, State > BEFORE, IN THE PRESENCE OF

opsis ὄψις 3799

opsis is a rare term denoting a person's "face" in John 11:44, and the "face" of the heavenly Christ in Rev 1:16.

stoma στόμα 4750

stoma is a term with the primary sense of "mouth" for most of its nearly eighty occurrences. In several places, however, ***stoma*** denotes a person's "face." The expression "face to face," indicating friendly social intercourse, is found in 3 John 14; 2 John 12.

- ▸ **16.** Body, Bodily Functions > MOUTH
- ▸ **31.** Kingdom, Empire, Rule, Military, Warfare > EDGE, EDGED

SEE ALSO

- ▸ **8.** Light, Darkness, Visible, Invisible, Color > APPEARANCE
  eidea

FINGER

daktylos δάκτυλος 1147

daktylos occurs eight times and denotes a "finger." References include Matt 23:4; Mark 7:33; Luke 11:46; 16:24; John 20:25, 27.

John 8:6 refers to Christ using his "finger" to write on the ground. Luke 11:20 contains an anthropomorphic reference to the "finger" of God as the agent of exorcising demons.

FLESH

sarx σάρξ 4561

sarx is the most common term for "flesh" in the NT, occurring about 150 times and meaning "flesh" throughout, with a number of related senses, both literal and metaphorical.

The expression "flesh and blood" indicates "humankind" or "mankind" in general (Matt 16:17; 1 Cor 15:50; Gal 1:16; Eph 6:12; Heb 2:14).

This sense of "humanity" in general is also evident in the meaning "flesh" in John 1:13; 3:6; 17:2; 1 Pet 1:24. Similarly, Christ's humanity is so indicated in Heb 5:7. In particular, the Holy Spirit is promised to be poured out on all "flesh" at the end of the age (Acts 2:17). This is a particular reference to all the people of God.

The phrase "one flesh" denotes the result of a union of two people in marriage (viz. husband and wife), constituting an intimate lifelong bonding of two persons (Matt 19:5ff.; Mark 10:8; 1 Cor 6:16; Eph 5:31).

General references to "flesh" as "human beings," "persons," are found in Matt 24:22; Luke 3:6; Rom 3:20; 1 Cor 1:29; Gal 2:16. In particular, the word of God is said to have become "flesh" (i.e., adopted a full human form) in John 1:14; 1 Tim 3:16; 1 John 4:2. Specific references to the human body as "flesh" are found in Eph 5:29; Heb 9:13; 1 Pet 3:21. Metaphorical references to "flesh" denoting "human weakness" are found in Matt 26:41; Phil 3:3. In Phil 3:4, however, "flesh" denotes "human accomplishment" in a positive sense.

References to literal human "flesh" are found in Luke 24:39; Rev 19:18, 21. 1 Cor 15:39 uses "flesh" in the general sense of a "physical being," with reference to man and animal alike (see also Rev 17:16). ***sarx*** also denotes the human "body" in contrast with the spirit (2 Cor 7:1, 5; 12:7). The body of Christ offered up in sacrifice for the sins of the world is designated as his "flesh" in John 6:51. Eating the "flesh" of Christ symbolically indicates the nurturing of one's absolute faith and dependence on him (John 6:52ff.). Other references to the "body" of Christ include Eph 2:15; Col 1:22; Heb 10:20.

sarx also denotes "flesh" in the sense of "sinful human nature" in Rom 7:5; 8:3ff.; Gal 3:3; 5:13ff.; Eph 2:3; Col 2:11ff.; 2 Pet 2:10; 1 John 2:16.

"Flesh" also denotes "racial kinship" in Rom 9:3ff., with reference to the Jewish people. See also Gal 6:13; Eph 2:11. Then, similarly, in Gal 4:23, 29, "flesh" denotes the "principle of human regeneration" (i.e., born in the ordinary human way).

SEE ALSO

- **14.** Animals > MEAT, FLESH
  kreas
- **57.** Evil, Wickedness, Sin > FLESHLY, CARNAL, WORLDLY
  sarkikos

FOOT

pous πούς 4228

pous is the most common term for "foot" in the NT, occurring about ninety times and referring to the feet of both human beings and beasts.

Literal references to the feet of people include those in Matt 15:30; Mark 7:25; Luke 24:39; John 11:2, 44; Acts 5:2; 14:10; 1 Tim 5:10. In particular, Jesus' action in washing his disciples' feet as a gesture of servanthood is described in John 13:5ff. With regard to the literal usage of ***pous***, a significant number of references denote the feet of Christ. See also 1 Cor 15:21ff.; Eph 6:15. Matt 7:6 refers to the feet of animals.

In the book of Revelation ***pous*** designates "feet" in a number of visionary contexts — for example, the "feet" of the heavenly Christ (Rev 1:15, 17; 2:18); the feet of angelic beings (Rev 10:1, 2; 19:10; 22:8); the feet of the saints (Rev 11:11; 12:1); and the feet of the sea beast — the satanic counterfeit messiah (Rev 13:2).

In particular, Matt 4:6; Luke 4:11 (citing Ps 91:11, 12) refer to God's protection of his Son, lest "he strike his foot against a stone."

Rom 16:20 states that "the God of peace will crush Satan under your feet," implying the messianic conquest of the devil. See also Eph 1:22; Heb 2:8.

The expression "shake the dust off one's feet" is a literal action that symbolically represents rejection (Matt 10:14; Mark 6:11; Luke 9:5; Acts 13:51).

The designation "feet" is sometimes used metaphorically to denote the whole person with reference, for example, to "guiding one's feet into the way of peace" (Luke 1:79). Acts 22:3 refers to Paul's pre-Christian vocation as a Pharisee, "sitting at the feet" of Gamaliel, his mentor.

SEE ALSO

- **20.** Illness, Disease, Health, Healing > FOOT
  basis
- **34.** Craftsmanship, Artisanship, Furniture, Implements > FOOTSTOOL
  hypopodion
- **86.** Movement Toward or Away From > WALK ON FOOT
  pezeuō

FOREHEAD

metōpon μέτωπον 3359

metōpon is a noun meaning "forehead" in all eight occurrences of the term — all of which are found in the visionary context of the book of Revelation.

Rev 7:3; 9:4 mention the seal of God on the "foreheads" of his protected people. Similarly, Rev 14:1; 22:4 refer to the name of God the Father branded on the "foreheads" of the elect 144,000.

Conversely, Rev 13:16; 14:9 refer to the mark of the beast, placed on either the right hand or "the forehead" of all those who worshiped the satanic figure. See also Rev 20:4.

Similarly, Rev 17:5 mentions the title "mystery, Babylon the great, the mother of harlots" written on "the forehead" of the symbolic woman epitomizing all moral evil.

GNASH, GNASHING, GRIND

brychō βρύχω 1031

brychō is a rare verb indicating "gnashing" one's teeth in anger in Acts 7:54.

brygmos βρυγμός 1030

brygmos is a noun denoting "gnashing" of teeth, all in the context of people expressing anguish in eternal torment (Matt 8:12; 13:42, 50; 22:13; 24:51; Luke 13:28).

trizō τρίζω 5149

trizō is a rare verb found only in Mark 9:18, meaning "to grind" one's teeth in the context of a demonic possession.

▸ **75.** Suffering, Distress, Sadness > GRINDING

GROAN, GROANING, SIGH

stenazō στενάζω 4727

stenazō means "groan" or "sigh" in most of its six occurrences.

In Mark 7:34, Jesus "sighs" before restoring the hearing of a deaf man, suggesting his "distress" over the plight of the disabled man before him.

In Rom 8:23; 2 Cor 5:2, 4 the people of God are said to "groan" under the limitations of their earthly existence while they eagerly await the liberation of life with God and Christ in glory.

anastenazō ἀναστενάζω 389

anastenazō is a rare variant of ***stenazō*** (above) denoting the "deep sighing" of Jesus as he laments the spiritual decline of his own generation in Mark 8:12.

systenazō συστενάζω 4959

systenazō is another rare variant of ***stenazō*** (above). It is found only in Rom 8:22 and refers to creation "groaning" like a woman in labor.

stenagmos στεναγμός 4726

stenagmos is a rare noun derived from ***stenazō*** (above) that is found only twice. Stephen's speech in Acts 7:34 refers to the "groaning" of the Israelites during their bondage in Egypt. In an unusual use of the term in Rom 8:26, ***stenagmos*** denotes the "groanings" of the Holy Spirit, symbolically alluding to the Spirit's identification with the believers he indwells, interceding with God the Father on their behalf.

HAIR

thrix θρίξ 2359

This term also refers to human and animal hair. ***thrix*** is found in about a dozen contexts. Animal hair is indicated in Matt 3:4; Mark 1:6. Human hair in a general sense is referred to, for example, in Matt 5:36. In a number of instances, ***thrix*** is used in a metaphorical expression that indicates a greatly reassuring divine protection, whereby it is declared that the person in distress or danger will not lose a "single hair on his head." The inference, of course, is that God is watching over his people (Luke 12:7; 21:18; Matt 10:30; Acts 27:34). The word is also found in texts where a devout or penitent women washes Jesus' feet with her hair — constituting an act of worship (Luke 7:38, 44; John 11:2).

komē κόμη 2864

The sole reference here is to a woman's hair as a symbol of her glory in 1 Cor 11:15.

HAND

cheir χείρ 5495

cheir occurs around 180 times and means "hand" in a physical sense, as well as conveying the metaphorical ideas of human and divine help or agency. ***cheir*** also refers to divine power and authority in determining the destinies of various people.

The literal, mundane sense of "hand" is found, for example, in Matt 8:15; Mark 1:31; Luke 6:1; John 11:21; Acts 12:7; 1 Cor 4:12; Phlm 9; 1 John 1:1. The physical sense of "hand(s)" is also found in contexts where Jesus performs miracles with his hands (e.g., Matt 8:3; Mark 6:2; Luke 4:40; 5:13), as do his disciples (Acts 3:7; 5:12; 9:12; 19:11).

cheir is also found in other literal expressions such as "to lay hands on (someone)" in the sense of physical assault or arrest (Mark 14:46; Luke 21:2). In relation to Jesus, it is recorded that no person could lay hands on him, in this sense, during his ministry prior to his appointed time of arrest (John 7:44; 10:39). This same phrase is also used in conjunction with the ceremony of initiation for the Holy Spirit's anointing (Acts 8:17; 19:6); and also for the rite of ordination for ministry (Acts 13:3 [Saul and Barnabas]; 1 Tim 4:14; 2 Tim 1:6; Heb 6:2). 1 Tim 2:8 also records lifting up one's hands in worship.

In the numerous metaphorical expressions in which the term ***cheir*** is found, there is a focus on both divine and human agency. First of all, there is the idea of the "hand(s) of God" as the instrument of divine judgment against humankind (e.g., Matt 3:12; Luke 3:17); and against his people (Rom 10:21). See also 1 Pet 5:6; Heb 10:31. Acts 7:35 describes the "hand of God, or the angel" as the instrument of divine deliverance. This term is also found with reference to the hands of theophanic figures in the visions of the book of Revelation — for example, the hands of Christ (Rev 1:16ff.; 6:5); of the angel (Rev 8:4; 10:2; 14:14; 20:1, 4); and of the Babylonian "whore" (Rev 19:2). The concept of the "hand of the Lord" is also used positively in the context of divine favor. Most notable of these is Luke 23:46, where Jesus on the cross repeats the words of Ps 31:5, "Into your hands I commit my spirit," in fulfillment of that prophetic cry. See also Luke 1:66; John 10:28; Acts 11:21. The motif of the authority of God is also conveyed by the use of this phrase in John 3:35; 13:3.

cheir also conveys human power and authority in being delivered over "into the hands of (one's enemies)." It is predicated of Jesus in his betrayal (Matt 17:20; 26:45; Mark 9:31; 14:41; Luke 9:44; 24:7), and in his crucifixion (Acts 2:23). It also occurs in reference to the Herodian persecution of the early church in Acts 12:1; and to Paul's being handed over to the Romans in Acts 28:17.

cheir also refers to the phenomenon of creativity: firstly of God in creation (Heb 1:10; 2:7); and secondly of human beings in Acts 7:41; 19:26. This latter sense is wholly negative, however, for the reference is to idol making.

HEAD

kephalē κεφαλή 2776

This noun is found approximately eighty times with the principal meaning "head." ***kephalē*** conveys a varied range of nuances associated with the concept of "head," both literal and metaphorical. The literal meaning is self-explanatory, but the metaphorical sense refers to "headship," suggesting that which is supreme, whether it be in the civil, ritual, or familial sphere of human relationships. In the NT, ***kephalē*** has a particular significance regarding the standing of Jesus Christ as head of the church, functioning both as its divine founder and ongoing sustainer, through the person of the Holy Spirit.

With the literal meaning of a human head ***kephalē*** is found, for example, in Matt 5:36; 10:30; Mark 6:24ff.; Luke 7:38ff.; John 13:9; Acts 18:18. Matt 8:20; Luke 9:58 refer to Christ having nowhere to lay his head — that is, having no permanent home. John 19:2; Matt 27:29 refer to the wounds inflicted on Jesus' head prior to his crucifixion. John 19:30 refers to Jesus bowing his head at the point of death, as an act of submission to his Father.

The metaphorical usage of ***kephalē*** is quite extensive. The phrase "blood upon one's head" constitutes a symbolic reference to one's condemnation and guilt (Acts 18:6). To "heap coals of fire upon one's head" is an action cited in Rom 12:20 which alludes to the aggravation of personal guilt as a consequence of rendering to one's enemy good for evil.

kephalē also refers to the phenomenon of "headship," from both a human and divine perspective. Within the sphere of the family, for example, 1 Cor 11:3 speaks of a fundamental divine ordering: the head of man is Christ; the head of woman is man, and the head of Christ is God (Eph 5:23). 1 Cor 11:5, 10 maintain that a woman uncovering her head amounts to a dishonoring of her head, violating her symbolic submission to both her husband and to Christ. The argument is also adduced (1 Cor 11:7) that because the man is "then head of his wife" and made in the image of God, his head is not to be covered. The term ***kephalē*** here is used symbolically to refer not to respective values of man and woman in the sight of God, but rather to their relative functions in the divinely ordered sphere of family and worship.

kephalē also conveys a divine perspective on headship. For example, reference to Jesus Christ as the chief cornerstone, the one rejected by the builder, is interpreted by the Gospel writers as a fulfillment of the OT prophecy in Ps 18:22 (Matt 21:42; Mark 12:10; Luke 20:17). References to Christ as head of the church are found in Eph 1:22; 4:15; 5:23; Col 1:18; 2:19. In addition, Christ is depicted as the head of all rulers in the kingdom of God, the supreme figure of universal authority (Col 2:10).

Significant metaphorical usage of the term ***kephalē*** is also found throughout the book of Revelation. The visionary head of Christ is depicted, for example, in Rev 1:14 (see also Rev 10:1). Rev 14:14 refers to the head of the "Son of man"; and Rev 19:12 speaks of the head of the messianic white rider, who has many crowns on his head. Rev 4:4 refers symbolically to the heads of the heavenly creatures around God's throne (see also Rev 12:1). Heads of locusts are also depicted in the apocalyptic vision of judgment in Rev 9:7. Similarly, the head of the dragon (i.e., Satan) is described in Rev 12:3, and the head of the sea beast (i.e., the false messiah, antichrist) in Rev 13:1. The head of the scarlet woman, the great "whore of Babylon," symbolizing all the godless nations of the world, is also mentioned in Rev 17:3ff. Those who witness the destruction of the city of Babylon in this context are described as sprinkling dust on their heads — a sign of anguish at the fall of the great city (Rev 18:19).

HEEL

pterna πτέρνα 4418

The only occurrence of this term in the NT is found in John 13:18, where Jesus refers to Judas opposing him (i.e., lifting up his heel against him) on the occasion of the Last Supper, prior to his crucifixion.

ITCH

knēthō κνήθω 2833

knēthō is found only in 2 Tim 4:3, where it refers to people having "itching ears." The term refers to those refusing to countenance sound teaching, only listening to what they want to hear.

KNEE, KNEEL

gony γόνυ 1119

gony occurs twelve times in all and refers to worship, or an act of deference, in most of these contexts.

gony is utilized in the expression "bow the knee" three times with specific reference to worship. In Rom 11:4, Paul refers to those in Israel who in the past had not "bowed the knee" to Baal. Rom 14:11; Phil 2:10 indicate the worship of God and Christ respectively through the phrase "bow the knee." See also Mark 15:19; Luke 5:8; Eph 3:14.

In the remaining contexts, ***gony*** is used in the verbal sense of "kneel down," with reference to prayer in Acts 7:60; 9:40; 20:36; 21:5; Luke 22:41. Heb 12:12 also mentions "feeble knees" in reference to weakness of spirit.

LEG

skelos σκέλος 4628

skelos is found only three times, referring to the legs of Jesus and the two men crucified with him at Golgotha. John 19:31, 32, 33 state that the legs of the two criminals were broken by the Roman soldiers in order to hasten death. But, on coming to Jesus, they found him already dead, so they did not break his legs.

LIP

cheilos χεῖλος 5491

cheilos occurs only seven times and is translated "lips" with reference to speaking in six of these contexts.

Matt 15:8; Mark 7:6 refer to the false worship of the Jewish people, in Jesus' quotation of the passage from Isa 29:13, "These people honor me with their lips, but their hearts are far from me." Deceitful speech is indicated in Rom 3:13; and 1 Pet 3:10 warns against such expression. True worship of God as the appropriate "fruit of (one's) lips" is indicated in Heb 13:15. Foreign languages are mentioned in 1 Cor 14:21.

▸ **9.** Land, Geography, Topography > SHORE, SEASHORE

MEMBER, JOINT

haphē ἁφή 860

haphē occurs only in Eph 4:16; Col 2:19, referring to physical joints of the human body. The context of each occurrence, however, is metaphorical, for in both Ephesians and Colossians, Paul uses the metaphor of the human body to illustrate the ideal harmony of believers in union with Christ as "members" of his body, the church.

harmos ἁρμός 719

harmos is found only in Heb 4:12, referring, as does ***haphē*** (above), to the joints of the human body. In this context, ***harmos*** is used metaphorically to indicate the impact of the word of God on the human heart as that which penetrates to the "joints and marrow," to the very depths, of the soul.

melos μέλος 3196

melos is a noun occurring around thirty times with the universal meaning "member," referring primarily to parts of the human body in a literal sense (Matt 5:29ff.; Rom 6:13, 19; 7:5, 23; Rom 12:4ff.; 1 Cor 12:12ff.; Jas 3:5ff.).

melos is also used metaphorically to refer to the believer as a "member with Christ," joined to him by faith (1 Cor 6:15; Eph 4:25; 5:30). See also Col 3:5; Jas 4:1.

MOUTH

stoma στόμα 4750

stoma is a noun found approximately eighty times with the predominant sense of "mouth" in a variety of contexts.

When predicated of human beings, ***stoma*** is most commonly used to signify human speech of various kinds. For example, the mouth is said to reflect in speech what is truly on the hearts of human beings, whether good or evil (Matt 12:34; 15:11, 18; Luke 6:45; Eph 4:29; Col 3:8; Jas 3:10). See also Rev 14:5. Other kinds of speech coming from people's mouths include false worship (Matt 15:8); evidence against wrongdoers (Matt 18:16; 2 Cor 13:1); genuine praise to God (Matt 21:16; Rom 15:6); confession of the person of Jesus (Rom 10:9ff); cursing by unbelievers (Rom 3:14); and preaching the gospel (Eph 6:19). References to prophetic revelation are found in allusions to the "mouth of the prophets" (Luke 1:70; Acts 3:18ff.); including "the mouth of David" (Acts 1:16; 4:25). There is also reference to the prophetic testimony of the two "heavenly witnesses" in Rev 11:5. Literal, mundane references to "mouth" are found in Luke 1:64; Acts 11:8.

stoma also refers metaphorically to the "mouth of God." In Matt 4:4, Jesus cites the affirmation of Deut 8:3: "Man shall live . . . by every word . . . from the mouth of God." Rev 3:16 declares that God will vomit out (i.e., spit out of his mouth) those who are lukewarm in their faith in the congregation at Laodicea.

Acts 8:32 refers to the prophecy of Isa 53:7, declaring that the messianic Servant would not open his mouth before his tormentors.

With reference to the person of Jesus Christ, ***stoma*** also refers to his "mouth," in the context of his teaching. Luke 4:22 declares that words from Jesus' mouth amazed his hearers. The message, or word of commissioning, to the apostle Paul from the "mouth" of the risen Christ is recorded in Acts 22:14. At his final return, the Lord Jesus Christ will slay his enemies with "the breath of his mouth." 1 Pet 2:22 declares that no guile is to be found on the lips, or mouth, of Christ. The book of Revelation mentions "the sword of his mouth" as the ultimate weapon of the heavenly Christ, which he will use to judge the wicked (Rev 1:16; 2:16; 19:15, 21). See also Matt 5:2; 13:35; John 19:29.

With regard to animals, ***stoma*** refers to the "mouth" of a fish (Matt 17:27); to "mouths" of lions, both literally and metaphorically (Heb 11:33; Rev 13:2ff., respectively); to horses' mouths (Jas 3:3); to the (symbolic) mouths of the apocalyptic beasts (Rev 9:17ff.); and also to the mouth of the dragon, the embodiment of satanic opposition to God and his people (Rev 16:13). See also Rev 12:16.

▸ **16.** Body, Bodily Functions > FACE

▸ **31.** Kingdom, Empire, Rule, Military, Warfare > EDGE, EDGED

NECK

trachēlos τράχηλος 5137

trachēlos is the only term for "neck" in the NT. It occurs seven times with both literal and symbolic force.

Literal references to "neck" are found in Luke 15:20; Acts 20:37. Both texts indicate people weeping as they embrace a person very dear to them, literally "falling upon their necks."

In metaphorical contexts, Matt 18:6; Mark 9:42; Luke 17:2 refer to the implied terrible fate set aside for those who cause young believers to stumble in their faith. Such a fate is worse than "having a millstone placed around their neck" and being cast into the sea. Making unfair and unreasonable demands on newly converted Gentile believers is likened in Acts 15:10 to "putting a yoke on the neck" of these disciples. In Rom 16:4, Paul praises the courage of those "who risked their necks" for his life.

SHOULDER

ōmos ὦμος 5606

ōmos is a noun referring to the "shoulders" of human beings. It is found only in Matt 23:4; Luke 15:5.

SIDE

pleura πλευρά 4125

pleura is a noun found in five places meaning "right side" (i.e., of the body), referring to Christ's crucifixion wound (John 19:34; 20:20ff.); and to Peter (Acts 12:7).

SEE ALSO

▸ **6.** Location, Position, Direction, Extension > RIGHT, RIGHT HAND, RIGHT SIDE
dexios

THIGH

mēros μηρός 3382

mēros is a noun found only in Rev 19:16, referring to the "thigh" of Christ, the divine warrior, bearing the name "King of kings and Lord of lords" as he rides forth to overthrow all the armies of Satan.

THROAT

pnigō πνίγω 4155

pnigō is a rare verb denoting the action of "seizing by the throat" (Matt 18:18).

larynx λάρυγξ 2995

larynx is another rare noun, found only in Rom 3:3, where Paul cites the refrain from Ps 5:9, describing the "throat" of the wicked as an "open grave."

TONGUE

glōssa γλῶσσα 1100

glōssa is a noun occurring fifty times with the meaning "tongue" throughout, with differing nuances.

Literal references to the tongue as the organ of speech are found in Mark 7:33ff.; Luke 16:24; Jas 3:5ff.; Rev 16:10. It is used to praise God in Acts 2:6; Rom 14:11; Phil 2:11; and is also capable of sinful use (Rom 3:13).

Metaphorically, ***glōssa*** also means "human language." The contexts for this usage involve the direct influence of the Spirit of God (Acts 2:4, 11; 10:46; Rev 5:9; 7:9; 10:11; 13:7; 14:6; 17:15). In Acts 19:6; 1 Cor 12:10, 28ff.; 13:1, 8; 14:2ff., the use of ***glōssa*** is often thought to indicate non-human discourse, or ecstatic utterance that bears no relation to ordinary human language. However, there would appear to be no compelling reason to reject the straightforward translation of "human language" in these contexts.

In Acts 2:3, ***glōssa*** refers to the appearance of "tongues" of fire, as a consequence of the Holy Spirit coming down upon the apostles on the Day of Pentecost.

SEE ALSO

▸ **63.** Speak, Tell, Declare, Call > TONGUE
dialektos, heteroglōssos

TOOTH

odous ὀδούς 3599

odous is a noun found in twelve places with consistent reference to a "tooth" or "teeth."

The old covenant law of retaliation ("eye for eye, tooth for tooth"), or *lex talionis*, is indicated in Matt 5:38. ***odous*** refers to animal teeth in Rev 9:8.

Most commonly, ***odous*** is found in the expression "gnashing one's teeth," indicating profound physical and mental anguish (Matt 22:13; 25:30; Mark 9:18; Luke 13:28; Acts 7:54).

VOMIT

emeō ἐμέω 1692

emeō is a verb found only in Rev 3:16, referring to Yahweh's threat to "vomit up" the lukewarm congregation of the church at Laodicea.

exerama ἐξέραμα 1829

exerama is a noun denoting "vomit," found only in 2 Pet 2:22.

17. Senses, Actions, Abilities, Disabilities

BLIND, MAKE BLIND

typhloō τυφλόω 5186

typhloō is a rare verb found three times with the meaning "to make blind."

John 12:40 cites the divine judgment against Israel whereby God "blinded their eyes" (Isa 6:10), a symbolic reference to the reality of a withdrawal of genuine spiritual understanding and insight.

Similarly, in another context, Satan is said to "have blinded the minds" of unbelievers to the truth of the gospel (2 Cor 4:4).

typhlos τυφλός 5185

The adjective ***typhlos*** occurs around fifty times with the meaning "blind," "blind man."

There are a number of references to blind men who experienced healing at the hands of Jesus (Matt 9:27ff.; 20:30; Mark 8:22ff.; 10:46ff.; Luke 18:35; John 9:1ff.). Other general references allude to "the blind" as a class of people (e.g., Matt 11:5; 15:30ff.; 21:4; Luke 6:39; 14:13; John 5:3; 9:39; 10:21).

Elsewhere ***typhlos*** denotes those who are "spiritually blind" (Rom 2:19; 2 Pet 1:9; Rev 3:17). In particular, Jesus denounces hypocritical, self-righteous Pharisees who were a hindrance to God's people attaining true godliness (Matt 23:14ff.).

In Acts 13:11, Elymas the sorcerer is afflicted with blindness as a judgment from God.

DEAF, MUTE

kōphos κωφός 2974

kōphos is an adjective found fourteen times in all denoting the disabilities of "muteness" (or "dumbness") and "deafness." References to those who are "deaf" include Matt 11:5; Mark 7:32, 37; Luke 7:22, all in contexts where the power of God in Christ guarantees their healing. In Mark 9:25 Jesus commands a "deaf and mute spirit" to leave a man it had been controlling.

▸ **17.** Senses, Actions, Abilities, Disabilities >
MUTE, VOICELESS, DUMB

FEEL

ginōskō γινώσκω 1097

ginōskō is a common verb found over two hundred times with the primary meaning "to know," as well as a variety of related senses. In Mark 5:29 ***ginōskō*** is translated "feel," referring to the woman healed of her hemorrhage when she "felt" that the disease had left her body.

▸ **51.** Knowledge, Wisdom, Remember, Forget >
KNOW, KNOWLEDGE, MAKE KNOWN

HEAR, HEARING, LISTEN

akouō ἀκούω 191

This is a common NT verb, occurring around 450 times with the primary sense of "hear," as well as associated senses such as "listen," "give heed to," "comprehend."

With people as subject, ***akouō*** refers to the literal sense of hearing as auditory perception in a number of contexts. For example, aural witness is very important to the life of Jesus (John 3:32; 1 John 1:1), and to his teaching ministry (Matt 21:45; Mark 6:2; Luke 5:1; John 9:40). As part of the record of Saul's conversion experience, Acts 9:4ff.; 22:7; 26:14 all refer to his hearing the voice of Jesus en route to Damascus. Rom 10:14 affirms the indispensability of hearing the word of the Lord in order to be saved. Jesus' miraculous restoration of hearing to the deaf is recorded in Matt 11:5; Mark 7:37. Various references are also made to hearing the voice of God or angels in episodes of divine visitation (Luke 2:20; Acts 10:46; 2 Cor 12:4; Rev 5:11; 10:8; 11:12; 14:2). See also Acts 2:6ff.

akouō also has the sense of "hearing about," such as news or information. General references in a mundane sense are found, for example, in Matt 12:24; Luke 1:58; Acts 7:12; 23:16; 1 Cor 11:18; Gal 1:23; 2 Thess 3:11; Jas 5:11. Mark 6:55; John 12:18 also refer to people hearing about Jesus and his miracle working. John the Baptist hears about the ministry of Jesus in Matt 11:2. Paul's delight in hearing about the faith of his fellow believers is noted in Col 1:4; Phlm 5.

Hearing in the sense of "understanding" is also indicated in the usage of ***akouō***. Specific blessings that result from genuine spiritual understanding (viz. "hearing") are mentioned in Matt 13:16; Mark 4:20; Luke 11:28; John 5:24. This includes hearing that leads to conversion (Acts 4:4; 10:44; 18:8; Eph 1:13). In the Sermon on the Mount, Jesus says, "You have heard that it was said . . ." several times (Matt 5:21ff.). This new legislation transcends the mere outward formality of the old covenant law, and here Jesus expounds the true inner requirement of divine law, contrasting the external mode of the Mosaic law code.

akouō also conveys the idea of "listen carefully, pay heed to." Its predominant usage in the NT focuses on the importance of carefully heeding the teaching of Jesus. Note the expression "He who has ears to hear, let him hear . . ." in Matt 11:15; Rev 2:7ff.; 3:6ff.; 13:9. See also Matt 17:5; Mark 9:7; Luke 16:29; Acts 2:22. In Mark 12:29, Jesus cites the command of Deut 6:4: "Hear, O Israel, the Lord our God, the Lord is one." Other related contexts stress the importance of hearing the word of God in worship (Acts 13:44); hearing the law of Moses (Gal 4:21); heeding the words of the apostle Paul (2 Tim 1:13); and hearing God's voice and obeying him (Heb 3:7, 15; 4:7). Negative connotations are also associated with the use of ***akouō***. Failing to hear (i.e., understand, or give close attention to) the word of God in the proclamation of the gospel leads inevitably to spiritual dullness, and hardness of heart (Matt 13:13, 15; Mark 4:12; Acts 28:27). This is a central theme of the parable of the sower (Luke 8:12ff.), where the seed falling on the path symbolizes the terrible reality of nonproductive hearing. See also John 8:47; Rom 11:8. Conversely, keen hearing in the sense of acute spiritual perception constitutes a profound blessing (Matt 13:16; 1 Cor 2:9).

Jesus is also portrayed as the unique "hearer" of God's word (John 8:40; 15:15); and he thanks his heavenly Father for hearing him (John 11:41).

Infrequently, God is portrayed as the subject of this verb, as one who has heard the groans and pleas of his people and has responded to them with mercy and grace (Acts 7:34; 1 John 5:14).

akoē ἀκοή 189

akoē is the noun derived from ***akouō*** (above). It occurs about twenty-five times and means "hearing" in about half of these contexts.

There is a literal reference to the process of hearing as a means to true spiritual understanding in Matt 13:14; Rom 10:17; Gal 3:25; 1 Thess 2:13.

akoē is also found in contexts of judgment, where God's people have become "hard of hearing" and are placed under divine judgment (Acts 28:26; Heb 5:11).

Mundane references to hearing as auditory perception are found in 1 Cor 12:17; 2 Pet 2:8.

- ▸ **16.** Body, Bodily Functions > EAR
- ▸ **52.** Status, Identity, Reputation, Honor, Shame > FAME
- ▸ **63.** Speak, Tell, Declare, Call > REPORT, FAME
- ▸ **63.** Speak, Tell, Declare, Call > RUMOR

IMPEDIMENT

mogilalos μογιλάλος 3424

mogilalos occurs only in Mark 7:32, referring to a man who was afflicted with deafness and a speech impediment. This man was brought to Jesus, who subsequently cured him.

- ▸ **17.** Senses, Actions, Abilities, Disabilities > SPEAK, SPEECH, TALK

LAME

chōlos χωλός 5560

chōlos is an adjectival form (occurring fifteen times) that refers primarily to the physical condition of lameness.

In Jesus' ministry of miracle working, the healing of the lame was a prominent feature (Matt 11:5; 15:30ff.; Mark 9:45; Luke 7:22; John 5:3). Likewise, the apostles continued with their own healing ministry after the ascension of Christ (Acts 3:2, 11; 8:7; 14:8). Luke 14:13, 21 refer generally to the lame or crippled.

chōlos is used metaphorically in Matt 18:8, where Jesus refers to the consequences of "cutting off one's limbs." The declared intention is that it is better to enter heaven "maimed" than to be thrown into hell with all hands and feet intact — emphasizing the necessity of self-denial and turning from sin. Heb 12:13 refers to spiritual healing through the metaphor of deliverance from lameness.

MUTE, VOICELESS, DUMB

alalos ἄλαλος 216

alalos is an adjective found in three places, all referring to the condition of speechlessness. The "mute" (or "dumb") are designated in Mark 7:37 as the objects of Christ's miraculous power when they are given back their voices. Mark 9:17, 25 both refer to demonic spirits who afflict their victims with muteness and who are designated as "mute" (or "dumb") spirits.

aphōnos ἄφωνος 880

aphōnos is another adjectival form meaning "mute," "voiceless," or "dumb" in four places, referring not to people but to idols (1 Cor 12:2); to a lamb "silent" (or "dumb") before its shearer (Acts 8:32); and the "speechless" (or "dumb") donkey associated with Balaam which was given a voice by God to rebuke the pagan seer (2 Pet 2:16 [citing Num 22:21–30]). The term is also translated "without meaning" in 1 Cor 14:10.

kōphos κωφός 2974

kōphos is an adjective meaning "mute," "speechless" (i.e., without voice), "dumb" throughout its twelve occurrences. ***kōphos*** is also translated "deaf."

A "mute" demoniac is noted in Matt 9:32ff.; 12:22; Luke 11:14. Christ's healing of the "mute" (or "dumb") is recorded in Matt 12:22; 15:30ff. The "mute" condition of Zechariah the priest, father of John the Baptist, is indicated in Luke 1:22.

- ▸ **17.** Senses, Actions, Abilities, Disabilities > DEAF, MUTE

ONE-EYED

monophthalmos μονόφθαλμος 3442

monophthalmos is a rare adjectival form denoting the disability of having only "one eye" (Matt 18:9; Mark 9:47).

SEE ALSO

- ▸ **16.** Body, Bodily Functions > EYE
  ophthalmos, omma
- ▸ **34.** Craftsmanship, Artisanship, Furniture, Implements > EYE
  trymalia, trypēma

SEE, LOOK, BEHOLD, GAZE

horaō ὁράω 3708
eidon, oida εἶδον, οἶδα 1492

horaō is a verb found in nearly seven hundred places meaning "see" in the majority of these contexts, with a variety of nuances. The terms ***eidon*** and ***oida*** are past tense forms of this verb. These forms also express the meaning "know," which is closely related to "seeing," in the context of mental perception.

References to "seeing" in the physical realm of visual perception include those in Mark 1:10; Luke 9:36; John 1:39; Acts 6:15; 1 Cor 2:9; Col 2:1. In particular, John 6:36 refers to people seeing or watching Christ perform miraculous signs.

In John 14:9 Christ declares that "to see" him is equivalent to "seeing" the Father — clearly implying spiritual perception. Seeing, or beholding, the glory of God or a vision from God is indicated, for example, in Luke 1:22; Acts 7:55; Rev 20:11ff. See also Rev 4:4; 7:1ff.; 18:1ff. Other contexts declare that human beings cannot "see" God in his essential being (John 1:18; 5:37; 6:46; 1 John 4:20; 1 Tim 6:16). Luke 2:30 refers to Simeon "seeing" the salvation of God when he was introduced to the infant Jesus and blessed him. John declares that he saw a vision of the "new heavens and the new earth" in Rev 21:1, 2. See also Matt 3:16; 16:28.

horaō means "see" in a number of other senses — for example, "take heed" (Matt 8:4; Acts 22:6; 1 Thess 5:15); "bear witness to" or "recognize," in the context of affirming Jesus Christ as the Son of God (John 1:34; 4:45; 19:35); "realize" or "perceive" (John 6:23; Acts 8:23; Jas 2:24; Gal 2:7). In particular, Christ "sees" into the heart of human beings (Luke 9:47) and then "perceives" faith in their hearts (Matt 9:2; Mark 2:5). ***horaō*** also refers to not "seeing" (i.e., experiencing) death (Luke 2:26; Heb 11:5) or "seeing" corruption (Acts 2:27ff.). Luke 9:27; John 3:3 refer to "seeing" the kingdom of God.

theōreō θεωρέω 2334

theōreō is a verb occurring about sixty times meaning "see," "look," or "behold" in most of these contexts.

The sense of "looking at or on," as a spectator, is indicated in Matt 27:55; Mark 12:41. In particular, Christ declares that he saw Satan fall like lightning from heaven (Luke 10:18).

The nuance of "inspect" or "examine" is evident in Matt 28:1 in relation to the tomb of Jesus.

Other senses of ***theōreō*** include that of "perceive," "realize" (John 4:19; Acts 17:22); "experience" (John 8:51, explicitly denying that any believer will ever "see" eternal death); and "consider" or "assess" (Heb 7:4).

The plain sense of "seeing" as visual perception is indicated in Mark 3:11; Luke 24:37; John 17:24; Acts 7:56; 10:11.

blepō βλέπω 991

blepō is a fairly common verb occurring about 130 times. It means "see," "look," along with a variety of associated nuances, predicated of both God and human beings.

Matt 5:28; 14:30 refer to people "looking on, or at" in the sense of "observe," or "watch." Matt 18:10 speaks of "observing" the face of God. Acts 8:6 refers to "witnessing" apostolic miracles. See also Acts 2:33. The action of "looking back" is noted in Luke 9:62.

Matt 12:22; John 9:25 refer to "seeing" after being healed from blindness. Ordinary visual perception is noted in Mark 13:2. The nuance of "impact" or "examine" is evident in Rev 5:4.

In a number of contexts, ***blepō*** expresses the idea of "seeing" as "understanding," or "realizing," especially in relation to spiritual truth (Matt 13:13ff.; Mark 8:18; Luke 8:10; John 9:39; Acts 28:26; Rom 11:10; Heb 2:9; 2 Cor 7:8).

The meaning "see," with the sense of "take heed," "take care," is evident in Matt 24:4; Mark 4:24; 1 Cor 3:10; Eph 5:15.

Where God is concerned, ***blepō*** indicates the divine action of "seeing" in the sense of "observing" or "taking note" (Matt 6:4ff.; 7:3).

anablepō ἀναβλέπω 308

anablepō is a variant form of ***blepō*** (above) meaning "look up," "receive one's sight," to see again after healing from blindness. The term is found in approximately twenty-five contexts.

References to the blind "receiving their sight" and seeing again are found, for example, in Matt 11:5; Mark 10:51; Luke 7:22; John 9:11ff.; Acts 9:12ff.

The action of "looking, or glancing up" in general is indicated in Mark 8:24; Luke 21:1. Matt 4:19; Mark 6:41; Luke 9:16 describe "raising one's glance" to heaven.

▸ **20.** Illness, Disease, Health, Healing > RECEIVE SIGHT

periblepō περιβλέπω 4017

periblepō, another variant form of ***blepō***, is a verb found in seven contexts with the literal meaning "to look around" (Mark 3:5, 34; 5:32; 9:8; 10:23; 11:11; Luke 6:10).

emblepō ἐμβλέπω 1689

The verb ***emblepō***, also related to ***blepō***, is found twelve times in all and means "look, or gaze upon."

Matt 6:26 contains Jesus' exhortation to "consider," or focus attention on, the birds of the air and note how God cares for them.

Christ is said to "look intently" at those to whom he was ministering (Mark 10:21, 27; Luke 20:17; 22:61; John 1:42). See also Mark 8:25; John 1:36. Acts 1:11 refers to the disciples "looking up" towards heaven, in the wake of Jesus' departure from the earth.

Acts 22:11 refers to Paul's temporary blindness in the aftermath of his dramatic conversion.

atenizō ἀτενίζω 816

atenizō is a verb found in fourteen contexts with the underlying sense of "to look intently at" or "gaze or stare at," "fix one's eyes on" (Luke 4:20; Acts 1:10; 6:15; 13:9; 23:1; 2 Cor 3:7). In particular, 2 Cor 3:13 speaks of God's people being denied the opportunity to "see" the fading glory on the face of Moses after his descent from Sinai.

parakyptō παρακύπτω 3879

parakyptō is a verb that occurs five times. It means "look into" in two of these contexts, both of them metaphorical. Jas 1:25 refers to "looking into" the law of liberty. 1 Pet 1:12 refers to angels longing "to look into" the fulfillment of God's redemptive purposes revealed to the prophets of old.

skopeō σκοπέω 4648

skopeō is a verb found eight times, meaning "look" in the sense of "take note of" in Rom 16:17; Phil 3:17. In 1 Cor 4:18, ***skopeō*** is translated "fix one's eyes on" in relation to spiritual realities that are not discerned by normal human means.

aphoraō ἀφοράω 872

aphoraō is a rare verb found only twice, meaning "see" in the sense of "consider," "assess," or "determine" how things will turn out (Phil 2:23). In Heb 12:2 it indicates "looking" to Jesus, or focusing attention upon him, as the one who brings our salvation to fulfillment.

SEE ALSO

- **56.** Folly, Ignorance > SHORT-SIGHTED ***myōpazō***

SILENCE, SILENT, QUIETNESS

siōpaō σιωπάω 4623

siōpaō is a verb found in twelve contexts with the consistent meanings "to keep silent," "hold one's peace" (Matt 20:31; 26:63; Mark 3:4; 9:34; 10:48; 14:61; Luke 18:39; 19:40; Acts 18:9). Luke 1:20 expresses the sense of "be silent" in the context of being struck dumb, unable to speak.

hēsychazō ἡσυχάζω 2270

hēsychazō is a term synonymous with ***siōpaō*** (above) found in five places and meaning "hold one's peace," "keep quiet," "keep silent" (e.g., Luke 14:4; Acts 11:18).

- **20.** Illness, Disease, Health, Healing > REST
- **60.** Virtues > PEACE, PEACEFUL, QUIET

hēsychia ἡσυχία 2271

hēsychia is a noun derived from ***hēsychazō*** (above) found in four places. It is translated "silence" or "quietness" and is also used as an adjective. Acts 22:2 refers to the silence of a crowd. The quiet submissiveness of women in the context of public worship is indicated in 1 Tim 2:11f. 2 Thess 3:12 contains the injunction to "work in quietness."

sigaō σιγάω 4601

Another synonym for ***siōpaō*** (above), ***sigaō*** occurs nine times and means "keep silence," "hold one's peace" (Luke 9:36; 20:26; Acts 12:17; 15:12ff.; 1 Cor 14:28ff.).

sigē σιγή 4602

sigē is a rare noun meaning "silence" in Acts 21:40; Rev 8:1.

phimoō φιμόω 5392

phimoō is a verb found eleven times meaning "(put to) silence," "hold one's peace," "muzzle" (i.e., animals).

The meaning "(put to) silence" is found in contexts where the aim is to prevent someone from speaking (Matt 22:34; 1 Pet 2:15). See also Luke 4:35. Mark 1:25 records the command of Christ to the demon to be silent, or quiet, just prior to his being cast out from the man he had previously "possessed."

The Mosaic command forbidding the "muzzling" of an ox is found in 1 Cor 9:9; 1 Tim 5:8.

SMELL

osphrēsis ὄσφρησις 3750

osphrēsis is a rare noun indicating a "sense of smell," found only in 1 Cor 12:17.

SEE ALSO

- **41.** Sacrifice, Offering, Worship, Praise > SMELL, AROMA ***euōdia***

SPEAK, SPEECH, TALK

mogilalos μογιλάλος 3424

mogilalos is a rare adjectival form denoting a "speech impediment" in Mark 7:32.

- **17.** Senses, Actions, Abilities, Disabilities > IMPEDIMENT

logos λόγος 3056

logos is a common noun found 331 times with the predominant meanings "word," "saying." ***logos*** also denotes "speech" in the sense of a "discourse" in Acts 20:7; 1 Cor 2:1ff.; 4:19; Col 4:6; Titus 2:8.

The faculty of "speech" is indicated in 2 Cor 10:10; 11:6.

- **32.** Law, Justice, Jurisprudence, Judgment > CAUSE, REASON, GROUND
- **63.** Speak, Tell, Declare, Call > WORD, SAYING, SPEECH
- **65.** Teach, Exhort, Rebuke, Discipline > DOCTRINE
- **66.** Ask, Answer, Discuss, Learn > QUESTION, INTERROGATE

syllaleō συλλαλέω 4814

syllaleō is a verb meaning "talk with," "speak with," or "confer." It occurs six times (Matt 17:3; Mark 9:4; Luke 4:36; 9:30; 22:4; Acts 25:12).

homileō ὁμιλέω 3656

homileō is synonymous with ***syllaleō*** (above) and means "talk with," "discuss" in four places (Luke 24:14, 15; Acts 20:11; 24:26).

synomileō συνομιλέω 4926

synomileō is a variant form of ***homileō*** (above). It is found only in Acts 10:27, meaning "talk with."

lalia λαλιά 2981

lalia is a noun occurring four times denoting the faculty of "speech" (Matt 26:73; Mark 14:7). References to "speech" in the sense of discourse are found in John 4:42; 8:43.

SEE ALSO

- **58.** Vices > FOOLISH TALKING ***mōrologia***

VOICE

phōnē φωνή 5456

phōnē is a noun occurring around 140 times with the primary sense of "voice," accounting for the large majority of its usage.

phōnē refers to the human voice of prophecy in Matt 2:18; 3:3; Mark 1:3; Luke 3:4; John 1:23. Other references to voices include those in Mark 1:26; Luke 1:42ff.; Acts 2:14; Rev 18:23. The voice of God is heard from heaven, as noted in Matt 3:17; Luke 3:22; John 12:28ff.; 2 Pet 1:17ff. It is also evident in theophanic visions (Acts 10:13ff.; 11:7ff.); and is heard in heaven itself (Rev 16:17; 18:4; 21:3).

The voice of the Holy Spirit is indicated in Heb 3:7, 15; 4:7.

The voice of the archangel is heard at the return of Christ (1 Thess 4:16). The voices of angels in heaven are heard in Rev 5:2; 10:3ff.; 18:2. See also Rev 6:10; 19:1, 6. In contrast, the voices of demons cry out in terror at their confrontation with Christ in Luke 4:33. See also Acts 8:7.

The voice of Christ is heard commanding Lazarus to rise from the dead in John 11:43. His "sheep," his followers, also recognize his voice (John 10:3ff.). The voice of the risen Christ in heaven is likewise recorded in Rev 1:10ff.; 3:20; 4:1; 14:13. He also addresses Saul in the context of his conversion in Acts 9:4ff.; 22:7ff.

▸ **63.** Speak, Tell, Declare, Call > SOUND

18. Strength, Weakness, Capability

FAINT

eklyō ἐκλύω 1590

eklyō is a verb found six times meaning "to faint" throughout.

Matt 15:32; Mark 8:3 mention people in danger of "fainting" (with hunger). Exhortations not to "faint," or lose heart, are found in Gal 6:9; Heb 12:3, 5.

FORCE

bebaios βέβαιος 949

bebaios is an adjective found in nine places with the primary meanings "sure," "firm." In Heb 9:17, ***bebaios*** refers to a last will and testament being "in force" only on the death of the testator.

SEE ALSO

- ▸ **75.** Suffering, Distress, Sadness > SUFFER
  biazō
- ▸ **76.** Force, Harm, Oppress > VIOLENCE, FORCE
  harpazō

STRENGTH, STRONG, POWER, POWERFUL, MIGHT, MIGHTY

ischys ἰσχύς 2479

ischys is a term denoting "strength," "power," "might" throughout the eleven contexts in which it is found.

Mark 12:30ff.; Luke 10:27 record the command to love God with all one's "strength" (i.e., with one's whole being). 1 Pet 4:11 affirms that God supplies strength to his people. See also 2 Pet 2:11.

The "might" or "power" of God is indicated in Eph 1:19; 6:10; 2 Thess 1:9; Rev 7:12. The "strength" of the Lamb, referring to the heavenly Christ, is indicated in Rev 5:12.

▸ **68.** Ability, Possibility, Effort, Succeed, Fail > ABILITY, ABLE

ischyros ἰσχυρός 2478

ischyros is an adjective derived from ***ischys*** (above) meaning "strong," "mighty" throughout nearly all thirty occurrences.

Jesus Christ is designated as "mighty" (Matt 3:11; Mark 1:7; Luke 3:16); as is God (Rev 18:8). 1 Cor 1:25 declares that the weakness of God is stronger than human strength, in a context that is clearly hyperbolic.

People are described as "strong" in Matt 12:29; Luke 11:21ff.; Rev 19:18. ***ischyros*** describes strength of character in 1 John 2:14; 1 Cor 4:10. Other general uses of ***ischyros*** include those in 1 Cor 1:27; 2 Cor 10:10; Heb 5:7.

kratos κράτος 2904

kratos is a noun synonymous with ***ischys*** (above) denoting "strength," "force," "power."

References to the "strength" or "power" of God include those in Luke 1:51; Eph 6:10; Col 1:11; 1 Tim 6:16; 1 Pet 5:11; Jude 25; Rev 1:6; 5:13.

kratos indicates the "power" of death in Heb 2:14; and 1 Pet 4:11 refers to the "dominion" of Christ.

The word of God is described as growing in "force" in Acts 19:20.

▸ **54.** Rule, Authority, Command, Obedience > DOMINION, LORD OVER

stereoō στερεόω 4732

stereoō is a verb found three times meaning "be made strong" in Acts 3:7, 16, with reference to healing a crippled man. In Acts 16:5, it refers to churches strengthened in their faith.

▸ **83.** Set, Put, Place, Prepare, Establish > ESTABLISH, FIX, GROUND, STRENGTHEN

dynamis δύναμις 1411

dynamis is the most common term in the NT denoting the qualities of "power," "might," "strength" in 120 contexts.

dynamis refers to the "power" of God (Matt 6:13; 22:29; Mark 12:24; 1 Cor 1:18; Eph 1:19; Rev 11:17); and to the power of the Son of Man coming in glory (Matt 24:30; Mark 13:26; Luke 21:27).

References to the "mighty deeds" (i.e., the miracles) of Christ include those in Matt 11:20ff.; Mark 6:5; Luke 10:13; Acts 2:22; 10:38. Similarly, "mighty works" performed by Jesus' followers are noted in Matt 7:12; 13:54ff.; 14:2; Acts 19:11. Rev 1:16; 5:12 refer to the power of the heavenly Christ.

The power of the Holy Spirit is indicated in Luke 4:14; Acts 1:8; Rom 15:13; as is the "powers of the heavens" in Matt 24:29; Mark 13:25; Luke 21:26. Angelic power is noted in 2 Pet 2:11. Luke 9:1 speaks of power over demons.

Rom 8:38 indicates demonic powers, and 2 Thess 2:9 refers to the power of Satan. Sin's power is described in 1 Cor 15:56.

The resurrection body is said to be "raised in power" in 1 Cor 15:43. The power of the resurrection is noted in Phil 3:10; and the power of the gospel in 1 Thess 1:5.

The power of John the Baptist is metaphorically designated as the "power of Elijah" in Luke 1:17.

- ▸ **47.** Show, Persuade, Confidence, Doubt > SIGN
- ▸ **68.** Ability, Possibility, Effort, Succeed, Fail > ABILITY, STRENGTH, POWER

dynatos δυνατός 1415

dynatos is an adjective derived from ***dynamis*** (above) meaning "powerful," "mighty," "strong." The term is found thirty-five times.

dynatos describes God as "mighty" (Luke 1:49), and also Moses (Acts 7:22; see also Acts 18:24). Jesus Christ is designated a "mighty prophet" in Luke 24:19. People are described as being "strong" in character in Rom 15:11; 2 Cor 12:10; 13:9.

dynatos expresses the nominal sense of "power" with reference to divine power in Rom 9:22; 2 Cor 10:4.

▸ **68.** Ability, Possibility, Effort, Succeed, Fail > POSSIBLE

dynateō δυνατέω 1414

dynateō is a rare verb found only in 2 Cor 13:3 with reference to the presence of Christ's Spirit "being powerful" among the Corinthian congregation.

WEAK, WEAKNESS, POWERLESS

asthenēs ἀσθενής 772

asthenēs is an adjective with the dual senses of "weak," "sick," often overlapping in meaning.

The meaning "weak" has a variety of connotations. General bodily weakness is indicated in Matt 26:41; Mark 14:38; 2 Cor 10:10. Women are referred to in 1 Pet 3:7 as the weaker sex. The designation "weak" refers to a lack of character (1 Cor 4:10); to one's conscience lacking in conviction (1 Cor 8:7ff.); to parts of the body lacking in importance (1 Cor 12:22); and to the law, which is described in Heb 7:18 as "weak," or lacking in effective power to deal absolutely with sin.

The weakness of people in relation to a spiritual impotence is indicated in Rom 5:6; 1 Thess 5:14. The designation "weak" is also applied to everything in the world that has no reputation (1 Cor 1:27; 9:22; Gal 4:9).

asthenēs is also used hyperbolically to indicate that the "weakness" of God is stronger than human strength (1 Cor 1:25).

▸ **20.** Illness, Disease, Health, Healing > SICK, SICKNESS

astheneō ἀσθενέω 770

astheneō is a verb occurring around forty times with the meanings "to be sick, or weak."

"Being weak in one's faith" is indicated in Rom 14:1ff. A passive use is indicated in Rom 8:3, where the law is said to be "weakened" by the sinful nature, or rendered unable to deal effectively with sin. Other references to "being weak" include those in 2 Cor 11:21ff., where Paul is said to be lacking in personal presence; and in 2 Cor 12:10, where his weakness denotes a lack of power and strength. In 2 Cor 13:3, Christ is designated specifically as one who is "not weak."

▸ **20.** Illness, Disease, Health, Healing > SICK, SICKNESS

astheneia ἀσθένεια 769

astheneia is a noun found in around twenty-five contexts meaning "sickness," "weakness," "disease."

"Weakness" in the sense of lack of strength or courage is indicated in 1 Cor 2:3; Heb 11:34. Bodily weakness is noted in 1 Cor 15:43, where the expression "sown in weakness" indicates the finite limitations of the human body (see also Heb 4:15; 5:2; 7:28). Such "weakness" describes the physical distress of Christ on the cross (2 Cor 13:4).

"Weakness" is also linked with illness and powerlessness in 2 Cor 11:30; 12:5ff.

▸ **20.** Illness, Disease, Health, Healing > DISEASE, PLAGUE
▸ **20.** Illness, Disease, Health, Healing > SICK, SICKNESS

adynatos ἀδύνατος 102

adynatos is an adjective found in ten places with the primary meaning "impossible" in the sense of "impotent," "powerless." ***adynatos*** also means "weak" in relation to those who are weak in their faith (Rom 15:1).

▸ **68.** Ability, Possibility, Effort, Succeed, Fail > IMPOSSIBLE

WEAK-WILLED

gunaikarion γυναικάριον 1133

gunaikarion is a rare noun found only in 2 Tim 3:6, as a term of mild disdain, denoting "weak-willed women."

SEE ALSO

▸ **15.** Gender, Reproduction, Youth, Aging > WOMAN
gynē, agamos, thēlys, gastēr, presbyteros, presbytis

19. Mind, Spirit, Emotions, Feelings, Desires

AMAZEMENT, ASTONISHMENT, BE AMAZED

ekstasis ἔκστασις 1611

The noun ***ekstasis*** is found in seven different places. In four of these it denotes the "astonishment," "amazement" of people in response to miraculous signs from God (Mark 5:42; 16:8; Luke 5:26; Acts 3:10).

thambos θάμβος 2285

thambos is synonymous with ***ekstasis*** (above) and also denotes "wonder," "amazement" as a response to miraculous signs. It is found only three times (Luke 4:36; 5:9; Acts 3:10).

thambeō θαμβέω 2284

The verb ***thambeō*** occurs four times, meaning "to be amazed, astonished" in reaction to the teaching ability of Jesus Christ (Mark 1:27; 10:24, 32; also Acts 9:6).

ekthambeō ἐκθαμβέω 1568

ekthambeō is a variant of ***thambeō*** (above) found in four places, again with the sense of "be amazed." In two of these instances, however, the astonishment may be linked to fear and alarm. (See also Mark 9:15; 14:33.)

ekthambos ἔκθαμβος 1569

ekthambos is a rare adjectival form found only in Acts 3:11 referring to people's "astonishment" or "wonder" at the healing of the crippled man by Peter and John at the gate of the temple.

ekplēssō ἐκπλήσσω 1605

The verb ***ekplēssō*** means "to be astonished, amazed" in fourteen contexts, mostly in reaction to the authority of Jesus' teaching (Matt 7:28; 13:54; 19:25; 22:33; Mark 1:22; 6:2; 10:26; 11:28; Luke 2:48; 4:32; 9:43). The people react similarly when Jesus heals a deaf mute (Mark 7:37). See also Acts 13:12.

existēmi ἐξίστημι 1839

existēmi is a verb largely synonymous with the entries above, found seventeen times in all, with the primary sense of "be amazed, astonished" in over half these contexts. The word describes amazement at the miracles and authority of Jesus in Matt 12:23; Mark 2:12; 5:42; 6:51; Luke 2:47; 8:56. Other such expressions of astonishment at the power of God are found in Acts 2:7, 12; 8:13; 10:45; 12:16. See also Luke 24:22; Acts 8:11ff.; 9:21.

ANGER, ANGRY, WRATH

orgē ὀργή 3709

The noun ***orgē*** occurs around forty times in a variety of contexts, meaning "anger," "wrath" throughout.

Divine "wrath" to be poured out on wicked humankind at the end of the age is indicated in Matt 3:7; Luke 3:7; 21:23; Rom 9:22; Eph 5:6; Col 3:6; 1 Thess 2:15; Rev 11:18; 14:10; 16:19; 19:15. The death of Christ removes such wrath, as noted in Rom 5:9; 1 Thess 1:10; 5:9. In particular, the "wrath" of the Lamb (i.e., the heavenly Christ) is described in Rev 6:16ff.

Jesus' anger at his skeptical audience's hardness of heart is noted in Mark 3:5. Human anger is referred to in Eph 4:31; Col 3:8; 1 Tim 2:8; Jas 1:19ff.

orgizō ὀργίζω 3710

The verb ***orgizō*** is found eight times with the meaning "to be angry" throughout. Human anger is in view for most of the contexts (Matt 5:22; 18:34; 22:7; Luke 14:21; 15:28; Rev 11:18). In Eph 4:26 there is an exhortation "to be angry" without sinning. Rev 12:17 mentions the dragon's wrath at the symbolic woman, the mother of the universal child-king (i.e., the Messiah).

parorgizō παροργίζω 3949

parorgizō is a rare verb found only twice with the meaning "to anger," "provoke to anger." Rom 10:19 describes God provoking his people to anger with another nation. Eph 6:4 contains the injunction to fathers not to anger their children.

cholaō χολάω 5520

cholaō is a rare verb found only in John 7:23 with reference to the Pharisees "being angry" at Jesus for healing a man on the Sabbath.

orgilos ὀργίλος 3711

orgilos is a rare adjective found only in Titus 1:7 denoting the vice of being "prone to anger" or "quick-tempered."

thymos θυμός 2372

thymos is a noun occurring eighteen times with the meaning "wrath" or "anger" throughout.

The wrath of God aimed at the wicked is noted in Rom 1:18; Rev 15:1, 7; 16:1. Metaphorical references to the "cup, or wine of God's wrath" are found in Rev 14:10; 16:19; 18:3; 19:15 ("the winepress of God's wrath" in Rev 14:19). The "anger" of the devil is indicated in Rev 12:12.

Human anger is depicted as a vice to be shunned in 2 Cor 12:20; Gal 5:20; Eph 4:31; Col 3:8. See also Heb 11:27.

CARE, WORRY, ANXIETY

merimna μέριμνα 3308

The noun ***merimna*** denotes "care," "worry," or "anxiety" in six places. In each context, the "cares" of this life are indicated (Matt 13:22; Mark 4:19; Luke 8:14; 21:34; 2 Cor 11:28; 1 Pet 5:7).

merimnaō μεριμνάω 3309

This verb occurs around twenty times with the underlying sense of "take care," "be careful."

The negative sense of "take no thought for" (i.e., don't be anxious about) is found in Matt 6:25, 34; 10:19; Luke 12:11, 22ff.; Phil 4:6.

The meaning "be anxious about" occurs in Matt 6:27ff.; Luke 10:41 in relation to the necessities of life. It is also used with this meaning in the context of the demands of Christian ministry (1 Cor 7:32ff.). See also Phil 2:20.

In 1 Cor 12:25 the term means "to care for someone."

SEE ALSO

- ▸ **46.** Wait, Hope, Be Vigilant, Pay Attention To > CAREFUL ***phrontizō***
- ▸ **62.** Care For, Protect, Guard, Watch > CARE ABOUT, CARE FOR, TAKE CARE OF ***melei, epimeleomai***

DESIRE

eudokia εὐδοκία 2107

eudokia is a noun found nine times with the predominant sense of "good will," "good pleasure." In Rom 10:1, however, ***eudokia*** denotes Paul's heartfelt "desire" to see his fellow countrymen saved.

▸ **48.** Will, Purpose, Decide, Advise > WILL, WILLING

epipothēsis ἐπιπόθησις 1972

epipothēsis is a rare noun denoting "earnest longing" in 2 Cor 7:7, 11.

epithymeō ἐπιθυμέω 1937

epithymeō is a verb found in eighteen places meaning "desire," denoting both a legitimate longing as well as a perverse "lusting" or "coveting."

Immoral "lusting" after a woman is noted in Matt 5:28. "Longing" to gain insight into spiritual truth is indicated in Matt 13:17; 1 Pet 1:12. General references to "desire" are found in Luke 15:16; 16:21 in relation to food. See also Rev 9:6; 1 Tim 3:1. The "desire" to witness the coming of the Son of Man is noted in Luke 17:22. Christ's "desire" to eat the Passover with his disciples is indicated in Luke 22:15.

Illegitimate "desire" or "coveting" is noted in Acts 20:33; Rom 7:7; 13:9; 1 Cor 10:16; Jas 4:2. Gal 5:17 refers to the "desires" of the flesh being in conflict with the desires of the Spirit.

▸ **19.** Mind, Spirit, Emotions, Feelings, Desires > LUST, YEARN

oregō ὀρέγω 3713

oregō is a verb found in three places meaning "desire," with both a positive and negative connotation. 1 Tim 3:1 affirms that to "desire" the office of bishop is a noble aspiration. 1 Tim 6:10 refers to the sin of "lusting, craving after" money. The believer's "desire" for a better country (i.e., a heavenly one) is noted in Heb 11:16.

DESIRE, LONGING

epithymia ἐπιθυμία 1939

epithymia is a noun denoting "desire" largely in relation to "inordinate craving" or "lust" as well as legitimate longing.

Christ's "strong desire" to eat the Passover meal with his disciples before his crucifixion is indicated in Luke 22:15.

John 8:44 describes the perverted "desires" of the evil one. References to the immoral "lusts" of the natural human being and the wicked are found in Rom 1:24; 6:12; 7:7ff.; Gal 5:16, 24; Eph 2:3; 4:22; Col 3:5; 1 Thess 4:5; 1 Tim 6:9; 2 Tim 2:22; 3:6; Titus 2:12; 3:3; Jas 1:14ff.; 1 Pet 2:11; 4:2ff.; 2 Pet 1:4; 2:10, 18; 1 John 2:16ff.; Jude 16ff.

Paul indicates his longing to depart this life and be with God in Phil 1:23. Other legitimate "desires" are noted in 1 Thess 2:17.

▸ **19.** Mind, Spirit, Emotions, Feelings, Desires > LUST, YEARN

FEAR, AFRAID, TERROR, FRIGHTEN, TERRIFY

phobos φόβος 5401

phobos is a noun denoting "fear," "terror" throughout its nearly fifty occurrences.

General references to the emotion of "fear" or "terror" in a human context are found in Matt 14:26; Rom 8:15; 1 Cor 2:3; Eph 6:5; 1 Pet 3:14. 1 John 4:18 affirms that perfect love casts out "fear." In particular, "fear" of the Jews is indicated in John 7:13; 19:38; 20:19; and the "fear" of death in Heb 2:15. See also Rev 18:10, 15.

Expressing "fear" in the presence of an angel is recorded in Matt 28:4; Luke 1:12; 2:9. The emotion of "fear" in response to a miraculous sign is indicated in several contexts — for example, on the occasion of Christ's resurrection (Matt 28:8); and in response to Christ's miracles (Mark 4:41; Luke 5:26; 8:37). See also Acts 2:43.

Luke 21:26 describes "fear" or "terror" at the signs of the world's end.

Experiencing the "fear" of God is indicated in Acts 5:5, 11; 9:31; 19:17; 2 Cor 5:11; 7:1, 5; Phil 2:12; Rev 11:11. The absence of the "fear" of God is recorded in Rom 3:18.

"Fear" in the sense of "reverence" or "respect," in the context of paying respect to civil authorities, is indicated in Rom 13:7. "Reverence" for Christ is noted in Eph 5:21; 1 Pet 3:15; and "respect" for one's master in 1 Pet 2:18.

phoberos φοβερός 5398

phoberos is a rare adjective found in only three places, meaning "fearful," "terrible." The "fearful" prospect of falling under divine judgment is noted in Heb 10:27, 31. The "terrifying" impact of the Sinai theophany on Moses is indicated in Heb 12:21.

ekphobos ἔκφοβος 1630

ekphobos is a rare adjective meaning "very (much) afraid," found only in Mark 9:6; Heb 12:21. Both texts speak of humanity's fear in the face of a divine revelation.

aphobōs ἀφόβως 870

aphobōs is an adverb found only four times, meaning "without fear."

Serving God "without fear" is indicated in Luke 1:74; as is speaking the word of God "without fear" in Phil 1:14. False prophets acting "without fear" are depicted in Jude 12. See also 1 Cor 16:10.

phobeō φοβέω 5399

phobeō is a verb found nearly one hundred times with the principal meanings "to fear," "be afraid."

Divine exhortations for people "not to fear" in the face of theophanic revelations include those in Matt 1:20; 28:5ff.; Mark 5:36; Luke 1:13; 2:10; John 6:20; Rev 1:17. See also Matt 10:26ff.; John 12:15; Heb 11:23.

General references to people "being afraid" include Matt 2:22; Luke 19:21; John 19:8; Acts 5:26; 2 Cor 12:20; Gal 2:12; 1 John 4:18. In particular, Matt 27:54; Mark 4:41; Luke 2:9; 8:35; 9:34; John 6:19 record people's fear at the manifestation of signs and miracles.

Luke 1:50; Acts 10:2, 22; Col 3:22; 1 Pet 2:17; Rev 14:7 describe the positive phenomenon of expressing "fear" towards God. In contrast, Luke 12:5 contains a warning to "fear" God, who is able to cast one into hell. See also Luke 23:40. An exhortation to "fear" the civil authorities for their power to wield the sword in judicial execution is noted in Rom 13:4.

The meaning "to respect" is indicated in the context of a wife's appropriate attitude to her husband in Eph 5:33.

eulabeia εὐλάβεια 2124

eulabeia is a rare noun denoting "godly fear," found only in Heb 5:7; 12:28.

deilia δειλία 1167

deilia is a rare noun found only in 2 Tim 1:7 denoting "fear" or "timidity."

deilos δειλός 1169

deilos is an adjective found only three times, meaning "fearful," "afraid." In Matt 8:26; Mark 4:40, Christ rebukes his disciples for being "afraid" and having no faith. Rev 21:8 refers to the "cowardly."

entromos ἔντρομος 1790

entromos is an adjectival form meaning "trembling with fear," found only in Acts 7:32; 16:29; Heb 12:21.

▸ **19.** Mind, Spirit, Emotions, Feelings, Desires > TREMBLE

ptoeō πτοέω 4422

ptoeō is a rare verb, found only in Luke 21:9; 24:37, meaning "to terrify," "be afraid."

ekphobeō ἐκφοβέω 1629

ekphobeō is another rare verb meaning "to frighten" or "terrify" and is found only in 2 Cor 10:9.

GLADLY

hēdeōs ἡδέως 2234

hēdeōs is an adverb found only five times meaning "gladly," "with pleasure" in the context of human emotion (Mark 6:20; 12:37; 2 Cor 11:19; 12:9, 15).

HATE, ABHOR

apostygeō ἀποστυγέω 655

apostygeō is a rare verb, found only in Rom 12:19, constituting an injunction to "abhor" or "hate" what is evil.

bdelyssō βδελύσσω 948

bdelyssō is another rare verb referring to the "abhorring" or "despising" of idols in Rom 2:22. In Rev 21:8 it is used participially to refer to those who are "abhorrent" (i.e., vile, abominable) to God.

HEART

kardia καρδία 2588

kardia occurs around 160 times, in a number of different contexts, and refers primarily to the heart as the center of the human will, mind, emotion, and soul or spirit. ***kardia*** does not refer at all to the heart as a physical organ, and is therefore wholly metaphorical in its usage.

With reference to the human heart as the center or seat of inner being and passions, ***kardia*** is found in a variety of contexts. 1 Cor 14:25, for example, refers to the secrets of the heart, and in Luke 2:19, 51, the heart is indicated as the location of one's deepest thoughts. The "pure in heart" are singled out as blessed by God (Matt 5:8f.; 1 Tim 3:5; 2 Tim 2:22; Jas 4:8; 1 Pet 1:22); as are those whose hearts are obedient to God (Rom 6:17). The "forgiving" heart is likewise commended in Matt 18:35. Blessing is also indicated in a heart that rejoices (John 16:22; Acts 2:26). The orientation of one's heart will determine whether one will have lasting spiritual "treasure" or merely temporary earthly riches. The ideal of humility is perfectly modeled in the "heart" of Jesus in Matt 11:29.

Exhortations concerning the human heart are also found in connection with this term. Jesus exhorts his disciples not to let their hearts be troubled in John 14:1. Paul expresses a strong desire that believers receive encouragement in their hearts in serving the Lord (2 Thess 2:17; Col 2:2); and that they demonstrate gratitude in their hearts towards God (Col 3:16). Peter urges his readers to sanctify their hearts in 1 Pet 3:15. By far the most profound exhortation is the command to love the Lord God with all one's heart in Matt 22:37; Mark 12:30; Luke 10:27, where Jesus cites Deut 6:4 from which this all-embracing commandment is drawn.

kardia is also found in contexts where the human heart is viewed in a negative light. For example, Luke 1:51 speaks of the vain imagination of the human heart. The wickedness of the human heart is cited in Matt 9:4; 12:34; 13:15; Mark 7:21; the sin of lust in one's heart is indicated in Matt 5:28; Rom 1:24. There are also solemn declarations that the human heart may constitute the object of satanic invasion, as in the case of Judas (John 13:2) and Ananias (Acts 5:3). Finally, Jesus declares that in many cases the heart of his people is far removed from God (Matt 15:8; Mark 7:6).

In more general terms, the human heart is portrayed as the object of the knowledge of God in Luke 16:15, and as the object of divine blessing in 1 Cor 2:9. ***kardia*** also refers to the heart as the "mind" of human beings, where reasoning takes place (Mark 2:6; Luke 5:22; 2 Cor 9:7).

Another significant aspect of the meaning of ***kardia*** is reflected in the concept of the heart as the receptor of divine revelation. There are a number of contexts that demonstrate this usage. For example, in the parable of the sower, the various soils represent various attitudes of the human heart that will either inhibit growth and spiritual blessing or promote it (Matt 13:19; Mark 4:15; Luke 8:12, 15). In the new covenant, the law of God is written on the heart of the believer (Heb 8:10; 10:16; Rom 2:15). The great miracle of conversion is sometimes described as the opening of the heart of faith in the life of a new believer — for example, Lydia (Acts 16:14) and the Ethiopian eunuch (Acts 8:3). See also Mark 11:23; Acts 15:9. Eph 3:17 affirms that Christ dwells in the heart of the believer by faith. Such a phenomenon is evidently a new covenant manifestation of the old covenant motif of "heart circumcision" (Rom 2:29). Conversely, the NT also refers to the phenomenon of a hardened heart (Mark 3:5; 6:52; 8:17; 2 Cor 3:15; Rom 1:21; John 12:40). The curse of the "uncircumcised heart" is also alluded to here. See also 2 Cor 3:3; Luke 24:25; Eph 4:18. Heb 3:8, 12, 15; 4:7 issue a solemn plea not to harden one's heart against the promptings of God's Spirit. For as Gal 4:6 also declares, the human heart is the location (metaphorically speaking) of the indwelling Spirit of God in the life of the believer (see also Rom 10:8).

JEALOUS, JEALOUSY

parazēloō παραζηλόω 3863

parazēloō occurs four times and is translated "provoke to jealousy" on each occasion. In Rom 10:19, Paul cites the text of Deut 32:21, where Yahweh issues the threat that he will make his people jealous of a pagan people far less significant than they. The context is one of covenant curse invoked against Israel. Similarly, Rom 11:11, 14 state that as a result of Israel's sins, salvation has come to the Gentiles, with the consequence that Israel is provoked to jealousy against them. 1 Cor 10:22 alludes to the familiar theme of God being driven to jealousy as a result of idolatrous attitudes and actions on the part of his people.

zēlos ζῆλος 2205

zēlos occurs nine times and means both "zeal" and "envy" or "jealousy." In John 2:17 the two senses overlap, where Jesus' anger boils over at the money changers in the temple, reminding his disciples of Ps 69:9 — "Zeal for your house will consume me."

The remaining usage of ***zēlos*** focuses on jealousy among human beings — for example, Acts 13:45 records the envy of the Jews against Paul and Barnabas. In Rom 13:13 there is an exhortation to refrain from the expression of jealousy and other vices. Jealousy is also indicated as one of the besetting sins of the Corinthian congregation (1 Cor 3:3; 2 Cor 12:20). See also Gal 5:20; Jas 3:14, 16. In a positive sense, Paul expresses his jealousy for the well-being of the Corinthian congregation whom he had established in their faith (2 Cor 11:2).

▸ **19.** Mind, Spirit, Emotions, Feelings, Desires > ZEAL, ZEALOUS

zēloō ζηλόω 2206

zēloō is the verb form from which ***zēlos*** (above) is derived. ***zēloō*** occurs twelve times and is translated "to be jealous" in five of these contexts. This term also has the sense of "be zealous."

Concerning the human action depicted in the use of this term, Acts 7:9 refers to the jealousy of Joseph's brothers towards their precocious younger sibling (cited from Gen 39ff.). Acts 17:5 records the jealousy of the Thessalonian Jews towards Paul's success in convincing Jewish people that Jesus was the Messiah. 1 Cor 13:4 declares that genuine love is wholly devoid of any jealousy. Jas 4:2 declares that coveting is a vice to be avoided — here the idea of coveting overlaps with the sense of being jealous.

▸ **19.** Mind, Spirit, Emotions, Feelings, Desires > ZEAL, ZEALOUS

JOY, JOYFUL, REJOICE, GLADNESS

chairō χαίρω 5463

chairō is a verb found on approximately seventy occasions with the sense of "rejoice," "be glad" in the majority of contexts in which it occurs. ***chairō*** is used in a whole range of situations in which the emotion of joy is evoked. Predominant in the usage of this term is the focus on rejoicing over the redemptive deeds of God that come to fruition in the gospel in the person of the Messiah, Jesus Christ.

A general feeling of delight and well-being is noted, for example, in Luke 23:8; John 3:29; Rom 12:15. Rejoicing at God's fulfillment of his promise to provide a messianic deliverer for his people is noted in Matt 2:10 (the reaction of the magi at seeing the divinely guided star); in John 8:56 (Jesus' claim that Abraham rejoiced at seeing his day); and in Luke 1:14. Frequently, joy is expressed at the prospect of heaven and eternal life (Matt 5:12; Luke 6:23; John 4:36; Rom 12:12). Delight in God's goodness to his people is noted (Acts 11:23; Rom 16:19; 2 Cor 7:7), as is joy in the faithfulness of believers (Col 2:5; 1 Thess 3:9; 2 John 4; 3 John 3). As a corollary to this, rejoicing in the repentance of sinners is described in 2 Cor 7:9. In Acts 8:39; 13:48; Rev 19:7, salvation is the focus of people's delight. Paul declares in 1 Cor 13:6 that love rejoices in righteousness, and he rejoices at the spread of the gospel in Phil 1:18. Joy is found even in traumatic circumstances — for example, in Acts 5:41; Col 1:24; 1 Pet 4:13, which contain evidence of joy experienced in the midst of persecution on account of the gospel, as well as an exhortation to so rejoice. Similarly, 2 Cor 6:10 records the apostle Paul's joy in the midst of sorrow.

Regarding the person and work of Christ, the joy of the Jewish people in witnessing the miracles of Jesus is noted (Luke 13:17; 19:37). The disciples rejoice at the Lord's resurrection in John 20:20. The apostle Paul exhorts his readers to rejoice in the Lord in Phil 3:1; 4:4, 10. In the parable depicting the immeasurable value of the kingdom of God, joy is expressed in the discovery of the lost sheep, a symbol of that infinite value (Matt 18:13; Luke 15:5).

In a number of negative contexts, wicked people express an evil delight — for example, those who are anticipating the destruction of Jesus Christ through his betrayal at the hands of Judas (Mark 14:11; Luke 22:5). And in Rev 11:10 the wicked rejoice over the death of the two prophets.

▸ **63.** Speak, Tell, Declare, Call > FAREWELL
▸ **63.** Speak, Tell, Declare, Call > GREET, GREETING

chara χαρά 5479

chara is the noun derived from ***chairō*** (above). It occurs around sixty times and is consistently translated "joy," "gladness." The range of contexts is quite similar to that of ***chairō***.

Regarding the person and work of God, ***chara*** denotes joy at Yahweh's fulfillment of his promise concerning the Messiah, the birth of Christ (Matt 2:10; Luke 1:14; 2:10). Joy in receiving God's word is highlighted in Matt 13:20; Mark 4:16; Luke 8:13. Experiencing the power of God also results in great joy (Luke 10:17; Acts 8:8). The indwelling of the Holy Spirit causes joy (Acts 13:52; Rom 14:17; 15:13); and joy itself is a fruit of the Spirit (Gal 5:22). Joy is also found in relationship with Christ (John 15:11; 17:13; 1 Pet 1:8); and the greatest delight is experienced by those who are party to the resurrection of Jesus (Matt 28:8; Luke 24:52). Christ himself has a deep, inner joy in anticipating his ascension to the Father (Heb 12:2).

In more general contexts, joy is a reward for service (Matt 25:21; Heb 13:17). There is joy in heaven over every sinner that repents (Luke 15:7, 10). John 16:21 refers to joy in childbirth. Fellowship yields joy (Rom 15:32; 2 Cor 1:24); as does affliction (2 Cor 8:2); and prayer (Phil 1:4). There is joy in discovering the riches of the kingdom (Matt 13:44), and in perseverance (Col 1:11). Paul signals his joy in seeing spiritual growth within his congregations (Phil 1:25; 1 Thess 2:19); as does John (3 John 4).

agalliaō ἀγαλλιάω 21

agalliaō occurs eleven times and signifies a heightened degree of gladness, meaning "to rejoice greatly," "exult."

This term also refers frequently to the person of God and Christ. In general terms, ***agalliaō*** refers to rejoicing in God as Savior (Luke 1:47), and to rejoicing in the Holy Spirit (Luke 10:21, predicated of Jesus). See also Acts 2:26. Similarly, exultation in regard to Christ is noted in 1 Pet 1:18. The Philippian jailer rejoices at his salvation in Acts 16:34. Jesus speaks of Abraham's delight at "seeing" the day of Christ in John 8:56. 1 Pet 4:13 mentions rejoicing in sharing in the sufferings of Christ. Rejoicing at the prospect of heaven is found in Matt 5:12; 1 Pet 1:6; Rev 19:7.

agalliasis ἀγαλλίασις 20

agalliasis is the noun derived from ***agalliaō*** (above), occurring only five times with the sense of "joy," "exultation."

Luke 1:14, 44 refer to joy at the anticipated birth of Christ. Acts 2:46 speaks of the joy in the fellowship of the early church. God anoints Christ his Son with the "oil of gladness" (Heb 1:9). And Jude 24 affirms joy in the presence of God.

skirtaō σκιρτάω 4640

skirtaō is a rare verb found only three times, meaning "leap for joy." It refers twice to the baby in Elizabeth's womb (John the Baptist),who leapt for joy at the greeting of Mary (Luke 1:41, 44). ***skirtaō*** is also found in Luke 6:23, where Jesus exhorts his followers to leap for joy at the prospect of reward in heaven for suffering for the gospel.

▸ **87.** Movement Upward or Downward > LEAP

euphrosynē εὐφροσύνη 2167

euphrosynē is found only twice and means "gladness" or "joy." In Acts 2:28, joy is experienced in the presence of God. In Acts 4:17, joy in people's hearts is bestowed by a caring God, who meets all of our needs.

synchairō συγχαίρω 4796

synchairō is a variant form of ***chairō*** meaning "to rejoice with, in." It is found in only six places. Luke 1:58; 15:6, 9; 1 Cor 12:26; Phil 2:17, 18 speak of rejoicing together with someone. 1 Cor 13:6 refers to rejoicing in the truth.

euphrainō εὐφραίνω 2165

euphrainō is a verb occurring fourteen times, meaning "to be glad," "rejoice."

The sense of "be glad," in the context of enjoying "the good life," is found in Luke 12:19; 15:23ff. 2 Cor 2:2 refers to the apostle Paul's gladness in a general sense.

The specific meaning "rejoice" is indicated in Rom 15:10, with reference to celebrating the salvation wrought by God on behalf of his people. In a similar fashion, ***euphrainō*** is used metaphorically in Rev 12:12, as an exhortation to the heavens to rejoice. Note also the injunction to God's people in Rev 18:20 to rejoice over the victory gained over the enemies of God. Gal 4:27 mentions rejoicing over the gift of children.

Acts 7:41 refers to the people of Israel rejoicing in their idolatry at Mount Sinai. In Rev 11:10, the wicked rejoice over the martyrdom of two servants of God.

kauchaomai καυχάομαι 2744

kauchaomai is a verb found in nearly forty places with the primary meaning "to boast," "glory (in)." In several of these contexts, the sense of "rejoice" is indicated. Rom 5:2 speaks of rejoicing in the hope of sharing in God's glory. Paul rejoices in his suffering in Rom 5:3 and rejoices in God in Rom 5:11.

▸ **63.** Speak, Tell, Declare, Call > BOAST, BOASTING

LAUGH, LAUGHTER

gelaō γελάω 1070

gelaō occurs only twice and refers to the action of laughing in a non-specific context. Luke 6:21 refers to one of the Beatitudes, "Blessed are you that weep now, for you shall laugh." The converse is recorded in Luke 6:25: "Woe to you that laugh now, for you shall mourn and weep." The thought here is that only those who truly appreciate the seriousness of their rebellion against God and mourn over their sin will enjoy ultimate happiness and laughter, through a relationship of faith and trust in Jesus Christ.

gelōs γέλως 1071

gelōs is the noun derived from ***gelaō*** (above). It is found only in Jas 4:9, where sinners are exhorted to turn their "laughter" into mourning, humbling themselves before God. The thought here is essentially the same as that expressed by ***gelaō*** in Luke's Gospel (see above).

SEE ALSO

▸ **45.** Faith, Belief, Trust, Promise > UNBELIEVING, LAUGH AT, LAUGH TO SCORN
katagelaō

▸ **58.** Vices > COARSE JESTING
eutrapelia

LUST, YEARN

epithymeō ἐπιθυμέω 1937

epithymeō occurs around twenty times and is translated variously as "desire," "long for," "covet," as well as "lust." ***epithymeō*** refers to desires that are both legitimate and illegitimate.

With reference to human craving, ***epithymeō*** indicates lusting as perverted sexual desire. In Matt 5:28, Jesus equates lusting after a woman as equivalent to adultery. 1 Cor 10:6; Jas 4:2 express warnings against illegitimate craving. In Gal 5:17, the "lusting" of the sinful nature is opposed to the Spirit of God.

Elsewhere, ***epithymeō*** has the sense of "long for." Matt 13:17; 1 Pet 1:12 refer to the OT prophets' yearning for revelation from God. Longing for the coming of the days of the Son of Man is expressed in Luke 17:22. A legitimate aspiring to the office of elder is noted in 1 Tim 3:1. The translation "covet" is found in Acts 20:33, and Rom 7:7; 13:9 record commands against this attitude. General craving for food is indicated in Luke 15:16; 16:21.

epithymeō is used once with respect to Jesus (Luke 22:15), who expresses a desire to celebrate the Passover with his disciples.

▸ **19.** Mind, Spirit, Emotions, Feelings, Desires > DESIRE

epithymia ἐπιθυμία 1939

epithymia is the noun derived from ***epithymeō*** (above) and is likewise translated "desire," "craving," "lust," "longing." The term occurs around forty times.

When referring to the desires of human beings, ***epithymia*** occurs almost entirely in negative contexts. Generalized cravings that choke out, or prevent, fruitful spiritual life and service are mentioned in Mark 4:19; 1 Tim 6:9; 2 Tim 2:22; Jas 1:5; Jude 16, 18. The desires of the wicked are condemned in John 8:44; Rom 1:24; 6:12; and the vice of coveting is noted in Rom 7:7, 8; Col 3:5. The "lusts" of the sinful nature are listed in Rom 13:14; Gal 5:16, 24; Eph 2:3; 4:22; 1 Thess 4:5; Titus 2:12; 1 Pet 2:11; 4:3; 2 Pet 2:10, 18; 1 John 2:16. The noble desire to be with Christ is indicated in Phil 1:23.

▸ **19.** Mind, Spirit, Emotions, Feelings, Desires > DESIRE, LONGING

orexis ὄρεξις 3715

orexis is found only in Rom 1:17, where it refers to the perverted "lusting" or "passion" of men for each other.

pathos πάθος 3806

pathos is a participial form of ***paschō*** occurring in only three places and meaning "impure passions" or "lust," with reference to sexual desire (Rom 1:26; Col 3:5; 1 Thess 4:5).

hēdonē ἡδονή 2237

hēdonē is a noun denoting "(illicit) passion" in a general sense, in five contexts (Luke 8:14; Titus 3:3; Jas 4:1, 3; 1 Pet 2:13).

▸ **58.** Vices > PLEASURE, PASSION, LUST

epipotheō ἐπιποθέω 1971

epipotheō is a verb that expresses the basic meaning "yearn," "(earnestly) desire," in positive contexts. ***epipotheō*** occurs nine times.

Paul's longing to make contact with his congregation is expressed in Rom 1:11; Phil 1:8; 1 Thess 3:6; 2 Tim 1:4. See also Phil 2:26; 2 Cor 9:14. The believer's intense desire to enter the realm of heaven after a life of suffering is indicated in 2 Cor 5:2. Peter exhorts his readers to long for "pure spiritual milk" in 1 Pet 2:2. Finally, Jas 4:5 refers to the "jealous yearning" of God for the spiritual welfare of his people.

MIND

dianoia διάνοια 1271

dianoia occurs thirteen times in all and means "mind," indicating that faculty as the seat of human reason, understanding, emotion, and will. In most of the contexts in which it is found, ***dianoia*** may also be translated "heart."

The command to love God with all one's "mind" is linked to "heart" and "soul" as well. The clear implication is that one is to love God with one's whole being. It is the greatest command of all (Matt 22:37; Mark 12:30; Luke 10:27). Linked to this all-embracing command is the observation in Heb 8:10; 10:16 that God has placed his law within the hearts and minds of his people as part of the essence of the promised new covenant renewal, accomplished through the finished redemptive work of Christ. In these two texts, ***dianoia*** ("mind") is used synonymously with ***kardia*** ("heart"). In fact, Heb 8:10 speaks of God "placing" his law "in their minds," and "writing" it "on their hearts." In Heb 10:16, the writer switches the metaphorical images, describing God's promise to "put" his law "on their hearts" and "write" it "on their minds."

dianoia also refers to the human mind in a general sense as the seat of understanding, speaking of the spiritual enlightenment of believing hearts or minds (Eph 1:18), and the darkening or blinding of the mind of unbelievers (Eph 4:18). The unregenerate minds (or hearts) of human beings are indicated in Eph 2:3; Col 1:2. See also 1 Pet 1:13; 2 Pet 3:1; 1 John 5:20.

▸ **58.** Vices > IMAGINATION, (STUBBORN) THINKING

nous νοῦς 3563

nous is a noun synonymous with ***dianoia*** (above) that occurs around twenty times with the sense of "mind" in various contexts.

In Luke 24:45, Jesus is said to open the minds of his disciples so that they could understand the full meaning the Scriptures concerning himself. Here ***nous*** refers to the "mind" as the faculty of reasoning and understanding.

The mind as the seat human volitional, moral, and cognitive expression is indicated in several places (Rom 14:5; 1 Cor 14:14ff.; Col 2:18; 2 Thess 2:2). In particular, divine judgment is brought to bear on the mind of unbelievers, resulting in the debasing of their minds, rendering these faculties corrupt and futile in the sight of God, on account of their wickedness (Rom 1:28; Eph 4:17; 1 Tim 6:5; 2 Tim 3:8). ***nous*** also refers to the volitional orientation of the human mind in Rom 7:23, 25, where Paul declares that while his mind is oriented towards the law of God on the one hand, the effect of sin produces a tension which incites him to work against that divine law principle in his mind. Such tension illustrates the classic battle with sin in the life of the believer.

In more general terms, ***nous*** refers to the "mind" as equivalent to the "heart" — the seat of a person's innermost being: In Rom 12:2; Eph 4:23; Phil 4:7 the renewal of the believer's mind, produced by a divine work of grace, is in view. See also 1 Cor 1:10; Rev 13:18.

▸ **19.** Mind, Spirit, Emotions, Feelings, Desires > UNDERSTANDING

phronēma φρόνημα 5427

phronēma refers to the "mind" in the general sense of the volitional and rational center of the human being as well as the "mind" of the Spirit of God. ***phronēma*** occurs in only three contexts. Rom 8:6 declares that an orientation of the mind that is set on the flesh leads to death, but a focus of the mind on the Spirit leads to life. Rom 8:7 expands this by adding that the mind set on the flesh is hostile to God. Rom 8:27 refers to the "mind of the Spirit" as something accessible to the divine searcher of the hearts of humankind.

noēma νόημα 3540

noēma is a noun occurring six times meaning "mind" or "thought." "Mind" refers to the center of human reason and volition in 2 Cor 3:14; 4:4, indicating the hardening or blinding of the minds of unbelievers, including apostate Jews. Phil 4:7 refers to the peace of God that keeps the mind of believers focused on Christ.

SEE ALSO

▸ **47.** Show, Persuade, Confidence, Doubt > UNCERTAIN, DOUBLE-MINDED
dipsychos, metaballō

RAGE

phruassō φρυάσσω 5433

phruassō is a verb found only twice, occurring both times in Acts 4:25. It means "rage," referring to the pagan nations who oppose God and his ways with a "furious arrogance."

SEE ALSO

▸ **11.** Meteorology, Water > RAGE
klydōn

SOUL

psychē ψυχή 5590

psychē is an approximate dynamic equivalent for the Hebrew term *nephesh*, occurring around sixty times. ***psychē***, however, has a narrower semantic field than its Hebrew equivalent, and it is translated primarily as "soul," "life" in the large majority of these contexts.

This Greek term indicates, as does the Hebrew, that the "soul" is not to be distinguished from the "body" in an absolute sense, for the Scriptures teach that humans are whole, integral beings. There is, however, evidence clearly suggesting that there is a duality within a person's created constitution — humans have a physical body that will perish and decay as well as a "spirit" or "soul" that is immortal and subject to divine judgment for good or ill at the end of time.

This perspective is not as fully developed in the OT as it is in the NT. However, as with *nephesh* (at least by implication, if not explicitly), ***psychē*** indicates a human being's "soul" as a way of describing his or her unique essence as a being with an inner emotional, rational, and spiritual essence that sets him or her apart from other created (i.e., animal) life forms.

psychē refers to "souls" in the sense of persons, individuals in a number of places (Acts 2:41ff.; Rom 2:9; 13:1; 1 Pet 3:20; Rev 18:13.

More commonly, ***psychē*** also refers to the "soul" of a person, referring to his or her "life" — the animating life force, sustaining earthly existence. The "lives" of people are referred to this way in Matt 2:20; 16:25ff.; Mark 3:4; Luke 6:9; 12:20ff.; Acts 20:10; Rom 16:4. In particular, John 13:37ff.; 15:13 speak of the greatest of virtues as laying down one's life for others. Such nobility is, of course, attributed to the person of Christ, who gave up his "life" for the salvation of his people (Matt 20:28; Mark 10:45; John 10:11; 1 John 3:16).

psychē also indicates the "soul" as that unique, immortal essence of all human beings, equated in many ways to a person's "spirit," which has an eternal destiny. One's "soul" is seen as being clothed with a physical body that will decay after physical death (Matt 10:28; Acts 2:27; 13:17; Jas 1:21; 5:20; 1 Pet 1:9; 2:25; Rev 6:9; 20:4).

Related to the above sense is the meaning "soul" (in relation to people), indicating the inner spiritual, psychological, and emotional center of one's being. This is occasionally identified as the "heart" or "mind." The usage of ***psychē*** with this shade of meaning does not imply an eternal destiny, but rather an inner quality of life on earth.

Such a perspective is illustrated in the following contexts, where ***psychē*** refers to promised rest for one's "soul" (Matt 11:29); and to people's "soul" as "heart" or "mind" (Acts 14:2; 15:24; Eph 6:6; Phil 1:27, 2 Pet 2:8). Elsewhere, ***psychē*** refers to one's "soul" in relation to one's "entire being," in an undifferentiated sense — for example, in contexts advocating loving God with all one's "heart" (i.e., all one's soul or being) (Matt 22:37; Mark 12:30ff.; Luke 10:27). See also Luke 1:46; 12:19. In 1 Thess 5:23 there is a rare reference to one's "soul," as distinct from "body" and "spirit." The context here, however, would probably suggest an emphasis on the profound relationship between the human physical and spiritual constitution within the phenomenon of the "whole person," rather than indicating human beings merely as a composite of three separate parts. A similar reference is also made in Heb 4:12; 6:19.

References to the entire emotional being of Christ (i.e., his "soul") are found in Matt 26:38; John 12:27 in relation to his mental and spiritual anguish prior to his crucifixion, in the garden of Gethsemane.

In a slightly different setting, the expression "my soul" is also predicated of God, metaphorically referring to "himself" (e.g., Matt 12:18; Heb 10:38).

Elsewhere, ***psychē*** means "living being" in relation to the first man, Adam (1 Cor 15:45). In Rev 16:3, ***psychē*** means "living thing" in relation to marine life.

▸ **22.** Life, Renewal, Immortality > LIFE, LIVE, LIVING

TREMBLE

phrissō φρίσσω 5425

phrissō is a verb found only in Jas 2:19 with reference to demons who "tremble with fear" at the thought of God.

tremō τρέμω 5141

tremō is synonymous with ***phrissō*** (above). It is found several times meaning "tremble," "be afraid" (Mark 5:33; Luke 8:47).

entromos ἔντρομος 1790

entromos is an adjective derived from ***tremō*** (above) indicating the state of "trembling" in fear (Acts 7:32; 16:29; Heb 12:21).

▸ **19.** Mind, Spirit, Emotions, Feelings, Desires > FEAR, AFRAID, TERROR, FRIGHTEN, TERRIFY

tromos τρόμος 5156

tromos is a noun derived from ***tremō*** (above). It occurs four times and means "trembling," linked explicitly with fear (1 Cor 2:3; 2 Cor 7:15; Eph 6:5; Phil 2:12).

UNDERSTANDING

nous νοῦς 3563

nous is a noun found in around twenty-five places with the predominant meaning "mind." This sense also overlaps with that of "understanding." In Phil 4:7; Rev 13:18, ***nous*** is translated this way with reference to one's "rational ability," or "mind," being the faculty from which "understanding" emanates.

▸ **19.** Mind, Spirit, Emotions, Feelings, Desires > MIND

phrēn φρήν 5424

phrēn is a rare noun meaning "understanding" in the sense of one's faculty of reasoning and discernment, or "thinking" (1 Cor 14:20).

SEE ALSO

▸ **51.** Knowledge, Wisdom, Remember, Forget > UNDERSTAND, UNDERSTANDING ***synetos***

▸ **56.** Folly, Ignorance > STUPID, WITHOUT UNDERSTANDING ***asynetos***

UNREASONABLE

alogos ἄλογος 249

alogos is an adjectival form denoting that which is "unreasonable" or "irrational." It occurs only three times. Acts 25:27 speaks of taking an "unreasonable" course of action. 2 Pet 2:12; Jude 10 liken false teachers to "irrational" beasts.

WONDER, MARVEL AT

thaumazō θαυμάζω 2296

thaumazō is found in approximately fifty contexts with the primary sense of "wonder, or marvel at."

Christ is said to "marvel at" people's faith in him (Matt 8:10; Luke 7:9). Conversely, he is also "astonished" at the unbelief of his countrymen (Mark 6:6; Luke 7:9).

People are commonly said to "marvel at" the miraculous powers of Christ (Matt 8:27; Mark 5:20; Luke 8:25; 11:14); and they also express wonder at his words (Luke 4:22). People "marvel at" the news of the birth of the Christ child (Luke 2:18), and also at his resurrection (Luke 24:41). ***thaumazō*** is also found in Mark 15:44; Luke 1:63; 2:33; John 4:27; Acts 2:7; Gal 1:6. Visions of God also produce a reaction of amazement (Acts 7:31; Rev 13:3; 17:6ff.).

thaumazō also means "to wonder" in the sense of "be surprised" or even "puzzled at" (Luke 1:21).

SEE ALSO

▸ **2.** Supernatural Beings/Forces, Spiritual Realm > WONDER, MIRACLE, OMEN, SIGN
teras

▸ **88.** Qualities, Characteristics > WONDERFUL
thaumasios, thaumastos

ZEAL, ZEALOUS

zēlos ζῆλος 2205

zēlos is a noun found in seventeen places, primarily denoting "envy," "jealousy." It also means "zeal" in the sense of "passionate enthusiasm."

John 2:17 records the overwhelming "zeal" consuming Christ in relation to the house of God. "Zeal" for God in general terms is indicated in Rom 10:2; as is "zeal" for godliness in 2 Cor 7:11; and for good deeds in 2 Cor 9:2. Phil 3:6 refers to "zeal" for the law.

▸ **19.** Mind, Spirit, Emotions, Feelings, Desires > JEALOUS, JEALOUSY

zēlōtēs ζηλωτής 2207

zēlōtēs is an adjective found in five places with the sense of "zealous" or "having eager enthusiasm for." This description is applied to God's law in Acts 21:20 (see also Gal 1:14); to God himself in Acts 22:3; and to good deeds in Titus 2:14. See also 1 Cor 14:12.

zēloō ζηλόω 2206

zēloō is a verb signifying the attitude of "being jealous" in six of its twelve occurrences. The remaining usage expresses the sense of "be zealous, or eager."

"Being zealous" to obtain spiritual gifts is indicated in 1 Cor 12:31; 14:1, 39. The meaning "covet" is indicated in Jas 4:2. Gal 4:18; Rev 3:19 express zeal in a general non-specific sense.

▸ **19.** Mind, Spirit, Emotions, Feelings, Desires > JEALOUS, JEALOUSY

20. Illness, Disease, Health, Healing

BIND, DRESS A WOUND

katadeō καταδέω 2611

katadeō is a rare verb that refers to "binding (i.e., dressing)" a wound. It is found only in Luke 10:34.

SEE ALSO

- ▸ **55.** Bondage, Captivity, Servitude > BIND, BOUND, TIE UP ***deō, desmeuō, proteinō***
- ▸ **67.** Acknowledge, Confess, Profess, Swear > BIND UNDER OATH ***anathematizō***

DEED

euergesia εὐεργεσία 2108

euergesia is a rare noun denoting a "good deed" shown to a crippled man who was healed through the apostolic ministry in Acts 4:9.

DISEASE, PLAGUE

astheneia ἀσθένεια 769

astheneia is a noun denoting "disease," "sickness" in most of the twenty-four occurrences of the term.

The "infirmities" in Matt 8:17 refer symbolically to the "afflictions" or "weaknesses" of God's people borne by the Suffering Servant-Messiah, as cited in Isa 53:4.

References to people's "diseases," eradicated by the miraculous power of Christ, are found in Luke 5:15; 8:2; 13:11ff.; John 5:5; 11:4. Similarly, "diseases" cured by the apostles are noted in Acts 28:9. Other references to "bodily ailments" are found in Gal 4:13; 1 Tim 5:23.

- ▸ **18.** Strength, Weakness, Capability > WEAK, WEAKNESS, POWERLESS
- ▸ **20.** Illness, Disease, Health, Healing > SICK, SICKNESS

malakia μαλακία 3119

malakia is a rare noun denoting "disease" in Matt 4:23; 9:35; 10:1.

nosos νόσος 3554

The noun ***nosos*** is synonymous with ***malakia*** (above), denoting "disease," "sickness" in twelve places (Matt 4:23ff.; 8:17; 9:35; 10:1; Mark 1:34; 3:15; Luke 4:40; 6:17; 7:21; 9:1; Acts 19:12).

- ▸ **20.** Illness, Disease, Health, Healing > SICK, SICKNESS

mastix μάστιξ 3148

mastix refers to "disease" in four of the six occurrences of the term. In each of these cases, ***mastix*** refers to diseases that were cured by Jesus (Mark 3:10; 5:29, 34; Luke 7:21).

- ▸ **76.** Force, Harm, Oppress > WHIP, SCOURGE

plēgē πληγή 4127

plēgē has three meanings — "wound," "beating," "plague" (i.e., disease). ***plēgē*** is found twenty-one times, meaning "plague" or "disease" in twelve of these contexts (all in the book of Revelation). In each case, the reference is to "disease" that is inflicted by God on a sinful world (Rev 9:20; 11:6; 15:1, 6ff.; 16:9, 21; 18:4, 8; 21:9; 22:18). Although these references all occur in symbolic contexts, it is clear that they all describe the reality of divine punishment.

- ▸ **76.** Force, Harm, Oppress > WOUND

DYSENTERY

dysenterion δυσεντέριον 1420

dysenterion is a rare term denoting "dysentery," mentioned only in Acts 28:8.

EXERCISE

gymnasia γυμνασία 1129

gymnasia is a rare noun denoting physical "exercise" found only in 1 Tim 4:8.

SEE ALSO

- ▸ **54.** Rule, Authority, Command, Obedience > EXERCISE AUTHORITY ***exousiazō***

EYE SALVE

kollourion κολλούριον 2854

kollourion is a rare noun denoting the medicinal "eye salve" produced by the city of Laodicea, as noted in Rev 3:18.

FEVER

pyretos πυρετός 4446

pyretos occurs six times, denoting the medical condition of a "fever" in each case (Matt 8:15; Mark 1:31; Luke 4:38, 39; John 4:52; Acts 28:8).

pyressō πυρέσσω 4445

pyressō is a rare verb found only twice, meaning "to be sick with fever" in Matt 8:14; Mark 1:30.

- ▸ **20.** Illness, Disease, Health, Healing > SICK, SICKNESS

FOAM

aphrizō ἀφρίζω 875

aphrizō is a rare verb meaning "to foam (at the mouth)" in relation to a demon-possessed man in Mark 9:18; Luke 9:39.

SEE ALSO

- ▸ **11.** Meteorology, Water > FOAM
  epaphrizō

FOOT

basis βάσις 939

basis is a rare noun denoting a person's "feet" miraculously healed of paralysis, found only in Acts 3:7.

SEE ALSO

- ▸ **16.** Body, Bodily Functions > FOOT
  pous
- ▸ **34.** Craftsmanship, Artisanship, Furniture, Implements > FOOTSTOOL
  hypopodion
- ▸ **86.** Movement Toward or Away From > WALK ON FOOT
  pezeuō

HEAL, CURE

therapeuō θεραπεύω 2323

therapeuō occurs around forty times with the principal sense of "heal," "cure."

Literal use of this term in reference to Jesus' healing miracles is frequently found in the Synoptic Gospels. Cure from physical illness is mentioned, for example, in Matt 4:23; 12:10; Mark 1:30; 6:13; and healing from demonically induced sickness in Matt 8:16; 12:22; Luke 6:18. Other references to healing include that in Matt 17:16, where the disciples are unable to cure the demon-possessed boy. Luke 8:43 mentions the woman with hemophilia with no medical hope of a cure; Jesus subsequently heals her. In Acts 4:14; 5:16 the crippled man at the gate of the temple is miraculously cured through the agency of Peter and John. The healing ministry of Philip is cited in Acts 8:7; as is Paul's healing activity in Malta in Acts 28:9.

Finally, Rev 13:3, 12 record the counterfeit healing of the sea beast, mimicking the resurrection of Christ.

iaomai ἰάομαι 2390

iaomai is synonymous with ***therapeuō*** (above) and occurs approximately thirty times.

iaomai refers to the healing ministry of Jesus, both in regard to physical illness (Matt 8:8; Mark 5:29; Luke 5:17; John 4:47; Acts 10:38); as well as to demonic oppression (Luke 9:42). See also Luke 4:18.

iaomai also refers to God's regenerating activity, but in contexts that indicate a withholding of divine healing. Matt 13:15 speaks of God's judgment on Israel's hardness of heart and applies that judgment to unbelieving Jews in Jesus' day, stating that in the face of persistent unbelief their hearts will be hardened lest they turn and be healed (see also John 12:40; Acts 28:27). In contrast, 1 Pet 2:24 cites the saving power of the cross of Christ, specifically the wounds he bore by which his people have been healed (Isa 53:5).

Further examples of physical healing are mentioned in Acts 3:11; 9:34, with reference to Peter and John; and in Acts 28:8 (Paul). In Heb 12:13, healing is indicated in the sense of spiritual soundness; and Jas 5:16 records a prayer for healing.

sōzō σῴζω 4982

This verb has the virtually exclusive meaning "save," but sometimes refers to the action of healing, with the translation "make whole" on sixteen occasions. The ideas of "saving" and "healing" are closely linked in these texts.

In relation to Jesus' healing ministry, ***sōzō*** refers to physical illness (Matt 9:21ff.; Mark 5:23ff.; 6:56; 10:52; Luke 8:48, 50; 17:19; 18:42). Luke 8:36 refers to Jesus curing demon possession. ***sōzō*** is also found in connection with the healing activity of Peter and John in Acts 4:9; and of Paul in Acts 14:9. See also Jas 5:16.

- ▸ **44.** Repentance, Forgiveness, Mercy, Redeem, Save > SAVE, SALVATION, SAVIOR

diasōzō διασῴζω 1295

diasōzō occurs eight times, meaning "save" or "escape" in all but two of these texts, where it means "heal" (Matt 14:36; Luke 7:3). Both refer to the healing work of Christ.

- ▸ **44.** Repentance, Forgiveness, Mercy, Redeem, Save > SAVE, SALVATION, SAVIOR
- ▸ **74.** Safety, Peace, Danger, Escape > ESCAPE
- ▸ **74.** Safety, Peace, Danger, Escape > SAFE, SAFELY, SAFETY, SECURITY

HEMMORHAGE, FLOW OF BLOOD

haimorroeō αἱμορροέω 131

haimorroeō is a rare verb found only in Matt 9:20, meaning "to suffer from a hemorrhage, a flow of blood."

SEE ALSO

- ▸ **16.** Body, Bodily Functions > BLOOD
  haima
- ▸ **38.** Covenant, Law, Rites, Roles > BLOOD
  haimatekchysia

LEPER

lepros λεπρός 3015

All nine occurrences of the word ***lepros*** are found in the Synoptic Gospels and refer primarily to lepers who were cured by Christ (Matt 8:2; 10:8; 11:5; Mark 1:40; Luke 7:22; 17:12). Luke 4:27 refers to Naaman the Syrian, who was cured of his leprosy during the ministry of Elisha the prophet. Two references to Simon the leper are found in Matt 26:6; Mark 14:3.

LEPROSY

lepra λέπρα 3014

lepra is the equivalent Greek term for the Hebrew *ṣāraʿat* and is translated "leprosy" in all four contexts in which it is found. All references indicate people who were cured of this disease by the direct intervention of Christ (Matt 8:3; Mark 1:42; Luke 5:12, 13).

MAD, MADNESS

mainomai μαίνομαι 3105

This verb occurs in five contexts and means "to be mad, rave like a madman." Jesus is accused of such in John 10:20, as is the servant girl, Rhoda, in Acts 12:15 when she initially reported Peter's miraculous escape from prison. Paul is likewise accused of speaking like a madman in his defense before the governor Festus. See also 1 Cor 14:23.

mania μανία 3130

mania is the noun derived from ***mainomai*** (above) and is found only in Acts 26:24, where Festus asserts that Paul's great learning has led him into "madness."

SEE ALSO

- ▸ **56.** Folly, Ignorance > MAD, MADNESS
  anoia, paraphronia

MAIMED

anapēros ἀνάπηρος 376

anapēros is found only twice, referring both times to those who are "maimed," whom Jesus healed of their physical disabilities (Luke 14:13, 21).

kyllos κυλλός 2948

kyllos occurs four times and is synonymous with ***anapēros*** (above). It likewise refers to those who are "maimed," referring to severe physical disability (Matt 15:30, 31; 18:8; Mark 9:43).

MYRRH

smyrnizō σμυρνίζω 4669

smyrnizō is a verb meaning "to mix with myrrh." It is found only in Mark 15:23, referring to the drink offered to Christ on the cross — wine mingled with myrrh, as a form of anesthetic.

SEE ALSO

- ▸ **13.** Plants, Trees, Flora > MYRRH
  smyrna

OIL

elaion ἔλαιον 1637

elaion is the sole term for "oil" in the NT, occurring eleven times.

General references to oil as a household commodity are found in Matt 25:3ff.; Luke 16:6; Rev 6:6; 18:13. ***elaion*** also refers to oil as a healing ointment, or medication (Mark 6:13; Luke 10:34; Jas 5:14); and as a cosmetic lotion (Luke 7:46). It is used metaphorically in Heb 1:9 to refer to God anointing his Son with "the oil of joy."

PARALYZED

paralytikos παραλυτικός 3885

paralytikos is an adjective occurring ten times that describes physical paralysis, a condition that was frequently cured by Jesus during his teaching ministry. Those who were "paralyzed" and subsequently healed by Jesus are described in Matt 4:24; 8:6; 9:2, 6; Mark 2:3ff.

paralyō παραλύω 3886

The verb ***paralyō*** expresses the condition of suffering from paralysis. It occurs in five contexts, with all but one use indicating this sense (Luke 5:18, 24; Acts 8:7; 9:33). Heb 12:12 refers to "weakness" in the knees.

PERFECT HEALTH

holoklēria ὁλοκληρία 3647

holoklēria is a noun found only in Acts 3:16, referring to the "perfect health" of a crippled man, cured of his affliction through the apostolic healing ministry of Peter and John.

SEE ALSO

- ▸ **61.** Integrity, Innocence, Piety >
  PERFECT, PERFECTION, COMPLETE
  teleios, teleioō, katartizō, teleiotēs
- ▸ **84.** Do, Make, Accomplish, Occur > PERFECTING
  teleiōsis
- ▸ **88.** Qualities, Characteristics > ACCURATELY
  akribēs

PHYSICIAN

iatros ἰατρός 2395

iatros is the sole term for "physician" in the NT. It is found seven times (Matt 9:12; Mark 2:17; 5:26; Luke 4:23; 5:31; 8:43; Col 4:14).

POUR

epicheō ἐπιχέω 2022

epicheō occurs only in Luke 10:34, with reference to "pouring" oil on wounds to speed their healing.

SEE ALSO

- ▸ **80.** Related to Liquids > POUR, POUR OUT
  ekcheō, katacheō, ballō, kerannymi

RECEIVE SIGHT

anablepō ἀναβλέπω 308

anablepō is a verb found in nearly thirty places, meaning "to receive one's sight" in more than half of these occurrences.

The expression "to receive one's sight" occurs exclusively in contexts where miraculous healing is given to the blind. Matt 20:34; Mark 10:51ff.; Luke 18:41ff.; John 9:11ff. refer to those so cured during the earthly ministry of Christ. Saul, in the immediate aftermath of his dramatic conversion, was cured of his blindness and received back his sight through the intercession of Ananias (Acts 9:12ff.; 22:13). The phenomenon of people receiving back their sight is also declared by Jesus as one of the irrefutable evidences that the Messiah had indeed come to live among his people (Matt 11:5; Luke 7:22).

▸ **17.** Senses, Actions, Abilities, Disabilities > SEE, LOOK, BEHOLD, GAZE

SEE ALSO

▸ **24.** Dwell, Live, Gather, Hospitality > RECEIVE, WELCOME
prosdechomai, eisdechomai, hypodechomai

▸ **41.** Sacrifice, Offering, Worship, Praise > TITHE, PAYMENT
dekatoō

▸ **70.** Give, Take, Seize, Touch > RECEIVE, ACCEPT, WELCOME
dechomai, lambanō, paradechomai, apolambanō, proslambanō, paralambanō, metalambanō, metalēmpsis, lēmpsis, apodechomai, epidechomai, anadechomai, komizō, apechō, nomotheteō

RECOVERY OF SIGHT

anablepsis ἀνάβλεψις 309

anablepsis is a noun found only in Luke 4:18, referring to the mission of the messianic Servant of Yahweh in giving "recovery of sight" to the blind — a mission espoused by, and embodied in, the person of Christ.

REFRESH

anapauō ἀναπαύω 373

anapauō is a verb with the primary sense of "rest" in most of its twelve occurrences. In 1 Cor 16:18, however, Paul commends his friends for "having refreshed" his spirit.

▸ **20.** Illness, Disease, Health, Healing > REST

synanapauomai συναναπαύομαι 4875

synanapauomai is found only in Rom 15:32, with reference to Paul's desire "to be refreshed" in the fellowship of the Roman congregation.

anapsychō ἀναψύχω 404

anapsychō occurs only once, in 2 Tim 1:16, where Paul offers thanks to the household of Onesiphorus who often "refreshed" him through their hospitality.

anapsyxis ἀνάψυξις 403

anapsyxis is a noun derived from ***anapsychō*** (above) meaning "refreshing." It is found only in Acts 3:19, with reference to spiritual refreshment coming from God upon those who turn to him in repentance.

REST

anapauō ἀναπαύω 373

anapauō is a verb found twelve times with the central meanings "give rest," "take refreshment, or one's ease."

Christ promises to give his followers "rest" in Matt 11:28, indicating total peace and freedom from all pain and trauma. Rev 14:13 depicts the saints of God enjoying their heavenly rest, totally free from all earthly toil. 1 Pet 4:14 speaks of the Spirit of God coming to rest on one's life. Taking rest in the sense of physical refreshment, or falling asleep, is indicated in Matt 26:45; Mark 6:31; 14:41. Taking one's ease in the sense of "relax" and "enjoy" is mentioned in Luke 12:19. Finally, ***anapauō*** expresses the idea of "rest," in the sense of "refresh one's spirit," in 1 Cor 16:18; 2 Cor 7:13; Phlm 7, 20.

▸ **20.** Illness, Disease, Health, Healing > REFRESH

anapausis ἀνάπαυσις 372

anapausis is the noun derived from ***anapauō*** (above), occurring in five places and meaning "rest."

"Rest," in the sense of "peace," "freedom from guilt, fear," is that state promised by Christ to his followers in Matt 11:29. Matt 12:43; Luke 11:24; Rev 14:11, however, deny rest for the wicked.

In the sense of "cessation from work," ***anapausis*** refers to "rest" in Rev 4:8, where the saints in heaven are said to never rest from their worship of God.

katapausis κατάπαυσις 2663

katapausis is a noun derived from ***katapauō*** (below) meaning "rest," used with reference to the "rest" granted by God to his people in the promised land of Canaan (Heb 3:11, 18; 4:3, 5), which in turn anticipates the heavenly "rest" prepared by God for those who belong to him (Heb 4:1ff.). See also Acts 7:49.

katapauō καταπαύω 2664

katapauō is a rare verb found in only four places, meaning "to rest" in three of these contexts. Heb 4:4 refers to God "taking rest" on the seventh day, after his creative endeavors of the previous six. Heb 4:8 speaks of Joshua "giving rest" to the people of God. In Heb 4:10, ***katapauō*** refers to believers "resting" (i.e., ceasing) from their labors.

▸ **49.** Allow, Accept, Approve, Refuse > RESTRAIN

anesis ἄνεσις 425

anesis is a noun found five times, meaning "rest" or "relief" in all but one of these contexts.

The "resting" of mind and body is noted in 2 Cor 2:13; 7:5 in the negative sense of "no rest."

Rest or relief from troubles and burdens is indicated in 2 Cor 8:13; 2 Thess 1:7.

sabbatismos σαββατισμός 4520

sabbatismos is a rare noun found only in Heb 4:9, referring to the "Sabbath rest" remaining for the people of God.

hēsychazō ἡσυχάζω 2270

hēsychazō is a verb found in five places. It means "to rest" only in Luke 23:56, with reference to resting on the Sabbath.

▸ **17.** Senses, Actions, Abilities, Disabilities > SILENCE, SILENT, QUIETNESS

▸ **60.** Virtues > PEACE, PEACEFUL, QUIET

SEE ALSO

▸ **85.** Movement, Position, State > REST
epanapauomai, episkēnoō

SICK, SICKNESS

kakōs κακῶς 2560

kakōs is an adverbial form used both adjectivally and verbally meaning "be sick, ill" or "diseased" in most of the sixteen contexts in which it is found (Matt 4:24; 14:35; Mark 1:32ff.; 2:17; Luke 5:31; 7:2).

▸ **57.** Evil, Wickedness, Sin > EVIL, EVILDOER, WICKED, WICKEDNESS, LAWLESS

astheneō ἀσθενέω 770

astheneō is a verb found thirty-five times with the sense of "to be sick" or "be weak (i.e., from disease, illness)" in most contexts (Matt 10:8; Mark 6:56; Luke 4:40; John 5:3ff.; Acts 9:37; Rom 14:2; Jas 5:14).

▸ **18.** Strength, Weakness, Capability > WEAK, WEAKNESS, POWERLESS

asthenēs ἀσθενής 772

asthenēs is an adjective derived from ***astheneō*** (above) found in twenty-five places and meaning "sick" or "weak" (i.e., from disease). See Matt 25:43ff.; Mark 14:38; Luke 10:9; Acts 4:9; 5:15ff.; 1 Cor 11:30.

▸ **18.** Strength, Weakness, Capability > WEAK, WEAKNESS, POWERLESS

astheneia ἀσθένεια 769

astheneia is a noun derived from ***astheneō*** (above). It is translated "illness," "disease," or "sickness" throughout the twenty or so occurrences (Matt 8:17; Luke 5:15; 8:2; 13:11, 12; John 11:4; Acts 28:9; Rom 8:26; 2 Cor 12:5ff.; Gal 4:13; 1 Tim 5:13; Heb 4:15).

▸ **18.** Strength, Weakness, Capability > WEAK, WEAKNESS, POWERLESS

▸ **20.** Illness, Disease, Health, Healing > DISEASE, PLAGUE

pyressō πυρέσσω 4445

pyressō is a verb found only twice, meaning "to be sick with fever" (Matt 8:14; Mark 1:30).

▸ **20.** Illness, Disease, Health, Healing > FEVER

arrōstos ἄρρωστος 732

arrōstos is an adjective meaning "sick," "ill" in all five occurrences (Matt 14:14; Mark 6:5, 13; 16:18; 1 Cor 11:30).

kamnō κάμνω 2577

kamnō is a rare verb found in only three places, indicating the sense of "to grow weary," "be sick." The latter sense is found only in Jas 5:15.

▸ **20.** Illness, Disease, Health, Healing > WEARY

nosos νόσος 3554

nosos is synonymous with ***astheneia*** (above), meaning "sickness," "disease" throughout all twelve occurrences of the term (Matt 4:23ff.; 10:1; Mark 1:34; Luke 4:40; Acts 9:12).

▸ **20.** Illness, Disease, Health, Healing > DISEASE, PLAGUE

SLEEP, ASLEEP, FALL ASLEEP

katheudō καθεύδω 2518

katheudō is a verb with the underlying sense of "sleep," "be asleep." The term is used both literally and metaphorically and occurs around twenty times.

Literal references to "being asleep," "sleeping" include Matt 8:24; 26:40ff.; Mark 4:27, 38; 14:37ff.; Luke 22:46; 1 Thess 5:6ff.

katheudō is also used metaphorically to refer to "death" — the "sleep" of death prior to resurrection. Texts include a resurrection miracle performed by Christ, plus the Christian hope of eternal life following physical death (Matt 9:24; Mark 5:39; Luke 8:52; Eph 5:14; 1 Thess 5:10).

koimaō κοιμάω 2837

koimaō is a verb synonymous with ***katheudō*** (above) found nearly twenty times with the meaning "sleep," "fall asleep," "be asleep." Usage is both literal and metaphorical, though the latter predominates.

Literal references include Matt 28:13; Luke 22:45; Acts 12:6. Elsewhere, ***koimaō*** denotes the action of "falling asleep" with reference to physical death as the precursor to eternal life in glory (Matt 27:52; John 11:11ff.; Acts 7:60; 13:36; 1 Cor 7:39 [here, literally translated "dies"]; 11:30; 15:6, 18ff., 51; 1 Thess 4:13ff.; 2 Pet 3:4).

▸ **21.** Die, Perish, Kill, Destroy > DIE, DEAD, PUT TO DEATH, DEADLY

aphypnoō ἀφυπνόω 879

aphypnoō is a rare verb found only in Luke 8:23 with reference to Christ "falling asleep."

exypnos ἔξυπνος 1853

exypnos is an adjectival form found only in Acts 16:27 describing the jailer as one "being awoken from sleep."

hypnos ὕπνος 5258

hypnos is a noun denoting "sleep" in each of the five occurrences of the term. Literal sleep is indicated in Matt 1:24; Luke 9:32; John 11:13; Acts 20:9. In Rom 13:11, believers are exhorted to awake from their "sleep." The usage is metaphorical, referring to an obligation to be on one's "spiritual guard" awaiting the "day" of the Lord's return.

SEE ALSO

▸ **22.** Life, Renewal, Immortality > AWAKEN, WAKE UP
exypnizō

SOUND, HEALTHY

hygiainō ὑγιαίνω 5198

hygiainō is a verb found in twelve contexts with the sense of "to be well, in good health" (i.e., sound). The term is also used adjectivally to refer to that which is trustworthy or accurate.

The expression "safe and sound" (i.e., in good health) is indicated in Luke 15:27; as is the meaning "to be well" in Luke 5:31; 7:10.

Elsewhere, "sound doctrine," that which is in accordance with the principles of revealed Scripture as given through God and Christ, is indicated in 1 Tim 1:10; 2 Tim 4:3; Titus 1:9, 13. Similarly, the "sound words" of Christ and the apostles are noted in 1 Tim 6:3; 2 Tim 1:13.

▸ **20.** Illness, Disease, Health, Healing > WHOLE

SEE ALSO

▸ **29.** Boats, Fishing, Maritime Activity > SOUND, TAKE A SOUNDING
bolizō

▸ **63.** Speak, Tell, Declare, Call > SOUND
phōnē, salpizō, ēchos

WASH, WASHING

niptō νίπτω 3538

niptō denotes the literal action of "washing" in all seventeen occurrences.

niptō refers to "washing" one's face (Matt 6:17); one's hands (Matt 15:2, Mark 7:3); and one's feet (John 13:5ff.; 1 Tim 5:10). In a miraculous cure of blindness performed by Christ, a man is commanded to "wash off" the clay from his eyes (John 9:7ff.).

baptizō βαπτίζω 907

baptizō is a verb found in approximately ninety contexts with the primary sense of "baptize." However, in Mark 7:4; Luke 11:38, the term refers to the ritual of "handwashing" prior to eating.

▸ **38.** Covenant, Law, Rites, Roles > BAPTISM, BAPTIST, BAPTIZE

SEE ALSO

▸ **39.** Clean, Pure, Holy > WASHING, CLEANSING
loutron

▸ **80.** Related to Liquids > WASH, BATHE, WASHING, WETTING
aponiptō, brechō, louō, apolouomai, plynō, baptismos

WEARY

kamnō κάμνω 2577

kamnō is a verb found three times meaning "grow weary" (Heb 12:3; Rev 7:3); and also "be sick" (Jas 5:15).

▸ **20.** Illness, Disease, Health, Healing > SICK, SICKNESS

SEE ALSO

▸ **60.** Virtues > (NOT) GROW WEARY
ekkakeō

▸ **75.** Suffering, Distress, Sadness > WEAR DOWN, WEAR OUT
hypōpiazō

▸ **84.** Do, Make, Accomplish, Occur > TOIL
kopiaō

WHOLE

hygiainō ὑγιαίνω 5198

hygiainō is a verb meaning "to be sound," "be whole," as well as related senses. It occurs in twelve places.

The meaning "be whole" (i.e., healthy, well) is indicated in Luke 5:31; 7:10; 3 John 2. The term is also used adjectivally in the expression "safe and sound" (Luke 15:27).

hygiainō means "sound," in the sense of "genuine," in relation to the teaching of Christ (1 Tim 6:3), and to sound doctrine in general (1 Tim 1:10; 2 Tim 1:13; 4:3; Titus 2:1). Titus 1:13; 2:2 refer to being "sound" in the faith.

▸ **20.** Illness, Disease, Health, Healing > SOUND, HEALTHY

hygiēs ὑγιής 5199

hygiēs is an adjectival form derived from ***hygiainō*** (above). It is found in fourteen contexts with the primary senses of "whole," "sound," in predominantly literal contexts.

The meaning "whole" in the sense of "restored," "healed" occurs in the context of Christ's healing ministry. Here ***hygiēs*** refers, for example, to the restoration of a man's withered hand (Matt 12:13; Mark 3:5; Luke 16:10); to healing a man paralyzed from birth (John 5:6; 7:23); and to the eradication of disease in general (Mark 5:34; John 5:4). This sense is also found in the context of the apostolic healing ministry (Acts 4:10).

hygiēs is also translated "wholesome," "pure" in relation to speech (Titus 2:8).

21. Die, Perish, Kill, Destroy

ABOLISH, NULLIFY

katargeō καταργέω 2673

katargeō is a verb occurring around thirty times with a variety of meanings centered around the idea of depriving a person or thing of influence, force, or existence. Primary meanings include "abolish," "nullify," "destroy," "make void."

The sense of "nullify," "make void" is hypothetically applied to the faithfulness of God in Rom 3:3. Rom 7:2 affirms that death "nullifies" the marriage bond. This same metaphorical sense is applied to one's obligation to the law after one's conversion (Rom 7:16).

The meaning "abolish" or "nullify" occurs with reference to the law of God, which may never be "nullified" or "abolished" by faith (Rom 3:31). Conversely, the bondage of the law is declared to be "abolished" by the death of Christ (Eph 2:15). The promises of God are deemed to be "nullified" or "abolished" only if salvation were ever to come via the law, i.e., an impossible scenario. Therefore the promises of God are certain to stand. There is also, in Gal 3:17, the outright claim that the promises of God may never be abolished. Sin is depicted as "abolished" in Rom 6:6; Gal 5:11.

katargeō can also suggest the closely related nuance of "destroy." The abolition or destruction of our human bodies at the hand of God is in view in 1 Cor 6:13. 1 Cor 15:24 affirms that all human rule and authority will be destroyed by God; as is death itself in 1 Cor 15:26; 2 Tim 1:10. The "veil of unbelief " is abolished (i.e., removed, destroyed) only through Christ (2 Cor 3:14). Likewise, the "lawless one" in 2 Thess 2:8, and the devil in Heb 2:14, are both destroyed solely through the work of Christ.

katargeō also expresses the sense of "put away," "discard" in 1 Cor 13:11 with reference to "childish things."

▸ **44.** Repentance, Forgiveness, Mercy, Redeem, Save > RESCUE, DELIVER, SET FREE

BEHEAD

apokephalizō ἀποκεφαλίζω 607

apokephalizō is a verb meaning "to behead." It is found in five places, all in the context of the execution of John the Baptist (Matt 14:10; Mark 6:16, 27; Luke 9:9).

pelekizō πελεκίζω 3990

pelekizō is a rare verb found only in Rev 20:4, referring to believers who "were beheaded" for their faith in Christ. The term literally means "to cut off with an ax."

BIER

soros σορός 4673

soros is a rare noun found only in Luke 7:14, denoting a "bier" — that is, a funeral carriage on which the dead were transported to their place of burial.

BURIAL, BURY

entaphiasmos ἐνταφιασμός 1780

entaphiasmos is a rare noun signifying a "burying" or "burial" in the context of preparing the body for burial, specifically Christ's own body (Mark 14:8; John 12:7).

taphē ταφή 5027

taphē is a term found only in Matt 27:7 denoting a "burial" place for strangers.

entaphiazō ἐνταφιάζω 1779

entaphiazō is a rare verb with the meaning "bury" in the sense of "preparing a body for burial," again with reference to Christ (Matt 26:12; John 19:40).

thaptō θάπτω 2290

thaptō is a verb that is consistently translated "bury" throughout its eleven occurrences (Matt 8:21ff.; 14:12; Luke 9:59ff.; 16:22; Acts 2:29; 5:6ff.; 1 Cor 15:4).

synthaptō συνθάπτω 4916

synthaptō is a verb used only metaphorically and passively in relation to being "buried together with Christ" in baptism.

CAST DOWN

katalyō καταλύω 2647

katalyō is a verb found twenty times with the primary sense of "destroy," as well as "throw down," "overthrow."

Jesus affirms in Matt 24:2; Mark 13:2; Luke 21:6 that there will be no stone left standing in the temple that "will not be thrown down" on the day of judgment. See also Acts 5:39.

▸ **21.** Die, Perish, Kill, Destroy > DESTROY, DESTROYER, DESTRUCTION

▸ **24.** Dwell, Live, Gather, Hospitality > GUEST, GUEST ROOM

kathaireō καθαιρέω 2507

kathaireō is a verb found eleven times with the meanings "take down," "destroy," which may also imply the sense of "cast down," "overthrow." God is said to have "cast down" the mighty from their thrones in Luke 1:52. Similarly, God is said to have "destroyed" (i.e., "overthrown") the Canaanite nations in Acts 13:19. See also Acts 19:27. In 2 Cor 10:5, Paul refers to "destroying" arguments that seek to discredit the gospel.

▸ **70.** Give, Take, Seize, Touch > TAKE, TAKE HOLD OF, TAKE UP, TAKE DOWN, TAKE AWAY, SNATCH

SEE ALSO

▸ **29.** Boats, Fishing, Maritime Activity > CAST, THROW OVERBOARD *aporiptō*

- ▸ **79.** Throw, Send, Drive, Mix, Remove > THROW, THROW OUT, CAST, CAST OUT
  ballō, rhiptō, apoballō, ekballō, emballō, kataballō, epiriptō

CONSUME, CONSUMING

analiskō ἀναλίσκω 355

analiskō is a rare verb found in three places, meaning "consume" in the underlying sense of "destroy." Luke 9:54 mentions destruction by fire. Gal 5:15 warns believers not to quarrel and thereby be metaphorically "consumed" (i.e., destroyed) by one another. 2 Thess 2:8 describes the fate of the antichrist (the "lawless one") in terms of the Lord Jesus "slaying" him with the breath of his mouth.

katanaliskō καταναλίσκω 2654

katanaliskō is a rare variant of ***analiskō*** (above) found only in Heb 12:29 and denoting God as a "consuming" fire in the context of divine judgment.

CORPSE, DEAD BODY

ptōma πτῶμα 4430

ptōma is a noun found in five places with the meaning "dead body," "corpse," or "carcass." Matt 24:28 refers to a carcass (whether human or animal is uncertain). Human corpses are noted in Mark 6:29; Rev 11:8ff.

SEE ALSO

- ▸ **16.** Body, Bodily Functions > BODY, BODILY
  sōma, sōmatikos, sōmatikōs, syssōmos, chrōs

CORRUPT, CORRUPTION

diaphtheirō διαφθείρω 1311

diaphtheirō is a verb with the underlying sense of "corrupt." It is translated in various ways.

The meaning "destroy," "ruin" refers literally to the destructive activity of moths on personal possessions (Luke 12:33). It refers to ships in Rev 8:9; and to the earth in Rev 11:18.

The meaning "waste away" refers to the physical deterioration, or corrupting, of one's human form in 2 Cor 4:16.

The adjectival sense of "corrupt" or "depraved" minds is noted in 1 Tim 6:5.

- ▸ **21.** Die, Perish, Kill, Destroy > DECAY
- ▸ **21.** Die, Perish, Kill, Destroy > DESTROY, DESTROYER, DESTRUCTION

phthora φθορά 5356

phthora is a noun denoting "corruption," "decay" for most of the nine occurrences of the term.

The meaning "decay" in the sense of physical and spiritual corruption in relation to created human existence is noted in Rom 8:21; Gal 6:8.

phthora denotes the sense of "perishable" or "subject to corruption" in relation to the human body in 1 Cor 15:42; 50; and with general reference to all things earthly in Col 2:22.

Moral "corruption" is indicated in 2 Pet 1:4; 2:19. 2 Pet 2:12 indicates the "destruction" of false teachers.

diaphthora διαφθορά 1312

diaphthora is a variant form of ***phthora*** (above) meaning "corruption" or "decay," with the sense of physical decay associated with human corpses. The term is found in only six places, referring to the "decay" of David's body in Acts 13:36. The remaining contexts declare that there is no such corruption associated with the person of Jesus Christ, whose body did not decay because God raised him from the dead (Acts 2:27, 31; 13:34ff.).

phthartos φθαρτός 5349

phthartos is an adjective denoting that which is "corruptible," or "perishable," "mortal," "subject to decay."

Rom 1:23 refers to mortal human beings. Human nature is described as "perishable" in 1 Cor 15:53ff.; 1 Pet 1:23. 1 Cor 9:25; 1 Pet 1:18 both speak of "perishable" things in general.

aphanizō ἀφανίζω 853

aphanizō is a verb meaning to "make disappear" or "put out of sight." It is translated "corrupt" or "destroy" with general reference to the destructive activity of moths and corrosion in Matt 6:19, 20.

- ▸ **21.** Die, Perish, Kill, Destroy > PERISH

SEE ALSO

- ▸ **22.** Life, Renewal, Immortality > INCORRUPTIBLE
  aphtharsia, aphthartos
- ▸ **57.** Evil, Wickedness, Sin > CORRUPT
  phtheirō, kataphtheirō

CROSS, CRUCIFY

stauros σταυρός 4716

The noun ***stauros*** means "cross" throughout the nearly thirty occurrences of the term.

"Cross" is used as a symbolic term for suffering in contexts where followers of Christ are exhorted to "take up their cross" and follow him, being ready to completely identify with him (Matt 10:38; 16:24; Mark 8:34; 10:21; Luke 9:23; 14:27).

Literal references to a wooden "cross" are found in relation to the execution of Christ. Simon of Cyrene carries one for Christ to the place of crucifixion (Matt 27:32; Mark 15:21; Luke 23:26). The "cross" as the instrument of Christ's death is noted in Matt 27:40ff.; Mark 15:30ff.; John 19:17ff.; Phil 2:8; Heb 12:2.

Metaphorically speaking, the "cross of Christ" is the primary symbol of the spiritual effectiveness of the gospel (1 Cor 1:17ff.; Gal 6:12ff.; Eph 2:16; Col 1:20; 2:14). The "cross of Christ" is also depicted as the symbolic "stumbling block" for the acceptance of the gospel in Gal 5:11. Phil 3:18 refers to the enemies of the "cross of Christ."

stauroō σταυρόω 4717

The verb ***stauroō*** means "to crucify" throughout the nearly fifty occurrences of the term.

Most of the occurrences refer to Christ's crucifixion (Matt 20:19; 27:22ff.; 28:5; Mark 15:13ff.; Luke 23:21ff.; 24:7, 20; John 19:6ff.; Acts 2:36; 4:10; 1 Cor 1:23; 2:8; 2 Cor 13:4; Gal 3:1). See also Matt 23:34; 1 Cor 1:13; Rev 11:8.

Gal 5:24 records a metaphorical use of ***stauroō*** affirming that those who belong to Christ "have crucified" the flesh, determining to put to death ungodly passions and desires.

systauroō συσταυρόω 4957

systauroō is a variant form of ***stauroō*** (above) meaning "to crucify along with," referring to the two criminals executed alongside Christ (Matt 27:44; Mark 15:32; John 19:32). The term also refers metaphorically to the "old self" of the natural human being "having been crucified" with Christ, so that the new believer would no longer be a slave to sin.

anastauroō ἀνασταυρόω 388

anastauroō is a verb found only in Heb 6:6, used metaphorically to describe apostasy as the act of "crucifying afresh" the Son of God.

prospēgnymi προσπήγνυμι 4362

prospēgnymi is a verb found only in Acts 2:23, describing the death of Christ in terms of wicked people "nailing him to the cross."

CUT TO PIECES

dichotomeō διχοτομέω 1371

dichotomeō is a rare verb found only twice, referring symbolically to the act of divine judgment against the wicked and faithless and describing their fate as "being cut to pieces" (Matt 24:51; Luke 12:46).

SEE ALSO

- ▸ **10.** Earth, Dust, Rocks, Minerals, Metals, Stones > CUT ***latomeō, laxeutos***
- ▸ **28.** Agriculture, Viticulture, Animal Husbandry > BREAK OFF, CUT, CUT OFF ***koptō***
- ▸ **76.** Force, Harm, Oppress > CUT, CUT OFF ***katakoptō, aphaireō***
- ▸ **78.** Act Upon, Push, Pull, Break, Cut > CUT OFF, CUT DOWN ***apokoptō, ekkoptō***

DEATH

thanatos θάνατος 2288

thanatos is a common noun denoting "death" throughout its nearly 120 occurrences in a variety of contexts.

Literal references to "death" include Matt 15:4; 26:38; Mark 7:10; Luke 9:27; John 11:4; Rom 8:38; Phil 1:20; Heb 7:23; 11:5; Jas 1:15; Rev 9:6. "Death" by judicial execution is noted in Acts 23:29; 28:18. A martyr's "death" is indicated in John 21:19; Rev 2:10; 12:11. The action of handing someone over to death is noted in Matt 10:21; Luke 2:26; Acts 22:4; Rev 2:23.

The record of Christ being condemned to death is found in Matt 20:18; 26:66; Mark 10:33; Luke 24:20; Acts 13:28; as is the prospect of his death in John 12:33; 18:32. In significant theological contexts the death of Christ is declared to result in justification for the people of God, releasing them from the results of sin and eternal death (Acts 2:24; Rom 5:10; 6:3ff.; Phil 2:8; Col 1:22; Heb 2:9; 9:15). The significance of Christ's death in relation to the Lord's Supper is indicated in 1 Cor 11:26.

Metaphorical usage of ***thanatos*** includes references to the "shadow of death" in relation to spiritual darkness in Matt 4:16; Mark 9:1; Luke 1:79. The "law of sin and death" is mentioned in Rom 8:2. 1 Cor 15:26, 54ff. affirm that the last enemy to be destroyed is "death." See also Rev 21:4; 2 Cor 4:11.

In other places, "death" signifies the horrifying reality of eternal judgment. The expression "second death" is the most profound symbol of eternal separation from God (Rev 2:11; 20:6; 21:8). General references to eternal death include John 5:24; Rom 1:32; Jas 5:20; 1 John 3:14; 5:16. The abolition of such a death through the work of Christ is indicated in 2 Tim 1:10; Heb 2:14ff. See also John 8:51ff. "Death" as the consequence of the "fall" of human beings, in both a literal and spiritual sense, is indicated in Rom 5:12ff.; 6:16ff.; 1 Cor 15:21; 2 Cor 3:7; 7:10. The primary feature of "spiritual death" is alienation from God. The name "Death" is given to the symbolic rider bringing divine judgment to wicked humankind in Rev 6:8. See also Rev 20:13.

epithanatios ἐπιθανάτιος 1935

epithanatios is a rare adjectival form, found only in 1 Cor 4:9, referring to people "sentenced to death."

anairesis ἀναίρεσις 336

anairesis is a rare noun denoting "death" in the context of the public execution of Stephen, the first Christian martyr, found only in Acts 8:1.

teleutē τελευτή 5054

teleutē is a rare noun, found only in Matt 2:15, referring to the "death" of King Herod.

DECAY

diaphtheirō διαφθείρω 1311

The verb ***diaphtheirō*** is found six times, meaning "destroy" with several nuances.

The "decaying," "destructive" effect of moths on material possessions is indicated in Luke 12:33.

2 Cor 4:16 refers to the "wasting away," the "corruption" of the human frame. 1 Tim 6:5 refers to human minds "being depraved." The literal "destroying" of ships is indicated in Rev 8:9; and the destruction of people in Rev 11:18.

▸ **21.** Die, Perish, Kill, Destroy > CORRUPT, CORRUPTION

▸ **21.** Die, Perish, Kill, Destroy > DESTROY, DESTROYER, DESTRUCTION

SEE ALSO

▸ **5.** Old, New, First, Last > DECAY, WEAR OUT, GROW OBSELETE *palaioō*

DESOLATE, DESOLATION

erēmoō ἐρημόω 2049

erēmoō is a verb found in five places with the consistent sense of "make desolate," "lay waste," or "bring to ruin."

In Matt 12:25; Luke 11:17, Christ declares that every kingdom that is divided against itself is guaranteed "to be made desolate, laid waste" by its enemies. God's judgment in "laying waste" the devil and his servants — both individual and corporate — is indicated in Rev 17:16; 18:17, 19.

erēmōsis ἐρήμωσις 2050

erēmōsis is a rare term meaning "desolation" in the sense of "desecration," in relation to the pagan altar erected in the Jerusalem temple by the Seleucid ruler Antiochus Epiphanes (the Hebrew term *šāmēm* in Dan 8:13; 9:27; 11:31; 12:11).

It is clear from the occurrences of ***erēmōsis*** in Matt 24:15; Mark 13:14, where Christ refers to this "abomination of desolation," that this flagrant desecration of the temple functions as an apocalyptic sign, one that will be repeated in the future, signifying the imminence of Christ's return on the final day of God's judgment on the earth. Luke 21:20 refers to the imminent "desolation" (i.e., destruction) of Jerusalem at the hands of the Roman army — an invasion and devastation predicted by Christ during his public ministry.

DESTROY, DESTROYER, DESTRUCTION

apollymi ἀπόλλυμι 622

apollymi is a verb found nearly ninety times with the primary meaning "perish," "lose," "destroy."

The meaning "destroy," in the sense of "kill," is indicated in relation to Herod's plan to eradicate the infant Jesus (Matt 2:13). It is also used in relation to the Pharisees' attempt to have Jesus killed (Matt 12:14; 27:20; Mark 3:6; Luke 19:47). The prospect of God "destroying" both body and soul in hell is noted in Matt 10:28. Luke 17:27 refers to the Noahic flood having "destroyed" the inhabitants of the earth.

General references to people being "destroyed" (i.e., killed) are found in Matt 21:41; 22:7; Mark 9:22; Luke 6:9; Jas 4:12. Divine judgment on the rebellious Israelites in the wilderness is indicated in 1 Cor 10:9 with reference to their being "destroyed" by serpents. See also Jude 5.

Christ "destroying" or "eliminating" demons is indicated in Mark 1:24; Luke 4:34. ***apollymi*** also refers to "destroying" property in John 10:10.

God's promise to "destroy" (i.e., render null and void) the wisdom of the wise is recorded in 1 Cor 1:19.

▸ **21.** Die, Perish, Kill, Destroy > PERISH

▸ **72.** Need, Gain, Loss, Advantage, Seek, Find > LOSE, LOSS, LOST

lyō λύω 3089

lyō is a verb found about forty times, meaning "loose," "release." Once, in 1 John 3:8, it refers to the Son of God "destroying" the works of the devil.

▸ **12.** Fire, Heat, Smoke, Burning > DISSOLVE, MELT
▸ **55.** Bondage, Captivity, Servitude > RELEASE
▸ **78.** Act Upon, Push, Pull, Break, Cut > BREAK

katalyō καταλύω 2647

The verb ***katalyō*** means "destroy," in addition to having related nuances, in most of its seventeen occurrences.

Christ denies having come to earth in order to "destroy" (i.e., "abolish") the Law and the Prophets — rather, he came to fulfill them (Matt 5:17).

Christ prophesies that the temple will be "destroyed" or "thrown down" in Matt 24:2; 26:61; 27:40; Mark 13:2; 14:58; 15:29; Luke 21:6; Acts 6:14.

A warning against "destroying" the work of God, nullifying its impact, is issued in Rom 14:20. See also Gal 2:18.

▸ **21.** Die, Perish, Kill, Destroy > CAST DOWN
▸ **24.** Dwell, Live, Gather, Hospitality > GUEST, GUEST ROOM

olothreuō ὀλοθρεύω 3645

olothreuō is a rare verb found only once, used in a participial form with reference to the angel of death as the "destroyer" of the Egyptian firstborn (Heb 11:28).

phtheirō φθείρω 5351

phtheirō is a verb with the predominant sense of "corrupt" for most of the eight occurrences of the term. However, 1 Cor 3:17 warns against anyone who might want to "destroy" the temple — God would "destroy" such a person himself.

▸ **57.** Evil, Wickedness, Sin > CORRUPT

diaphtheirō διαφθείρω 1311

diaphtheirō is a variant form of ***phtheirō*** (above) occurring six times with the meanings "corrupt" and "destroy."

Rev 8:9 refers to "destroying" ships, and Rev 11:18 to "destroying" the earth.

▸ **21.** Die, Perish, Kill, Destroy > CORRUPT, CORRUPTION
▸ **21.** Die, Perish, Kill, Destroy > DECAY

olethros ὄλεθρος 3639

olethros is a noun found in four places, denoting "destruction" in each of them.

The "destruction" of the flesh in relation to church discipline is noted in 1 Cor 5:5. The "destruction" of the wicked, implying eternal judgment, is noted in 1 Thess 5:3; 2 Thess 1:9; 1 Tim 6:9.

apōleia ἀπώλεια 684

apōleia is a noun denoting "ruin," "destruction" for most of the twenty occurrences of the term.

Eternal "destruction" visited on the ungodly is indicated in Matt 7:13; Rom 9:22; Phil 1:28; 3:19; 1 Tim 6:19; Heb

10:39; 2 Pet 2:1ff. In particular, the final "destruction" of Satan and his minions is indicated in 2 Thess 2:3; Rev 17:8, 11.

portheō πορθέω 4199

portheō is a rare verb meaning "destroy" in relation to Paul's attempt to eradicate the infant Christian church prior to his conversion (Gal 1:13, 23).

DIE, DEAD, PUT TO DEATH, DEADLY

nekros νεκρός 3498

nekros is an adjectival form meaning "dead" throughout the nearly 130 occurrences of the term, but it is used predominantly as a noun in both literal and metaphorical contexts.

General references to "the dead" are found in Matt 8:22; 22:32; Luke 9:60; 24:5; John 5:25; Rev 20:5. More commonly, references to the miraculous "raising or the resurrection of the dead" are found in Matt 10:8; 11:5; Mark 9:10; 12:25ff.; Luke 7:22; 9:7; 15:24; 20:35ff.; John 5:21; 12:1, 9, 17; Acts 23:6; Phil 3:11; Heb 6:2; 11:19. The promise that the Son of Man will be "raised from the dead" is noted in Matt 17:9; Mark 9:9; Luke 24:46; John 20:9. The reports of Christ's resurrection are found, for example, in Matt 27:64; 28:7; John 2:22; Acts 3:15; 13:30, 34; 26:23; Rom 1:4; 6:4, 9; 7:4; 8:11; Gal 1:1; Eph 1:20; Col 2:12; 1 Thess 1:10; Heb 13:20; 1 Pet 1:3, 21; Rev 2:8. In Rom 4:17, God is said to give life to the dead.

Christ is designated as "Lord of the dead" in Rom 14:9. The "dead" are designated as the objects of divine judgment in Acts 10:42; 2 Tim 4:1; 1 Pet 4:5; Rev 11:18; 20:12ff. 1 Cor 15:12–52 is a significant passage which sets out the supreme significance of Christ's resurrection from the dead as the firstfruits of the general resurrection for believers. The certainty of resurrection from the dead is dependent on the fact of Christ's resurrection, without which there is no hope for believers. See also Col 1:18; Rev 1:5. God is designated as the one who "raises the dead" in 2 Cor 1:9. 1 Thess 4:16 affirms that "the dead in Christ" shall rise first when Christ returns. See also Rom 6:13.

The adjectival sense of "dead" refers to the physically deceased in Matt 23:27; Luke 7:15; Acts 5:10; 20:19; 28:6; Rev 1:17; 16:13.

Elsewhere, the adjective "dead" refers to bodies that have been fatally affected by sin in Rom 8:10; 10:9; Eph 2:1, 5; Col 2:13. Rev 3:1 describes the "spiritually dead." Jas 2:17, 26 affirm that "faith without works is dead." Rom 7:8 refers to sin "lying dead" apart from the law. Heb 6:1; 9:14 mention "dead works," or deeds or actions that are ineffective in gaining merit in the sight of God.

nekroō νεκρόω 3499

nekroō is a rare verb found in only three places, meaning "to be dead" in a literal sense in Rom 4:19. Col 3:5 contains the exhortation to "put to death" one's fleshly desires. In Heb 11:12 the term is used metaphorically, referring to Abraham's physiological inability to father a child — his body "being as good as dead."

thanatoō θανατόω 2289

thanatoō is a verb found in seventeen contexts with the principal meaning "put to death," "kill."

The meaning "have someone put to death" is indicated in Matt 10:21; 13:12; Luke 21:16. See also Rom 8:36; 2 Cor 6:9. The plot to have Jesus "put to death" is recorded in Matt 26:59; 27:1; Mark 14:55.

thanatoō has a metaphorical sense in 1 Pet 3:18 with reference to believers "being put to death" in the flesh but made alive in the Spirit. Similarly, Rom 7:4 refers to believers "having died to the law" through being linked to Christ through faith.

▸ **21.** Die, Perish, Kill, Destroy > KILL, MURDER, SLAY, SLAUGHTER

thanatēphoros θανατηφόρος 2287

thanatēphoros is a rare adjectival form denoting "deadly" poison, found only in Jas 3:8.

thanasimos θανάσιμος 2286

thanasimos is a rare synonym for ***thanatēphoros*** (above) also denoting "deadly" poison (Mark 16:18).

hēmithanēs ἡμιθανής 2253

hēmithanēs is an adjective found only in Luke 10:30 referring to a man left "half dead" by robbers on a desolate road.

apagō ἀπάγω 520

apagō is a verb found fifteen times with the primary meaning "to lead away." In a number of places it refers to Christ being "led away" to be crucified. In Acts 12:19 the term specifically indicates King Herod's orders that certain prison guards "be put to death."

▸ **71.** Lead, Guide, Follow > LEAD, LEAD OUT, LEAD AWAY

thnēskō θνήσκω 2348

thnēskō is a verb occurring fifteen times with the meaning "die," "be dead."

References to people who are dead include Matt 2:20; Mark 15:44; Luke 7:12; 8:49; John 11:21, 39ff.; 12:1; 19:33; Acts 14:19; 25:19. 1 Tim 5:6 refers metaphorically to the pleasure-seeking women who had rendered themselves spiritually insensitive as "being dead."

apothnēskō ἀποθνήσκω 599

apothnēskō is a common verb meaning "die," "be dead," "perish" throughout the more than one hundred occurrences of the term, and in a variety of significant contexts.

General references to "perishing," "dying" are found in relation to animals (Matt 8:32; Rev 16:3); and to people (Matt 9:24; Mark 5:35ff.; Luke 8:52ff.; 20:28ff.; John 6:49ff.; 8:52ff.; Acts 9:37; Rom 7:2; Heb 9:27). In particular, people "dying" as a result of divine judgment is mentioned in Rev 8:11; a judgment that also includes Christ (Mark 15:44). John 12:24; 1 Cor 15:31 refer to a seed "dying."

The appearance of "death" is noted in Mark 9:26. Resurrection to life is guaranteed to believers after their physical death in John 11:25ff. "Spiritual death" is indicated in John

8:21, 24. The state of being "dead to sin" is predicated of the believer, justified by faith in Christ, in Rom 6:2ff.

Reference to the principle that it is better for one person to die for the people than for the whole nation to perish, indicating the approaching death of Christ, is found in John 11:50ff. Specific references to the certainty of Christ's coming death are found in John 12:33; 18:32; 19:7.

The redemptive impact of Christ's substitutionary death for the ungodly is indicated in Rom 5:6ff.; 8:13; 14:9, 15; 1 Cor 8:11; 15:3; 2 Cor 5:14, 15; 1 Thess 4:14; 5:10.

The universal condemnation of the human race to death as the consequence of the sin of Adam is noted in Rom 5:15; 1 Cor 15:22.

The impact of the law on an individual brings about that person's death, unless its strangle hold is broken by the grace of God through saving faith (Rom 7:9; 8:13). In this regard, Gal 2:10 bears testimony to Paul's experience of "dying to the law." See also 1 Cor 15:31. 2 Cor 5:14; Col 2:20; 3:3 refer metaphorically to the spiritual identification of all believers in the death of Christ, indicating that in him "they all died."

Paul expresses the unthinkable hypothesis in Gal 2:21 that, "if righteousness could be gained through the law, then Christ died for nothing."

The prospect of living with Christ for eternity leads Paul to the conclusion that "to die" is far better (Phil 1:21).

synapothnēskō συναποθνήσκω 4880

synapothnēskō is a rare variant of ***apothnēskō*** (above) meaning "die together with" someone (Mark 14:31; 2 Cor 7:3). In 2 Tim 2:11 the term is used metaphorically, affirming that those who "have died" with Christ (i.e., in self-denial) shall also live with him.

teleutaō τελευτάω 5053

The verb ***teleutaō*** is synonymous with ***thnēskō*** and ***apothnēskō*** (above) and means "die, be dead" throughout its ten occurrences, mostly concerning people (Matt 2:19; 15:4; Mark 7:10; Luke 7:2; Acts 2:29; 7:15; Heb 11:22).

koimaō κοιμάω 2837

koimaō is a verb with the primary meaning "sleep" throughout its nearly twenty occurrences. It is used both literally and metaphorically. Metaphorically, it denotes the "sleep" of death in Matt 27:52; John 11:11ff.; Acts 7:60; 13:36; 1 Cor 11:30; 15:6, 18, 20, 51; 1 Thess 4:13ff.; 2 Pet 3:4.

▸ **20.** Illness, Disease, Health, Healing > SLEEP, ASLEEP, FALL ASLEEP

apoginomai ἀπογίνομαι 581

apoginomai is a rare verb found only in 1 Pet 2:24 with the metaphorical sense of "being dead" to sin.

DROWN

katapinō καταπίνω 2666

katapinō is a verb found seven times with the primary meaning "to swallow." In Heb 11:29 the related sense of "drown" is indicated in connection with the Egyptian army that was "swallowed up" by the waters of the Re(e)d Sea.

▸ **23.** Food, Drink, Cooking > SWALLOW

katapontizō καταποντίζω 2670

katapontizō is another rare verb meaning "to be drowned" in connection with the preferred punishment prescribed by Christ for any who prevented little children from coming to faith in him.

▸ **29.** Boats, Fishing, Maritime Activity > SINK

FADE AWAY

marainō μαραίνω 3133

marainō is a verb found only in Jas 1:11, referring to the rich man "fading away" in the middle of his exploits, indicating his inevitable perishing or destruction.

SEE ALSO

▸ **82.** Change, Exchange, Transform > UNFADING ***amarantos***

GIVE UP THE GHOST

ekpneō ἐκπνέω 1606

ekpneō is a rare verb found three times with reference to Christ "breathing his last" (lit., "giving up the ghost") on the cross.

ekpsychō ἐκψύχω 1634

ekpsychō is rare synonym for ***ekpneō*** (above) referring to people "breathing their last" or "giving up the ghost" in Acts 5:5, 10; 12:23.

GRAVE, TOMB

abyssos ἄβυσσος 12

abyssos is a term consistently denoting the "abyss" or "bottomless pit" as the symbolic designation for the location and confinement of Satan and demonic spirits (Luke 8:31; Rev 9:1, 2, 11; 11:7; 17:8; 20:1ff.). In Rom 10:7, however, the term is a symbolic designation for the "grave."

▸ **1.** Celestial Realm, Earthly Realm > PIT, ABYSS, DEEP

mnēmeion μνημεῖον 3419

mnēmeion is a noun denoting a "grave" or "tomb" throughout its nearly forty occurrences. All the references are literal (e.g., Matt 8:28; 27:52ff.; 28:8; Mark 5:2ff.; 16:2ff.; Luke 11:44ff.; 24:2ff.; John 11:17, 31, 38; 19:41ff.; 20:1ff.; Acts 13:29).

mnēma μνῆμα 3418

mnēma is a variant form of ***mnēmeion*** (above) denoting a "grave" or "tomb" in each of its seven occurrences (Mark 5:5; Luke 8:27; 23:53; 24:1; Acts 2:29; 7:16; Rev 11:9).

taphos τάφος 5028

taphos is a synonym for ***mnēmeion*** and ***mnēma*** (above). It is found in seven places, denoting "tombs," "graves" throughout (Matt 23:27ff.; 27:61ff.; 28:1). In Rom 3:13, ***taphos*** is used symbolically to denote the mouth of the ungodly as an "open grave" that produced poisonous, libelous speech.

HANG

apanchō ἀπάγχω 519

This word occurs only in Matt 27:5, where it refers to Judas going out and hanging himself.

SEE ALSO

▸ **85.** Movement, Position, State > HANG
kremannymi, perikeimai

KILL, MURDER, SLAY, SLAUGHTER

phoneuō φονεύω 5407

phoneuō is a verb occurring about twelve times with the consistent meaning "kill," in the sense of "murder" or "slay."

General references to killing others are found in Jas 4:2; 5:6. The murder of the prophets in earlier Israelite history is recorded in Matt 23:31, 35.

Reaffirmation of the sixth commandment prohibiting murder is found in Matt 5:21; 19:18; Mark 10:19; Luke 18:20; Rom 13:9; Jas 2:11.

apokteinō ἀποκτείνω 615

This verb is the most common NT term for "kill," "slay," "put to death." ***apokteinō*** occurs around eighty times.

The meaning "kill," in a general sense, is found in a number of places. Matt 10:28; Luke 12:4 contain Jesus' exhortation to his listeners not to fear those who can kill the body, but the one who can cast both body and soul into hell. Accidental catastrophe is indicated in Luke 13:4, which describes the death of eighteen people when the tower in Siloam fell on them. Other general references are found in Mark 3:4, John 8:22; Rev 13:10.

The action of execution, or being put to death, is also evident in the usage of ***apokteinō*** — or, more accurately, the anticipation of that procedure. The term is used in reference to Jesus' approaching death as he predicts his suffering to come (Matt 16:21; 17:23; Mark 8:31; 9:31; 10:34; Luke 9:22; 18:33). ***apokteinō*** is also used in reference to the plot to kill Jesus (Matt 26:4; Mark 14:1; Luke 13:31; John 7:1, 19, 20, 25; 11:53). Two passages refer back to Jesus' execution (Acts 3:15; 1 Thess 2:15).

apokteinō also anticipates the execution or violent death of John the Baptist (Matt 14:5; Mark 6:19); Lazarus (John 12:10); and the disciples of Jesus (Matt 24:9; John 16:2). The book of Revelation mentions the prospective deaths of the wicked at the hands of God (Rev 2:23; 6:8; 9:15, 18; 11:5, 13; 19:21).

apokteinō also has the specific sense of "murder" in a number of places. In the parables of Jesus, for example, it refers to vineyard tenants who slay the servants of the owner (Matt 21:35; Mark 12:5); and also the owner's son (Matt 21:38, 39; Mark 12:7, 8; Luke 20:14, 15). See also Matt 22:6. The NT also speaks of the callous way in which many of Israel's prophets had been murdered by their own people in the past (Matt 23:37; Luke 11:47, 48, 49; 13:34; Acts 7:52; Rom 11:3). During Paul's lifetime, several attempts were made to kill him (Acts 21:31; 23:12, 14; 27:42). See also Rev 2:13; 11:7; 13:15.

apokteinō is also used metaphorically. Paul speaks of himself being put to death by the effect of sin and the law in his life (Rom 7:11). Similarly, Paul refers to the lethal impact of the law (2 Cor 3:6). Eph 2:16 refers to Christ slaying the enemy of sin and death.

thyō θύω 2380

This term is translated "kill," in the sense of "sacrifice" or "slaughter," in all but one context. ***thyō*** occurs thirteen times.

The slaughter of animals is in view for a festive celebration in Matt 22:4; Luke 15:23, 27, 30; Acts 10:13; 11:7. The sacrifice of the Passover lamb is mentioned in Mark 14:12; Luke 22:7; and Jesus' sacrifice as "our Passover Lamb" is referred to in 1 Cor 5:7.

There is a non-specific use of ***thyō***, "to kill," in reference to the action of a thief in John 10:10.

▸ **41.** Sacrifice, Offering, Worship, Praise > SACRIFICE

diacheirizomai διαχειρίζομαι 1315

diacheirizomai is rare, occurring only twice and indicating the act of killing. Acts 5:30 refers to Jesus being slain and hung on a "tree" (i.e., a cross). Acts 26:21 describes the abortive attempt of a Jewish mob to kill the apostle Paul.

thanatoō θανατόω 2289

thanatoō is found on eleven occasions and is usually translated "put to death," both literally and metaphorically.

In reference to literal slaying, several texts indicate the actions of children in having their parents put to death (Matt 10:21; Mark 13:12; Luke 21:16). The plot to have Jesus put to death is recorded in Matt 26:59; 27:1; Mark 14:55. 1 Pet 3:18 speaks of Jesus having been put to death in the flesh but made alive by the Spirit.

In a metaphorical context, ***thanatoō*** refers to putting to death sinful misdeeds, which, if undertaken by the Spirit, will lead to life (Rom 8:13). In an illustration of hyperbole, Rom 8:36 describes the extreme suffering of the apostle Paul in terms of "being killed all day long . . ." (see also 2 Cor 6:9). Rom 7:4 speaks of the believer "dying to the law" through the body of Christ.

▸ **21.** Die, Perish, Kill, Destroy >
DIE, DEAD, PUT TO DEATH, DEADLY

anaireō ἀναιρέω 337

anaireō occurs around twenty times meaning "kill" in the sense of "slay," "put to death" on all but one occasion, where it signifies "abolish" (Heb 10:9).

Matt 2:16 refers to slaying infants according to Herod's decree to have all male children below the age of two put to death as an attempt to get rid of the Christ child, whom he viewed as a potential claimant to the Jewish throne. Other references to the act of murder are found in Acts 5:36; 7:28; 12:2.

anaireō also conveys the meaning "to execute" in several contexts, such as the death of Stephen, the first Christian martyr (Acts 22:20); the thieves on the cross alongside Christ (Luke 22:32); and the death of Jesus Christ himself (Acts 2:23; 10:39; 13:28). Acts 26:10 also speaks of Christians persecuted for their faith by Saul of Tarsus, who voted for their execution.

anaireō is also found in contexts where the intent to kill is expressed, as is the case with ***apokteinō*** (above). Examples of this usage are found in relation to the plot to kill Paul (Acts 9:23, 29; 23:15, 21, 27; 25:3); and also Jesus (Luke 22:2). Acts 5:33 refers to the intention to have Peter and other apostles killed. Acts 16:27 mentions the attempted or threatened suicide of the Philippian jailer.

sphazō σφάζω 4969

Another synonym for the preceding terms, ***sphazō*** also means "kill," "slay," where a violent death is in view. This verb is found ten times.

sphazō, with the sense of "murder," is found in 1 John 3:12 (twice) in regard to Cain killing his brother Abel. In Rev 6:4, in relation to the universal judgment of God against wickedness, ***sphazō*** indicates slaughter with the sword.

The sense of "put to death" or "execute" is also evident in the usage of ***sphazō***. It is used in Rev 5:6, 9, 12; 13:8 to refer to Christ as the Lamb of God; and in Rev 6:9; 18:24 to refer to Christian martyrs.

sphazō is also found in a metaphorical context in Rev 13:3, indicating the "fatal wounding" of the sea beast. As the satanic counterpart to the Son of God in this "unholy trinity" in Rev 12 and 13, the sea beast mimics the resurrection of Christ from the dead in his recovery from this fatal assault.

sphagē σφαγή 4967

sphagē is a noun occurring three times with reference to "slaughter" in relation to Jesus Christ's crucifixion (Acts 8:32), and the persecuted saints (Rom 8:36). See also Jas 5:5.

phonos φόνος 5408

This term occurs ten times with predominant literal references to "murder" (Matt 15:19; Mark 7:21; Luke 23:19; Acts 9:1; Rom 1:29; Rev 9:21).

kopē κοπή 2871

kopē is a rare noun found only in Heb 7:1 with reference to the "slaughter" of battle.

LINEN

othonion ὀθόνιον 3608

othonion refers exclusively to the pieces of linen cloth, or "linen strips," used to wrap the bodies of the deceased prior to burial. In the NT, this term is found on five occasions, referring only to the funerary garments of Jesus (Luke 24:12; John 19:40; 20:5ff.).

SEE ALSO

▸ **35.** Clothing, Adornment, Textiles > LINEN, FLAX
sindōn, byssos, linon, byssinos

MIXTURE

migma μίγμα 3395

migma occurs only in John 19:39 with reference to a blend of spices — a "mixture of myrrh and aloes" — brought by Nicodemus to prepare Jesus' body for burial after his crucifixion.

SEE ALSO

▸ **79.** Throw, Send, Drive, Mix, Remove > MIX, MINGLE
synkerannymi, mignymi

MORTAL

thnētos θνητός 2349

thnētos is an adjective that is translated "mortal" in the sense of "liable to death and decay." It occurs six times and refers exclusively to our mortal bodies (Rom 6:12; 8:11; 1 Cor 15:53, 54; 2 Cor 4:11; 5:4). All texts except Rom 6:12 promise that our mortality will be exchanged for immortality in the light of the finished redemptive work of Christ and his resurrection from the dead.

NOISE, UPROAR

rhoizēdon ῥοιζηδόν 4500

rhoizēdon is a rare noun found only in 2 Pet 3:10, referring to the "loud noise" associated with cosmic dissolution at the end of time.

SEE ALSO

▸ **27.** Community, Partnership, Unity, Discord > TROUBLE, UPROAR, RIOT
thorybos, thorybeō, stasis, syncheō

PERISH

apollymi ἀπόλλυμι 622

apollymi has the primary meanings "perish," "destroy," or "lose" in the majority of the ninety or so contexts in which it is found. The meaning "destroy" for ***apollymi*** is causative in force with the literal sense of "to cause to perish."

apollymi refers to the body "perishing" (Matt 5:29, 30); and to people in general (Matt 8:25; 26:52; Mark 4:38; Luke 13:5; Acts 5:37; Rom 2:12; 1 Cor 1:18; 2 Cor 2:15). In particular, the godless are said to perish in 2 Cor 4:3; 2 Thess 2:10; Jude 11, as are the people of God in 1 Cor 15:18. This fate is predicated of individuals in Luke 11:51; 13:33; 15:17. In several contexts, there are declarations that people are to be spared from spiritual death — they will not perish by virtue of their faith and trust in God and his son (John 3:15, 16; 10:28; 11:50). In 2 Pet 3:9, the writer reveals God's desire that none should perish but that all should come to repentance.

apollymi is also used impersonally to refer to those things that "perish" or "will perish," in the sense of "being ruined" — including wineskins (Matt 9:17; Mark 2:22; Luke 5:37); food (John 6:27); gold (1 Pet 1:17); the beauty of flowers (Jas 1:11); and heaven and earth (Heb 1:11; 2 Pet 3:6).

▸ **21.** Die, Perish, Kill, Destroy > DESTROY, DESTROYER, DESTRUCTION

▸ **72.** Need, Gain, Loss, Advantage, Seek, Find > LOSE, LOSS, LOST

aphanizō ἀφανίζω 853

aphanizō is a rare verb found in only five places. It is translated variously as "destroy," "disfigure," "vanish" and once, in Acts 13:41, as "perish." The underlying sense of the term is "to bring about a state of decay," both literal and metaphorical, resulting in either disappearance or destruction.

▸ **21.** Die, Perish, Kill, Destroy > CORRUPT, CORRUPTION

synapollymi συναπόλλυμι 4881

synapollymi is found only in Heb 11:31 and is used negatively, referring to sparing Rahab the harlot's life, for she "did not perish" along with the other citizens of Jericho on account of her faith and trust in Yahweh.

ROLL

apokyliō ἀποκυλίω 617

This term refers exclusively to "rolling away (or back)" the stone across the entrance of the tomb where Christ's body was placed. ***apokyliō*** is found only in Matt 28:2; Mark 16:3, 4; Luke 24:2.

proskyliō προσκυλίω 4351

proskyliō is a verb related to ***apokyliō*** (above) meaning "roll towards." It is found only twice, with reference to "rolling" the stone across the entrance to the tomb containing the body of Christ (Matt 27:60; Mark 15:46).

SEE ALSO

▸ **82.** Change, Exchange, Transform > ROLL UP
helissō

SHED

haimatekchysia αἱματεκχυσία 130

haimatekchysia is a noun found only in Heb 9:22, referring to "the shedding" of blood, without which (in the ritual sense) there is no remission of sins.

▸ **38.** Covenant, Law, Rites, Roles > BLOOD

SEE ALSO

▸ **80.** Related to Liquids > SHED, SPILL
ekcheō

SKULL

kranion κρανίον 2898

kranion is the dynamic equivalent of the Aramaic term "Golgotha," referring to the hill near Jerusalem designated as the site of Christ's crucifixion, translated "the place of the skull" (Matt 27:33; Mark 15:22; Luke 23:33; John 19:17).

SPECTACLE

theōria θεωρία 2335

theōria is found only in Luke 23:48, denoting the "spectacle" of Christ on the cross, as seen by the assembled Jerusalem crowd, who watched him die.

SEE ALSO

▸ **45.** Faith, Belief, Trust, Promise > SIGHT
eidos

▸ **64.** Reveal, Explain, Hiddenness, Secrecy > VISION
horama, horasis, optasia

SPICE, PERFUME

arōma ἄρωμα 759

arōma is a noun found four times, meaning "spice," "perfume," used in the preparation of a funeral blend for "anointing" corpses in connection with the burial ritual. In the NT, this usage focuses exclusively on the body of Christ. The Gospels refer to the group of women who had prepared this perfumed blend of spices, intending to anoint the body of Christ recently laid in the tomb. This action was never performed, since Christ had by then risen from the grave (Mark 16:5; Luke 23:56; 24:1; John 19:40).

STONE

lithazō λιθάζω 3034

This verb occurs eight times, meaning "to stone," "pelt with stones" — either to wound or to kill. John 10:31ff.; 11:8 record the unsuccessful attempt to have Jesus stoned. See also Acts 5:26; 4:19; 2 Cor 11:25; Heb 11:37.

lithoboleō λιθοβολέω 3036

lithoboleō is a verb synonymous with ***lithazō*** (above) meaning "to kill by stoning" in Matt 21:35; Luke 13:34; John 8:5; Acts 7:58ff.; Heb 12:20. See also Mark 12:4.

SEE ALSO

▸ **10.** Earth, Dust, Rocks, Minerals, Metals, Stones > STONE
lithos, lithinos, psēphos, petrōdēs

SWIFT

oxys ὀξύς 3691

oxys is an adjective with the primary meaning "sharp." However, in Rom 3:15 it means "swift," describing how quickly the wicked move to shed blood.

▸ **88.** Qualities, Characteristics > SHARP

tachinos ταχινός 5031

tachinos is an adjective that refers to the "swift" destruction that will come upon false teachers.

SEE ALSO

- ▸ **60.** Virtues > SWIFT (TO LISTEN)
  tachys

THROW TO THE GROUND

edaphizō ἐδαφίζω 1474

edaphizō is a rare verb found only in Luke 19:44, meaning "throw to the ground" in the context of the threatened destruction of Jerusalem.

SEE ALSO

- ▸ **9.** Land, Geography, Topography > GROUND
  edaphos, chamai
- ▸ **83.** Set, Put, Place, Prepare, Establish > ESTABLISH, FIX, GROUND, STRENGTHEN
  themelioō

TREAD

pateō πατέω 3961

pateō is a verb meaning "tread," "tread down" in all five occurrences of the term. Luke 10:19 speaks of treading on serpents. Jerusalem is said to be trodden down by the Gentiles in Luke 21:24; Rev 11:2. The treading of the winepress in Rev 14:20; 19:15 indicates divine judgment.

SEE ALSO

- ▸ **28.** Agriculture, Viticulture, Animal Husbandry > TREAD
  aloaō

WRAP

entylissō ἐντυλίσσω 1794

entylissō is a rare verb meaning to "wrap up," "roll together." Matt 27:59; Luke 23:53 refer to "wrapping up" Jesus' body in a shroud. See also John 20:7.

systellō συστέλλω 4958

systellō is a rare verb referring to "wrapping up" a body in preparation for burial (Acts 5:6).

eneileō ἐνειλέω 1750

eneileō is a rare synonym for ***entylissō*** (above) referring to "wrapping up" the body of Jesus for burial in Mark 15:46.

SEE ALSO

- ▸ **35.** Clothing, Adornment, Textiles > WRAP
  sparganoō

22. Life, Renewal, Immortality

AWAKEN, WAKE UP

exypnizō ἐξυπνίζω 1852

exypnizō is a rare verb found only in John 11:11 with reference, in a metaphorical sense, to Christ "awakening" Lazarus "from his sleep" — bringing him back to life.

SEE ALSO

- ▸ **20.** Illness, Disease, Health, Healing > SLEEP, ASLEEP, FALL ASLEEP
katheudō, koimaō, aphypnoō, exypnos, hypnos

BE BORN AGAIN

anagennaō ἀναγεννάω 313

anagennaō is a rare verb found three times with the meaning "to be born again," referring to one's spiritual awakening to the word of God through his Spirit (1 Pet 1:3, 23).

SEE ALSO

- ▸ **15.** Gender, Reproduction, Youth, Aging > BEGET, GIVE BIRTH, BE BORN
gennaō, genesis, gennētos, artigennētos, apokyeō, ektrōma, tiktō, prōtotokos

IMMORTAL, IMMORTALITY, IMPERISHABLE

athanasia ἀθανασία 110

athanasia is one of the several specific NT Greek terms for immortality. It occurs three times. 1 Cor 15:53, 54 speak of the ultimate "reclothing" of the perishable human nature with an immortal, undying nature. 1 Tim 6:16 affirms that God alone possesses immortality as one of his innate perfections.

aphtharsia ἀφθαρσία 861

aphtharsia occurs seven times, and in all but one of these contexts is translated "immortality," "imperishable," emphasizing both never-ending life and ultimate purity in that eternal state.

Rom 2:7 indicates that those who with patient, godly living strive for immortality will be granted eternal life. 1 Cor 15:42, 50ff. affirm that in the process of becoming immortal, the believer will discard the old earthly nature and assume a nature that will not only be eternally enduring (i.e., ***athanasia***, see above), but also incorruptible or imperishable (i.e., ***aphtharsia***). Eph 6:24 contains the phrase "loving . . . imperishably," which is usually translated "undying love" with reference to the believer's devotion to Christ. 2 Tim 1:10 declares that immortality is an inevitable consequence of the light of the gospel.

▸ **22.** Life, Renewal, Immortality > INCORRUPTIBLE

aphthartos ἄφθαρτος 862

aphthartos is the adjectival form derived from ***aphtharsia*** (above) and is found in six contexts. The term is translated "incorruptible" and "immortal." Rom 1:23; 1 Tim 1:17 refer to God as incorruptible. 1 Cor 9:25 refers to the "imperishable" wreath as the "prize" for the believer who perseveres to the end (see also 1 Pet 1:4). 1 Cor 15:52 speaks of the dead in Christ being raised incorruptible. 1 Pet 1:23 affirms that believers have been born of the "imperishable seed" of the word of God. 1 Pet 3:4 contains a metaphorical reference to the "imperishable jewel" of a quiet spirit.

▸ **22.** Life, Renewal, Immortality > INCORRUPTIBLE

SEE ALSO

- ▸ **3.** Periods of Time, Duration, Frequency, Speed > IMMORTAL, IMMORTALITY
eis tōn aiōna

INCORRUPTIBLE

aphtharsia ἀφθαρσία 861

aphtharsia is a term denoting that which is "incorruptible" or "immortal" throughout most of the eight occurrences of the term.

The designation "incorruptible" is equated with the "immortal" state of the renewed body in glory after the resurrection (Rom 2:7; 1 Cor 15:42, 50ff.). A general reference to immortality is found in 2 Tim 1:10, 11.

▸ **22.** Life, Renewal, Immortality > IMMORTAL, IMMORTALITY, IMPERISHABLE

aphthartos ἄφθαρτος 862

aphthartos is an adjective meaning "incorruptible," "immortal" in seven places. Rom 1:23; 1 Tim 1:17 describe God as "incorruptible." The "incorruptible," "immortal" condition of the resurrected believer is noted in 1 Cor 9:25; 1 Pet 1:23. The "incorruptible" or "imperishable" inheritance of eternal life is indicated in 1 Pet 1:4; 1 Cor 9:25. See also 1 Pet 3:4.

▸ **22.** Life, Renewal, Immortality > IMMORTAL, IMMORTALITY, IMPERISHABLE

SEE ALSO

- ▸ **21.** Die, Perish, Kill, Destroy > CORRUPT, CORRUPTION
diaphtheirō, phthora, diaphthora, phthartos, aphanizō
- ▸ **57.** Evil, Wickedness, Sin > CORRUPT
phtheirō, kataphtheirō

LIFE, LIVE, LIVING

psychē ψυχή 5590

psychē is found in about one hundred contexts with the primary sense of "life," "soul." With regard to the meaning "life," ***psychē*** indicates the animating principle (or breath) of life that God gives to both humans and animals.

When referring to human beings, ***psychē*** refers to "life" in a general sense (Matt 2:20; 6:25; Mark 3:4; Luke 12:22, 23; John 12:25; Acts 20:24; Rom 16:4). Phil 2:30 speaks of risking one's life for the sake of Christ. Peter's promise to lay down his life for Jesus is recorded in John 13:37. In John 15:13, Jesus refers to the greatest act of love, that of laying down one's life for one's friend.

In reference to Christ, ***psychē*** also refers to his life, given as a ransom for many (Matt 20:28; Mark 10:45). In John 10:11ff.; 1 John 3:16, Christ is said to lay down his life for his "sheep" (i.e., his people).

▸ **19.** Mind, Spirit, Emotions, Feelings, Desires > SOUL

zōē ζωή 2222

zōē is another of the crucial NT terms for "life." ***zōē*** refers to life that is of the highest quality, having reached the fullest potential in the people of God through the finished redemptive work of Christ. In a large number of cases, it refers to "eternal life" — not only to heavenly reality, but also to that quality of life initiated by the Spirit of God at conversion. ***zōē*** occurs around 130 times.

Concerning human life, ***zōē*** refers first of all to life of the highest quality, as God had intended it (Matt 7:14; Luke 12:15; John 6:33; Acts 2:28; 11:18; Rom 6:4; 2 Cor 2:16; 1 Pet 3:7). Rev 2:7; 22:2, 14 refer to the "tree of life."

In relation to life as embodied in the person of Christ, ***zōē*** refers to several aspects of this phenomenon. Jesus is the "bread of life" (John 6:48); the "resurrection and the life" (John 11:25); and "the way, the truth and the life" (John 14:6).

"Eternal life" is implied in Matt 18:8ff.; Mark 9:43; and made explicit in John 17:3; Acts 13:46. Enquiries about eternal life are made in Matt 19:16; Mark 10:17; Luke 10:25; 18:18; as are promises of such in Matt 19:29; Mark 10:30; Luke 18:30; John 3:15, 16; Rom 6:22; 1 Tim 1:16; Titus 1:2; Jas 1:12; 1 John 2:25. Certainty of the resurrection to life is indicated in John 5:29. Jesus is noted as the source of eternal life in John 10:28. The "book of life" is referred to in Phil 4:3; Rev 3:5; 13:8; 17:8; 20:12, 15; 21:27. Eternal life is granted by God in Rom 2:7; 6:23; 1 John 5:11, 20, and brought about by the work of Christ (Rom 5:17ff.; 8:2, 6; Gal 6:8; 2 Tim 1:10). The water of (eternal) life is indicated in Rev 21:6; 22:1, 17.

bios βίος 979

bios is a noun meaning "life," "living" in eight contexts.

Referring to "living" in the sense of the sum total of one's possessions, ***bios*** is found in Mark 12:44; Luke 21:4 with respect to the generosity of the impoverished widow who gave all she had to the temple treasury. Similarly, the term is also found in regard to the inherited wealth of the "prodigal son" (Luke 15:12, 30).

"Life" in general is indicated by the term ***bios*** in Luke 8:14, with reference to the "pleasures of life." In 1 John 2:16 ***bios*** designates the "pride of life." Leading a quiet life is indicated in 1 Tim 2:2; 2 Tim 2:4.

▸ **30.** Money, Business, Wealth, Poverty > GOODS, PROPERTY, POSSESSIONS

zaō ζάω 2198

zaō is the verb from which ***zōē*** (above) is derived and likewise sometimes means "live," "be alive" in a normal sense. Usually, however, ***zaō*** describes living a life that fulfills the potential God has intended for those who live for him, both here on earth and for eternity. This term is predicated of both God and human beings. The participial form is also used in a nominal or adjectival sense, "living." ***zaō*** occurs around 130 times.

The meaning "to live" refers to people in a variety of contexts. Matt 4:4; Luke 4:4 declare that human beings shall live by the word of God alone. A number of people are miraculously "restored to life" through the power of Christ — for example, Jairus' daughter (Matt 9:18; Mark 5:23); and the son of a royal official (John 4:50ff.). To live with the highest quality of life, implying eternal life, is indicated in Luke 10:28; Rom 1:17. Other texts anticipate the experience of eternal life (John 6:58; 11:25; Rom 8:3; Rev 20:4).

With respect to this life, ***zaō*** refers to living in direct dependence on God and his power (Acts 17:28; 2 Cor 13:14). Gal 5:25 refers to living by the Spirit, and Heb 10:38 to living by faith. ***zaō*** refers to living for the glory of God (Rom 6:10; 14:8; Gal 2:19); and for Christ's glory (2 Cor 5:15; Gal 2:20; Phil 1:21). The ideal of living by the righteousness of the law as a means to life is put forward in Rom 10:5; Gal 3:11.

zaō also indicates the process of living with respect to Jesus Christ, who is said to live in dependence on God in John 6:57. Gal 2:20 declares that Christ lives in us. And Heb 7:25 affirms that Christ lives in the presence of his Father to make intercession for us.

Similarly, this term is also applied to God. Rom 14:11 records the divine affirmation, ". . . as I live." In Rev 4:9; 10:6; 15:7, God is portrayed as living forever on his throne.

In a nominal sense, ***zaō*** refers to people in general as "the living," usually in contrast with "the dead" (Matt 22:32; Mark 12:27; Luke 20:38; Acts 10:42; Rom 14:9; 2 Tim 4:1; 1 Pet 4:5).

As an adjective, ***zaō*** indicates "the living God" — for example in Matt 16:16, in the context of Peter's confession. See also Matt 26:63; Acts 14:15; Rom 9:26; 2 Cor 3:3; 6:16; 1 Thess 1:9; 1 Tim 3:15; Heb 3:12; 10:13; Rev 7:2. Human beings are described likewise as "living beings" in 1 Cor 15:45. The adjectival form of ***zaō*** is also used in relation to the person of Christ, describing him, for instance, as "living water" (John 4:10, 11; 7:38; Rev 7:17) and "living bread" (John 6:51).

zōogoneō ζῳογονέω 2225

zōogoneō occurs only twice, meaning "to preserve life" in both instances. Luke 17:33 refers to those who by "losing" their life (i.e., in self-denial) will in fact "preserve" it for eternity. Acts 7:19 refers to the cruel edict of the Egyptian Pharaoh at the time of Israel's enslavement, who passed an edict requiring all Israelite parents to expose their infant male children, leaving them for dead (lit., that they might not be kept alive).

▸ **22.** Life, Renewal, Immortality > PRESERVE

syzaō συζάω 4800

syzaō means "to live (together) with" and occurs three times. Rom 6:8; 2 Tim 2:11 promise that believers will one day live with Christ in glory. 2 Cor 7:3 refers to the spirit of Christian community and fellowship whereby believers are said to live together.

makrochronios μακροχρόνιος 3118

makrochronios is adjectival in form but has the verbal sense of "live long." It is found only in Eph 6:3, where it refers to the promise of living long on the earth, made to those who honor their parents.

anazaō ἀναζάω 326

anazaō occurs five times and is translated on each occasion "to come alive," "come to life again," or "revive," in both a literal as well as a metaphorical sense.

With literal reference to the resurrection, Rom 14:9 declares that Christ came back to life in order to be Lord of both the dead and the living. Rev 20:5 refers to the rest of the dead (i.e., the wicked) being brought back to life after the completion of Christ's thousand-year reign.

In metaphorical contexts, ***anazaō*** refers first of all to the prodigal son returning to his father, viewed by the latter as a return to life "from the dead," so to speak (Luke 15:24, 32). In Rom 7:9, Paul declares that when the law was given, sin "came back to life" within him and he "died" (i.e., became a slave to sin).

SEE ALSO

- **34.** Craftsmanship, Artisanship, Furniture, Implements > LIFELESS
  apsychos
- **58.** Vices > LUXURY
  tryphaō
- **61.** Integrity, Innocence, Piety > LIVE
  politeuomai, eirēneuō

PRESERVE

zōogoneō ζῳογονέω 2225

zōogoneō is a verb found only in two places, meaning "preserve," "(keep) alive." Luke 17:33 contains the famous proverbial truth uttered by Christ: ". . . whoever loses his life will preserve it."

- **22.** Life, Renewal, Immortality > LIFE, LIVE, LIVING

SEE ALSO

- **62.** Care For, Protect, Guard, Watch > PRESERVE
  syntēreō

QUICKEN, MAKE ALIVE

zōopoieō ζῳοποιέω 2227

zōopoieō is a verb that means "to quicken" in the sense of "give life," "make alive" — an action that is largely wrought by the power of God. ***zōopoieō*** is found in twelve contexts.

The senses of "give life," "be made alive," are found almost exclusively in the context of divine power bringing the dead back to life. John 5:21; Rom 4:17; 1 Cor 15:22; 1 Tim 6:13 refer to God "quickening." "Quickening" is a consequence of the movement of God's Spirit in John 6:63; Rom 8:11; 2 Cor 3:6; 1 Pet 3:18.

zōopoieō is also used adjectivally in 1 Cor 15:45 to refer to Christ as the "last Adam, a life-giving spirit."

In a mundane reference, ***zōopoieō*** refers to seed "coming to life" in 1 Cor 15:36.

syzōopoieō συζωοποιέω 4806

syzōopoieō is a verb found only twice, with the sense of "quicken together with" or "make alive together with." In Eph 2:5; Col 2:13, God makes believers alive together with Christ.

RAISE

synegeirō συνεγείρω 4891

synegeirō is another verb related to ***egeirō***, meaning "to raise (up) with," "raise together with." It is found only three times, all with reference to the believer "being raised up together with" Christ from death to the heavenly realm (Eph 2:6; Col 2:12; 3:1).

SEE ALSO

- **87.** Movement Upward or Downward > ARISE, RISE UP, RAISE UP
  exegeirō

REGENERATION, RENEW, RENEWAL, RE-CREATION

palingenesia παλιγγενεσία 3824

palingenesia refers to "regeneration" or "renewal." It is a rare term, occurring only twice in the NT, but with very significant implications. ***palingenesia*** occurs only in Matt 19:28 with reference to God's ultimate "renewal" of the cosmos, and in Titus 3:5 in regard to the regeneration effected by the Holy Spirit. The underlying sense of ***palingenesia*** is that of "renewal," "re-creation" — a radical change of heart and mind resulting in renewed devotion to God and Christ.

anakainoō ἀνακαινόω 341

anakainoō is found only twice. 2 Cor 4:16; Col 3:10 refer to the "renewing" of the believer through the Holy Spirit.

ananeoō ἀνανεόω 365

ananeoō is a verb found only in Eph 4:23, describing the "renewing" of the believer's mind.

anakainōsis ἀνακαίνωσις 342

anakainōsis is a noun derived from ***anakainoō*** (above) meaning "renewing," "renewal" in only two contexts. Rom 12:2 describes the "renewing" of the believer's mind. Titus 3:5 speaks of the "renewal" of the believer wrought by the Holy Spirit.

RESURRECTION

anastasis ἀνάστασις 386

anastasis is a noun meaning "resurrection" in most of its approximately forty occurrences.

General references to the "resurrection for the dead" include those in Matt 22:23ff.; Mark 12:18ff.; Luke 4:14; 20:27ff.; John 5:29; 11:24ff.; Acts 23:8; 24:15ff.; 2 Tim 2:18; Heb 6:2; 11:35.

Acts 1:6; 4:33; Rom 1:4; 6:5; Phil 3:10; 1 Pet 3:21 refer to the resurrection of Christ.

Several texts specifically allude to preaching the reality of the resurrection from the dead (Acts 4:2; 17:32; 23:6; 1 Cor 15:12ff.).

exanastasis ἐξανάστασις 1815

exanastasis is a rare variant of ***anastasis*** (above) found only in Phil 3:11, with reference to the "resurrection" from the dead.

egersis ἔγερσις 1454

egersis is another rare term found only in Matt 27:53, with reference to the resurrection of Christ.

23. Food, Drink, Cooking

ABSTINENCE

asitia ἀσιτία 776

asitia is a rare noun found only in Acts 27:21, referring to "abstinence" from food.

SEE ALSO

▸ **41.** Sacrifice, Offering, Worship, Praise > ABSTAIN, REFRAIN
apechomai

BARLEY

krithinos κρίθινος 2916

krithinos is a rare adjectival form referring to loaves "made of barley" in John 6:9, 13.

SEE ALSO

▸ **28.** Agriculture, Viticulture, Animal Husbandry > BARLEY
krithē

BREAD

artos ἄρτος 740

The noun ***artos***, meaning "bread," occurs about one hundred times. Literal references to "bread" as food include Matt 4:3ff.; 14:17ff.; 16:5ff.; Mark 3:20; 8:24ff.; Luke 4:3ff.; 9:13ff.; John 6:5ff.; 13:18; Acts 2:42ff.; 20:7ff.; 2 Cor 9:10.

The "bread of the presence," or ceremonial bread displayed in the temple, is described in Mark 2:6; Luke 6:4; Heb 9:2.

artos also refers to "manna," the staple food miraculously provided by Yahweh for his people during their sojourn in the wilderness (John 6:31).

"Bread" in a metaphorical sense is indicated in John 6:32ff., where Jesus claims to be the "bread of life," or God's provision from heaven to meet humankind's deepest spiritual need for reconciliation with God and intimate fellowship with him. In this passage Christ claims that he fulfills the spiritual significance of the manna, given by his Father to the Israelites in the wilderness.

Christ gives new significance to the bread of the Passover meal in the company of his disciples (1 Cor 10:16ff.; 11:23, 26ff.). This bread symbolizes his broken body that hung on the cross, metaphorically signifying his agony and suffering.

SEE ALSO

▸ **40.** Holy Days, Feasts, Festivals > UNLEAVENED BREAD
azymos

BREAK BREAD

klaō κλάω 2806

klaō is a verb found in fifteen places with the consistent meaning "to break bread" in two contexts. Christ uses the word in the Lord's Supper, symbolizing the suffering he would endure on the cross (Matt 26:26; Mark 14:22; Luke 22:19; 1 Cor 10:16; 11:24). The other use of the term is found in the context of eating a meal (Matt 14:19; 15:36; Mark 8:6, 19; Luke 24:30; Acts 2:46; 20:7, 11; 27:35).

kataklaō κατακλάω 2622

kataklaō is a rare variant of ***klaō*** (above) indicating the action of "breaking" loaves of bread in preparation for eating (Mark 6:41; Luke 9:16).

klasis κλάσις 2800

klasis is a rare noun denoting the "breaking of bread," or sharing a meal (Luke 24:35; Acts 2:42).

SEE ALSO

▸ **28.** Agriculture, Viticulture, Animal Husbandry > BREAK OFF, CUT, CUT OFF
ekklaō

▸ **58.** Vices > STEAL, BREAK IN, BURGLE
dioryssō

▸ **75.** Suffering, Distress, Sadness > BREAK
synthryptō

▸ **76.** Force, Harm, Oppress > BREAK
katagnymi

▸ **78.** Act Upon, Push, Pull, Break, Cut > BREAK
lyō, syntribō, diarrēgnymi, synthlaō

CUP

potērion ποτήριον 4221

The noun ***potērion*** denotes a "cup" (i.e., a drinking vessel) throughout its nearly thirty occurrences.

Literal references to "cups" in general contexts include Matt 10:42; 23:25ff.; Mark 7:4; 9:41; Luke 11:39. The "Passover cup" drunk by Jesus and his disciples on the evening prior to his death is indicated in Mark 14:23; Luke 22:17, 20.

The remaining usage of ***potērion*** is metaphorical. The "cup" symbolizing the anticipation of Christ's suffering on the cross denotes the "judgment of God" in Matt 20:22ff.; 26:39ff.; Mark 10:38ff.; 14:36; Luke 22:42; John 18:11. Specific mention of the "cup" of God's anger is found in Rev 14:10; 16:19; 18:6. Babylon's "cup of abominations" is noted in Rev 17:4. In a positive sense, the "cup of blessing" is mentioned in 1 Cor 10:16, 21; 11:25ff., denoting the wine drunk at the Lord's Supper, symbolizing the blood Christ shed for the forgiveness of sins.

DISH

tryblion τρύβλιον 5165

tryblion is a noun denoting a household "dish," found only in Matt 26:23; Mark 14:20.

DRINK, DRINKING, GIVE DRINK, BE DRUNK

poma πόμα 4188

poma is a rare noun denoting "drink" in a general sense in Heb 9:10. 1 Cor 10:4 refers to the "supernatural drink" provided by God for his people in the wilderness.

posis πόσις 4213

posis is a noun found in three contexts denoting "drink" in a general sense in Col 2:16; Rom 14:17. John 6:55 refers to Christ's blood as "drink," symbolizing spiritual nourishment for the believer alongside his flesh, designated as "food."

sikera σίκερα 4608

sikera is a rare noun denoting "strong drink," found only in Luke 1:15.

pinō πίνω 4095

pinō is a verb found in approximately seventy places meaning "to drink," used both literally and figuratively.

Literal references to "drinking" include Matt 6:25; 11:18ff.; 24:38; 27:34; Mark 2:16; 15:23; Luke 1:15; 5:30ff.; 12:19; John 4:7ff.; Acts 9:9; 23:12; 1 Cor 11:22. "Drinking" the cup of the Lord's Supper is indicated in 1 Cor 10:21; 11:25ff.

A significant metaphorical usage of ***pinō*** is found in Matt 20:22ff.; 26:42; Mark 10:38ff., with reference to Christ "drinking the cup" that will be given to him. This refers to his approaching arrest, trial, and crucifixion. Luke 22:30; John 18:11 refer to eating and drinking in the heavenly kingdom of Christ as a metaphor for enjoying his fellowship.

Christ asks his disciples "to drink" the cup of the Passover meal with him, signifying his blood of the covenant which is soon to be poured out for the forgiveness of the sins of many people (Matt 26:27ff.; Mark 14:23ff.). See also John 6:53ff.

Associated with Christ's request for drinking water from the Samaritan woman is his own "offer" to the woman. He affirms that if she "drinks" the water he gives to her she will never thirst again. This is the "water of life," a symbol for everlasting peace with God gained through Christ. (John 4:14). See also John 7:37. In the context of judgment, Rev 14:10 declares that the wicked will be forced "to drink" the wine of God's wrath. See also Rev 16:6; 18:3. 1 Cor 10:4 refers to Israel "drinking" the water provided by Yahweh in the wilderness.

methyō μεθύω 3184

methyō is a verb found seven times with the primary meaning "to be drunk" as a consequence of taking excessive amounts of wine (Matt 24:49; John 2:10; Acts 2:15; 1 Cor 11:21; 1 Thess 5:7). Metaphorical usage of the term is found in Rev 17:2 in relation to the kings of the earth having become "drunk" on the immorality of the "Babylonian whore," symbolizing the kingdom of Babylon. The same symbolic whorish figure is said to "be drunk" with the blood of the martyrs.

potizō ποτίζω 4222

potizō is a verb found fifteen times, meaning "provide water," "give to drink" throughout.

The act of "giving a drink of water" to someone is indicated in Matt 10:42; 25:35ff.; 27:48; Mark 9:41; 15:36; Rom 12:20. The act of "watering" animals is noted in Luke 13:15. The "giving of milk to drink" is indicated in 1 Cor 3:2.

The remaining use of ***potizō*** is metaphorical. The act of "watering" in 1 Cor 3:6ff. refers to the cultivation and enrichment of one's ministry. Believers are said to "have been made to drink" of the one Spirit, signifying their spiritual union with Christ on the occasion of their baptism. Rev 14:8 refers to Babylon "making the nations drink the wine of her adulteries."

hydropoteō ὑδροποτέω 5202

hydropoteō is a rare verb found only in 1 Tim 5:23, referring to "drinking water."

▸ **23.** Food, Drink, Cooking > WATER

EAT, EATING

esthiō ἐσθίω 2068

esthiō is a verb found about sixty times, meaning "to eat" and used only in the present tense form. ***esthiō*** is to be compared with ***phagō*** (below).

Mundane references to people "eating" include Matt 9:11; 12:1; Mark 1:6; 7:2ff.; Luke 5:30ff.; 7:33ff.; 17:27ff.; Rom 14:2ff.; 1 Cor 9:7, 13; 11:22, 34; 2 Thess 3:10ff. 1 Cor 8:7, 10 refer to "eating" food offered to idols, and in 1 Cor 10:25ff. there is a reference to consuming food that may possibly have been so presented.

"Eating" the various items of the Lord's Supper (i.e., the bread and the wine), in remembrance of Christ's death and resurrection, is indicated in 1 Cor 11:26ff.

In Heb 10:27 the use of ***esthiō*** is metaphorical, referring to the fury of God's wrath that will "consume" his enemies.

phagō φάγω 5315

phagō is an alternate form of ***esthiō*** (above) used in tenses other than the present (***esthiō*** is used exclusively in the present). ***phagō*** is found nearly one hundred times and is translated "eat" throughout.

Mundane references to "eating" food include Matt 6:25; 15:32ff.; Mark 6:31ff.; 8:1ff.; Luke 4:2; 7:26; John 4:31ff.; 6:23ff.; Acts 10:13ff.; Rom 14:21ff.; 1 Cor 8:8, 13; 15:32; 2 Thess 3:8. Eating food sacrificed to idols is noted in Rev 2:14, 20. Jesus eats the Passover meal with his disciples in Matt 26:17, 26; Mark 14:12ff.; Luke 22:8ff.; John 18:28. Other references to eating the Lord's Supper include 1 Cor 11:20ff. The manna miraculously provided by God for his people in the wilderness, described as "bread from heaven," is noted in John 6:31, 49. See also 1 Cor 10:13. In John 6, however, there is a distinctive play on words employed by Christ, who compares and contrasts the literal "heavenly bread" (i.e., manna) with the true "spiritual bread from heaven," or his own person and teaching that is eternally satisfying to those who partake of it (John 6:49ff.).

phagō is used metaphorically in Jas 5:3, referring to the spiritually harmful effect of wealth on those who idolize it as something that will "eat" their flesh. Elsewhere, the term refers to "eating" the fruit of the tree of life in the heavenly Jerusalem, symbolically designating the purification of its inhabitants (Rev 2:7). See also Rev 2:17. Rev 10:10 refers to the apostle John "eating" the scroll of judgment against humankind, handed to him by the angel in his vision. The destruction of the Babylonian "whore" in Rev 17:16 is recorded in terms of her flesh being "devoured." See also Rev 19:18.

trōgō τρώγω 5176

trōgō is a rare synonym of ***esthiō*** (above) found six times and meaning "eat." Most of these occurrences are metaphorical, referring in John 6:54ff. to "eating" the flesh of Christ — an allusion to the spiritual significance of the Passover bread (or meal) when consumed in an attitude of genuine faith. John 6:58 refers to "eating" the Passover bread. Matt 24:38 speaks of "eating" in a mundane, literal sense.

geuomai γεύομαι 1089

geuomai is a verb found in twenty places and meaning "taste." The mundane sense of "eating" food is indicated only in Acts 23:14.

▸ **23.** Food, Drink, Cooking > TASTE

bibrōskō βιβρώσκω 977

bibrōskō is a rare verb found only in John 6:13, referring to the physical act of eating.

katesthiō κατεσθίω 2719

katesthiō is a synonym for ***phagō*** and ***esthiō*** (above) with the primary meanings "devour," "eat" in both literal and metaphorical contexts — though the latter usage predominates. The literal meaning "devour" is found in the contexts of birds consuming seed in Matt 13:4; Mark 4:4; Luke 8:5.

The remaining use of ***katesthiō*** is metaphorical. The "devouring" (i.e., "buying up") of widows' houses by callous religious leaders is indicated in Matt 23:14; Mark 12:40; Luke 20:47. The sense of "devour," denoting the act of "destroying," is used in relation to the enemies of God and his people (Rev 11:5; 12:4; 20:9). Zeal for the temple is said to "consume" Christ in John 2:17. The apostle John's symbolic "eating" of a scroll is recorded in Rev 10:9. See also 2 Cor 11:20; Gal 5:15.

korennymi κορέννυμι 2880

korennymi is a rare verb indicating "eating one's fill," "sating oneself," found only in Acts 27:38; 1 Cor 4:8.

synesthiō συνεσθίω 4906

synesthiō is a variant form of ***esthiō*** (above) meaning "to eat with someone" in all five occurrences of the term (Luke 15:2; Acts 10:41; 11:3; 1 Cor 5:11; Gal 2:12).

SEE ALSO

▸ **41.** Sacrifice, Offering, Worship, Praise > EATING
brōsis

FASTING

nēstis νῆστις 3523

nēstis is a rare noun denoting "fasting" in the sense of "refraining from eating" and is translated "hungry" in Matt 15:32; Mark 8:3.

SEE ALSO

▸ **42.** Prayer, Intercession, Fasting > FAST, FASTING
nēsteia, nēsteuō

FEED, NOURISH

trephō τρέφω 5142

trephō is a verb meaning "feed," "nourish" throughout its eight occurrences. References to God "feeding" his creatures are found in Matt 6:26; Luke 12:24. Rev 12:6, 14 refer to the divine "nourishing" of the symbolic woman in the wilderness. Matt 25:37 mentions "feeding" people. See Jas 5:5 for another symbolic usage.

▸ **25.** Family, Marriage, Adoption, Inheritance > BRING UP, RAISE, NURTURE

psōmizō ψωμίζω 5595

psōmizō is a rare verb, expressing the sense of "feeding" someone in Rom 12:20.

SEE ALSO

▸ **28.** Agriculture, Viticulture, Animal Husbandry > FEED, TEND
boskō, poimainō

FLOUR

semidalis σεμίδαλις 4585

semidalis is a rare noun found only once, denoting "fine flour" in Rev 18:13.

aleuron ἄλευρον 224

aleuron is a rare term also denoting "flour," found only in Matt 13:33; Luke 13:21.

FOOD

trophē τροφή 5160

trophē is a general term for "food," found in sixteen places (e.g., Matt 3:4; 6:25; Luke 12:23; John 4:8; Acts 2:46; 27:33ff.; Heb 5:12ff.; Jas 2:15).

diatrophē διατροφή 1305

diatrophē is a rare variant of ***trophē*** (above) found only in 1 Tim 6:8, also denoting "food" in a general sense.

brōsis βρῶσις 1035

brōsis is a noun found eleven times, denoting "food" in both a literal and metaphorical sense in most of these occurrences.

"Food" in a general sense is indicated in John 6:27a; Rom 14:17; 2 Cor 9:10; Col 2:16.

brōsis also denotes "food" in the metaphorical sense of "spiritual nourishment," intimately associated with the person of Christ and his teaching in John 6:27b. In particular, Christ declares that his flesh is "food" in John 6:55, indicating that genuine spiritual life is dependent on "nourishing" oneself on his body — on believing in and committing oneself wholly to Christ.

▸ **41.** Sacrifice, Offering, Worship, Praise > EATING

brōma βρῶμα 1033

brōma is a noun found seventeen times, denoting "food" in both a literal and symbolic sense throughout.

General references to "food" include those in Matt 14:15; Mark 7:19; Rom 14:20; 1 Cor 6:13; 1 Tim 4:3; Heb 9:10. In particular, ***brōma*** denotes the food God supernaturally supplied to his people in the wilderness (1 Cor 10:3).

Elsewhere, the sense of "food" is metaphorical. Christ affirms in John 4:34 that his "food" is to do the will of his Father. In this context, "food" denotes the innermost desire of his being, his fundamental purpose in life. In 1 Cor 3:2, "solid food" signifies teaching from the word that is instrumental in maturing people in their faith.

HONEY

meli μέλι 3192

This term is rare, occurring only four times. ***meli*** signifies honey as food in Matt 3:4; Mark 1:6. In Rev 10:9, 10 it refers to the sweet honey taste of the angelic scroll given to John to eat, which afterwards turns sour in his stomach.

JAR

keramion κεράμιον 2765

keramion is rare in the NT, occurring only twice. In both instances the term indicates a jar or pitcher of water (Mark 14:13; Luke 12:10).

hydria ὑδρία 5201

hydria is likewise a rare form, found only three times in John 2:6, 7; 4:28 — all with reference to large stone water jars.

▸ **23.** Food, Drink, Cooking > WATER

MEASURE

choinix χοῖνιξ 5518

choinix occurs only in Rev 6:6, signifying a "measure of wheat." The term refers specifically to a dry measure of approximately one liter.

SEE ALSO

▸ **7.** Quantity, Amount, Number, Size, Measure > MEASURE, QUANTITY, STANDARD, CRITERION
metron, hyperperissōs, metreō

MILK

gala γάλα 1051

gala is found in only five contexts in the NT, meaning "milk" used in a metaphorical sense in all but one of these places.

In these four texts, 1 Cor 3:2; Heb 5:12, 13; 1 Pet 2:2, "milk" refers to elementary or basic spiritual truths. Only 1 Pet 2:2 uses the term in a positive sense, referring to the "spiritual milk" that will feed and nourish "infant believers." The other three uses constitute rebukes for believers who have become "stunted" in their growth, failing to move beyond the elementary teachings of the faith to greater maturity where they should be partaking of "solid food." Literal reference to milk is found in 1 Cor 9:7.

OVEN

klibanos κλίβανος 2823

klibanos is a rare noun, occurring only twice. Both references indicate an "oven" in the literal sense of an earthen vessel for baking bread (Matt 6:30; Luke 12:28).

PLATE, PLATTER

paropsis παροψίς 3953

paropsis is a term found only twice, in Matt 23:25, with reference to "plate" as a household utensil.

pinax πίναξ 4094

pinax refers to a "large platter" or "plate." It occurs only five times. Matt 14:8, 11; Mark 6:25, 28 refer to the platter on which was placed the severed head of John the Baptist. In Luke 11:39, ***pinax*** refers to a common "plate" or "dish."

SALT

halas ἅλας 217

halas is a noun found eight times with reference to "salt" in each case. ***halas*** emphasizes the preserving effect of salt in both a literal sense, in relation to food, as well as in a metaphorical sense, in relation to the wholesome influence of godly people in a sinful world (Matt 5:13; Mark 9:50; Luke 14:34; Col 4:6).

halizō ἁλίζω 233

halizō is the verb from which ***halas*** (above) is derived and is found only twice. In Matt 5:13 ***halizō*** is used passively to indicate the hypothetical process of salt "having its saltiness restored" (lit., "salt . . . being salted"), something that is in reality impossible. Mark 9:49 refers metaphorically to the terrible fate of the wicked who, as part of their torment, are depicted as being "salted" with fire.

analos ἄναλος 358

analos is an adjectival form derived from the noun ***halas*** (above). It is found only once, with a "negative prefix," and is translated literally as "unsalted" or "without salt," though in the context of Mark 9:50 it refers to salt "losing its saltiness."

SEE ALSO

- ▸ **11.** Meteorology, Water > SALT, SALT WATER
halykos

SIT

synanakeimai συνανάκειμαι 4873

synanakeimai is a verb found in nine places referring to being seated at a meal (Matt 9:10; 14:9; Mark 2:15; Luke 14:10, 15; John 12:2).

kataklinō κατακλίνω 2625

kataklinō is a verb found in only three places, meaning "sit down" (i.e., to eat) (Luke 9:14; 14:8; 24:30).

anapiptō ἀναπίπτω 377

The verb ***anapiptō*** is synonymous with the preceding entries. It is found in ten places and means "sit down" in the context of taking a meal (Matt 15:35; Mark 6:40; Luke 11:37; 14:10; 17:7; 22:14; John 6:10; 13:12).

SEE ALSO

- ▸ **85.** Movement, Position, State > SIT, SIT DOWN, SIT UP
kathēmai, synkathēmai, kathizō, synkathizō, anakathizō, parakathizō, anakeimai, katakeimai, anaklinō, kathezomai

SPARE

perisseuō περισσεύω 4052

perisseuō is a verb found in about forty contexts with the underlying meaning "to have an abundance of." In Luke 15:17, ***perisseuō*** expresses the idea of having enough (food) to spare.

- ▸ **7.** Quantity, Amount, Number, Size, Measure > ABOUND, INCREASE, EXCEED, OVERFLOW, ABUNDANCE
- ▸ **7.** Quantity, Amount, Number, Size, Measure > EXCEED, EXCEEDINGLY
- ▸ **7.** Quantity, Amount, Number, Size, Measure > INCREASE, GROW
- ▸ **85.** Movement, Position, State > REMAIN, STAY, ABIDE, DWELL

SEE ALSO

- ▸ **62.** Care For, Protect, Guard, Watch > SPARE
pheidomai

SWALLOW

katapinō καταπίνω 2666

katapinō is a verb found in seven contexts meaning "swallow," "drink," "devour" in predominantly metaphorical contexts.

The expression "swallow a camel" indicates the act of ignoring very obvious faults or flaws in one's behavior (Matt 23:24). Rev 12:16 speaks of the earth swallowing up a river. 1 Cor 15:54 refers to death being swallowed up in the victory of Christ over sin. Similarly, mortal life is swallowed up to eternal life in 2 Cor 5:4. The state of being swallowed up (or overwhelmed) by emotion is indicated in 2 Cor 2:7. Heb 11:29 speaks of being swallowed up by water, or drowned.

- ▸ **21.** Die, Perish, Kill, Destroy > DROWN

TASTE

geuomai γεύομαι 1089

geuomai is the sole term in the NT indicating the experience of "tasting." It occurs fifteen times and is used both literally and metaphorically.

Literal references to "tasting" food and drink are found in Matt 27:34; Luke 14:24; John 2:9; Acts 23:14. Col 2:21 refers to the avoidance of "tasting" certain foods.

Elsewhere, ***geuomai*** is used metaphorically, especially in the context of "tasting" (i.e., experiencing) death. Mention is made of those who "will not taste death" before Christ returns to his heavenly glory, after his resurrection (Matt 16:28; Mark 9:1; Luke 9:27). See also John 8:52. In particular, Jesus Christ is said to have tasted death for every person in Heb 2:9.

Other contexts refer to people "tasting" the heavenly gift (Heb 6:4); the word of God (Heb 9:5); and the kindness of the Lord (1 Pet 2:3).

- ▸ **23.** Food, Drink, Cooking > EAT, EATING

THIRST, THIRSTY

dipsaō διψάω 1372

dipsaō is found in eighteen places and means "to thirst," "be thirsty."

The experience of literally "being thirsty" is noted in Matt 25:35ff.; John 4:13ff.; 19:28; Rom 12:20; 1 Cor 4:11; Rev 7:16. ***dipsaō*** is also used metaphorically, indicating "thirsting after" true righteousness and godly living (Matt 5:6). John 6:35 guarantees that those who believe in Christ shall never thirst again — they shall be satisfied forever in every aspect of their being. See also Rev 21:6; 22:7.

dipsos δίψος 1373

dipsos is a rare noun, found only in 2 Cor 11:27 with reference to "thirst."

VINEGAR, SOUR WINE

oxos ὄξος 3690

oxos refers to the "vinegar," or "sour wine," offered to Jesus on the cross (Matt 27:34, 48; Mark 15:36; Luke 23:36; John 19:29, 30).

WATER

hydria ὑδρία 5201

hydria is a rare noun denoting "water pots" in John 2:6ff.; 4:28.

▸ **23.** Food, Drink, Cooking > JAR

hydropoteō ὑδροποτέω 5202

hydropoteō is a rare verb referring to "drinking" water in 1 Tim 5:23.

▸ **23.** Food, Drink, Cooking > DRINK, DRINKING, GIVE DRINK, BE DRUNK

SEE ALSO

▸ **11.** Meteorology, Water > WATER
hydōr, anydros

WINE

oinos οἶνος 3631

oinos denotes "wine" throughout its approximately thirty occurrences, in both a literal and figurative sense.

Literal references to "wine" include those in Matt 9:17; Mark 15:23; Luke 1:15; 5:37ff.; John 2:3ff.; Rom 14:21; 1 Tim 5:23; Rev 6:6; 18:13. Injunctions not to get drunk with wine, or be addicted to it, are found in Eph 5:18; 1 Tim 3:8; Titus 2:3.

oinos also denotes "wine" symbolizing the wrath of God in Rev 14:10; 16:19. In Rev 14:8; 17:2; 18:3, ***oinos*** denotes the "wine" of Babylonian "adulteries" (i.e., pagan idolatry).

gleukos γλεῦκος 1098

gleukos is a rare noun found only in Acts 2:13, denoting "new wine."

YEAST, LEAVEN

zymē ζύμη 2219

zymē is a noun denoting "leaven" or "yeast," in both literal and figurative contexts.

Literal references are found in Matt 13:33; Luke 13:21.

More significantly, ***zymē*** refers to "the leaven of the Pharisees," denoting their hypocrisy, as recorded in Matt 16:6ff.; Mark 8:15; Luke 12:1. "Leaven" also signifies the invisible effect of sin in the life and heart of the believer (1 Cor 5:6ff.; Gal 5:9).

zymoō ζυμόω 2220

zymoō is a verb found in four places indicating the action of "leavening" or "mixing with yeast." It refers literally to baking bread in Matt 13:33; Luke 13:21. Metaphorically, the action of "leavening" designates infecting one's life with evil intent (1 Cor 5:6; Gal 5:9).

24. Dwell, Live, Gather, Hospitality

ABIDE, STAY, REMAIN

menō μένω 3306

menō is a common verb found in 120 different places with the primary senses of "abide," "remain," or "stay," both literal and metaphorical.

Literal references to "staying" include "lodging as a guest" in someone's home (Matt 10:11; Luke 1:56; John 4:40; Acts 9:43; 21:7ff.); "remaining" in someone's company (Matt 26:38; John 14:25; Luke 24:29); "remaining" in the same geographic location (John 7:9; 10:40; Acts 27:31; 2 Tim 4:20); "remaining" in the same physical position, in particular with reference to the Spirit of God on the person of Christ in John 1:32ff. (see also John 19:31). In John 1:38ff. ***menō*** means "reside" or "live."

The verb also means to "remain" in the sense of "endure," "continue," or "last" in a number of places. It is used hypothetically, for example, of the city of Sodom in Matt 11:23; Mark 14:34. Jesus declares that "heavenly food," figuratively speaking, "lasts forever" in John 6:27. Paul encourages those who are unmarried to "remain" in their single state in 1 Cor 7:8ff. 1 Cor 13:13; Heb 13:1 speak of the "enduring" qualities of faith, hope, and love. The "veil" of unbelief is said to "remain" over the minds of unbelievers in 2 Cor 3:14 (see also John 9:41; 12:46 for related nuances). The "lasting" nature of a person's life and ministry will be assessed on the day of judgment (1 Cor 3:14). Rom 9:11 notes the eternal qualities of God's purposes in election. John 8:35; 12:34 mention Christ, the Son, who "continues" or "lives" forever. Then the priest-king Melchizedek is said to be a priest who "remains" forever in that position in Heb 7:23; as is Christ, who fulfills that role (Heb 7:24). The word of God is said to "remain" forever in 1 Pet 1:23ff.; and God himself is described thus in 2 Tim 2:13 (see also Heb 12:27). For this meaning see also Acts 5:4; 1 Cor 5:6.

There are a number of places where the meaning "abide" or "remain" expresses a significant theological nuance. When the word of God "remains" in the life of the believer, it has a significant sanctifying effect on that person's life (John 5:38; see also 1 John 2:27). The phenomenon of "abiding (or remaining) in Christ" indicates an intimate spiritual relationship with Christ on the part of the believer (John 6:56; 1 John 2:6ff.). The same phenomenon is evident in John 15:4ff., which describes the believer's intimate relationship with Christ via the metaphor of "branches" and "the vine." The love of God is said to "remain" in the life of the believer in 1 John 3:17. John 8:31 refers to the state of continuing to live by the word of God. See also 1 John 2:6ff.

John 3:36 expresses the metaphorical sense of "rest upon," where the anger of God is said to "rest upon" unbelievers.

Other metaphorical uses of ***menō*** are found in connection with the person of God, who "dwells" in Christ (John 14:10; 1 John 4:15) and also in the believer (1 John 3:24; 4:12ff.). The Holy Spirit is also promised to the believer, guaranteeing to "remain" with him or her forever (John 14:16ff.) See also John 1:2; 1 John 4:16; 2 John 9.

▸ **4.** Beginning, Continuing, Finishing, Postponing > CONTINUE, REMAIN

▸ **4.** Beginning, Continuing, Finishing, Postponing > ENDURE, REMAIN

▸ **24.** Dwell, Live, Gather, Hospitality > DWELL, DWELLING

▸ **85.** Movement, Position, State > REMAIN, STAY, ABIDE, DWELL

epimenō ἐπιμένω 1961

epimenō is a related form of ***menō*** (above) occurring nineteen times with the meanings "abide," "stay," "remain," and "continue."

The sense of "remain" or "abide" is found in Acts 10:48; 21:4, 10; 28:12ff.; 1 Cor 16:7ff.; Gal 1:18. In each case the intended meaning is that of "staying over" as a guest.

▸ **4.** Beginning, Continuing, Finishing, Postponing > CONTINUE, REMAIN

paramenō παραμένω 3887

paramenō is a rare synonym for ***menō***, found in only three places and meaning "abide" or "stay," in the sense of "spending time" as a guest in 1 Cor 16:6.

▸ **4.** Beginning, Continuing, Finishing, Postponing > CONTINUE, REMAIN

hypomenō ὑπομένω 5278

hypomenō is another variant of ***menō*** with the primary sense of "endure" evident in the majority of the eighteen occurrences of the term. In Luke 2:43; Acts 17:14, however, the term expresses the meaning "stay behind" or "remain."

▸ **60.** Virtues > ENDURE, BEAR, FORBEAR

diatribō διατρίβω 1304

diatribō is a verb found in ten contexts with the consistent meaning "remain," "spend time" in a particular location (John 3:22; 11:54; Acts 12:19; 14:3, 28; 15:35; 16:12; 20:6; 25:6, 14).

aulizomai αὐλίζομαι 835

aulizomai is a rare verb found only twice, in both places referring to "lodging" or "spending the night" (Matt 21:17; Luke 21:37).

▸ **24.** Dwell, Live, Gather, Hospitality > LODGE, LODGING

ASSEMBLE, ASSEMBLY

synerchomai συνέρχομαι 4905

synerchomai is a verb found in around thirty contexts, signifying the action of "coming together" with several different nuances. One of these is "gathering together," the "assembling" of a group of people for particular purposes (e.g., Mark 3:20; 14:53; Luke 5:15; Acts 1:6; 2:6; 5:16; 10:27; 28:17). In particular, 1 Cor 11:17ff.; 14:23ff. refer explicitly to "coming together" for worship.

▸ **85.** Movement, Position, State > ACCOMPANY

SEE ALSO

- **27.** Community, Partnership, Unity, Discord > EXPEL, EXCOMMUNICATE
  aposynagōgos
- **38.** Covenant, Law, Rites, Roles > RULER OF THE SYNAGOGUE
  archisynagōgos
- **41.** Sacrifice, Offering, Worship, Praise > GATHER, ASSEMBLE, ASSEMBLY, SYNAGOGUE, CHURCH
  ekklēsia, panēgyris, synagōgē, episynagōgē

BANQUET, FEAST

dochē δοχή 1403

dochē is found only in Luke 5:29; 14:13 and denotes a "banquet," "feast" in a general context.

SEE ALSO

- **40.** Holy Days, Feasts, Festivals > FEAST, FESTIVAL
  heortē, heortazō, deipnon, agapē

CITY

polis πόλις 4172

The noun ***polis***, meaning "city" or "town," occurs about 160 times.

Literal references to "city" include Matt 2:23; Mark 1:45; Luke 1:26; 10:8ff.; John 4:5ff.; Acts 8:5ff.; 16:12ff.; Rom 16:23; 2 Cor 11:26ff.; Jas 4:13; 2 Pet 2:6. The "city" of Jerusalem is noted in Matt 5:35. Rev 11:2 refers to Jerusalem as the "holy city."

Metaphorical references to the "heavenly city" of Jerusalem are found in Heb 11:10, 16; 12:22; 13:14; Rev 3:12; 14:20; 21:2, 10ff.

Metaphorical references to the "city" of Babylon (the symbolic embodiment of godlessness) are found in Rev 14:8; 17:18; 18:10ff.

CROWD, THRONG

ochlos ὄχλος 3793

ochlos is a noun denoting a "crowd" or "throng" of people for most of the 175 occurrences of the term.

Literal references to "crowds" include Matt 4:25; 15:30ff.; Mark 2:4; 8:1ff.; Luke 5:15ff.; 9:11ff.; John 6:2ff.; 12:9ff.; Acts 13:45; 21:27, 34.

Acts 11:24 refers to a "large company of people" converted under the apostolic preaching of the gospel. The "throng" of the saints in heaven is noted in Rev 7:9; 17:15; 19:1ff.

- **24.** Dwell, Live, Gather, Hospitality > MULTITUDE

ochlopoieō ὀχλοποιέω 3792

ochlopoieō is a rare verb found only in Acts 17:5 meaning to "gather a crowd."

plēthos πλῆθος 4128

plēthos is a noun synonymous with ***ochlos*** (above) denoting a "multitude," "crowd" throughout the nearly thirty occurrences of the term.

References to "crowds" of people include Mark 3:7ff.; Luke 6:17; 19:37; John 5:3; Acts 2:6; 6:5. Acts 5:14 describes the crowds converted under apostolic preaching.

plēthos also denotes the heavenly "host" of angelic beings praising God (Luke 2:13).

epikeimai ἐπίκειμαι 1945

The verb ***epikeimai*** means "lie on," "lay upon" for most of the seven occurrences of the term. However, in Luke 5:1 the term describes people "crowding in upon" Jesus.

dēmos δῆμος 1218

dēmos is a noun found four times with the meaning "people" in the contexts of a crowd (Acts 12:22; 17:5; 19:30, 33).

DWELL, DWELLING

oikeō οἰκέω 3611

oikeō is a verb occurring nine times, meaning "to dwell" throughout, largely in a metaphorical sense.

Sin is described as "dwelling" in the life of believers in Rom 7:17ff.; underscoring their ongoing struggle. Conversely, the person of the Holy Spirit is said to "dwell" in the heart of the believer in 1 Cor 3:16. 1 Cor 7:12ff. refers to an unbelieving spouse being content to "live" with their believing partner. 1 Tim 6:16 mentions God who "dwells" in unapproachable light.

katoikeō κατοικέω 2730

katoikeō is a verb found in nearly fifty places, meaning "live" or "dwell" throughout.

Literal references to "living," "dwelling" in various localities include Matt 2:23; 4:13; Luke 13:4; Acts 1:19; 2:5ff.; 7:2ff.; 9:22ff.; 19:10ff. References to people "dwelling" on earth include Rev 3:10; 6:10; 8:13; 13:8ff.; 14:6; 17:2ff.

All other uses of ***katoikeō*** are metaphorical. Demons "dwelling" in their human hosts are noted in Matt 12:45; Luke 11:26. God is said to "dwell" in the tabernacle and temple in Matt 23:21; Heb 11:9 — though in an absolute sense God can never truly "dwell" in houses made by human beings (Acts 7:48; 17:24ff.). Christ "dwelling" in the hearts of believers is mentioned in Eph 3:17. Col 1:19; 2:9 affirm that God "dwells" in his fullness in the person of Christ. The Holy Spirit is said to "dwell" in the believer in Jas 4:5. The phenomenon of righteousness "dwelling" in the new heavens and the earth is described in 2 Pet 3:13.

enoikeō ἐνοικέω 1774

enoikeō is another variant of ***oikeō*** (above) and indicates the phenomenon of a spiritual inhabiting or "indwelling."

References to the Holy Spirit "indwelling" the believer are found in Rom 8:11; 2 Tim 1:14. The phenomenon of

God "living" among his people is noted in 2 Cor 6:16; as is the word of Christ in Col 3:16. See also 2 Tim 1:5.

synoikeō συνοικέω 4924

synoikeō is a rare verb meaning "to live together with" in relation to husbands and wives, found only in 1 Pet 3:7.

menō μένω 3306

menō is a common verb found 120 times with the predominant senses of "stay," "remain," with related nuances, including the meaning to "live," "dwell" in literal general contexts (e.g., Luke 1:56; 8:27; John 1:39; Acts 18:3; 28:16, 30).

Elsewhere, the meaning "dwell" is metaphorical. John 14:10 refers to God "dwelling" in Christ. The Spirit of God is said to "dwell" in the believer in John 14:17.

- ▸ **4.** Beginning, Continuing, Finishing, Postponing > CONTINUE, REMAIN
- ▸ **4.** Beginning, Continuing, Finishing, Postponing > ENDURE, REMAIN
- ▸ **24.** Dwell, Live, Gather, Hospitality > ABIDE, STAY, REMAIN
- ▸ **85.** Movement, Position, State > REMAIN, STAY, ABIDE, DWELL

skēnoō σκηνόω 4637

skēnoō is a verb found in five places with the underlying meaning "to live in a tent." It is translated "to dwell" with reference to Christ "living" among men in John 1:14. In this text the use of this particular term draws a theological connection between the glory cloud of the ancient tabernacle and its redemptive-historical fulfillment in the person of Christ, who embodies and incarnates the divine glory cloud; hence the significance of the possible translation here: "and the Word . . . tabernacled among us." References to those who "dwell" in heaven with God are found in Rev 12:12; 13:6; 21:3.

GATHER, GATHERING

synagō συνάγω 4863

synagō is found in approximately sixty contexts meaning "to gather (together)," "assemble" as well as the corresponding passive sense "be gathered."

Matt 2:4; 13:2; Mark 5:21 refer to "gathering" or "calling" people together in mundane senses.

Matt 3:12; Luke 15:13; John 6:12; 15:6 refer to "gathering" produce, or material goods.

Christ's action in "gathering" people to himself for the purpose of making them his own is indicated in Matt 12:30; 25:32; Luke 11:23; John 11:52.

In several contexts, "gathering wheat" is equated with the final assembling of believers in glory (Matt 13:30; Luke 3:17).

As in the OT, people often "gather" or "assemble" for a specific purpose — for example, to worship (Matt 18:20; Acts 20:7; 1 Cor 5:4); to plot to kill Jesus (Matt 26:3; Acts 4:27); to see and hear Jesus speak (Mark 2:2); to attempt to humiliate Jesus in public (Mark 7:1); to force the disciples to stop preaching (Acts 4:6); to gather against the Lord (Acts 4:26); to wait to receive the Holy Spirit (Acts 4:31); to hear the preaching of the word of God (Acts 13:44); to hear about the spread of the gospel (Acts 14:27); and to face God on the great and final day of battle (Rev 16:14ff.; 19:19; 20:8). See also Rev 19:17.

Vultures "gather" around a corpse prior to feeding on it in Luke 17:37.

episynagō ἐπισυνάγω 1996

episynagō is a variant form of ***synagō*** (above) occurring nine times and meaning "gather together" throughout.

Jesus expresses the desire to "gather his children together," as a hen gathers her chickens under her wings, referring to the wayward people of Jerusalem (Matt 23:37; Luke 13:34). The prospect of God "gathering together" his elect from all over the world is noted in Matt 24:31; Mark 13:27.

Mundane references to people "gathering together" include those in Mark 1:33; Luke 12:1.

synathroizō συναθροίζω 4867

synathroizō is a verb found only three times, meaning "to gather, call together" people (Luke 24:33; Acts 12:12; 19:25).

SEE ALSO

- ▸ **28.** Agriculture, Viticulture, Animal Husbandry > GATHER, HARVEST, PICK, PLUCK
  syllegō, trygaō
- ▸ **41.** Sacrifice, Offering, Worship, Praise > GATHER, ASSEMBLE, ASSEMBLY, SYNAGOGUE, CHURCH
  episynagōgē
- ▸ **69.** Have, Possess, Hold, Grasp, Bear, Carry > GATHER
  systrephō

GUEST, GUEST ROOM

katalyō καταλύω 2647

katalyō is a verb found seventeen times with the predominant meanings "destroy," "cast down," but in Luke 9:12; 19:17 it has the meaning "to lodge as a guest." Although this meaning appears unrelated, ***katalyō*** also has the sense, outside the NT, of "to unloose, untie." The meaning "lodge as a guest" probably developed from the practice of prospective guests at a lodging place untying the straps from their beasts of burden (i.e., unharnessing them) prior to their entry.

- ▸ **21.** Die, Perish, Kill, Destroy > CAST DOWN
- ▸ **21.** Die, Perish, Kill, Destroy > DESTROY, DESTROYER, DESTRUCTION

katalyma κατάλυμα 2646

katalyma is a rare noun denoting an "inn" or a "guest room," found only in Mark 14:14; Luke 2:7; 22:11.

- ▸ **24.** Dwell, Live, Gather, Hospitality > INN

INN

xenia ξενία 3578

xenia occurs only twice and refers in both contexts to a place of lodging. Acts 28:23 refers to Paul's lodgings in Rome, where he was under house arrest. In Phlm 22, Paul requests his prospective host to provide him with a guest room on his arrival.

▸ **24.** Dwell, Live, Gather, Hospitality > LODGE, LODGING

katalyma κατάλυμα 2646

katalyma is synonymous with ***xenia*** (above) and refers to either an inn or a guest room. The term is found three times. Mark 4:14; Luke 22:11 refer to the guest room requested by the disciples of Jesus for the celebration of the Passover. Luke 2:7 refers to the lack of accommodation for Joseph and Mary in Bethlehem.

▸ **24.** Dwell, Live, Gather, Hospitality > GUEST, GUEST ROOM

pandocheion πανδοχεῖον 3829

pandocheion is found only in Luke 10:34, referring to the inn in the parable of the good Samaritan.

INVITE

kaleō καλέω 2564

kaleō is a term occurring around 150 times with the primary meaning "call." In one text, however, ***kaleō*** is translated "invite" as a particular application of the meaning "to call." In the parable of the marriage feast in Matt 22:9, an invitation is given to all and sundry to come to the banquet.

▸ **63.** Speak, Tell, Declare, Call > CALL, CALLED, CALLING, SUMMON, NAME

phōneō φωνέω 5455

phōneō occurs around forty times and is usually translated "call (out)" or "crow" (i.e., of a cock). However, in Luke 14:12 it is translated "invite" in the negative context of not inviting someone to come to a feast.

▸ **63.** Speak, Tell, Declare, Call > CALL, CALLED, CALLING, SUMMON, NAME

antikaleō ἀντικαλέω 479

This term occurs only in Luke 14:12 and signifies "to offer an invitation" in return for receiving one, again in the context of a banquet.

LODGE, LODGING

kataskēnoō κατασκηνόω 2681

kataskēnoō means "lodge" or "dwell." In three of the four contexts in which it is found, it refers to birds "making their nests" (i.e., "lodging") in trees (Matt 13:32; Mark 4:32; Luke 13:19). In Acts 2:26, ***kataskēnoō*** refers metaphorically to David "dwelling" in hope, in fellowship with God.

▸ **14.** Animals > NEST

aulizomai αὐλίζομαι 835

aulizomai occurs only twice and indicates Jesus "lodging" or "spending the night" in Bethany (Matt 21:17) and on the Mount of Olives (Luke 21:37).

▸ **24.** Dwell, Live, Gather, Hospitality > ABIDE, STAY, REMAIN

xenizō ξενίζω 3579

xenizō is found in ten contexts, and in the majority of these it means "to lodge," and also "to offer hospitality."

References to "lodging" as a guest in someone's house are found in Acts 10:6, 18, 23, 32; 21:16; 28:7. Heb 13:2 contains the instruction not to neglect offering hospitality to strangers.

xenia ξενία 3578

xenia is the noun derived from ***xenizō*** (above). It occurs only in Acts 28:23; Phlm 22, meaning "lodging" or "guest room."

▸ **24.** Dwell, Live, Gather, Hospitality > INN

xenodocheō ξενοδοχέω 3580

xenodocheō is a verb derived from ***xenizō*** (above) and means "to entertain strangers as guests." It occurs only in 1 Tim 5:10.

MULTITUDE

ochlos ὄχλος 3793

ochlos is a common noun denoting "crowds" or "multitudes" of people.

References to "multitudes" or "crowds" of people include those in Matt 4:25; 21:8ff.; Mark 5:21ff.; 8:1ff.; Luke 5:1ff.; John 6:2ff.; Acts 8:6; 14:11ff.

Metaphorical references to the assembled "multitudes" of believers in heaven are found in Rev 7:9; 19:1, 6. The gathered "masses" of earth's inhabitants are noted in Rev 17:15.

▸ **24.** Dwell, Live, Gather, Hospitality > CROWD, THRONG

NEIGHBOR

perioikos περίοικος 4040

perioikos is found only in Luke 1:58 and refers to the neighbors of Elizabeth, mother of John the Baptist, in the sense of those who lived near her.

geitōn γείτων 1069

geitōn is a noun found only four times, meaning "neighbor" in the sense of those who live close by (Luke 14:12; 15:6, 9; John 9:8).

SEE ALSO

▸ **26.** Nations, Identities, People Groups > NEIGHBOR
plēsion

RECEIVE, WELCOME

prosdechomai προσδέχομαι 4327

prosdechomai is found fourteen times and in three cases means "receive" in the sense of "welcome" (Luke 15:2; Rom 16:2; Phil 2:9).

- ▸ **46.** Wait, Hope, Be Vigilant, Pay Attention To > WAIT
- ▸ **49.** Allow, Accept, Approve, Refuse > ACCEPT

eisdechomai εἰσδέχομαι 1523

eisdechomai is found only in 2 Cor 6:17 and means "receive" in the context of God's promise to "welcome" his people when they come out of captivity in Babylon. This Corinthian text cites the prophetic declaration of Isa 52:11.

hypodechomai ὑποδέχομαι 5264

hypodechomai means "receive," with the sense of "to welcome as a guest," in each of its four occurrences (Luke 10:38; 19:6; Acts 17:7; Jas 2:25).

SEE ALSO

- ▸ **20.** Illness, Disease, Health, Healing > RECEIVE SIGHT
  anablepō
- ▸ **41.** Sacrifice, Offering, Worship, Praise > TITHE, PAYMENT
  dekatoō
- ▸ **70.** Give, Take, Seize, Touch > RECEIVE, ACCEPT, WELCOME
  dechomai, lambanō, paradechomai, apolambanō, proslambanō, paralambanō, metalambanō, metalēmpsis, lēmpsis, apodechomai, epidechomai, anadechomai, komizō, apechō, nomotheteō

RECLINE, SHARE A MEAL

anakeimai ἀνάκειμαι 345

anakeimai is a verb with the underlying meaning "lie down, recline at a table." The contexts all indicate the partaking of hospitality. ***anakeimai*** occurs fourteen times. In Matt 22:10ff.; 26:7; Luke 7:37; 22:27, ***anakeimai*** has the explicit sense of "sharing a meal as a guest."

- ▸ **85.** Movement, Position, State > SIT, SIT DOWN, SIT UP

ROOM

chōreō χωρέω 5562

This verb occurs twelve times, meaning "receive," "contain." In Mark 2:2, however, ***chōreō*** indicates negatively that there is "no room" for any more people to enter the house where Jesus is teaching.

topos τόπος 5117

topos is a noun occurring about ninety times, with the dominant sense of "place." But in Luke 14:22 ***topos*** may be translated "room" in the sense of "space" remaining, in relation to the availability of room left for a banquet.

- ▸ **9.** Land, Geography, Topography > PLACE

SEE ALSO

- ▸ **33.** Architecture > ROOM
  anagaion, hyperōon

VILLAGE, TOWN

kōmē κώμη 2968

kōmē is a noun that occurs approximately thirty times and means "village," "town" (e.g., Matt 9:35; Mark 6:6, 36, 56; 8:23ff.; Luke 9:6ff.; John 7:42; Acts 8:25).

kōmopolis κωμόπολις 2969

kōmopolis is a rare variant of ***kōmē*** (above) referring to "towns" or "villages" in Mark 1:38.

VISIT, VISITATION

historeō ἱστορέω 2477

historeō is a verb found only in Gal 1:18 meaning "to pay a visit to" or "see (someone)."

SEE ALSO

- ▸ **32.** Law, Justice, Jurisprudence, Judgment > VISIT (IN JUDGMENT)
  episkopē
- ▸ **62.** Care For, Protect, Guard, Watch > VISIT
  episkeptomai

25. Family, Marriage, Adoption, Inheritance

ADOPTION

hyiothesia υἱοθεσία 5206

The noun ***hyiothesia*** is found five times, with the underlying sense of "adoption" in each case, all referring to the status of believers as children, sons adopted by God in and through Christ (Rom 8:15, 23; 9:4; Gal 4:5; Eph 1:5).

BETROTH, PROMISE IN MARRIAGE

mnēsteuō μνηστεύω 3423

mnēsteuō is a rare verb found three times, used only in the passive sense of "be promised in marriage" (i.e., betrothed). It is used only in relation to Mary the mother of Christ, as one "betrothed" to Joseph (Matt 1:18; Luke 1:27; 2:5).

harmozomai ἁρμόζομαι 718

harmozomai is a rare verb found only in 2 Cor 11:2, used metaphorically in relation to the apostle Paul's action in "betrothing" the Corinthian congregation to Christ as their (corporate) spiritual Lord.

BIRTHRIGHT

prōtotokia πρωτοτόκια 4415

prōtotokia is a rare noun denoting the "birthright" of Esau, who foolishly sold it to his brother Jacob for a hearty meal (Heb 12:16).

BRIDE, BRIDEGROOM

nymphē νύμφη 3565

nymphē is a noun occurring eight times denoting both a "bride" and a "daughter-in-law."

John 3:29 contains a literal reference to a "bride." The term is more commonly used metaphorically, denoting the church as a "bride," the people of God in glory, joined to Christ her "bridegroom" (Rev 21:9; 22:17).

▸ **25.** Family, Marriage, Adoption, Inheritance > DAUGHTER, DAUGHTER-IN-LAW

nymphios νυμφίος 3566

nymphios denotes a "bridegroom" throughout the sixteen occurrences of the term.

The "bridegroom" is cited several times throughout the teaching and parables of Christ (Matt 9:15; 25:1ff.; Mark 2:19; Luke 5:34, 35). Other literal references to a "bridegroom" are found in John 2:9; Rev 18:23.

In John 3:29 the use of ***nymphios*** is metaphorical. Here Christ anticipates the heavenly spiritual union of himself (the "bridegroom") with his people, the church (the "bride").

BRING UP, RAISE, NURTURE

trephō τρέφω 5142

trephō is a verb found eight times with the primary sense of "feed," "nourish." However, in Luke 4:16 it refers to Jesus having been "brought up" (i.e., raised as a child) in Nazareth.

▸ **23.** Food, Drink, Cooking > FEED, NOURISH

anatrephō ἀνατρέφω 397

anatrephō is a variant of ***trephō*** (above) meaning "bring up" in the sense of "raise, nurture" (a child). It refers to Moses in Acts 7:20ff.; and to Paul in Acts 22:3.

ektrephō ἐκτρέφω 1625

ektrephō is a rare variant of ***anatrephō*** (above) found in three places. Eph 6:4 enjoins fathers to "bring up" their children to love and fear the Lord.

teknotropheō τεκνοτροφέω 5044

teknotropheō is a rare verb found only in 1 Tim 5:10, meaning "to bring up children."

SEE ALSO

▸ **15.** Gender, Reproduction, Youth, Aging > CHILD, OFFSPRING
paidarion, nepiazō, teknogoneō, enkyos

▸ **27.** Community, Partnership, Unity, Discord > CHILDREN
teknion

BROTHER

adelphos ἀδελφός 80

adelphos is a noun found about 350 times, translated "brother" and used both literally and metaphorically.

Literal references to "brother" in a familial sense are found, for example, in Matt 1:2, 11; 12:46ff.; Mark 1:16ff.; 6:17ff.; Luke 8:19ff.; John 1:40ff.; 11:21ff.; Jude 1.

"Brother" in the sense of a friend or fellow countryman is indicated in Matt 5:22ff.; Luke 6:41ff.; Acts 7:23ff.; 10:23; Rom 11:25.

More commonly, the term "brother" constitutes a form of address for fellow believers (e.g., Acts 3:17ff.; 23:1ff.; Rom 7:1ff.; 1 Cor 1:10ff.; 2 Cor 8:18ff.; Gal 5:11ff.; Eph 6:21ff.; Col 1:1ff.; 4:7ff.; 1 Thess 2:1, 9; Heb 3:12; Jas 1:9; 1 Pet 5:12; 1 John 2:7ff.; Rev 1:9). Significantly, the term "brothers" is recorded as being used by Christ with reference to his followers (Heb 2:11ff.).

SEE ALSO

▸ **27.** Community, Partnership, Unity, Discord > BROTHER, BROTHERHOOD
pseudadelphos, adelphotēs

CHILD

teknon τέκνον 5043

teknon is one of the common terms for "child" or "children" found in about one hundred contexts.

Literal references to children include Matt 2:18; Mark 10:29; Luke 1:7; 20:31; Acts 7:5; 1 Cor 7:14; Eph 6:1ff.; Col 3:20ff.; 1 Tim 3:4; Titus 1:6.

Christ referred to his disciples as "children" as a term of endearment (Mark 10:24). Other metaphorical uses of the term include references to Abraham's spiritual descendants as "children" in Luke 3:8; John 8:39. "Children" of wisdom are noted in Luke 7:35. Several texts describe believers as "children" of God (e.g., John 1:12; 11:52; Rom 8:16ff.; 9:7ff.; Gal 4:27ff.; Eph 5:1; 1 Tim 1:2; 1 John 3:10; 2 John 1). In 1 Cor 4:14, Paul uses "children" as a term of endearment for his congregation in Corinth. Gal 4:25 refers to "children" as a symbol for the nation of Israel under the old covenant. The phrase "children of wrath" designates those under divine condemnation in Eph 2:3. The infant Messiah is described as a "child" in the vision of Rev 12:4ff.

pais παῖς 3816

The noun ***pais*** means "servant," "child." The former sense is the most common.

General references to "child," including "boy," are found in Matt 17:18; 21:15; Luke 9:42. In particular, Luke 2:43; Acts 4:27, 30 refer to the "child" Jesus.

▸ **55.** Bondage, Captivity, Servitude > SERVANT, SLAVE

paidion παιδίον 3813

paidion is a diminutive form of ***pais*** (above) meaning "little child," "young child" throughout its nearly fifty occurrences.

The literal sense of "little child" is indicated in Matt 2:8ff.; 18:2ff.; 19:13ff.; Luke 1:59, 66, 76; 2:17ff. The term "little children" refers metaphorically to one's congregation in 1 John 2:13, 18.

Elsewhere ***paidion*** denotes "child," "children" in general contexts (e.g., Matt 14:21; Mark 5:39ff.; 10:13ff.; Luke 11:27; 18:16ff.; John 16:21; Heb 11:23).

Jesus uses ***paidion***, "children," as a term of endearment for his disciples (John 21:5). It is also a designation for the people of God in Heb 2:13.

▸ **15.** Gender, Reproduction, Youth, Aging > GIRL, MAID, MAIDEN

nēpios νήπιος 3516

nēpios is found in fourteen places with primary reference to "babies," "infant children." ***nēpios*** is used literally in Matt 11:25; 21:16; Luke 10:21. It is used metaphorically to refer to "babes in Christ" (i.e., immature believers) in 1 Cor 3:1; Eph 4:14; Heb 5:13 (see also 1 Cor 13:11). The meaning "child" in a general sense is indicated in Gal 4:1ff.

▸ **15.** Gender, Reproduction, Youth, Aging > CHILD, INFANT, BABE

SEE ALSO

▸ **15.** Gender, Reproduction, Youth, Aging > CHILD, OFFSPRING
paidarion, nepiazō, teknogoneō, enkyos

▸ **27.** Community, Partnership, Unity, Discord > CHILDREN
teknion

DAUGHTER, DAUGHTER-IN-LAW

thygatēr θυγάτηρ 2364

The noun ***thygatēr*** occurs around thirty times with the meaning "daughter," in both literal and metaphorical contexts.

Jesus uses the term as a courteous title for a woman, in the context of a healing (Matt 9:22; Mark 5:34; 7:26ff.; Luke 8:48).

The literal sense of "daughter" is indicated in Matt 10:35ff.; Mark 5:35; Luke 1:5; 2:36; 12:53; Acts 2:17; 7:21; 21:9; Heb 11:24. Reference to "daughters" denoting the "female descendants" of Abraham is found in Luke 13:16.

The expression "daughter of Zion" is a metaphorical reference to the city of Jerusalem and its population (Matt 21:5; John 12:15).

Similarly, the phrase "daughters of Jerusalem" denotes the female inhabitants of the city in Luke 23:28. Reference to "daughters" in 2 Cor 6:18 describes women as children of God.

thygatrion θυγάτριον 2365

thygatrion is a rare diminutive form of ***thygatēr*** (above) denoting a "little daughter." It is found only in Mark 5:23; 7:25.

nymphē νύμφη 3565

The noun ***nymphē*** denotes both a "bride" and "daughter-in-law" in the eight occurrences of the term. The latter meaning is found only in Matt 10:35; Luke 12:53.

▸ **25.** Family, Marriage, Adoption, Inheritance > BRIDE, BRIDEGROOM

SEE ALSO

▸ **15.** Gender, Reproduction, Youth, Aging > UNMARRIED
parthenos

DESCENT, ANCESTRY

agenealogētos ἀγενεαλόγητος 35

agenealogētos is a rare adjective found only in Heb 7:3, denoting Melchizedek as a man "without descent," or without record of mother or father (citing the account of the patriarch Abraham's mysterious priestly royal visitor in Gen 14).

▸ **25.** Family, Marriage, Adoption, Inheritance > GENEALOGY

genealogeō γενεαλογέω 1075

genealogeō is a rare verb found only in Heb 7:6 with the sense of "trace one's descent, or ancestry."

- ▶ **25.** Family, Marriage, Adoption, Inheritance > GENEALOGY

SEE ALSO

- ▶ **87.** Movement Upward or Downward > DESCEND, COME DOWN
  katabainō, katerchomai

DIVORCE

apolyō ἀπολύω 630

apolyō is a common verb found in nearly ninety places with the primary senses of "release," "let go," "dismiss."

In several places, however, ***apolyō*** refers to the action or process of "divorcing" one's wife (Matt 1:19; 5:31ff.; 19:3ff.; Mark 10:2ff.; Luke 16:18).

- ▶ **25.** Family, Marriage, Adoption, Inheritance > PUT AWAY
- ▶ **44.** Repentance, Forgiveness, Mercy, Redeem, Save > FORGIVE, FORGIVENESS, RELEASE
- ▶ **49.** Allow, Accept, Approve, Refuse > ALLOW
- ▶ **55.** Bondage, Captivity, Servitude > RELEASE
- ▶ **79.** Throw, Send, Drive, Mix, Remove > SEND, SEND AWAY, SEND OUT

apostasion ἀποστάσιον 647

apostasion is a noun found only in Matt 5:31; 19:7; Mark 10:4, denoting a "bill of divorce" in each case.

FAMILY, HOUSEHOLD, LINEAGE

oikos οἶκος 3624

oikos is a common noun occurring over one hundred times with the primary meanings "house," "home."

In several places, however, the sense of "household" or "family" is indicated. The "house of David," denoting the ruler's lineage, is indicated in Luke 1:27, 69; 2:4; as is that of Jacob in Luke 1:40; the "house of Israel" in Acts 2:36; 7:42; Heb 8:10; and the "house of Judah" in Heb 8:8. General references to a "household" or "family" are indicated in Luke 11:17; Acts 10:2; 1 Cor 1:16; 1 Tim 3:5, 12; 2 Tim 1:16; Heb 11:7. In reference to the community of believers, ***oikos*** denotes the "household" or "family" of God in 1 Tim 3:15; 1 Pet 4:17.

- ▶ **33.** Architecture > HOUSE

patria πατριά 3965

patria is a rare noun found in three places. It refers to the "lineage" or "family" of David in Luke 2:4; the "families" of the earth in Acts 3:25; and a general reference to a "family" in Eph 3:15.

FATHER, ANCESTOR

patēr πατήρ 3962

patēr is translated "father" throughout its more than four hundred occurrences.

References to one's biological father predominate (e.g., Matt 2:22; 10:37; 19:5; Mark 7:10ff.; Luke 1:59ff.; 15:12ff.; Acts 16:1; Eph 5:31; 6:2ff.; 1 Tim 5:1; Heb 12:7ff.).

patēr, like its Hebrew equivalent *'āb*, also signifies "father" in the sense of "ancestor," with references to Abraham (Matt 3:9; Luke 1:73; 16:24; John 8:39; Rom 4:11ff.; Jas 2:21); to David (Mark 11:10; Luke 1:32); and to Israel's ancestors in general (Matt 23:30; Luke 11:47ff.; John 4:12; Acts 3:22; Rom 9:5; 1 Cor 4:15; Heb 1:1). References to God as the "Father" of his people are found in Matt 5:16, 45; 10:29ff.; Mark 11:25ff.; Luke 11:2; Acts 1:4ff.; Rom 8:15; Eph 3:14; Eph 2:11; 1 Thess 1:3; Titus 1:4; 1 Pet 1:2; 2 Pet 1:17. The designation "Father" in the context of the relationship between God and Christ his Son is indicated, for example, in Matt 11:27; 16:17; 18:19; 26:39ff.; Mark 14:36; Luke 2:49; 24:49; John 1:14, 18; 3:35; 4:23; 5:17ff.; 6:32ff.; 8:16ff.; 12:26ff.; 14:2ff.; 15:1ff.; 16:3ff.; 17:1ff.; Rom 15:6; Gal 1:1ff.; Eph 1:2, 3; Col 1:3; 1 Pet 1:3; 1 John 2:22ff.; Rev 2:27; 3:5, 21; 14:1. The term "Father" also occurs with the other persons of the Godhead (viz. Son and Holy Spirit) in Matt 28:19; Mark 8:38. Luke 9:26 refers to God as the "Father" of the Son of Man.

apatōr ἀπάτωρ 540

apatōr is a rare adjective found only in Heb 7:3 referring metaphorically to Melchizedek as one "without father or mother," whose parents are not recorded in any genealogy.

patroparadotos πατροπαράδοτος 3970

patroparadotos is a rare adjectival form found only in 1 Pet 1:18, referring to ways "inherited from one's fathers."

FATHER-IN-LAW

pentheros πενθερός 3995

pentheros is a noun meaning "father-in-law," found only in John 18:13 with reference to the high priest Caiaphas' relative.

GENEALOGY

genealogia γενεαλογία 1076

genealogia is a rare noun found only twice, denoting a "genealogy" in the sense of a "record of family descent" (1 Tim 1:4; Titus 3:9).

genealogeō γενεαλογέω 1075

genealogeō is a rare verb found only in Heb 7:6 meaning "to trace one's family lineage."

- ▶ **25.** Family, Marriage, Adoption, Inheritance > DESCENT, ANCESTRY

agenealogētos ἀγενεαλόγητος 35

agenealogētos is a rare adjective found only in Heb 7:3, describing Melchizedek as a priest-king "without genealogy" — that is, there is no record of his parentage.

- ▶ **25.** Family, Marriage, Adoption, Inheritance > DESCENT, ANCESTRY

genesis γένεσις 1078

genesis is a rare noun denoting the "genealogy" of Jesus Christ in Matt 1:1.

▸ **15.** Gender, Reproduction, Youth, Aging > BIRTH

GENERATION

genea γενεά 1074

genea is a noun found about forty times with the primary meaning "generation," denoting a "natural grouping of family descent," as well as associated nuances.

Matt 7:11 lists the "generations" in a stylized genealogy tracing the descent of Jesus Christ from the very origins of the Israelite people of God.

"Generation" in the sense of a community of people living at the same period of time, at the national or local level, is noted in Matt 11:16; 12:39ff.; 23:36; Mark 8:12, 38; 9:19; Luke 7:31; 9:41; 11:29ff.; Acts 2:40; Phil 2:15; Heb 3:10 (all of which refer to a wicked and unbelieving generation).

The term is used in a neutral sense in Matt 24:34; Luke 1:48ff.; 16:8; Acts 8:33; 13:36; 14:16; 15:21; Eph 3:5.

gennēma γέννημα 1081

gennēma is a noun found in nine places meaning "generation" in the sense of that which is born or begotten. It is used metaphorically in Matt 3:7; 12:34; 23:33; Luke 3:7 to refer to hypocritical, self-righteous Pharisees as a "brood" of vipers.

▸ **28.** Agriculture, Viticulture, Animal Husbandry > FRUIT, FRUITFUL

HEIR

klēronomos κληρονόμος 2818

klēronomos occurs about fifteen times and means "heir" in the conventional sense of one who receives his allotted property from an inheritance. It also conveys the same meaning in a messianic sense, referring to Christ as one who benefits from his status as God's Son. It is most commonly applied to believers as heirs with Christ.

The conventional sense of "heir" is observed in Matt 21:38; Mark 12:7; Luke 24:14; Gal 4:1. In Rom 4:14, ***klēronomos*** refers to Abraham as the "heir" of the world, identifying him as the recipient of the covenant promises.

In the metaphorical, spiritual sense, believers are described as heirs of God and co-heirs with Christ (Gal 4:7; Rom 8:17; 1 Pet 3:7). Gal 3:29; Heb 6:17 add that believers are heirs according to the promise (i.e., of the covenant). Heb 11:7 describes Noah as the "heir of righteousness"; and in Jas 2:5 believers are designated "heirs of the kingdom." Finally, in Heb 1:2 ***klēronomos*** indicates that Christ is the divinely appointed "heir of all things."

synklēronomos συγκληρονόμος 4789

This term is a partial synonym for ***klēronomos*** (above) and emphasizes the phenomenon of a shared inheritance. ***synklēronomos*** is translated "joint heir," "fellow heir" and occurs only four times, always with a spiritual sense. In Rom 8:17 believers are described as "joint heirs" with Christ; and Eph 3:6 includes Gentiles in this designation. Heb 11:9 refers to Abraham, Isaac, and Jacob as fellow heirs of the covenant promise. Then 1 Pet 3:7 indicates that husband and wife are "heirs together" of the gift of life.

▸ **25.** Family, Marriage, Adoption, Inheritance > JOINT, FELLOW

HUSBAND

anēr ἀνήρ 435

This term is usually translated "man." ***anēr*** occurs around two hundred times, but the meaning "husband" is found in about fifty places.

Matt 1:16; Luke 2:36; John 4:16ff.; Acts 5:9, 10 refer to specific husbands. "Husbands" in general are referred to in Mark 10:12; Rom 7:2, 3; 1 Cor 7:2ff.; Gal 4:27; Eph 5:23, 33. Christ is declared to be "husband" to the church in Eph 5:25ff.

▸ **15.** Gender, Reproduction, Youth, Aging > MAN, MALE
▸ **27.** Community, Partnership, Unity, Discord > FELLOW

INHERIT, INHERITANCE

klēronomeō κληρονομέω 2816

klēronomeō is found in eighteen contexts and is consistently translated "inherit," and in one instance "obtain by inheritance."

Matt 5:5 says, "Blessed are the meek for they shall inherit the earth." Heb 12:16, 17 record the incident of Esau rejecting his birthright and afterwards pleading to inherit this blessing again, but to no avail.

The blessing of inheriting eternal life is indicated in Matt 19:29; Mark 10:17; Luke 10:25; 18:18; Heb 1:14; Rev 21:7. Similarly, Matt 25:34 refers to the blessed destiny of all believers in inheriting the kingdom of God for eternity. Heb 1:4 affirms that Jesus Christ has obtained by inheritance a more excellent name than the angels.

klēronomeō is also used in a number of negative contexts. The following groups of people do not inherit the kingdom of God: the unrighteous (1 Cor 6:9ff.; Gal 5:21); "flesh and blood" (i.e., mere mortal human beings) (1 Cor 15:50); "the son of the slave woman" (i.e., those outside of God's chosen people) (Gal 4:30).

klēroō κληρόω 2820

klēroō occurs only once, in Eph 1:11, where it refers to the believer's inheritance of salvation having been obtained in and through the person of Christ.

klēronomia κληρονομία 2817

klēronomia is a noun derived from ***klēronomeō*** (above) and is consistently translated "inheritance." The term occurs fourteen times.

klēronomia refers to inheritance as a human legacy (Matt 21:38; Mark 12:7, 13; Luke 20:14; Acts 7:5). The term also refers to the inheritance of the land of Canaan as promised to Abraham, in Heb 11:8.

klēronomia also refers to the "inheritance" of salvation, which is the destiny of those who are sanctified by God's grace and true servants of Jesus Christ (Acts 20:32; Col 3:24). Gal 3:18 refers to this inheritance being accessed not through the law, but by means of grace. Heb 9:15 affirms that the guarantee of the promised eternal inheritance is made certain by Christ's mediatorial role under the new covenant; and 1 Pet 1:4 refers to the imperishable inheritance of eternal life. Similarly, Eph 1:14, 18 indicate that it is the Holy Spirit who is the guarantee of our eternal inheritance.

The sole negative context for ***klēronomia*** is found in Eph 5:5, which declares that no idolatrous or immoral person has any inheritance in the kingdom of God.

klēros κλῆρος 2819

klēros refers to that which is obtained by lot, and the process of casting lots, in most of the thirteen contexts in which it is found. On two occasions, however, ***klēros*** refers to the inheritance of salvation to be enjoyed by the people of God (Acts 26:18; Col 1:12).

- ▸ **27.** Community, Partnership, Unity, Discord > SHARE, PART, ALLOTMENT, PARTAKE
- ▸ **70.** Give, Take, Seize, Touch > LOT, ALLOTMENT, SHARE, CAST LOTS

JOIN

syzeugnymi συζεύγνυμι 4801

syzeugnymi is only found twice, and in both of these texts refers to the process of being joined together in marriage — a lifelong bond that may not be broken (Matt 19:6; Mark 10:9).

proskollaō προσκολλάω 4347

proskollaō occurs only three times, and on each occasion refers to the institution of marriage in which a man leaves his father and mother and is joined to his wife. The idea here is one of intimate union (Matt 19:5; Mark 10:7; Eph 5:31).

SEE ALSO

- ▸ **27.** Community, Partnership, Unity, Discord > JOIN ***kollaō, synarmologeō***

JOINT, FELLOW

synklēronomos συγκληρονόμος 4789

synklēronomos refers to a "joint heir" or "fellow heir." It occurs only four times. Rom 8:17 speaks of believers as "joint heirs" with Christ, as does Eph 3:6, with particular reference to Gentile converts. Heb 11:9 cites Isaac and Jacob as "fellow heirs" of the covenant promise given to their father and grandfather Abraham.

- ▸ **25.** Family, Marriage, Adoption, Inheritance > HEIR

SEE ALSO

- ▸ **16.** Body, Bodily Functions > MEMBER, JOINT ***haphē, harmos***

KIN, KINSMAN, KINSWOMAN, RELATIVE

syngenēs συγγενής 4773

syngenēs occurs twelve times and exclusively means "kin," "kinsman," "kinswoman." General references are found in Mark 6:4; Luke 2:44; 14:12; 21:16; John 18:26; Acts 10:24; Rom 9:3; 16:7, 11, 21. In Luke 1:36 the term refers to Elizabeth, mother of John the Baptist and cousin of Mary, mother of Jesus.

MARRY, MARRIAGE, GIVE IN MARRIAGE

gamos γάμος 1062

gamos means "wedding banquet," "marriage feast," and occurs sixteen times. The term is frequently found in Jesus' parables concerning the celebratory feast at the end of the age described in terms of a wedding banquet (Matt 22:2ff.; 25:10; Luke 12:36). In Matt 22:11, ***gamos*** is used in conjunction with ***endyma*** to describe a wedding garment. General references to marriage feasts in a literal sense are found in Luke 14:8; John 2:1, 2. Heb 13:4 refers to the sanctity of the marriage bed. Rev 19:7, 9 refer to the consummate eschatological feast of the "marriage supper of the Lamb."

gamiskō, gamizō γαμίσκω, γαμίζω 1061

gamiskō and ***gamizō*** are variant forms of the same verb, which means "to give in marriage." These terms are found in only six contexts. Matt 24:38; Luke 17:27; 1 Cor 7:38 speak of marriage in the natural, human context. Mark 12:25; Matt 22:30; Luke 20:35 refer to the denial of marriage status to heavenly beings such as angels, and the resurrected saints in glory.

gameō γαμέω 1060

gameō is the more common NT term signifying "to marry," "give in marriage." In the majority of cases, the term relates to the human custom of marriage (Matt 5:32; 19:9ff.; 22:25ff.; 24:38; Mark 6:17; 10:11ff.; Luke 14:20; 16:18; 17:27; 20:34; 1 Cor 7:9ff.; 1 Tim 4:3; 5:11ff.). Then, in three contexts, like ***gamizō*** (above), ***gameō*** refers to the denial of marriage status to angels and resurrected saints in heaven (Matt 22:30; Mark 12:25; Luke 20:35).

epigambreuō ἐπιγαμβρεύω 1918

epigambreuō occurs only in Matt 22:24 and refers to a man marrying the childless widow of his brother who has recently died. This verb is the NT dynamic equivalent of the Hebrew term *yābam*, which signified the custom of levirate marriage in ancient Israel. Matt 22:24 is actually citing and summarizing the Mosaic legislation dealing with this custom.

MOTHER

mētēr μήτηρ 3384

mētēr is found approximately ninety times meaning "mother" in both a literal and metaphorical sense.

mētēr frequently refers to mothers of specific persons, including a number of references to Mary the mother of Jesus (Matt 1:18; 2:11ff.; 12:46ff.; Mark 3:31ff.; Luke 2:34, 43ff.; John 2:1ff.; 19:25ff.; Acts 1:14). See also Matt 14:8; 20:20; Mark 5:40; Luke 7:12ff.; Acts 12:12; Rom 16:13; 2 Tim 1:5.

mētēr also refers to "mother" in non-specific, generalized contexts. There is the command to honor one's father and mother in Matt 15:4; 19:19; Mark 7:10; Luke 18:20; Eph 6:2. Blessing is promised to those who leave father and mother for the sake of the gospel in Matt 19:29; Mark 10:29ff. The necessity of leaving father and mother in order to marry is indicated in Matt 19:5; Mark 10:7, 19; Eph 5:31. Matt 10:35ff.; Luke 14:26 affirm that love for one's mother and father is to be subservient to the love of Christ. In confronting the necessity of "new birth," Nicodemus had great difficulty in grasping what Jesus meant. His question in John 3:4 illustrates this: "How can a man enter his mother's womb a second time and be born again?" Paul, in Gal 1:15, declares that God had called him to be his servant prior to his birth, or literally, "from his mother's womb."

mētēr is also found in metaphorical contexts. In several contexts, Jesus declared that his disciples, and all those who obey the word of God, are his "mother and brothers," that is, his true spiritual family (Matt 12:48ff.; Mark 3:33ff.; Luke 8:21). Gal 4:26 mentions the heavenly Jerusalem as the "mother" of the church of Christ. In Rev 17:5, the city of Babylon is declared to be the "mother of harlots," supreme in her idolatry.

MOTHER-IN-LAW

penthera πενθερά 3994

penthera occurs five times and means "mother-in-law" in each instance. The "mother-in-law" of the apostle Peter is specifically mentioned in the context of her illness and subsequent cure by Jesus (Matt 8:14; Mark 1:30; Luke 4:38). The other references to "mother-in-law" are found in Matt 10:35; Luke 12:53, indicating that the impact of the gospel on families will inevitably entail some division among family members — between those who believe and those who do not.

ORPHAN, FATHERLESS

orphanos ὀρφανός 3737

orphanos is a rare adjectival form denoting "those who are without fathers" (i.e., orphans) in John 14:18; Jas 1:17.

POSSESSIONS

peripoiēsis περιποίησις 4047

peripoiēsis is a noun derived from the verb ***peripoieō*** ("to purchase"), meaning "(purchased) possessions" and found only in Eph 1:14. In this context it refers to the heavenly inheritance of the people of God, whose salvation has been obtained through the redemptive work of Christ on the cross.

- ▸ **69.** Have, Possess, Hold, Grasp, Bear, Carry > OBTAIN

SEE ALSO

- ▸ **2.** Supernatural Beings/Forces, Spiritual Realm > POSSESS, POSSESSION
  daimonizomai
- ▸ **30.** Money, Business, Wealth, Poverty > GOODS, PROPERTY, POSSESSIONS
  ktēma

PUT AWAY

apolyō ἀπολύω 630

apolyō is a verb found nearly ninety times with the primary meaning "to release," including the more common senses of "let go," "send away," "put away."

The action of "putting away" refers to divorcing one's wife, or at least the intention to do so (Matt 1:19; 5:31ff.; 19:3, 7ff.; Mark 10:2ff.; Luke 16:18; 1 Cor 7:12).

- ▸ **25.** Family, Marriage, Adoption, Inheritance > DIVORCE
- ▸ **44.** Repentance, Forgiveness, Mercy, Redeem, Save > FORGIVE, FORGIVENESS, RELEASE
- ▸ **49.** Allow, Accept, Approve, Refuse > ALLOW
- ▸ **55.** Bondage, Captivity, Servitude > RELEASE
- ▸ **79.** Throw, Send, Drive, Mix, Remove > SEND, SEND AWAY, SEND OUT

SEE ALSO

- ▸ **54.** Rule, Authority, Command, Obedience > PUT IN SUBJECTION
  hypotassō
- ▸ **79.** Throw, Send, Drive, Mix, Remove > PUT OFF, PUT AWAY, CAST ASIDE
  apotithēmi, apekdyomai
- ▸ **83.** Set, Put, Place, Prepare, Establish > PUT, PLACE, LAY
  tithēmi, paratithēmi, epitithēmi, peritithēmi, epiballō

SISTER

adelphē ἀδελφή 79

adelphē occurs around twenty-five times and means "sister" both in the literal sense of one's siblings and as a term of endearment.

Literal references to "sisters" include those in Matt 13:56; Mark 10:29ff.; John 11:1ff.; Acts 23:16; Rom 16:15. Other contexts indicate the sense of "sister" as a platonic term of endearment for a woman, reflecting her status as part of the family of believers (Matt 12:50; Mark 3:35; Rom 16:1; 1 Cor 7:15; Jas 2:15; 2 John 13).

SON, CHILD

huios υἱός 5207

huios occurs nearly four hundred times. It means "son," "child(ren)" throughout its usage, and is used both literally and metaphorically. ***huios*** refers generally to "son" in the literal sense of a male child (e.g., Matt 7:9; Luke 1:31; John 4:46ff.; Rom 9:9; Gal 4:22; Heb 11:24).

huios also refers to Jesus, the "son" of Mary and Joseph (Matt 1:21ff.; Mark 6:3; Luke 1:13; John 1:45). Matt 1:1 uses the word "son" in a genealogical context. The "sons" of Levi are referred to in Heb 7:5.

Believers are often spoken of as "children," or "sons," of God (Matt 5:9; Rom 8:14; Gal 4:6). 1 Thess 5:5 refers to believers as "children of light." Matt 13:48 speaks of "children, or sons of the kingdom." The expression "sons of Abraham" is found in Gal 3:7. Conversely, unbelievers are referred to as "sons of disobedience" in Eph 5:6; Col 3:6. The antichrist figure is described in 2 Thess 2:3 as "the son of perdition."

Elsewhere, the term "Son" refers to Christ. The phrase "Son of God" is commonly used in reference to Christ (e.g., Matt 4:3ff.; 16:16; Mark 3:11; Luke 1:35; 15:11ff.; John 10:36; Acts 8:37; Rom 1:4; 2 Cor 1:19; Gal 2:20; Eph 4:13; Heb 4:14ff.; 1 John 5:10ff.; Rev 2:18). In addition, Christ is often referred to simply as "the Son" (Matt 11:27; Mark 1:1; John 1:18; 5:22ff.; 1 Cor 15:28; Heb 1:8; 1 John 2:22ff.). John 3:16 refers to Christ as "the only begotten Son." Luke 1:32 describes him as the "Son of the Most High." The title "Son of Man" is self-consciously taken by Christ as an expression of his fulfillment of the messianic "Son of Man" figure of Dan 7 (Matt 8:20; 20:28; Mark 2:10; Luke 5:25; John 1:51; Acts 7:56; Rev 1:13; 14:14). Christ is also described as the embodiment of the messianic "Son of David" (Matt 9:27; 12:23; 22:42ff.; Luke 18:38ff.).

God himself refers to Jesus Christ as "my (beloved) Son" in a number of places (Matt 3:17; Mark 1:11; 9:7; Luke 3:22; 2 Pet 1:17; Acts 13:33). In Heb 1:5; 5:5, this designation is expanded with the words ". . . whom I have begotten."

UNMARRIED

agamos ἄγαμος 22

agamos is an adjective found in four contexts, used nominally to refer to those who are unmarried, both men and women (1 Chr 7:8, 11, 32, 34).

▸ **15.** Gender, Reproduction, Youth, Aging > UNMARRIED

WIDOW

chēra χήρα 5503

chēra is a noun occurring around thirty times. It means "widow" in both literal and figurative contexts, though the latter use is rare.

General references to "widows" as a social class are found in Matt 23:14; Mark 12:40ff.; Luke 4:25ff.; Acts 6:1; 1 Cor 7:8; 1 Tim 5:3ff.; Jas 1:27; and individual women in this category are described in Luke 2:37; 18:3ff.; 21:2.

chēra is also used metaphorically to refer to the city of Babylon in Rev 18:7, indicating that it is stripped of all power and authority.

WIFE

gunē γυνή 1135

gynē is a noun found in over two hundred contexts with the dual meanings of "woman" and "wife." There is overlap between these two senses.

Literal references to individual women as wives include those in Matt 1:20; 5:31; Mark 6:18. Other general references to wives are found in Matt 22:24ff.; Mark 12:20; Luke 20:29; Rom 7:21; 1 Cor 5:1. The creation ordinance of marriage in which "a husband is joined to his wife" is referred to in Matt 19:5; Mark 10:7.

"Levirate marriage" is referred to in Matt 22:24ff.; Mark 12:9ff.; Luke 20:28ff. This cultural practice advocated the remarriage of a childless widowed woman to the closest eligible male relative of her deceased husband, so that she could have children by him in order to preserve the family line of her first husband (Eph 5:22; Col 3:18ff.; 1 Pet 3:1).

gynē is used metaphorically in Rev 19:7; 21:9, referring to the church as the "bride," the "wife" of Christ, the Lamb.

26. Nations, Identities, People Groups

CHRISTIAN

Christianos Χριστιανός 5546

Christianos is a rare noun transliterated as "Christian," denoting those who are followers of Jesus Christ. It is found only in Acts 11:26; 26:28; 1 Pet 4:16.

FOREIGNER, STRANGER, SOJOURNER ALIEN

allotrios ἀλλότριος 245

The noun ***allotrios*** occurs fourteen times with the senses of "other," "stranger and alien," or "foreigner." The term is also used adjectivally.

The meaning "stranger," merely in the sense of "someone else" or "other people" who may or may not be known, is indicated in Matt 17:25, 26; Luke 16:12; John 10:5; Rom 14:4; 15:20; 2 Cor 10:15, 16; 1 Tim 5:22. In Heb 9:25, the specific reference to the blood of the high priest's sacrifice that "does not belong to him" literally designates it as "the blood of others." In Heb 11:9, ***allotrios*** is used nominally to refer to Abraham, likening him to a "foreigner" in the land of promise. In Heb 11:34 the usage is adjectival, denoting "foreign" armies; and in Acts 7:6 ***allotrios*** refers to a "foreign" land.

paroikos πάροικος 3941

paroikos is a noun occurring four times meaning "stranger," "foreigner," or "sojourner." It refers to the Israelites in Egypt (Acts 7:6, 29); and to believers on earth (Eph 2:19; 1 Pet 2:11).

paroikia παροικία 3940

paroikia is a rare noun with the sense of "sojourner" or "stranger" found only in Acts 13:17, with reference to the Israelites in Egypt.

GENTILE, GREEK

ethnos ἔθνος 1484

ethnos is a noun found over 160 times with the dominant meanings "Gentiles," "nations" throughout.

The term "Gentile" denotes pagan peoples in Matt 4:15; Luke 22:25; Acts 14:2; Rom 2:14; 1 Cor 5:1; Gal 2:2ff.; 1 Pet 4:3.

ethnos refers to the Romans in Matt 20:19; Mark 10:33; Luke 18:32; Acts 4:27.

The Gentile nations are the objects of divine mercy and saving revelation in Luke 2:32; Acts 21:19ff.; Rom 1:13; 9:24; 15:9ff.; Col 1:27; 2 Tim 4:17. In particular, they are said to be the recipients of the Holy Spirit in Acts 10:45; 11:1, 18; Eph 2:11; 3:6ff. Similarly, the Gentiles are also said to receive the "light" of the gospel in Acts 13:47ff.; and their conversion is noted in Acts 15:3ff.; 26:23; Rom 11:11ff.

The expression "times of the Gentiles" refers to the time when the world will come to an end and God's final judgment is imminent (Luke 21:24). Similarly, the phrase "fullness of the Gentiles" refers to the time when the greatest number of pagan peoples will be brought into the kingdom of God (Rom 11:25).

▸ **26.** Nations, Identities, People Groups > NATION

ethnikos ἐθνικός 1482

ethnikos is a rare noun denoting a "pagan, or Gentile man," found only in Matt 6:7; 18:17.

ethnikōs ἐθνικῶς 1483

ethnikōs is a rare adverbial form meaning "like a Gentile" (i.e., after the custom of the Gentiles), found only in Gal 2:14.

hellēn Ἕλλην 1672

hellēn is a noun found nearly thirty times denoting those of Greek nationality. In the NT the "Greeks" are synonymous with the Gentiles (e.g., John 12:20; Acts 14:1; 18:4; Rom 1:14ff.; 2:9ff.; 10:12; 1 Cor 1:22ff.; Gal 2:3; Col 3:11).

JEW, HEBREW

Hebraios Ἑβραῖος 1445

This term is rare in the NT, occurring only five times. ***Hebraios*** refers in all cases to the Jewish people or nation in distinction from others (Acts 6:1; 13:25; 2 Cor 11:22; Phil 3:5 [twice]).

Ioudaios Ἰουδαῖος 2453

Ioudaios refers to a Jew, a person belonging to the Jewish race. The term occurs around two hundred times.

Mundane usage in narrative description is found in Matt 28:15; Mark 7:3; Luke 7:3; John 3:1. The magi in Matt 2:2 refer to Jesus as "King of the Jews"; the same title is used in Jesus' trial before Pontius Pilate (Matt 27:11; Mark 15:2ff.; Luke 23:3; John 18:33). The crowd mocks Jesus with this title (Matt 27:29); and a sign with this ascription is placed on the cross above Jesus' head (Matt 27:37; Mark 15:26; Luke 23:38; John 19:19ff.). During the earthly ministry of Jesus, Jewish people were often hostile towards him (John 2:18; 5:16ff.; 6:41; 7:1; 10:31ff.; 19:7). John 4:9 mentions the Jews' hatred of Samaritans.

Jewish opposition to the missionary enterprise of the apostle Paul is frequently alluded to in the book of Acts (Acts 9:23; 13:45; 14:19; 20:3; 21:27; 23:12; 25:7). The early Christians were likewise despised by the Jewish community on the whole (Acts 14:2; 17:1). Ironically, the Jewish people were initially the sole targets, or recipients, of Paul's gospel preaching (Acts 11:19; 13:5; 17:7). According to Paul, genuine "Jewishness" requires the process of "heart circumcision" to take place — that is, renewal of one's heart attitude to God as revealed in the person of Christ (Rom 2:29). Rom 10:12; Gal 3:28 make it clear that there is no distinction between Jew and Gentile believers in the sight of God, who accepts all who call upon him in genuine faith, Jew and Gentile alike.

NATION

ethnos ἔθνος 1484

ethnos is found in approximately 160 contexts with the meanings "nation" and "Gentile" (predominantly in the plural). ***ethnos*** refers to "nation" in a general sense and also indicates a pagan or Gentile people group.

ethnos refers to "nation(s)" in a general sense in Matt 21:43; 24:7; Mark 11:17; Luke 12:30; Acts 2:5; 17:26. Jesus declares in Matt 24:9 that his followers will be hated by "all nations." The nations are depicted as the object of divine judgment, including both the righteous and the wicked (Matt 25:32). Several texts declare that divine judgment or wrath is poured out on the nations (Luke 21:25; Acts 7:7; 13:19; Rev 11:18; 16:19). The nations are described as inflicting temporary victory over the people of God (Rev 11:2, 9; 13:7). In the latter context, the rule of the "sea beast," or the satanic counterfeit messiah, is in view. In Rev 18:23, the nations are said to be deceived by the city of Babylon; and they are depicted as the object of satanic deception in Rev 20:8.

In a much more positive context, the nations are designated as the object of Christian missionary endeavor, that they might become baptized disciples of Christ (Matt 28:19). Several texts indicate that the gospel is to be preached to "all nations" (Mark 13:10; Luke 24:47; Rom 1:5 [implied]; Rev 14:6). The spiritual blessing of salvation is designated for the nations through the covenant promises to Abraham in Gal 3:8, 14. Rev 15:4 affirms that all nations will ultimately worship God; and Rev 21:24 declares that the redeemed nations shall be illuminated by the heavenly city. Rev 22:2 refers to the nations receiving healing from the tree of life in the heavenly city.

Israel is described as a nation in Luke 23:2; John 11:48; 18:35; Acts 10:22; 24:2; 26:4; 28:19. Believers in Christ are declared to be a "holy nation" in 1 Pet 2:9, according to the promise given to the old covenant people of Israel. Rev 2:26 indicates that believers are to be given power over the nations by Christ. Rev 5:9; 7:9 record that people "from every nation" are delivered from the penalty of sin and death by means of the death of Christ, which constitutes a ransom for sin. In Rev 12:5; 19:15, Christ is portrayed as the ruler of the nations.

▸ **26.** Nations, Identities, People Groups > GENTILE, GREEK

NAZARENE

nazōraios Ναζωραῖος 3480

It is uncertain whether the NT term ***nazōraios*** derives from Hebrew *nāzîr* (which refers primarily to an Israelite man or woman who undertook a special vow of separation or holiness, dedicating himself/herself to Yahweh for a specified period, up to and including the whole of one's life) or whether ***nazōraios*** is simply an adjective referring to the town of Nazareth.

nazōraios is translated "Nazarene" twice. Matt 2:23 contains a cryptic reference to an otherwise unknown OT prophecy referring to the Messiah: "He shall be called a Nazarene." In this context, it is clear that the statement refers to Jesus in relation to Nazareth, the town of his upbringing. In Acts 24:25 Jesus is described as the ringleader of the "Nazarene sect."

All other uses of ***nazōraios*** refer to Jesus "of Nazareth" (Matt 26:71; Mark 10:47; Luke 18:37; 24:19; John 18:5ff.; 19:19; Acts 2:22; 3:6; 4:10; 6:14; 22:8; 26:9).

NEIGHBOR

plēsion πλησίον 4139

plēsion is a general term for "neighbor," expressing the idea of one's fellow human being. In addition, for Jews, the term indicates any member of the Hebrew race; and for Christians, it refers to fellow believers. ***plēsion*** occurs in seventeen contexts.

The general sense of "neighbor" as one's fellow human being is indicated in Matt 5:43; 19:19; 22:39; Mark 12:31ff.; Luke 10:27ff.; Rom 13:9ff.; 15:2; Gal 5:14; Jas 2:8.

The other senses of "neighbor" occur much less frequently. Acts 7:27 refers to the "neighbor" of Moses, or his fellow Hebrew, whose beating at the hands of an Egyptian task master he avenged by slaying the latter. Eph 4:25; Heb 8:11 refer to one's fellow Christian believers as "neighbors."

SEE ALSO

▸ **24.** Dwell, Live, Gather, Hospitality > NEIGHBOR
perioikos, geitōn

PEOPLE

laos λαός 2992

laos is a noun occurring around 140 times, meaning "people." This meaning overlaps with that of "nation" in a number of places.

The meaning "people(s)," with the sense of "Gentiles" or "nation(s)," is indicated in Luke 2:31; Acts 4:21; Rev 10:11; 11:19; 14:6; 17:15. Acts 15:14 refers to a "people" chosen from out of the Gentiles, for his name (i.e., God's name). See also Rev 7:9.

The bulk of the usage of ***laos*** refers to the people of Israel, the people belonging to God. References to the people of Israel are found, for example, in Matt 2:6; 15:8; Mark 7:6; Acts 4:8; 13:17; Rom 10:21; Heb 5:3; 7:27; Jude 5. John 18:14 records the significant statement of Caiaphas the high priest that it would be expedient if one man should die for the people (or nation). 1 Pet 2:9, 10; Rev 5:9 specifically allude to a people belonging to God. In a more general context, ***laos*** refers to people, focusing on the population of Jerusalem (Matt 2:4; 21:23; 26:5; 27:25; Luke 1:10, 21; Acts 5:20). Several texts indicate the meaning "people" in the sense of a crowd of Jewish citizens (Luke 18:43; 20:9; Acts 3:11).

There are several significant references to "his people," indicating those who belong to Christ (Matt 1:21); and those who belong to God in the context of God redeeming his people from their sin (Luke 1:68, 77; 7:16; Rom 11:2). Also recorded in several places is the expression "my people," referring to those who belong to God — both Jew and Gentile (Rom 9:25; Rev 18:4). In 2 Cor 6:16; Heb 8:10, these words are found in the context of the writers citing the old covenant formula: "I will be your God and you shall be my people." See also Rev 21:3.

TRIBE

phylē φυλή 5443

phylē is a noun found in twenty-five contexts meaning "tribe(s)" throughout.

References to the "tribes" of Israel include those in Matt 19:28; Luke 2:36; 22:36; Acts 13:21; Rom 11:1; Phil 3:5; Heb 7:13ff.; Rev 5:5; 7:14ff.; 21:12.

More generally, the "tribes" of the earth, referring to the nations at large, are mentioned in Matt 24:30; Rev 7:1; 5:9; 7:9; 11:9; 13:7; 14:6.

27. Community, Partnership, Unity, Discord

ACCESS

prosagōgē προσαγωγή 4318

prosagōgē is a noun found three times, denoting "access" to God made possible through the saving work of Christ through faith (Rom 5:2; Eph 2:18; 3:12).

AGREE, AGREEMENT

symphōneō συμφωνέω 4856

symphōneō is a verb found in seven contexts, each of which expresses the meaning "to agree," "come to an agreement" (Matt 18:19; 20:2, 13; Luke 5:36; Acts 5:9; 15:15).

phroneō φρονέω 5426

The verb ***phroneō*** is found in nearly forty different contexts, with the primary meaning of "think," plus related senses. One of these is "to agree," "be of one mind or like-minded" (Rom 12:16; 15:5; 2 Cor 13:11; Phil 2:2; 4:2).

- ▸ **51.** Knowledge, Wisdom, Remember, Forget > SET ONE'S MIND ON
- ▸ **51.** Knowledge, Wisdom, Remember, Forget > THINK, THOUGHT

syntithēmi συντίθημι 4934

syntithēmi is a verb with the meaning "to agree," "make a formal pledge." It is found in only four places (Luke 22:5; John 9:22; Acts 23:20; 24:9).

- ▸ **27.** Community, Partnership, Unity, Discord > AGREEMENT, COVENANT

synkatathesis συγκατάθεσις 4783

synkatathesis is a rare noun denoting an "agreement" in the sense of "that which is compatible." It is found only in 2 Cor 6:16, where Paul asks the rhetorical question: "What agreement is there between the temple of God and idols?" The implicit answer is "None."

AGREEMENT, COVENANT

syntithēmi συντίθημι 4934

syntithēmi is a verb found in four places with the meaning "to enter into an agreement," "make plans." The contexts are all mundane and refer only to human participants (Luke 22:5; John 9:22; Acts 23:20; 24:9).

- ▸ **27.** Community, Partnership, Unity, Discord > AGREE, AGREEMENT

SEE ALSO

- ▸ **38.** Covenant, Law, Rites, Roles > COVENANT, TESTAMENT
  diathēkē, diatithēmi

ALIENATE

apallotrioō ἀπαλλοτριόω 526

The verb ***apallotrioō*** is found three times, meaning "to be alienated" or "separated" and referring to estrangement from God or his people (Eph 2:12; 4:18; Col 1:21).

SEE ALSO

- ▸ **26.** Nations, Identities, People Groups > FOREIGNER, STRANGER, SOJOURNER ALIEN
  allotrios

BOND

syndesmos σύνδεσμος 4886

syndesmos is a noun found four times with the largely metaphorical sense of "bond," or that which "binds" people together for good or ill.

Acts 8:23 refers to the evil desire for power that had overtaken Simon the magician who tried to buy the gift of the Holy Spirit. Peter rebuked him as one who was "captive to sin" (lit., "in the bond of iniquity"). Eph 4:3 enjoins believers to maintain the "bond of peace," or the spirit of unity that will maintain their strong fellowship. There is a similar expression in Col 3:14 — "the bond of perfect harmony."

In Col 2:19, ***syndesmos*** refers to the "ligaments" of the human body that give it a uniform structure and function. The context is a metaphorical description of the importance of the unity of the body of Christ, the fellowship of Christian believers.

SEE ALSO

- ▸ **32.** Law, Justice, Jurisprudence, Judgment > CHAIN, BOND
  desmios
- ▸ **55.** Bondage, Captivity, Servitude > BOND, CHAIN
  desmos, halysis

BROTHER, BROTHERHOOD

pseudadelphos ψευδάδελφος 5569

pseudadelphos denotes a "false brother," or one who professes to be a Christian but whose life contradicts his testimony (2 Cor 11:26). Gal 2:4 contains the additional observation that such "false brethren" are also guilty of false teaching.

adelphotēs ἀδελφότης 81

adelphotēs is a rare noun meaning "brotherhood" or "brethren" in the sense of the community of believers in general terms (1 Pet 2:17; 5:9)

SEE ALSO

- ▸ **25.** Family, Marriage, Adoption, Inheritance > BROTHER
  adelphos

CHILDREN

teknion τεκνίον 5040

teknion is a noun meaning "little child." Each of its nine occurrences refers metaphorically to one's congregation and/or fellow believers under one's pastoral care (John 13:33; Gal 4:19; 1 John 2:1, 12, 28; 3:7, 18; 4:4; 5:21).

SEE ALSO

- ▸ **15.** Gender, Reproduction, Youth, Aging > CHILD, OFFSPRING
  paidarion, nepiazō, teknogoneō, enkyos
- ▸ **25.** Family, Marriage, Adoption, Inheritance > CHILD
  teknon, pais, paidion, nēpios, teknotropheō

COMPLAINT

momphē μομφή 3437

momphē is a rare noun denoting a "complaint" against someone, found only in Col 3:13.

SEE ALSO

- ▸ **58.** Vices > COMPLAIN, MURMUR, MUTTER, GRUMBLE
  mempsimoiros

CONFUSION, DISORDER

akatastasia ἀκαταστασία 181

akatastasia is a noun found in five contexts with the general sense of "confusion," "disorder." Luke 21:9 refers to "revolutions" in the context of social upheaval and war; as does 2 Cor 6:5, specifically mentioning "riots." Confusion and disorder in general are noted in 2 Cor 12:20; Jas 3:16. 1 Cor 14:33 affirms that God is not a God of "confusion."

synchysis σύγχυσις 4799

synchysis is a rare noun found only in Acts 19:29 denoting "confusion" in the sense of civil unrest.

SEE ALSO

- ▸ **45.** Faith, Belief, Trust, Promise > CONFOUND, CONFUSE, CONFUSION
  syncheō

DISAGREEMENT

asymphōnos ἀσύμφωνος 800

asymphōnos is a rare adjectival term found only in Acts 28:25 with reference to a "disagreement."

isos ἴσος 2470

The adjective ***isos*** occurs in eight contexts and expresses the meaning "equal" in most of them. In Mark 14:56, 59, however, the term is used negatively in the sense of "not agreeing" with reference to the false testimony given against Christ at his trial.

- ▸ **88.** Qualities, Characteristics > EQUAL

DIVIDE, DIVISIVE, DIVISION

schizō σχίζω 4977

schizō is a verb found eleven times with the primary sense of "to bear." There is also, however, the associated metaphorical sense of "divide," found in Acts 14:4; 23:7, referring to two contrasting points of view held by two opposing groups of people within a community — a people "divided."

- ▸ **35.** Clothing, Adornment, Textiles > TEAR
- ▸ **85.** Movement, Position, State > OPEN

diamerismos διαμερισμός 1267

diamerismos is a rare noun found only in Luke 12:51 denoting "division" in the sense of "strife."

dichostasia διχοστασία 1370

dichostasia is a noun found in two places referring to "divisions" in the sense of "quarreling," "dissension" in Rom 16:17; Gal 5:20.

schisma σχίσμα 4978

schisma is a noun found eight times denoting "division" in the sense of "dispute," "argument" in John 7:43; 9:16; 10:19. In particular, Paul exhorts the Corinthian congregation not to engage in "factional arguments or disputes" in 1 Cor 1:10; 11:18; 12:25.

hairetikos αἱρετικός 141

hairetikos occurs only once, in Titus 3:10, and refers to a person who is a schismatic, who divides a congregation with false teaching. Such a one is to be isolated from the community.

EXPEL, EXCOMMUNICATE

aposynagōgos ἀποσυνάγωγος 656

aposynagōgos is an adjective denoting "one who is expelled from the synagogue" or "excommunicated." It is found three times (John 9:22; 12:42; 16:2).

SEE ALSO

- ▸ **24.** Dwell, Live, Gather, Hospitality > ASSEMBLE, ASSEMBLY
  synerchomai
- ▸ **38.** Covenant, Law, Rites, Roles > RULER OF THE SYNAGOGUE
  archisynagōgos
- ▸ **41.** Sacrifice, Offering, Worship, Praise > GATHER, ASSEMBLE, ASSEMBLY, SYNAGOGUE, CHURCH
  ekklēsia, panēgyris, synagōgē, episynagōgē

FELLOW

anēr ἀνήρ 435

anēr is a common noun occurring over two hundred times with the principal meaning "man," "husband." In Acts 17:5, however, ***anēr*** refers to wicked "fellows," troublemakers inciting a civil riot.

▸ **15.** Gender, Reproduction, Youth, Aging > MAN, MALE
▸ **25.** Family, Marriage, Adoption, Inheritance > HUSBAND

FELLOWSHIP, COMMUNION, PARTNER

koinōnia κοινωνία 2842

koinōnia is a noun denoting "fellowship," "communion" throughout most of its twenty occurrences. It emphasizes the worth of Christian community bound together by faith and trust in Christ (Acts 2:42; 1 Cor 1:9).

In particular, ***koinōnia*** refers to the "participation," the "communion" made possible through the symbolic meal signifying the body and blood of Christ in 1 Cor 10:16; Gal 2:9; 1 John 1:3ff.

A general reference to "fellowship" in the sense of a "partnership" is found in 2 Cor 6:14; Phil 1:5. The bond of "fellowship" between the believer and the Holy Spirit is indicated in 2 Cor 13:14; Phil 2:1; the "fellowship" or "sharing" of Christ's sufferings in Phil 3:10; and the "sharing" of one's faith in Phlm 6.

koinōnos κοινωνός 2844

koinōnos is a variant of ***koinōnia*** (above) denoting a "partner," or one who shares in a bond, commitment, or common task.

The murderous "partnership" of godless Israelites who had brought about the death of prophets is indicated in Matt 23:30.

Various "partnerships" are referred to: business comrades (Luke 5:10); fellow worshipers (1 Cor 10:18); demon worshipers (1 Cor 10:20); partners in Christ's sufferings (2 Cor 1:7); gospel ministry (2 Cor 8:23; Phlm 17); suffering in persecution (Heb 10:33).

Being a "partaker" of divine glory is indicated in 1 Pet 5:1; and a "partaker" of the divine nature in 2 Pet 1:4.

▸ **27.** Community, Partnership, Unity, Discord > SHARE, PART, ALLOTMENT, PARTAKE

koinōneō κοινωνέω 2841

koinōneō is a verb found in eight places signifying the action of "making oneself a partner," "sharing in."

"Sharing in" the spiritual blessings of God's people is indicated in Rom 15:27. The act of "sharing" material goods with the teachers of God's word is noted in Gal 6:6. "Entering into a partnership" of gospel ministry is indicated in Phil 4:15. A warning against "participating" in another person's sin is recorded in 1 Tim 5:22. The privilege of "sharing in" Christ's sufferings is noted in 1 Pet 4:13. See also Rom 12:13; 2 John 11.

▸ **27.** Community, Partnership, Unity, Discord > SHARE, PART, ALLOTMENT, PARTAKE

synkoinōneō συγκοινωνέω 4790

synkoinōneō is a synonym for ***koinōneō*** (above) found in only three places. A warning to "take no part in" the works of darkness and the sins of others is found in Eph 5:11; Rev 18:4. Phil 4:4 refers to "sharing" one's trouble.

▸ **27.** Community, Partnership, Unity, Discord > SHARE, PART, ALLOTMENT, PARTAKE

FRIEND, FRIENDSHIP

philos φίλος 5384

philos is a noun occurring about thirty times with the consistent meaning "friend."

The meaning "friend" in the sense of a "genuine companion" is predicated of Christ in his relationship with the outcasts of Jewish society (Matt 11:19; Luke 7:34).

References to "friends" in general human relationships are found in Luke 7:6; 11:5ff.; 14:10ff.; 16:9; John 3:29; 15:13; Acts 10:24; 19:31; 27:3. Jesus refers to his disciples as his "friends" in Luke 12:4; and also all those who devote themselves to him (John 15:14ff.). In Jas 2:23 Abraham is designated the "friend of God." Caesar's "friend" in John 19:12 denotes one who is a loyal citizen of the empire, and obedient to the emperor.

In a metaphorical context, ***philos*** denotes the secular, godless person as a "friend" of the world.

philia φιλία 5373

philia is a rare variant of ***philos***. It is found only in Jas 4:4 and equates enmity with God with "friendship" with the world.

hetairos ἑταῖρος 2083

hetairos is a noun meaning "friend," found in Matt 20:13; 22:12; 26:50. The sense here denotes the polite form of address "Sir."

HERESY, HERETICAL

hairesis αἵρεσις 139

This noun occurs nine times with the predominant sense of "sect." However, in 2 Pet 2:1, the word refers to "(destructive) heresies" perpetrated by false teachers within the church, whose punishment from God will be swift and inevitable.

▸ **27.** Community, Partnership, Unity, Discord > SECT, FACTION, PARTY

JOIN

kollaō κολλάω 2853

kollaō occurs eleven times and means "join together with" in over half of these contexts.

In the context of employment in Luke 15:15, the prodigal son "joins himself to" the owner of a swineherd in order to obtain work feeding the pigs and so avoid starvation.

kollaō is also used in the context of worship. 1 Cor 6:17 mentions a spiritual union with God, being joined to him.

Acts 5:13 records that no one initially dared to "join together with" the early Christians in worship, out of fear at the signs performed by the apostles. Then Acts 9:26 explains that Paul's attempt to "join together with" the disciples in Jerusalem was thwarted at first, on account of their fear of him. Acts 17:4 speaks of Jewish converts in Thessalonica who "joined together with" Paul and Silas in fellowship.

In another quite different context, 1 Cor 6:16 spells out the sobering consequences of "joining oneself together with" a prostitute in becoming one in body with her.

synarmologeō συναρμολογέω 4883

This is a rare term, occurring only twice and meaning "to be joined together." The underlying sense is that of a perfect fit. Eph 2:21 speaks metaphorically of the new covenant community of God's people as a building whose cornerstone is Jesus Christ. It is this "building" that is perfectly built, or "joined together," as an appropriate symbolic expression for the perfection of the church. Similarly, ***synarmologeō*** also describes the body image of the church in Eph 4:16, referring to Christ as the one from whom the whole body is (perfectly) joined together.

SEE ALSO

▸ **25.** Family, Marriage, Adoption, Inheritance > JOIN
syzeugnymi, proskollaō

KISS

phileō φιλέω 5368

phileō is a verb that occurs approximately thirty times, with the predominant meaning "love." On three occasions, however, it refers to Judas' kiss of betrayal when he effectively handed Jesus over to his enemies through this action (Matt 26:48; Mark 14:44; Luke 22:47).

▸ **48.** Will, Purpose, Decide, Advise > LOVE

philēma φίλημα 5370

philēma is a noun derived from ***phileō*** (above) with the exclusive sense of "kiss." It is found in seven places.

Luke 7:45 indicates kissing in the context of a social greeting. In a number of places in the Pauline correspondence, the apostle refers to the kiss of greeting among believers, exhorting his readers to engage in it (Rom 16:16; 1 Cor 16:20; 2 Cor 13:12; 1 Thess 5:26; 1 Pet 5:14).

Judas' kiss of betrayal with respect to Jesus is mentioned in Luke 22:48.

kataphileō καταφιλέω 2705

kataphileō is a verb related to ***phileō*** (above), but with the exclusive sense of "kiss." ***kataphileō*** occurs six times.

kataphileō refers to the action of kissing not merely as a kiss of greeting, but as an action filled with emotions such as devotion, joy, sadness, and treachery — but not sexual passion.

Matt 26:49; Mark 14:45 mention Judas' kiss of treachery against Jesus. Luke 7:38 describes the action of the sinful woman, who was overcome by her sins and came to express her devotion to Christ by kissing his feet and anointing them with expensive perfume. Luke 15:20 describes the emotional reunion of the rebellious son with his father in Jesus' parable, as the father threw his arms around his son and kissed him on his return. Paul's farewell to the Ephesian elders was likewise an emotional parting when the leaders of the church wept and kissed him (Acts 20:37).

RECONCILE, RECONCILIATION, ATONEMENT

katallagē καταλλαγή 2643

katallagē is a noun derived from ***katallassō***, found in four places with the meaning "reconciliation." However, in each instance it is clear from the context that such "reconciliation" of sinners with God has come about only as a result of Christ's work of atonement through his death on the cross (Rom 5:11; 11:15; 2 Cor 5:18, 19).

apokatallassō ἀποκαταλλάσσω 604

apokatallassō is a verb found in only three places, all referring to Christ's work of reconciliation in restoring harmony between God and humankind. Eph 2:16 refers to God's intention to reconcile both Jew and Gentile to himself through the redemptive sacrifice of his Son on the cross. A like purpose is also indicated in Col 1:20, 21.

katallassō καταλλάσσω 2644

katallassō is a synonym for ***apokatallassō*** (above) meaning "to reconcile" in each of the five occurrences of the term.

katallassō usually refers to the redemptive work of Christ in bringing about a full reconciliation between human beings and God, through Christ's substitutionary atonement for sinful humanity on the cross (Rom 5:10; 2 Cor 5:18ff.). 1 Cor 7:18 refers to Paul's instruction concerning wives who separate from their husbands. They must either remain single, or be reconciled to their husband.

diallassomai διαλλάσσομαι 1259

diallassomai is a verb found only in Matt 5:24, with reference to Christ's command to be reconciled with one's brother (with whom there is a problem) before offering one's gift to the Lord at the altar.

hilaskomai ἱλάσκομαι 2433

hilaskomai is a term found only twice in the NT, meaning "to make atonement" in the sense of bringing about reconciliation between God and sinful humankind. This meaning occurs in Heb 2:17 with reference to the saving work of Christ, who turns aside the wrath of God against human beings through his sacrifice on the cross. In Luke 18:13, ***hilaskomai*** means "be merciful."

▸ **44.** Repentance, Forgiveness, Mercy, Redeem, Save > MERCY, MERCIFUL, COMPASSION, PITY

RESTORE

katartizō καταρτίζω 2675

katartizō is a verb found thirteen times with the primary sense of "to perfect," "mend." In one context, the term refers to the believer's obligation to attempt to "restore" his brother who has fallen into sin, returning him to the congregation as a member in good standing, having (presumably) repented of his sin.

▸ **61.** Integrity, Innocence, Piety > PERFECT, PERFECTION, COMPLETE

▸ **83.** Set, Put, Place, Prepare, Establish > PREPARE, MAKE READY

SEE ALSO

▸ **82.** Change, Exchange, Transform > RESTORE
apokathistēmi

SECT, FACTION, PARTY

hairesis αἵρεσις 139

hairesis is a noun found in nine contexts meaning "sect," in the sense of a religious or political party or faction. It also has the connotation of "heresy" or "false teaching."

The meaning "sect" in the sense of "party" is found in a number of contexts. It is evident in the general sense of a "faction" in 1 Cor 11:19; Gal 5:20. ***hairesis*** refers to the Sadducean "party" (Acts 5:17); the Pharisaic "party" (Acts 15:5; 26:5); the "sect" of the Nazarenes (Acts 24:5); and the "sect" of the Christians (Acts 28:22).

In Acts 24:14; 2 Pet 2:1, ***hairesis*** is translated "heresy" or "false teaching," referring in the latter text to the false prophets that threatened the spiritual well-being of the first-century church.

▸ **27.** Community, Partnership, Unity, Discord > HERESY, HERETICAL

SEPARATE

apodiorizō ἀποδιορίζω 592

apodiorizō is a rare verb found only in Jude 19 meaning "to separate" or "cause division."

SEE ALSO

▸ **79.** Throw, Send, Drive, Mix, Remove > SEPARATE, DIVIDE
aphorizō, chōrizō

SHARE, PART, ALLOTMENT, PARTAKE

klēros κλῆρος 2819

klēros is a noun occurring thirteen times, meaning "lot," "inheritance," in most of these contexts. In several places, however, ***klēros*** has the nuance of "allotted share." It refers, for example, to the traitor Judas Iscariot, who originally "shared" in the ministry of the twelve apostles (Acts 1:17), and also to Matthias, who succeeded him as the result of a ballot (Acts 1:25ff.). Acts 8:21 denies Simon Magus a "share" or "part" in the apostolic ministry, on account of his greed in imagining that he could purchase the gift of the Holy Spirit with money.

▸ **25.** Family, Marriage, Adoption, Inheritance > INHERIT, INHERITANCE

▸ **70.** Give, Take, Seize, Touch > LOT, ALLOTMENT, SHARE, CAST LOTS

metechō μετέχω 3348

metechō is a verb found eight times, meaning "to become a partaker of," "have a share in."

It refers, for example, to one's right "to share" in material blessings as a remuneration for ministry (1 Cor 9:10ff.). 1 Cor 10:17ff. refers to "sharing" or "partaking" of one bread. Christ is said to "share" our human nature in Heb 2:14.

metochos μέτοχος 3353

metochos is an adjective occurring six times meaning "sharing in," "partaker of." It is also used nominally to mean "partner."

metochos refers to believers "sharing" in a heavenly call (Heb 3:1) and "sharing" in godly discipline (Heb 12:8). Heb 3:14 speaks of those who "share" in Christ; and Heb 6:4 mentions those who "share" in the Holy Spirit.

symmetochos συμμέτοχος 4830

symmetochos is a synonym for ***metochos*** (above). It is twice used as a noun meaning "partaker," or "one who shares in." Eph 3:6 refers to those who share in the promise of salvation through Jesus Christ. Eph 5:7 warns against "sharing" in fellowship with the ungodly.

koinōneō κοινωνέω 2841

koinōneō is a verb found in eight contexts with the underlying sense of "come into communion or fellowship with" or "become a sharer in."

koinōneō refers to sharing in the spiritual blessings of the Gentiles (Rom 15:27); sharing in material blessings (Gal 6:6); and sharing in the sufferings of Christ (1 Pet 4:13). 1 Tim 5:22 warns against sharing, or participating in, someone else's sins. See also 2 John 11.

▸ **27.** Community, Partnership, Unity, Discord > FELLOWSHIP, COMMUNION, PARTNER

koinōnos κοινωνός 2844

koinōnos is a noun derived from ***koinōneō*** (above) occurring ten times and meaning "one who shares in" — a partner or companion.

Partners in ministry are indicated in 2 Cor 8:23; Phlm 17. "Sharers" (i.e., companions) in suffering for the gospel are noted in 2 Cor 1:7; Heb 10:33. "Those who share" in eternal glory are indicated in 1 Pet 5:1. See also 2 Pet 1:4; 1 Cor 10:18, 20. A mundane usage is found in Luke 5:10 with reference to "partners" in commerce.

▸ **27.** Community, Partnership, Unity, Discord > FELLOWSHIP, COMMUNION, PARTNER

synkoinōnos συγκοινωνός 4791

This term is derived from ***koinōnos*** with the same meaning — "one who shares with" or a "partaker of."

synkoinōnos occurs in a significant metaphorical context in Rom 11:17, which speaks of Gentile believers who were grafted on to the "olive tree," symbolizing the "elect people" of Israel. They were subsequently designated literally as "partakers of" the spiritual richness of that tree, focusing on Christ. In related contexts, see also 1 Cor 9:10; Phil 1:7, which speak of "sharing" in gospel ministry.

synkoinōneō συγκοινωνέω 4790

synkoinōneō is a variant form of ***koinōneō*** (above) occurring three times and meaning "to have fellowship with, or in," "to have a share, or part in."

Eph 5:11 warns against having a share, or part, in the works of darkness. See also Rev 18:4 in this regard. And in Phil 4:14 Paul speaks of "sharing" in his trouble.

▸ **27.** Community, Partnership, Unity, Discord > FELLOWSHIP, COMMUNION, PARTNER

symmerizō συμμερίζω 4829

This is a rare verb found only in 1 Cor 9:13 with reference to "those who share in" the sacrificial offerings presented at the temple altar.

meris μερίς 3310

meris is a noun found five times, meaning "part," "portion," or "share." It refers to a participation in the ministry of the kingdom (Acts 8:21), and to the inheritance of the saints (Col 1:12). See also 2 Cor 6:15, where Paul asks what a believer "shares" or "has in common" with an unbeliever.

synkakopatheō συγκακοπαθέω 4777

This verb is found only in 2 Tim 1:8, meaning "to share in suffering" for the gospel.

metalambanō μεταλαμβάνω 3335

metalambanō is a verb occurring six times, meaning "to partake of food," "to be a partner." In two of these contexts, the term indicates the sense of "to have (first) share" of the crops (2 Tim 2:6), and "to share in" the holiness of God (Heb 2:10).

▸ **70.** Give, Take, Seize, Touch > RECEIVE, ACCEPT, WELCOME

STIR UP

synkineō συγκινέω 4787

synkineō is a rare verb found only in Acts 6:12, with reference to "stirring up commotion," "causing a disturbance."

epegeirō ἐπεγείρω 1892

epegeirō is a rare verb, synonymous with ***synkineō*** (above) and meaning "to stir up strife," "cause a civil disturbance" in Acts 14:2.

saleuō σαλεύω 4531

saleuō is a verb with the primary sense of "shake," occurring fifteen times. In Acts 17:13, however, it refers to "stirring up" or "inciting" a crowd to uproar.

▸ **85.** Movement, Position, State > SHAKE

anaseiō ἀνασείω 383

anaseiō is a verb found on only two occasions. It means "to stir up," "excite" a crowd (Mark 15:11; Luke 23:5).

SEE ALSO

▸ **78.** Act Upon, Push, Pull, Break, Cut > STIR UP, PROVOKE
erethizō

STRIFE, QUARREL

eris ἔρις 2054

eris denotes "strife," "contention," or "quarreling" in the majority of its nine occurrences (Rom 1:29; 13:13; 1 Cor 1:11; 2 Cor 12:20; Phil 1:15; 1 Tim 6:4).

eritheia ἐριθεία 2052

eritheia is a synonym for ***eris*** (above) found in seven contexts and mostly meaning "strife," "dissension," "discord" (Rom 2:8; 2 Cor 12:20; Gal 5:10; Phil 1:16). The sense of "selfish ambition" is indicated in Phil 2:3; Jas 3:14, 16, emphasizing that such an attitude causes disunity and discord among believers.

philoneikia φιλονεικία 5379

philoneikia is found only in Luke 22:24 with reference to a "dispute" or "quarrel."

logomachia λογομαχία 3055

logomachia is a term found only in 1 Tim 6:4 with reference to "controversy" in the context of "quarreling over words."

▸ **58.** Vices > ARGUE, ARGUMENT, DISPUTE, QUARREL, STRIVE

machē μάχη 3163

machē is a noun found in four places denoting "quarrels" or "fights" (2 Cor 7:5; 2 Tim 2:23; Titus 3:9; Jas 4:1).

▸ **77.** Resist, Oppose, Fight, Rebel > FIGHT

TROUBLE, UPROAR, RIOT

ektarassō ἐκταράσσω 1613

ektarassō is another rare verb meaning to "trouble" or "throw into uproar." It is found only in Acts 16:20.

thorybos θόρυβος 2351

thorybos is a noun found seven times with the consistent meaning "uproar," in the context of a "riotous crowd" or a threatened riot (Matt 26:5; 27:24; Mark 14:2; Acts 20:1; 21:34; 24:18). In addition, Mark 5:38 refers to an "uproar" not in the sense of a riot, but an "outburst of wailing" among the crowd at the death of Jairus' daughter.

thorybeō θορυβέω 2350

thorybeō is a verb occurring only four times. In two of these contexts, it means "making a loud noise" in mourning the dead (Matt 9:23; Mark 5:39). Then, in Acts 17:5, ***thorybeō*** indicates the act of "starting a riot." In Acts 20:10 it means "being alarmed," expressed as a negative command.

stasis στάσις 4714

stasis is a noun expressing the general sense of "uproar" in most of its usage (nine times), with several differing nuances.

"Insurrection" or "revolt," in a political sense, usually involves violence of some kind. The term is used in connection with Barabbas, who was spared execution and whose place on the cross was taken by Jesus Christ (Mark 15:7; Luke 23:19, 25).

stasis also indicates a "riot" or "civil disturbance" (Acts 19:40; 23:7ff.). The apostle Paul is falsely accused of stirring up "riots" in Acts 24:5.

Finally, ***stasis*** denotes a "quarrel" or "argument" in Acts 15:2. The setting of this dispute involves the legalistic "Judaizing party" (probably a Pharisaic group) in conflict with the followers of the apostle Paul.

syncheō συγχέω 4797

syncheō is a verb occurring five times, meaning "to be in confusion," "stir up confusion" with respect to agitating a crowd (Acts 19:32; 21:27, 31).

▸ **45.** Faith, Belief, Trust, Promise > CONFOUND, CONFUSE, CONFUSION

SEE ALSO

▸ **21.** Die, Perish, Kill, Destroy > NOISE, UPROAR
rhoizēdon

UNITY

henotēs ἑνότης 1775

henotēs is a rare noun signifying the "unity" of the Spirit (Eph 4:3), and the "unity" of the faith (Eph 4:13). In both contexts, such a unity, embracing the peace and knowledge of God, is affirmed as a goal to which all believers should aspire within the community of God's people.

homophrōn ὁμόφρων 3675

homophrōn is a rare adjectival form meaning "harmonious," "being of one mind." It is found in 1 Pet 3:8 as an exhortation: "Live in unity (i.e., be at peace) with one another."

WORK TOGETHER, FELLOW WORKER

synergeō συνεργέω 4903

synergeō is a verb found in five places, meaning "to work together with," and referring to people working together in ministry (Mark 16:20; 1 Cor 16:16; 2 Cor 6:1; Jas 2:22). ***synergeō*** also refers to things "working together" for the gospel in accord with the purposes of God (Rom 8:28).

synergos συνεργός 4904

synergos is a noun occurring thirteen times, denoting "fellow workers" in gospel ministry (Rom 16:3ff.; 1 Cor 3:9; 2 Cor 1:24; 8:23; Phil 2:25; 4:3; Col 4:11; Phlm 1, 24; 3 John 8).

SEE ALSO

▸ **28.** Agriculture, Viticulture, Animal Husbandry > WORKING, TILLING
geōrgeō

▸ **30.** Money, Business, Wealth, Poverty > GAIN, PROFIT
ergasia

▸ **84.** Do, Make, Accomplish, Occur > WORK, LABOR, PRODUCE, BRING ABOUT, DEED
ergazomai, katergazomai, ergon, ergatēs, energeō, energeia, poiēma, praxis, kopos

28. Agriculture, Viticulture, Animal Husbandry

AX

axinē ἀξίνη 513

axinē is a rare noun denoting an "ax," found only in Matt 3:10; Luke 3:9.

BARLEY

krithē κριθή 2915

krithē is a rare noun found only in Rev 6:6 with reference to "barley" grain, priced at three measures for a denarius (i.e., a day's wages).

SEE ALSO

- ▸ **23.** Food, Drink, Cooking > BARLEY
  krithinos

BARN, STOREHOUSE

apothēkē ἀποθήκη 596

apothēkē is a noun denoting "barn," "storehouse" for grain, food, or other goods (Matt 3:12; 6:26; 13:30; Luke 3:17; 12:18, 24).

BEAR, BRING FORTH

karpophoreō καρποφορέω 2592

karpophoreō is a verb found in eight places with the universal sense of "bear, bring forth fruit."

The term is used literally in Matt 13:23; Mark 4:20, 28. It refers metaphorically to the manifestation of godly virtue in Luke 8:15; Rom 7:4; Col 1:10. There is a negative usage in Rom 7:5, where the impact of sinful passion aroused by the law in the life of the believer are portrayed as "bearing fruit for death." Then, in Col 1:6, mention is made of the gospel "bearing fruit" throughout the world.

- ▸ **28.** Agriculture, Viticulture, Animal Husbandry > FRUIT, FRUITFUL

SEE ALSO

- ▸ **60.** Virtues > ENDURE, BEAR, FORBEAR
  hypopherō, stegō, anechomai
- ▸ **69.** Have, Possess, Hold, Grasp, Bear, Carry > BEAR, CARRY
  bastazō, pherō, anapherō, ekpherō, phoreō, dysbastaktos

BIT, BRIDLE

chalinos χαλινός 5469

chalinos is a rare noun denoting a horse's "bit" and "bridle." Reference to a horse's "bit" is found in Jas 3:3; and to a horse's "bridle" in Rev 14:20.

SEE ALSO

- ▸ **60.** Virtues > BRIDLE, RESTRAIN
  chalinagōgeō

BREAK OFF, CUT, CUT OFF

ekklaō ἐκκλάω 1575

ekklaō is a verb found three times with the meaning "break off" in relation to branches, referring solely to the metaphorical scenario of God "cutting off" some of the Israelites from the stock of the people of God, so that Gentiles may be grafted in (Rom 11:17ff.).

koptō κόπτω 2875

koptō is a verb found in ten places with the predominant senses of "lament," "wail." In Matt 21:8; Mark 11:8, however, the term indicates the "cutting" of branches from a tree.

- ▸ **75.** Suffering, Distress, Sadness > LAMENT, LAMENTATION, MOURN, MOURNING

SEE ALSO

- ▸ **10.** Earth, Dust, Rocks, Minerals, Metals, Stones > CUT
  latomeō, laxeutos
- ▸ **21.** Die, Perish, Kill, Destroy > CUT TO PIECES
  dichotomeō
- ▸ **76.** Force, Harm, Oppress > CUT, CUT OFF
  katakoptō, aphaireō
- ▸ **78.** Act Upon, Push, Pull, Break, Cut > CUT OFF, CUT DOWN
  apokoptō, ekkoptō

CHAFF

achyron ἄχυρον 892

achyron is a rare noun denoting "chaff," the stalk of produce from which the grain has been harvested, found only in Matt 3:12; Luke 3:17.

CLEAR

diakatharizō διακαθαρίζω 1245

diakatharizō is a verb meaning "clear," in the sense of "clean" (i.e., remove all refuse), in the metaphorical context of Christ preparing his threshing floor to gather in his "wheat" with his people and burn the "chaff" (i.e., his enemies) (Matt 3:12; Luke 3:17).

SEE ALSO

- ▸ **39.** Clean, Pure, Holy > CLEAN, PURE
  katharos, katharizō, katharismos, katharotēs, ekkathairō, hagnos, hagnotēs, hagnismos, hagnizō

FAMINE, HUNGER

limos λιμός 3042

limos denotes "famine," "hunger," in twelve places. Specific references to "famine" are noted as evidence that the world's end is nigh in Matt 24:7; Mark 13:8; Luke 21:11; Rev 18:18.

General references to "famine" or "(extreme) hunger" are found in Luke 4:25; 15:14ff.; Acts 7:11; 11:28; Rom 8:35; 2 Cor 11:27; Rev 6:8.

FARMER

geōrgos γεωργός 1092

geōrgos is a noun found in nineteen places with the primary sense of "tenant," suggesting the sense of hired land workers. However, in two places the term specifically denotes a "farmer" (2 Tim 2:6; Jas 5:7).

▸ **28.** Agriculture, Viticulture, Animal Husbandry > VINE, VINEDRESSER

FEED, TEND

boskō βόσκω 1006

boskō is a verb found nine times meaning "feed" in both a literal and metaphorical sense in most of these contexts.

The description of animals "feeding" is recorded in Matt 8:30; Mark 5:11; Luke 8:32; 15:15.

Christ's injunction to Peter to "feed my sheep" has the metaphorical sense of "nurture God's people in the word" (John 21:15, 17).

poimainō ποιμαίνω 4165

poimainō is a verb meaning "feed," "tend," "rule" throughout its eleven occurrences.

The literal meaning "tending" cattle or sheep includes the responsibility of "feeding" them, among other things (Luke 17:7; 1 Cor 9:7). Christ's figurative exhortation to Peter to "feed my sheep" is an injunction to attend to the spiritual needs of his people (John 21:16). See also Acts 20:28; 1 Pet 5:2; Rev 7:17.

▸ **54.** Rule, Authority, Command, Obedience > RULE, RULER

SEE ALSO

▸ **23.** Food, Drink, Cooking > FEED, NOURISH
trephō, psōmizō

FIELD, FIELD OF GRAIN, CORNFIELD

agros ἀγρός 68

agros is a noun signifying "field" throughout its nearly forty occurrences.

agros refers to a "field" as a plot of agricultural land, cultivated or uncultivated, in Matt 6:28ff.; 13:24ff.; 27:7ff.; Mark 13:6; Luke 12:28; 15:15, 25; Acts 4:37.

▸ **9.** Land, Geography, Topography > COUNTRY, LAND

chōra χώρα 5561

chōra is a noun found nearly thirty times with the primary senses of "country," "region," "land" throughout. In two places, the term denotes a "field" ready for harvesting (John 4:35; Jas 5:4).

▸ **9.** Land, Geography, Topography > COUNTRY, LAND
▸ **9.** Land, Geography, Topography > REGION

chōrion χωρίον 5564

chōrion is a diminutive form of ***chōra*** (above) denoting a "field" in the ten occurrences of the term (John 4:5; Acts 1:18; 4:34; 28:7). Acts 1:19 specifically refers to the "field of blood."

▸ **9.** Land, Geography, Topography > PLACE

sporimos σπόριμος 4702

sporimos is a noun found three times denoting a "field of grain" in Matt 12:1; Mark 2:23; Luke 6:1.

geōrgion γεώργιον 1091

geōrgion is a rare noun found only in 1 Cor 3:9, referring to the sphere and object of God's work of redemption among people as his "field."

FIG

sykon σῦκον 4810

sykon is a noun denoting "figs" in four contexts, all of them literal (Matt 7:16; Mark 11:13; Luke 6:44; Jas 3:12).

olynthos ὄλυνθος 3653

olynthos is a rare noun occurring only in Rev 6:13, referring to an "unripe fig."

FIRSTFRUIT

aparchē ἀπαρχή 536

aparchē is a noun denoting "firstfruits" in eight contexts. Its usage is metaphorical in all but one of these contexts.

Rom 8:23 refers to the "firstfruits" of the Spirit in the context of the believer's assurance of salvation as a consequence of the Spirit's indwelling. In other contexts the designation "firstfruits" refers to the initial converts in Asia (Rom 16:5); and in Achaia (1 Cor 16:15). In Rev 14:4 the redeemed people of God, the "144,000," are described in heaven as the "firstfruits" for God and the Lamb. See also Jas 1:18.

In 1 Cor 15:20, 23 Christ himself is referred to as the "firstfruits" of those who have been raised from the dead, indicating that he is the first of many who would likewise rise from the dead and live with him eternally in glory. Rom 11:16 contains the sole literal reference to bread dough offered as "firstfruits" to God in ritual worship.

FRUIT, FRUITFUL

karpos καρπός 2590

karpos is a noun found nearly seventy times meaning "fruit," in several different contexts with differing nuances.

karpos is used metaphorically to denote "fruit" in the sense of "moral characteristics" in Matt 3:8, 10; 7:16ff.; Luke 3:8ff. "Fruit" in the sense of "tangible results of gospel ministry" such as conversions and spiritual maturity in the lives of believers is indicated in Rom 1:13. "Fruit" in a literal sense is indicated, for example, in Matt 12:33; 21:19ff.; Mark 4:7ff.; Luke 6:43ff.; 12:17; John 12:24; 1 Cor 9:7; Jas

5:17ff. Children are designated as "fruit" of the womb in Luke 1:42. See also Acts 2:30.

The metaphorical expression "to harvest crops (or fruit) for eternal life" denotes cultivating a godly lifestyle that will lead to the enjoyment of eternal peace with God (John 4:36). In a similar context, ***karpos*** also denotes "fruit," referring to those spiritual characteristics that derive from a relationship of faith and trust in the person of Christ (John 15:24ff.). The metaphor of "fruit" is here linked to the metaphor of a "vine," referring to Christ himself. A listing of "fruit" (i.e., virtues) as the produce of the work of the Spirit in the life of the believer is found in Gal 5:22. See also Eph 5:9; Phil 1:11; Heb 12:11; Jas 3:17ff. for a similar usage.

In other contexts, praising God is the "fruit" of one's lips (Heb 13:15). Rev 22:2 refers to the tree of life in the heavenly city that yielded its "fruit" for the healing of the nations.

karpophoros καρποφόρος 2593

karpophoros is a rare adjectival form found only in Acts 14:17, referring to "fruitful" seasons that result in a good harvest.

karpophoreō καρποφορέω 2592

karpophoreō is a verb found eight times, meaning "to bear fruit," "be fruitful" in predominantly figurative contexts.

The literal sense of "bearing fruit" in relation to the production of crops is indicated in Mark 4:28.

The rest of the usage is figurative. The nurturing of godly virtues as a result of exposure to the word of God is described as the process of "bearing fruit" in Matt 13:23; Mark 4:20; Luke 8:15. Similarly, the phenomenon of the gospel "bearing fruit," acting as a catalyst for genuine godliness, is indicated in Col 1:6, 10. See also Rom 7:4, 5 for a similar context.

▸ **28.** Agriculture, Viticulture, Animal Husbandry > BEAR, BRING FORTH

akarpos ἄκαρπος 175

akarpos is an adjective found six times meaning "unfruitful," usually in a figurative sense.

The meaning "unfruitful" in Matt 13:22; Mark 4:19 expresses the sense of "unproductive," in reference to spiritual maturity extinguished by the cares of the world. Both of these contexts concern the parable of the sower. 1 Cor 14:14 refers to an "unfruitful" mind in the context of praying in tongues. The meaning here focuses on the inability of the mind to grasp the meaning of an unknown language.

"Spiritual ineffectiveness" is indicated by the term "unfruitful" in 2 Pet 1:8; Titus 3:14. Eph 5:11 speaks of the "unfruitful" works of darkness, denoting deeds that have no positive value whatsoever.

References to trees "without fruit" are found in Jude 12.

gennēma γέννημα 1081

gennēma is a rare noun found nine times meaning "generation," "fruit," "harvest" throughout.

gennēma denotes the "fruit" of the vine, referring to wine drunk by Christ and his disciples at the Passover feast (Matt 26:29; Mark 14:25; Luke 22:18). 2 Cor 9:10 refers to a "harvest" of righteousness, signifying significant growth in godliness in the life of the believer.

In Luke 12:18 ***gennēma*** denotes "produce" or "grain," signifying the fruits of a person's labor.

▸ **25.** Family, Marriage, Adoption, Inheritance > GENERATION

SEE ALSO

▸ **30.** Money, Business, Wealth, Poverty > FRUIT
opōra

GATHER, HARVEST, PICK, PLUCK

syllegō συλλέγω 4816

syllegō is a verb found eight times, meaning "gather," "pick," and used exclusively in relation to fruit and plants.

"Gathering" or "picking" grapes is noted in Matt 7:16; and figs in Luke 6:44. Matt 13:28ff. refers to "harvesting" weeds.

trygaō τρυγάω 5166

trygaō is a rare verb, synonymous with ***syllegō*** (above), found only three times. It signifies "gathering" or "harvesting" grapes in a literal sense in Luke 6:44; and metaphorically in Rev 14:18, 19 (referring to "harvesting" both the righteous and the wicked).

therismos θερισμός 2326

therismos occurs thirteen times with the exclusive meaning "harvest," in a metaphorical sense. The term is found, for example, in Matt 9:37, 38; Luke 10:2; John 4:35, with reference to the gathering of converts to Christ. There is also a symbolic reference to "harvest" as the eschatological time of the final judgment when the righteous will be gathered to hear of their eternal blessing, and the ungodly of their doom (Matt 13:30, 39; Mark 4:39; Rev 14:15).

tillō τίλλω 5089

tillō is a verb found in only three places, meaning "plucking" or "picking" heads of grain (or, archaically, ears of corn) (Matt 12:1; Mark 2:23; Luke 6:1).

GRAPE

staphylē σταφυλή 4718

staphylē is a rare noun found only three times, denoting "grapes" in each context (Matt 7:16; Luke 6:44; Rev 14:18).

GRIND

alēthō ἀλήθω 229

alēthō is a rare verb found only twice, indicating the action of "grinding" at a mill (Matt 24:41; Luke 17:35).

SEE ALSO

- ▸ **75.** Suffering, Distress, Sadness > GRINDING
  trizō

GROW, SPROUT, SPRING UP

synauxanō συναυξάνω 4885

synauxanō is a rare verb found only in Matt 13:30 and referring to weeds and plants "growing together."

anabainō ἀναβαίνω 305

anabainō has the meanings "come, go up," "ascend," as well as a variety of nuances. In two places, the term means "spring up," "grow," in relation to thorns (Mark 4:7) and mustard seed (Mark 4:32).

- ▸ **86.** Movement Toward or Away From > ENTER, ENTRANCE, ENTRY
- ▸ **87.** Movement Upward or Downward > ARISE, RISE UP, RAISE UP

mēkynō μηκύνω 3373

mēkynō is a rare verb meaning "sprout," "grow up" in relation to seed in Mark 4:27.

SEE ALSO

- ▸ **85.** Movement, Position, State > GROW, INCREASE
  auxanō, hyperauxanō

HEAD OF GRAIN, EAR OF CORN

stachys στάχυς 4719

stachys denotes a literal "head of grain" (or, archaically, "ear of corn") in Matt 12:1; Mark 2:23; 4:28; Luke 6:1.

HEDGE, FENCE

phragmos φραγμός 5418

This noun signifies a "hedge," "fence," and occurs only four times. ***phragmos*** refers three times to a literal hedge in the parables of Jesus (Matt 21:33; Mark 12:1; Luke 14:23), and once to the "wall of partition" in Eph 2:14 that kept Jews and Gentiles separate. In this latter context, ***phragmos*** indicates first of all the literal, physical partition in the temple that strictly divided worship areas for Jews and God-fearing Gentiles. It also alludes metaphorically to the barrier that prevented Gentiles from participating in the blessings of the new covenant age. The person and work of Jesus Christ have broken down this barrier.

HUSK, POD

keration κεράτιον 2769

keration occurs only once and refers to the fruit or pod of the carob tree. These pods are shaped like horns and sweet tasting, and are a traditional food for fattening pigs. The term is used in the parable of the lost son (Luke 15:16), where he is reduced through poverty to eating these pods, or "husks."

MANGER, STALL

phatnē φάτνη 5336

phatnē occurs four times and means "manger" or "stall" in each case. Luke 2:7, 12, 16 all refer to the "manger" as the place where the infant Jesus was laid after his birth. ***phatnē*** refers literally to a feeding trough for animal use, which is the meaning indicated in Luke 13:15.

MANURE, DUNG

koprion κόπριον 2874

koprion is a rare noun found in Luke 14:35 referring to a "manure pile." See also Luke 13:8.

MILL, MILLSTONE

mylos μύλος 3458
lithos λίθος 3037

mylos occurs five times and refers in each case to a "millstone." Matt 18:6; Luke 17:2 refer to the desired fate of those who cause little children and/or those "young in the faith" to stumble and sin in their Christian walk. That is, it would be better for such deceivers to have a large millstone placed around their necks and be cast into the sea. (Note that ***lithos*** refers to this same phenomenon in Mark 9:42.)

Rev 18:21 refers to an angel throwing a great stone "like a millstone" into the sea in order to symbolically demonstrate and illustrate the violent overthrow of the city of Babylon through the savage judgment of God. Rev 18:22 declares that the sound of a millstone would never again be heard in the city of Babylon, indicating, along with other things, the total destruction of that civilization.

mylos describes the situation in Matt 24:41, whereby two women will be grinding at a "mill." One will be taken up to glory to be with God in heaven; the other will be left behind.

PASTURE

nomē νομή 3542

nomē occurs in only two places. John 10:9 mentions "pasture" in the metaphorical context of ample spiritual "nourishment" for those who belong to Christ. The other reference to ***nomē*** is found in 2 Tim 2:17, where it is used in conjunction with the verb ***echō*** to convey the meaning "to spread." The context is that of false teaching, which is said to "spread like gangrene."

PLOW

arotron ἄροτρον 723

arotron is found only in Luke 9:62, referring to a "plow."

arotriaō ἀροτριάω 722

arotriaō is the verb expressing the action of plowing, and is found only twice (Luke 17:7; 1 Cor 9:10).

PRESS

piezō πιέζω 4085

piezō is a verb found only in Luke 6:38 with reference to a measure of grain (implied), "pressed down" and running over, so as to reflect generosity.

SEE ALSO

▸ **68.** Ability, Possibility, Effort, Succeed, Fail > PRESS ON
diōkō

REAP, REAPER

therizō θερίζω 2325

therizō means "to reap" in each of its twenty-four occurrences. Its use is both literal and metaphorical.

Literal references to reaping the harvest are found in Matt 6:26; Luke 12:24; 19:21ff.; Jas 5:4.

Metaphorically, ***therizō*** refers to the blessing of reaping a harvest of eternal life (John 4:36ff.; 2 Cor 9:6); and reaping material benefits in the course of one's ministry (1 Cor 9:11). Gal 6:7 affirms the universal principle that one will always reap the consequences of one's actions — good and bad. Illustrating this principle, Gal 6:8 goes on to affirm that if we "sow" to please our sinful nature, we shall "reap" corruption. Conversely, if we "sow" to please the Spirit of God, we shall "reap" eternal life from the Spirit. See also Gal 6:9.

Rev 14:15, 16 refer to divine "reaping," where the earth is said to be harvested. In this context, divine judgment on a wicked earth is indicated.

theristēs θεριστής 2327

theristēs is the noun derived from ***therizō*** (above); it occurs only twice and means "reaper" in both instances. In Matt 13:30, 39, Jesus refers to "reapers" in one of his kingdom parables, whose role is to separate the "wheat" (i.e., the godly) and the "chaff" (i.e., the ungodly). These "reapers" are identified as angels who serve as instruments of divine judgment.

RIPE

xērainō ξηραίνω 3583

xērainō is a verb occurring sixteen times with the principal meanings "wither," "dry up." However, in Rev 14:15, ***xērainō*** refers to the harvest of the earth as "ripe" (i.e., ready for judgment).

▸ **88.** Qualities, Characteristics > DRY, DRY UP, WITHER, WITHERED

akmazō ἀκμάζω 187

akmazō is a verb found only in Rev 14:18 with reference to the grapes of the earth being "ripe" for harvest (i.e., for judgment).

SEED, SOW

sperma σπέρμα 4690

sperma occurs around forty times, in various contexts, with the underlying sense of "seed," as well as associated nuances.

Seed for planting is indicated, for example, in Matt 13:24ff.; Mark 4:31; 2 Cor 9:10 (see also 1 Cor 15:38).

More commonly, ***sperma*** refers to "seed" as "progeny" or "children." General references include those in Matt 22:24ff.; Mark 12:19ff.

As with the corresponding Hebrew term, ***sperma*** refers to the "posterity" granted by God to Abraham under the promises of the old covenant (Luke 1:55; John 8:33; Rom 4:13ff.; 9:7ff.; 11:1; Heb 11:11, 18). Similar mention is made of David's "seed" in John 7:42; Rom 1:3; 2 Tim 2:8. ***sperma*** likewise refers to the "nation" of Israel in Gal 3:29; Heb 2:16. In a redemptive-historical sense, ***sperma*** indicates that Jesus Christ is the one "seed" of Abraham — the culmination of all of God's redemptive purposes.

speirō σπείρω 4687

speirō is a verb occurring about fifty times with the principal meaning "to sow seed," or, with a nominal sense, "sower."

Literal references to "sowing" (i.e., scattering) seed for planting include those in Matt 6:26; 13:3ff.; Mark 4:3ff., 31; Luke 8:5; John 4:36. References to the "sower" are made in the parable of the sower in Matt 13:3ff.; Mark 4:3ff.; Luke 8:5.

The expression "one reaps what one sows" is found in Matt 25:24; Luke 12:24; 1 Cor 15:37; Gal 6:7, 8. 1 Pet 3:18 declares that those who "sow" in peace reap a harvest of righteousness.

speirō is used metaphorically to indicate "sowing the seed" of God's word in the hearts of human beings (Matt 13:19ff.; Mark 4:14ff.; John 4:36ff.). Similarly, 1 Cor 9:11 refers to "sowing" truth in the lives of believers.

The contrast between the earthly and heavenly body of the believer is described with reference to that which is "sown" perishable, but raised imperishable (1 Cor 15:37ff.).

sinapi σίναπι 4615

sinapi is a noun found in five contexts, referring in each case to a "mustard seed" (Matt 13:31; 17:20; Mark 4:31; Luke 13:19; 17:6).

▸ **13.** Plants, Trees, Flora > MUSTARD

sporos σπόρος 4703

sporos is a noun occurring five times, referring literally to "seed (for sowing)" in Mark 4:26f.; Luke 8:5; 2 Cor 9:10. Luke 8:11 refers to the word of God as "seed."

spora σπορά 4701

spora is a noun found only in 1 Pet 2:3 with the metaphorical meaning "seed" in the sense of "physical and finite human existence."

SHEAR, SHAVE

keirō κείρω 2751

keirō is found in four contexts. There is one reference to "sheep shearing" (Acts 8:32), with the remaining references signifying the "shaving" of one's head (Acts 18:18; 1 Cor 11:6).

SHEPHERD, PASTOR

poimēn ποιμήν 4166

poimēn is a noun occurring eighteen times meaning "shepherd," "pastor."

Literal references to shepherds include those in Matt 25:32; Luke 2:8, 15ff.; John 10:2.

The remaining uses of ***poimēn*** are all metaphorical. Matt 9:36; Mark 6:34 refer to spiritual leaders as "shepherds." Eph 4:11 refers to "pastors" of a congregation. Christ is depicted as "the good shepherd" in John 10:11ff.; Heb 13:20; 1 Pet 2:25.

archipoimēn ἀρχιποίμην 750

archipoimēn is a variant of ***poimēn*** (above) found only in 1 Pet 5:4, referring to Christ as the "chief shepherd."

▸ **38.** Covenant, Law, Rites, Roles > SHEPHERD

SIFT

siniazō σινιάζω 4617

siniazō is a verb found only in Luke 22:31, referring to Peter being "sifted" like wheat, signifying a severe trial of his faith.

TREAD

aloaō ἀλοάω 248

aloaō is a rare verb referring to oxen "treading out the grain" in 1 Cor 9:9; 1 Tim 5:18.

SEE ALSO

▸ **21.** Die, Perish, Kill, Destroy > TREAD
pateō

UPROOT

ekrizoō ἐκριζόω 1610

ekrizoō is a verb found in four contexts, meaning "uproot."

There are two figurative contexts of divine judgment in which the metaphor of plants being uprooted by God signifies the destruction of the wicked (Matt 15:13; Jude 12). The remaining two texts refer in a metaphorical sense to "wheat" (i.e., the righteous) being safeguarded against "uprooting" for judgment (Matt 13:29). Luke 17:6 mentions a sycamore tree "being uprooted" as a sign of genuine faith. The usage here is evidently hyperbolic.

SEE ALSO

▸ **13.** Plants, Trees, Flora > ROOTED
rhizoō

VINE, VINEDRESSER

ampelos ἄμπελος 288

ampelos is a noun denoting a "vine" in all eight occurrences of the term.

A general reference to the "grape vine" is found in Jas 3:12. Jesus refers to the "fruit of the vine" at the celebration of the Passover with his disciples, indicating that he will not share it with them again until the consummation of the kingdom of God (Matt 26:29; Mark 14:25; Luke 22:18). In John 15:1ff., Christ testifies that he is "the true vine," the source of eternal life for all who would entrust themselves to him. Rev 14:19 refers to the harvesting of "the vine of the earth," alluding to gathering the wicked for judgment.

geōrgos γεωργός 1092

geōrgos is a noun found only in John 15:1 designating God as the "vinedresser," who "tends" his Son Jesus Christ, the "true vine."

▸ **28.** Agriculture, Viticulture, Animal Husbandry > FARMER

ampelourgos ἀμπελουργός 289

ampelourgos is synonymous with ***geōrgos*** (above). It too is rare, referring to a "vinedresser" only in Luke 13:7.

VINEYARD

ampelōn ἀμπελών 290

ampelōn denotes a literal "vineyard" in each of its approximately twenty-five occurrences (Matt 20:1ff.; 21:28ff.; Mark 12:1ff.; Luke 20:9ff.; 1 Cor 9:7).

WEED

zizanion ζιζάνιον 2215

zizanion is a noun found in eight places denoting "weeds" throughout. ***zizanion*** most likely refers to "darnel," a plant that resembles wheat in its early stages of growth (Matt 13:25ff.).

WILD

agrios ἄγριος 66

agrios is a rare adjective referring to "wild" or "uncultivated" honey in Matt 3:4; Mark 1:6.

agrielaios ἀγριέλαιος 65

agrielaios is a rare noun denoting a "wild olive tree," used metaphorically to refer to all Gentile believers who have been brought into the kingdom of God, "grafted onto the olive tree" that represents the Israelite nation (Rom 11:17, 24).

▸ **13.** Plants, Trees, Flora > OLIVE, OLIVE TREE

SEE ALSO

▸ **14.** Animals > WILD
thērion

WINEPRESS

lēnos ληνός 3025

lēnos is a noun denoting a "winepress" in Matt 21:33. In Rev 14:19, 20; 19:15, ***lēnos*** refers metaphorically to a "winepress" as the vehicle for the expression of the wrath of God against the wicked.

WORKING, TILLING

geōrgeō γεωργέω 1090

geōrgeō is a rare verb designating the action of "working" or "tilling" the ground, found only in Heb 6:7.

SEE ALSO

▸ **27.** Community, Partnership, Unity, Discord >
WORK TOGETHER, FELLOW WORKER
synergeō, synergos

▸ **30.** Money, Business, Wealth, Poverty >
GAIN, PROFIT
ergasia

▸ **84.** Do, Make, Accomplish, Occur >
WORK, LABOR, PRODUCE, BRING ABOUT, DEED
ergazomai, katergazomai, ergon, ergatēs, energeō, energeia, poiēma, praxis, kopos

YIELD

didōmi δίδωμι 1325

didōmi is a common verb found in more than four hundred contexts with the primary meaning "give," along with several related senses. One of these is "yield" or "bear," with reference to the cultivation of grain (Mark 4:7, 8).

▸ **70.** Give, Take, Seize, Touch >
GIVE, GIVE UP, GIVE OVER, GRANT

apodidōmi ἀποδίδωμι 591

apodidōmi is a variant of ***didōmi*** (above) found in fifty places with the dominant senses of "pay," "give," "render," in a variety of contexts. However, ***apodidōmi*** denotes trees "yielding" or "bearing" fruit in Rev 22:2. It also refers metaphorically to discipline "yielding" or "producing" the fruit of righteousness in the lives of believers (Heb 12:11).

▸ **30.** Money, Business, Wealth, Poverty > PAY, RENDER

▸ **73.** Blessing, Curse, Reward, Punishment >
REWARD, RECOMPENSE

YOKE

zygos ζυγός 2218

zygos is a noun signifying a "yoke" in a figurative sense throughout all six occurrences.

zygos denotes a "yoke" in reference to a "burden" placed by Christ on his people — a burden that is easy to bear. This signifies a commitment to serve him with one's whole being (Matt 11:29ff.). Acts 15:10 refers to an unwarranted "yoke," a burden of legal obligations placed by Jewish believers onto Gentile converts. In Gal 5:1, the "yoke" referred to is the law, from which Christians have been delivered. In 1 Tim 6:1, the "yoke" is the bond of slavery.

▸ **30.** Money, Business, Wealth, Poverty >
BALANCE, SCALES

heterozygeō ἑτεροζυγέω 2086

heterozygeō is a rare verb found only in 2 Cor 6:14 as part of an injunction to believers not "to be unequally yoked together" in marriage with unbelievers.

29. Boats, Fishing, Maritime Activity

ALLOW

proseaō προσεάω 4330

proseaō is a rare verb found only in Acts 27:7 with reference to the wind "not allowing" a boat to proceed from its anchorage.

SEE ALSO

- **49.** Allow, Accept, Approve, Refuse > ALLOW
  epitrepō, apolyō, aphiēmi, eaō

ANCHOR

ankyra ἄγκυρα 45

The noun ***ankyra*** is found in four places, denoting a ship's "anchor" in Acts 27:29ff. It is used metaphorically in Heb 6:19 for the certainty of God's promises in salvation, an anchor for the soul.

BOARD, EMBARK

embainō ἐμβαίνω 1684

embainō is a verb found in eighteen places with the exclusive sense of "board (a boat)," that is, to get into or enter it (Matt 8:23; 9:1; 13:2; 14:22; 15:39; Mark 4:1; 5:18; 6:45; 8:10ff.; Luke 5:3; 8:22, 37; John 6:17, 24; 21:3; Acts 21:6).

SEE ALSO

- **86.** Movement Toward or Away From > ENTER, ENTRANCE, ENTRY
  eiserchomai, syneiserchomai, pareiserchomai, eisporeuomai, anabainō, epibainō, eiseimi, eisodos

BOAT, SHIP

ploion πλοῖον 4143

The noun ***ploion*** is found about seventy times with the consistent literal meaning "ship," "boat" (e.g., Matt 4:21ff.; Mark 1:19; 6:15ff.; Luke 5:2ff.; John 6:17ff.; 21:3ff.; Acts 21:2ff.; Jas 3:4; Rev 8:9; 18:17, 19).

ploiarion πλοιάριον 4142

ploiarion is a diminutive form of ***ploion*** (above) found in five places, denoting a "small boat," "little ship" in Mark 3:9; 4:36; John 6:22ff.; 21:8.

skaphē σκάφη 4627

skaphē is a rare synonym for ***ploion*** and ***ploiarion*** (above) designating a "ship" or "boat" in Acts 27:16, 30, 32.

CAPTAIN

kybernētēs κυβερνήτης 2942

kybernētēs is a noun denoting a ship's "captain" in Acts 27:11; Rev 18:17.

SEE ALSO

- **31.** Kingdom, Empire, Rule, Military, Warfare > CAPTAIN, COMMANDER, OFFICER
  chiliarchos, stratēgos
- **38.** Covenant, Law, Rites, Roles > AUTHOR, CAPTAIN, PRINCE
  archēgos

CAST, THROW OVERBOARD

aporiptō ἀπορίπτω 641

aporiptō is a rare verb found only in Acts 27:43 indicating the action of "throwing oneself overboard."

SEE ALSO

- **21.** Die, Perish, Kill, Destroy > CAST DOWN
  katalyō, kathaireō
- **79.** Throw, Send, Drive, Mix, Remove > THROW, THROW OUT, CAST, CAST OUT
  ballō, rhiptō, apoballō, ekballō, emballō, kataballō, epiriptō

CATCH

piazō πιάζω 4084

piazō is a verb found twelve times with the primary senses of "take," "seize." In two places, the meaning "catch" is indicated: John 21:3, 10 make reference to catching fish.

- **70.** Give, Take, Seize, Touch > APPREHEND, SEIZE, CAPTURE, ARREST

SEE ALSO

- **70.** Give, Take, Seize, Touch > CATCH
  harpazō, agreuō, thēreuō

DANGEROUS

episphalēs ἐπισφαλής 2000

episphalēs is an adjective found only in Acts 27:9 denoting a "dangerous" sea voyage.

SEE ALSO

- **32.** Law, Justice, Jurisprudence, Judgment > DANGER, LIABILITY
  enochos
- **74.** Safety, Peace, Danger, Escape > DANGER
  kindyneuō

DRIVE ALONG

pherō φέρω 5342

pherō is a verb found about sixty times with the primary meanings "bear," "carry," "bring," as well as related nuances. Acts 27:15, 17 refer to a ship "being driven along" by a storm wind.

- ▸ **69.** Have, Possess, Hold, Grasp, Bear, Carry > BEAR, CARRY
- ▸ **86.** Movement Toward or Away From > BRING, BROUGHT
- ▸ **86.** Movement Toward or Away From > REACH, REACH OUT

SEE ALSO

- ▸ **76.** Force, Harm, Oppress > DRIVE OUT
  ekdiōkō, exōtheō
- ▸ **79.** Throw, Send, Drive, Mix, Remove > DRIVE, DRIVE OUT
  ekballō, elaunō

ESCAPE

diapheugō διαφεύγω 1309

diapheugō is a rare verb found only in Acts 27:42, denoting the action of "escaping" from the perils of shipwreck.

SEE ALSO

- ▸ **74.** Safety, Peace, Danger, Escape > ESCAPE
  pheugō, apopheugō, ekpheugō, diasōzō, ekbasis

FISH, FISHERMAN

halieus ἁλιεύς 231

halieus is a noun found in five places denoting a "fisherman" in a literal sense in Matt 4:18; Mark 1:16; Luke 5:2. Matt 4:19; Mark 1:17 both contain Jesus' assertion that he would make his disciples "fishers of men" (i.e., evangelists engaged in winning people for Christ).

halieuō ἁλιεύω 232

halieuō is a rare verb found only in John 21:3, meaning "to go fishing."

SEE ALSO

- ▸ **14.** Animals > FISH
  ichthys, ichthydion, opsarion

HARBOR, HAVEN

limēn λιμήν 3040

limēn is a rare term, occurring only three times in Acts 27:8, 12, indicating a safe haven or harbor, a refuge from storms.

HOOK

ankistron ἄγκιστρον 44

This word is found only in Matt 17:27 with reference to a fish hook.

NET

amphiblēstron ἀμφίβληστρον 293

amphiblēstron occurs only twice, both with literal reference to fishing nets (Matt 4:18; Mark 1:16).

sagēnē σαγήνη 4522

sagēnē is found only in Matt 13:47, likening the kingdom of God to a "net" that is thrown into the sea and gathers fish of every kind.

diktyon δίκτυον 1350

diktyon is a noun found in twelve contexts with exclusive reference to fishing nets as used by Jesus' disciples (Matt 4:20ff.; Mark 1:18ff.; Luke 5:2ff.; John 21:6ff.).

OWNER

nauklēros ναύκληρος 3490

nauklēros occurs only in Acts 27:11, where it refers to "the owner of a ship."

SEE ALSO

- ▸ **69.** Have, Possess, Hold, Grasp, Bear, Carry > OWNER
  kyrios

PULL, DRAW

anabibazō ἀναβιβάζω 307

anabibazō is a rare verb found only in Matt 13:48 referring to people "drawing" or "pulling" a boat to shore.

SEE ALSO

- ▸ **76.** Force, Harm, Oppress > DRAW
  spaō
- ▸ **79.** Throw, Send, Drive, Mix, Remove > DRAW, DRAG
  helkō, exelkō, syrō, anaspaō
- ▸ **80.** Related to Liquids > DRAW
  antleō
- ▸ **86.** Movement Toward or Away From > COME, DRAW NEAR
  engizō

RUN UNDER, RUN AGROUND

hypotrechō ὑποτρέχω 5295

hypotrechō is a verb meaning "to run under the lee." It occurs only in Acts 27:16 in a nautical context, referring to a boat sailing past a shoreline protected from the wind.

epikellō ἐπικέλλω 2027

epikellō is found only in Acts 27:41, referring to a boat that "ran aground" on a rocky shoreline.

SEE ALSO

- ▸ **7.** Quantity, Amount, Number, Size, Measure > OVERFLOW, RUN OVER
  hyperekchynnō
- ▸ **85.** Movement, Position, State > RUN
  trechō, episyntrechō, syntrechō, peritrechō, protrechō
- ▸ **86.** Movement Toward or Away From > RUN, RUN TOWARD, RUN DOWN
  prostrechō, eistrechō, katatrechō, hormaō

SAIL, SET SAIL

pleō πλέω 4126

pleō is a verb found in five places, meaning "to sail" (Luke 8:23; Acts 21:3; 27:2, 6, 24).

parapleō παραπλέω 3896

parapleō, a derivative of ***pleō*** (above), is found only in Acts 20:16 and means "sail by."

apopleō ἀποπλέω 636

apopleō, also derived from ***pleō*** (above), is found four times and means "set sail," "sail away" (Acts 13:4; 14:26; 20:15; 27:1).

ekpleō ἐκπλέω 1602

ekpleō is another variant form of ***pleō***. It occurs three times and means "sail," "sail away" (Acts 15:39; 18:18; 20:6).

hypopleō ὑποπλέω 5284

hypopleō is a variant of ***pleō*** (above). It occurs only twice and means "sail under" (Acts 27:4, 7).

diapleō διαπλέω 1277

diapleō is found only in Acts 27:5, meaning "sail over," "sail across."

paralegomai παραλέγομαι 3881

paralegomai is found in only two places and means "sail close" (i.e., to the shore) (Acts 27:8, 13).

anagō ἀνάγω 321

anagō is a verb occurring around twenty-five times with the dual meanings "to bring, lead up," and "to launch, set sail." The latter sense is indicated in Luke 8:22; Acts 18:21; 20:3, 13; 21:1, 2; 27:2, 4, 12, 21; 28:10, 11.

▸ **71.** Lead, Guide, Follow > LEAD, LEAD OUT, LEAD AWAY

SAILOR

nautēs ναύτης 3492

nautēs is a noun found three times, meaning "sailor" (Acts 27:27ff.; Rev 18:13).

SHIPWRECK

nauageō ναυαγέω 3489

nauageō is a verb found only twice, meaning "to suffer shipwreck," "make shipwreck," in 2 Cor 11:25; 1 Tim 1:19.

SINK

katapontizō καταποντίζω 2670

katapontizō is a verb occurring only twice, meaning "sink" or "drown" (Matt 14:30; 18:6).

▸ **21.** Die, Perish, Kill, Destroy > DROWN

bythizō βυθίζω 1036

bythizō is a rare verb referring to ships "beginning to sink" (Luke 5:7).

SOUND, TAKE A SOUNDING

bolizō βολίζω 1001

bolizō is a verb, a nautical term, found twice with the exclusive sense of "to sound," "take a sounding," to ascertain water depth beneath a ship (Acts 27:28).

SEE ALSO

▸ **20.** Illness, Disease, Health, Healing > SOUND, HEALTHY
hygiainō

▸ **63.** Speak, Tell, Declare, Call > SOUND
phōnē, salpizō, ēchos

30. Money, Business, Wealth, Poverty

ACCOUNT

ellogeō ἐλλογέω 1677

ellogeō is a rare verb found only twice, meaning "impute" or "charge to one's account." The term is used literally in Phlm 18 with reference to Paul's own financial "account," and symbolically in Rom 5:13 in relation to sin "not being imputed" (i.e., charged to one's "spiritual account") where there is no law.

▸ **30.** Money, Business, Wealth, Poverty > IMPUTE

BALANCE, SCALES

zygos ζυγός 2218

zygos is found in six places and refers mostly to a "yoke" in both a literal and metaphorical sense. However, in Rev 6:5 it denotes a "pair of scales" or a "balance" held by the rider of the black horse and symbolizing economic ruin for humankind — a judgment from God.

▸ **28.** Agriculture, Viticulture, Animal Husbandry > YOKE

BEG, BEGGAR

epaiteō ἐπαιτέω 1871

epaiteō is a rare verb found only in Luke 16:3 with the meaning "to beg" (i.e., for a living).

prosaiteō προσαιτέω 4319

prosaiteō is a variant form of ***epaiteō*** (above) that is found in three places. It also expresses the sense of "beg (for a living)" (Mark 10:46; Luke 18:35; John 9:8).

ptōchos πτωχός 4434

ptōchos is an adjective occurring about thirty-five times with the primary sense of "poor." There is occasional overlap in meaning with the sense of "beggars" (e.g., Luke 16:20ff.).

▸ **30.** Money, Business, Wealth, Poverty > POOR

BORROW

daneizō δανείζω 1155

daneizō is a verb found four times with the meaning "to borrow" in Matt 5:42; and "to lend" in Luke 6:34, 35. All contexts suggest the borrowing and lending of money.

▸ **30.** Money, Business, Wealth, Poverty > LEND

BUY, PURCHASE

agorazō ἀγοράζω 59

agorazō is a verb translated "buy" in its approximately thirty occurrences.

Literal references to "buying" include the purchase of property in Matt 13:44; 27:7; Luke 14:18; of goods and merchandise in Matt 14:15; 25:9ff.; Mark 6:36ff.; Luke 9:13; 22:36; John 4:8; 13:29; 1 Cor 7:30; Rev 13:17; 18:11; and of a precious pearl in Matt 13:46.

▸ **44.** Repentance, Forgiveness, Mercy, Redeem, Save > REDEEM, REDEMPTION

ōneomai ὠνέομαι 5608

ōneomai is a rare noun found only in Acts 7:16 with the meaning "purchase" in relation to a tomb.

CRAFT, TRADE, BUSINESS

ergasia ἐργασία 2039

ergasia is a noun denoting a "craft" or "business" in Acts 19:25. Elsewhere it refers to the monetary gains derived from business (Acts 16:16, 19; 19:24).

▸ **30.** Money, Business, Wealth, Poverty > GAIN, PROFIT

homotechnos ὁμότεχνος 3673

homotechnos is a rare adjectival form denoting one who was "of the same trade (or business)" in Acts 18:3.

meros μέρος 3313

The noun ***meros*** usually means "part," "portion" (approximately forty times). However, in Acts 19:27 the term denotes the "trade" or "business" of the idol manufacturers in Ephesus.

▸ **81.** Forms, Groups, Patterns, Order > PART, PORTION, SECTION, PIECE, GROUP

ergazomai ἐργάζομαι 2038

ergazomai is a verb found in forty contexts with the primary meanings "to work," "labor." However, in a few contexts it means "to trade" in the context of business (Matt 25:16; Rev 18:17).

▸ **84.** Do, Make, Accomplish, Occur > WORK, LABOR, PRODUCE, BRING ABOUT, DEED

diapragmateuomai διαπραγματεύομαι 1281

This verb is found only in Luke 9:15, referring to "gaining through trading."

▸ **30.** Money, Business, Wealth, Poverty > GAIN, PROFIT

DEBT, DEBTOR

opheilē ὀφειλή 3782

opheilē is a noun found only twice. It denotes "debt" in Matt 18:32. In Rom 13:7 the term refers to "that which is owed" in the context of paying government taxes.

opheilēma ὀφείλημα 3783

opheilēma is a rare synonym for ***opheilē*** (above) denoting "that which is due" to someone, in the context of one's wages, in Rom 4:4. In Matt 6:12 the term is part of the text of the Lord's Prayer. Its meaning is most likely metaphorical, referring to people's "sins" or "offenses."

opheiletēs ὀφειλέτης 3781

opheiletēs is a noun found seven times referring to a person bound by some obligation or duty. Negatively, the term denotes a "sinner" or an "offender" in Matt 6:12; Luke 13:4. In Matt 18:24 it refers to a "debtor" owing a huge sum of money to a creditor.

Positively, ***opheiletēs*** denotes a person under moral obligation in several contexts. In Rom 1:14 Paul sees himself as "under obligation" to Gentiles on account of the gospel; and in Rom 8:12 the obligation is to live according to the dictates of the Holy Spirit. Gal 5:3 affirms that everyone who is circumcised "is bound" to keep the whole law. See also Rom 15:27.

opheilō ὀφείλω 3784

opheilō is a verb found nearly forty times with the underlying meaning "ought," "owe." The latter sense embraces several nuances.

The literal sense of "owing" money, or being in the grip of debt, is indicated in Matt 18:28ff.; Luke 7:41; 16:5ff.; Rom 13:8; Phil 1:18.

Elsewhere, ***opheilō*** means "being bound by an oath" or "being under a moral obligation." It is found with this meaning in Matt 23:16, 18, referring to a solemn ritual oath. 2 Thess 1:3; 2:13 refer to the solemn "obligation" to give thanks to God.

▸ **30.** Money, Business, Wealth, Poverty > OWE

daneion δάνειον 1156

daneion is a rare noun denoting a monetary "debt" in Matt 18:27.

chreopheiletēs χρεοφειλέτης 5533

chreopheiletēs is a noun denoting a "debtor," in the literal sense of "one who owes money," found only in Luke 7:41; 16:5.

DENARIUS

dēnarion δηνάριον 1220

The term ***dēnarion*** is of Latin origin and is sometimes translated, now archaically, as "penny," "pence," though it is more often transliterated as "denarius." It was the principal silver coin of the Roman Empire. ***dēnarion*** is found sixteen times, each time referring to literal currency (Matt 18:28; 20:2ff.; 22:19; Mark 6:37; 12:15; 14:5; Luke 7:41; 10:35; 20:24; John 6:7; 12:5; Rev 6:6).

DEPOSIT, PLEDGE, EARNEST

arrabōn ἀρραβών 728

arrabōn is a term originally denoting "earnest money" deposited by the purchaser and forfeited if the purchase was not completed. It was probably a Phoenician word introduced into Greece. In general usage it came to denote a "pledge" or "earnest" of any sort. In the NT it is used only of that which is assured by God to believers. It is predicated of the Holy Spirit, who is described as the divine "pledge" of all future blessedness (2 Cor 5:5). In Eph 1:14, the term refers particularly to their eternal inheritance.

▸ **45.** Faith, Belief, Trust, Promise > GUARANTEE

FREE OF CHARGE

adapanos ἀδάπανος 77

adapanos is a rare adjectival form meaning "free of charge" (i.e., at no cost), found only in 1 Cor 9:18.

SEE ALSO

▸ **32.** Law, Justice, Jurisprudence, Judgment > CHARGE, COMPLAINT
aitia, aitiōma, enklēma, enkaleō

▸ **54.** Rule, Authority, Command, Obedience > CHARGE, INSTRUCT
parangelia, diamartyromai, diastellomai, embrimaomai, exorkizō, horkizō

FRUIT

opōra ὀπώρα 3703

opōra is a rare noun found only in Rev 18:4, meaning "fruit" in a figurative sense, denoting "material wealth" which the city of Babylon yearned for but failed to acquire.

SEE ALSO

▸ **28.** Agriculture, Viticulture, Animal Husbandry > FRUIT, FRUITFUL
karpos, karpophoros, karpophoreō, akarpos, gennēma

GAIN, PROFIT

diapragmateuomai διαπραγματεύομαι 1281

diapragmateuomai is a rare verb found only in Luke 19:15, denoting the action of "gaining" a living through business.

▸ **30.** Money, Business, Wealth, Poverty > CRAFT, TRADE, BUSINESS

ergasia ἐργασία 2039

ergasia is a noun denoting "trade" or "business," as well as "profits" gained from such enterprise. Acts 16:16ff. refers to "profitable gain" derived from one's business or work. Acts 19:24ff. refers generally to "business," "work," or "trade."

▸ **30.** Money, Business, Wealth, Poverty > CRAFT, TRADE, BUSINESS

SEE ALSO

▸ **27.** Community, Partnership, Unity, Discord > WORK TOGETHER, FELLOW WORKER
synergeō, synergos

▸ **28.** Agriculture, Viticulture, Animal Husbandry > WORKING, TILLING
geōrgeō

▸ **84.** Do, Make, Accomplish, Occur > WORK, LABOR, PRODUCE, BRING ABOUT, DEED
ergazomai, katergazomai, ergon, ergatēs, energeō, energeia, poiēma, praxis, kopos

GOODS, PROPERTY, POSSESSIONS

hyparxis ὕπαρξις 5223

hyparxis is a rare noun denoting "goods," "property," in Acts 2:45.

bios βίος 979

bios is a noun found eleven times with the primary meaning "life" or "living." In 1 John 3:17, however, it denotes "goods" in the sense of "possessions."

▸ **22.** Life, Renewal, Immortality > LIFE, LIVE, LIVING

skeuos σκεῦος 4632

skeuos is a noun denoting a "vessel," "container" for most of the twenty or so occurrences of the term. However, in Matt 12:29; Mark 3:27; Luke 17:31 it refers to a person's "goods" or "possessions."

▸ **34.** Craftsmanship, Artisanship, Furniture, Implements > VESSEL, ARTICLE, UTENSIL, BASKET, FLASK

hyparchonta ὑπάρχοντα 5224

hyparchonta is the most common NT noun denoting "goods," "property," "possessions." It occurs fourteen times (Matt 19:21; 24:47; Luke 11:21; 12:15, 44; 16:1; 19:8; Acts 4:32; 1 Cor 13:3; Heb 10:34).

ousia οὐσία 3776

ousia is a rare term denoting "goods," "property" in Luke 15:12, 13.

ktēma κτῆμα 2933

ktēma is a noun found in only four places, meaning "possession(s)" in the sense of one's property, wealth, and personal belongings (Matt 19:22; Mark 10:22; Acts 2:45; 5:1).

SEE ALSO

▸ **2.** Supernatural Beings/Forces, Spiritual Realm > POSSESS, POSSESSION
daimonizomai

▸ **25.** Family, Marriage, Adoption, Inheritance > POSSESSIONS
peripoiēsis

IMPUTE

ellogeō ἐλλογέω 1677

ellogeō is a verb occurring only twice and meaning "impute," "set to one's account." Rom 5:13 affirms that where there is no law, sin is not imputed. In Phlm 18, Paul asks Philemon to charge to the apostle's account any money owed him by Onesimus, his servant.

▸ **30.** Money, Business, Wealth, Poverty > ACCOUNT

SEE ALSO

▸ **51.** Knowledge, Wisdom, Remember, Forget > IMPUTE
logizomai

INTEREST

tokos τόκος 5110

tokos occurs only in Matt 25:27; Luke 19:23. Both of these texts refer to the parable of the lazy servant, who failed to invest his master's money left in his trust. The man simply buried it in the ground, and he was condemned for doing so. The point is made that at least he could have left the money with the bankers to gain interest.

LEND

daneizō δανείζω 1155

daneizō is found only four times. Three times it refers to the action of lending, and once to borrowing. Luke 6:34, 35 speak of the practice of lending, referring firstly to such a practice among pagans. The latter text contains Jesus' exhortation to his followers to lend freely to their enemies, expecting nothing in return.

▸ **30.** Money, Business, Wealth, Poverty > BORROW

MARKET, MARKETPLACE

agora ἀγορά 58

agora is a noun found in ten contexts, referring to "market," "marketplace," where people would gather to buy and sell in towns and cities (Matt 11:16; 23:7; Mark 6:56; 7:4; 12:38; Luke 7:32; 11:43; 20:46; Acts 17:17). In Matt 20:3, the marketplace is also designated as a location where employment is sought. In Acts 16:19, it is cited as the location of the municipal courts, where Paul and Silas were taken in Philippi.

MERCHANT

emporos ἔμπορος 1713

emporos is a noun meaning "merchant," "trader" found in five places (Matt 13:45; Rev 18:3, 11, 15, 23).

MITE, PENNY, COIN

lepton λεπτόν 3016

lepton refers to a small copper coin, translated "mite," which was worth only a fraction of a cent. ***lepton*** is found in only three contexts, two of which refer to the classic "widow's mite," the offering of a poverty-stricken woman (Mark 12:42; Luke 21:2). ***lepton*** is also found in Luke 12:59, referring to "the very last mite" demanded by a magistrate from a hapless victim of a lawsuit.

kerma κέρμα 2772

kerma refers to "coins" or "pieces of money." It occurs only in John 2:15 in the context of trading in the temple.

SEE ALSO

▸ **31.** Kingdom, Empire, Rule, Military, Warfare > TAX, TRIBUTE, TOLL
nomisma

MONEY

chalkos χαλκός 5475

chalkos refers to various items made of brass, including money. ***chalkos*** occurs five times and indicates money in three of these contexts. See Matt 10:9; Mark 6:8, where Jesus instructs his disciples not to take any gold, silver, or brass with them on their evangelistic mission. Mark 12:41 refers to the rich placing large sums of money in the temple treasury.

▸ **10.** Earth, Dust, Rocks, Minerals, Metals, Stones > BRONZE, BRASS

chrēma χρῆμα 5536

chrēma is found in seven contexts and means "riches," "money." The sense of "money" as a "sum of money" is found in Acts 4:37; 8:18, 20; 24:26.

▸ **30.** Money, Business, Wealth, Poverty > RICH, RICHES

philargyria φιλαργυρία 5365

philargyria occurs only in 1 Tim 6:10 and refers to the sin of the "love of money" as the root of all evil.

SEE ALSO

▸ **31.** Kingdom, Empire, Rule, Military, Warfare > TAX, TRIBUTE, TOLL
nomisma

MONEY CHANGER

kermatistēs κερματιστής 2773

kermatistēs means "money changer" and occurs only in John 2:14, with reference to the people trading in the Jerusalem temple.

SEE ALSO

▸ **31.** Kingdom, Empire, Rule, Military, Warfare > TAX, TRIBUTE, TOLL
nomisma

OWE

opheilō ὀφείλω 3784

opheilō is a verb that occurs about forty times. It is translated "to owe," in the sense of "be under obligation," "be in debt." The contexts for the translation "owe" primarily involve financial indebtedness (Matt 18:28ff.; Luke 7:41; 16:5ff.; Phlm 18). In Rom 13:8, an obligation is laid on believers to avoid financial indebtedness to one another.

The general sense of being under a solemn obligation, bound by an oath, is illustrated in Matt 23:16ff.

▸ **30.** Money, Business, Wealth, Poverty > DEBT, DEBTOR

prosopheilō προσοφείλω 4359

prosopheilō is a rare variant verb form of ***opheilō*** (above), also translated "to owe" and found only in Phlm 19.

PAY, RENDER

teleō τελέω 5055

teleō is a verb that expresses the primary meaning "finish," "fulfill," as well as associated meanings. It is found in twenty-six places. On two occasions, ***teleō*** conveys the meaning "pay" in the context of paying taxes (Matt 17:24; Rom 13:6).

▸ **4.** Beginning, Continuing, Finishing, Postponing > FINISH, COMPLETE, FULFILL, BRING TO AN END, COME TO AN END

▸ **84.** Do, Make, Accomplish, Occur > CARRY OUT, COMPLETE, FULFILL, ACCOMPLISH

apodidōmi ἀποδίδωμι 591

The verb ***apodidōmi*** primarily means "pay," in addition to the associated senses of "give," "render," "reward." The term is found in approximately fifty places. ***apodidōmi*** is translated "pay" in the sense of repaying a debt in Matt 5:26; 18:25ff.; Luke 7:42; 12:59; 19:8. In Matt 5:33, the meaning indicated is that of "fulfilling or performing" a vow. Matt 20:8; Rom 2:6 refer to paying wages. In the latter text, it is the spiritual sense of "recompense," the intangible but very real divine payment for deeds done in one's life, whether good or bad. Several texts exhort believers to pay their rightful taxes to the governing authorities (Matt 22:21; Mark 12:17; Luke 20:25; Rom 13:7).

▸ **28.** Agriculture, Viticulture, Animal Husbandry > YIELD

▸ **73.** Blessing, Curse, Reward, Punishment > REWARD, RECOMPENSE

SEE ALSO

▸ **41.** Sacrifice, Offering, Worship, Praise > TITHE, PAYMENT
dekatoō

POOR

ptōchos πτωχός 4434

ptōchos is the most common term in the NT for "poor." While adjectival in form, ***ptōchos*** is used mainly as a noun. The term is found around thirty-five times.

ptōchos means "poor" in the sense of being economically destitute in Matt 11:5; 26:11; Mark 14:5; Luke 4:18; 16:20ff.; John 12:5; Rom 15:26; Gal 2:10; Jas 2:2ff.

One interesting use of ***ptōchos*** is found in Matt 5:3, where Jesus blesses those who are "poor in spirit." The expression refers to the quality of genuine humility, recognizing that one lacks worldly status and honor, which leads to a faithful dependence on God.

▸ **30.** Money, Business, Wealth, Poverty > BEG, BEGGAR

penichros πενιχρός 3998

penichros is an adjective found only in Luke 21:2, with reference to a "poor" widow.

ptōcheuō πτωχεύω 4433

ptōcheuō is the verb from which the adjective ***ptōchos*** (above) is derived. It is found only in 2 Cor 8:9, where it refers to the selfless action of Christ, who "became poor" for our sake, that we might become rich in spiritual relationship with him.

penēs πένης 3993

penēs is an adjective found only in 2 Cor 9:9, with reference to "the poor," who benefit from divine giving.

PRICE

timē τιμή 5092

timē is a noun with the primary sense of "honor" in the majority of the forty or so contexts in which it is found. However, it means "price" in two places. In Matt 27:9 it refers to the price of thirty pieces of silver paid by the religious leaders of Judea to Judas for the betrayal of Jesus. 1 Cor 6:20; 7:23 refer to the truth that all believers have been "bought with a price" (i.e., the sacrifice of Christ in his death and resurrection).

▸ **52.** Status, Identity, Reputation, Honor, Shame > HONOR

RICH, RICHES

plousios πλούσιος 4145

plousios is an adjective found in approximately thirty contexts, also used as a noun, and meaning "rich," "rich person." In addition to its literal use, ***plousios*** is used metaphorically to indicate spiritual wealth, or an abundance of Christian virtue and spiritual blessing.

The literal sense of "rich person" is indicated, for example, in Matt 19:23ff.; Luke 12:16; 16:1, 19ff.; Jas 2:6. It is used adjectivally in Mark 12:41; Luke 19:2; 1 Tim 6:17; Rev 3:17.

plousios is used metaphorically to refer to Christ as "rich" in divine attributes (2 Cor 8:9); and to designate God as "rich" in mercy (Eph 2:4). Believers are described as "rich" in faith in Jas 2:5; Rev 2:9.

plouteō πλουτέω 4147

plouteō is a verb occurring twelve times, meaning "to be rich," "to enrich," or "make rich."

Luke 1:53; Rev 18:3, 15, 19 refer to "the wealthy" as a clan of people.

In metaphorical contexts, the term ***plouteō*** is used adjectivally in Luke 12:21; Rev 3:17 to indicate that the selfish rich are not "rich" towards God. 1 Tim 6:9 warns against the desire to be rich. ***plouteō*** also refers to heavenly, or spiritual, "riches" (Rom 10:12; 1 Cor 4:8; 2 Cor 8:9; Rev 3:18). 1 Tim 6:18 refers to those who are "rich" in good deeds.

ploutizō πλουτίζω 4148

ploutizō is a synonym for ***plouteō*** (above) found in four places and meaning "to make rich," "enrich" in a spiritual sense. 1 Cor 1:5 refers to being enriched in Christ; and 2 Cor 6:10 (twice); 9:11 describe the experience of being made rich through spiritual blessings.

ploutos πλοῦτος 4149

ploutos is a noun found in twenty-two places, meaning "riches."

Literal references to material wealth include those in Matt 13:22; Mark 4:19; Luke 8:14; Jas 5:2; Rev 18:17.

Metaphorically, ***ploutos*** refers to the "riches" of God's kindness (Rom 2:4); his glory (Rom 9:23; Eph 1:18; 3:16; Col 1:27); and his grace (Eph 1:7; 2:7). Spiritual "riches" are noted in Col 2:2; 1 Tim 6:17; Heb 11:26; Rom 11:12. The "riches" of Christ are declared in Eph 3:8; Phil 4:19; Rev 5:12. 2 Cor 8:2 speaks of the "riches" of people's generosity.

chrēma χρῆμα 5536

chrēma is a noun found in seven contexts meaning "riches" or "money." The former sense is found in Mark 10:23, 24; Luke 18:24, referring to material abundance. The latter meaning is found in Acts 4:37; 8:18, 20; 24:26.

▸ **30.** Money, Business, Wealth, Poverty > MONEY

SELL, SELLER

pōleō πωλέω 4453

pōleō is a verb that occurs around twenty times and means "sell." It refers to birds and animals (Matt 10:29; Luke 12:6; John 2:14ff.); one's possessions (Matt 13:44; 19:21; Luke 18:22); merchandise (Matt 21:21; Mark 11:15; Luke 19:45; Rev 13:17); food (1 Cor 10:25); clothing (Luke 22:36); and property (Acts 4:34ff.; 5:1).

porphyropōlis πορφυρόπωλις 4211

porphyropōlis is a rare noun found only in Acts 16:14 with reference to Lydia, a "seller of purple cloth."

SPEND

dapanaō δαπανάω 1159

dapanaō is a verb found in five contexts, meaning "to spend." Mark 5:26; 15:14 refer to people spending all that they have, exhausting their monetary resources. Acts 21:24 refers to "paying one's expenses." See also 2 Cor 12:15; Jas 4:3.

prosdapanaō προσδαπανάω 4325

prosdapanaō is found only in Luke 10:35, meaning "to spend more money."

SEE ALSO

▸ **3.** Periods of Time, Duration, Frequency, Speed > SPEND TIME
chronotribeō

▸ **55.** Bondage, Captivity, Servitude >
SPEND COMPLETELY, GIVE ONESELF
ekdapanaō

TREASURE

thēsauros θησαυρός 2344

thēsauros is a noun found approximately twenty times meaning "treasure" in the sense of "valuables" in Matt 2:11; 6:19; 13:44; Heb 11:26. Metaphorical references to the "treasure" of the heart include those in Matt 12:35; Luke 6:45; 12:34. Heavenly "treasure" is indicated in Matt 6:20; Mark 10:21; Luke 18:22; 2 Cor 4:7. Col 2:3 affirms that all the "treasures" of wisdom and knowledge are hidden in Christ.

thēsaurizō θησαυρίζω 2343

thēsaurizō is a verb meaning "lay up," "store up" in relation to wealth or riches in several contexts. Matt 6:19; Luke 12:21; Jas 5:3 refer to "laying up" earthly riches; and Matt 6:20 refers to heavenly riches.

gaza γάζα 1047

gaza is a rare noun found only in Acts 8:27 with reference to "the treasures" of royalty.

SEE ALSO

▸ **41.** Sacrifice, Offering, Worship, Praise > TREASURY
korbanas, gazophylakion

WAGES

opsōnion ὀψώνιον 3800

opsōnion is a noun occurring four times denoting "wages" or "financial support." Luke 3:14 refers to a soldier's wages, or allowance. See also 1 Cor 9:7. 2 Cor 11:8 refers to "financial support" provided by churches to the apostle Paul. Rom 6:23 refers metaphorically to death as the "wages of sin."

misthos μισθός 3408

misthos is a noun denoting a "reward" in most of its thirty occurrences. In several places, however, the meaning "wages" is indicated. Literal references include those in Matt 20:8; Luke 10:7; John 4:36; Rom 4:4; 1 Cor 3:8; 1 Tim 5:18; Jas 5:4. 2 Pet 2:15 refers to the "wages of unrighteousness" desired by Balaam, in relation to his greed and deception.

▸ **73.** Blessing, Curse, Reward, Punishment >
REWARD, RECOMPENSE

31. Kingdom, Empire, Rule, Military, Warfare

ARMS, WEAPONS, ARMOR, ARM

hoplon ὅπλον 3696

hoplon is a noun found in six places, four of which explicitly refer to "arms" or "weapons." John 18:3 indicates literal weaponry. Rom 6:13 makes reference to the spiritual "armor" of light; 2 Cor 6:7 speaks of the "armor" of righteousness; and 2 Cor 10:4 describes the "(spiritual) weapons" of divine "warfare."

▸ **34.** Craftsmanship, Artisanship, Furniture, Implements > INSTRUMENT

hoplizō ὁπλίζω 3695

hoplizō is a rare verb found only in 1 Pet 4:1 referring to the symbolic act of "arming" ourselves with the Christlike attitude of willingness to suffer for righteousness' sake.

panoplia πανοπλία 3833

panoplia is a noun denoting "armor" in all three occurrences of the term. In Luke 11:22 the literal "armor" of a soldier is indicated. However, Eph 6:11, 13 both refer to the metaphor of "the armor of God" — weaponry used in the spiritual warfare waged by the believer.

kathoplizō καθοπλίζω 2528

kathoplizō is a rare verb, found only in Luke 11:21 with the meaning "to supply with arms, or weapons."

ARMY

strateuma στράτευμα 4753

strateuma is a noun occurring eight times, meaning "army" as well as "soldiers," "men of war."

References to "armies" include those in Matt 22:7; Rev 9:16. ***strateuma*** also refers to the apocalyptic armies of the heavenly Christ-King and those of the evil one (Rev 19:14, 19).

In addition, "soldiers" are mentioned in Luke 23:11; Acts 23:10, 27.

▸ **31.** Kingdom, Empire, Rule, Military, Warfare > WAR, BATTLE, FIGHT

stratopedon στρατόπεδον 4760

stratopedon is a rare noun occurring only in Luke 21:20 with reference to "armies" that will surround Jerusalem.

parembolē παρεμβολή 3925

parembolē is a noun found in ten contexts, referring primarily to "army barracks" in Acts 21:34ff.; 22:24; 23:10, 16, 32. Heb 13:11 makes specific reference to "foreign armies."

ARROW, DART

belos βέλος 956

belos is a rare noun referring solely and symbolically to the fiery "arrows" (or "darts") of the devil — those demonic weapons designed to destroy the people of God.

BAND, REGIMENT

speira σπεῖρα 4686

speira is a noun found seven times, referring to a "band" or "regiment" of soldiers in Matt 27:27; Mark 15:16; John 18:3, 12; Acts 10:1; 27:1.

BOW

toxon τόξον 5115

toxon is a rare noun found only in Rev 6:2 denoting a "bow" as a weapon.

BREASTPLATE

thōrax θώραξ 2382

The noun ***thōrax*** denotes a "breastplate." Metaphorical reference to spiritual defense against satanic attack (i.e., the "breastplate" of righteousness) is found in Eph 6:14; as is reference to the "breastplate" of faith and love in 1 Thess 5:8. Rev 9:9, 17 refer to the "breastplates" worn by the demonic locust-like creatures of John's apocalyptic vision, bent on destruction of the wicked.

CAPTAIN, COMMANDER, OFFICER

chiliarchos χιλίαρχος 5506

chiliarchos is a noun occurring about twenty times with literal reference to the commander of 1,000 soldiers, and is translated "captain" or "commander" throughout its usage. This military sense is indicated in Mark 6:21; John 18:12; Acts 21:31ff.; 22:24ff.; 23:10, 15ff.; 24:22; 25:23; Rev 6:15; 19:18.

stratēgos στρατηγός 4755

stratēgos is a synonym for ***chiliarchos*** (above) denoting the supreme civil officers, or commanders (or captains), of the Jerusalem temple (Luke 22:4, 52; Acts 4:1; 5:24, 26). It also refers to "civil magistrates" (Acts 16:20ff.).

SEE ALSO

▸ **29.** Boats, Fishing, Maritime Activity > CAPTAIN ***kybernētēs***

▸ **38.** Covenant, Law, Rites, Roles > AUTHOR, CAPTAIN, PRINCE ***archēgos***

CHARIOT

harma ἅρμα 716

harma is a rare noun found in only four places denoting a "chariot" in each case. Three of these are literal references (Acts 8:28ff.); and a symbolic reference is found in Rev 9:9.

rheda ῥέδη 4480

rheda is a rare noun of Latin origin denoting a "chariot," found only in Rev 18:13.

CHIEF

prōtos πρῶτος 4413

prōtos is an adjectival term with the primary sense of "first" for most of the hundred or so occurrences of the term. In several places it means "chief," referring to the "chief" civil rulers of the Jews in Luke 19:47; Acts 13:50; 25:2; 28:17. Acts 16:12 refers to Philippi as the "chief" or "leading" city of Macedonia. See also Acts 17:4; 28:7; 1 Tim 1:15.

- ▸ **5.** Old, New, First, Last > FORMER, PREVIOUS
- ▸ **7.** Quantity, Amount, Number, Size, Measure > FIRST

SEE ALSO

- ▸ **33.** Architecture > CORNERSTONE
  akrogōniaios
- ▸ **38.** Covenant, Law, Rites, Roles > SHEPHERD
  archipoimēn

DELEGATION

presbeia πρεσβεία 4242

presbeia is a rare noun found only twice and meaning "message" in the sense of a "delegation" in Luke 14:32; 19:14.

SEE ALSO

- ▸ **43.** Prophecy, Preaching, Proclamation > AMBASSADOR
  presbeuō

EDGE, EDGED

stoma στόμα 4750

stoma is a noun found nearly eighty times with the predominant sense of "mouth." However, in Luke 21:24; Heb 11:34, ***stoma*** denotes the "edge" of a sword.

- ▸ **16.** Body, Bodily Functions > FACE
- ▸ **16.** Body, Bodily Functions > MOUTH

distomos δίστομος 1366

distomos is a rare adjective referring to a "two-edged" sword in Heb 4:12; Rev 1:16; 2:12.

GOVERNOR

hēgemōn ἡγεμών 2232

hēgemōn is a noun found around twenty times with the predominant meaning "governor." General references to "governors" as civil rulers are found in Matt 10:18; Mark 13:9; 1 Pet 2:14. Specifically, Matt 27:2ff. mentions the Roman governor Pontius Pilate, and Acts 23:24ff. refers to Felix, another Roman governor.

- ▸ **54.** Rule, Authority, Command, Obedience > RULE, RULER

hēgemoneuō ἡγεμονεύω 2230

hēgemoneuō is a rare verb meaning "to be governor," found only in Luke 2:2; 3:1.

ethnarchēs ἐθνάρχης 1481

ethnarchēs is a rare synonym for ***hēgemōn*** (above) denoting the "governor" of Damascus in 2 Cor 11:32.

GUARD

koustōdia κουστωδία 2892

koustōdia is a noun of Latin origin denoting a "unit of guards" (i.e., a watch). The term is found only three times, referring in each case to the Roman guards assigned to watch over the tomb where Christ was buried (Matt 27:65ff.; 28:11).

SEE ALSO

- ▸ **32.** Law, Justice, Jurisprudence, Judgment > GUARD
  phylax
- ▸ **62.** Care For, Protect, Guard, Watch > GUARD, GUARDIAN, WATCH OVER, PROTECT
  phylassō, diaphylassō, phroureō

HELMET

perikephalaia περικεφαλαία 4030

This term is only found twice, in Eph 6:17; 1 Thess 5:8. In both texts the use is metaphorical, referring to the "helmet of salvation" as a symbol of the Christian's hope, drawing on the use of the equivalent Hebrew term *kôba'* in Isa 59:17.

KING

basileus βασιλεύς 935

basileus is consistently translated "king." It occurs around 120 times and refers to human kingship as well as to the royal office of God and Christ.

General references to kings in the NT are found in Matt 10:18; 17:25; Mark 13:9; Luke 21:12; Acts 4:26; 9:15; 1 Tim 2:2; Rev 1:5; 6:15. In 1 Pet 2:13, 17 believers are commanded to render obedience to earthly kings. In Rev 17:2, 10, 18; 18:9; 19:18, 19, kings of the earth are depicted as objects of divine wrath on account of their wickedness. Conversely, Rev 21:24 cites the regenerate kings of the earth among the citizens of heaven. Kings are also frequently mentioned in the parables of Jesus (Matt 18:23; 22:2, 11, 13; Luke 14:31).

A number of specific royal figures are also cited such as Herod (Matt 2:1ff.; Mark 6:14, 22ff.; Acts 12:1), Agrippa (Acts 25:13ff., 24; 25:26; 26:2ff.); Aretas of Damascus (2 Cor 11:32); the demonic king, Apollyon (Rev 9:11); as well as kings from the Israelite theocracy such as Saul (Acts 13:21), the king of Egypt (Heb 11:23), and the mysterious Melchizedek (Heb 7:12).

Christ's role and position as "King of the Jews" is frequently indicated throughout the NT. There is the affirmation first of all that Jesus Christ is the fulfillment of the messianic king figure of OT prophecy. This is made clear on the occasion of Jesus' triumphal return to Jerusalem (Matt 21:5; Luke 19:38; John 12:13, 15). Jesus' action fulfills to the letter the prophecy contained in Zech 9:9. During

Jesus' trial, Pilate asks him, "Are you the King of the Jews?" (Matt 27:11; Mark 15:2ff.; Luke 23:3; John 18:33), to which Jesus replies in the affirmative (John 18:37ff.). The sign on the cross testifying to Jesus' status as King of the Jews is deliberately placed there at the behest of Pilate (Matt 27:37; Mark 15:26; Luke 23:38; John 19:19). The soldiers, who had no idea of the truth of the words they uttered in scorn: "Hail, King of the Jews!" use this title to mock Christ during his pretrial ordeal (Mark 15:18; John 19:3).

In an interesting corollary to this context, John 6:15 records Jesus' refusal to be made king, on the grounds that it was not yet his time to do so. Christ's kingship is then given explicit expression in 1 Tim 6:15, which contains the titles, "Lord of Lords," and "King of kings," as does Rev 17:14; 19:16.

Believers are declared to be "kings" reigning with Christ, pointing to their spiritual, royal status in union with him (Rev 1:6; 5:10).

KINGDOM

basileia βασιλεία 932

basileia is the only Greek term for "kingdom," occurring around 150 times and consistently translated as such. Two particularly significant phrases containing the term ***basileia*** are "kingdom of heaven" and "kingdom of God." These phrases are functionally synonymous and both refer to the dominion of God on earth and incorporate the heavenly realm as well. This kingdom is brought to a climax through the person and work of Jesus Christ, and maintained through the indwelling presence of the Holy Spirit in the lives of believers. The phrase "kingdom of heaven" is frequently associated with the parables of Jesus.

General references to the kingdom of heaven are found in Matt 5:19, 20; 7:21; 10:7; 18:1ff.; 19:12, 14, 23; 23:13. The kingdom of heaven requires repentance as a prerequisite for entry (Matt 3:2; 4:17). This realm is the destiny of the "poor in spirit" (Matt 5:3; Luke 6:20); and those who are persecuted (Matt 5:10). The consummation of the kingdom of heaven is destined to take place at the end of the age (Matt 8:11). Matt 13:11 affirms that this kingdom is a repository of mysteries, accessible only by divine grace. In Matt 16:19, the authority of the kingdom is said to be vested in the symbol of the apostolic "keys." In the parables of Jesus in Matthew's Gospel, the consistent refrain "the kingdom of heaven is like . . ." opens each symbolic story (Matt 13:24, 31, 33, 44ff.; 18:23; 20:1; 22:2; 25:1).

In several contexts, references to the "kingdom of God" are very similar to those made in relation to the "kingdom of heaven." For example, the consummation of the kingdom of God is also destined to take place at the end of this world (Mark 14:25; Luke 21:31; 22:30; Rev 12:10). Similarly, the secrets of the kingdom of God are given to the disciples as an act of divine grace, so that they might understand them (Mark 4:11; Luke 8:10). The phrase, "the kingdom of God is like . . ." is also found at the outset of Jesus' parables, but much less frequently than the corresponding formula in relation to the "kingdom of heaven" parables in Matthew's Gospel (Mark 4:26; Luke 13:29).

Other aspects of the "kingdom of God" are indicated in varying contexts. The priority of the kingdom is demanded in Matt 6:33. It is said to be victorious over the demonic kingdom in Matt 12:28; and the power of the kingdom is indicated explicitly in Mark 9:1; 1 Cor 4:20. The kingdom of God is also declared to be essentially one of righteousness and peace (Rom 14:17), which cannot be inherited by mere human effort (1 Cor 15:50). In this regard, access to the kingdom of God is only possible on the basis of the "new birth," as Jesus explains in John 3:3ff.; thus making it difficult to enter, as indicated in Mark 10:24; Luke 18:24. It is an everlasting kingdom (Luke 1:33; Heb 12:28); and God calls his people to enter in (1 Thess 2:12). Jesus himself expresses the desire for God's kingdom to come (i.e., in its fullness) in the prayer he taught his disciples (Luke 11:2; also Matt 26:29). General references to the kingdom of God are found in Matt 13:43; 19:24; Mark 1:15; 12:34; Luke 7:28; 18:29; Acts 1:3; 19:8; Gal 4:11; Heb 1:8. It is spoken of as the inheritance of God's people in Matt 25:34; Luke 18:16 (of little children); but denied to the world in Eph 5:5. The "gospel of the kingdom" is mentioned in Matt 4:23; 9:35; Mark 1:15; Luke 4:43; 8:1; 16:16.

References to the kingdom of the world from a purely human perspective are found in Mark 3:24; Luke 4:5; 12:32; Heb 11:33; Rev 16:10; 17:12ff.

The NT also refers to the divine kingdom as belonging to Jesus Christ (John 18:36; Col 1:13; 2 Tim 4:1; 2 Pet 1:11; Rev 11:5). While Jesus is viewed as God's appointed ruler, he also recognizes that he holds it "in trust," so to speak, from his Father. 1 Cor 15:24 affirms that Christ will hand the kingdom back to the Father, once his work of redemption is completed.

LEGION

legiōn λεγιών 3003

legiōn is translated "Legion" and occurs only four times. Three times it refers to the symbolic name of the demon-possessed man exorcised by Jesus, "Legion," indicating that he had a multitude of evil spirits within him (Mark 5:9, 15; Luke 8:30). In Matt 26:53, Jesus affirms that, should he so desire, God would send to his aid "twelve legions of angels" to deliver him from the cross.

QUEEN

basilissa βασίλισσα 938

basilissa is the only term for "queen" in the NT and is found in four contexts. Matt 12:42; Luke 11:31; Acts 8:27 refer to historical figures. Rev 18:7 refers symbolically to the city of Babylon as the idolatrous self-styled "queen" (i.e., "queen of heaven").

ROYAL

basilikos βασιλικός 937

basilikos is an adjective found in five places with the underlying sense of "belonging to the nobility." It is translated "royal" in Jas 2:8 with reference to "royal" law, and in Acts 12:21 it refers to "royal" apparel.

basileios βασίλειος 934

basileios is an adjectival form synonymous with ***basilikos***. It occurs only in 1 Pet 2:9 and refers to the "royal" priesthood of believers.

SHIELD

thyreos θυρεός 2375

thyreos is a term found only in Eph 6:16, referring metaphorically to a "shield" of faith.

SOLDIER

stratiōtēs στρατιώτης 4757

stratiōtēs is a noun occurring thirty times, meaning "soldier" throughout.

stratiōtēs frequently refers to the "(common) soldier" (e.g., Matt 8:9; Mark 15:16; Luke 7:8; John 19:2, 23ff.; Acts 10:7; 12:4ff.; 21:32).

A metaphorical reference to a "soldier" as a devout follower of Christ is found in 2 Tim 2:3.

SWORD

machaira μάχαιρα 3162

machaira is found in around thirty places and consistently denotes a "sword" in both literal and metaphorical contexts.

Matt 26:5ff.; Mark 14:43ff.; Luke 22:36, 52; John 18:10; Acts 12:2 contain literal references to swords as weapons. Heb 11:37 refers to being slain by the sword, indicating a savage persecution.

The "sword" is held up in a number of places as symbolic of strife, war, or divine judgment (Matt 10:34; Luke 21:24; Rev 13:10). Rom 13:4 alludes to the authority of governments, given by God, to "exercise the sword" as a means of judicial punishment.

Eph 6:17 refers to the word of God as the "sword of the Spirit." In Heb 4:12, the word of God is declared to be sharper than any two-edged sword.

rhomphaia ῥομφαία 4501

rhomphaia is a noun synonymous with ***machaira*** (above) denoting a "sword" in all seven occurrences.

rhomphaia is used exclusively in metaphorical and visionary contexts. Luke 2:35 refers to a "sword piercing the soul," indicating the prospect of a terrible calamity.

The remaining uses of ***rhomphaia*** are all found in the context of John's visionary Apocalypse, where the term consistently indicates a "two-edged sword," symbolizing the exercising of divine judgment (Rev 1:16; 2:12, 16; 6:8; 19:15, 21).

TAX, TRIBUTE, TOLL

nomisma νόμισμα 3546

nomisma is found only in Matt 22:19 and refers to money collected for the purposes of taxation.

phoros φόρος 5411

phoros is a term denoting "tribute" or "tax" in Luke 20:22; 23:2; Rom 13:6, 7.

didrachmon δίδραχμον 1323

didrachmon denotes a "half-shekel tax," found only in Matt 17:24 (twice).

kēnsos κῆνσος 2778

kēnsos refers to "taxes," or a "toll," and is found only in Matt 17:25; 22:17, 29; Mark 12:14.

WAR, BATTLE, FIGHT

polemos πόλεμος 4171

polemos is a noun denoting "battle," "war," or "fight" in eighteen contexts.

General references to "wars" are found in Matt 24:6; Mark 13:7; Luke 14:31; Jas 4:1. Heb 11:34 refers to those who are mighty in "warfare." The process of preparing for "battle" is described in 1 Cor 14:8.

The book of Revelation makes a number of references to "war." Here ***polemos*** refers to war waged by Satan and his demonic servants against the people of God (Rev 12:17; 13:7; 16:14; 20:8), including against the Messiah himself (Rev 19:19); and to war in the heavenly realm between the archangel Michael and the dragon (Rev 12:7). Rev 9:7ff.; 11:7 depict demonic beasts arrayed for battle.

strateuomai στρατεύομαι 4754

This verb occurs in seven contexts with the primary sense of "to make war," "go to war," used in both literal and figurative contexts. 1 Cor 9:7 describes "going to war" (i.e., serving as a soldier). 2 Cor 10:3 refers to "waging war" in a literal sense. ***strateuomai*** refers to figuratively waging war against the spiritual forces of evil in 1 Tim 1:18. Also in figurative contexts, ungodly passions are said to be "at war" in the hearts of believers (Jas 4:1; 1 Pet 2:11).

strateuomai is also given nominal force (i.e., in participial form) in Luke 3:14; 2 Tim 2:4, referring to "soldiers" (i.e., those who go to war).

strateuma στράτευμα 4753

strateuma is a noun derived from ***strateuomai*** (above) meaning "soldier," "man of war," or "army." It is found in eight contexts.

References to army "troops" or "soldiers" are found in Matt 22:7; Luke 23:11; Acts 23:10, 27. Rev 9:16 refers to visionary "men of war," and Rev 19:14, 19 refer to the "armies" of heaven.

▸ **31.** Kingdom, Empire, Rule, Military, Warfare > ARMY

polemeō πολεμέω 4170

polemeō is a verb found seven times denoting the figurative action of "make war" or "fight."

The general sense of "fight" or "quarrel" is found in Jas 4:2. The heavenly Christ gives a warning to "wage war" against the godless Nicolaitans of Pergamum in Rev 2:16. The archangel Michael "wages war" against the dragon in Rev 12:7. Rev 13:4 notes the futility of human "opposition" against the satanic sea beast. Rev 17:14 denotes the armies of Satan seeking "to make war" against the Lamb (i.e., the Messiah). And the messianic rider on the white horse "engages in war" against the enemies of God and his people in Rev 19:11.

32. Law, Justice, Jurisprudence, Judgment

ACCUSE, ACCUSATION, ACCUSER

aitia αἰτία 156

The noun ***aitia*** occurs twenty times with the principal meanings "cause," "reason." In several places, however, the meaning "accusation" or "charge" is evident — all in relation to legal indictments applied to Christ at his trial (Matt 27:37; Mark 15:26); and to Paul (Acts 23:28; 25:18, 27).

- ▸ **32.** Law, Justice, Jurisprudence, Judgment > CAUSE, REASON, GROUND
- ▸ **32.** Law, Justice, Jurisprudence, Judgment > CHARGE, COMPLAINT

aitiōma αἰτίωμα 157

aitiōma is a rare synonym for ***aitia*** (above) referring to the "charges" brought against Paul in Acts 25:7.

- ▸ **32.** Law, Justice, Jurisprudence, Judgment > CHARGE, COMPLAINT

enklēma ἔγκλημα 1462

enklēma is another rare synonym for ***aitia*** and ***aitiōma*** (above). It is found only in Acts 23:29; 25:16, with reference to "legal charges" or "accusations."

- ▸ **32.** Law, Justice, Jurisprudence, Judgment > CHARGE, COMPLAINT

katēgoria κατηγορία 2724

The noun ***katēgoria*** is found in four places with the technical sense of a "legal charge" in Luke 6:7; John 18:29. It has a more general sense of "accusation" in 1 Tim 5:19; Titus 1:6.

katēgoreō κατηγορέω 2723

The verb ***katēgoreō*** is found in approximately twenty-five different contexts with the consistent meaning "accuse," "bring an accusation against." The usage is primarily one of legal indictment (e.g., Matt 12:10; 27:12; Mark 3:2; 15:3; Luke 11:54; 23:2, 10, 14; John 5:45; 8:6; Acts 22:30; 24:2ff.; 25:5ff.).

Then, in Rom 2:15, ***katēgoreō*** refers to people's consciences "accusing" them. In Rev 12:10, ***katēgoreō*** is used nominally (i.e., participially) to refer to Satan as "the accuser."

katēgoros κατήγορος 2725

katēgoros is a participial noun derived from ***katēgoreō*** (above) occurring six times with the meaning "accuser."

There are general references to "those who accuse," "accusers," in Acts 23:30, 35; 24:8; 25:16, 18. In Rev 12:10, Satan is implicitly referred to as the "accuser" of the saints.

diaballō διαβάλλω 1225

diaballō is a rare verb found only in Luke 16:1 with the meaning "accuse," "bring an accusation against."

enkaleō ἐγκαλέω 1458

The verb ***enkaleō*** is synonymous with ***katēgoreō*** and ***diaballō*** (above) and means "bring charge(s), accusation(s) against" in seven places (Acts 19:38ff.; 23:28ff.; 26:2ff.; Rom 8:33).

- ▸ **32.** Law, Justice, Jurisprudence, Judgment > CHARGE, COMPLAINT

sykophanteō συκοφαντέω 4811

sykophanteō is a rare verb found only in Luke 3:14, with the meaning "falsely accuse," and in Luke 19:8, where it describes the act of "defrauding" (i.e., taking by false accusation).

SEE ALSO

- ▸ **58.** Vices > ACCUSATION
  krisis, diabolos

ACT

dikaiōma δικαίωμα 1345

The noun ***dikaiōma*** occurs ten times with the senses of "righteousness," "judgment," "justification." In Rom 5:18 the term denotes precisely "an act of righteousness," viz. the atoning work of Christ.

- ▸ **32.** Law, Justice, Jurisprudence, Judgment > JUDGMENT
- ▸ **32.** Law, Justice, Jurisprudence, Judgment > JUSTIFICATION
- ▸ **59.** Justice, Righteousness, Truth > RIGHTEOUS, RIGHTEOUSNESS, JUST, JUSTIFY, JUSTIFICATION

ANSWER

apologeomai ἀπολογέομαι 626

The verb ***apologeomai*** is found in eleven places with the primary meaning of "answer for oneself" in the sense of "making a defense" in a judicial context (Luke 12:11; 21:14; Acts 19:33; 25:8; 26:1ff.; Rom 2:15; 2 Cor 12:19).

- ▸ **32.** Law, Justice, Jurisprudence, Judgment > DEFENSE
- ▸ **49.** Allow, Accept, Approve, Refuse > EXCUSE

apologia ἀπολογία 627

apologia is the noun derived from ***apologeomai*** (above) found eight times in all, with the meaning "defense," in a judicial context, where one has to "answer for oneself" (Acts 22:1; 25:16; 1 Cor 9:3; 2 Tim 4:16). In 1 Pet 3:15; Phil 1:7 the context is that of the defense of the gospel.

- ▸ **32.** Law, Justice, Jurisprudence, Judgment > DEFENSE

SEE ALSO

- ▸ **66.** Ask, Answer, Discuss, Learn > ANSWER
  apokrinomai, apokrisis, antapokrinomai, chrēmatismos, hypolambanō

APPEAL

epikaleō ἐπικαλέω 1941

epikaleō is a verb found in around thirty contexts with the primary senses of "be called (i.e., named)," "call upon."

In several places, however, ***epikaleō*** expresses the sense of "appeal" in the judicial context of Paul's appeal to Caesar (Acts 25:11ff.; 26:32; 28:19).

- ▸ **63.** Speak, Tell, Declare, Call > CALL, CALLED, CALLING, SUMMON, NAME

CAUSE, REASON, GROUND

aitia αἰτία 156

The noun ***aitia*** means "cause," "reason" in several of the twenty occurrences of the term.

Matt 19:3 refers to the "cause" or "reason" for divorce. The "cause," or legal ground, for capital punishment is noted in Acts 13:28; 28:18.

- ▸ **32.** Law, Justice, Jurisprudence, Judgment > ACCUSE, ACCUSATION, ACCUSER
- ▸ **32.** Law, Justice, Jurisprudence, Judgment > CHARGE, COMPLAINT

aition αἴτιον 158

aition is a rare variant of ***aitia*** (above) denoting the total absence of a "cause" (i.e., reason) for capital punishment in relation to Christ at his trial (Luke 23:22). The absence of a "reason" or "cause" for a riot is noted in Acts 19:40.

- ▸ **32.** Law, Justice, Jurisprudence, Judgment > FAULT, FAULTLESS

logos λόγος 3056

logos is a common term denoting "word," "saying," or "speech" in most of the 331 occurrences of the term. In Matt 5:32, however, ***logos*** denotes a "cause" (i.e., legal ground) of adultery, validating a divorce.

- ▸ **17.** Senses, Actions, Abilities, Disabilities > SPEAK, SPEECH, TALK
- ▸ **63.** Speak, Tell, Declare, Call > WORD, SAYING, SPEECH
- ▸ **65.** Teach, Exhort, Rebuke, Discipline > DOCTRINE
- ▸ **66.** Ask, Answer, Discuss, Learn > QUESTION, INTERROGATE

CHAIN, BOND

desmios δέσμιος 1198

The noun ***desmios*** is found in sixteen places referring to a "prisoner" as one who is "kept in bonds, chains" (Matt 27:15ff.; Mark 15:6; Acts 16:25ff.; 28:16ff.; Eph 3:1; 4:1; 2 Tim 1:8; Phlm 1, 9; Heb 13:3).

- ▸ **32.** Law, Justice, Jurisprudence, Judgment > PRISON, PRISONER, IMPRISONMENT

SEE ALSO

- ▸ **27.** Community, Partnership, Unity, Discord > BOND
  syndesmos
- ▸ **55.** Bondage, Captivity, Servitude > BOND, CHAIN
  desmos, halysis

CHARGE, COMPLAINT

aitia αἰτία 156

aitia is a noun occurring in twenty contexts with the primary meaning "cause" or "reason," as well as "charge," "accusation."

The meaning "charge" in a legal sense is indicated in a number of places with reference to the accusation against Christ as "the King of the Jews" (Matt 27:37; Mark 15:26); other contexts recording "(legal) accusation" include Acts 23:28; 25:27. In John 19:4ff. Pilate fails to find any "(legal) grounds" for prosecution against Christ. See also Acts 13:28; 25:18.

- ▸ **32.** Law, Justice, Jurisprudence, Judgment > ACCUSE, ACCUSATION, ACCUSER
- ▸ **32.** Law, Justice, Jurisprudence, Judgment > CAUSE, REASON, GROUND

aitiōma αἰτίωμα 157

aitiōma is a rare noun denoting a legal "charge" or "complaint" in Acts 25:7.

- ▸ **32.** Law, Justice, Jurisprudence, Judgment > ACCUSE, ACCUSATION, ACCUSER

enklēma ἔγκλημα 1462

enklēma is a rare synonym for ***aitia*** and ***aitiōma*** (above) denoting a "(legal) charge" in judicial contexts. It is found only in Acts 23:29; 25:16.

- ▸ **32.** Law, Justice, Jurisprudence, Judgment > ACCUSE, ACCUSATION, ACCUSER

enkaleō ἐγκαλέω 1458

enkaleō is a verb found in seven places with the meaning "accuse," "lay a charge against" in each of these contexts (Acts 19:38ff.; 23:28ff.; 26:2ff.; Rom 8:33).

- ▸ **32.** Law, Justice, Jurisprudence, Judgment > ACCUSE, ACCUSATION, ACCUSER

SEE ALSO

- ▸ **30.** Money, Business, Wealth, Poverty > FREE OF CHARGE
  adapanos
- ▸ **54.** Rule, Authority, Command, Obedience > CHARGE, INSTRUCT
  parangelia, diamartyromai, diastellomai, embrimaomai, exorkizō, horkizō

CONDEMN, CONDEMNATION

kataginōskō καταγινώσκω 2607

kataginōskō is a rare verb found only three times, with the meaning "condemn" in each case. It refers to Paul's assessment of Peter, who stood "condemned" in the former's sight because the latter had compromised his integrity in the gospel by refusing to have fellowship with Gentile believers out of fear of the so-called "Jewish party," who disapproved of such interaction. In 1 John 3:20, 21 ***kataginōskō*** refers metaphorically to the heart of the believer "condemning" him in the face of sinful action(s) or a sinful attitude.

katadikazō καταδικάζω 2613

katadikazō is a verb occurring six times and translated "condemn." The act of judicial "condemnation" is indicated both directly and indirectly in Matt 12:7, 37; Jas 5:6. In Luke 6:37 the term is used in a general sense, affirming that if one does not condemn others without just cause, then one will escape condemnation from the hand of God.

krinō κρίνω 2919

krinō is a common verb with the primary meaning "judge" throughout the approximately 110 occurrences of the term. In several contexts, however, the sense of "condemn" is expressed. John 3:17, 18 speak of both the absence and presence of divine condemnation. The culpable action of the Jewish leaders in condemning Christ during his lifetime is indicated in Acts 13:27. Rom 14:22 describes self-condemnation.

▸ **32.** Law, Justice, Jurisprudence, Judgment > JUDGE

▸ **32.** Law, Justice, Jurisprudence, Judgment > SENTENCE

katakrinō κατακρίνω 2632

katakrinō is a verb found in nineteen places with the predominant sense of "condemn," "pass judgment on," throughout its usages.

The meanings "condemn," "pass judgment on" in circumstances precipitated by moral outrage are noted in Matt 12:41ff.; Luke 11:31ff.; John 8:10 (see also Rom 8:34).

Such an action is taken against Christ by the spiritual and civil authorities of Jerusalem who sought to be rid of him (Matt 20:18; Mark 10:33). Christ himself is said to "have condemned" sin in his own body through his death on the cross. The passive sense of "being condemned" describes Judas, who stood morally culpable, aware of his heinous crime in betraying Jesus to the authorities (Matt 27:3). God is said to have condemned Sodom and Gomorrah to destruction, as recorded in 2 Pet 2:6.

A number of references depict people "condemned by God" for unbelief (Mark 16:16; 1 Cor 11:32). Jas 5:9 contains a warning against being "exposed to divine judgment." Heb 11:7 refers to Noah having "condemned" the world by his righteousness. In John 8:11, Jesus refuses to "pass judgment" on the woman caught in adultery. "Self-condemnation" is evident in Rom 2:1; 14:23.

katakrima κατάκριμα 2631

katakrima is a variant form found in only three places and denoting the universal "condemnation" of humankind brought about by the sin of Adam and Eve (Rom 5:16, 18). Rom 8:1 declares that there is no "divine condemnation" for those who are joined to Christ in faith.

katakrisis κατάκρισις 2633

katakrisis is a rare synonym for ***katakrima*** (above) denoting the "condemnation" wrought by the law on humankind in 2 Cor 3:9. 2 Cor 7:3 refers to "passing judgment" on someone in general terms.

autokatakritos αὐτοκατάκριτος 843

autokatakritos is a rare adjective found only in Titus 3:11, denoting one who is "self-condemned."

akatagnōstos ἀκατάγνωστος 176

akatagnōstos is a rare adjectival form found only in Titus 2:8, denoting noble character that "cannot be condemned."

COURT, CASE

agoraios ἀγοραῖος 60

agoraios is a rare adjectival form used nominally in Acts 19:38 to denote a "court of law."

kritērion κριτήριον 2922

kritērion refers to the means of judgment, or to the process of coming to a judicial decision — a "case." It is found only three times. 1 Cor 6:2 refers to the competency of the Corinthian congregational leaders to "try" cases of church discipline. Here ***kritērion*** is translated in a verbal mode. In 1 Cor 6:4, ***kritērion*** indicates the actual "cases" of disciplinary matters coming before the church. In Jas 2:6, ***kritērion*** refers to the "courtroom" itself.

SEE ALSO

▸ **51.** Knowledge, Wisdom, Remember, Forget > JUDGMENT
aisthēsis, gnōmē

DANGER, LIABILITY

enochos ἔνοχος 1777

enochos is an adjective found ten times meaning "in danger of" in the sense of "being liable" to judgment and punishment in a legal forensic sense in Matt 5:21ff.; 26:66; Mark 14:64; Jas 2:10. Such "danger" — "liability," or "guilt" in the context of punishment for sin — is indicated in Mark 3:29 in relation to blasphemy against the Holy Spirit; and in 1 Cor 11:27 in relation to profaning the body and blood of Christ at the Lord's Supper. See also Jas 2:15.

▸ **32.** Law, Justice, Jurisprudence, Judgment > GUILT, GUILTY

▸ **32.** Law, Justice, Jurisprudence, Judgment > WORTHY

▸ **55.** Bondage, Captivity, Servitude > SUBJECT, SUBJECTION, SUBMIT, SUBMISSION

SEE ALSO

▸ **29.** Boats, Fishing, Maritime Activity > DANGEROUS
episphalēs

▸ **74.** Safety, Peace, Danger, Escape > DANGER
kindyneuō

DEFENSE

apologia ἀπολογία 627

apologia is a noun found in eight places with the underlying sense of a "verbal defense," or a reasoned statement offered as a defense in the face of threatened legal prosecution.

Formal legal "defenses" undertaken by the apostle Paul before his opponents are noted in Acts 22:1; 25:16; 1 Cor 9:3; Phil 1:7; 2 Tim 4:16.

The non-judicial sense of a defense is indicated in 2 Cor 7:11 in relation to the Corinthian congregation's successful attempt at their "vindication" in the context of a moral dilemma. 1 Pet 3:15 stresses that believers must be able to offer a "reasoned defense" of their faith to any who might challenge them.

- ▸ **32.** Law, Justice, Jurisprudence, Judgment > ANSWER

apologeomai ἀπολογέομαι 626

apologeomai is a verb found in eleven places, meaning "to make, offer a defense," primarily in a judicial setting (Luke 12:11; 21:14; Acts 19:33; 25:8; 26:1, 2, 24). The non-judicial sense of "defending oneself " is indicated in Rom 2:15; 2 Cor 12:11.

- ▸ **32.** Law, Justice, Jurisprudence, Judgment > ANSWER
- ▸ **49.** Allow, Accept, Approve, Refuse > EXCUSE

EXAMINE, EXAMINATION, INVESTIGATION

anakrisis ἀνάκρισις 351

anakrisis is a rare noun denoting the "(judicial) examination, or investigation" of Paul before King Agrippa in Acts 25:26.

anakrinō ἀνακρίνω 350

anakrinō is a verb found in sixteen places, meaning "to examine" as well as having several related nuances.

The act of "examining" a person in a judicial sense is indicated in Luke 23:14; Acts 4:9; 12:19; 28:18; 1 Cor 9:3. In a similar context, the meaning "judge" is indicated in 1 Cor 4:3. See also 1 Cor 14:24. The citizens of Berea are commended for their eagerness to "search," or "examine," the Scriptures in Acts 17:11.

The divine prerogative of "judging" or "examining" a person is acknowledged by Paul in 1 Cor 4:4.

- ▸ **32.** Law, Justice, Jurisprudence, Judgment > JUDGE
- ▸ **51.** Knowledge, Wisdom, Remember, Forget > DISCERN
- ▸ **66.** Ask, Answer, Discuss, Learn > ASK, REQUEST, BEG, PLEAD
- ▸ **66.** Ask, Answer, Discuss, Learn > QUESTION, INTERROGATE

anetazō ἀνετάζω 426

anetazō is a rare verb meaning "to examine" in a judicial context in Acts 22:29.

SEE ALSO

- ▸ **46.** Wait, Hope, Be Vigilant, Pay Attention To > EXAMINATION, EXAMINE
  dokimazō, peirazō

FAULT, FAULTLESS

aition αἴτιον 158

aition is a noun found four times meaning "fault" (i.e., crime) in Luke 23:4, 14, 22; and denoting a "reason" in Acts 19:40.

- ▸ **32.** Law, Justice, Jurisprudence, Judgment > CAUSE, REASON, GROUND

SEE ALSO

- ▸ **50.** Love, Hate, Please, Be Pleased With > FAULT
  memphomai, elenchō

GUARD

phylax φύλαξ 5441

phylax is a noun denoting a "prison guard or sentry," found only three times (Acts 5:23; 12:6, 19).

SEE ALSO

- ▸ **31.** Kingdom, Empire, Rule, Military, Warfare > GUARD
  koustōdia
- ▸ **62.** Care For, Protect, Guard, Watch > GUARD, GUARDIAN, WATCH OVER, PROTECT
  phylassō, diaphylassō, phroureō

GUILT, GUILTY

enochos ἔνοχος 1777

enochos is an adjective found ten times, meaning "liable to," "guilty of" in relation to peoples' deeds that were open to judicial indictment (Matt 5:21, 22; 26:66; Mark 3:29; 14:64; Jas 2:10). It also has a spiritual connotation in 1 Cor 11:27, where those who partake of the Lord's Supper in an unworthy way are deemed "guilty" of despising the body and blood of the Lord.

- ▸ **32.** Law, Justice, Jurisprudence, Judgment > DANGER, LIABILITY
- ▸ **32.** Law, Justice, Jurisprudence, Judgment > WORTHY
- ▸ **55.** Bondage, Captivity, Servitude > SUBJECT, SUBJECTION, SUBMIT, SUBMISSION

JAILER

desmophylax δεσμοφύλαξ 1200

This term is rare, occurring only three times with the meaning "jailer" or "prison keeper" on each occasion. All occurrences are found in Acts 16, with reference to the jailer of Paul and Silas in Philippi (Acts 16:23, 27, 36).

- ▸ **32.** Law, Justice, Jurisprudence, Judgment > KEEPER
- ▸ **32.** Law, Justice, Jurisprudence, Judgment > PRISON, PRISONER, IMPRISONMENT

JUDGE

krinō κρίνω 2919

krinō is the predominant NT term designating the judicial function of "judging." This verb occurs around ninety times, though not exclusively in formal judicial settings. ***krinō*** refers to the act of judging predicated of human beings, Christ, and God.

As far as human beings are concerned, the contexts of judicial function involving the use of ***krinō*** are varied. There are instructions not to judge unjustly or in hypocritical self-righteousness (Matt 7:1; Rom 2:1, 3; 14:3ff.). John 18:31; Acts 4:19 allude to the civil function of Jewish judges. Matt 7:2 affirms the principle that our criteria in judging others will be applied in the same measure by God towards us. The valid right of church leaders to judge those within the church is spelled out in 1 Cor 5:3, 12. Matt 19:28; Luke 22:30 refer to the anticipated heavenly privilege of judging the twelve tribes of Israel, as well as angels (1 Cor 6:2ff.). Gentile judges are mentioned in 1 Cor 6:1, 6.

In "non-judicial" contexts, ***krinō*** refers to judging in the sense of passing an opinion or considering an issue (Acts 13:46; 1 Cor 10:15, 29; 2 Cor 5:14; Col 2:16). It also expresses the idea of judging in the sense of one who exercises discernment, whether it be commendation (Luke 7:43), or condemnation (Luke 19:22; Rom 2:27; 2 Thess 2:12).

When speaking of Christ as the agent of judging, ***krinō*** indicates in John 3:17; 12:47 that his mission lay not in "judging" (i.e., condemning) the world, but in rescuing it. Then, John 5:22, 30; 8:26 affirm that all divine judgment is given to the Son by God. 2 Tim 4:1 declares that Christ's act of judgment will be consummated at his appearing. John 8:16; Rev 19:11 declare that Christ's judgment is perfect.

krinō also refers to God as the agent of judging. Such divine action is universal in its effect and includes his people as well as the nations (John 8:50; Acts 7:7; 1 Cor 5:13; Heb 10:30). The phenomenon of divine judgment at the end of time is highlighted with respect to "the evil ruler of this world" (John 16:11; Rev 18:8, 20) and to the world in general on the great day of judgment (Acts 17:31; Rom 3:6; Heb 13:4; 1 Pet 4:5; Rev 11:18). God is also said to judge his people in the sense of chastising them, to avoid their ultimate condemnation (1 Cor 11:32). Several texts also declare that God judges justly (1 Pet 2:23; Rev 16:5; 19:2).

▸ **32.** Law, Justice, Jurisprudence, Judgment > CONDEMN, CONDEMNATION

▸ **32.** Law, Justice, Jurisprudence, Judgment > SENTENCE

kritēs κριτής 2923

kritēs is the noun derived from ***krinō*** (above) and is translated "judge" in all seventeen occurrences. Like the verb from which it is derived, ***kritēs*** refers to a judge in a judicial as well as a general, non-judicial sense (i.e., one who passes an opinion or a judgment on someone else).

In the context of society, and of Israelite society in particular, ***kritēs*** refers to a judge or judicial officer in Matt 5:25; Luke 12:58; and in Acts 24:10, where Felix the governor of Judea is mentioned. In a non-specific sense, ***kritēs*** refers to a judge in Matt 12:27; Acts 18:15; Jas 2:4. Acts 13:20 refers to "the judges" as that unique Spirit-anointed class of military and civil leaders during the early period of Israelite settlement in Canaan.

When referring to God, ***kritēs*** refers to him as the judge of the living and the dead in Acts 10:42; Heb 12:23. 2 Tim 4:8 portrays God as the righteous judge; and Jas 5:9 utilizes the term "judge" as a title for God.

anakrinō ἀνακρίνω 350

anakrinō is a variant form of ***krinō*** (above), occurring sixteen times with the primary meanings "examine" and "judge," reflecting the sense of investigation, interrogation, and estimation, and other related nuances.

anakrinō indicates "examination" in a judicial sense with Jesus before Pilate (Luke 23:14); and with Peter and John before the Sanhedrin (Acts 4:9). ***anakrinō*** is also used in a non-judicial sense (Acts 12:19; 1 Cor 9:3; 14:24); and in the sense of "search" or "inquiry," when the Bereans are commended for examining the Scriptures in Acts 17:11.

anakrinō means "accusation" in Acts 24:8; 28:18, where Paul is accused by the Jews and the Romans, respectively. ***anakrinō*** also means "spiritual discernment" (1 Cor 2:14, 15); "judging" in a judicial sense (1 Cor 4:3, 4); and "questioning" (1 Cor 10:25, 27).

▸ **32.** Law, Justice, Jurisprudence, Judgment > EXAMINE, EXAMINATION, INVESTIGATION

▸ **51.** Knowledge, Wisdom, Remember, Forget > DISCERN

▸ **66.** Ask, Answer, Discuss, Learn > ASK, REQUEST, BEG, PLEAD

▸ **66.** Ask, Answer, Discuss, Learn > QUESTION, INTERROGATE

SEE ALSO

▸ **51.** Knowledge, Wisdom, Remember, Forget > JUDGE
dikastēs, diakrinō

JUDGMENT

krisis κρίσις 2920

krisis is the principal noun derived from ***krinō***, occurring around fifty times with the primary sense of "judgment," as well as several related nuances in a variety of contexts. Again, it is a term that refers to both human and divine actions.

When referring to human beings, ***krisis*** indicates "judgment" in the legal sense of judicial condemnation for crimes (Matt 5:21; 1 Tim 5:24; Jas 2:13). Pharisaical neglect of justice is indicated in Matt 23:23; Luke 11:42. John 7:24 commands that righteous judgment be executed.

When divine judgment is in view, ***krisis*** is found in a number of contexts. God's righteous judgment in a general sense is indicated (2 Thess 1:5; Rev 16:7; 19:2); as is his judgment against human beings (John 3:19; Heb 9:27; 2 Pet 2:9, 11). References to the great day of judgment are found in Matt 10:15; 11:22, 24; John 5:29; 12:31; 1 John 4:17; Rev 14:7. Damnation for the wicked is threatened and invoked on the wicked — on the Pharisees (Matt 23:33; Mark 3:29); the ungodly (Jude 15); and on Babylon (Rev 18:10).

Judgment is also a function assigned to Christ (John 5:30; 8:16), whose judgment is perfect; and in a negative sense to the archangel Michael, from whom no judgment may be personally directed against the devil.

▸ **58.** Vices > ACCUSATION

krima κρίμα 2917

krima is another noun derived from ***krinō***. It also embraces the sense of "judgment," but with the dominant emphases on judicial sentencing, condemnation, and penal judgment. ***krima*** occurs thirty times in reference to God and human beings.

In the context of human judgment, ***krima*** has a general meaning in Matt 7:2; 1 Pet 4:17; and also refers to judicial condemnation (Rom 13:2); to a lawsuit (1 Cor 6:7); and to capital punishment (Luke 23:40). Luke 24:20 refers to the condemnation of Jesus under the jurisdiction of Pilate.

Judgment attributed to God in the sense of assessment is indicated in John 3:1. His decrees or statutes are mentioned in Rom 11:33; Heb 6:2. Divine condemnation is directed against the Pharisees (Matt 23:14; Mark 12:40; Luke 20:47); against evildoers (Rom 2:23; 5:16; Gal 5:16; Jude 14); and against those who abuse the Lord's Supper (1 Cor 11:29, 34) In reference to the judgment of Christ, John 9:39 speaks of action that is both redemptive and punitive.

The task of judgment is committed to heavenly beings in Rev 20:4.

praitōrion πραιτώριον 4232

This term (derived from the Latin *praetorium*) refers to the governor's residence (or palace) or headquarters of the Roman commander-in-chief. The ***praitōrion*** was used as a civil court, and thus the usual translation "hall of judgment." It is found seven times in relation both to the place of Jesus' trial (Matt 27:27; Luke 15:16; John 18:28, 33; 19:9); and to the setting for Paul's trial and imprisonment (Acts 23:35; Phil 1:13).

- ▸ **33.** Architecture > PALACE, PRAETORIUM

bēma βῆμα 968

bēma refers to the official seat of a judge or to the tribunal, or court itself. ***bēma*** occurs thirteen times, with all but three of these referring to judgment of some kind.

The judgment seat of Pilate is indicated in Matt 27:19; John 19:13 in a literal sense; and in spiritual contexts Rom 14:10 mentions God's judgment seat and 2 Cor 5:10 refers to the judgment seat of Christ. The tribunal of Gallio, proconsul of Achaia, is indicated in Acts 18:12, 16, 17, as is that of Festus, governor of Judea, in Acts 25:6, 10, 17.

- ▸ **32.** Law, Justice, Jurisprudence, Judgment > SEAT
- ▸ **34.** Craftsmanship, Artisanship, Furniture, Implements > THRONE

dikē δίκη 1349

dikē is found four times meaning "judgment" in the sense of a judicial sentence (Jude 7; Acts 25:15; 2 Thess 1:9) or principle of justice (Acts 28:4).

- ▸ **73.** Blessing, Curse, Reward, Punishment > PUNISH, PUNISHMENT

dikaiōma δικαίωμα 1345

dikaiōma occurs ten times and means "ordinance," "justification." It also means "judgment" on two occasions. In Rom 1:32 ***dikaiōma*** indicates the divine decree, whereby God's judgment of eternal condemnation will be poured out on those whose lifestyles embody the very antithesis of holiness. Rev 15:4 speaks of the revelation of God's "judgments," which will bring forth worship from the nations. The term here suggests that God's righteous acts of deliverance throughout history are in view. The force of ***dikaiōma*** clearly indicates a divine initiative and source.

- ▸ **32.** Law, Justice, Jurisprudence, Judgment > ACT
- ▸ **32.** Law, Justice, Jurisprudence, Judgment > JUSTIFICATION
- ▸ **59.** Justice, Righteousness, Truth > RIGHTEOUS, RIGHTEOUSNESS, JUST, JUSTIFY, JUSTIFICATION

dikaiokrisia δικαιοκρισία 1341

dikaiokrisia is only found in Rom 2:5, which speaks of the revelation of God's righteous judgments.

SEE ALSO

- ▸ **51.** Knowledge, Wisdom, Remember, Forget > JUDGMENT
  aisthēsis, gnōmē

JUSTIFICATION

dikaiōsis δικαίωσις 1347

dikaiōsis is one of the two nouns derived from ***dikaioō***. While the latter term is fairly common in the NT, this corresponding noun only occurs twice, in Romans. ***dikaiōsis*** refers in Rom 4:25 to the resurrection of Christ in conjunction with his death as the ground for our justification. It is this concrete expression of divine grace that results in the acquittal of people's guilt and the declaration of their righteousness in his sight. In Rom 5:18, the same term indicates that Christ's one act of righteousness (i.e., his death and resurrection, considered as one event) leads to our justification as an antidote to the one trespass of Adam that brought humankind into the bondage of sin and death.

- ▸ **59.** Justice, Righteousness, Truth > RIGHTEOUS, RIGHTEOUSNESS, JUST, JUSTIFY, JUSTIFICATION

dikaiōma δικαίωμα 1345

dikaiōma is also derived from ***dikaioō***. However, of the ten contexts in which ***dikaiōma*** is found, only Rom 5:18 explicitly refers to justification as the "free gift" following many sins. This free gift is the finished work of Christ in his death and resurrection, as indicated by the context of Romans 5.

- ▸ **32.** Law, Justice, Jurisprudence, Judgment > ACT
- ▸ **32.** Law, Justice, Jurisprudence, Judgment > JUDGMENT
- ▸ **59.** Justice, Righteousness, Truth > RIGHTEOUS, RIGHTEOUSNESS, JUST, JUSTIFY, JUSTIFICATION

JUSTIFY

dikaioō δικαιόω 1344

dikaioō means "justify" and may also be translated "declare righteous." It occurs in about forty contexts and usually refers to God's action.

On the rare occasions that ***dikaioō*** refers to the practice of justifying in the human arena, it refers either to justifying oneself, as in Luke 10:29 concerning the lawyer's motive in asking Jesus the question, "Who is my neighbor?"; or to declaring that God's way is right (i.e., "justifying" him; Luke 7:29). In a unique metaphorical reference to the commendation of godly living, wisdom is said to be justified by her deeds (Matt 11:19) and her children (Luke 7:35).

Elsewhere, "justifying" is an action wholly predicated of God. For example, 1 Tim 3:16 declares that Jesus is justified by God in the Spirit. In relation to human beings being declared righteous by God, there is the absolute statement in Rom 8:33 that it is God who justifies. Matt 12:37 indicates that God uses one's words as a means of either condemnation or acquittal (i.e., justification).

Similarly, it is by the actions of human beings that God will evaluate their standing before him. In Luke 18:14, for example, it is the repentance of the tax collector in Jesus' parable that brings about his justification.

Rom 2:3 affirms that, by keeping the law perfectly, one will be justified before God. However, it is clear that no mere mortal is able to do so (Rom 3:20; Gal 3:11; 5:4 [implied]). As a corollary to this reality, Rom 4:2 declares that Abraham was justified not by his works, but by his faith and trust in God. Hence, faith and trust in Christ in the new covenant era become the criterion by which one is declared righteous before God (Acts 13:39; Rom 3:26ff.; 4:5; 5:1; Gal 2:16; 3:8, 24). The overarching ground of justification is divine grace, as affirmed in Rom 3:24; Titus 3:7, in relation to which faith is an instrument of justification, as is the blood of Christ (Rom 5:9). The divinely applied sequence in the application of redemption has the divine calling immediately preceding the believer's justification.

A special note is appropriate in relation to the teaching of Jas 2:21–25. Here, James is affirming by way of a corollary argument what is implicit in the teaching of the apostle Paul. James wants to emphasize that faith, without the accompanying evidence of good works, is not true faith at all. Here he claims that Abraham and Rahab (for example) were justified by their works. This is not to contradict the Pauline doctrine of justification by grace through faith alone. Rather, James is declaring that faith must be accompanied by, not replaced by, works, if that faith is to be a genuine means of one's justification.

▸ **55.** Bondage, Captivity, Servitude > FREE, FREEDOM, SET FREE, LIBERTY

▸ **59.** Justice, Righteousness, Truth > RIGHTEOUS, RIGHTEOUSNESS, JUST, JUSTIFY, JUSTIFICATION

KEEPER

desmophylax δεσμοφύλαξ 1200

This term is rare, occurring only three times, with reference to a "keeper of the prison," or a jailer (Acts 16:23, 27, 36).

▸ **32.** Law, Justice, Jurisprudence, Judgment > JAILER

▸ **32.** Law, Justice, Jurisprudence, Judgment > PRISON, PRISONER, IMPRISONMENT

LAWFUL

exesti ἔξεστι 1832

exesti is a verb form which is translated impersonally "it is lawful." ***exesti*** occurs around thirty times, and in the majority of contexts it is concerned with appropriate or inappropriate behavior in response to the demands of God's law. The appropriate behavior is that which conforms to the principles of the law. Conversely, inappropriate behavior has to do with that which is not permitted under the law. In some cases, however, what is expressed as "not lawful" is a contradiction — not of God's law, but of the misguided Pharisaic interpretation of the law. It is this latter illegality that Jesus and the disciples were sometimes accused of by the Pharisees and others of the Jewish religious hierarchy.

The ascription "not lawful," in accordance with Pharisaic tradition, is recorded in Matt 12:2; Mark 2:24; Luke 6:2; John 5:10. Such a designation is also predicated of Mosaic ritual legal requirements (Matt 12:4; Mark 2:26; Luke 6:4). Unlawful behavior, in violation of the moral law, is indicated in Matt 14:4; 27:6; Mark 6:18. A general sense of illegality, unrelated to the law of God, is referred to in Matt 20:15; John 18:31; Acts 16:21; 22:25.

Occasionally, ***exesti*** is found in the context of an inquiry, for example "Is it lawful?" in Matt 12:10; Mark 3:4; Luke 6:9; 14:3, where Jesus is asked: "Is it lawful to heal on the Sabbath?" A similar question is asked with reference to divorce (Matt 19:3; Mark 10:2), and paying taxes to Caesar (Matt 22:17; Mark 12:14; Luke 20:22).

The positive affirmation of lawful behavior, behavior that is in full accord with God's law, is illustrated in Matt 12:12 concerning doing good on the Sabbath, and 1 Cor 6:12; 10:23, where Paul expresses his liberty in Christ, declaring that all things are lawful for him.

MAGISTRATE

archōn ἄρχων 758

archōn is a noun occurring around twenty times with the principal meaning "ruler" or "commander." It is a general term for a civil, spiritual leader. However, on one occasion, the term refers to a civil magistrate (Luke 12:58).

▸ **54.** Rule, Authority, Command, Obedience > RULE, RULER

NAIL

prosēloō προσηλόω 4338

prosēloō is a rare verb found only in Col 2:14. Here it refers metaphorically to Christ "nailing" to the cross the legal indictment of the sin of his people. This sin would otherwise have condemned them, had not Christ freely offered himself as a substitutionary atonement for that sin.

SEE ALSO

▸ **34.** Craftsmanship, Artisanship, Furniture, Implements > NAIL
hēlos

OFFICER, OFFICIAL

hypēretēs ὑπηρέτης 5257

hypēretēs means "officer" or "official" in a number of places. The term is found twenty times, with the sense of "officer" evident in half of these contexts.

hypēretēs most frequently refers to a "legal officer" charged with the responsibility of carrying out the judicial sentence of the courts or the maintenance of law and order, similar to a modern member of the police force. Many of these instances occur in the context of Christ's arrest, trial, and crucifixion (John 7:32, 45, 46; 18:3, 12, 18, 22; 19:6). See also Matt 5:25; Acts 5:22, 26. In addition, ***hypēretēs*** refers to a "synagogue attendant or official" in Luke 4:20.

▸ **55.** Bondage, Captivity, Servitude > SERVANT, SLAVE

praktōr πράκτωρ 4233

praktōr, a synonym for ***hypēretēs*** (above), occurs only in Luke 12:58, referring twice in that verse to an "officer" of the jail system.

PRISON, PRISONER, IMPRISONMENT

phylakē φυλακή 5438

phylakē is a term meaning "prison," "imprisonment" in the large majority of its nearly fifty occurrences.

Literal references to imprisonment are found, for example, in Matt 5:25; Mark 6:17; Luke 3:20; 23:19ff.; John 3:24; Acts 16:23ff.; Heb 11:36; Rev 2:10.

Two significant metaphorical uses of ***phylakē*** are to be noted. 1 Pet 3:19 refers to the Spirit of Christ in Noah (i.e., by implication), who preached to the "spirits in prison" in the days prior to the great flood. The expression "spirits in prison" refers to those who were held in spiritual bondage by their willful rejection of God. Rev 20:7 refers to the momentary release of Satan from "his prison," heralding a brief flurry of satanic activity prior to his doom.

desmios δέσμιος 1198

desmios consistently means "prisoner" in each of its sixteen occurrences (Matt 27:15ff.; Mark 15:6; Acts 16:25ff.; Eph 3:1; 4:1; 2 Tim 1:8; Heb 13:3).

▸ **32.** Law, Justice, Jurisprudence, Judgment > CHAIN, BOND

desmōtērion δεσμωτήριον 1201

desmōtērion occurs only four times, referring to a "prison" (Matt 11:2; Acts 5:21, 23; 16:26).

desmophylax δεσμοφύλαξ 1200

desmophylax occurs in only three places, referring to "the keeper of the prison," or the "jailer" (Acts 16:23, 27, 36).

▸ **32.** Law, Justice, Jurisprudence, Judgment > JAILER
▸ **32.** Law, Justice, Jurisprudence, Judgment > KEEPER

desmōtēs δεσμώτης 1202

desmōtēs occurs only in Acts 27:1, 42, referring to "prisoners."

tērēsis τήρησις 5084

tērēsis is a noun with the underlying sense of "keeping." It occurs only three times and refers to a place of confinement, a prison, in two of these contexts (Acts 4:3; 5:18).

PROVE

apodeiknymi ἀποδείκνυμι 584

apodeiknymi is a verb found only in four places, meaning "show," "approve," and "prove." The latter meaning occurs only in Acts 25:7, referring to Paul's enemies, who were unable to prove charges against him.

▸ **49.** Allow, Accept, Approve, Refuse > APPROVE, APPROVED

QUESTION

zētēma ζήτημα 2213

zētēma is a noun meaning "question" in a legal context in all five occurrences of the term. The sense of "legal matter" underlies the references to "questions" (Acts 15:2; 18:15; 23:29; 25:19). In Acts 26:3, the sense of ***zētēma*** is less clear, though the translation "question" is possible, along with that of "controversy," with reference to Jewish customs that are difficult to understand.

SEE ALSO

▸ **66.** Ask, Answer, Discuss, Learn > QUESTION, INTERROGATE
syzēteō, logos, anakrinō, eperōtaō

REQUIRE

ekzēteō ἐκζητέω 1567

ekzēteō is a verb found in seven contexts meaning "require" in two of these. Luke 11:50, 51 refer to God "holding accountable" the present generation of Israelites for killing the prophets in ages past. The reason for such condemnation is that this current generation venerates their forbears, who actually put the prophets to death. The literal sense of this accusation reads: ". . . the blood of the prophets will be required of this generation."

▸ **72.** Need, Gain, Loss, Advantage, Seek, Find > SEEK, SEARCH

apaiteō ἀπαιτέω 523

apaiteō is a rare verb, occurring only twice. It means "require" in the sense of "demand" in the parable of the rich fool, where God says to this man: "Tonight your soul shall be required of you" (Luke 12:20).

▸ **66.** Ask, Answer, Discuss, Learn > ASK, REQUEST, BEG, PLEAD

SEE ALSO

▸ **54.** Rule, Authority, Command, Obedience > BE REQUIRED
zēteō

SEAT

bēma βῆμα 968

bēma is a noun occurring thirteen times with the predominant sense of "judgment seat" or "throne" in contexts where justice is administered from this vantage point — both human and divine.

The "judgment seat" of Pontius Pilate during the time of Christ is indicated in Matt 27:19; John 19:13. The divine "judgment seat" of Christ, before which all believers will stand, is noted in Rom 14:10; 2 Cor 5:10.

bēma refers to "the throne" of Herod Agrippa (Acts 12:21), and to the Roman "tribunal" (i.e., the official Roman court of justice) in Acts 18:12ff.; 25:6, 10, 17.

- ▸ **32.** Law, Justice, Jurisprudence, Judgment > JUDGMENT
- ▸ **34.** Craftsmanship, Artisanship, Furniture, Implements > THRONE

SEE ALSO

- ▸ **34.** Craftsmanship, Artisanship, Furniture, Implements > SEAT, CHAIR
  kathedra, prōtokathedria

SENTENCE

krinō κρίνω 2919

krinō is a verb with the predominant sense of "judge," found over one hundred times. It also has the sense of "pass judicial sentence" on.

- ▸ **32.** Law, Justice, Jurisprudence, Judgment > CONDEMN, CONDEMNATION
- ▸ **32.** Law, Justice, Jurisprudence, Judgment > JUDGE

epikrinō ἐπικρίνω 1948

epikrinō is a rare variant form of ***krinō*** (above) found only in Luke 23:24 and meaning "to give, or pass judicial sentence," in the context of the trial of Christ under the control of the Roman procurator, Pontius Pilate.

apokrima ἀπόκριμα 610

apokrima is a rare noun derived from ***krinō*** (above) meaning "sentence" in relation to a metaphorical "sentence of death" and found only in 2 Cor 1:9.

SHUT UP, CONFINE

katakleiō κατακλείω 2623

This verb is found only twice, in Luke 3:20; Acts 26:10, where it refers to being "shut up" or "confined" in prison.

SEE ALSO

- ▸ **85.** Movement, Position, State > SHUT
  kleiō, apokleiō

VISIT (IN JUDGMENT)

episkopē ἐπισκοπή 1984

episkopē is a noun denoting both "the office of a bishop" and the "visitation," or "coming," of God. The term occurs four times, with the latter meaning evident in two contexts. One of these contexts refers to "the coming" of God to judge the world (1 Pet 2:12); the other in Luke 19:44 refers to the more immediate "coming" of God among his people that will result in the destruction of the temple.

- ▸ **38.** Covenant, Law, Rites, Roles > OFFICE, POSITION

SEE ALSO

- ▸ **24.** Dwell, Live, Gather, Hospitality > VISIT, VISITATION
  historeō
- ▸ **62.** Care For, Protect, Guard, Watch > VISIT
  episkeptomai

WITNESS, TESTIMONY

pseudomartys ψευδόμαρτυς 5575

pseudomartys is a noun found only in Matt 26:60; 1 Cor 15:15 denoting a "false witness."

pseudomartyreō ψευδομαρτυρέω 5576

pseudomartyreō is a verb occurring six times meaning "to bear false witness." It is found in contexts rehearsing the ninth commandment in relation to "lying" (Matt 19:18; Mark 10:19; Luke 18:20; Rom 13:9); and also in connection with presenting "false testimony" in a court of law against Christ (Mark 14:56ff.).

pseudomartyria ψευδομαρτυρία 5577

pseudomartyria is a rare noun found twice. In Matt 15:19 it denotes "false testimony" as a vice, and in Matt 26:59 it indicates the "false testimony" presented in relation to Christ at his trial.

SEE ALSO

- ▸ **58.** Vices > BEAR WITNESS AGAINST, PERJURE
  katamartyreō
- ▸ **63.** Speak, Tell, Declare, Call > WITNESS, BEAR WITNESS, TESTIFY, TESTIMONY
  martyreō, martyria, martyrion, martys, amartyros, symmartyreō, diamartyromai

WORTHY

enochos ἔνοχος 1777

enochos is an adjectival form found ten times with the primary sense of "in danger of" as well as "guilty, or deserving of." The latter sense is found in Matt 26:66; Mark 14:64, where Christ is declared "worthy" of death by the hostile Jerusalem population.

- ▸ **32.** Law, Justice, Jurisprudence, Judgment > DANGER, LIABILITY
- ▸ **32.** Law, Justice, Jurisprudence, Judgment > GUILT, GUILTY
- ▸ **55.** Bondage, Captivity, Servitude > SUBJECT, SUBJECTION, SUBMIT, SUBMISSION

SEE ALSO

- ▸ **53.** Value, Worth > WORTHY, UNWORTHY
  hikanos, axios, axioō, kataxioō, axiōs

33. Architecture

BUILD, BUILDER, BUILDING

oikodomeō οἰκοδομέω 3618

oikodomeō is a verb found in approximately thirty contexts indicating the action of "building" in both a literal and metaphorical sense. The term is also translated nominally as "builder." General references to the act of "building" are found, for example, in Matt 7:24ff.; Mark 12:1; Luke 6:48ff.; 17:28. References to the construction of the temple are found in John 2:20; Acts 7:47ff.

oikodomeō is used metaphorically in Matt 16:18, where Christ promises Peter to build his (i.e., Christ's) church on the rock, referring to himself as the foundation of the worldwide community of believers. Elsewhere, Jesus promises to "rebuild" the temple in three days, referring to his own person as the resurrected Messiah (Matt 26:61; Mark 14:50). See also Matt 27:40; Mark 15:29. In other contexts, ***oikodomeō*** is translated "edify," "build up" (i.e., to strengthen and nurture one's faith) (Acts 9:31; 1 Thess 2:11; 1 Pet 2:5). True love is said to produce this effect in 1 Cor 8:1 (see also 1 Cor 14:4). Similarly, the task of "building" one's gospel ministry in the sense of developing and maintaining it is noted in Rom 15:20 (see also Gal 2:18).

oikodomeō in the sense of "builder" is also used metaphorically to refer to the unbelieving leaders of God's people throughout history who rejected the servants of Yahweh including, ultimately, Christ himself (Matt 21:42; Mark 12:10; Luke 20:17; Acts 4:11; 1 Pet 2:7).

▸ **65.** Teach, Exhort, Rebuke, Discipline >
EDIFICATION, EDIFY

anoikodomeō ἀνοικοδομέω 456

anoikodomeō is a rare variant of ***oikodomeō*** (above) meaning "rebuild." It is found only in Acts 15:16, which cites the prophecy of Amos 9:11, 12, where God promises "to rebuild the fallen tent of David" — to restore the kingdom of Israel to his people.

epoikodomeō ἐποικοδομέω 2026

epoikodomeō is another variant of ***oikodomeō*** (above). It signifies "build up," "build upon" and is found in eight contexts, all metaphorical. The meaning "build up" in the sense of encouraging or strengthening one's faith is indicated in Acts 20:32; Col 2:7; Jude 20. In 1 Cor 3:10ff. this term means to "build upon," in the sense of developing and furthering one's gospel ministry. In particular, Eph 2:20 speaks of the church "(having been) built on" the foundation of Christ and the apostles.

synoikodomeō συνοικοδομέω 4925

This word is another rare variant of ***oikodomeō*** (above) and signifies "to build together." It is found only in Eph 2:22 and is used passively to indicate the continuing spiritual process of believers "being built together" into the community of God's people worldwide, joined together by the spirit of God in Christ.

kataskeuazō κατασκευάζω 2680

The verb ***kataskeuazō*** is found thirteen times and means to "prepare" or "build." The underlying sense for both of these meanings is that of "to make ready," "construct." Jesus is designated indirectly as "the builder" (lit., "one who builds") of the "house," referring to the church, the community of God's people in Heb 3:3. God is described as the ultimate "builder" in Heb 3:4. Heb 9:2 refers to the "building" or "construction" of the tabernacle, and Heb 11:7; 1 Pet 3:20 refer to Noah's ark.

▸ **83.** Set, Put, Place, Prepare, Establish >
PREPARE, MAKE READY

oikodomē οἰκοδομή 3619

oikodomē is a noun derived from ***oikodomeō*** (above) found in eighteen contexts and denoting a "building" in both a literal and metaphorical sense.

Literal references to the temple "buildings" are found in Matt 24:1; Mark 13:1ff.

The metaphorical sense of "building up" or "edification," in the sense of the spiritual maturing of one's faith, is indicated in Rom 14:19; 15:2; 1 Cor 14:3ff.; 2 Cor 10:8; 12:19; 13:10; Eph 4:12, 16, 29.

The expression "God's building" is an indirect metaphorical reference to the church community of God's people, both in the earthly and heavenly contexts (1 Cor 3:9; 2 Cor 5:1; Eph 2:21).

▸ **65.** Teach, Exhort, Rebuke, Discipline >
EDIFICATION, EDIFY

technitēs τεχνίτης 5079

technitēs is a rare noun denoting a "builder," designating God as the "builder" of the heavenly city in Heb 11:10.

▸ **34.** Craftsmanship, Artisanship, Furniture, Implements >
CRAFTSMAN

architektōn ἀρχιτέκτων 753

architektōn is used only once, in 1 Cor 3:10, to refer to Paul's description of himself as a skilled "master builder," equipped by God for the task of founding churches.

COMPLETION

apartismos ἀπαρτισμός 535

apartismos is a rare noun found only in Luke 14:28 denoting the "completion" of a tower.

SEE ALSO

▸ **61.** Integrity, Innocence, Piety >
PERFECT, PERFECTION, COMPLETE
artios

▸ **84.** Do, Make, Accomplish, Occur >
CARRY OUT, COMPLETE, FULFILL, ACCOMPLISH
epiteleō

CORNERSTONE

akrogōniaios ἀκρογωνιαῖος 204

akrogōniaios is a rare term denoting Christ as the "chief cornerstone" of the heavenly temple in Eph 2:20; 1 Pet 2:6. This is a metaphor for Christ's status as the foundation of the kingdom of God.

SEE ALSO

- ▸ **6.** Location, Position, Direction, Extension > CORNER, CORNERSTONE
  gōnia
- ▸ **31.** Kingdom, Empire, Rule, Military, Warfare > CHIEF
  prōtos
- ▸ **35.** Clothing, Adornment, Textiles > CORNER
  archē
- ▸ **38.** Covenant, Law, Rites, Roles > SHEPHERD
  archipoimēn

COURT

aulē αὐλή 833

aulē is a noun denoting "palace," "hall" in most of the twelve occurrences of the term. In Rev 11:2, however, the term denotes the "outer court" of the temple in John's apocalyptic vision.

- ▸ **33.** Architecture > PALACE, PRAETORIUM

basileion βασίλειον 933

basileion is a rare noun denoting a "royal court" (or palace) found only in Luke 7:25.

SEE ALSO

- ▸ **32.** Law, Justice, Jurisprudence, Judgment > COURT, CASE
  agoraios

DOOR

thyra θύρα 2374

The noun ***thyra*** designates a "door" or "gate" throughout its nearly forty occurrences.

Literal references to "doors" include Matt 6:6; 25:10; Mark 11:4; 15:46; Luke 11:7; John 10:1ff.; 18:16; Acts 3:2; 12:6; 16:26ff.

Elsewhere, ***thyra*** refers metaphorically to a "door" of opportunity for ministry in 1 Cor 16:9; 2 Cor 2:12; Col 4:3. The "door" of the heavenly kingdom is indicated in Rev 3:8; 4:1; and similarly, Jas 5:9 refers to the symbolic "doors" of heaven, at which the judge of all the earth stood ready to pronounce his judgment.

FOUNDATION, LAY A FOUNDATION

themelios θεμέλιος 2310

themelios is a noun found sixteen times with the consistent meaning "foundation."

Literal references to the "foundations" of a house are found in Luke 6:48ff.; to the "foundation" of a tower in Luke 14:29; and to the "foundations" of a prison in Acts 16:26.

Elsewhere, ***themelios*** is used in metaphorical contexts. The "foundation" of a man's ministry is indicated in Rom 15:20; 1 Cor 3:10ff. In particular, Jesus Christ is depicted as the "foundation" of gospel ministry in 1 Cor 3:11; and in Eph 2:20 the household or family of God is said to be built on the "foundation" of the apostles and prophets, with Christ himself as the chief cornerstone.

In 1 Tim 6:19, ***themelios*** denotes a "foundation" in the sense of a "spiritual guarantee" of eternal life. Heb 6:10 refers to the "foundation" of repentance in the sense of a "fundamental set of teachings" as prerequisite for a godly life. See also 2 Tim 2:19.

Heb 11:10; Rev 21:4, 19 refer to the "foundations" of the heavenly city.

themelioō θεμελιόω 2311

themelioō is a verb found six times meaning "found," "ground," "establish," as well as "lay a foundation." The sense of "setting a foundation," both literal and metaphorical, is common to each reference.

Matt 7:25; Luke 6:48 both refer to the efficient "founding," or erection, of a house that can withstand the impact of wind and rain. Eph 3:17 mentions believers being "grounded" in love. Col 1:23 refers to the blessing of a steadfast, or well-grounded, faith. 1 Pet 5:10 contains the promise that God will "establish" his people in their faith. Finally, Heb 1:10 affirms that God "has laid the foundation of the earth" at the beginning of time.

- ▸ **83.** Set, Put, Place, Prepare, Establish > ESTABLISH, FIX, GROUND, STRENGTHEN

SEE ALSO

- ▸ **4.** Beginning, Continuing, Finishing, Postponing > FOUNDATION
  katabolē

GATE

pylē πύλη 4439

pylē denotes a "gate" in all ten of its occurrences, in both a literal and figurative sense. Literal references to the "gate" of a city are found in Luke 7:12; Acts 9:24; 12:10; Heb 13:12. The temple gate known as "Beautiful" is noted in Acts 3:10.

pylē is also used metaphorically, denoting a "gate" as a symbolic access point to the dual destinies of eternal blessing and judgment. Matt 7:13 refers to the "narrow gate," that leads to eternal life with God, and also to the "wide gate," that leads to destruction. The same "narrow gate" is found in Matt 7:14; Luke 13:24. In Matt 16:18 Jesus declares that the "gates of hell" shall not prevail against his church.

pylōn πυλών 4440

pylōn is a variant form of ***pylē*** (above) also denoting a "gate" in both a literal and figurative sense.

The "gates" of domestic residences are noted in Luke 16:20; Acts 10:17; 12:13ff. See also Matt 26:71. City "gates" are indicated in Acts 14:13.

In Rev 21:12ff.; 22:14 there are several allusions to the "gates" of the heavenly city.

probatikos προβατικός 4262

probatikos is an adjectival form found only in John 5:2, with reference to the "Sheep Gate" in Jerusalem.

SEE ALSO

- ▸ **14.** Animals > SHEEP
  probaton

HOUSE

oikos οἶκος 3624

oikos occurs around one hundred times and is consistently translated "house," "household," in a variety of contexts.

Indicating an ordinary home or dwelling, ***oikos*** is found in Matt 9:6; 23:38; Mark 2:1; Luke 22:54; John 7:53. The term also refers to a palace in Matt 11:8.

oikos refers to the nation of God's people in the expression "house of Israel" in Matt 10:6; 15:24; Luke 1:33; Acts 2:36; 7:42; Heb 8:8, 10. The "house of David" also refers to God's people in Luke 1:69; 2:4.

In relation to the temple, the expression "house of God" occurs in Mark 2:26; Luke 6:4; John 2:17; Acts 7:47; Heb 3:2, 5. See also Matt 21:13; Mark 11:17; Luke 19:46, where Jesus refers to God's designation of the temple as "My house . . ."

oikos also refers to family or household (Luke 12:52; Acts 7:10; 10:22; 1 Cor 1:16; 1 Tim 3:4, 12; 2 Tim 1:16). In Luke 13:35, the term "house" refers to the city of Jerusalem. And the phrase "house of God" in Heb 10:21; 1 Pet 2:5; 4:17 refers to the people of God.

- ▸ **25.** Family, Marriage, Adoption, Inheritance > FAMILY, HOUSEHOLD, LINEAGE

oikia οἰκία 3614

oikia is a synonym for ***oikos*** (above) occurring with nearly the same frequency (found in about ninety places). It is likewise translated "house," "household" in a variety of contexts.

In reference to "house" as a literal dwelling ***oikia*** is found, for example, in Matt 2:11; 7:24ff.; Mark 1:29; Luke 17:31; Acts 12:12. It designates a "household" in Mark 3:25; Luke 18:29; John 4:53; 1 Cor 16:15; Phil 4:22; 2 Tim 3:6. Jesus refers to the heavenly dwelling as "my Father's house" in John 14:2.

PALACE, PRAETORIUM

aulē αὐλή 833

aulē refers to the uncovered courtyard surrounding a dwelling. By extension, it indicates the courtyards and buildings associated with the temple complex in Jerusalem. The term occurs twelve times.

Specifically, ***aulē*** indicates the dwelling of the high priest, referred to as a "palace" in Matt 26:3, 58, 69 (implied); Mark 14:54, 66; John 18:5. It also refers in Mark 15:16 to the palace built by Herod the Great (located southwest of the temple area), which is also known as the "Praetorium" (see ***praitōrion,*** below).

- ▸ **33.** Architecture > COURT

praitōrion πραιτώριον 4232

praitōrion is the term given to the Herodian palace near the Jerusalem temple that was used in the first century A.D. as the palatial residence of successive Roman governors in Judea, including Pontius Pilate during the time of Christ. It served not only as a residence but also as a judicial court, and was the setting for the Roman trial of Jesus. ***praitōrion*** occurs eight times. It is sometimes transliterated as "Praetorium" or "Pretorium" and sometimes rendered "palace" or "hall of judgment" (Matt 27:27; Mark 15:16; John 18:28ff.; 19:9; Acts 23:35; Phil 1:13).

- ▸ **32.** Law, Justice, Jurisprudence, Judgment > JUDGMENT

PAVEMENT

lithostrōtos λιθόστρωτος 3038

lithostrōtos is found only in John 19:13 as a title for a place of judgment (or judicial court) at or near the Praetorium in Jerusalem. The term is usually translated as "the stone pavement," or simply "the pavement."

PILLAR

stylos στῦλος 4769

stylos is a term found in only four places, referring metaphorically in each case to a "pillar." Gal 2:9 refers to Peter, James, and John as reputed "pillars" of the church. 1 Tim 3:15 describes the church of God as the "pillar" of the truth. Rev 3:12 declares that the faithful believer will be constituted by the living Christ as a "pillar" in God's temple. In Rev 10:1, the legs of a powerful angel are likened to "pillars" of fire.

PINNACLE

pterygion πτερύγιον 4419

pterygion is a term found only in Matt 4:5; Luke 4:9. In each place it refers to the "pinnacle" of the Jerusalem temple, meaning the top of the building. It is here that Satan took Jesus during his period of trial and temptation prior to the commencement of his public ministry.

PITCH

pēgnymi πήγνυμι 4078

pēgnymi is a verb found only in Heb 8:2 with reference, metaphorically speaking, to the Lord "setting up" (lit., "pitching") the heavenly tabernacle.

PORCH

stoa στοά 4745

stoa is a noun meaning "porch" in each of the four contexts in which it occurs. It refers to the porches of the pool of Bethesda (John 5:2); and to the porches of Solomon's temple (John 10:23; Acts 3:11; 5:12).

ROOF

stegē στέγη 4721

stegē is found in only three places, referring to the "roof" of a house (Matt 8:8; Mark 2:4; Luke 7:6).

ROOM

anagaion ἀνάγαιον 508

anagaion occurs only twice, referring to the "upper room" where Jesus shared the Passover meal with his disciples (Mark 14:15; Luke 22:12).

hyperōon ὑπερῷον 5253

hyperōon is synonymous with ***anagaion*** (above) and refers to the highest part of a house as an "upper room" (Acts 1:13; 9:37, 39; 20:8).

SEE ALSO

▸ **24.** Dwell, Live, Gather, Hospitality > ROOM
chōreō, topos

TABERNACLE, BOOTH, DWELLING

skēnē σκηνή 4633

skēnē is found approximately twenty times with the meaning "tent" or "tabernacle," in both literal and figurative contexts.

Literal references to the "tabernacle" of the old covenant era are found in Acts 7:44; 15:16; Heb 8:5; 13:10. Linked to these references in a theological sense are those which refer to the heavenly "tabernacle" as the true spiritual reality to which the earthly structure pointed (Acts 8:2; Heb 9:2ff.; Rev 13:6; 15:5).

skēnē is also translated "booth" or "shelter" in Matt 17:4; Mark 9:5; Luke 9:33, where Peter proposes (quite irrationally) to have three "shelters" erected to "house" Jesus, Moses, and Elijah, and thus prolong indefinitely their visionary appearance to the disciples on the "Mount of Transfiguration."

Luke 16:9 refers to the eternal "dwelling place" of believers. In Heb 11:9, ***skēnē*** denotes the ordinary sense of "house."

skēnos σκῆνος 4636

skēnos is a rare variant of ***skēnē*** (above) that is found only twice. In 2 Cor 5:1, 4 it refers metaphorically to the human body as a "tabernacle," a temporary dwelling place and a prelude to the eternal house prepared for the believer in glory.

skēnōma σκήνωμα 4638

skēnōma is another less common variant of ***skēnē*** (above). It refers to the "dwelling" of God in Acts 7:46, citing the old covenant tabernacle. In 2 Pet 1:13, 14, the term refers metaphorically to the body as a "tabernacle," a temporary dwelling for the spirit of the believer, to be released at death to be with Christ.

SEE ALSO

▸ **40.** Holy Days, Feasts, Festivals > TABERNACLES
skēnopēgia

TEMPLE, SANCTUARY, SHRINE

hieron ἱερόν 2411

hieron is a noun meaning "temple" throughout its approximately seventy occurrences. It usually refers to the temple at Jerusalem (Matt 4:5; 21:12ff.; Mark 11:11ff.; Luke 2:27; 19:45ff.; John 2:14, 15; 8:20; Acts 2:46; 5:20ff.; 21:26ff.; 1 Cor 9:13). It also refers to the temple of Artemis in Ephesus (Acts 19:27).

naos ναός 3485

naos is a synonym for ***hieron*** (above) meaning "temple" throughout its forty-five occurrences. ***naos*** refers primarily to the inner sanctuary (i.e., the holy place) of the temple complex. It also denotes the structure as a whole.

References to the inner sanctuary of the Jerusalem temple include those in Matt 23:16ff.; Mark 14:58; Luke 1:9, 21; John 2:19ff.; 2 Thess 2:4; Rev 3:12; 11:1, 2. In particular, Matt 27:51; Mark 15:38; Luke 23:45 refer to tearing the veil separating the "holy of holies" from the rest of the temple at the time of Christ's crucifixion. ***naos*** refers to the temple as a whole (Matt 26:61; 27:5), and also to the pagan "shrine" for the Greek goddess Diana (Acts 19:24). See also Acts 17:24.

naos is also used metaphorically in John 2:21 to refer to the "temple" of Jesus' body. Believers are declared to be "temples" of God's Spirit in 1 Cor 3:16ff.; 6:19; 2 Cor 6:16; Eph 2:21. The book of Revelation contains a number of references to the heavenly "temple," which constitutes the consummate reality of the true "inner sanctuary" (Rev 7:15; 11:19; 14:15ff.; 15:5ff.; 16:1, 17; 21:22).

eidōleion εἰδωλεῖον 1493

eidōleion is found only in 1 Cor 8:10, indicating an idol's "temple," or a temple consecrated for idolatrous worship.

TOWER

pyrgos πύργος 4444

pyrgos is a term indicating a "tower" in only four places (Matt 21:33; Mark 12:1; Luke 13:4; 14:28).

WALL

teichos τεῖχος 5038

teichos is a noun found in nine contexts, denoting a "city wall" throughout. References to a literal structure include those in Acts 9:25; 2 Cor 11:33; Heb 11:30. In Rev 21:12ff., ***teichos*** is used figuratively to refer to "the wall" surrounding the heavenly city of Jerusalem.

mesotoichon μεσότοιχον 3320

mesotoichon is a rare noun found only in Eph 2:14, referring to the "dividing wall" of hostility that has hitherto kept Jew and Gentile from worshiping God together. Now, through the person and work of Christ, that "wall" has been broken down.

WINDOW

thyris θυρίς 2376

thyris is a rare noun denoting the "windows" of a house in Acts 20:9; 2 Cor 11:33.

34. Craftsmanship, Artisanship, Furniture, Implements

ARK

kibōtos κιβωτός 2787

kibōtos is a noun found in six places, with reference to both Noah's "ark" at the time of the great flood (Matt 24:38; Luke 17:27; Heb 11:7; 1 Pet 3:20); and also the ark of the covenant in Heb 9:4; Rev 11:19.

BED

klinē κλίνη 2825

klinē occurs ten times, with the literal sense of "bed" (Matt 9:2ff.; Mark 4:21; 7:30; Luke 5:18; 8:16; 17:34; Acts 5:15; Rev 2:22).

koitē κοίτη 2845

The noun ***koitē*** means "bed" in two places. It is literal in Luke 11:7; and Heb 13:4 contains the injunction "to keep the marriage bed undefiled." Here the exhortation relates to maintaining sexual fidelity in marriage.

BOX

alabastron ἀλάβαστρον 211

alabastron is a noun found in four places meaning a "box" or "flask" made of alabaster designed to carry perfume (Matt 26:7; Mark 14:3; Luke 7:37).

CRAFTSMAN

technitēs τεχνίτης 5079

technitēs is a noun denoting a "craftsman" in Acts 19:24, 38; Heb 11:10; Rev 18:22.

▸ **33.** Architecture > BUILD, BUILDER, BUILDING

SEE ALSO

▸ **30.** Money, Business, Wealth, Poverty > CRAFT, TRADE, BUSINESS
ergasia, homotechnos, meros

ENGRAVE

entypoō ἐντυπόω 1795

entypoō is a rare verb found only in 2 Cor 3:7 and meaning "engrave," referring to the old covenant law that had been "engraved" in letters on stone tablets. Paul refers to this as a ministry of death.

EYE

trymalia τρυμαλιά 5168

trymalia is a rare noun denoting the "eye" of a needle in Mark 10:25; Luke 18:25.

trypēma τρύπημα 5169

trypēma is a rare variant of ***trymalia*** (above) denoting the "eye" of a needle in Matt 19:24.

SEE ALSO

▸ **16.** Body, Bodily Functions > EYE
ophthalmos, omma

▸ **17.** Senses, Actions, Abilities, Disabilities > ONE-EYED
monophthalmos

FOOTSTOOL

hypopodion ὑποπόδιον 5286

hypopodion is a noun found nine times, meaning "footstool" throughout. Matt 5:35; Acts 7:49 refer to the earth as God's "footstool" (i.e., symbolizing his sovereignty over all nations). Specific references to the vanquished enemies of God as his footstool are found in Matt 22:44; Mark 12:36; Luke 20:43; Acts 2:35; Heb 1:13; 10:13. Most of these references are citations of OT texts. See also Jas 2:3.

SEE ALSO

▸ **16.** Body, Bodily Functions > FOOT
pous

▸ **20.** Illness, Disease, Health, Healing > FOOT
basis

▸ **86.** Movement Toward or Away From > WALK ON FOOT
pezeuō

FORM, MOLD

morphoō μορφόω 3445

morphoō is a rare verb found only in Gal 4:19, used passively with reference to Christ "being formed" in his congregation as followers come to a Christlike spiritual maturity.

plassō πλάσσω 4111

plassō is another rare verb found only twice, meaning "to form," with the underlying senses of "mold" or "shape." Rom 9:20 refers to the literal action of the potter "molding" his artistic creation. 1 Tim 2:13 declares that Adam "was formed" (i.e., fashioned, created) by God prior to Eve.

plasma πλάσμα 4110

plasma is a rare derivative noun from ***plassō*** (above) found only in Rom 9:20, with the generalized sense of "that which is formed" by its maker, denoting (from the context) an earthen pot fashioned by the potter.

SEE ALSO

▸ **81.** Forms, Groups, Patterns, Order > FORM, SHAPE
morphē, morphōsis, eidos

▸ **81.** Forms, Groups, Patterns, Order > THING, MATTER
pragma

GLASS

hyalos ὕαλος 5194

hyalos is a rare noun found only twice. In Rev 21:18, 21 it denotes "glass" in a simile referring to the heavenly Jerusalem as a city "clear as glass."

hyalinos ὑάλινος 5193

hyalinos is a rare adjectival form derived from ***hyalos*** (above) found only in Rev 4:6; 15:2 and referring to a visionary sea "of glass."

INSTRUMENT

hoplon ὅπλον 3696

hoplon refers to a tool, implement, or instrument in both literal and metaphorical contexts. The term is found six times.

Indicating weaponry, ***hoplon*** is found in John 18:3 with reference to the armed mob coming to arrest Jesus. In 2 Cor 10:4 it refers to spiritual weapons, and in 2 Cor 6:7 it speaks of the weapons of righteousness. Rom 13:12 mentions believers putting on the "armor of light." Rom 6:13 urges believers to yield members of their bodies to God as instruments of righteousness, not wickedness.

▸ **31.** Kingdom, Empire, Rule, Military, Warfare > ARMS, WEAPONS, ARMOR, ARM

IVORY

elephantinos ἐλεφάντινος 1661

elephantinos occurs only in Rev 18:16, with reference to articles of ivory.

KEY

kleis κλείς 2807

kleis occurs six times and refers to "key" only in a metaphorical sense, but with powerful symbolism in each context. In Matt 16:19, Jesus promises to give Peter the "keys" of the kingdom as a sign of his apostolic authority. In Luke 11:52, the ***kleis*** refers to the "key" of knowledge which the Israelite lawyers had removed and deprived many people of the opportunity to enter into the kingdom of heaven. The supreme spiritual authority of Jesus the Messiah-King is indicated by the risen Christ holding the "keys" to death and Hades (Rev 1:18), and the "key of David" (Rev 3:7). In Rev 9:1; 20:1, ***kleis*** refers to the "key" of the bottomless pit as one of the symbols for the place of eternal punishment.

LAMPSTAND

lychnia λυχνία 3087

lychnia occurs in twelve contexts, referring mostly to the "lampstand" of the temple, in its earthly as well as its heavenly location. In addition, ***lychnia*** refers to a "lampstand" or "candlestick" in a mundane sense (Matt 5:15; Mark 4:21; Luke 8:16; 11:33).

Regarding the use of ***lychnia*** with reference to the lampstands in the temple, Heb 9:2 lists it among a general description of the Solomonic temple furniture. The remaining references to ***lychnia*** are found in the book of Revelation. In Rev 1:12, 13, 20, the apostle John records his vision of the risen Christ standing among seven golden lampstands. The heavenly throne room of the celestial temple is in view here, of which the earthly sanctuary is but a pale shadow (Heb 9:1, 2). Rev 2:1 makes further allusion to this phenomenon. Rev 2:5 indicates that the church at Ephesus, in view of its failings, is in danger of having its lampstand removed from the heavenly sanctuary. This reference links the function of the lampstands to the spiritual vitality of the seven churches to whom John is writing.

LIFELESS

apsychos ἄψυχος 895

apsychos is an adjectival form meaning "lifeless." It occurs only in 1 Cor 14:7, with reference to "lifeless" instruments such as the flute or harp.

SEE ALSO

▸ **22.** Life, Renewal, Immortality > LIFE, LIVE, LIVING
psychē, zōē, bios, zaō, zōogoneō, syzaō, makrochronios, anazaō

▸ **58.** Vices > LUXURY
tryphaō

▸ **61.** Integrity, Innocence, Piety > LIVE
politeuomai, eirēneuō

MIRROR

esoptron ἔσοπτρον 2072

esoptron refers to a "mirror" in only two contexts. Paul uses the term metaphorically in 1 Cor 13:12, where he likens our earthly spiritual perception to looking in a dull mirror with poor reflections. Jas 1:23 mentions someone looking at his face in a mirror.

NAIL

hēlos ἧλος 2247

hēlos is found in only one verse in the NT, which refers twice to the prints of the iron "nails" used in the crucifixion of Christ, seen in the hands of his resurrection body (John 20:25).

SEE ALSO

▸ **32.** Law, Justice, Jurisprudence, Judgment > NAIL
prosēloō

NEEDLE

rhaphis ῥαφίς 4476

rhaphis is found only three times in the NT, and on each occasion it refers to "needle" in the expression "the eye of a needle." The phrase is found in the context of Jesus' warning to the wealthy, affirming hyperbolically that, such is the attraction of worldly riches, it is "easier for a camel to go through the eye of a needle" than for a rich person to enter heaven (Matt 19:24; Mark 10:25; Luke 18:25).

OVERSHADOW

kataskiazō κατασκιάζω 2683

kataskiazō is a verb found only in Heb 9:5, referring to the wings of the golden cherubim "overshadowing" the ark of the covenant.

SEE ALSO

- **8.** Light, Darkness, Visible, Invisible, Color > SHADOW, SHADE
  skia, aposkiasma

POT

xestēs ξέστης 3582

xestēs is another term referring to a "pot" as a general household utensil, found only in Mark 7:4.

SEE ALSO

- **41.** Sacrifice, Offering, Worship, Praise > POT, URN
  stamnos

POTTER

kerameus κεραμεύς 2763

kerameus is a term referring to a "potter," found in only three places (Matt 27:7, 10; Rom 9:21).

ROD, STAFF, SCEPTER

rhabdos ῥάβδος 4464

This noun means "scepter," "staff," "rod."

rhabdos refers literally to a "staff" for walking, or support, in Matt 10:10; Mark 6:8; Luke 9:3; Heb 11:21. It also refers to Aaron's "rod," the symbol of his high priestly authority in Heb 9:4.

All other uses of ***rhabdos*** are metaphorical. It is translated "rod" and used as a symbol of chastisement in 1 Cor 4:21. The meaning "scepter" is symbolic of the rule of the Messiah (Rev 2:27; 12:5; 19:15); and of God's kingdom (Heb 1:8).

SEAT, CHAIR

kathedra καθέδρα 2515

kathedra is a rare noun found only three times and meaning "seat" or "chair." It refers literally in Matt 21:12; Mark 11:15 to the seats of the money changers in the temple. A metaphorical usage is found in Matt 23:2, referring to "the seat" of Moses, which signified his position of leadership in Israel. This "seat" is now occupied by the Pharisees, the religious leaders of Israel at the time of Jesus Christ.

prōtokathedria πρωτοκαθεδρία 4410

prōtokathedria is a noun occurring four times, referring to the "best seats" (i.e., seats of chief honor) in the synagogues, that were the prime choice of the Pharisees and other religious leaders of the day (Matt 23:6; Mark 12:39; Luke 11:43; 20:46).

SEE ALSO

- **32.** Law, Justice, Jurisprudence, Judgment > SEAT
  bēma

SILVERSMITH

argyrokopos ἀργυροκόπος 695

argyrokopos is found only in Acts 19:24, where it refers to a "silversmith."

SEE ALSO

- **10.** Earth, Dust, Rocks, Minerals, Metals, Stones > SILVER
  argyros, argyrion, argyrous

TABLE

trapeza τράπεζα 5132

trapeza occurs thirteen times and refers to "tables" in a variety of contexts.

References to "tables" in the context of eating are found in Matt 15:27; Luke 16:21; 22:21; Acts 6:2; Rom 11:9. The tables of the money changers in the temple are noted in Matt 21:12; Mark 11:15; John 2:15. Heb 9:2 refers to the "table of the presence" in the tabernacle.

In metaphorical contexts, ***trapeza*** refers to God setting up a table in his heavenly kingdom, symbolizing his intention to establish an intimate fellowship with his people there (Luke 22:30). 1 Cor 10:21 refers to the "table of the Lord," indicating the location for the Lord's Supper.

THRONE

thronos θρόνος 2362

thronos is translated "throne" throughout its nearly sixty occurrences, most of which are located in the book of Revelation.

General references to human beings on "thrones" are found in Luke 1:52; Col 1:16. There are also thrones reserved for the saints in glory, as indicated in Luke 22:30; Rev 11:16; 20:4.

There are several references to the satanic "throne" — in a general context (Rev 2:13); to the "throne of the dragon" (Rev 13:2); and to the "throne of the beast" (Rev 16:10).

In metaphorical contexts, ***thronos*** denotes the "throne of David," designated as the throne of the Messiah in Luke 1:32; Acts 2:30.

Most commonly, ***thronos*** refers to the heavenly "throne of God" (Matt 5:34; Acts 7:49; Heb 4:16; Rev 1:4; 4:2ff.; 5:1ff.; 7:9ff.; 8:3; 12:5; 14:3ff.; 19:4ff.; 22:1ff.). Rev 20:11 depicts the "great white throne" judgment of God against the wicked.

thronos also denotes the throne of the Son of Man, referring to the royal standing of the risen Christ in heaven (Matt 19:28; 25:31; Heb 1:8; 8:1; Rev 3:21; 5:6).

bēma βῆμα 968

bēma is a noun occurring thirteen times meaning "throne," "judgment seat."

The "throne" of Herod is noted in Acts 12:21. More commonly, ***bēma*** means "judgment seat" or "tribunal" in connection with the high office of leading Roman officials (Matt 27:19; John 19:13; Acts 18:12ff.; 25:6ff.).

bēma also denotes the "throne of Christ" in Rom 14:10; 2 Cor 5:10.

▸ **32.** Law, Justice, Jurisprudence, Judgment > JUDGMENT
▸ **32.** Law, Justice, Jurisprudence, Judgment > SEAT

hilastērion ἱλαστήριον 2435

hilastērion is a rare noun, occurring only twice. In Rom 3:25 the term indicates "atonement" for sin. The other occurrence of ***hilastērion*** is found in Acts 9:5, where it denotes the "atonement cover" of the ark of the covenant, or the earthly, symbolic location of God's throne, pointing to the existence of the divine throne in heaven.

▸ **41.** Sacrifice, Offering, Worship, Praise > PROPITIATION

VESSEL, ARTICLE, UTENSIL, BASKET, FLASK

angeion ἀγγεῖον 30

angeion is a rare noun denoting a "flask" for carrying lamp oil (Matt 25:4), and a "basket" for sorting fish (Matt 13:48).

skeuos σκεῦος 4632

skeuos is a noun found in approximately twenty places primarily meaning "goods," "household utensils." The former sense is found in Matt 12:29; Luke 17:31; 2 Tim 2:20. See also Rev 18:12. Household utensils are indicated in Luke 8:16; John 19:29; Rev 2:27. Heb 9:21 refers to the "articles" or "utensils" of the Jerusalem temple under the old covenant.

skeuos is also used figuratively in a number of places. Persons chosen by God for a particular task are designated as "vessels" or "instruments" (Acts 9:15; 2 Tim 2:21), as are those ordained for a particular destiny (Rom 9:21ff.). The expression "vessels made of clay" in 2 Cor 4:7 symbolizes the fragility and purely temporal condition of the human body. The term "vessel" is also a symbol for one's wife in 1 Thess 4:4; 1 Pet 3:7.

▸ **30.** Money, Business, Wealth, Poverty > GOODS, PROPERTY, POSSESSIONS

chalkion χαλκίον 5473

chalkion is a rare noun found only in Mark 7:4 with reference to a "brass pot, or container," a household utensil.

▸ **10.** Earth, Dust, Rocks, Minerals, Metals, Stones > BRONZE, BRASS

35. Clothing, Adornment, Textiles

BAG, PURSE

glōssokomon γλωσσόκομον 1101

glōssokomon is a rare noun denoting "bags" or "purses" used for carrying money. It is found only in John 12:6; 13:29.

ballantion βαλλάντιον 905

ballantion is a noun found only in Luke 12:33 with reference to a "money bag."

pēra πήρα 4082

The noun ***pēra*** is found in six places, all denoting a "traveling bag" for taking one's personal possessions on a journey (Matt 10:10; Mark 6:8; Luke 9:3; 10:4; 22:35, 36).

BASKET

kophinos κόφινος 2894

kophinos is a noun found in six contexts, all referring to the large "baskets" used to collect the scraps of food left over after the miraculous feeding of thousands of people performed by Christ as a demonstration of his divine power (Matt 14:20; 16:9; Mark 6:43; 8:19; 9:17; John 6:13).

spyris σπυρίς 4711

spyris is a synonym for ***kophinos*** (above) also denoting a "basket," most likely made of reeds, and plaited. ***spyris*** is found five times and usually refers to the baskets used to collect food scraps after Christ's feeding miracle, as recorded in Matt 15:37; 16:10; Mark 8:8, 20. In Acts 9:25, ***spyris*** refers to the "basket" used to lower the apostle Paul down the wall of the city of Damascus, allowing him to escape the clutches of a hostile crowd.

sarganē σαργάνη 4553

sarganē is a rare synonym for ***spyris*** (above) found only in 2 Cor 11:33, referring to the "basket" Paul used to escape from his enemies in Damascus.

BELT, SASH, GIRDLE

zōnē ζώνη 2223

zōnē denotes a "belt" in most of the eight occurrences of the term. Most of these refer to the literal item of clothing (Matt 3:4; 10:9; Mark 1:6; 6:8; Acts 21:11). In Rev 1:13; 15:6 ***zōnē*** denotes the golden "sashes" worn by the heavenly Christ and angelic beings.

BOWL

phialē φιάλη 5357

phialē is a noun fond in twelve places denoting a "(broad, shallow) bowl" — all in the context of John's vision of the heavenly city in the book of Revelation. In this sense, all occurrences are symbolic. Golden "bowls" filled with incense are noted in Rev 5:8. "Bowls" filled with the wrath of God are noted in Rev 15:7; 16:1ff.; 17:1; 21:9.

CLOTH, HANDKERCHIEF

rhakos ῥάκος 4470

rhakos is a rare noun denoting a piece of woven "cloth" in Matt 9:16; Mark 2:21.

soudarion σουδάριον 4676

A rare term found only four times, ***soudarion*** indicates a "cloth" or "handkerchief" used for personal hygiene and as a cloth wrapping. In Luke 19:20, the term refers to a wrapping for a sum of money hidden away. Acts 19:12 refers to "handkerchiefs" used in connection with Paul's healing miracles. John 11:44 refers to the cloth binding around the face of Lazarus at the time of his burial (see also John 20:7 concerning Jesus' body in the tomb).

CLOTHING, GARMENT

himation ἱμάτιον 2440

himation is a noun found about sixty times, with the predominant senses of "garment," "clothing" plus associated senses.

General references to "garment(s)," "piece(s) of clothing," "clothes" are found in Matt 9:16ff.; 27:35; Mark 2:21; Luke 5:36; 8:27; 19:35ff.; John 13:4, 12; 19:23, 24; Acts 22:20ff.; Heb 1:11; Jas 5:2; 1 Pet 3:3; Rev 3:4ff.

The high priest's "clothes" are described in Matt 26:65. In Mark 9:3 the "clothes" of Christ shine brilliantly white at his transfiguration. In Rev 19:13, 16, ***himation*** denotes the "garment" or "robe" dipped in blood and worn by the heavenly Christ.

endyma ἔνδυμα 1742

endyma is a noun found in eight places meaning "garment," "clothing" throughout. References to a "garment" (i.e., an article of clothing) include Matt 3:4; 22:11, 12. "Clothing" in a general sense is indicated in Matt 6:25ff.; 7:15; Luke 12:23. Matt 28:3 describes angelic "clothing," brilliant and gleaming.

esthēs ἐσθής 2066

esthēs is a noun found in seven contexts with the meanings "robe," "clothing" throughout. The latter sense occurs in Acts 1:10; 10:30; Jas 2:2, 3.

stolē στολή 4749

stolē is found eight times with reference to "robes" or "clothing" (see Mark 12:38; 16:5; Luke 15:22; 20:46). In particular, it denotes the heavenly white "robes" of the saints in glory (Rev 6:11; 7:9, 13, 14).

CORD, ROPE

schoinion σχοινίον 4979

schoinion is a rare noun denoting "cords," "ropes," found only in John 2:15; Acts 27:32.

CORNER

archē ἀρχή 746

archē is a noun with the primary meaning "beginning." In two places, however, the term denotes the "corners" of a sheet that the apostle Peter saw in a vision (Acts 10:11; 11:5).

▸ **4.** Beginning, Continuing, Finishing, Postponing > BEGIN, BEGINNING

SEE ALSO

▸ **6.** Location, Position, Direction, Extension > CORNER, CORNERSTONE
gōnia

COVER, VEIL, CURTAIN, MANTLE

katakalyptō κατακαλύπτω 2619

The verb ***katakalyptō*** means "to cover (one's head) with a veil," and it is found only in 1 Cor 11:6, 7.

peribolaion περιβόλαιον 4018

peribolaion is a noun describing a woman's hair as the "covering" for her head. The term also denotes a "mantle" in 1 Cor 11:15.

kalymma κάλυμμα 2571

kalymma denotes a "veil" for covering the face. It is found in four contexts, referring literally in 2 Cor 3:13 to the veil used by Moses to cover himself after his meeting with God on Mount Sinai.

kalymma is also used figuratively in that same passage, referring to the "veil" of spiritual blindness that covers the hearts and minds of unbelieving Jews who refuse to believe in the person of Christ. Only when saving faith in the Son of God is granted to them is that "veil" removed (2 Cor 3:14ff.).

katapetasma καταπέτασμα 2665

katapetasma denotes the two "curtains," or "veils," that separate the holy place from the outer court of the temple, and the holy of holies from the holy place. This term is found in six contexts, each of them highly significant.

Matt 27:51; Mark 15:38; Luke 23:45 constitute the three Synoptic Gospel references to the tearing of the veil that separated the most holy place from the remainder of the sanctuary. The occasion of this shearing of the "veil, or curtain" was the death of Christ — a sacrifice that signaled the effective end of the old covenant legislation. The ritual requirements maintained the strict sanctity of the holy of holies, allowing only the high priest to draw back that veil just once a year in order to offer sacrifice for the people of Israel before the ark of the covenant. This inner sanctuary constituted the symbolic (though very real) dwelling place of God on earth. When this curtain was torn in two at the crucifixion of Christ, it signaled the end of restricted access to God. Now all who trust in the redemptive work of the Savior can gain unrestricted access to the very throne room of God in heaven.

Heb 6:19; 9:3; 10:20 refer to this temple "veil" in contexts that explain the full significance of Christ's sacrificial death and ongoing, eternal high priestly ministry in heaven on behalf of his peoples. In Heb 9:3 it is clear (by implication) that ***katapetasma*** also refers to the outer curtain separating the priestly holy place from the general areas of temple worship.

CROWN

stephanos στέφανος 4735

The noun ***stephanos*** denotes a "crown" in all eighteen occurrences, in a number of contexts that are primarily metaphorical.

References to a "crown" of thorns, placed on the head of Christ prior to his crucifixion, are found in Matt 27:29; Mark 15:17; John 19:2, 5.

The metaphorical sense of "wreath," "crown" refers symbolically to the believer's eternal reward in glory (1 Cor 9:25; Phil 4:1; 1 Thess 2:19; Jas 1:12; 1 Pet 5:4; Rev 2:10; 3:11; 4:4). See also Rev 9:7. In particular, 2 Tim 4:8 refers to the "crown of righteousness."

The crown is the symbol of the supreme authority of the messianic king, leading the army of heaven against the armies of Satan (Rev 6:2; and also Rev 14:14). See also Rev 12:1.

stephanoō στεφανόω 4737

stephanoō is a verb found four times with the meaning "to crown." An athlete is crowned with a wreath in 2 Tim 2:5. Heb 2:7, 9 speak of Christ "crowned" with glory by God.

diadēma διάδημα 1238

diadēma is a noun found in three places meaning "crown." Rev 12:3; 13:1 speak of the crowns worn by the two satanic beasts in John's visions. By contrast, Rev 19:12 refers to the many "crowns" worn by the messianic King of kings.

FRINGE, HEM, BORDER

kraspedon κράσπεδον 2899

kraspedon is a noun denoting the "border" of a garment — the "fringe" or "hem" (Matt 9:20; 14:36; 23:5; Mark 6:56; Luke 8:44).

LINEN, FLAX

sindōn σινδών 4616

sindōn occurs six times and indicates a "linen cloth" used both as a garment (Mark 14:51, 52); and as a shroud for wrapping the body of Jesus (Matt 27:59; Mark 15:46; Luke 23:53).

byssos βύσσος 1040

byssos is derived from the Hebrew word *bûṣ* and refers to linen produced from a species of Egyptian flax. The term only occurs in Luke 16:19; Rev 18:12.

linon λίνον 3043

linon occurs only twice, indicating "flax" in Matt 12:20 and "linen" in Rev 15:6, with reference to the clothing of angels.

byssinos βύσσινος 1039

byssinos is the adjectival form of ***byssos*** (above) but is translated nominally in all three contexts in which it is found. "Fine linen" in Rev 18:16 refers to the garb of the city of Babylon. In Rev 19:6, the "bride of the Lamb" is depicted as one "dressed in fine linen," metaphorical clothing that represents her imputed righteousness — for the immediate context says that such clothing was "given her to wear." Rev 19:14 describes the armies of heaven as clothed in "fine linen."

SEE ALSO

- **21.** Die, Perish, Kill, Destroy > LINEN
  othonion

NAKED, NAKEDNESS, BARE

gymnos γυμνός 1131

gymnos is an adjectival form occurring fifteen times with the predominant sense of "naked" or "bare."

In the context of those who are vulnerable and destitute, such people are said to be "naked" and in dire need of aid (Matt 25:36; Jas 2:15; Rev 3:17). In the sense of shameful exposure, ***gymnos*** indicates nakedness (Rev 16:15) and refers metaphorically of the city of Babylon (Rev 17:16) in the context of God's judgment against that people. Literal references to nakedness in non-judgmental, or neutral, contexts are found in Mark 14:51, 52; John 21:7; Acts 19:6 (although this latter reference speaks of men who had their clothes torn off after being assaulted by a demon-possessed man, resulting in their running away naked and bleeding).

In metaphorical contexts, ***gymnos*** is used first of all in 1 Cor 15:37 to refer literally to a "bare seed" from which substantial growth will come. The context here deals with the subject of the heavenly bodies of believers, which they will inherit at the resurrection. 2 Cor 5:3 contains an implied reference to our disembodied souls after death as being "naked," prior to our being "clothed" with our "heavenly bodies." In Heb 4:13, the writer declares that all people are "laid bare" to God's inscrutable gaze — that is, nothing can be hidden from him.

gymnotēs γυμνότης 1132

gymnotēs is a noun occurring only three times, meaning "nakedness." It is used in Rom 8:35; 2 Cor 11:25 to refer to a state of exposure (i.e., being without clothes), among other trials and tribulations. In Rev 3:18, "nakedness" is indicated as a shameful condition.

NEW, UNSHRUNK

agnaphos ἄγναφος 46

agnaphos is an adjective found only twice, meaning "new" in both contexts. Matt 9:16; Mark 2:21 refer to "new" cloth in the sense of material that is unprocessed or "unshrunk."

SEE ALSO

- **5.** Old, New, First, Last > NEW, NEWNESS
  kainos, kainotēs, neos, prosphatos
- **40.** Holy Days, Feasts, Festivals > NEW MOON
  neomēnia

PIECE, PATCH

epiblēma ἐπίβλημα 1915

epiblēma refers to a "piece" of cloth used as a patch sewn on to cover a tear. The term is found four times (Matt 9:16; Mark 2:21; Luke 5:36).

PILLOW

proskephalaion προσκεφάλαιον 4344

proskephalaion is only found in Mark 4:38, referring to a "pillow" used by Jesus in the fishing boat belonging to his disciples.

RING

daktylios δακτύλιος 1146

daktylios is a rare noun, found only in Luke 15:22 with reference to an ornament for the hand.

chrysodaktylios χρυσοδακτύλιος 5554

chrysodaktylios is a variant form of ***daktylios*** (above) occurring only in Jas 2:2 and indicating "rings" as part of the personal jewelry of the rich.

ROBE

chlamys χλαμύς 5511

chlamys is found only twice, referring to the scarlet "robe" draped around Christ by the Roman soldiers prior to his crucifixion, in mockery of his claim to be King of the Jews (Matt 27:28, 31).

SANDAL

sandalion σανδάλιον 4547

sandalion occurs only in Matt 6:9; Acts 12:8, referring to "sandals."

TAKE OFF, STRIP

ekdyō ἐκδύω 1562

ekdyō is a verb referring to the "taking off," or "stripping," of clothes. It occurs in five places, most of which refer to divesting Christ's garments prior to his crucifixion (Matt 27:28, 31; Mark 15:20; Luke 10:30). In 2 Cor 5:4 ***ekdyō*** is used adjectivally, referring to the supposed intermediate state of the believer between death and resurrection to life, describing the person as "unclothed."

SEE ALSO

- ▸ **70.** Give, Take, Seize, Touch > TAKE, TAKE HOLD OF, TAKE UP, TAKE DOWN, TAKE AWAY, SNATCH ***lambanō, paralambanō, analambanō, epilambanō, proslambanō, harpazō, apairō, kathaireō***
- ▸ **79.** Throw, Send, Drive, Mix, Remove > TAKE AWAY, REMOVE ***aphaireō, periaireō, parapherō***
- ▸ **85.** Movement, Position, State > TAKE WITH ***symparalambanō***

TEAR

schizō σχίζω 4977

schizō is a verb found ten times with the predominant meaning "tear" (i.e., divide in two).

Reference is made to the veil of the temple being "torn in two" at the moment of Christ's death on the cross, signifying the climactic end of the old covenant, with unhindered access to the holy of holies opened for all (Matt 27:51; Mark 15:38; Luke 23:45).

Other general references to "tearing" cloth include those in Luke 5:36; John 19:24.

- ▸ **27.** Community, Partnership, Unity, Discord > DIVIDE, DIVISIVE, DIVISION
- ▸ **85.** Movement, Position, State > OPEN

WEAR, PUT ON CLOTHES, CLOTHE

amphiennymi ἀμφιέννυμι 294

amphiennymi is a verb found in four places and meaning "clothe" throughout. The term is used metaphorically in Matt 6:30; Luke 12:28, where God is said to "clothe" the grass of the field. In Matt 11:8; Luke 7:25, ***amphiennymi*** is used in the literal sense of a man "clothed" in fine apparel.

endyō ἐνδύω 1746

The verb ***endyō*** occurs about thirty times with the consistent meaning "to put on clothes," "clothe."

General references to "putting on" clothes are found in Matt 6:25; Mark 1:6; 15:17ff.; Luke 12:22; 15:22. The "putting on" of royal apparel is noted in Acts 12:21.

The remaining usage of ***endyō*** is metaphorical. The heavenly Christ is described as being "clothed" in a long white robe in Rev 1:13. The saints are likewise "clothed" in pure white linen in Rev 15:6. Luke 24:49 refers to being "clothed" with power from on high.

In Rom 13:12 the term indicates the symbolic action of "putting on" the (spiritual) armor of light. Similarly, Eph 6:11, 14; 1 Thess 5:8 describe "putting on" the whole armor of God — spiritual weapons against satanic attacks. ***endyō*** also indicates the act of "embracing" the Lord Jesus Christ as Lord of one's life through faith and repentance (Rom 13:14; Gal 3:27). "Putting on" the imperishable nature of immortality, referring to the appearance of the believer in glory, is noted in 1 Cor 15:53ff.; 2 Cor 5:3. Eph 4:24; Col 3:10ff. describe the act of "putting on" the new person (i.e., embarking on a godly lifestyle).

ependyomai ἐπενδύομαι 1902

ependyomai is a verb derived from ***endyō*** (above) and is found only in 2 Cor 5:2, 3, with the passive sense of "be clothed" in the context of the believer's longing to put on heavenly "clothing" after death.

endidyskō ἐνδιδύσκω 1737

endidyskō is a rare synonym for ***endyō*** (above) found only in Luke 8:27; 16:19, with the meaning "wear, put on clothes."

himatizō ἱματίζω 2439

The verb ***himatizō*** is also synonymous with the entries above, meaning "to be clothed" in Mark 5:15; Luke 8:35.

periballō περιβάλλω 4016

periballō is a verb found in approximately thirty contexts with the underlying meaning "to clothe," plus several related nuances.

The general sense of "wear," "put on clothes," "dress oneself" is evident in Matt 6:31; Mark 14:51; 16:5; Acts 12:8. References to "clothing" other people are found in Matt 25:36ff.; Luke 23:11. See also John 19:2.

Metaphorical reference to the "clothing" of the lilies of the field is found in Luke 12:27. The saints are declared "to be clothed" in white garments in heaven in Rev 3:5, 18; 4:4; 7:9ff.; 19:8. The heavenly Christ is described as "being clothed" in a robe dipped in blood.

phoreō φορέω 5409

phoreō is a verb expressing the dual meanings "wear" and "bear."

Matt 11:8; Jas 2:3 refer to "wearing" clothing, and Christ "wears" the crown of thorns in John 19:5.

- ▸ **69.** Have, Possess, Hold, Grasp, Bear, Carry > BEAR, CARRY

perithesis περίθεσις 4025

perithesis is a rare noun referring to "wearing" jewelry (1 Pet 3:3).

WRAP

sparganoō σπαργανόω 4683

sparganoō is a verb found only in Luke 2:7, 12, referring to "wrapping up" the infant Jesus in strips of cloth.

SEE ALSO

- ▸ **21.** Die, Perish, Kill, Destroy > WRAP ***entylissō, systellō, eneileō***

36. Reading, Writing

BACK

opisthen ὄπισθεν 3693

opisthen is an adjectival form translated "behind" or "after" in most of the seven occurrences of the term. However, in Rev 5:1 it denotes the reverse side or "back" of a scroll sealed with seven seals of divine judgment.

SEE ALSO

▸ **16.** Body, Bodily Functions > BACK
nōtos

BOOK, SCROLL

biblos βίβλος 976

biblos is a noun found thirteen times denoting a "book" (or "scroll") in a variety of contexts.

The genealogical records of Christ are indicated in Matt 1:1. Matt 12:26 refers to the covenant law of Moses. The prophet Isaiah is noted in Luke 3:4; and the Psalter in Luke 20:42; Acts 1:20. The prophetic writings in general are indicated in Acts 7:42; and in Rev 22:19 the book of Revelation is explicitly indicated. Acts 19:19 refers to magic books and occult manuscripts.

The "book of life," which contains all the names of God's people destined for glory, is specifically mentioned in Phil 4:3; Rev 3:5; 13:8; 20:15.

biblion βιβλίον 975

biblion is a noun found about thirty times, a diminutive form of ***biblos*** (above) denoting "book" (or "scroll"). It can also refer to a "document" or "bill."

General references to "books" are indicated in John 21:25; Rev 1:11; 6:14. In the context of John's vision in the book of Revelation, ***biblion*** refers to the "scroll" containing the expression of divine judgment and condemnation of sin, a document fastened with seven seals that only Christ, the Lamb of God, is able to open (Rev 5:1ff.). The "book" of Revelation itself is indicated in Rev 22:7ff. Metaphorical reference to the "book of life" (see above) is indicated in Rev 17:8; 21:27. The "book" containing the legal indictment of the wicked, to be used at the last judgment, is noted in Rev 20:12.

Elsewhere, ***biblion*** denotes the "book" of Isaiah the prophet in Luke 4:17ff.; John's Gospel in John 20:30; and the law covenant in Gal 3:10; 2 Tim 4:13; Heb 9:19; 10:7. Then, Matt 19:7; Mark 10:4 both refer to a "bill of divorce" that constituted a legal document in biblical times.

biblaridion βιβλαρίδιον 974

This noun is a diminutive of ***biblion*** (above) meaning "little book" or "scroll." ***biblaridion*** occurs four times and is found exclusively in Revelation, where the angel hands over a "little book" to the apostle which he is commanded to eat. This book symbolizes and contains the judgment of God against the godless nations of the world (Rev 10:2ff.).

ENGRAVE

engraphō ἐγγράφω 1449

engraphō is a verb found only in 2 Cor 3:2, 3, referring to the faithful, true hearts of believers "engraved" with the Spirit of God.

INK

melas μέλας 3188

melas occurs three times, all with reference to writing in ink (2 Cor 3:3; 2 John 12; 3 John 13).

▸ **8.** Light, Darkness, Visible, Invisible, Color > BLACK

INSCRIPTION, SUPERSCRIPTION

epigraphē ἐπιγραφή 1923

epigraphē is a noun that indicates a "superscription" or "inscription," and occurs five times. Matt 22:20 refers to Caesar's superscription on a coin (also Mark 2:16; Luke 20:24). Mark 15:16; Luke 23:38 refer to the inscription placed over the head of Jesus as he hung on the cross: "This is the King of the Jews."

JOT, LETTER

iōta ἰῶτα 2503

iōta occurs only in Matt 5:18. It refers to the tenth letter of the Hebrew alphabet — the *yod*, which is the smallest Hebrew character. Jesus affirms here that not one "jot" will disappear from the law until all is fulfilled in him.

LETTER, EPISTLE

epistolē ἐπιστολή 1992

epistolē is a noun found approximately twenty times, meaning "letter" or "epistle."

General references to literary correspondence are found in Acts 9:2; 15:30; 22:5; Rom 16:22; 1 Cor 16:3; 2 Cor 3:1. The letters of Paul are indicated in 1 Cor 5:9; 2 Cor 7:8; 10:9ff.; Col 4:16; 1 Thess 5:27; 2 Thess 2:2, 15; 3:14, 17; 2 Pet 3:16; as are the letters of Peter in 2 Pet 3:1.

epistolē is used metaphorically in 2 Cor 3:2 to denote the Corinthian congregation as his "letters of recommendation" bearing testimony to the world of their worthy spiritual qualifications. Similarly, 2 Cor 3:3 refers to the Corinthian believers as a "letter" from Christ "written" by the Spirit of God. This is a metaphorical description of the spiritual transformation of a person from pagan to believer.

PAPER

chartēs χάρτης 5489

chartēs is found only in 2 John 12, referring to the apostle John's disinclination to communicate with his audience fully in writing, in "paper" and ink.

PARCHMENT

membrana μεμβράνα 3200

membrana occurs only in 2 Tim 4:13, referring to Paul's "parchments," his personal collection of "books."

PEN

kalamos κάλαμος 2563

kalamos is a noun occurring twelve times, meaning "reed" or "rod" in all but one of these contexts. In 3 John 13, ***kalamos*** refers to an ordinary writing pen.

▸ **13.** Plants, Trees, Flora > REED

READ, READING

anaginōskō ἀναγινώσκω 314

anaginōskō is the only term in the NT meaning "to read." It is found thirty-three times.

General references to the Scriptures being read are found in Acts 13:27; 15:21; 2 Cor 3:15.

In a number of places, Jesus asks of his audience, "Have you not read . . . ?," inquiring about their knowledge of the (OT) Scriptures (Matt 12:3ff.; 19:4; 21:16, 42; 22:31; Mark 2:25; 12:10, 26; Luke 6:3; 10:26). Jesus also exhorts the reader of the Scriptures to pay close attention to what he is pointing out (Matt 24:15; Mark 13:14). Jesus' own reading of the Isaiah scroll in the synagogue at Nazareth is recorded in Luke 4:16. John 19:20 mentions the Jerusalem inhabitants reading the inscription placed above the head of Christ on the cross: "The King of the Jews." The incident of the Ethiopian royal official reading the book of Isaiah is recorded in Acts 8:28ff.

General references to the early church congregations reading the letters of Paul are found in Acts 23:34; 2 Cor 1:13; Eph 3:4; Col 4:16; 1 Thess 5:27. Acts 15:31 refers to the church at Antioch reading the letter of the Jerusalem Council to Gentile believers. A specific blessing is promised to all who read the words of the book of Revelation (Rev 1:3).

Finally, ***anaginōskō*** refers metaphorically to "reading" the hearts of true believers (2 Cor 3:2).

anagnōsis ἀνάγνωσις 320

anagnōsis is the noun derived from ***anaginōskō*** (above). It occurs in only three places and refers literally to "reading." ***anagnōsis*** refers to reading the Law and the Prophets (Acts 13:15); to reading the old covenant (2 Cor 3:14); and to the public reading of Scripture (1 Tim 4:13).

SCRIBE

grammateus γραμματεύς 1122

grammateus is the primary term for "scribe" in the NT, occurring nearly seventy times. It refers to the teachers, interpreters, and preservers of the Hebrew Scriptures. In the NT, "scribes" are often associated with the priests and/or the Pharisees.

Scribes are specifically referred to in Matt 2:4; 7:29; 8:19; 12:38; Mark 1:22; 12:35; Luke 5:30; John 8:3; Acts 4:5; 6:12; 23:9. In particular, the scribes bear the brunt of Jesus' wrath on account of their hypocrisy (Matt 23:13ff.; Luke 11:44).

General references to scribes are found in Matt 13:52; 1 Cor 1:20.

SCRIPTURE

graphē γραφή 1124

graphē is a noun with the underlying sense of "writing." However, in the fifty or so occurrences of the term, it refers almost exclusively to "Scripture(s)," or the sacred, canonical writings of the old covenant people of Israel. In at least one place, ***graphē*** also refers to the unique canonical authority of the NT "Scriptures."

The Scriptures, or the old covenant canonical writings, are affirmed by Jesus Christ in the course of his teaching ministry (Matt 21:42; 26:54; Mark 12:10; 14:49; Luke 4:21; 24:27; John 5:39; 7:38).

The Hebrew Scriptures are similarly viewed by the Gospel writers (Matt 26:56; Luke 24:45; John 2:22; 20:19). They are also declared to be uniquely authoritative, and are quoted by other apostolic writers (Acts 1:16; 8:35; Rom 1:2; 11:2; 1 Cor 15:3ff.; Gal 3:8, 22; 1 Tim 5:18; 2 Tim 3:16; Jas 2:8; 4:5; 1 Pet 2:6).

General references to the OT Scriptures are found in Acts 17:11; 18:24, 28. 2 Pet 3:16 mentions the NT writings of Paul as "Scripture."

gramma γράμμα 1121

gramma is a noun occurring fourteen times, with the sense of "writing," "letters," "learning," in most of these. In 2 Tim 3:15, ***gramma*** refers to the "sacred writings," or the old covenant Scriptures.

▸ **36.** Reading, Writing > WRITE, WRITING

TABLET

pinakidion πινακίδιον 4093

pinakidion is a rare noun denoting a "writing tablet" in Luke 1:63.

WRITE, WRITING

graphō γράφω 1125

graphō occurs around two hundred times, in a variety of contexts, and is consistently translated "write" throughout this usage.

General references to writing activity include those in Luke 1:63; 16:6; 23:38; John 8:6ff.; 19:19ff.; Acts 15:23. Letter writing is indicated in Rom 16:22; 1 Cor 5:9; 2 Cor 1:13; Gal 1:20; Eph 3:1; 1 Tim 3:14; 2 Pet 3:1. Mark 10:4 records the action of writing a certificate of divorce. Luke 1:3 affirms that Luke the physician wrote his Gospel for Theophilus. There are several references to Moses, who wrote down the old covenant law of God (Mark 12:19; Luke 20:28; John 5:46). See also 1 John 2:7ff.

The expression "it is written" constitutes virtually a technical formula denoting a canonical source from the OT. The expression varies somewhat in places, but the meaning is consistent (Matt 4:4ff.; 26:24, 31; Mark 9:12ff.; Luke 2:23; 4:4ff.; 24:44; John 2:7; 12:14ff.; Acts 1:20; Rom 3:4, 10; 1 Cor 1:19; 15:45, 54; Gal 3:10; Heb 10:7).

A divine command is given "to write" to the seven churches of Asia Minor (Rev 2:1–3:7). See also Rev 21:5; 22:18. A scroll is "inscribed" by God in Rev 5:1. Names of believers "are written" in the Lamb's "book of life," as noted in Rev 13:8; 17:8; 20:15; 21:27. (In this regard, see also Exod 32:32; Ps 69:28; Isa 4:3.) Similarly, the name of God the Father "is written" on the foreheads of his people in Rev 14:1. See also Rev 17:5.

epistellō ἐπιστέλλω 1989

epistellō is a rare verb meaning "to write," in the context of communicating instructions (Acts 15:20; 21:25; Heb 13:22).

epigraphō ἐπιγράφω 1924

epigraphō is a verb found in five places meaning "to write upon," "inscribe" (Mark 15:26; Acts 17:23; Rev 21:12). There is also a metaphorical reference to God "writing" his law on the hearts and minds of believers (Heb 10:16).

prographō προγράφω 4270

prographō is a verb meaning "to write before," in a temporal sense, referring twice to the Hebrew Scriptures in Rom 15:4, and once to prior correspondence in Eph 3:3.

gramma γράμμα 1121

gramma is a noun found in fifteen contexts denoting various kinds of "writing."

gramma refers to a commercial bill or account (Luke 16:6ff.); an inscription (Luke 23:38); letters or other correspondence (Acts 28:21); and handwriting (Gal 6:11). The canonical "writings" of Scripture (i.e., the OT) are indicated in John 5:47; Rom 2:27; 7:6; 2 Cor 3:6; 2 Tim 3:15.

▸ **36.** Reading, Writing > SCRIPTURE

37. Music, Singing, Dancing

CYMBAL

kymbalon κύμβαλον 2950

kymbalon is a rare noun found only in 1 Cor 13:1 denoting a "cymbal" that clanged noisily.

DANCE, DANCING

choros χορός 5525

choros is a rare noun found only in Luke 15:25 denoting "dancing" as part of general festivity.

orcheomai ὀρχέομαι 3738

orcheomai is a verb occurring six times, meaning "to dance" in the context of celebration in Matt 14:6; Mark 6:22; and with reference to an individual girl in Matt 11:17; Luke 7:32.

HARP

kithara κιθάρα 2788

kithara is found four times, indicating the harp as a musical instrument in a general sense (1 Cor 14:7); and as a heavenly instrument used in singing praises to God in glory (Rev 5:8; 14:2; 15:2).

HYMN

hymnos ὕμνος 5215

hymnos only occurs in Eph 5:19; Col 3:16, where it refers to singing hymns in the context of worship.

hymneō ὑμνέω 5214

hymneō refers to the activity of singing hymns — that is, psalm singing, or singing praise to God. It occurs four times. Jesus and his disciples sing in Matt 26:30; Mark 14:26, probably a selection from Pss 113–118. See also Acts 16:25; Heb 2:12.

▸ **37.** Music, Singing, Dancing > SING, SONG
▸ **41.** Sacrifice, Offering, Worship, Praise > PRAISE

MUSIC, MUSICIAN

mousikos μουσικός 3451

mousikos is found only in Rev 18:22 with reference to "musicians."

symphōnia συμφωνία 4858

symphōnia is found only in Luke 15:25 with reference to music in a general sense.

PIPE, FLUTE

aulos αὐλός 836

aulos refers to the "pipe" or "flute." It is found only in 1 Cor 14:7.

auleō αὐλέω 832

auleō is the verb from which ***aulos*** (above) is derived. It occurs only three times and means "to play the pipe, flute" (Matt 11:17; Luke 7:32; 1 Cor 14:7).

aulētēs αὐλητής 834

aulētēs is translated "flute player" and is found only in Matt 9:23; Rev 18:22.

SING, SONG

hymneō ὑμνέω 5214

hymneō is a verb occurring four times, meaning "sing a hymn," "sing praise" to God (Matt 26:30; Mark 14:26; Acts 16:25; Heb 2:12).

▸ **37.** Music, Singing, Dancing > HYMN
▸ **41.** Sacrifice, Offering, Worship, Praise > PRAISE

psallō ψάλλω 5567

psallō is a verb found in five contexts, meaning "sing" in relation to psalm singing or making music in the context of praising God (Rom 15:9; 1 Cor 14:15 [twice]; Jas 5:13; Eph 5:19).

adō ᾄδω 103

adō is a verb meaning "sing" in relation to praising God in Eph 5:19; Col 3:16; Rev 5:9; 14:3; 15:3.

ōdē ᾠδή 5603

ōdē is a noun derived from ***adō*** (above) meaning "song" in the same five contexts (i.e., Eph 5:19; Col 3:16; Rev 5:9; 14:3; 15:3).

TRUMPETER

salpistēs σαλπιστής 4538

salpistēs is a rare noun denoting "trumpeters" in Rev 18:22.

SEE ALSO

▸ **63.** Speak, Tell, Declare, Call > TRUMPET
salpinx, salpizō

38. Covenant, Law, Rites, Roles

ANOINT, ANOINTING, CONSECRATE

chriō χρίω 5548

chriō is a verb found five times with the meaning "anoint," primarily in the sense of "commission" or "consecrate."

Christ is described as having been "anointed" with the Spirit of God as an indispensable prerequisite for his ministry. This phenomenon is depicted as a supernatural investiture (Luke 4:18; Acts 4:27; 10:38). 2 Cor 1:21 specifically notes the action of God in "consecrating" his apostles for ministry. Heb 1:9 affirms that God "has anointed" his Son with "the oil of gladness," equipping him for ministry.

chrisma χρῖσμα 5545

chrisma is a rare noun found only in 1 John 2:20, 27 with reference to the "anointing" of the Holy Spirit for ministry.

enkainizō ἐγκαινίζω 1457

enkainizō is a rare verb meaning "consecrate" in respect of the old covenant law in Heb 9:18. The underlying sense is that of "put into effect."

SEE ALSO

- ▶ **40.** Holy Days, Feasts, Festivals > DEDICATION
  enkainia

APOSTLE, APOSTLESHIP

apostolos ἀπόστολος 652

The noun ***apostolos*** occurs in about eighty contexts with the consistent meaning of "apostle," a divinely appointed messenger or representative.

References to the twelve apostles chosen by Christ can be found in Matt 10:2; Mark 6:30; Luke 17:5; Acts 1:2; 15:2ff.; 1 Cor 15:7ff.; Gal 1:17ff.; Eph 2:20; 1 Pet 1:1; 2 Pet 1:1; Jude 17; Rev 21:14.

Other references to "apostles" as divinely appointed messengers and representatives of Christ are found in Luke 11:49; John 13:16; Acts 11:1; 2 Cor 8:23; Eph 3:5; Phil 2:25; 1 Thess 2:6. The unique apostleship of Paul is indicated in Rom 1:1; 1 Cor 1:1; 2 Cor 1:1; Gal 1:1; Eph 1:1; Col 1:1; 1 Tim 1:1; 2 Tim 1:1; Titus 1:1. The office of "apostle" in the church is noted in 1 Cor 12:28ff.; Eph 4:11; Rev 18:20. Self-styled (i.e., false) apostles are referred to in 2 Cor 11:5, 13; 12:11; Rev 2:2. In Heb 3:1 Jesus is described as the supreme "apostle."

apostolē ἀποστολή 651

apostolē is a noun found in four places, denoting the "office of an apostle" or "apostleship" (Acts 1:25; Rom 1:5; 1 Cor 9:2). See also Gal 2:8.

AUTHOR, CAPTAIN, PRINCE

archēgos ἀρχηγός 747

archēgos is found only four times in the NT. It refers metaphorically to Jesus as the "author" of the Christian's life in Acts 3:15; as the "author" of salvation in Heb 2:10; and as the "author" of the faith of God's people in Heb 12:2. Each context indicates Jesus' role and function as the one who provides the foundation and impetus for each phenomenon. The older translation "captain" in Heb 2:10 is now somewhat archaic. In Acts 5:31, ***archēgos*** refers to Jesus as "Prince," seated next to God's right hand.

SEE ALSO

- ▶ **29.** Boats, Fishing, Maritime Activity > CAPTAIN
  kybernētēs
- ▶ **31.** Kingdom, Empire, Rule, Military, Warfare > CAPTAIN, COMMANDER, OFFICER
  chiliarchos, stratēgos

BAPTISM, BAPTIST, BAPTIZE

baptisma βάπτισμα 908

baptisma is a noun occurring around twenty times, meaning "baptism." It indicates submerging or immersing people in water for ritual purposes.

John's "baptism" of repentance is indicated in Matt 3:7; 21:25; Mark 1:4; 11:30; Luke 3:3; 7:29; 20:4; Acts 1:22; 10:37; 13:24; 18:25; 19:3ff.

References to the "baptism" of Christ are metaphorical when denoting his suffering and death on the cross (Matt 20:22ff.; Mark 10:38ff.; Luke 12:50).

Elsewhere, ***baptisma*** denotes the baptism of believers performed in the name of Christ, depicted metaphorically as a baptism into his death and resurrection (Rom 6:4; Col 2:12).

General references to baptism include Eph 4:5; 1 Pet 3:21.

baptismos βαπτισμός 909

baptismos is a variant form of ***baptisma*** (above) found only four times. It denotes "washing" in the sense of a purification ritual for sacred utensils (Mark 7:4, 8) and also for priestly purification and preparation for service in the temple (Heb 6:2; 9:10).

- ▶ **80.** Related to Liquids > WASH, BATHE, WASHING, WETTING

baptistēs βαπτιστής 910

The noun ***baptistēs*** signifies "baptizer" (i.e., "one who baptizes"). The term is used in the NT exclusively as a surname for John, the forerunner of Christ — John the Baptist (Matt 3:1; 11:11ff.; 14:2ff.; 17:13; Mark 6:24ff.; 8:28; Luke 7:20ff.; 9:19).

baptizō βαπτίζω 907

The verb ***baptizō*** is found about ninety times in the NT, with a very significant theological sense. Its root meanings are "dip," "immerse," "submerge" in water, and it is found in the context of John the Baptist's ministry of "baptizing" for the forgiveness of sin, as well as Christian baptism. The latter usage has to do both with Christ's own personal trauma surrounding his death, as well as with the ritual applied to his followers signifying their spiritual union with him through the symbolism of immersion in water. The ritual of baptism is also associated with the outpouring of the Holy Spirit.

References to "baptizing" for the confession of sin in relation to the ministry of John the Baptist include Matt 3:6ff.; Mark 1:4ff.; Luke 3:7ff.; 7:29ff.; John 1:25ff.; 3:23ff.; 10:40; Acts 19:3ff. Some of these references describe John baptizing Jesus. In reality, Christ needed no baptism to cleanse him from sin, because by nature he was perfect. However, his submission to John's baptism indicates the divine intention for him to be identified with human beings.

baptizō is used passively and metaphorically in relation to Christ "being baptized," or suffering in the course of his crucifixion and death (Matt 20:22ff.; Mark 10:38ff.; Luke 12:50). Jesus' own ministry of baptism is indicated in John 3:22; 4:12, though it is clear that it is the disciples, not Christ, who actually perform the rite. Then there is Christ's promise to "baptize" his followers with the Holy Spirit (Luke 3:16; John 1:33; Acts 1:5; 11:16). The followers of Christ are commanded to baptize disciples in the name of the Father, Son, and Holy Spirit (Matt 28:19). In Acts 2:38, Peter exhorts his large audience "to repent and be baptized." In other very significant contexts, salvation applied through the expression of saving faith is attested by the sign of baptism (Mark 16:16; Acts 2:41; 8:12ff., 36ff.; 9:18; 10:47ff.; 16:15, 33; 18:8; 19:5; 22:16). The apostle Paul's ministry of baptism is noted in 1 Cor 1:13ff.

baptizō also denotes the act of "ritual bathing, or washing," referring to the Pharisaic tradition whereby one could maintain ceremonial purity (Mark 7:4). It also refers to the tradition of "washing" prior to taking a meal (Luke 11:38).

"Being baptized" into Christ, symbolizing the believer's identification with him in his death and resurrection, is indicated in Rom 6:3; Gal 3:27.

The phenomenon of Israel "being baptized" into Moses in the cloud and the sea is noted in 1 Cor 10:2. ***baptizō*** is used metaphorically here to refer to Israel's dependence upon and submission to Moses as their spiritual leader and deliverer. The "cloud" refers to the divine mode of guidance through the wilderness; and the "sea" refers to the miraculous deliverance of Israel from the pursuing Egyptian army at the Re(e)d Sea. In both cases it is Moses who functions as the people's prophet, mediator, and leader, chosen and appointed by God for that purpose. The parallel with Christian baptism is clear. Just as the Israelites identified themselves with God though Moses, so Christian believers identify themselves with God through Christ, in the sacrament of baptism. Baptism is the "mechanism" by which the Holy Spirit constitutes all believers as members of the "one body" of Christ (1 Cor 12:13).

There is also a cryptic reference to the practice of "baptizing" people on behalf of the dead in 1 Cor 15:29. This is not mentioned or explained anywhere else in the NT.

▸ **20.** Illness, Disease, Health, Healing > WASH, WASHING

SEE ALSO

▸ **80.** Related to Liquids > DIP, IMMERSE
baptō, embaptō

BISHOP, OVERSEER

episkopos ἐπίσκοπος 1985

The noun ***episkopos*** is found six times with the consistent meaning "bishop" or "overseer." The term exclusively denotes one who is given the spiritual charge (i.e., oversight) of a local congregation or group of congregations (Acts 20:28; Phil 1:1; 1 Tim 3:2; 2 Tim 4:22; Titus 1:7; 3:15). In 1 Pet 2:25, ***episkopos*** refers to Christ as the supreme "overseer" of our souls.

This term, though distinctive in its usage, is functionally synonymous with the spiritual offices of both "pastor" and "elder."

BLOOD

haimatekchysia αἱματεκχυσία 130

haimatekchysia is a rare noun found only in Heb 9:22, denoting the "shedding of blood" and affirming the necessity of such bloodletting as the divinely ordained means of forgiveness for sin under the terms of the old covenant law.

▸ **21.** Die, Perish, Kill, Destroy > SHED

SEE ALSO

▸ **16.** Body, Bodily Functions > BLOOD
haima

▸ **20.** Illness, Disease, Health, Healing > HEMMORHAGE, FLOW OF BLOOD
haimorroeō

CIRCUMCISE, CIRCUMCISION, UNCIRCUMCISED

peritomē περιτομή 4061

peritomē is a noun denoting "circumcision" throughout the nearly forty occurrences of the term.

Literal references to the old covenant rite of circumcision are found in John 7:22ff.; Rom 2:25ff.; 3:1, 30; 4:9ff.; 1 Cor 7:19; Gal 5:6, 11; 6:15; Col 3:11. The "covenant of circumcision" is indicated in Acts 7:8.

The designation "uncircumcised" is a metaphorical reference to Gentile unbelievers in Gal 2:7. References to "circumcised believers" (i.e., Jewish Christians) are found in Acts 10:45; Col 4:11. The term "circumcised" constitutes a metaphorical reference to the Jewish nation in Gal 2:9. See also Col 4:11.

References to the "circumcision party" — a virtual technical term denoting those strict observers of Mosaic law who prized circumcision as an important element in one's justification before God — are found in Acts 11:2; Gal 2:12; Titus 1:10. Reference to spiritual "circumcision," denoting true heart renewal, is made in Rom 2:29. This condition is clearly distinguished from the mere ritual of circumcision. In Phil 3:3, genuine followers of Christ are designated as the "true circumcision."

There is a significant usage of ***peritomē*** in Col 2:11, where the "circumcision of Christ" is indicated. This phrase is generally regarded technically as a "subjective genitive." This grammatical form indicates here that the circumcision mentioned is something performed by Christ and not simply as something belonging to him. The "circumcision" referred to here is the work of salvation accomplished by Christ on the cross.

peritemnō περιτέμνω 4059

peritemnō is a verb meaning "circumcise" throughout the approximately twenty occurrences of the term, referring to the removal of the foreskin by a sharpened flint.

Literal references to ritual circumcision include Luke 1:59; 2:21; John 7:22; Acts 16:3; 21:21; 1 Cor 7:18; Gal 2:3; 5:2ff.; 6:12.

In Acts 7:8; 15:1, 5, 24; 6:13 the desire to be circumcised is linked to the erroneous belief that it is necessary for salvation.

For the metaphorical usage of ***peritemnō*** in Col 2:11, see ***peritomē*** (above).

aperitmētos ἀπερίτμητος 564

aperitmētos is a rare adjective meaning "uncircumcised" found only in Acts 7:51. The use is metaphorical, referring to those who are "uncircumcised" in heart — possessing an unbelieving heart and a rebellious attitude towards God.

akrobystia ἀκροβυστία 203

akrobystia is a noun denoting "uncircumcision" — the state of being uncircumcised. It is found in twenty contexts.

References to "uncircumcised men" are found in Acts 11:3. The "uncircumcised" in Gal 2:7; Eph 2:11 are unbelievers. See also Col 2:13 in this regard.

The state of being uncircumcised is indicated in Rom 2:25ff.; 4:9ff.; 1 Cor 7:18ff.; Gal 5:6; 6:15; Col 3:11.

epispaomai ἐπισπάομαι 1986

epispaomai is a rare verb found only in 1 Cor 7:18 with the meaning "to remove the marks of circumcision."

COMMAND, COMMANDMENT

entolē ἐντολή 1785

entolē is a noun denoting "commandment" throughout its nearly seventy occurrences. Its primary usage centers on the commandments of the Mosaic law covenant.

General references to the law given by God include Matt 5:19; 19:17; 22:36ff.; Mark 7:8ff.; Luke 1:6; 1 Cor 7:19; 14:35; Heb 7:5; 9:19; 2 Pet 2:21; Rev 12:17; 14:12. In particular, Rom 7:8ff. mentions the lethal effect of the law on the heart of human beings. Transgressing God's "law" is noted in Matt 15:3ff. Explicit mention of the Decalogue is made in Mark 10:19; 12:28ff.; Luke 18:20; 23:56; Rom 13:9; Eph 6:2. The curse of the "commandments" is declared abolished by the death of Christ in Eph 2:15. The outmoded uselessness of the old "commandment" in making people perfect, set aside by God in favor of the new covenant, is noted in Heb 7:18. The importance of keeping God's "commandments," thus demonstrating one's genuine love for him, is indicated in 1 John 2:3ff.; 4:21; 5:3; 2 John 4ff.

Christ's "new command" to his disciples to love one another is recorded in John 13:34; 15:12. General references to the binding nature of the commandments Christ gave to his disciples are found in John 14:15, 21; 15:10. The specific "charge" or "command" given by God to Christ, granting him authority to take up his own life again after death, is recorded in John 10:18 (see also John 12:49ff.).

Human "commands" or "instructions" are noted in Luke 15:29; John 11:57; Acts 17:15; Col 4:10; Titus 1:14.

SEE ALSO

▸ **54.** Rule, Authority, Command, Obedience > COMMAND, COMMANDMENT, DIRECT, ORDER
diatagma, entalma, epitagē

COVENANT, TESTAMENT

diathēkē διαθήκη 1242

diathēkē is a significant term found approximately thirty times meaning "covenant" throughout, referring to both the old and new covenant bonds. In one or two places it also denotes a human "(last) will and testament."

Reference to the inauguration of the new covenant is noted in Rom 11:27. See also Eph 2:12; Heb 13:20.

New covenant forgiveness is anticipated on the occasion of the Last Supper over which Jesus presides on the eve of his crucifixion. At that meal he affirms that his blood, about to be shed, constitutes the blood of "the covenant" effective for the forgiveness of sins (Matt 26:28; Mark 14:24). See also 1 Cor 11:25; Heb 10:29. Heb 9:15; 12:24 affirm Christ as the mediator of a new covenant. General references to the "covenant" promises made to the patriarchs of old are found in Luke 1:72; Acts 3:25; Rom 9:4.

Acts 7:8 refers to the "covenant of circumcision" given to Abraham, and 2 Cor 3:14; Gal 3:17; Heb 8:9; 9:15, 20 refer to the old covenant.

The characteristic and distinctive spiritual nature of the new covenant is recorded in 2 Cor 3:6.

diathēkē may also be translated "last will" or "testament" in the context of a human disposition. It is found with this meaning first of all in Gal 3:15. Paul uses ***diathēkē*** to illustrate a binding promise or guarantee on the earthly plane that is mirrored in essence in the divine-human covenant that is likewise binding on both God and humankind. The apostle's primary intention here is to stress the certainty that such promises made by God to his people will never be broken. Such a sense is also indicated in Heb 9:16, 17.

Reference to both the old and new covenants in an allegorical context is made in Gal 4:24. The "new covenant" is declared better than the old in Heb 7:22; 8:6.

The divine promise to establish a "new covenant" that would be characterized by a spiritual internalizing of the law of God in the believer's heart is recorded in Heb 8:8, 10; 10:16. The "ark of the covenant" is noted in Heb 9:4; Rev 11:19.

diatithēmi διατίθημι 1303

diatithēmi is a verb found in seven places with the primary sense of "make a covenant." The term refers to a person making a last will and testament in Heb 9:16, 17 (translated here "testator"), as well as to God making a covenant (both old and new) in Acts 3:25; Heb 8:10; 10:16.

SEE ALSO

- ▸ **27.** Community, Partnership, Unity, Discord > AGREEMENT, COVENANT
  syntithēmi

DEACON, MINISTER, SERVANT, SERVE

diakonos διάκονος 1249

The noun ***diakonos*** denotes the general sense of "minister," "servant" in around thirty contexts. In Rom 16:1, 27; Phil 1:1; 1 Tim 3:8, 12, however, the term specifically denotes "deacons" as officers in the early church, entrusted with the day-to-day administration of Christian ministry both to those within and without the community of God's people.

- ▸ **55.** Bondage, Captivity, Servitude > SERVANT, SLAVE

diakoneō διακονέω 1247

diakoneō is a verb with the general sense of "serve" throughout most of the nearly forty occurrences of the term. However, in 1 Tim 3:10, 13 the term specifically expresses the meaning "to serve as deacons."

- ▸ **55.** Bondage, Captivity, Servitude > SERVE, SERVICE

DISCIPLE

mathētēs μαθητής 3101

mathētēs is a noun denoting "disciple" throughout all occurrences of the term (approximately 270).

References to Jesus' twelve disciples include Matt 5:1; 8:21ff.; 26:17ff.; Mark 8:1ff.; 14:12ff.; Luke 6:13ff.; 19:39; John 1:35ff.; 2:11ff.; 6:11ff.; 18:15ff. The followers of Jesus, the broader circle of his "disciples," are noted in John 13:35; 15:8; 19:38.

Other general references to "disciples" are found in Matt 10:24; Luke 6:40; 14:26ff. The term specifically refers to the early Christians as "disciples" in Acts 6:1ff.; 9:1, 10; 11:26; 14:20ff.

The "disciples" of John the Baptist are noted in Matt 9:14; Mark 2:18; Luke 7:18; John 3:25. "Disciples" of Moses are indicated in John 9:28.

mathētria μαθήτρια 3102

mathētria is a rare feminine variant of ***mathētēs*** (above) referring to the "disciple" in Acts 9:36.

mathēteuō μαθητεύω 3100

mathēteuō is a verb meaning to "make disciples" in Matt 28:19, referring to Jesus' last instructions to his own disciples. The activity of "making disciples" is indicated in Acts 14:21. In Matt 27:57 the term is translated "to be a disciple."

ELDER

sympresbyteros συμπρεσβύτερος 4850

sympresbyteros is a rare noun denoting a "fellow elder." It is found only in 1 Pet 5:1.

presbyterion πρεσβυτέριον 4244

presbyterion denotes the "council of the elders" of the Jewish people in Luke 22:66; Acts 22:5; 1 Tim 4:14.

SEE ALSO

- ▸ **15.** Gender, Reproduction, Youth, Aging > ELDER, OLDER, OLD MAN
  presbyteros

ENACT, ESTABLISH

nomotheteō νομοθετέω 3549

nomotheteō is a rare verb found only twice. In Heb 7:11 it refers to "providing" the law to the Israelite people at Sinai. In Heb 8:6 it refers to "enacting" or "establishing" the new covenant on better promises, indicating its superiority over the old.

- ▸ **70.** Give, Take, Seize, Touch > RECEIVE, ACCEPT, WELCOME

EVANGELIST

euangelistēs εὐαγγελιστής 2099

euangelistēs is a noun denoting the office of "evangelist," or a messenger bearing the good news of the gospel (Acts 21:8; 2 Tim 4:5).

EXORCIST

exorkistēs ἐξορκιστής 1845

exorkistēs is a rare noun found only in Acts 19:13, denoting itinerant Jewish "exorcists."

LAW

nomos νόμος 3551

nomos is the only term in the NT that refers to the concept of "law" in a variety of contexts. It has both a general and specific usage relating primarily to the law established by God and brought to fulfillment in Christ.

nomos occurs around two hundred times and refers exclusively to the law of God.

In general terms, ***nomos*** indicates the law of God in relation to the pentateuchal traditions and their application throughout the OT. General references to this law include those in Matt 12:5; Luke 2:2; 24:44; John 18:31; Acts 6:13; Rom 3:28; 7:12ff.; 8:4; 1 Cor 9:8; Gal 5:14; Eph 2:15; Jas 2:8.

More particularly, ***nomos*** refers to the Torah (i.e., the Pentateuch) as distinct from the Prophets in a canonical sense (Matt 7:12; Luke 16:16; John 1:45; Acts 13:15). The Jewish privilege of being instructed in the law is noted in Rom 2:18, 20, as is their condemnation for violating the law in Rom 2:23, 25. In a broader context, the condemnation on people brought by the law through the knowledge of sin is made clear in Rom 3:19, 20; 4:15; 5:20; 1 Cor 15:56; Gal 3:10ff.; Jas 2:12. Similarly, "the law of sin" is said to be at work in the human heart in Rom 7:23, 25, although Rom 8:32 declares that believers are set free from that law by the "law" of the Spirit. The obligation of obedience to God "under the law" is indicated in 1 Cor 9:20; Gal 3:23, 24; 4:4ff.; 5:3; Heb 9:22. Laws relating to marriage for the believer are noted in Rom 7:2ff.; 1 Cor 7:39.

In distinctively positive contexts, there is divine approval expressed for keeping the law in Rom 2:27. Rom 3:21 affirms that the righteousness of God is manifested apart from the law; and Rom 6:14, 15; 7:6 declare that Christians are not under the curse of the law, but under grace. Heb 8:10; 10:16 refer to the law of God as written on the hearts of believers. Christ's fulfillment of the law is indicated in Matt 5:17, 18; John 15:25; Rom 10:4.

In addition to the above, ***nomos*** refers to the divine law, revealed in the OT, as God's source of judicial assessment for his people in particular, and for humankind in general. These contexts are all found in Rom 2. The judgment of humankind in general by the law is indicated in Rom 2:12. Rom 2:13 affirms that doers of the law will be justified. Finally, Rom 2:15 declares that the law is written on the hearts of the Gentiles.

nomodidaskalos νομοδιδάσκαλος 3547

nomodidaskalos occurs only three times, referring to a "teacher of the (Mosaic) law" (Luke 5:17; Acts 5:34; 1 Tim 1:7).

▸ **65.** Teach, Exhort, Rebuke, Discipline > TEACH, TEACHER, TEACHING

anomōs ἀνόμως 460

anomōs is an adverbial expression that signifies "without the law," indicating lack of knowledge of the law, ignorance of its demands. ***anomōs*** occurs only twice, in Rom 2:12.

LAWGIVER

nomothetēs νομοθέτης 3550

nomothetēs occurs only in Jas 4:12, with reference to God as "lawgiver" and judge.

LAWYER

nomikos νομικός 3544

nomikos is a noun derived from the principal term for "law" in the NT, ***nomos***. ***nomikos*** occurs nine times and has the principal meaning "lawyer," in the sense of one who is trained in the interpretation of the Mosaic law and is responsible for teaching that law to the people of Israel.

nomikos refers to the lawyers whom Jesus confronted during his earthly ministry. In all of these situations, such people were antagonistic towards Christ, seeking (unsuccessfully) to trap him in debate (Matt 22:35; Luke 10:25; 14:3); or rejecting him outright (Luke 7:30). Elsewhere, they suffer the sting of Jesus' rebukes, as Jesus castigates them for the huge barriers they place in the way of those who genuinely seek after God (Luke 11:45, 46, 52).

A positive general reference to a lawyer is found in Titus 3:13; and in Titus 3:9, ***nomikos*** is translated by the adverbial phrase "about the law," in the context of fruitless wrangling over legal matters.

MEDIATOR

mesitēs μεσίτης 3316

mesitēs is the sole term utilized in the NT (six times in all) to convey the precise sense of mediator. It is used in Gal 3:19, 20 to refer implicitly to Moses as the mediator of the old covenant. In 1 Tim 2:5; Heb 8:6; 9:15; 12:24, ***mesitēs*** refers to Christ as the unique mediator of the new covenant.

OFFICE, POSITION

hierateia ἱερατεία 2405

hierateia is found only in Luke 1:9; Heb 7:5, where it refers to the "custom" or "office" of the priesthood.

▸ **38.** Covenant, Law, Rites, Roles > PRIEST, PRIESTHOOD

episkopē ἐπισκοπή 1984

episkopē occurs only four times, referring twice to divine "visitation" and twice to an "office" or "position of leadership." Acts 1:20 refers to Judas' position of leadership being given to another (Matthias) on account of his betrayal of Christ. 1 Tim 3:1 refers to the "office" of a bishop as a noble ambition for a Christian man to aspire to.

▸ **32.** Law, Justice, Jurisprudence, Judgment > VISIT (IN JUDGMENT)

PREACHER

kēryx κῆρυξ 2783

kēryx is a noun occurring only three times and meaning "preacher," with the underlying sense of a "herald" (1 Tim 2:7; 2 Tim 1:11; 2 Pet 2:5).

SEE ALSO

▸ **43.** Prophecy, Preaching, Proclamation > PREACH, PREACHING
kēryssō, kērygma, euangelizō, diangellō, katangellō, parrēsiazomai, laleō

PRIEST, PRIESTHOOD

archiereus ἀρχιερεύς 749

archiereus is a common term in the NT, designating the office of "chief priest" or "high priest." ***archiereus*** occurs over 120 times, with references to "chief" priests and "high" priests divided fairly equally.

References to "chief priests" — that group of priestly leaders immediately below the rank of "high priest," are found, for example, in Matt 2:4; 21:15; 27:1ff.; Mark 11:18, 27; 15:1ff.; Luke 9:22; 22:2ff.; John 18:3; 19:15ff.; Acts 5:24; 9:14; 19:14. As a group, along with the elders of the Jewish Sanhedrin, these men were implacably opposed to the person and work of Jesus Christ, whom they regarded as a serious threat to their privileged status in the Jewish community.

The "high priest" is also frequently mentioned (Matt 26:57ff.; Mark 14:47ff.; Luke 22:50ff.; John 11:49ff.; 18:10ff.; Acts 4:6). Other references to the office of the high priest are found in Heb 5:1; 7:27ff.; 8:3; 9:7, 25; 13:11.

The most significant theological usage of ***archiereus*** is found in the book of Hebrews, with reference to Christ's heavenly ministry as the great high priest of his people (Heb 2:17; 3:1; 4:14, 15; 7:26; 8:1; 9:11). In particular, Heb 5:5, 10; 6:20 speak of Jesus' eternal high priestly ministry as one patterned after the order of Melchizedek, without beginning or end.

hiereus ἱερεύς 2409

hiereus means "priest" in each of the thirty-two contexts in which it is found. It refers primarily to the ceremonial officials of Jesus' day and is also a metaphor for believers in terms of their intimate relationship with God. ***hiereus*** also refers to Christ's heavenly high priestly ministry.

References to priests as Jewish ministers in the first century include those in Matt 8:4; 12:4ff.; Mark 1:44; 2:26; Luke 1:5; 5:14; John 1:19; Acts 4:1; 6:7; Heb 7:23; 9:6; 10:11. There is also one reference to a priest of the cult of Zeus (the patron god of the city of Lystra) in Acts 14:13.

hiereus also refers to the high priestly role of Jesus, whose ministry of intercession is patterned after the priesthood of Melchizedek, the ancient priest-king of Salem mentioned in Gen 14 (Heb 5:6; 7:1ff.).

hiereus also refers to the saints in heaven as "priests" of God in the eternal kingdom (Rev 1:6; 5:10; 20:6).

hierōsynē ἱερωσύνη 2420

hierōsynē means "priesthood" in each of the four contexts where it occurs. On three occasions, ***hierōsynē*** refers to the Levitical priesthood (Heb 7:11ff.). Heb 7:24 refers to the eternal "priesthood" of the heavenly Christ.

hierateia ἱερατεία 2405

hierateia is a synonym for ***hierōsynē*** (above) found only twice and meaning "priestly office" in both contexts (Luke 1:9; Heb 7:5).

▸ **38.** Covenant, Law, Rites, Roles > OFFICE, POSITION

hierateuma ἱεράτευμα 2406

hierateuma occurs only twice, referring on each occasion to the body of Christ, the people of God, as a holy and royal "priesthood" belonging to God (1 Pet 2:5, 9).

hierateuō ἱερατεύω 2407

hierateuō is a verb found only in Luke 1:8, meaning "to serve as a priest" and referring to Zechariah, the father of John the Baptist.

PROPHET

prophētēs προφήτης 4396

prophētēs is the standard term for "prophet" in the NT and occurs nearly 150 times. ***prophētēs*** (when it refers to genuine prophetic activity) describes those individuals who were raised up and equipped by God to communicate his plan and purposes to his people and to the world at large.

General designations of people as "prophets" are found in Matt 13:57; Mark 6:4; Luke 4:24. Other general references to OT prophets include those in Matt 1:22; 2:15ff.; 3:3; John 1:23; 12:38 — all of which refer to revelation as that "which was spoken by the prophets." Luke 1:70; Heb 1:1; Jas 5:10 refer to the prophets as God's spokesmen. "The prophets" are referred to as a distinct group of people in the old covenant in Matt 5:17; 7:12; 23:29ff.; Luke 10:24; 13:28. Rev 10:7; 11:18 refer to the prophets of old as the servants of God. ***prophētēs*** refers on numerous occasions to the canonical prophets (Matt 22:40; 26:56; Mark 1:2; Luke 3:4; 24:27, 44; John 1:45; 6:45; Acts 3:18; 8:28ff.; 13:15; Rom 1:2; Eph 2:20; 3:5).

Jesus is occasionally referred to as a prophet (Matt 21:11, 46; Luke 7:16; 24:19; John 4:19); as is John the Baptist (Luke 1:76; 20:6). Groups of itinerant NT prophets are noted in Acts 11:27; 13:1; 21:10. Prophets in the new covenant church are indicated in 1 Cor 12:28ff.; 14:29ff.; Eph 4:11.

prophētis προφῆτις 4398

prophētis is the feminine form of ***prophētēs*** (above). It is found in only two places, meaning "prophetess" (Luke 2:36; Rev 2:20).

pseudoprophētēs ψευδοπροφήτης 5578

pseudoprophētēs is a variant form of ***prophētēs*** (above). It occurs eleven times and means "false prophet."

Matt 7:15 warns against false prophets. Matt 24:11, 24; Mark 13:22 predict the emergence of false prophets in the last days. Other references to false prophets are found in Luke 6:26; Acts 13:6; 2 Pet 2:1; 1 John 4:1. The designation "false prophet" is also applied metaphorically to the third member of the "unholy trinity" in Rev 16:13; 19:20; 20:10. These texts refer to the dragon, the sea beast, and the earth beast — all satanic counterfeits of the Godhead: Father, Son, and Holy Spirit.

SEE ALSO

- ▸ **43.** Prophecy, Preaching, Proclamation > PROPHECY, PROPHESY, PROPHETIC ***prophēteuō, prophēteia, prophētikos***

RULER OF THE SYNAGOGUE

archisynagōgos ἀρχισυνάγωγος 752

archisynagōgos is a noun occurring nine times denoting "the ruler of the synagogue." This is the position held by Jairus (Mark 5:22ff.; Luke 8:49); Crispus (Acts 18:8); and Sosthenes (Acts 18:17). Other references include those in Luke 13:14; Acts 13:15.

- ▸ **54.** Rule, Authority, Command, Obedience > RULE, RULER

SEE ALSO

- ▸ **24.** Dwell, Live, Gather, Hospitality > ASSEMBLE, ASSEMBLY ***synerchomai***
- ▸ **27.** Community, Partnership, Unity, Discord > EXPEL, EXCOMMUNICATE ***aposynagōgos***
- ▸ **41.** Sacrifice, Offering, Worship, Praise > GATHER, ASSEMBLE, ASSEMBLY, SYNAGOGUE, CHURCH ***ekklēsia, panēgyris, synagōgē, episynagōgē***

SHEPHERD

archipoimēn ἀρχιποίμην 750

archipoimēn is a rare term denoting Christ as the "chief shepherd," found only in 1 Pet 5:4.

- ▸ **28.** Agriculture, Viticulture, Animal Husbandry > SHEPHERD, PASTOR

SEE ALSO

- ▸ **31.** Kingdom, Empire, Rule, Military, Warfare > CHIEF ***prōtos***
- ▸ **33.** Architecture > CORNERSTONE ***akrogōniaios***

STANDARD

kanōn κανών 2583

kanōn is a noun denoting a "rule" in the sense of a "standard," "principle," or "law" explicitly set by God (2 Cor 10:13; Gal 6:16; Phil 3:16).

UNLAWFUL, LAWLESS

athemitos ἀθέμιτος 111

athemitos is an adjective denoting that which is "unlawful" or "lawless," in the context of the revealed standards of God's statutes. It occurs only twice. In Acts 10:28, Peter protests to the Lord that it would be "unlawful" for him to associate with a Gentile in any way. 1 Pet 4:3 refers to the "lawless" idolatry of the Gentiles.

- ▸ **53.** Value, Worth > ABOMINABLE, ABOMINATION, DETESTABLE

39. Clean, Pure, Holy

CLEAN, PURE

katharos καθαρός 2513

katharos is an adjective denoting that which is "clean," "pure." It is found in nearly thirty contexts.

References to the "pure in heart," or those who are morally upright, are made in Matt 5:8; 1 Tim 1:5; 2 Tim 2:22. A "pure" conscience is indicated in 1 Tim 3:9; 2 Tim 1:3.

To be "clean" in the sense of being free from moral impurity is indicated in Matt 23:26; John 13:10; Rom 14:20; Titus 1:15; Jas 1:27. The state of righteousness in relation to having been "made clean" is indicated in John 15:3. "Clean" in the sense of "innocent" is the meaning indicated in Acts 20:26.

hagnos ἁγνός 53

hagnos is an adjective found in eight contexts with the underlying sense of "pure."

"Pure" in the sense of "chaste" is indicated in 2 Cor 11:2 with metaphorical reference to the church as Christ's "bride." The sense of "guiltless" is indicated in 2 Cor 7:11. General references to moral purity are noted in Phil 4:8; 1 Tim 5:22; Titus 2:5; 1 Pet 3:2. Divine wisdom is described as "pure," or "without corruption," in Jas 3:17. See also 1 John 3:3.

SEE ALSO

▸ **28.** Agriculture, Viticulture, Animal Husbandry > CLEAR *diakatharizō*

CLEANSE, PURIFY

katharizō καθαρίζω 2511

katharizō is a verb meaning "cleanse," "purify," plus related senses, throughout the nearly forty occurrences of the term.

The meaning "make clean," "cleanse" is evident in contexts describing Christ's healing ministry. For example, lepers are "healed," or "cleansed," in Matt 8:2ff.; 11:5; Mark 1:40ff.; Luke 4:27; 5:12ff.; 7:22; 17:17. References to people "healed" or "cleansed" of various diseases are found in Matt 10:8; Luke 17:14.

The literal sense of "cleanse" in relation to the outside of a cup is used symbolically in Matt 23:25ff.; Luke 11:39 to denote the superficial cleanliness of the Pharisees and imply their hypocrisy.

God makes a declaration of ceremonial cleanness in Acts 10:15; 11:9. In Acts 15:9 God is said to "cleanse" the heart by faith.

The "purifying" effect of blood in the old covenant ritual sacrificial system is recorded in Heb 9:22, 25. The process of "cleansing oneself" from (moral) defilement is indicated in 2 Cor 7:1.

1 John 1:7, 9 affirm that the blood of Christ "cleanses" one from all sin. Eph 5:26 contains the declaration that Christ "has cleansed" the church by the spiritual application of God's word. In Titus 2:14 Christ is said to "purify" a people for himself. Heb 9:14 declares that the consciences of believers are "purged" or "purified" by the blood of Christ.

ekkathairō ἐκκαθαίρω 1571

ekkathairō is a rare verb meaning "to thoroughly cleanse" in the metaphorical context of 1 Cor 5:7, where the believer is exhorted to rid himself of all "leaven" (i.e., a godless lifestyle). 2 Tim 2:21 refers generally to people "purifying" themselves from what is ignoble.

hagnizō ἁγνίζω 48

hagnizō is a verb meaning "to purify oneself" in a ritual, ceremonial context in John 11:55; Acts 21:24ff. The word has a general moral, spiritual emphasis in Jas 4:8; 1 Pet 1:2; 1 John 3:3.

SEE ALSO

▸ **28.** Agriculture, Viticulture, Animal Husbandry > CLEAR *diakatharizō*

CLEANSING, PURIFICATION

katharismos καθαρισμός 2512

katharismos is a noun meaning "cleansing," "purification" and found in eight places. Ritual "cleansing" is indicated in Mark 1:44; Luke 2:22; John 2:6; 3:25. Heb 1:3 refers to Christ "having made purification" for the sins of his people. 2 Pet 1:9 describes the reality of "being cleansed" from one's sins.

katharotēs καθαρότης 2514

katharotēs is a rare noun found only in Heb 9:13 referring to the "(ritual) purification" of the Levitical covenant.

hagnismos ἁγνισμός 49

hagnismos is a rare noun referring to ritual "purification" only in Acts 21:26.

SEE ALSO

▸ **28.** Agriculture, Viticulture, Animal Husbandry > CLEAR *diakatharizō*

DEFILE

koinoō κοινόω 2840

koinoō is a verb with the predominant meaning "defile," "pollute" throughout its fifteen occurrences. The act of "defiling" in a moral sense is described in Matt 15:11ff.; Mark 7:15ff., where Jesus affirms that it is not what goes into people that defiles them, but rather what comes out of them — their speech and actions. Moral impurity in a general sense is indicated in Rev 21:27.

In a ceremonial context, the "defiling" of the holy place of the temple is indicated in Acts 21:28. Heb 9:13 mentions people who are ritually unclean.

miainō μιαίνω 3392

The verb ***miainō***, meaning "defile," is found five times. John 18:28 describes the contraction of "ritual uncleanness," with the result of being "defiled." The process of "becoming corrupted or defiled" in a moral sense is mentioned in relation to the wicked (Titus 1:15); as a warning to believers (Heb 12:15); and in connection with false prophets (Jude 8).

molynō μολύνω 3435

molynō is a verb found three times with the passive sense of "being defiled" in relation to weak consciences in 1 Cor 8:7. Rev 3:4 refers to believers who "have not defiled" their garments with sinful corruption. Rev 14:4 describes the saints who "have not defiled themselves" with women.

spiloō σπιλόω 4695

spiloō is a rare synonym for the entries listed above. Jas 3:6 describes the tongue as an organ that "defiles" the whole body. Jude 23 speaks of a piece of clothing "stained" by the flesh with reference to ritual contamination.

DEFILEMENT, DEFILING

miasma μίασμα 3393

miasma is a rare noun denoting the moral "defilement" or "corruption" of the world, found only in 2 Pet 2:20.

miasmos μιασμός 3394

miasmos is a rare variant of ***miasma*** (above) found only in 2 Pet 2:10, denoting a "morally defiling" passion.

molysmos μολυσμός 3436

molysmos is a rare noun found only in 2 Cor 7:1 and denoting moral "defilement" in a general sense.

FILTH, FILTHINESS, FILTHY, DIRTY

perikatharma περικάθαρμα 4027

perikatharma is a rare noun denoting "filth" or "rubbish" in 1 Cor 4:13, referring symbolically to the attitude of hatred and disgust directed at the apostle Paul by his enemies.

rhypos ῥύπος 4509

rhypos is another rare noun denoting "filth" in the literal sense of "dirt" in 1 Pet 3:21.

rhypainō ῥυπαίνω 4510

rhypainō is a rare verb found only twice, meaning "to be vile, filthy" in a moral sense in Rev 22:11.

rhyparos ῥυπαρός 4508

rhyparos is a rare adjective found only in Jas 2:2, referring to a poor man's "dirty" or "shabby" clothing.

rhyparia ῥυπαρία 4507

rhyparia is a noun found only in Jas 1:21 denoting moral "filthiness."

aischrotēs αἰσχρότης 151

aischrotēs is a term occurring only in Eph 5:4, referring to the vice of "obscenity," "moral filth."

HOLINESS, HOLY, SANCTIFY

hagios ἅγιος 40

hagios is an adjective that commonly refers to those persons and things that are "holy" in the sense of being set apart for divine redemptive purposes. When predicated of God, ***hagios*** refers to his purity of character and is applied as part of the designation for the third person of the Godhead, the Holy Spirit. ***hagios*** is commonly translated "saint" with reference to the people of God. The term occurs around 230 times.

References to the Holy Spirit abound in the NT in connection with this term (e.g., Matt 1:18ff.; Mark 1:8; Luke 1:15, 67; John 20:22; Acts 1:2ff.; 13:2ff.; Rom 5:5; 1 Cor 2:14; Eph 1:13; 1 Thess 5:26; Heb 6:4; 1 Pet 1:12; 1 John 5:7; Jude 20).

Concerning "holy things" in general contexts, ***hagios*** occurs in Matt 7:6; Rom 12:1; 2 Pet 1:18. In particular, the "holy" city of Jerusalem is indicated in Matt 4:5; 27:53 in the earthly sense, whereas in Rev 21:2, 10; 22:19 it is spoken of with reference to the heavenly city of Jerusalem to be revealed at the end of the age with the return of Christ. Matt 24:15; Acts 21:28; Eph 2:21 refer to the holy place in the temple. In addition, "holy" angels are mentioned in Matt 25:31; Mark 8:38; Luke 9:26; Rev 14:10.

"Saints" in general are also commonly designated by the term ***hagios*** (e.g., Matt 27:52; Acts 9:13, 32; Rom 12:13; 1 Cor 6:2; 2 Cor 9:1; Eph 2:19; Phil 1:1; Col 1:2, 12; 2 Thess 1:10; 1 Tim 5:10; Heb 6:10; Rev 5:8; 19:8).

Various other contexts also use the term "holy" to describe Jesus, as the "Holy One of God" (Mark 1:24; Luke 1:35; Rev 3:7); the apostles (Eph 3:5; Rev 18:20); the prophets (Luke 1:70; Acts 3:21; Rev 22:6); the covenant (Luke 1:72); God as "Holy Father" (John 17:11); the Scriptures (Rom 1:2); the commandments (Rom 7:12; 2 Pet 2:21); children (1 Cor 7:14); the church (Eph 5:27); God's people (Col 1:22; 1 Pet 1:16; 2:9); a kiss of greeting (1 Thess 5:26; 1 Cor 15:20); and holiness as a characteristic of God (1 Pet 1:16; Rev 4:8; 6:10).

HOLINESS, SANCTIFICATION

hagiasmos ἁγιασμός 38

hagiasmos is a noun that is translated "sanctification" or "holiness." The term occurs ten times.

"Godly living" is signified by the use of this term in Rom 6:19; Heb 12:14; 1 Tim 2:15; 1 Thess 4:7. Sanctification is designated as the fruit or consequences of one's salvation in Rom 6:22; 1 Thess 4:3. Paul, in 1 Cor 1:30, declares that God has made Jesus our sanctification. The process of sanctification by the Spirit of God is affirmed in 2 Thess 2:13; 1 Pet 1:2.

hosiotēs ὁσιότης 3742

hosiotēs is a rare noun, occurring only twice and meaning "holiness." In Luke 1:75 the term is found together with "righteousness," indicating that the coming of Christ was intended to bring about an attitude of renewed faith and obedience towards God in the lives of the people of God. Eph 4:24 refers to the new nature of all believers in Christ who have been re-created in righteousness and holiness for the same purpose.

hagiōsynē ἁγιωσύνη 42

This term is a synonym for both ***hosiotēs*** and ***hagiasmos*** (above). ***hagiōsynē*** occurs only three times. In Rom 1:4, the word is applied to the Spirit of God (viz. "Spirit of holiness"), who was instrumental in bringing Jesus back from the dead. 2 Cor 7:1 exhorts believers to holiness of life (see also 1 Thess 3:13).

hagiotēs ἁγιότης 41

hagiotēs occurs only once, in Heb 12:10, and refers to the divine holiness which is the ultimate purpose for which the Lord disciplines us throughout our lives.

HOLY, PURE

hosios ὅσιος 3741

hosios is an adjective describing people and things as "holy," or morally and religiously pure. The term occurs six times.

The title "Holy One" is applied to Christ in Acts 2:27; 13:35 as one whose coming was anticipated by the ruler David (Ps 16:8–11). In Rev 16:5, the same title is applied to God (see also Rev 15:4). The adjective "holy" is also applied to Christ as our great high priest in Heb 7:26. The "holy and sure blessings of David," given to him by God for his faithfulness, are referred to in Acts 13:34. 1 Tim 2:8 describes "lifting holy hands" as an appropriate attitude for prayer. Titus 1:8 lists holiness as an indispensable character trait for a prospective pastor or elder.

PURITY

hagnotēs ἁγνότης 54

hagnotēs is a rare noun denoting "purity" of life found only in 2 Cor 6:6.

SEE ALSO

▸ **28.** Agriculture, Viticulture, Animal Husbandry > CLEAR
diakatharizō

SANCTIFY

hagiazō ἁγιάζω 37

This verb is found in about thirty contexts and means "to sanctify" in most of these. The translation of ***hagiazō*** will occasionally vary — for example, "consecrate" or "be, make holy." But the underlying sense of "sanctify," or to set apart people and things for the service of God, remains.

The process or action of sanctifying, in general contexts, is illustrated in Matt 23:17; 1 Cor 7:14; 1 Tim 4:5; 2 Tim 2:21; Rev 22:11. The action and attitude of "sanctifying the name of God," or maintaining a holy reverence towards him, is evident in Luke 11:2; Matt 6:9, where Christ begins his paradigm prayer: "Our Father in heaven, holy be your name . . ." 1 Pet 3:15 speaks of "sanctifying" Christ as Lord, or treating him with reverence.

The other uses of ***hagiazō*** all relate explicitly to the actions of God and Christ. For instance, Jesus "consecrates" himself for the sake of his disciples (John 17:19); and also sanctifies his church (Eph 5:26) and his disciples, setting them apart for ministry (John 17:17). God is declared to have sanctified the person and mission of Christ (John 10:36); and also his people (Acts 20:32; Heb 3:11; 10:10; 1 Thess 5:23; 1 Cor 6:11).

UNCLEAN, DEFILED

koinos κοινός 2839

koinos is an adjective with the dual senses of "common" and "defiled," "unclean." It is found in twelve places.

The meaning "unclean" in a ritual sense is indicated in relation to unwashed hands in Mark 7:2. General references to that which is unclean are found in Rom 14:14.

The designation "common" in the sense of "unclean" refers to food shown to the apostle Peter in a vision — an opinion for which God rebuked the apostle (Acts 10:14, 28; 11:8). The term is used in a moral sense in Heb 10:29, where terrible judgment is threatened for anyone who has treated the blood of Christ's sacrifice as an "unclean thing" (i.e., through unbelief).

The meaning "common" in the sense of something held in common is indicated in Acts 2:44; Titus 1:4; Jude 3.

▸ **39.** Clean, Pure, Holy >
UNCLEAN, UNCLEANNESS, IMPURITY

UNCLEAN, UNCLEANNESS, IMPURITY

akathartos ἀκάθαρτος 169

akathartos is an adjective found in thirty contexts with the consistent meaning "unclean" throughout, in both a ceremonial and a moral sense. The moral connotation is prominent, referring to "unclean" (i.e., demonic) spirits (Matt 10:1; 12:43; Mark 1:23ff.; 5:2ff.; Luke 4:33ff.; 9:42; Acts 5:16; Rev 16:13; 18:2). Eph 5:5 refers to moral impurity.

Ritual uncleanness is also indicated in Acts 10:14, 28; 11:8; 2 Cor 6:17. In 1 Cor 7:14, the designation "unclean" is applied to the children of unbelievers.

koinos κοινός 2839

koinos is an adjective found ten times meaning "unclean," "defiled," usually in a ceremonial sense.

The designation "unclean" refers to unwashed hands (Mark 7:2); to food (Acts 10:14; 11:8); and to men (Acts 10:28). See also Rom 14:4.

A notable use of ***koinos*** is found in Heb 10:29, which denounces all those who would treat the blood of Christ as an "unclean" (or profane) thing — referring to all who reject Christ.

▸ **39.** Clean, Pure, Holy > UNCLEAN, DEFILED

akatharsia ἀκαθαρσία 167

akatharsia is a noun found in ten contexts meaning "uncleanness," "impurity," primarily in a moral sense.

Moral uncleanness is predicated of the Pharisees, who are condemned by Christ during his public ministry (Matt 23:27). Morally depraved men and women are so described in Rom 1:24; 6:19; 2 Cor 12:21.

The general sense of "uncleanness" or "impurity" as a characteristic (or "fruit") of the unbeliever is indicated in Gal 5:19; Eph 4:19; 5:3; Col 3:5. See also 1 Thess 2:3; 4:7.

UNDEFILED

amiantos ἀμίαντος 283

amiantos is an adjective found four times meaning "undefiled" in the sense of being "free from any impurity or flaw."

The designation "undefiled" is applied to the high priestly ministry of Christ in Heb 7:26. Heb 13:4 contains the injunction to keep the marriage bed undefiled. Pure religion is described as undefiled (Jas 1:27); as is the eternal inheritance of the unbeliever (1 Pet 1:4).

WASHING, CLEANSING

loutron λουτρόν 3067

loutron is a rare noun denoting the metaphorical action of "washing" or "bathing" in two places. Eph 5:25 mentions "washing" (i.e., "cleansing") the church by the word of God. Titus 3:5 describes conversion as "the washing" of regeneration, through the Holy Spirit.

SEE ALSO

▸ **20.** Illness, Disease, Health, Healing > WASH, WASHING
niptō, baptizō

▸ **80.** Related to Liquids >
WASH, BATHE, WASHING, WETTING
aponiptō, brechō, louō, apolouomai, plynō, baptismo

40. Holy Days, Feasts, Festivals

DEDICATION

enkainia ἐγκαίνια 1456

enkainia is a rare noun found only in John 10:22 referring to the "Feast of Dedication," celebrating the cleansing of the temple by Judas Maccabeus in the middle of the second century B.C., following its desecration by Antiochus Epiphanes IV — the cruel, despotic, and anti-Semitic Seleucid ruler.

SEE ALSO

- ▸ **38.** Covenant, Law, Rites, Roles > ANOINT, ANOINTING, CONSECRATE
  enkainizō

FEAST, FESTIVAL

heortē ἑορτή 1859

heortē is a noun found nearly thirty times meaning "feast," "festival" throughout, indicating specific celebrations in the Jewish religious calendar.

The Feast of Passover is indicated in Matt 26:5; 27:15; Mark 14:2; 15:6; Luke 2:41; John 2:23; 6:4; 11:56; 12:12, 20. The Feast of Tabernacles is noted in John 7:2ff.

General references to an unidentified feast are found in John 5:1; Col 2:16.

heortazō ἑορτάζω 1858

heortazō is a rare verb found only in 1 Cor 5:8, exhorting the people "to celebrate the festival" of Passover in sincerity and truth.

- ▸ **40.** Holy Days, Feasts, Festivals > KEEP

deipnon δεῖπνον 1173

deipnon is a noun denoting a "banquet," "feast," or "meal" in both a ritual and non-ritual sense. The term occurs sixteen times. The sense of "banquet" or "feast" is found in Matt 23:6; Mark 6:21; Luke 14:12ff.

Ritual "festivals" are in view in Mark 12:39; Luke 20:46; John 13:2ff.; 21:20. The Lord's "supper" is mentioned in 1 Cor 11:21. An ordinary "meal" is indicated in John 12:2.

Rev 19:9, 17 refer metaphorically to the marriage "supper" of the Lamb at the end of time.

agapē ἀγάπη 26

agapē is a common term denoting "love," "affection" throughout its nearly 120 occurrences. In particular, ***agapē*** denotes a "love feast" in Jude 16.

- ▸ **48.** Will, Purpose, Decide, Advise > LOVE

SEE ALSO

- ▸ **24.** Dwell, Live, Gather, Hospitality > BANQUET, FEAST
  dochē

KEEP

poieō ποιέω 4160

The verb ***poieō*** is common, occurring about six hundred times with the primary sense of "do," "make." However, in Matt 26:18, ***poieō*** is translated "keep" in reference to Jesus' intention to observe the Passover with his disciples.

- ▸ **83.** Set, Put, Place, Prepare, Establish > APPOINT, ORDAIN, ASSIGN
- ▸ **84.** Do, Make, Accomplish, Occur > EXECUTE
- ▸ **84.** Do, Make, Accomplish, Occur > DO, MAKE, MAKER

heortazō ἑορτάζω 1858

heortazō is found only in 1 Cor 5:8 and refers to keeping the feast of the Passover in sincerity and truth.

- ▸ **40.** Holy Days, Feasts, Festivals > FEAST, FESTIVAL

SEE ALSO

- ▸ **69.** Have, Possess, Hold, Grasp, Bear, Carry > KEEP
  tēreō, phylassō, katechō, diatēreō, phroureō

NEW MOON

neomēnia νουμηνία 3561

neomēnia occurs only in Col 2:16 with reference to the Jewish "new moon" festival.

SEE ALSO

- ▸ **1.** Celestial Realm, Earthly Realm > MOON
  selēnē
- ▸ **5.** Old, New, First, Last > NEW, NEWNESS
  kainos, kainotēs, neos, prosphatos
- ▸ **35.** Clothing, Adornment, Textiles > NEW, UNSHRUNK
  agnaphos

PASSOVER

pascha πάσχα 3957

pascha refers about thirty times to the celebration of the Passover festival (Matt 26:2, 17ff.; Mark 14:14ff.; Luke 22:1ff.; John 2:13; 6:4; 12:1; 13:1; 18:28, 39; Acts 12:4; 1 Cor 5:7; Heb 11:28).

PENTECOST

pentēkostē πεντηκοστή 4005

pentēkostē is transliterated "Pentecost" in reference to the "fiftieth day" after the Sabbath of the Passover week, or the "day of Pentecost." This is the Greek equivalent of the second of the three great annual Jewish festivals — the Feast of Weeks, or Harvest. ***pentēkostē*** occurs only three times, referring to the festival of Pentecost itself (1 Cor 16:8) and to the day of Pentecost (Acts 2:1; 20:16).

PREPARATION

paraskeuē παρασκευή 3904

paraskeuē is a noun meaning "preparation." ***paraskeuē*** occurs only six times and refers to the day of "preparation," prior to the Sabbath (i.e., Saturday) at the time of Jesus' trial and crucifixion (Matt 27:62; Mark 15:42; Luke 23:54; John 19:14, 31, 42).

SEE ALSO

▸ **83.** Set, Put, Place, Prepare, Establish > PREPARE, MAKE READY
hetoimazō, proetoimazō, kataskeuazō, katartizō

SABBATH

sabbaton σάββατον 4521

sabbaton is the Greek transliteration of the Hebrew word *shabbātôn* and is found in approximately seventy contexts. ***sabbaton*** refers to the "Sabbath day" in the majority of these contexts.

General references to the "Sabbath day" include those in Matt 24:20; Mark 6:2; 16:1ff.; Luke 23:54; John 5:9ff.; 7:22ff.; Acts 1:12; 1 Cor 16:2; Col 2:16.

The remaining usage of ***sabbaton*** focuses on the healing ministry of Jesus, that sometimes took place on the Sabbath, and which drew sharp criticism from the Pharisees. Jesus responded by drawing attention to the Pharisees' own hypocrisy on this issue (Matt 12:1ff.; Mark 3:2ff.; Luke 6:6ff.; 13:14ff.; 14:3ff.; John 5:16ff.; 9:14ff.). See also Mark 2:23ff.; Luke 6:1ff.; 13:10. Jesus declared himself to be "the Lord of the Sabbath."

▸ **3.** Periods of Time, Duration, Frequency, Speed > WEEK, WEEKS

TABERNACLES

skēnopēgia σκηνοπηγία 4634

skēnopēgia occurs only in John 7:2 with reference to the "Feast of Tabernacles," specifically indicating the activity of building "shelters" or "tents." This festival celebrated God's protection and guidance of his people during their period of wandering in the wilderness, when they lived in "tents," characteristic of a nomadic lifestyle.

SEE ALSO

▸ **33.** Architecture > TABERNACLE, BOOTH, DWELLING
skēnē, skēnos, skēnōma

UNLEAVENED BREAD

azymos ἄζυμος 106

azymos denotes "unleavened bread" and is used only in ritual contexts. The Feast of Unleavened Bread is the festival that followed Passover and lasted for seven days (Matt 26:17; Mark 14:1, 2; Luke 22:1; Acts 12:3; 20:6). The Day of Unleavened Bread, or Passover, is noted in Luke 22:7.

SEE ALSO

▸ **23.** Food, Drink, Cooking > BREAD
artos

41. Sacrifice, Offering, Worship, Praise

ABSTAIN, REFRAIN

apechomai ἀπέχομαι 567

apechomai is a verb found in six contexts with the consistent sense of "abstain (i.e., refrain) from" idol worship and immorality (Acts 15:20, 29; 1 Thess 4:3; 5:22; 1 Tim 4:3; 1 Pet 2:11).

SEE ALSO

▸ **23.** Food, Drink, Cooking > ABSTINENCE
asitia

ALTAR

thysiastērion θυσιαστήριον 2379

thysiastērion usually denotes the sacrificial altar of the temple. The term occurs around twenty times (e.g., Matt 5:23ff.; 23:18ff.; Luke 11:51; 1 Cor 9:13; Heb 7:13). In Rev 6:9; 8:5; 11:1; 14:18; 16:7, ***thysiastērion*** denotes the visionary altar in the heavenly temple as seen by the apostle John.

Elsewhere, the term refers to the golden altar of incense that stood in front of the veil enclosing the holy of holies (Luke 1:11; Rev 8:3; 9:13). Heb 13:10 makes mention of the "heavenly altar" at which the people of God now "serve" in anticipation of the coming consummation of the Lord in his glory. Jas 2:21 refers to the primitive altar Abraham built when he prepared to offer up his son Isaac to Yahweh.

bōmos βωμός 1041

bōmos is a rare noun found only in Acts 17:23 with reference to an elevated high place, a pagan altar.

BOW, KNEEL

kamptō κάμπτω 2578

This verb occurs four times with the meaning to "bow down" in worship, with primary reference to the worship of God (Rom 14:11; Eph 3:14; Phil 2:10). Rom 11:4 uses ***kamptō*** in a negative sense to refer to those who, at the time of the prophet Elijah, "had not bowed the knee to Baal."

gonypeteō γονυπετέω 1120

gonypeteō is a verb occurring four times with the underlying sense of "bow the knee," or kneel down, fall on one's knees — either in an act of worship or in order to make a special plea.

A man falls on his knees before Jesus to plead for healing for his son (Matt 17:14). Similarly, a leper "bows down" to Jesus, begging for healing in Mark 1:40. In Mark 10:17 a man "kneels before" Jesus and asks him what the requirements are for inheriting eternal life. Matt 27:29 records the action of those who mock Christ on the cross by "falling on their knees" pretending to worship him.

▸ **87.** Movement Upward or Downward > KNEEL

SEE ALSO

▸ **87.** Movement Upward or Downward >
BOW, BOW DOWN
klinō

EATING

brōsis βρῶσις 1035

brōsis is a noun denoting "food," "meat" for most of its eleven occurrences. However, in 1 Cor 8:4 it designates "eating" food offered to idols.

▸ **23.** Food, Drink, Cooking > FOOD

SEE ALSO

▸ **23.** Food, Drink, Cooking > EAT, EATING
esthiō, phagō, trōgō, geuomai, bibrōskō, katesthiō, korennymi, synesthiō

GATHER, ASSEMBLE, ASSEMBLY, SYNAGOGUE, CHURCH

ekklēsia ἐκκλησία 1577

The noun ***ekklēsia*** occurs over one hundred times, meaning "church," with the sense of a gathered community of God's people assembled for worship. The word has only a few exceptional "secular" uses.

General references to the "church" as the new covenant community of believers include Matt 18:17; Acts 2:47; 8:1ff.; 15:38; Rom 16:1ff.; 1 Cor 11:16ff.; 14:4ff.; 2 Cor 8:18ff.; Eph 3:10; Phil 3:6; Col 4:15ff.; Jas 5:14. In particular, Acts 7:38 makes reference to the old covenant community of God's people as "the church in the wilderness." And Heb 12:23 refers to "the assembly of the firstborn, enrolled in heaven."

Elsewhere, specific references to "the church(es) of God" are found in Acts 20:28; 1 Cor 1:2; 10:32; 11:22; 15:9; 2 Cor 1:1; Gal 1:3; 1 Tim 3:5; 2 Thess 1:4. ***ekklēsia*** refers to the letters to the seven churches of Asia in Rev 1:4, 11, 20; 2:1ff.; 3:1ff.; 22:16. Christ is depicted as head of the church, his "body," in Eph 1:22; Col 1:18, 24. ***ekklēsia*** is also used metaphorically of the church, portrayed as a community "wedded" to Christ and the object of his love and devotion (Eph 5:23ff).

ekklēsia is also found in several places with the "profane" sense of a "crowd" or "mob" in Acts 18:22; 19:32ff.

panēgyris πανήγυρις 3831

panēgyris is a rare noun, found only in Heb 12:22, denoting the company of countless angels in "joyful assembly."

synagōgē συναγωγή 4864

synagōgē denotes the place where Jewish people gathered for worship and instruction from the Hebrew Scriptures. The synagogue also served as the initial focus and location for Jewish evangelism by the early apostles. The synagogue constitutes a meeting place for the gathering of

God's people for worship. The term is found only in the NT, though the origin of the synagogue dates most likely from the time of the return from captivity in Babylon. There is, however, no scholarly consensus on this matter.

synagōgē is found about sixty times in the NT. The synagogue itself as a place of worship is indicated, for example, in Matt 6:2ff.; 23:34; Mark 13:9; Luke 12:11; Acts 6:9; 9:2; 17:1, 10. It is the place where Jesus preached his first public sermon (Luke 4:15ff.); and where he often taught during the course of his public ministry (Matt 4:23; Mark 1:21ff.; Luke 6:6; John 6:59; 18:20).

The term is also used metaphorically in Rev 2:9; 3:9 with reference to the "synagogue of Satan," indicating a spiritually corrupt, or apostate, congregation. ***synagōgē*** is also translated "assembly" in Jas 2:2, indicating an explicitly Christian gathering.

episynagōgē ἐπισυναγωγή 1997

episynagōgē is a noun that is found only twice. In 2 Thess 2:1 it signifies the prospect of "being gathered" to the Lord in glory. Heb 10:25 contains an admonition to believers not to abandon their "assembling together" for worship.

▸ **41.** Sacrifice, Offering, Worship, Praise > GATHER, ASSEMBLE, ASSEMBLY, SYNAGOGUE, CHURCH

SEE ALSO

▸ **24.** Dwell, Live, Gather, Hospitality > ASSEMBLE, ASSEMBLY
synerchomai

▸ **24.** Dwell, Live, Gather, Hospitality > GATHER, GATHERING
synagō, episynagō, synathroizō

▸ **27.** Community, Partnership, Unity, Discord > EXPEL, EXCOMMUNICATE
aposynagōgos

▸ **28.** Agriculture, Viticulture, Animal Husbandry > GATHER, HARVEST, PICK, PLUCK
syllegō, trygaō

▸ **38.** Covenant, Law, Rites, Roles > RULER OF THE SYNAGOGUE
archisynagōgos

▸ **69.** Have, Possess, Hold, Grasp, Bear, Carry > GATHER
systrephō

GLORIFY

doxazō δοξάζω 1392

The verb ***doxazō*** occurs about sixty times with the dominant meanings "glorify," "give glory, praise to," in a variety of contexts.

References to people "glorifying" God or "giving praise" include those in Matt 5:16; Luke 5:25ff.; Acts 4:21; 11:18; Rom 15:6ff. In particular, praise to God is offered in the aftermath of healing received from Christ (Luke 17:15; 18:43). And, in Luke 23:47, the Roman centurion who witnessed the death of Christ "praised" God by declaring that Jesus was innocent. See also 2 Cor 9:13; Gal 1:24; 1 Pet 2:12; 4:16. In Luke 4:15 people "offer praise" to Jesus. Matt 6:2; Mark 2:12 refer to people "giving praise" to other people.

doxazō is used passively in relation to the coming of the Holy Spirit, who would not be revealed until Christ "was glorified," or received his heavenly, glorious status at the right hand of the Father upon returning to heaven (John 7:39). See also John 12:16, 23.

Other references to God "glorifying" or "giving supreme honor to" his Son include those in John 8:54; 11:4; 12:28; 17:1; Acts 3:13. Conversely, God is said to "be glorified" in and through his Son in John 13:31ff.; 14:13; 15:8; 17:1ff.; 21:19; 1 Pet 4:11. See also Heb 5:5. Rom 1:21 describes the refusal of human beings to "glorify" or "honor" God. God is said to "glorify" those whom he has chosen — to grant them the status of a heavenly citizen freed forever from the penalty of sin and death (Rom 8:30). See also 1 Pet 4:14.

endoxazō ἐνδοξάζω 1740

endoxazō is a rare variant of ***doxazō*** (above) found only twice and used passively in both places. 2 Thess 1:10, 12 refer to Christ "being glorified" in his saints, or receiving honor and praise for redeeming them.

SEE ALSO

▸ **52.** Status, Identity, Reputation, Honor, Shame > GLORY, GLORIOUS, GLORIFY
syndoxazō

HALLELUJAH

hallēlouia ἀλληλουϊά 239

A term of praise directed to God in an attitude of thanksgiving for his greatness and goodness, ***hallēlouia*** is a transliteration of the Hebrew phrase *halalû yāh*. This term is rare in the NT, being found only a few times in Rev 19:1, 3, 4, 6. On each occasion the term is heard from the mouths of the saints in heaven, as well as from the twenty-four elders and the four creatures before the divine throne.

HOSANNA

hōsanna ὡσαννά 5614

This Greek term, which occurs six times in the NT, is the transliterated equivalent of the Aramaic phrase *hôsha' nā'*, "save, please!" In each case, ***hōsanna*** is used by the Jerusalem population as a cry of adulation directed at Jesus Christ during his triumphal entry into Jerusalem in the last week of his earthly life and ministry (Matt 21:9 [twice], 15; Mark 11:9, 10; John 12:13).

IDOL, IDOLATRY, IDOLATER

eidōlon εἴδωλον 1497

eidōlon is translated "image," "idol" and occurs eleven times.

A review of Israel's past sin of idolatry is recorded in Acts 7:41. Commands to abstain from idolatry are found in Acts 15:20; 1 John 5:21. The abhorrence of idols is indicated in Rom 2:22; 2 Cor 6:16.

The use of ***eidōlon*** in 1 Cor 8:4, 7; 10:19ff. introduces an important distinction. On the one hand, in 1 Cor 8 idols are dismissed as nonentities. However, the context of 1 Cor 10:19 indicates that behind the facade of the idol lies the real world of demonic power.

The powerful influence of idols over those who engage in such worship is indicated in 1 Cor 12:2; Rev 9:20; while 1 Thess 1:9 cites deliverance from idolatry, which was of profound significance for the Thessalonian converts to Christianity.

eidōlothyton εἰδωλόθυτον 1494

eidōlothyton refers not so much to idols themselves, but to that which was offered to idols in sacrificial worship. The term occurs ten times.

In Acts 15:29; 21:25, ***eidōlothyton*** refers to "food offered to idols" from which Gentile believers are required to abstain. General references to the subject of eating food offered to idols are found in 1 Cor 8:1ff.; 10:19, 28. Allusion to Israel's past sin in engaging in this practice is found in Rev 2:14. The same sinful activity is mentioned in regard to the church at Thyatira (Rev 2:20).

▸ **41.** Sacrifice, Offering, Worship, Praise > OFFERING
▸ **41.** Sacrifice, Offering, Worship, Praise > SACRIFICE

eidōlolatrēs εἰδωλολάτρης 1496

This term is found on seven occasions and is always translated "idolater." Paul issues a command to the Corinthian church not to associate with idolaters within the congregation (1 Cor 5:10, 11). The eternal doom of idolaters is mentioned in 1 Cor 6:9; Eph 5:5; Rev 21:8; 22:15.

eidōlolatria εἰδωλολατρία 1495

This general term for idolatry is found on fourteen occasions. 1 Cor 10:14 contains a command to shun idols. Idolatry is one of the fruits of the sinful person (Gal 5:20). In Col 3:5, covetousness is equated with idolatry. Idolatry is also declared as characteristic of the pagan lifestyle in 1 Pet 4:3.

kateidōlos κατείδωλος 2712

kateidōlos occurs once, referring to the city of Athens as "full of idolatry" in Acts 17:16.

INCENSE

thymiama θυμίαμα 2368

thymiama is found in six contexts, meaning "incense" and "odor." Luke 1:10 refers to the "hour of incense," which indicates the occasion of ritual worship. Luke 1:11 mentions the "altar of incense" located in the holy place before the veil of the holy of holies; and Rev 5:8; 8:3, 4 indicate the "golden bowls full of incense," depicting the heavenly reality to which the earthly altar of incense points. In Rev 18:13, "incense" is included in the inventory of the merchants of the earth in the context of the destruction of the great harlot, the city of Babylon.

thymiaō θυμιάω 2370

thymiaō occurs only once, in Luke 1:9. It refers to the customary ritual of the priest Zechariah, in offering incense at the altar in the Jerusalem temple.

▸ **12.** Fire, Heat, Smoke, Burning > BURN, BURNING, LIGHT, SET ON FIRE

thymiatērion θυμιατήριον 2369

thymiatērion is found only in Heb 9:4, referring to the golden altar of incense in the earthly tabernacle/ temple.

MINT

hēdyosmon ἡδύοσμον 2238

hēdyosmon is the term for the fragrant herb "mint," found only in Matt 23:23; Luke 11:42, referring to the tithing practices of the Pharisees.

OFFERING

eidōlothyton εἰδωλόθυτον 1494

eidōlothyton is a term that consistently conveys the sense of "that which is sacrificed to idols," referring to food in each of the ten contexts in which it is found. The principle of abstaining from such food is laid down by the Jerusalem Council in Acts 15:29; 21:25. Paul refers to this contentious practice in 1 Cor 8:1ff.; 10:19, 28. The term is also found in Rev 2:14, 20 where it refers to this practice wrongly tolerated by members of the church at Thyatira.

▸ **41.** Sacrifice, Offering, Worship, Praise > IDOL, IDOLATRY, IDOLATER
▸ **41.** Sacrifice, Offering, Worship, Praise > SACRIFICE

spendomai σπένδομαι 4689

spendomai is a verb found only twice. The sense of the term is metaphorical, indicating the idea of "being offered up" or "poured out as a drink offering." In Phil 2:17 Paul refers to himself in these terms, indicating the likelihood that he will have to surrender his life for his faith. 2 Tim 4:6 reinforces this perspective, for here Paul refers to his approaching death (i.e., by execution) in terms of "already being poured out as a drink offering" or "on the point of being sacrificed."

prosphora προσφορά 4376

prosphora is a general term for "offering," with both a literal as well as a metaphorical sense. The term occurs nine times.

Acts 21:26; 24:17 refer to an offering or vow of purification taken by the apostle Paul and some of his associates. Heb 10:5, 8 refer to old covenant offerings in general, indicating that merely presenting such sacrifices in and of themselves was insufficient as a means of gaining favor with God. Rather, it was only the offering up of Christ himself to God through his death on the cross as an act of substitutionary atonement that accomplished salvation and forgiveness for his people (Eph 5:2; Heb 10:10, 14). Heb 10:18 speaks generally of an "offering" for sin.

holokautōma ὁλοκαύτωμα 3646

holokautōma is a noun with the general meaning "burnt offering" in a literal, ceremonial sense. It is found only in Mark 12:33; Heb 10:6, 8.

POT, URN

stamnos στάμνος 4713

stamnos indicates a "pot" or "urn." It is found only in Heb 9:4, referring to the golden urn containing the manna.

SEE ALSO

▸ **34.** Craftsmanship, Artisanship, Furniture, Implements > POT
xestēs

PRAISE

ainos αἶνος 136

ainos is a rare noun, found only in Matt 21:16; Luke 18:43 with reference to "praise" offered to God.

aineō αἰνέω 134

aineō is the verb from which ***ainos*** (above) is derived and is consistently translated "to offer praise" (to God) in each of the ten occurrences in which it occurs (Luke 2:13, 20; 19:37; 24:53; Acts 2:47; 3:8, 9; Rev 19:5).

epainos ἔπαινος 1868

epainos is a noun found in eleven contexts, meaning "praise" in the sense of "commendation" given and received, as well as "adoration" offered to God.

The sense of "commendation," given to human beings by other human beings, is found in Rom 13:3; 2 Cor 8:18; Phil 4:8; 1 Pet 2:14. 1 Cor 4:5 mentions "praise" or "commendation" given to human beings by God.

epainos also means "praise" in the context of adoration given to God (Rom 2:29; Eph 1:6, 12, 14; Phil 1:11; 1 Pet 1:7).

epaineō ἐπαινέω 1867

epaineō is the verb from which ***epainos*** (above) is derived, meaning "commend," "offer praise." The term is found in only five places, four of which indicate the human attitude of "commending." Two of these speak of positive commendation (Luke 16:8; 1 Cor 11:2). In 1 Cor 11:17, 22, the apostle Paul refuses to commend the Corinthian congregation, on account of their carnality. Rom 15:11 is the only text in which ***epaineō*** indicates giving praise to God.

ainesis αἴνεσις 133

ainesis is a noun derived from ***aineō*** (above) referring to "praise" offered to God in Heb 13:5.

hymneō ὑμνέω 5214

hymneō is a verb expressing the underlying sense of "singing." It occurs only four times, referring explicitly to "singing praise" to God in Acts 16:25; Heb 2:12. It speaks implicitly of "singing praise" to God in Matt 26:30; Mark 14:26, with reference to "singing hymns."

▸ **37.** Music, Singing, Dancing > HYMN
▸ **37.** Music, Singing, Dancing > SING, SONG

PROPITIATION

hilasmos ἱλασμός 2434

The noun ***hilasmos*** is found only twice. 1 John 2:2; 4:10 refer to the "propitiation" affected by the sacrificial death of Christ on the cross, whose atoning work eradicated the sin of human beings and appeased the wrath of God.

hilastērion ἱλαστήριον 2435

hilastērion is found only three times in the NT. Each occurrence has a great deal of theological significance and refers to the "atoning sacrifice" of Jesus Christ. It is this sacrifice that paid the penalty for the sins of the people of God in their entirety — past, present, and future. This substitutionary atonement appeased, or "propitiated," the wrath of God once and for all (Rom 3:25; 1 John 2:2; 4:10).

▸ **34.** Craftsmanship, Artisanship, Furniture, Implements > THRONE

SACRIFICE

thysia θυσία 2378

thysia is a noun found in approximately thirty places, meaning "sacrifice" in a variety of contexts.

General references to the ritual of sacrifice include those in Phil 2:17; Heb 10:26. In Matt 9:13; 12:7; Mark 12:33; Heb 10:5, 8, the ritual of sacrifice is subordinated to demonstrating a merciful, compassionate spirit towards others, and a genuine love for God. Metaphorical references to a "sacrifice" of praise to God that is pleasing to him are found in Heb 13:15, 16.

References to sacrificial ritual under the old covenant are found in Luke 2:24; Acts 7:41, 42; Heb 11:4. In particular, Heb 5:1; 7:27; 8:3; 9:9 all refer to the priestly role in offering sacrifices under the Mosaic law. Heb 10:1, 11 point out that the old covenant was utterly incapable — by deliberate divine intention — of removing sin and making perfect those who offered sacrifices.

The presentation of sacrificial offerings in the NT era is noted in Luke 13:1; 1 Cor 10:18. In the latter text, idolatrous sacrifice is in view.

The superior quality of new covenant offerings is affirmed in Heb 9:23, speaking of "better sacrifices." In significant metaphorical language, Paul exhorts believers to present their whole lives as "living sacrifices" to God (Rom 12:1; 1 Pet 2:5). See also Phil 4:18. Christ's work of atonement is designated as a "sacrifice" to God in Eph 5:2, supremely effective in doing away with sin (Heb 9:26; 10:12).

thyō θύω 2380

thyō is a verb found fourteen times, referring to the action of "sacrificing" or "slaughtering" for sacrifice in about half of these contexts.

thyō refers to the sacrifice of the Passover lamb (Mark 14:12; Luke 22:7); pagan sacrifice (Acts 14:13; 1 Cor 10:20); and to Christ as the lamb sacrificed for the sins of his people (1 Cor 5:7).

▸ **21.** Die, Perish, Kill, Destroy > KILL, MURDER, SLAY, SLAUGHTER

eidōlothyton εἰδωλόθυτον 1494

eidōlothyton is an adjectival form used nominally with the sense of "that which is offered in sacrifice to idols," usually in reference to food.

Gentile believers are prohibited from consuming food that had undergone such a ritual (Acts 15:29; 21:25). See also Rev 2:14, 20.

Paul considers that eating such food, however, is a matter for one's individual conscience (1 Cor 8:1ff.; 10:28). See also 1 Cor 10:19.

▸ **41.** Sacrifice, Offering, Worship, Praise > IDOL, IDOLATRY, IDOLATER

▸ **41.** Sacrifice, Offering, Worship, Praise > OFFERING

SERVE, SERVICE, WORSHIP

latreuō λατρεύω 3000

latreuō is a verb found about twenty times, meaning "serve" in the primary sense of "worship, or officiate in a ritual ceremony."

latreuō refers to "serving" or worshiping God in general terms in Matt 4:10; Luke 1:74; Acts 26:7; Rom 1:9; Phil 3:3; 2 Tim 1:3; Heb 9:14; 12:28. The contrasting activity of "serving" idols is indicated in Acts 7:42; Rom 1:25.

In particular, ***latreuō*** refers to "serving" at the temple, indicating the process of conducting and guiding worship there (Acts 7:42; Rom 1:25).

latreia λατρεία 2999

latreia is a noun derived from ***latreuō*** (above). It occurs five times, only in ceremonial contexts, and means "service" or "worship" (John 16:2; Rom 9:4; Heb 9:1, 6). Rom 12:1 contains a metaphorical ceremonial reference, as Paul exhorts his readers to present themselves as living sacrifices to God as an expression of reasonable "worship."

proskyneō προσκυνέω 4352

The verb ***proskyneō*** is found in sixty-five places, meaning "worship" throughout, in various contexts.

Worship offered to God by human beings is indicated in John 4:20ff.; 1 Cor 14:25; Rev 4:10; 5:14; 7:11; 11:16; 14:7; 15:4; 19:4, 10. Various people offer worship to the infant Christ in Matt 2:2ff. See also Heb 1:6. Christ is also portrayed as the object of worship in Matt 8:2; 14:33; Mark 5:6; John 9:38. Satan attempts, without success, to entice Christ to worship him in Matt 4:9; Mark 4:7. Idolatrous worship is undertaken in Rev 9:20; 13:4ff.; 14:9ff.; 16:2; 19:20; 20:4; 22:9.

There are general commands for all to "worship" God alone in Matt 4:10; Mark 4:8. Worship, incorporating the action of "bowing or kneeling down" before Christ, is indicated in Matt 18:26; 20:20; Mark 15:19.

sebomai σέβομαι 4576

sebomai is a verb found in ten places meaning "to worship." It also has the adjectival sense of "devout."

The act of worshiping God is indicated in Acts 16:4; 18:7, 13; and "vain worship" is noted in Matt 15:9; Mark 7:7. The idolatrous worship of the created order is noted in Rom 1:25. See also Acts 19:27.

Believers are described as "devout" or "God-fearing" in Acts 13:50; 17:4, 17.

▸ **61.** Integrity, Innocence, Piety > DEVOUT

eusebeō εὐσεβέω 2151

eusebeō is a rare verb meaning "to worship" in Acts 17:23 in connection with the "unknown god" of the Athenians. 1 Tim 5:4 refers to "practicing religious observance."

ethelothrēskeia ἐθελοθρησκία 1479

ethelothrēskeia is a rare noun found only in Col 2:23, referring to "arbitrary, self-imposed worship," which is formulated not for the glory of God but for one's own self-glorification. As such, it is condemned by the apostle.

sebasma σέβασμα 4574

sebasma is a rare noun found only in Acts 17:23; 2 Thess 2:4, denoting an "object of worship." Idolatry is involved in both instances.

theosebēs θεοσεβής 2318

theosebēs is a rare adjective denoting anyone "who worships God." It is found only in John 9:31.

proskynētēs προσκυνητής 4353

proskynētēs is a rare noun denoting a "worshiper" of God in John 4:23.

thrēskeia θρησκεία 2356

thrēskeia is a noun indicating "religion," "religious worship." It is found in four places.

Pure "religion" is commended in Jas 1:26, 27; and the "religion" of the Pharisees is noted in Acts 26:5, in relation to Paul's pre-conversion vocation. Col 2:18 refers to the ritualistic "religious worship" of angels.

SMELL, AROMA

euōdia εὐωδία 2175

euōdia is a rare noun found in three places, referring metaphorically to a "sweet smell" or "fragrant aroma." 2 Cor 2:15 refers to believers as a "sweet aroma" of Christ to God. Eph 5:2 declares that Christ gave himself as a "fragrant offering" to God. Gifts from the Philippian church are described as a "fragrant offering" to God (Phil 4:18).

SEE ALSO

▸ **17.** Senses, Actions, Abilities, Disabilities > SMELL ***osphrēsis***

SPRINKLE

rhantizō ῥαντίζω 4472

rhantizō is a verb meaning to "sprinkle" in all four occurrences of the term.

In relation to the sprinkling of blood, ***rhantizō*** refers to the sin offering (Heb 9:13); to the covenant ratification ceremony (Heb 9:19); and to hearts "sprinkled clean" from an evil conscience (Heb 10:22). See also Heb 9:21.

rhantismos ῥαντισμός 4473

rhantismos is a noun derived from ***rhantizō*** (above) found only twice. Heb 12:24; 1 Pet 2:5 refer to the "sprinkled" blood of Christ that has eradicated sin once and for all.

TITHE, PAYMENT

dekatoō δεκατόω 1183

dekatoō is a verb found in only two contexts. It means "to receive tithes" in Heb 7:6, referring to the gift Abraham gave to Melchizedek, king of Salem (Gen 14:18ff.). It means to "pay tithes" in Heb 7:9, referring symbolically to the "tithes paid" by Levi (the great-grandson of Abraham) to one greater than Abraham — Melchizedek, who typologically represents Christ as the eternal high priest.

apodekatoō ἀποδεκατόω 586

apodekatoō is a verb found in four places meaning "to give, pay a tithe," all in the context of worship (Matt 23:23; Luke 11:42; 18:12; Heb 7:5).

TREASURY

korbanas κορβᾶν 2878

korbanas refers to the "sacred treasury" of the temple in Matt 27:6. It also indicates a gift to God, referred to as "corban" in Mark 7:11.

gazophylakion γαζοφυλάκιον 1049

gazophylakion is a noun referring five times to the "treasury" of the temple (Mark 12:41ff.; Luke 21:1; John 8:20).

SEE ALSO

▸ **30.** Money, Business, Wealth, Poverty > TREASURE
thēsauros, thēsaurizō, gaza

42. Prayer, Intercession, Fasting

FAST, FASTING

nēsteia νηστεία 3521

nēsteia is a noun denoting the practice of "fasting" in eight places (Matt 17:21; Mark 9:29; Luke 2:37; Acts 14:23; 1 Cor 7:5; 2 Cor 6:5; 11:27). In particular, Acts 27:9 refers to the "fast" associated with the Day of Atonement festival.

nēsteuō νηστεύω 3522

nēsteuō is a verb found around twenty times with the consistent meaning "to fast."

Jesus' own "fasting" in the wilderness prior to the beginning of his public ministry is noted in Matt 4:2.

Elsewhere, ritual "fasting" is indicated in Matt 6:16ff.; 9:14ff.; Mark 2:18ff.; Luke 5:33ff.; 18:12; Acts 10:30; 13:2ff.

SEE ALSO

▸ **23.** Food, Drink, Cooking > FASTING
nēstis

INTERCEDE, INTERCESSION

entynchanō ἐντυγχάνω 1793

entynchanō means "intercede," "make intercession for," and "petition" in five contexts.

Acts 25:24 refers to the Jewish people petitioning Festus (the Roman procurator who succeeded Pontius Pilate in Judea), complaining of the evangelistic activities of the apostle Paul. Elsewhere, intercession is spoken of as the ministry of the Spirit of God in making the needs and requests of the saints known to God (Rom 8:27). Rom 11:2 refers to Elijah pleading with God against Israel (1 Kgs 19:10, 14). Rom 8:34; Heb 7:25 speak of the high priestly mediatorial role of Christ in heaven, who intercedes at God's right hand on our behalf.

hyperentynchanō ὑπερεντυγχάνω 5241

This verb is a variation of ***entynchanō*** (above). ***hyperentynchanō*** occurs only in Rom 8:26, where it refers to the Spirit of God interceding for his people when they find it very difficult to pray in times of suffering.

enteuxis ἔντευξις 1783

enteuxis is a rare noun derived from ***entynchanō*** (above) and occurring twice. In 1 Tim 2:1 it refers to the need for Timothy, as an elder, to pray for all people, making intercession for them before God. In 1 Tim 4:5, ***enteuxis*** refers to consecrating God's created order through prayer, as well as through the word of God.

▸ **42.** Prayer, Intercession, Fasting > PRAY, PRAYER

PRAY, PRAYER

proseuchomai προσεύχομαι 4336

proseuchomai is the most common verb in the NT referring to the activity of praying. It is translated "to pray," "offer prayer" in each of its nearly ninety occurrences.

General references to prayer are found in Matt 24:20; Mark 11:24ff.; Luke 1:10; Acts 9:11; 22:17; 1 Cor 11:4ff.; 14:13ff. Other texts allude to the posture of praying, as in Matt 6:5ff.; 1 Tim 2:8. A prescribed paradigm for praying is indicated with regard to the "Lord's Prayer," as recorded in Luke 11:2.

Exhortations to pray are found in Mark 13:18; Eph 6:18; 1 Thess 5:17; Jude 20. In particular, Jesus exhorts his followers to pray for those who persecute them (Matt 5:44; Luke 6:28).

proseuchomai also refers to praying for guidance (Acts 1:24); praying for the healing of the sick (Jas 5:13ff.); and intercessory prayer (Rom 8:26; Phil 1:9; Col 1:3, 9; 4:3; 2 Thess 1:11; 3:1; Heb 13:8). Praying as an act of commissioning for ministry, associated with the laying on of hands, is indicated in Acts 6:6; 8:15; 13:3; 14:23. Hypocritical praying is condemned in Matt 23:14; Mark 12:40; Luke 20:47.

A number of texts refer to Jesus praying (Matt 14:23; Mark 1:35; 6:46; Luke 3:21; Luke 5:16; 6:12; 9:18). The most dramatic and poignant of these episodes is the agony of Jesus' prayer in the garden of Gethsemane the night before his crucifixion. Matt 19:13 refers specifically to Jesus praying for the sick in order to bring about their healing (see also Paul in Acts 28:8).

proseuchē προσευχή 4335

proseuchē is the noun derived from ***proseuchomai*** (above) and means "prayer" in all thirty-seven occurrences of the term.

General references to prayer are found in Matt 17:21; Acts 2:42; Rom 1:9; 1 Cor 7:5; Eph 1:16; 1 Pet 3:7.

Prayer associated with temple worship is recorded in Matt 21:13; Mark 11:17; Luke 19:46; Acts 3:1. A number of contexts refer to intercessory prayer (Acts 12:5; Eph 6:18; Phil 4:6; Col 4:12; 1 Thess 1:2; 1 Tim 2:1; Phlm 4, 22; Jas 5:17). In particular, the intercessory prayers of the saints are indicated in Rev 5:8; 8:3, 4. An exhortation to pray is contained in Col 4:2. Acts 16:13, 16 refer to a "place of prayer" beside the river in Philippi. There were so few Jews in the city, specifically an insufficient number of men, that a synagogue could not be established. References to Jesus' prayer life are found in Luke 6:12; 22:45.

euchomai εὔχομαι 2172

euchomai is a verb related to ***proseuchomai*** (above), but it occurs far less frequently. ***euchomai*** occurs seven times and means "pray," "wish." In five contexts, ***euchomai*** refers to the action of earnest, intercessory prayer (Acts 27:29; 2 Chr 13:7, 9; Jas 5:16; 3 John 2).

euchē εὐχή 2171

euchē is a rare term, found only three times. Twice it refers to a "vow," and once, in Jas 5:15, to a "prayer" of faith.

▸ **67.** Acknowledge, Confess, Profess, Swear > VOW

enteuxis ἔντευξις 1783

enteuxis is another rare noun meaning "prayer," referring to intercessory prayer (1 Tim 2:1) and to prayer in a general sense (1 Tim 4:5).

▸ **42.** Prayer, Intercession, Fasting > INTERCEDE, INTERCESSION

deomai δέομαι 1189

deomai is a verb with the underlying meanings "beseech," "beg," "make a request." These senses account for more than half of its twenty-two occurrences. In nine places, however, ***deomai*** specifically indicates the offering up of intercessory prayer (Matt 9:38; Luke 10:2; 21:36; 22:32; Acts 4:31; 8:22, 24; 10:2; 1 Thess 3:10).

deēsis δέησις 1162

deēsis is a noun derived from ***deomai*** (above) meaning "prayer," "entreaty" in each of its nineteen occurrences.

Prayer in a general sense is indicated in Luke 5:33; Acts 1:14; Rom 10:1; 2 Cor 1:11; 9:14. Prayers of entreaty or "supplication" are mentioned in Eph 6:18; Phil 4:6; 1 Tim 2:1; 5:5; Jas 5:6. Heb 5:7 refers to the supplication of Christ. Intercessory prayer is indicated in Phil 1:4, 9; 2 Tim 1:3. Prayer associated with worship is noted in Luke 2:37, and prayer heard and accepted by God in Luke 1:13; 1 Pet 3:12.

▸ **42.** Prayer, Intercession, Fasting > SUPPLICATION

SUPPLICATION

deēsis δέησις 1162

deēsis is a noun meaning "prayer" or "supplication" in most of its nineteen occurrences (Acts 1:14; Eph 6:18; Phil 4:6; 1 Tim 2:1; 5:5).

▸ **42.** Prayer, Intercession, Fasting > PRAY, PRAYER

hiketēria ἱκετηρία 2428

hiketēria is a rare noun found only in Heb 5:7 with reference to "supplication" or "earnest prayer" offered by Christ to God during his time on earth.

43. Prophecy, Preaching, Proclamation

AMBASSADOR

presbeuō πρεσβεύω 4243

presbeuō is a rare verb meaning "to act as an ambassador." It is found only twice, in 2 Cor 5:20; Eph 6:20, both referring to Paul as a representative of the gospel of Christ.

SEE ALSO

▸ **31.** Kingdom, Empire, Rule, Military, Warfare > DELEGATION
presbeia

GOSPEL, GOOD NEWS

euangelion εὐαγγέλιον 2098

euangelion is the distinctive NT Greek term for the "gospel," the good news of the consummation of God's plan of salvation, forgiveness for sin and promise of eternal life and peace with God gained through the sacrifice of Jesus Christ. The term occurs nearly eighty times and is used with several distinctive nuances.

The "gospel" of the kingdom (of God), emphasizing the omnipotent rule or control of God over his people, is noted in Matt 4:23; 24:14; Mark 1:14. The message of the "gospel" in an unqualified sense is described in Matt 26:13; Mark 8:35; 16:15; Acts 15:7; Rom 10:16; 1 Cor 4:15; 15:1; Gal 1:11; Eph 1:13; Phil 1:5ff.; Col 1:5; Rev 14:6.

References to the "gospel of (Jesus) Christ" are found in Mark 1:1; Rom 1:16; 15:19; 1 Cor 9:12; 2 Cor 2:12; Gal 1:7; 1 Thess 3:2; 2 Thess 2:14. Acts 20:24 mentions the "gospel of the grace of God," emphasizing the merciful expression of divine compassion in effecting the salvation of his people.

General references to the "gospel of God" are found in Rom 1:1; 15:16; 2 Cor 11:7; 1 Thess 2:2; 1 Pet 4:17; to the "gospel of his (i.e., God's) Son" in Rom 1:9; and to the "gospel of peace" in Eph 6:15. In a negative context, Paul condemns Jewish false teachers who are proclaiming a "false gospel" and deceiving many (Gal 1:6).

The phrase "mystery of the gospel" in Eph 6:19 refers to the hidden nature of God's plan of salvation prior to the revelation of Jesus Christ, now proclaimed by the apostle Paul.

euangelizō εὐαγγελίζω 2097

euangelizō is the verb corresponding to ***euangelion*** (above). It is found nearly sixty times, with the primary meaning "preach the gospel" throughout most of the usage (approximately fifty occurrences) — for example, Matt 11:5; Luke 4:18; 8:1; Acts 8:25; 14:21; 2 Cor 11:7; Gal 1:11; 4:13; Heb 4:2, 6; 1 Pet 1:12; 4:6; Rev 14:6. Then Gal 1:8ff. refers to the "proclamation" of a false gospel.

euangelizō is also translated to "bring, preach good news" (1 Thess 3:6).

In many of these contexts, however, the sense of "gospel" is implied (Luke 1:19; 2:10; 16:16; Acts 8:12; Rom 1:15; 1 Cor 1:17; 9:16ff.; 15:1ff.).

In addition, ***euangelizō*** is also simply translated "to preach." In Acts 5:42; 8:35; 17:18, Jesus is the direct object of the verb.

"Preaching the word" is indicated in Acts 8:4; 15:35. "Preaching" Christ is noted in Eph 3:8. See also Gal 1:23; Eph 2:17.

▸ **43.** Prophecy, Preaching, Proclamation > PREACH, PREACHING

PREACH, PREACHING

kēryssō κηρύσσω 2784

kēryssō is a verb meaning "preach." The underlying sense is that of making proclamation after the manner of a herald. ***kēryssō*** is found in approximately sixty contexts.

General references to preaching are found in Mark 13:10; Luke 24:47; Rom 2:21; 10:8, 14ff.; Gal 2:2; Col 1:23; 2 Tim 4:2; 1 Pet 3:19.

kēryssō describes the preaching ministry of John the Baptist (Matt 3:1; Mark 1:4ff.; Luke 3:3; Acts 10:37); Jesus' preaching activity (Matt 4:17, 23; 11:1; Mark 1:14, 39; Luke 4:18ff.; 8:1); and the apostolic proclamation of the gospel (Matt 10:7; Mark 3:14; Luke 9:2; Acts 8:5; 19:13; 20:25).

The usage of ***kēryssō*** indicates that Christ is the focus of NT preaching (1 Cor 1:23; 15:12; 2 Cor 1:19; 4:5; 11:4; Phil 1:15; 1 Tim 3:16).

kērygma κήρυγμα 2782

kērygma is a noun derived from ***kēryssō*** (above) meaning "preaching" in all eight occurrences of the term. ***kērygma*** refers to the content of the proclamation of God's word in the OT and the gospel of Christ in the NT.

kērygma refers to the preaching of Jonah (Matt 12:41; Luke 11:32); to the "preaching of Jesus Christ" (i.e., Jesus as the content of the preaching) (Rom 16:25); and to the apostolic preaching of the gospel (1 Cor 1:21; 2:4; 15:14; 2 Tim 4:17; Titus 1:3).

euangelizō εὐαγγελίζω 2097

euangelizō is a synonym for ***kēryssō*** (above), likewise meaning "preach" in all of the fifty-five contexts in which it occurs. ***euangelizō*** conveys the sense of "proclaiming or bringing the good news" of God's plan of salvation, culminating in the person and work of Christ.

The general sense of preaching the gospel, or bringing good news, is indicated in Luke 1:19; 2:10; Acts 13:32; Rom 10:15; 1 Thess 3:6; 1 Pet 1:12; Rev 14:6.

euangelizō refers to Jesus' own preaching to his people in general terms (Luke 3:18; 4:18; 7:22; 20:1); and specifically to his proclamation of the kingdom of God (e.g., Luke 4:43; 8:1; Acts 8:12). Matt 11:5 refers specifically to preaching to the poor.

The apostolic preaching of Christ is indicated in Luke 9:6; Acts 5:42; 8:4, 25, 35; Rom 1:15; 1 Cor 1:17; 9:16ff.; 2 Cor 11:7; Gal 1:8ff. A variation on this theme is found in Eph 2:17, which mentions the preaching of peace.

▸ **43.** Prophecy, Preaching, Proclamation > GOSPEL, GOOD NEWS

diangellō διαγγέλλω 1229

diangellō is a verb found in only three places with the underlying sense of "declare." However, in Luke 9:60; Rom 9:17, ***diangellō*** conveys the specific meaning "preach" or "proclaim" with respect to the kingdom of God and the name of Yahweh, respectively.

katangellō καταγγέλλω 2605

katangellō is a verb found ten times with the predominant sense of "preach" or "proclaim."

The preaching of the resurrection of Christ is noted in Acts 4:2; 17:3. Proclaiming the gospel, preaching Christ, is indicated in 1 Cor 9:14; Phil 1:16, 18; Col 1:28. ***katangellō*** also refers specifically to "preaching" the word of God (Acts 13:5; 15:36; 17:13; 1 Cor 2:1); the forgiveness of sins (Acts 13:38); the way of salvation (Acts 16:17; 17:23); the light of the Gentiles (Acts 26:23); and, finally, the declaration of the faith of the Roman believers (Rom 1:8).

parrēsiazomai παρρησιάζομαι 3955

parrēsiazomai is a verb with the predominant meaning "to speak boldly." In most of its nine occurrences, ***parrēsiazomai*** conveys the sense of "preaching boldly" in the name of Christ (Acts 9:27, 29; 14:3; 18:26; 19:8; Eph 6:20; 1 Thess 2:2).

▸ **47.** Show, Persuade, Confidence, Doubt > BOLD, BOLDNESS, BOLDLY, CONFIDENT, CONFIDENCE

laleō λαλέω 2980

laleō is a common verb occurring nearly three hundred times with the dominant sense of "speak." In five of these contexts, the explicit sense of "preaching" the word is indicated (Mark 2:2; Acts 16:6; Acts 8:25; 13:42; 14:25).

▸ **63.** Speak, Tell, Declare, Call > SAY, SPEAK

▸ **63.** Speak, Tell, Declare, Call > TELL

SEE ALSO

▸ **38.** Covenant, Law, Rites, Roles > PREACHER
kēryx

PROPHECY, PROPHESY, PROPHETIC

prophēteuō προφητεύω 4395

prophēteuō is a verb meaning "to be a prophet," "prophesy" in all thirty occurrences of the term.

There are general references to prophetic activity in Matt 7:22; 26:68; Mark 14:65; Luke 22:64; Rev 10:11. In John 11:51, Caiaphas prophesies that one man would die for the nation.

John the Baptist represents continuity with the OT prophetic tradition (Matt 11:13). ***prophēteuō*** refers to the activity of the old covenant prophets, including Isaiah (Matt 15:7; Mark 7:6) and the prophets in general (1 Pet 1:10). Prophetic ministry at the time of Christ's appearing is noted in Luke 1:67 with respect to Zechariah, the father of John the Baptist.

Acts 2:17, 18 cite the prophecy uttered in Joel 2:28 regarding the outpouring of the Holy Spirit on all "flesh." Prophetic activity as a consequence of Holy Spirit baptism is noted in Acts 19:6; and the ministry of prophets in the first-century church is referred to in Acts 21:9; 1 Cor 11:4ff.; 13:9; 14:1ff., 39.

prophēteia προφητεία 4394

prophēteia is the primary noun meaning "prophecy" in the NT. It occurs nineteen times.

The prophecy of Isaiah is indicated in Matt 13:14. There are a number of references to the gift of prophecy in the new covenant community (Rom 12:6; 1 Cor 12:10; 13:2, 8; 14:6, 22; 1 Thess 5:20; 1 Tim 1:18; 4:14). The "prophecy of Scripture" in a general sense is indicated in 2 Pet 1:20ff. Rev 19:10 speaks of the "spirit of prophecy" in relation to Jesus.

The book of Revelation is itself described as a "prophecy" (Rev 1:3; 22:7ff.); and the prophesying activity of the visionary prophets in Revelation is noted in Rev 11:6.

prophētikos προφητικός 4397

prophētikos is an adjectival form meaning "prophetic." The term is rare, found only twice (Rom 16:26; 2 Pet 1:19) in relation to the "prophetic word."

SEE ALSO

▸ **38.** Covenant, Law, Rites, Roles > PROPHET
prophētēs, prophētis, pseudoprophētēs

SPREAD

dianemō διανέμω 1268

dianemō is a verb occurring only once, in Acts 4:17, in relation to "spreading" the message of the Christian gospel.

SEE ALSO

▸ **63.** Speak, Tell, Declare, Call > SPREAD
diaphēmizō

▸ **79.** Throw, Send, Drive, Mix, Remove > SPREAD OUT
strōnnymi

44. Repentance, Forgiveness, Mercy, Redeem, Save

COVER, FORGIVE

epikalyptō ἐπικαλύπτω 1943

epikalyptō is a rare verb found in Rom 4:7, where it refers passively to the happy state of the person whose sins "are covered" (i.e., forgiven).

SEE ALSO

- ▸ **35.** Clothing, Adornment, Textiles > COVER, VEIL, CURTAIN, MANTLE ***katakalyptō, peribolaion***
- ▸ **64.** Reveal, Explain, Hiddenness, Secrecy > HIDE, CONCEAL, COVER ***synkalyptō***
- ▸ **85.** Movement, Position, State > COVER, COVER UP ***kalyptō, perikalyptō***

FORGIVE, FORGIVENESS, RELEASE

aphiēmi ἀφίημι 863

aphiēmi is a common verb occurring nearly 150 times with the meaning "to leave," with a variety of associated senses. This term is also translated "forgive" in about one-third of its occurrences.

A plea for God to "forgive" is found in Matt 6:12a; Luke 11:4a; Acts 8:22. However, people who do not forgive one another will not be offered forgiveness themselves (Mark 11:26). God's action of "forgiving" is noted in Matt 6:15; Mark 3:28; Jas 5:15; 1 John 1:9; 2:12.

References to the act of human forgiveness, including the requirement to forgive, are found in Matt 6:12b; 18:21ff.; Mark 11:25; Luke 11:4b; 17:3.

Jesus' right to forgive sin is recorded in Matt 9:2, 6; Mark 2:5ff.; Luke 5:20ff.; 7:49. At his crucifixion, Jesus asks God his Father to "forgive" those who were tormenting him (Luke 23:34).

General references to the act of "forgiving" are found in Matt 9:5; 12:31; Rom 4:7.

The sin of blaspheming the Holy Spirit is designated as the one sin that will not be forgiven, as noted in Matt 12:31ff.; Luke 12:10.

- ▸ **49.** Allow, Accept, Approve, Refuse > ALLOW
- ▸ **86.** Movement Toward or Away From > LEAVE, GO AWAY, LEAVE BEHIND, ABANDON

aphesis ἄφεσις 859

aphesis is the noun derived from ***aphiēmi*** (above), denoting "forgiveness (of sin)" in all but one occurrence.

One of the specific purposes for which Jesus was to die, the forgiveness of people's sins, is recorded in Matt 26:28; Acts 5:31.

John's baptism was designed as a ritual of repentance leading to forgiveness of sin, as noted in Mark 1:4; Luke 3:3.

Those who blaspheme against the Holy Spirit are denied "forgiveness" (Mark 3:29). Heb 9:22 affirms that without the shedding of blood there can be no "forgiveness" of sins.

References to the "forgiveness of sins" for the people of God, granted through the person of Christ, are found in Luke 1:77; 24:47; Acts 10:43; 13:38; 26:18; Eph 1:7; Col 1:14; Heb 10:18. Exhortations to repent and be baptized for the "forgiveness" of sins are found in Acts 2:38.

aphesis denotes "release" for captives in Luke 4:18.

charizomai χαρίζομαι 5483

charizomai is synonymous with ***aphiēmi*** (above) and is found around twenty times, meaning "freely give" and "forgive." This term refers primarily to the act of forgiving in a human context, as indicated in Luke 7:42ff.; 2 Cor 2:7, 10; 12:13; Eph 4:32a; Col 3:13. This term also refers to God's act of "forgiving" the sin of his people in Eph 4:32; Col 2:13.

- ▸ **70.** Give, Take, Seize, Touch > GIVE, GIVE UP, GIVE OVER, GRANT

apolyō ἀπολύω 630

apolyō is a verb found in nearly ninety places with various meanings including "let go," "release," "divorce," "send," and "forgive." The latter use is rare, found only in Luke 6:37 with an injunction to "forgive" so that forgiveness might be received back.

- ▸ **25.** Family, Marriage, Adoption, Inheritance > DIVORCE
- ▸ **25.** Family, Marriage, Adoption, Inheritance > PUT AWAY
- ▸ **49.** Allow, Accept, Approve, Refuse > ALLOW
- ▸ **55.** Bondage, Captivity, Servitude > RELEASE
- ▸ **79.** Throw, Send, Drive, Mix, Remove > SEND, SEND AWAY, SEND OUT

GRACE, FAVOR

charitoō χαριτόω 5487

charitoō is a rare verb found only twice. In Luke 1:28 it is used adjectivally to refer to Mary as one "favored" by God. In Eph 1:6, God is said "to have freely granted" grace to his people through the person of Christ his Son.

charis χάρις 5485

charis is found about 150 times and denotes "favor," "grace," as well as having a variety of related nuances, throughout its usages. The large majority of occurrences indicate "grace" originating from God. This "grace" denotes the limitless kindness and mercy of God that is freely given to human beings undeserved.

The blessing of finding "favor" with God is noted in Luke 1:30; Acts 7:46. Jesus is explicitly said to have found "favor" with both God and human beings in Luke 2:52.

Specific references to the "grace of God" granted to human beings include those in Luke 2:40; John 1:16; Acts 4:33; 11:23; Rom 1:5; 2 Cor 6:1; Jude 4. In particular, God's "grace" is indicated as the specific catalyst initiating a person's salvation in Rom 3:24; 4:16; 5:15ff.; 11:5; Gal 5:4; Eph 1:7; 2:5ff.; Titus 2:11; 3:7.

Reference to Christ as the incarnate Word of God, "full of grace and truth," indicates that his being was full of divine goodness and favor intended for the blessing of God's people (John 1:14, 17; 1 Pet 1:13). Divine "grace" is also predicated of Jesus Christ in Acts 15:11; Gal 1:6; 2 Tim 2:1.

The "grace of God" is noted as part of a benediction in Rom 1:7; 1 Cor 1:3; 2 Cor 8:9; Gal 1:3; Eph 1:2; Phil 1:2; Col 1:2; 1 Thess 1:1; 1 Tim 1:2; Heb 13:25; 1 Pet 1:2; Rev 1:4; 22:21.

"Grace" in the sense of "divine enabling, or gift" is indicated in Rom 12:3ff.; 1 Cor 3:10; Eph 4:7; Heb 2:9; 1 Pet 4:10. "Favor" in the sense of "goodwill" among people is indicated in Acts 2:47; 7:10. "Favor" in the sense of an "act of kindness" is indicated in Acts 25:3; 2 Cor 8.

MERCY, MERCIFUL, COMPASSION, PITY

eleeō ἐλεέω 1653

eleeō occurs around thirty times meaning "to have mercy," "show mercy," again with the accompanying senses of "compassion" and "pity."

The practice of "showing mercy" is indicated in Rom 12:8. The obligation to show compassion or mercy is presented in the parable of the ungrateful servant, who received mercy from his master by canceling a huge debt, but who in turn failed to show the same compassion to a colleague who owed him a pittance (Matt 18:33).

The remaining uses of ***eleeō*** are found in contexts where the source of mercy is located in God or Jesus Christ. The beatitude of Matt 5:7 promises that mercy will be extended to those who are merciful to others. On a number of occasions, those who are diseased or disabled plead for mercy from Jesus during his earthly ministry — for example, those who are blind (Matt 9:27; 20:30ff.; Mark 10:47ff.; Luke 18:38ff.); and lepers (Luke 17:13). See also Matt 15:22; 17:15; Luke 16:24. Other recipients of divine mercy include the Gadarene demoniac exorcised by Jesus (Mark 5:19); and the apostle Paul (1 Tim 1:13, 16). Other texts speak of the sovereign divine exercise and initiative of mercy (Rom 9:15ff., "I will have mercy on whom I will have mercy . . ."; 11:30ff.; 1 Cor 7:25; 2 Cor 4:1; Phil 2:27; 1 Pet 2:10).

eleos ἔλεος 1656

eleos is the noun derived from ***eleeō*** (above) and has the primary sense of "mercy" that also includes "compassion," "kindness," "pity." ***eleos*** occurs in approximately thirty contexts and is likewise predicated of God and human beings.

Concerning human "mercy," God desires this quality to be manifested in the life of his people (Matt 9:13; 12:7). The crime of neglecting to show mercy, kindness, or compassion to others forms part of Jesus' condemnation of the Pharisees in Matt 23:23. The practice of showing mercy is mentioned in Luke 10:37; and commendation for doing so is indicated in Jas 2:13.

As far as God is concerned, his mercy is given to those who fear him (Luke 1:50ff.). The phrase "vessels of mercy" is found in Rom 9:23, referring to those people whom God has destined to be the recipients of his mercy and grace. The fact of divine mercy being granted to the Gentiles is indicated in Rom 11:31; 15:9. The invocation of divine mercy is found in Gal 6:16; 1 Tim 1:2; Jude 2; 2 Tim 1:2, 16, 18; Titus 1:4; Heb 4:16; 2 John 3. Mercy is affirmed as a quality of the divine being in Eph 2:4; Titus 3:5; Jas 3:17; 1 Pet 1:3; Jude 21.

eleēmōn ἐλεήμων 1655

eleēmōn is an adjectival form from ***eleeō*** and ***eleos*** (above) occurring only twice. In Matt 5:7 it refers to the blessed condition of those who are "merciful" by nature and who will in turn receive mercy from the Lord. Heb 2:17 refers to Jesus Christ as our merciful and faithful high priest.

oikteirō οἰκτείρω 3627

oikteirō is a synonym for ***eleeō*** and means "to have compassion or pity on." It is found only in Rom 9:15 and refers to the divine intervention and expression of compassion towards his chosen people: "I will have compassion on whom I will have compassion. . . ."

▸ **62.** Care For, Protect, Guard, Watch > COMPASSION

oiktirmos οἰκτιρμός 3628

oiktirmos is the noun derived from ***oikteirō*** (above) and is translated "mercy" or "compassion" in all five contexts in which it is found.

oiktirmos refers to the "mercies" of God (Rom 12:1; 2 Cor 1:13), and similarly to the kindness and compassion of Christ (Phil 2:1). Mercy as a godly quality is commended to the believer in a list of Christlike virtues in Col 3:12. Heb 10:28 refers to the penal sanction of the Mosaic covenant whereby a person found guilty of a capital offense under the law was put to death "without mercy" on the evidence of two or three witnesses.

oiktirmōn οἰκτίρμων 3629

oiktirmōn is the adjectival form derived from ***oikteirō*** and ***oiktirmos*** (above) occurring in only three places and meaning "merciful." Luke 6:36 contains the injunction to be merciful just as God is merciful; and Jas 5:11 affirms that God is both compassionate and "merciful."

hilaskomai ἱλάσκομαι 2433

hilaskomai is only found in two places and is translated "to be merciful" in Luke 18:13 with reference to the prayer of the tax-collector in the parable of Christ: "Be merciful to me a sinner . . ." In Heb 2:18, ***hilaskomai*** is translated "to make reconciliation, or expiation" for sins with reference to the atoning sacrifice of Christ on the cross.

▸ **27.** Community, Partnership, Unity, Discord > RECONCILE, RECONCILIATION, ATONEMENT

hileōs ἵλεως 2436

hileōs is an adjectival term that occurs only twice. In Heb 8:12 is it translated "merciful," with respect to God's compassionate determination to forgive the sins of his people. However, in Matt 16:22, the term is translated as an interjection: "Be it far from me."

RANSOM

lytron λύτρον 3083

lytron is a rare term, occurring only twice and meaning "ransom." In Matt 20:28; Mark 10:45, ***lytron*** refers to the "ransom" offered by Jesus Christ for the salvation of many — that is, he gave his life freely as a substitutionary sacrifice for sin.

antilytron ἀντίλυτρον 487

antilytron is a rare synonym for ***lytron*** (above) occurring only in 1 Tim 2:6 and referring to Jesus Christ offering himself as a "ransom" for all.

RECONCILE, MAKE PEACE

eirēnopoieō εἰρηνοποιέω 1517

eirēnopoieō occurs only in Col 1:20, meaning "to make peace" or "reconcile." The context here is the reconciliation of the world to God through the agency of Jesus Christ.

SEE ALSO

▸ **60.** Virtues > PEACE, PEACEFUL, QUIET
eirēneuō

▸ **74.** Safety, Peace, Danger, Escape > PEACE
eirēnē

REDEEM, REDEMPTION

exagorazō ἐξαγοράζω 1805

exagorazō is a verb found in only four places. It is translated "redeem" on each occasion, but with two distinct senses.

Gal 3:13; 4:5 refer to Christ "redeeming" his people from the curse of the law so as to reconcile them to God and remove the impact of divine judgment against them. The underlying sense here would appear to be that of "deliver" or "rescue" rather than "buy back."

In Eph 5:16; Col 4:5, ***exagorazō*** occurs in the expression "redeem the time" with the sense of "make the most of every opportunity" to serve the Lord, because the days are evil.

lytroō λυτρόω 3084

lytroō is a verb meaning "redeem." It is found in three contexts with the sense of "deliver" or "rescue" (as with ***exagorazō***; see above).

Luke 24:21 refers to Christ as the hoped-for redeemer of Israel. Titus 2:14 speaks more particularly of Christ's self-sacrifice, given to "redeem" his people from all iniquity. 1 Pet 1:18 refers to the unique manner of the believer's redemption, in that they have been "redeemed" or "delivered" from sin and death (implied here) by means of the shed blood of Christ on the cross. Being redeemed "not with perishable things such as silver and gold . . ." has given rise to the translation "ransom" for ***lytroō*** in this text, suggesting that the blood of Christ was the price paid in order to effect the release of his people from the penalty of sin. While this is a possible meaning, the context of the NT vocabulary for "redemption" does not give unambiguous support for such a rendering.

lytrōsis λύτρωσις 3085

lytrōsis is a noun derived from ***lytroō*** meaning "redemption" in all three occurrences of the term. In each case, the phenomenon of "salvation" (i.e., deliverance) is in view.

lytrōsis refers to the "redemption" of God's people in Heb 9:12 as having been secured by the blood of Christ. Luke 2:38 mentions the "redemption" of Jerusalem to be ultimately won by the power of God. Luke 1:68 speaks of the God of Israel having gained "redemption" for his people.

agorazō ἀγοράζω 59

agorazō is a verb with the literal sense of "buy," as in a commercial transaction, in the large majority of its nearly thirty occurrences. In several places, however, the term refers metaphorically to "purchasing" people for God by means of the blood of Christ's atoning sacrifice. 1 Cor 6:20; 7:23 both contain the expression "bought with a price" — a metaphorical reference to the successful impact of Christ's death on his people being released from the curse of sin and death (see also 2 Pet 2:1).

Rev 5:9 mentions Christ having "purchased" people for God with his blood — an unambiguous allusion to his substitutionary atonement for sin. See also Rev 14:3, 4.

▸ **30.** Money, Business, Wealth, Poverty > BUY, PURCHASE

apolytrōsis ἀπολύτρωσις 629

apolytrōsis is a noun closely related to ***lytrōsis*** (above). It occurs ten times, with the primary meaning "redemption" in the sense of "deliverance." It is synonymous with ***lytrōsis*** in Rom 8:23; 1 Cor 1:30; Eph 1:14; 4:30. "Deliverance" or "release" (i.e., from death) is explicitly indicated in Heb 11:35. The person of Christ and his shed blood are the sole means of accomplishing salvation for his people (Rom 3:24; Eph 1:7; Col 1:14; Heb 9:15).

REPENT

metanoeō μετανοέω 3340

metanoeō is a verb occurring around thirty-five times, meaning "repent" and referring exclusively to "turning from one's sin."

Matt 3:2; Mark 1:15; Luke 13:3, 5; Acts 2:38; 17:30; 26:30 contain exhortations to repent. General references to repenting are found in Luke 16:30; 17:3ff.; Rev 2:22. Luke 10:13; Matt 11:21 refer to a hypothetical repentance. Matt 12:41; Luke 11:32 speak of the repentance of the Ninevites under the preaching of Jonah. Luke 15:7ff. declares the joy in heaven at the repentance of a sinful person. ***metanoeō*** also refers to people's refusal or failure to repent (Matt 11:20; 2 Cor 12:21; Rev 2:21; 9:20, 21; 16:9, 11).

metanoia μετάνοια 3341

metanoia is a noun derived from ***metanoeō*** (above) found in approximately twenty-five contexts, referring exclusively to renouncing and turning from one's sin (with one possible exception).

The fruit of repentance are indicated in Matt 3:8; Luke 3:8. John's baptism for repentance is noted in Matt 3:11; Mark 1:4; Luke 3:3; Acts 13:24; 19:4. General references to repentance are found in Luke 5:32; 15:7; Acts 20:21; Rom 2:4; 2 Cor 7:9, 10; Heb 6:1; as is the preaching of repentance in Luke 24:47; Acts 26:20. Acts 5:31; 11:18; 2 Tim 2:5 speak of repentance as the gift of God to both Jew and Gentile alike. In contrast, the impossibility of repentance after apostasy is indicated in Heb 6:6. 2 Pet 3:9 indicates God's desire that all people should come to repentance, reflecting his divine benevolence.

One text may imply "repentance" as "a change of mind." Heb 12:17 refers to Esau's abortive attempt to reclaim the blessing he had voluntarily forfeited to his brother Jacob. Esau sought to "produce a change of mind" (i.e., presumably in his father, Isaac), though such was not forthcoming and he lost the blessing of the firstborn forever.

metamelomai μεταμέλομαι 3338

metamelomai is a synonym for ***metanoeō*** (above) found in six places. It means "to repent" in several different contexts.

It refers first of all to "changing one's mind" in Matt 21:29; 27:3. The latter text refers to Judas' decision to return the thirty pieces of silver (the price paid for the betrayal of Jesus) to the religious authorities. This was an action fraught with bitter regret, but it did not constitute godly repentance. Heb 7:21 speaks of God refusing to "change his mind" in regard to assigning to Christ an eternal priesthood after the order of Melchizedek.

metamelomai is also found in the context of refusing to repent of one's sins (Matt 21:32).

This term also expresses the attitude of "regret" in 2 Cor 7:8.

ametamelētos ἀμεταμέλητος 278

ametamelētos is an adjectival form derived from ***metamelomai*** (above) found only twice. In Rom 11:29 it refers to God's call as "irrevocable" (i.e., incapable of being altered). 2 Cor 7:10 refers to a repentance (i.e., ***metanoia,*** see above) that "leaves no regret."

RESCUE, DELIVER, SET FREE

eleutheroō ἐλευθερόω 1659

eleutheroō is a verb found twelve times with the predominant meaning "set free," with the sense of "being rescued, or delivered from."

John 8:32, 36 refer to "setting free" the believer from the darkness of unbelief. Rom 6:18, 22 affirm the experience of "being set free (i.e., delivered)" from the power and sentence of sin. Positively, Rom 8:2 affirms that the work of Jesus Christ "sets (people) free" from the law of sin and death. See also Gal 5:1. Rom 8:21 declares that creation "will be delivered" (i.e., liberated) from bondage to decay.

▸ **55.** Bondage, Captivity, Servitude > FREE, FREEDOM, SET FREE, LIBERTY

exaireō ἐξαιρέω 1807

exaireō is a verb found eight times with the predominant sense of "set free," "rescue," "deliver."

Acts 7:10 refers to Joseph, whom God "rescued" or "delivered" from his troubles. Acts 7:34 notes that God had intended to set Israel free from the Egyptian bondage. Peter reports that God "had set him free" from prison in Acts 12:11. See also Acts 26:17; 23:27. Gal 1:4 affirms that Christ's sacrificial death "has rescued" his people from the present evil age.

katargeō καταργέω 2673

katargeō is a verb with the primary meanings "destroy," "abolish," as well as related nuances, in about thirty places. In Rom 7:6, however, the term is used passively — affirming that believers "have been released" (i.e., delivered) from the law as a consequence of the redemptive work of Christ.

▸ **21.** Die, Perish, Kill, Destroy > ABOLISH, NULLIFY

rhyomai ῥύομαι 4506

The verb ***rhyomai*** means "deliver" throughout its nearly twenty occurrences.

Matt 6:13; Luke 11:4 record appeals to God to "deliver" his people from temptation. The act of rescuing from death is indicated in Matt 27:43; Luke 1:74; Rom 7:24. Then, the experience of being "rescued" from one's enemies is recorded in Rom 15:31; 2 Thess 3:2.

rhyomai is also used in a nominal sense denoting the "deliverer," with reference to the coming Messiah, in Rom 11:26.

Christ is said to "rescue" his people from the coming wrath in 1 Thess 1:10. References to God having "delivered" his people from the judgment of sin are found in 2 Cor 1:10; Col 1:13. 2 Cor 1:10; 2 Tim 4:18; 2 Pet 2:9 also promise deliverance.

lytrōtēs λυτρωτής 3086

lytrōtēs is a rare noun found only in Acts 7:35, referring to Moses as the "deliverer" of the Israelites from Egypt.

SEE ALSO

▸ **70.** Give, Take, Seize, Touch > DELIVER, DELIVER OVER, HAND OVER, BETRAY ***anadidōmi, epididōmi, paradidōmi***

SACKCLOTH

sakkos σάκκος 4526

sakkos is a noun found in only four contexts, all with reference to "sackcloth." Matt 11:21; Luke 10:13 mention the hypothetical repentance of ancient Sodom and Gomorrah "in sackcloth and ashes," had they witnessed the same kinds of miraculous signs given to the towns of Bethsaida and Chorazin, who rejected Jesus outright. Rev 16:12 refers metaphorically to the darkness of the sun at the end of time, likened to the blackness of "sackcloth." Rev 11:3 refers to sackcloth worn by the two witnesses, faithful to their Christian testimony to the point of death. In this context, wearing sackcloth expresses penitence for the sin of the people of God, as the two witnesses are identified as the priestly and royal intercessors for the people of God.

SAVE, SALVATION, SAVIOR

sōtēria σωτηρία 4991

sōtēria is the only NT term for "salvation," "deliverance." It occurs fifty times, with these meanings in the large majority of these texts. In each of these contexts, the salvation is predicated of God and/or Christ, either explicitly or implicitly.

General references to "salvation" include those in 2 Cor 7:10; Phil 1:19; 1 Thess 5:8; Heb 1:14; 6:9; 2 Pet 3:15. More explicit references to the salvation granted by God to his people are found in Luke 1:77; John 4:22; Acts 4:12; 13:26; Phil 1:28; 2 Thess 2:13. In particular, the consummate "day of salvation" is noted in 2 Cor 6:2. Other references to the salvation to be revealed at the end of time include those in Rom 13:11; 1 Pet 1:5, 9.

Particular references to salvation having come to God's people in the person of Christ are found in Luke 2:30; 19:9; 1 Thess 5:9; 2 Tim 2:10; 3:15; Heb 2:3, 10; 5:9; 9:28; 1 Pet 1:10; Jude 3. Acts 16:7 refers to the "way of salvation" in connection with the proclamation of the gospel of Christ. God and Christ are praised and glorified as the source of the salvation of their people in Rev 7:10; 12:10; 19:1.

The gospel is declared to be the power and vehicle of salvation in Rom 1:16; Eph 1:13.

Acts 13:47; 28:28 proclaim God's people to be the bearers of the message of salvation to the world at large. Rom 11:11; Titus 2:11 declare that salvation is to be granted to the Gentiles.

The expression "horn of salvation" refers metaphorically to Jesus Christ the Messiah in Luke 1:69. The "helmet of salvation" is mentioned as part of the believer's spiritual armor in Eph 6:13.

sōzō σῴζω 4982

sōzō is the most common verb in the NT meaning "save." The term occurs around 110 times in a variety of contexts, although the most common of these refers to being saved, or delivered, from the penalty of sin and death.

General references to "saving one's life," in the sense of preserving it, are found in Matt 16:25; Mark 3:4; 8:35; 9:24; Luke 17:33; 1 Tim 2:15; Jas 5:15.

The saving work of Jesus Christ is explicitly alluded to in Matt 1:21; 18:11; Luke 19:10 — referring to Christ as the one who saves his people, or the lost, from their sin. Christ expresses his intention to save the world — sinners — in John 12:47; 1 Tim 1:15. In other contexts, there is the taunt, directed at Christ on the cross, to "save himself" (Matt 27:40; Mark 15:30ff.; Luke 23:35ff.). Appeals to Christ for literal physical rescue are found in Matt 8:25; 14:30.

In relation to the great hope of the believer, a number of texts refer to "being saved" through the work of Christ, or being delivered from the penalty of sin and its terrible consequences (John 3:17; 10:9; Acts 4:12; Rom 5:9; 10:9; 1 Cor 1:18, 21; 2 Cor 2:15; Eph 2:5, 8; 2 Tim 1:9; Titus 3:5; Heb 7:25; 1 Pet 3:21). In contrast, the impossibility of "being saved" by the law of Moses is indicated in Acts 15:1.

Other contexts indicate the hope and reality of "being saved" by God, in the sense of being delivered from destruction and being granted eternal life (Matt 24:22; Mark 10:26; 13:20; Luke 7:50; Acts 2:47; 16:30; Rom 9:27; 11:14, 26; 1 Cor 3:15; 7:16; 1 Tim 2:4; 4:16; Jas 1:21; 5:20; Jude 5). Promises of deliverance or salvation are also found in Matt 10:22; 24:13; Mark 13:13, contingent on the believer enduring to the end.

▸ **20.** Illness, Disease, Health, Healing > HEAL, CURE

diasōzō διασῴζω 1295

diasōzō is a verb occurring eight times and meaning "escape," "bring to safety." It is with this sense that the term is translated "to save" in Acts 27:43, with reference to the plan to save Paul from being assassinated; and in 1 Pet 3:20, in relation to Noah and his family "having been saved" at the time of the great flood.

▸ **20.** Illness, Disease, Health, Healing > HEAL, CURE
▸ **74.** Safety, Peace, Danger, Escape > ESCAPE
▸ **74.** Safety, Peace, Danger, Escape > SAFE, SAFELY, SAFETY, SECURITY

sōtēr σωτήρ 4990

sōtēr is found in approximately twenty-five contexts and is consistently translated "savior" (as one who saves, delivers, or rescues).

Mary declares God to be "my Savior" in Luke 1:47; and his people declare God to be "our Savior" in Titus 1:3; 2:10; 3:4; 2 Pet 3:2; Jude 25.

Christ is declared to be the "Savior" of his people Israel (Luke 2:11; Acts 5:31; 13:23); of the world (John 4:42; 1 Tim 4:10; 1 John 4:14); and of the church (Eph 5:23). He is described as "our Savior" in 1 Tim 1:1; 2:3; 2 Tim 1:10. The title "Savior" in a general sense is recorded in Phil 3:20.

45. Faith, Belief, Trust, Promise

ASSURANCE

plērophoria πληροφορία 4136

plērophoria is a noun occurring four times, meaning "full assurance, conviction" in matters relating to the believer's hope of salvation (Col 2:2; 1 Thess 1:5; Heb 6:11; 10:22).

hypostasis ὑπόστασις 5287

hypostasis is a noun found in five contexts, most of which indicate the meaning "confidence," "assurance." Heb 3:14 speaks of the believer's confidence in Christ; and in Heb 11:1 "assurance" is linked with the definition of faith. See also 2 Cor 9:4; 11:17.

▸ **45.** Faith, Belief, Trust, Promise > CONFIDENCE

BELIEVE

pisteuō πιστεύω 4100

The verb ***pisteuō*** occurs around 250 times with the underlying meaning "believe." Included in this usage is the very significant nuance of "have faith, put one's trust in" the person of Christ, as the means by which God applies salvation to his people.

pisteuō most commonly means "believe" in reference to saving faith in Christ. Examples of this meaning include Matt 8:13; Mark 9:24; Luke 22:67; John 1:7; 3:15ff., 36; 4:39ff.; 6:29ff.; 7:38ff.; 11:25ff.; 16:27ff.; Acts 2:44; 4:4, 32; 11:17, 21; 15:5ff.; Rom 1:16; 4:24; 10:4ff.; 1 Cor 1:21; Gal 2:16; Eph 1:13; 1 Thess 2:10ff.; 1 Tim 3:16; 1 Pet 1:8; 2:6; 1 John 3:23; 5:1ff. The serious consequences of not believing in Christ are noted in John 10:26. References to Abraham's "belief" (i.e., his saving faith) in God as a model of genuine saving trust are found in Rom 4:3ff., 11, 17ff.; Gal 3:6, 22; Jas 2:23. Jesus commands belief in the gospel in Mark 1:15; John 10:38; 14:1. The need to believe in God for answer to prayer is expressed in Matt 21:22; Mark 11:23ff. Luke 1:45; 24:25; John 2:22 refer to believing in the prophetic word of God. Heb 11:6; Jas 2:19 address the need to believe in God. The command not to believe false teaching is found in Matt 24:26. General references to "believe" with the sense of "accept as true," both positive and negative, are found in Matt 21:32; Mark 16:13; 1 Cor 11:18; 13:7.

apisteō ἀπιστέω 569

apisteō is the negative form of ***pisteuō*** (above) and is found seven times with the meaning "not to believe" or "have no faith," "be unfaithful." The sense of "refuse to believe" in the gospel and/or the true significance of Christ and his works is found in Mark 16:11, 16; Acts 28:24. See also Luke 24:11, 41. The sense of "be unfaithful" to Christ and the gospel is indicated in Rom 3:3; 2 Tim 2:13.

apeitheō ἀπειθέω 544

apeitheō is a negative variant of ***peithō*** meaning "not to believe" and "be disobedient." The two occasionally overlap in meaning.

A refusal to believe in Christ is indicated in John 3:36; Acts 14:2; 17:5; 19:9; Rom 15:31; 1 Pet 2:7. The refusal to obey the word or truth of the gospel is indicated in Rom 2:8; 10:21; 11:30ff.; Heb 3:18; 11:31; 1 Pet 2:8; 3:1, 20; 4:17.

▸ **45.** Faith, Belief, Trust, Promise > UNBELIEF, UNBELIEVER, UNBELIEVING

▸ **54.** Rule, Authority, Command, Obedience > DISOBEY, DISOBEDIENCE, DISOBEDIENT

CONFIDENCE

pepoithēsis πεποίθησις 4006

pepoithēsis is a noun found six times and means "confidence," "trust."

Confidence (in the sense of certainty) is indicated in 2 Cor 1:5. Confidence or trust in human nature (i.e., "flesh") is noted in 2 Cor 8:22; 10:2; Phil 3:4. Confidence (i.e., hope, trust) in Christ is indicated in 2 Cor 3:4; Eph 3:12.

hypostasis ὑπόστασις 5287

hypostasis is a noun denoting "confidence," "assurance" in four of the five occurrences of the term.

"Confidence" associated with boasting is indicated in 2 Cor 9:4; 11:7. One's "confidence" (i.e., hope of salvation) in Christ is noted in Heb 3:14.

The "assurance" (i.e., certainty) of things hoped for is part of a definition of faith in Heb 11:1.

▸ **45.** Faith, Belief, Trust, Promise > ASSURANCE

CONFOUND, CONFUSE, CONFUSION

syncheō συγχέω 4797

syncheō is a verb found in five places with the underlying sense of "confound," "confuse," as well as a few related nuances.

The "bewilderment" of a crowd is indicated in Acts 2:6, denoting a "confused amazement." The newly converted Saul of Tarsus is said to have "confounded" the Jewish population of Damascus by proving that Jesus was the Christ.

The "confusion" of crowds elsewhere points to civil rioting and unrest (Acts 19:32; 21:27, 31).

▸ **27.** Community, Partnership, Unity, Discord > TROUBLE, UPROAR, RIOT

SEE ALSO

▸ **27.** Community, Partnership, Unity, Discord > CONFUSION, DISORDER
akatastasia, synchysis

CONVERSION

epistrophē ἐπιστροφή 1995

epistrophē is a rare noun found only in Acts 15:3, referring to the "conversion" of the Gentiles from their pagan religion to faith in Christ.

DOUBT

diakrinō δῐακρίνω 1252

diakrinō is a verb found over twenty times with the primary meaning "judge," "discern." In several places ***diakrinō*** also means "to doubt," referring in Matt 21:21; Mark 11:23 to the importance of "not doubting" the power of God. Jas 1:6; Rom 14:23 affirm that the person who doubts is condemned. See also Jude 22.

▸ **51.** Knowledge, Wisdom, Remember, Forget > JUDGE

distazō διστάζω 1365

distazō is a rare verb meaning "doubt" in relation to the wavering of one's faith and trust in God and Christ (Matt 14:31; 28:17).

FAITH, FAITHFULNESS

pistis πίστις 4102

pistis is the most common term denoting "faith" in the NT, with the underlying senses of "belief," "trust," and "conviction" in the person of God and Christ as the only means of salvation, forgiveness of sin, and guarantee of eternal life. In most cases, the meanings "belief" and "faith" are interchangeable.

The designation "faith" in the general sense of belief and trust in Christ or God is indicated in Matt 17:20; Luke 8:25; Acts 14:9, 27; Rom 1:8, 17; Eph 6:16; 1 Thess 3:2ff.; 1 Tim 1:19; 2 Tim 1:13; Titus 2:2; Heb 10:22; 11:1; Jas 1:3; 2:14ff.; 1 Pet 1:5ff.; 2 Pet 1:5.

The exercise of faith in Christ as a prerequisite for healing is noted in Matt 8:10; 9:29; 15:28; Mark 2:5; 10:52; Luke 5:20; Acts 3:16; and as the specific prerequisite for salvation in Acts 3:22ff.; Rom 5:1ff.; 10:17; 1 Cor 15:14ff.; Gal 2:16, 20; 3:2ff.; Eph 1:15; 2:8; Phil 3:9; Rev 14:12. Related to this is the corresponding quality of faith in God under the old covenant (Rom 4:5ff.; Gal 3:7; 1 Tim 3:13; Heb 11:2ff.). Heb 4:2 notes that this quality was totally lacking in the Israelite people when they first approached the borders of Canaan. Non-specific references to "faith" include those found in Matt 23:23; Acts 6:5; Rom 1:5; 14:1; 1 Cor 13:1, 13; 2 Cor 5:7.

Specific references to "the faith" as a designation for Christianity as a system of belief centered on the person of Christ are found in Acts 13:8; 14:22; 2 Cor 13:5; Gal 1:23; Eph 4:13; Phil 1:25ff.; Col 1:23; 2:7; 1 Tim 1:2; 4:1; 2 Tim 4:7; Titus 1:13; Jas 2:1; Jude 3; Rev 13:10. See also Eph 4:5. "Faith" is described specifically as a gift of God in 1 Cor 12:9.

pistis denotes "assurance" in the sense of the conviction of a certain outcome in relation to salvation in Acts 17:31.

The attribute of "faithfulness" is predicated of God in Rom 3:3; and is listed as a fruit of the Spirit in Gal 5:22.

The specific sense of "belief" in the truth of the gospel is indicated in 2 Thess 2:13.

oligopistos ὀλιγόπιστος 3640

oligopistos is a rare adjective found only in Matt 6:30 denoting doubting believers as people "of little faith."

FAITHFUL, FAITHLESS

pistos πιστός 4103

pistos is the standard adjectival term in the NT for "faithful," found about seventy times.

The meaning "faithful" in the sense of "devoted to duty" is predicated of servants in Matt 24:45; 25:21ff.; Luke 12:42; 16:10ff.; 1 Cor 4:2; 1 Tim 3:11; 1 Pet 5:12, and of Moses in Heb 3:5.

Believers who are "faithful" are described in Acts 16:15; 1 Cor 4:17; Eph 1:1; 6:21; Col 1:2, 7; 4:7ff.; 2 Tim 2:2; Titus 1:6; Rev 1:5; 2:10ff.; 3:14; 17:14. See also Gal 3:9; 1 Tim 1:12. God is described as "faithful," implying the consistent honoring of his promises, in 1 Cor 1:9; 10:13; 2 Cor 1:18; 1 Thess 5:24; 2 Tim 2:13; Heb 10:23; 11:11; 1 John 1:9. He is described as the "faithful" Creator in 1 Pet 4:19.

References to "faithful" or "sure" sayings are found in 1 Tim 1:15; 2 Tim 2:11; Rev 22:6.

Jesus Christ is described as a "faithful" high priest in Heb 2:17; and as a "faithful" Son to his Father in Heb 3:2; and he is given the name "Faithful" in Rev 19:11.

apistos ἄπιστος 571

apistos is an adjective found in around twenty contexts meaning "unfaithful," "faithless," "unbelieving" throughout.

▸ **45.** Faith, Belief, Trust, Promise >
UNBELIEF, UNBELIEVER, UNBELIEVING

FALL AWAY, APOSTATIZE, APOSTASY

parapiptō παραπίπτω 3895

parapiptō is a rare verb found only in Heb 6:6, referring to those who "fall away" or "commit apostasy."

aphistēmi ἀφίστημι 868

aphistēmi is a verb meaning "draw away," "depart" in most of its fifteen occurrences. However, in Luke 8:13 the term refers to those who hear the word of God with initial eagerness but then "fall away" from the faith in a time of temptation.

▸ **86.** Movement Toward or Away From >
LEAVE, GO AWAY, LEAVE BEHIND, ABANDON

apostasia ἀποστασία 646

apostasia is a rare noun denoting "apostasy," or rebellion against God, and is found only twice. Acts 21:21 contains the accusation against Paul, charging him with inciting Jewish people literally to "teach rebellion" against Moses, dissuading them from having their children circumcised. 2 Thess 2:3 refers to the anticipated "apostasy" or "rebellion" of the last days when many would abandon the faith.

GUARANTEE

engyos ἔγγυος 1450

engyos is a rare term found only in Heb 7:22, designating Jesus Christ as the "guarantee" (i.e., the pledge) of a better covenant.

arrabōn ἀρραβών 728

arrabōn is found in only three places and denotes the Holy Spirit's outpouring in the hearts of new covenant believers as the "guarantee" (i.e., deposit, down payment) of one's eternal inheritance in the kingdom of heaven (2 Cor 1:22; 5:5; Eph 1:14).

▸ **30.** Money, Business, Wealth, Poverty > DEPOSIT, PLEDGE, EARNEST

PROMISE

epangelia ἐπαγγελία 1860

epangelia is a noun that is consistently translated "promise" in the fifty or so contexts in which it is found. ***epangelia*** is usually concerned with promises given by God.

In the context of giving divine promises, ***epangelia*** refers, for example, to the promised coming of the Spirit (Luke 24:49; Acts 1:4; 2:33, 39; Gal 3:14; Eph 1:13); and to the covenant promises made to Abraham (Acts 7:17; Rom 4:13ff.; Heb 6:15ff.; 7:6; 11:9, 17). In particular, Rom 9:8ff.; Gal 3:16ff.; 4:23, 28; Eph 2:12 indicate that all believers are to be reckoned as spiritual descendants of Abraham. Other contexts speak of the covenant promises given to the patriarchs and the heroes of the faith (Acts 26:6; Rom 9:4; 15:8; Heb 11:13, 33, 39). See also 2 Cor 7:1; Eph 6:2. Reflections on the promise of heavenly rest are found in Heb 8:6; 9:15; 10:36.

The promise of the savior, referring to Christ himself, is indicated in Acts 13:23, 32; 2 Cor 1:20; Gal 3:22; Eph 3:6; 2 Tim 1:1. The promise of Jesus' return is affirmed in 2 Pet 3:4, 9. Heb 4:1; 6:12 speak of the promise of entering heavenly rest; and 1 John 2:25 mentions the promise of eternal life.

A general reference to promises made by people is found in Acts 23:21; and a reference is made to an undefined promise in 1 Tim 4:8.

epangellomai ἐπαγγέλλομαι 1861

epangellomai is a verb meaning "to promise" in most of the fifteen occurrences of the term.

As with the noun ***epangelia*** (above), ***epangellomai*** refers primarily to promises made by God. Heb 10:23 contains a general reference to such activity. A number of texts refer to the covenant promise made to Abraham (Acts 7:5; Rom 4:21; Gal 3:19; Heb 6:13; 11:11). Eternal life is pronounced by God in Titus 1:2; Jas 1:12; 1 John 2:25. Heb 12:26 refers to judgment against the wicked, promised by God. Mark 14:11 mentions promises made by people, in general terms.

proepangellomai προεπαγγέλλομαι 4279

proepangellomai is a verb found only in Rom 1:2, meaning "to promise beforehand" and referring to God's revelation through the prophets.

homologeō ὁμολογέω 3670

homologeō is a verb meaning "confess" in the majority of the twenty-four contexts in which it occurs. In Matt 14:7, however, ***homologeō*** means "to promise."

▸ **67.** Acknowledge, Confess, Profess, Swear > CONFESS, CONFESSION, PROFESS, PROFESSION, ACKNOWLEDGE

epangelma ἐπάγγελμα 1862

epangelma is a noun found in only two places, referring to the promises God has given to his people regarding their hope of a heavenly inheritance (2 Pet 1:4; 3:13).

SIGHT

eidos εἶδος 1491

eidos is a noun expressing the sense of "appearance," "form" in most of its five occurrences. Only in 2 Cor 5:7 does ***eidos*** mean "sight." Here Paul declares that believers "walk by faith, not by sight," affirming that the exercise of one's physical and rational faculties of perception is not adequate for maintaining a vital relationship with God.

▸ **81.** Forms, Groups, Patterns, Order > FORM, SHAPE

SEE ALSO

▸ **21.** Die, Perish, Kill, Destroy > SPECTACLE
theōria

▸ **64.** Reveal, Explain, Hiddenness, Secrecy > VISION
horama, horasis, optasia

TRUST

elpizō ἐλπίζω 1679

elpizō is a verb found around thirty times, in a variety of contexts, with the predominant sense of "hope" or "trust." There is also a distinct overlap in meaning between these two senses in several contexts.

elpizō refers to placing trust (i.e., putting one's hope in) in Moses (John 5:45); in Christ (Rom 15:12; 2 Cor 1:10; Phil 2:19); in the living God (1 Tim 4:10; 5:5); and in wealth (1 Tim 6:17; 1 Pet 3:5).

elpizō also means "trust" or "hope" in the sense of "earnestly desire" or "wish for" (2 Cor 5:11; 13:6; 2 John 12).

▸ **46.** Wait, Hope, Be Vigilant, Pay Attention To > HOPE

peithō πείθω 3982

peithō is a verb indicating the predominant sense of "persuade" in most of its approximately sixty occurrences. However, in several places ***peithō*** is also translated "to trust."

Matt 27:43; Gal 5:10; Phil 1:14; Heb 2:13 refer to trusting in the Lord. 2 Cor 10:7 speaks of being confident in belonging to Christ. Putting trust in one's wealth is noted in Mark 10:24, and in one's armor in Luke 11:22. In Phlm 12, Paul describes his "confidence" in the obedience of Philemon. Phil 3:3ff. disdains any confidence being placed in the "flesh" (i.e., human nature).

▸ **47.** Show, Persuade, Confidence, Doubt > PERSUADE, PERSUASION

▸ **54.** Rule, Authority, Command, Obedience > OBEDIENCE, OBEDIENT, OBEY

SEE ALSO

▸ **65.** Teach, Exhort, Rebuke, Discipline > DEPOSIT, TRUST
parathēkē

UNBELIEF, UNBELIEVER, UNBELIEVING

apistia ἀπιστία 570

apistia is a noun with the consistent meaning "unbelief" in each of the twelve contexts in which it occurs. The sense underlying "unbelief" is that of a lack or absence of saving faith and trust in Christ and/or God (Matt 13:58; 17:20; Mark 6:6; 9:24; 16:14; Rom 3:3; 4:20; 11:20ff.; 1 Tim 1:13; Heb 3:12, 19).

apeitheia ἀπείθεια 543

apeitheia is translated as both "unbelief" and "disobedience." The two meanings are clearly linked. Logically, the mindset of "unbelief" may be said to pave the way for the action of "disobedience." ***apeitheia*** is found in six places with this ambiguity (Rom 11:30ff.; Eph 2:2; 5:6; Col 3:6; Heb 4:6, 11).

apistos ἄπιστος 571

apistos is an adjective meaning "faithless" or "unbelieving," with respect to a lack of saving trust in God or Christ. ***apistos*** is also used nominally to refer to "unbelievers." The term occurs around twenty-five times.

The adjectival sense of "unbelieving" is applied to Jesus' Jewish audience on several occasions (Matt 17:17; Mark 9:19; Luke 9:41). See also John 20:27; Titus 1:15.

General references to "unbelievers" include those in Luke 12:46; 1 Cor 6:6; 7:12ff.; 10:27; 14:22ff.; 2 Cor 4:4; 6:14ff.; 1 Tim 5:8; Rev 21:8.

▸ **45.** Faith, Belief, Trust, Promise > FAITHFUL, FAITHLESS

apeitheō ἀπειθέω 544

As with ***apeitheia*** (above), ***apeitheō*** is a verb that conveys the dual, related senses of "disobey" and "refuse, withhold belief" (i.e., not to believe). ***apeitheō*** is found in sixteen contexts.

In John 3:36 ***apeitheō*** has the sense of "reject" in the context of spurning Christ. The same translation is found in Rom 2:8.

The ambiguity between "disobeying" and "refusing to believe" the gospel, or the word of God, is preserved in Rom 11:30, 31; Heb 3:18; 11:31; 1 Pet 2:7, 8; 3:1.

Other references to unbelieving Jews are found in Acts 14:2; 19:9; Rom 15:31.

▸ **45.** Faith, Belief, Trust, Promise > BELIEVE

▸ **54.** Rule, Authority, Command, Obedience > DISOBEY, DISOBEDIENCE, DISOBEDIENT

UNBELIEVING, LAUGH AT, LAUGH TO SCORN

katagelaō καταγελάω 2606

katagelaō occurs three times and is translated "laugh to scorn" on each occasion. Matt 9:24; Mark 5:40; Luke 8:53 refer to the incident where the crowd mocks Jesus for his claim that the dead girl before him, Jairus' daughter (whom he was about to bring back to life), was only sleeping.

SEE ALSO

▸ **19.** Mind, Spirit, Emotions, Feelings, Desires > LAUGH, LAUGHTER
gelaō, gelōs

▸ **58.** Vices > COARSE JESTING
eutrapelia

46. Wait, Hope, Be Vigilant, Pay Attention To

CAREFUL

phrontizō φροντίζω 5431

phrontizō is a rare verb found only in Titus 3:8, meaning "be careful" in relation to doing good works.

SEE ALSO

- ▸ **19.** Mind, Spirit, Emotions, Feelings, Desires > CARE, WORRY, ANXIETY
  merimna, merimnaō
- ▸ **62.** Care For, Protect, Guard, Watch > CARE ABOUT, CARE FOR, TAKE CARE OF
  melei, epimeleomai

DILIGENCE, DILIGENT, DILIGENTLY

spoudē σπουδή 4710

spoudē is a noun found twelve times with the primary sense of "haste," "diligence."

The meaning "diligence" in the sense of "earnest zeal" is indicated in Rom 12:8, 11; 2 Cor 7:11, 12; 8:7ff.; Heb 6:11 — all in the context of living out godly lives.

- ▸ **3.** Periods of Time, Duration, Frequency, Speed > HASTE, HASTEN, HURRY, QUICKLY

spoudazō σπουδάζω 4704

The verb ***spoudazō*** means "to be diligent," in the sense of "strive," "do one's best," in most of the eleven occurrences of the term.

The sense of "striving" to arrange meetings is indicated in 1 Thess 2:17; 2 Tim 4:9, 21; Titus 3:12. "Being diligent" in the pursuit of godly living is noted in Gal 2:10; Eph 4:3; 2 Tim 2:15. In particular, Heb 4:11 exhorts believers to "strive" to enter their heavenly "rest." There is a similar exhortation in 2 Pet 2:10 for believers "to be zealous" or "diligent" to confirm their call and election.

- ▸ **68.** Ability, Possibility, Effort, Succeed, Fail > EFFORT, ENDEAVOR
- ▸ **68.** Ability, Possibility, Effort, Succeed, Fail > STRIVE

spoudaios σπουδαῖος 4705

spoudaios is a rare adjective found only in 2 Cor 8:22 denoting a "diligent," "earnest" believer.

spoudaioteros σπουδαιότερος 4706

spoudaioteros is an adverb meaning "diligently" in relation to Onesiphorus' earnest drive to find Paul in Rome (2 Tim 1:17).

epimelōs ἐπιμελῶς 1960

epimelōs is a rare adverb, synonymous with ***spoudaioteros*** (above), denoting a woman's "diligent" search for a coin (Luke 15:8).

akribōs ἀκριβῶς 199

akribōs is an adverb meaning "diligently" in relation to Herod's careful search for the infant Jesus in Matt 2:8.

- ▸ **88.** Qualities, Characteristics > ACCURATELY

exeraunaō ἐξεραυνάω 1830

exeraunaō is a rare verb found only in 1 Pet 1:10 referring to the prophets of old who "had searched diligently" concerning the fulfillment of God's plan of salvation embodied in the coming of the Messiah, Jesus Christ.

EXAMINATION, EXAMINE

dokimazō δοκιμάζω 1381

dokimazō is a verb found nearly thirty times, with the principal meanings "prove," "approve," "discern." In several places, however, the meaning "examine" is evident.

The action of "examining" one's newly acquired oxen is noted in Luke 14:19. The exhortation to let a person "examine" himself or herself prior to taking the Lord's Supper is recorded in 1 Cor 11:28. Another exhortation to "test" or "examine" oneself to see if one is holding to the faith is noted in 2 Cor 13:5. See also Gal 6:4; 1 Thess 5:21. The "testing" or "examining" of potential deacons to determine their suitability for office is indicated in 1 Tim 3:10. The charge to "test" or "examine" the spirits to see whether they are of God is found in 1 John 4:1.

- ▸ **49.** Allow, Accept, Approve, Refuse > APPROVE, APPROVED
- ▸ **51.** Knowledge, Wisdom, Remember, Forget > TEST, TEMPT, TEMPTATION

peirazō πειράζω 3985

peirazō is a verb found in approximately forty contexts with the predominant meaning "tempt" or "test." In one context, however, ***peirazō*** means "examine." 2 Cor 13:5 contains the exhortation to "examine" oneself to see whether one is still holding to the faith.

- ▸ **51.** Knowledge, Wisdom, Remember, Forget > TEST, TEMPT, TEMPTATION

SEE ALSO

- ▸ **32.** Law, Justice, Jurisprudence, Judgment > EXAMINE, EXAMINATION, INVESTIGATION
  anakrisis, anakrinō, anetazō

EXPECT, EXPECTATION, ANTICIPATION

ekdechomai ἐκδέχομαι 1551

ekdechomai is a verb found eight times with the predominant meaning "to wait for." In 1 Cor 16:11, however, the verb indicates the sense of "expect" in the context of anticipating someone's return.

ekdochē ἐκδοχή 1561

ekdochē is a rare noun derived from ***ekdechomai*** (above) meaning "prospect" or "expectation" in the context of a terrible anticipation of judgment.

prosdokaō προσδοκάω 4328

prosdokaō is a verb found eighteen times, meaning "wait for," "look for," "expect." There is occasionally some overlap in meaning.

The meaning "expect" is found in the context of John the Baptist's question of Jesus, asking him if he is the Messiah, or if they should "expect" someone else (Matt 11:3; Luke 7:19ff.).

The general sense of "expecting" or "looking for" someone is indicated in Matt 24:50; Luke 3:15; 12:46; Acts 3:5. In Acts 28:6, after Paul had been bitten by an adder, his companions "were expecting" him to swell up.

▸ **46.** Wait, Hope, Be Vigilant, Pay Attention To > WAIT

prosdokia προσδοκία 4329

prosdokia is a rare noun derived from ***prosdokaō*** (above) found only in Luke 21:26; Acts 12:11, meaning "expectation," "anticipation," and, in the former text, "foreboding."

apokaradokia ἀποκαραδοκία 603

apokaradokia is a rare noun meaning "eager or anxious expectation, or longing." It is used metaphorically in Rom 8:19, referring to the "eager expectation" of creation for the revealing of the final day when God's people will experience the climax of their redemption. Phil 1:20 refers to Paul's "eager expectation" of his salvation.

HEED, GIVE ATTENTION TO

prosechō προσέχω 4337

The verb ***prosechō*** occurs about twenty times with the meanings "beware," "give heed to," or "give attention to." The latter sense is indicated in contexts where particular care is advised in specific circumstances — for example, in the public reading of Scripture (1 Tim 4:13); the appropriate response to the word of the prophets (2 Pet 1:19); and, negatively, in a refusal to give heed to "Jewish myths" or human traditions (Titus 1:14).

HOPE

elpis ἐλπίς 1680

In virtually all of the approximately fifty contexts in which this noun is found, it is translated "hope," with a number of underlying emphases. ***elpis*** indicates that the Christian hope is not based on mere wishful thinking, but on a certain outcome of blessing that is grounded in the finished redemptive work of Jesus Christ.

The believer's explicit hope in God's finished work of salvation through Christ constitutes the dominant usage of ***elpis*** (e.g., Rom 5:5; 1 Cor 9:10; 2 Cor 3:12; Eph 1:18; Phil 1:20; Col 1:23, 27; 1 Thess 5:8; Heb 3:6; 1 Pet 3:15; 1 John 3:3). Related to this theme is the Christian hope of resurrection from the dead (Acts 23:6), and also hope in the promises of God for salvation (Acts 26:6, 7; Rom 4:18; 8:20).

Other uses of the term indicate the hope of sharing God's glory (Rom 5:2); hope as a Christian virtue (Rom 5:4; 1 Cor 13:13). See also 2 Cor 1:7; 1 Thess 2:19; Gal 5:5. The tragedy of the unbeliever who has no hope is cited in Eph 2:12; 1 Thess 4:13.

elpizō ἐλπίζω 1679

This verb form has the same sense of "hope" as ***elpis*** (above), its nominal derivative. The action of hoping has nothing to do with a speculative desire. It is, rather, a fully confident anticipation of deliverance, won through the person and work of Christ. ***elpizō*** occurs about thirty times.

The confident hope or expectation of salvation is illustrated in Matt 12:21; Luke 24:21; Acts 26:7; Rom 8:24; 2 Cor 1:10; 1 Tim 4:10; 5:5; 1 Pet 1:13. Note also Paul's affirmation of a "hypothetical hopelessness," if Christ had not risen from the dead, in 1 Cor 15:19. The classic definition of faith as ". . . the assurance of things hoped for" is found in Heb 11:1.

False hope in earthly riches is indicated in 1 Tim 6:17, as is trust in the Mosaic law for salvation in John 5:45.

There is also a mundane usage of ***elpizō*** in relation to general human circumstances in Luke 6:34; Rom 15:24; Phil 2:23; 1 Tim 3:14.

▸ **45.** Faith, Belief, Trust, Promise > TRUST

MARANATHA

maranatha μαράναθα 3134

maranatha is an expression that occurs only in 1 Cor 16:22, translated as the invocation "Our Lord, come!"

OBSERVE

tēreō τηρέω 5083

tēreō is a verb occurring seventy-five times with the primary meanings "keep," "keep watch." It also means "observe" in the broad sense of "keep" or "give attention to."

▸ **69.** Have, Possess, Hold, Grasp, Bear, Carry > KEEP

PATIENTLY

makrothymōs μακροθύμως 3116

makrothymōs is an adverb, found only in Acts 26:3, with reference to listening "patiently."

SEE ALSO

▸ **60.** Virtues > PATIENCE, PATIENT
makrothymeō, makrothymia, hypomonē, anexikakos

READY, PREPARED

hetoimos ἕτοιμος 2092

hetoimos is an adjective with the primary meaning "ready" in the sense of "being prepared." It is found in seventeen contexts.

Exhortations to be ready for the coming of the Son of Man are found in Matt 24:44; Luke 12:40. In 1 Pet 3:15, the apostle urges his readers to be ready to offer a defense of their faith. Peter professes his readiness to suffer persecution for the sake of Christ in Luke 22:33. Acts 23:15, 21 record the readiness of Paul's enemies to assassinate him. Readiness to attend a feast is a prominent theme in several parables taught by Christ during his earthly ministry (Matt 22:4, 8; 25:10; Luke 14:17). See also Mark 14:15; 2 Cor 9:5; 10:6. Finally, God declares his readiness to reveal the climax of redemption for his people at the last day in 1 Pet 1:5.

WAIT

prosdechomai προσδέχομαι 4327

prosdechomai is a verb meaning "look for," "wait for" with expectancy. It is used in fourteen places. It refers to the coming kingdom of God, for example, in Mark 15:43; Luke 23:51. Luke 2:25 refers to the anticipation of the coming Messiah. Similar expectancy is expressed in relation to the redemption of Jerusalem (Luke 2:38); and to the hope of Christ's return in glory (Titus 2:13; Jude 21). See also Luke 12:36; Acts 23:21.

▸ **24.** Dwell, Live, Gather, Hospitality > RECEIVE, WELCOME

▸ **49.** Allow, Accept, Approve, Refuse > ACCEPT

apekdechomai ἀπεκδέχομαι 553

apekdechomai is synonymous with ***prosdechomai*** (above). It is found in five places. Rom 8:19ff. refers to believers waiting for the consummation of redemption of the sons of God. "Waiting for" the revelation of Jesus Christ in glory at his return is indicated in 1 Cor 1:7; Phil 3:20; Heb 9:28. See also Gal 5:5.

prosdokaō προσδοκάω 4328

prosdokaō is another verb meaning "wait, or look for" in a variety of contexts. The term occurs eighteen times. General references to "waiting for" people to come, or arrive, are found in Luke 1:21; 12:46; Acts 10:24. See also Acts 3:5.

prosdokaō also refers to waiting expectantly for the coming of the Messiah (Matt 11:3). See also Matt 24:50. The anticipation of the day of salvation is noted in Luke 7:19ff.; 2 Pet 3:12ff.

▸ **46.** Wait, Hope, Be Vigilant, Pay Attention To > EXPECT, EXPECTATION, ANTICIPATION

SEE ALSO

▸ **74.** Safety, Peace, Danger, Escape > TRAP, AMBUSH, LIE IN WAIT *enedreuō*

WAKE

grēgoreō γρηγορέω 1127

grēgoreō is a verb with the predominant meaning "to watch" in the sense of "keep awake," "give close attention to." It is found around twenty times.

Jesus exhorts his disciples in Gethsemane to "watch" and pray with him (Matt 26:38ff.; Mark 14:34ff.). Elsewhere, Jesus commands his hearers to "watch" for the day of the Lord's return (Matt 24:42ff.; Mark 13:34ff.; Luke 12:37ff.). See also Acts 20:31.

There are general exhortations to believers to "keep watch," "keep awake," and safeguard their relationship with the Lord (1 Cor 16:13; 1 Thess 5:6; 1 Pet 5:8; Rev 3:2ff.; 16:15).

▸ **46.** Wait, Hope, Be Vigilant, Pay Attention To > WATCH

WATCH

grēgoreō γρηγορέω 1127

grēgoreō is a verb occurring around twenty times with the primary meaning "watch," as well as a variety of related nuances.

"Watching" in the sense of "be vigilant" or "pay close attention to" is indicated in the context of waiting for the Day of the Lord (Matt 24:42; 25:13; Mark 13:35); and also in relation to "guarding" one's house (Matt 24:43; Mark 13:34; Luke 12:39).

Elsewhere, ***grēgoreō*** means "keep watch" in the sense of "be watchful, alert." Christ pleads with his disciples to "keep watch" with him in Gethsemane during his agony there (Matt 26:38ff.; Mark 14:34ff.). Such an exhortation is also given in relation to maintaining one's faith (Acts 20:31; 1 Cor 16:13; 1 Thess 5:6; 1 Pet 5:8; Rev 3:2; 16:15). Col 4:2 contains an injunction to be watchful in prayer.

grēgoreō means "to be, keep awake" in 1 Thess 5:10.

▸ **46.** Wait, Hope, Be Vigilant, Pay Attention To > WAKE

agrypneō ἀγρυπνέω 69

agrypneō is a verb meaning "keep watch," "be vigilant, alert." It is found in four places. Mark 13:33; Luke 21:36 exhort believers to be vigilant in waiting for the return of the Lord. Eph 6:18 enjoins believers "to be alert" in prayer. "Keeping watch" over the people of God in a pastoral context is indicated in Heb 13:17.

paratēreō παρατηρέω 3906

paratēreō is a verb found in six places meaning "watch," "closely observe."

The Pharisees watched Jesus to see if he would heal on the Sabbath (Mark 3:2; Luke 6:7). See also Luke 14:1; 20:20. The enemies of Paul are said to "keep a close watch" on the city gates of Damascus in order to waylay him (Acts 9:24). Gal 4:10 refers to "keeping" or "observing" ritual festivals.

47. Show, Persuade, Confidence, Doubt

BOLD, BOLDNESS, BOLDLY, CONFIDENT, CONFIDENCE

tharreō θαρρέω 2292

tharreō is a verb found in six places with the meaning "be bold, confident."

The sense of "be confident of, have confidence in" is indicated in relation to one's intimate relationship with God being characterized by peace (2 Cor 5:6ff.; Heb 13:6). 2 Cor 7:16 speaks of "having confidence" in one's friends in Christ. Having confidence, or being bold in the presence of people, is noted in 2 Cor 6:1ff.

parrēsiazomai παρρησιάζομαι 3955

parrēsiazomai is a verb found nine times with the meaning "to speak boldly" in the context of preaching the gospel (Acts 9:27ff.; 13:46; 14:3; 18:26; 19:8; 26:26; Eph 6:20; 1 Thess 2:2).

▸ **43.** Prophecy, Preaching, Proclamation > PREACH, PREACHING

parrēsia παρρησία 3954

parrēsia is a noun found in thirty places meaning "boldness," "confidence" in about half of these contexts. It is also used adverbially in several places with the sense of "boldly."

"Boldness" or "confidence" in preaching is indicated with respect to apostolic preachers in Acts 4:13, 29ff.; 28:31; 2 Cor 3:12; Eph 6:19; Phil 1:20.

2 Cor 7:4 refers to "having confidence" in fellow believers. The same state of mind is also noted in relation to the day of judgment in 1 John 4:17; and to Christ and one's salvation in Eph 3:12; 1 Tim 3:13; Phlm 8; Heb 3:6; 10:19, 35; 1 John 2:28; 3:21; 5:14.

The adverbial meaning "boldly" describes preaching in Acts 2:29; and approaching God in prayer in Heb 4:16.

tolmaō τολμάω 5111

tolmaō is a verb found eighteen times with the primary meaning "to dare." The related senses of "to be bold," "show boldness" are indicated in 2 Cor 10:2; 11:21. In Phil 1:14 the demonstration of boldness is specifically related to speaking the word of God without fear.

▸ **48.** Will, Purpose, Decide, Advise > DARE, DARING

apotolmaō ἀποτολμάω 662

apotolmaō is a rare variant of ***tolmaō*** (above) found only in Rom 10:20.

tolmēroterōs τολμηροτέρως 5112

tolmēroterōs is a rare adverbial form found only in Rom 15:15 with the meaning "very boldly."

DEMONSTRATION

apodeixis ἀπόδειξις 585

apodeixis is a rare noun denoting the "demonstration" of the Holy Spirit's power, found only in 1 Cor 2:4.

endeixis ἔνδειξις 1732

endeixis is a noun denoting "proof" or "demonstration" in four contexts. Rom 3:25, 26 speak of Christ's atonement as a "demonstration" of God's justice. The "proof" or "demonstration" of Christian love is noted in 2 Cor 8:24. A "token" or "proof" of the imminent destruction of the wicked is indicated in Phil 1:28.

EVIDENCE, EVIDENT

tekmērion τεκμήριον 5039

tekmērion is a rare noun denoting the "convincing proofs" or "evidence" provided by Christ to people of the region that he had indeed risen from the dead (Acts 1:3).

dēlos δῆλος 1212

dēlos is an adjective meaning "clear," "evident" in two places.

The meaning "apparent," "obvious" in the impersonal expression "it is evident that . . ." is indicated in 1 Cor 15:27; Gal 3:11.

katadēlos κατάδηλος 2612

katadēlos is a rare adjectival form, an intensive form of ***dēlos*** (above) meaning "thoroughly plain or evident" in Heb 7:15.

prodēlos πρόδηλος 4271

prodēlos is another rare adjectival variant of ***dēlos*** (above), meaning "obvious," "evident" as a description of the sins of humankind in 1 Tim 5:1; and also as a designation of good deeds in 1 Tim 5:25. The general sense of "clear" or "evident" in the expression "it is clear that . . ." is indicated in Heb 7:14, explaining that Jesus Christ was a direct descendant from the tribe of Judah.

EYEWITNESS

autoptēs αὐτόπτης 845

autoptēs is a rare noun denoting an "eyewitness" to the ministry of Christ in Luke 1:2.

epoptēs ἐπόπτης 2030

epoptēs is a rare synonym for ***autoptēs*** (above) denoting "eyewitnesses" to the majesty of Christ through his miraculous signs in 2 Pet 1:16.

PERSUADE, PERSUASION

peithō πείθω 3982

peithō is a verb meaning "persuade" in about half of the approximately sixty occurrences in which it is found.

The meaning "persuade" indicates, first of all, the sense of inducing someone to change his or her course of action or way of thinking (Matt 27:20; Acts 14:19; 21:14).

peithō is also used passively in the sense of "being persuaded" or "being convinced" (Luke 16:31; 20:6; Acts 18:4; 26:26; Rom 8:38; 14:14; 15:14; 2 Tim 1:5, 12; Heb 6:9). In Acts 17:4, this passive usage refers to those who come to faith, or who believe. The active sense of "persuading" or "convincing" occurs in Acts 26:28, likewise with reference to coming to faith. Acts 19:8, 26; 28:23; 2 Cor 5:11 express the active sense of "persuade," referring to the process of convincing people through reasoned debate.

In Acts 13:43, ***peithō*** means "persuade" in the sense of "urge" or attempting to persuade.

- ▸ **45.** Faith, Belief, Trust, Promise > TRUST
- ▸ **54.** Rule, Authority, Command, Obedience > OBEDIENCE, OBEDIENT, OBEY

plērophoreō πληροφορέω 4135

plērophoreō is a verb with the underlying sense of making something fully known — by a process of reasoning, persuasion, or proclamation. ***plērophoreō*** occurs only six times and is translated "to be fully persuaded, or convinced" in two of these contexts. Rom 4:21 speaks of being fully convinced of God's promises, and Rom 14:5 refers to being fully persuaded in one's own mind.

- ▸ **84.** Do, Make, Accomplish, Occur > CARRY OUT, COMPLETE, FULFILL, ACCOMPLISH

anapeithō ἀναπείθω 374

anapeithō is a derivative verb from ***peithō*** (above) and is likewise translated "persuade." It is found in Acts 18:13.

peismonē πεισμονή 3988

peismonē is a noun derived, presumably, from ***peithō*** (above). It means "persuasion" and occurs only in Gal 5:8, with reference to a negative enticement to abandon one's faith in Christ alone.

SHOW

hypodeiknymi ὑποδείκνυμι 5263

This verb occurs seven times and means "to warn," "show." In Acts 9:16, it means "show" in the sense of "reveal" or "explain." In Acts 20:35, the translation is "show" in the sense of "teach."

- ▸ **65.** Teach, Exhort, Rebuke, Discipline > WARN

endeiknymi ἐνδείκνυμι 1731

The verb ***deiknymi*** means "show," "show forth" in most of its twelve occurrences.

The sense of "point out," or "prove," is illustrated in Rom 2:15; 2 Cor 8:24. The nuance of "demonstrate" is indicated in Titus 2:10; 3:2; Heb 6:10ff. with reference to people.

God is said to "show" or "demonstrate" his divine power in relation to the hardening of Pharaoh's heart (Rom 9:17); his wrath against wickedness (Rom 9:22); and the riches of his grace (Eph 2:7).

Christ is said to "show forth" or "display" his patience in the hearts of his people in order to sustain them for eternal life (2 Tim 1:16).

paristēmi παρίστημι 3936

paristēmi is a verb occurring around forty times with the predominant meaning "stand by," along with a number of related senses. One of these associated nuances is that of "to show" in the sense of "present oneself," as noted in Acts 1:3, where the resurrected Christ is said to "have presented himself" alive to his disciples. Also, in 2 Tim 2:15, Paul gives an exhortation to Timothy "to present himself" to God as a competent teacher of the holy Scriptures.

- ▸ **70.** Give, Take, Seize, Touch > PRESENT
- ▸ **85.** Movement, Position, State > STAND

SEE ALSO

- ▸ **64.** Reveal, Explain, Hiddenness, Secrecy > SHOW, DISCLOSE, MANIFEST ***deiknymi, anadeiknymi, phaneroō, emphanizō***

SHOW, DEMONSTRATE, PROVE

epideiknymi ἐπιδείκνυμι 1925

epideiknymi is a verb meaning "to show" in each of its nine occurrences.

epideiknymi refers to "showing" a sign from heaven (Matt 16:1) and "showing" the truth of the Scriptures (Acts 18:28), both in the sense of "demonstrate."

The sense of "disclose," "reveal," or "point out" is indicated in Matt 22:19; 24:1; Luke 24:40; Acts 9:39.

The sense of "present oneself" is evident in Luke 17:14.

SEE ALSO

- ▸ **64.** Reveal, Explain, Hiddenness, Secrecy > SHOW, DISCLOSE, MANIFEST ***deiknymi, anadeiknymi, phaneroō, emphanizō***

SIGN

sēmeion σημεῖον 4592

sēmeion is found in approximately eighty contexts in the NT, with the primary senses of "sign" or "miracle," ranging in meaning from a "distinguishing mark" to a significant "divine revelation" usually, though not always, accompanied by a miraculous omen.

The general sense of "sign" as a confirming gesture is illustrated in Matt 26:48 with reference to Judas' kiss of betrayal identifying Jesus Christ to the Jewish authorities. The meaning "sign" as a "mark" or "signature" is indicated in 2 Thess 3:17.

The meaning "sign" in the general sense of a confirmation of divine authority is indicated in 1 Cor 1:22; 14:22. Such signs were demanded of Jesus by the Jewish population (John 2:18; 6:30); by the Pharisees (Matt 12:38ff.; 16:1ff.; Mark 8:11; Luke 11:16, 29ff.); and were expected by King Herod (Luke 23:8). Highly significant in this regard are the "signs" or miraculous deeds performed by Jesus as indicators of his divine person and authority — although these could only be truly understood through the eyes of faith (John 2:11, 23; 3:2; 4:48, 54; 6:2, 14, 26, 30; 7:31; 11:47; Acts 2:22). John 12:37, in contrast, records a "sign" of unbelief in spite of Jesus' miracles. The early apostles were also granted power to perform miracles, testifying to the divine authority they had received through the Spirit of God (Acts 2:43; 4:16ff.; 5:12, 6:8; Rom 5:19; 2 Cor 2:12).

One of the great miraculous "signs" of the NT is the birth of Jesus Christ, clearly portrayed as a fulfillment of OT prophecy (Luke 2:12, 34).

References to Yahweh's miraculous "signs" in Egypt are found in Acts 7:36 (see also Heb 2:4). Circumcision, as the "sign" or "seal" of the old covenant, is noted in Rom 4:11. In contrast, the reality of satanic power and authority is indicated with reference to demonic "signs" or "miracles" in 2 Thess 2:9; Rev 16:14; 19:20.

Jesus' disciples ask him for "signs" of the approaching end of the world (Matt 24:3, 24, 30; Mark 13:4, 22; 16:17ff.; Luke 21:7ff.). ***sēmeion*** also refers to "signs" as symbolic apocalyptic references to the coming final judgment of God against the wicked, and at the same time the vindication and fulfillment of his redemptive purposes in Christ. These are all found in the book of Revelation (Rev 12:1, 3; 13:13, 14; 15:1).

enneuō ἐννεύω 1770

enneuō is a rare verb found only in Luke 1:62 with reference to people "making signs," or "gesturing" with face and hands in order to communicate.

dynamis δύναμις 1411

dynamis is a fairly common noun with the primary sense of "power," "strength" in the majority of its 120 occurrences. In a few places, however, ***dynamis*** is translated "mighty works" as well as "miracle" or "sign." In essence, these two meanings are synonymous.

References to "mighty works" or "signs" performed by Christ include those in Matt 11:20ff.; 13:54ff.; Mark 6:2ff.; Luke 19:37; Acts 2:22 (see also Matt 7:22).

References to "miracles" performed by the apostles are found in Acts 8:13; 19:11; 2 Cor 9:12. This gift is also said to be given to some in the church (1 Cor 12:10, 28ff.; Heb 2:4; Gal 3:5).

▸ **18.** Strength, Weakness, Capability > STRENGTH, STRONG, POWER, POWERFUL, MIGHT, MIGHTY
▸ **68.** Ability, Possibility, Effort, Succeed, Fail > ABILITY, STRENGTH, POWER

UNCERTAIN, DOUBLE-MINDED

dipsychos δίψυχος 1374

dipsychos occurs only in Jas 1:8, 4:8 as an adjective meaning "double-minded" or "wavering," "uncertain."

▸ **7.** Quantity, Amount, Number, Size, Measure > DOUBLE, DOUBLE-MINDED

metaballō μεταβάλλω 3328

metaballō is found only in Acts 28:6 meaning "to change one's mind."

▸ **82.** Change, Exchange, Transform > CHANGE, EXCHANGE

SEE ALSO

▸ **19.** Mind, Spirit, Emotions, Feelings, Desires > MIND
dianoia, nous, phronēma, noēma

48. Will, Purpose, Decide, Advise

ADVICE

gnōmē γνώμη 1106

The noun ***gnōmē*** is found in nine contexts with the meanings "mind," "opinion," "purpose," and "advice." It denotes the human faculty of rational knowledge in general.

The sense of "purpose" or "intention" is indicated in Acts 20:3; 1 Cor 1:10; Rev 17:13, 17. Other texts make reference to "advice," "opinion," or "judgment" (1 Cor 7:25, 40; 2 Cor 8:10). Then, in Phlm 14, ***gnōmē*** denotes "consent" or "permission."

▸ **51.** Knowledge, Wisdom, Remember, Forget > JUDGMENT

boulē βουλή 1012

The noun ***boulē*** is found twelve times with the consistent meaning of "counsel" or "will" throughout, except for Acts 27:12, where the term refers to "advice" given regarding the commencement of an ocean journey.

▸ **48.** Will, Purpose, Decide, Advise > COUNSEL, COUNSELOR

CHOOSE, CHOSEN

eklegomai ἐκλέγομαι 1586

eklegomai is a verb occurring about twenty times and meaning "choose."

In the context of divine election, God is said to "choose" his people in Mark 13:20; Acts 13:17; 15:7; Eph 1:4. In 1 Cor 1:27ff. God is said to "choose" the foolish things of the world to shame the wise.

Jesus "choosing" his disciples is recorded in Luke 6:13; John 6:70; 13:18; 15:16ff.; Acts 1:2, 24.

Other general references to people exercising choice are found in Luke 10:42; 14:7; Acts 15:22, 25. Acts 6:5 refers to "choosing" deacons in the early church.

epilegō ἐπιλέγω 1951

epilegō is a rare verb with the meaning "choose" in Acts 15:40 in relation to Paul's choice of a traveling companion.

haireomai αἱρέω 138

haireomai is a rare verb synonymous with ***eklegomai*** and ***epilegō*** (above), again meaning "choose" and occurring in only three places.

The choice of human beings is indicated in Phil 1:22. Moses' choosing to side with the people of Israel is recorded in Heb 2:13. God's elective "choosing" of believers is noted in 2 Thess 2:13.

hairetizō αἱρετίζω 140

hairetizō is a rare verb found only in Matt 12:18 with reference to God having "chosen" his Servant Son.

procheirotoneō προχειροτονέω 4401

procheirotoneō is a rare verb meaning "choose (beforehand)" in the context of God having already chosen those who would witness the post-resurrection appearances of Christ (Acts 10:41).

eklektos ἐκλεκτός 1588

eklektos is an adjective meaning "elect," "chosen" throughout its approximately twenty occurrences.

The process of "being chosen" by God in the context of being joined to his people is noted in Matt 20:16; 22:14. Christ is designated as God's "chosen one" in Luke 23:35; 1 Pet 2:4ff. Believers are described as a "chosen generation" in 1 Pet 2:9.

The "elect" (i.e., chosen by God) specifically refers to the body of believers worldwide (Matt 24:22ff.; Mark 13:20ff.; Luke 18:7; Rom 8:33; Col 3:12; 2 Tim 2:10; Titus 1:1; 1 Pet 1:2; 2 John 1, 13; Rev 17:14). "Elect" angels are noted in 1 Tim 5:21.

▸ **48.** Will, Purpose, Decide, Advise > ELECT, ELECTION

eklogē ἐκλογή 1589

eklogē is a noun denoting "election," referring to God choosing his people. It is found seven times.

The term is used adjectivally in Acts 9:15, where God designates Paul as his "chosen" instrument to preach the gospel.

The phenomenon of divine "election," of God having "chosen" his people according to his redemptive purposes, is evident in Rom 9:11; 11:5ff., 28; 1 Thess 1:4; 2 Pet 1:10.

▸ **48.** Will, Purpose, Decide, Advise > ELECT, ELECTION

COUNCIL

symboulion συμβούλιον 4824

symboulion is a noun denoting both a "council" and "counsel" (i.e., advice given). Reference to a "council," or formal gathering, is found in Matt 12:14 (describing the Pharisees' determination to be rid of Jesus). The "council" of Festus, the Roman governor of Judea, is noted in Acts 25:12.

▸ **48.** Will, Purpose, Decide, Advise > COUNSEL, COUNSELOR

synedrion συνέδριον 4892

synedrion is a noun found about twenty times with the meaning "council." In some contexts, ***synedrion*** is transliterated "Sanhedrin" — the great Jewish council in Jerusalem composed of civil and religious leaders, which was the highest judicial court in the land.

The "Sanhedrin" itself is indicated in Matt 5:22; 26:59; Mark 14:55; Luke 22:66; John 11:47; Acts 4:15; 5:21ff.; 6:12ff.; 22:30; 23:1ff. The more general sense of "councils" is found in Matt 10:17; Mark 13:9.

COUNSEL, COUNSELOR

boulē βουλή 1012

boulē is a noun found in twelve places denoting "counsel" in the sense of "advice" or "purpose."

The meaning "counsel," denoting the "will" or "purpose" of God, is indicated in Luke 7:30; Acts 13:36; 20:27. In particular, Acts 2:23 speaks of Jesus Christ having been delivered up to death by God's explicit "counsel" or "plan." Eph 1:11; Heb 6:17 refer to God's "will" controlling all things.

The "counsel," "purpose," or "plan" of human beings is indicated in Luke 23:51; Acts 4:28; 5:38; 27:42; and 1 Cor 4:5 refers to the "counsel" of people's hearts.

▸ **48.** Will, Purpose, Decide, Advise > ADVICE

bouleuō βουλεύω 1011

bouleuō is a verb found ten times meaning "to plan" throughout — all in the context of human determination (Luke 14:31; John 12:10; Acts 5:33; 15:37; 27:39; 2 Cor 1:17).

symboulos σύμβουλος 4825

symboulos is a rare noun denoting a "counselor" in a general sense in Rom 11:34, hypothetically questioning who would be the Lord's "counselor."

symboulion συμβούλιον 4824

symboulion is a noun denoting "counsel" or "advice" in the eight occurrences of the term. The Sanhedrin "takes counsel" (i.e., makes plans) for the purpose of destroying Jesus (Matt 22:15; 27:1; Mark 3:6; 15:1). See also Matt 27:7; 28:12.

▸ **48.** Will, Purpose, Decide, Advise > COUNCIL

symbouleuō συμβουλεύω 4823

The verb ***symbouleuō*** means "to take counsel," "give counsel," "plot" in five contexts. In Matt 26:4; John 11:53; 18:14 the object of the Sanhedrin's deliberations or "plans" is the destruction of Jesus. Acts 9:23 records the "plot" to kill Paul. Rev 3:18 contains the divine "counsel" or "advice" for the members of the congregation at Laodicea to seek after true godliness.

DARE, DARING

tolmaō τολμάω 5111

tolmaō is a verb meaning "to dare," "be bold" throughout the eighteen occurrences of the term.

The meaning "dare" is used mostly in the negative, indicating the sense of "being unwilling to act through moral conviction, fear, or embarrassment." In order to avoid public humiliation, people often "dared not" ask Jesus any more questions (Matt 22:46; Mark 12:34; Luke 20:40; John 21:12). Other similar uses are found in Acts 5:13; 7:32; Rom 15:18; 2 Cor 10:12; Jude 9.

The positive sense of "be bold," "take courage" is indicated in Mark 15:43; Rom 5:7; 1 Cor 6:1; 2 Cor 10:2; 11:21. In particular, Phil 1:14 refers to the disciples "being bold" to speak the word of God fearlessly.

▸ **47.** Show, Persuade, Confidence, Doubt > BOLD, BOLDNESS, BOLDLY, CONFIDENT, CONFIDENCE

SEE ALSO

▸ **58.** Vices > BOAST, BOASTING, ARROGANCE
tolmētēs

DETERMINE, PREDETERMINE, FOREORDAIN

horizō ὁρίζω 3724

horizō is a verb found in eight places meaning "determine" in relation to exercising sovereign divine purpose and intent.

The handing over of Christ to death by crucifixion, and his subsequent resurrection and ascension to glory, resulting in his return to heavenly power and authority, are a series of events "determined" or "decreed" by the explicit intention and plan of God, indicated in Luke 22:22; Acts 2:23; 10:42; 17:31; Rom 1:4. The divine "determination" of the boundaries and circumstances of humankind is noted in Acts 17:26. In Heb 4:7, God is said to have "determined" or "set" a certain day for the proclamation of the gospel in a call for repentance and the expression of saving faith.

▸ **63.** Speak, Tell, Declare, Call > DECLARE, DECLARATION
▸ **83.** Set, Put, Place, Prepare, Establish > APPOINT, ORDAIN, ASSIGN

proorizō προορίζω 4309

proorizō is a significant verb found in seven places meaning "predetermine," "foreordain," or "predestine" — relating to God's sovereign purposes in relation to humankind.

General references to God's "predetermined" purposes and plan are found in Acts 4:28; Eph 1:11. The action of God in "predetermining" people for salvation is noted in Rom 8:29, 30; Eph 1:5. The secret wisdom of God "decreed" before the beginning of time and now revealed to God's people in Christ is noted in 1 Cor 2:7.

ELECT, ELECTION

eklektos ἐκλεκτός 1588

eklektos is an adjective found in approximately twenty places with the predominant meaning "elect" or "chosen" throughout.

References to the "elect" denoting the "chosen people of God" are found in Matt 20:16; 24:22ff.; Mark 13:20ff.; Luke 18:7; Rom 8:33; Col 3:12; 2 Tim 2:10; Titus 1:1; 1 Pet 1:2. In particular, "elect" individuals chosen by God include angels in heaven in 1 Tim 5:21; and the Messiah, under the guise of the "chief cornerstone" of the temple, in 1 Pet 2:4ff. See also 1 Pet 5:13; 2 John 1, 13.

▸ **48.** Will, Purpose, Decide, Advise > CHOOSE, CHOSEN

eklogē ἐκλογή 1589

eklogē is a noun denoting the phenomenon of divine "election" in Rom 9:11; 11:5ff., 28; 2 Thess 1:4; 2 Pet 1:10.

▸ **48.** Will, Purpose, Decide, Advise > CHOOSE, CHOSEN

FOREKNOW, FOREKNOWLEDGE

proginōskō προγινώσκω 4267

proginōskō is a verb found in five contexts meaning "to know beforehand," "foreknow," "foreordain." Acts 8:29; Rom 11:2 speak of God "foreknowing" those whom he has redeemed. 1 Pet 1:20 affirms that Christ was "foreordained" (i.e., chosen by God) prior to the foundation of the world. The sense of "knowing someone beforehand" is indicated in Acts 26:5; 2 Pet 3:17.

prognōsis πρόγνωσις 4268

prognōsis is a rare noun derived from ***proginōskō*** (above) denoting divine "foreknowledge" in Acts 2:23; 1 Pet 1:2. Both of these contexts imply divine election.

LOVE

agapaō ἀγαπάω 25

agapaō occurs around 140 times and is consistently translated "to love," in a variety of contexts. Such an action and attitude is predicated of human beings, God, and Christ. Human love, as indicated by ***agapaō*** in positive contexts, is a noble affection. It is characterized by a concern, not for oneself, but for others. Yet on other occasions it refers to the love of that which is evil and unprofitable. When God and Christ are said to love, ***agapaō*** conveys the idea of a deep, limitless compassion that is given through the supreme self-sacrificial actions of Christ on the cross in association with the mercy and kindness of God.

Where ***agapaō*** refers to the love of human beings, several contexts indicate the mandatory nature of its expression. For example, there is the command to love one's neighbor (Matt 5:43ff.; 19:19; 22:39; Mark 12:31ff.; Luke 6:27; Rom 13:9; Gal 5:14); and the command to love one another (John 13:34; 15:12, 17; 1 Thess 4:9; 1 John 3:23; 2 John 5). Affirmations of love for each other are found in Rom 13:8; 1 Pet 1:22; 1 John 2:10; 3:18. See also Luke 7:42. The command to love God with all one's heart is recorded in Matt 22:37; Mark 12:30; Luke 10:27. Declaration of love for Christ is indicated in Eph 6:24. God is the object of human love in Rom 8:28; 1 Cor 2:9; Jas 1:12; and God's love for us is the ground of our love for others (1 John 4:19). See also 1 John 5:2.

Other references to ***agapaō*** in the human sphere include that in John 3:19, where unbelievers are declared to love darkness rather than light. Similarly, John 12:43 refers to those who love the praise of human beings rather than God. The illegitimate love of money is noted in 2 Pet 2:15. Paul affirms a love for his congregation in 2 Cor 12:15 and mentions the importance of a man's love for his wife in Eph 5:28; Col 3:19.

Love displayed by Christ is noted in a number of different contexts. There is, for example, his deeply compassionate regard for individuals such as the rich young ruler (Mark 10:21); Martha (John 11:5); and his disciples (John 13:23; 21:7). Jesus' love for his own people is expressed in John 13:1; 14:21, 23; 15:9; Gal 2:20; Eph 5:25; Rev 1:5; 3:9. In particular, Eph 5:2 emphasizes the self-sacrificial nature of that love. Love for his Father is noted in John 14:31; 15:9. Jesus' question of Peter, "Do you love me?" is found in John 21:15, 16. Heb 1:9 indicates Christ's love of righteousness.

With respect to God, ***agapaō*** refers to his love for the world (John 3:16); for his Son (John 3:35; 10:7; 17:24); and for his people in particular (John 17:24; Rom 8:37; Eph 2:4; 2 Thess 2:16; Heb 12:6; 1 John 4:10). See also Rom 9:13, where God's love for Jacob is expressed as a predestined choice, at the expense of Esau his brother, who is described (with a sense of hyperbole) as one "hated" by God.

agapē ἀγάπη 26

agapē is the noun derived from ***agapaō*** (above) and also means "love," with the same emphases and nuances as the verb. ***agapē*** occurs around 120 times.

As a human attitude and emotion, ***agapē*** indicates "love" in a generalized sense in Matt 24:12; Rom 12:9; 13:10; 1 Cor 8:1. In Gal 5:22, "love" is listed first among the fruit of the Spirit. The underlying essence of ***agapē*** as a supremely self-sacrificing love is indicated in 1 Cor 13:4, 8, 13; 1 John 4:10, 18; 2 John 6 (see also 2 Cor 6:6; 8:7ff.). One of the great illustrations of ***agapē*** love is giving up one's life for a friend (John 15:13). See also 1 John 3:16; 1 Cor 14:1. Paul expresses his love for his Corinthian congregation in 1 Cor 16:24; 2 Cor 2:4. The reality of the love of Christ controlling our lives is indicated in 2 Cor 5:14. Mutual love for one another is noted in John 13:35. In a negative context, Luke 11:42 records Christ's censure of the Pharisees for their neglect of the love and justice of God. Similarly, 1 John 2:15; 3:17 declare that those who love the world cannot love God.

In relation to the believer, ***agapē*** refers to love given by God and shaped by the Spirit of Christ as the guiding principle of Christian living. It is a common theme, expressed both in the Pauline correspondence and other General Epistles (e.g., Eph 1:15; Phil 1:9; Col 1:4; 1 Tim 1:5; Heb 6:10; 1 Pet 4:8; 1 John 2:5). In Rev 2:4, the Ephesian church is rebuked for having abandoned her first love (i.e., love for Christ).

When predicated of Christ, ***agapē*** indicates his love as impregnable and unassailable (Rom 8:35, 39); and surpassing knowledge (Eph 3:19). John 15:9, 10 contain the command to abide in the love of Christ.

In regard to love as a quality of the divine being, ***agapē*** is found in a number of places. John 15:10 affirms Christ abiding in God's love. Paul declares in Rom 5:5 that God's love is poured out into our hearts. That love makes us alive with Christ (Eph 2:4; 3:17; 1 John 4:9) and makes us his children (1 John 3:1). See also Gal 5:6. The unique quality of divine love is strikingly illustrated in Rom 5:8, which states that Christ died for us while we were still sinners. God is described as "love" in 1 John 4:8, 16, and he is given the title "God of love" in 2 Cor 13:11. The benediction, ". . . love of God," is found in 2 Cor 13:14; 2 Thess 3:5; 2 John 3; Jude 2.

▸ **40.** Holy Days, Feasts, Festivals > FEAST, FESTIVAL

phileō φιλέω 5368

phileō is a verb synonymous with ***agapaō*** (above) that is also translated "to love," but not usually with that same sublime quality of unselfishness as indicated by ***agapaō***, except perhaps when predicated of God. ***phileō*** indicates the action of "loving" as a strong desire to act, or to express affection to another person.

In regard to human beings, ***phileō*** often indicates the meaning "love" in the sense of "like to do." Such is the case with the Pharisees, who are described in Matt 6:5 as "loving" to show their piety in public. They also "love" to have the place of honor in public and private gatherings (Matt 23:6), and they generally have a great fondness for recognition (Luke 20:46).

In terms of "love" as affection, ***phileō*** is found in John 15:19; Titus 3:15. Love for one's family is indicated in Matt 10:37. The paradoxical statement "he who loves his life will lose it" is found in John 12:25. Peter expresses his love for Christ in John 21:15, 16, 17, using the verb ***phileō***, not ***agapaō***. In John 21:17, when Jesus asks Peter for the third time if he loves him, he uses ***phileō*** rather than ***agapaō***, as he did on the first two occasions.

phileō expresses divine love in John 5:20, where God is said to love the Son, and in John 16:27, which indicates God's love for his people.

With regard to love expressed by Jesus, ***phileō*** indicates the great affection he has for individuals — for example, Lazarus (John 11:3, 36), and John (John 20:2). Rev 3:19 affirms that Jesus loves his people, but that he will also chasten them.

▸ **27.** Community, Partnership, Unity, Discord > KISS

SEE ALSO

▸ **50.** Love, Hate, Please, Be Pleased With > LOVE
philadelphia

LOVER

philautos φίλαυτος 5367
philēdonos φιλήδονος 5369
philotheos φιλόθεος 5377
philoxenos φιλόξενος 5382
philagathos φιλάγαθος 5358

These NT terms, each of which occurs only once or a few times, all refer to people as "lover(s) of . . ." In each case, the reference is to those people who are passionately devoted to the object of their affection.

philautos refers to "lovers of self," ***philēdonos*** to "lovers of pleasure," ***philotheos*** to "lovers of God," ***philoxenos*** to "lover of hospitality," "given to hospitality," and ***philagathos*** to "lovers of good men."

PURPOSE, PLAN

prothesis πρόθεσις 4286

prothesis is found twelve times, referring mainly to God's "purpose" in his plan of salvation (Rom 8:28; 9:11; Eph 1:11; 3:11; 2 Tim 1:9).

boulēma βούλημα 1013

boulēma is a term found only twice. In Acts 27:43 it refers to the "plan" or "purpose" to have Paul and the other prisoners killed to prevent their escape from a shipwreck.

▸ **48.** Will, Purpose, Decide, Advise > WILL, WILLING

protithēmi προτίθημι 4388

protithēmi is a verb found on only three occasions. In two of these contexts, it refers to the expression of one's purpose, or intent. Rom 1:13 speaks of Paul's determined purpose to visit the church in Rome. In Eph 1:9, ***protithēmi*** refers to the expression of God's purpose in the person of Christ in relation to the divine plan of salvation.

WILL, WILLING

thelō θέλω 2309

The underlying sense of ***thelō*** is that of "to be willing," "desire," "want," or "wish." When used in the negative, this term is translated "be unwilling," "refuse."

thelō occurs in a number of places with the general negative sense of "be unwilling," "refuse" (Matt 1:19; 21:29; Luke 15:28; 18:13; 1 Cor 12:1; Gal 1:7; 1 Thess 2:18). In particular, John 5:40 speaks of a refusal to come to Christ. Heb 10:5ff. affirms that God "does not want" sacrifices and offerings without an accompanying godly motive.

Elsewhere, ***thelō*** is used positively to indicate the desire to see something done, and is translated thus "to want, or wish." Such a desire is predicated of human beings in Matt 5:40ff.; 12:23; Mark 6:19; Luke 8:20; 9:23ff.; John 5:6; 8:44; Acts 7:28. In particular, Rom 7:15ff. refers to Paul's dilemma in not doing what he "wants to do" (see also Gal 5:17); and 2 Tim 3:12 refers to people "wanting" to live a godly life.

thelō is also used in relation to Christ (Matt 8:2ff.; Mark 3:13; John 21:23). In particular, Christ is said to yield to the "will" and purpose of the Father (Mark 14:36). Luke 4:6 affirms that Christ delivers authority to whomever "he wills"; and John 5:21 declares that he gives life to whomever "he wills." See also John 17:24.

God is said, for example, to "desire" mercy (Matt 12:7). Rom 9:18 declares that God has mercy on whomever he "wills." 1 Tim 2:4 expresses God's general "desire" that all people will be saved. Phil 2:13 refers to God's "will" (or purpose) in nurturing believers in a life that will please him. See also Acts 18:21; 1 Cor 4:19; Jas 4:15.

thelō also refers metaphorically to the wind in John 3:8, where Christ declares that it blows "wherever it wills."

thelēma θέλημα 2307

thelēma is a noun derived from ***thelō*** (above) found in around sixty contexts with the primary meaning "will." The term refers primarily to "that which is desired or intended" and is predicated of both human beings and God. ***thelēma*** has primary reference, however, to the will of God.

References to God's "will," "purpose," or "intent" are varied. Matt 6:10; Luke 11:2; Acts 21:14 plead for God's will to be done. Those who do "the will" of God are noted in Matt 7:21; Mark 3:35; Eph 6:6; 1 John 2:17. And Matt 26:42; Luke 22:42 refer to Christ's submission to "God's will" in Gethsemane. Christ's determination to do his Father's "will" is expressed in John 4:34; 5:30; 6:3ff.; Heb 10:9. The "will" of God in relation to the plan of salvation is expressed in Eph 1:5ff. Knowing the "will of God" is indicated in Rom 2:18; 12:2. Being called to service by "the will of God" is noted in 1 Cor 1:1; Eph 1:1; Col 1:1; 2 Tim 1:1. See also 1 Thess 4:3; 1 Pet 2:15; Rev 4:11.

Luke 12:47 refers generally to the "will" of humankind in relation to "desire." See also John 1:13. The evil "purpose" of the Jewish religious leaders plotting to do away with Christ is noted in Luke 23:25.

thelēsis θέλησις 2308

thelēsis is a rare variant of ***thelēma*** (above) found only in Heb 2:4 with reference to the "will" of God that determines the distribution of spiritual gifts to his people.

boulomai βούλομαι 1014

boulomai is a synonym for ***thelō*** (above). It occurs about thirty times and expresses the underlying meaning "to will" in the sense of "express a purpose, intention, or desire." It is occasionally used in the negative.

The meaning "to be unwilling" is indicated in Matt 1:19 in relation to human beings. With respect to God, 2 Pet 3:9 declares that he is "not willing" that any should perish. In this case, the divine attitude is thought to be characterized by a general desire rather than an explicit purpose.

The meaning "to will" in the sense of "choose," "make a choice," is predicated of Christ in Matt 11:27; Luke 10:22. In 1 Cor 12:11, God "chooses" to give various gifts to this people.

The meaning "be willing" or "wish" is predicated of people in general terms (Mark 15:15; Acts 17:20; Jas 4:4) and also of God (Luke 22:42; Heb 6:17).

boulomai is also translated "to be determined," "intend" with reference to people (Acts 5:28) and God (Jas 1:18).

boulēma βούλημα 1013

boulēma is a rare noun meaning "will" or "purpose." The people's "purpose" (or intention) is indicated in Acts 27:43. God's will or purpose is said to be irresistible in Rom 9:19.

▸ **48.** Will, Purpose, Decide, Advise > PURPOSE, PLAN

eudokeō εὐδοκέω 2106

eudokeō is a verb found around twenty times with the underlying sense of "be pleased with" or "be willing" (i.e., take pleasure in).

The meaning "be pleased with" refers to God's estimation of his Son, Jesus Christ (Matt 3:17; 12:18; 17:5; Mark 1:11; Luke 3:22; 2 Pet 1:17).

Elsewhere, ***eudokeō*** is translated "to be willing" with the sense of "take pleasure in doing." This attitude is predicated of God in Luke 12:32 in relation to his desire to grant his kingdom to his people; and in 1 Cor 1:21 in relation to saving people from their sin. Heb 10:6ff. affirms that God "takes no pleasure" in offerings presented by people who do not have a right spirit of worship. The "desire" to be "at home with the Lord" rather than to remain in the body is expressed in 2 Cor 5:8. See also 1 Thess 2:3; 3:1.

▸ **50.** Love, Hate, Please, Be Pleased With > PLEASE, BE PLEASED

eudokia εὐδοκία 2107

eudokia is a noun derived from ***eudokeō*** (above). It is found in nine contexts and means "good will" or "good pleasure," as well as "desire."

God's "good pleasure" is indicated in Phil 2:13; Matt 11:26. Luke 2:14 refers specifically to God's "good will" toward humankind (see also Luke 10:21; Eph 1:5). This attitude is predicated of people in Phil 1:15.

The meaning "will" or "desire" is indicated in Rom 10:1 with regard to Paul's deep longing that people should be saved.

▸ **19.** Mind, Spirit, Emotions, Feelings, Desires > DESIRE

hekōn ἑκών 1635

hekōn is a rare adjective with the sense of "one's own will." In Rom 8:20 creation is subjected to futility "not of its own will," but by God himself. ***hekōn*** refers to Paul's own will in 1 Cor 9:17.

akōn ἄκων 210

akōn is a rare adjective found only in 1 Cor 9:7, referring to something done "against one's will."

prothymos πρόθυμος 4289

prothymos is an adjective found only three times meaning "willing," "ready."

Matt 26:41; Mark 14:38 refer to a "willing spirit." A "willing desire" to preach the gospel is noted in Rom 1:15.

49. Allow, Accept, Approve, Refuse

ACCEPT

prosdechomai προσδέχομαι 4327

prosdechomai is a verb found in fourteen places with the primary meanings "wait for," "receive." A couple of occurrences, however, express the meaning "accept." Heb 10:34 refers to believers who willingly "accepted" the trauma of persecution; and Heb 11:35 specifically mentions martyrs who refused to "accept" a release from death so that they could rise again to a better life.

- ▸ **24.** Dwell, Live, Gather, Hospitality > RECEIVE, WELCOME
- ▸ **46.** Wait, Hope, Be Vigilant, Pay Attention To > WAIT

SEE ALSO

- ▸ **50.** Love, Hate, Please, Be Pleased With > ACCEPTABLE, ACCEPTANCE
  dektos, apodektos, euprosdektos, euarestos, apodochē

ALLOW

epitrepō ἐπιτρέπω 2010

The verb ***epitrepō*** occurs nineteen times in a variety of contexts with the primary meaning "persist," "allow" throughout.

In a number of places, people ask Jesus to "allow" them a number of things — to bury their loved ones, for example (Matt 8:21; Luke 9:59), or to say farewell to family (Luke 9:61). Even demons beg permission of him to be sent away into a herd of swine (Matt 8:31; Mark 5:13; Luke 8:32).

Other contexts where permission is granted include Jesus "allowing" people to get divorced (Matt 19:8; Mark 10:4). Pilate "allows" the disciples of Christ to take his body down from the cross (John 19:38). Permission to speak is both sought and granted in Acts 21:39ff.; 26:1; 1 Cor 14:34. Women are refused permission to teach in 1 Tim 2:12. See also Acts 27:3; 28:16; 1 Cor 16:7; Heb 6:3.

- ▸ **49.** Allow, Accept, Approve, Refuse > PERMIT

apolyō ἀπολύω 630

The verb ***apolyō*** is found in about ninety contexts, and in about sixty of these it means "release," with the sense of "permitting, allowing to leave."

- ▸ **25.** Family, Marriage, Adoption, Inheritance > DIVORCE
- ▸ **25.** Family, Marriage, Adoption, Inheritance > PUT AWAY
- ▸ **44.** Repentance, Forgiveness, Mercy, Redeem, Save > FORGIVE, FORGIVENESS, RELEASE
- ▸ **55.** Bondage, Captivity, Servitude > RELEASE
- ▸ **79.** Throw, Send, Drive, Mix, Remove > SEND, SEND AWAY, SEND OUT

aphiēmi ἀφίημι 863

aphiēmi is a verb found in more than 150 contexts with the predominant sense of "forgive," "leave" in most of these occurrences.

The general sense of "permit," "let," or "allow" something to happen is evident in Matt 7:4; 8:22; 13:30; Luke 6:42; 9:60. In particular, Matt 19:14; Luke 10:14 make reference to Jesus' request to "allow" little children to come to him for blessing. The exhortation "let it be" (i.e., allow to happen) is found in Matt 3:15. See also Mark 11:6; John 11:44.

The negative use of ***aphiēmi***, indicating a "refusal to allow," is evident in Matt 23:13, where Jesus indicts the Pharisees for refusing to allow people to enter the kingdom of heaven (see also Mark 7:12). In Mark 1:34 Jesus refuses demons permission to speak. See also Mark 5:37; 11:16; Rev 11:9.

- ▸ **44.** Repentance, Forgiveness, Mercy, Redeem, Save > FORGIVE, FORGIVENESS, RELEASE
- ▸ **86.** Movement Toward or Away From > LEAVE, GO AWAY, LEAVE BEHIND, ABANDON

eaō ἐάω 1439

eaō is a verb expressing the meaning "allow," "permit" in most of its thirteen occurrences.

eaō is predicated of God in Acts 14:16, where he is said to "have granted permission" (or allowed) the nations to go their own way in the past. In 1 Cor 10:13, the promise is made that God "will not allow" his people to be tempted beyond their strength. There is an indictment in Rev 2:20 against the church at Thyatira for "tolerating" an ungodly prophetess (i.e., allowing her to minister) within the congregation.

General references to a refusal to allow or permit include Matt 24:43; Acts 19:30; 28:4. Christ refuses to allow demons to speak in Luke 4:41. In Acts 16:7, the Spirit of Christ refuses to allow Paul and his companions to journey into Bithynia.

SEE ALSO

- ▸ **29.** Boats, Fishing, Maritime Activity > ALLOW
  proseaō

APPROVE, APPROVED

dokimazō δοκιμάζω 1381

dokimazō is a verb occurring nearly thirty times. It expresses the meanings "approve" and "prove" along with several related nuances.

The meaning "approve" in the sense of "examine," "impact" is indicated in relation to cattle in Luke 14:19; the value of people's ministry to be tested by fire at the last judgment in 1 Cor 3:13; self-examination in 2 Cor 13:5; Gal 6:4. In 1 John 4:1, believers are exhorted to "test" the spirits to see whether they are of God.

The capacity for "approving" ("discerning") what pleases God in relation to his law and will is noted in Rom 2:18; 12:2; Eph 5:10; Phil 1:10; 1 Thess 5:21 (Rom 14:22 in relation to what is morally right).

The "approving" of people for ministry in the sense of deeming them worthy of commendation is indicated in 1 Cor 16:3; 1 Tim 3:10.

The status of being "approved" by God is mentioned in 1 Thess 2:4 in the context of gospel ministry; and in 1 Pet 1:7 in relation to one's life work, to be tested by fire at the final judgment.

▸ **46.** Wait, Hope, Be Vigilant, Pay Attention To > EXAMINATION, EXAMINE

▸ **51.** Knowledge, Wisdom, Remember, Forget > TEST, TEMPT, TEMPTATION

apodeiknymi ἀποδείκνυμι 584

apodeiknymi is a verb found in four contexts, with the meaning "exhibit," "put on display" in all but one of these. In Acts 2:22, it means to "approve" in the sense of "attest," "accredit" with reference to Jesus Christ as one "approved," "attested" by God among the people of Israel.

▸ **32.** Law, Justice, Jurisprudence, Judgment > PROVE

dokimos δόκιμος 1384

dokimos is an adjectival form derived from ***apodeiknymi*** (above) with the meaning "approved" in several different senses. It occurs seven times.

The state of being "approved," "commended" by human beings refers to one's acceptability and worthiness for gospel ministry in Rom 14:18; 16:10. 1 Cor 11:19; 2 Cor 10:18 refer explicitly to those who are "commended" by God.

dokimos also refers to those who "have been approved," that is, to those who have been subject to assessment and deemed satisfactory (2 Cor 13:7). Similarly, Jas 1:12 affirms that those who "have stood the test" will receive the crown of life in the state hereafter.

Finally, 2 Tim 2:15 describes a worker in the word of God as one who is "approved," who demonstrates competence in accurately teaching its content.

AVOID

ekklinō ἐκκλίνω 1578

ekklinō is a rare verb meaning "avoid," found in Rom 16:17 referring to opponents of the gospel message, whom Paul instructs the Roman believers to avoid. The sense of "turn away from" is indicated in Rom 3:12; 1 Pet 3:11.

ektrepō ἐκτρέπω 1624

ektrepō is a verb synonymous with ***ekklinō*** (above) with the primary meaning "turn aside, turn away from" (1 Tim 1:6; 5:15; 2 Tim 4:4; Heb 12:13). In 1 Tim 6:20, it is translated "avoid" in the context of Paul's admonition to Timothy to "keep away from" godless chatter.

paraiteomai παραιτέομαι 3868

paraiteomai is a verb found in nine contexts. For the most part it is translated "refuse," "have nothing to do with." In two places, it means "avoid": 2 Tim 2:23 contains the injunction to "avoid" senseless controversies; and in Titus 3:10 there is an admonition to "avoid" any troublemaker in the church who refuses to accept rebuke.

▸ **49.** Allow, Accept, Approve, Refuse > EXCUSE

▸ **49.** Allow, Accept, Approve, Refuse > REFUSE

periistēmi περιΐστημι 4026

periistēmi is a verb translated "shun," "avoid" in 2 Tim 2:16; Titus 3:9 in relation to stupid, foolish, or profane talk.

▸ **85.** Movement, Position, State > STAND

CONSENT

synkatatithēmi συγκατατίθημι 4784

synkatatithēmi is a rare verb found only in Luke 23:5, referring to Joseph of Arimathea's refusal "to consent" (i.e., give approval) to the Sanhedrin's decision to seek the execution of Christ.

syneudokeō συνευδοκέω 4909

The verb ***syneudokeō*** is found in six places and means "consent," "give approval to." Christ condemns the Pharisees' "approval" of their ancestors killing the prophets in Luke 11:48. Similar culpable "consenting" to evil deeds is noted in Rom 1:32. Saul's "giving consent" to the execution of Stephen, the first Christian martyr, is indicated in Acts 8:1; 22:20. References to an unbelieving spouse "consenting" to live with his/her partner are found in 1 Cor 7:12ff.

DENY

arneomai ἀρνέομαι 720

arneomai is a verb with the predominant sense of "deny," with a variety of nuances, throughout the nearly thirty occurrences of the term.

References to "denying" in the sense of "disown" are found regarding those who "deny" Christ, or refuse to recognize him as Lord and bear testimony to him before human beings (Matt 10:33; Luke 12:9; 2 Tim 2:12; 1 John 2:22ff.; 2 Pet 2:21; Jude 4; Rev 2:13; 3:8). "Denying" God is noted in Titus 1:16. The action of "denying" in the sense of "refusing to acknowledge or admit the truth" is indicated in Matt 26:70ff.; Mark 14:68ff.; Luke 8:45; 22:57; John 18:25ff. Acts 3:13ff. refers to the Jews "denying" or "disowning" Christ and handing him over to Pilate.

Acts 4:16 describes the impossibility of "denying" a miracle.

The action of "denying" (i.e., rejecting) one's faith is recorded in 1 Tim 5:8, as is "denying" the power of godliness in 2 Tim 3:5. The impossibility of Christ "denying" (i.e., "disowning") himself is described in 2 Tim 2:13.

▸ **49.** Allow, Accept, Approve, Refuse > REFUSE

aparneomai ἀπαρνέομαι 533

aparneomai is a variant form of ***arneomai*** (above) meaning "deny" throughout the fourteen occurrences of the term.

Matt 16:24; Mark 8:34; Luke 9:23 speak of the importance of "denying" oneself to take up one's cross and follow Christ.

Peter's action in "denying" Christ on the eve of his trial, refusing to acknowledge him as master and friend, is noted in Matt 26:34ff., 75; Mark 14:30ff., 72; Luke 22:34, 61; John 13:38.

Luke 12:9 affirms that whoever "denies" Christ before others will be denied before the angels in heaven.

antilegō ἀντιλέγω 483

antilegō is a verb occurring ten times with the underlying sense of "speak against." It specifically means "deny" in Luke 20:27 where the Sadducees are said to "deny" (i.e., refuse to believe in) the resurrection.

ENDURE

tropophoreō τροποφορέω 5159

tropophoreō is a rare verb found only in Acts 13:18, referring to God "enduring" the ill conduct of his people in the desert for forty years.

SEE ALSO

- ▸ **4.** Beginning, Continuing, Finishing, Postponing > ENDURE, REMAIN
  menō
- ▸ **60.** Virtues > ENDURE, BEAR, FORBEAR
  hypomenō

EXCUSE

apologeomai ἀπολογέομαι 626

apologeomai is a verb found eleven times, meaning "answer," "excuse," "defend." The former meaning is predominant.

The meaning "excuse" is found in Rom 2:15, referring to the phenomenon of a person's conscience "excusing" him. In 2 Cor 12:19 the apostle asks his readers whether they think he and his companions were "defending" themselves.

- ▸ **32.** Law, Justice, Jurisprudence, Judgment > ANSWER
- ▸ **32.** Law, Justice, Jurisprudence, Judgment > DEFENSE

anapologētos ἀναπολόγητος 379

anapologētos is a rare adjective found only twice (Rom 1:20; 2:1), referring to godless people who are "without excuse" in feigning ignorance of God.

paraiteomai παραιτέομαι 3868

paraiteomai is a verb found nine times, meaning "excuse," "refuse."

Luke 14:18, 19 refer to a man "making excuses" in refusing an invitation to a feast and also requesting to "have himself excused" from such an obligation.

- ▸ **49.** Allow, Accept, Approve, Refuse > AVOID
- ▸ **49.** Allow, Accept, Approve, Refuse > REFUSE

prophasis πρόφασις 4392

prophasis is a noun occurring seven times, meaning "pretext" in most of these contexts. John 15:22, however, mentions people "having no excuse" for their sin.

FORBID, HINDER, PREVENT

kōlyō κωλύω 2967

kōlyō is a verb occurring about twenty times with the senses of "hinder," "forbid," "prevent" throughout.

The meaning "forbid" with the underlying sense of people expressing a negative command is indicated in Mark 9:38ff.; Luke 9:49ff.; 23:2; 1 Cor 14:39; 1 Tim 4:3; Acts 10:47.

The Holy Spirit is said to "have forbidden" the apostle Paul to enter Asia in Acts 16:6.

Jesus exhorts his disciples not to "hinder" little children from coming to him in Matt 19:14; Mark 10:14; Luke 18:16. He also denounces Jewish lawyers for "hindering" those seeking to enter the kingdom of heaven by keeping knowledge of the truth from them (Luke 11:52). Heb 7:23 refers to priests "being prevented" by death from continuing in office. Other occurrences of the meaning "hinder" or "prevent" include those in Acts 8:36; 1 Thess 2:16.

OFFENSE, OFFEND

skandalizō σκανδαλίζω 4624

skandalizō is a verb found in thirty-five contexts with the underlying sense of bringing about someone's downfall as a consequence of sin. ***skandalizō*** is variously translated "cause to sin," "bring about one's downfall," "fall away," "offend," "take (or give) offense." The latter two meanings are found in seven contexts.

The meaning "take offense" is found in the context of Jesus' person and ministry. For example, not to take offense at Jesus is considered worthy of praise (Matt 11:6; Luke 7:23). Conversely, those who do take offense at Jesus for what he does and says are condemned (Matt 13:57; 15:12; Mark 6:3). The question of taking offense at Jesus' teaching is raised in John 6:61. The meaning "offend" in the context of giving offense to people is found in Matt 17:27.

- ▸ **57.** Evil, Wickedness, Sin > SIN, SINNER, CAUSE TO SIN

OVERLOOK

hypereidō ὑπερείδω 5237

hypereidō is found only in Acts 17:30 where it means "overlook," referring to God taking no notice of humanity's ignorance in the past.

PERMIT

epitrepō ἐπιτρέπω 2010

epitrepō is a verb that is variously translated as "let," "allow," "give leave," "permit" — although all of these meanings are virtually interchangeable. ***epitrepō*** occurs nineteen times.

The concept of "permitting" occurs first of all in the context of requesting permission to do something. In Matt 8:21; Luke 9:57, people ask permission of Jesus to bury their dead before becoming his disciples. Similarly, in Luke 9:61, potential disciples ask permission to say farewell to their families.

More frequently, ***epitrepō*** indicates the action of allowing a certain event, or transaction, to take place. Matt 19:8; Mark 10:4 refer to Moses allowing divorce to take place in the old covenant era. Mark 5:13; Luke 8:32 relate the incident in which Jesus permitted the evil spirits that had formerly possessed the man to enter a herd of pigs. In John 19:38, Pilate gives permission for Joseph of Arimathea to remove the body of Jesus from the cross. Acts 21:39 refers to Paul's request to be allowed to speak to the Jerusalem crowd (see also Acts 26:1; 27:3; 28:16). In 1 Cor 14:34, Paul refuses to give women permission to speak in church (see also 1 Tim 2:12).

Finally, 1 Cor 16:7; Heb 6:3 contain the formulaic expression "If God permits . . . " or "God willing . . ."

▸ **49.** Allow, Accept, Approve, Refuse > ALLOW

REFUSE

paraiteomai παραιτέομαι 3868

paraiteomai is a verb found only nine times, with the underlying sense of "have nothing to do with." It is translated "refuse" (twice) in Heb 12:25 in the context of an injunction not to refuse (or reject) the spoken word of God.

▸ **49.** Allow, Accept, Approve, Refuse > AVOID
▸ **49.** Allow, Accept, Approve, Refuse > EXCUSE

arneomai ἀρνέομαι 720

arneomai is a verb occurring about thirty times, meaning "deny" in most of these contexts. In two places, however, it is translated "refuse" — in Heb 11:24, and also in Acts 7:35, with the sense of "reject" in reference to Moses, who was unsuccessfully challenged by the rebellious Levitical family of Korah (Num 16).

▸ **49.** Allow, Accept, Approve, Refuse > DENY

apoblētos ἀπόβλητος 579

apoblētos is a noun derived from the verb ***apoballō*** (to cast away, off), meaning "that which is refused." It is found only in 1 Tim 4:4, in the admonition not to refuse, or reject, anything that is created by God.

REJECT

atheteō ἀθετέω 114

atheteō is a verb occurring sixteen times and meaning "despise," "reject" in most of these contexts. The underlying sense is that of "cast aside" or "spurn." ***atheteō*** is predicated only of human beings.

The Pharisees are said to have rejected the law of God (Mark 7:9), and the purpose of God for their lives (Luke 7:30). Luke 10:16; John 12:48 warn against rejecting the person of Christ. A similar warning with respect to the law of God is found in 1 Thess 4:8. 1 Tim 5:12 refers to rejecting one's promise to God, in the sense of casting it aside. Jude 8 refers to false prophets rejecting duly instituted civil authority.

▸ **54.** Rule, Authority, Command, Obedience > DESPISE

apodokimazō ἀποδοκιμάζω 593

apodokimazō is a verb found in nine places and meaning "reject" or "repudiate" in each of these contexts.

Christ refers to the OT (i.e., Ps 118:22, 23), indicating that the stone rejected by the builders has now become the chief cornerstone (Matt 21:42; Mark 12:10; Luke 20:17; 1 Pet 2:4, 7). This allusion refers to the emerging supremacy of the Messiah, notwithstanding the attempts by an unbelieving people to recognize his true divine authority. In other places, Jesus refers to his imminent arrest and crucifixion by indicating to his disciples that the Son of Man is soon to be "rejected" by the religious authorities in Israel (Mark 8:31; Luke 9:22; 17:25).

Heb 12:17 speaks of Esau's rejection by God, the divine refusal to grant him afresh the birthright he had despised by handing it over to his brother, Jacob.

RENOUNCE

apeipomēn ἀπειπόμην 550

apeipomēn is a verb found only in 2 Cor 4:2, which speaks of "renouncing" or "casting aside" deceitful practices in undertaking gospel ministry.

RESTRAIN

katapauō καταπαύω 2664

katapauō is a verb found only four times, and in three of these contexts it means "rest." However, in Acts 14:18, ***katapauō*** refers to "restraining" people from offering sacrifices to Paul and Barnabas.

▸ **20.** Illness, Disease, Health, Healing > REST

50. Love, Hate, Please, Be Pleased With

ACCEPTABLE, ACCEPTANCE

dektos δεκτός 1184

dektos is an adjective meaning "accepted," "acceptable," and is found in five contexts. Luke 4:19 refers to the "acceptable" year of the Lord (i.e., the divinely ordained time for the coming of the Messiah and the kingdom of God). Acts 10:35 and Phil 4:18 describe the condition of being "acceptable" to God. See also Luke 4:24; 2 Cor 6:2.

apodektos ἀπόδεκτος 587

apodektos is synonymous with ***dektos*** (above) and is found twice only, indicating "that which is acceptable" to God in 1 Tim 2:3; 5:4.

euprosdektos εὐπρόσδεκτος 2144

euprosdektos is another synonym for ***dektos*** and ***apodektos*** (above) and is found in five contexts. Rom 15:16; 1 Pet 2:5 refer to the state of being "acceptable" to God. Rom 15:31 refers to Christian service deemed "acceptable" to the saints in Jerusalem. See also 2 Cor 6:2; 8:12.

euarestos εὐάρεστος 2101

euarestos is an adjective used to describe "that which is well-pleasing or acceptable." It occurs nine times.

Devoted service, or commitment, to God is "well pleasing" to him in Rom 12:1ff.; 14:18; 2 Cor 5:9; Eph 5:10; Phil 4:18; Heb 13:21. In particular, children's obedience to their parents and a slave's submission to his master are "pleasing" to God (Col 3:20; Titus 2:9).

▸ **50.** Love, Hate, Please, Be Pleased With > PLEASING

apodochē ἀποδοχή 594

apodochē is a rare noun denoting that which is worthy of full "acceptance" in the eyes of God (1 Tim 1:15; 4:9).

SEE ALSO

▸ **49.** Allow, Accept, Approve, Refuse > ACCEPT
prosdechomai

BELOVED

agapētos ἀγαπητός 27

agapētos is an adjectival form occurring around sixty times with the meaning "(dearly) beloved," "well-loved."

God designates Christ as "my beloved Son" (Matt 3:17; 12:18; 17:5; Mark 1:11; 9:7; Luke 3:22; 9:35; 2 Pet 1:17). In 1 Cor 4:17, Paul refers to Timothy as his "beloved son" since he was converted under the apostle's ministry. In Luke 20:13, ***agapētos*** refers to a person in the parable, though in reality it is applied to Christ as the Son of God.

People are deemed "highly esteemed" or "beloved" in general contexts in Acts 15:25; Rom 16:5ff.; Eph 5:1; 6:21; 1 Tim 6:2. Rom 1:7; 11:28 designate people as "beloved of God."

The term "beloved" is also a form of address or greeting in Rom 12:19; 1 Cor 10:14; 2 Cor 7:1; Phil 2:12; Phlm 2; Heb 6:9; 1 Pet 2:11; 2 Pet 3:14ff.; 1 John 4:1ff.; Jude 3, 17, 20.

DELIGHT IN

synēdomai συνήδομαι 4913

synēdomai is a rare verb found only in Rom 7:22 describing Paul's "delighting" in the law of God.

ENJOYMENT

apolausis ἀπόλαυσις 619

apolausis is a rare noun found only twice, denoting the "enjoyment" of the pleasures of sin in Heb 11:25. 1 Tim 6:19 refers to the blessings of God given to his people for their "enjoyment."

SEE ALSO

▸ **84.** Do, Make, Accomplish, Occur > EXPERIENCE, ENJOY
tynchanō

FAULT

memphomai μέμφομαι 3201

memphomai is a rare verb meaning "find fault" (i.e., attribute blame) in Rom 9:19; Heb 8:8.

elenchō ἐλέγχω 1651

elenchō is a verb occurring seventeen times with the primary meanings "rebuke," "reprove." In Matt 18:15, however, it is translated "to show someone's fault to them," or to expose their fault or blame.

▸ **64.** Reveal, Explain, Hiddenness, Secrecy > CONVICT
▸ **64.** Reveal, Explain, Hiddenness, Secrecy > EXPOSE
▸ **65.** Teach, Exhort, Rebuke, Discipline > REBUKE

SEE ALSO

▸ **32.** Law, Justice, Jurisprudence, Judgment > FAULT, FAULTLESS
aition

LOVE

philadelphia φιλαδελφία 5360
philadelphos φιλάδελφος 5361

philadelphia occurs six times and means "brotherly love," "love of the brethren" (Rom 12:10; 1 Thess 4:9; Heb 13:1; 1 Pet 1:22; 2 Pet 1:7). The variant form ***philadelphos*** occurs in 1 Pet 3:8 with the same meaning.

SEE ALSO

▸ **48.** Will, Purpose, Decide, Advise > LOVE
agapaō, agapē, phileō

PLEASE, BE PLEASED

areskō ἀρέσκω 700

areskō is a verb meaning "to please" in each of the seventeen settings in which it occurs.

The general sense of "pleasing" someone conveys the idea of making a favorable impression on others. This usage is evident in Acts 6:5; Rom 15:2; 1 Cor 7:33ff.; 10:33; Gal 1:10; 2 Tim 2:4. Rom 15:3 states that Christ chose not to please himself during his life on earth. The same idea is indicated with respect to human beings pleasing God in 1 Cor 7:32; 1 Thess 4:1. The impossibility of unbelievers pleasing God is indicated in Rom 8:8; 1 Thess 2:15. Rom 15:1 records the exhortation not to please oneself (see also 1 Thess 2:4). In Matt 14:6; Mark 6:22, a unique use of ***areskō*** suggests that Herodias' dancing before her stepfather king Herod may have pleased him in an erotic way.

euaresteō εὐαρεστέω 2100

euaresteō is a synonym for ***areskō*** (above) and occurs only three times, meaning "to please." Heb 11:5 refers to the patriarch Enoch, who was said to have pleased God. Heb 13:16 affirms that a selfless concern for other people constitutes a sacrifice that is pleasing to God. Heb 11:6 claims that it is impossible to please God without the possession of saving faith.

eudokeō εὐδοκέω 2106

eudokeō is a verb meaning "to be (well) pleased," "please," or "take pleasure in" in most of its twenty-one occurrences.

When predicated of God, ***eudokeō*** refers to God being pleased with his Son Jesus, expressed through explicit divine testimony at the outset of, and during, the public ministry of Christ (Matt 3:17; 12:18; 17:5; Mark 1:11; Luke 3:22; 2 Pet 1:17). In contrast, God was not pleased with most of the Israelite people during their sojourn in the wilderness en route to the land of Canaan (1 Cor 10:5). See also Heb 10:38. In other contexts, God is said to be pleased with, or to take pleasure in, giving the kingdom to his followers (Luke 12:32); saving people through the preaching of the gospel (1 Cor 1:21); and revealing himself in his Son (Gal 1:15; Col 1:19). But God takes no pleasure in formalized worship or sacrifices (Heb 10:6, 8).

As far as human beings are concerned, the godless are said to take pleasure in unrighteousness in 2 Thess 2:12. Paul refers to those who "were pleased" to make a significant contribution to the plight of the poor in Rom 15:26ff.

▸ **48.** Will, Purpose, Decide, Advise > WILL, WILLING

SEE ALSO

▸ **58.** Vices > PLEASURE, PASSION, LUST
hēdonē, philēdonos

PLEASING

arestos ἀρεστός 701

arestos is an adjective referring to those things that are pleasing. The term occurs four times and expresses this meaning in three of these contexts. John 8:29 speaks of Jesus being committed to do what is "pleasing" to his Father; and 1 John 3:22 refers to the willingness of believers to do what is pleasing to God.

areskeia ἀρεσκεία 699

areskeia is a noun that occurs only in Col 1:10, where the believer is exhorted to live a life wholly "pleasing" to God.

euarestos εὐάρεστος 2101

euarestos is an adjective that is consistently translated "acceptable" or "(well) pleasing" in each of the nine contexts in which it occurs.

The majority usage of ***euarestos*** centers on those things that are "pleasing" to God, such as wholehearted service to God (Rom 12:12; Phil 4:18; Heb 13:21); and also service to Christ (Rom 14:18). 2 Cor 5:9; Eph 5:10 contain exhortations to live lives pleasing to God. The obedient submission of children to parents, and slaves to masters, evokes a pleasing response from God in Col 3:20; Titus 2:9, respectively.

▸ **50.** Love, Hate, Please, Be Pleased With > ACCEPTABLE, ACCEPTANCE

SEE ALSO

▸ **58.** Vices > PLEASURE, PASSION, LUST
hēdonē, philēdonos

THANK, THANKS, THANKSGIVING

eucharistia εὐχαριστία 2169

eucharistia is a noun found in fifteen places and meaning "thanks," "thanksgiving," "thankfulness" throughout — primarily in relation to God.

Thanksgiving to God in worship is noted in 1 Cor 14:16; Rev 4:9; 7:2. Other general contexts for the expression of gratitude include those in 2 Cor 4:15; Phil 4:6; Col 2:7; 1 Tim 2:1; 4:3ff.

exomologeō ἐξομολογέω 1843

exomologeō is a verb expressing the primary meaning "confess." However, in two of the eleven occurrences of the term, the meaning indicated is "give thanks" in relation to Jesus' gratitude to God for making his revelation known not to the proud, who called themselves "wise," but to the "little children," or those who showed genuine faith and dependence on God for all their needs (Matt 11:25; Luke 10:21).

▸ **67.** Acknowledge, Confess, Profess, Swear > CONFESS, CONFESSION, PROFESS, PROFESSION, ACKNOWLEDGE

eucharistos εὐχάριστος 2170

eucharistos is an adjectival form found only in Col 3:15 meaning "thankful" in relation to the believer's gratitude for his saving relationship with Christ.

anthomologeomai ἀνθομολογέομαι 437

This is a rare verb found only in Luke 2:38 in the context of "giving thanks" to God.

eucharisteō εὐχαριστέω 2168

eucharisteō is a verb meaning "give thanks," "be thankful," primarily in the context of giving thanks to God.

Jesus expresses such thankfulness to the Father in Matt 15:36; Mark 8:6; John 6:11; 11:41. In particular, he does so at the Passover festival (Matt 26:27; Mark 14:23; Luke 22:17ff.). See also 1 Cor 11:24.

People give thanks to Christ for healing them in Luke 17:16.

General references to thanks being offered up to God include those in Luke 18:11; Acts 28:15; Rev 11:17. In Rom 1:21, unbelievers refuse to give thanks to God. Paul gives thanks to God for the salvation offered in Christ (Rom 1:8; 7:25; 1 Cor 1:4; Eph 5:20; Col 1:3). See also Acts 27:35; Eph 1:16; 1 Thess 1:2; Phlm 4.

51. Knowledge, Wisdom, Remember, Forget

CONSCIENCE

syneidēsis συνείδησις 4893

syneidēsis is the sole term in the NT denoting the human "conscience" as the created moral faculty for discerning between good and evil.

General references to one's conscience are found in 1 Cor 10:29; 2 Cor 4:2; 5:11; Heb 9:9, 14. A "good, clear conscience" is noted in Acts 23:1; 24:16; 1 Tim 1:5; 3:9; 2 Tim 1:3; Heb 10:2, 22; 13:18; 1 Pet 3:16, 21. A "seared or defiled conscience" is indicated in 1 Cor 8:7; 1 Tim 4:2; Titus 1:15. Rom 2:15 mentions one's "conscience" working to either excuse or accuse. The condition of having a "weak conscience" is indicated in 1 Cor 8:10ff. The vindication of one's conscience is noted in Rom 9:1. 1 Tim 1:19 refers to "rejecting one's conscience." Acting for the sake of one's conscience, or avoiding morally dubious behavior, is mentioned in Rom 13:5; 1 Cor 10:25.

CONSIDER

noeō νοέω 3539

noeō is a verb found in around twenty contexts with the primary sense of "understand." However, in 2 Tim 2:7 the term expresses the meaning "consider" in the sense of "think over" or "reflect on," referring to Paul's injunction to Timothy to carefully consider the apostle's teaching.

▸ **51.** Knowledge, Wisdom, Remember, Forget > UNDERSTAND, UNDERSTANDING

katanoeō κατανοέω 2657

katanoeō is a verb meaning "consider" in the sense of "perceive," "notice," and "reflect on" in most of the fourteen occurrences of the term.

It refers to the action of "considering" or "noticing" one's own faults (Matt 7:3; Luke 6:41); as well as another's craftiness (Luke 20:23).

Elsewhere, Christ's advice to his listeners to "ponder" or "reflect on" the birds of the air and the flowers of the field, who have no need to worry, is found in Luke 12:24ff. Paul affirms in Rom 4:19 that Abraham, while "considering" the aged condition of his own body, had not weakened in his faith. Heb 3:1 contains an appeal to "reflect on" the person of Christ. See also Heb 10:24.

anatheōreō ἀναθεωρέω 333

anatheōreō is a rare verb found only twice. It means "observe" in Acts 17:23, and "consider" in the sense of "reflect on" in Heb 13:7. This latter reference contains the exhortation to "consider" the lifestyle of one's spiritual leaders and imitate their faith.

analogizomai ἀναλογίζομαι 357

analogizomai is a verb found only in Heb 2:3 expressing the admonition to "consider" (i.e., "ponder," "reflect on") the suffering endured by Christ.

logizomai λογίζομαι 3049

logizomai is a verb found about forty times, translated various ways, with the underlying connotation of mental "reasoning" or "calculating." It often means "to count," "consider," or "reckon."

The meaning "count" in the sense of "consider" or "regard" is found in a number of places. "Regarding" uncircumcision as circumcision, as in the case of Gentiles who were devout followers of the Jewish law, is the meaning indicated in Rom 2:26. To "consider" someone justified by faith rather than works of the law is a position indicated in Rom 3:28. This assessment applies especially to Abraham in Rom 4:3ff.; Gal 3:6; Jas 2:23. "Regarding" oneself as dead to sin is a state of mind indicated in Rom 6:11. Believers "considered" as sheep to be slaughtered are indicated in the context of persecution in Rom 8:36. In Rom 9:8, children of Abraham are "reckoned" as children of God. God refuses to "count" the sins of his people against them in 2 Cor 5:19.

Other occurrences include those in 1 Cor 4:1; 2 Cor 12:6; Phil 3:13; 2 Tim 4:16; Heb 11:19.

▸ **51.** Knowledge, Wisdom, Remember, Forget > IMPUTE
▸ **51.** Knowledge, Wisdom, Remember, Forget > RECKON
▸ **52.** Status, Identity, Reputation, Honor, Shame > NUMBER

katamanthanō καταμανθάνω 2648

katamanthanō is a rare verb found only in Matt 6:28 referring to Christ's injunction to his listeners not to worry, and hence to "consider" the lilies of the field — to "reflect" on the fact that they are cared for by their Creator without the need for anxiety.

COUNT

hēgeomai ἡγέομαι 2233

The verb ***hēgeomai*** is found in thirty places and means "count," "think," "consider," as well as having some related nuances.

The action of "counting" in the sense of "consider," "reckon" is indicated in Phil 3:7ff., referring to "counting" gain as loss for the sake of Christ. See also Heb 11:26; Acts 26:2.

hēgeomai means to "judge someone faithful" in 1 Tim 6:1. "Esteeming" people highly is indicated in 1 Thess 5:13. To "consider" the blood of Christ as useless is a heinous offense in the sight of God (Heb 10:29). Other references include 2 Thess 3:15; Heb 11:11; 13:7; Jas 1:2; 2 Pet 1:13; 2:13.

Referring to Christ, Paul affirms in Phil 2:6 that the Lord "did not count" equality with God something to be grasped.

▸ **54.** Rule, Authority, Command, Obedience > RULE, RULER

DISCERN

anakrinō ἀνακρίνω 350

anakrinō is a verb found sixteen times with the principal meanings "judge," "examine." In 1 Cor 2:14, however, the term refers to the unspiritual person's inability to "discern" spiritual things.

- ▸ **32.** Law, Justice, Jurisprudence, Judgment > EXAMINE, EXAMINATION, INVESTIGATION
- ▸ **32.** Law, Justice, Jurisprudence, Judgment > JUDGE
- ▸ **66.** Ask, Answer, Discuss, Learn > ASK, REQUEST, BEG, PLEAD
- ▸ **66.** Ask, Answer, Discuss, Learn > QUESTION, INTERROGATE

diakrisis διάκρισις 1253

diakrisis is a rare noun denoting the capacity for "discerning" between good or evil in Heb 5:14; and for "discerning" spirits in 1 Cor 12:10. The latter practice required an assessment of whether spirits were godly or demonic.

- ▸ **66.** Ask, Answer, Discuss, Learn > REASON, DEBATE, DISPUTE

DISPUTE

syzētētēs συζητητής 4804

syzētētēs is a rare noun found only in 1 Cor 1:20, denoting a "philosopher," or one who "debates," who engages in disputes or discussions concerning human life. In this context the reference is negative, indicating the person who extols only human wisdom and ignores the wisdom of God.

- ▸ **51.** Knowledge, Wisdom, Remember, Forget > PHILOSOPHER, PHILOSOPHY

syzēteō συζητέω 4802

syzēteō is a verb found ten times with the sense of "dispute," "argue," or "debate" in most of these contexts. Specific references to "disputing" or "arguing" include Mark 1:27; 8:11; 9:10ff.; 12:28; Acts 6:9; 9:29. Neutral contexts where "questioning" or "discussion" is involved are found in Luke 22:23; 24:15.

- ▸ **66.** Ask, Answer, Discuss, Learn > QUESTION, INTERROGATE

SEE ALSO

- ▸ **58.** Vices > ARGUE, ARGUMENT, DISPUTE, QUARREL, STRIVE
  logomachia, diaparatribē
- ▸ **66.** Ask, Answer, Discuss, Learn > REASON, DEBATE, DISPUTE
  antilogia, diakrisis

FORGET

epilanthanomai ἐπιλανθάνομαι 1950

epilanthanomai is a verb found in nine places meaning "forget" throughout, with several different nuances.

"Forgetting" in the sense of "failure to do something" is indicated in Matt 16:5; Mark 8:14, in relation to providing food.

The impossibility of God "forgetting" or "overlooking" the needs of his creation is noted in Luke 12:6; as is his determination not to "forget" or "overlook" the service of the saints in Heb 6:10.

Phil 3:13 refers to Paul's determination to "forget" (i.e., put aside from his mind) what lies behind him.

Heb 13:2 contains an injunction not to "forget" (i.e., neglect) to show hospitality to strangers; and Heb 13:16 contains a more generalized exhortation not to "forget" (i.e., neglect) to do good.

Jas 1:24 describes the phenomenon of a person looking into a mirror and then "forgetting" what he looks like — that is, failing to recall the image in his memory. See also Jas 1:25.

eklanthanomai ἐκλανθάνομαι 1585

A rare variant of ***epilanthanomai*** (above), ***eklanthanomai*** means "forget," in the sense of "fail to recall," in Heb 12:5.

IMPUTE

logizomai λογίζομαι 3049

logizomai is found approximately forty times and is translated "reckon," "count," "impute." There is an underlying rational element to all the meanings associated with this verb, including the sense of "to reason" in a number of contexts.

Paul poses the question in Rom 2:26 as to whether those who are uncircumcised will be reckoned by God as circumcised if they keep the law of God. The exercise of faith is imputed as righteousness to those who so believe (Rom 4:3ff., 22ff.; Gal 3:6; Jas 2:23), with Abraham as the paradigm for imputed righteousness. In a corollary context, 2 Cor 5:19 declares that God was in Christ reconciling the world to himself, not imputing the sins of human beings against them. As a consequence, believers are "to reckon" themselves as dead to sin, as stated in Rom 6:11.

Other general occurrences of ***logizomai*** indicate that wages are "reckoned" as a person's due (Rom 4:4). In a metaphorical sense, talking about the realities of persecution, believers may often be "considered" as sheep to be slaughtered.

- ▸ **51.** Knowledge, Wisdom, Remember, Forget > CONSIDER
- ▸ **51.** Knowledge, Wisdom, Remember, Forget > RECKON
- ▸ **52.** Status, Identity, Reputation, Honor, Shame > NUMBER

SEE ALSO

- ▸ **30.** Money, Business, Wealth, Poverty > IMPUTE
  ellogeō

JUDGE

dikastēs δικαστής 1348

dikastēs occurs only in Acts 7:27, 35, with reference to a judge in a general sense and not in a formal, official capacity.

diakrinō διακρίνω 1252

diakrinō is a verb with several senses, including "discerning," "interpreting," "doubling," and "judging." Of its approximately twenty occurrences, the term is translated "to judge" on four occasions. 1 Cor 11:31; Jas 2:4 refer to the process of "judging" in a general, informal sense. 1 Cor 6:5; 14:29 indicate the practice of making a judgment within the church among believers.

▸ **45.** Faith, Belief, Trust, Promise > DOUBT

SEE ALSO

▸ **32.** Law, Justice, Jurisprudence, Judgment > JUDGE
krinō, kritēs, anakrinō

JUDGMENT

aisthēsis αἴσθησις 144

aisthēsis occurs once, referring to judgment in the sense of "discernment" in Phil 1:9.

gnōmē γνώμη 1106

gnōmē occurs nine times and means "judgment" in most of these contexts. The underlying sense is that of one's mind, advice, or opinion.

Acts 20:3 records Paul's "decision" to travel through Macedonia. In 1 Cor 1:10, Paul exhorts the Corinthian congregation to be united in "mind." Rev 17:13 records the one "purpose" of the ten horns of the symbolic beast ridden by the Babylonian harlot, giving their authority to the satanic beast (Rev 12; 13).

In the remaining contexts, ***gnōmē*** means "opinion" in Paul's Corinthian correspondence (1 Cor 7:25, 40; 2 Cor 8:10). The notion of "consent" is referred to in Phil 1:14.

▸ **48.** Will, Purpose, Decide, Advise > ADVICE

SEE ALSO

▸ **32.** Law, Justice, Jurisprudence, Judgment > JUDGMENT
krisis, krima, praitōrion, kritērion, bēma, dikē, dikaiōma, dikaiokrisia

KNOW, KNOWLEDGE, MAKE KNOWN

ginōskō γινώσκω 1097

ginōskō is one of the most common verbs in the NT, conveying the sense of "knowing" in a variety of contexts, and a whole range of associated senses.

The meaning "know" in the general sense of "be aware" is found in a number of places (e.g., Matt 6:3; 24:50; Mark 8:17; Luke 2:43; John 12:9; Acts 19:35; Rom 7:7; 2 Cor 2:4; Phil 1:12; 2 Tim 1:18; Jas 1:3; 1 John 3:19; Rev 2:23). It functions as a euphemism for sexual intercourse in Matt 1:5.

Another significant aspect of the usage of ***ginōskō*** lies in the meaning "understand." It refers to understanding the law of God (Rom 7:1); the mind of God (1 Cor 2:16); the mysteries of heaven (Matt 13:11; Mark 4:11; Luke 8:10); and the spiritual aspects of God's revealed truth (John 7:17; 8:28, 32; 14:20; 2 Tim 3:1; 2 Pet 1:20). From a negative viewpoint, Jesus points out Nicodemus' failure to understand spiritual truth in John 3:10. General lack of spiritual understanding is indicated in John 8:27; 10:6; 1 Cor 2:14.

With regard to the person of Christ as the object of humanity's knowledge, ***ginōskō*** is found in a variety of contexts. Knowing Christ in the sense of having a relationship of faith and trust in him, based on a recognition of his divine person, is indicated, for example, in John 10:14, 15, where Jesus declares that his followers (i.e., his "sheep") know him and he knows them. In Phil 3:10, Paul affirms his desire to know Christ and the power of his resurrection. Other references to this knowledge include those in John 14:17; 2 Cor 8:9; Eph 3:19; Heb 8:11; 1 John 2:3ff., 13ff. There is also an intriguing reference in Acts 19:15 to an evil spirit knowing, or recognizing, Jesus.

Concerning God as the object of knowledge, ***ginōskō*** refers to knowing him personally in John 17:3, 25; Gal 4:9; 1 John 4:7. 1 John 4:2 speaks of knowing God as the Spirit of truth. Rom 1:21 also refers to people knowing God, but only in a superficial sense of merely acknowledging his existence. In contrast, several references indicate the world's ignorance of God — that is, they have not known him (John 16:3; 17:25; 1 Cor 1:21; 1 John 3:1; 4:8; 5:20).

When predicated of God, ***ginōskō*** indicates the absolute knowledge of every thought and desire of the human heart (Luke 16:15; 1 Cor 3:20; 1 John 3:20). 1 Cor 8:3 speaks of the reality of being known by God through loving him. Similarly, ***ginōskō*** refers to Christ knowing our inner being in intimate, omniscient detail (John 2:25; 5:42; 6:15; 16:19; 21:17). A stark contrasting perspective is found in Matt 7:23, where Jesus declares that he will inform unbelievers on the day of judgment that he never knew them.

▸ **17.** Senses, Actions, Abilities, Disabilities > FEEL

epiginōskō ἐπιγινώσκω 1921

epiginōskō is a synonym for the more common ***ginōskō*** (above). ***epiginōskō*** likewise has the primary sense of "know" in a variety of contexts, with several related meanings. The term occurs around forty times.

Where human knowledge is concerned, ***epiginōskō*** refers to the state of being aware, or realizing (Acts 22:29; 25:10; Rom 1:32; 2 Cor 13:5). It also has the sense of "acknowledge" (1 Cor 14:37; 16:18; 2 Cor 1:14); "understand" (1 Cor 1:13); and "being acquainted with" the way of righteousness (2 Pet 2:21). Quite a few texts reflect the meaning "know," in the sense of "recognize" — for example, Matt 7:16, 20 contain Jesus' affirmation that people shall be known or recognized by their "fruit," or their actions. See also Matt 14:35; Mark 6:33; Luke 1:4; Acts 3:10; 12:14; 19:34. Luke 24:16 refers to the Emmaus disciples being kept from initially recognizing Jesus — a little later they finally recognize him (Luke 24:31).

epiginōskō also indicates the extent and nature of Christ's knowledge. Matt 11:27 declares that no one knows the Father except the Son. Mark 2:8; Luke 5:22 indicate that Christ knows intimately the hearts, minds, and thoughts of people. The sense of "be aware" is evident in Mark 5:30, where Christ realizes that power has left him when a sick woman touched the hem of his garment.

epignōsis ἐπίγνωσις 1922

epignōsis is a noun derived from ***epiginōskō*** (above) and refers to knowledge of moral and ethical values as well as of sin. It also refers to intimate acquaintance with God. The term occurs around twenty times.

Concerning a person's knowledge of God, ***epignōsis*** refers to knowledge of the Son (Eph 4:13); knowledge of God's will (Phil 1:9; Col 1:9; 2 Pet 1:2, 3); and knowledge of the mystery of Christ (Col 2:2; 2 Pet 1:8; 2:20). See also Eph 1:17; Col 1:10; 3:10. Rom 1:28 refers to absence of the knowledge of God, as Paul declares that the wicked refuse to acknowledge God. In Rom 10:2 the Israelites are said to exhibit zeal for God, but it is not based on knowledge.

Knowledge of sin is expressed in Rom 3:20, and knowledge of the truth in 1 Tim 2:4; 2 Tim 2:25; 3:7; Titus 1:1; Heb 10:26.

gnōsis γνῶσις 1108

gnōsis is another noun derived from ***epiginōskō*** (above), a synonym for ***epignōsis*** (above). ***gnōsis*** is translated "knowledge," with particular reference to understanding and appreciation of the spiritual truths of the Christian faith. ***gnōsis*** occurs around thirty times.

gnōsis is concerned primarily with human knowledge. Luke 1:77; 11:52; Rom 15:14; 1 Cor 8:7; 12:8 express the knowledge of salvation. Rom 2:20 refers to knowledge gained from the law. Rom 11:33; 2 Cor 4:6; 10:5 mention human knowledge of God; and 2 Cor 2:14; Phil 3:8; 2 Pet 3:18 speak of the knowledge of Christ.

A number of references point to knowledge in an unspecified way (e.g., Rom 15:14; 1 Cor 13:2, 8; 2 Cor 6:6; 8:7; Eph 3:19; 2 Pet 1:5, 6). 1 Cor 14:6 speaks of spiritual truth, and Col 2:3 cites knowledge that is derived from Christ.

gnōstos γνωστός 1110

gnōstos is an adjective derived from ***ginōskō*** (above) and is translated "known" in most of its fifteen occurrences.

Several texts speak of people known to one another (Luke 2:44; 23:49; John 18:15, 16; Acts 1:19). ***gnōstos*** is also used in contexts where people are made aware of certain information by others (Acts 2:14; 4:10; 13:38; 28:28). God is also said to "make known" (i.e., reveal) his plan of salvation in Acts 15:18. The human being's potential knowledge of God is indicated in Rom 1:19, where it is said that what can be known about God is evident to humans in general, although the ungodly deny God's existence.

gnōrizō γνωρίζω 1107

gnōrizō is found in about twenty contexts, meaning "make known," "gain knowledge of."

When referring to God, ***gnōrizō*** indicates revealing (i.e., making known) his divine purposes in several contexts: he reveals his purposes to angels concerning Jesus' birth (Luke 2:15); and he also reveals the mystery of his will (Eph 1:9; 3:3, 5; 6:19); his wisdom (Eph 3:10); his wrath (Rom 9:22); and the riches of his glory (Rom 9:23; Col 1:27). See also Acts 2:28. Similarly, Christ makes known the teaching of his Father to his disciples (John 15:15; 17:26).

The meaning "gain knowledge of," in reference to human beings, is indicated in 2 Cor 8:1, where the grace of God is the object of that knowledge. Gal 1:11 claims that the knowledge of the gospel is not something gleaned from human beings.

The idea of "making known" or "informing" is indicated in Eph 6:21; Col 4:7, 9. In Phil 4:6, believers are exhorted to make their requests known to God. 2 Pet 1:16 refers to Peter making his readers aware of the power and coming of the Lord Jesus Christ.

anagnōrizomai ἀναγνωρίζομαι 319

anagnōrizomai occurs only in Acts 7:13, meaning "make known" or "recognize."

oida οἶδα 1492

oida is a verb in the perfect tense, meaning "know," "understand," with various nuances. It is predicated of both human beings and God and occurs in about three hundred contexts.

In reference to God, ***oida*** indicates his knowing all things, including our need (Matt 6:8, 32; Luke 12:30); and the mind of the Spirit (Rom 8:27). Such knowledge is similarly predicated of Christ, who knows everything in the hearts and minds of his hearers (Matt 9:4; John 8:55), including his enemies (Matt 27:18; Mark 12:15; Luke 6:8; John 13:11). Christ is also one who knows perfectly his Father's mind and intention for his people (John 11:22; 13:18); as well as God's will for his own life, in relation to his approaching death (John 13:1). Jesus is aware of the truth of God's revelation to him (John 5:32; 12:50); and knows the Father intimately (John 7:29; 8:14). The omniscience of Christ in general is indicated in John 16:30; 18:4; 19:28; 21:17.

oida is also commonly used in the context of human knowledge. The primary sense is that of "being aware." General references to this phenomenon are found, for example, in Luke 8:53; John 4:10; 21:15ff.; Acts 3:17; Phil 1:19. ***oida*** refers to human awareness or knowledge of, for example, the Scriptures (2 Tim 3:15); the uniqueness of Jesus' person and work (John 7:28; 1 Cor 2:2; 2 Tim 1:12); the truth of the gospel (John 19:35; 21:24); spiritual truth (Rom 5:3; Gal 2:16; 1 Thess 1:4); the power of God in Christ (Mark 2:10; 5:33; Acts 12:11); and personal knowledge of God (1 John 5:19).

To "know" in the sense of "believe in" is indicated with reference to the coming of the Messiah (John 4:25, 42); to the resurrection of Jesus (John 11:24; Rom 6:9); to the return of Christ (1 John 3:2); and to the assurance of salvation (1 John 5:13). See also Rom 8:28; 1 Cor 8:4.

oida also refers to one knowing in the sense of "being (personally) acquainted with" (John 6:42; Acts 3:16; 7:18). John 10:4 speaks of sheep knowing their shepherd, referring to the followers of Jesus. This kind of knowledge is even predicated of demons, who are described as knowing (i.e., recognizing) Christ as the Son of God (Mark 1:24, 34; Luke 4:34ff.).

A number of contexts indicate the negative sense of ***oida***. Matt 13:14, for example, refers to those who will not understand the teaching of Jesus, as a consequence of divine judgment on them. John 15:21; 1 Thess 4:5; 2 Thess 1:8 refer to those who have no saving knowledge of God. Several texts point to the ignorance of human beings in a number of ways — for example, in respect of the timing of the Day of the Lord (Matt 24:36; Mark 13:22ff.); the person of Christ (John 1:31; 9:30); and spiritual matters (1 Cor 5:6; 6:2ff.). See also Matt 20:22; Mark 10:38; Luke 23:34; John 4:22; Rom 8:26. In addition, people deny a saving relationship with Christ (i.e., refuse to know him) (Matt 25:12; Luke 13:27); and deny acquaintance with Christ, in the case of Peter's rejection of Jesus (Matt 26:70ff.; Mark 14:68ff.; Luke 22:34, 57, 60).

epistamai ἐπίσταμαι 1987

epistamai, a form of the verb ***ephistēmi***, means "know," "understand." ***epistamai*** occurs thirteen times and is used only in reference to human knowledge.

The sense of "know" or "be aware" is indicated in Acts 18:25; 19:25; 20:18; 22:19; 26:26. Acts 19:15 refers to "knowing" in terms of personal acquaintance.

epistamai means "understand" in Acts 10:28; 15:7. It is otherwise used negatively — for example, with respect to Peter's denial of Jesus (Mark 14:68); our ignorance of tomorrow (Jas 4:14); the ignorance of false teachers (1 Tim 6:4; Jude 10); and Abraham's ignorance of his destination when God called him to leave Ur of the Chaldees (Heb 11:8).

synesis σύνεσις 4907

synesis occurs seven times and means "knowledge" in respect of various phenomena, including human knowledge of Christ (Col 2:2; Eph 3:4); and of God (Col 1:9); and spiritual understanding (2 Tim 2:7). Loving God with all one's understanding is indicated in Mark 12:33. 1 Cor 1:19 affirms that worldly understanding will be destroyed by God. Luke 2:47 records people's amazement at the boy Jesus' prodigious understanding of the law.

phaneros φανερός 5318

phaneros is an adjectival form signifying "made known," "manifest." It occurs around twenty times.

That which is known about God is referred to in Rom 1:19. Information is made known as Paul witnesses in prison (Phil 1:13); about the secrets of one's heart (1 Cor 14:25); and about one's earthly service on the day of judgment (1 Cor 3:13). See also Acts 7:13. In two places, Jesus instructs those whom he has just healed not to make him known (Matt 12:16; Mark 3:12).

▸ **64.** Reveal, Explain, Hiddenness, Secrecy > APPEAR, APPEARING, APPARENT

SEE ALSO

▸ **56.** Folly, Ignorance > IGNORANT, IGNORANCE, UNAWARE ***agnoeō, agnōsia***

PHILOSOPHER, PHILOSOPHY

syzētētēs συζητητής 4804

syzētētēs is found only in 1 Cor 1:20 and refers to a learned man trained in the art of sophistry, or eloquent persuasive argument.

▸ **51.** Knowledge, Wisdom, Remember, Forget > DISPUTE

philosophos φιλόσοφος 5386

philosophos is found only in Acts 17:18 with reference to the philosophers among the Epicureans — scholars who formed part of the audience at the Areopagus listening to the apostle Paul.

philosophia φιλοσοφία 5385

philosophia refers literally to the "love of wisdom." The term occurs only in Col 2:8, referring to the system of human knowledge that is opposed to the knowledge and wisdom of God.

RECKON

logizomai λογίζομαι 3049

logizomai occurs about forty times with the underlying sense of logical, rational expression. Meanings include "reckon," "think," and "count." The meaning "reckon" conveys several nuances.

Luke 22:37 refers to Isa 53:12, declaring that the Suffering Servant-Messiah was to be "reckoned" (i.e., "numbered" or "counted") with the transgressors. This prophecy finds fulfillment in the person of Christ.

More frequently, ***logizomai*** is translated "reckon" with the sense of "consider" or "regard." For example, Rom 4:4 affirms that wages are to be "considered" as one's due. Rom 6:11 commands believers to "reckon" (i.e., regard) themselves dead to sin. See also Rom 2:26; 8:36; 1 Cor 4:1; Phil 3:13.

logizomai also means "reckon" with the sense of "impute." In several places, it is affirmed that genuine faith in God is "imputed" as righteousness. Abraham is the classic recipient of such divine favor (Rom 4:3, 9ff., 22ff.; Gal 3:6; Jas 2:23). Rom 4:5ff., 24 declare this to be true for all believers. 2 Cor 5:19 declares the person blessed against whom the Lord will not "impute" his sin.

▸ **51.** Knowledge, Wisdom, Remember, Forget > CONSIDER
▸ **51.** Knowledge, Wisdom, Remember, Forget > IMPUTE
▸ **52.** Status, Identity, Reputation, Honor, Shame > NUMBER

REMEMBER, REMEMBRANCE, MEMORY

mnēmoneuō μνημονεύω 3421

mnēmoneuō is a verb found around twenty times, meaning "remember" in most of these contexts.

Most commonly this term refers to the act of remembering as mental recall (Matt 16:19; Luke 17:32; John 15:20; Acts 20:31, 35; Eph 2:11; 2 Thess 2:5).

Elsewhere, ***mnēmoneuō*** means "remember" in the sense of "be mindful of." Each of the following contexts contains injunctions to exercise such a recall — for example, the poor (Gal 2:10); Paul's imprisonment (Col 4:18); the resurrection of Christ from the dead as an essential component of the gospel (2 Tim 2:8); one's spiritual leaders (Heb 13:7); and the fate from which one has been delivered (Rev 2:5). See also Rev 3:3.

Where God is concerned, ***mnēmoneuō*** refers once to the divine "remembering" of the sins of the nations of Babylon with a view to punishment (Rev 18:5).

mnaomai μνάομαι 3415

mnaomai is a verb found in approximately twenty places meaning "remember," as well as associated senses.

As with ***mnēmoneuō*** (above), ***mnaomai*** refers primarily to people remembering as an act of mental recall (e.g., Matt 5:23; 27:63; Luke 16:25; John 2:17, 22; Acts 11:16; 2 Tim 1:4; 2 Pet 3:2; Jude 17).

The meaning "remember" also indicates the sense of "be mindful of," with a view to acting in a certain way. The penitent thief on the cross, for example, pleads for Christ to remember him in paradise (Luke 23:42). Paul commends the Corinthian congregation for "remembering" the traditions of the gospel he had passed onto them (1 Cor 11:2).

When predicated of God, ***mnaomai*** refers to divine remembering in the anthropomorphic sense of initiating an aspect of his redemptive purposes. Luke 1:54 speaks of God "remembering" to be merciful (see also Acts 10:31). Luke 1:72 affirms that God will remember his covenant. Heb 8:12; 10:17 promise that God will remember the sins of his people no more. God is said to remember Babylon in Rev 16:19, with a view to punishing her for her sins.

mimnēskō μιμνήσκω 3403

mimnēskō is a rare verb found in only two places, meaning "remember," "be mindful of." Heb 2:6 refers to God being mindful of humankind. Heb 13:3 enjoins believers to remember those who are in prison for the sake of the gospel.

hypomimnēskō ὑπομιμνήσκω 5279

hypomimnēskō is a verb, a variant of ***mimnēskō*** (above) found in six contexts meaning "remember," "bring to remembrance."

The term means mental recall in Luke 22:6. In John 14:26, Jesus declares that the Holy Spirit will "bring to remembrance" in the hearts of true believers all that Jesus had taught.

The meaning "remind" (lit., "cause to remember") is also found in several places. The apostolic writers remind their readers of the need to trust in the salvation won by Christ (2 Tim 2:14; 2 Pet 1:12). Paul reminds Titus of the need to submit to governing authorities (Titus 3:1). See also Jude 5.

anamimnēskō ἀναμιμνήσκω 363

anamimnēskō is a synonym for ***mimnēskō*** and ***hypomimnēskō*** (above) occurring six times and meaning "remember," "bring to remembrance."

The process of mental recall is indicated in Mark 11:21; 14:72; Heb 10:32. The meaning "remind" in the sense of "bring to remembrance" is indicated in 1 Cor 4:17, with reference to Timothy reminding the Corinthian church of Paul's ways in Christ (see also 2 Cor 7:15). Paul reminds Timothy to rekindle God's gift to him (2 Tim 1:6).

anamnēsis ἀνάμνησις 364

anamnēsis is a noun derived from ***mimnēskō*** (above). It occurs four times, with the meaning "remembrance."

The instruction to celebrate the Lord's Supper in remembrance of Christ who died on the cross is found in Luke 22:19; 1 Cor 11:24, 25. Heb 10:3 declares that ritual sacrifices are an annual reminder of sins under the old covenant.

mneia μνεία 3417

mneia is a noun found in seven places meaning "remembrance," or "memory," "remembering."

In all but one occurrence of the term, ***mneia*** refers to remembering others in one's prayers (Rom 1:9; Eph 1:16; Phil 1:3; 1 Thess 1:2; 2 Tim 1:3; Phlm 4). In 1 Thess 3:6, ***mneia*** refers to the fond "memories" of people's generosity.

mnēmē μνήμη 3420

mnēmē is a noun occurring only in 2 Pet 1:15, with reference to the apostle's readers being able to "recall" his teaching (lit., "to call these things to remembrance").

mnēmosynon μνημόσυνον 3422

mnēmosynon is a noun found in only three places, indicating the sense of "memory" or "memorial." Christ commends the woman who anointed his feet with perfume by declaring that this deed will be told the world over as a "memorial" to her (Matt 26:13; Mark 14:9). The prayers of the Roman centurion Cornelius are described in Acts 10:4 as a "memorial" having ascended to God.

SET ONE'S MIND ON

phroneō φρονέω 5426

phroneō is a verb occurring around forty times with the primary meaning "think," in various senses. The phrase "set one's mind on" in Col 3:2 refers to the desired focus of the believer's heart on preparing himself for eternal life in the hereafter.

▸ **27.** Community, Partnership, Unity, Discord > AGREE, AGREEMENT

▸ **51.** Knowledge, Wisdom, Remember, Forget > THINK, THOUGHT

SEE ALSO

▸ **1.** Celestial Realm, Earthly Realm > SET
dynō

▸ **83.** Set, Put, Place, Prepare, Establish > SET
tithēmi, paratithēmi, peritithēmi, histēmi, keimai, prokeimai, epibibazō

TEST, TEMPT, TEMPTATION

peirazō πειράζω 3985

peirazō is a verb occurring about forty times, with the primary meanings "tempt," "put to the test," in the sense of ascertaining the validity or integrity of one's faith in God. The term is used in a variety of contexts.

Satan is depicted as "tempting" Christ in the wilderness — attempting, without success, to have him betray his trust in God (Matt 4:13; Mark 1:13; Luke 4:2; Heb 2:18; 4:15). 1 Cor 7:5 also describes Satan's active tempting of Christian couples to violate their marriage vows through sexual misconduct. 1 Thess 3:5 refers to the devil tempting believers in general.

The Pharisees are frequently described as "tempting" Christ during his earthly ministry, deliberately seeking to trap or ensnare him so as to bring an accusation against him (Matt 16:1; 19:3; 22:18, 35; Mark 8:11; 10:2; 12:15; Luke 11:16; John 8:16).

Warnings against being tempted to sin are given in Gal 6:1; and the reality of that state is found in Jas 1:14. Jas 1:13 affirms that God is never directly the agent of tempting. The Israelites' sin of "tempting" God in the wilderness is noted in 1 Cor 10:9; Heb 3:9. In Acts 5:9, the sin of Ananias and Sapphira in lying to the apostles about the sale of property is described as "tempting (i.e., putting to the test) the Spirit of the Lord" — a sin for which they were struck dead. 1 Cor 10:13 records the promise that God will keep his people from being "tempted" or "tested" beyond their capacity to cope.

▸ **46.** Wait, Hope, Be Vigilant, Pay Attention To > EXAMINATION, EXAMINE

peirasmos πειρασμός 3986

peirasmos is a noun derived from ***peirazō*** (above), occurring around twenty times with the consistent meaning "temptation," primarily in the context of incitement to sin. The term is also translated "trial."

The prayer that God will not lead his people into temptation is recorded in Matt 6:13; Luke 11:14. Luke 8:13 mentions those who fall away, having given in to temptation. Matt 26:41; Mark 14:38; Luke 22:40, 46 contain exhortations to keep away from temptation. See also 1 Tim 6:9.

Satan fails completely to ensnare Christ in the temptation to act on his own initiative rather than place his trust in God (Luke 4:13). 1 Cor 10:13 contains the promise that God will always provide a way of escape for the believer from succumbing to various "temptations" or "trials."

▸ **51.** Knowledge, Wisdom, Remember, Forget > TRIAL, TESTING

ekpeirazō ἐκπειράζω 1598

ekpeirazō is a verb found only four times, meaning "tempt" or "put to the test." Matt 4:7; Luke 4:12 refer to Jesus' rebuke of the devil, appealing to the scriptural command that God must not be tempted. That sin is attributed to the Israelite people during their wandering in the wilderness, who did in fact put God to the test (1 Cor 10:9).

apeirastos ἀπείραστος 551

apeirastos is an adjectival form meaning "cannot be tempted," found only in Jas 1:13 with reference to God.

dokimazō δοκιμάζω 1381

dokimazō is a verb found thirty times meaning "prove," "examine," "test" throughout.

The process of "testing" (i.e., proofing, or assessing) that which is good is described in Rom 12:2; Phil 1:10; 1 Thess 5:2. Such a process is also indicated in relation to one's love for God (2 Cor 8:8); and concerning one's suitability for the office of deacon (1 Tim 3:10). ***dokimazō*** is also used in this sense in relation to the life work of the believer, which will be "tested" on the day of judgment.

dokimazō also means "test" with the underlying sense of "to scrutinize" or "examine." This is evident in 1 John 4:1 in relation to believers "testing the spirits," to see whether they are of God. It also refers to the Lord's Supper, as believers are exhorted to "examine" themselves prior to taking the sacrament. See also 2 Cor 13:5; Gal 6:4.

Heb 3:9 refers to the sinful action of the Israelites in putting God to the test.

▸ **46.** Wait, Hope, Be Vigilant, Pay Attention To > EXAMINATION, EXAMINE

▸ **49.** Allow, Accept, Approve, Refuse > APPROVE, APPROVED

THINK, THOUGHT

dokeō δοκέω 1380

dokeō is a verb with the general meaning "to think" throughout most of its nearly sixty occurrences, in a variety of contexts. The underlying sense is that of "making a rational assessment" or "giving consideration to."

General references to such a process are found in Matt 6:7; 22:17. "Thinking" in the sense of "believing" is indicated in Matt 17:25; Luke 19:11; John 11:56; Acts 26:9; 1 Cor 4:9; 8:2; 12:23. Matt 22:42 refers to thinking about or believing in Jesus Christ.

dokeō also means "think" in the sense of "suppose" (Mark 6:49; Luke 8:18; 10:36; John 11:13; 2 Cor 12:19; Jas 4:5).

dialogismos διαλογισμός 1261

dialogismos is a noun found fourteen times with the general meaning "thoughts," as well as associated nuances (e.g., "doubts," as well as "thinking," i.e., the process of human reasoning itself).

"Thoughts" in general are indicated in Luke 2:35; 1 Cor 3:20. Evil thoughts in particular are noted in Matt 15:19; Mark 7:21; Jas 2:4. "Doubts" (i.e., "questioning thoughts") are mentioned in Luke 5:22; 6:8; 9:47; 24:38. Luke 9:46; Phil 2:14 refer to "arguments."

Rom 1:21 contains the theologically significant affirmation that sin has rendered human "thinking" (i.e., our very thought processes) futile in a moral and spiritual sense.

▸ **56.** Folly, Ignorance > FUTILE THINKING, VAIN IMAGINATION

nomizō νομίζω 3543

nomizō is a verb found in fifteen places meaning "think" or "suppose" (Matt 5:17; 20:10; Luke 2:44; Acts 7:25; 17:29; 1 Cor 7:36).

hyponoeō ὑπονοέω 5282

hyponoeō is a verb found only three times, meaning "think," "suppose" (Acts 13:35; 25:18; 27:27).

phroneō φρονέω 5426

phroneō is a verb with a number of meanings, including "think," "agree," "to be like-minded," "regard." ***phroneō*** occurs about forty times. The meaning "think" includes a number of related nuances.

Acts 28:22 means "think" with the sense of "express a view or opinion." In Rom 12:3; 1 Cor 4:6, ***phroneō*** means "think" with the idea of estimating the level of one's own importance. 1 Cor 13:11 speaks of "thinking" or "reasoning" like a child.

▸ **27.** Community, Partnership, Unity, Discord > AGREE, AGREEMENT

▸ **51.** Knowledge, Wisdom, Remember, Forget > SET ONE'S MIND ON

dianoēma διανόημα 1270
epinoia ἐπίνοια 1963

These two nouns are rare synonyms for ***dialogismos*** (above) meaning "thoughts." ***dianoēma*** is found only in Luke 11:17, and ***epinoia*** only in Acts 8:22.

enthymeomai ἐνθυμέομαι 1760

enthymeomai is a verb found three times meaning "think" in the sense of "ponder," "think about," focusing on one's inner thoughts (Matt 1:20; 9:4; Acts 10:19).

enthymēsis ἐνθύμησις 1761

This noun is derived from ***enthymeomai*** (above). It is found in four contexts, meaning "thought" in the sense of the innermost thoughts of one's heart (Matt 9:4; 12:25; Acts 17:29; Heb 4:12).

oimai οἶμαι 3633

oimai is a verb meaning "think" in the sense of "suppose," found only in John 21:25; Phil 1:16; Jas 1:7.

TRIAL, TESTING

dokimion δοκίμιον 1383

dokimion is a noun found only in Jas 1:3; 1 Pet 1:7. It refers to "trying," "proving," or "trial" in relation to one's faith.

peirasmos πειρασμός 3986

peirasmos is a noun found in around twenty contexts meaning "trial," "testing," "temptation."

Luke 4:13 refers to Jesus' "trial" or "temptation" by Satan in the wilderness. Heb 3:8 refers to Israel's "trial" in the wilderness. The prayer that God will not lead his people into "trial" or "temptation" is recorded in Matt 6:13; Luke 11:4 (see also Matt 26:41). General references to times of "trial" or "testing" are found in Luke 8:13; 1 Tim 6:19. In particular, times of "testing" for followers of Christ are recorded in Luke 22:28ff.; Acts 20:19; 1 Cor 10:13; 1 Pet 1:6; 2 Pet 2:9; Rev 3:10.

▸ **51.** Knowledge, Wisdom, Remember, Forget > TEST, TEMPT, TEMPTATION

SEE ALSO

▸ **75.** Suffering, Distress, Sadness > TRIAL
dokimē, pyrōsis

UNDERSTAND, UNDERSTANDING

syniēmi συνίημι 4920

syniēmi is a verb with the consistent meaning "understand" throughout its approximately twenty-five occurrences. The dominant sense is that of rational and spiritual comprehension, or discernment, of the word of God and the gospel. ***syniēmi*** refers to people "being granted insight" into God's word, the truth of the gospel (Matt 13:23; Luke 24:45; Rom 15:21). Conversely, people are declared to be incapable of discerning spiritual truth (e.g., Matt 13:13ff.; Mark 8:21; Luke 2:50; 18:30; Acts 7:25). Such lack of understanding or comprehension is sometimes deemed to be the result of divine judgment (Mark 4:12; Luke 8:10; Acts 28:26ff.); and is also viewed as one of the characteristics of the wicked (Rom 3:11; 2 Cor 10:12). Matt 15:10; Mark 7:14 contain exhortations to understand the word of God; and Eph 5:17 refers to understanding the will of God. General references to "understanding" in the sense of "realize" or "perceive" are found in Matt 16:12; 17:13.

noeō νοέω 3539

noeō is a verb occurring fourteen times meaning "to understand" in the sense of "perceive with the mind," "realize." General references to the activity of rational perception or discernment include those in Matt 15:17; 16:9ff.; Mark 7:18; 8:17. In particular, Rom 1:20 indicates the potential capacity for every person to "realize" (i.e., understand) that God is both real and eternally sovereign in his knowledge and power. ***noeō*** is also translated "understand" with the underlying sense of "comprehend the significance of" or "interpret." This use of the term is indicated in Matt 24:15; Mark 13:14 in relation to the signs of the times. This sense is also evident in Heb 11:3, where the "understanding" that the world has been created by the word of God is only possible through the exercise of faith. Divine judgment is said to prevent people from being able to understand or discern spiritual truth (John 12:40). In contrast, Eph 3:4 affirms the God-given ability of the believer to understand the significance of the person of Christ.

▸ **51.** Knowledge, Wisdom, Remember, Forget > CONSIDER

dysnoētos δυσνόητος 1425

dysnoētos is a rare adjective found only in 2 Pet 3:16, referring to some of the teaching of the apostle Paul, which Peter regards as "hard to understand."

synetos συνετός 4908

synetos is an adjectival form found in four places with the meaning "intelligent" in Matt 11:25; Luke 10:21; Acts 13:7; 1 Cor 1:19.

SEE ALSO

- ▸ **19.** Mind, Spirit, Emotions, Feelings, Desires > UNDERSTANDING
  nous, phrēn
- ▸ **56.** Folly, Ignorance > STUPID, WITHOUT UNDERSTANDING
  asynetos

WISDOM, WISE

sophia σοφία 4678

sophia is consistently translated "wisdom" throughout its fifty or so occurrences. ***sophia*** denotes both human and divine wisdom with knowledge, intelligence, and understanding.

sophia generally designates "wisdom" as a gift of God, given to specific individuals in order to equip them to live godly lives. Such "wisdom" includes intelligence and deep understanding. ***sophia*** refers to the wisdom of Solomon (Matt 12:42; Luke 11:31); Joseph (Acts 7:10); and Moses (Acts 7:22). The people of Jesus' day attributed wisdom to him during his earthly ministry, although not all may have accepted that it came from God (Matt 13:54; Mark 6:2).

Godly wisdom is given to Christ's disciples and followers (Luke 21:15; Acts 6:3, 10; 1 Cor 2:6; Col 1:9; Jas 3:13, 17; 2 Pet 3:15). In Col 4:5, believers are exhorted to ask God for wisdom. Godly wisdom is required for intelligent understanding of spiritual realities (Rev 13:18; 17:9). Such wisdom is also implicitly attributed to Christ in his boyhood years (Luke 2:40, 52).

Wisdom as a divine attribute is indicated in Luke 11:49; Rom 11:33; 1 Cor 1:21, 24; Eph 3:10; Rev 7:12. Col 2:3 indicates that "all the treasures of wisdom" are hidden in Christ. And Rev 5:12 declares that God gives wisdom. Christ is designated as "our wisdom" in 1 Cor 1:30; Col 3:16, wrought by God in the lives of his people. In Matt 11:19; Luke 7:35, "wisdom" is personified as a woman of noble and godly virtue.

Human wisdom is described as "folly" in the eyes of God (1 Cor 1:17ff.; 2:1ff.; 3:19; Col 2:23; Jas 3:15).

sophos σοφός 4680

sophos is an adjectival form derived from ***sophia*** (above) meaning "wise," "skilled." It occurs around twenty times, referring to both human beings and God in a variety of contexts. ***sophos*** is also used nominally.

Matt 11:25; Luke 10:21; Rom 1:14 refer to "the wise," "wise ones," indicating that such people see themselves as wise by human standards alone. Matt 23:34 refers to godly "wise people."

The adjectival sense of "wise" is found in Rom 1:22; 1 Cor 1:19ff.; 3:18ff., referring to the folly of human wisdom. In contrast, ***sophos*** also refers to those who are "wise" in the godly sense of being spiritually discerning (Rom 16:19; 1 Cor 6:5; Eph 5:15; Jas 3:13). This attribute is predicated of God in Rom 16:27.

The meaning "skilled" refers to a "master builder" in 1 Cor 3:10.

phronimos φρόνιμος 5429

phronimos is an adjective found in fourteen places meaning "wise" in the sense of "intelligent" or "prudent," careful to maintain one's own interests in a noble sense.

This characteristic is predicated of people, denoting them as "wise" or "intelligent," capable of insight and understanding (Matt 7:24; 10:16; 25:2ff.; Luke 12:42; 16:8; 1 Cor 10:15).

phronimos is also used in a negative sense, where "wise" has the connotation of "conceit" (Rom 11:25; 12:16).

phronimos also refers to "wisdom" in the context of sarcastic condemnation of foolish people (1 Cor 4:10; 2 Cor 11:19).

phronēsis φρόνησις 5428

phronēsis is a rare noun denoting "(godly) wisdom" in Luke 1:17, and divine "wisdom" in Eph 1:8.

SEE ALSO

- ▸ **2.** Supernatural Beings/Forces, Spiritual Realm > WISE MAN, SORCERER, MAGICIAN
  magos

52. Status, Identity, Reputation, Honor, Shame

ASHAMED

aischynomai αἰσχύνομαι 153

aischynomai is a verb found five times with the meaning "to be ashamed." The term is used positively in Luke 16:3 to refer to a person's shame at the prospect of having to beg. Elsewhere it is used negatively. In 1 Pet 4:16 there is the exhortation "not to be ashamed" for suffering as a Christian. Phil 1:20; 1 John 2:28 both refer to a desire not to be ashamed on the day of judgment. See also 2 Cor 10:8.

epaischynomai ἐπαισχύνομαι 1870

epaischynomai is a variant form of ***aischynomai*** (above) with the sense of "be ashamed" throughout all eleven occurrences of the term.

Mark 8:38; Luke 9:26 both contain the solemn declaration that Christ "will be ashamed" at the last judgment of those who "are ashamed" of him and his teaching during this life. Paul affirms in Rom 1:16; 2 Tim 1:12 that he is "not ashamed" of the gospel of Christ, and he exhorts others to be of the same mind in 2 Tim 1:8. The attitude of "being ashamed" of one's sinful past is indicated in Rom 6:21. Heb 2:11 declares that Christ is "not ashamed" to call his people his "brothers"; and Heb 11:16 declares that God is "not ashamed" to be called the God of his people.

entrepō ἐντρέπω 1788

entrepō is a verb found nine times, and in over half of these contexts it means "to fear" or "reverence." In the remaining places, however, it means "to be ashamed," i.e., "humiliated," "disgraced" (1 Cor 4:14; 2 Thess 3:14; Titus 2:8).

anepaischyntos ἀνεπαίσχυντος 422

anepaischyntos is a rare adjectival form found only in 2 Tim 2:15, referring to a preacher of the word who "has no need to be ashamed," for he knows how to accurately interpret the word of God.

kataischynō καταισχύνω 2617

kataischynō occurs thirteen times, meaning "to put to shame," "dishonor," "be ashamed" in most of these contexts, with various nuances.

The meaning "be ashamed" refers to Jesus' opponents in Luke 13:17. To actively shame or humiliate is the meaning indicated in 1 Cor 11:22.

With the underlying sense of "dishonor," God is said to shame the wise (1 Cor 1:27). A man praying with his head covered "dishonors" his head (1 Cor 11:4). Conversely, a woman praying with her head uncovered "dishonors" herself (1 Cor 11:5).

Those who persecute followers of Christ are said to "be put to shame" (1 Pet 3:16). Those who do trust in Christ, however, will not be put to shame (Rom 9:33; 10:11; 1 Pet 2:6). See also 2 Cor 7:14.

▸ **52.** Status, Identity, Reputation, Honor, Shame > PUT TO SHAME, TREAT SHAMEFULLY

DESPISE

periphroneō περιφρονέω 4065

The verb ***hybrizō*** is found in five contexts with the predominant meaning to "treat cruelly, or shamefully" in the contexts of physical assault (Matt 22:6; Luke 18:32; Acts 14:5; 1 Thess 2:2).

atimos ἄτιμος 820

periphroneō is a rare verb found only in Titus 2:15 in relation to Paul's exhortation to his young protégé not to allow anyone to "despise" him — that is, to disregard him, or view him as unimportant.

▸ **52.** Status, Identity, Reputation, Honor, Shame > DISHONOR

SEE ALSO

▸ **54.** Rule, Authority, Command, Obedience > DESPISE
atheteō

▸ **77.** Resist, Oppose, Fight, Rebel > DESPISE, DISDAIN
exoutheneō, kataphroneō

DISHONOR

atimia ἀτιμία 819

atimos is an adjectival form meaning "without honor" in relation to a prophet in Matt 13:57; Mark 6:4. 1 Cor 12:23 refers to private parts of the body that are deemed "less honorable." The sense of "being despised" (i.e., held in disrepute) is indicated in 1 Cor 4:10.

▸ **52.** Status, Identity, Reputation, Honor, Shame > SHAME

atimos ἄτιμος 820

atimos is an adjective found four times referring to people who are "without honor" in Matt 13:57; Mark 6:4; 1 Cor 4:10. It also denotes body parts that are "less honorable" than others in 1 Cor 12:23.

▸ **52.** Status, Identity, Reputation, Honor, Shame > DESPISE

atimazō ἀτιμάζω 818

atimazō is a verb occurring six times, meaning "to treat shamefully," "dishonor," and "suffer dishonor."

Luke 20:11; John 8:49; Jas 2:6 refer to treating people shamefully. The experience of believers "suffering dishonor" in the course of persecution is indicated in Acts 5:41. "Breaking the law" is identified with "dishonoring" God in Rom 2:23. Rom 1:24 refers to "dishonoring" one's body through sexual impurity.

▸ **52.** Status, Identity, Reputation, Honor, Shame > PUT TO SHAME, TREAT SHAMEFULLY

▸ **52.** Status, Identity, Reputation, Honor, Shame > SHAME

EXALT, EXALTED

hypsoō ὑψόω 5312

hypsoō is a verb found in approximately twenty places meaning "to exalt," "lift on high."

The state of "being exalted, lifted up" to heaven is indicated in Matt 11:23; Luke 10:15. The arrogant act of "exalting oneself" is indicated in Matt 23:12; Luke 14:11; 18:14.

God's action in "exalting" the poor and downtrodden, "lifting" their fortunes, is noted in Luke 1:52. See also 2 Cor 11:7; Jas 4:10; 1 Pet 5:6. The significant parallel between Christ "being lifted up" on the cross and Moses "lifting up" the serpent in the wilderness (and healing the plague-ridden Israelites) is indicated in John 3:14; 8:28; 12:32ff. The point of this comparison is to emphasize the unique effectiveness of Christ's substitutionary atonement, removing the sins of his people once and for all in a supreme act of spiritual healing. As a sequel to this phenomenon, Acts 2:33; 5:31 refer to Christ being "exalted" at the right hand of God after his ascension to heaven.

The sense of God "exalting" his people in Egypt carries the underlying meaning of "to make great" in Acts 13:17.

hyperypsoō ὑπερυψόω 5251

hyperypsoō is a rare variant of ***hypsoō*** (above) denoting God's action in "highly exalting" his Son, Jesus Christ, granting to him the name that is greater than any other name.

hyperairō ὑπεραίρω 5229

hyperairō is a rare verb found in three places. The meaning "be exalted," in the sense of being affected by a supreme feeling of elation, is indicated in 2 Cor 12:7, referring twice to the apostle Paul's experience of a heavenly vision. The arrogant and idolatrous action of "exalting oneself" before God, seeking to supplant him, is predicated of the "man of lawlessness" in 2 Thess 2:4.

EXCEL, EXCELLENT

kratistos κράτιστος 2903

kratistos is an adjective found in four places with the superlative sense of "most excellent" used as a title, a form of address for royalty or nobility (Luke 1:3; Acts 23:26; 24:3; 26:25).

▸ **52.** Status, Identity, Reputation, Honor, Shame > NOBLE, NOBLEMAN

prōteuō πρωτεύω 4409

prōteuō is a rare verb found only in Col 1:18, meaning "to be preeminent" in the sense of holding the primary place of power and status.

philoprōteuō φιλοπρωτεύω 5383

philoprōteuō is a rare variant of ***prōteuō*** (above) found only in 3 John 9, meaning "to love to have the preeminence," or to strive for a position of excellence.

SEE ALSO

▸ **7.** Quantity, Amount, Number, Size, Measure > EXCEED, EXCEEDINGLY
hyperbolē

▸ **53.** Value, Worth > EXCEL, EXCELLENT
hyperballō, diaphoros

FAME

akoē ἀκοή 189

akoē is a noun occurring nearly twenty-five times, meaning "hearing" in most of these contexts. In several contexts, however, ***akoē*** signifies the "fame" of Christ in relation to his performing miraculous signs, as noted in Matt 4:24; 14:1; Mark 1:28.

▸ **16.** Body, Bodily Functions > EAR
▸ **17.** Senses, Actions, Abilities, Disabilities > HEAR, HEARING, LISTEN
▸ **63.** Speak, Tell, Declare, Call > REPORT, FAME
▸ **63.** Speak, Tell, Declare, Call > RUMOR

SEE ALSO

▸ **63.** Speak, Tell, Declare, Call > REPORT, FAME
phēmē

GLORY, GLORIOUS, GLORIFY

syndoxazō συνδοξάζω 4888

syndoxazō is a rare verb found only in Rom 8:17, where it refers to the believer's certain hope of "being glorified" with Christ.

doxa δόξα 1391

doxa denotes "glory" in most of its nearly 170 occurrences in a variety of contexts and with different nuances.

The "glory" of world kingdoms (their wealth, power, and prestige) is indicated in Matt 4:8; Luke 4:6, in the context of Satan's temptation of Jesus in the wilderness.

The created "glory" of the universe is indicated in 1 Cor 15:41; 1 Pet 1:24; and the "glory" of the heavenly realm in 1 Cor 15:43; Col 3:4. Heb 2:7ff. declares that God has crowned human beings with "glory" and honor, and also includes the implicit crowning of Christ with such "glory." "Glory" in the sense of "beauty" is indicated in relation to Solomon in Matt 6:29; Luke 12:27; and in the sense of a literal radiance in relation to Moses' transfigured face after his meeting with God on Mount Sinai in 2 Cor 3:7.

The heavenly "glory" of God is indicated in Matt 16:27; Mark 8:38; Luke 2:9; 1 Thess 2:12; 2 Thess 1:9; as is that of Christ upon his return to earth in Matt 24:30; Mark 13:26; Luke 9:26; 21:27. Christ's own heavenly "glory" is glimpsed on the Mount of Transfiguration in Luke 9:31ff. Jesus' miracles are also described as a manifestation of his "glory" in John 2:11.

doxa is also used adjectivally to denote the "glorious" throne of God in Matt 19:28.

General references to "the glory" of God include those in John 11:4; Acts 7:2; Rom 1:23; 3:23; 1 Cor 10:31; 2 Cor 3:18; 4:6; Rev 21:23. In particular, the expression "glory of God" refers to the "glory cloud" in the heavenly temple.

The "glory" of the new covenant is indicated in 2 Cor 3:10ff.

"Glory" is ascribed to God in Luke 2:14; John 9:24; Rom 11:36; Eph 1:12ff.; Phil 4:20; 1 Tim 1:17; 1 Pet 1:7; 2 Pet 3:18; Jude 25; Rev 1:6; 4:9ff.; 5:12ff.; 19:1.

Jesus Christ is declared to be the embodiment of divine glory in Luke 2:32; John 1:14; Phil 2:11; Col 1:27; Heb 1:3; 3:3. Such glory was anticipated by the prophet Isaiah (John 12:41). God is said to "give glory" to Christ his Son in 1 Pet 1:21. "Glory," denoting the privileged state of heavenly intimate relationship with God in Christ, is indicated in John 5:44; Rom 9:4, 23; 2 Thess 2:14; 1 Tim 2:10; 1 Pet 5:1. In particular, 1 Pet 5:4 describes the believer's "crown of glory."

Human "glory" in the sense of pride, power, accomplishment, and status is noted in John 7:18; Phil 3:19; 1 Thess 2:6 — all with negative connotations.

Jesus' explicit claim for "divine glory" is found in John 17:5, 22. 2 Cor 4:4 also refers to the "glory" of Christ. NT churches are depicted as the "glory of Christ" in 2 Cor 8:23. Christ is said to receive "glory" from God the Father in 2 Pet 1:17.

Believers striving for "(heavenly) glory" in their desire to know and serve God forever are noted in Rom 2:7; 8:18.

A women's hair is said to be her "glory" in 1 Cor 11:15, denoting her "crowning beauty."

endoxos ἔνδοξος 1741

endoxos is a rare adjectival form found only four times. Luke 7:25 refers to the "glorious" (i.e., beautiful, gorgeous) clothing worn by the rich. Luke 13:17 refers to "glorious" things done by Christ (i.e., his miracles). Believers are said to be "held in honor" in 1 Cor 14:10. Eph 5:27 describes the "glorious" or "splendid" state of the church.

HONOR

timē τιμή 5092

This noun occurs around forty times and refers predominantly to "honor" that is given in recognition of one's service or rank. It can also refer to the "price" or "value" of a person or thing. 1 Tim 1:17; 6:16; Rev 4:9, 11; 7:12; 19:1 refer to ascribing honor to God in the context of praise or worship. Likewise, "honor" to Christ is indicated in Heb 2:7, 9; 3:3; 2 Pet 1:17; Rev 5:12, 13.

In the context of honor among people, ***timē*** refers to respect or recognition in a number of places — for example, showing deference or honor to one's wife (1 Pet 3:7; 1 Tim 4:14); granting double honor for elders (1 Tim 5:17); and bestowing parts of the body with honor (1 Cor 12:23, 24). See also Rom 2:7; 12:10; Acts 28:10; 1 Tim 6:1. Respect for government authority ordained of God is commanded in Rom 13:7.

timē also has the sense of "value" as "worth" in Rom 9:21, where high value is set on a beautiful pot. Merely human regulations have no value in restraining sexual immorality, as affirmed in Col 2:23.

Rev 21:24 refers to the glory and honor of the redeemed kings of the earth brought into heaven. Similarly, Rev 21:26 describes carrying the glory and honor of the nations into the heavenly city.

▸ **30.** Money, Business, Wealth, Poverty > PRICE

timaō τιμάω 5091

timaō is the verb from which ***timē*** (above) is derived. It is found approximately twenty times and signifies primarily the action of "honoring" in a number of different contexts. It can also mean "to price."

Honoring God in the sense of worshiping and reverencing him in a right spirit is affirmed in John 5:23. This attitude is perfectly illustrated by Jesus' honoring his heavenly Father in John 8:49. Conversely, in John 12:26, God is said to honor his faithful servants. Hypocritical worship, or mere lip service, is condemned by Christ in Matt 15:8 (Isa 29:13; Mark 7:6).

God's people are required to give honor to their parents (Matt 15:4, 6; 19:19; Mark 7:10; 10:19; Luke 18:20; Eph 6:2); and also to widows, who are to be treated kindly and with respect (1 Tim 5:3). Respect for the king or emperor is also demanded in 1 Pet 2:17.

▸ **53.** Value, Worth > VALUABLE, VALUE

HUMBLE, LOWLY

tapeinoō ταπεινόω 5013

The verb ***tapeinoō*** refers to the action of humbling or being humbled, as well as a number of related meanings in a variety of contexts. The term also describes the literal action of "lowering the height" of an object. ***tapeinoō*** occurs around seventeen times.

Christ commends the attitude of humbling oneself in Matt 18:4; 23:12; Luke 14:11; 18:14. Paul refers to his experience of being humbled in 2 Cor 11:7; Phil 4:12. And, in 2 Cor 12:21, he affirms that God had specifically humbled him. Exhortations to humble oneself before God are found in Jas 4:10; 1 Pet 5:6. The voluntary humbling of Jesus Christ to the will of his Father is recorded in Phil 2:8.

tapeinos ταπεινός 5011

tapeinos is the adjectival form derived from ***tapeinoō*** (above) and means "lowly in heart" (i.e., humble) and "of low status." The word occurs eight times.

The quality of lowliness or humility of heart is predicated of Christ (Matt 11:29); of Paul (2 Cor 10:1); and of believers (Jas 1:9; 4:6; 1 Pet 5:5). Lowliness of one's status or rank is indicated in Luke 1:52; 12:16; 2 Cor 7:6.

tapeinōsis ταπείνωσις 5014

tapeinōsis is a noun that indicates one's low or humble status, or humiliation, and occurs four times. It is found in connection with Mary, the mother of Christ, in Luke 1:48. Christ's own humiliation, anticipated through the sufferings of the Servant of Yahweh, is indicated in Acts 8:33. Phil 3:21 refers to the transformation of our "lowly" bodies at the end of the age. Jas 1:10 refers to the humiliation of the rich.

SEE ALSO

▸ **60.** Virtues > HUMILITY
tapeinophrosynē

MAJESTY, GREATNESS

megaleiotēs μεγαλειότης 3168

megaleiotēs occurs only three times, with the underlying sense of "greatness." In Luke 9:43, Jesus' healing of the demon-possessed boy gave rise to the people's reaction of astonishment at the "majestic power" of God. A similar comment is made by Peter in his second letter, where he refers to the disciples as eyewitnesses of the "majesty" of Jesus Christ during his lifetime. In a quite different context, Acts 19:27, ***megaleiotēs*** refers to the "majesty" or "greatness" of the Ephesian goddess, Artemis.

megalōsynē μεγαλωσύνη 3172

megalōsynē is a noun that explicitly refers to the divine "majesty." It occurs in three places only. In Heb 1:3; 8:1, the term is used as a title for God, the "Majesty on high" or "in heaven." In Jude 25 it is used as an ascription of praise to God: ". . . to the only God . . . be glory, majesty . . ."

NAME

onoma ὄνομα 3686

onoma is a noun found in approximately two hundred places, with the consistent meaning "name." It is used of people, places, and objects, and refers also to both God and Christ.

onoma refers to naming people in mundane literal contexts in Matt 27:32; Mark 3:16; 5:22; Luke 1:5, 13, 27; 8:41; John 1:6; Acts 5:1. Elsewhere the term refers to the names of the twelve disciples (Matt 10:2). Luke 10:20; Phil 4:3; Rev 3:5, 8 all declare in some way that the names of all believers are recorded in heaven. John 10:3 records that Jesus calls his "sheep" (i.e., his followers) by name. In a metaphorical context, Rev 21:12ff. declares that the names of the twelve tribes of Israel are written on the gates of the heavenly Jerusalem.

The term "name" also refers to places (e.g., Luke 24:13; Mark 14:32; Luke 1:26; Rev 3:12); and once it refers to a symbolic star with the name "Wormwood," from which will emanate a catastrophic judgment on humankind (Rev 8:11).

With reference to Christ, ***onoma*** is found in a variety of contexts. General references to the "name of Jesus" are indicated in Matt 1:21, 25; Luke 1:31; 2:21; Acts 9:15 (implied); Phil 2:10. Several texts declare that Jesus is given the name that is above every name (Eph 1:21; Phil 2:9; Heb 1:4); and Rev 3:12; 19:12ff. record that Christ is given a new name in heaven. The prophetic name of Immanuel is determined for the Christ child in Matt 1:23.

Jesus uses the phrase "for my name's sake" in the sense of "for my cause," and it is found primarily in contexts where Jesus warns his followers that they will be hated and persecuted for being associated with him (Matt 10:22; 24:9; Mark 13:13; Luke 21:12, 17; Acts 9:16; 1 Pet 4:14; Rev 2:3). See Rom 1:5; 1 John 2:12 for use of this expression in the third person.

The expression "in the name of Jesus Christ" is used in the context of baptism in Acts 2:36; 8:16; 10:48. It is also found in contexts where the name of Christ is invoked as a prelude to a miraculous cure (Acts 3:6; 4:10, 30; 16:18). The phrase "in his name" is equivalent to the concept "in him," indicating the person of Christ. It is found in Matt 12:21 with reference to the Gentiles, who "hope in his name." John 1:12 declares that those who believe "in his name" will be granted the status of children of God. General references to believing in his name are found in John 2:23; 20:31; Acts 3:16; 8:12; 1 John 3:23; 5:3. Similarly, Jesus' own words "in my name" have a similar significance (Matt 18:5; 24:5; Mark 9:37; 13:6; Luke 9:48; John 14:13, 26; 15:16; 16:23ff.). See also Luke 10:17.

onoma is also applied directly to God. John 12:28; Rom 15:9; Rev 15:4 refer to glorifying the name of God. The sanctifying of God's name is enjoined in the Lord's Prayer in Matt 6:9; Luke 11:2. The practice of baptizing in the name of the Father, Son, and Holy Spirit is mentioned in Matt 28:19. Mary, the mother of Jesus, affirms that God's name is holy in Luke 1:49. Jesus is said to have come and worked in the name of his Father (John 5:43; 10:25); and he speaks of making known to his disciples the name of his Father in his prayer recorded in John 17:6, 26. The sin of blaspheming the name of God is indicated in Rom 2:24 and warned against in 1 Tim 6:1. Rev 14:1; 22:4 refer to the Father's name and the name of the lamb written on the foreheads of the saints in glory.

The expression "the name of the Lord" is found in a number of significant contexts. The hymn of praise for Christ as he enters Jerusalem in triumph at that fateful Passover festival is recorded in Matt 21:9; 23:9; Mark 11:9; Luke 13:35; 19:38; John 12:13 — "Blessed is he who comes in the name of the Lord." The guarantee that "he who calls on the name of the Lord shall be saved" is found in Acts 2:21; Rom 10:13. The practice of baptizing believers "in the name of the Lord (Jesus)" is noted in Acts 8:16; 19:5. Preaching and prophesying "in the name of the Lord Jesus" is indicated in Acts 9:29; Jas 5:10. Praising the name of the Lord Jesus is mentioned in Acts 19:17. Acts 21:13 refers to Paul's willingness to die "for the name of the Lord Jesus." 1 Cor 6:11 declares that the believer is justified "in the name of the Lord Jesus Christ." See also Acts 19:13; Col 3:17; Jas 5:14 for other uses of the expression.

onoma also refers to the names of evil spirits, such as "Legion" (Mark 5:9; Luke 8:30); Apollyon the demonic ruler of the abyss (Rev 9:11); the blasphemous name of the sea beast (Rev 13:1); the name of the earth beast (Rev 13:17; 14:11); and the name of the city of Babylon, "the mother of harlots" (Rev 17:5).

onoma is translated "name" in the sense of "reputation" in Rev 3:1. Here the congregation of Sardis falsely assumes that they have a "name" for being alive. But, in reality, they are spiritually dead.

onomazō ὀνομάζω 3687

onomazō is the verb from which the noun ***onoma*** (above) is derived. ***onomazō*** is found in only ten places and is translated "to name" or "call."

onomazō refers to the process of naming individuals (Luke 6:13, 14); to naming Christ in the sense of proclaiming the gospel (Rom 15:20); to naming believing families in the sense of their spiritual identification (Eph 3:15; also Eph 1:21); and to naming the name of the Lord (2 Tim 2:19) in the sense of confessing him as Savior and Lord.

To "name" in the sense of "mention" is the meaning found in 1 Cor 5:1; Eph 5:3, with reference to immorality of varying kinds. Acts 19:13 refers to Jewish exorcists "pronouncing" the name of the Lord Jesus, attempting the exorcism of evil spirits.

In 1 Cor 5:11, ***onomazō*** conveys the sense of "be called" or "bear the name of" with respect to those who wanted to be known as "brothers" in Christ, but whose sinful lifestyle denied the integrity of their profession.

NOBLE, NOBLEMAN

eugenēs εὐγενής 2104

eugenēs is a rare term found in only three contexts. In Luke 19:12 it refers in general terms to a "nobleman." In 1 Cor 1:26 the term is used adjectivally to describe the Berean Christians as "more noble" than those in Thessalonica. The qualities indicated here are those of purity of motive and devotion to Christ and his word. 1 Cor 1:26 also records an adjectival usage, referring to nobility of birth.

kratistos κράτιστος 2903

kratistos occurs only four times in the NT. On each occasion it serves as a form of address to men of high political or regal status. Luke 1:3 contains Luke's greeting to a "most noble Theophilus." ***kratistos*** similarly addresses Felix the Roman governor of Judea (Acts 23:26; 24:3); and his successor, Festus (Acts 26:25). ***kratistos*** may also be translated "most excellent" in these contexts.

▸ **52.** Status, Identity, Reputation, Honor, Shame > EXCEL, EXCELLENT

NUMBER

logizomai λογίζομαι 3049

logizomai is a verb occurring about forty times with the primary meanings "reckon," "impute." However, in Mark 15:28, the term is translated "number" with reference to the quotation from Isa 53, identifying Jesus as the fulfillment of that prophecy in which the Suffering Servant was to be "numbered with the transgressors."

▸ **51.** Knowledge, Wisdom, Remember, Forget > CONSIDER
▸ **51.** Knowledge, Wisdom, Remember, Forget > IMPUTE
▸ **51.** Knowledge, Wisdom, Remember, Forget > RECKON

SEE ALSO

▸ **7.** Quantity, Amount, Number, Size, Measure > NUMBER
arithmos, arithmeō, katarithmeō

PUT TO SHAME, TREAT SHAMEFULLY

kataischynō καταισχύνω 2617

kataischynō is another variant form of the entries listed above, with the meanings "to shame," "put to shame," "disgrace," "dishonor," in several different contexts.

The general meaning "put to shame" in the sense of "embarrass," "humiliate" is indicated, for example, in Luke 13:17; 1 Cor 11:22; 2 Cor 7:14; 9:4; 1 Pet 3:16. Where God is the subject of the verb, he is said to "shame" both the wise and strong of this world (1 Cor 1:27).

The negative use of ***kataischynō*** in Rom 5:5 indicates that the hope of the gospel does "not put the believer to shame"; and those who believe in Christ will likewise "not be put to shame" (Rom 9:33; 10:11; 1 Pet 2:6).

The meaning "dishonor" or "disgrace" is indicated in 1 Cor 11:4, 5, where it is affirmed that men who pray and prophesy with their heads covered, and women who do so with their heads uncovered, serve to "dishonor" their heads. This suggests that they act inappropriately in worship and thereby fail to bring glory to God.

▸ **52.** Status, Identity, Reputation, Honor, Shame > ASHAMED

atimazō ἀτιμάζω 818

atimazō is a verb synonymous with the entries listed above, occurring six times with the meanings "put to shame," "suffer shame," "dishonor."

The sense of "treat shamefully" (i.e., mistreat cruelly) is indicated in Luke 20:11. The action of "dishonoring" Christ and God the Father is noted in John 8:49; Rom 2:23. Acts 5:41 speaks of "suffering shame" for the name of Christ. Rom 1:24 refers to the "dishonoring" of one's body through immorality; and Jas 2:6 to the "shameful despising" of the poor.

▸ **52.** Status, Identity, Reputation, Honor, Shame > DISHONOR
▸ **52.** Status, Identity, Reputation, Honor, Shame > SHAME

paradeigmatizō παραδειγματίζω 3856

atimia is a noun found in seven contexts with the consistent sense of "shame," "dishonor" throughout.

The term is used adjectivally in Rom 1:26 to denote "shameful" sexual relations. The meaning "shame" or "dishonor" in a personal sense is indicated in 1 Cor 11:14; 15:43; 2 Cor 6:8; 11:21. The same meaning is applied in non-personal contexts to household utensils with the sense of "menial" or "common."

hybrizō ὑβρίζω 5195

paradeigmatizō is a rare verb occurring only twice, with the meaning "to put to open shame" or "hold up to contempt." It is found in Matt 1:19 in relation to Joseph's unwillingness to publicly disgrace Mary, his betrothed, after finding out she was pregnant. It is also found in Heb 6:6 in relation to Christ being publicly disgraced as a consequence of his death by crucifixion.

▸ **52.** Status, Identity, Reputation, Honor, Shame > SHAME

SEE ALSO

▸ **76.** Force, Harm, Oppress > TREAT SHAMEFULLY
atimoō

REPROACH

oneidos ὄνειδος 3681

oneidos is a noun found only in Luke 1:25 with reference to Elizabeth (the mother of John the Baptist) rejoicing in her pregnancy, declaring that God had taken away her "reproach" (i.e., shame) among her countrymen.

oneidizō ὀνειδίζω 3679

oneidizō is a verb occurring eleven times and meaning "reproach" in two distinct senses.

In the first place, ***oneidizō*** is translated "reproach" with the underlying sense of "to cast insult(s)." In this regard, the disciples of Christ are declared blessed on account of people "reproaching" and persecuting them for their faith (Matt 5:11; Luke 6:22; 1 Pet 4:14). In other contexts, the thief on the cross reproaches Christ by hurling insults at him (Matt 27:44), as does the crowd watching his agony (Mark 15:32).

Secondly, ***oneidizō*** means "reproach" in the sense of "rebuke" or "denounce." Christ is said to reproach unbelieving hearers in this manner (Matt 11:20). Even his disciples are so chastised in Mark 16:14. Rom 15:3 declares that Christ bore the reproach (i.e., disgrace or rejection) of God on the cross. Jas 1:5 affirms God's generosity in giving blessings to people, "without reproach" (i.e., without finding fault).

oneidismos ὀνειδισμός 3680

oneidismos, along with ***oneidos*** (above), is a noun form derived from ***oneidizō*** (above), meaning "reproach" in all five occurrences of the term.

Rom 15:3; Heb 13:13 refer to the "reproach" (i.e., disgrace, shame) borne by Christ. 1 Tim 3:7 warns against falling into "reproach" (i.e., disgrace). Heb 10:33 refers to the "reproach" (i.e., abuse) suffered by believers at the hand of their enemies. Heb 11:26 speaks of Moses suffering "reproach" or "abuse" for the sake of Christ.

SEE ALSO

▸ **58.** Vices > REPROACH, INSULT, ABUSE
loidoria, loidoreō

REPUTATION, REPUTE

martyreō μαρτυρέω 3140

martyreō is a verb found in about eighty contexts with the primary meanings "witness," "testify," as well as a number of associated senses. One of these is the meaning "to have a good reputation," "be of good repute," applied to individuals in several contexts (Acts 6:3; 10:22; 22:12; Heb 11:2; 3 John 12).

▸ **63.** Speak, Tell, Declare, Call >
WITNESS, BEAR WITNESS, TESTIFY, TESTIMONY

martyria μαρτυρία 3141

martyria is the noun derived from ***martyreō*** (above) and means "witness," "testimony" in most of its nearly forty occurrences. In 1 Tim 3:7, however, it means "of good reputation" with reference to one of the prerequisite qualities of an elder.

▸ **63.** Speak, Tell, Declare, Call >
WITNESS, BEAR WITNESS, TESTIFY, TESTIMONY

dysphēmia δυσφημία 1426

dysphēmia is a noun found solely in 2 Cor 6:8, referring to the quality of a "bad reputation."

SHAME

aischynē αἰσχύνη 152

aischynē is a noun found six times, meaning "shame," "disgrace," "dishonor." It refers to the "disgrace" arising from the practice of idolatry (Phil 3:19); to the shame of "crucifixion" (Heb 12:2); and to a dissolute lifestyle (Jude 13).

Metaphorically, ***aischynē*** refers to the "shame" of one's spiritual nakedness, or bankruptcy (Rev 3:18).

More positively, ***aischynē*** expresses "humility" in Luke 14:9.

aischron αἰσχρόν 149

aischron is a noun synonymous with ***aischynē*** (above) found in three places with the general sense of "shame," "disgrace" (1 Cor 11:6; Eph 5:12). 1 Cor 14:35 indicates that it is shameful for a woman to speak in church.

entropē ἐντροπή 1791

entropē is a rare noun denoting "shame" (i.e., "humiliation," "embarrassment") found only in 1 Cor 6:5; 15:34.

atimia ἀτιμία 819

atimia is a noun found seven times, denoting "dishonor" and "shame," as well as related nuances.

The term is used adjectivally in Rom 1:26 to refer to "vile" or "shameful" passions. In Rom 9:21 the term refers metaphorically to vessels constructed for "common" or "menial" use. See also 2 Tim 2:20.

Personal "shame" or "dishonor" is indicated in 1 Cor 11:14; 2 Cor 6:8; 11:21.

The humble condition of the human body, referred to metaphorically as having been "sown in dishonor," is noted in 1 Cor 15:43.

▸ **52.** Status, Identity, Reputation, Honor, Shame >
DISHONOR

atimoō ἀτιμόω 821

atimoō is a verb found only in Mark 12:4, meaning "to treat shamefully."

▸ **76.** Force, Harm, Oppress > TREAT SHAMEFULLY

atimazō ἀτιμάζω 818

atimazō is a verb found six times, with the meaning "to treat shamefully" or "dishonor" as well as associated senses.

The sense of "treat shamefully" (i.e., with contempt) is found in Luke 20:11; Rom 1:24; Jas 2:6.

atimazō refers to "dishonoring" Christ (John 8:49) and God (Rom 2:23), as a consequence of breaking the law.

The meaning "to suffer shame" is indicated in Acts 5:41 in relation to the persecution of Christ's disciples.

▸ **52.** Status, Identity, Reputation, Honor, Shame > PUT TO SHAME, TREAT SHAMEFULLY

▸ **52.** Status, Identity, Reputation, Honor, Shame > DISHONOR

hybrizō ὑβρίζω 5195

hybrizō is a term synonymous with ***atimazō*** (above). It occurs five times and means "to treat shamefully, or with contempt" (Matt 22:6; Luke 18:32; Acts 14:5; 1 Thess 2:2). In Luke 11:45, it means "reproach."

▸ **52.** Status, Identity, Reputation, Honor, Shame > PUT TO SHAME, TREAT SHAMEFULLY

53. Value, Worth

ABOMINABLE, ABOMINATION, DETESTABLE

athemitos ἀθέμιτος 111

athemitos is a rare adjective found only twice. It designates as "unlawful" any association between Jew and Gentile, as noted in Acts 10:28. In 1 Pet 4:3 the term refers to idolatries as "abominable."

▸ **38.** Covenant, Law, Rites, Roles > UNLAWFUL, LAWLESS

bdelyktos βδελυκτός 947

bdelyktos is a rare adjective describing the deeds of false teachers as "abominable" or "detestable."

bdelygma βδέλυγμα 946

bdelygma is a noun found in six different contexts with the consistent meaning "abomination."

The idolatrous altar placed in the Jerusalem temple, known as "the abomination of desolation," is referred to in Matt 24:15; Mark 13:14. Human wickedness, designated as "abomination(s)" is indicated in Luke 16:15; Rev 17:4ff.; 21:27.

EXCEL, EXCELLENT

hyperballō ὑπερβάλλω 5235

hyperballō is a verb found five times, meaning "surpass," denoting the underlying sense of "excel," "be exceedingly great" on three of these occasions. 2 Cor 3:10 speaks of the glory of the new covenant that "surpasses" the glory of the old. In Eph 3:19, the love of Christ is said to "surpass" all human knowledge. 2 Cor 9:14 speaks of the "surpassing" grace of God indwelling the lives of the Corinthian congregation, describing it as something of exquisite excellence. In the remaining texts, ***hyperballō*** is used adjectivally to refer in Eph 1:19 to the "immeasurable" or "excellent" greatness of God's power; and in Eph 2:7 to the "immeasurable" riches of God's grace.

diaphoros διάφορος 1313

diaphoros is an adjectival form found in two places, meaning "excellent." Heb 1:4 refers to the name of Christ that is "more excellent" than that of the angels. In Heb 8:6 the ministry of Christ in the new covenant is described as "more excellent" than that of the old covenant.

SEE ALSO

▸ **7.** Quantity, Amount, Number, Size, Measure > EXCEED, EXCEEDINGLY
hyperbolē

▸ **52.** Status, Identity, Reputation, Honor, Shame > EXCEL, EXCELLENT
kratistos, prōteuō, philoprōteuō

GOOD

agathos ἀγαθός 18

agathos is an adjectival form denoting "good things" in a number of contexts. A question as to what "good thing" one must do to gain eternal life is put to Christ in Matt 19:16. "Doing good" is commended in Eph 6:8. The possession of "every good thing" in Christ is noted in Phlm 6. See also John 1:46; Gal 4:18; 2 Tim 1:14; Heb 13:9.

The negative sense of "nothing good" is indicated in relation to human nature in Rom 7:18.

▸ **88.** Qualities, Characteristics > GOOD, EXCELLENT, ADMIRABLE, WELL

SEE ALSO

▸ **81.** Forms, Groups, Patterns, Order > THING, MATTER
pragma

LEAST

elachistos ἐλάχιστος 1646

elachistos is a superlative form of the adjective *elachys* ("short"), with the primary meaning "least," as well as "smallest," "very little." ***elachistos*** occurs thirteen times.

The meaning "least (in rank)" is found in Matt 2:6 with reference to Bethlehem, as the least among the towns of Judah. Matt 5:19 refers to the least of the commandments; and Paul describes himself as the least of the apostles in 1 Cor 15:9. See also Matt 25:40ff.

elachistos also means "least" in the sense of "very little." Luke 16:10; 19:17 point to the quality of being faithful in "very little." See also Luke 12:26; 1 Cor 4:3; Jas 3:4. 1 Cor 6:2 refers to legal cases that are "trivial" or "least," in the sense "of little consequence."

▸ **7.** Quantity, Amount, Number, Size, Measure > LITTLE, SMALL, LEAST, FEW

elachistoteros ἐλαχιστότερος 1647

elachistoteros is a comparative form of ***elachistos*** (above) meaning "last of all," "very least." It occurs only in Eph 3:8, where Paul refers to himself as the "very least" of the saints.

mikros μικρός 3398

mikros is an adjectival form meaning "small," "little." However, six of the thirty contexts in which this term is found indicate the sense of "least."

The meaning "least," in the sense of "smallest," is found in Matt 13:32. The sense of "least (in rank)" is indicated in Luke 9:48; Acts 8:10; Heb 8:11. Matt 11:11; Luke 7:28 refer to those who are designated "least in the kingdom of heaven."

▸ **7.** Quantity, Amount, Number, Size, Measure > LITTLE, SMALL, LEAST, FEW

LUKEWARM

chliaros χλιαρός 5513

chliaros occurs only in Rev 3:16, referring to the "lukewarm" spirit of devotion to Christ in the Laodicean church. For such an attitude, they will have to endure being "vomited out" of God's mouth if there is no change in their condition.

SPLENDOR

phantasia φαντασία 5325

phantasia is a rare noun found only in Acts 25:23 indicating the "splendor" of King Agrippa.

UNWORTHY, UNWORTHILY

anaxiōs ἀναξίως 371

anaxiōs is an adverb found on two occasions meaning "unworthily" (1 Cor 11:27, 29). Here it refers to the sin of profaning the body and blood of Christ by eating the bread and drinking the cup of the Lord's Supper "in an unworthy manner," or participating in the sacrament of the Lord's Supper with an impure motive or unconfessed sin.

anaxios ἀνάξιος 370

anaxios is a rare adjectival form meaning "unworthy" in the sense of "incompetent" in 1 Cor 6:2.

VAIN, MAKE VAIN, MAKE VOID

matēn μάτην 3155

matēn is an adverb that depicts the hypocritical worship of the Pharisees as being "in vain" (i.e., of no value) (Matt 15:9; Mark 7:7).

kenos κενός 2756

kenos is an adjective meaning "vain," "empty." It also has the adverbial sense "in vain."

The designation "vain" or "futile" is applied to speech (Eph 5:6; Col 2:8), and to human beings (Jas 2:20), indicating their foolishness.

kenos is also used adverbially. The nations plotting "in vain" against God are noted in Acts 4:25 (citing Ps 2:2). Paul affirms in 1 Cor 15:10 that the grace of God is never offered "in vain," for no purpose (see also 1 Cor 15:10, 58). Gal 2:2; Phil 2:16 warn of the danger of running the race of the Christian life "in vain" (i.e., without receiving the prize of eternal life). See also 1 Thess 2:1; 3:5.

▸ **7.** Quantity, Amount, Number, Size, Measure > EMPTY, EMPTY-HANDED

mataioō ματαιόω 3154

mataioō is a rare verb found only in Rom 1:21 which declares that unbelievers "have become vain (i.e., futile)" in their thinking.

mataios μάταιος 3152

mataios is the adjective derived from ***mataioō*** (above) and denotes that which is "vain" or "useless." ***mataios*** refers to idols (Acts 14:15); to human thoughts (1 Cor 3:20); and to religion without love (Jas 1:26). See also 1 Cor 15:17; Titus 3:9; 1 Pet 1:18.

mataiologia ματαιολογία 3150

mataiologia is a rare noun occurring only in 1 Tim 1:6 with reference to "vain" or "worthless" talk.

mataiologos ματαιολόγος 3151

mataiologos is a noun found only in Titus 1:10 denoting a "vain talker," or one who utters senseless words.

kenōs κενῶς 2761

kenōs is an adverb meaning "in vain," found only in Jas 4:5 as a mistaken assessment of the Scriptures being "without reason."

kenoō κενόω 2758

kenoō is a verb occurring in five places and meaning primarily "to make vain," "render useless, null and void."

Rom 4:14 declares that faith "is rendered useless" if people are justified by the law. The power of the cross of Christ is also "rendered useless" without the accompanying proclamation of the gospel. See also 1 Cor 9:15; 2 Cor 9:3.

A special use of ***kenoō*** is indicated in Phil 2:7, which speaks of Christ "having emptied himself " (i.e., made himself nothing), so that he might submit to the humiliation of assuming a human form, simultaneously laying aside his heavenly position for a time in order to do so.

▸ **7.** Quantity, Amount, Number, Size, Measure > EMPTY, EMPTY-HANDED

eikē εἰκῆ 1500

eikē is an adverb meaning "in vain," in the sense of "without reason" or "for nothing." It occurs in seven places.

Rom 13:4 refers to national governments who "do not use the sword in vain" exercising just punishment. 1 Cor 15:2 declares that people have believed "in vain" if they do not hold firmly to the message of the gospel. See also Gal 3:4; 4:11; Col 2:18.

dōrean δωρεάν 1432

dōrean is an adverb with the dominant sense of "freely" in most of the nine contexts in which it is found. In Gal 2:21, the death of Christ is said to be "in vain" (i.e., useless, futile) if justification is to be gained through the law.

▸ **88.** Qualities, Characteristics > FREELY

VALUABLE, VALUE

timaō τιμάω 5091

timaō is a verb found in around twenty places with the principal meaning "to honor." Twice, however, it means "set a value, or price on" (Matt 27:29).

▸ **52.** Status, Identity, Reputation, Honor, Shame > HONOR

timios τίμιος 5093

timios is an adjective derived from ***timaō*** (above) meaning "precious," "valuable" in most of its fourteen occurrences. It is applied to gemstones (1 Cor 3:12; Rev 17:4; 18:12ff.; 21:11, 19); to one's faith (1 Pet 1:7); to the blood of Christ (1 Pet 1:19); and to God's promises (2 Pet 1:4). See also Acts 20:24; Jas 5:7.

barytimos βαρύτιμος 927

barytimos is a rare adjectival form found only in Matt 26:7 denoting ointment or perfume that is "very precious (i.e., expensive)."

entimos ἔντιμος 1784

entimos is another adjective meaning "prized," "precious." Luke 7:2 refers to a valued slave. Christ the "living stone" is deemed "precious" in God's sight in 1 Pet 2:4ff. See also Luke 14:8.

isotimos ἰσότιμος 2472

Another rare variant of the above words, ***isotimos*** is found only in 2 Pet 1:1 and refers to a faith "of equal value."

polytimos πολύτιμος 4186

Another adjectival variant of the above entries, ***polytimos*** is found in two places. It indicates a pearl "of great value" in Matt 13:46, and "very expensive" perfume in John 12:3.

polytelēs πολυτελής 4185

polytelēs is an adjective synonymous with ***polytimos*** (above). It is found three times with the general meaning "precious," "valuable" in relation to perfume (Mark 14:3); garments (1 Tim 2:9); and to an intangible (yet very real), gentle, and quiet spirit (1 Pet 3:4).

ōphelimos ὠφέλιμος 5624

ōphelimos is an adjective denoting that which is "profitable" (i.e., "of value") in varying degrees. It occurs four times, describing good deeds (Titus 3:8) and bodily fitness and godliness (1 Tim 4:8). 2 Tim 3:16 declares that all Scripture is "profitable" for teaching.

euchrēstos εὔχρηστος 2173

euchrēstos is an adjective synonymous with ***ōphelimos*** (above) denoting in three places those who are "useful" in Christian ministry (2 Tim 2:21; 4:11; Phlm 11).

diapherō διαφέρω 1308

diapherō is a verb meaning "to be more valuable, of more value," found in five contexts (Matt 6:26; 10:31; 12:12; Luke 12:7, 24).

WEIGHT, WEIGHTY

baros βάρος 922

baros is a noun found six times with the predominant sense of "burden," but it is translated "weight" in a figurative context in 2 Cor 4:17. The context here refers to the glorious destiny of the believer in heaven that far "outweighs" all earthly afflictions during this life.

▸ **75.** Suffering, Distress, Sadness > BURDEN

barys βαρύς 926

barys is an adjective found in six places meaning "weighty" in the sense of "important," "significant," in Matt 23:23; 2 Cor 10:10.

▸ **88.** Qualities, Characteristics >
HEAVY, WEIGHTY, BURDENSOME

WORTHLESS, USELESS

achreioō ἀχρειόω 889

achreioō is a verb found only in Rom 3:12, referring to all people "becoming worthless, or unprofitable."

achreios ἀχρεῖος 888

achreios is an adjective found in only two places (Matt 25:30; Luke 17:10), describing servants as "worthless," "useless," "good-for-nothing."

achrēstos ἄχρηστος 890

achrēstos is a rare adjective found only in Phlm 11, indicating the former status of Onesimus as "useless" or "worthless" to his master Philemon.

anōphelēs ἀνωφελής 512

anōphelēs is another rare adjectival form referring to "worthless" or "unprofitable" argument over the law in Titus 3:9. It also describes as "useless" the former statute of priestly law under the old covenant that could never effectively remove sin and guilt in the life of the Israelite people (Heb 7:18).

WORTHY, UNWORTHY

hikanos ἱκανός 2425

hikanos is an adjective occurring around forty times with the primary senses of "many," "much," "enough." However, the term also means "worthy," although in the NT it occurs only in the negative — with the sense of "unworthy" (Matt 3:11; 8:8; Mark 1:7; Luke 3:16; 7:6).

axios ἄξιος 514

axios is an adjective found in around forty contexts with the dominant sense of "worthy," with varying nuances.

The meaning "worthy" in the sense of "deserving" is indicated in Rev 3:4 in relation to a few members of the congregation at Sardis who are deemed "worthy of praise." Deeds "worthy of repentance" are noted in Matt 3:8; Luke 3:8; Acts 26:20. Matt 10:10; Luke 10:7; 1 Tim 5:8 affirm that a laborer is "worthy of his hire." Sin "deserving" death is referred to in Rom 1:32. See also Matt 10:13; Luke 7:4; 12:48; 23:15; 1 Tim 1:15; 4:9. God is deemed "worthy" to receive praise in Rev 4:11; 5:12. The negative sense of "unworthy," "undeserving," is indicated in Matt 22:8; Luke 15:19ff. In several places, people are said to be "unworthy" of Christ (Matt 22:8; Luke 15:19ff.; Acts 13:25; 23:29; Heb 11:38).

▸ **73.** Blessing, Curse, Reward, Punishment > REWARD, RECOMPENSE

axioō ἀξιόω 515

axioō is a verb found in five contexts, meaning "to count, or consider worthy." 2 Thess 1:11 refers to "being counted worthy" of one's calling by God himself. In 1 Tim 5:17, Paul expresses the desire that elders "be counted worthy" of double honor. Heb 3:3 affirms that Jesus should be counted worthy of a greater glory than Moses. See also Heb 10:29.

kataxioō καταξιόω 2661

The verb ***kataxioō*** is a derivative form of ***axios*** (above). It is found in several contexts, meaning "to judge, or count worthy." Luke 20:35 affirms that believers are "counted worthy" to attain eternal life. In Acts 5:41, the apostles are "judged worthy" to suffer persecution for Christ's sake. See also 2 Thess 1:5.

axiōs ἀξίως 516

axiōs is an adverbial form meaning "worthy," in the context of leading a life "worthy" of one's calling (Eph 4:1; Phil 1:27; Col 1:10; 1 Thess 2:12).

SEE ALSO

▸ **32.** Law, Justice, Jurisprudence, Judgment > WORTHY
enochos

54. Rule, Authority, Command, Obedience

AUTHORITY, POWER, RIGHT

exousia ἐξουσία 1849

exousia is a noun found in approximately one hundred contexts with the predominant sense of "authority" or "right," and "power." "Authority" constitutes the inherent "right" and principal foundation of "power"; and the exercise of "power" is evidence of a duly grounded "authority." "Power" and "authority" are neutral in and of themselves. It is the moral contexts from which these phenomena derive that determine whether "power" and "authority" are good or evil. The scriptural context makes it clear that all "power" and "authority" derives from God — and may be justly utilized, or abused. In any case, God will in the end judge their use or abuse. The meanings "power" and "authority" often overlap, although there is no one English term that describes the fusion of these two senses.

General references to "authority" include Luke 19:17; Rom 9:21. Civil authority or jurisdiction is indicated in Luke 23:7; John 19:10; Acts 9:14; 26:10ff. Such authority is specifically said to be granted by God in John 19:11; Rom 13:1ff. A soldier recognizes his obligation to submit to a superior "authority" in Matt 8:9; Luke 7:8. Civil authorities, or magistrates, are noted in Luke 12:11; Titus 3:1. References to "heavenly authorities" in general are found in Col 1:16; Eph 3:10; 1 Pet 3:22.

In particular, God's "authority" in general terms is indicated in Acts 1:7; Jude 25. General references to "authority" given to human beings by God include Matt 9:8; Eph 1:21; and apostolic "authority" is evident in 2 Cor 10:8; 13:10.

Elsewhere, Christ's "authority" is both implicitly and explicitly declared to be given by God. Explicit indications of Christ's God-given authority are noted in Matt 28:18; Col 2:10. In particular, Christ affirms that he has been given authority to forgive sin in Matt 9:6; Mark 2:10; 6:7; Luke 5:24; to exorcise demonic spirits in Matt 10:1; Mark 1:27; Luke 9:1; and to execute divine judgment in John 5:27.

General references to God's power are found in Acts 8:19; and in Rev 6:8; 9:3, 10; 12:10; 16:9 such power is manifested in the execution of divine judgment on sinful humanity. See also Luke 12:5. Divine power is said to be given to Christ in John 10:18; 17:2, and to angels in Rev 14:18. John 1:12 affirms that God gives power to his people to become his "adopted" children. Such a "power" is linked with "right" or "privilege."

Luke 22:53; 1 Cor 15:24, Eph 2:2; 6:12; Rev 13:2ff.; 17:12ff. refer to evil, or demonic, power. Christ destroys such power (Col 1:13; 2:15).

exousia can also mean "right." 1 Cor 9:4ff.; 2 Thess 3:9 make reference to the "right" to derive material support from one's ministry in the gospel. In Rev 22:14 the saints in heaven are given the "right" to access the tree of life.

epitagē ἐπιταγή 2003

epitagē is a noun found seven times with the meaning "command," "commandment" in all but one context. In Titus 2:15 the term denotes the "authority" associated with the pastoral office.

▸ **54.** Rule, Authority, Command, Obedience > COMMAND, COMMANDMENT, DIRECT, ORDER

exousiazō ἐξουσιάζω 1850

exousiazō is a verb meaning "have power, authority over."

The exercise of royal power or authority is indicated in Luke 22:25. In 1 Cor 6:12 Paul declares that he will not "be enslaved" by anything (i.e., brought under its power). 1 Cor 7:4 makes several references to the principle or "rule" that the husband does not have power (or rule) over his own body, but over rather his wife, and vice versa.

▸ **54.** Rule, Authority, Command, Obedience > EXERCISE AUTHORITY

katexousiazō κατεξουσιάζω 2715

katexousiazō is a variant form of ***exousiazō*** (above) with the meaning "exercise authority" or "wield power" over. It is found only twice (Matt 20:25; Mark 10:42).

authenteō αὐθεντέω 831

authenteō is a rare verb, found only in 1 Tim 2:12 with reference to the apostle's refusal to allow a woman "to have authority over" a man.

BE REQUIRED

zēteō ζητέω 2212

zēteō is a common verb meaning "seek" in most of its nearly 120 occurrences. However, in Luke 12:48; 1 Cor 4:2 it is used passively to indicate that which is required (i.e., demanded) of faithful servants of God.

▸ **66.** Ask, Answer, Discuss, Learn > INQUIRE
▸ **72.** Need, Gain, Loss, Advantage, Seek, Find > SEEK, SEARCH

SEE ALSO

▸ **32.** Law, Justice, Jurisprudence, Judgment > REQUIRE
ekzēteō, apaiteō

CHARGE, INSTRUCT

parangelia παραγγελία 3852

parangelia is a noun denoting a "charge" or "instruction" in Acts 16:24; 1 Tim 1:18.

diamartyromai διαμαρτύρομαι 1263

diamartyromai is a verb meaning "testify" in most of the fifteen occurrences of the term. The term also means "to charge" in the sense of "to give a solemn instruction or exhortation" as found in 1 Tim 5:21; 2 Tim 2:14; 4:1; Heb 2:6.

▸ **63.** Speak, Tell, Declare, Call > WITNESS, BEAR WITNESS, TESTIFY, TESTIMONY

diastellomai διαστέλλω 1291

diastellomai is a verb found nine times with the meaning "to charge" in the sense of "issue strict instructions." It is used in the context of Jesus' exhortations to his disciples (Matt 16:20; Mark 5:43; 9:9). See also Acts 15:24; Heb 12:20.

embrimaomai ἐμβριμάομαι 1690

The verb ***embrimaomai*** means to "give a solemn charge, or instruction" and is found in Matt 9:30; Mark 1:43.

exorkizō ἐξορκίζω 1844

exorkizō is a rare verb meaning "to charge" or "to issue a solemn injunction" found only in Matt 26:63.

horkizō ὁρκίζω 3726

horkizō is a verb found in three places meaning to "give a solemn charge to" (Mark 5:7; Acts 19:13; 1 Thess 5:27)

SEE ALSO

- ▸ **30.** Money, Business, Wealth, Poverty > FREE OF CHARGE ***adapanos***
- ▸ **32.** Law, Justice, Jurisprudence, Judgment > CHARGE, COMPLAINT ***aitia, aitiōma, enklēma, enkaleō***

COMMAND, COMMANDMENT, DIRECT, ORDER

diatassō διατάσσω 1299

diatassō is a verb found in sixteen places, meaning "command," "charge."

The meaning "command" in the sense of "give a charge, instruction(s)" is found in Luke 8:55; 17:9ff.; Acts 18:2; 20:13; 23:31; 24:23; 1 Cor 11:34; 16:1; Titus 1:5.

Acts 7:44 describes God "giving instructions" to Moses on how to construct the tabernacle. In 1 Cor 9:14, Paul affirms that the Lord "has commanded" that those who preach the gospel should earn their living from the gospel.

epitassō ἐπιτάσσω 2004

epitassō is a variant form of ***diatassō*** (above) found in ten contexts, meaning "command," "charge."

The "giving of orders" in a military context is indicated in Mark 6:27. The household context of a master "giving instructions" to his servant is noted in Luke 14:22. In a civil context, Acts 23:2 records the high priest "issuing instructions" to his servants. In the apostolic context, Paul "gives an instruction" to Philemon in Phlm 8.

Christ "issues a command" to evil spirits to abandon their victims in Mark 1:27; 9:25; Luke 4:36; 8:31; and in Mark 6:39 he "instructs" the crowd to be seated. In Luke 8:25, he "commands" the natural elements of wind and sea to obey him.

prostassō προστάσσω 4367

The verb ***prostassō*** is synonymous with ***diatassō*** and ***epitassō*** (above). It is found seven times, meaning "command," "instruct" throughout.

God is said to "issue commands" coming through the old covenant law of Moses in Matt 8:4; Mark 1:44; Luke 5:14. There is also direct "instruction" from God in Acts 10:33; and in Acts 10:48 Peter "gives instructions" for new converts to be baptized. The angel of the Lord "gives instructions" to Joseph to take Mary his wife home in Matt 1:24. Matt 21:6 refers to Christ "instructing" his disciples.

syntassō συντάσσω 4929

syntassō is a rare variant for the above entries. It is found twice in Matt 26:19, where Christ "directs" his followers to make preparations for the Passover. Matt 27:10 cites Jer 32:6ff. in regard to the Lord's "instruction" to the prophet to purchase the field at Anathoth.

keleuō κελεύω 2753

keleuō is another synonym for the entries above, indicating the action of "commanding," "directing," or "instructing" people to perform certain actions. Jesus instructs the crowds following him in Matt 8:18; 14:9, 19; 15:35; and he "commands" a blind man to be brought to him (Luke 18:40). Peter asks Jesus to "command him" to walk on water in Mark 14:28.

General references to people "giving orders" are found in Matt 18:25; 27:58, 64; Acts 4:15; 27:43. Elsewhere, the "giving of orders" in a judicial context is noted in Acts 12:15; 16:22; 21:33ff.; 22:30; 24:8; 25:6, 17, 21ff.

entellō ἐντέλλω 1781

entellō is a verb meaning "command," "give orders" throughout the nearly twenty occurrences of the term.

God is said to "give commands" concerning his angels in Matt 4:6; Luke 4:10; in relation to honoring one's parents in Matt 15:4; concerning divorce in Matt 19:7; through Moses in Mark 10:3; John 8:5; and to his Son in John 14:31. God also "directs" his servants to be a light for the Gentiles in Acts 13:47. He issues a command with respect to keeping the covenant in Heb 9:20.

Jesus "gives commands" to his disciples in Matt 17:9; 28:20; John 15:14, 17. See also Acts 1:2.

Other general references to "giving orders" include Mark 13:34; Heb 11:22.

parangellō παραγγέλλω 3853

parangellō is a verb found in about thirty places, with the primary meaning "command."

The meanings "charge," "give a solemn order to" are found in relation to the disciples being forbidden to preach the gospel of Christ in Acts 4:18; 5:28, 40. Paul "instructs" husbands and wives not to separate in 1 Cor 7:10. Christian converts are commanded in Acts 15:5 to keep the law of Moses and to be circumcised — an order contrary to the gospel and to new covenant practice. Commands are given to evil spirits in the process of their exorcism in Acts 16:18. Instructions relating to godly living and gospel ministry are noted in 1 Tim 1:3; 4:11; 6:17. See also Acts 16:23; 2 Thess 3:4ff.

In relation to the ministry of Christ, Jesus "gives instruction" to his disciples in Matt 10:5; Mark 6:8; Acts 1:4; and to the crowds following him in Mark 8:6. He "commands" his followers to preach the gospel in Acts 10:42; and he "orders" unclean spirits to leave their victims in Luke 8:29. See also Luke 9:21.

Acts 17:30 contains the divine command for all people everywhere to repent.

diatagma διάταγμα 1297

diatagma is a rare noun found only in Heb 11:27, referring to the Egyptian king's "edict" or "command" to have all male Hebrew infants slain at birth so as to prevent the expansion of the Israelite people.

entalma ἔνταλμα 1778

entalma is a rare noun denoting the "precepts" or "commandments" of human beings in the sense of "human traditions." The term is found only in Matt 15:9; Mark 7:7; Col 2:22, and the connotation is wholly negative. All three references indicate that such traditions are wholly useless in attracting the favor of God.

epitagē ἐπιταγή 2003

epitagē is a noun denoting the general sense of "command" in seven contexts. General references to the command of God are found in Rom 16:26; 1 Cor 7:25; 1 Tim 1:1; Titus 1:3; 2:15.

References to human commands are found in 1 Cor 7:6; 8:8.

▸ **54.** Rule, Authority, Command, Obedience > AUTHORITY, POWER, RIGHT

SEE ALSO

▸ **38.** Covenant, Law, Rites, Roles > COMMAND, COMMANDMENT
entolē

DECREE, ORDINANCE

dogma δόγμα 1378

dogma is a noun found in five places denoting "ordinances," "decrees."

Luke 2:1 refers to the "decree" issued by Caesar Augustus for a universal census throughout the Roman Empire — the catalyst for events leading up to the birth of Christ. Caesar's "decrees" in general are noted in Acts 17:17. Acts 16:4 refers to the "ordinances" or "decisions" of the apostolic council. Eph 2:15; Col 2:14 refer to the "decrees" or "ordinances" of the law covenant, whose curse and penalty have been abolished through the death of Christ.

DESPISE

atheteō ἀθετέω 114

atheteō is a verb with the primary meaning "reject." In Heb 10:28, however, the term refers to the act of "despising" the law of Moses — "violating" it, or treating it with contempt through disobedience.

▸ **49.** Allow, Accept, Approve, Refuse > REJECT

SEE ALSO

▸ **52.** Status, Identity, Reputation, Honor, Shame > DESPISE
periphroneō, atimos

▸ **77.** Resist, Oppose, Fight, Rebel > DESPISE, DISDAIN
exoutheneō, kataphroneō

DISOBEY, DISOBEDIENCE, DISOBEDIENT

apeithēs ἀπειθής 545

apeithēs is an adjective found in six places, all referring to "disobedience."

General references to "disobedient" people are found in Luke 1:17; Titus 1:16; 3:3. Paul acknowledges in Acts 26:19 that he was "not disobedient" to the heavenly vision. Those disobedient to their parents are mentioned in Rom 1:30; 2 Tim 3:2.

parakoē παρακοή 3876

parakoē is a noun denoting "disobedience" in all three occurrences of the term. The "disobedience" of Adam and its terrible impact on the whole human race are noted in Rom 5:19. Other references to "disobedience" are found in 2 Cor 10:6; Heb 2:2.

apeitheō ἀπειθέω 544

apeitheō is a verb occurring sixteen times. Approximately half of these contexts reflect the negative sense of "to not obey" or "be disobedient." In the remaining usage it means "not to believe," "be unbelieving."

Rom 2:8 refers to those who do not obey the truth. Similarly, 1 Pet 2:8; 3:1, 20 refer to those who disobey the word of God; and 1 Pet 4:17 to those who disobey the gospel of God. In Rom 10:21, Israel is described as a disobedient people.

▸ **45.** Faith, Belief, Trust, Promise > BELIEVE

▸ **45.** Faith, Belief, Trust, Promise > UNBELIEF, UNBELIEVER, UNBELIEVING

DOMINION, LORD OVER

kratos κράτος 2904

kratos is a noun found in twelve places with the primary sense of "power" or "strength." In several places, however, the term also denotes the "dominion" or "rule" of God — all in the context of invoking such divine authority (1 Pet 4:11; 5:11; Jude 25; Rev 1:6; 5:13).

▸ **18.** Strength, Weakness, Capability > STRENGTH, STRONG, POWER, POWERFUL, MIGHT, MIGHTY

kyrieuō κυριεύω 2961

kyrieuō is a verb with the principal meaning "have dominion, power over," "be lord over" throughout its nine occurrences.

The exercise of human royal dominion or authority is indicated in Luke 22:25. Death is declared to no longer have dominion over Christ in Rom 6:9. Similarly, sin is declared to no longer exercise any dominion over the believer, who has passed from law to grace. The binding effect of the power or "dominion" of the law is noted in Rom 7:1. Rom 14:9 declares that Christ "is Lord of both the dead and the living" (Rom 14:9). See also 2 Cor 1:24; 1 Tim 6:15.

katakyrieuō κατακυριεύω 2634

katakyrieuō is a variant form of ***kyrieuō*** (above) found in four places and meaning "exercise dominion, rule over," in the sense of "lord (it) over someone." Such an attitude and action is predicated of the Gentiles in Matt 20:25; Mark 10:42. The denial of a "domineering stance" towards the members of one's congregation is noted in 1 Pet 5:3. The meaning "overpower" is found in Acts 19:16.

kyriotēs κυριότης 2963

kyriotēs is a noun derived from ***kyrieuō*** (above) denoting "dominion," "civil authority" in a general sense in only four places (Eph 1:21; Col 1:16; 2 Pet 2:10; Jude 8).

EXERCISE AUTHORITY

exousiazō ἐξουσιάζω 1850

exousiazō is a verb found four times with the underlying sense of "have power, rule over." Luke 22:25 refers to the Gentile rulers "exercising authority" over their people.

▸ **54.** Rule, Authority, Command, Obedience > AUTHORITY, POWER, RIGHT

SEE ALSO

▸ **20.** Illness, Disease, Health, Healing > EXERCISE ***gymnasia***

LORD, OVERLORD

kyrios κύριος 2962

The term ***kyrios*** is found around seven hundred times in the NT and usually refers to Jesus Christ as God incarnate. The title "Lord," when applied to the Messiah, signifies his divine nature. As the NT Greek equivalent of the Hebrew term *YHWH*, normally transliterated as Yahweh, it transfers to the person of Christ all those characteristics that the Hebrew title attributes to the person of God. In approximately five hundred places, ***kyrios*** refers to Jesus as "Lord," "the Lord Jesus," "the Lord Jesus Christ," or "Jesus Christ our Lord" (including slight variations in word order).

The term ***kyrios*** is also used in the expression "angel of the Lord" on twelve occasions (Matt 1:20, 24; 2:13, 19; 28:2; Luke 1:11; 2:9; Acts 5:19; 7:30; 8:26; 12:7, 23). Only in Matt 1:24 is the definite article used to specify "*the* angel of the Lord" as the divine messenger to Joseph, instructing him to take Mary as his wife.

kyrios explicitly refers to God as "the Lord" in a number of places. Many of these are quotations from OT sources — for example, Matt 22:37 (Deut 6:4ff.); Luke 3:4 (Isa 40:1ff.); Luke 4:12 (Deut 6:16); Acts 7:33 (Exod 3:5); Rom 10:16 (Isa 53:1); Heb 8:8 (Jer 31:31); Heb 10:30 (Ps 135:14).God is described as "the Lord of heaven and earth" in Matt 11:25. The Day of the Lord is indicated in Acts 2:20. Jas 5:4 affirms that God is "Lord of hosts." He is declared the "Lord of the harvest" in Matt 9:30; Luke 10:2. The title "Lord God" is frequently cited in the book of Revelation (Rev 4:8, 11; 11:17; 15:3ff.; 16:7; 18:8; 19:1, 6; 21:22; 22:6). Other general references to God as Lord are found in Mark 16:20; Luke 1:16; Acts 2:21; Rom 4:8; Heb 1:10.

At the human level, ***kyrios*** indicates an "overlord" or "master" (Matt 6:24; 18:34; Mark 13:35; Luke 12:36; Acts 16:16; Gal 4:1; Col 4:1; 1 Pet 3:6).

▸ **54.** Rule, Authority, Command, Obedience > MASTER
▸ **69.** Have, Possess, Hold, Grasp, Bear, Carry > OWNER

despotēs δεσπότης 1203

despotēs is found on ten occasions and refers to a "lord" or "master," at both the human and divine level.

despotēs refers to God by the title "sovereign Lord," in the context of prayer offered to him (Luke 2:29; Acts 4:24; Rev 6:10).

Human overlords or masters are indicated in 1 Tim 6:1, 2; 2 Tim 2:21; 1 Pet 2:18, and Paul exhorts those who are in service to pay due respect to their masters.

In 2 Pet 2:1; Jude 4, ***despotēs*** refers to Jesus Christ as "Master," whom false teachers have denied.

▸ **54.** Rule, Authority, Command, Obedience > MASTER

MASTER

kyrios κύριος 2962

kyrios is the most common term in the NT for "Lord," in relation to the divine title given to Jesus Christ. It occurs nearly seven hundred times in this context.

However, on several occasions ***kyrios*** refers to "master" in the sense of "slave owner," "master of the household" (Acts 16:16, 19; Eph 6:5, 9; Col 3:22; 4:1). The term also refers once to the Lord Christ as our "Master in heaven" in Eph 6:9. Matt 6:24; Luke 16:13 refer in a general sense to one's "master," of whom there can only be one — God or money — for a person can serve only one master.

▸ **54.** Rule, Authority, Command, Obedience > LORD, OVERLORD
▸ **69.** Have, Possess, Hold, Grasp, Bear, Carry > OWNER

epistatēs ἐπιστάτης 1988

epistatēs is a term of address, "Master," indicating one who has a position of authority and leadership. It occurs only six times and is used of Jesus Christ by his disciples on all occasions except one (Luke 5:5; 8:24, 45; 9:33, 49). In Luke 17:13, a group of lepers addresses Jesus this way.

despotēs δεσπότης 1203

despotēs is another term meaning "lord" and "master," in ten contexts. Some contexts refer to either God or Christ. In other contexts, ***despotēs*** refers to human overlords (1 Tim 6:1, 2; 2 Tim 2:21; Titus 2:9; 1 Pet 2:18).

▸ **54.** Rule, Authority, Command, Obedience > LORD, OVERLORD

OBEDIENCE, OBEDIENT, OBEY

hypakoē ὑπακοή 5218

hypakoē occurs fifteen times and is consistently translated "obedience" with respect to both human beings and Christ.

In several places, ***hypakoē*** refers to the "obedience" of faith, or to a positive response of faith and trust in Christ (Rom 1:5; 15:18 [implied]; 16:26). In Rom 6:16, ***hypakoē*** refers to obedience leading to righteousness. 1 Pet 1:2 indicates that believers are destined to live lives of obedience to Christ; and 1 Pet 1:14 refers to obedient children of God, literally "children of obedience."

hypakoē refers to Christ's obedience in undertaking and carrying out the plan of salvation that God sent him to earth to accomplish (Rom 5:19; Heb 5:8). In general terms, the obedience of Christ is recognized and affirmed in Rom 16:19; 2 Cor 7:15; 10:5, 6; Phlm 21.

hypakouō ὑπακούω 5219

hypakouō is the verb from which ***hypakoē*** (above) is derived and is translated "to obey," "be obedient," in almost every context in which it is found. ***hypakouō*** occurs around twenty times.

Regarding inanimate forces and objects, the wind and waves are said to obey the voice of Christ in his miraculous calming of the storm in Matt 8:27; Mark 4:41; Luke 8:25 (see also Luke 17:6).

In Mark 1:27, demonic spirits are said to obey the command of Christ, and they are compelled to abandon the minds and bodies of those they previously possessed.

Concerning the human response of obedience, Acts 6:7 indicates that many Jewish priests were obedient to the call of the gospel as the number of believers multiplied in the early days of apostolic preaching. In contrast, ***hypakouō*** is used in the negative to indicate a response of unbelief (Rom 10:16; 2 Thess 1:8; 3:14). Rom 6:17; Phil 2:12 speak of the believer's deliverance from sin so that one becomes obedient to a new standard of righteousness in Christ. Likewise, Paul exhorts his readers not to allow sin to cause them to yield to, or obey, their sinful passions (Rom 6:12, 16).

Children are enjoined to obey their parents (Eph 6:1; Col 3:20), and slaves to obey their masters (Eph 6:5; Col 3:22). Heb 11:8 records Abraham's obedience in his faithful dependence upon God, leading him to leave his homeland in Ur. 1 Pet 3:6 refers to Sarah's obedience to Abraham, her husband, as characteristic of her life. Heb 5:9 affirms that obeying Christ will lead to eternal salvation.

hypēkoos ὑπήκοος 5255

hypēkoos is an adjectival form derived from ***hypakoē*** and ***hypakouō*** (above). ***hypēkoos*** is found in only three places, meaning "obedient." Acts 7:39 uses the term negatively, noting the Israelite people's rejection of Moses in the wilderness, refusing to obey him. 2 Cor 2:9 refers to Paul's testing the Corinthian congregation, to establish whether they are obedient to their new calling. Phil 2:8 indicates Christ's humble submission to the will of his Father, becoming obedient to the point of death.

peitharcheō πειθαρχέω 3980

peitharcheō occurs four times with the explicit meaning "obey" in three of these contexts. Acts 5:29 affirms the necessity of obeying God as the primary obligation over all other priorities. Acts 5:32 indicates that those who obey God are recipients of the Holy Spirit. Titus 3:1 contains the apostolic injunction to be obedient to civil rulers and authorities. In Acts 27:21 ***peitharcheō*** is translated "to listen to," but the underlying sense is that of "obey." Paul argues here that his traveling companions should not have ignored his warning not to set sail from Crete so late in the year when the risk of bad weather was much greater.

peithō πείθω 3982

peithō is a verb found in approximately sixty contexts with the primary meanings "persuade," "trust," as well as related senses. However, ***peithō*** is translated "obey" in three places. Gal 5:7 refers to the importance of "obeying" the truth, which the Galatians had ceased to do. Heb 13:7 instructs people to obey their spiritual leaders, whom God has ordained to act as overseers of his people in local congregations. Jas 3:3 mentions the bits placed in the mouths of horses as a means of rendering them obedient to their riders.

- ▸ **45.** Faith, Belief, Trust, Promise > TRUST
- ▸ **47.** Show, Persuade, Confidence, Doubt > PERSUADE, PERSUASION

PUT IN SUBJECTION

hypotassō ὑποτάσσω 5293

hypotassō is a verb found nearly fifty times with the predominant meanings "be subject to," "submit." It also has the active sense of "put under, in subjection to." 1 Cor 15:27ff.; Heb 2:8 refer to God "having put all things in subjection" under his feet, and under the feet of Christ (Eph 1:22).

- ▸ **54.** Rule, Authority, Command, Obedience > SUBJECT, SUBJECTION, SUBMIT, SUBMISSION

SEE ALSO

- ▸ **25.** Family, Marriage, Adoption, Inheritance > PUT AWAY ***apolyō***
- ▸ **79.** Throw, Send, Drive, Mix, Remove > PUT OFF, PUT AWAY, CAST ASIDE ***apotithēmi, apekdyomai***
- ▸ **83.** Set, Put, Place, Prepare, Establish > PUT, PLACE, LAY ***tithēmi, paratithēmi, epitithēmi, peritithēmi, epiballō***

REIGN

basileuō βασιλεύω 936

basileuō occurs about twenty times, with the exclusive meaning "to reign" in the sense of "to be king." It is used metaphorically in both human and divine contexts.

basileuō refers to the reign of the Herodian dynasty in first-century Judea in Matt 2:22. General references to royal rule are found in Luke 19:14, 27.

Luke 1:33 refers to Christ reigning as King; and in 1 Cor 15:25 the reference to the reign of Christ points to the elimination of all the enemies of God. Rev 11:15 speaks of the eternal reign of Christ. The heavenly reign of God is affirmed in 1 Tim 6:15; Rev 11:17; 19:6.

basileuō is used metaphorically in a number of contexts. All of God's people are said to reign on earth in Rev 5:10. Similarly, it is said that believers will reign with Christ for one thousand years as a prelude to the eternal kingdom of God and Christ (Rev 20:4, 6). Rev 22:5 speaks of the eternal reign of all believers in glory. Rom 5:14, 17 refer to the "reign of death," as it impacts the whole of the human race. Rom 6:12 refers to the reign of sin in one's body. 1 Cor 4:8 employs the phrase "to reign as kings," indicating a rise to a position of power and influence in society.

hēgemonia ἡγεμονία 2231

hēgemonia is found only in Luke 3:1, referring to the reign of the emperor Tiberius Caesar.

archō ἄρχω 757

archō is a verb found only twice, referring to those who "reign" (or rule) over the Gentiles (Mark 10:42; Rom 15:12).

▸ **54.** Rule, Authority, Command, Obedience > RULE, RULER

symbasileuō συμβασιλεύω 4821

symbasileuō is a variant form of ***basileuō*** (above) meaning "to reign together with." It is found only in 1 Cor 4:8; 2 Tim 2:12.

RINGLEADER

prōtostatēs πρωτοστάτης 4414

prōtostatēs is a noun found only in Acts 24:5, accusing Paul of being a "ringleader" of the sect of the Nazarenes.

RULE, RULER

archō ἄρχω 757

archō is a verb found in only two places, meaning "to rule over," "reign over." Mark 10:12; Rom 15:12 refer to ruling over the Gentiles.

▸ **54.** Rule, Authority, Command, Obedience > REIGN

archōn ἄρχων 758

archōn is a participial noun derived from ***archō*** (above) meaning "ruler," "commander," "chief." The term is found in approximately forty contexts.

The general sense of "ruler" is indicated in Acts 3:17; 4:26; 7:27; Rom 13:8; 1 Cor 2:6, 8. Matt 20:25 mentions the rulers of the Gentiles. Luke 12:58 refers to a "ruler" who is a magistrate (see also Luke 18:18).

In the religious or ceremonial sphere, ***archōn*** also denotes a "ruler" of the synagogue, as in the case of Jairus (Matt 9:18ff.; Luke 8:41). Other likely references to synagogue rulers include those in Luke 23:13, 15; 24:20; John 7:48; 12:42; Acts 4:5ff.; 13:27. Luke 14:1 refers to a "ruler" of the Pharisees.

archōn refers to Satan as the "ruler" or "prince" of demons (Matt 9:34; 12:24; Mark 3:22; Luke 11:15; Eph 2:2). The title "ruler of this world" is also applied to Satan in John 12:31; 14:30; 16:11.

archōn refers to Christ as "the ruler" of kings in Rev 1:5.

▸ **32.** Law, Justice, Jurisprudence, Judgment > MAGISTRATE

politarchēs πολιτάρχης 4173

politarchēs is found only in Acts 17:6, 8, with reference to the "ruler of the city."

poimainō ποιμαίνω 4165

poimainō is a verb meaning to "feed" or "tend" (animals) in the majority of its eleven occurrences. However, in several of these places, ***poimainō*** means "rule" or "govern."

Matt 2:6 refers to the one who will come to "govern" the people of God (i.e., Christ). Rev 2:21 speaks of the "rule" of Christ in the heavenly kingdom. Rev 12:5; 19:15 refer to the universal rule of Christ over all nations — a reign characterized by the use of a rod of iron.

▸ **28.** Agriculture, Viticulture, Animal Husbandry > FEED, TEND

proistēmi προΐστημι 4291

proistēmi is a verb found in eight contexts, meaning "rule," "govern," "watch, or preside over" in most of these.

Rom 12:8 mentions ruling as a leader in an unspecified way. 1 Thess 5:12; 1 Tim 5:17 speak of the "ruling" function of pastors and elders in the church, as those who "watch over" the congregation of God's people. The responsibility of "governing" one's household is affirmed in 1 Tim 3:4ff., 12.

kathistēmi καθίστημι 2525

kathistēmi is a verb occurring about twenty times and meaning "to appoint as a ruler," "to watch over" in several of these contexts.

The sense of "to appoint as a ruler" is indicated in Matt 24:45ff.; 25:21ff.; Luke 12:42ff., all of which refer to a servant placed in authority over his master's household. Acts 7:10 refers to Joseph being appointed as "governor" of Egypt. A general reference to this action is found in Acts 7:27, 35.

▸ **83.** Set, Put, Place, Prepare, Establish > APPOINT, ORDAIN, ASSIGN

hēgeomai ἡγέομαι 2233

hēgeomai is found in approximately thirty contexts with the primary meanings "think," "consider." However, in several places, the term is used nominally to refer to a "ruler" or "governor."

Luke 22:26 mentions a "leader" or "ruler" in a general sense. Matt 2:6 refers to the messianic "ruler" of the people of God. Acts 7:10 refers to Joseph as a "governor" or "ruler" of Egypt. In the context of congregational leadership, Heb 13:7, 17, 24 refer to elders as those "having authority" or "ruling" over their churches.

▸ **51.** Knowledge, Wisdom, Remember, Forget > COUNT

hēgemōn ἡγεμών 2232

hēgemōn is a participial noun derived from ***hēgeomai*** (above) meaning "ruler" or "governor."

The general meaning "ruler," referring to the "kings" of Judah, is indicated in Matt 2:6.

More commonly, ***hēgemōn*** means "governor." General references to this office are found in Matt 10:18; Mark 13:9; Luke 21:12; 1 Pet 2:14. In particular, Matt 27:2ff.; 28:14; Luke 20:20 refer to Pilate as Roman "governor" of Judea. Felix, one of Pilate's successors, is likewise referred to by his official title of "governor" in Acts 23:24ff.; 24:1.

▸ **31.** Kingdom, Empire, Rule, Military, Warfare > GOVERNOR

brabeuō βραβεύω 1018

This verb is used figuratively and found only in Col 3:15 in the exhortation: "Let the peace of Christ 'rule' in your hearts." Here ***brabeuō*** expresses the underlying sense of "having the role of greatest influence."

archisynagōgos ἀρχισυνάγωγος 752

archisynagōgos is found in nine places, meaning "ruler of the synagogue" (Mark 5:22, 35ff.; Luke 8:49; 13:14ff.; Acts 18:8, 17).

▸ **38.** Covenant, Law, Rites, Roles > RULER OF THE SYNAGOGUE

kosmokratōr κοσμοκράτωρ 2888

kosmokratōr is a noun found only in Eph 6:12, referring to the demonic "rulers" of the present dark age, or spiritual powers of darkness, satanic "authorities" arrayed in opposition against heavenly, angelic "rulers."

SUBJECT, SUBJECTION, SUBMIT, SUBMISSION

hypotassō ὑποτάσσω 5293

hypotassō is a verb occurring about forty times with the senses of "subject to," "submit to," "bring into subjection," as well as related nuances.

The meaning "submit," "be subject to" has the underlying sense of "to obey," "be obedient" in a variety of contexts. Jesus willingly submits to his parents' directions in Luke 2:51. There are exhortations to submit to governing authorities in Rom 13:1; Titus 3:1; 1 Pet 2:13. Women are to "submit" to their husbands (1 Cor 14:24; Eph 5:22; Col 3:18; Titus 2:5; 1 Pet 3:1, 5). Slaves are enjoined to "submit" to their masters (Titus 2:9; 1 Pet 2:18). Demons are said to "be subject to" (i.e., under the control of) the apostles during their evangelistic mission (Luke 10:17ff.). The unregenerate human mind does not submit itself to the law of God (Rom 8:7).

Several texts affirm that God "has subjected" all things under his rule (1 Cor 15:27ff.; Eph 1:22; Phil 3:21; Heb 2:8). 1 Pet 3:22 affirms that all things "are subject" to Christ. The church's "submission" to her Lord is noted in Eph 5:24. Creation is said to "be subjected" to futility by the will of God in Rom 8:20.

Other general references to the attitude or stance of "submission," "subjection" include those in 1 Cor 14:32; Eph 5:21; Heb 12:9; Jas 4:7; 1 Pet 5:5.

▸ **54.** Rule, Authority, Command, Obedience > PUT IN SUBJECTION

SEE ALSO

▸ **55.** Bondage, Captivity, Servitude > SUBJECT, SUBJECTION, SUBMIT, SUBMISSION
enochos, doulagōgeō, hypotagē

TRANSGRESS, TRANSGRESSION, TRANSGRESSOR, TRESPASS, VIOLATE, VIOLATION

parabainō παραβαίνω 3845

parabainō is a verb denoting the act of "transgressing or violating the law," referring to both the traditions of human beings as well as the commandments of God (Matt 15:2ff.; Acts 1:25; 2 John 9).

parabasis παράβασις 3847

parabasis is a noun derived from ***parabainō*** (above) found in seven places and meaning "transgression" or "violation" in relation to the commands of God (Rom 2:23; 4:15; 5:14; Gal 3:19; Heb 2:2; 9:15).

parabatēs παραβάτης 3848

parabatēs is another noun derived from ***parabainō*** (above) meaning "lawbreaker," "transgressor," with exclusive reference to the law of God (Rom 2:25ff.; Gal 2:18; Jas 2:9ff.).

anomos ἄνομος 459

anomos is a noun synonymous with ***parabatēs*** (above) meaning "transgressor," "lawbreaker" (i.e., against God).

General references to such people include those in Mark 15:28; Acts 2:23; 1 Tim 1:9. In Luke 22:37, Christ's identification with "transgressors" in no way implies the existence of wickedness in his person. 2 Thess 2:8 mentions "the lawless one" (i.e., the antichrist). ***anomos*** also refers to "lawless deeds" in 2 Pet 2:8.

In a special use of ***anomos*** in 1 Cor 9:21, the term refers to "those outside the law" (i.e., Gentiles). Paul, in his determination to win these people for Christ, is intent on identifying with them and describes himself as "outside the law." This does not implicate him in any culpable attitude or action toward God.

▸ **57.** Evil, Wickedness, Sin > EVIL, EVILDOER, WICKED, WICKEDNESS, LAWLESS

paraptōma παράπτωμα 3900

paraptōma is a noun found in around twenty places meaning "trespass," "sin," "offense," as well as related senses.

Offenses committed by people against other people are indicated in Matt 6:14ff.; 18:35, emphasizing the importance of forgiving one another's trespasses.

General references to trespass against God include those in Matt 6:14ff.; Mark 11:25ff.; and see also 2 Cor 5:19; Gal 6:1; Jas 5:16. Forgiveness offered by God for "trespass" against him is described in Rom 11:11ff.; and sin or trespass leading to spiritual death, from which we are delivered in Christ, is noted in Eph 2:1ff.; Col 2:13.

Christ's atoning death for our "trespasses" is noted in Rom 4:25. The "trespass" of one man (i.e., Adam) leading to the condemnation of the entire human race is described in Rom 5:15ff. Forgiveness for humankind's "sins" is guaranteed by the finished redemptive work of Christ on the cross, as explained in Eph 1:7.

55. Bondage, Captivity, Servitude

BIND, BOUND, TIE UP

deō δέω 1210

deō is a verb found in approximately forty contexts meaning "bind," "tie up," plus associated nuances — both literal and metaphorical.

The literal sense of "bind" or "tie up" is found in connection with people (Matt 12:29; 14:3; Mark 3:27; 15:1; John 11:44; Acts 9:2; 21:11ff.); bundles of weeds (Matt 13:30); and a donkey (Matt 21:2; Mark 11:2ff.; Luke 19:30). Satan is also said to be bound by angels in Rev 20:2. See also Rev 9:14. The state of imprisonment is described as "being in bonds" in Col 4:3.

Other uses of ***deō*** are metaphorical. In Matt 16:19; 18:18, the sense of "bind" indicates a "bringing into subjection, under control." Acts 20:22 specifically mentions being brought under the control of the Holy Spirit. Luke 13:16 refers to bondage, the affliction of suffering, as the expression of satanic control. Several texts refer to "being bound" by the law, or being under legal obligation (Rom 7:2; 1 Cor 7:27, 39). The latter text refers explicitly to the bond of marriage. ***deō*** is used negatively in 2 Tim 2:9, which affirms that the word of God is "not bound," that is not restricted, in its effect.

desmeuō δεσμεύω 1195

The verb ***desmeuō*** is found in two places with the meaning "bind," "tie up." It refers literally in Acts 22:4 to tying people up in order to restrict their movement. In Matt 23:4 it is used metaphorically to refer to Jewish religious leaders who "tie up heavy burdens" (make intolerable demands) and impose them callously onto the common people.

proteinō προτείνω 4385

proteinō is a rare synonym for ***desmeuō*** (above) meaning "tie up" (with rope). It is found only in Acts 22:25.

SEE ALSO

- ▸ **20.** Illness, Disease, Health, Healing > BIND, DRESS A WOUND *katadeō*
- ▸ **67.** Acknowledge, Confess, Profess, Swear > BIND UNDER OATH *anathematizō*

BOND, CHAIN

desmos δεσμός 1199

desmos is a noun found about twenty times with the underlying meaning "bonds" signifying restriction of movement in the literal sense of "chains," and the metaphorical sense of "imprisonment" or "crippling disease."

Literal references to "chains" include Luke 8:29; Acts 26:29; Col 4:18; 2 Tim 2:9. "Chains" broken by divine power are noted in Acts 16:26, and prisoners are released by the civil authorities in Acts 22:30.

A metaphorical reference to the satanic "bondage" of a crippling disease from which a woman was healed by Jesus is noted in Luke 13:16. Other metaphorical references to "imprisonment" include Acts 20:23; 23:29; 26:31; Phil 1:7, 13ff.; Phlm 10ff.; Heb 10:34; 11:36. There is another symbolic usage of ***desmos*** in Jude 6, which mentions "eternal chains" that keep fallen angels bound in darkness until the judgment day.

halysis ἅλυσις 254

halysis is a noun found eleven times referring to "chains" as a means of restricting one's movement in several different contexts.

Chains restraining the Gadarene demoniac are noted in Mark 5:3ff.; Luke 8:29. Acts 12:6ff.; 21:33; 28:20; Eph 6:20; 2 Tim 1:16 refer to prisoners' "chains." In Rev 20:1, the angel holds "chains" to restrain the activity of Satan, who will be released for a short time prior to the final judgment.

SEE ALSO

- ▸ **27.** Community, Partnership, Unity, Discord > BOND *syndesmos*
- ▸ **32.** Law, Justice, Jurisprudence, Judgment > CHAIN, BOND *desmios*

BONDAGE, SLAVERY

katadouloō καταδουλόω 2615

katadouloō is a verb found four times meaning to "bring into bondage, slavery." It is used literally in 2 Cor 11:20 and figuratively in Gal 2:4 in relation to the old covenant law.

CAPTIVE, CAPTIVITY, CAPTURE

aichmalōsia αἰχμαλωσία 161

The noun ***aichmalōsia*** denotes "captivity" in a spiritual sense in Eph 4:8; and in a visionary context in Rev 13:10.

aichmalōteuō αἰχμαλωτεύω 162

The verb ***aichmalōteuō*** means "to make, take captive" and is found in Eph 4:8 with reference to Christ's activity in "capturing" his enemies at the point of his ascension. In 2 Tim 3:6 the term is used metaphorically with reference to false teachers who prey on, harass, and manipulate weak and vulnerable women — this activity is described as "leading them into captivity."

aichmalōtizō αἰχμαλωτίζω 163

aichmalōtizō is a synonym for ***aichmalōteuō*** (above) with the meaning "to take captive" in three contexts. It is used literally in Luke 21:24. Rom 7:23 contains a figurative usage, referring to the law of his mind "making him captive" to the law of sin. Then, 2 Cor 10:5 speaks of "taking every thought captive" to obey Christ.

aichmalōtos αἰχμάλωτος 164

aichmalōtos is a rare noun denoting a "captive" found only in Luke 4:18.

zōgreō ζωγρέω 2221

zōgreō is a rare verb meaning to "catch," "take captive." In Luke 5:10 the term is used metaphorically to refer to the evangelizing activity of "catching" people for the kingdom of God. 2 Tim 2:26 refers to "being captured" by the devil to do his will.

FREE, FREEDOM, SET FREE, LIBERTY

eleutheros ἐλεύθερος 1658

eleutheros is an adjectival form occurring nearly twenty-five times with the predominant meaning "free," with several different nuances.

The meaning "free" is evident in Matt 17:26 in relation to the non-payment of taxes, that is, being "exempt" from payment. "Freedom" from slavery in a literal sense is indicated in 1 Cor 7:21; 12:13; Gal 3:28; Eph 6:8; Col 3:11; Rev 6:15; 13:16; 19:18. The state of being "set free" from spiritual bondage through the agency of Christ is indicated in John 8:33ff.; Rom 6:20; 1 Cor 7:22.

Freedom from the law is indicated in Rom 7:3; 1 Cor 7:39 in relation to the marriage bond being dissolved by death, thus setting the surviving party free to remarry.

The state of freedom in the gospel, in relationship with Christ, is noted in 1 Cor 9:1, 19; 1 Pet 2:16. The metaphorical designation of "free woman" is applied to Sarah, Abraham's wife, in Gal 4:22ff. — a description identifying Sarah as a woman sealed through the gift of a son, favored by God as the recipient of covenant blessing.

eleutheroō ἐλευθερόω 1659

eleutheroō is a verb found seven times, meaning "to set free" and conveying the significant nuance of being liberated from the power of sin through the person and work of Christ.

In John 8:32, 36 Jesus declares that he, the Son, who embodies ultimate truth, "will make free" any who put their trust in him. Rom 6:18, 22; 8:2 contain the significant statements that believers "have been set free" from sin and death through the person of Christ in his redemptive work. Rom 8:21 offers a similar expression of truth, claiming that the creation itself "will be set free" from its bondage to decay. Gal 5:1 also affirms that Christ "has set his people free" from enslavement to sin.

▸ **44.** Repentance, Forgiveness, Mercy, Redeem, Save > RESCUE, DELIVER, SET FREE

eleutheria ἐλευθερία 1657

eleutheria is the noun derived from ***eleutheros*** and ***eleutheroō*** (above) denoting "liberty," "freedom" throughout its eleven occurrences.

eleutheria denotes "liberty" or "freedom" in the context of deliverance from the bondage of sin and death (Rom 8:21; Gal 2:4; 5:1). Elsewhere, "liberty" denotes "freedom of conscience" in 1 Cor 10:29; 1 Pet 2:16.

In 2 Cor 3:17, ***eleutheria*** denotes "freedom" in the general sense of a lifestyle liberated by the indwelling Holy Spirit in the life of the believer, a "freedom" to serve God wholeheartedly. See also Gal 5:13 for a similar context. Such a "freedom" is identified in Jas 1:25; 2:12 as the "law of liberty."

False "freedom" proclaimed by false teachers is indicated in 2 Pet 2:19.

apeleutheros ἀπελεύθερος 558

apeleutheros is a rare variant of ***eleutheros*** (above) found only in 1 Cor 7:22, referring to the Lord's "freedman" — a metaphorical reference to the paradox of the believer's standing before God. Only as a "slave" to God in Christ does one become truly "free."

dikaioō δικαιόω 1344

dikaioō is a verb meaning "to justify" throughout its nearly forty occurrences. However, in one context, Rom 6:7, ***dikaioō*** is translated passively "to be freed" in relation to being liberated from sin.

▸ **32.** Law, Justice, Jurisprudence, Judgment > JUSTIFY
▸ **59.** Justice, Righteousness, Truth > RIGHTEOUS, RIGHTEOUSNESS, JUST, JUSTIFY, JUSTIFICATION

SEE ALSO

▸ **88.** Qualities, Characteristics > FREELY
dōrean

RELEASE

apolyō ἀπολύω 630

apolyō is a verb found about ninety times with the underlying sense of "to release," along with several associated nuances.

The specific meaning "release," in the sense of restoring the liberty of those in prison, or of those held in custody after arrest, is indicated, for example, in Matt 27:15ff.; Mark 15:6ff.; Luke 23:18ff.; John 18:39; Acts 4:21ff.; Heb 13:23. Luke 23:16 refers to Pilate's failed attempt to have Jesus released from his custody after scourging. ***apolyō*** means "release" in the non-judicial sense of "let go" in Luke 14:4.

▸ **25.** Family, Marriage, Adoption, Inheritance > DIVORCE
▸ **25.** Family, Marriage, Adoption, Inheritance > PUT AWAY
▸ **44.** Repentance, Forgiveness, Mercy, Redeem, Save > FORGIVE, FORGIVENESS, RELEASE
▸ **49.** Allow, Accept, Approve, Refuse > ALLOW
▸ **79.** Throw, Send, Drive, Mix, Remove > SEND, SEND AWAY, SEND OUT

lyō λύω 3089

lyō is a verb with the primary meaning "loose" in the majority of the approximately forty contexts in which it is found. The underlying sense of ***lyō*** is "untie" or "release." It is translated "release" in about half of the occurrences of the term.

The meaning "release" in the sense of a judicial remission of a penalty is evident in Matt 16:19; 18:18.

lyō also refers literally to releasing or untying ropes that bind an animal, such as the colt required by Jesus (Matt 21:2; Mark 11:2ff.; Luke 13:15; 19:30ff.), or a man (Acts 22:30). Metaphorically, the term refers to releasing bound angels (Rev 9:14ff.); and also to the temporary "untying" or "loosing" of Satan at the end of time (Rev 20:3, 7). Luke 13:16 refers to a person's "release" from an illness.

▸ **12.** Fire, Heat, Smoke, Burning > DISSOLVE, MELT
▸ **21.** Die, Perish, Kill, Destroy > DESTROY, DESTROYER, DESTRUCTION
▸ **78.** Act Upon, Push, Pull, Break, Cut > BREAK

SERVANT, SLAVE

paidiskē παιδίσκη 3814

paidiskē occurs twelve times and refers to female domestic servants (Matt 26:69; Mark 14:66ff.; Luke 12:45; 22:56; John 18:17; Acts 12:13; 16:16). The term can be translated "maid," "servant girl," and "slave girl."

In Galatians, Paul refers to Hagar as the "slave woman" (***paidiskē***), in contrast to Sarah as the "free woman" — symbolizing two contrasting destinies. Sarah alone is the beneficiary of the covenant promise given to Abraham, whose wife was the one chosen by God to bear the child of promise.

doulos δοῦλος 1401

doulos is a noun found about 125 times meaning "servant" or "slave" in all of these contexts, both literal and metaphorical.

Literal references to "servant" include those in Matt 8:9; 13:27ff.; Luke 7:2ff.; Eph 6:5; Col 3:11; 1 Tim 6:1; Rev 13:16.

References to the "servant(s)" of God are found in Luke 2:29; Acts 2:18; 4:29; Jas 1:1; 1 Pet 2:16; Rev 10:7; 11:18.

The following passages refer to the "servant" of Jesus Christ (e.g., Rom 1:1; 1 Cor 7:22; Gal 1:10; Eph 6:6; 2 Tim 2:24; 2 Pet 1:1; Rev 1:1; 2:20).

doulos is used metaphorically to indicate the condition of being a "slave" to sin (John 8:34; Rom 6:16) and a "slave" of corruption (2 Pet 2:19).

douloō δουλόω 1402

douloō is a verb that is translated "to bring into slavery or bondage," "to become, make a servant" in each of the eight contexts in which it is found.

The meaning "to be under bondage (i.e., obligation)" is indicated in 1 Cor 7:15.

Acts 7:6 refers to Israel being "brought into slavery" in Egypt. In 1 Cor 9:19, Paul speaks of "making himself a slave or servant" to all human beings. Rom 6:18 refers to one "becoming a slave" of righteousness; 2 Pet 2:19 to becoming a "slave" to passion. See also Gal 4:3; Titus 2:3. Rom 6:22 refers to "becoming servants" of God.

pais παῖς 3816

pais is a noun with the primary meanings "servant," "child," in around twenty-five occurrences.

The meaning "servant," in the literal sense of "a person bonded as a slave," is indicated in Matt 8:6ff.; 12:18; 14:2; Luke 7:7; 12:45; 15:26.

The designation "servant" is applied to Israel (Luke 1:54); and to David (Luke 1:69; Acts 4:25).

▸ **25.** Family, Marriage, Adoption, Inheritance > CHILD

diakonos διάκονος 1249

diakonos is a noun found in thirty contexts and meaning "servant" or "minister," and also "deacon." The usage is varied.

The general sense of "servant" as "one who serves or ministers" is indicated in Matt 20:26; 23:11; Mark 9:35; 10:43. Household slaves are mentioned in Matt 22:13; John 2:5, 9.

diakonos refers to servants as "deacons" (1 Tim 3:8, 12); as "deaconesses" (Rom 16:1, 27); and as "servants" of the church (Col 1:25; 1 Tim 4:6).

The meaning "servant" of Christ is indicated in John 12:26; 1 Cor 3:5; 2 Cor 11:23; Eph 6:21; Col 1:7; and "servant" of God in Rom 13:4; 2 Cor 6:4; 1 Thess 3:2. Christ himself is described as a "servant" to the circumcised in Rom 15:8. In stark contrast, ***diakonos*** refers to "servants" of Satan in 2 Cor 11:15.

diakonos refers also to "ministers" of the new covenant (2 Cor 3:6); and to "ministers" of the gospel (Eph 3:7; Col 1:23).

▸ **38.** Covenant, Law, Rites, Roles > DEACON, MINISTER, SERVANT, SERVE

syndoulos σύνδουλος 4889

syndoulos is a noun that is consistently translated "fellow servant" in each of the ten contexts in which it is found. Literal references are indicated in Matt 18:28ff.; 24:49; Col 1:7. References are made to one's "fellow servant" in the Lord in Col 4:7; Rev 6:11; 19:10; 22:9.

therapōn θεράπων 2324

therapōn is a rare term found only in Heb 3:5 with reference to Moses as a faithful "servant" in God's house.

misthōtos μισθωτός 3411
misthios μίσθιος 3407

Both of these terms are translated "hired servant." ***misthōtos*** is found three times (Mark 1:20; John 10:12f.). ***misthios*** occurs only in Luke 15:17, 19.

hypēretēs ὑπηρέτης 5257

hypēretēs occurs about twenty times with the principal meanings "guard," "officer" in most of these contexts. However, ***hypēretēs*** twice refers to the "servants" of Christ (John 18:36; 1 Cor 4:1).

▸ **32.** Law, Justice, Jurisprudence, Judgment > OFFICER, OFFICIAL

oiketēs οἰκέτης 3610

oiketēs is a noun found five times meaning "servant" in the sense of a "bonded slave" (Luke 16:13; Acts 10:7; Rom 14:4; Phlm 25; 1 Pet 2:18).

SERVE, SERVICE

douleuō δουλεύω 1398

douleuō is a verb found in twenty-five contexts meaning "serve," "do service," "be a slave."

The general sense of "serve" in relation to "being in bond service to a master" is noted in Matt 6:24; Luke 16:13; John 8:33; Acts 7:7; 1 Tim 6:2. See also Luke 15:29. Metaphorically, the state of "being in bondage" to sin is evident in Rom 6:6; Titus 3:3. See also Gal 4:8, 9.

"Serving" God in a general sense is indicated in Matt 6:24; Luke 16:13; Acts 20:19; Rom 7:6, 25; 12:11; Eph 6:7. Similarly, Rom 14:18; Col 3:24 refer to "serving" in gospel ministry.

diakoneō διακονέω 1247

diakoneō is a verb occurring about forty times with the primary meaning "to minister" or "serve" in most of these contexts.

"Serving" in the general sense of offering hospitality or particular service and help is recorded in Matt 4:11; 8:15; Mark 1:13; Luke 8:3; John 12:2; 2 Tim 1:18; Heb 6:18. Matt 20:28; Mark 10:45 speak of the purpose of Christ — not to be served, but to serve. Acts 6:2 refers to "serving" tables in the early Christian community.

John 12:26 refers to "serving" Christ; and 1 Tim 3:10ff. refers to the "service" of deacons.

▸ **38.** Covenant, Law, Rites, Roles >
DEACON, MINISTER, SERVANT, SERVE

diakonia διακονία 1248

diakonia is the noun derived from ***diakoneō*** (above). It is found in approximately thirty-five contexts and means "ministry" or "service," "serving."

"Serving" as the exercise of hospitality is noted in Luke 10:40; Rom 12:7.

diakonia means "ministry" in numerous contexts, referring to ministry in general (1 Cor 12:5; 2 Cor 9:13; Rev 2:19); ministry of the word (Acts 6:4); apostolic ministry (Acts 1:17, 25); gospel ministry (Acts 12:25; 2 Cor 4:1; 5:18; Eph 4:12; 1 Tim 1:2); and the ministry of the Spirit (2 Cor 3:8ff.). See also 2 Cor 3:8, 9 which contrast the ministry of life in the Sprit with the "ministry of death."

hypēreteō ὑπηρετέω 5256

hypēreteō is a verb found in only three places, meaning "to serve" or "minister." David is said to "serve" the purpose of God in Acts 13:36; and the noble action of "ministering to one's needs" is described in Acts 20:34; 24:23.

leitourgia λειτουργία 3009

leitourgia is a noun found six times, meaning "service," "ministry."

Service in association with temple worship is indicated in Luke 1:23; Heb 9:21. "Ministry" in general is cited in Phil 2:30. The "ministry" of generous giving is indicated in 2 Cor 9:12.

Metaphorical reference to one's "service" or sacrifice for the gospel is found in Phil 2:17. The more excellent "ministry" of Christ through the new covenant is described in Heb 8:6.

SEE ALSO

▸ **41.** Sacrifice, Offering, Worship, Praise >
SERVE, SERVICE, WORSHIP
latreuō, latreia

SPEND COMPLETELY, GIVE ONESELF

ekdapanaō ἐκδαπανάω 1550

ekdapanaō is a verb found only in 2 Cor 12:15 with reference to "spending oneself wholly" (i.e., to sacrificially give oneself to the welfare of others).

SEE ALSO

▸ **3.** Periods of Time, Duration, Frequency, Speed >
SPEND TIME
chronotribeō

▸ **30.** Money, Business, Wealth, Poverty > SPEND
dapanaō, prosdapanaō

STEWARD, OVERSEER, DIRECTOR, TRUSTEE, GUARDIAN

oikonomos οἰκονόμος 3623

oikonomos is a noun denoting "one who oversees or manages household or civic affairs." This is usually, though not always, the function of a slave. The term is used both literally and metaphorically, and is found in ten contexts.

The literal sense of "manager" or "steward" is found in Luke 12:42; 16:1ff. In Rom 16:23, the likely translation of ***oikonomos*** is "director of public works."

Metaphorical reference to "stewards" is found in 1 Cor 4:1ff., where ***oikonomos*** designates the apostles as "custodians" of the gospel message, which is the full account of the mysteries of God's revelation.

Elsewhere, the metaphor of "steward" or "trustee" relates to the role of the old covenant law in the life of God's people, prior to the coming of Christ (Gal 4:2). Titus 1:7 speaks of the bishop as a "steward of God," and 1 Pet 4:10 alludes to the "stewards" of God's gifts.

oikonomeō οἰκονομέω 3621

oikonomeō is a rare verb, found only in Luke 16:2 in relation to "holding the office of a steward."

oikonomia οἰκονομία 3622

oikonomia is a noun derived from ***oikonomeō*** (above) and is found in seven places.

The term denotes "the office of a steward" in a literal sense in Luke 16:2ff. In addition, it refers to "the divine plan," involving the outworking of God's purposes in salvation and the spread of the message of redemption (1 Cor 9:17; Eph 1:10; 3:2; Col 1:25).

epitropos ἐπίτροπος 2012

epitropos is a noun occurring three times, synonymous with ***oikonomos*** (above), in relation to a "steward" or "manager" of a household (Matt 20:8; Luke 8:3).

It is also used metaphorically to denote a "guardian" or "tutor" in relation to the function of the old covenant law for the people of God prior to the coming of Christ (Gal 4:2).

▸ **62.** Care For, Protect, Guard, Watch > GUARD, GUARDIAN, WATCH OVER, PROTECT

SUBJECT, SUBJECTION, SUBMIT, SUBMISSION

enochos ἔνοχος 1777

enochos is an adjective meaning "in danger of," "liable to" in most of its ten occurrences. However, in Heb 2:15, ***enochos*** indicates the state of "being held in slavery" (i.e., subject to bondage) through the fear of death.

▸ **32.** Law, Justice, Jurisprudence, Judgment > DANGER, LIABILITY

▸ **32.** Law, Justice, Jurisprudence, Judgment > GUILT, GUILTY

▸ **32.** Law, Justice, Jurisprudence, Judgment > WORTHY

doulagōgeō δουλαγωγέω 1396

doulagōgeō is a rare verb found only in 1 Cor 9:27 with reference to "subduing" the body (i.e., bringing it under control).

hypotagē ὑποταγή 5292

hypotagē is a noun denoting "subjection" in the sense of "submission," "obedience." It occurs four times, signifying obedience to the gospel (2 Cor 9:13) and children obeying their parents (1 Tim 3:4). See also Gal 2:5; 1 Tim 2:11.

SEE ALSO

▸ **54.** Rule, Authority, Command, Obedience > SUBJECT, SUBJECTION, SUBMIT, SUBMISSION ***hypotassō***

56. Folly, Ignorance

FALSE KNOWLEDGE

pseudōnymos ψευδώνυμος 5581

pseudōnymos is a rare adverb found only in 1 Tim 6:20 denoting knowledge that is "falsely named."

SEE ALSO

▸ **58.** Vices > FALSE, FALSEHOOD
pseudēs

FOLLY

anoia ἄνοια 454

anoia is a rare noun denoting "folly" in the sense of "moral ineptitude," "senselessness," of minds closed to the truth.

▸ **56.** Folly, Ignorance > MAD, MADNESS

aphrosynē ἀφροσύνη 877

aphrosynē is a noun found four times denoting "folly" as one of several vices listed as characteristic of the human heart. In 2 Cor 11:1, 17, 21 Paul uses this term as hyperbole, referring to his hypothetical "foolishness" in the face of his detractors.

FOOL, FOOLISH, FOOLISHNESS

aphrōn ἄφρων 878

aphrōn is a noun found in eleven places denoting a "fool," and is always used as a term of reproach to describe those who are morally and spiritually corrupt at worst, or naïvely stupid at best.

Jesus designates hypocritical and self-righteous Pharisees as "fools" in the worst sense of spiritual and moral corruption in Luke 11:40. He similarly denounces the rich "fool" in the parable in Luke 12:20.

The designation "fool" in the sense of naïve ignorance or stupidity is found in Rom 2:20; 1 Cor 15:36; 2 Cor 11:16ff.; 12:6, 11; Eph 5:17; 1 Pet 2:15.

mōros μωρός 3474

mōros is an adjective found in thirteen contexts with the meanings "foolish," "stupid" throughout.

The sense of "foolish," denoting "senseless stupidity," is indicated in relation to Jesus' indictment of the Pharisees in Matt 5:22; 23:17ff. Similarly, Paul exhorts his fellow believers to avoid engaging in "foolish" controversies or arguments in 2 Tim 2:23; Titus 3:9. People lacking spiritual discernment are described as "foolish" in Matt 7:26; 25:2ff.

In several contexts ***mōros*** is used hyperbolically, referring for example to the "foolishness" of God in 1 Cor 1:25 as that which is "wiser than human wisdom." The point here is that God's wisdom is infinitely superior to that of human beings. 1 Cor 1:27 claims that God has chosen the "foolish" things of the world (viz. things, people deemed worthless) to shame the wise (viz. the self-sufficient, the arrogant). The experience of becoming "fools" for the sake of Christ and the gospel is noted in 1 Cor 3:18; 4:10.

mōrainō μωραίνω 3471

mōrainō is a rare verb meaning "become fools" in Rom 1:22, referring to ungodly people who had wholly turned their backs on God and his revealed moral code. 1 Cor 1:20 affirms that God "has made foolish" the wisdom of the world — that is, he has nullified it.

mōria μωρία 3472

mōria is a noun derived from ***mōrainō*** (above) denoting "folly," "foolishness" in each of the five occurrences of the term.

The message of the gospel is said to be "folly" in the eyes of unbelievers (i.e., nonsense fantasy) in 1 Cor 1:18, 23. Similarly, in 1 Cor 1:21 there is the ironic affirmation that God chose to save people through the "folly" of preaching. In 1 Cor 2:14 the gifts of the Spirit are said to be "folly" to the unspiritual person — that is, incapable of being understood. 1 Cor 3:19 declares that the wisdom of the world is "folly" to God — that is, despised by him as of no account.

anoētos ἀνόητος 453

anoētos is an adjective meaning "foolish" throughout the six occurrences of the term, in several different contexts.

The designation "foolish" implies "lack of spiritual insight or perception" in Luke 24:25; Rom 1:14; Gal 3:1, 3. 1 Tim 6:9 refers to "foolish" (i.e., senseless, morally questionable) desires. See also Titus 3:3 for a similar sense.

asynetos ἀσύνετος 801

asynetos is an adjectival term found five times, signifying people as "foolish" who are "without understanding," "lacking spiritual insight" (Matt 15:16; Mark 7:18; Rom 1:21, 31; 10:19).

▸ **56.** Folly, Ignorance >
STUPID, WITHOUT UNDERSTANDING

FUTILE THINKING, VAIN IMAGINATION

dialogismos διαλογισμός 1261

dialogismos occurs only in Rom 1:21 and refers to the vain imagination or futile thinking of Gentiles in their darkened minds.

▸ **51.** Knowledge, Wisdom, Remember, Forget >
THINK, THOUGHT

SEE ALSO

▸ **58.** Vices > IMAGINATION, (STUBBORN) THINKING
dianoia

▸ **77.** Resist, Oppose, Fight, Rebel > CONSPIRE, IMAGINE
meletaō

IGNORANCE, IGNORANT

agnoeō ἀγνοέω 50

agnoeō occurs around twenty times with the principal meaning "be ignorant" in the sense of not knowing or understanding.

Luke 9:45 records the disciples' failure to understand the words of Jesus, and Acts 13:27 records the people of Jerusalem's failure to recognize Jesus' true identity as Messiah. Paul observes the Athenians' folly in worshiping an "unknown" God in Acts 17:23.

General references to being ignorant or "not knowing" are found, for example, in Rom 1:13; 6:3; 1 Cor 10:1; 14:38; 2 Cor 1:8; 1 Thess 4:13. Rom 10:3 mentions the ignorance of the Jews in failing to acknowledge that righteousness comes from God. Destruction of ignorant false teachers is indicated in 2 Pet 2:12. 1 Tim 1:13 refers to Paul having acted in ignorance and unbelief prior to his conversion. Heb 5:2 indicates that the ignorant and wayward are dealt with gently by the high priest, who is himself beset with human weakness.

▸ **56.** Folly, Ignorance >
UNAWARE, UNKNOWN

agnoia ἄγνοια 52

agnoia refers to the state of ignorance and is found in only four contexts. Acts 3:17 speaks of the ignorance of the Jewish people in bringing about the death of Jesus. Acts 17:30 refers to God having overlooked times of human ignorance under the old covenant.

The culpable ignorance of the Gentiles due to their hardness of heart is cited in Eph 4:18. 2 Pet 1:14 offers a similar perspective.

agnōsia ἀγνωσία 56

agnōsia occurs only twice and means "ignorance" or "lack of knowledge." 1 Cor 15:34 refers to some having no knowledge of God, and 1 Pet 2:15 speaks of the ignorance of foolish people.

SEE ALSO

▸ **51.** Knowledge, Wisdom, Remember, Forget >
KNOW, KNOWLEDGE, MAKE KNOWN
ginōskō, epiginōskō, epignōsis, gnōsis, gnōstos, gnōrizō, anagnōrizomai, oida, epistamai, synesis, phaneros

MAD, MADNESS

anoia ἄνοια 454

anoia occurs only twice and conveys the sense of "folly" or "madness" in both contexts. In Luke 6:11, the term refers to the anger of the Pharisees directed towards Jesus after he had got the better of them in a confrontation, healing a crippled man on the Sabbath. ***anoia*** thus has the connotation of a "mad" rage or fury here. 2 Tim 3:9 refers to the "folly" of false teachers, similarly suggesting a "madness of folly."

▸ **56.** Folly, Ignorance > FOLLY

paraphronia παραφρονία 3913

paraphronia is found only in 2 Pet 2:16, referring to the "madness" of the prophet Balaam who was restrained by the rebuke of the donkey, supernaturally effected by the hand of Yahweh. The "madness" of the prophet refers to Balaam's insatiable greed.

SEE ALSO

▸ **20.** Illness, Disease, Health, Healing > MAD, MADNESS
mainomai, mania

SHORT-SIGHTED

myōpazō μυωπάζω 3467

myōpazō is a rare verb found only in 2 Pet 1:9. It describes the condition of "being short-sighted" or seeing dimly in a spiritual sense — being unable to grasp the implications of being granted new life and godliness.

SEE ALSO

▸ **17.** Senses, Actions, Abilities, Disabilities >
SEE, LOOK, BEHOLD, GAZE
horaō, theōreō, blepō, anablepō, periblepō, emblepō, atenizō, parakyptō, skopeō, aphoraō

STUPID, WITHOUT UNDERSTANDING

asynetos ἀσύνετος 801

asynetos is an adjective found in five contexts meaning "foolish," "without understanding."

Matt 15:16; Mark 7:18 describe people as "foolish," or "stupid." In Rom 1:21, 31; 10:19, ***asynetos*** refers to people as "foolish" in the sense of "morally inept."

▸ **56.** Folly, Ignorance > FOOL, FOOLISH, FOOLISHNESS

SEE ALSO

▸ **19.** Mind, Spirit, Emotions, Feelings, Desires >
UNDERSTANDING
nous, phrēn

▸ **51.** Knowledge, Wisdom, Remember, Forget >
UNDERSTAND, UNDERSTANDING
synetos

UNAWARE, UNKNOWN

agnoeō ἀγνοέω 50

agnoeō is a verb expressing the negative sense of "to not know" or "be ignorant," "not understand." ***agnoeō*** is found in twenty-five contexts.

Mark 9:32; Luke 9:45 refer to Jesus' disciples' failure to understand that Jesus was to be betrayed and lose his life. The unbelief of the Jewish population in Jerusalem led to their failure to understand Jesus' real nature (Acts 13:27).

agnoeō also refers to people acting in ignorance in 1 Cor 14:38; 2 Cor 2:11. Acting ignorantly in unbelief is mentioned in 1 Tim 1:13; 2 Pet 2:12. The Athenians' ignorant worship of idols, specifically adoration of "the unknown God," is indicated in Acts 17:23. Ignoring righteousness that comes from God is mentioned in Rom 10:3.

The meaning "be unaware" is also evident in the usage of ***agnoeō*** (Rom 6:3; 7:1; 1 Cor 12:1; 2 Cor 1:8). Rom 2:4 speaks of the contempt shown towards the riches of God's kindness when people are unaware that God's goodness is intended to lead to repentance.

agnoeō is also translated "be unknown" in Gal 1:22, referring to the fact that Paul was unknown to the Galatian churches.

In a nominal usage of ***agnoeō*** in Heb 5:2, the writer refers to God dealing gently with those who are ignorant.

▸ **56.** Folly, Ignorance > IGNORANCE, IGNORANT

SEE ALSO

▸ **51.** Knowledge, Wisdom, Remember, Forget > KNOW, KNOWLEDGE, MAKE KNOWN
ginōskō, epiginōskō, epignōsis, gnōsis, gnōstos, gnōrizō, anagnōrizomai, oida, epistamai, synesis, phaneros

57. Evil, Wickedness, Sin

CORRUPT

phtheirō φθείρω 5351

phtheirō is a verb found eight times meaning "ruin," "destroy." The sense of "ruin" incorporates the meaning "corrupt" in a number of these contexts. 1 Cor 15:33 speaks of bad company "corrupting" good morals. The "corrupting" of one's mind and old nature is indicated in 2 Cor 11:3; Eph 4:22. The senses "ruin," "destroy" refer to the corrupting of the earth in Rev 19:2 and the corruption of evil people in Jude 10. See also 2 Cor 7:2.

- ▸ **21.** Die, Perish, Kill, Destroy > DESTROY, DESTROYER, DESTRUCTION

kataphtheirō καταφθείρω 2704

kataphtheirō is a rare variant verb of ***phtheirō*** (above) used adjectivally in 2 Tim 3:8 to refer to "corrupt (i.e., morally depraved) minds." 2 Pet 2:12 speaks of the hand of God "destroying" evil people.

SEE ALSO

- ▸ **21.** Die, Perish, Kill, Destroy > CORRUPT, CORRUPTION ***diaphtheirō, phthora, diaphthora, phthartos, aphanizō***
- ▸ **22.** Life, Renewal, Immortality > INCORRUPTIBLE ***aphtharsia, aphthartos***

CURSE

ara ἀρά 685

ara is a rare noun found only in Rom 3:14, denoting "cursing" in general terms alongside the spirit of bitterness.

SEE ALSO

- ▸ **67.** Acknowledge, Confess, Profess, Swear > CURSE, CURSED ***anathematizō, katathematizō***
- ▸ **73.** Blessing, Curse, Reward, Punishment > CURSE, CURSED, CURSING, ACCURSED ***anathema, katathema, katara, kataraomai, epikataratos***
- ▸ **77.** Resist, Oppose, Fight, Rebel > CURSE, MALIGN ***kakologeō***

ENTICE, SEDUCE

deleazō δελεάζω 1185

deleazō is a rare verb found in only three places, meaning "seduce," "entice," indicating an inciting to sin in each case. Jas 1:14 contains a general recognition that people are "enticed" into sinning by innate sinful desire. 2 Pet 2:14, 18 condemn false teachers for "enticing" others into doctrinal error and immorality.

ERR, GO ASTRAY, LEAD ASTRAY

planaō πλανάω 4105

planaō is a verb occurring about fifty times, meaning "err" with the nuances "lead astray," "go astray" in a moral sense.

Matt 18:12, 13 refer literally to sheep "going astray" (i.e., getting lost); Heb 11:38 refers to people.

The meaning "err" in the sense of "be mistaken, wrong" is found in Matt 22:29; Mark 12:24, 27.

Warnings against "being led astray" in a moral sense are found in Matt 24:4; Mark 13:5; Luke 21:8. See also Titus 3:3. Likewise, the meaning "be deceived" is found in 1 Cor 15:33; Gal 6:7; Jas 1:16.

Similarly, the practice of "deceiving," "leading (people) astray" in the sense of morally corrupting them is indicated in Matt 24:5, 11; Mark 13:6; John 7:12; 1 John 2:26; Rev 12:9; 13:14; 19:20; 20:3, 8, 10. See also Matt 24:24; John 7:47.

The sense of "going astray" indicating disobedience against God is noted in Heb 3:10. The danger and practice of "wandering" from the truth is noted in Jas 5:19; 1 Pet 2:25; 2 Pet 2:15.

- ▸ **58.** Vices > DECEIT, DECEITFUL, DECEPTION, DECEIVE, DECEIVER, DECEITFULLY

apoplanaō ἀποπλανάω 635

apoplanaō is a rare variant of ***planaō*** (above) found only twice. It means "lead astray" in the context of "wandering" from the faith (Mark 13:22; 1 Tim 6:10).

astocheō ἀστοχέω 795

astocheō is a rare synonym for ***planaō*** and ***apoplanaō*** (above) meaning "erring" or wandering, in the context of abandoning the faith in 1 Tim 6:21. In 2 Tim 2:18, ***astocheō*** refers to "wandering away" from the truth.

ERROR

planē πλάνη 4106

planē is a noun found in ten places, meaning "error" or "deceit."

"Error" in the sense of "fraud" or "deception" is indicated in Matt 27:64; "delusion" in 2 Thess 2:11; and "false doctrine" in 1 John 4:6.

planē denotes "error" in the sense of moral perversion in Rom 1:27; 2 Pet 2:18; 3:17; Jude 11; 1 Thess 2:3; and the general sense of "sin" in Jas 5:20.

The "deceit" of false teaching is indicated in Eph 4:14.

- ▸ **58.** Vices > DECEIT, DECEITFUL, DECEPTION, DECEIVE, DECEIVER, DECEITFULLY

agnoēma ἀγνόημα 51

agnoēma is a rare noun, found only in Heb 9:7, denoting the Jewish people's "errors" or "sins."

EVIL, EVILDOER, WICKED, WICKEDNESS, LAWLESS

kakos κακός 2556

kakos is an adjectival form found in approximately fifty places and meaning "evil," "wicked." It is used both adjectivally and nominally. The term denotes "wicked people" in a general sense in Matt 21:41; Phil 3:2; Titus 1:12; Rev 2:2.

kakos is used adjectivally to refer to a "wicked" servant in Matt 24:48; and to "evil" thoughts in Mark 7:21. In 2 Cor 5:10, the term refers to the good or "bad" done in the body which will be adjudicated at the judgment seat of Christ.

kakos denotes "evil" in a moral, nominal sense in Matt 27:23; Mark 15:14; Luke 16:25; John 18:23; Acts 9:13; Rom 1:30; 9:11; 12:17ff.; 13:3ff.; 1 Cor 10:6; Col 3:5; 1 Thess 5:15; 1 Tim 6:10; Heb 5:14; Jas 1:13; 1 Pet 3:9ff. The meaning "harm" in the sense of "physical injury" is indicated in Acts 28:5; and in the sense of "hurt" in a psychological, emotional context.

kakia κακία 2549

kakia is a noun derived from the adjective ***kakos*** (above) denoting "evil," "wickedness" in the generalized sense of "moral depravity" throughout the eleven occurrences of the term (Matt 6:34; Acts 8:22; Rom 1:29; 1 Cor 5:8; 14:20; Eph 4:31; Col 3:8; Titus 3:3; Jas 1:21; 1 Pet 2:1, 16).

kakōs κακῶς 2560

kakōs is an adverbial form found in sixteen places with the primary meaning "ill," "sick." However, in Acts 23:5, the term occurs in the context of an injunction not to speak "evil" of a civil ruler.

▸ **20.** Illness, Disease, Health, Healing > SICK, SICKNESS

ponēros πονηρός 4190

ponēros is an adjectival form synonymous with ***kakos*** and ***kakia*** (above) found nearly eighty times with the meaning "evil," "wicked."

"Evil" in the sense of "harm, injury" is indicated in Matt 5:11.

The general sense of moral "evil" is evident in Matt 5:37ff.; 7:11ff.; Mark 7:22ff.; Luke 3:19; John 3:19; 7:7; Rom 12:9; Eph 5:16; 1 Thess 5:22; Jas 4:16.

ponēros is used nominally to denote the devil as "the evil one" in Matt 13:19, 38; John 17:15; Acts 19:12ff.; Eph 6:16; 1 John 2:13ff.; 3:12; 5:18ff.

ponēros also denotes wicked people in general in Matt 13:49; Luke 6:45; Acts 17:5; 1 Cor 5:13; "evil" (i.e., "immoral") thoughts are noted in Matt 15:19; Jas 2:4; "evil" spirits in Luke 7:21; 8:2; the current "evil" age in Gal 1:4; Eph 6:13; an "evil" conscience in Heb 10:22.

The adjectival sense of "wicked" or "evil" describes people in Matt 16:4; 18:32; 25:26; Luke 11:29; 19:22; Heb 3:12.

phaulos φαῦλος 5337

phaulos is an adjective found in four places, denoting "(moral) evil" in a nominal sense in John 3:20; 5:29. The adjectival sense of "evil," "wicked" is found in Titus 2:8; Jas 3:16.

kakopoios κακοποιός 2555

kakopoios is an adjectival form used nominally in only five places, denoting "evildoer," "those who do practice evil" (John 18:30; 1 Pet 2:12ff.; 3:16; 4:15).

kakopoieō κακοποιέω 2554

kakopoieō is a verb meaning "to do wrong," "harm" in the general sense of "moral evil" in 1 Pet 3:17; 3 John 11. Mark 3:4; Luke 6:9 refer to "doing harm" on the Sabbath.

anomos ἄνομος 459

anomos is an adjective occurring ten times with the fundamental sense of "lawless," referring to those who violate the law of God. It may also be rendered "wicked" and is used both nominally and adjectivally.

Acts 2:23; 2 Pet 2:8 refer generally to that which is "lawless" or "wicked." Nominal references to "the wicked" or "lawless ones" are found in Mark 15:28; Luke 22:37; 1 Cor 9:21; 1 Tim 1:9. In particular, 2 Thess 2:8 refers to "the antichrist" as "the lawless one."

▸ **54.** Rule, Authority, Command, Obedience > TRANSGRESS, TRANSGRESSION, TRANSGRESSOR, TRESPASS, VIOLATE, VIOLATION

athesmos ἄθεσμος 113

athesmos is a rare noun found only twice. In 2 Pet 2:7; 3:17 it refers to "wicked, or lawless people" and to morally depraved, false teachers, respectively.

ponēria πονηρία 4189

ponēria is a noun denoting "wickedness" with several different nuances in the seven occurrences of the term. A general designation of "depravity" or "iniquity" underlying the sense of "wickedness" is evident in Mark 7:22; Luke 11:39; Rom 1:29; 1 Cor 5:8. "Lawlessness" in the context of rebellion against God is indicated in Acts 3:26. Matt 22:18 refers to "wickedness" in the sense of "malice." "Wickedness" is also predicated of demonic spirits in Eph 6:12.

FLESHLY, CARNAL, WORLDLY

sarkikos σαρκικός 4559

sarkikos is an adjectival form meaning "fleshly," "carnal" (i.e., belonging to this world), as well as "material," with reference to earthly possessions. The term occurs eleven times.

The meaning "carnal" in the sense of "worldly," denoting a sinful lifestyle, is indicated in Rom 7:14; 1 Cor 3:1ff.; 1 Pet 2:11. "Earthly" wisdom is indicated in 2 Cor 1:12; and "earthly," "carnal" weapons are indicated in 2 Cor 10:4. See also Heb 7:16.

sarkikos refers to "material" blessings in Rom 15:27; 1 Cor 9:11.

SEE ALSO

- ▸ **14.** Animals > MEAT, FLESH
  kreas
- ▸ **16.** Body, Bodily Functions > FLESH
  sarx

GOD-HATER

theostygēs θεοστυγής 2319

theostygēs occurs only once and refers to "God-haters" in Rom 1:30.

SEE ALSO

- ▸ **77.** Resist, Oppose, Fight, Rebel > HATE, HATEFUL
  miseō, stygētos

HARDENING, HARDNESS, HARDHEARTEDNESS

sklērotēs σκληρότης 4643

sklērotēs occurs only once, referring to the hardheartedness of the Jewish people in Rom 2:5.

pōrōsis πώρωσις 4457

This noun is rare, occurring only three times. ***pōrōsis*** primarily denotes a "hardening," hence the translation "hardness." The meaning suggests a dullness of perception with an underlying intention or unwillingness to accept what is otherwise plain. Therefore, the conditions of "stubbornness" and "blindness" are also indicated (e.g., Mark 3:5). Here Jesus expresses his anger at the hardheartedness of the Pharisees in their response to his healing the man with the withered hand. In Rom 11:25 the term means "blindness," with reference to the Jews' refusal to believe in Christ and his work. Here it is associated with hardness of heart. See Eph 4:18 for a similar usage.

pōroō πωρόω 4456

pōroō is the verb from which the noun ***pōrōsis*** (above) derives. Like ***sklērotēs*** (above), it refers primarily to hardening, associated with hardheartedness and spiritual blindness. It occurs six times.

Mark 6:52; 8:17 refer to the disciples' hardness of heart, indicating their failure to understand the significance of Jesus' miracles and his teaching at this specific point in time. John 12:40 indicates God's action in hardening the hearts of unbelieving Jews (see also Rom 11:7). In 2 Cor 3:14, Paul mentions the curse of spiritual blindness that will remain on unbelievers until the Spirit of God removes the veil of unbelief that leaves them devoid of spiritual understanding.

sklērynō σκληρύνω 4645

sklērynō is the verb form associated with ***sklērotēs*** (above) and is synonymous with ***pōroō*** (above) and its associated forms. ***sklērynō*** occurs six times.

Acts 19:9; Rom 9:14 indicate the divine judgment of hardening on those who refuse to heed the message of the gospel. The remaining occurrences of ***sklērynō*** are found in the book of Hebrews, which solemnly warns its readers to guard against hardening their hearts and turning away from allegiance to Christ (Heb 3:8, 13, 15; 4:7).

SEE ALSO

- ▸ **88.** Qualities, Characteristics >
  HARD, DIFFICULT, HARSH, SEVERE
  sklēros

INIQUITY

anomia ἀνομία 458

anomia means "lawlessness" (literally, "without law"), and is translated "iniquity," "wickedness," indicating the violation of God's law. ***anomia*** occurs thirteen times. 1 John 3:4 equates sin and lawlessness. The utter incompatibility of righteousness and iniquity is affirmed in 2 Cor 6:14. Matt 24:12 indicates the growth of iniquity in a person's heart. Those who are guilty of persistent, unrepentant iniquity are to be removed from the kingdom of God (Matt 13:41). Heb 1:9 declares Jesus Christ's hatred of iniquity. And Jesus' command for "evildoers" to leave him on the day of judgment is recorded in Matt 7:23. Jesus levels the charge of iniquity against the Pharisees in Matt 23:38. 2 Thess 2:7 makes it clear that the mystery of iniquity is at work in the world; yet is fully subject to God's control.

In a positive context, Rom 4:7 guarantees blessing for those whose iniquities are forgiven. Christ's role in redeeming his people from iniquity is portrayed in Titus 2:14. Then there is God's refusal to remember the sins of his people as a consequence of Christ's work (Heb 8:12).

adikia ἀδικία 93

adikia is a synonym for ***anomia*** (above) and refers likewise to the action of violating God's law. ***adikia*** occurs twenty-five times and is translated "iniquity," "unrighteousness," in most of these contexts.

Divine wrath against iniquity and wickedness is indicated in Rom 1:18; 2:8; 3:5; 2 Thess 2:10, 12; 2 Pet 2:13. Paul also declares in Rom 1:29 that iniquity is characteristic of all unbelievers. Acts 8:23 affirms that iniquity brings about a profound moral and spiritual enslavement. An unjust judge is specifically mentioned in one of Jesus' parables in Luke 18:6. Judas' monetary reward for his iniquitous act of betrayal is mentioned in Acts 1:18. Luke 13:27 contains a terrible pronouncement against all "workers of iniquity," to be issued by Christ on the final day of judgment. Other general references to iniquity are found in 1 Cor 13:6; 2 Cor 12:13; 2 Tim 2:19; Jas 3:6; 2 Pet 2:15; 1 John 5:17.

In contrast, John 7:18; Rom 9:14 declare that the persons of God and Christ are absolutely free of iniquity. With respect to human sinfulness, Heb 8:12 declares God's determination to be merciful toward the iniquity of his people. 1 John 1:9 contains the divine promises to cleanse his people from iniquity on the basis of the finished work of Christ. Rom 6:13 commands us not to use our bodies as instruments of iniquity.

- ▸ **57.** Evil, Wickedness, Sin > WRONG, INJUSTICE

PERVERSE, PERVERT

diastrephō διαστρέφω 1294

diastrephō is a verb expressing the primary meaning "pervert," as well as, in its participial form, the adjectival sense of "perverse" or "morally corrupt," "crooked." It is found in seven places.

Acts 13:10 records Paul's accusation against Elymas, the Jewish sorcerer — that he perverted the straight paths of the Lord. The remaining usage of ***diastrephō*** is adjectival, referring to those who are morally corrupt, or perverse (Matt 17:17; Luke 9:41; Acts 20:30; Phil 2:15). See also Luke 23:2; Acts 13:8.

▸ **86.** Movement Toward or Away From > TURN, TURN AROUND, TURN TOWARD, TURN AWAY, TURN BACK

metastrephō μεταστρέφω 3344

metastrephō is a verb found in only three places. In two of these, the meaning is "turn (around)"; and in Gal 1:7 it refers to those who "pervert" the gospel of Christ. The underlying sense is that these people seek to "overturn" the gospel so as to place it on a different foundation than that intended by God.

▸ **82.** Change, Exchange, Transform > TURN INTO

REBELLION

parapikrasmos παραπικρασμός 3894

parapikrasmos is a term found only twice. On both occasions it refers to the period of Israel's rebellion against God during her times of wandering in the wilderness (Heb 3:8, 15).

SIN, SINNER, CAUSE TO SIN

hamartia ἁμαρτία 266

hamartia is found in approximately 170 places, with the sense of "sin" throughout, primarily with reference to failing to meet God's revealed moral, ethical, and ritual standards.

The meaning "sin" in the general sense of "violating God's law" is indicated in Matt 1:21; Mark 1:5; John 8:2ff.; 1 Tim 5:24; Heb 10:3ff.; Jas 2:9. The power of sin and its impact, leading to death, is expressed in Rom 3:9; 5:12ff., 20ff.; 7:5; Gal 3:22; Eph 2:1; Heb 10:3ff. The importance of the law in fully eradicating sin is described in Heb 10:4ff. The so-called "man of sin" (i.e., the antichrist) is described in 2 Thess 2:3.

Mark 1:4; Luke 3:3 refer to John the Baptist's baptism for the forgiveness of sins. Heb 8:12; 10:17 contain God's promise to remember the sins of his people no more. John 16:8 refers to the role of the Holy Spirit in convicting people of sin.

hamartia also refers to Jesus' claim to forgive sin (Matt 9:2ff.; Mark 2:5, 9ff.; Luke 5:20ff.; 7:47ff.). The perfection of Christ's nature, being "without sin," is indicated in Heb 4:15; 1 Pet 2:22. His eradication of the deadly power of sin is recorded frequently in the NT (e.g., Matt 26:28; Acts 2:38; 10:43; 22:16; Rom 4:7ff.; 6:6ff.; 8:2ff.; Gal 1:4; Heb 1:3; 9:26ff.; 1 Pet 3:18; 1 John 1:7ff.; Rev 1:5).

hamartanō ἁμαρτάνω 264

hamartanō is the principal verb in the NT meaning "to sin." It occurs around fifty times and has the underlying sense of missing the mark that God has established as a standard for his people to follow.

The general sense of human beings "sinning" against God is predominant (Matt 27:4; Luke 15:18ff.; John 8:11; Rom 2:12; 3:23; 5:12ff.; Heb 3:17). Angels are said to sin against God (2 Pet 2:4); as does Satan (1 John 3:18). Eph 4:26 records an exhortation "not to sin."

Sinning against another person is noted in Matt 18:21; Luke 17:4; 1 Cor 8:12; as is sinning against one's own body in 1 Cor 6:18. 1 John 3:9 refers to the destruction of sin in the life of the believer.

hamartōlos ἁμαρτωλός 268

hamartōlos is a noun derived from ***hamartanō*** (above) meaning "sinner" throughout its fifty occurrences (Matt 9:10ff.; Mark 2:15ff.; Luke 5:30ff.; John 9:16, 24ff.; Rom 3:7; Gal 2:15ff.; 1 Tim 1:9; Heb 12:3; 1 Pet 4:1ff.).

hamartēma ἁμάρτημα 265

hamartēma is a synonym for ***hamartia*** (above) that is translated "sin" in all four occurrences (Mark 3:28; 4:12; Rom 3:25; 1 Cor 6:18).

skandalizō σκανδαλίζω 4624

skandalizō is a verb found in thirty-five contexts with the primary meaning "to offend," "cause offense." In certain contexts, the underlying sense is that of "causing someone to sin" (e.g., Matt 5:29ff.; 18:6ff.; Mark 9:42ff.; Rom 14:21; 1 Cor 8:13).

▸ **49.** Allow, Accept, Approve, Refuse > OFFENSE, OFFEND

SEE ALSO

▸ **61.** Integrity, Innocence, Piety > SINLESS
anamartētos

STUMBLING BLOCK

proskomma πρόσκομμα 4348

proskomma is a noun occurring six times. The term denotes a "stumbling block" with reference to an obstacle that causes people to sin if they are not wary of it. 1 Pet 2:8; Rom 9:32f. refer to Christ "the stumbling stone" (citing Isa 8:14) who, if rejected by unbelievers, will bring about their spiritual ruin.

The meaning "stumbling block" in the sense of causing people to sin is evident in Rom 14:13, 20; 1 Cor 8:9. These contexts warn against placing such an obstacle in the way of another believer.

skandalon σκάνδαλον 4625

skandalon is a noun synonymous with ***proskomma*** (above) denoting a "stumbling block," "offense" or "temptation to sin." The term is found in fifteen contexts.

The meaning "stumbling block" is indicated in Matt 13:41; 16:23; Rom 11:9; 1 Cor 1:23. In particular, Gal 5:11 refers to the "stumbling block" of the cross. References to Christ as the "rock of offense" are found in Rom 9:33; 1 Pet 2:8.

The sense of "temptation to sin" is evident in Matt 18:7; Luke 17:1; Rom 14:13; 1 John 2:10.

UNGODLINESS, UNGODLY

asebēs ἀσεβής 765

asebēs is an adjectival form found nine times meaning "ungodly," referring to all who are devoid of any faith commitment or devotion to God. They are consistently singled out for judgment (Rom 4:5; 5:6; 1 Tim 1:9; 1 Pet 4:18; 2 Pet 2:5; 3:7; Jude 14, 15).

asebeō ἀσεβέω 764

asebeō is a rare verb found in only two places, meaning "to live ungodly lives," "be ungodly" (2 Pet 2:6; Jude 15).

asebeia ἀσέβεια 763

asebeia is a noun meaning "ungodliness," denoting a lifestyle devoid of any reverence towards God (Rom 1:18; 11:26; 2 Tim 2:16; Titus 2:12; Jude 15, 18).

UNRIGHTEOUS, UNJUST

adikos ἄδικος 94

adikos is an adjective occurring twelve times meaning "unrighteous," "unjust."

General references to the "unjust," or those who have violated the divinely ordained principles of honesty and integrity, include those in Matt 5:45; Luke 16:10ff.; 18:11; Acts 24:15; 1 Cor 6:1. Other references to the "wicked," the "unrighteous," who will be denied entry into the kingdom of God and condemned, are found in 1 Cor 6:9; 2 Pet 2:9. 1 Pet 3:18 declares, remarkably, that Christ died for the "unrighteous." Rom 3:5 denounces as illegitimate any attempt to charge God with "injustice." See also Heb 6:10.

WRONG, INJUSTICE

adikia ἀδικία 93

adikia is a noun found in twenty-five contexts with the underlying sense of "moral wrong" throughout. It is translated in various ways.

The meaning "iniquity," in the sense of a violation of God's law, is indicated in Luke 13:27; 16:9; Acts 1:18; Rom 1:18, 29; 2:8; 2 Thess 2:10ff.; 2 Tim 2:19; Heb 8:12; Jas 3:6; 2 Pet 2:13ff.; 1 John 1:9; 5:17.

adikia also denotes "injustice" in Luke 16:8; 18:6; Rom 9:14. It is also used adjectivally, meaning "false" (John 7:18), and "(morally) wrong" (2 Cor 12:13).

▸ **57.** Evil, Wickedness, Sin > INIQUITY

adikeō ἀδικέω 91

adikeō is a verb found about thirty times meaning "do wrong," "hurt," "suffer wrong," as well as having related nuances.

General references to "doing wrong" or "hurting" include those in Matt 20:13; Acts 7:26; 25:10ff.; 2 Cor 7:12; Rev 6:6; 7:2ff.; 9:4; 22:11. The related sense of "treat unjustly" is indicated in 1 Cor 6:8; Col 3:25; Phlm 18. There are also denials of such action in 2 Cor 7:2; Gal 4:12. Rev 2:11 speaks of "being harmed, or hurt" by the "second death." The meaning "injure" (i.e., to physically hurt) is indicated in Rev 9:10, 19; 11:5. The sense of "suffer wrong" is found in Acts 7:24; 1 Cor 6:7.

▸ **75.** Suffering, Distress, Sadness > SUFFER

SEE ALSO

▸ **75.** Suffering, Distress, Sadness >
WRONGFULLY, UNJUSTLY
adikōs

58. Vices

ACCUSATION

krisis κρίσις 2920

The noun ***krisis*** occurs about fifty times with the primary meaning "judgment." In 2 Pet 2:11; Jude 9, however, the term denotes a "slanderous accusation."

▸ **32.** Law, Justice, Jurisprudence, Judgment > JUDGMENT

diabolos διάβολος 1228

diabolos is the standard term in the NT for "the devil," occurring nearly forty times. In several places, however, it denotes those who "slander" (i.e., who spread "false accusations"; 1 Tim 3:11; 2 Tim 3:3; Titus 2:3).

▸ **2.** Supernatural Beings/Forces, Spiritual Realm > DEVIL
▸ **58.** Vices > SLANDER, SLANDERER

SEE ALSO

▸ **32.** Law, Justice, Jurisprudence, Judgment > ACCUSE, ACCUSATION, ACCUSER
aitia, aitiōma, enklēma, katēgoria, katēgoreō, katēgoros, diaballō, enkaleō, sykophanteō

ADULTERY, ADULTERER

moichos μοιχός 3432

The noun ***moichos*** is found in four places, meaning "adulterer" in each case. Three of these contexts make a literal reference to those who are guilty of marital infidelity (Luke 18:11; 1 Cor 6:9; Heb 13:4). In Jas 4:4, the term "adulterer" is metaphorical, referring to the people of God who have "betrayed" their allegiance to Christ by being ensnared by the world.

moichalis μοιχαλίς 3428

moichalis is the feminine form of ***moichos*** (above). It is found in seven contexts with the meanings "adulteress," "adultery," and "adulterous."

moichalis is used adjectivally and metaphorically by Christ in Matt 12:39; 16:4; Mark 8:38 to refer to his unbelieving, hostile, and skeptical hearers as an "adulterous" and evil generation.

The literal meaning "adulteress" is found in Rom 7:3; and in Jas 4:4 it refers metaphorically to faithless, backslidden believers.

In 2 Pet 2:14, ***moichalis*** refers to the sin of "adultery."

moicheia μοιχεία 3430

The noun ***moicheia*** is found in four places referring to the physical sin of "adultery" (Matt 15:19; Mark 7:21; John 8:3; Gal 5:19).

moichaō μοιχάω 3429

The verb ***moichaō*** refers to the act of "committing adultery" in six contexts (Matt 5:32 [twice]; 19:9 [twice]; Mark 10:11, 12).

moicheuō μοιχεύω 3431

moicheuō is a synonym for ***moichaō*** (above). It occurs around twenty times, with the consistent literal physical sense of "commit adultery" (Matt 5:27ff.; 19:18; Mark 10:19; Luke 16:18; 18:20; John 8:4; Rom 2:22; 13:9; Jas 2:11). The term is used metaphorically in Rev 2:22, where it signifies the act of adultery in relation to idol worship.

ARGUE, ARGUMENT, DISPUTE, QUARREL, STRIVE

logomachia λογομαχία 3055

logomachia is a rare noun found only in 1 Tim 6:4, denoting "quarrels, or disputes over words" — a practice condemned by the apostle.

▸ **27.** Community, Partnership, Unity, Discord > STRIFE, QUARREL

diaparatribē διαπαρατριβή 3859

diaparatribē is a rare noun denoting unprofitable "wrangling," "arguments," or "disputes" as practiced by false teachers, whom Paul denounces as depraved in mind and lifestyle. ***diaparatribē*** is found only in 1 Tim 6:5.

machomai μάχομαι 3164

machomai is a verb found four times meaning "fight," primarily in the sense of "arguing," or "quarreling" (John 6:52; Acts 7:26; 2 Tim 2:24; Jas 4:2).

▸ **77.** Resist, Oppose, Fight, Rebel > FIGHT

logomacheō λογομαχέω 3054

logomacheō is a rare verb found only in 2 Tim 2:14 meaning "to quarrel about words."

SEE ALSO

▸ **63.** Speak, Tell, Declare, Call > WORD, SAYING, SPEECH
logos, rhēma, angelia

BEAR WITNESS AGAINST, PERJURE

katamartyreō καταμαρτυρέω 2649

katamartyreō is a verb found four times meaning "testify against," "bear witness against," referring to those enemies of Christ at his trial who perjured themselves against him (Matt 26:62; 27:13; Mark 14:60; 15:4).

SEE ALSO

▸ **32.** Law, Justice, Jurisprudence, Judgment > WITNESS, TESTIMONY
pseudomartys, pseudomartyreō, pseudomartyria

▸ **63.** Speak, Tell, Declare, Call > WITNESS, BEAR WITNESS, TESTIFY, TESTIMONY
martyreō, martyria, martyrion, martys, amartyros, symmartyreō, diamartyromai

BITE, TEAR APART

daknō δάκνω 1143

daknō is a rare verb used metaphorically with the meaning "bite" in the sense of "tear people apart" with unkind words or vicious slander. It is found only in Gal 5:15.

BITTERNESS

pikria πικρία 4088

pikria is a rare noun denoting "bitterness" in the sense of "anger," "disillusionment" in Acts 8:23; Rom 3:14; Eph 4:31; Heb 12:15.

SEE ALSO

- ▸ **75.** Suffering, Distress, Sadness > BITTERLY
  pikrōs
- ▸ **88.** Qualities, Characteristics > BITTER, BRACKISH, EMBITTER
  pikros, pikrainō

BLASPHEME, BLASPHEMY, BLASPHEMER, BLASPHEMOUS

blasphēmia βλασφημία 988

blasphēmia is a noun occurring about twenty times with the consistent meaning "blasphemy," "slander."

General references to blasphemy include Matt 15:19; Mark 3:28; 7:22; John 10:33; Rev 2:9. The "slandering" of people is condemned in Eph 4:31; Col 3:8; 1 Tim 6:4. Blasphemy against the devil, equivalent to cursing him, is noted in Jude 9.

Explicit blasphemy against God is indicated in Matt 12:31; Mark 2:7; Rev 13:1ff.; 17:3. In Matt 26:65; Mark 14:64; Luke 5:21, Jesus is wrongfully accused of such an offense. Matt 12:31 mentions "blasphemy" against the Holy Spirit. This is designated as the unforgivable sin — the hardness of heart resulting from a persistent refusal to acknowledge God's rightful place in one's life. Here, in the case of the Pharisees, such a crime also involves attributing the work of God to the devil.

blasphēmeō βλασφημέω 987

blasphēmeō is a verb found in about forty places, meaning "to speak blasphemy (against)," "slander," "speak scornfully (of someone)."

General references to the blaspheming of God are found in Mark 3:28; Acts 26:11; Rom 2:24; 1 Tim 1:20; Jas 2:7; Rev 13:6ff.; 16:21. The blaspheming of idols is noted in Acts 19:37. Such activity is wrongfully attributed to Jesus in Matt 9:3; 26:65; John 10:36. The blaspheming of the Holy Spirit is indicated in Mark 3:29; Luke 12:10 (see the discussion under ***blasphēmia***, above).

Matt 27:39; Mark 15:29; Luke 22:65; Acts 13:45; Rom 3:8; 1 Cor 4:13; Titus 3:2; 1 Pet 4:4, 14 all refer to scornful and mocking speech. See also 2 Pet 2:10; Jude 8ff.

The word of God is said to "be defamed" or "discredited" in Titus 2:5, as is the Christian way of life in 2 Pet 2:2.

▸ **58.** Vices > SLANDER, SLANDERER

blasphēmos βλάσφημος 989

blasphēmos is an adjective meaning "blasphemous," as well as a noun denoting a "blasphemer."

Stephen, the first Christian martyr, is wrongfully accused of blasphemous speech against God in Acts 6:11ff. 1 Tim 1:13 refers to Paul's pre-Christian activity as a blasphemer. More generally, ***blasphēmos*** refers to "abusive" speech in 2 Tim 3:2; 2 Pet 2:11.

BLEMISH

mōmos μῶμος 3470

mōmos is a rare noun found only in 2 Pet 2:13 with reference to the "blemishes" (i.e., disgraceful behavior) of false teachers.

BOAST, BOASTING, ARROGANCE

katakauchaomai κατακαυχάομαι 2620

katakauchaomai is a rare word meaning "boast" in Rom 11:18; Jas 3:14, both of which warn against "vain boasting."

megalaucheō μεγαλαυχέω 3166

megalaucheō is a rare verb found only in Jas 3:5 with reference to the tongue, which "boasts of great things."

alazōn ἀλαζών 213

alazōn is a rare noun found only twice, denoting "those who boast" with arrogance and insolence (Rom 1:30; 2 Tim 3:2).

alazoneia ἀλαζονεία 212

alazoneia is a rare noun denoting "arrogant boasting, or pride," found only in Jas 4:16; 1 John 2:16.

▸ **58.** Vices > PRIDE, PROUD

tolmētēs τολμητής 5113

tolmētēs is an adjectival form found only in 2 Pet 2:10 and denoting people who are "bold" in an arrogant sense.

SEE ALSO

- ▸ **48.** Will, Purpose, Decide, Advise > DARE, DARING
  tolmaō

COARSE JESTING

eutrapelia εὐτραπελία 2160

eutrapelia occurs only once, in Eph 5:4, where it refers to the vice of "levity" or "coarse jesting."

SEE ALSO

- ▸ **19.** Mind, Spirit, Emotions, Feelings, Desires > LAUGH, LAUGHTER
  gelaō, gelōs
- ▸ **45.** Faith, Belief, Trust, Promise > UNBELIEVING, LAUGH AT, LAUGH TO SCORN
  katagelaō

COMPLAIN, MURMUR, MUTTER, GRUMBLE

mempsimoiros μεμψίμοιρος 3202

mempsimoiros is a rare noun found only in Jude 16 referring to "those who complain or grumble."

gongyzō γογγύζω 1111

gongyzō is a verb occurring eight times in all, with the senses of "murmur," "mutter," "grumble."

The general meaning "complain" is found in Matt 20:11 where, in Jesus' parable, workers are dissatisfied with their wage.

The Pharisees complain forthrightly against Jesus' disciples for keeping company with social outcasts, or "sinners" (Luke 5:30).

The Jewish audience mutters in disbelief at Jesus' teaching concerning his claim to be "the bread of life" (John 6:41, 43). Even his disciples "murmured" at this difficult teaching (John 6:61).

The Pharisees are very disturbed at some people's "muttering" about their official denial of Jesus' messianic identify. Clearly, the impact of Jesus' signs was not lost on a number of his hearers (John 7:32).

A historical reference to the sin of Israel's murmuring in the wilderness is noted in 1 Cor 10:10.

diagongyzō διαγογγύζω 1234

diagongyzō is a variant form of ***gongyzō*** (above) with reference to the Pharisees' "murmuring" against Jesus. The term occurs only in Luke 15:2; 19:7, where it indicates the religious leaders' indignation and disgust at Jesus for fraternizing with people whom they regarded as the refuse of society.

gongystēs γογγυστής 1113

gongystēs is a noun, likewise derived from ***gongyzō*** (above). It is found only in Jude 16 and refers to "grumblers," one of the many godless traits of false prophets and teachers.

gongysmos γογγυσμός 1112

gongysmos is another derivative noun form from ***gongyzō*** (above) and means "murmuring," "complaining." It is found only four times. John 7:12 refers to people "muttering" about Jesus as to whether is a genuine or false teacher. Acts 6:1 records the "complaining" of Greek believers against Jewish Christians for neglecting the widows in the Gentile Christian community. Phil 2:14; 1 Pet 4:9 exhort believers to do all things "without complaint."

COVETOUS, COVETOUSNESS, GREED, GREEDY

pleonexia πλεονεξία 4124

pleonexia is a noun denoting "covetousness," "greed" throughout the ten occurrences of the term (Mark 7:22; Luke 12:15; Rom 1:29; 2 Cor 9:5; Eph 4:19; Col 3:5; 2 Pet 2:3, 4).

pleonektēs πλεονέκτης 4123

pleonektēs is a noun denoting a "covetous (or greedy) man" in 1 Cor 5:10, 11; 6:10; Eph 5:5.

philargyros φιλάργυρος 5366

philargyros is an adjective denoting those who are "lovers of money" in Luke 16:14; 2 Tim 3:2.

SEE ALSO

▸ **60.** Virtues > FREE OF THE LOVE OF MONEY
aphilargyros

DECEIT, DECEITFUL, DECEPTION, DECEIVE, DECEIVER, DECEITFULLY

apatē ἀπάτη 539

apatē is a noun found in seven places, meaning "deceit," "deception" and used metaphorically throughout.

The "deceitfulness" of riches is indicated in Matt 13:22; Mark 4:19. Similarly, Eph 4:22 speaks of the "deceitful" lusts of life, and Heb 3:13 refers to the "deceitfulness" of sin. 2 Thess 2:10 indicates the "deception" of wickedness with reference to the wicked.

apataō ἀπατάω 538

apataō is a verb meaning "deceive" in all five occurrences.

Eph 5:6 contains an exhortation not to allow unbelievers to deceive God's people with empty words. 1 Tim 2:14 refers to the serpent "deceiving" Adam and Eve in Eden. The moral and spiritual danger of "deceiving" one's heart is indicated in Jas 1:26.

exapataō ἐξαπατάω 1818

exapataō is a synonym for ***apataō*** (above) meaning "deceive" throughout.

Rom 7:11 notes the "deceiving" effect of sin in one's life. The deceptive activities of false teachers are indicated in Rom 16:18. 1 Cor 3:18 records warnings against self-deception; and 2 Thess 2:3 warns against being deceived by false teaching. 2 Cor 11:3 speaks of the serpent deceiving Eve in the garden of Eden.

phrenapataō φρεναπατάω 5422

phrenapataō is a rare synonym for the entries above, found only in Gal 6:3 and referring to the folly of those who "deceive" themselves into thinking they are of importance when in fact they are not.

dolos δόλος 1388

dolos is a noun denoting "deceit," "stealth," or "craftiness" throughout the twelve occurrences of the term.

"Deceit" is listed as a general vice in Mark 7:22; John 1:47; Acts 13:10; Rom 1:29; 1 Thess 2:3; 1 Pet 2:1; 3:10. 1 Pet 2:22 affirms that "no deceit" was found on the lips of Christ. See also 2 Cor 12:16.

The process and action of arresting Christ by "stealth" is noted in Matt 26:4; Mark 14:1.

dolios δόλιος 1386

dolios is a rare adjective found only in 2 Cor 11:13, referring to false teachers as "deceitful workmen."

dolioō δολιόω 1387

dolioō is a rare verb found only in Rom 3:13, referring to sinful humanity who "practice deceit" with their tongues.

doloō δολόω 1389

doloō is a rare variant of ***dolioō*** (above) found only in 2 Cor 4:2 and referring to the apostle Paul's refusal to "handle the word of God deceitfully."

▸ **70.** Give, Take, Seize, Touch > TOUCH, HANDLE, FEEL

planaō πλανάω 4105

planaō is a verb found about fifty times, meaning "deceive" in addition to related nuances.

Matt 24:4; Mark 13:5; Luke 21:8 warn the disciples not to be deceived by others.

The activity of false christs in deceiving many is recorded in Matt 24:5, 11; Mark 13:6 — except for the elect, as noted in Matt 24:24.

General references to the activity of "deceiving" are found in John 7:12, 47; 2 Tim 3:13. Rev 12:9; 13:14; 19:20; 20:3ff. describe Satan "deceiving" the whole world. See also Rev 18:23.

General exhortations for believers "not to be deceived" or "be led astray" in relation to spiritual truth and holy living are found in 1 Cor 6:9; 15:33; Gal 6:7; 1 John 3:7.

The state of "being deceived" by one's ungodly lifestyle is indicated in Titus 3:3.

The folly of "deceiving oneself " in relation to being without sin is noted in 1 John 1:8.

▸ **57.** Evil, Wickedness, Sin > ERR, GO ASTRAY, LEAD ASTRAY

paralogizomai παραλογίζομαι 3884

paralogizomai is a rare verb, occurring only twice and meaning "deceive." In Col 2:4 it refers to the apostolic intention to have the Colossian church well-instructed in the gospel lest they "be deceived" by pagan thinking. Jas 1:22 warns about "deceiving oneself" in relation to having God's word without acting upon it.

planē πλάνη 4106

planē is a noun found in ten places meaning "error," as well as the derivative sense of "deceit."

Eph 4:14 refers to the "deceitful schemes" (lit., "schemes of deceit") of the wicked.

▸ **57.** Evil, Wickedness, Sin > ERROR

planos πλάνος 4108

planos is an adjective used primarily in the nominal sense of "deceiver." Matt 27:63 contains a blasphemous reference to Christ as a "deceiver" — an epithet given to him by his enemies. "Deceivers" in the sense of "impostors," referring to false teachers, are noted in 2 Cor 6:8; 2 John 7. "Deceitful" spirits of satanic origin are noted in 1 Tim 4:1.

phrenapatēs φρεναπάτης 5423

phrenapatēs is a rare noun found only in Titus 1:10 denoting the "deceivers," the false teachers belonging to the so-called fanatical "Jewish circumcision party," whose members opposed the apostolic gospel message of salvation through Christ's sacrifice alone, apart from the law.

DEFRAUD

apostereō ἀποστερέω 650

apostereō is a verb found seven times with the primary sense of "defraud," "keep back by fraudulent means."

Mark 10:19 lists some of the ten commandments repeated by Christ. One of them is "Do not defraud," a variation on the crime of "stealing." The action of "defrauding" or "acquiring by fraudulent means" is indicated in 1 Cor 6:7, 8. In Jas 5:4 ***apostereō*** means "keep back, withhold by fraudulent means."

pleonekteō πλεονεκτέω 4122

pleonekteō is a verb found in five contexts with the underlying sense of "gain advantage over" someone in the context of fraudulent acts and motives. Such action is predicated of Satan in 2 Cor 2:11. Denial of such an action is noted in 2 Cor 7:2; 12:17, 18. 1 Thess 4:6 contains a warning against such action.

▸ **58.** Vices > TAKE ADVANTAGE OF

DRUNK, DRUNKENNESS, DRUNKARD

methyskō μεθύσκω 3182

methyskō is a form of ***methyō*** with the specific meaning "get drunk," "become intoxicated," found only in Luke 12:45; Eph 5:18; 1 Thess 5:7.

methysos μέθυσος 3183

methysos is a rare noun, a variant form denoting a "drunkard" and found only in 1 Cor 5:11; 6:10.

methē μέθη 3178

methē is a noun found only three times, signifying the state of "drunkenness" in Luke 21:34; Rom 13:13; Gal 5:21.

paroinos πάροινος 3943

paroinos is an adjective denoting the vice of those "given to drunkenness," a characteristic forbidden to those aspiring to the office of elder (1 Tim 3:3; Titus 1:7).

oinophlygia οἰνοφλυγία 3632

oinophlygia is a rare synonym for ***methē*** and ***paroinos*** (above) found only in 1 Pet 4:3 and denoting the vice of "drunkenness" in relation to orgies and debauchery.

ENVY, ENVIOUS, JEALOUSY

phthonos φθόνος 5355

phthonos is a noun found nine times, denoting the emotion and attitude of "envy" or "jealousy" throughout. "Envy" is the dominant emotion motivating the Jewish leaders who sought to have Jesus handed over to the Roman courts in Matt 27:18; Mark 15:10. "Envy" is listed among a number of vices in Rom 1:29; Gal 5:21; 1 Tim 6:4; Titus 3:3; 1 Pet 2:1. Phil 1:15 affirms that some false teachers preach Christ out of "envy."

phthoneō φθονέω 5354

phthoneō is a rare verb found only in Gal 5:26, meaning "to be envious" (of someone).

EXTORTION, EXTORTIONER, ROB, ROBBER, PLUNDER

harpagē ἁρπαγή 724

harpagē is a noun found three times, denoting the crime of "extortion" by illegal and oppressive means as perpetrated by the religious leaders of the Jewish people against the poor and powerless in that society (Matt 23:35; Luke 11:39). The "plundering" of property is indicated in Heb 10:34.

▸ **58.** Vices > SPOIL

harpax ἅρπαξ 727

harpax is an adjectival form found five times, translated nominally as "extortioners" in Luke 8:11, and as "robbers" in 1 Cor 5:10, 11; 6:10. See also Matt 7:15, where the term refers metaphorically to false prophets as "ravenous" wolves.

sylaō συλάω 4813

sylaō is found only in 2 Cor 11:8 with reference to Paul metaphorically "robbing" churches by accepting support from them.

▸ **58.** Vices > STEAL, BREAK IN, BURGLE

lēstēs λῃστής 3027

lēstēs is a term found in fifteen places meaning "robber," "thief."

Jesus refers to the profaning of the temple in Matt 21:13; Mark 11:17; Luke 19:46 (see also Jer 7:11). He describes it as a "den of robbers," because of the corrupt activity of those conducting business in the outer court.

General references to "robbers" include those in Matt 26:55; Luke 10:30ff.; John 10:1, 8; 2 Cor 11:26.

kleptēs κλέπτης 2812

This noun occurs sixteen times, meaning "thief" or "robber" (Matt 6:19ff.; Luke 12:33; John 10:1; 1 Cor 6:10; 1 Pet 4:15). In Rev 3:3; 16:15, the return of Christ is described as being "like a thief."

FALSE, FALSEHOOD

pseudēs ψευδής 5571

pseudēs is an adjectival form found in only three places, denoting "false" witnesses in Acts 6:13; and "liars" (i.e., those who bear false witness) in Rev 2:2; 21:8.

▸ **58.** Vices > LIE, LYING, LIAR

pseusma ψεῦσμα 5582

pseusma occurs only in Rom 3:7 and refers to "falsehood" as a hypothetical moral failing on the part of Paul.

SEE ALSO

▸ **61.** Integrity, Innocence, Piety > UNABLE TO LIE
apseudēs

FIERCE, SAVAGE

anēmeros ἀνήμερος 434

anēmeros is a rare adjective found only in 2 Tim 3:3, denoting false teachers as "fierce" (or "savage") — one moral flaw in a long list of vices.

SEE ALSO

▸ **76.** Force, Harm, Oppress > FIERCE
chalepos

FOOLISH TALKING

mōrologia μωρολογία 3473

mōrologia is a noun occurring only once, in Eph 5:4, indicating the sense of "foolish (or silly) talking."

SEE ALSO

▸ **17.** Senses, Actions, Abilities, Disabilities > SPEAK, SPEECH, TALK
syllaleō, homileō, synomileō, lalia

FORNICATION, SEXUAL IMMORALITY, PROSTITUTE

porneia πορνεία 4202

porneia is a noun occurring around twenty-five times with the general meaning "fornication," expressing the underlying sense of "sexual immorality" in a variety of contexts.

porneia denotes the vice of "sexual immorality" in the context of marriage in Matt 5:32; 19:9; John 8:41; Acts 15:20, 29; 1 Cor 5:1; 6:13, 18; 7:2. A specific reference to "sexual immorality" outside the confines of a marital context is found in Rev 2:21.

General references to "immorality," implying "moral perversity" and signifying more than marital infidelity, are found in Matt 15:19; Rom 1:29; 1 Cor 5:1; 6:13, 18; 7:2; Gal 5:19; Eph 5:3; Col 3:5; Rev 9:21.

porneia expresses the sense of "sexual immorality" in a number of metaphorical contexts in the book of Revelation with reference to the symbolic woman "Babylon," portrayed as a prostitute. In these contexts, her "sexual immorality" denotes the sin of "idolatry," frequently described through the symbol of moral impurity. It is the sin of idolatry that most distresses God as it challenges and undermines his unique authority and majesty in the hearts of those who commit such sin (Rev 14:8; 17:2, 4; 18:3; 19:2).

pornos πόρνος 4205

pornos is a noun found ten times with the general sense of an "immoral person" throughout, referring both to sexual misconduct as well as to moral perverseness in general. References to "immoral men," denoting people who are sexually immoral, are found in 1 Cor 5:9ff.; Eph 5:5; Heb 13:4; Rev 22:15 (implied).

General references to "the immoral" in the broad sense of "the morally perverse" are found in 1 Cor 6:9; 1 Tim 1:10; Heb 12:16; Rev 21:8.

pornē πόρνη 4204

pornē is a variant of ***pornos*** (above) denoting a "(female) prostitute" in both literal and metaphorical contexts. The term occurs twelve times. Literal references to a "harlot" or "prostitute" include those in Matt 21:31ff.; Luke 15:30; 1 Cor 6:15ff.; Heb 11:31; Jas 2:25.

The godless city of Babylon is depicted metaphorically as a "whore" in Rev 17:1ff.; 19:2, denoting her rank idolatry and opposition against God.

▸ **58.** Vices > HARLOT

porneuō πορνεύω 4203

porneuō is a verb found eight times meaning "to practice, indulge in immorality" in a sexual sense in 1 Cor 6:18f.; 10:8; Rev 2:14, 20. In Rev 17:2; 18:3, 9 ***porneuō*** signifies the committing of adultery in a metaphorical sense, with reference to the peoples of the earth engaging in morally culpable business with the archetypal evil nation Babylon. Such symbolic "adultery" most likely takes the form of idolatry — a practice universally evident throughout the nations of the world and frequently equated with "immoral living" (symbolically speaking) in the prophetic canon of Scripture.

ekporneuō ἐκπορνεύω 1608

ekporneuō is a rare verb found only in Jude 7, referring to the citizens of Sodom and Gomorrah who had "given themselves over to sexual immorality."

GANGRENE

gangraina γάγγραινα 1044

gangraina is a rare noun found only in 2 Tim 2:17 denoting "gangrene" in a figurative context. Here the impact of foolish talk is likened to the spreading condition of rotting flesh.

GOSSIP, WHISPER

psithyristēs ψιθυριστής 5588

psithyristēs is a rare noun, found only in Rom 1:29 with reference to those who "whisper" (i.e., gossip) about others.

psithyrismos ψιθυρισμός 5587

psithyrismos is another rare noun found only in 2 Cor 12:20, referring to "whisperings" or "gossip."

HARLOT

pornē πόρνη 4204

pornē occurs twelve times with the sole meaning "prostitute." It has both a literal and a metaphorical sense. ***pornē*** refers to the moral crime of fornication, whether for economic gain or for passion. Metaphorically, the word refers to those who commit idolatry.

The literal sense of ***pornē*** is indicated in Matt 21:13ff.; Luke 15:30; Heb 11:30; Jas 2:5. In 1 Cor 6:15, 16, however, the term points to the spiritual harm done to one's relationship with Christ as a consequence of sexual immorality with a prostitute. Rev 17:1, 5, 15, 16; 19:2 all refer allegorically to Babylon as the "great whore," the universal biblical symbol for crass idolatry.

▸ **58.** Vices >
FORNICATION, SEXUAL IMMORALITY, PROSTITUTE

HEARTLESS, MERCILESS, RUTHLESS

astorgos ἄστοργος 794

astorgos is an adjectival form that occurs only twice, meaning "heartless" or "inhuman" but literally conveying the sense of "without natural affection" (Rom 1:31; 2 Tim 3:3).

aneleēmōn ἀνελεήμων 415

aneleēmōn is an adjective found only in Rom 1:31, describing the wicked as "merciless" or "ruthless."

HYPOCRISY, HYPOCRITE

hypokrisis ὑπόκρισις 5272

This term refers to the practice of dissimulation or hypocrisy, with the Pharisees being the target of Christ's public condemnation during his earthly ministry. ***hypokrisis*** occurs seven times and is translated "hypocrisy" in all but one text, Jas 5:12, where it is translated as "condemnation." It is also found in Matt 23:28; Mark 12:15; Luke 12:1; Gal 2:13; 1 Tim 4:2; 1 Pet 2:1.

hypokritēs ὑποκριτής 5273

hypokritēs occurs twenty times and is consistently translated "hypocrite." ***hypokritēs*** always comes from the mouth of Christ, and is largely directed at the Pharisees (Matt 6:2, 5, 16; 15:17; 16:3; 22:18; 23:13ff.; Mark 7:6; Luke 11:44; 12:56; 13:15). Matt 7:5; 24:51; Luke 6:12 express general condemnation of hypocrites.

IDLE, LAZY

argos ἀργός 692

argos is an adjective occurring six times with the primary sense of "idle," "lazy" in all but one of these contexts. Matt 12:36 refers to an "idle (i.e., careless) word." Matt 20:3, 6 speak of idleness in the work place. Paul condemns "idle busybodies" in 1 Tim 5:13, and refers to Cretans as "lazy gluttons" in Titus 1:12.

IMAGINATION, (STUBBORN) THINKING

dianoia διάνοια 1271

dianoia occurs twelve times, once meaning "imagination" in the sense of "vain, stubborn thinking," in Luke 1:51.

▸ **19.** Mind, Spirit, Emotions, Feelings, Desires > MIND

SEE ALSO

▸ **56.** Folly, Ignorance > FUTILE THINKING, VAIN IMAGINATION ***dialogismos***

▸ **77.** Resist, Oppose, Fight, Rebel > CONSPIRE, IMAGINE ***meletaō***

INSOLENCE

hybristēs ὑβριστής 5197

hybristēs occurs only twice. In Rom 1:30 it indicates the vice of "insolence" as characteristic of the wicked who refuse to acknowledge God's rightful place in their lives. 1 Tim 1:13 refers to Paul's practice of "insulting" God prior to his conversion, when he actively and aggressively persecuted Christians — implying insolence towards both God and humankind.

LIE, LYING, LIAR

pseustēs ψεύστης 5583

pseustēs is a noun that consistently refers to "liars," or those who are deceptive and totally untrustworthy. ***pseustēs*** occurs ten times.

The devil is referred to as a "liar" and the "father of lies" in John 8:44. General references to people as liars are found in Rom 3:4; 1 Tim 1:10; Titus 1:12. 1 John 2:4; 4:20 indicate that those who profess to know God, but who do not show love to others, show themselves to be liars; as are those who deny that Jesus is the Christ (1 John 2:22). More blatantly, failure to acknowledge our sinfulness and failure to believe in Jesus as sent by God create the impression that God himself is a liar.

pseudēs ψευδής 5571

pseudēs is the adjectival form derived from ***pseudomai*** (below) and is translated "lying," "deceitful," "false." ***pseudēs*** occurs three times. Acts 1:13 refers to "false witnesses" who wrongly accused Stephen, the first Christian martyr, of blasphemy. Rev 2:2 describes false prophets in the church at Ephesus. Rev 21:8 contains a nominal use of ***pseudēs***, in which "liars" are included in the list of the wicked set aside for judgment.

▸ **58.** Vices > FALSE, FALSEHOOD

pseudos ψεῦδος 5579

pseudos is a noun found in nine contexts, meaning "lie" or "lying."

Lying is a natural expression of Satan's character (John 8:44). ***pseudos*** refers to the embodiment of the evil one in the person of "the lawless one" in 2 Thess 2:9, 11. Rom 1:25 refers to the fundamental attitude underlying the sin of idolatry — exchanging the truth of God for a lie. Rev 21:27; 22:15 refer to those who utter lies as having no part whatever with the people living in the heavenly city. Eph 4:25 contains the exhortation to put away all lying or deceit from one's character. 1 John 2:21, 27 affirm the absolute truth of the teaching given by God in Christ — that is, there is no lie in it.

pseudomai ψεύδομαι 5574

pseudomai is a verb consistently translated "to lie" and occurs twelve times.

The lying activity of individuals is indicated in Matt 5:11; Acts 5:3, 4; Rev 3:9; 1 John 1:6. Paul's strong denial of any lying is recorded in Rom 9:1; 2 Cor 11:31; Gal 1:20; 1 Tim 2:7. Exhortations to keep from speaking lies are found in Col 3:9; Jas 3:14. The impossibility of deceit residing in God is affirmed in Heb 6:18.

SEE ALSO

▸ **61.** Integrity, Innocence, Piety > UNABLE TO LIE ***apseudēs***

LUXURY

tryphaō τρυφάω 5171

tryphaō is found only in Jas 5:5, meaning "live in luxury."

SEE ALSO

▸ **22.** Life, Renewal, Immortality > LIFE, LIVE, LIVING ***psychē, zōē, bios, zaō, zōogoneō, syzaō, makrochronios, anazaō***

▸ **34.** Craftsmanship, Artisanship, Furniture, Implements > LIFELESS ***apsychos***

▸ **61.** Integrity, Innocence, Piety > LIVE ***politeuomai, eirēneuō***

MOCK, MOCKER, MOCKING, SCOFF, SCOFFER, SCORN

empaizō ἐμπαίζω 1702

empaizō occurs in thirteen contexts and means "to mock" or "scorn."

The primary usage of ***empaizō*** is found in relation to the Roman soldiers and the Jewish religious and civil authorities mocking Christ (Matt 20:19; 27:29ff., 41; Mark 10:34; 15:20, 31; Luke 18:32; 22:63; 23:11, 36). See also Luke 14:29.

empaiktēs ἐμπαίκτης 1703

empaiktēs is a noun derived from ***empaizō*** (above). It refers to "mockers" or "scoffers" who will appear in the last days prior to the return of Christ, deriding the idea of his return. The word occurs only in 2 Pet 3:3; Jude 18.

empaigmos ἐμπαιγμός 1701

empaigmos is another noun derived from ***empaizō*** (above) and has the abstract sense of "mocking." It occurs only in Heb 11:36, with reference to the persecution suffered by God's people down through the ages, who were scorned by the enemies of God.

chleuazō χλευάζω 5512

chleuazō is a synonym for ***empaizō*** (above) and means "mock," "deride," or "jeer." It is found only twice. Acts 2:13 mentions those who mocked the disciples' speaking in foreign languages under the influence of the Holy Spirit. The skeptical crowd believed the disciples to be drunk. Acts 17:32 refers to the Athenians, who mocked Paul for his belief in the resurrection from the dead.

myktērizō μυκτηρίζω 3456

myktērizō occurs only in Gal 6:7 with the sense of "mock." It is used in the negative, expressing the serious warning that God is not to be mocked, lest one incur his judgment.

PLEASURE, PASSION, LUST

hēdonē ἡδονή 2237

hēdonē refers to "pleasure" in the sense of "passion" or "lust" in an unwholesome sense, as a characteristic of a godless lifestyle. The term occurs five times (Luke 8:14; Titus 3:3; Jas 4:1, 3; 2 Pet 2:13).

▸ **19.** Mind, Spirit, Emotions, Feelings, Desires > LUST, YEARN

philēdonos φιλήδονος 5369

philēdonos is an adjectival form derived from ***hēdonē*** (above) meaning "lovers of pleasure" (i.e., passion, or lust). It occurs only in 2 Tim 3:4.

SEE ALSO

▸ **50.** Love, Hate, Please, Be Pleased With > PLEASING
arestos, areskō, areskeia, euaresteō, euarestos, eudokeō

PRIDE, PROUD

hyperēphania ὑπερηφανία 5243

hyperēphania is a noun found only in Mark 7:22 with reference to the human vice of "pride."

hyperēphanos ὑπερήφανος 5244

hyperēphanos is an adjective found in only five contexts, meaning "proud." This quality inevitably draws down the judgment of God upon those who manifest it (Luke 1:51; Rom 1:30; 2 Tim 3:2; Jas 4:6; 1 Pet 5:5).

typhoō τυφόω 5187

typhoō is a verb meaning "to be proud" or "filled with pride." It is found only three times (1 Tim 3:6; 6:4; 2 Tim 3:4).

alazoneia ἀλαζονεία 212

alazoneia is a noun meaning "pride," "boasting." It occurs only twice, in Jas 4:16; 1 John 2:16.

▸ **58.** Vices > BOAST, BOASTING, ARROGANCE

REPROACH, INSULT, ABUSE

loidoria λοιδορία 3059

loidoria is a noun derived from the verb ***loidoreō*** (below), found only three times and meaning "insult" on each occasion (1 Tim 5:14; 1 Pet 3:9 [twice]).

loidoreō λοιδορέω 3058

loidoreō is a verb found in only four places, meaning "reproach" with the sense of "heap abuse on" (John 9:28; Acts 23:4; 1 Cor 4:12; 1 Pet 2:23).

SEE ALSO

▸ **52.** Status, Identity, Reputation, Honor, Shame > REPROACH
oneidos, oneidizō, oneidismos

SLANDER, SLANDERER

blasphēmeō βλασφημέω 987

blasphēmeō is a verb with the predominant sense of "blaspheme" (i.e., against God) in nearly all of its forty or so occurrences. In addition, ***blasphēmeō*** means "speak evil" or "slander" (Matt 27:39; Mark 15:29; Acts 13:45; Rom 3:8; Titus 3:2; 2 Pet 2:2; Jude 8ff.).

▸ **58.** Vices > BLASPHEME, BLASPHEMY, BLASPHEMER, BLASPHEMOUS

diabolos διάβολος 1228

diabolos is a common term for "devil" found in about forty contexts. ***diabolos*** is also occasionally translated as "slanderer," "accuser," in relation to people (2 Tim 3:3; Titus 2:3).

▸ **2.** Supernatural Beings/Forces, Spiritual Realm > DEVIL
▸ **58.** Vices > ACCUSATION

SPOIL

diarpazō διαρπάζω 1283

diarpazō is a verb found twice, referring to "plundering" or "spoiling" one's property (Matt 12:29; Mark 3:27).

harpagē ἁρπαγή 724

harpagē is a noun found three times meaning "to extort." In Heb 10:34 it refers to "spoiling" or "plundering" one's goods.

▸ **58.** Vices > EXTORTION, EXTORTIONER, ROB, ROBBER, PLUNDER

STEAL, BREAK IN, BURGLE

dioryssō διορύσσω 1358

The verb ***dioryssō*** means to "break in" in the sense of "burgle" a house (Matt 6:19ff.; 24:43; Luke 12:39).

kleptō κλέπτω 2813

kleptō is a verb meaning "to steal," "rob" in each of the thirteen occurrences of the term (Matt 6:19ff.; 27:64; 28:13; John 10:10; Rom 2:21; Eph 4:28). The commandment "do not steal" is noted in Matt 9:18; Mark 10:19; Luke 18:20; Rom 13:9.

sylaō συλάω 4813

sylaō is a verb found only in 2 Cor 11:9, referring metaphorically to Paul "robbing" churches by accepting monetary support from them. This statement is tinged with sarcasm.

▸ **58.** Vices > EXTORTION, EXTORTIONER, ROB, ROBBER, PLUNDER

STUBBORN, OBSTINATE

sklērotrachēlos σκληροτράχηλος 4644

sklērotrachēlos is a rare adjectival form found only in Acts 7:51, denoting people who are "stubborn," "stiff-necked," or "obstinate" — an accusation directed at the Jewish religious leaders by Stephen, the first Christian martyr.

TAKE ADVANTAGE OF

pleonekteō πλεονεκτέω 4122

pleonekteō is a verb found in five places with the meaning "to gain, take advantage of." The contexts all reflect the underlying sense of "wrong" or "defraud" (2 Cor 2:11; 7:2; 12:17, 18; 1 Thess 4:6).

▸ **58.** Vices > DEFRAUD

SEE ALSO

▸ **72.** Need, Gain, Loss, Advantage, Seek, Find > ADVANTAGE, PROFIT
perissos, ophelos, ōpheleia, ōpheleō

TRAITOR

prodotēs προδότης 4273

prodotēs is a rare noun found in only three places meaning "traitor." Luke 6:16 refers to Judas Iscariot, who betrayed Christ to the authorities. Acts 7:52 refers to the traitors who had Christ put to death. See also 2 Tim 3:4.

VENOM

ios ἰός 2447

ios is a noun found three times. In two of these contexts, it refers figuratively to the "venom" of serpents in relation to the wicked (Rom 3:13). Jas 3:8 speaks of the "venom" of the untamed human tongue.

WASTE, SQUANDER

diaskorpizō διασκορπίζω 1287

diaskorpizō is a verb with the dominant sense of "scatter," "scatter abroad." However, in two places it refers to "wasting" or squandering one's wealth or property (Luke 15:13; 16:1).

▸ **79.** Throw, Send, Drive, Mix, Remove > SCATTER, DISPERSE

59. Justice, Righteousness, Truth

RIGHTEOUS, RIGHTEOUSNESS, JUST, JUSTIFY, JUSTIFICATION

dikaios δίκαιος 1342

dikaios is an adjectival form that is also used nominally, found in approximately eighty contexts with the primary meanings "righteous," "just." There is a clear overlap in meaning between the two in many places.

When predicated of people, ***dikaios*** describes them as "righteous" in the sense of "fair" or "just," indicating their moral purity (Matt 1:19; 13:17; Acts 10:22; Titus 1:8; Jas 5:16). There are exhortations to judge "rightly" or "with justice" in John 7:24; Col 4:1.

dikaios also refers to "the just," indicating that class of people who are godly (Matt 5:45; 25:37; Luke 1:6; 14:14; Heb 12:23; 1 Pet 3:12; Gal 3:11). Rom 1:17 contains the declaration that "the just shall live by faith" (citing the OT declaration of Hab 2:4).

In negative contexts, the attitude of the "self-righteous" is condemned (Matt 9:13; 10:41; Mark 2:17). And Rom 3:10 denies that there are any who are truly "righteous" before God in their natural condition.

Christ is also frequently described as one who is uniquely "just" or "righteous," in the sense of being completely innocent of all wrong (Matt 27:19, 24; Luke 23:47; Acts 3:14; 7:52; 22:14; 1 Pet 3:18; 1 John 2:1). In John 5:30, his judgment is described as "just."

God is likewise declared to be "righteous" in the sense of "morally perfect," "just" (John 17:25; Rom 3:26; 1 John 1:9; Rev 15:3; 16:5ff.). His judgment is likewise deemed "righteous" in 2 Thess 1:5; 2 Tim 4:8; Rev 19:2.

Rom 5:19 is a significant theological statement whereby, through an act of God, many will be constituted "righteous" in his sight (i.e., justified, declared guiltless before him) as a consequence of the atoning work of Christ. See also Heb 11:4, where Abel's sacrifice, presented in a wholehearted attitude of faith and trust in God, was the means by which he was approved by God as righteous.

dikaiosynē δικαιοσύνη 1343

dikaiosynē is the most common term in the NT for "righteousness," with all its significant theological connotations. It is found approximately eighty times.

First of all, ***dikaiosynē*** means "righteousness" in the sense of "meeting the demands of God's law." In general terms, Christ's desire to manifest this kind of righteousness is indicated in Matt 3:15 with regard to his baptism by John. Paul's pre-Christian conversion concept of righteousness under the law is indicated in Phil 3:6. The phenomenon of the "way of righteousness" is noted in Matt 21:32; 2 Pet 2:21. In relation to Christ himself, his righteousness is identified in Rom 5:21 with his act of obedient submission to death on the cross. References to "our righteousness" in Christ, or "the righteousness of God" in Christ, illustrate the doctrine of imputed righteousness for the believer (1 Cor 1:30; 2 Cor 5:21; 2 Pet 1:1).

In a more general sense, the meaning "righteousness" indicates the state of being acceptable to God in every way (Matt 5:30; John 16:8, 10; 2 Cor 6:14; 2 Tim 3:16). Phil 1:11; Heb 12:11; Jas 3:18 refer to the "fruits of righteousness" in Christ. Rom 6:13ff.; 1 Tim 6:11; 2 Tim 2:22; 1 Pet 2:24 affirm that attaining such a state is the great goal of all believers. See also Matt 5:6 in this regard. In addition, Eph 6:14 contains the apostolic injunction to all believers to don the "breastplate of righteousness." There is also, in contrast, an invalid "righteousness" based on the pursuit of lawful obedience apart from Christ (Rom 9:31; Titus 3:5).

dikaiosynē also means "righteousness" in the sense of "justification," or the judicial declaration of innocence under the law. The grounds for such an acquittal is the completed redemptive work of Christ on the cross, and the instrument for applying such righteousness to the believer is saving faith in the person of God under the old covenant, and trust in the person of Christ in the new. The patriarch Abraham is used by the apostle Paul as the classic old covenant illustration of this phenomenon (Rom 4:3ff.; 5:17; 9:30; 10:4, 6, 10; Gal 2:21; 3:6; Phil 3:9; Heb 11:7; Jas 2:23).

When applied to the person of God, ***dikaiosynē*** signifies divine righteousness as one of his essential characteristics (Matt 6:33; Rom 1:17; 3:5, 21ff.; 10:3; 2 Cor 9:9; Eph 4:24; Jas 1:20). Acts 17:31 speaks of God's perfect judgment of the world through Christ, "in righteousness."

Similarly, in relation to Christ, his love of "righteousness" is indicated in Heb 1:9. In Rev 19:11, he is described as the one who judges in righteousness, with perfect justice. The mysterious Melchizedek is given a typological significance through his name, "king of righteousness," anticipating the eternal nature of Jesus Christ's high priestly ministry (Heb 7:2 [citing Gen 14]).

dikaioō δικαιόω 1344

dikaioō is a verb found forty times in the NT with the consistent meaning "to justify," with a variety of nuances. With respect to humankind's standing before God, this action is wholly a divine one, with the underlying sense of "declaring righteous" those who have humbled themselves before him, in repentance and faith. And for those living at the time of the earthly ministry of Christ (and afterwards), such a declaration is made for all who so commit themselves to the person of the Messiah. As a consequence, all who regard the person of God and Christ in this manner are adjudged innocent of all guilt under the law of Moses, for that sin has been borne by Christ through his substitutionary death on the cross.

General references to such a declaration by God include those in Luke 18:14; Acts 13:39 (see also Rom 2:13).

Classic references to being justified by grace through faith in the person and work of Christ include those in Rom 3:20, 24ff.; 4:5; 5:1, 9; 8:30, 33; 1 Cor 6:11; Gal 2:16ff.; 3:8, 24; Titus 3:7. The "justifying" of Abraham through his faith, mentioned in Rom 4:2, applies the identical principle as indicated in each of the above texts. Even though Christ was not the object of the patriarch's trust in his own time and experience, his explicit faith in Yahweh is deemed to be identical in essence. Such was the case with all old covenant believers.

James' teaching on justification requires a point of clarification: for faith to be genuine, James argues that it must be accompanied by good works. James is not contradicting the Pauline perspective here. Rather, he is complementing it by emphasizing good works as the inevitable fruit of genuine faith, and not as the ground of our right standing with God (Jas 2:21ff.).

Christ himself is "declared righteous," or "justified," "vindicated" by the Spirit of God, who enabled him to validate his claim to the divine nature through his miracles, and ultimately through his resurrection from the dead (1 Tim 3:16). Other references to the action of "justifying" or "declaring righteous" include those in Matt 11:19; Luke 7:35, where "Wisdom" (a personification of a divine attribute) is justified by her deeds.

The act of justifying in the sense of "granting an acquittal" is indicated in Matt 12:37; Rom 3:4; 1 Cor 4:4. Luke 10:29; 16:15 refer to justifying oneself in the sense of "making oneself appear to be in the right." Luke 7:29 refers to "justifying" God in the sense of "acknowledging his ways as right."

▸ **32.** Law, Justice, Jurisprudence, Judgment > JUSTIFY
▸ **55.** Bondage, Captivity, Servitude > FREE, FREEDOM, SET FREE, LIBERTY

dikaiōma δικαίωμα 1345

dikaiōma is a noun derived from ***dikaioō*** (above) found ten times and meaning "righteousness," "ordinance," "decree," "justification." This term refers to actions or a state of heart and mind that conform to the law of God.

The usage of ***dikaiōma*** with reference to God's "righteous" decrees, or judgments, is indicated in Luke 1:6; Rom 2:26. God's "righteous acts" are noted in Rev 15:4. In Rom 1:32, the context is that of a divine decree that threatens judgment upon those that flout God's law. ***dikaiōma*** also refers to the "just requirements" of the law in Rom 8:4.

"Justification" is the explicit meaning of ***dikaiōma*** in Rom 5:16, referring to the righteous standing before God imputed to his people through the redemptive work of Christ.

The "righteous deeds" of the saints are noted in Rev 19:8. And the climactic "act of righteousness" performed by Christ that brought life to all humankind is indicated in Rom 5:18.

Finally, ***dikaiōma*** refers to "regulations" for worship in Heb 9:1, 10. The sense here is that such regulations are in full accord with the law of ritual worship.

▸ **32.** Law, Justice, Jurisprudence, Judgment > ACT
▸ **32.** Law, Justice, Jurisprudence, Judgment > JUDGMENT
▸ **32.** Law, Justice, Jurisprudence, Judgment > JUSTIFICATION

dikaiōs δικαίως 1346

dikaiōs is an adverbial form occurring five times, derived from the adjective ***dikaios*** (above) and meaning "righteously," "justly," or "blameless." The term refers to human behavior in Luke 23:11; 1 Cor 15:34; 1 Thess 2:10; Titus 2:12. In 1 Pet 2:23, ***dikaiōs*** refers to God as one who judges "justly."

dikaiōsis δικαίωσις 1347

dikaiōsis is a rare noun derived from ***dikaioō*** (above). It is found only twice and means "justification" in both cases. ***dikaiōsis*** refers, as do the synonymous terms discussed above, to the judicial declaration of righteousness by God, granted to his people on the basis of Christ's finished work of redemption (Rom 4:25; 5:18).

▸ **32.** Law, Justice, Jurisprudence, Judgment > JUSTIFICATION

euthytēs εὐθύτης 2118

euthytēs is a term found only in Heb 1:8, referring to the scepter of "righteousness" belonging to God.

TRUE, TRUTH, TRULY

alēthēs ἀληθής 227

alēthēs is an adjectival form found in twenty-five contexts meaning "true" in a variety of settings.

The quality of being "true" in the sense of being "endowed with integrity, honesty" describes Christ (Matt 22:6; Mark 12:14; John 7:18); God (John 8:26; Rom 3:4); and human beings (2 Cor 6:8).

In a number of places, ***alēthēs*** denotes the quality "true" in the sense of "that which is in accord with truth" (e.g., John 5:31ff.; 8:13ff.; Phil 4:8; Titus 1:13; 1 John 2:8, 27).

Similarly, the meaning "true" also signifies that which is "genuine" (e.g., 2 Pet 2:22; 3 John 12), including the grace of God (1 Pet 5:12).

alēthinos ἀληθινός 228

alēthinos is another adjectival form meaning "true" throughout its nearly thirty occurrences, indicating various related nuances.

The designation "true" is applied to "that which is genuine" in a number of places. It refers, for example, to eternal, spiritual wealth (Luke 16:11); to the spiritual light embodied in the person of Christ (John 1:9; 1 John 2:8); to the believer's heart (Heb 10:22); to the bread of life, indicating the word of God (John 6:32); to the vine representing Christ as the source of eternal life (John 15:1); and to the tabernacle in heaven, anticipated by the earthly dwelling place of God (Heb 8:2; 9:24). See also Rev 19:11.

alēthinos also means "true," designating "that which is in accord with truth" (i.e., the absolute virtue of truth). It is applied to the judgments of God (Rev 19:2); to the word of God (Rev 3:7; 19:9; 21:5); to God himself (John 7:28; 17:3; 1 Thess 1:9; 1 John 5:20; Rev 6:10); and to apostolic testimony (John 19:35).

alētheia ἀλήθεια 225

alētheia is the primary term for "truth" in the NT, occurring about 110 times in a variety of contexts.

Truth as a virtue, describing "that which accords with reality," is noted in general in Matt 22:16; Mark 5:33; John 8:40ff.; Rom 1:18, 25; Eph 4:25; 1 John 1:6. Truth as the characteristic of God's word is indicated in John 17:17ff.; 2 Tim 2:15; as is the truth of the gospel (Gal 2:5, 14; Eph 1:13; 2 Thess 2:12; 1 Tim 2:4; Heb 10:26).

alētheia is also used with the adverbial sense of "truly" in Col 1:5.

Truth as an element of the divine character, denoting absolute integrity, is embodied in Christ (John 1:14ff.; 5:33; 14:6; 2 Cor 11:10; Eph 4:21); designated as a trait of the Holy Spirit (John 14:17; 15:26; 16:13); and is also a characteristic of God (Rom 3:7; 15:8).

alēthōs ἀληθῶς 230

alēthōs is an adverb meaning "truly," "surely" in nearly twenty contexts (e.g., Matt 14:33; Mark 14:70; John 4:42; 17:8; Acts 12:11).

alētheuō ἀληθεύω 226

alētheuō is a verb meaning to "tell the truth." It occurs only in Gal 4:16; Eph 4:15.

▸ **63.** Speak, Tell, Declare, Call > TELL

gnēsios γνήσιος 1103

gnēsios is an adjective found in four places meaning "true" or "genuine" in relation to Christian love (2 Cor 8:8) and to people (Phil 4:3; 1 Tim 1:2; Titus 1:4).

60. Virtues

BRIDLE, RESTRAIN

chalinagōgeō χαλιναγωγέω 5468

chalinagōgeō is a rare verb with the metaphorical sense of "bridle," or keep in check, restrain. Jas 1:26 notes the dangers of "not bridling" one's tongue. "Bridling" the whole body is a metaphor for mature self-control in Jas 3:2.

SEE ALSO

- ▸ **28.** Agriculture, Viticulture, Animal Husbandry > BIT, BRIDLE
  chalinos

ENDURE, BEAR, FORBEAR

hypopherō ὑποφέρω 5297

hypopherō is a rare verb found three times with the meaning "bear up" in the sense of "patiently endure." God's promise to enable his people to "bear up" under trials and tribulation is noted in 1 Cor 10:13. In 2 Tim 3:11; 1 Pet 2:19, general references are made to "enduring" various trials.

stegō στέγω 4722

The verb ***stegō*** is found six times with the meaning "bear" in the sense of "endure," "suffer." General references to "enduring" or "forbearing" are found in 1 Cor 9:12; 1 Thess 3:1ff. Love is said to "endure all things" in 1 Cor 13:7.

anechomai ἀνέχομαι 430

anechomai is a verb found nearly twenty times with the meaning "endure," "bear with," "forbear."

Most commonly, ***anechomai*** expresses the sense of "bear with someone" (i.e., be patient with) in Matt 17:17; Luke 9:41; 2 Cor 11:1, 19ff.; Eph 4:2; Col 3:13; Heb 13:22.

Elsewhere, ***anechomai*** is translated "bear," "endure persecution" (1 Cor 4:12; 2 Thess 1:4). Then 2 Tim 4:3 mentions the refusal of people to "bear" or "endure" sound teaching.

hypomenō ὑπομένω 5278

hypomenō is a verb found in eighteen contexts with the primary meanings "endure," "bear patiently."

References to the perseverance of believers who "stand firm (i.e., endure) to the end" are found in Matt 10:22; 24:13; Mark 13:13. See also Jas 5:11. The exhortation "to be patient" under persecution is found in Rom 12:12; Heb 12:7. Christ himself is said to "have endured" much persecution, including death on the cross. "Suffering, or enduring affliction, persecution" is indicated in 2 Tim 2:10ff.; Heb 10:32; Jas 1:12. The virtue of love is said to "endure" all things in 1 Cor 13:7.

- ▸ **24.** Dwell, Live, Gather, Hospitality > ABIDE, STAY, REMAIN

SEE ALSO

- ▸ **4.** Beginning, Continuing, Finishing, Postponing > ENDURE, REMAIN
  menō
- ▸ **49.** Allow, Accept, Approve, Refuse > ENDURE
  tropophoreō

EQUALITY, FAIRNESS

isotēs ἰσότης 2471

isotēs is a rare noun denoting "equality" in the context of shared material prosperity in 2 Cor 8:14. In Col 4:1 the meaning "equality" carries the sense of "fairness" in relation to the just treatment of slaves.

SEE ALSO

- ▸ **88.** Qualities, Characteristics > EQUAL
  isos

FREE OF THE LOVE OF MONEY

aphilargyros ἀφιλάργυρος 866

aphilargyros is an adjective denoting those who are "free from the love of money" (1 Tim 3:3; Heb 13:5).

SEE ALSO

- ▸ **58.** Vices > COVETOUS, COVETOUSNESS, GREED, GREEDY
  pleonexia, pleonektēs, philargyros

GENTLE, GENTLENESS

epieikēs ἐπιεικής 1933

epieikēs is a rare adjectival form meaning "gentle" in relation to a kindly, patient disposition of spirit (1 Tim 3:3; Titus 3:2; Jas 3:17; 1 Pet 2:18).

ēpios ἤπιος 2261

ēpios is a rare synonym for ***epieikēs*** (above) meaning "gentle" in 1 Thess 2:7; 2 Tim 2:24.

epieikeia ἐπιείκεια 1932

epieikeia is a rare variant form of ***epieikēs*** (above) denoting the "gentleness" of Christ in Acts 24:4.

GOOD, GOODNESS, DO GOOD

agathōsynē ἀγαθωσύνη 19

agathōsynē is a rare noun found four times, indicating the virtue of "goodness" in the sense of "(moral) uprightness of heart" in Rom 15:14; Gal 5:22; Eph 5:9. See also 2 Thess 1:11.

agathopoieō ἀγαθοποιέω 15

agathopoieō is a verb found eleven times, meaning "to do good" throughout. There are a couple of nuances to note.

"Doing good" in the sense of performing an act of kindness for someone is indicated in Mark 3:4; Luke 6:9, 33ff.

"Doing good" is also predicated of God in the sense of "bestowing material blessing" on his people in Acts 14:17.

agathopoieō also means "doing good" in the sense of "living righteous lives" in accordance with God's precepts in 1 Pet 2:15ff.; 3:6, 17; 3 John 11.

agathoergeō ἀγαθοεργέω 14

agathoergeō is a rare variant of ***agathopoieō*** (above) meaning "do good" in the general sense of "acting uprightly," found only in 1 Tim 6:18.

eupoiia εὐποιΐα 2140

eupoiia is a rare noun found only in Heb 13:16, denoting the action of "doing good" in the sense of acting generously, kindly toward others.

aretē ἀρετή 703

aretē is a noun found five times denoting "virtue," "good(ness)" in Phil 4:8; 2 Pet 1:3ff.

SEE ALSO

▸ **88.** Qualities, Characteristics > GOOD, EXCELLENT, ADMIRABLE, WELL ***agathos, kalos, kalōs, eu***

HUMILITY

tapeinophrosynē ταπεινοφροσύνη 5012

tapeinophrosynē is a noun meaning "humility (of heart and mind)," "lowliness (of heart and mind)." It is found seven times.

Acts 20:19; Eph 4:2; Phil 2:3; Col 2:18; 3:12; 1 Pet 5:5 refer to the virtue of humility. A "show" of humility is mentioned in Col 2:23, in relation to corrupted human traditions of worship.

SEE ALSO

▸ **52.** Status, Identity, Reputation, Honor, Shame > HUMBLE, LOWLY ***tapeinoō, tapeinos, tapeinōsis***

KIND, KINDNESS

philanthrōpia φιλανθρωπία 5363

philanthrōpia occurs only twice, meaning "kindness." In Acts 28:2, the inhabitants of Malta show kindness to the shipwrecked party that includes the apostle Paul. Titus 3:4 speaks of the kindness of God.

chrēstos χρηστός 5543

chrēstos occurs seven times, meaning "kindness" in three of these contexts. Luke 6:35 refers to God's kindness to the ungrateful. Rom 2:4 speaks of the riches of God's kindness. Eph 4:32 contains the Pauline exhortation to be kind to one another.

chrēsteuomai χρηστεύομαι 5541

chrēsteuomai is found only in 1 Cor 13:4, where Paul declares that "love is kind."

chrēstotēs χρηστότης 5544

chrēstotēs occurs ten times and in all but one of these contexts is translated "kindness." The kindness of God is spoken of in Rom 2:4, where Paul declares that such benevolence is intended to lead one to repentance (Rom 11:22; Titus 3:4). In Eph 2:7, Paul affirms that God's kindness is supremely demonstrated to us in the person of Jesus Christ. 2 Cor 6:6; Col 3:12 refer to the virtue of human kindness, and Gal 5:22 describes such a virtue as a fruit of the Spirit.

LONG-SUFFERING

makrothymia μακροθυμία 3115

makrothymia is translated "patience," "long-suffering," with an emphasis on patient endurance in the face of provocation.

The explicit patient forbearance of God is indicated in Rom 2:4; 9:22; 1 Pet 3:20; 3:15, in the face of human sinfulness. As with the usage of the Hebrew word *'erek* in the OT with reference to God being "slow (to anger)," there is no suggestion in the usage of ***makrothymia*** that God ever waives punishment for sin. Such forbearance is also predicated of Christ in 1 Tim 1:16.

Elsewhere, ***makrothymia*** refers to the virtue of "long-suffering" or "patience" in God's people. ***makrothymia*** is included in a list of other such godly characteristics in 2 Cor 6:6; Gal 5:22; Eph 4:2; Col 1:11; 3:12. Paul declares that Timothy is aware of the apostle's patient perseverance in suffering in 2 Tim 3:10, and he exhorts him to do likewise in 2 Tim 4:2. See also Heb 6:12.

▸ **60.** Virtues > PATIENCE, PATIENT

makrothymeō μακροθυμέω 3114

makrothymeō is the verb form embodying the attitude "to be patient," "have patience," "be long-suffering." The term occurs nine times.

In one of Jesus' parables, the servant who would subsequently be condemned as ungrateful and wicked initially begs his master to be patient with him and allow him time to pay his massive debt (Matt 18:26). Another servant then approached this first servant and begged him to also be patient in allowing a much smaller debt to be repaid over time (Matt 18:29). Abraham is declared in Heb 6:15 to have "patiently endured" and so obtained the promise of covenant blessing. Love is said to "be patient" in 1 Cor 13:4. Exhortations to be "patient (in suffering)" are found in 1 Thess 5:14; Jas 5:7, 8.

makrothymeō also speaks of divine forbearance and long-suffering in Luke 18:7; 2 Pet 3:9.

▸ **60.** Virtues > PATIENCE, PATIENT

MEEK, MEEKNESS

praus πραΰς 4239

praus is an adjectival form conveying the sense of "meek," indicating an attitude of quiet, reverent, and humble submission to the will and purpose of God. ***praus*** occurs only three times. In Matt 5:5, those who are "meek" are promised the inheritance of the earth as their reward. Matt 21:5 refers to Jesus as one who is "meek" (or "humble") riding into Jerusalem on a donkey, in fulfillment of the prophecy found in Zech 9:9. In 1 Pet 3:4, the apostle commends the person in possession of a "meek" and quiet spirit, which is precious in the sight of God.

prautēs πραΰτης 4240

The noun ***prautēs*** occurs twelve times and designates the quality of "meekness," the gentle, quiet spirit of selfless devotion to God that is also translated "gentleness."

"Meekness" is the very antithesis of arrogant pride. "Meekness" appears in lists of Christian virtues in Gal 5:23; Col 3:12; 1 Tim 6:11. A "spirit of gentleness (or meekness)" is referred to in 1 Cor 4:21; Gal 6:1. Cultivating an attitude of meekness towards one another is enjoined upon believers in Eph 4:2; 2 Tim 2:25; Titus 3:2; 1 Pet 3:15. The meekness of Christ is alluded to in 2 Cor 10:1. Jas 3:13 indicates that the quality of "meekness" originates as a by-product of wisdom in the life of the believer. James also exhorts his readers to receive the word of God with "meekness."

(NOT) GROW WEARY

ekkakeō ἐκκακέω 1573

ekkakeō is a verb found six times meaning "be weary" in the sense of "grow tired" or "lose heart" (i.e., give up all hope of accomplishing one's goal or maintaining one's faith). The term is always used in the negative.

The concept of never "losing heart" or "giving up" is found in Luke 18:1; 2 Cor 4:1, 16; Eph 3:13. The virtue of never growing weary in well doing is noted in Gal 6:9; 2 Thess 3:13.

SEE ALSO

- ▸ **20.** Illness, Disease, Health, Healing > WEARY
  kamnō
- ▸ **75.** Suffering, Distress, Sadness > WEAR DOWN, WEAR OUT
  hypōpiazō
- ▸ **84.** Do, Make, Accomplish, Occur > TOIL
  kopiaō

PATIENCE, PATIENT

makrothymeō μακροθυμέω 3114

makrothymeō is a verb with the primary sense of "have patience," "be patient" in most of the occurrences in which it is found.

With regard to human beings, Matt 18:26, 29; 1 Thess 5:14 contain a plea to be patient with others. In Jas 5:7ff., the apostle exhorts his readers to be patient while awaiting the coming of the Lord. Heb 6:15 contains an exhortation to be patient in enduring persecution. 2 Pet 3:9 speaks of God's patient forbearance towards all people. Patience is listed in 1 Cor 13:4 as a key characteristic of love.

▸ **60.** Virtues > LONG-SUFFERING

makrothymia μακροθυμία 3115

makrothymia is the noun derived from ***makrothymeō*** (above), meaning "long-suffering" or "patience" in each of the fourteen places in which it is found.

"Patience" or "long-suffering" is predicated of God as one of his perfections (Rom 2:4; 9:22; 1 Pet 3:20); and also of Christ (1 Tim 1:16; 2 Pet 3:15). Such a characteristic is also true of genuine believers (2 Cor 6:6; Eph 4:2; Col 1:11; 3:12; 2 Tim 3:10; 4:2; Heb 6:12; Jas 5:10).

▸ **60.** Virtues > LONG-SUFFERING

hypomonē ὑπομονή 5281

hypomonē is a noun found in around thirty contexts meaning "patience" or "endurance."

Such a quality is predicated of believers as a key factor in producing spiritual growth and hope for the future (Luke 8:15; Rom 2:7; 5:3; 2 Cor 12:12; 1 Tim 6:11; Titus 2:2; Heb 12:1; Jas 1:4; 2 Pet 1:6). Believers are also urged to cultivate patience in the face of persecution (2 Cor 1:6; Col 1:11; Heb 10:36; Rev 1:9; 3:10; 14:12). God is likewise described as a God of patience in Rom 15:5.

anexikakos ἀνεξίκακος 420

anexikakos is an adjective meaning "patient." It occurs only in 2 Tim 2:24, with reference to teachers.

SEE ALSO

- ▸ **46.** Wait, Hope, Be Vigilant, Pay Attention To > PATIENTLY
  makrothymōs

PEACE, PEACEFUL, QUIET

eirēneuō εἰρηνεύω 1514

eirēneuō is a verb found in four contexts. On each occasion it means "to live peaceably" or "be at peace" and is used as a command or exhortation (Mark 9:50; Rom 12:18; 2 Cor 13:11; 1 Thess 5:13).

▸ **61.** Integrity, Innocence, Piety > LIVE

hēsychazō ἡσυχάζω 2270

hēsychazō is a verb found on five occasions meaning "to hold one's peace," "rest," as well as having associated meanings. In 1 Thess 4:11 it means "to live quietly" or to live at peace with one's neighbors.

- ▸ **17.** Senses, Actions, Abilities, Disabilities > SILENCE, SILENT, QUIETNESS
- ▸ **20.** Illness, Disease, Health, Healing > REST

ēremos ἤρεμος 2263

ēremos is an adjective found only in 1 Tim 2:2. It means "quiet," in the sense of "peaceful," in regard to one's lifestyle.

hēsychios ἡσύχιος 2272

hēsychios is an adjectival form occurring only twice, derived from ***hēsychazō*** (above). It means "quiet" or "peaceful" in 1 Tim 2:2; 1 Pet 3:4.

SEE ALSO

▸ **88.** Qualities, Characteristics > QUIET, CALM
katastellō

SELF-CONTROL, TEMPERANCE, SOBRIETY

enkrateia ἐγκράτεια 1466

enkrateia is a noun found in three contexts indicating the virtue of "temperance," "restraint," or "self-control." It is used in a general sense in Acts 24:25, and it is listed as a fruit of the Spirit in Gal 5:23; 2 Pet 1:6.

enkratēs ἐγκρατής 1468

enkratēs is an adjective found only in Titus 1:8, referring to the personal quality of "self-control," "temperance."

enkrateuomai ἐγκρατεύομαι 1467

enkrateuomai is a rare verb found only in 1 Cor 7:9, 25, referring to the exercise of self-control — the former in relation to sexual desire, the latter in regard to the lifestyle of the athlete.

sōphrōn σώφρων 4998

sōphrōn is an adjective, synonymous with ***enkratēs*** (above) and denoting the quality of "self-control" in 1 Tim 3:2; Titus 1:8; 2:2, 5.

sōphroneō σωφρονέω 4993

sōphroneō is a verb found seven times, meaning "to be in (one's) right mind" and "to be self-controlled." The latter sense is indicated in Titus 2:6; 1 Pet 4:7.

nēphō νήφω 3525

nēphō is another verb synonymous with ***enkrateuomai*** and ***sōphroneō*** (above). It likewise indicates "exercising self-control" or "being temperate, or sober." ***nēphō*** occurs seven times (1 Thess 5:6ff.; 2 Tim 4:5; 1 Pet 1:13; 4:7; 5:8).

nēphalios νηφάλιος 3524

nēphalios is another adjective synonymous with ***enkratēs*** and ***sōphrōn*** (above) and likewise signifyies the quality of "sobriety," "temperance," "self-control" (1 Tim 3:2, 11; Titus 2:2).

SWIFT (TO LISTEN)

tachys ταχύς 5036

tachys is an adjective found only in Jas 1:19, which contains the exhortation to be "swift to hear, and slow to speak."

SEE ALSO

▸ **21.** Die, Perish, Kill, Destroy > SWIFT
oxys, tachinos

TENDERHEARTED

eusplanchnos εὔσπλαγχνος 2155

eusplanchnos is an adjective meaning "tenderhearted" (Eph 4:32; 1 Pet 3:8).

SEE ALSO

▸ **13.** Plants, Trees, Flora > TENDER
hapalos

61. Integrity, Innocence, Piety

BLAMELESS, FAULTLESS

mōmaomai μωμάομαι 3469

mōmaomai is a rare verb meaning "to blame," "find fault with" in 2 Cor 8:20. In 2 Cor 6:3, however, the term is used negatively to mean "be blameless," "without fault."

amōmos ἄμωμος 299

amōmos is an adjective found in nine places with the consistent sense of "blameless," "without fault." This status is God's intention and purpose for his chosen people (Eph 1:4; 5:27; Phil 2:15; Col 1:22; 2 Pet 3:15; Jude 24). The saints in heaven are described as "flawless" in Rev 14:5. Heb 9:14; 1 Pet 1:19 both affirm the person of Christ as one "without blemish."

amemptos ἄμεμπτος 273

The adjective ***amemptos*** is synonymous with ***mōmaomai*** and ***amōmos*** (above) and means "blameless," "faultless."

Luke 1:6; Phil 3:6 refer to those who live "blameless" lives in accordance with God's ordinances. Heb 8:7 describes the hypothetical "blameless" nature of the first covenant. "Blameless" lives are clearly indicated as God's purpose for his people in Phil 2:15; 1 Thess 3:13.

▸ **61.** Integrity, Innocence, Piety > INNOCENCE, INNOCENT

anaitios ἀναίτιος 338

anaitios is a rare adjective synonymous with ***mōmaomai***, ***amōmos***, and ***amemptos*** (above) and denoting those who are "blameless" or "without guilt" under the law (Matt 12:5, 7).

▸ **61.** Integrity, Innocence, Piety > INNOCENCE, INNOCENT

anepilēmptos ἀνεπίλημπτος 423

The adjective ***anepilēmptos*** is found in three places denoting those who are "without reproach," "blameless" in their lifestyle — a prerequisite for those who aspire to positions of leadership in the church (1 Tim 3:2; 5:7; 6:14).

▸ **61.** Integrity, Innocence, Piety > INNOCENCE, INNOCENT

anenklētos ἀνέγκλητος 410

anenklētos is an adjective found in five places meaning "blameless," or unable to be accused. Such is the moral destiny of the people of God, made possible by the work and person of Christ (1 Cor 1:8; Col 1:22). It is also the quality required of spiritual leaders in the local congregation of believers (1 Tim 3:10; Titus 1:6, 7).

▸ **61.** Integrity, Innocence, Piety > INNOCENCE, INNOCENT

amemptōs ἀμέμπτως 274

amemptōs is an adverbial form found only twice, meaning "blameless," "without fault" — a characteristic of true believers (1 Thess 2:10; 5:23).

▸ **61.** Integrity, Innocence, Piety > INNOCENCE, INNOCENT

DEVOUT

eulabēs εὐλαβής 2126

eulabēs is an adjective meaning "devout" in all three occurrences of the term. It describes those who are godly, whose lives are characterized by wholehearted, pure worship of God (Luke 2:25; Acts 2:5; 8:2).

eusebēs εὐσεβής 2152

eusebēs is an adjectival form synonymous with ***eulabēs*** (above) referring to "devout" believers in Acts 10:2, 7; 22:12; 2 Pet 2:9.

▸ **61.** Integrity, Innocence, Piety > GODLINESS, GODLY, PIETY

sebomai σέβομαι 4576

sebomai is a verb meaning "worship" for the majority of the ten occurrences of the term. On four occasions the term is used in the participial nominal sense of "God-fearing ones," the "devout" (Acts 13:43, 50; 17:4, 17).

▸ **41.** Sacrifice, Offering, Worship, Praise > SERVE, SERVICE, WORSHIP

GODLINESS, GODLY, PIETY

eusebeia εὐσέβεια 2150

eusebeia is a noun occurring fifteen times with the predominant sense of "godliness," "piety," denoting devotion to God characterized by a life of conformity to his will, or godly living.

This virtue of "piety," "godly living" is indicated in Acts 3:12; 1 Tim 2:2; 4:7ff.; 6:3ff., 11; Titus 1:1; 2 Pet 1:3ff. 2 Tim 3:5 refers to false believers who merely adopt the form of "godliness" but deny its power.

eusebēs εὐσεβής 2152

eusebēs is a rare adjective found in four places with the consistent sense of "devout" or "godly" (Acts 10:2, 7; 22:12; 2 Pet 2:9).

▸ **61.** Integrity, Innocence, Piety > DEVOUT

eusebōs εὐσεβῶς 2153

eusebōs is a rare adverbial form of ***eusebēs*** (above) found only twice, with the sense of "godly," "devout" in 2 Tim 3:12; Titus 2:12.

HARMLESS, GUILELESS

akeraios ἀκέραιος 185

This rare term occurs only three times, meaning "harmless." Matt 10:16 signifies the desirable attitude and manner of "gentleness" and "non-hostility," through the simile "harmless as doves." Paul expresses a similar thought in

Rom 16:19: "(be) harmless concerning evil" (see also Phil 2:15).

akakos ἄκακος 172

This is another rare term that means "without evil, or harm, or guile" — that is, "harmless." ***akakos*** only occurs twice. Rom 16:18 refers to those who are "without guile," or void of harmful intent toward others. Heb 7:26 refers to Jesus as our high priest, who is totally innocent of any deceitful attitude or action.

INNOCENCE, INNOCENT

athōos ἀθῷος 121

athōos is an adjective occurring only twice, meaning "innocent," "guiltless." With reference to taking innocent blood, Matt 27:4 indicts Judas with respect to Jesus, and Matt 27:24 involves Pilate's claim to be innocent of the blood of Christ.

anaitios ἀναίτιος 338

anaitios is an adjective occurring only twice, meaning "innocent." Matt 12:5, 7 refer to priests and the "innocent" in Israel.

▸ **61.** Integrity, Innocence, Piety > BLAMELESS, FAULTLESS

amemptos ἄμεμπτος 273

amemptos is a synonym for ***athōos*** and ***anaitios*** (above) occurring five times with the underlying sense of "blameless," "faultless," "innocent."

This quality is predicated of Zechariah and Elizabeth (Luke 1:6); and of believers (Phil 2:15; 1 Thess 3:13). In Phil 3:6 it is Paul who, prior to his conversion, was accounted "blameless" or "innocent" in the eyes of Jewish law and tradition. Heb 8:7 offers the hypothesis that if nothing had been wrong with the first covenant (i.e., if it had been "innocent"), then God would not have sought to replace it with another. But that first covenant was in fact defective and needed to be superseded if full salvation was to be awarded to the people of God.

▸ **61.** Integrity, Innocence, Piety > BLAMELESS, FAULTLESS

amemptōs ἀμέμπτως 274

amemptōs is the adverbial form of ***amemptos*** (above). It is translated "blameless" or "innocent" in 1 Thess 5:23.

▸ **61.** Integrity, Innocence, Piety > BLAMELESS, FAULTLESS

anenklētos ἀνέγκλητος 410

anenklētos is another synonym for the entries above and is also translated "blameless," "innocent," with the particular underlying sense of "beyond reproach," unable to be rightfully accused of wrongdoing. ***anenklētos*** occurs five times. 1 Cor 1:18; Col 1:22 declare that true believers will be kept blameless on the final judgment day. Such a quality is also a requirement for elders and deacons (1 Tim 3:10; Titus 1:6, 7).

▸ **61.** Integrity, Innocence, Piety > BLAMELESS, FAULTLESS

anepilēmptos ἀνεπίλημπτος 423

This term is a precise synonym for ***anenklētos*** (above) and is found on three occasions. 1 Tim 3:2 lists a "blameless" or "innocent" lifestyle as an indispensable quality for appointment to the office of elder or deacon. Similarly, such a virtue is declared to be the desired goal of all of God's people in 1 Tim 5:7. 1 Tim 6:14 contains the apostle Paul's charge to Timothy to remain "beyond reproach" in carrying out his pastoral duties.

▸ **61.** Integrity, Innocence, Piety > BLAMELESS, FAULTLESS

amōmētos ἀμώμητος 298

This term occurs twice, meaning "blameless," "irreproachable" in Phil 2:15; 2 Pet 3:14, describing God's people in general.

INTEGRITY

aphthoria ἀφθορία 90

aphthoria occurs only in Titus 2:7, meaning "integrity" in the sense of a godly lifestyle consistent with one's teaching.

LIVE

politeuomai πολιτεύομαι 4176

politeuomai basically means "to live one's life" in accordance with a particular set of high moral values, or as a good citizen. This term only occurs twice and refers in both cases to living one's life worthy of the calling of God. Acts 23:1 refers to Paul's claim that he has lived before God with a clear conscience. Phil 1:27 contains the exhortation to live a life worthy of the gospel of Christ.

eirēneuō εἰρηνεύω 1514

eirēneuō means "to be, live in peace" (i.e., with others) and is found in only four places (Mark 9:50; Rom 12:18; 2 Cor 13:11; 1 Thess 5:13).

▸ **60.** Virtues > PEACE, PEACEFUL, QUIET

SEE ALSO

▸ **22.** Life, Renewal, Immortality > LIFE, LIVE, LIVING
psychē, zōē, bios, zaō, zōogoneō, syzaō, makrochronios, anazaō

▸ **34.** Craftsmanship, Artisanship, Furniture, Implements > LIFELESS
apsychos

▸ **58.** Vices > LUXURY
tryphaō

PERFECT, PERFECTION, COMPLETE

artios ἄρτιος 739

artios is a rare noun found only in 2 Tim 3:17 referring to a person of God being "complete," or equipped for every good work.

teleios τέλειος 5046

teleios is an adjective with the primary sense of "perfect" with a number of related nuances in the nineteen contexts in which it is found.

Matt 5:48 contains a dramatic command emphasizing the necessity for the believer to emulate divine perfection through cultivating consummate human integrity and virtue.

Matt 19:21 contains Jesus' command to the rich young ruler to sell all his possessions to the poor if he wants to become "perfect," to align himself in total conformity with God's will.

In Rom 12:2, Paul describes the will of God as perfect, lacking in nothing.

More commonly, ***teleios*** describes as "perfect" those who manifest a "mature Christian character" (1 Cor 2:6; 14:20; Eph 4:13; Phil 3:15; Col 1:28; Heb 5:14; Jas 1:4; 3:2).

Finally, the ascription "perfect" is applied to that which is flawless or complete in its expression or construction. This is predicated of the heavenly tabernacle (Heb 9:11; 1 Cor 13:10); of every gift from God (Jas 1:17); and of the law of God (Jas 1:25). And, in 1 John 4:18, the apostle declares that "perfect love casts out fear."

teleioō τελειόω 5048

teleioō is a verb with the primary meaning "to make perfect," with the senses of "complete," "accomplish," "fulfill."

In John 17:23, Jesus prays that his followers may be brought to "complete" or "perfect" unity. The apostle Paul affirms in 2 Cor 12:9 that power is "made perfect" in weakness. Heb 10:14; 11:40; 12:23 refer to the perfecting of the saints through the redemptive work of Christ. Jas 2:22 refers to the perfecting, or completion, of faith. The work of perfecting love in the life of the believer is noted in 1 John 2:5; 4:12ff. The possibility of attaining to moral perfection is denied in the earthly state in Phil 3:12. The law is declared powerless to make anyone perfect in Heb 7:19; 9:9; 10:1. Finally, several texts affirm that Christ has been made perfect through his suffering on behalf of his people (Heb 2:10; 5:9; 7:28).

▸ **4.** Beginning, Continuing, Finishing, Postponing > FINISH, COMPLETE, FULFILL, BRING TO AN END, COME TO AN END

▸ **84.** Do, Make, Accomplish, Occur > CARRY OUT, COMPLETE, FULFILL, ACCOMPLISH

katartizō καταρτίζω 2675

katartizō is a verb that is translated "restore," "mend," "repair," as well as "perfect," "make perfect." The term occurs fifteen times.

katartizō is used adverbially in 1 Cor 1:10 in the expression "perfectly joined together," referring to Paul's exhortation to the Corinthian congregation to manifest a greater unity of spirit. 2 Cor 13:11 contains another exhortation to the church at Corinth to "aim for perfection."

▸ **27.** Community, Partnership, Unity, Discord > RESTORE

▸ **83.** Set, Put, Place, Prepare, Establish > PREPARE, MAKE READY

teleiotēs τελειότης 5047

teleiotēs is a rare noun derived from ***teleioō*** (above) meaning "perfection." It is found only in Col 3:14, with reference to the "perfect harmony" among believers, and in Heb 6:1 referring to the state of "spiritual maturity."

SEE ALSO

▸ **20.** Illness, Disease, Health, Healing > PERFECT HEALTH
holoklēria

▸ **84.** Do, Make, Accomplish, Occur > PERFECTING
teleiōsis

▸ **88.** Qualities, Characteristics > ACCURATELY
akribēs

SINLESS

anamartētos ἀναμάρτητος 361

anamartētos is an adjective found only in John 8:7, meaning "without sin."

SEE ALSO

▸ **57.** Evil, Wickedness, Sin > SIN, SINNER, CAUSE TO SIN
hamartia, hamartanō, hamartōlos, hamartēma, skandalizō

UNABLE TO LIE

apseudēs ἀψευδής 893

apseudēs is an adjective occurring only in Titus 1:2 and translated as an adjectival clause, "who cannot lie," predicated of God.

SEE ALSO

▸ **58.** Vices > LIE, LYING, LIAR
pseustēs, pseudēs, pseusma, pseudos, pseudomai

62. Care For, Protect, Guard, Watch

CARE ABOUT, CARE FOR, TAKE CARE OF

melei μέλει 3199

melei is a verb found in thirteen places with the meaning to "care about" or "care for."

The meaning "care about" (i.e., "have a compassionate interest in") is found in Mark 4:38; Luke 10:40; 1 Cor 9:9; 1 Pet 5:7.

By way of contrast, the negative sense of "have no care for" (i.e., pay no attention to) is indicated in Acts 8:17.

epimeleomai ἐπιμελέομαι 1959

epimeleomai is a rare verb found in three places, a synonym for ***melei*** (above) meaning "to take care of" in the sense of to "see to someone's personal needs" in Luke 10:34ff. The responsibility of "caring for" the church of God is indicated in 1 Tim 3:5.

SEE ALSO

- ▸ **19.** Mind, Spirit, Emotions, Feelings, Desires > CARE, WORRY, ANXIETY
  merimna, merimnaō
- ▸ **46.** Wait, Hope, Be Vigilant, Pay Attention To > CAREFUL
  phrontizō

COMFORT, COMFORTER, CONSOLATION, ENCOURAGEMENT

parakaleō παρακαλέω 3870

parakaleō is a verb occurring over one hundred times with the primary meanings "exhort" and "comfort."

The meaning "offer comfort" is indicated in several contexts. Such comfort is forthcoming in the face of persecution or catastrophe in Matt 2:18; 5:4; 2 Cor 1:4ff. The penitent sinner benefits from such comfort in 2 Cor 2:7.

There are exhortations to "comfort" or "encourage" one's fellow believers in 1 Thess 4:18; 5:11.

The passive sense of "be comforted" is indicated in relation to the support received through the faith of one's congregation in 1 Thess 3:7. The experience of comfort is offered in the aftermath of suffering in Luke 16:25; Acts 20:12. 2 Cor 7:13 mentions "being comforted" by God.

In 2 Cor 7:6 God is said to "comfort" the downcast.

- ▸ **65.** Teach, Exhort, Rebuke, Discipline > EXHORT, EXHORTATION, BESEECH, URGE
- ▸ **66.** Ask, Answer, Discuss, Learn > ASK, REQUEST, BEG, PLEAD

paraklēsis παράκλησις 3874

paraklēsis is a noun derived from ***parakaleō*** (above) denoting "consolation," "encouragement," "comfort."

Metaphorical reference to the "consolation of Israel" denotes the coming Messiah, who would bring comfort to Israel (Luke 2:25).

The designation "Son of Encouragement" is a name for Barnabas recorded in Acts 4:36.

paraklēsis denotes the literal sense of "(material) comfort" in Luke 6:24.

Elsewhere, this term denotes comfort that is intangible or spiritual. For example, Phil 2:1 describes the "comfort" and encouragement found in Christ. The spiritual "comfort" of the Holy Spirit is noted in Acts 9:31, as well as that offered by God in 2 Cor 1:3, 7; 2 Thess 2:16. "Comfort" derived from the Scriptures is indicated in Rom 15:4. "Comfort" gained from Christian fellowship is noted in 2 Cor 7:7, 13; Phlm 7.

- ▸ **65.** Teach, Exhort, Rebuke, Discipline > EXHORT, EXHORTATION, BESEECH, URGE

paraklētos παράκλητος 3875

paraklētos is a rare noun derived from ***parakaleō*** (above) referring mainly to the person of the Holy Spirit. A precise translation of ***paraklētos*** is difficult to determine. The underlying sense of the term is that of "one who stands alongside another in order to offer encouragement, comfort." It is generally conceded that the legal connotation of "advocate" also constitutes a likely understanding of ***paraklētos***. The four contexts in which this term appears (John 14:16, 26; 15:26; 16:7) suggest that the role attributed to the Holy Spirit is that of either "Counselor" or "Advocate." Christ describes the Holy Spirit's mission as one of revealing truth, convicting of sin, and applying the context of Jesus' teaching to the lives of his disciples. Clearly the function of the Holy Spirit is to enable the people of God, individually and corporately, to maintain a vital relationship with God through his personal indwelling presence. Thus the designations "Advocate" and "Counselor," while accurate, are not comprehensive. No one English term expresses the full semantic range of ***paraklētos***.

paramythia παραμυθία 3889

paramythia is a rare term denoting "comfort" as one of the intended consequences of genuine prophecy for those who listened. It is found only in 1 Cor 14:3.

paramytheomai παραμυθέομαι 3888

paramytheomai is a verb found only four times, meaning offer "comfort" or "consolation" in the case of a bereavement in John 11:19, 31, and "encourage" in the general sense of "offer helpful advice" in 1 Thess 2:11; 5:14.

parēgoria παρηγορία 3931

parēgoria is a rare noun denoting "comfort" in the sense of "encouragement" found only in Col 4:11.

COMPASSION

oikteirō οἰκτείρω 3627

oikteirō is a rare verb found only twice, in Rom 9:15, as part of the promise that God will have compassion on whom he will have compassion — that is, affirming God's sovereignty in the dispensing of his mercy.

- ▸ **44.** Repentance, Forgiveness, Mercy, Redeem, Save > MERCY, MERCIFUL, COMPASSION, PITY

splanchnizomai σπλαγχνίζομαι 4697

splanchnizomai is a verb found in twelve places with the consistent sense of "have compassion," "be moved with compassion."

People "moved with compassion" for others are noted in Matt 18:27; Luke 10:33; 15:20.

Christ is depicted as one "moved with compassion" for the crowds following him in Matt 9:36; 14:14; 15:32; Mark 6:34; 8:2; as well as for those afflicted with illness or incapacity prior to healing (Matt 20:34; Mark 1:41). See also Luke 7:13. In Mark 9:22, a demon-possessed man pleads for Jesus to have pity and help him.

DEFEND

amynō ἀμύνω 292

amynō is a rare verb found only in Acts 7:24, referring to Moses "defending" his fellow countryman against assault by an Egyptian soldier.

GUARD, GUARDIAN, WATCH OVER, PROTECT

phylassō φυλάσσω 5442

phylassō is a verb meaning "guard," "keep watch over," "keep under guard," as well as the general sense of "keep," "obey."

Luke 2:8 refers to "keeping watch over" a flock of sheep.

Luke 8:29 refers to an outcast demoniac "being kept under guard." The "guarding" of prisoners is indicated in Acts 12:4; 23:35; 28:16.

The precaution of "guarding" one's house and property is indicated in Luke 11:21.

▸ **69.** Have, Possess, Hold, Grasp, Bear, Carry > KEEP

diaphylassō διαφυλάσσω 1314

diaphylassō is a rare variant of ***phylassō*** (above). It is found only in Luke 4:10 and means "to guard" in relation to the divine promise that God will give his angels the task of "watching over," or protecting, his people.

phroureō φρουρέω 5432

phroureō is a verb found only four times, expressing the literal sense of "guarding" the city of Damascus in 2 Cor 11:32. The rest of the usage is metaphorical. Gal 3:23 refers to believers "being guarded" under the law until faith "released" them from that confinement. Phil 4:7 affirms that the peace of God "will guard" (i.e., protect) the hearts and minds of believers in Christ. In 1 Pet 1:5, believers are said to "be guarded" through faith in readiness for their future salvation in glory.

▸ **69.** Have, Possess, Hold, Grasp, Bear, Carry > KEEP

epitropos ἐπίτροπος 2012

epitropos is a rare noun found in three places denoting both a "steward" and a "guardian." The latter sense is indicated only in Gal 4:2, referring to legal "guardians" placed as supervisors of those who have not yet become eligible for their inheritance. The sense of "steward" may also imply a role of guardianship or care for members of a family, or a household (Matt 20:8; Luke 8:3).

▸ **55.** Bondage, Captivity, Servitude > STEWARD, OVERSEER, DIRECTOR, TRUSTEE, GUARDIAN

HELP, HELPER

boētheō βοηθέω 997

This verb occurs eight times, meaning "help," "bring help" in all instances.

In 2 Cor 6:2 Paul quotes from Isa 49:8, affirming that God had extended help to his people in former times. Acts 16:9 records an angelic plea from the "man of Macedonia" for Paul to come and bring help to the Macedonian church.

In reference to the person and work of Christ, several places in the Gospels record pleas to Jesus for help (Matt 15:25; Mark 9:22, 24). Heb 2:18 mentions Jesus' ability to help his people as their great high priest.

Acts 21:28 refers to a plea for Jews to help ruin the ministry of Paul. And in Rev 12:14, in a spectacular vision of spiritual and earthly conflict, the earth comes to the help of the woman under attack from the dragon.

antilambanō ἀντιλαμβάνω 482

This verb is rare, occurring only three times and meaning "help" or "support" in two of these contexts. Luke 1:54 records that God's help is given to Israel; and Acts 20:35 contains Paul's exhortation for believers to help the weak.

syllambanō συλλαμβάνω 4815

syllambanō means "to take," "seize," or "conceive" in the majority of its sixteen occurrences. On two occasions it means "help." Luke 5:7 refers to help being given to pull in a huge catch of fish. Phil 4:3 records Paul's request to the Philippians to help those who labor in the gospel.

▸ **15.** Gender, Reproduction, Youth, Aging > CONCEIVE
▸ **70.** Give, Take, Seize, Touch > APPREHEND, SEIZE, CAPTURE, ARREST

synantilambanō συναντιλαμβάνω 4878

This term is also rare, occurring only twice. In Luke 10:40 it refers to Martha's demand for her sister, Mary, to help her. In Rom 8:26 Paul indicates that the Spirit of God helps us in our weakness.

boēthos βοηθός 998

boēthos is found only in Heb 13:6, where it refers to the Lord as our helper.

NEGLECT, NEGLIGENCE, NEGLIGENT

ameleō ἀμελέω 272

ameleō is a rare verb found in only four places, meaning "to neglect," "show negligence," "be negligent." Human negligence is indicated in Matt 22:5; and Heb 8:9 refers to divine negligence of Israel — a deliberate act of judicial neglect for the people's violation of their covenant responsibilities towards God. In 1 Tim 4:14, Paul instructs

Timothy not to neglect the gifts of ministry given to him by the Spirit of God. Heb 2:3 warns of the dire spiritual consequences of neglecting one's salvation in Christ.

paratheōreō παραθεωρέω 3865

paratheōreō occurs only in Acts 6:1, referring to the Hellenistic believers' complaint that the widows in their community were being neglected in the daily distribution of food.

PRESERVE

syntēreō συντηρέω 4933

syntēreō is a verb found in four places, meaning "preserve" in Matt 9:17 with reference to the preservation of fresh wineskins.

SEE ALSO

- ▸ **22.** Life, Renewal, Immortality > PRESERVE
  zōogoneō

PROVIDE FOR, TAKE CARE OF

pronoeō προνοέω 4306

This verb form occurs only three times with the meaning "provide for" in the sense of "take care of" one's family in 1 Tim 5:8. Rom 12:7 refers to "being careful" not to repay evil for evil.

SPARE

pheidomai φείδομαι 5339

pheidomai is a verb found twelve times with the primary meaning "spare," with the underlying sense of "keeping from harm, or emotional hurt" (1 Cor 7:28; 2 Cor 1:23).

The term is also used negatively to indicate a desire not to preserve from harm. For example, Acts 20:29 refers to cruel leaders of God's people who will abuse (i.e., "not spare") the flock. Rom 8:32 affirms that God refused to spare his own Son from death in order to fully accomplish his plan of salvation for humankind. See also 2 Pet 2:4, 5.

SEE ALSO

- ▸ **23.** Food, Drink, Cooking > SPARE
  perisseuō

VISIT

episkeptomai ἐπισκέπτομαι 1980

episkeptomai is a verb meaning "visit" in several different senses. It occurs eleven times and refers to "paying someone a visit" in order to offer care, support, and help for the sick or imprisoned (Matt 25:36, 43; Acts 15:36; Jas 1:27); or to ascertain their well-being, as was Moses' intention in "visiting" his own people in Egypt (Acts 7:23). God is also said to "care for" human beings, his own creation (Heb 2:6).

God is said to "have visited his people" by sending them his son, Jesus Christ, to accomplish their salvation (Luke 1:68; 7:16) as well as the salvation of a people chosen from the Gentiles (Acts 15:14).

SEE ALSO

- ▸ **24.** Dwell, Live, Gather, Hospitality > VISIT, VISITATION
  historeō
- ▸ **32.** Law, Justice, Jurisprudence, Judgment > VISIT (IN JUDGMENT)
  episkopē

63. Speak, Tell, Declare, Call

ANNOUNCE, MAKE KNOWN

anangellō ἀναγγέλλω 312

anangellō is a verb occurring eighteen times with the underlying meaning "tell" in the sense of "announce," "make known," "report."

The action of "making known," "announcing (information)" is indicated in several places, with reference to spreading the news of Jesus' miraculous signs in Mark 5:14, 19; the deeds of God in Acts 14:27; 15:4; the "whole counsel of God" in Acts 20:27; and "reporting" to the authorities in Acts 16:38. See also Rom 15:21.

The phenomenon of the "revealing," "announcing" of all things by the Messiah is indicated in John 4:25. In related contexts, spiritual truth is said to be "revealed" to the believer by the Holy Spirit (John 16:13ff.; 1 Pet 1:12). See also 1 John 1:5.

▸ **63.** Speak, Tell, Declare, Call > TELL

BOAST, BOASTING

kauchaomai καυχάομαι 2744

kauchaomai is a verb occurring around forty times with the senses of "glory in," "boast about," "rejoice in." These three meanings overlap to some degree. This term indicates both positive and negative connotations of boasting.

"Boasting" about one's faithful observance of Jewish law as ameans of gaining right standing before God is an attitude condemned in Rom 2:17, 23. 2 Cor 5:12 condemns boasting in one's self-righteousness. 1 Cor 1:29 warns against boasting in the presence of God. Vain or arrogant boasting is noted in 2 Cor 11:12, 16ff., 30; Gal 6:13; Eph 2:9; Jas 4:16.

In positive contexts, 1 Cor 1:31; 10:13ff.; Gal 6:14 speak of "boasting" in the goodness of God. Phil 3:3 refers to "rejoicing" or "boasting" in Christ. Similarly, "rejoicing" (or boasting) in one's growth in grace, as a blessing from God, is indicated in 2 Cor 7:14; 9:2; 2 Thess 1:4. Paradoxically, Paul "boasts" of his own weakness in 2 Cor 12:9.

Other general references to boasting are found in 1 Cor 3:21; 2 Cor 10:16; 12:1ff.; Jas 1:9.

▸ **19.** Mind, Spirit, Emotions, Feelings, Desires > JOY, JOYFUL, REJOICE, GLADNESS

kauchēma καύχημα 2745

kauchēma is a noun found eleven times meaning "boasting" or "rejoicing in."

Boasting from a purely human perspective, and therefore illegitimate in God's sight, is indicated in 1 Cor 5:6. By way of contrast, legitimate "boasting" or "rejoicing in" the goodness of God is referred to in 2 Cor 1:14; 5:12; 9:3; Phil 1:26; 2:16; Heb 3:6. Other general references include 1 Cor 9:15ff.; Gal 6:4.

kauchēsis καύχησις 2746

kauchēsis is synonymous with ***kauchēma*** (above) and denotes the act of "boasting" or "rejoicing" in twelve contexts. Boasting in one's righteousness is rendered null and void on the principle of faith in Rom 3:27. Vain, arrogant boasting is indicated in Jas 4:16.

Positively expressed, "rejoicing" in one's ministry in Christ is noted in Rom 15:17; 2 Cor 1:12. 1 Cor 15:31 speaks of "boasting" or "rejoicing" in Christ. "Rejoicing" in the spiritual growth and maturity of one's flock, or congregation, and one's fellow workers, is a characteristic of the apostle Paul's letters in 2 Cor 7:4, 14; 8:24; 11:10; 1 Thess 2:19. See also 2 Cor 11:17.

SEE ALSO

▸ **58.** Vices > BOAST, BOASTING, ARROGANCE
katakauchaomai, megalaucheō, alazōn, alazoneia

CALL, CALLED, CALLING, SUMMON, NAME

kaleō καλέω 2564

kaleō is a verb found around 150 times indicating the primary sense of "call" with several related nuances in a variety of contexts. It is used of both human beings and God.

Commonly, ***kaleō*** expresses the meaning "call" in the sense of "giving someone or something a name." The "naming" of Jesus is indicated in Matt 1:21ff.; 2:23; Luke 1:31ff. In particular, he is "called" the "Son of God" in Luke 1:35; "Faithful and True" in Rev 19:1; and "Word of God" in Rev 19:13. See also Luke 1:13, 60 in relation to John the Baptist. Peacemakers are called "sons of God" in Matt 5:9. Reference is made to Abraham being called the "friend of God" in Jas 2:23. See also John 1:42. Satan is given the alternate name of "Beelzebub" in Matt 10:25. The naming of places and towns is indicated, for example, in Luke 7:11; 23:33; Acts 1:12; 9:11; Rev 12:9.

Another common denotation for this verb is that of "summon," "invite." General references to this usage include Matt 22:3ff.; Luke 14:7ff.; John 2:22; Acts 4:18; 1 Cor 10:27. With this sense Christ is said to "call" the righteous to repentance in Matt 9:13; Mark 2:17; Luke 5:32; and he "calls" people to follow him as his disciples in Mark 1:20. See also John 10:3. Elsewhere, God is the subject of ***kaleō*** — for example, Heb 11:8 refers to God "calling" Abram out of Ur. God also "calls" his people to peace in 1 Cor 7:15. Paul notes his "calling" to be an apostle in 1 Cor 15:9, with the implication of divine calling.

Other uses of ***kaleō*** with God as the subject include God "calling" things into existence, or employing his creative power, in Rom 4:17. Of particular significance are references to God "calling" people into a relationship with himself, initiating the conversion experience (Rom 8:30; 9:11, 24; 1 Cor 1:9; Gal 1:6, 15; Eph 4:1ff.; 1 Thess 2:12; 2 Thess 2:14; 1 Tim 6:12; 2 Tim 1:9; Heb 9:15; 1 Pet 1:15; 2:9; 5:10). Then, in Rom 9:25ff. (citing Hos 2), God is said to "call" his people (i.e., give them a new name) and restore them to divine favor.

The meaning "cry out" is indicated in Matt 4:21.

▸ **24.** Dwell, Live, Gather, Hospitality > INVITE

epikaleō ἐπικαλέω 1941

epikaleō is a verb found thirty times with the senses of "call on, upon" and "be called" (i.e., be given a name).

References to "calling upon" the name of the Lord in the contexts of worship and prayer are found in Acts 2:21; 7:59; 9:14; 22:16; Rom 10:12ff.; 2 Tim 2:22; 1 Pet 1:17. "Calling on" the name of Christ is noted in Acts 9:21; 1 Cor 1:2. Paul exercises his prerogative to "call upon" or "make (legal) appeal to" Caesar in Acts 25:11ff.; 28:19. "Making appeal" to God is noted in 2 Cor 1:23.

epikaleō also indicates the passive sense of "be called" (i.e., "named") in relation to people in Acts 10:18, 32; 12:12, 25; 15:22. In Heb 11:16 it is affirmed that God is not ashamed "to be called" the God of his people.

▸ **32.** Law, Justice, Jurisprudence, Judgment > APPEAL

metakaleō μετακαλέω 3333

metakaleō is a verb found four times with the meaning "to call for" or "summon" individuals (Acts 7:14; 10:32; 20:17; 24:25).

proskaleomai προσκαλέομαι 4341

The verb ***proskaleomai***, a synonym for ***metakaleō*** (above), is found in thirty places with the meaning "to call to," "summon" people for a particular purpose. Jesus "calls" people to himself in Matt 15:10, 32; 18:2; 20:25; Mark 3:13; Luke 18:16. Acts 2:39 refers to God "calling" people to himself. The Spirit of God is said to "call" Saul and Barnabas into the work of the gospel in Acts 13:2; 16:10.

General references to people "calling others to themselves" are found in Matt 18:32; Luke 7:19; Acts 5:40; 6:2; 20:1; Jas 5:14.

synkaleō συγκαλέω 4779

synkaleō is another synonym for the above entries, meaning "call together," "assemble" in the contexts of summoning people. It is found eight times (Mark 15:16; Luke 9:1; 15:6ff.; 23:13; Acts 5:21; 10:24; 28:17).

phōneō φωνέω 5455

phōneō is a verb occurring about forty times with the predominant meaning to "call, cry out" as well as to "summon."

The sense of "call, cry out" is indicated, for example, in Matt 20:32; Mark 15:35; Luke 8:8; 23:46; John 1:48; Acts 16:28; Rev 14:18.

The action of "summoning" people is indicated in Mark 9:35; 14:12; Luke 19:5; John 2:9; 4:16; Acts 9:41. Jesus' action of "calling Lazarus up from the dead" is noted in John 12:17.

▸ **24.** Dwell, Live, Gather, Hospitality > INVITE

legō λέγω 3004

legō is a common verb occurring over 1,300 times with the dominant sense of "say," "speak." However, in a number of cases ***legō*** means "call," primarily in the passive sense of "be called," "named."

General references to peoples' names are noted in Matt 4:18; 10:2; Acts 9:36; and particular reference to the naming of Christ is made in Matt 1:16; John 9:11; Col 4:11; Heb 7:11; 11:24. Rev 8:11 mentions the naming of the star "Wormwood." See also 1 Cor 8:5.

Elsewhere, general references to the naming of places include Matt 27:16; John 4:5; 19:13ff.; Acts 3:2. Other uses of ***legō*** with this sense are found in relation to Gethsemane in Matt 26:36; to the Passover feast in Luke 22:1; and to the holy place of the temple in Heb 9:2ff.

There is a metaphorical use of ***legō*** in Eph 2:11 where Gentiles are "called" the "uncircumcision."

▸ **63.** Speak, Tell, Declare, Call > SAY, SPEAK
▸ **63.** Speak, Tell, Declare, Call > TELL

klēsis κλῆσις 2821

klēsis is a noun derived from ***kaleō*** (above) found in eleven contexts and denoting the primary sense of "calling" or "vocation."

The meaning "vocation," "call" in a general sense is found in 1 Cor 7:20.

More significantly the "calling" of God, that is the irresistible summons of God extended to those whom he desires to save, is indicated in Rom 11:29; 1 Cor 1:26; Eph 1:18; 4:1ff.; Phil 3:14; 2 Tim 1:9; Heb 3:1; 2 Pet 1:10.

klētos κλητός 2822

klētos is an adjective derived from the verb ***kaleō*** (above) found eleven times with the meaning "called."

The state of being "called" by God, implying sovereign divine election in the context of salvation, is indicated in Matt 20:16; 22:14; Rom 1:6ff.; 8:28; Jude 1; Rev 17:14. Then, in Rom 1:1; 1 Cor 1:1ff., 24, Paul indicates that he was "called" by God to be an apostle.

DECLARE, DECLARATION

exēgeomai ἐξηγέομαι 1834

exēgeomai is a verb found in six places, meaning "report," "make a declaration." It is used in relation to narrating events or circumstances in Luke 24:35; Acts 10:8. Acts 15:12, 14; 21:19 record the "declaring" or "reporting" of God's miraculous deeds and signs among his people. Specifically, John 1:18 affirms that God has "made Jesus known" to the world — that is, he has made Christ the subject of a divine declaration.

horizō ὁρίζω 3724

horizō is a verb found in eight contexts with the primary sense of "ordain," "predetermine" throughout. However, in Rom 1:4 the apostle affirms that Jesus Christ "was declared" by God to be his Son through his resurrection from the dead.

▸ **48.** Will, Purpose, Decide, Advise > DETERMINE, PREDETERMINE, FOREORDAIN
▸ **83.** Set, Put, Place, Prepare, Establish > APPOINT, ORDAIN, ASSIGN

FAREWELL

chairō χαίρω 5463

chairō is a verb with the primary sense of "rejoice," as well as related nuances, for most of its nearly eighty occurrences. However, in 2 Cor 13:11 ***chairō*** expresses the salutation "farewell" or "goodbye."

- ▸ **19.** Mind, Spirit, Emotions, Feelings, Desires > JOY, JOYFUL, REJOICE, GLADNESS
- ▸ **63.** Speak, Tell, Declare, Call > GREET, GREETING

apotassomai ἀποτάσσομαι 657

apotassomai is a verb found six times, meaning "bid farewell," "take leave" in most of these contexts. Such farewells are found in Mark 6:46; Luke 9:61; Acts 18:18ff.; 2 Cor 2:13.

GREET, GREETING

aspazomai ἀσπάζομαι 782

aspazomai is a verb found in sixty places with the dominant sense of "greet."

"Greeting" one's fellow believers is indicated in Matt 5:47; Acts 21:7; 1 Pet 5:13. Exhortations to do so are found in Rom 16:3ff.; 2 Cor 13:12; Phil 4:21ff.; Col 4:15; 1 Pet 5:14. "Extending a greeting" to a household is indicated in Matt 10:12.

References to "greeting" people in general contexts are found in Mark 9:15; Luke 1:40; Acts 25:13.

aspazomai also denotes the action of "calling out" or "addressing" someone. The soldiers' mocking salutation of Christ, "Hail, King of the Jews," is recorded in Mark 15:18.

The term is translated "take leave of" or "say goodbye" in Acts 20:1, implying the act of embracing in the ritual of farewell.

aspasmos ἀσπασμός 783

aspasmos is the noun derived from ***aspazomai*** (above) and denotes "greetings" throughout the ten occurrences of the term (Matt 23:7; Mark 12:38; Luke 1:29, 41ff.; 11:43; 20:46). In particular, 1 Cor 16:21; Col 4:18; 2 Thess 3:17 refer to Paul writing his own greeting.

chairō χαίρω 5463

chairō is a verb with the predominant meaning "to rejoice" throughout its nearly eighty occurrences. However, in Acts 15:23; 23:26; Jas 1:1, the term denotes the expression of a formal greeting in literary correspondence.

- ▸ **19.** Mind, Spirit, Emotions, Feelings, Desires > JOY, JOYFUL, REJOICE, GLADNESS
- ▸ **63.** Speak, Tell, Declare, Call > FAREWELL

LANGUAGE

dialektos διάλεκτος 1258

dialektos is the sole term in the NT referring to the phenomenon of language. It occurs six times and is translated "language," "tongue," "speech."

Acts 1:19 refers to the language of Aramaic in the expression *akeldama*, indicating the "field of blood" where Judas threw away the thirty pieces of silver gained as the price of betraying Jesus Christ to the Jewish authorities. Specific human languages are indicated in Acts 2:6, 8 on the occasion of the Pentecost miracle, where many nations simultaneously heard the sermon of Peter in their own tongue. The Hebrew language is referred to in Acts 21:40; 22:2, where Paul's speech to the Jerusalem crowd is recorded; and also in Acts 26:14 in Christ's words to Saul during his conversion experience on the road to Damascus.

- ▸ **63.** Speak, Tell, Declare, Call > TONGUE

REPORT, FAME

phēmē φήμη 5345

phēmē is a rare noun occurring only twice and denoting "fame" in the sense of "news" or a "report" that emerged in the wake of Jesus raising the synagogue ruler's daughter from the dead (Matt 9:26). A general "report" of Jesus' unique activity and ministry is indicated in Luke 4:14.

akoē ἀκοή 189

akoē is a noun found approximately twenty-five times with the primary sense of "hearing," as well as a number of associated meanings, one of which is "report." This meaning is found twice, in John 12:38; Rom 10:16, where it refers to the message proclaimed by the prophet Isaiah (Isa 53:1).

- ▸ **16.** Body, Bodily Functions > EAR
- ▸ **17.** Senses, Actions, Abilities, Disabilities > HEAR, HEARING, LISTEN
- ▸ **52.** Status, Identity, Reputation, Honor, Shame > FAME
- ▸ **63.** Speak, Tell, Declare, Call > RUMOR

apangellō ἀπαγγέλλω 518

apangellō is a verb with the primary sense of "tell" in the large majority of its fifty occurrences. However, in a number of places it is translated "report," with the underlying sense of "convey a message." There is considerable overlap in meaning with that of "tell" (Acts 4:23; 5:22; 16:36; 23:16ff.; 1 Thess 1:9).

- ▸ **63.** Speak, Tell, Declare, Call > TELL

RUMOR

akoē ἀκοή 189

akoē is a noun found in approximately twenty-five contexts with the fundamental sense of "hearing." It is derived from the verb ***akouō*** and is variously translated as "hearing," "news," "fame," "report," "rumor."

The meaning "rumor" indicates essentially the same sense as "report," though with the less formal nuance of "hearsay." This usage is illustrated in Matt 24:6; Mark 13:7, in the context of Jesus' discourse on the signs of the end times where he warns that there will be, among other things, "wars and rumors of war."

- ▸ **16.** Body, Bodily Functions > EAR

- ▸ **17.** Senses, Actions, Abilities, Disabilities > HEAR, HEARING, LISTEN
- ▸ **52.** Status, Identity, Reputation, Honor, Shame > FAME
- ▸ **63.** Speak, Tell, Declare, Call > REPORT, FAME

SAY, SPEAK

legō λέγω 3004

legō occurs over 1,300 times with the primary meanings "say," "speak," divided in usage between human and divine verbal communication.

The verbal expression of God is illustrated in the context of passing judgment on the wicked (Luke 12:20); speaking to Moses (Mark 12:26); and commending Christ as his Son (Matt 17:5; 22:44; Luke 3:22).

Christ addresses Satan in rebuke (Matt 4:7; Luke 4:8). He also speaks to those whom he cures of disease or raises back to life (Matt 8:13; Mark 10:52; John 11:39; Luke 7:14); to his disciples in the course of their instruction (Matt 14:16); to the crowds listening to his teaching discourses (Matt 19:11ff.; Mark 6:4; John 13:31); to those who are prospective disciples (Matt 8:22; Mark 1:17); and to those he seeks to evangelize (John 4:17). He also personally addresses his Father in prayer (John 11:41; 17:1); and he prays for the forgiveness of those who put him to death (Luke 23:34).

legō also indicates angelic verbal communication with human beings, especially in relation to announcing Christ's birth to Mary (Luke 1:30ff.). See also Luke 1:13; 2:10; Acts 12:8; Rev 4:1; 17:7. Satan himself also engages Christ in conversation during the time of the latter's "trial" in the wilderness (Matt 4:3; Luke 4:6).

The phrase "It is said . . ." refers in Heb 4:7; 11:18 to the authority of Scripture.

In a number of contexts, various individuals address Jesus Christ. For example, people ask him questions in Matt 8:19ff.; Mark 2:16; Luke 6:2. Peter speaks with the risen Christ in a vision in Acts 10:2. The Pharisees blaspheme against him in Matt 9:34; Luke 11:15. Judas speaks in order to betray him in Matt 26:25. A request for salvation is made of him in Luke 23:42.

Ordinary human discourse is indicated in Matt 20:4, Mark 1:37; Luke 9:9; Acts 2:13.

- ▸ **63.** Speak, Tell, Declare, Call > CALL, CALLED, CALLING, SUMMON, NAME
- ▸ **63.** Speak, Tell, Declare, Call > TELL

laleō λαλέω 2980

laleō is a synonym for ***legō*** (above). It occurs around three hundred times with the primary sense of "speak," "say." Again the usage is divided between divine and human verbal expression.

God is declared to have spoken to Moses (John 9:29); to the patriarchs (Luke 1:55); and to the prophets (Acts 3:21; 23:9; Luke 1:70). In Heb 1:1, the fulfillment of God's spoken word is expressed in the person of his Son, Jesus Christ. The angel of the Lord speaks to Philip the evangelist in Acts 8:26 in order to redirect his ministry.

In the context of Christ's teaching ministry, he speaks to the people of Israel (Matt 26:47; John 8:12, 30). He also speaks in parables (Matt 13:33ff.; 22:1; Mark 4:33). Jesus speaks to his Father in prayer in John 17:1.

Human verbal discourse is indicated in Acts 6:10, with reference to speaking godly wisdom; and in Acts 19:6; 1 Cor 14:5, in relation to speaking in tongues. Acts 4:31 refers to the disciples of Christ speaking the word of God boldly. John 12:41 indicates that Isaiah spoke of Christ. See also Acts 16:13.

- ▸ **43.** Prophecy, Preaching, Proclamation > PREACH, PREACHING
- ▸ **63.** Speak, Tell, Declare, Call > TELL

phēmi φημί 5346

phēmi is a synonym for ***legō*** and ***laleō*** (above), a verb with the primary sense of "say" or "declare," found in around sixty places. The contexts often suggest an underlying nuance of a solemn affirmation or declaration borne of deep conviction or divine authority.

In relation to Christ speaking, for example, Matt 4:7 affirms the authority of the written word of God, as Christ's rebuke to Satan. Christ is said to instruct his people in the gospel (Matt 19:21); and he is involved in teaching his disciples (Matt 17:26). He is recorded as speaking a prophetic word (Matt 26:34); and he acknowledges his royal status to Pilate (Matt 27:11).

References to general human discourse are found in Matt 13:28; 14:8; Luke 22:58. Instances of preaching are found in Acts 2:38; 7:2; 17:22. Peter affirms his loyalty to Christ in Mark 14:29. A profession of faith in Christ is indicated in John 9:38. The formula "It is said . . ." in relation to the authority of Scripture is indicated in 1 Cor 6:16.

SEND FOR

metapempō μεταπέμπω 3343

metapempō is a verb found eight times meaning "send for" or "call for someone" (Acts 10:5, 22, 29; 11:13; 24:24, 26; 25:3).

SEE ALSO

- ▸ **11.** Meteorology, Water > SEND RAIN
  brechō
- ▸ **79.** Throw, Send, Drive, Mix, Remove > SEND, SEND AWAY, SEND OUT
  apostellō, exapostellō, synapostellō, pempō, anapempō, sympempō, ekballō, apolyō

SHOUT

epiphōneō ἐπιφωνέω 2019

epiphōneō is a verb found three times, meaning "cry," "shout out," in each case. The angry shout of a crowd demanding punishment for Jesus Christ at his trial is indicated in Luke 23:21; and also in Acts 22:24 in relation to Paul. See also Acts 12:22.

- ▸ **16.** Body, Bodily Functions > CRY, CRY OUT, SHOUT

keleusma κέλευσμα 2752

keleusma is a rare noun found only in 1 Thess 4:16, referring to the "shout" of the archangel announcing the return of the Lord on the final day of judgment.

SOUND

phōnē φωνή 5456

phōnē is a noun found in approximately 140 places with the dominant sense of "voice." In a few contexts, however, it is translated "sound." ***phōnē*** refers to a trumpet sound (Matt 24:31); to the sound of a trumpet likened to a "voice" (Rev 1:10; 4:1); to the "sound" of the wind (John 3:8); and to the "sound" of the Holy Spirit coming upon the disciples of Christ, likened to a rushing wind (Acts 2:6). See also Rev 1:15; 9:9.

▸ **17.** Senses, Actions, Abilities, Disabilities > VOICE

salpizō σαλπίζω 4537

salpizō is a verb occurring twelve times, referring to "sounding a trumpet" in Matt 6:2; 1 Cor 15:52. In Rev 8:6ff.; 9:1, 13; 11:15, trumpets are "sounded" by angels in a cycle of judgment against the wickedness of humankind.

▸ **63.** Speak, Tell, Declare, Call > TRUMPET

ēchos ἦχος 2279

ēchos is a rare noun, occurring three times with reference to "sound" or "noise" in Acts 2:2 (rushing wind); Heb 12:19 (a trumpet).

SEE ALSO

▸ **20.** Illness, Disease, Health, Healing > SOUND, HEALTHY
hygiainō

▸ **29.** Boats, Fishing, Maritime Activity > SOUND, TAKE A SOUNDING
bolizō

SPREAD

diaphēmizō διαφημίζω 1310

diaphēmizō is a verb occurring three times with the primary sense of "spread abroad." It refers to spreading fame (Matt 9:31); and news, or a report (Matt 28:15; Mark 1:45).

SEE ALSO

▸ **43.** Prophecy, Preaching, Proclamation > SPREAD
dianemō

▸ **79.** Throw, Send, Drive, Mix, Remove > SPREAD OUT
strōnnymi

TELL

legō λέγω 3004

legō is a common verb occurring over 1,300 times with the dominant senses of "say," "speak." However, the meaning "tell" is evident in a number of places.

legō means "tell" in relation to conveying news and messages in Matt 10:27; Mark 1:30; Luke 24:10; Phil 3:18; 2 Thess 2:5. In Acts 17:21, ***legō*** describes the process of "discussing" novel philosophies in the context of Athenian society.

legō also means "tell" with the underlying sense of "state," "declare." In Matt 10:27; Mark 8:30, Jesus issues a command to his followers to tell no one that he is the Christ. Then, in Mark 10:32, Jesus "informs" his disciples what will happen to him as he comes to the end of his earthly life. Jesus also frequently declares, "I tell you . . ." (Luke 12:51; 13:3; 18:8; 22:67; John 13:19; 16:7).

legō also means "tell" in the sense of "explain" in Mark 11:33; Luke 20:8, where Jesus refuses to reveal the true source of his authority to the unbelieving Pharisees.

▸ **63.** Speak, Tell, Declare, Call > CALL, CALLED, CALLING, SUMMON, NAME

▸ **63.** Speak, Tell, Declare, Call > SAY, SPEAK

apangellō ἀπαγγέλλω 518

apangellō is a verb with the primary meanings "tell," "report," as well as several related senses.

In general contexts, ***apangellō*** indicates the sense of "bring news of" or "report" (e.g., Matt 2:8; 8:33; 28:9ff.; Mark 6:30; Luke 7:18; 8:36; John 4:51; Acts 12:14). A more formal sense of "bring a report" is indicated in Acts 4:23; 5:22; 28:21; 1 Thess 1:9.

The term also means "tell" with the nuance of "declare" or "explain" (Luke 8:47; Acts 11:13; 1 Cor 14:25; Heb 2:12).

▸ **63.** Speak, Tell, Declare, Call > REPORT, FAME

anangellō ἀναγγέλλω 312

anangellō is a synonym for ***apangellō*** (above) meaning "tell," "declare" in most of its eighteen occurrences.

The idea of "reporting" is noted in Mark 5:14; John 5:15; Acts 16:38; 1 Pet 1:12. The nuance of "declare" or "affirm" is found in Acts 14:27; 15:4; 20:27; 1 John 1:5. And the sense of "relate," "recount" is evident in Mark 5:19.

▸ **63.** Speak, Tell, Declare, Call > ANNOUNCE, MAKE KNOWN

laleō λαλέω 2980

laleō is a synonym for ***legō*** (above) occurring around three hundred times and likewise translated "speak," "say." The variant sense of "tell" is found in several places.

The sense of "inform" is found in Luke 12:17; Acts 9:6. ***laleō*** also expresses the sense of "proclaim" in relation to the message of the gospel (Acts 11:14); and to the shepherds' account of Jesus' birth (Luke 2:18ff.) Jesus' claim to "proclaim" the truth is noted in John 8:40.

▸ **43.** Prophecy, Preaching, Proclamation > PREACH, PREACHING

▸ **63.** Speak, Tell, Declare, Call > SAY, SPEAK

diēgeomai διηγέομαι 1334

diēgeomai is a verb found in eight places meaning "tell," "declare." The concept of "bringing a report" or "giving an account of" an incident or news is indicated in Mark 5:16; 9:9; Luke 9:10; Acts 9:27; 12:17; Heb 11:32. ***diēgeomai*** also has the sense of "declare" or "proclaim" (Luke 8:39). See also Acts 8:33.

eklaleō ἐκλαλέω 1583

eklaleō occurs only in Acts 23:22 (in the negative), meaning "tell" in the sense of "divulge" or "inform."

alētheuō ἀληθεύω 226

alētheuō is found only in Gal 4:16; Eph 4:15 meaning to "tell the truth."

▸ **59.** Justice, Righteousness, Truth > TRUE, TRUTH, TRULY

TONGUE

dialektos διάλεκτος 1258

dialektos is a noun with the consistent sense of "human language" evident in the translation "tongue" throughout each of its six occurrences (Acts 1:19; 2:6, 8; 21:40; 26:14).

▸ **63.** Speak, Tell, Declare, Call > LANGUAGE

heteroglōssos ἑτερόγλωσσος 2084

heteroglōssos is a rare noun found only in 1 Cor 14:21, referring to "one who speaks a foreign tongue (i.e., language)."

SEE ALSO

▸ **16.** Body, Bodily Functions > TONGUE
glōssa

TRUMPET

salpinx σάλπιγξ 4536

salpinx is a noun denoting a "trumpet" throughout its eleven occurrences.

References to the trumpet heralding the return of Jesus Christ are found in Matt 24:31; 1 Cor 15:52; 1 Thess 4:16. The sounding of the trumpet at the Sinai theophany is noted in Heb 12:19. A trumpet is sounded in heaven in the presence of the risen Christ-King in Rev 1:10. See also 1 Cor 14:8.

In metaphorical contexts, ***salpinx*** is found in Rev 4:1, referring to a voice that sounds like a trumpet. A trumpet heralds a cycle of divine judgment against wicked humanity in Rev 8:6, 13; 9:14.

salpizō σαλπίζω 4537

salpizō is a verb meaning "to sound a trumpet," occurring thirteen times.

The sounding of a trumpet announcing the return of Christ is noted in 1 Cor 15:52. Trumpet blasts indicating the outpouring of divine wrath against humankind are recorded in Rev 8:6ff.; 9:1, 13; 11:17. See also Rev 10:7.

▸ **63.** Speak, Tell, Declare, Call > SOUND

SEE ALSO

▸ **37.** Music, Singing, Dancing > TRUMPETER
salpistēs

WITNESS, BEAR WITNESS, TESTIFY, TESTIMONY

martyreō μαρτυρέω 3140

martyreō is a verb found in around eighty places with the dominant meanings "to testify," "bear witness against," as well as related senses.

The meaning "bear witness to" or "testify" is evident in a variety of contexts. Luke 11:48 refers to testifying to the sins of the fathers of Israel; and John 3:11; 21:24; Rev 22:16 refer to testimony to the deeds of Jesus. See also John 1:7ff.; Rev 1:2. Elsewhere, Jesus denies "bearing witness to himself" (John 8:13, 14; 15:26). The works of Christ "bear witness to" his divine nature and origin (John 5:36; 10:25). The Scriptures are said to "bear witness to Christ" (John 5:39; Acts 10:43; Rom 3:21). God the Father is said to "bear witness to" the Son (John 8:18; 1 John 5:10). See also John 18:37.

The meaning "testify" is also used in a general sense in relation to "speaking well of" people (Luke 4:22; Acts 6:3; 10:22; Heb 11:39); "reporting" an incident (John 4:39); and general "declaration" (John 7:7; Acts 26:22; 1 Cor 15:15; Heb 7:17; John 4:14). See also Acts 23:11.

martyreō is also used nominally to refer to the "witness" the disciples must give of Christ and his works (John 15:27).

▸ **52.** Status, Identity, Reputation, Honor, Shame > REPUTATION, REPUTE

martyria μαρτυρία 3141

martyria is a noun derived from ***martyreō*** (above). It occurs in around forty contexts and means "witness," "testimony" throughout, in a variety of contexts.

The meaning "testimony" in the general sense of a "report" is indicated in John 1:19; Acts 22:18; Titus 1:13. ***martyria*** refers to God's "testimony" concerning his Son (1 John 5:9ff.); to Jesus' "testimony" about himself (John 5:31ff.; 8:13ff.; Rev 1:2, 9); and to general "testimony" or "witness" concerning the person and work of Christ (John 3:11, 33; 19:35; 21:24; Rev 6:9; 11:7; 12:11, 17; 20:4). John 1:7 refers to "witness" to Christ as "the light of the world."

The legal sense of "testimony," "evidence" is used in connection with Jesus at his trial (Mark 14:55ff.; Luke 22:71).

▸ **52.** Status, Identity, Reputation, Honor, Shame > REPUTATION, REPUTE

martyrion μαρτύριον 3142

martyrion is a noun synonymous with ***martyria*** (above) meaning "witness," "testimony" throughout.

martyrion refers to the "testimony" or "witness" of the gospel to all nations (Matt 24:14); to the "witness" to the life of Christ (1 Cor 1:6; 2 Thess 1:10); and to the "testimony" to the perfect ransom provided by Christ to the Father (1 Tim 2:6). See also Heb 3:5; Jas 5:3.

"Testimony" in the sense of "proof" or "evidence" is indicated in relation to ceremonial cleansing (Mark 1:44; Luke 5:14); to divine rejection (Mark 6:11; Luke 9:5); to the resurrection of Christ (Acts 4:33); and to the presence of godly sincerity in one's conscience (2 Cor 1:12). Courtroom "testimony" or "evidence" is indicated in Mark 13:9; Luke 21:13.

Acts 7:44; Rev 15:5 refer to the "tent of testimony" (i.e., the tabernacle containing the ark of the covenant), with the latter text indicating the heavenly sanctuary.

martys μάρτυς 3144

martys is a noun denoting a "witness" in a legal, historical sense, as one who bears testimony to significant persons and phenomena. The term occurs around thirty times.

martys refers to a "witness" in the legal sense of presenting testimony in a judicial context in Matt 18:16; 26:25; Mark 14:63; Acts 7:58; 2 Cor 13:1; 1 Tim 5:19; Heb 10:28.

Acts 1:8, 22; 5:32; 10:39ff.; 22:15; 26:16; 1 Pet 5:1; Rev 1:5 mention those who are "witnesses" to the life of Christ and, for following generations in particular, to his death and resurrection.

The apostle Paul occasionally invokes God as his "witness" in order to validate his declaration (e.g., Rom 1:9; 2 Cor 1:23; Phil 1:8; 1 Thess 2:5).

Reference to a "witness" in general contexts as one who makes a claim is found in 1 Thess 2:10; 1 Tim 6:2. "False witnesses" are noted in Acts 6:13 in the trial of Stephen, the first recorded Christian martyr. In Rev 3:14, Christ himself is declared as the "faithful and true witness."

martys is also translated "martyr" in a number of places, referring to those who give their lives for the cause of the gospel (Acts 22:20; Heb 12:1 [implied]; Rev 2:13; 17:6). See also Rev 11:3.

amartyros ἀμάρτυρος 267

amartyros is a rare adjective found only in Acts 14:17 meaning "without a witness" or "unattested." It is predicated of God, of whom it is said that he did not leave himself without a witness.

symmartyreō συμμαρτυρέω 4828

symmartyreō is a verb found four times, meaning "bear joint witness to" (Rom 2:15; 8:16; 9:1). See also Rev 22:18.

diamartyromai διαμαρτύρομαι 1263

diamartyromai is a verb expressing the sense of "to testify," "(solemnly) affirm." It occurs fifteen times.

The meaning "testify" in the sense of "warn" is found in Luke 16:28; 1 Thess 4:6. A solemn charge or exhortation is expressed in Acts 2:40; 1 Tim 5:21; 2 Tim 2:14; 4:1; Heb 2:6.

Acts 8:25 refers to "bearing witness to" the words of the Lord. Acts 10:42 "declares" that Jesus Christ will be the judge of all humankind. Acts 20:21ff. contains the solemn declaration that the central element of the gospel constitutes repentance toward God, and faith in Christ. Acts 18:5; 23:11; 28:23 also contain the unambiguous "declaration" that Jesus is the Christ.

▸ **54.** Rule, Authority, Command, Obedience > CHARGE, INSTRUCT

SEE ALSO

▸ **32.** Law, Justice, Jurisprudence, Judgment > WITNESS, TESTIMONY
pseudomartys, pseudomartyreō, pseudomartyria

▸ **58.** Vices > BEAR WITNESS AGAINST, PERJURE
katamartyreō

WORD, SAYING, SPEECH

logos λόγος 3056

logos signifies "word(s)," "saying," "speech" in the majority of its over three hundred occurrences.

The "words" of human beings are indicated in the context of preaching (e.g., Matt 10:4; Acts 2:22, 40ff.; 4:4; 2 Cor 1:18). See also Matt 8:8; 12:37; Luke 3:4. In particular, the "word of the kingdom" signifies gospel preaching (Matt 13:19ff.; Mark 2:2; 4:14ff.; Acts 6:2ff.; 8:4). In Luke 8:11ff., the "word of God" is equated with the "seed" in the parable of the sower.

The "words of Christ" express the content of his public preaching and teaching. General references to these sayings are found in Matt 7:24ff.; Mark 10:24; Luke 4:32ff.; 9:26; 10:39; John 2:22; 8:31, 37ff.; 1 Tim 6:3. Christ's "words" effect miraculous healing (Matt 8:16); bind people to follow him in obedience and faith (John 14:23; Col 3:16ff.); and are said to be eternally enduring (Matt 24:35; Mark 13:31; Luke 21:33).

Specific reference to the "word of God" is found in a variety of contexts. It summarizes the obligation of God's people to obey the commandments of the Lord, and to turn to Christ (Mark 7:13; Luke 11:28; John 5:24, 38; 17:6, 14ff.; Gal 6:6; Jas 1:22; 1 John 2:5, 14). The "word of God" is equated with the teaching of Christ (Luke 5:1); revealed through the Hebrew Scriptures (John 15:25; Rom 9:16ff.; 2 Cor 4:2); and equated with gospel preaching (Acts 8:14; 11:1; 17:11ff.; Eph 1:13; Col 1:15; 1 Thess 1:5ff.; 2 Tim 2:11; Heb 4:2, 12; 1 Pet 1:23; Rev 6:9; 20:4). In 2 Pet 3:5, the "word of God" is depicted as the agent of creation.

In particular, the person of Christ, identified as "the Word," is equated with God the divine being (John 1:1, 14; 1 John 1:1; Rev 19:13).

The "word" or "message" of wisdom and knowledge is indicated in 1 Cor 12:8. In 2 Cor 5:19, the "word of reconciliation" is equated with the gospel. In Rev 1:3; 22:6ff., "words of prophecy" are identified with the book of Revelation. "Words" taught by the Spirit are indicated in 1 Cor 2:13. See also Luke 1:20.

Metaphorically speaking, the "word of the cross" in 1 Cor 1:18 points to the message of Christ's crucifixion, his atoning sacrifice.

▸ **17.** Senses, Actions, Abilities, Disabilities > SPEAK, SPEECH, TALK

▸ **32.** Law, Justice, Jurisprudence, Judgment > CAUSE, REASON, GROUND

▸ **65.** Teach, Exhort, Rebuke, Discipline > DOCTRINE

▸ **66.** Ask, Answer, Discuss, Learn > QUESTION, INTERROGATE

rhēma ῥῆμα 4487

rhēma is a synonym for ***logos*** (above). It occurs seventy times and means "word," "utterance," "saying," "speech."

rhēma refers to "words" spoken by God as part of the divine revelation to humankind (Matt 4:14; Luke 2:29; 3:2). In Eph 6:17, the "word of God" is identified with the "sword of the spirit." In Heb 11:3, God's "word" or "command" is identified as the agent of creation.

rhēma also refers generally to "words" uttered by human beings (Matt 12:36; 18:16; Acts 6:11ff.); and to "words" uttered in the context of apostolic preaching (Acts 2:14; 10:37, 44; Rom 10:8; 1 Pet 1:25).

Elsewhere, ***rhēma*** denotes the "words" of Jesus in the context of his public teaching and preaching ministry (Matt 26:75; Mark 9:32; 14:72; Luke 18:34; 24:8; John 5:47; 12:47ff.). These words are equated with gospel preaching (Eph 5:26; Heb 1:3); and they reflect the very words of God (John 3:34; 8:47; 18:8). See also John 6:68.

rhēma also metaphorically denotes "words" of creation that proclaim the glory of God (Rom 10:18).

angelia ἀγγελία 31

angelia is a rare noun, found only in 1 John 3:11, indicating the sense of "message" in the context of divinely revealed principles.

SEE ALSO

▸ **58.** Vices >
ARGUE, ARGUMENT, DISPUTE, QUARREL, STRIVE
logomacheō

64. Reveal, Explain, Hiddenness, Secrecy

APPEAR, APPEARING, APPARENT

phainō φαίνω 5316

The verb ***phainō*** is found in about thirty contexts with the dual senses of "appear," "shine" throughout.

The meaning "appear" is found in a variety of contexts. There is reference, for example, to an angel of the Lord appearing to Joseph bringing news of the birth of the Messiah and accompanying circumstances (Matt 1:20; 2:13, 19). The appearance of the sign of the final coming of the Son of Man is noted in Matt 24:30. The appearance of the star indicating the birthplace of the Messiah in Bethlehem is recorded in Matt 2:7. Mark 16:9 records the appearance of the resurrected Christ before Mary Magdalene. Matt 23:26ff. describes the phenomenon of self-righteousness Pharisees appearing as hypocrites.

Other uses of ***phainō*** with this meaning include Matt 13:26; Luke 9:8; Rom 7:13; 2 Cor 9:8; Heb 11:3; Jas 4:14; 1 Pet 4:18.

▸ **8.** Light, Darkness, Visible, Invisible, Color > SHINE

epiphainō ἐπιφαίνω 2014

epiphainō is a verb found in only four places. In three of these it expresses the meaning "appear." Acts 27:20 mentions the non-appearance of the sun and stars in the context of bad weather. Titus 2:11 speaks of the appearance of the grace of God for salvation; and Titus 3:4 refers to the appearance of God's goodness and kindness.

anaphainō ἀναφαίνω 398

anaphainō is another rare variant form of ***phainō*** (above) with the meaning "appear" in reference to the coming kingdom of God in Luke 19:11.

phaneroō φανερόω 5319

The verb ***phaneroō*** occurs about sixty times with the consistent meanings of "reveal" (i.e., cause to appear), "appear" throughout.

The passive sense "to be revealed" is found in a number of places, occurring with reference to God's work in the lives of human beings (John 9:3); the righteousness of God (Rom 3:21); the love of God (John 4:9); eternal life through God's word (Titus 1:3); the life of Jesus in the bodies, lives of believers (2 Cor 4:10ff.; Col 3:4); and the mystery of Christ and the gospel, communicated to the saints (Col 1:26; 1 Tim 3:16; 2 Tim 1:10; 1 Pet 1:20; 1 John 1:2). The revelation of Christ to Israel is indicated in John 1:31; and to the world at large at the end of the age in 1 Pet 5:4; 1 John 2:28; 3:2.

The active meaning "to reveal" (in the sense of "cause to appear") is found in relation to Christ's glory during his earthly ministry (John 2:11). John 17:6 affirms that Christ reveals God's name to God's people. Rom 1:19 declares that God reveals himself to humankind. The sense of "make clear, plain" is also evident in the use of this term (2 Cor 11:6; Col 4:4; 1 John 2:19).

The specific sense of "appear" is noted in the context of the risen Christ showing himself to his disciples prior to his ascension to heaven (Mark 16:12ff.; John 21:1, 14). All believers are set to "appear" before the judgment seat of Christ as indicated in 2 Cor 5:10. Heb 9:26; 1 John 3:5, 8 affirm that Jesus "has appeared" to take away sin once and for all. The phenomenon of "becoming visible" in the glare of light is indicated in Eph 5:13.

▸ **64.** Reveal, Explain, Hiddenness, Secrecy > SHOW, DISCLOSE, MANIFEST

phaneros φανερός 5318

phaneros is an adjective found in around twenty contexts with the meanings "apparent," "evident" (in the sense of being clearly recognized) in about half of these texts.

General reference to all things being "made evident" on the day of judgment is indicated in Luke 8:17. The general knowledge of God as Creator is said to "be made plain" to all people in Rom 1:19. Humankind's work on the day of judgment will also "be made plain" to God as noted in 1 Cor 3:13. See also 1 Cor 14:25 for a related usage. Gal 5:19 declares that the works of the flesh are "plain" (i.e., "apparent"). See also Acts 4:16.

▸ **51.** Knowledge, Wisdom, Remember, Forget > KNOW, KNOWLEDGE, MAKE KNOWN

epiphaneia ἐπιφάνεια 2015

epiphaneia is a noun found six times, with the meaning "appearing" in all but one of these places, referring solely to the manifestation of Jesus Christ at his return to earth at the end of the age (1 Tim 6:14; 2 Tim 1:10; 4:18; Titus 2:13).

emphanizō ἐμφανίζω 1718

The verb ***emphanizō*** means "appear," "reveal" in about half of the ten contexts in which it occurs.

The meaning "appear" in the sense of "show oneself in public view" occurs in Matt 27:53. It is also predicated of Christ, who now "appears" in heaven to intercede before God on behalf of his people (Heb 9:24).

emphanizō also expresses the meaning "reveal" in the sense of "make oneself known," and is applied to Christ in John 14:21ff., where it is claimed he will "manifest" himself to those who love him, along with God the Father.

▸ **64.** Reveal, Explain, Hiddenness, Secrecy > SHOW, DISCLOSE, MANIFEST

CONVICT

elenchō ἐλέγχω 1651

The verb ***elenchō*** means to "convict," "reprove," in addition to associated nuances, throughout the nearly twenty occurrences of the term.

The meaning "be convicted" in relation to sin is indicated in John 8:9; 1 Cor 14:24; Jas 2:9. Then, the active sense of "convict" (i.e., of sin) is found in John 8:46; 2 Tim 4:2. John 16:8 specifically mentions the Holy Spirit's role in convicting the world of sin.

The associated senses of "reprove," "expose," in the context of rebuking people of sin, are found in Matt 18:15;

Luke 3:19ff.; Eph 5:11; 1 Tim 5:20; Titus 1:9, 13; 2:15; Heb 12:5.

▸ **50.** Love, Hate, Please, Be Pleased With > FAULT
▸ **64.** Reveal, Explain, Hiddenness, Secrecy > EXPOSE
▸ **65.** Teach, Exhort, Rebuke, Discipline > REBUKE

exelenchō ἐξελέγχω 1827

exelenchō is a rare verb found only in Jude 15, referring to "convicting" the ungodly of their lawlessness.

DREAM

onar ὄναρ 3677

onar is a noun denoting "dream" in all six occurrences of the term, most of which indicate divine presence and intention in the dream and have to do with protecting the infant Jesus and those who were venerating him (Matt 1:20; 2:12ff.). Matt 27:19 refers to the disturbing dream of Pilate's wife, which moved her to warn her husband to have nothing to do with Jesus.

enypnion ἐνύπνιον 1798

enypnion is a rare noun denoting "dreams," found only in Acts 2:17.

enypniazō ἐνυπνιάζομαι 1797

enypniazō is a verb found only twice, designating the experience of "dreaming" in Acts 2:17; Jude 8.

EXPOSE

elenchō ἐλέγχω 1651

elenchō is a verb occurring eighteen times, meaning "convict," "rebuke," "expose."

The meaning "expose" is used mainly in the context of bringing people's sin to light (John 3:20; Eph 5:11).

See also Eph 5:13, where the general sense of "exposing" hidden objects to the light is indicated.

▸ **50.** Love, Hate, Please, Be Pleased With > FAULT
▸ **64.** Reveal, Explain, Hiddenness, Secrecy > CONVICT
▸ **65.** Teach, Exhort, Rebuke, Discipline > REBUKE

HIDE, CONCEAL, COVER

synkalyptō συγκαλύπτω 4780

synkalyptō is a rare verb found only in Luke 12:2 with the sense of "cover up," "conceal" in a general sense.

kryptō κρύπτω 2928

This verb means "to hide," "conceal," "keep secret." ***kryptō*** occurs in sixteen contexts.

The concealing of persons is indicated in Heb 11:23, which cites the incident of the baby Moses hidden in the reeds of the Nile (Exod 2). John 8:59; 12:36 refer to Jesus hiding himself in order to avoid premature arrest or containment by the crowd. The concealment of various objects is described in Matt 5:14; 13:44; 25:25; Rev 2:17. 1 Tim 5:25 contains the reassuring observation that good deeds cannot remain hidden (presumably from God, although this is not made explicit).

As a manifestation of divine judgment, divine mysteries are kept secret, or hidden from human view, in Matt 13:35. Similarly, understanding is hidden from the disciples in Luke 18:34, and from the people of Jerusalem in Luke 19:42. Rev 6:15, 16 again affirm the futility of seeking to hide from the judgment of God.

Finally, in a profound symbolic context, Col 3:3 refers to the life of the believer being hidden with Christ.

▸ **64.** Reveal, Explain, Hiddenness, Secrecy > SECRET, SECRETLY

apokryptō ἀποκρύπτω 613

This term is synonymous with ***kryptō*** (above) and is found six times meaning "hide," "conceal."

The physical concealment of money is indicated in Matt 25:18 — the only literal use of ***apokryptō***. The term is used metaphorically in Matt 11:25; Luke 10:21, where divine wisdom is hidden from the "wise" and given to "babes," or those who readily submit to the authority of God and obey him unquestioningly. Then, in 1 Cor 2:7; Eph 3:9; Col 1:26, Paul declares that the secret wisdom of God, kept hidden for centuries, has now been made available to believers through the ministry of Christ and the Holy Spirit.

enkryptō ἐγκρύπτω 1470

A rare synonym with the preceding two verbs, ***enkryptō*** is found only in Matt 13:33; Luke 13:21, referring to the parable in which a woman hid yeast in three measures of flour.

kalyptō καλύπτω 2572

kalyptō is found on seven occasions and means "cover," as well as "hide," "conceal." The latter sense is only specifically mentioned in 2 Cor 4:3, where the phenomenon of "veiling" is indicated. This infers that the truth of the gospel is hidden from the hearts and minds of those who continue to reject it. The sense of "cover" in Jas 5:20; 1 Pet 4:8 overlaps with that of "hide."

▸ **85.** Movement, Position, State > COVER, COVER UP

lanthanō λανθάνω 2990

lanthanō means "be hidden" in three of the six contexts in which it occurs.

Mark 7:24 refers to the inability of Jesus to remain hidden from the public in a house in the region of Tyre and Sidon. Luke 8:47 points to the woman suffering from hemophilia who could not remain hidden in her approach to Jesus. Acts 26:26 then refers to King Agrippa's awareness of the significance of Jesus Christ's death, resurrection, ascension, and the emergence of the Christian community of believers. Paul claims here in his public defense that nothing was hidden from the king.

apokryphos ἀπόκρυφος 614

This adjectival form is also rare, occurring only three times and meaning "hidden" or "kept secret." Col 2:3 refers to Jesus Christ as the one in whom is hidden all treasures of wisdom and knowledge. Mark 4:22; Luke 8:17 affirm the desirability of bringing into public view that which may have been hidden away, such as a lamp on a lampstand.

▸ **64.** Reveal, Explain, Hiddenness, Secrecy > SECRET, SECRETLY

INSPIRATION

theopneustos θεόπνευστος 2315

theopneustos is found only in 1 Tim 3:16, literally meaning "God-breathed." The term refers to the divine origin of the Scriptures as coming not from the initiative of human beings, but from God. The translation "inspiration" is misleading in a way, for it suggests the idea of "taking breath into . . . ," whereas what is indicated is the product of God's "breathed-out word." However, this popular meaning of the term (viz. "inspiration") to describe the divine foundation of the sacred writings remains, notwithstanding the looseness of the translation of ***theopneustos.***

MYSTERY

mystērion μυστήριον 3466

mystērion is a term found in approximately thirty places, meaning "mystery" or "secret" in each instance. The underlying sense of this term in the majority of contexts refers to that which has been kept secret by God in the past, but which he has now chosen to make plain. The revelation of this "mystery" centers on the appearance of Jesus Christ in human history as the messianic King of kings.

The "mysteries" of the kingdom of heaven are said to be given to Jesus' disciples in Matt 13:11; Mark 4:11; Luke 8:10. The context of this affirmation by Christ is that the intent of his teaching in parables was first of all to illuminate the spiritual understanding of his followers concerning God's plan of salvation. For those who rejected Christ, however, there would be no such insight, and they would learn nothing from hearing the parables.

Understanding the mystery of God's plan of salvation, whereby Israel's full salvation will only take place when all the Gentile peoples have been saved in accordance with the divine plan, is the goal of the apostle Paul for his readers in Rom 11:25.

The revelation of the divine mystery centers on the disclosure of Jesus as the Christ — a phenomenon that remained hidden for a long time in the past until now. This climactic "unveiling" of the "mystery" of God's plan of salvation is a common motif in the NT writings (Rom 16:25; 1 Cor 2:7; 4:1; Eph 1:9; 3:3ff.; 5:32; 6:19; Col 1:26ff.; 2:2; 4:3; 1 Tim 3:9, 16; Rev 10:7).

The "mysteries of God" in a general sense, implying the understanding of the significance of the person of Christ, are referred to in 1 Cor 13:2; 14:2.

The "mystery" involving the transformation of our earthly bodies into heavenly ones is indicated in 1 Cor 15:51. The "mystery of lawlessness" in 2 Thess 2:7 refers to the time of the unveiling of the antichrist in the last days prior to the Lord's return.

The term ***mystērion*** also indicates the sense of "mystery" with reference to a riddle, or puzzle. In Rev 1:20, for example, the "mystery" of the seven stars in the right hand of the heavenly Christ refers to the angels of the seven churches addressed in the opening chapters of the book of Revelation. Rev 17:5 mentions the "mysterious" title given to the city of Babylon, "Babylon the Great, the mother of prostitutes and of the abominations of the earth." See also Rev 17:7.

ORACLE

logion λόγιον 3051

logion is a noun related to ***logos***, which is translated "oracle." It occurs only four times. In each instance ***logion*** is linked to the person of God, indicating the "oracles of God" or the "word of God." Acts 7:38; Rom 3:2 utilize this phrase in relation to the Mosaic covenant. This meaning is also implied in 1 Pet 4:11. In Heb 5:12 ***logion*** may also be understood as the "word" of God.

REVEAL, REVELATION

apokalyptō ἀποκαλύπτω 601

apokalyptō is a verb occurring about twenty-five times with the exclusive meaning "reveal" in the sense of "uncovering, or laying open what has previously been hidden."

The general, passive use of ***apokalyptō***, referring to that which is revealed, is found in John 12:28 (citing Isa 40:5); 1 Cor 14:30. In particular, Matt 10:26; Luke 12:3 affirm that all shall be revealed in the last days. Similarly, 1 Cor 3:13 declares that a person's life work will be revealed to God on the day of judgment. The revealing of divine glory at the end of time is described in Rom 8:18; 1 Pet 5:1. 2 Thess 2:3ff. warns that the man of lawlessness will be revealed before the return of Christ.

Where God is concerned, ***apokalyptō*** is found in contexts where he reveals spiritual truth or knowledge to those with a childlike devotion to, and trust in, him (Matt 11:25; 16:17; Luke 10:21; 1 Cor 2:10; Eph 3:5; Phil 3:15; 1 Pet 1:12). Rom 1:17 declares that the righteousness of God is revealed through faith; and 1 Pet 1:5 affirms that salvation will be revealed in the last time. In contrast, Rom 1:18 states that the wrath of God is revealed from heaven against all wickedness. Gal 1:16 declares that God reveals his Son to humankind.

Concerning Christ himself, Matt 11:27; Luke 10:22 declare that he reveals God the Father to humankind. Luke 17:30 says that the Son of Man is to be revealed on the last day.

apokalypsis ἀποκάλυψις 602

apokalypsis is the noun derived from ***apokalyptō*** (above) and has the consistent meaning "revelation" in each of its eighteen occurrences. All references speak of revelation as that which emanates from God or Christ.

General, non-specific references to revelation include those in 1 Cor 14:6, 26; Gal 2:2; Eph 1:17; 3:3.

apokalypsis refers to giving and receiving revelation in contexts including conveying the light of the gospel to the Gentiles (Luke 2:32); the revelation of the mystery of the gospel (Rom 16:25); the revelation of God's judgment at the last day (Rom 2:5); and unveiling the sons of God at the end of time (Rom 8:19). The revelation of the Lord Jesus Christ himself is indicated in 1 Cor 1:7; 2 Thess 1:7; 1 Pet 1:7, 13 (see also 1 Pet 4:13). Gal 1:12; 2 Cor 12:1, 7; Rev 1:1 refer to the revelation given by Christ to his people. Rev 1:1 indicates the canonical book of Revelation.

chrēmatizō χρηματίζω 5537

chrēmatizō is a verb found in nine places, meaning "warn" in most of these contexts. In Luke 2:26, ***chrēmatizō*** means "reveal" with reference to the godly Israelite Simeon, to whom God had revealed that he would not die before he had seen the Messiah.

▸ **64.** Reveal, Explain, Hiddenness, Secrecy > WARN
▸ **65.** Teach, Exhort, Rebuke, Discipline > WARN

SECRET, SECRETLY

kryptos κρυπτός 2927

kryptos is an adjective occurring about twenty times, also used adverbially, meaning "secret," "in secret," and indicating "that which is hidden."

Practicing piety "in secret" will earn the favor of God who sees "in secret" (Matt 6:4, 6, 18). See also John 7:4. Nothing can remain hidden (i.e., secret) from God (Matt 10:26; Mark 4:22; Luke 8:17; 12:2).

kryptos is used nominally in Rom 2:16; 1 Cor 4:5; 14:25 to refer to the "secrets" of human beings to be judged by God.

Jesus Christ denies having said anything "in secret," with a view to deceive (John 18:20).

kryptō κρύπτω 2928

kryptō is a verb found in sixteen contexts with the dominant sense "to hide." However, in John 19:38, ***kryptō*** is used adverbially to refer to the "secret" discipleship of Joseph of Arimathea.

▸ **64.** Reveal, Explain, Hiddenness, Secrecy > HIDE, CONCEAL, COVER

apokryphos ἀπόκρυφος 614

apokryphos is an adjective found in only three contexts, meaning "secret" (i.e., "kept hidden"). It is used negatively in Mark 4:22; Luke 8:17, indicating that nothing can be kept secret or hidden from the scrutiny of God. See also Col 2:3.

▸ **64.** Reveal, Explain, Hiddenness, Secrecy > HIDE, CONCEAL, COVER

kryphē κρυφῇ 2931

kryphē is an adverb found only in Eph 5:12 with reference to shameful things done "in secret."

lathra λάθρᾳ 2977

lathra is an adverb found in four places, meaning "secretly" in the sense of "quietly" or "discreetly" (Matt 1:19; 2:7; John 11:28; Acts 16:37).

SHOW, DISCLOSE, MANIFEST

deiknymi δείκνυμι 1166

deiknymi is a verb found about thirty times, meaning "show" with a number of associated nuances.

The meaning "show" in the sense of "manifest" or "reveal" is indicated in Matt 4:8; Mark 14:15; Luke 4:5; John 20:20; Acts 7:3; Rev 21:10; 22:1ff. In particular, in John 14:8ff. there is a plea for God to "show himself" to his disciples. Heb 8:5 refers to God showing the pattern of the tabernacle to Moses.

The sense of "to present oneself (before another)" is noted in Matt 8:4; Mark 1:44; Luke 5:14.

The action of "showing" in the sense of "disclosing" or "explaining" is noted in Matt 16:21; Acts 10:28; Jas 2:18; Rev 1:1; 4:1; 17:1.

Divine power is indicated in John 2:18; 5:20; 10:32, where God "shows" signs or works of redemption.

anadeiknymi ἀναδείκνυμι 322

This variant of ***deiknymi*** (above) is found only twice. In Acts 1:24 it is translated "show" in the sense of "disclose" or "reveal."

▸ **83.** Set, Put, Place, Prepare, Establish > APPOINT, ORDAIN, ASSIGN

phaneroō φανερόω 5319

phaneroō is a verb occurring around sixty times meaning "to (make, be) manifest," "show," with a number of nuances.

General references to "show" in the sense of "present oneself," "demonstrate," or "prove" are found in John 7:4; 2 Cor 3:3.

God is said to "manifest" or "reveal" his works in the lives of human beings (John 9:3); and to manifest his general revelation to humankind (Rom 1:9).

Christ is said to "show" or "manifest" himself as the "chief shepherd" (1 Pet 5:4); to show his glory to human beings (John 2:11); to show his name (John 17:6); and his life (2 Cor 4:10ff.). John 21:1 describes the risen Christ "showing" himself to his disciples. 1 John 3:8 declares that Christ "is revealed" to destroy the work of the devil.

▸ **64.** Reveal, Explain, Hiddenness, Secrecy > APPEAR, APPEARING, APPARENT

emphanizō ἐμφανίζω 1718

emphanizō is a verb occurring ten times, with the varying senses of "inform," "make known," "manifest," "show."

John 14:21 speaks of Christ's promise to "show" or "reveal" himself to the one who keeps his commandments. In the next verse (i.e., John 14:22), Christ is said to "reveal" himself to his disciples.

▸ **64.** Reveal, Explain, Hiddenness, Secrecy > APPEAR, APPEARING, APPARENT

SEE ALSO

▸ **47.** Show, Persuade, Confidence, Doubt > SHOW, DEMONSTRATE, PROVE
epideiknymi, hypodeiknymi, endeiknymi, paristēmi

TRANSLATE, INTERPRET, INTERPRETATION

methermēneuō μεθερμηνεύω 3177

This verb form occurs seven times and has the primary sense of "translate" (from one language to another).

methermēneuō refers to the translation of the Hebrew term *'immānû'ēl*, which is "God with us" in Matt 1:23, and that of the Aramaic command *Talitha kûm* (i.e., "Little girl, arise,"), which was uttered by Jesus in raising Jairus' daughter from the dead in Mark 5:41. Mark 15:22 refers to Golgotha, which is translated "place of the skull." Jesus' cry from the cross, *Eloi, Eloi lama sabachthani*, is translated "My God, my God, why have you forsaken me?" in Mark 15:34. In John 1:4, the term Messiah is translated "Christ." Acts 4:36 records that the name Barnabas means "son of encouragement"; and in Acts 13:8 Elymas is translated "magician."

hermēneuō ἑρμηνεύω 2059

hermēneuō is a synonym for ***methermēneuō*** (above) occurring four times with the primary sense of "translate." In John 1:38 the meaning "teacher" is given for the term "Rabbi," and Cephas is translated "Peter" in John 1:42. John 9:17 indicates that the name of the Pool of Siloam means "sent." And the mysterious figure of Melchizedek, mentioned in Heb 7:2 (citing Gen 14:18), is to be understood as the "king of righteousness."

diermēneuō διερμηνεύω 1329

diermēneuō is another synonym for ***methermēneuō*** and ***hermēneuō*** (above), occurring six times. However, in addition to the meaning "translate," it has the expanded sense of "interpret," signifying "to expound, or explain."

In Luke 24:27, for example, Jesus interprets for his disciples all things concerning himself as the fulfillment of all that is in the Hebrew Scriptures. In Acts 9:38, the name Tabitha is translated "Dorcas." Then, in 1 Cor 12:30; 14:5, 13, 27, ***diermēneuō*** refers to the "interpretation" of speaking in tongues.

▸ **65.** Teach, Exhort, Rebuke, Discipline > EXPOUND

hermēneia ἑρμηνεία 2058

hermēneia is a noun derived from ***hermēneuō*** (above) and signifies "interpretation" of that which has been expressed or spoken by others. It only occurs twice, in 1 Cor 12:10; 14:26, and on both occasions refers to interpreting words spoken in tongues.

epilysis ἐπίλυσις 1955

epilysis is only found in 2 Pet 1:20, where it refers to an individual's interpretation (lit., "unraveling" or "unloosing") of prophecy. The point of the text is to deny that any prophecy of Scripture ever came about by a "private interpretation" (i.e., from the prophet himself). Rather, all prophecy originates from God, through the Spirit, who mediates that revelation through the human author.

UNVEIL

anakalyptō ἀνακαλύπτω 343

anakalyptō is a verb meaning "unveil" or "draw back," "uncover" with the use of a veil. It is used figuratively in both contexts in which it occurs. 2 Cor 3:14 refers in a negative context to the mind and heart of the unbeliever that remains "veiled" (lit., "not unveiled") to the truth of the gospel until the Spirit of God removes the "veil" of unbelief. 2 Cor 3:18 mentions the blessed state of the believer who is able to contemplate the glory of God with an "unveiled face." This expression refers metaphorically to a saving understanding of gospel truth, after release from spiritual blindness.

VISION

horama ὅραμα 3705

horama is a noun denoting a "vision" in the sense of a revelation from God that is both seen and heard. It is found in twelve contexts.

A vision of God or Christ is indicated in Matt 17:9, with reference to Christ's transfiguration. Acts 7:31 refers to Moses' "vision" of the burning bush. Visions are also granted to Ananias, who sees the risen Christ in Acts 9:10ff. Peter receives a vision from God (Acts 11:5), as does Cornelius (Acts 10:3, 17, 19). See also Acts 12:9; 16:9ff.; 18:9.

horasis ὅρασις 3706

horasis is a variant form of ***horama*** (above) found only three times. It denotes supernatural visions of God (Acts 2:17; Rev 9:17) and an "appearance" of God that resembles the radiance of precious gemstones (Rev 4:3).

optasia ὀπτασία 3701

optasia is a noun that also denotes "visions" from heaven, found in four contexts (Luke 24:23; Acts 26:19; 2 Cor 12:1). Luke 1:22 refers to a vision of an angel bearing the news to the priest Zechariah that his wife would bear a son named John, the forerunner of the Messiah.

SEE ALSO

▸ **21.** Die, Perish, Kill, Destroy > SPECTACLE
theōria

▸ **45.** Faith, Belief, Trust, Promise > SIGHT
eidos

WARN

chrēmatizō χρηματίζω 5537

chrēmatizō is a verb found nine times with the sense of "being warned (by God)" in about half of these contexts.

In Matt 2:12, God warns the magi not to return to Herod after seeing the Christ child, but to go home another way. In Matt 2:22, Joseph is similarly warned in a dream not to return to Judea with Mary and Jesus. Heb 11:7 speaks of God warning Noah of the impending universal flood. See also Heb 12:25.

▸ **64.** Reveal, Explain, Hiddenness, Secrecy > REVEAL, REVELATION
▸ **65.** Teach, Exhort, Rebuke, Discipline > WARN

SEE ALSO

▸ **65.** Teach, Exhort, Rebuke, Discipline > WARN
prolegō, noutheteō, hypodeiknymi

65. Teach, Exhort, Rebuke, Discipline

ADMONITION

nouthesia νουθεσία 3559

The noun ***nouthesia*** is found in three contexts with the meanings "admonition," "instruction" in relation to divine teaching in 1 Cor 10:11; Eph 6:4; and "warning" in Titus 3:10.

ALLEGORY

allēgoreō ἀλληγορέω 238

allēgoreō is a rare verb found only in Gal 4:24 with the meaning "to speak allegorically" or simply "to be an allegory."

CHASTEN, CHASTENING, DISCIPLINE

paideuō παιδεύω 3811

paideuō is a verb found in fifteen places with the sense of "chasten," "chastise" as well as "learn," "instruct."

In Luke 23:16, 22, the meaning "chastise" conveys the sense of "flog with a whip," utilized in the context of Christ's pre-crucifixion suffering at the hands of the Romans.

The meaning "to chasten" in the sense of "exercise discipline" or "punish" is used exclusively in the contexts of divine punishment directed towards his people (1 Cor 11:32; 2 Cor 6:9; Heb 12:6ff.; Rev 3:19).

▸ **65.** Teach, Exhort, Rebuke, Discipline > INSTRUCT, INSTRUCTION, INSTRUCTOR

▸ **66.** Ask, Answer, Discuss, Learn > LEARN

paideia παιδεία 3809

paideia is a noun derived from ***paideuō*** (above) found in six places with the sense of "chastening" or "discipline" from the Lord (Heb 12:5ff.).

▸ **65.** Teach, Exhort, Rebuke, Discipline > INSTRUCT, INSTRUCTION, INSTRUCTOR

CORRECTION

epanorthōsis ἐπανόρθωσις 1882

epanorthōsis is a rare noun denoting "correction" in the sense of moral reformation, found only in 2 Tim 3:16 as one of the divinely ordained purposes of Holy Scripture.

DEPOSIT, TRUST

parathēkē παραθήκη 3866

parathēkē is a rare noun found in 2 Tim 1:12 meaning a "deposit" or "trust," signifying a body of teaching concerning the purity of the gospel which has been entrusted to Timothy by Paul and the other apostles.

SEE ALSO

▸ **45.** Faith, Belief, Trust, Promise > TRUST
elpizō, peithō

DOCTRINE

didachē διδαχή 1322

didachē is a noun found thirty times to mean "doctrine," "teaching." The "teaching" of Christ during his public ministry is indicated in Matt 7:28; 22:33; Mark 1:22, 27; 4:2; 12:38; John 7:16ff.; 18:19.

The "teaching" of the Pharisees is noted in Matt 16:12, and the apostolic "teaching" of the early church in Acts 2:42; 5:28; 17:19. In particular, the "teaching" of the Lord is mentioned in Acts 13:12; and the "teaching" of Christ in 2 John 9.

The liberating "teaching" of the gospel in general terms is noted in Rom 6:17; 16:17; Titus 1:9; 2 Tim 4:2; 2 John 10. See also 1 Cor 14:6, 26. In contrast, strange or heretical "teaching" is indicated in Heb 13:9; Rev 2:14, 15, 24.

didaskalia διδασκαλία 1319

didaskalia is a synonym for ***didachē*** (above) denoting "doctrine" or "teaching" throughout the nearly twenty occurrences of the term.

The necessity for "sound teaching," based on the apostolic doctrine of the gospel tradition, is indicated in 1 Tim 1:10; 4:6, 13ff.; 5:17; 6:1ff.; 2 Tim 3:10ff.; 4:3; Titus 1:9; 2:1ff. There is also one reference to demonic teaching or "doctrines" in 1 Tim 4:1.

logos λόγος 3056

logos is a common term denoting "word," as well as various nuances, throughout its 331 occurrences. In Heb 6:1, however, ***logos*** is translated "doctrine" or "teaching" in relation to "the elementary teaching of Christ."

▸ **17.** Senses, Actions, Abilities, Disabilities > SPEAK, SPEECH, TALK

▸ **32.** Law, Justice, Jurisprudence, Judgment > CAUSE, REASON, GROUND

▸ **63.** Speak, Tell, Declare, Call > WORD, SAYING, SPEECH

▸ **66.** Ask, Answer, Discuss, Learn > QUESTION, INTERROGATE

EDIFICATION, EDIFY

oikodomē οἰκοδομή 3619

oikodomē is a noun found in eighteen contexts with the primary meaning "building" in both a literal and metaphorical sense. The meaning "edification" in the sense of "being built up, strengthened in one's faith" is indicated, for example, in Rom 14:19; 15:2; 1 Cor 14:3ff., 12, 25; 2 Cor 10:8; 12:19; 13:10; Eph 4:12; 16.

Symbolic references to the people of God as his "building" are found in 1 Cor 3:9; 2 Cor 5:1; Eph 2:21.

▸ **33.** Architecture > BUILD, BUILDER, BUILDING

oikodomeō οἰκοδομέω 3618

oikodomeō is a verb with the principal meaning "to build" in most of its approximately thirty occurrences, used in both literal and metaphorical contexts.

The meaning "to edify," in the sense of "build up, encourage, nurture one's faith," is evident in relation to the church in Acts 9:31; 1 Cor 4:4; 1 Pet 2:5; and to the individual in 1 Cor 8:1; 14:4, 17; 1 Thess 5:11.

▸ **33.** Architecture > BUILD, BUILDER, BUILDING

ENCOURAGE

protrepō προτρέπω 4389

protrepō is a rare verb found only in Acts 18:27, meaning "to encourage" in the context of exhorting fellow believers.

▸ **65.** Teach, Exhort, Rebuke, Discipline > EXHORT, EXHORTATION, BESEECH, URGE

EXHORT, EXHORTATION, BESEECH, URGE

parakaleō παρακαλέω 3870

parakaleō is a common verb with the primary meanings "beseech" and "comfort," as well as "exhort" and some related nuances.

The meanings "beseech" and "exhort" are related in contexts where pleas are made in order to produce a certain response or avoid a course of action. The sense of "urge" is indicated in Luke 3:8; Acts 2:40; 11:23; Rom 12:8; 1 Thess 2:11; 1 Tim 2:1; 2 Tim 4:2; Titus 2:6, 15; Heb 3:13; 1 Pet 5:1, 12. In particular, "exhortations" are frequently made in the name of the Lord Jesus (1 Thess 4:1; 2 Thess 3:12).

▸ **62.** Care For, Protect, Guard, Watch > COMFORT, COMFORTER, CONSOLATION, ENCOURAGEMENT

▸ **66.** Ask, Answer, Discuss, Learn > ASK, REQUEST, BEG, PLEAD

paraklēsis παράκλησις 3874

paraklēsis is a noun derived from ***parakaleō*** (above) found in approximately thirty places, with the principal meanings "comfort," "consolation," and "exhortation." There is, however, some overlap in meaning between all these senses in several contexts. The meaning "exhortation" in the context of teaching and preaching the word of God is evident in Acts 13:15; Rom 12:8ff.; 1 Tim 4:13. The related sense of "encouragement" is found, for example, in Acts 15:31; Rom 15:4; 1 Cor 14:3; Heb 12:5. See also 2 Cor 8:17 for the meaning "appeal," "exhortation" in a general context.

▸ **62.** Care For, Protect, Guard, Watch > COMFORT, COMFORTER, CONSOLATION, ENCOURAGEMENT

paraineō παραινέω 3867

paraineō is a rare verb found only twice, meaning "urge," "exhort" in Acts 27:9, 22.

▸ **65.** Teach, Exhort, Rebuke, Discipline > WARN

protrepō προτρέπω 4389

protrepō is a rare verb found only in Acts 18:27, meaning "exhort" or "encourage" in relation to welcoming friends.

▸ **65.** Teach, Exhort, Rebuke, Discipline > ENCOURAGE

EXPLAIN

phrazō φράζω 5419

phrazō is a rare verb found only twice, meaning "explain" in Matt 13:36; 15:15, referring to the disciples' request to Jesus to "explain" the parable of the weeds to them.

EXPOUND

ektithēmi ἐκτίθημι 1620

ektithēmi is a rare verb found in several places, meaning to "expound" in the sense of "explain" or "interpret." The activity of "expounding" the word of God is indicated in Acts 18:26; 28:23. In Acts 11:4 ***ektithēmi*** means "explain."

epilyō ἐπιλύω 1956

epilyō is a rare verb found only once, meaning "expound" in the context of Jesus "explaining" the significance of his teaching to his disciples.

diermēneuō διερμηνεύω 1329

diermēneuō is a verb found in six places, meaning "expound," "interpret" throughout. Luke 24:27 refers to Jesus' response to his disciples in "expounding" or "interpreting" for them the christological focus of the entire OT canon, which points unambiguously to him as its fulfillment.

▸ **64.** Reveal, Explain, Hiddenness, Secrecy > TRANSLATE, INTERPRET, INTERPRETATION

INSTRUCT, INSTRUCTION, INSTRUCTOR

katēcheō κατηχέω 2727

katēcheō is found in eight contexts with the consistent meaning "to instruct," "teach" (Acts 21:21, 24).

Luke writes to Theophilus to convince him of the truthfulness of the elements of the Christian faith in which he has been instructed (Luke 1:4). Acts 18:5 records Apollos' instruction in the "way of the Lord." Rom 2:18 indicates that Jewish people have been instructed in the law. In 1 Cor 14:19, Paul mentions his desire to instruct others clearly in gospel truth. Gal 6:16 expounds the principle that the teachers of God's word derive financial support from those they teach.

▸ **65.** Teach, Exhort, Rebuke, Discipline > TEACH, TEACHER, TEACHING

paideuō παιδεύω 3811

paideuō indicates the sense of "chasten," "chastise," as well as the meaning "instruct." ***paideuō*** occurs fifteen times and is translated "instruct," "learn" in about a third of these contexts. Acts 7:22 indicates that Moses was instructed in all of the knowledge of the Egyptians. Acts 22:3 mentions the fact that Paul was educated (i.e., instructed) at the feet of the great rabbinical scholar Gamaliel. 1 Tim 1:20 records that Paul had to discipline Hymenaeus and Alexander so that they would "learn" not to blaspheme. In 2 Tim 2:25, Paul advises Timothy to instruct, or correct, his opponents gently. Titus 2:12 affirms that the grace of God "teaches" the people of God to renounce ungodliness.

▸ **65.** Teach, Exhort, Rebuke, Discipline > CHASTEN, CHASTENING, DISCIPLINE
▸ **66.** Ask, Answer, Discuss, Learn > LEARN

symbibazō συμβιβάζω 4822

symbibazō is found in six contexts and has the underlying sense of bringing or joining together, both literally and metaphorically. The term is translated "join together," and by extension "prove," "conclude"; and, in one instance, "instruct." 1 Cor 2:16 poses the question: "Who has known the mind of the Lord so as to instruct him?" Clearly no one is capable of achieving such insight, since no one is capable of grasping the totality of the divine mind — a perspective suggested by the usage of ***symbibazō.***

paidagōgos παιδαγωγός 3807

paidagōgos is a term referring to a tutor, or schoolmaster (i.e., one who instructs). This role was performed by trusted slaves whose job it was to teach and supervise the moral development of young boys in both Greek and Roman culture. In the NT, ***paidagōgos*** occurs only three times. In 1 Cor 4:15, it refers to the countless spiritual instructors in the service of the Corinthian congregation. In Gal 3:24, 25, ***paidagōgos*** is used metaphorically of the law, depicted as a harsh "tutor" for God's people, until true freedom came along in the person of Christ.

paideia παιδεία 3809

paideia is a term that indicates the entire process of nurturing, educating, and disciplining, applied to believers as well as to children. It is found six times and is translated "instruction" in 2 Tim 3:16 in reference to the Scriptures, being suitable among other things, for instruction (or training) in righteousness.

▸ **65.** Teach, Exhort, Rebuke, Discipline > CHASTEN, CHASTENING, DISCIPLINE

paideutēs παιδευτής 3810

paideutēs occurs only twice, referring to an "instructor" of the foolish in Rom 2:20, and in Heb 12:9 to earthly fathers who disciplined their children (lit., "our fathers whom we have as instructors").

PARABLE

parabolē παραβολή 3850

parabolē is translated "parable" in most of the fifty occurrences in which it is found. It refers predominantly to the stories Jesus told, which were at the heart of his teaching ministry. These narratives have symbolic content with a profound spiritual application (e.g., Matt 13:3ff.; 21:33, 45; Mark 4:2ff.; 13:28; Luke 8:4ff.; 12:16, 41; 20:9, 19). See also Heb 9:9; 11:19.

REBUKE

epiplēssō ἐπιπλήσσω 1969

epiplēssō is a verb found only in 1 Tim 5:1, where Paul instructs Timothy not to rebuke an older man, but rather to exhort him as a father.

elenchō ἐλέγχω 1651

elenchō is a verb meaning "rebuke," "reprove" in seven of the seventeen contexts in which it occurs.

In several places, believers are exhorted to rebuke those who have sinned against them so that they might be restored to fellowship with each other and with God (Matt 18:15; 1 Tim 5:20; 2 Tim 4:2; Titus 1:13; 2:15). John the Baptist rebukes Herod the Tetrarch of Judea for improperly taking Herodias, his sister-in-law, as his wife (Luke 3:19).

elenchō also refers to God, who is said to rebuke (i.e., discipline, chasten) those he loves (Heb 12:5; Rev 3:19).

▸ **50.** Love, Hate, Please, Be Pleased With > FAULT
▸ **64.** Reveal, Explain, Hiddenness, Secrecy > CONVICT
▸ **64.** Reveal, Explain, Hiddenness, Secrecy > EXPOSE

elenxis ἔλεγξις 1649

elenxis is a noun derived from ***elenchō*** (above). It occurs only in 2 Pet 2:16 and refers to the divine rebuke given to Balaam for his greed through the mouth of his donkey.

elenchos ἔλεγχος 1650

elenchos is another noun derived from ***elenchō*** (above). It is found only in 2 Tim 3:16 as a variant reading meaning "rebuke," designated as one of the divinely ordained purposes of the "God-breathed" Scriptures.

REBUKE, REPROVE

epitimaō ἐπιτιμάω 2008

epitimaō is a verb meaning "to rebuke" in the majority of its nearly thirty occurrences. The underlying sense is that of "censure," "reprove."

In the course of Christ's earthly ministry, he was occasionally moved to offer a rebuke in a variety of contexts. For example, he rebukes the storm elements of wind and sea, resulting in immediate calm (Matt 8:26; Mark 4:39; Luke 8:24). Demons are also subject to his divine rebuke, immediately prior to their exorcism from individuals under their control (Matt 17:18; Mark 1:25; 9:25; Luke 4:35, 41 [see also Luke 4:39]; 9:42). Peter receives a stern rebuke for daring to question Jesus' destiny to face betrayal, death, and subsequent resurrection (Mark 8:31). The apostolic band as a whole earn a rebuke from their Lord in Luke 9:55.

epitimaō also refers to humans giving rebukes in a number of contexts. For example, the disciples rebuke the crowds when they bring children to Jesus in order to be blessed (Matt 19:13; Mark 10:13; Luke 18:15). In another context, the crowd tries to censure those who continually cry out for Jesus to have mercy on them (Matt 20:31; Mark 10:13, 48; Luke 18:39 [see also Luke 23:40]). Luke 17:3; 2 Tim 4:2 contain general exhortations to rebuke one's fellow believer for his sin.

Jude 9 records that Michael the archangel asks the Lord to rebuke Satan for (presumably) wanting to tamper with the body of Moses. And in Luke 19:39, the Pharisees demand (quite inappropriately) that Jesus rebuke his disciples for praising him as the coming messianic king.

TEACH, TEACHER, TEACHING

didaskō διδάσκω 1321

didaskō is the most common verb meaning "to teach" in the NT. The term occurs around one hundred times.

The teaching ministry of Christ is described throughout the Gospels and Acts (e.g., Matt 4:23; 5:2; 13:54; Mark 4:1ff.; Luke 13:22; 20:1; John 6:59; 7:28ff.; Acts 1:1). Paul indicates in Gal 1:12 that he was not taught the gospel message by any human source, but by the risen Christ himself in a revelation.

General references to human teaching are found in Matt 5:19; 15:9; Acts 15:1; Rev 2:14, 20. See also 1 Cor 11:14. Jesus' command to his disciples to teach others the gospel and disciple them is found in Matt 28:20. The teaching ministry of the apostles is also frequently indicated (e.g., Mark 6:30; Luke 11:1; Acts 4:2; 5:21; 1 Cor 4:17; Eph 4:21; Col 1:28; 2 Thess 2:15; 1 Tim 4:11). Mutual edification (i.e., teaching) among believers is indicated in Col 3:16; Heb 5:12. Paul's refusal to admit women to the teaching office in the church is recorded in 1 Tim 2:12.

The ministry of the Holy Spirit in teaching the people of God is noted in Luke 12:12; John 14:26.

katēcheō κατηχέω 2727

katēcheō is a verb occurring eight times meaning "instruct," "inform," or "teach." The usage is largely passive. Being instructed in, or taught, the word of God is a process indicated in Luke 1:4; Acts 18:25; Rom 2:18; Gal 6:6. General references to "being informed" are found in Acts 21:21ff. The active sense of "teach" or "instruct" is noted in 1 Cor 14:19.

▸ **65.** Teach, Exhort, Rebuke, Discipline > INSTRUCT, INSTRUCTION, INSTRUCTOR

heterodidaskaleō ἑτεροδιδασκαλέω 2085

heterodidaskaleō is a verb found only twice. 1 Tim 1:3; 6:3 refer to those who "teach a different doctrine" to that of the apostolic tradition of the gospel.

didaktikos διδακτικός 1317

didaktikos is an adjective signifying the quality of being "apt to teach" or "skilled in teaching." It occurs only in 1 Tim 3:2; 2 Tim 2:24 as part of a list of prerequisite characteristics for those aspiring to the office of elder.

didaskalos διδάσκαλος 1320

didaskalos is a noun derived from ***didaskō*** (above) occurring around sixty times with the primary sense of "teacher," applied most often as a title for Jesus Christ during his earthly ministry.

The title "teacher" is frequently given to Jesus in the Gospel narratives (e.g., Matt 8:19; 22:16, 24, 36; Mark 4:38; 10:17ff.; Luke 3:12; 11:45; 12:13; John 1:38; 3:2).

References to the teachers of the Jewish people include those in Luke 2:46; John 3:10; Acts 13:1. 1 Tim 2:7; 2 Tim 1:11 refer to apostolic teachers, appointed by God for the edification of the church. 1 Cor 12:28ff.; Eph 4:11 refer to teachers who are gifted by the Spirit of God, again for the benefit of God's people.

General references to teachers include those in Matt 10:24ff.; Luke 6:40; Rom 2:20; 2 Tim 4:3; Heb 5:12; Jas 3:1

nomodidaskalos νομοδιδάσκαλος 3547

nomodidaskalos is a term denoting the specific office of "teacher of the law," found only three times (Luke 5:17; Acts 5:34; 1 Tim 1:7).

▸ **38.** Covenant, Law, Rites, Roles > LAW

kalodidaskalos καλοδιδάσκαλος 2567

kalodidaskalos is an adjective found only in Titus 2:3, referring to those who "teach what is good."

pseudodidaskalos ψευδοδιδάσκαλος 5572

pseudodidaskalos is a term denoting "a false teacher," found only in 2 Pet 2:1.

rhabbi ῥαββί 4461

rhabbi is the Greek transliteration of a Hebrew term that denotes a "teacher" of the law of Moses. It is used seventeen times in the NT as a courtesy title for Jesus (e.g., Matt 23:7ff.; Mark 9:5; 14:65; John 1:38, 49; 4:31; 11:8).

TRADITION

paradosis παράδοσις 3862

paradosis means "tradition" throughout its thirteen occurrences. The underlying literal sense of ***paradosis*** refers to "that which is handed down," indicating the huge repository of Jewish oral interpretation of the Mosaic law that had accumulated over the centuries. Though in theory this "tradition" was of a lesser standing than Scripture itself, in practice it became equally authoritative and binding. The Pharisees frequently criticized Jesus for failing to observe the "tradition" of the elders. He responded by rebuking them for transgressing the law of God for the sake of that tradition (Matt 15:2ff.; Mark 7:3ff.). See also Col 2:8; Gal 1:14.

More positively, "tradition" in the NT can also refer to the "tradition" of the gospel handed on by the apostles (1 Cor 11:2; 2 Thess 2:15; 3:6).

WARN

paraineō παραινέω 3867

paraineō is a rare verb found only twice, with the meaning "warn" in the context of physical danger in Acts 27:9, and "urge" or "exhort" in Acts 27:22.

▸ **65.** Teach, Exhort, Rebuke, Discipline > EXHORT, EXHORTATION, BESEECH, URGE

chrēmatizō χρηματίζω 5537

The verb ***chrēmatizō*** has the primary sense of "warned by God" for the majority of the nine occurrences of the term (Matt 2:12, 22; Acts 10:22; Heb 8:5; 11:7).

▸ **64.** Reveal, Explain, Hiddenness, Secrecy > REVEAL, REVELATION

▸ **64.** Reveal, Explain, Hiddenness, Secrecy > WARN

prolegō προλέγω 4302

prolegō is a verb occurring three times meaning "warn," "issue a warning." 2 Cor 13:2 refers to Paul warning the Corinthian congregation about a painful visit from him if they do not change their sinful ways. Gal 5:21 warns that those who manifest a consistently sinful lifestyle will not inherit the kingdom of God. 1 Thess 3:4 contains Paul's recollection of the warning he had previously given to this congregation that they would suffer persecution.

noutheteō νουθετέω 3560

This verb occurs eight times, meaning "warn," "admonish," "instruct." There is some overlap in meaning here, for in certain contexts "warning" and "admonishing" appear to be identical. In Acts 20:31, for example, Paul reports that he "has exhorted" or "admonished" the Ephesian congregation for three years with tears to maintain their faith in Christ. A similar use is evident in 1 Cor 4:14; Col 1:28; 1 Thess 5:12ff.; 2 Thess 3:15. In other contexts, admonition is linked to instruction (Rom 15:14; Col 3:16).

hypodeiknymi ὑποδείκνυμι 5263

hypodeiknymi is a verb occurring in six contexts and meaning "warn" or "show" throughout. People are warned to flee from the coming judgment of God in Matt 3:7; Luke 3:7. Jesus warns his hearers to fear God, who can cast someone into hell (Luke 12:5).

▸ **47.** Show, Persuade, Confidence, Doubt > SHOW

SEE ALSO

▸ **64.** Reveal, Explain, Hiddenness, Secrecy > WARN
chrēmatizō

66. Ask, Answer, Discuss, Learn

ANSWER

apokrinomai ἀποκρίνομαι 611

The common verb ***apokrinomai*** occurs 250 times with the consistent meaning "to answer."

Christ gives answers to questions in various contexts (e.g., concerning John the Baptist in Matt 3:15; 11:4; about himself in John 1:48; about eternal life in John 3:5ff.; from his disciples in John 6:70; 14:23). In addition, he responds to questions in the course of explaining the significance of his parables (Matt 12:48; 13:37). Jesus also "answers" various challenges (e.g., from his disciples showing lack of faith [Mark 9:19]; from religious leaders [Mark 12:28ff.]; from unbelievers or hostile Jewish leaders [Matt 12:39, 15:3; Mark 11:30ff.; Luke 5:22; John 5:17ff.; 8:19, 49; 18:5, 20ff.]; from Satan [Matt 4:3]; and from his accusers at trial [i.e., he gave no answer; Matt 27:12ff.]).

Examples of people responding to other people include Matt 20:13; Luke 3:16; John 1:21; Acts 3:12; Col 4:6. People also answer Christ in the context of a confession of belief and faith (John 1:49; Saul on the road to Damascus [Acts 22:8]). Other examples of this usage include Matt 8:8; 25:37; Mark 9:17; John 16:31; Acts 9:13.

Luke 1:19 records the angels' "answer" to the inquiries of human beings.

apokrisis ἀπόκρισις 612

apokrisis is a noun derived from ***apokrinomai*** (above). In each of the four contexts where it is found, it means "answer." In Luke 2:47; 20:26 people express their amazement at the answers Jesus gave to their questions. In John 1:22 people question John the Baptist, asking him for an answer as to his identity. John 19:9 records Jesus' refusal to give an answer to his accusers at his trial.

antapokrinomai ἀνταποκρίνομαι 470

antapokrinomai is a rare variant of ***apokrinomai*** (above) with the meaning "to answer back" — to reply in contradiction to the speaker. It is found only in Luke 14:6; Rom 9:20. The latter reference affirms that such a stance may not be taken against God.

chrēmatismos χρηματισμός 5538

chrēmatismos is a rare noun found only in Rom 11:4 denoting an "answer" from God.

hypolambanō ὑπολαμβάνω 5274

hypolambanō is a verb occurring four times. It expresses the meaning "to answer" in the context of Jesus responding to a question by telling the story of the good Samaritan.

SEE ALSO

▸ **32.** Law, Justice, Jurisprudence, Judgment > ANSWER
apologeomai, apologia

ASK, REQUEST, BEG, PLEAD

aiteō αἰτέω 154

The verb ***aiteō*** is found in approximately seventy places with the predominant meanings "ask," "desire" throughout most of the usage.

The underlying sense of ***aiteō*** is that of "making request." General references include Matt 14:7; 27:58; Mark 6:22; Luke 1:63; John 4:9ff.; Acts 3:14. ***aiteō*** describes requests for money or food in Matt 5:42; Luke 6:30. 1 Cor 1:22 declares that Jews "ask" or "make demands" for miraculous signs.

Petitioning God in prayer is also indicated in the semantic range of ***aiteō***, most commonly in relation to material needs (Matt 6:8; 7:7ff.; Mark 11:24; Luke 11:9ff.; John 11:22; 16:23ff.; Eph 3:20; Jas 1:5ff.; 1 John 3:22; 5:14ff.). Incorporated in these references is the willingness of God to grant these requests when they are made with due recognition of his name (i.e., in accord with the divine will and purpose). Allied with these texts are those that contain references to requests made of Christ. In John 14:13ff.; 15:7, 16, Jesus affirms that he will do whatever his people ask of him in his name. Elsewhere, some of his disciples "make an (illegitimate) request" of him that is denied to them (Mark 10:35ff.). In Col 1:9 the apostle Paul, in prayerful request on behalf of the Colossian believers, "asks" for them to be filled with spiritual knowledge.

apaiteō ἀπαιτέω 523

apaiteō is a rare verb found only twice. In Luke 6:30 it means "to ask again, a second time." In Luke 12:20 it is used passively in the context of a rich man's soul "being required of him" by God.

▸ **32.** Law, Justice, Jurisprudence, Judgment > REQUIRE

erōtaō ἐρωτάω 2065

The verb ***erōtaō*** occurs about sixty times with the underlying sense of "ask" and includes various nuances such as "ask a question," "beg," "make a request," and "sue for peace."

The action of "asking (with earnestness)" in the sense of "beg," "plead" is indicated, for example, where Jesus is begged to respond to various crisis situations, usually involving a need for healing (Matt 15:23; Mark 7:26; Luke 4:38; 7:3; John 4:47). "Begging" for money is noted in Acts 3:3. Apostolic exhortations to live for God in accordance with his revealed ways are found in 1 Thess 4:1; 5:12; 2 Thess 2:1; 2 John 5.

General references to "asking a question" include John 1:19ff.; 5:12; 9:15ff. In particular, ***erōtaō*** describes questions posed by the hearers of Jesus and by Jesus himself (Matt 16:3; 21:24; Mark 4:10; Luke 5:3; 20:3; John 9:2; 16:19). In Luke 9:45, the disciples are afraid to ask Jesus questions because of their ignorance and confusion.

References to "making a request" are found in Luke 14:18ff.; John 4:40; 12:21; 19:31, 38; Acts 10:48; 23:18. Jesus himself makes requests of his Father on behalf of his people in John 14:16; 16:23; 17:9ff.

The meaning "sue for peace" is indicated in Luke 14:32.

eperōtaō ἐπερωτάω 1905

eperōtaō is a variant form of ***erōtaō*** (above) occurring about sixty times with the consistent sense of "ask a question."

General references include John 18:7; Acts 5:27; 1 Cor 14:35. More commonly, the term denotes questions asked of Jesus by his hearers, and of them by him (Matt 12:10; 22:23, 35ff.; Mark 7:5; 9:11ff.; 10:2, 17; 14:60ff.; 15:2ff.; Luke 2:46; 17:20). Mark 12:34 records the incident where no one dared ask Jesus any more questions in order to save further embarrassment. Then, in Mark 5:9; Luke 20:40, specific mention is made of Christ's interrogation of a demon.

▸ **66.** Ask, Answer, Discuss, Learn > QUESTION, INTERROGATE

pynthanomai πυνθάνομαι 4441

pynthanomai, found in twelve places, is synonymous with the entries listed above. All but one indicate the meaning "ask" in the sense of either "demand" or "inquire" (Matt 2:4; Luke 15:26; 18:36; John 4:52; 13:24; Acts 4:7; 10:18, 29, 33; 21:33; 23:19ff.).

▸ **66.** Ask, Answer, Discuss, Learn > INQUIRE

exetazō ἐξετάζω 1833

exetazō is a rare verb found in only three places with the meaning "make an inquiry" in Matt 10:11; and "ask a question" in John 21:12. See also Matt 2:8, where the translation "search diligently" presupposes stringent inquiries being made.

anakrinō ἀνακρίνω 350

anakrinō is a verb found sixteen times in all with the primary meaning of "examine," as well as the subsidiary senses of "ask," "judge."

▸ **32.** Law, Justice, Jurisprudence, Judgment > EXAMINE, EXAMINATION, INVESTIGATION
▸ **32.** Law, Justice, Jurisprudence, Judgment > JUDGE
▸ **51.** Knowledge, Wisdom, Remember, Forget > DISCERN
▸ **66.** Ask, Answer, Discuss, Learn > QUESTION, INTERROGATE

parakaleō παρακαλέω 3870

parakaleō is a verb occurring around one hundred times with the dual meanings "to comfort" and "plead with" (i.e., ask in earnestness, beg, exhort). This latter sense predominates.

General references to the action of "pleading" and associated nuances include Matt 18:29; Acts 13:42; 16:9; 21:12; 2 Cor 2:8; 9:5; Phlm 9, 10. Urgent appeals to Christ for healing are made in Matt 8:5; 14:36; Mark 1:40; 5:23; 8:22. Paul "pleads with" God for the removal of his "thorn in the flesh" in 2 Cor 12:8. Demons "beg" Christ to send them into a herd of swine in Matt 8:31ff.; Mark 5:10ff.; Luke 8:32. There are numerous strong appeals for God's people to maintain a vital, faithful, and dependent relationship with him in their Christian life (e.g., Acts 11:23; 15:32; Rom 12:1; 15:3; 1 Cor 1:10; Eph 4:1; Phil 4:2; 1 Thess 4:1; 2 Thess 3:12; 1 Tim 6:2; Titus 2:6; Heb 3:13; 13:19ff.; 1 Pet 2:11; 5:1; Jude 3). Then, in Acts 2:40; 2 Cor 5:20, people are "urged" to be reconciled to God.

In Matt 26:53 Christ declares his capacity "to make an appeal" to his Father to rescue him from the cross, should he so desire.

▸ **62.** Care For, Protect, Guard, Watch > COMFORT, COMFORTER, CONSOLATION, ENCOURAGEMENT
▸ **65.** Teach, Exhort, Rebuke, Discipline > EXHORT, EXHORTATION, BESEECH, URGE

aitēma αἴτημα 155

aitēma is a rare noun, occurring only three times and meaning "request" or "petition." Luke 23:24 refers to Pilate bowing to the pressure of the Jerusalem mob, yielding to their "request" (i.e., demand) that Jesus be crucified. Phil 4:6; 1 John 5:15 refer to "requests" made known to God in prayer.

INQUIRE

pynthanomai πυνθάνομαι 4441

pynthanomai occurs twelve times, and in each of these contexts it may be translated "ask" or "inquire of," with the aim of finding out certain information.

In Matt 2:4, Herod makes inquiries concerning the whereabouts of Christ's birth. Peter inquires of Jesus as to who would betray him in John 13:24. Acts 4:7 describes the Sanhedrin's inquiry, set up to investigate the preaching activity of Peter and John. In Acts 21:33 the Roman commander makes an inquiry concerning Paul's claim to be a Roman citizen in the wake of the Jerusalem riot that saw the apostle taken into custody. See also Luke 15:26; 18:26; John 4:52; Acts 10:18, 29; 23:19ff.

▸ **66.** Ask, Answer, Discuss, Learn > ASK, REQUEST, BEG, PLEAD

akriboō ἀκριβόω 198

akriboō occurs only twice, meaning "to inquire, or investigate diligently" in Matt 2:7, where Herod tries to find out from the wise men what time the star in the east had appeared.

zēteō ζητέω 2212

zēteō commonly indicates "to seek" and occurs over one hundred times with that meaning. Twice, however, ***zēteō*** expresses the sense of "inquire after" in the sense of gaining information — once by Jesus from the disciples (John 16:19), and once by Ananias from the newly converted Saul of Tarsus (Acts 9:11).

▸ **54.** Rule, Authority, Command, Obedience > BE REQUIRED
▸ **72.** Need, Gain, Loss, Advantage, Seek, Find > SEEK, SEARCH

LEARN

manthanō μανθάνω 3129

manthanō is the principal verb in the NT meaning "learn." It occurs around twenty-five times. The underlying sense is that of increasing one's knowledge.

Where the learning of men and women is concerned, ***manthanō*** indicates that the true meaning of devotion to God lies in learning mercy, not sacrifice (Matt 9:13). ***manthanō*** refers to learning in a number of contexts: learning doctrine (Rom 16:17; 1 Cor 4:6; 14:31; Phil 4:9; 2 Tim 3:14); learning from Christ, the master teacher (Matt 11:29; see also Eph 4:20); learning from God the Father (John 6:45; Col 1:7); learning in a general sense (Acts 23:27; Phil 4:11; 1 Tim 2:11; Titus 3:14; Rev 14:3); and learning from the object lesson of the fig tree (Matt 24:32; Mark 13:28). In John 7:15, the degree of Jesus' great learning is questioned.

Heb 5:8 declares that Christ learned obedience through what he suffered.

paideuō παιδεύω 3811

paideuō is found thirteen times and has the principal meaning "chasten," "chastise." However, in 1 Tim 1:20, the term signifies "to learn," referring to Paul's disciplinary action against Hymenaus and Alexander, that they might learn not to blaspheme.

- ▸ **65.** Teach, Exhort, Rebuke, Discipline > CHASTEN, CHASTENING, DISCIPLINE
- ▸ **65.** Teach, Exhort, Rebuke, Discipline > INSTRUCT, INSTRUCTION, INSTRUCTOR

QUESTION, INTERROGATE

syzēteō συζητέω 4802

syzēteō is a verb that occurs ten times and means "to question" in four of these contexts.

In Mark 1:27; 9:10; Luke 22:23, ***syzēteō*** means "to question" in a group setting with the sense of "questioning one another." Mark 8:11 refers to Jesus questioning the Pharisees.

- ▸ **51.** Knowledge, Wisdom, Remember, Forget > DISPUTE

logos λόγος 3056

logos is a common NT term meaning "word," "saying," "speech," as well as a variety of related senses, in the 331 occurrences of the term. In Mark 11:20, ***logos*** is translated "question," referring to Jesus' inquiry to the spiritual leaders of Israel.

- ▸ **17.** Senses, Actions, Abilities, Disabilities > SPEAK, SPEECH, TALK
- ▸ **32.** Law, Justice, Jurisprudence, Judgment > CAUSE, REASON, GROUND
- ▸ **63.** Speak, Tell, Declare, Call > WORD, SAYING, SPEECH
- ▸ **65.** Teach, Exhort, Rebuke, Discipline > DOCTRINE

anakrinō ἀνακρίνω 350

anakrinō is a verb occurring sixteen times, meaning "to question" in six of these contexts. Other meanings include "to judge," "search," or "discern."

The sense of "question" in the context of a legal inquiry or examination is indicated in Luke 23:14; Acts 12:19; 28:18; 1 Cor 9:3. The action of withholding a question is noted in 1 Cor 10:25, 27, where Paul advises his readers not to raise questions about pagan religious ceremonies associated either with meat sold in the market or meat served to them in the homes of unbelievers.

- ▸ **32.** Law, Justice, Jurisprudence, Judgment > EXAMINE, EXAMINATION, INVESTIGATION
- ▸ **32.** Law, Justice, Jurisprudence, Judgment > JUDGE
- ▸ **51.** Knowledge, Wisdom, Remember, Forget > DISCERN
- ▸ **66.** Ask, Answer, Discuss, Learn > ASK, REQUEST, BEG, PLEAD

eperōtaō ἐπερωτάω 1905

eperōtaō is a verb meaning "ask" in the large majority of its nearly sixty occurrences. On several occasions, however, the term is translated "to question" or "ask a question" in the sense of "interrogate" (Luke 2:46; 23:9; Acts 5:29).

- ▸ **66.** Ask, Answer, Discuss, Learn > ASK, REQUEST, BEG, PLEAD

SEE ALSO

- ▸ **32.** Law, Justice, Jurisprudence, Judgment > QUESTION *zētēma*

REASON, DEBATE, DISPUTE

antilogia ἀντιλογία 485

antilogia is a noun found four times with the various senses of "opposition," "rebellion" and "strife," or "dispute." The latter meaning is indicated in Heb 6:16; 7:7.

diakrisis διάκρισις 1253

diakrisis is a noun denoting "disputes" over various opinions in Rom 14:1.

- ▸ **51.** Knowledge, Wisdom, Remember, Forget > DISCERN

dialogizomai διαλογίζομαι 1260

dialogizomai is a verb found sixteen times, with the principal meaning "to reason (together)" found in most of these contexts. The underlying sense of ***dialogizomai*** is that of engaging in discussion, questioning, or debate over a difficult question to resolve, from the perspective of the participants.

References to reasoning involving general discussion include those in Matt 16:7ff.; Mark 8:16ff.; Luke 20:14. Matt 21:25 refers to the reasoned discussion of the spiritual leaders of Israel earnestly seeking, but failing to find, a solution to the difficult question put to them by Jesus.

dialogizomai also refers to the unbelieving questioning taking place in the hearts and minds of the Pharisees and scribes who witnessed Jesus' healing of the young paralytic. They were skeptical of his intentions and accused him of blasphemy for claiming to have the authority to forgive sins (Mark 2:6ff.; Luke 5:21ff.).

In Mark 9:33, ***dialogizomai*** refers to Jesus' disciples "arguing among themselves" as to who was the greatest.

syllogizomai συλλογίζομαι 4817

syllogizomai is a rare synonym for ***dialogizomai*** (above) found only in Luke 20:5, referring to the reasoned discussion of the scribes and Pharisees seeking in vain to discover a satisfactory response to the question put to them by Jesus.

dialegomai διαλέγομαι 1256

dialegomai is a verb found in thirteen places with the primary meanings "to dispute," "argue," "reason with," found in most of these contexts.

dialegomai refers to the disciples "arguing" over who is the greatest among them (Luke 9:46).

Most commonly, ***dialegomai*** refers to Paul "debating" or "reasoning" with the Jews from the Hebrew Scriptures over the identity of Jesus Christ as the Messiah (Acts 17:2, 17; 18:4, 19; 19:8ff.).

Jude 9 contains the enigmatic reference to the archangel Michael disputing with the devil over the body of Moses.

diamachomai διαμάχομαι 1264

diamachomai is a rare verb found only in Acts 23:9 meaning "to argue, dispute" vigorously.

SEE ALSO

- ▸ **58.** Vices >
  ARGUE, ARGUMENT, DISPUTE, QUARREL, STRIVE
  machomai
- ▸ **68.** Ability, Possibility, Effort, Succeed, Fail > STRIVE
  agōnizomai, spoudazō

67. Acknowledge, Confess, Profess, Swear

BIND UNDER OATH

anathematizō ἀναθεματίζω 332

anathematizō is a verb occurring four times with the meaning "to bind oneself under a solemn oath" in Acts 23:12ff.

- ▸ **67.** Acknowledge, Confess, Profess, Swear > CURSE, CURSED
- ▸ **67.** Acknowledge, Confess, Profess, Swear > OATH

SEE ALSO

- ▸ **20.** Illness, Disease, Health, Healing > BIND, DRESS A WOUND
  katadeō
- ▸ **55.** Bondage, Captivity, Servitude > BIND, BOUND, TIE UP
  deō, desmeuō, proteinō

CONFESS, CONFESSION, PROFESS, PROFESSION, ACKNOWLEDGE

homologeō ὁμολογέω 3670

The verb ***homologeō*** is found about twenty-five times with the underlying sense of "confess" throughout, with several associated nuances.

The meaning "confess" in the sense of "acknowledge" is evident in relation to those confessing Christ before others, whom Christ will likewise confess before God (Matt 10:32; Luke 12:8). The act of "confessing" Christ as God is indicated in 1 John 2:23; 4:2ff., 15. In John 1:20 John the Baptist refuses to "confess" that he is the Christ. "Confessing" one's sins before God is described in 1 John 1:9. "Acknowledging" the reality of the resurrection is indicated in Acts 23:8. Heb 13:15 refers to "acknowledging" the name of God.

General references to "identifying" Jesus as the Christ are found in John 9:22; 12:42.

The meaning "confess" in the sense of "profess," "admit," "declare" is found in Paul's "declaration" that he is a believer or follower of the way in Acts 24:14. See also 1 Tim 6:12. The act of "confessing" Jesus as Lord is recorded in Rom 10:9ff. The affirmation of "pressing" to know God is indicated in Titus 1:16. See also Heb 11:13.

- ▸ **45.** Faith, Belief, Trust, Promise > PROMISE

exomologeō ἐξομολογέω 1843

exomologeō is a variant form of ***homologeō*** (above) meaning "confess" in all eleven occurrences of the term, with one or two related senses.

"Confessing" one's sins is indicated in Matt 3:6; Mark 1:5; Acts 19:18; Jas 5:16. The act of "giving thanks, or praise" to God is indicated in Matt 11:25; Luke 10:21; Rom 14:11; 15:9. Paul "declares that Christ is Lord" in Phil 2:11. In Rev 3:5 Christ is depicted as "acknowledging" the names of the saints before God.

- ▸ **50.** Love, Hate, Please, Be Pleased With > THANK, THANKS, THANKSGIVING

homologia ὁμολογία 3671

homologia is a noun found six times denoting both "confession" and "profession."

The "confession" (i.e., declaration) of the gospel is noted in 2 Cor 9:13; 1 Tim 6:12, 13; Jesus is described in Heb 3:1 as the apostle and high priest of our "confession" (i.e., indicating the gospel). See also Heb 4:14; 10:23 for related contexts.

CURSE, CURSED

anathematizō ἀναθεματίζω 332

anathematizō is a verb found in four places meaning "to curse" or "invoke a curse" in Mark 14:71; and "to bind oneself a solemn oath" in Acts 23:12ff., referring to the attempt to murder Paul.

- ▸ **67.** Acknowledge, Confess, Profess, Swear > BIND UNDER OATH
- ▸ **67.** Acknowledge, Confess, Profess, Swear > OATH

katathematizō καταναθεματίζω 2653

katathematizō is a rare variant of ***anathematizō*** (above) found only in Matt 26:74 referring to Peter "invoking a curse" in the course of denying his relationship.

SEE ALSO

- ▸ **57.** Evil, Wickedness, Sin > CURSE
  ara
- ▸ **73.** Blessing, Curse, Reward, Punishment > CURSE, CURSED, CURSING, ACCURSED
  anathema, katathema, katara, kataraomai, epikataratos
- ▸ **77.** Resist, Oppose, Fight, Rebel > CURSE, MALIGN
  kakologeō

OATH

horkos ὅρκος 3727

horkos is a noun that occurs ten times meaning "oath," predicated of both God and human beings.

As far as human beings are concerned, Matt 5:23 contains the command to fulfill one's oaths made to God. General references to sworn oaths are found in Matt 14:7, 9; Mark 6:26; Heb 6:16. An oath equivalent to a curse is indicated in Matt 26:72 in the context of Peter's third denial of Christ, where the apostle utters an oath following two previous denials of his master, in quick succession. There is an injunction in Jas 5:12, forbidding believers to swear an oath.

Where God is involved with this phenomenon, Luke 1:73; Heb 6:17 refer to the oath of the covenant given by

God to Abraham. Acts 2:30 mentions the oath sworn to David by God, granting him an unending royal lineage.

anathematizō ἀναθεματίζω 332

anathematizō is a verb indicating the action of "invoking a curse" and "binding oneself under an oath." The term occurs in four contexts.

Mark 14:71 refers to Peter invoking an oath, or a curse, in denying Jesus. Acts 23:12, 14, 21 refer to a group of Paul's Jewish enemies who "conspired under oath" (unsuccessfully) to assassinate the apostle.

▸ **67.** Acknowledge, Confess, Profess, Swear > BIND UNDER OATH
▸ **67.** Acknowledge, Confess, Profess, Swear > CURSE, CURSED

horkōmosia ὁρκωμοσία 3728

horkōmosia is a noun derived from ***horkos*** (above). It occurs four times meaning "oath." Heb 7:20, 21, 28 refer to the divine oath that led to the appointment of the risen Christ as the great high priest. The context also notes that no such divine oath accompanied the inauguration of the Levitical priesthood.

SWEAR

omnyō ὀμνύω 3660

omnyō is a verb found in thirty contexts with the consistent meaning "to swear."

Matt 5:34ff.; Jas 5:16 command human beings not to swear (Matt 23:16ff.). "Invoking a curse" is noted in Matt 26:74; Mark 14:71. The action of swearing an oath is indicated in Mark 6:23; Heb 6:16.

With reference to "divine oaths," God is said to grant his people the land of Canaan under the terms of his covenant "promise" (Luke 1:73; Acts 7:17; Heb 6:13). Acts 2:30 mentions the Davidic covenant oath. See also Heb 7:21; Rev 10:6.

omnyō is also used in the context of God bringing a solemn curse against his people by denying them rest in Canaan (Heb 3:11, 18; 4:3).

TRULY, AMEN

amēn ἀμήν 281

amēn indicates the solemn affirmation of the divine will and purpose in about one-third of the nearly 150 occurrences of the term. The remaining uses of the term yield the adverbial meaning "truly."

The sense of "truly" indicates an affirmation of genuineness or sincerity and is found throughout the Gospel narratives (e.g., Matt 5:18; 18:13; Mark 8:12; Luke 13:35; John 3:3ff.; 5:19ff.; 8:51).

The "amen" also expresses worship and praise of God's person and majesty (Rom 1:25; 9:5; 11:36; Eph 3:21; 1 Tim 1:17; 6:16ff.; Rev 1:6ff.; 5:14; 7:12; 19:4; 22:20ff.). It also concludes a blessing or benediction (e.g., Rom 15:33; 16:20ff.; 1 Cor 16:24; 2 Cor 3:14; Gal 6:18; Eph 6:24; Phil 4:20ff.; Col 4:18; 1 Thess 5:28; Heb 13:21; 1 Pet 5:11ff.; Jude 25). "Amen" is also a metaphorical name for Christ in Rev 3:14.

VOW

euchē εὐχή 2171

euchē is a noun denoting a "vow" in two places, referring to a vow of an indeterminate nature undertaken by Paul and several of his companions (Acts 18:18; 21:23).

▸ **42.** Prayer, Intercession, Fasting > PRAY, PRAYER

68. Ability, Possibility, Effort, Succeed, Fail

ABILITY, ABLE

ischys ἰσχύς 2479

ischys is a noun found in eleven different places, meaning "strength," "power," "ability."

The meaning "strength" is indicated in Mark 12:30ff.; Luke 10:27 with reference to the "force of one's entire being" in the context of being devoted to loving and serving God.

The "power" of God is indicated in the use of ***ischys*** in general terms in Eph 1:19; 6:10; 2 Thess 1:9. Divine power is given to the people of God for godly living, as noted in 1 Pet 4:11; and also to "the Lamb" (i.e., the heavenly Christ on the throne of God) in Rev 5:12. In Rev 7:12, the heavenly saints ascribe power to God. The power of angels is attested in 2 Pet 2:11.

▸ **18.** Strength, Weakness, Capability > STRENGTH, STRONG, POWER, POWERFUL, MIGHT, MIGHTY

ischyō ἰσχύω 2480

ischyō is a less common synonym for ***dynamai*** (below) found in approximately thirty places with the meanings "to be able" or "to exercise power (or strength) over."

With regard to human ability, Phil 4:13 declares that all things "are possible" for the believer through the indwelling strength of Christ. More frequently, ***ischyō*** is used in the negative, to indicate humankind's inability in certain areas (Mark 5:4; 9:18; 14:37; Luke 6:48; 14:29ff.; John 21:6; Acts 15:10). Jas 5:16, however, affirms that the prayer of a righteous person "is powerful" in its effects. The physical sense of "overpower" is evident in Acts 19:16.

In Acts 19:20, the word of God is said to have a powerful impact on those who hear it.

dynamai δύναμαι 1410

dynamai is a common verb found over two hundred times with the primary meanings "can" and "be able," used both positively and negatively.

The "ability" of God is indicated in several contexts. For example, God is able to keep believers from falling away in Jude 24; and has a supreme ability to forgive sin (Mark 2:7; Luke 5:21). See also Matt 3:9; Luke 3:8; Eph 3:20. Then, 2 Tim 2:13 affirms that God is "unable" to deny himself.

Where the person of Christ is concerned, several contexts refer to his ability to effect miraculous cures (Matt 8:2; 9:28; Mark 1:40ff.; Luke 5:12). In his role as eternal high priest, he is able to help those of his people who are tempted (Heb 2:18), and is always able to intercede on their behalf before the throne of God (Heb 7:25). There is also the false accusation that he is unable to save himself from death by crucifixion (Matt 27:42). In addition, John 5:19 declares that Christ is incapable of doing anything independently of his Father.

In the human sphere, ***dynamai*** refers positively to humankind's ability (or capacity) to receive spiritual insight, as noted in Matt 19:12. Elsewhere, God is said to give human beings the ability to overcome temptation and satanic attack (1 Cor 10:13; Eph 6:11ff.). Examples of negative contexts include the innate inability of human beings to please God by their own merit (Rom 8:8); to see the kingdom of God without the new birth (John 3:3ff.; 6:44, 65; Acts 15:1; 1 Cor 15:56). Elsewhere, specific inability is indicated with respect to speaking (Luke 1:20); to hearing and understanding the word of God (John 8:43; 1 Cor 2:14); to casting out demons (Mark 9:28; Luke 9:40). See also Matt 6:24ff.; 16:3; Luke 16:13; John 10:29; Acts 5:39; Heb 3:19; Rev 5:3.

dynamai also speaks of ability and inability with reference to inanimate, though highly significant, phenomena. For example, Jesus declares in Mark 3:24ff. that any kingdom divided against itself is unable to stand, and that the word of God is incapable of being broken (John 10:35). Paul affirms in Rom 8:39 that nothing is able to separate God's people from his love. Positively, the word of God is able to build up one's spiritual vitality (Acts 20:32), and to save one's soul (Jas 1:21; 2:14).

ABILITY, STRENGTH, POWER

dynamis δύναμις 1411

dynamis is a noun with the primary meaning of "power," emphasizing "strength" and "ability" in most of its 120 occurrences. ***dynamis*** can also suggest the sense of "miracle." In addition, ***dynamis*** also signifies "mighty works" or "deeds."

References to "power" or "strength" are varied. The power of God is indicated in a number of general contexts (Matt 22:29; Mark 12:24; Luke 1:35; Acts 8:10; 1 Cor 2:5; 2 Cor 6:7; Rev 4:11; 19:1). In a related context, ***dynamis*** signifies a "word of power" in Heb 1:3, denoting a divine catalyst for creation. The term also refers to the "power" of the Son of Man in Matt 24:30; Mark 13:26; Luke 21:27; and to the person of Christ in Mark 5:30; Luke 4:36; 1 Cor 5:4; 2 Cor 12:9. Specifically, Christ's power is manifested in his resurrection as noted in Phil 3:10 (see also Rev 5:12). There is a general reference to the power of the Spirit in Luke 4:14. 1 Cor 4:20 and Rev 12:10 speak of the power of the kingdom of God. In negative contexts, ***dynamis*** denotes the "power" of sin in 1 Cor 15:56 and refers to the power of the dragon in Rev 13:2 (see also Rev 17:13). References to the "powers" of natural, cosmic forces include Matt 24:29; Mark 13:25; Luke 21:26. Other general references to "power" include those in Acts 3:12; 2 Tim 3:5; Heb 11:11; Rev 1:16; 3:8; 15:8.

Elsewhere, ***dynamis*** has particular reference to the "power of God" in significant theological contexts. This power is declared effective for salvation in Rom 1:16; 1 Cor 1:18, 24; 1 Pet 1:5; for the reality of resurrection in 1 Cor 6:14; 15:43; and for godly living in 2 Cor 13:4; Eph 1:19; 2 Pet 1:13. This divine power is given to the disciples for exorcising demons in Luke 9:1; for gospel ministry in Acts 4:33; 2 Tim 1:8; and for performing miraculous signs in Acts 6:8.

God equips the disciples for ministry with the "power" of the Spirit in 1 Thess 1:5; 2 Thess 1:11. Christ also receives the Spirit's power, as noted in Acts 10:38; Rom 1:4, as do the believers (Rom 15:13; 2 Tim 1:7). Such a power is promised to the disciples in Luke 24:49; Acts 1:8. God also provides the Spirit's power for effective gospel ministry in 1 Cor 2:4; Eph 3:7, 20.

dynamis also denotes "powers" with reference to "spiritual forces" of darkness in Rom 8:38; 1 Cor 15:24; Eph 1:21; 2 Thess 2:9; and to the heavenly "powers" in Heb 6:5; 1 Pet 3:22.

dynamis indicates a sense of "ability," with reference to natural talent, in Matt 25:15. Conversely, ***dynamis*** is also used to describe the "inability" to cope with overwhelming persecution in 2 Cor 1:8.

Elsewhere, ***dynamis*** refers to "miracles" (i.e., signs of power from God) in Acts 2:4, 22; 8:13; 19:11; 1 Cor 12:10, 28ff.; Gal 3:5.

▸ **18.** Strength, Weakness, Capability > STRENGTH, STRONG, POWER, POWERFUL, MIGHT, MIGHTY

▸ **47.** Show, Persuade, Confidence, Doubt > SIGN

EFFORT, ENDEAVOR

spoudazō σπουδάζω 4704

spoudazō is a verb found twelve times, meaning "endeavor" in the senses of "be eager, diligent," "make every effort" to do something. General references include Gal 2:10; 1 Thess 2:17; 2 Tim 2:15; 4:9, 21. In particular, the term constitutes an appeal to "do one's best," to present oneself as one approved in the art of explaining/interpreting God's word (2 Tim 2:15). Eph 4:3 contains the exhortation "to make every effort" to maintain the unity of the Spirit; in Heb 4:11 the same exhortation is expressed in relation to believers entering their eternal rest; and in 2 Pet 1:10 with reference to making one's calling and election sure. See also 2 Pet 3:14.

▸ **46.** Wait, Hope, Be Vigilant, Pay Attention To > DILIGENCE, DILIGENT, DILIGENTLY

▸ **68.** Ability, Possibility, Effort, Succeed, Fail > STRIVE

FAIL

ekleipō ἐκλείπω 1587

ekleipō is a verb found in three only places meaning "fail" in each instance. Luke 16:9 refers to worldly wealth "failing" (i.e., ceasing to exist).

In Luke 22:32 Jesus promises to pray for Peter, that his faith may not fail. Heb 1:12 affirms that the years belonging to God will never fail (i.e., will never end).

SEE ALSO

▸ **72.** Need, Gain, Loss, Advantage, Seek, Find > FAIL
anekleiptos

GOAL, MARK

skopos σκοπός 4649

skopos is found only in Phil 3:14, where it refers to Paul's desire to strive for the "mark" or "goal" of a heavenly calling into the eternal presence of God, based on Christ's finished work of redemption.

SEE ALSO

▸ **76.** Force, Harm, Oppress > SCAR, MARK
stigma

▸ **81.** Forms, Groups, Patterns, Order > MARK, STAMP, BRAND
charagma

IMPOSSIBLE

adynateō ἀδυνατέω 101

This verb is rare, occurring only twice and meaning "be impossible," indicating utter inability or lack of strength or power. In both instances, however, the context positively stresses what is possible. In speaking of faith in Matt 17:20, Jesus answers his listeners that if their faith is genuine, nothing they desire to do will be impossible for them. Luke 1:37 contains the declaration that with God nothing is impossible.

adynatos ἀδύνατος 102

adynatos, an adjective, is more common than the verb form ***adynateō*** (above), from which it derives. ***adynatos*** occurs ten times, meaning "impossible" in the sense of "impotent," "powerless," or "disabled."

Human impotence is indicated in Matt 19:26; Mark 10:27; Luke 18:27, affirming that what is impossible with human beings is possible with God. Acts 14:8 refers to a disabled man for whom walking was impossible. Rom 8:3; Heb 10:14 refer to the law's utter inability to bring about the permanent removal of sin. Heb 6:4 contains the sobering warning that for those who have resolutely and absolutely turned their backs on God, there is no possibility of restoration to repentance. And finally, Heb 11:6 declares the impossibility of pleasing God without the exercise of faith.

▸ **18.** Strength, Weakness, Capability > WEAK, WEAKNESS, POWERLESS

anendektos ἀνένδεκτος 418

This term occurs only in Luke 17:1 with the idea that temptation to sin will certainly emerge, but those through whom the incitement comes will be held responsible. The sense of "impossible" is expressed negatively. The verse literally reads: "It is impossible for offenses not to come, but woe . . ."

OVERCOME

hēttaomai ἡττάομαι 2274

hēttaomai is a rare verb, found in only three places. In two of these contexts it means "overcome." 2 Pet 2:19, 20 refer to the perils of those who, having made a profession of faith in Christ, are then "overcome" afresh by the corruption of sin.

OVERCOME, PREVAIL, CONQUER

nikaō νικάω 3528

nikaō is a verb occurring twenty-five times with the principal meanings "overcome," "conquer," or "prevail." ***nikaō*** is predominantly used in a metaphorical sense.

In a literal context, ***nikaō*** is translated "overcome" in the sense of being overwhelmed in physical combat by a superior opponent (Luke 11:22).

More commonly, ***nikaō*** means "overcome" in the spiritual sense of "to win a victory." Several contexts are in view. Such an action is predicated of Christ, who is said to "overcome" the world, indicating that he has conquered the satanic opposition inherent in a sinful, fallen humanity (John 16:33; Rev 5:5). Elsewhere, believers are also said to "overcome," or they are exhorted to do so. The context here is likewise that of a spiritual victory over the sinful snare of a wicked world, promised to those who truly belong to Christ and who persevere in their relationship with him to the end (1 John 5:4, 5; Rev 2:7, 11, 17, 26; 3:5, 12, 21). Rom 12:21 exhorts believers not to be overcome by evil, but to overcome evil with good. 1 John 2:13, 14; 4:4 refer to overcoming the "evil one." Rom 3:4 refers to "prevailing" in the sense of escaping divine judgment.

POSSIBLE

dynatos δυνατός 1415

dynatos is an adjective with the underlying sense of "powerful" or "mighty," as well as "possible." ***dynatos*** is found thirty-five times, meaning "possible" in nearly half of these.

In several places there is the affirmation that with God "all things are possible" (Matt 19:26; Mark 10:27; Luke 18:27). See also Mark 9:23.

Hypothetical situations are occasionally introduced by the words "if possible . . ."This is illustrated in particular with reference to the elect going astray (Matt 24:24; Mark 13:22); and to Christ avoiding the cross (Matt 26:39; Mark 14:35, 36).

▸ **18.** Strength, Weakness, Capability > STRENGTH, STRONG, POWER, POWERFUL, MIGHT, MIGHTY

PRESS ON

diōkō διώκω 1377

diōkō is a verb with the dominant sense of "persecute," with the subsidiary meaning "to follow," occurring in over forty contexts. In Phil 3:14, however, ***diōkō*** is translated "to press on," indicating Paul's determination to attain eternal life with Christ.

▸ **71.** Lead, Guide, Follow > FOLLOW, ACCOMPANY, PURSUE

▸ **76.** Force, Harm, Oppress > PERSECUTE, PURSUE

SEE ALSO

▸ **28.** Agriculture, Viticulture, Animal Husbandry > PRESS *piezō*

RACE, COURSE

stadion στάδιον 4712

stadion is a noun referring primarily to the linear measurement of approximately 600 feet, or 185 meters — the standard length of athletic running courses in ancient Greece. In five of the six occurrences of this term in the NT, ***stadion*** reflects this meaning. In 1 Cor 9:24, ***stadion*** refers to the actual running of the race itself.

agōn ἀγών 73

agōn refers primarily to a "fight" or "conflict." It occurs six times, and on one occasion it refers metaphorically to a "race," or the challenge that life presents to the follower of Christ (Heb 12:1).

▸ **77.** Resist, Oppose, Fight, Rebel > FIGHT

dromos δρόμος 1408

dromos is found in only three places. In two of these it means "race," referring metaphorically to the course of one's life (Acts 20:24; 2 Tim 4:7). In Acts 13:25, ***dromos*** refers with the same metaphorical force to one's "course," or "life's work."

STRIVE

agōnizomai ἀγωνίζομαι 75

agōnizomai is a verb found seven times, meaning "strive" in the sense of "put in a great effort to obtain a result" in the majority of these contexts.

The attitude of "striving" in order to gain salvation is indicated in Luke 13:24; 1 Tim 6:12; 2 Tim 4:7. See also John 18:36.

Col 1:29 refers to the "struggle" to present people mature in Christ.

▸ **77.** Resist, Oppose, Fight, Rebel > FIGHT

spoudazō σπουδάζω 4704

spoudazō is a verb meaning "to strive" in the sense of "make every effort." It is synonymous with ***agōnizomai*** (above) and occurs eleven times.

Eph 4:3 refers to "striving to maintain the unity of the Spirit." 2 Tim 2:15 advocates making the effort to be an accurate and faithful teacher of God's word. 2 Pet 1:10 refers to striving to make one's calling and election sure, and Heb 4:11 refers to the struggle to enter into one's eternal rest.

Other general references include those in 1 Thess 2:17; 2 Tim 4:9; Titus 3:12; 2 Pet 1:12; 3:14.

- ▸ **46.** Wait, Hope, Be Vigilant, Pay Attention To > DILIGENCE, DILIGENT, DILIGENTLY
- ▸ **68.** Ability, Possibility, Effort, Succeed, Fail > EFFORT, ENDEAVOR

SEE ALSO

- ▸ **58.** Vices > ARGUE, ARGUMENT, DISPUTE, QUARREL, STRIVE *machomai*
- ▸ **66.** Ask, Answer, Discuss, Learn > REASON, DEBATE, DISPUTE *diamachomai*

TRIUMPH

thriambeuō θριαμβεύω 2358

thriambeuō is a rare verb found only twice. 2 Cor 2:14 contains the affirmation that God in Christ always "leads (his people) in triumph." Col 2:15 then declares that Christ "has triumphed" over his enemies on the cross.

VICTORY

nikos νῖκος 3534

nikos is a noun denoting "victory" in all four occurrences of the term. Establishing "victory" over injustice as part of the charter of the messianic king is indicated in Matt 12:20. The remaining contexts speak of the "victory" over death and sin won by Christ through his own death and resurrection (1 Cor 15:54ff.).

nikē νίκη 3529

nikē is a rare variant form of ***nikos*** (above) denoting the believer's "victory" over the world, won by faith (1 John 5:4).

WRESTLING, STRUGGLING

palē πάλη 3823

palē is a rare noun denoting the "wrestling" or "struggle" of the believer against spiritual powers of darkness (Eph 6:12).

69. Have, Possess, Hold, Grasp, Bear, Carry

ATTAIN, LAY HOLD OF

katantaō καταντάω 2658

katantaō is a verb found in thirteen places with the primary meaning "come to." In most of these contexts, the sense is that of reaching, or arriving at, a particular destination. In two places, however, the meaning "come to" carries the additional sense of "attain" — "to come to the point of experiencing." In Eph 4:12 the aim is to "attain to the unity of the faith"; and in Phil 3:11 the apostle's goal is "to attain (i.e., experience) the resurrection from the dead."

▸ **86.** Movement Toward or Away From > ARRIVE

katalambanō καταλαμβάνω 2638

The verb ***katalambanō*** is found in fifteen contexts, expressing the underlying sense of "lay hold of," "take," "apprehend," plus other related nuances. One of these nuances is "attain" or "obtain," as in Rom 9:30, in relation to the Gentiles "obtaining" righteousness. 1 Cor 9:24 refers to believers striving to "obtain" or "win" the prize of eternal life. In addition, ***katalambanō*** indicates the sense of "attain to understanding" or "comprehend," "understand" in relation to perceiving spiritual truth (Acts 10:34; Eph 3:18).

▸ **69.** Have, Possess, Hold, Grasp, Bear, Carry > OBTAIN
▸ **70.** Give, Take, Seize, Touch > APPREHEND, SEIZE, CAPTURE, ARREST

BEAR, CARRY

bastazō βαστάζω 941

The verb ***bastazō*** means "bear," "carry" throughout its usages.

References to "bearing" or "carrying" people include Matt 3:11; Mark 14:13; Luke 10:4; John 20:15; Acts 3:2; 21:35; Rev 17:7 (Gal 6:17). Matt 8:17 refers to sorrows "borne" by the messianic Suffering Servant (Isa 53:4). Exhortations to "bear one another's burdens" are found in Rom 15:1; Gal 6:2. The "bearing" of children in the womb is indicated in Luke 11:27. In the context of the spread of the gospel, the task of "bearing" or "carrying" the name of Christ to the Gentiles is indicated in Acts 9:15. John 19:17 describes Christ as literally "carrying" his cross to his place of execution. In Luke 14:27, the expression "to carry one's cross" is used symbolically to indicate a person's desire to identify with the sufferings of Christ.

The meaning "bear" in the sense of "receive" is found in connection with the appropriating of the teachings of Christ (John 16:12).

bastazō is also translated "support" in relation to a tree's root system "bearing" or "supporting" the branches (Rom 11:18).

Elsewhere the meaning "bear" signifies "to endure," "tolerate." The Ephesian congregation is commended for refusing to "tolerate" evil men in Rev 2:2, and for "enduring" persecution in Rev 2:3.

pherō φέρω 5342

The verb ***pherō*** occurs around sixty times with the primary sense of "bring." A few contexts indicate the meaning "bear" or "carry."

The capacity of a branch to "bear" fruit is indicated in John 15:2ff. in both a literal and metaphorical sense. The literal phenomenon of "fruit bearing" is used as an analogy for the manifestation of godly character in the life of the believer, brought about by the Holy Spirit.

The meaning "bear" is found in Heb 13:13 in reference to sharing in the disgrace Christ experienced as a means of identifying with him in his suffering.

pherō is also predicated of God when he is said to "endure" or "bear" wickedness with patience (Rom 9:22).

▸ **29.** Boats, Fishing, Maritime Activity > DRIVE ALONG
▸ **86.** Movement Toward or Away From > BRING, BROUGHT
▸ **86.** Movement Toward or Away From > REACH, REACH OUT

anapherō ἀναφέρω 399

anapherō is a variant of ***pherō*** (above) found twelve times with the senses of "offer up" (i.e., sacrifices) and "carry" or "bear."

Luke 24:51 affirms that Christ was carried up to heaven by angels. In Heb 9:28; 1 Pet 2:24, Christ is declared to "have borne" the sins of many people in his atoning death on the cross.

▸ **70.** Give, Take, Seize, Touch > OFFER

ekpherō ἐκφέρω 1627

ekpherō is a verb found in nine places, with the primary meaning "carry out." The term refers to the literal, physical removal of dead bodies from a house in Acts 5:6ff.; and to the impossibility of "carrying out" anything of this world into the next (1 Tim 6:7).

phoreō φορέω 5409

phoreō is a verb found five times, with the meanings "wear" and "bear."

Rom 13:4 refers to the civil ruler as one who "bears the sword of justice." 1 Cor 15:49 refers to God's people "bearing" both the image of man as a created being and also the image of the man in heaven.

▸ **35.** Clothing, Adornment, Textiles > WEAR, PUT ON CLOTHES, CLOTHE

dysbastaktos δυσβάστακτος 1419

dysbastaktos is an adjective found only twice, with the meaning "hard to bear." Both Matt 23:4; Luke 11:46 refer to intolerable burdens the religious leaders placed on the Israelite people.

SEE ALSO

- ▸ **28.** Agriculture, Viticulture, Animal Husbandry > BEAR, BRING FORTH
  karpophoreō
- ▸ **60.** Virtues > ENDURE, BEAR, FORBEAR
  hypopherō, stegō, anechomai

GATHER

systrephō συστρέφω 4962

systrephō is a rare verb found only in Acts 28:3, referring to Paul "gathering" some firewood.

SEE ALSO

- ▸ **24.** Dwell, Live, Gather, Hospitality > GATHER, GATHERING
  synagō, episynagō, synathroizō
- ▸ **28.** Agriculture, Viticulture, Animal Husbandry > GATHER, HARVEST, PICK, PLUCK
  syllegō, trygaō
- ▸ **41.** Sacrifice, Offering, Worship, Praise > GATHER, ASSEMBLE, ASSEMBLY, SYNAGOGUE, CHURCH
  episynagōgē

HOLD, GRASP, HAVE

echō ἔχω 2192

echō primarily means "have," as well as a number of related senses, in the approximately six hundred contexts in which it is found. On seven occasions, however, ***echō*** is translated "hold," with various nuances.

Matt 21:26; Mark 11:32 record that the Israelite population "held" (i.e., considered) John the Baptist to be a prophet. The same is predicated of Jesus in Matt 21:46. In Acts 20:24, Paul does not consider (lit., "hold") his own life as precious to himself. 1 Tim 3:9 contains the exhortation to "hold to" (i.e., believe in) the mystery of the faith; and in 2 Tim 1:13 a similar injunction is given with respect to the pattern of sound teaching. ***echō*** is translated "hold" in the sense of "possessing" in 2 Tim 3:5.

katechō κατέχω 2722

This verb is found in about twenty places meaning "keep," "take possession," "hold." With the latter meaning and several related senses, ***katechō*** occurs nine times.

The meaning "take hold of," in the sense of "seize," is found in Matt 21:38 with respect to persons. Metaphorically speaking, ***katechō*** is translated "hold," in the sense of "hold down" or "suppress," in relation to the stifling of truth in the human consciousness. More commonly ***katechō*** reflects the idea of "holding fast (i.e., clinging tenaciously) to" a number of things such as the word of the gospel (1 Cor 15:2); that which is good (1 Thess 5:21); confidence in Christ (Heb 3:6); and one's confession of faith (Heb 10:23). 2 Thess 2:6, 7 refer to holding back, or restraining, the man of lawlessness.

▸ **69.** Have, Possess, Hold, Grasp, Bear, Carry > KEEP

krateō κρατέω 2902

krateō occurs around fifty times and is translated "hold" in a variety of contexts with several nuances. Two predominant meanings are "take hold of," in the sense of "grasp" or "seize"; and "hold fast to," signifying "remain true to" or "observe."

The idea of "grasp" or "seize" is primarily literal in the following texts, where the following objects are laid hold of — for example, sheep (Matt 12:11); a hand (Mark 1:31); seven stars in the hand of Christ (Rev 2:1); and the four winds of heaven, by angelic hands (Rev 7:1). People are also seized upon in the following passages — for example, John the Baptist (Matt 14:3, Mark 6:17); a servant (Matt 18:28); and a young man wearing a linen cloth (Mark 14:51). An unsuccessful attempt to seize Jesus is made in Mark 12:12. But, in the garden of Gethsemane, Jesus is finally arrested (Matt 26:48ff.; Mark 14:44ff.). Heb 6:18 encourages believers to grasp the hope of salvation set before them.

krateō also reflects the meaning "hold fast to" in the sense of "observe." Mark 7:3ff., for example, reports the Pharisees' strict observance of the traditions of the elders. 2 Thess 2:15 contains Paul's exhortation to hold fast to the apostle's teaching. See also Heb 4:14; Rev 2:14, 15; 3:11.

Reflecting the idea of restraint, Acts 2:24 refers to the impossibility of death "holding" Jesus.

▸ **70.** Give, Take, Seize, Touch > APPREHEND, SEIZE, CAPTURE, ARREST

epilambanō ἐπιλαμβάνω 1949

This term occurs around twenty times with the primary sense of "take." In about half of these contexts, however, ***epilambanō*** is translated "take hold of."

In Luke 20:20, 26, ***epilambanō*** refers to taking hold of Jesus' words. Luke 23:26; Acts 16:19; 21:30, 33 describe "seizing" people. "Seeking after" eternal life is described in 1 Tim 6:12, 19. And Heb 8:9 refers to God "taking hold of" the hand of his people to lead them out of Egypt.

- ▸ **70.** Give, Take, Seize, Touch > APPREHEND, SEIZE, CAPTURE, ARREST
- ▸ **70.** Give, Take, Seize, Touch > TAKE, TAKE HOLD OF, TAKE UP, TAKE DOWN, TAKE AWAY, SNATCH

KEEP

tēreō τηρέω 5083

tēreō is a verb found seventy-five times and means "keep" in the sense of "obey," "preserve," as well as associated nuances.

The meaning "obey" is found primarily in the context of keeping the commandments of God (Matt 19:17) and Christ (Matt 28:20; John 14:15 [implied]). Acts 15:5 expresses the requirement to keep the law of Moses. See also 1 Tim 6:14. In addition, affirmations of obedience to such commandments are found in John 8:51ff.; 14:21; 17:6; Jas 2:10; 1 John 2:3; 5:2; Rev 1:3; 3:8; 12:17; 14:12; 22:7. Conversely, refusal or failure to obey is indicated in Mark 7:9, with reference to the Pharisees. In John 9:16, Jesus is falsely accused of failing to keep the Sabbath. See also John 14:24; 1 John 2:4.

tēreō also means "keep" in the sense of "guard," "watch over." Matt 27:36, 54 refer to guarding Jesus on the cross. Acts 12:5ff. refers to Peter being kept in prison, and Acts 24:23 refers to Paul in prison. Used participially, ***tēreō*** means "keeper" or "guard" in relation to those watching over Jesus' tomb.

tēreō expresses the idea of "keep" with the sense of "preserve" in a number of different contexts. Keeping the faith is indicated in 2 Tim 4:7. ***tēreō*** refers to believers being kept or preserved for the coming of the Lord, the eternal inheritance for the people of God (1 Thess 5:23; 1 John 5:18; Jude 1; 1 Pet 1:4). Jude 21 contains the commandment to keep oneself in the love of God. In Rev 3:10, the risen Christ promises to keep the church at Philadelphia safe from the "hour of trial" that will come upon the whole world. This is in response to their faithful endurance in obedience to his command. Several texts also indicate God's intention to preserve the wicked for the day of judgment (2 Pet 2:4, 9; 3:7; Jude 13). The command to keep oneself pure is found in 1 Tim 5:22; Jas 1:27; and the instruction to maintain the unity of the Spirit in Eph 4:3.

At a more mundane level, ***tēreō*** also refers to the action of preserving good wine (John 2:10), and perfume (John 12:7). 2 Cor 11:9 speaks of Paul keeping himself from being a financial burden to the Corinthian congregation.

▸ **46.** Wait, Hope, Be Vigilant, Pay Attention To > OBSERVE

phylassō φυλάσσω 5442

phylassō occurs around thirty times with the primary meaning "keep," as well as a number of related nuances that render the term a close synonym of ***tēreō*** (above).

With regard to the commands or statutes of God, ***phylassō*** is translated "keep" with the underlying sense of "obey." 1 Tim 5:21; 6:20 refer to the command to keep the divine laws. Obedience is acknowledged in Matt 19:20; Mark 10:20; Luke 18:21; Acts 21:24; Rom 2:26; Gal 6:13. The blessing for keeping these laws is affirmed in Luke 11:28. Conversely, an indictment for failing to keep them is found in Acts 7:53.

phylassō is also translated "keep watch over" or "protect" in Luke 2:8, in the context of caring for sheep. John 17:12 refers to Jesus protecting his disciples. In 2 Thess 3:3 Paul assures his Thessalonian congregation that God will protect them from the evil one. 2 Pet 2:5 records the historical observation that God protected Noah from the effects of the flood.

phylassō also means "keep," as in "guard." The experience of being kept under guard in chains is mentioned in relation to the Gadarene demoniac (Luke 8:29); and in relation to imprisonment (Acts 12:4; 23:35; 28:16). Luke 11:21 refers to guarding one's property. The exhortation to be on guard is indicated in Luke 12:15, where Jesus warns against cultivating such an attitude. In 2 Tim 4:15, Paul warns his readers to be on their guard against Alexander the coppersmith, who did him a great deal of harm. Similarly, Peter warns his readers against lawless men in 2 Pet 3:17.

phylassō is also translated "keep" in the sense of "retain." In John 12:25, Jesus declares that the one who "hates" his life in this world will retain it for eternal life. Acts 22:20 refers to retaining articles of clothing. The idea of "refrain from" is also evident in the usage of this term. ***phylassō*** occurs in Acts 25:25 with reference to Gentile converts being required to refrain from, or keep themselves from, ritual uncleanness. 1 John 5:21 expresses the command to keep oneself from idol worship.

phylassō also refers to "keeping" in the sense of "preserving." In 2 Tim 1:12, Paul communicates his assurance that God is able to preserve (or guard) the salvation promised to him. Jude expresses a similar assurance that God will keep him from falling away and thereby preserve him for the day of judgment (Jude 24).

▸ **62.** Care For, Protect, Guard, Watch >
GUARD, GUARDIAN, WATCH OVER, PROTECT

katechō κατέχω 2722

katechō occurs in about twenty places, meaning "keep" in the sense of "hold fast," "secure," "hold back" in about half of these contexts.

The sense of "hold back" is evident in Luke 4:42, where the crowds attempt to prevent Jesus from leaving them. Rom 1:18 speaks of the wicked attempting (in vain) to hold back (i.e., suppress) the truth of divine revelation in their own lives. 2 Thess 2:6, 7 describe the restraining of the antichrist, the lawless one, who will be held back by God until the time is right for his appearing.

katechō also conveys the sense of "holding fast" or "keeping with passionate conviction." ***katechō*** refers to holding fast to God's word (Luke 8:15); the traditions of the gospel (1 Cor 11:2); belief in the gospel (1 Cor 15:2); and our hope in Christ (Heb 3:6, 14; 10:23).

In Phlm 13 ***katechō*** conveys the sense of "retain," referring to Paul's desire to keep Onesimus, the runaway slave, as an assistant in the work of the gospel. However, he recognized that it was best to return Onesimus to his master Philemon.

▸ **69.** Have, Possess, Hold, Grasp, Bear, Carry >
HOLD, GRASP, HAVE

diatēreō διατηρέω 1301

diatēreō occurs only twice. Luke 2:51 refers to Jesus' mother keeping in her heart the insights she had gained from her son's encounter with the chief priests and elders in the Jerusalem temple. Acts 15:29 refers to the Jerusalem church leaders' instructions to recent Gentile converts to keep away from ritual and moral uncleanness.

phroureō φρουρέω 5432

phroureō occurs four times, referring to the process of "guarding" or "confirming." In 2 Cor 11:32 it refers literally to King Aretas placing the city of Damascus under guard in order to seize the apostle Paul. The remaining references are metaphorical, with a spiritual application. In Gal 3:23, Paul speaks of Christians being kept or confined under the law of Moses before their conversion to Christ, when they were freed from the law. Phil 4:17 refers to the peace of

God guarding or preserving our minds in Jesus Christ; and 1 Pet 1:5 indicates believers being guarded or preserved by God's power through faith in Christ.

▸ **62.** Care For, Protect, Guard, Watch > GUARD, GUARDIAN, WATCH OVER, PROTECT

SEE ALSO

▸ **40.** Holy Days, Feasts, Festivals > KEEP
poieō, heortazō

OBTAIN

tynchanō τυγχάνω 5177

tynchanō is a verb occurring thirteen times in all. The meaning "to obtain" is found in four of these contexts. In Acts 26:22 Paul testifies to having obtained help from God. 2 Tim 2:10 refers to the hope of the elect, who will obtain salvation in Christ for eternity. Heb 8:6 speaks of Christ having obtained a ministry that is far superior to that of the old covenant. Heb 11:35 refers to the hope of the martyrs, who look forward to gaining, or obtaining, a better resurrection.

▸ **84.** Do, Make, Accomplish, Occur > EXPERIENCE, ENJOY

katalambanō καταλαμβάνω 2638

katalambanō occurs fifteen times and means "take," "take hold of," "make one's own," "grasp." The meaning "gain," in the sense of "obtain," is found in two of these contexts. Rom 9:30 refers to the Gentiles having obtained righteousness through faith. 1 Cor 9:24 speaks of Paul's exhortation to the Corinthian believers to run the race that they might obtain the prize (i.e., of eternal life).

▸ **69.** Have, Possess, Hold, Grasp, Bear, Carry > ATTAIN, LAY HOLD OF

▸ **70.** Give, Take, Seize, Touch > APPREHEND, SEIZE, CAPTURE, ARREST

peripoiēsis περιποίησις 4047

peripoiēsis is a noun that refers to a "possession," "acquiring," "gaining," or "obtaining." The term occurs five times, with the latter sense evident in two places. 1 Thess 5:9 refers to the obtaining of our salvation through our Lord Jesus Christ; and in 2 Thess 2:14 Paul speaks of believers obtaining the glory of Christ as a consequence of their calling in the gospel.

▸ **25.** Family, Marriage, Adoption, Inheritance > POSSESSIONS

epitynchanō ἐπιτυγχάνω 2013

epitynchanō is a verb with the exclusive sense of "obtain," occurring five times. Rom 11:7 affirms that Israel failed to obtain the salvation they sought, but that it was gained by the elect. Heb 6:15 declares that Abraham obtained the promise given to him by God, as did the saints of old (Heb 11:33). In Jas 4:2 the point is made that human sinfulness makes it impossible for one to always get (or obtain) what one wants.

OWNER

kyrios κύριος 2962

kyrios commonly refers to a "lord" or "master" in the NT, primarily in the title "Lord," given to Jesus Christ by the authors of Scripture. However, on one occasion it means "owners," referring to those who had possession of the colt chosen by Jesus to carry him into Jerusalem at the beginning of the Passover festival (Luke 19:33).

▸ **54.** Rule, Authority, Command, Obedience > LORD, OVERLORD

▸ **54.** Rule, Authority, Command, Obedience > MASTER

SEE ALSO

▸ **29.** Boats, Fishing, Maritime Activity > OWNER
nauklēros

POSSESS, ACQUIRE

ktaomai κτάομαι 2932

ktaomai occurs seven times in all with the meaning "possess" in Luke 18:12; "acquire" or "buy" in Acts 1:18; 8:20; 22:28. See also Matt 10:9; Luke 21:19; 1 Thess 4:4.

70. Give, Take, Seize, Touch

APPREHEND, SEIZE, CAPTURE, ARREST

katalambanō καταλαμβάνω 2638

katalambanō is a verb found in fifteen contexts with the meanings "take," "overcome."

In several places where the term is translated "take," the thought of "seize" or "apprehend by force" is indicated (Mark 9:18). Elsewhere, ***katalambanō*** is translated "seize," in the sense of "take by surprise" (1 Thess 5:4). In John 8:3, 4 mention is made of the woman "caught" or "apprehended" in the very act of adultery.

- ▸ **69.** Have, Possess, Hold, Grasp, Bear, Carry > ATTAIN, LAY HOLD OF
- ▸ **69.** Have, Possess, Hold, Grasp, Bear, Carry > OBTAIN

piazō πιάζω 4084

piazō is a verb translated "seize" or "arrest" (i.e., apprehend by force) throughout most of the twelve occurrences of the term.

The action of "arresting," or at least attempting to arrest in a judicial sense, is indicated in John 7:30ff., 44; 8:20; 10:39; 11:57 — all with respect to Christ. See also Acts 12:4; 2 Cor 11:32.

The meaning "capture" is evident in Rev 19:20 in relation to the satanic "beast."

- ▸ **29.** Boats, Fishing, Maritime Activity > CATCH

synarpazō συναρπάζω 4884

synarpazō is a verb found in only four places, meaning "seize by force" or "catch" in each case. Three times, ***synarpazō*** refers to seizing people (Luke 8:29; Acts 6:12; 19:29); and once it refers to a ship being "caught" in a storm (Acts 27:15).

syllambanō συλλαμβάνω 4815

syllambanō is a verb found in sixteen contexts with the general meaning "take" in the senses of "seize," "capture" in most of these places.

The meaning "seize" in the sense of "capture" or "take by force" is indicated in Matt 26:55; Mark 14:48; Luke 22:54; John 18:24; Acts 1:16, with reference to the capture of Jesus the night before his crucifixion. See also Acts 23:27; 26:21.

- ▸ **15.** Gender, Reproduction, Youth, Aging > CONCEIVE
- ▸ **62.** Care For, Protect, Guard, Watch > HELP, HELPER

epilambanō ἐπιλαμβάνω 1949

epilambanō is a variant form of ***syllambanō*** (above) occurring twenty times with the general meaning "take" in various senses, including "lead," "guide," "seize" (i.e., take hold of).

The meaning "seize" in the sense of "capture," "take (violent) hold of" someone is indicated in Luke 23:26; Acts 16:19; 17:19; 18:17; 21:30.

- ▸ **69.** Have, Possess, Hold, Grasp, Bear, Carry > HOLD, GRASP, HAVE
- ▸ **70.** Give, Take, Seize, Touch > TAKE, TAKE HOLD OF, TAKE UP, TAKE DOWN, TAKE AWAY, SNATCH

krateō κρατέω 2902

krateō is a verb synonymous with ***synarpazō*** and ***syllambanō*** (above). It occurs about fifty times with the general meanings "take," "hold," in a number of contexts. ***krateō*** also means "seize" or "capture" in approximately half of these contexts (Matt 14:3; 22:6; 26:48ff.; Mark 3:21; 14:1, 4ff.; Acts 24:6).

- ▸ **69.** Have, Possess, Hold, Grasp, Bear, Carry > HOLD, GRASP, HAVE

CATCH

harpazō ἁρπάζω 726

harpazō is a verb found in thirteen places with the underlying sense of "take by force." However, in several places ***harpazō*** expresses the passive sense of "being caught up, away." Paul refers to his visionary experience of "being caught up into heaven" in 2 Cor 12:2ff. The experience of "being caught up" with the Lord at the end of time is recorded in 1 Thess 4:17. The child is said to "be caught up" to God in Rev 12:5.

- ▸ **70.** Give, Take, Seize, Touch > TAKE, TAKE HOLD OF, TAKE UP, TAKE DOWN, TAKE AWAY, SNATCH
- ▸ **76.** Force, Harm, Oppress > VIOLENCE, FORCE

agreuō ἀγρεύω 64

agreuō is a rare verb meaning "to catch." It is found only in Mark 12:13 with reference to the attempt by Jewish civil and religious leaders to "catch" or "entrap" Jesus in his words.

thēreuō θηρεύω 2340

thēreuō is a rare verb, synonymous with ***agreuō*** (above), describing the attempt by the enemies of Jesus to "catch" him in his speech in order to discredit him. It occurs only in Luke 11:54.

SEE ALSO

- ▸ **29.** Boats, Fishing, Maritime Activity > CATCH
  piazō

DELIVER, DELIVER OVER, HAND OVER, BETRAY

anadidōmi ἀναδίδωμι 325

anadidōmi is a rare verb found only in Acts 23:33, referring to a group of soldiers "delivering" a letter to the Roman governor.

epididōmi ἐπιδίδωμι 1929

epididōmi is another verb found in eleven places with the principal sense of "give." In Acts 15:30, however, the verb indicates the action of "delivering" a letter.

- ▸ **70.** Give, Take, Seize, Touch > GIVE, GIVE UP, GIVE OVER, GRANT

paradidōmi παραδίδωμι 3860

paradidōmi is a common verb found in approximately 120 contexts with the meaning "deliver," "betray."

The meaning "deliver" in the sense of "hand over" is evident in the context of arrest and delivering people to the courts (Matt 5:25; 10:17ff.; Mark 3:11). See also Matt 24:9. "Handing over" prisoners to the jailers is recorded in Matt 18:34; Acts 28:17. The Sanhedrin — the Jewish supreme civil court — "hand Jesus over" to Pilate for sentence in Mark 15:1; John 18:30ff. God is said to "hand over" wicked angels to gloomy dungeons to be held for judgment in 2 Pet 2:4. Pilate's action in "handing Jesus over" to be crucified is recorded in Matt 27:26; John 19:16. Blood money is "handed over" to Judas in Matt 26:15ff. for betraying Jesus.

paradidōmi is also translated "betray," a more specific nuance of "deliver," indicating the "handing over" of someone to a terrible fate. General references to "betrayal" include Matt 10:21; Mark 13:12; Acts 21:11. Christ's "betrayal" into the hands of humans is noted in Matt 17:22; 20:18ff.; 26:2, 23ff.; 27:18; Mark 9:31; 10:33; 14:41; Luke 9:44; 18:32; 24:2; Acts 3:13. Judas' role in this act of treachery is recorded in Mark 14:10ff.; Luke 22:4, 21ff.; John 6:71; 13:2; 18:5.

The passive sense of the term "be delivered up" is indicated in several contexts (e.g., Matt 11:27; Luke 10:22). Here all things are said to "be delivered up" by God to Christ, in the sense of committing them to him. Rom 4:25; 8:32 confirm that Christ "was delivered over to death" by God for our sins.

Other general references to the act of "delivering," in the sense of "hand over," "entrust to," include entrusting money or property to one's servants in Matt 25:14, 20. The "handing down" of the traditions of the gospel of Christ to future generations is a process indicated in Luke 1:2; Rom 6:17; 1 Cor 15:3; 2 Pet 2:21; Jude 3. God is said to "deliver over" the morally perverse to their lusts in Rom 1:24ff. The "handing over" of an immoral man to Satan — an action of ecclesiastical discipline — is noted in 1 Cor 5:5; 1 Tim 1:20. 1 Cor 15:24 affirms that Christ "will deliver" the heavenly kingdom to his Father at the end of the age.

▸ **70.** Give, Take, Seize, Touch >
GIVE, GIVE UP, GIVE OVER, GRANT

SEE ALSO

▸ **44.** Repentance, Forgiveness, Mercy, Redeem, Save >
RESCUE, DELIVER, SET FREE
eleutheroō, exaireō, katargeō, rhyomai, lytrōtēs

DIVIDE, DISTRIBUTE

diaireō διαιρέω 1244

diaireō is a verb found in only two places, meaning "divide" in the sense of "distribute." A man's inheritance is "divided" between his sons in Luke 15:12. The Holy Spirit is said to "apportion" ("distribute") gifts to all believers in 1 Cor 12:11.

diadidōmi διαδίδωμι 1239

diadidōmi is a verb found five times, meaning "divide" in the sense of "distribute." Luke 11:22 refers to the "dividing" or "distribution" of the spoils of war. "Distributing" money to the poor is noted in Luke 18:22; Acts 4:35; as is the "distribution" of food to the masses in John 6:11.

merizō μερίζω 3307

merizō is a verb found fifteen times with the underlying meaning "divide," including the dual senses of "split," and "distribute."

Matt 12:25ff.; Mark 3:24ff. refer to "dividing" a kingdom, signifying its breakup or disintegration leading to obliteration. The "distribution" of food is noted in Mark 6:41; and the "dividing" of an inheritance in Luke 12:13. The capacity of God to "distribute" or "assign" a measure of faith is indicated in Rom 12:3. See also 1 Cor 7:17. 1 Cor 1:13 refers to the impossibility of Christ "being divided."

SEE ALSO

▸ **27.** Community, Partnership, Unity, Discord >
DIVIDE, DIVISIVE, DIVISION
schizō

▸ **79.** Throw, Send, Drive, Mix, Remove >
SEPARATE, DIVIDE
diamerizō, merismos

GIFT

dōron δῶρον 1435

dōron is a noun found nineteen times with the primary meaning "gift" in a variety of contexts.

"Gifts" presented to the Christ child are noted in Matt 2:11.

Offering a "gift" at the altar in the context of worship is noted in Matt 5:23ff.; Luke 21:1, 4; Heb 5:1; 8:3ff.; 9:9; 11:4. A non-ritual reference to a "gift" is found in Rev 11:10.

In an intangible spiritual sense, ***dōron*** refers to saving faith as the "gift" of God in Eph 2:8.

dōrea δωρεά 1431

dōrea is a variant form of ***dōron*** (above) denoting a "gift" in all eleven occurrences of the term. The usage of ***dōrea*** is entirely spiritual. References to salvation and eternal life as "the gift" of God are found in John 4:10; Rom 5:15, 17; 2 Cor 9:15; Heb 6:4.

The "gift" of the Holy Spirit as the accompaniment to personal conversion is noted in Acts 2:38; 10:45; 11:17. See also Acts 8:20. Then, the divine "gift" of grace is indicated in Eph 3:7; 4:7.

dōrēma δώρημα 1434

dōrēma is a rare synonym for ***dōron*** and ***dōrea*** (above) denoting the "gift" of salvation in Rom 5:16; and a "gift" in the general sense of God's goodness to humankind in Jas 1:17.

doma δόμα 1390

doma is a noun found four times meaning "gifts" in a general, tangible sense in Matt 7:11; Luke 11:13; Eph 4:8; Phil 4:17.

charisma χάρισμα 5486

charisma is a noun denoting a "spiritual gift" throughout its seventeen occurrences.

The meaning "spiritual gift" as given by God in a general sense is indicated in Rom 1:11; 11:29; 12:6; 1 Cor 1:7; 7:7; 2 Tim 1:6; 1 Pet 4:10. Specific "gifts" granted by the Spirit of God are noted in 1 Cor 12:4, 9, 28ff.; 1 Tim 4:14.

charisma denotes the "free gift" of salvation in Rom 5:15, 16; 6:23.

merismos μερισμός 3311

merismos is a rare noun denoting the "gifts" of the Holy Spirit in Heb 2:4.

▸ **79.** Throw, Send, Drive, Mix, Remove > SEPARATE, DIVIDE

GIVE, GIVE UP, GIVE OVER, GRANT

didōmi δίδωμι 1325

didōmi is a common verb found in approximately four hundred places with the predominant meaning "to give" throughout, in a variety of contexts and with a variety of nuances.

The "granting" of a certificate of divorce is indicated in Matt 5:31; 19:7.

Mundane references to "giving" among people include those in Matt 5:42; Mark 6:37; Luke 6:38; John 4:12; Acts 20:35.

"Giving" praise or glory to God is indicated in Luke 18:43; John 9:24; Acts 12:23; Rom 4:20. Heb 7:4 mentions Abraham "giving" Melchizedek a tenth of the plunder from the victory over the Canaanite kings. People are said to "give" glory to the God of heaven in Rev 11:13.

Requests for God to "give" his people their daily needs are found in Matt 6:11; Luke 11:3. There are also other references to people requesting God to "grant" them their requests (e.g., Matt 7:7).

In particular, some of the disciples ask Christ to "grant" them the privilege of sitting next to him in glory in Mark 10:37.

God "gives" various things to his people, including civil authority (Matt 9:8); spiritual power over unclean spirits (Matt 10:1; Mark 6:7); insight into spiritual realities (Matt 13:11ff.; Mark 4:11; 13:11; Luke 8:10; John 3:27); knowledge of salvation (Luke 1:77); the kingdom of God (Luke 12:32); power to become children of God (John 1:12); the law to Moses (citing the Sinai narrative traditions, John 1:17); manna from heaven (John 6:31ff., again with reference to the wilderness narratives of the Pentateuch); the Holy Spirit as another counselor for his people (John 14:16; Acts 11:17); peace to his people (John 14:27); repentance to Israel (Acts 5:31); the covenant of circumcision to Abraham (Acts 7:8); and rain from heaven (Acts 14:17).

General references to God "giving" the Holy Spirit to his people include those in Acts 15:8; 1 John 3:24; 4:13; Rom 5:5; 1 Cor 12:7; 2 Cor 1:22. In a related sense, God is also said to "give" gifts to his church through the Spirit (1 Cor 12:8; Eph 4:11), as well as "grace" (1 Cor 3:10; Gal 2:9; Eph 3:7, 8; 2 Tim 1:9); and love (1 John 3:1). 1 John 5:11 declares that God "has given" his people eternal life.

Divine refusal to "give" is noted in Matt 12:39; Luke 11:29, with reference to a sign.

White robes are given to the saints in heaven (Rev 6:11). Jesus takes to himself the prerogative of "giving the keys of the kingdom" to Peter his disciple in Matt 16:19.

Jesus is said to "give his life as a ransom for many" (Matt 20:28; Mark 10:45; 1 Tim 2:6), and to "give" his people eternal life (John 10:28). Gal 1:4 affirms that Christ "gave himself" for the sins of his people. Eph 4:8 affirms that he "gave" gifts to people.

God himself is said to "give" divine authority to his Son in Matt 21:23; 28:18 (see also Mark 11:28); to "give" him the throne of David his ancestor (Luke 1:32); to "give" all things into his hand (John 3:35; 13:3). See also John 5:22ff.; 10:29; 18:11. In particular, John 17:2ff. refers to the people God had given to him. 1 Pet 1:21 declares that God "gave" glory to Jesus after raising him from the dead. John 3:16 records that God "gave" his Son to a lost world, that it may be redeemed and forgiven.

In non-personal contexts, Matt 24:29; Mark 13:24 refer to the light "given off" by the sun and moon. The devil promises to "give" Jesus all the kingdoms of the world if he will fall down and worship him (Matt 4:9; Luke 4:6).

Satanic beings "are given" power to harm humankind in Rev 9:5; 16:8. See also Rev 13:2ff. The sea and hell are said to "give up" the dead in Rev 20:13.

▸ **28.** Agriculture, Viticulture, Animal Husbandry > YIELD

epididōmi ἐπιδίδωμι 1929

epididōmi is a verb found twelve times with the primary senses of "give," "hand over (to)."

The literal act of "giving," or "handing" something over to someone, is indicated in Matt 7:9ff.; Luke 4:17; 11:11ff.; 24:30, 42; John 13:26.

▸ **70.** Give, Take, Seize, Touch > DELIVER, DELIVER OVER, HAND OVER, BETRAY

paradidōmi παραδίδωμι 3860

paradidōmi is a common verb meaning "betray," "deliver up (to)" in most of its 135 occurrences, with the underlying sense of "give over."

In several places, the explicit sense of "give over (to)" is indicated where God's judgment on the morally perverse results in him "giving them over" to their immorality in a permanent state of alienation from him (Rom 1:24ff.). Similarly, Eph 4:19 refers to the wicked "giving themselves over" to every kind of immorality.

Elsewhere, the use of ***paradidōmi*** is positive. In Gal 2:20, Paul affirms that Christ "gave himself" for him; and Eph 5:2, 25 declares that Christ "has given himself up" for his church, speaking of his supreme self-sacrifice.

▸ **70.** Give, Take, Seize, Touch > DELIVER, DELIVER OVER, HAND OVER, BETRAY

charizomai χαρίζομαι 5483

charizomai is a verb found over twenty times with the predominant sense of "forgive." The term also means "give" in several places.

Luke 7:21 refers to Jesus "giving (sight) back" to the blind.

The meaning "give (up)," "grant," in the sense of "hand (someone) over" or "deliver" is found in Acts 3:14; 25:11, 16. See also Phlm 22.

God is said to "have freely given" his people all things in Christ in Rom 8:32; 1 Cor 2:12. Specifically, Gal 3:18 declares that God "gave" Abraham the covenant promise of land and progeny. Phil 2:9 affirms that God "has given" to Christ a name that is above every name.

▸ **44.** Repentance, Forgiveness, Mercy, Redeem, Save > FORGIVE, FORGIVENESS, RELEASE

dōreō δωρέω 1433

dōreō is a rare verb found three times, meaning "give," "grant."

Mark 15:45 refers to Pilate "granting" Jesus' body to Joseph of Arimathea. 2 Pet 1:3ff. declares that God "has granted" much spiritual blessing to his people.

LOT, ALLOTMENT, SHARE, CAST LOTS

klēros κλῆρος 2819

klēros is a noun referring to objects that were used in casting or drawing lots — either a stone of some sort, or a small piece of wood. ***klēros*** is translated "lot," "allotment," "inheritance." Thus the term connotes both the means of casting lots and the process of allotment itself. ***klēros*** is used both literally and metaphorically and is found twelve times with these meanings.

Reference to the physical casting of lots is found in Matt 27:35; Luke 23:34; John 19:24, in regard to Jesus' clothing at the time of his crucifixion.

klēros also refers to an "(allotted) place, or share" in ministry, as in the case of Judas Iscariot, who is mentioned in Acts 1:17 as having had a legitimate place in the apostolic band of Jesus' disciples. In the aftermath of Judas' betrayal of Jesus and the subsequent death, burial, resurrection, and ascension of Christ, Acts 1:25, 26 refer to the one who would take "the (allotted) place" of Judas in that continuing ministry. It was Matthias, who was subsequently chosen "by lot" to assume that position. Acts 8:21 cites the case of one, Simon the sorcerer, who was refused a "share" or "place" in the apostolic ministry because of his greed.

Acts 26:18 records the words of the risen Christ who spoke to Saul during his conversion experience on the road to Damascus, promising the Gentiles a "share" or "lot" in the spiritual inheritance of God's people. Similarly, Col 1:12 refers to the spiritual "inheritance" of the saints of God.

▸ **25.** Family, Marriage, Adoption, Inheritance > INHERIT, INHERITANCE

▸ **27.** Community, Partnership, Unity, Discord > SHARE, PART, ALLOTMENT, PARTAKE

lanchanō λαγχάνω 2975

lanchanō is a verb meaning "to be chosen by lot," "obtain by lot," "to cast lots." It occurs only four times. Luke 1:9 refers to Zechariah, the father of John the Baptist, being "chosen by lot" to burn incense in the temple. John 19:24 describes the Roman soldiers casting lots for the clothing of Christ at his crucifixion, as the fulfillment of the prophecy recorded in Ps 22:18. Acts 1:17 refers to Judas Iscariot as "having been allotted" a place in the apostolic band of Christ. 2 Pet 1:1 uses the term ***lanchanō*** to indicate those who have "received" a faith as precious as the apostle's. The underlying thought is of granting a spiritual allotment, or a share in the blessing of eternal life and peace with God.

OFFER

prospherō προσφέρω 4374

prospherō occurs around fifty times with the predominant senses of "offer," "offer up," "bring to," "present." In approximately half of these contexts ***prospherō*** is translated "offer" with the sense of bringing gifts to God in worship.

Matt 2:11 records the worship of the magi in offering gifts to the infant Jesus. Offering sacrifices to God in general contexts is indicated in Heb 11:4, 17 with reference to Abel and Abraham, respectively. Offering one's gift at the temple is noted in Matt 5:23ff.; 8:4; Mark 1:44; Luke 5:14; Acts 21:26; and priestly activity in this regard is specifically mentioned in Heb 5:1ff.; 8:3ff.; 9:7; 10:1ff. ***prospherō*** also refers to the offering of Jesus Christ, who gave his own life as a once-for-all sacrifice for the sin of the world (Heb 9:14, 25ff.; 10:12).

Elsewhere, ***prospherō*** refers to those who offered vinegar to Jesus as he hung on the cross. Heb 5:7 refers to Jesus offering up prayers to his Father during his life on earth. Acts 8:18 refers to Simon Magus offering money to the apostles, vainly seeking to buy the gift of the Spirit of God from them.

anapherō ἀναφέρω 399

anapherō occurs twelve times, meaning "bring," "bear," "offer (up)." The latter sense is found in five of these contexts. Heb 7:27 refers to the sacrifices offered up by the high priest under the old covenant law, and also to the once-for-all sacrifice of Jesus Christ, who offered himself as the substitutionary atonement for the sins of humankind. Jas 2:21 speaks of Abraham's willingness to offer up his own son Isaac as a sacrifice in response to God's command, even though God never intended to allow the sacrifice to take place. 1 Pet 2:5 speaks of the believer's destiny to offer up spiritual sacrifices to God through godly living (see also Heb 13:15 in this regard).

▸ **69.** Have, Possess, Hold, Grasp, Bear, Carry > BEAR, CARRY

PRESENT

paristēmi παρίστημι 3936

paristēmi is a verb with the primary meanings "stand," "stand by," "present," as well as several other minor senses, in the forty or so contexts in which it is found.

Luke 2:22 speaks of Jesus' parents presenting him to the Lord in the temple at the time of his circumcision and consecration. Peter presents the young woman Tabitha alive after raising her from the dead (Acts 9:41). Paul is "presented" (i.e., handed over) to Felix, the governor of Judea, in Acts 23:33. Paul exhorts his readers to present their bodies as living sacrifices to the Lord in Rom 12:1. Paul's desire to present the Corinthian congregation as a "pure bride" to her "husband," the risen Christ, is recorded in 2 Cor 11:2 (see also Eph 5:27; Col 1:22, 28).

- ▸ **47.** Show, Persuade, Confidence, Doubt > SHOW
- ▸ **85.** Movement, Position, State > STAND

histēmi ἵστημι 2476

histēmi is a verb that is translated "to stand," as well as a number of related senses, in the great majority of its nearly 160 occurrences. In one place, however, ***histēmi*** means "to present" in the context of the benediction of Jude 24, whereby Christ is declared able to "present" us without fault to God himself in glory.

- ▸ **83.** Set, Put, Place, Prepare, Establish > APPOINT, ORDAIN, ASSIGN
- ▸ **83.** Set, Put, Place, Prepare, Establish > ESTABLISH, FIX, GROUND, STRENGTHEN
- ▸ **83.** Set, Put, Place, Prepare, Establish > SET
- ▸ **85.** Movement, Position, State > STAND

SEE ALSO

- ▸ **3.** Periods of Time, Duration, Frequency, Speed > PRESENT
  enistēmi
- ▸ **85.** Movement, Position, State > BE PRESENT, COME
  pareimi, paraginomai, sympareimi

RECEIVE, ACCEPT, WELCOME

dechomai δέχομαι 1209

dechomai is a verb meaning "to receive" in almost all of its nearly sixty occurrences. This meaning has several distinct connotations.

In a number of places, ***dechomai*** is translated "receive" in the sense of "welcome." General references to "receiving" people in this sense are found in Matt 10:40ff.; Luke 16:9; John 4:45; Acts 21:17; 2 Cor 7:15 (see also 2 Cor 11:16); Gal 4:14; Col 4:10. The courtesy of welcoming people as guests in one's town is noted in Luke 16:4. Also, Heb 11:31 refers to Rahab's faith in Yahweh and to her courage in welcoming the Israelite spies into her Jericho home and offering them protection. Mark 6:11; Matt 10:14; Luke 9:5 mention those who refuse to extend hospitality to the disciples of Jesus during their ministry "tour" of Judea. By refusing to "receive" the members of the apostolic band, such towns would incur divine displeasure. Matt 18:5; Mark 9:37; Luke 9:48 cite the importance of "receiving" (i.e., welcoming) little children into the kingdom of God unconditionally and without prejudice.

The sense of "receive" as "accept as true" is indicated, for example, in Matt 11:14, where Jesus affirms, for those willing to "accept" it, that John the Baptist is the "new Elijah" as foretold by the prophet Malachi. Luke 8:13; Acts 8:14; 17:11; 1 Thess 2:13; Jas 1:21 indicate the value of receiving (i.e., accepting) God's word as true. 2 Cor 11:4 warns against "receiving" a different gospel.

"Receiving" also expresses the idea of "discerning" in 1 Cor 2:14, where it is affirmed that unbelievers do not receive gifts from the Spirit of God because they are incapable of appreciating them.

Other contexts refer to the act of "receiving" in regard to human relationships with God. Acts 7:38, for example, cites Moses as the one who received from God the oracles of the law. In Acts 7:59, Stephen asks God to receive his Spirit at the point of his own death. 2 Cor 6:1 warns against receiving the grace of God in vain.

In mundane contexts, ***dechomai*** also refers to receiving letters (Acts 22:5; 28:21).

lambanō λαμβάνω 2983

lambanō is a verb occurring around 260 times, with the two primary meanings "take," "receive." The meaning "receive" is found in a variety of contexts.

lambanō refers literally to "receiving" with the sense of "acquire" or "gain." General references to such activity include those in Matt 10:8; John 13:30; Acts 3:5, including the oft-quoted maxim "It is more blessed to give than to receive" (Acts 20:35). ***lambanō*** also refers to receiving a wage (Matt 20:9; John 4:36; 1 Cor 3:8); a prize (1 Cor 9:24); tithes (Heb 7:8, 9); and civil authority (Acts 26:10; Rev 17:12).

lambanō indicates receiving blessing from God (John 1:16); a reward (1 Cor 3:14); a reward for faithful service to God (Matt 19:29; Mark 10:30); answers as a result of prayer (Matt 7:8; Mark 11:24; Luke 11:10; John 16:24; 1 John 3:22 [see also Jas 4:3]); and even the office of the priesthood (Heb 7:5). Heb 11:35 cites the blessing of receiving one's dead back to life. Rev 2:17 speaks of receiving a new name from the risen Christ in heaven.

With particular reference to the relationship between God and his people Israel, Heb 11:8 mentions the divine promise to Abraham that his descendants would receive the land of Canaan as an inheritance. Heb 11:13 refers to the list of old covenant saints who received the promises of God concerning his purposes in salvation. God promises that his new covenant people will receive their promised eternal inheritance (Heb 9:15, including mention of the "crown of life" in Jas 1:2).

In negative contexts, ***lambanō*** refers to people receiving punishment for sin (Matt 23:14; Mark 12:40; Luke 20:47; Rom 13:2; Heb 2:2). Rev 14:9, 11; 19:20 refer to the godless receiving the "mark of the beast" on their hands and foreheads. In contrast, Rev 20:4 refers to those believers who had not received this demonic "mark," declaring that they came to life and reigned with Christ for 1,000 years.

lambanō also refers to "receiving" a welcome that demonstrates genuine hospitality (Matt 10:41). In a "negative" context, 2 John 10 enjoins believers not to "receive" any false teacher into one's home. No welcome of any kind is to be extended to them.

As with ***dechomai*** (above), ***lambanō*** also refers to the act of "receiving" in terms of "accepting as true." This applies, for example, to receiving the word of God in John 17:8. Such a response to God's word is also indicated symbolically in the parable of the sower, where seed sown in fertile ground yields an abundant harvest (Matt 13:20). A lesser response is indicated in Mark 4:16, where the seed is received joyfully but, as it is sown on rocky ground, the results are only short lived. John 12:48 denounces and condemns those who refuse to receive God's word. Similar references to rejecting (i.e., "not receiving") apostolic testimony to the person of Christ are found in John 3:11, 32; 5:43. But see also John 3:33 for a wholehearted acceptance of such testimony.

Other examples of "receiving" include worshiping Christ as Savior and Lord, implicitly indicated in John 1:12; receiving forgiveness of sins (Acts 10:43; 26:18); and receiving circumcision (John 7:23; Rom 4:11; 5:11). Acts 20:24 refers to Paul receiving a ministry from the Lord; and Acts 1:5 to receiving the grace of God. The promise of receiving the Holy Spirit is noted in John 7:39 (in relation to this phenomenon, see also John 14:17; 1 John 2:27). There are also distinctive references to the early believers receiving the Holy Spirit in Acts 8:17; 10:47; 19:2 (see also Acts 8:19); Rom 8:15; 1 Cor 2:12; Gal 3:2, 14.

Jesus Christ is the one who "receives" a command from the Father (e.g., John 10:18); as well as honor and glory (2 Pet 1:17; Rev 4:11; 5:12); and power (Rev 2:27). Acts 2:33 declares that Jesus receives the promised Holy Spirit in the first instance from God the Father. In related contexts, Jesus invokes the pouring out of the Holy Spirit on his disciples in John 20:22 with the words "receive the Spirit," as an anticipation of the baptism of the Spirit in Acts 2. Acts 1:8 promises that the disciples will receive power at the coming of the Spirit (see also Acts 2:38).

▸ **70.** Give, Take, Seize, Touch > TAKE, TAKE HOLD OF, TAKE UP, TAKE DOWN, TAKE AWAY, SNATCH

paradechomai παραδέχομαι 3858

paradechomai is a verb closely related to the term ***dechomai*** (above) occurring in only five contexts and meaning "receive" in the sense of "accept." Mark 4:20 refers to those who hear the word of God and "receive" (i.e., accept) it as true. Acts 16:21 speaks of customs that Romans are unable to accept. Paul exhorts Timothy in 1 Tim 5:19 never to accept any charges against an elder except on the advice of two or three witnesses. Everyone whom God lovingly accepts as a son will be disciplined by him (Heb 12:6). See also Acts 22:18.

apolambanō ἀπολαμβάνω 618

apolambanō is a variant form of ***lambanō*** (above) occurring fourteen times and meaning "receive" in the general sense of "get back that which is due." The individual usage of the term is varied.

Luke 6:34 refers to the practice of receiving payment from a debtor. Luke 15:27 speaks of the grateful father in Jesus' parable who gets (i.e., receives) his son back home safely. Luke 16:25 speaks of receiving good things in this life (see also Luke 18:30). In Luke 23:41, the penitent thief on the cross beside Jesus admits to receiving due justice for his crime. This same fate awaits the godless, alluded to in Rom 1:27. Gal 4:5 cites the blessing of believers who receive adoption as God's children. Col 3:25; 2 John 8 refer to the blessing granted to the believer in Christ, who will receive eternal life as his reward.

proslambanō προσλαμβάνω 4355

proslambanō is a variant form of ***lambanō*** (above) found in fifteen contexts and meaning "take" or "receive." The meaning "receive" is found in seven contexts, all with the sense of "welcome" (Acts 28:2; Rom 14:1, 3; 15:7; Phlm 12, 17).

▸ **70.** Give, Take, Seize, Touch > TAKE, TAKE HOLD OF, TAKE UP, TAKE DOWN, TAKE AWAY, SNATCH

paralambanō παραλαμβάνω 3880

paralambanō is also a variant form of ***lambanō*** (above). It is found in fifty contexts, with the dominant meanings "take" and "receive." The former meaning is more common. The meaning "receive," by and large, expresses the underlying sense of "get," "acquire," or "obtain." It is used in various contexts.

Mark 7:4 refers to the fastidious practices of the Pharisees, who "received" (i.e., observed) many traditions under the law. 2 Thess 3:6 refers to receiving, or observing, the noble tradition of godly living which Paul commended to his congregation at Thessalonica. 1 Cor 15:1ff.; Gal 1:9ff. refer to receiving the gospel (see also Phil 4:9); and 1 Thess 2:13 refers to receiving the word of God. 1 Cor 11:23 refers to receiving instructions from the Lord, in the context of Paul laying down the essential elements for the observation of the Lord's Supper. Col 2:6 refers to receiving Christ as Lord. Col 4:17 speaks of Paul receiving a ministry from the Lord. Believers are described in Heb 12:28 as receiving a kingdom that is unshakable. John 1:11 uses ***paralambanō*** in a negative sense, with reference to Jesus not being received (i.e., accepted) by his fellow citizens of Nazareth.

Concerning Jesus, as one who also "receives," John 14:3 speaks of heaven as the place where Christ will one day receive his followers — meaning that he will "take them to himself."

▸ **70.** Give, Take, Seize, Touch > TAKE, TAKE HOLD OF, TAKE UP, TAKE DOWN, TAKE AWAY, SNATCH

metalambanō μεταλαμβάνω 3335

metalambanō is another variant form of the verb ***lambanō*** (above). It occurs six times; only once, however, does it mean "receive." Heb 6:7 speaks of land that drinks in the rain falling on it as receiving a blessing from God.

▸ **27.** Community, Partnership, Unity, Discord > SHARE, PART, ALLOTMENT, PARTAKE

metalēmpsis μετάλημψις 3336

metalēmpsis is a noun derived from ***metalambanō*** (above) occurring only in 1 Tim 4:3, with the force of a passive infinitive, "to be received." The context speaks of food which God created "to be accepted or received" with thanksgiving from his people.

lēmpsis λῆμψις 3028

lēmpsis is a noun derived from ***lambanō*** (above) with the sense of "receiving." It is an abstract term paired with the term "giving," referring to the generosity of the Philippian church in their relationship with Paul and other churches. ***lēmpsis*** occurs only in Phil 4:15.

apodechomai ἀποδέχομαι 588

apodechomai is a variant form of the verb ***dechomai*** (above). It occurs in only five places, meaning "receive" in the sense of "welcome," "accept" (i.e., believe to be true). The former sense of "welcome" is found in Luke 8:40, with respect to the crowd's reception of Jesus. Acts 15:4; 18:27; 28:30 refer to extending a welcome in terms of hospitality. Acts 2:41 refers to the believing response of the huge audience that listened to the apostle Peter preaching on the day of Pentecost and "received his word." See also Acts 24:3.

epidechomai ἐπιδέχομαι 1926

This variant form of ***dechomai*** (above) is found only twice. It refers to the refusal of Diotrephes to "receive" or "acknowledge" the authority of the apostle John. In 3 John 10, ***epidechomai*** means "receive" in the sense of "welcome."

anadechomai ἀναδέχομαι 324

anadechomai, a variant form of ***dechomai*** (above), is found in only two places and means "receive." In Acts 28:7 it describes the act of "welcoming a guest," and in Heb 11:17 it refers to Abraham as the one who "received" the covenant promises of God.

komizō κομίζω 2865

komizō is a verb meaning to "receive" in all but one of the eleven occurrences of the term.

Matt 25:27 refers to receiving interest from a bank loan. ***komizō*** refers in several places to receiving due recompense — either good or evil — for our actions in this life, from the judgment seat of Christ (2 Cor 5:10; Eph 6:8; Col 3:25; 2 Pet 2:13). Receiving the benefits of God's redemptive promises is a blessing indicated in Heb 10:36 (Heb 11:39; 1 Pet 1:9 [referring to salvation itself]; 1 Pet 5:4 [the crown of glory]). This miracle of Abraham "receiving Isaac back from the dead" — metaphorically speaking — is described in Heb 11:19.

apechō ἀπέχω 568

apechō is a verb found eleven times, meaning "receive" in several of these contexts. Matt 6:2ff.; Luke 6:24 speak of receiving a reward. The privilege of receiving payment, as a gift, is indicated in Phil 4:18. To receive someone back in the sense of welcoming them back is indicated in Phlm 15.

nomotheteō νομοθετέω 3549

nomotheteō is a verb meaning "to receive the law" in Heb 7:11, with regard to the people of God. The term occurs only twice, with the second meaning evident in Heb 8:6, "to enact."

▸ **38.** Covenant, Law, Rites, Roles > ENACT, ESTABLISH

SEE ALSO

▸ **20.** Illness, Disease, Health, Healing > RECEIVE SIGHT
anablepō

▸ **24.** Dwell, Live, Gather, Hospitality >
RECEIVE, WELCOME
prosdechomai, eisdechomai, hypodechomai

▸ **41.** Sacrifice, Offering, Worship, Praise >
TITHE, PAYMENT
dekatoō

TAKE, TAKE HOLD OF, TAKE UP, TAKE DOWN, TAKE AWAY, SNATCH

lambanō λαμβάνω 2983

lambanō is a verb occurring around 260 times with the primary senses of "receive" and "take." The latter meaning accounts for a little under half of its usage, including a variety of nuances.

The meaning "take away" or "remove" is indicated in relation to the loss of one's coat in a lawsuit (Matt 5:40). Pilate issues the command to have Jesus taken away in John 18:31; 19:6. John 19:40 records that Jesus' body was taken away for burial.

The sense of "take up" is evident in relation to the believer taking up his cross in identification with Christ in his suffering (Matt 10:38). Acts 1:25 refers to taking up a position for ministry. In John 10:17, Jesus declares that he will take up his life again after laying it down. See also Matt 16:9, 10.

lambanō refers to Christ "taking upon" himself the form of a man (Phil 2:7); as well as the sins and infirmities of his people (Matt 8:17).

Other nuances of ***lambanō*** associated with "taking" include "to accost," "grab hold of" (Matt 21:39); "take counsel," "seek advice" (Matt 27:7); "take courage" (Acts 28:15); and "take" a wife (i.e., marry) (Mark 12:19ff.; Luke 20:28ff.).

The general sense of "taking (hold of)" objects is illustrated in Matt 13:31; 26:52; Mark 14:22ff.; Luke 6:4; John 6:7; 1 Cor 11:24; Rev 5:7; 10:9ff.

▸ **70.** Give, Take, Seize, Touch >
RECEIVE, ACCEPT, WELCOME

paralambanō παραλαμβάνω 3880

paralambanō is a synonym for ***lambanō*** (above) with the primary meanings "take," "receive." The term occurs fifty times, with the meaning "take" evident in over half of these contexts.

The meaning "take" in the sense of "lead" or "bring" is applied to the infant Jesus being taken to Egypt by his parents in Matt 2:13ff. Satan is described taking Jesus to Jerusalem, to the pinnacle of the temple, in order to tempt him (Matt 4:5ff.). Other such general references include those in Matt 12:45; Mark 4:36; Luke 9:28; Acts 15:39.

Elsewhere, ***paralambanō*** refers to "taking" a wife (Matt 1:20); to Jesus being "taken away" to be crucified (John 19:16); and to persons being "taken up" into heaven (Matt 24:40; Luke 17:34).

▸ **70.** Give, Take, Seize, Touch > RECEIVE, ACCEPT, WELCOME

analambanō ἀναλαμβάνω 353

analambanō is a verb meaning "take," "take up" for most of its approximately thirteen occurrences.

The meaning "take up" relates to Christ ascending into heaven after his resurrection (Mark 16:19; Acts 1:2, 11, 22; 1 Tim 3:16). The visionary sheet laden with unclean food in Peter's vision is "taken up" into heaven in Acts 10:16. In Eph 6:13, 16 Paul exhorts his readers to "take up" the whole armor of God.

analambanō is also translated "take" in the sense of "get," "fetch" in Acts 23:31; 2 Tim 4:11.

epilambanō ἐπιλαμβάνω 1949

This verb, occurring approximately twenty times, means "take hold of" in the majority of cases.

"Taking hold of" people in the sense of "seizing" them is noted in Luke 23:26; Acts 21:30. Mark 8:29; Heb 8:9 speak of "taking hold of" someone's hand. An attempt to "take hold of" Jesus' words (i.e., to catch him out) is indicated in Luke 20:20. An exhortation to take hold of eternal life is found in 1 Tim 6:12, 19. See also Luke 9:47; 14:4; Acts 9:27.

▸ **69.** Have, Possess, Hold, Grasp, Bear, Carry > HOLD, GRASP, HAVE

▸ **70.** Give, Take, Seize, Touch > APPREHEND, SEIZE, CAPTURE, ARREST

proslambanō προσλαμβάνω 4355

proslambanō is a verb occurring fourteen times meaning "take," "take to oneself," "take (someone) aside" in over half of these contexts.

The action of "taking people aside" is indicated in the following contexts: for teaching (Acts 18:26); for rebuke (Matt 16:22; Mark 8:32); and the general context of Acts 17:5. Acts 27:33ff. refers to taking food to eat.

▸ **70.** Give, Take, Seize, Touch > RECEIVE, ACCEPT, WELCOME

harpazō ἁρπάζω 726

harpazō is a verb found in thirteen places meaning "take by force" in various settings.

"Take away" means "snatch away" in relation to Satan stealing the word of God from the hearts and minds of people who had initially received it (Matt 13:19). John 10:12 describes the action of the wolf snatching sheep away from the flock. John 10:28ff. contains the divine guarantee that no believer will ever "be snatched out" of the hand of Christ.

harpazō also refers to Paul "being caught (or taken) up" to the third heaven in 2 Cor 12:2ff. Similarly, believers are promised that they will be caught up with the dead in Christ to meet the Lord in the air when he returns (1 Thess 4:17; Rev 12:5).

harpazō also means "to take by force" in the context of violent action (Matt 11:12; John 6:15; Acts 23:10).

▸ **70.** Give, Take, Seize, Touch > CATCH

▸ **76.** Force, Harm, Oppress > VIOLENCE, FORCE

apairō ἀπαίρω 522

apairō is a verb found only three times, all referring to Jesus Christ as the "bridegroom" who one day "will be taken away" from his disciples (Matt 9:15; Mark 2:20; Luke 5:35).

kathaireō καθαιρέω 2507

This verb occurs in nine places, meaning "take down" in about half of these, all referring to the body of Christ being taken down from the cross (Mark 15:36, 46; Luke 23:53; Acts 13:29).

▸ **21.** Die, Perish, Kill, Destroy > CAST DOWN

SEE ALSO

▸ **35.** Clothing, Adornment, Textiles > TAKE OFF, STRIP
ekdyō

▸ **79.** Throw, Send, Drive, Mix, Remove > TAKE AWAY, REMOVE
aphaireō, periaireō, paraphero

▸ **85.** Movement, Position, State > TAKE WITH
symparalambanō

TOUCH, HANDLE, FEEL

psēlaphaō ψηλαφάω 5584

This a rare term, occurring four times and meaning "handle," "touch," "feel" in all but one of these contexts.

In Luke 24:39, Jesus invites his disciples to "touch" or "handle" him, to verify that he has a physical body after his resurrection. Heb 12:18 denies that the new Jerusalem can be physically handled or touched like the ancient Mount Sinai. 1 John 1:1 emphasizes the fact that John and the other disciples physically touched and handled the incarnate word of life in the person of Jesus Christ.

doloō δολόω 1389

This word occurs only once, in 2 Cor 4:2, in reference to handling the word of God deceitfully.

▸ **58.** Vices > DECEIT, DECEITFUL, DECEPTION, DECEIVE, DECEIVER, DECEITFULLY

haptomai ἅπτομαι 680

haptomai means "touch" throughout its usage, in a variety of contexts.

The action of "touching" in the sense of "making direct physical contact with" is found in a general sense in John 20:17. Christ's miraculous "touching," resulting in the healing of others, is recorded in Matt 8:3, 15; 9:20ff.; Mark 3:10; 5:28ff.; Luke 5:13; 8:44ff. "Touching" with intent to harm is indicated in 1 John 5:18. The exhortation to touch nothing unclean is found in 2 Cor 6:17 (see also Col 2:21). 1 Cor 7:1 refers to "touching" in the context of sexual relationships.

71. Lead, Guide, Follow

FOLLOW, ACCOMPANY, PURSUE

akoloutheō ἀκολουθέω 190

akoloutheō is a verb found about ninety times with the consistent meaning "to follow." It is used in a variety of contexts, with a number of nuances.

The meaning "follow after" with the underlying sense of "become devoted, attached to," involving a solemn commitment to a person, is evident in the disciples' relationship to Christ, their leader (Matt 4:20, 25; Mark 1:18; 2:14ff.; Luke 5:27ff.; John 1:37ff.).

Christ's command to his disciples to "follow" him is recorded in Matt 9:9; 19:21; John 12:26; 21:19, 22. Exhortations concerning such a "following" are found in Matt 10:38; 16:24; Mark 8:34; Luke 9:23; 18:22.

Such an action is also predicated of the crowds who "followed after" Jesus. But this following was motivated largely by curiosity, the desire to witness miraculous signs and, for some, the need for healing — rather than by a genuine commitment to him (Matt 4:25; 8:1, 10, 22; John 6:22). There is one exception, noted in Matt 21:9; Mark 11:9, where crowds had followed him to Jerusalem in order to offer him praise — though this would be short lived. It must also be noted that of those whom Jesus had healed, many chose to "follow" him with wholehearted devotion (Luke 9:11; 18:43). A promise to "follow" Jesus, offering him a solemn lifelong commitment, is given in Matt 8:19; Luke 9:59. Such promises, however, were inevitably halfhearted (but compare John 13:36ff.).

Mundane references to people "following" others include those in Matt 8:23; Luke 22:10; John 18:15. See also Matt 12:8, 9; Acts 13:43.

Metaphorical references to Christ's sheep "following" him denote his people in John 10:4, 5, 27. Elsewhere, 1 Cor 10:4 mentions the supernatural rock (viz. Christ), from which they drank, that "followed" the people of Israel through the wilderness. Rev 6:8 mentions Hades "following" the rider Death. Rev 14:4 refers to the martyrs in heaven who always "follow" the Lamb (i.e., Christ) with great devotion. Reference to the deeds of the saints in heaven "following" them is found in Rev 14:13. In Rev 19:14 the armies of heaven "follow" the messianic rider on a white horse, who is their heavenly leader victorious against the forces of Satan.

exakoloutheō ἐξακολουθέω 1811

exakoloutheō is a rare variant of ***akoloutheō*** (above) meaning "follow" in all three occurrences of the term. 2 Pet 2:15 refers to false teachers who had "followed the way of Balaam" (i.e., lived according to the dictates of greed). 2 Peter 1:16 contains the denial that Peter and the other apostles had ever "followed" cleverly devised fables in their proclamation of the gospel. 2 Pet 2:2 warns of the danger of "following" the way of immorality as practiced by the false teachers.

epakoloutheō ἐπακολουθέω 1872

epakoloutheō is another rare variant of ***akoloutheō*** (above). It is found in 1 Pet 2:21, exhorting believers to "follow" the example of Christ's suffering.

parakoloutheō παρακολουθέω 3877

parakoloutheō is another variant of ***akoloutheō*** (above). It is found in 1 Tim 4:6, where Paul affirms that Timothy had "followed" (i.e., devoted himself to) good biblical teaching throughout his life.

synakoloutheō συνακολουθέω 4870

This rare variant of ***akoloutheō*** (above) is found only twice, in Mark 5:37; Luke 23:49. In these texts, ***synakoloutheō*** means to "follow" in the sense of "accompany (someone)."

diōkō διώκω 1377

diōkō is a verb found nearly fifty times with the primary sense of "persecute." In several places, however, there is some overlap in meaning with the sense of "follow," "pursue." An exhortation not to "follow after" false messiahs is found in Luke 17:23.

Rom 9:30 contains the affirmation that Gentiles "did not pursue" righteousness. In the following verse it is claimed, by way of contrast, that Israel had indeed "pursued" righteousness — but one that was unattainable by law. Exhortations to "pursue" peace are found in Rom 14:19; Heb 12:14; 1 Pet 3:11. Similarly, 1 Cor 14:1 contains an injunction to "follow" (i.e., pursue) the way of love. See also 1 Thess 5:15; 1 Tim 6:11; 2 Tim 2:22.

▸ **68.** Ability, Possibility, Effort, Succeed, Fail > PRESS ON

▸ **76.** Force, Harm, Oppress > PERSECUTE, PURSUE

katadiōkō καταδιώκω 2614

katadiōkō is a rare variant of ***diōkō*** (above) found only in Mark 1:36 with the literal sense of "following after" or "pursuing" someone.

SEE ALSO

▸ **81.** Forms, Groups, Patterns, Order > IMITATE, IMITATOR, FOLLOW, FOLLOWER ***mimētēs***

GUIDE, DIRECT

hodēgos ὁδηγός 3595

hodēgos is a noun found in five contexts denoting a "guide" or "leader" throughout. Matt 15:14; 23:16, 24 refer to the Pharisees as "blind guides," condemned by Jesus for their hypocrisy. Acts 1:16 describes Judas Iscariot as the "guide" who had led the Jewish authorities to arrest Jesus. Rom 2:19 refers to a "guide" to the spiritually blind.

kateuthynō κατευθύνω 2720

kateuthynō is a verb found in three places meaning "guide," "direct." Each context is metaphorical. Luke 1:79 refers to John the Baptist as a future "guide" for God's people into the way of peace. 1 Thess 3:11 refers to God as one who "directs" or "guides" the circumstances of his people. 2 Thess 3:5 contains an appeal to God to "direct" the hearts of the congregation to the love of God.

LEAD, LEAD OUT, LEAD AWAY

anagō ἀνάγω 321

anagō is a verb found nearly twenty-five times meaning "lead," "bring up" for most of the usage.

References to the Spirit "leading Jesus up" into the wilderness to be tempted by the devil are found in Matt 4:1; Luke 4:5. Other references to people "being brought or led up" to various places are found in Luke 2:22; Acts 9:39; 12:4.

Rom 10:7; Heb 13:20 refer to God having brought Jesus up from the dead.

▸ **29.** Boats, Fishing, Maritime Activity > SAIL, SET SAIL

agō ἄγω 71

agō is a verb occurring around seventy times and is usually translated "bring," "lead," in a variety of contexts.

Meaning "to (physically) lead or bring," ***agō*** refers to both human beings and animals. Matt 21:2; Mark 11:2; Luke 19:30 refer to the colt being led to Jesus for the ride into Jerusalem. Many texts refer prophetically to the disciples of Jesus being led before councilors to be persecuted (Mark 13:9, 11; Luke 21:12; Acts 5:21, 27; 6:12; 18:12). People are led to Jesus for healing in Luke 4:40; 18:40. Jesus is led from Caiaphas' house to the governor's palace in John 18:28. Other general references to "leading" are found in Luke 4:29; 23:32; John 1:42; Acts 9:2; 17:15. A metaphorical reference to the death of the Messiah is made in Acts 8:32, where his demise is likened to a sheep being led to the slaughter.

agō also refers in a number of places to God leading. Jesus' temptation experience at the outset of his public ministry commences with the Holy Spirit leading him into the wilderness (Luke 4:1). Rom 8:14; Gal 5:18 describe the sons of God as those who are led by the Spirit of God. John 10:16 speaks of Jesus bringing his flock together from other peoples, leading them towards himself. A more indirect reference is found in Rom 2:4, where Paul affirms that the kindness of God is intended to lead to repentance.

agō also refers to the activity of Satan. Luke 4:9 observes that the devil led Jesus to the pinnacle of the temple in order to tempt him.

eispherō εἰσφέρω 1533

eispherō occurs seven times and is translated "lead into," "bring into." The specific sense of "lead," however, occurs only twice, referring to the petition of the Lord's Prayer ". . . lead us not into temptation" (Matt 6:13; Luke 11:4).

hodēgeō ὁδηγέω 3594

hodēgeō occurs five times and is translated "lead," "guide."

There is a metaphorical reference to the spiritual bankruptcy of the Pharisees in Matt 15:14; Luke 6:39, where they are referred to as "blind guides," who will ultimately lead others who are spiritually blind into eternal destruction. John 16:13 refers to the ministry of the Holy Spirit, who will guide believers into all truth. Similarly, Rev 7:14 speaks of the Lamb on the throne guiding the saints to springs of living water. In Acts 8:31, the Ethiopian eunuch, reading Isaiah 53, responds to Philip's question with his own, saying: "How can I [understand], unless someone guides me?"

apagō ἀπάγω 520

apagō is a verb derived from ***agō*** (above) that means "lead away," with particular emphasis on being taken to trial or punishment, both literally and metaphorically. The term occurs fifteen times.

Metaphorical reference to the narrow path that leads to eternal destruction is found in Matt 7:13, 14.

Physical leading away is indicated in Matt 26:57; 27:2, 31; Mark 14:44, 53; 15:16; John 18:13, referring to Jesus being led away to the various authorities at the time of his arrest, as well as to his death. Luke 13:15 mentions beasts of burden being led away to water.

Spiritual blindness is indicated in 1 Cor 12:2, where Paul refers to the heathen background of the Corinthian believers, citing their being "led astray by dumb idols."

▸ **21.** Die, Perish, Kill, Destroy >
DIE, DEAD, PUT TO DEATH, DEADLY

exagō ἐξάγω 1806

exagō is another verb derived from ***agō*** (above). ***exagō*** has the primary sense of "lead, bring out" and occurs thirteen times.

Physically leading people out is indicated in a general sense (Luke 24:50; John 10:3; Acts 5:19; 16:37, 39; 21:38); and refers to Jesus in particular (Mark 15:20) when he is taken away to be crucified.

With God as the agent of leading, ***exagō*** refers to Israel being led out of Egyptian captivity in Acts 7:36, 40; 13:17; Heb 8:9. In Acts 12:17, it refers to Peter's deliverance from prison.

cheiragōgeō χειραγωγέω 5496

cheiragōgeō means "to lead by the hand" and is found only in Acts 9:8; 22:11, where it refers to the newly converted Saul being led by the hand into Damascus.

72. Need, Gain, Loss, Advantage, Seek, Find

ADVANTAGE, PROFIT

perissos περισσός 4053

The adjective ***perissos*** occurs ten times and means "more," "abundant." In Rom 3:1, however, it expresses the sense of "advantage" in Paul's question as to what spiritual "advantage" belongs to the Jews.

▸ **7.** Quantity, Amount, Number, Size, Measure > ABOUND, INCREASE, EXCEED, OVERFLOW, ABUNDANCE

ophelos ὄφελος 3786

The noun ***ophelos*** is found only three times, meaning "profit" or "gain" in the non-material sense of an "advantage" (1 Cor 15:32; Jas 2:14, 16).

▸ **72.** Need, Gain, Loss, Advantage, Seek, Find > GAIN, ACQUIRE

ōpheleia ὠφέλεια 5622

The noun ***ōpheleia*** occurs twice and is synonymous with ***ophelos*** (above), with the same sense of non-material "profit" or "advantage" (Rom 3:1; Jude 16).

ōpheleō ὠφελέω 5623

ōpheleō is a verb found in nineteen places, usually with the sense of "gain," "profit" in both a material and non-material sense.

In Matt 15:5; Mark 7:11 ***ōpheleō*** means "to draw a financial gain from."

General references to "gaining an advantage" are found in Matt 16:26; Luke 9:25; 1 Cor 13:3; Heb 13:9. In particular, Heb 4:2 indicates that the unbelieving generation of Israelites who failed to enter the land of Canaan because of their unbelief had no spiritual gain.

ōpheleō also expresses the sense of "to be of value," used positively in relation to circumcision in Rom 2:25. The term also occurs in a negative context in Gal 5:2, where Christ is said to be of no spiritual advantage if one receives circumcision as a perceived means of becoming right with God.

▸ **72.** Need, Gain, Loss, Advantage, Seek, Find > GAIN, ACQUIRE

SEE ALSO

▸ **58.** Vices > TAKE ADVANTAGE OF
pleonekteō

FAIL

anekleiptos ἀνέκλειπτος 413

anekleiptos is a rare adjectival form found only in Luke 12:33 and referring to one's treasure in heaven that does not fail (i.e., it remains forever).

SEE ALSO

▸ **68.** Ability, Possibility, Effort, Succeed, Fail > FAIL
ekleipō

FIND

heuriskō εὑρίσκω 2147

heuriskō is a common verb found nearly 180 times meaning "find," in a variety of contexts with a number of different nuances.

The meaning "find" in the general sense of "discover" is indicated in Matt 2:8ff.; Mark 1:37; Luke 2:12; 11:9; John 1:41ff.; Acts 4:21; Rom 7:21; 2 Cor 2:13; 2 Tim 1:17; Rev 2:2; 9:6.

The passive sense of "be found" is indicated in relation to Mary's supernatural encounter with the Holy Spirit when it is recorded that she "was found" to be pregnant (Matt 1:18). Other passive uses include 1 Cor 15:15; 2 Cor 5:3; Gal 2:17; Phil 2:8; 1 Pet 2:22; Rev 5:4; 16:20; 20:11ff.

There is a significant metaphorical usage of "find" in Matt 10:39; 16:25, with the underlying sense of "take full possession of" in relation to people "finding" true life if they are prepared to deny themselves for the sake of the gospel.

heuriskō means "find" in the sense of "receive" in Luke 1:30, which speaks of Mary "finding favor" with God. Other references to people "finding" such divine favor include those in Acts 7:46; 2 Tim 1:18; Heb 4:16. See also Heb 9:12; 11:5.

The meaning "find" with the sense of "consider" or "make an assessment" of someone is indicated in Acts 24:5, with reference to Paul's enemies having "found" him to be a troublemaker. See also 1 Cor 4:2. Rev 3:2 mentions divine assessment of people.

"Find" has the sense of "measure" in Acts 27:28, in relation to taking soundings in deep water.

aneuriskō ἀνευρίσκω 429

aneuriskō is a rare variant of ***heuriskō*** (above) meaning "to find" as a result of searching. It is found in only two places (Luke 2:16; Acts 21:4).

GAIN, ACQUIRE

kerdainō κερδαίνω 2770

kerdainō is a verb meaning "to gain," "acquire" throughout most of its seventeen occurrences.

References to "gaining the whole world," in the sense of becoming materially prosperous, at the expense of one's spiritual life are found in Matt 16:26; Mark 8:36; Luke 9:25.

"Gaining" someone, in the sense of winning him or her over to a renewed relationship, is indicated in Matt 18:15; 1 Pet 3:1. In particular, 1 Cor 9:19ff. affirms Paul's desire to "win" or "gain" more converts.

References to "gaining" or "acquiring" money are found in Matt 25:17ff.; Jas 4:13.

In Phil 3:8 Paul refers to "gaining" Christ, or making his eternal salvation secure.

kerdos κέρδος 2771

kerdos is a rare noun derived from ***kerdainō*** (above) denoting "gain" in the sense of "material wealth" in Phil 3:7;

Titus 1:11. ***kerdos*** is used figuratively in Phil 1:21 in Paul's affirmation that to live is Christ and to die is "gain," or a decided advantage over physical life.

porismos πορισμός 4200

porismos is a rare noun denoting "gain" in the sense of "monetary remuneration" in 1 Tim 6:5; and referring to "spiritual benefit" in 1 Tim 6:6.

peripoieō περιποιέω 4046

peripoieō is another rare verb referring to deacons "gaining" a good reputation for themselves.

ophelos ὄφελος 3786

ophelos is a noun found only three times, always as part of the question "What profit is it?" or "What good is it?" (1 Cor 15:32; Jas 2:14, 16).

▸ **72.** Need, Gain, Loss, Advantage, Seek, Find > ADVANTAGE, PROFIT

ōpheleō ὠφελέω 5623

ōpheleō is a verb meaning "to be advantageous," "to be of value" in several of its nineteen occurrences.

Like the derivative noun ***ophelos*** (above), ***ōpheleō*** occurs in the question "What does it profit a person . . . ?" in Matt 16:26; Mark 8:36; Luke 9:25.

The sense of "bringing or gaining spiritual benefit" is found in John 6:63; 1 Cor 13:3; 14:6; Gal 5:2; Heb 4:2; 13:9.

▸ **72.** Need, Gain, Loss, Advantage, Seek, Find > ADVANTAGE, PROFIT

SEE ALSO

▸ **30.** Money, Business, Wealth, Poverty > GAIN, PROFIT
diapragmateuomai

LOSE, LOSS, LOST

apollymi ἀπόλλυμι 622

apollymi is found in nearly ninety contexts and is translated variously as "destroy," "perish," and has associated meanings, including "lose," "be lost." These two latter meanings constitute about a quarter of the usage of ***apollymi***. ***apollymi*** has an adjectival, as well as a verbal, sense.

With reference to people, ***apollymi*** signifies "to lose" one's life in Luke 17:33; John 12:25, with the corollary that he will "find" it. Only a life characterized by self-denial and humility will lead to real life in the sight of God. See also Luke 9:25. In 2 John 8, the apostolic writer warns against loss of reward. In another context, Jesus affirms that those who demonstrate genuine love and compassion to the needy will not lose their reward (Matt 10:42; Mark 9:41).

There is also an adjectival sense evident in the usage of ***apollymi*** in a number of contexts. A lost sheep is indicated in Luke 15:4; and a lost coin in Luke 15:8. See also John 6:12. In the story of the prodigal son, the wayward youth is described as one who was "lost" and then found again (Luke 15:24).With the exception of John 6:12, the preceding references all refer to the joy of rediscovery following a period in which an object, animal, or person was deemed to be lost. Matt 10:6; 15:24 refer to the "lost sheep of Israel," the object of Jesus' mission and concern. More seriously, 2 Cor 4:3 declares that the gospel is hidden to those who are "lost," who are therefore liable to destruction.

apollymi also means "lose" in relation to the ministry of Christ. John 6:39; 18:9 record that Jesus should lose nothing of what the Father had given him. The one exception to this was Judas Iscariot, who betrayed Jesus (John 17:12). The mystery of divine providence is evident here — Judas was accountable for his action, even though he was "destined to be lost."

▸ **21.** Die, Perish, Kill, Destroy > DESTROY, DESTROYER, DESTRUCTION
▸ **21.** Die, Perish, Kill, Destroy > PERISH

zēmioō ζημιόω 2210

zēmioō means "to lose," "suffer loss," and is found in six contexts. Matt 16:26; Mark 8:36; Luke 9:25 refer to Jesus' question, "What will it profit a man if he gains the whole world, but loses his own life?" Paul refers to the judgment of Christ on those who will "suffer loss" for their service, but who themselves will be saved (1 Cor 3:15). In Phil 3:8, Paul declares that he gladly "suffered the loss" of all that he had in order to gain Christ. See also 2 Cor 7:9.

▸ **72.** Need, Gain, Loss, Advantage, Seek, Find > SUFFER LOSS

zēmia ζημία 2209

zēmia is the noun derived from ***zēmioō*** (above) and is translated "loss" or "damage." It is found in four places. Acts 27:10, 21 refer to "damage" to a ship. In Phil 3:7, 8, Paul affirms that everything associated with his former life as a Pharisee was "loss," or utterly worthless, compared with the joy of knowing Christ.

apobolē ἀποβολή 580

apobolē is a rare noun, found only in two places. Acts 27:22 indicates that there will be no "loss" of life on the ship containing Paul and his companions on the way to Rome. Rom 11:15 refers to God "casting off" or "rejecting" the Jewish people for their denial of Christ.

NEED

chreia χρεία 5532

chreia is a noun occurring around fifty times with the primary senses of "need" (i.e., necessity of life) and as part of the expressions "to have need (of)," "to be in need."

The literal sense of "need," indicating a material necessity for life, is found in Acts 2:45; 4:35; 20:34; 28:10; Rom 12:13; Phil 2:25; 4:16; Titus 3:14. "Need" in a spiritual sense is indicated in Phil 4:19; 1 John 3:17.

chreia is also utilized in the expression "to be in need" in a general sense (Eph 4:28), and with reference to food (Mark 2:25), and healing (Luke 9:11).

The expression "to have need (of)" in a general sense is found in Matt 21:3; Luke 22:71; John 2:25; 13:29; 16:30; 1 Thess 1:8. The need to be baptized is indicated in Matt

3:14. Heb 10:36 speaks of the need for endurance; and Heb 5:2 indicates the need of immature believers for a teacher. Matt 26:65; Mark 14:63 refer to the need for witnesses. Jesus' need of a donkey is mentioned in Mark 11:3; Luke 19:31, 34. Matt 6:8 makes the claim that God knows what his people need. The expression "to have no need (of)" refers to material goods (Rev 3:17); to a physician (Matt 9:12; Mark 2:17; Luke 5:31); and to a teacher (1 John 2:27). The absence of any need for repentance is noted in Luke 15:7. And in a metaphorical context, Rev 21:23; 22:5 indicate that there is no need of the sun or moon in the heavenly city. In a quite different symbolic context, Paul deals with the metaphor of the human body in discussing the phenomenon of mutual interdependence in the fellowship of believers. In 1 Cor 12:21 he records a hypothetical "dialogue" between parts of the human body where one part says to the other: "I have no need of you." The point here is that such independence is both untenable and undesirable where genuine Christian community is in view.

chrēzō χρῄζω 5535

chrēzō is a verb found in only five contexts, meaning "to have need of."

Matt 6:32; Luke 12:30 speak of God's knowledge of the needs of his people. Awareness of what others may need is indicated in Luke 11:8; Rom 16:2. A question of need, as regards letters of commendation, arises in 2 Cor 3:1.

SEEK, SEARCH

zēteō ζητέω 2212

zēteō is found in approximately 120 contexts and means "seek" or "search for" in the great majority of these places.

zēteō refers to people "searching for" wisdom (1 Cor 1:22); spiritual blessing (Matt 7:7; Luke 11:19); rest (Matt 12:43); peace (1 Pet 3:11); a sign (Mark 8:11); and death (Rev 9:6). People are also said to "seek after" the kingdom of God (Matt 6:33; Luke 12:31; 13:24). See also Matt 2:13; Mark 16:6; Luke 13:6; 1 Cor 7:27.

The meaning "seek" in the sense of "attempt" is indicated in contexts where there is an intention to destroy or kill (Matt 2:20; 21:31). In particular, such an intent is recorded in connection with the campaign of the Jewish authorities to have Jesus Christ killed (Matt 21:46; Mark 11:18; Luke 19:47; John 5:16; 7:1, 19ff.; 8:37ff.). Elsewhere, ***zēteō*** refers to the "attempt" to obtain eternal life or glory (Rom 2:7; Col 3:1). See also Luke 17:33. It also refers to people touching Jesus in order to obtain a cure for disease (Luke 6:19).

Christ, as the Son of Man, "seeks" to do the will of God (John 5:44); and "seeks out" those who are spiritually lost in order to save them (Luke 19:10).God is said to seek those who will worship him in John 4:23.

▸ **54.** Rule, Authority, Command, Obedience > BE REQUIRED

▸ **66.** Ask, Answer, Discuss, Learn > INQUIRE

epizēteō ἐπιζητέω 1934

epizēteō is a variant form of ***zēteō*** (above) occurring fourteen times and meaning "seek after" or "search for" in most of these contexts.

People are described as "seeking after" material needs (Matt 6:32; Luke 12:30); a sign or miracle (Matt 12:39; 16:4; Mark 8:12; Luke 11:29); and salvation (Rom 11:7). Heb 11:14 speaks of the OT saints "looking for" a homeland. Believers are then described as "searching for" an eternal city (Heb 13:14). See also Acts 12:19.

ekzēteō ἐκζητέω 1567

ekzēteō is another variant form of ***zēteō*** (above), found eight times and meaning "seek after" in about half of these contexts.

The intention of "seeking after the Lord" is indicated in Acts 15:17; Heb 11:6. Rom 3:11 acknowledges that none seek after the Lord. Heb 12:17 refers to Esau's abortive attempt to seek a blessing after forfeiting his birthright to Jacob. 1 Pet 1:10 refers to those "searching for" the fulfillment of God's redemptive purposes for his people.

▸ **32.** Law, Justice, Jurisprudence, Judgment > REQUIRE

anazēteō ἀναζητέω 327

anazēteō is a rare verb found in only two places. Luke 2:44 refers to Jesus' parents "searching for" him among their friends and relatives. In Acts 11:25, Barnabas "looks for" Saul in Tarsus.

SUFFER LOSS

zēmioō ζημιόω 2210

zēmioō is a verb found six times meaning "to lose" and also "to suffer loss." The latter sense is indicated in 1 Cor 3:15, referring to the prospective loss of reward experienced by the believer on the final day of judgment. In Phil 2:8, Paul declares that he "has suffered the loss" of all things for the sake of Christ.

▸ **72.** Need, Gain, Loss, Advantage, Seek, Find > LOSE, LOSS, LOST

SEE ALSO

▸ **75.** Suffering, Distress, Sadness > SUFFER
paschō, adikeō

73. Blessing, Curse, Reward, Punishment

AVENGE, AVENGER, REVENGE, VENGEANCE

ekdikeō ἐκδικέω 1556

The verb ***ekdikeō***, meaning "avenge," "take revenge" predicated of God with respect to his enemies in Rev 6:10; 19:2, is found in six places. Believers are enjoined in Rom 12:19 not to avenge themselves against their enemies, that being God's prerogative alone. In Luke 18:3ff. the sense of ***ekdikeō*** is that of "vindicate," through a plea for justice against one's adversary.

ekdikos ἔκδικος 1558

ekdikos is an adjectival form derived from ***ekdikeō*** (above) denoting "one who takes revenge." It occurs only twice. In Rom 13:4 the term describes a God-ordained ruler as "an agent of (divine) wrath" (lit., "one who takes revenge on God's behalf"). In 1 Thess 4:6, God himself is described as "an avenger" — one who initiates punishment against the wicked.

ekdikēsis ἐκδίκησις 1557

ekdikēsis is a noun occurring ten times with the meaning "vengeance," "revenge," and related nuances.

In Luke 18:7, 8, mention is made of God "vindicating" his elect (lit., "taking revenge" on their behalf) against their enemies. The phrase "days of vengeance" is found in Luke 21:22 denoting a period of divine punishment. Rom 12:19; Heb 10:30 contain the declaration that "vengeance" belongs to God. "Vengeance" in the sense of "punishment" is indicated in 2 Thess 1:8; 1 Pet 2:14. See also Acts 7:24; 2 Cor 7:11.

▸ **73.** Blessing, Curse, Reward, Punishment >
PUNISH, PUNISHMENT

BLESS, BLESSED, BLESSING, BLESSEDNESS

eulogeō εὐλογέω 2127

The verb ***eulogeō*** is found in about forty places with the primary sense of "bless," often equated with the actions of "praise," "give thanks."

The meaning "bless" in the sense of "give thanks" is indicated in relation to thanking God for food (Matt 14:19; Mark 6:41; 14:22; Luke 9:16; 24:30); and for the cup of the Lord's Supper (1 Cor 10:16). See also Luke 1:64; 2:28, 34; Jas 3:9.

eulogeō also expresses the meaning "blessed" in the sense of "happy," "joyful." It is predicated of Christ in Matt 21:9; 23:39; Mark 11:9ff.; Luke 13:35; 19:38; John 12:13; of God's people in Matt 25:34; Luke 1:28, 42. Such blessing is also indicated in the context of receiving the gift of salvation (Gal 3:9; 1 Pet 3:9) and the fulfillment of the covenant promises (Heb 6:14).

Elsewhere, ***eulogeō*** conveys the sense of "giving a spiritual blessing." Christ is said to do this to his people in Mark 10:16; Luke 24:51; Acts 3:26. Similarly, God provides spiritual blessings for his people in Christ (Eph 1:3). Such blessing is also provided by Melchizedek for Abram (Heb 7:1, 6ff. [citing Gen 14]). Invoking a blessing on someone through prayer is indicated with respect to one's enemies in Luke 6:28; Rom 12:14; 1 Cor 4:12 (see also 1 Cor 14:16). Blessing through the covenant promises is also invoked in Heb 11:20ff.

eneulogeō ἐνευλογέω 1757

eneulogeō is a rare variant form of ***eulogeō*** (above). It is found only twice and used in the passive voice. The meaning "be blessed" is found in the context of receiving the promises of the Abrahamic covenant in relation to the nations of the world (Acts 3:25; Gal 3:8).

eulogētos εὐλογητός 2128

eulogētos is an adjectival form found eight times with the meaning "blessed." It is used as a title, "the Blessed (One)," predicated of God in Mark 14:61. The ascription of praise "blessed be God" is found in Luke 1:68; Rom 1:25; 9:5; 2 Cor 1:3; 11:31; Eph 1:3; 1 Pet 1:3.

eulogia εὐλογία 2129

The noun ***eulogia*** occurs sixteen times and means "blessing."

Blessing associated with belonging to Christ is indicated in Rom 15:29; Eph 1:13. The blessing of the Abrahamic covenant associated with the fulfillment of divine blessing to the Gentiles (i.e., the spread of the gospel) is noted in Gal 3:14. The "cup of blessing" associated with the Lord's Supper, commemorating the significance of his shed blood, is mentioned in 1 Cor 10:16. Blessing from God in a general sense is indicated in Heb 6:7; 12:17; Jas 3:10; 1 Pet 3:9.

Blessing in the sense of "praise" is attributed to the heavenly Christ in Rev 5:12, 13, and to God in Rev 7:12.

makarizō μακαρίζω 3106

makarizō is a verb found three times with the meaning "call someone blessed," "count someone happy" (Luke 1:48; Jas 5:11).

makarios μακάριος 3107

makarios is an adjective found in fifty places with the meaning "blessed," "happy."

The term is commonly used by Christ. He promises a state of "blessedness," "happiness" to all who live out the virtues of godly living as expressed in the "Beatitudes" (Matt 5:3ff.; Luke 6:20ff.). Christ also offers blessings to those who follow him and who genuinely seek after God in Matt 11:6; 13:16. In Matt 16:17, Peter is declared "blessed" when he acknowledges the true identity of Jesus as the Christ, the Son of God. See also Luke 1:45; 11:27ff.; 23:29; John 13:17; 20:29; Acts 20:35. Such blessing, or happiness, is also promised to servants who are faithful to their masters (Luke 12:37ff.). God is described as "blessed" in 1 Tim 1:11; 6:15 (i.e., worthy to be praised).

Blessings in the spiritual sphere are affirmed for those whose sins are forgiven (Rom 4:7ff.); and for those who will enjoy eternal life in glory (Rev 14:13; 19:9; 20:6; 22:7, 14). See also Rom 14:22; Jas 1:12, 25; 1 Pet 3:14; 4:14; Rev 1:3.

makarismos μακαρισμός 3108

The noun ***makarismos*** denotes "blessing" in Rom 4:6, 9; Gal 4:15.

CURSE, CURSED, CURSING, ACCURSED

anathema ἀνάθεμα 331

anathema is a noun found in six places with the underlying sense of a "curse." In most of these contexts the term is used adjectivally with the meaning "accursed." 1 Cor 16:22; Gal 1:8, 9 record the apostolic invocation "Let him be accursed," directed against false teachers and the faithless. 1 Cor 12:3 affirms that no true believer would ever express the invocation "Jesus be cursed." See also Rom 9:3. Acts 23:14 implies a "curse" by referring to a "solemn oath" taken by those who had sworn to assassinate the apostle Paul, and not to eat until they had accomplished that task.

katathema κατάθεμα 2652

katathema is a rare variant of ***anathema*** (above) denoting a "curse." It is found only in Rev 22:3, indicating the total absence of anything accursed in heaven.

katara κατάρα 2671

katara has the nominal sense of "curse," "cursing" in all but one of its six occurrences. Gal 3:10, 13 refer to the "curse" of the law. The practice of "cursing" is condemned in Jas 3:10. The adjectival sense of "cursed" is indicated in Heb 6:8; 2 Pet 2:14.

kataraomai καταράομαι 2672

kataraomai is a verb found in six places and translated "to curse" in each case. The action of cursing people is indicated in Matt 5:44; Luke 6:28; Rom 12:14; Jas 3:9. The wicked who are "cursed" by God are noted in Matt 25:41. Mark 11:21 mentions the fig tree "cursed" by Christ.

epikataratos ἐπικατάρατος 1944

epikataratos is an adjectival form found in three places, meaning "cursed" in each case. All of these contexts refer to "being cursed" by God (John 7:49; Gal 3:10, 13).

SEE ALSO

- ▸ **57.** Evil, Wickedness, Sin > CURSE
  ara
- ▸ **67.** Acknowledge, Confess, Profess, Swear > CURSE, CURSED
  anathematizō, katathematizō
- ▸ **77.** Resist, Oppose, Fight, Rebel > CURSE, MALIGN
  kakologeō

PRIZE

brabeion βραβεῖον 1017

brabeion is found only twice, meaning "prize." 1 Cor 9:24 refers to the literal prize given to the athlete who wins the race. In Phil 3:14, Paul uses the term to refer to his great goal — gaining the "prize" of his reward in heaven through the work of Jesus Christ.

PUNISH, PUNISHMENT

kolazō κολάζω 2849

kolazō is a verb found only twice, meaning "to punish," — once in the human sphere of legal action (Acts 4:21); and once in the realm of divine dealings with the wicked (2 Pet 2:9).

kolasis κόλασις 2851

kolasis is the noun derived from ***kolazō*** (above) and is found in only two places. ***kolasis*** refers to everlasting punishment in Matt 25:46 and to punishment in general in 1 John 4:18.

timōreō τιμωρέω 5097

timōreō is a verb meaning "punish" in the context of procuring a legal sanction against those who violate the law. It is found only in Acts 22:5; 26:11, with reference to Saul's fanatical pursuit of the early Christians prior to his conversion, with a view to bringing them to justice and having them punished.

timōria τιμωρία 5098

timōria is the noun derived from ***timōreō*** (above) and is found only in Heb 10:29, where it refers to the terrible divine punishment that will fall upon all those who spurn the Son of God and renounce their allegiance to him.

epitimia ἐπιτιμία 2009

epitimia is a term found only in 2 Cor 2:6, referring to "punishment" arising out of the context of church discipline.

dikē δίκη 1349

dikē is a noun occurring in four contexts with the underlying sense of a judicial sentence. It refers to such a punishment in Acts 25:15; 28:4. In 2 Thess 1:9; Jude 7, ***dikē*** refers to the sentence of eternal punishment handed down by God to unbelievers on the day of judgment.

▸ **32.** Law, Justice, Jurisprudence, Judgment > JUDGMENT

ekdikēsis ἐκδίκησις 1557

ekdikēsis is a noun with the primary meaning "revenge" or "vengeance" in all but one of the ten occurrences of the term. In 1 Pet 2:14 it refers to the legal prerogative of the civil authorities to punish those who break the law.

▸ **73.** Blessing, Curse, Reward, Punishment > AVENGE, AVENGER, REVENGE, VENGEANCE

REWARD, RECOMPENSE

misthos μισθός 3408

misthos is a noun found in around thirty contexts and means "reward" in most of these.

misthos often refers to a "reward" as a spiritual blessing from God, whether in a general sense (Matt 10:41ff.; Mark

9:41; 1 Cor 9:17ff.; 2 John 8; Rev 11:18; 22:12); or whether it refers specifically to one's reward in heaven (Matt 5:12, 46; Luke 6:23, 35; 1 Cor 3:14). Matt 6:1 threatens no reward from God. Negatively, as in the OT, "rewards" can also be the recompense for sin (Acts 1:18; 2 Pet 2:13).

In a few places, ***misthos*** also refers to "reward" as an earthly gain, or payment for labor (Matt 6:2, 16; Jude 11). See also 1 Tim 5:18.

▸ **30.** Money, Business, Wealth, Poverty > WAGES

apodidōmi ἀποδίδωμι 591

apodidōmi is a verb found in fifty contexts with the meanings "pay," "repay," and "reward." The underlying sense of the term is "rendering to people what is their due," in both a literal and metaphorical sense.

God is said to "reward" (i.e., give a spiritual blessing) to his people for their godly living (Matt 6:14ff.). The general sense of spiritual recompense for works done in this life is indicated in Matt 16:27; Rev 22:12. The negative sense of God "rewarding" punishment for sin is evident in 2 Tim 4:14; Rev 18:6.

In the sphere of human relationships, Rom 12:17; 1 Thess 5:15; 1 Pet 3:9 warn against "rewarding" (i.e., repaying) evil for evil.

▸ **28.** Agriculture, Viticulture, Animal Husbandry > YIELD

▸ **30.** Money, Business, Wealth, Poverty > PAY, RENDER

antapodosis ἀνταπόδοσις 469

antapodosis is a term found only in Col 3:24 with reference to receiving an eternal inheritance as a reward for serving Christ.

misthapodosia μισθαποδοσία 3405

misthapodosia is a noun occurring only three times, meaning "reward" in the sense of "due recompense" on each occasion. Heb 2:2 refers to a "reward" for wickedness, reflecting the idea of a "just retribution" from God. Heb 10:3ff.; 11:26 speak positively of reward as a spiritual blessing from God.

misthapodotēs μισθαποδότης 3406

misthapodotēs occurs only once, in Heb 11:6, referring to God as the one "who rewards" (i.e., a rewarder of) those who seek him.

axios ἄξιος 514

axios is an adjective found approximately forty times with the primary meaning "worthy." In Luke 23:41, however, ***axios*** is used as a noun meaning "due reward" in the sense of "penalty for sin."

▸ **53.** Value, Worth > WORTHY, UNWORTHY

74. Safety, Peace, Danger, Escape

DANGER

kindyneuō κινδυνεύω 2793

kindyneuō is a verb found in four places, meaning "to be in danger" in the context of facing physical danger (Luke 8:23; Acts 19:27, 40; 1 Cor 15:30).

SEE ALSO

- ▸ **29.** Boats, Fishing, Maritime Activity > DANGEROUS
  episphalēs
- ▸ **32.** Law, Justice, Jurisprudence, Judgment > DANGER, LIABILITY
  enochos

ENSNARE, ENTANGLE

pagideuō παγιδεύω 3802

pagideuō is a rare verb found only in Matt 22:15 with reference to the plans of the Pharisees seeking to "ensnare" or "trap" Jesus in his speech.

emplekō ἐμπλέκω 1707

emplekō is a rare verb found only twice, referring to the "entangling" or "ensnaring" of the soldier in civilian affairs in 2 Tim 2:4. 2 Pet 2:20 speaks of the danger of "becoming entangled" or "being trapped" in the corruption of the world.

ESCAPE

pheugō φεύγω 5343

pheugō is a verb occurring about thirty times with the primary meaning "to flee." In three places, however, ***pheugō*** expresses the explicit sense of "escape." Matt 23:33 refers to "escaping" from the sentence of hell. "Escaping" the edge of the sword is indicated in Heb 12:25. Failure to "escape" the judgment of God is noted in Heb 11:34.

- ▸ **74.** Safety, Peace, Danger, Escape > FLEE, FLIGHT

apopheugō ἀποφεύγω 668

apopheugō is a variant form of ***pheugō*** (above) meaning "escape," "escape from." References to "escaping" the corruption of the world are found in 2 Pet 1:4; 2:20. 2 Pet 2:18 mentions those who had barely "escaped" from the error of false teachers.

ekpheugō ἐκφεύγω 1628

ekpheugō is another variant form of ***pheugō*** (above) found eight times and meaning "escape."

References to "escaping" the judgment of God are found in Luke 21:36; Rom 2:3; Heb 2:3. The fear of prisoners "escaping" is noted in Acts 16:27. Paul's experience of "escaping" from his persecutors is recorded in 2 Cor 11:33.

- ▸ **74.** Safety, Peace, Danger, Escape > FLEE, FLIGHT

diasōzō διασῴζω 1295

diasōzō is a verb occurring eight times, meaning "save," "preserve" as well as "escape." Acts 27:44; 28:1, 4 refer to an "escape" from physical danger.

- ▸ **20.** Illness, Disease, Health, Healing > HEAL, CURE
- ▸ **44.** Repentance, Forgiveness, Mercy, Redeem, Save > SAVE, SALVATION, SAVIOR
- ▸ **74.** Safety, Peace, Danger, Escape > SAFE, SAFELY, SAFETY, SECURITY

ekbasis ἔκβασις 1545

ekbasis is a rare noun denoting the "way of escape" God promises to believers so that they will not be compelled to commit sin (1 Cor 10:13).

SEE ALSO

- ▸ **29.** Boats, Fishing, Maritime Activity > ESCAPE
  diapheugō

FALL AMONG

peripiptō περιπίπτω 4045

peripiptō is a rare verb referring to "falling among" thieves in Luke 10:30.

SEE ALSO

- ▸ **45.** Faith, Belief, Trust, Promise > FALL AWAY, APOSTATIZE, APOSTASY
  parapiptō, aphistēmi
- ▸ **87.** Movement Upward or Downward > FALL, FALL DOWN, FALL UPON, FALL INTO
  piptō, apopiptō, ekpiptō, empiptō, epipiptō, katapiptō, prospiptō

FLEE, FLIGHT

pheugō φεύγω 5343

pheugō is a verb found over thirty times with the consistent meaning "to flee."

The meaning "flee" in the literal sense of "escape (to)" is found in Matt 2:13; Mark 5:14; 13:14; Luke 8:34; John 10:12ff.; Acts 7:29; Heb 11:34; Rev 12:6. Sheep are said to "flee" in John 10:5. The devil is said to "flee" from those who submit themselves to God.

The metaphorical sense of "flee" in relation to "running away from" the judgment or wrath of God is evident in Matt 3:7; Luke 3:7; Heb 12:25. An exhortation to "flee" or "shun" immorality is found in 1 Cor 6:18. A like injunction is directed against idolatry in 1 Cor 10:14. See also 1 Tim 6:11; 2 Tim 2:22. In the context of executing divine wrath, death is said to "flee" from those who seek it (Rev 9:6). Similarly, at the end of time, elements of the cosmos are said "to have fled away," signifying the dissolution of the heavens and the earth (Rev 16:20; 20:11).

- ▸ **74.** Safety, Peace, Danger, Escape > ESCAPE

ekpheugō ἐκφεύγω 1628

ekpheugō is a variant form of ***pheugō*** (above) meaning "escape," "flee" in each of the eight occurrences of the term.

"Escaping" the judgment of God is a course of action indicated in Luke 21:36; Rom 2:3. Such an escape is denied in 1 Thess 5:3; Heb 2:3.

"Fleeing" from a dangerous situation is recorded in Acts 16:27; 19:16; 2 Cor 11:23.

- ▸ **74.** Safety, Peace, Danger, Escape > ESCAPE

katapheugō καταφεύγω 2703

katapheugō is another rare variant of ***pheugō*** (above) meaning "to flee (for refuge)" in Acts 14:6; Heb 6:18.

phygē φυγή 5437

phygē is a rare noun derived from ***pheugō***, found only in Matt 24:20 denoting "flight" in the sense of "escape" from danger.

SEE ALSO

- ▸ **77.** Resist, Oppose, Fight, Rebel > ROUT, PUT TO FLIGHT
  klinō

PEACE

eirēnē εἰρήνη 1515

eirēnē means "peace" in virtually all of its ninety occurrences and is found in a number of varying contexts.

eirēnē indicates "peace" first of all as a blessing, greeting, or farewell salutation to individuals, coming from human beings (Matt 10:13; John 20:19ff.); from Christ (Mark 5:34; John 20:19; Rev 1:4); and from God himself (Rom 1:7; Luke 2:29; 2 Cor 1:2; Eph 1:2; Phil 1:2; Col 3:15; 1 Thess 1:1; 2 Tim 1:2). See also Luke 19:38, where the context is offering praise to God.

eirēnē also refers to "peace" as a state of tranquility, an absence of conflict among people. It is given as a blessing from God through the person of Christ (Luke 2:14; Rom 2:10; 15:13). See also Matt 10:34; Luke 12:51. 1 Cor 7:15 affirms that God calls his people to manifest such a peace.

The "way of peace" is indicated in Luke 1:79; Rom 3:17 as a godly lifestyle, a consequence of devotion to God in Christ. The "gospel of peace" is alluded to in Eph 6:15. The title "king of peace" is noted in Heb 7:2 (citing Gen 14:18) as a secondary translation of the name Melchizedek, the mysterious priest-king of Salem.

The phrase "at peace" refers to the safety and security of property in Luke 11:21. Peace, with reference to the cessation of military conflict, is indicated in Luke 14:32; Acts 12:20.

As a specific blessing, or gift from Christ, peace is promised to his disciples and all his followers. This peace is unique in that it is everlasting and flawless, unlike any peace offered by the world (John 14:27; 16:33). Similarly, the spiritual peace of reconciliation with God as a direct consequence of saving faith in Christ is affirmed in Acts 10:36; Rom 5:1; 8:6; Eph 2:15. Christ is described as the supreme embodiment of peace in Eph 2:14. Peace is likewise described as a "fruit" of the spirit in Gal 5:22, and as a characteristic evident in the relationship among believers (Eph 4:3).

SEE ALSO

- ▸ **44.** Repentance, Forgiveness, Mercy, Redeem, Save > RECONCILE, MAKE PEACE
  eirēnopoieō
- ▸ **60.** Virtues > PEACE, PEACEFUL, QUIET
  eirēneuō

SAFE, SAFELY, SAFETY, SECURITY

diasōzō διασῴζω 1295

diasōzō is a verb with the underlying meaning "bringing to safety" in the sense of "make well" or "escape." It occurs eight times.

The explicit sense of "bring to safety" is found in Acts 23:24, referring to Paul's safe passage to Felix the governor. Acts 27:44 describes escaping safely to land from a shipwreck.

- ▸ **20.** Illness, Disease, Health, Healing > HEAL, CURE
- ▸ **44.** Repentance, Forgiveness, Mercy, Redeem, Save > SAVE, SALVATION, SAVIOR
- ▸ **74.** Safety, Peace, Danger, Escape > ESCAPE

asphalēs ἀσφαλής 804

asphalēs is an adjectival form occurring five times meaning "safe," "certain." The sense of "safe" in a nominal sense is found in Phil 3:1, where Paul refers to his writings as a "safeguard" for the Philippian congregation. Heb 6:19 refers metaphorically to the hope of the gospel as an anchor that is "safe."

asphalōs ἀσφαλῶς 806

asphalōs is an adverbial form found three times, translated "safely" in reference to physical security in Mark 14:44; Acts 16:23.

asphaleia ἀσφάλεια 803

asphaleia is a noun occurring three times, indicating people's "safety" or "security" in general terms in 1 Thess 5:3. Acts 5:3 speaks of a prison cell "securely locked" (lit., "locked with safety").

TRAP, AMBUSH, LIE IN WAIT

thēra θήρα 2339

thēra is a rare noun referring to a moral "trap" or "snare" in Rom 11:9.

brochos βρόχος 1029

brochos is a synonym for ***thēra*** (above) found only in 1 Cor 7:35.

enedreuō ἐνεδρεύω 1748
enedron ἔνεδρον 1749

enedreuō is a verb meaning "to lie in wait for," "set a trap, or ambush." It is found only twice. Luke 11:54 refers to the Pharisees "lying in wait" for Jesus, seeking to ensnare him through what he might say. Acts 23:21 refers to a literal ambush set for the apostle Paul.

The derivative noun ***enedron*** is found only in Acts 23:16 with reference to the ambush set for Paul.

SEE ALSO

▸ **46.** Wait, Hope, Be Vigilant, Pay Attention To > WAIT
prosdechomai, apekdechomai, prosdokaō

▸ **85.** Movement, Position, State > LIE, LIE DOWN, RECLINE
katakeimai, keimai

75. Suffering, Distress, Sadness

AFFLICT, AFFLICTION

kakopatheō κακοπαθέω 2553

The verb ***kakopatheō*** occurs in five places with the consistent sense of "endure affliction, or suffering." Jas 5:13 refers to this in general terms; and 2 Tim 2:3, 9; 4:5 all suggest the context of persecution.

▸ **75.** Suffering, Distress, Sadness > TROUBLE

kakopatheia κακοπάθεια 2552

kakopatheia is a rare noun derived from ***kakopatheō*** (above) and is found only in Jas 5:10, meaning "the suffering of affliction, or distress."

kakōsis κάκωσις 2561

kakōsis is a rare noun found only in Acts 7:34 with reference to the "affliction" the Israelites suffered in Egypt.

thlibō θλίβω 2346

The verb ***thlibō*** means "to trouble," "afflict," "oppress" in most of its ten occurrences.

The passive sense of "being afflicted, oppressed" in the content of tribulation or persecution is indicated in 2 Cor 1:6; 4:8; 7:5; 2 Thess 1:7; Heb 11:37. The allied sense of "suffering affliction" is evident in 1 Thess 3:4. The active sense of "to afflict, oppress or trouble" in relation to one's persecutors is found in 2 Thess 1:6. The participial, nominal sense of "those who are afflicted" is evident in 1 Tim 5:10.

thlipsis θλῖψις 2347

thlipsis is the noun derived from ***thlibō*** (above). It occurs around fifty times with the predominant sense of "affliction" or "tribulation," with an underlying sense of deep-seated anguish and suffering.

The general sense of "affliction" or "tribulation" giving rise to anguish is indicated, for example, in Matt 13:21; 24:9, 21, 29; Mark 13:9ff.; John 16:21, 33; Acts 7:11; Rom 8:35; 1 Cor 7:28; 2 Cor 1:4ff.; 1 Thess 3:3ff.; Jas 1:27. Acts 7:10; 20:23 refer to the "affliction" of individuals. Viewed as punishment from God, such "affliction" is evident in Rom 2:9; Rev 2:22. This kind of suffering is said to produce endurance in the life of the believer in Rom 5:3; 12:12; 2 Cor 6:4. The "afflictions" of Christ are noted in Col 1:24.

The specific nuance of persecution in "affliction" is evident in Acts 11:19; Heb 10:33; Rev 1:9; 2:9ff.; 7:14.

▸ **75.** Suffering, Distress, Sadness >
PERSECUTION, TRIBULATION

pathēma πάθημα 3804

The noun ***pathēma***, meaning "suffering," "affliction" is found sixteen times.

General references to "affliction" and "suffering," mostly linked to persecution, are found in Rom 8:18; 2 Cor 1:6ff.; Col 1:24; 2 Tim 3:11; Heb 2:10; 10:32; 1 Pet 5:9. In particular, the "suffering(s)" of Christ are indicated in 2 Cor 1:5; Phil 3:10; Heb 2:9; 1 Pet 1:11; 4:13; 5:1.

SEE ALSO

▸ **76.** Force, Harm, Oppress > HARM, MISTREAT, AFFLICT
kakoō, kakoucheō

ANGUISH

stenochōria στενοχωρία 4730

stenochōria is a noun found in four contexts denoting "anguish" or "distress" in each case. The "anguish" of the wicked is noted in Rom 2:9. The "anguish" or "distress" borne of persecution is indicated in Rom 8:35; 2 Cor 6:4; 12:10.

▸ **75.** Suffering, Distress, Sadness > DISTRESS, TORMENT

synechō συνέχω 4912

synechō is a verb found in twelve places, communicating the underlying sense of being caught in difficult circumstances — both physical and emotional.

The term is translated "to be taken sick, or afflicted with sickness" in Matt 4:24; Luke 4:38; Acts 28:8. The meaning "to be hard-pressed" in an emotional sense, indicating a state of anxiety or anguish, is evident in Luke 12:50; Phil 1:23.

synochē συνοχή 4928

synochē is a rare noun found only twice, with the meaning "distress" or "anguish" in Luke 21:25; 2 Cor 2:4.

▸ **75.** Suffering, Distress, Sadness > DISTRESS, TORMENT

odynaō ὀδυνάω 3600

The verb ***odynaō*** is found in four places with the consistent meaning "to suffer anguish," "be sorrowful" (Luke 2:48; 16:24, 25; Acts 20:38).

▸ **75.** Suffering, Distress, Sadness >
SAD, SORROW, SORROWFUL, GRIEF

BITTERLY

pikrōs πικρῶς 4090

pikrōs is a rare adverbial form with the meaning "bitterly" in the context of weeping with great anguish, inconsolable grief (Matt 26:75; Luke 22:62).

SEE ALSO

▸ **58.** Vices > BITTERNESS
pikria

▸ **88.** Qualities, Characteristics >
BITTER, BRACKISH, EMBITTER
pikros, pikrainō

BREAK

synthryptō συνθρύπτω 4919

synthryptō is a rare verb found only in Acts 21:13 and translated "break one's heart" with grief.

SEE ALSO

- ▸ **23.** Food, Drink, Cooking > BREAK BREAD
  klaō, kataklaō, klasis
- ▸ **28.** Agriculture, Viticulture, Animal Husbandry > BREAK OFF, CUT, CUT OFF
  ekklaō
- ▸ **58.** Vices > STEAL, BREAK IN, BURGLE
  dioryssō
- ▸ **76.** Force, Harm, Oppress > BREAK
  katagnymi
- ▸ **78.** Act Upon, Push, Pull, Break, Cut > BREAK
  lyō, syntribō, diarrēgnymi, synthlaō

BURDEN

baros βάρος 922

baros is a noun found six times with the general meaning of "burden" in different contexts.

Reference to the "burden" of a completed day's work is indicated in Matt 20:12. ***baros*** also denotes an "obligation" under the law described as a "burden" in Acts 15:28 (see also 1 Thess 2:6). 2 Cor 4:17 refers to a "weight" (i.e., burden) of glory. "Burdens" in the sense of "difficulty," "personal trauma" are noted in Gal 6:2; Rev 2:24.

▸ **53.** Value, Worth > WEIGHT, WEIGHTY

phortion φορτίον 5413

phortion is a noun denoting "burden" in the primary sense of an obligation under the law, and is found in five contexts. Christ promises his followers a light "burden" when they commit themselves to him (Matt 11:30). Jesus condemns the religious leaders of the day for imposing unjust, harsh "burdens" on the people of Israel (Matt 23:4; Luke 11:46). Gal 6:5 mentions a man's "burden" in reference to his own "responsibility."

SEE ALSO

- ▸ **76.** Force, Harm, Oppress > BURDEN
  epibareō, katabareō, katanarkaō

DESPAIR

exaporeō ἐξαπορέω 1820

exaporeō is a rare verb found only in 2 Cor 1:8; 4:8 with the meaning "despair" in the sense of "give up hope for living."

DISTRESS, TORMENT

anankē ἀνάγκη 318

anankē is a noun denoting "distress" or "anguish" in three places (Luke 21:23; 1 Cor 7:26; 1 Thess 3:7).

stenochōria στενοχωρία 4730

stenochōria is a noun denoting "distress," "anguish," or "calamity" — all in the context of the trauma of persecution (Rom 2:9; 8:35; 2 Cor 6:4; 12:10).

▸ **75.** Suffering, Distress, Sadness > ANGUISH

synochē συνοχή 4928

synochē is a rare noun denoting "anguish," "distress" in the sense of deep emotional turmoil in Luke 21:25; 2 Cor 2:4.

▸ **75.** Suffering, Distress, Sadness > ANGUISH

basanizō βασανίζω 928

basanizō is a verb found in twelve places meaning "to torment," in the sense of "cause great pain, and distress."

Matt 8:6 refers to the "distress" and pain of a terrible illness. Matt 8:29; Mark 5:7; Luke 8:28 refer to Christ "tormenting" demons. 2 Pet 2:8 notes Lot's "torment" or "distress" in response to the lawless deeds of the citizens of Sodom. The "distress" or "pain" of women in childbirth is indicated in Rev 12:2.

Inflicting pain, distress, or torment in the context of punishment is indicated in Rev 9:5; 11:10. In particular, Rev 14:10; 20:10 refer to God "tormenting" the wicked.

▸ **75.** Suffering, Distress, Sadness > PAIN

basanismos βασανισμός 929

basanismos is a noun found in six places. It denotes "torment," or the terrible anguish of distress in the context of divine punishment against the wicked (Rev 9:5; 14:11; 18:7, 10, 15).

basanos βάσανος 931

basanos is a noun denoting the "torment," "terrible anguish," or "distress" of eternal punishment in Luke 16:23, 28. Matt 4:24 refers to the "painful torments" of disease.

GRINDING

trizō τρίζω 5149

trizō is a rare verb found only in Mark 9:18, denoting the action of "grinding" one's teeth in anguish and suffering.

▸ **16.** Body, Bodily Functions > GNASH, GNASHING, GRIND

SEE ALSO

- ▸ **28.** Agriculture, Viticulture, Animal Husbandry > GRIND
  alēthō

HEAVY

adēmoneō ἀδημονέω 85

This rare verb is found in only three places, meaning "being heavy" with anguish, sorrow, or grief. It is used of Jesus in the garden of Gethsemane in Matt 26:37; Mark 14:33, and of Epaphroditus in Phil 2:26.

SEE ALSO

- ▸ **88.** Qualities, Characteristics > HEAVY, WEIGHTY, BURDENSOME
  bareō, barys

HOWL

ololyzō ὀλολύζω 3649

ololyzō is found only in Jas 5:1, where it refers to the rich being called upon to "howl" in anguish over the miseries that will come upon them.

LAMENT, LAMENTATION, MOURN, MOURNING

koptō κόπτω 2875

koptō is a verb found in seven contexts, meaning "lament" or "mourn" in five of these places.

Mourning as a social custom is mentioned in a generalized context in Matt 11:17. The peoples of the earth are said to mourn at the appearing of the Son of Man in glory at the end of the age. The context here suggests that it will involve a cry of dismay or anguish (Matt 24:30; Rev 1:7). On the occasion of the death of Jairus' daughter (whom Jesus subsequently bought back to life), the wailing of crowds in the street is noted in Luke 8:52. The wailing of a number of women accompanying Jesus on the way to his crucifixion is noted in Luke 23:27. Rev 18:9 contains a visionary description of the kings of the earth lamenting the demise of the city of Babylon.

▸ **28.** Agriculture, Viticulture, Animal Husbandry > BREAK OFF, CUT, CUT OFF

kopetos κοπετός 2870

kopetos is a noun derived from ***koptō***, occurring only in Acts 8:2 and referring to the "lamentation" made for Stephen at his martyrdom.

thrēneō θρηνέω 2354

thrēneō is a synonym for ***koptō*** (above). It is found in only four places, with general references to mourning or lamenting (Matt 11:17; Luke 7:32; John 16:20). Luke 23:27 refers to people following Jesus and mourning for him on the way to his crucifixion.

klauthmos κλαυθμός 2805

klauthmos occurs on nine occasions and refers to "wailing," "weeping," or "lamentation" in the context of severe anguish. It is the term used in the expression "wailing and gnashing of teeth," where "wailing" conveys the emotion of stark horror and despair at being denied entry into the eternal kingdom of God (Matt 8:12; 13:42, 50; 22:13; 24:51; 25:30; Luke 13:28). Lamentation or wailing in a more generalized context is indicated in Matt 2:18. In Acts 20:37, ***klauthmos*** refers to the weeping of the Ephesian elders as they bade farewell to the apostle Paul.

▸ **75.** Suffering, Distress, Sadness > WEEP, WEEPING, WAILING

odyrmos ὀδυρμός 3602

odyrmos refers to mourning and lamentation, expressing great sadness. The term occurs only in Matt 2:18; 2 Cor 7:7.

pentheō πενθέω 3996

pentheō is a verb occurring eleven times, meaning "mourn" in a number of contexts.

Mourning that expresses sorrow for sin is indicated in Matt 5:4, for which blessing shall be granted. 1 Cor 5:2 notes the absence of such an attitude. See also 2 Cor 12:21; Jas 4:9 in this regard. Mourning expressed at the death of Jesus is noted in Mark 16:10. Rev 18:11ff. records the outpouring of lamentation by the nations of the world at the destruction of the city of Babylon.

penthos πένθος 3997

penthos is the noun derived from ***pentheō*** and is translated "sorrow," "mourning." ***penthos*** is found in only four contexts.

Jas 4:9 exhorts sinners to mourn for their sin. Rev 18:7 refers to the arrogant boast of the Babylonian rulers, represented as a class by the metaphor of a "queen," who prides herself on the boast that she will never know any sorrow, or mourning. See also Rev 18:4. By way of stark contrast, Rev 21:4 promises the resurrected people of God that mourning shall be abolished forever in the heavenly kingdom.

▸ **75.** Suffering, Distress, Sadness > SAD, SORROW, SORROWFUL, GRIEF

MISERABLE, MISERY

eleeinos ἐλεεινός 1652

eleeinos is an adjectival form derived from ***eleos*** that is translated "miserable," "pitiable." It occurs only twice. In 1 Cor 15:19, ***eleeinos*** refers to the hypothetical miserable condition that would come upon all believers if Jesus Christ had not in fact risen from the dead. Rev 3:17 refers to, among other things, the miserable condition of the congregation at Laodicea.

talaipōria ταλαιπωρία 5004

talaipōria means "misery" in the sense of "hardship," "calamity," or "judgment." The term only occurs twice. In Rom 3:16, ***talaipōria*** refers to the misery wrought by the wicked on their victims; and in Jas 5:1 it indicates the miseries or calamities that await the rich and powerful who despise God and their fellow human beings. The context here is one of imminent divine judgment against them.

OPPRESS, CRUSH

thrauō θραύω 2352

thrauō is a rare verb found only in Luke 4:18 referring to the Spirit-anointed Christ setting free those who are "oppressed," suggesting deliverance for those who are crushed in their spirit.

SEE ALSO

▸ **76.** Force, Harm, Oppress > CRUSH
syntribō

▸ **78.** Act Upon, Push, Pull, Break, Cut > PRESS, CRUSH
apothlibō

PAIN

synōdinō συνωδίνω 4944

synōdinō is a verb found only in Rom 8:22. It refers metaphorically to the suffering of the world under the curse of sin, likening it to the pain of a woman in labor.

ponos πόνος 4192

ponos indicates "pain" in each of its three occurrences, all in the book of Revelation. Rev 16:10, 11 indicate the agony, both physical and mental, of the wicked on earth experiencing the wrath of God in a visitation of a terrible punishment on them. Rev 21:4 refers to the glorious abolition of all pain and suffering in the eternal kingdom of God.

basanizō βασανίζω 928

basanizō is a verb meaning to "torment," inflicting pain in various contexts. The term occurs twelve times.

The affliction of illness is described as terrible pain in Matt 8:6.

Elsewhere, ***basanizō*** refers to the tormenting impact of evil spirits in the lives of individuals who were subsequently exorcised by Jesus (Matt 8:29; Mark 5:7; Luke 8:28).

Rev 9:5; 14:10; 20:10 refer to inflicting pain in the context of God's terrible judgment on the wicked, including the devil (see also Rev 11:10).

basanizō also refers to the pain of a woman in labor in Rev 12:2. In this case the woman is a visionary representative of the mother of the Christ child.

▸ **75.** Suffering, Distress, Sadness > DISTRESS, TORMENT

ōdin ὠδίν 5604

ōdin is a noun occurring only four times. It is always used metaphorically. In Matt 24:8; Mark 13:8, the term refers to the onset of the tribulation in the last days prior to the Lord's return as the beginning of "birth pangs." Similarly, in 1 Thess 5:3 such a judgment is explicitly defined in terms of a woman's pain in childbirth. Acts 2:24 refers to the miraculous display of divine power in raising Jesus from the dead, defining it as a "freeing from the agony of death."

PERSECUTION, TRIBULATION

diōgmos διωγμός 1375

diōgmos is a noun occurring only in Matt 13:21 and referring to "persecution" that comes upon a new "convert," causing him to fall away from the faith.

thlipsis θλῖψις 2347

thlipsis is a noun found in approximately fifty places with the primary senses of "tribulation," "persecution," and "affliction."

References to "tribulation" that are largely synonymous with persecution of the Christian church include those in Matt 13:21; 24:2ff.; Acts 11:19; 14:22; Rom 2:9; 12:12; Rev 1:9; 2:9ff.; 7:14.

▸ **75.** Suffering, Distress, Sadness > AFFLICT, AFFLICTION

PIERCE

dierchomai διέρχομαι 1330

dierchomai is commonly translated "to go, pass, walk through" in the forty or so contexts in which it occurs. In Luke 2:35, however, it is translated "pierce" — referring to the sorrow that will come upon Mary the mother of Jesus. Simeon foretells here that a sword will pierce Mary's heart, anticipating the agony of her son's suffering.

▸ **85.** Movement, Position, State > PASS, PASS BY, PASS THROUGH, CROSS OVER
▸ **85.** Movement, Position, State > TRAVEL, TRAVELER
▸ **85.** Movement, Position, State > GO, WALK, GO BEFORE

peripeirō περιπείρω 4044

peripeirō is another rare verb meaning "pierce through" in the context of torturing oneself with many sorrows. This describes those who have wandered from the faith, who "have pierced themselves with many sorrows."

SEE ALSO

▸ **76.** Force, Harm, Oppress > PIERCE
nyssō, ekkenteō, diikneomai

SAD, SORROW, SORROWFUL, GRIEF

syllypeō συλλυπέω 4818

syllypeō is a rare verb with the passive sense of "be grieved," referring to Christ's "distress" at the hardness of people's hearts, found only in Mark 3:5.

skythrōpos σκυθρωπός 4659

skythrōpos is a rare adjective found only twice and meaning "sad," describing a facial expression (Matt 6:16; Luke 24:17).

stygnazō στυγνάζω 4768

stygnazō is a rare verb found only twice. In Mark 10:22 it describes a "falling" countenance, in relation to the rich young ruler who rejected Jesus' call to give away his wealth to the poor, resulting in him becoming sad or dejected. See also Matt 16:3, where ***stygnazō*** is used metaphorically, referring to the "threatening" appearance of a stormy sky.

lypē λύπη 3077

lypē is a noun found sixteen times meaning "sorrow," "grief" in the majority of these contexts (Luke 22:45; John 16:6, 20, 22; Rom 9:2; 2 Cor 2:3). 2 Cor 7:10 speaks of "sorrow" leading to repentance. In John 16:21, ***lypē*** is translated "pain" in relation to childbirth.

lypeō λυπέω 3076

lypeō is a verb found around twenty times with a variety of meanings such as "to cause grief," "sorrow," "make sorrowful," "affect with sadness," "be sorry."

lypeō means "to be sorry" (Matt 14:9; 18:31); "be sorrowful, very sad" (Matt 19:22; 26:22; Mark 10:22; John 16:20); "cause grief, anguish" (2 Cor 2:2ff.; 7:8ff.). Eph 4:30 contains the admonition not "to grieve" the Holy Spirit. See also 1 Thess 4:13.

perilypos περίλυπος 4036

perilypos is an adjective found in five contexts meaning "very sad," "sorrowful" in Matt 26:38; Mark 6:26; 14:34; Luke 18:23, 24.

penthos πένθος 3997

penthos is a noun meaning "sorrow," "mourning" in Jas 4:9; Rev 18:7, 8; 21:4.

▸ **75.** Suffering, Distress, Sadness > LAMENT, LAMENTATION, MOURN, MOURNING

odynē ὀδύνη 3601

odynē is a rare noun found only in Rom 9:2; 1 Tim 6:10, meaning "profound sorrow, grief."

odynaō ὀδυνάω 3600

odynaō is a verb found four times, meaning "to cause sorrow, torment," "be in anguish," in Luke 2:48; 16:24, 25; Acts 20:38.

▸ **75.** Suffering, Distress, Sadness > ANGUISH

STRUGGLE

athlēsis ἄθλησις 119

athlēsis is a rare noun denoting the "struggle" with suffering, found only in Heb 10:32.

SEE ALSO

▸ **77.** Resist, Oppose, Fight, Rebel > FIGHT
agōn, agōnizomai, pykteuō, machomai, thēriomacheō, machē, theomachos

SUFFER

biazō βιάζω 971

biazō is a rare verb meaning "to endure, suffer violence" in the cause of the kingdom of heaven (Matt 11:12). Luke 16:16 refers to people "forcing their way" into the kingdom of heaven.

paschō πάσχω 3958

paschō is a verb found in around forty places meaning "to suffer," referring to enduring both physical and emotional trauma.

paschō frequently refers to the "suffering" borne by Christ. Christ's suffering on the cross is anticipated in Matt 16:21; 17:12; Mark 8:31; 9:12; Luke 9:22; 17:25; 22:15. Reflection on his ordeal after the event but prior to his ascension is found in Luke 24:26. The prophetic prediction of his suffering is recorded in Luke 24:46; Acts 3:18. Mention of his "passion" as a matter of history is noted in Acts 1:3; Heb 2:18; 5:8; 9:26; 13:12; 1 Pet 2:21. Paul's determination to demonstrate to his fellow countrymen that the OT prophets had actually predicted the suffering of Christ and his subsequent resurrection is indicated in Acts 17:3.

Elsewhere, human suffering is noted in relation to psychological torment (Matt 27:19); to illness (Mark 5:26); to the agony of persecution (Luke 13:2; Phil 1:29; 1 Thess 2:14; 1 Pet 2:19ff.; 3:17; 4:1; Rev 2:10); and to suffering in general (1 Cor 12:26).

adikeō ἀδικέω 91

adikeō is a verb found nearly thirty times with the predominant sense of "hurt," "do wrong." However, Acts 7:24 refers to Moses having seen one of his Israelite countrymen "suffering wrong" at the hands of an Egyptian overseer.

▸ **57.** Evil, Wickedness, Sin > WRONG, INJUSTICE

SEE ALSO

▸ **72.** Need, Gain, Loss, Advantage, Seek, Find > SUFFER LOSS
zēmioō

TEAR, TEARS

dakryon δάκρυον 1144

dakryon is a noun occurring ten times with the consistent sense of "tears." General references to "tears" shed in grief include those in Acts 20:19, 31; 2 Cor 2:4; 2 Tim 1:4; Rev 7:17; 21:4. Tears shed as a consequence of a penitent spirit are noted in Heb 12:17. Christ shed tears during his life on earth as he earnestly prayed to the Father on behalf of his people (e.g., Heb 5:7).

TRIAL

dokimē δοκιμή 1382

dokimē is a noun indicating the primary meanings "proof," "evidence." In 2 Cor 8:2, however, the term means "trial," referring to an experience of undefined suffering.

pyrōsis πύρωσις 4451

pyrōsis is a noun with the underlying sense of "burning," used metaphorically in 1 Pet 4:12 to refer to a "fiery trial."

▸ **12.** Fire, Heat, Smoke, Burning > BURN, BURNING, LIGHT, SET ON FIRE

SEE ALSO

▸ **51.** Knowledge, Wisdom, Remember, Forget > TRIAL, TESTING
dokimion, peirasmos

TROUBLE

kakopatheō κακοπαθέω 2553

kakopatheō is a verb meaning "to endure hardship" or "suffer trouble" (2 Tim 2:3, 9; 4:5; Jas 5:13).

▸ **75.** Suffering, Distress, Sadness > AFFLICT, AFFLICTION

throeō θροέω 2360

throeō is a verb found in only three places, meaning to be "troubled," "anxious," or "frightened." It is used only in the negative as an exhortation (Matt 24:6; Mark 13:7; 2 Thess 2:2).

diatarassō διαταράσσω 1298

diatarassō is a rare verb found only in Luke 1:29, meaning "to be troubled, disturbed."

tyrbazō τυρβάζω 5182

tyrbazō is a synonym for ***diatarassō*** (above). It is found only in Luke 10:41 and describes the troubled state of mind of Mary, the sister of Lazarus.

SEE ALSO

- ▸ **27.** Community, Partnership, Unity, Discord > TROUBLE, UPROAR, RIOT
  ektarassō
- ▸ **76.** Force, Harm, Oppress > TROUBLE, IRRITATE, BOTHER, ANNOY
  kopos, skyllō, parenochleō, parechō, enochleō

TROUBLE, TROUBLED, DISTURBED

tarassō ταράσσω 5015

tarassō is a verb found in approximately twenty contexts meaning "trouble," "cause distress," as well as "be troubled, fearful, or anxious."

The mental state of anxiety is predicated of human beings in Matt 2:3; Mark 6:50; Luke 1:12; John 11:33; 14:1, 27; 1 Pet 3:14. Such a condition is also noted in relation to Christ's apprehension at his approaching death (John 12:27; 13:21).

tarassō refers to causing trouble in Acts 15:24; 17:8; Gal 1:7; 5:10. And in John 5:4ff., ***tarassō*** means "troubling," or agitating, stirring up the water of a pool.

SEE ALSO

- ▸ **27.** Community, Partnership, Unity, Discord > TROUBLE, UPROAR, RIOT
  ektarassō
- ▸ **76.** Force, Harm, Oppress > TROUBLE, IRRITATE, BOTHER, ANNOY
  kopos, skyllō, parenochleō, parechō, enochleō

WEAR DOWN, WEAR OUT

hypōpiazō ὑπωπιάζω 5299

hypōpiazō is a verb meaning "wear out" or "wear down" as a result of verbal harassment in Luke 18:5. In 1 Cor 9:27, ***hypōpiazō*** refers to the metaphorical "beating" of one's body in the context of self-discipline. There is arguably some overlap in meaning here.

SEE ALSO

- ▸ **20.** Illness, Disease, Health, Healing > WEARY
  kamnō
- ▸ **60.** Virtues > (NOT) GROW WEARY
  ekkakeō
- ▸ **84.** Do, Make, Accomplish, Occur > TOIL
  kopiaō

WEEP, WEEPING, WAILING

klaiō κλαίω 2799

klaiō is a verb found in approximately forty contexts meaning "weep" in relation to "mourning" and "suffering."

klaiō refers to the outpouring of grief in weeping in a variety of contexts, including the loss of loved ones (Matt 2:18; 5:38ff.; Luke 7:13; 8:52; John 11:31ff.); bitter remorse for sin (Matt 26:75; Mark 14:72; Luke 7:38); Christ's compassion for the rebellious city of Jerusalem (Luke 19:41); and the grief of the disciples over the loss of their Master (John 16:20). Other general references to weeping are found in Luke 6:21ff.; 7:32; 23:28.

klauthmos κλαυθμός 2805

klauthmos is a noun denoting "weeping" or "wailing" in nine places.

Matt 2:18 refers to "mourning" the loss of loved ones. "Weeping" as a consequence of suffering the judgment of God is recorded in Matt 13:42; 22:13; 25:30; Luke 13:28. "Weeping" over the parting of friends and fellow believers is noted in Acts 20:37.

- ▸ **75.** Suffering, Distress, Sadness > LAMENT, LAMENTATION, MOURN, MOURNING

WRONGFULLY, UNJUSTLY

adikōs ἀδίκως 95

adikōs is an adverb found only in 1 Pet 2:19 with reference to suffering "wrongfully" or "unjustly."

SEE ALSO

- ▸ **57.** Evil, Wickedness, Sin > WRONG, INJUSTICE
  adikia, adikeō

76. Force, Harm, Oppress

BEAT

derō δέρω 1194

The verb ***derō*** is found fifteen times with the primary sense of "beat" or "strike," in the context of giving someone a beating.

General references to this action are found in Matt 21:35; Mark 12:3ff.; Luke 12:47ff.; Acts 5:40; 22:19; 2 Cor 11:20. Christ is subject to such treatment in Luke 22:63; John 18:23. 1 Cor 9:26 refers to the actions of a boxer who practices his art by "beating" the air.

▸ **76.** Force, Harm, Oppress > STRIKE, SLAP

typtō τύπτω 5180

The verb ***typtō*** is synonymous with ***derō*** (above). It is found in fourteen places with the meaning "beat," "strike," as in giving a beating (Matt 24:49; Luke 12:45; Acts 18:17; 21:32). The specific act of "striking" is indicated in Matt 27:30; Mark 15:19; Luke 6:29; 22:64; Acts 23:2ff. The phrase "beat one's breast" is found in Luke 18:13; 23:48, expressing a penitent humility.

▸ **76.** Force, Harm, Oppress > STRIKE, SLAP

rhabdizō ῥαβδίζω 4463

rhabdizō is a rare verb with the meaning "to beat with rods," found only in Acts 16:22; 2 Cor 11:25.

BLOW

rhapisma ῥάπισμα 4475

rhapisma is a noun found in three places meaning to strike someone with the hand, to strike them with a "blow." Mark 14:65; John 18:22; 19:3 all describe the actions of some officials of the high priest in assaulting Jesus at the time of his trial.

▸ **76.** Force, Harm, Oppress > STRIKE, SLAP

BREAK

katagnymi κατάγνυμι 2608

katagnymi is a verb occurring five times with the literal meaning to "break" a leg in John 19:31ff.

SEE ALSO

▸ **23.** Food, Drink, Cooking > BREAK BREAD
klaō, kataklaō, klasis

▸ **28.** Agriculture, Viticulture, Animal Husbandry > BREAK OFF, CUT, CUT OFF
ekklaō

▸ **58.** Vices > STEAL, BREAK IN, BURGLE
dioryssō

▸ **75.** Suffering, Distress, Sadness > BREAK
synthryptō

▸ **78.** Act Upon, Push, Pull, Break, Cut > BREAK
lyō, syntribō, diarrēgnymi, synthlaō

BRING

epagō ἐπάγω 1863

The verb ***epagō*** means "to bring upon" — to cause something evil to happen to someone. In Acts 5:28 the religious leaders of Jerusalem expressed the fear that the preaching of the gospel by the early Christians would "bring the blood of Christ upon the nation of Israel."

2 Pet 2:1 refers to the hand of God "bringing" swift destruction upon false teachers. 2 Pet 2:5 refers to the ancient flood that God "brought upon" the wicked world during the time of Noah.

SEE ALSO

▸ **25.** Family, Marriage, Adoption, Inheritance > BRING UP, RAISE, NURTURE
trephō, anatrephō, ektrephō

▸ **86.** Movement Toward or Away From > BRING, BROUGHT
pherō, katagō, proagō, prosagō

BRUISE, BREAK, SHATTER, TEAR

syntribō συντρίβω 4937

syntribō is the one NT term translated "bruise" as well as "break," "shatter," plus related nuances. It occurs eight times.

Matt 12:20 cites the OT promise, referring to the coming Messiah's gentleness, that he will not break a reed that is "bruised" (Isa 42:1ff.). ***syntribō*** also refers to those who are "brokenhearted" in Luke 4:18.

The term refers literally to the "tearing apart" of chains in Mark 5:4 (see also Luke 9:39). The meaning "shatter" or "break" is applied to a pot of expensive perfume in Mark 14:3 (see also Rev 2:27). John 19:36 refers to the promise in Ps 34:20 that not one of the bones of the Messiah would be "broken." Rom 16:20 describes how God will "crush" Satan under his feet.

▸ **76.** Force, Harm, Oppress > CRUSH

▸ **78.** Act Upon, Push, Pull, Break, Cut > BREAK

BURDEN

epibareō ἐπιβαρέω 1912

epibareō is a verb found three times with the meaning "to be a burden" or to put people to inconvenience (1 Thess 2:9; 2 Thess 3:8).

katabareō καταβαρέω 2599

katabareō is synonymous with ***epibareō*** (above) and is found only in 2 Cor 12:16.

katanarkaō καταναρκάω 2655

katanarkaō is another synonym for ***epibareō*** and ***katabareō*** (above), also signifying "to be a burden" on someone. It is always used in a negative context (2 Cor 11:9; 12:13ff.).

SEE ALSO

- ▸ **75.** Suffering, Distress, Sadness > BURDEN
  baros, phortion

CRUSH

syntribō συντρίβω 4937

syntribō is a verb found eight times meaning "break," "shatter," "crush." Matt 12:20 refers to a "crushed" reed. Rom 16:20 predicts that God will soon "crush" Satan under the feet of his people.

- ▸ **76.** Force, Harm, Oppress > BRUISE, BREAK, SHATTER, TEAR
- ▸ **78.** Act Upon, Push, Pull, Break, Cut > BREAK

SEE ALSO

- ▸ **75.** Suffering, Distress, Sadness > OPPRESS, CRUSH
  thrauō
- ▸ **78.** Act Upon, Push, Pull, Break, Cut > PRESS, CRUSH
  apothlibō

CUT, CUT OFF

katakoptō κατακόπτω 2629

katakoptō is a verb found only in Mark 5:5, describing the actions of a demon-possessed man "cutting" himself with stones.

aphaireō ἀφαιρέω 851

The verb ***aphaireō*** is found in eleven places meaning "take away," "cut off." The latter sense is found in Matt 26:51; Mark 14:47; Luke 22:50, all referring to Peter's action in "cutting off " the right ear of the high priest's servant.

- ▸ **79.** Throw, Send, Drive, Mix, Remove > TAKE AWAY, REMOVE

SEE ALSO

- ▸ **10.** Earth, Dust, Rocks, Minerals, Metals, Stones > CUT
  latomeō, laxeutos
- ▸ **21.** Die, Perish, Kill, Destroy > CUT TO PIECES
  dichotomeō
- ▸ **28.** Agriculture, Viticulture, Animal Husbandry > BREAK OFF, CUT, CUT OFF
  koptō
- ▸ **78.** Act Upon, Push, Pull, Break, Cut > CUT OFF, CUT DOWN
  apokoptō, ekkoptō

DRAW

spaō σπάω 4685

spaō is a rare verb found only in Mark 14:47; Acts 16:27, referring to "drawing" a sword.

SEE ALSO

- ▸ **29.** Boats, Fishing, Maritime Activity > PULL, DRAW
  anabibazō
- ▸ **79.** Throw, Send, Drive, Mix, Remove > DRAW, DRAG
  helkō, exelkō, syrō, anaspaō
- ▸ **80.** Related to Liquids > DRAW
  antleō
- ▸ **86.** Movement Toward or Away From > COME, DRAW NEAR
  engizō

DRIVE OUT

ekdiōkō ἐκδιώκω 1559

ekdiōkō is a rare verb meaning "persecute" in Luke 11:49. In 1 Thess 2:15 the term is translated "drive out," referring to Jews persecuting the early Christians.

- ▸ **76.** Force, Harm, Oppress > PERSECUTE, PURSUE

exōtheō ἐξωθέω 1856

exōtheō is a rare verb indicating God's redemptive action in "driving out" the pagan peoples of Canaan. It is found with this meaning only in Acts 7:45. In Acts 27:39, the term expresses the sense of "run aground" with reference to a boat.

SEE ALSO

- ▸ **29.** Boats, Fishing, Maritime Activity > DRIVE ALONG
  pherō
- ▸ **79.** Throw, Send, Drive, Mix, Remove > DRIVE, DRIVE OUT
  ekballō, elaunō

FIERCE

chalepos χαλεπός 5467

chalepos is a rare adjectival form describing the Gadarene demoniac as "fierce" (i.e., frightening in behavior and appearance) in Matt 8:28.

SEE ALSO

- ▸ **58.** Vices > FIERCE, SAVAGE
  anēmeros

HARM, MISTREAT, AFFLICT

kakoō κακόω 2559

kakoō is a verb found in seven places with the meaning "to treat harmfully," "mistreat." With this sense, the meaning "afflict" is evident in Acts 7:6; 18:10; 1 Pet 3:13. (See also Acts 7:19; 12:1; 14:2.)

- ▸ **76.** Force, Harm, Oppress > ILL-TREAT

kakoucheō κακουχέω 2558

kakoucheō is a rare verb with the meaning "oppress," "afflict" in the sense of "mistreat," "harm" found in Heb 11:37; 13:3.

SEE ALSO

- ▸ **75.** Suffering, Distress, Sadness > AFFLICT, AFFLICTION
  kakopatheō, kakopatheia, kakōsis, thlibō, thlipsis, pathēma

ILL-TREAT

kakoō κακόω 2559

kakoō is a verb found in seven places, meaning to "ill-treat," "harm" in three of these contexts (Acts 7:6; 18:10; 1 Pet 3:13).

▸ **76.** Force, Harm, Oppress > HARM, MISTREAT, AFFLICT

SEE ALSO

▸ **57.** Evil, Wickedness, Sin > EVIL, EVILDOER, WICKED, WICKEDNESS, LAWLESS ***kakos, kakia, kakōs, ponēros, phaulos, kakopoios, kakopoieō***

OPPRESS

katadynasteuō καταδυναστεύω 2616

katadynasteuō is a verb found only twice. In both instances it means "to oppress" with the underlying sense of being harassed or tormented. In Acts 10:38 such activity is predicated of the devil. Jas 2:8 accuses the rich of such behavior towards the poor.

kataponeō καταπονέω 2669

kataponeō is also a rare verb that is found only twice. It means "oppress" in the sense of "treating harshly" (Acts 7:24), and "causing distress" (2 Pet 2:7).

PERSECUTE, PURSUE

diōkō διώκω 1377

diōkō is a verb found in around fifty contexts meaning "persecute," "follow," or "pursue." Unlike in the case of the Hebrew word *rādaph*, which demonstrates a significant overlap in meaning between "persecute" and "pursue," there is no such blurring of these meanings in the use of ***diōkō***, with the possible exception of Rev 12:13. In other words, ***diōkō*** clearly and unambiguously refers to "persecution."

General references to persecution are found in Matt 23:34; Gal 4:29; 6:12. In several places persecution is viewed as a blessing, since it will result in true believers gaining possession of the kingdom of heaven (Matt 5:10, 44; 23:34; Luke 21:12). Rom 12:14 exhorts believers to bless those who persecute them. The reality of persecution for the followers of Jesus Christ is indicated in Matt 10:23; John 15:20; 1 Cor 4:12; 2 Cor 4:9; Gal 5:11; 2 Tim 3:12. Acts 7:52 speaks of the persecution of Yahweh's prophets by the Israelites of old. Paul refers to his persecution of the first generation of Christians following the resurrection of Christ, prior to his own conversion (Acts 22:4; 26:11; 1 Cor 15:9; Gal 1:13, 23; Phil 3:6).

Jesus himself was persecuted by his fellow countrymen, as recorded in John 5:16. In the divine revelation to Saul (later Paul) at his conversion experience, the risen Christ declares that the zealous Pharisee was in fact persecuting him through the harassment of the Christian community (Acts 9:4, 5; 22:7, 8; 26:14, 15).

▸ **68.** Ability, Possibility, Effort, Succeed, Fail > PRESS ON

▸ **71.** Lead, Guide, Follow > FOLLOW, ACCOMPANY, PURSUE

ekdiōkō ἐκδιώκω 1559

ekdiōkō is a rare verb, found only twice. It means "to persecute" in Luke 11:49 and "to drive out" or "banish" in 1 Thess 2:15.

▸ **76.** Force, Harm, Oppress > DRIVE OUT

diōktēs διώκτης 1376

diōktēs is a noun derived from ***diōkō*** (above) and is found only in 1 Tim 1:13, where Paul admits that he was once a "persecutor."

SEE ALSO

▸ **75.** Suffering, Distress, Sadness > PERSECUTION, TRIBULATION ***diōgmos***

PIERCE

nyssō νύσσω 3572

nyssō is found only in John 19:34, referring to the Roman soldiers "piercing" the body of Jesus on his side as he hung on the cross.

ekkenteō ἐκκεντέω 1574

ekkenteō is found only in John 19:37; Rev 1:7. The term is a synonym for ***nyssō*** (above) and refers in each text to "piercing" Christ on the cross.

diikneomai διϊκνέομαι 1338

diikneomai is used metaphorically in Heb 4:12 to refer to the word of God as a two-edged sword that "pierces" deep into the soul and spirit of a person.

SEE ALSO

▸ **75.** Suffering, Distress, Sadness > PIERCE ***dierchomai, peripeirō***

SCAR, MARK

stigma στίγμα 4742

stigma occurs only once, in Gal 6:17, where it refers to the "marks" or "scars" on the body of Christ as a consequence of his crucifixion.

SEE ALSO

▸ **68.** Ability, Possibility, Effort, Succeed, Fail > GOAL, MARK ***skopos***

▸ **81.** Forms, Groups, Patterns, Order > MARK, STAMP, BRAND ***charagma***

STRIKE, SLAP

typtō τύπτω 5180

typtō is a verb meaning "strike," "beat," "wound" throughout its usage (fourteen times).

The action of "beating" one's servants is noted in Matt 24:49; Luke 12:45. "Striking" someone on the face is indicated in Luke 6:29; 22:64; Acts 23:2ff. See also Matt 27:30; Mark 15:19.

"Striking or beating one's breast" is a sign of repentance in Luke 18:13; 23:48.

▸ **76.** Force, Harm, Oppress > BEAT

patassō πατάσσω 3960

patassō means "to strike" in several different contexts. The verb occurs ten times.

It is used metaphorically in the expression "to strike the shepherd" with reference to Christ's imminent death (Matt 26:31; Mark 14:27; Luke 22:50).

General references to people "striking" include the use of a sword in Matt 26:51; Luke 22:49. See also Acts 7:24; 12:7.

God is said to strike (or afflict) the earth with plagues in the visionary context of Rev 11:6. See also Rev 19:15. An angel of God is said to "strike" King Herod with a fatal illness in Acts 12:23.

derō δέρω 1194

derō is a verb meaning to "beat," "give a beating" (i.e., a physical assault). The term is found in fifteen contexts (Matt 21:35; Mark 12:3ff.; Luke 12:47ff.; Acts 5:40; 22:19).

derō also refers to the accusers of Christ at his trial "striking" him on the face (John 18:23). See also 2 Cor 11:20; 1 Cor 9:26.

▸ **76.** Force, Harm, Oppress > BEAT

paiō παίω 3817

paiō is a verb found in five places and meaning "strike," "sting."

Mark 14:47; John 18:10 refer to striking someone with a sword. ***paiō*** refers to "striking" Christ on the face in Luke 22:64; Matt 26:68, in the context of his humiliating treatment at his trial. The "strike" or "sting" of a scorpion is mentioned in Rev 9:5.

rhapizō ῥαπίζω 4474

rhapizō is a verb meaning "to slap" (with the hand) in reference to striking the face (Matt 5:39; 26:67).

rhapisma ῥάπισμα 4475

rhapisma is a term denoting a "blow or slap on the face," given with the hand (Mark 14:65; John 18:22; 19:3).

▸ **76.** Force, Harm, Oppress > BLOW

THREAT, THREATEN

apeileō ἀπειλέω 546

apeileō is a verb found only in 1 Pet 2:23, meaning "threaten" (used here in the negative).

prosapeileō προσαπειλέω 4324

prosapeileō is a variant of ***apeileō*** (above) meaning "threaten further" in Acts 4:21.

apeilē ἀπειλή 547

apeilē is a noun (derived from ***apeileō***, above) referring to "threats" in three places (Acts 4:29; 9:1; Eph 6:9).

TRAMPLE, TREAD

katapateō καταπατέω 2662

katapateō is a verb denoting the action of "trampling," "treading down," "treading under foot" in five contexts. In Luke 8:5, the seed of God's word is trampled under foot and fails to take root in the hearts of those who hear it. Heb 10:29 speaks of people "trampling" the Son of God, indicating their utter rejection of him. Literal references to "trampling" are found in Matt 5:13; 7:6; Luke 12:1.

TREAT SHAMEFULLY

atimoō ἀτιμόω 821

atimoō is found only in Mark 12:4, with the meaning "treat shamefully" (i.e., cruelly).

▸ **52.** Status, Identity, Reputation, Honor, Shame > SHAME

SEE ALSO

▸ **52.** Status, Identity, Reputation, Honor, Shame > ASHAMED
aischynomai, epaischynomai, kataischynō, entrepō, anepaischyntos, atimazō, paradeigmatizō, hybrizō

TROUBLE, IRRITATE, BOTHER, ANNOY

kopos κόπος 2873

kopos is a noun denoting the state of "trouble" or "annoyance." It is used primarily, however, with verbal force, translated "to bother, annoy" in Matt 26:10; Mark 14:6; Luke 11:7; 18:5.

▸ **84.** Do, Make, Accomplish, Occur > WORK, LABOR, PRODUCE, BRING ABOUT, DEED

skyllō σκύλλω 4660

skyllō is a verb meaning "to trouble," "bother," or "annoy" in Mark 5:35; Luke 7:6; 8:49.

parenochleō παρενοχλέω 3926

parenochleō is a rare verb found only in Acts 15:19, meaning "to trouble," "make difficult."

parechō παρέχω 3930

parechō is a verb found in five contexts meaning "to cause trouble," "irritate," or "bother," often used in the negative (Matt 26:10; Mark 14:6; Luke 11:7; 18:5; Gal 6:17).

enochleō ἐνοχλέω 1776

enochleō is a rare term, found only in Heb 12:15, meaning to "cause trouble" in a spiritual sense.

SEE ALSO

▸ **27.** Community, Partnership, Unity, Discord > TROUBLE, UPROAR, RIOT
ektarassō

▸ **75.** Suffering, Distress, Sadness > TROUBLE, TROUBLED, DISTURBED
tarassō, kakopatheō, throeō, diatarassō, tyrbazō

VIOLENCE, FORCE

harpazō ἁρπάζω 726

harpazō is a verb found thirteen times with the predominant meaning "seize" or "catch," with several nuances.

In several places, ***harpazō*** also means "take by force." Matt 11:12 refers to people "taking the kingdom of heaven by force." The meaning here is unclear, but it may suggest feverish human attempts to gain favor with God. John 6:15 records the Jewish crowd's abortive attempt to "take Jesus by force" and make him king over them. See also Acts 23:10.

▸ **70.** Give, Take, Seize, Touch > CATCH

▸ **70.** Give, Take, Seize, Touch > TAKE, TAKE HOLD OF, TAKE UP, TAKE DOWN, TAKE AWAY, SNATCH

bia βία 970

bia is a noun denoting "violence" or "force" in relation to people in Acts 5:26; 21:35. Acts 27:41 refers to the "force" of the breaking surf.

hormēma ὅρμημα 3731

hormēma refers to the "violence" of the destruction of Babylon in Rev 18:21.

WHIP, SCOURGE

mastigoō μαστιγόω 3146

mastigoō is a verb found seven times meaning "to scourge" or "whip."

Most commonly, ***mastigoō*** refers to "scourging" or "whipping" as a judicial punishment (Matt 10:17; 20:19; 10:34; Luke 18:33; John 19:1).

The term is used metaphorically in Heb 12:6 concerning the disciplinary action of God in "whipping" or "scourging" his children.

mastizō μαστίζω 3147

mastizō is a rare verb found only in Acts 22:25, meaning "scourge" or "whip" in the literal sense of judicial punishment.

mastix μάστιξ 3148

mastix is a noun that occurs six times, referring to the practice of "scourging" or "flogging" as corporal punishment (Acts 22:24; Heb 11:36).

▸ **20.** Illness, Disease, Health, Healing > DISEASE, PLAGUE

phragelloō φραγελλόω 5417

phragelloō is a verb found only twice, referring to the "scourging" or "whipping" of Christ prior to his crucifixion (Matt 27:26; Mark 15:15).

phragellion φραγέλλιον 5416

phragellion is a rare noun derived from ***phragelloō*** (above) and is found only in John 2:15, with reference to a "whip."

WOUND

plēgē πληγή 4127

plēgē is a noun occurring around twenty times meaning "wound," "blow," as well as "plague." The sense of "wound" as the result of a beating is indicated in Luke 10:30; Acts 16:23; 2 Cor 6:5.

plēgē also metaphorically denotes a mortal "wound" inflicted on the satanic beast in Rev 13:3, 12ff.

▸ **20.** Illness, Disease, Health, Healing > DISEASE, PLAGUE

kephalaioō κεφαλαιόω 2775

kephalaioō is a rare verb found only in Mark 12:4 meaning "to wound in the head."

traumatizō τραυματίζω 5135

traumatizō is a verb found twice, meaning "to inflict a wound" (Luke 20:12; Acts 19:16).

trauma τραῦμα 5134

trauma is a noun denoting a "wound," found only in Luke 10:34.

77. Resist, Oppose, Fight, Rebel

ADVERSARY, OPPONENT

antidikos ἀντίδικος 476

antidikos is a noun found five times with the underlying senses of "adversary." In Matt 5:35; Luke 12:58 (twice); 18:3, the term designates a "legal opponent." In 1 Pet 5:8 the devil is described as an "adversary" prowling around like a roaring lion.

antikeimai ἀντίκειμαι 480

antikeimai is a verb with the underlying sense of "to oppose," "set over against." It is found in eight contexts.

In the majority of its usage, ***antikeimai*** occurs in a participial noun with the sense of "enemy," "opponent" in general (Luke 13:17; 21:15; 1 Cor 16:9; Phil 1:28). In 1 Tim 5:14 it designates the devil as "the enemy" in particular.

The sense of "be opposed to" is found in the context of the antipathy between the flesh and the Spirit in Gal 5:17. See also 2 Thess 2:4; 1 Tim 5:10.

hypenantios ὑπεναντίος 5227

hypenantios is a rare adjectival form found only twice. In Col 2:14 it refers to the impact of the law standing "against" the people of God, which Christ removed by his death. In Heb 10:27 the term is used nominally to refer to "the enemies" who will be consumed by the fiery judgment of God.

CONSPIRE, IMAGINE

meletaō μελετάω 3191

This verb occurs only in Acts 4:25, meaning "imagine" in the sense of "conspire." Such an attitude is predicated of the Gentiles, who conspire in vain to overthrow the purposes of God — that is, they "imagine" vain things against him.

SEE ALSO

- ▸ **56.** Folly, Ignorance > FUTILE THINKING, VAIN IMAGINATION ***dialogismos***
- ▸ **58.** Vices > IMAGINATION, (STUBBORN) THINKING ***dianoia***

CURSE, MALIGN

kakologeō κακολογέω 2551

kakologeō is a verb found four times with the underlying sense of "speak evil of." Matt 15:4; Mark 7:10 refer to "cursing" one's parents — a capital offense under the Mosaic law. The act of "maligning" someone is noted in Mark 9:39; Acts 19:9.

SEE ALSO

- ▸ **57.** Evil, Wickedness, Sin > CURSE ***ara***
- ▸ **67.** Acknowledge, Confess, Profess, Swear > CURSE, CURSED ***anathematizō, katathematizō***
- ▸ **73.** Blessing, Curse, Reward, Punishment > CURSE, CURSED, CURSING, ACCURSED ***anathema, katathema, katara, kataraomai, epikataratos***

DESPISE, DISDAIN

exoutheneō ἐξουθενέω 1848

exoutheneō is a verb found in thirteen places with the general meaning "despise," including several related nuances.

"Despising" others in the sense of "viewing with disdain" is indicated in Luke 18:19; Rom 14:3, 10; 1 Cor 1:28. The allied sense of "esteeming people as worthless" is evident in 1 Cor 6:4. See also 2 Cor 10:10; 1 Thess 5:10. The sense of "treat with contempt" is noted in Luke 23:11; 1 Cor 16:11; Gal 4:14.

The OT reference to the stone "rejected" by the builders — a messianic allusion — is recorded in Acts 4:11.

kataphroneō καταφρονέω 2706

kataphroneō is a synonym for ***exoutheneō*** (above) meaning "despise" throughout the eleven occurrences of the term.

"Despise" in the sense of "reckon to be of no value or importance" is indicated in Matt 6:24; Luke 16:13; 1 Tim 4:12.

The sense of "view with disdain" is indicated in relation to the warning against "despising" little children, keeping them from entering the kingdom of heaven (Matt 18:10). The same attitude in relation to the mercy of God is indicated in Rom 2:4. See also 1 Tim 6:2.

The action of "treating people with contempt" is noted in 1 Cor 11:22. Treating civil authority with contempt is indicated in 2 Pet 2:10.

Heb 12:2 refers to Christ "despising" the shame of the cross, indicating his determination to "set it at naught," emptying it of its potency.

SEE ALSO

- ▸ **52.** Status, Identity, Reputation, Honor, Shame > DESPISE ***periphroneō, atimos***
- ▸ **54.** Rule, Authority, Command, Obedience > DESPISE ***atheteō***

ENEMY, ENMITY

echthros ἐχθρός 2190

echthros is an adjectival term with the nominal sense of "enemy" or "foe" throughout the thirty or so occurrences of the term with a variety of nuances, both literal and spiritual.

The meaning "enemy" in the general sense of one's personal adversary is evident in Matt 5:43ff.; 13:25ff.; Mark 12:36; Rom 12:20; Luke 6:27, 35; Gal 4:16; 2 Thess 3:15; Rev 11:5. The sense of "enemy" as one who opposes everything that is right is indicated in Rom 5:10.

echthros also denotes the "enemies" of God's people, Israel, in Luke 1:71, 74. See also Rom 11:28; Rev 11:12. In spiritual contexts, this term also refers directly and indirectly to Satan as the great "enemy" of God's people (Luke 10:19).

In a related context, ***echthros*** denotes the defeat of the "enemies" of Christ in Acts 2:35; 1 Cor 15:25; Phil 3:18; Heb 1:13; 10:13. Unbelievers are designated as "enemies" of God in Rom 5:10; Col 1:21; Jas 4:4.

Metaphorically, ***echthros*** denotes "death" as the last enemy to be destroyed in 1 Cor 15:26.

echthra ἔχθρα 2189

echthra is a variant form of ***echthros*** found in only six places with the predominant sense of "enmity" or "hatred." It most commonly refers to "enmity" with God, as in Rom 8:7; Eph 2:16; Jas 4:4. "Hostility" among individuals is noted in Luke 23:12. The vice of "hatred" is indicated in Gal 5:20.

FIGHT

agōn ἀγών 73

agōn is a noun found six times, meaning "conflict," "fight," in both literal and metaphorical contexts.

General references to "conflict" among people are found in Phil 1:30; Col 2:1; 1 Thess 2:2. Metaphorical references to "fighting the good fight" in relation to living out the Christian life are found in 1 Tim 6:12; 2 Tim 4:7. The Christian life is described as a "race" in Heb 12:1, with the underlying inference of a struggle.

▸ **68.** Ability, Possibility, Effort, Succeed, Fail > RACE, COURSE

agōnizomai ἀγωνίζομαι 75

agōnizomai is a verb found seven times, meaning "to strive," "fight," and used both literally and metaphorically.

An exhortation to "strive" to enter the narrow door that leads to salvation is found in Luke 13:24.

A general reference to people "fighting" in a physical sense is found in John 18:36. The athlete's "striving" for self-control is noted in 1 Cor 9:25. The apostle Paul's "toiling" in the context of gospel ministry is indicated in Col 1:29. Paul describes "laboring earnestly" in prayer in Col 4:12. The stance of "fighting the good fight" in relation to the struggle of Christian living is indicated in 1 Tim 6:12; 2 Tim 4:7.

▸ **68.** Ability, Possibility, Effort, Succeed, Fail > STRIVE

pykteuō πυκτεύω 4438

pykteuō is a rare verb found only in 1 Cor 9:26 meaning "to fight" as a boxer.

machomai μάχομαι 3164

machomai is a verb found four times meaning "strive," "quarrel." References to people "arguing," "quarreling" among themselves are found in John 6:52; Acts 7:26; 2 Tim 2:24. Jas 4:2 refers generally to "fighting."

▸ **58.** Vices > ARGUE, ARGUMENT, DISPUTE, QUARREL, STRIVE

thēriomacheō θηριομαχέω 2341

thēriomacheō is a rare verb meaning "to fight with wild beasts," found only in 1 Cor 15:32.

▸ **14.** Animals > BEAST, LIVING CREATURE, ANIMAL

machē μάχη 3163

machē is a noun derived from ***machomai*** (above) denoting "fighting," "quarreling" in four contexts. Three of these contexts indicate "quarreling" among believers. In 2 Cor 7:5 ***machē*** denotes "fighting" in the probable sense of "physical harassment" in the context of persecution.

▸ **27.** Community, Partnership, Unity, Discord > STRIFE, QUARREL

theomachos θεομάχος 2314

theomachos is a rare adjectival form describing those "who fight against God."

SEE ALSO

▸ **75.** Suffering, Distress, Sadness > STRUGGLE
athlēsis

HATE, HATEFUL

miseō μισέω 3404

miseō occurs about forty times with the exclusive sense of "hate." For the most part it occurs with a literal meaning, indicating animosity towards people, God, or particular attitudes. The term is also used in a non-literal sense, though this is rare.

The literal meaning of bearing ill will towards another person or persons is found in the majority of texts (e.g., Matt 5:43, 44; 6:24; Luke 1:71; John 7:7; 17:14; Titus 3:3; 1 John 2:9ff.; Rev 17:16). The world's hatred for the people of God is expressed in Luke 1:71; John 7:7; 15:18; 17:14; 1 John 3:13. Matt 10:22; 24:9; Mark 13:13; Luke 21:17 describe suffering hatred for the cause of the gospel.

In Luke 14:26, a non-literal use of ***miseō*** refers to "hating one's father and mother." This is a hyperbolic and symbolic use of the verb. Our love for God, for Christ, and for the cause of the gospel should so exceed all other loyalties that, compared with our earthly love for those in our family, our love for the Lord should make our mortal attachment to our loved ones seem like hatred. Explicit malice towards our families is, of course, in no way intended.

John 12:25 describes "hating one's life in order to save or keep it." A similar perspective is found in Luke 14:26. Hate in this text is not literal malice towards oneself, but rather indicates symbolically the most sublime expression of selflessness, expressed hyperbolically as "hatred." Eph 5:29 also contains a strong expression of self-denial defined as hate.

Hatred of God, an attitude predicated of the wicked, is mentioned in John 15:24, as is the attitude of hating that which is good in John 3:20.

miseō also indicates hatred of sin in Heb 1:9; Jude 23; Rev 2:6, 15. Rom 7:15 mentions the apostle Paul's personal dilemma in which he wrestles with conflicting desires of hatred of sin and an attraction to that which is evil. The paradox of God's attributes and decrees is revealed in Rom 9:13, where he declares that he loved Jacob, but hated Esau.

stygētos στυγητός 4767

This term is only found in Titus 3:3, meaning "hateful," or bearing malice against one another.

SEE ALSO

▸ **57.** Evil, Wickedness, Sin > GOD-HATER
theostygēs

RESIST, WITHSTAND

anthistēmi ἀνθίστημι 436

anthistēmi occurs fourteen times with the sense "to resist" or "withstand."

There is, for example, the injunction by Christ not to resist an evil person in Matt 5:13. Then there is a strong exhortation to resist the devil in Eph 6:13; Jas 4:7; 1 Pet 5:9. Rom 9:19 affirms the impossibility of resisting God's will. Rom 13:2 declares that resisting the civil authorities is equated with resisting God. See also Luke 21:15; Acts 6:10.

The meaning "resist" also includes the sense of "oppose." Acts 13:8 refers to Elymas the magician opposing Paul's ministry. Paul himself opposes Peter for inappropriate behavior towards Gentile believers. See also 2 Tim 3:8; 4:15.

antipiptō ἀντιπίπτω 496

antipiptō is a verb found only in Acts 7:51 with reference to "resisting" the Holy Spirit, or opposing his influence in the life of the believer.

antitassomai ἀντιτάσσομαι 498

antitassomai is a synonym for ***antipiptō*** (above) occurring five times and meaning "resist" (Acts 18:6; Rom 13:2; Jas 5:6). Such action is also predicated of God, who "resists" the proud (Jas 4:6; 1 Pet 5:5).

antikathistēmi ἀντικαθίστημι 478

antikathistēmi is found only in Heb 12:4 with reference to "resisting" (i.e., withstanding the pressure of) sin to the point of shedding blood.

RISE AGAINST

synephistēmi συνεφίστημι 4911

synephistēmi is a rare verb found only in Acts 16:22 with reference to a hostile crowd "rising up against" Paul and his companions to attack them.

SEE ALSO

▸ **84.** Do, Make, Accomplish, Occur >
HAPPEN, TAKE PLACE, COME TO PASS, ARISE
ginomai, eiserchomai

▸ **87.** Movement Upward or Downward >
ARISE, RISE UP, RAISE UP
anistēmi, exanistēmi, egeirō, diegeirō, anabainō, anatellō

ROUT, PUT TO FLIGHT

klinō κλίνω 2827

klinō is a verb with the primary meanings "lay," "bow (down)" throughout its seven occurrences. However, in Heb 11:34 it means "rout," "put to flight," referring to one's enemies.

▸ **87.** Movement Upward or Downward >
BOW, BOW DOWN

SEE ALSO

▸ **74.** Safety, Peace, Danger, Escape > FLEE, FLIGHT
phygē

78. Act Upon, Push, Pull, Break, Cut

BREAK

lyō λύω 3089

lyō is a verb found in forty places with the primary sense of "loose," "release." However, in several contexts the verb is translated "to break."

Matt 5:19 refers to "breaking" the commandments of God. Jesus is wrongly accused of "breaking" the Sabbath in John 5:18; 7:23. ***lyō*** is used negatively in John 10:35, asserting that Scripture "cannot be broken." See also Acts 13:43; 27:41.

lyō is used metaphorically in Eph 2:14 to describe how the work of Christ "breaks down" the wall of hostility between Jew and Gentile.

- ▸ **12.** Fire, Heat, Smoke, Burning > DISSOLVE, MELT
- ▸ **21.** Die, Perish, Kill, Destroy > DESTROY, DESTROYER, DESTRUCTION
- ▸ **55.** Bondage, Captivity, Servitude > RELEASE

syntribō συντρίβω 4937

syntribō is a verb found in eight places with the meanings "break in pieces," "shatter." It is used literally with reference to chains in Mark 5:4; to a flask, or pot in Mark 14:3; Rev 2:27. In John 19:36 there is the affirmation that the Messiah would never suffer a broken bone.

- ▸ **76.** Force, Harm, Oppress > BRUISE, BREAK, SHATTER, TEAR
- ▸ **76.** Force, Harm, Oppress > CRUSH

diarrēgnymi διαρρήγνυμι 1284

diarrēgnymi is a verb found five times with the meaning "break," "tear." The "breaking" of chains is literally indicated in Luke 8:29, where the Gadarene demoniac tears off his fetters. Luke 5:6 refers to "breaking" fishing nets.

synthlaō συνθλάω 4917

synthlaō is a rare verb with the meaning "break in pieces," "crush," found only in Matt 21:44; Luke 20:18 in relation to the fate of those who attempt to confound the messianic "stone" of God's appointing.

SEE ALSO

- ▸ **23.** Food, Drink, Cooking > BREAK BREAD
  klaō, kataklaō, klasis
- ▸ **28.** Agriculture, Viticulture, Animal Husbandry > BREAK OFF, CUT, CUT OFF
  ekklaō
- ▸ **58.** Vices > STEAL, BREAK IN, BURGLE
  dioryssō
- ▸ **75.** Suffering, Distress, Sadness > BREAK
  synthryptō
- ▸ **76.** Force, Harm, Oppress > BREAK
  katagnymi

CUT OFF, CUT DOWN

apokoptō ἀποκόπτω 609

apokoptō is a verb meaning "cut off," "mutilate" throughout the nine occurrences of the term. Mark 9:43ff. refers metaphorically to "cutting off" one's hands and feet, symbolizing the need to remove those things that give rise to sin. John 18:10, 26 record the action of Peter who "cut off" the ear of the high priest's servant on the occasion of Jesus' arrest. Acts 27:32 refers to "cutting away" a ship's ropes. In Gal 5:12 Paul gives vent to his rage and frustration at the false teachers, the so-called "Judaizers," expressing the wish that they should mutilate themselves.

ekkoptō ἐκκόπτω 1581

ekkoptō means "cut off," "cut down," "cut out" for most of its sixteen occurrences.

The literal action of "cutting down" trees is indicated in Matt 3:10; 7:19; Luke 3:9; 13:7, 9.

The rest of the usage is metaphorical. In Matt 5:30; 18:8, ***ekkoptō*** refers to the need to symbolically "amputate" one's hands or feet should they cause one to sin — that is, remove those features that produce sinful attitudes and behavior. Rom 11:22 refers to eternal judgment in terms of being "cut off" from God. Rom 11:24 describes Gentile believers being "cut out" of a wild olive tree and grafted onto the cultivated olive tree (symbolizing the people of Israel).

SEE ALSO

- ▸ **10.** Earth, Dust, Rocks, Minerals, Metals, Stones > CUT
  latomeō, laxeutos
- ▸ **21.** Die, Perish, Kill, Destroy > CUT TO PIECES
  dichotomeō
- ▸ **28.** Agriculture, Viticulture, Animal Husbandry > BREAK OFF, CUT, CUT OFF
  koptō
- ▸ **76.** Force, Harm, Oppress > CUT, CUT OFF
  katakoptō, aphaireō

DASH, STRIKE

proskoptō προσκόπτω 4350

proskoptō is a verb found in eight places with the predominant sense of "stumble." In two places, however, the term means "dash" in the context of "striking one's foot against a stone" (Matt 4:6; Luke 4:11).

- ▸ **87.** Movement Upward or Downward > STUMBLE

DIG

oryssō ὀρύσσω 3736

oryssō is a verb found in three places denoting the "digging" of the ground in Matt 25:18, and digging a pit for a winepress in Matt 21:33; Mark 12:1.

skaptō σκάπτω 4626

skaptō is a verb found three times indicating the action of "digging" the ground in Luke 6:48; 13:8; 16:3.

KICK

laktizō λακτίζω 2979

laktizō occurs only once, referring to the action of "kicking" in a metaphorical sense. In Acts 26:14, Christ uses the term in Saul's vision on the occasion of his conversion. The Lord questions the persecutor of his people and makes the point that it is hard for Saul "to kick against the goads." The allusion is to an ox that tries to break free of the yoke and only succeeds in kicking against the iron spikes of the plow.

KNOCK

krouō κρούω 2925

krouō occurs nine times and means "knock at the door (or gate)."

In a literal context, ***krouō*** refers to Peter knocking on the door of John Mark's family home after his miraculous escape from prison (Acts 12:13, 16).

The remaining usage of ***krouō*** is metaphorical. In reference to petitionary prayer, if one "asks and knocks," God will hear and answer (Matt 7:7, 8; Luke 11:9, 10). In the context of a parable, Luke 12:36 illustrates the same principle. Those who place themselves outside of a saving relationship of faith and trust in God are denied entry into the kingdom of God, symbolized by a narrow door. In this context, persistent "knocking at the door," once the "owner" has closed it, is fruitless (Luke 13:25). The risen Christ's offer to the congregation at Laodicea is to "open the door" of their lives when he "knocks," so that he might enter and have fellowship with them (Rev 3:20).

PRESS, CRUSH

apothlibō ἀποθλίβω 598

apothlibō is a rare verb found only in Luke 8:45, meaning "press" or "crush" in the context of a crowd "pressing" in on Christ and his disciples.

SEE ALSO

- **75.** Suffering, Distress, Sadness > OPPRESS, CRUSH
  thrauō
- **76.** Force, Harm, Oppress > CRUSH
  syntribō

STIR UP, PROVOKE

erethizō ἐρεθίζω 2042

erethizō is a verb meaning "stir up" or "provoke" in only two contexts.

In 2 Cor 9:2, the connotation is a positive one. Paul refers to the Corinthian congregation having "provoked" others to good works in generous giving. Col 3:21 contains the admonition to fathers not to "provoke" (or stir up) their children to wrath.

SEE ALSO

- **27.** Community, Partnership, Unity, Discord > STIR UP
  synkineō, epegeirō, saleuō, anaseiō

79. Throw, Send, Drive, Mix, Remove

DRAW, DRAG

helkō ἕλκω 1670

helkō is a verb found eight times with the meaning "draw," "drag."

In literal contexts, the term refers to the "drawing (i.e., unsheathing)" of a sword (John 18:10). The "dragging" or "hauling" in of a net full of fish is indicated in John 21:6, 11. The physical action of "dragging" people away is noted in Acts 16:19; 21:30. See also Jas 2:6.

Metaphorically, ***helkō*** also describes the divine act of "drawing people" to God — causing them to come to him in faith and trust (John 6:44; 12:32).

exelkō ἐξέλκω 1828

exelkō is a rare variant of ***helkō*** (above) found only in Jas 1:14 and referring symbolically to people "being dragged away (i.e., lured)" by their own lust.

syrō σύρω 4951

syrō is a synonym for the entries above, meaning "draw," "drag" in literal contexts. John 21:8 describes the disciples "dragging" a net full of fish. Elsewhere, the term denotes the physical "removal" or "dragging" of people from one location to another.

anaspaō ἀνασπάω 385

anaspaō is a rare verb referring to "drawing or pulling up" an animal or person that had fallen into a well in Luke 14:5. In Acts 11:10, the sheet laden with food in Peter's vision is "drawn up" into heaven.

SEE ALSO

- ▸ **29.** Boats, Fishing, Maritime Activity > PULL, DRAW
  anabibazō
- ▸ **76.** Force, Harm, Oppress > DRAW
  spaō
- ▸ **80.** Related to Liquids > DRAW
  antleō
- ▸ **86.** Movement Toward or Away From > COME, DRAW NEAR
  engizō

DRIVE, DRIVE OUT

ekballō ἐκβάλλω 1544

ekballō is a verb with the primary meaning "cast out," "throw out." The sense of "drive out" is virtually synonymous.

- ▸ **79.** Throw, Send, Drive, Mix, Remove > THROW, THROW OUT, CAST, CAST OUT
- ▸ **79.** Throw, Send, Drive, Mix, Remove > SEND, SEND AWAY, SEND OUT

elaunō ἐλαύνω 1643

elaunō is a verb found five times with the meaning "drive" in a couple of different contexts. Luke 8:29 refers to a man possessed by a demon "being driven" into the wilderness by that evil spirit. Jas 3:4 refers to large ships "being driven" by fierce winds. 2 Pet 2:17 mentions false teachers symbolically depicted as "mists driven by a storm."

SEE ALSO

- ▸ **29.** Boats, Fishing, Maritime Activity > DRIVE ALONG
  pherō
- ▸ **76.** Force, Harm, Oppress > DRIVE OUT
  ekdiōkō, exōtheō

MIX, MINGLE

synkerannymi συγκεράννυμι 4786

synkerannymi means "combine together," "mix." This verb is only found in two places. In 1 Cor 12:24, God is said to have "combined together" the various parts of the human body to form a integrated whole. Heb 4:2 indicates the absence of a believing response in the hearts of the ancient people of Israel on the border of Canaan in the wilderness. These people heard the message of the gospel, a divine command and promise to take the land of Canaan, but they refused to "combine" the message with saving faith, to "mix them together."

mignymi μίγνυμι 3396

mignymi means to "mix," "mingle" and occurs four times. Matt 27:34 refers to "wine mixed with gall," a potion offered to Christ on the cross, which he tasted but did not drink. Luke 13:1 refers to killing Galilean Jews, slaughtered by the Roman procurator, Pontius Pilate, who is described as having "mingled" their blood with the sacrifices they were offering. Rev 8:7 describes, in an apocalyptic metaphor, one of the plagues inflicted by an angel on the world population as "hail and fire mixed with blood." In another metaphorical description of heaven, Rev 15:2 refers to a "sea of glass mingled with fire."

SEE ALSO

- ▸ **21.** Die, Perish, Kill, Destroy > MIXTURE
  migma

PUT OFF, PUT AWAY, CAST ASIDE

apotithēmi ἀποτίθημι 659

This verb has the primary metaphorical sense of "put away, off," "cast aside" in the eight occurrences of the term.

Most of these occurrences consist of exhortations to "put off," "cast aside" sinful attitudes and lifestyles (Rom 13:12; Eph 4:22ff.; Col 3:8; Heb 12:1; Jas 1:21; 1 Pet 2:1).

Acts 7:58 refers to people "laying down" their clothes at the feet of Saul.

apekdyomai ἀπεκδύομαι 554

apekdyomai is a rare verb found in Col 3:9 that describes the believer "having put off" or "cast aside" the old nature.

SEE ALSO

- ▸ **25.** Family, Marriage, Adoption, Inheritance > PUT AWAY
  apolyō
- ▸ **54.** Rule, Authority, Command, Obedience > PUT IN SUBJECTION
  hypotassō
- ▸ **83.** Set, Put, Place, Prepare, Establish > PUT, PLACE, LAY
  tithēmi, paratithēmi, epitithēmi, peritithēmi, epiballō

REMOVE, REMOVAL

paropherō παραφέρω 3911

parapherō is a verb found only twice, in the context of Jesus' prayer asking God that, if possible, he could remove from him the cup of suffering involving his ordeal on the cross (Mark 14:36; Luke 22:42).

▸ **79.** Throw, Send, Drive, Mix, Remove > TAKE AWAY, REMOVE

methistēmi μεθίστημι 3179

methistēmi is a verb found in five places meaning "remove." In Acts 13:22 it refers to King Saul's expulsion from the throne of Israel by a solemn divine intervention in response to Saul's rebellion against Yahweh.

kineō κινέω 2795

kineō is a verb found in eight places, with the underlying sense of "move." In Rev 2:5, however, Christ warns that he will "remove the lampstand" representing the church of Ephesus from its place in the heavenly realm.

metathesis μετάθεσις 3331

metathesis is a noun occurring three times, referring to the "removal" of created things at the end of this age (Heb 12:27).

▸ **82.** Change, Exchange, Transform > CHANGE, EXCHANGE

SCATTER, DISPERSE

diaskorpizō διασκορπίζω 1287

diaskorpizō is a verb with the primary meanings "scatter," "disperse," "winnow." It is found eleven times.

The meaning "winnow" is expressed in Matt 25:24, 26. The "scattering" of the flock refers to those who will abandon Christ at the time of his trial (Matt 26:31; Mark 14:27). God is said to scatter the proud in Luke 1:51. John 11:52 refers generally to the scattering of God's children. See also Acts 5:37.

▸ **58.** Vices > WASTE, SQUANDER

skorpizō σκορπίζω 4650

skorpizō is related to ***diaskorpizō*** (above) and means "scatter abroad," "disperse" in all five occurrences. Matt 12:23; Luke 11:23; John 10:12 all warn that the opponents of Christ will scatter his people. John 16:32 also warns that the followers of Jesus Christ will "scatter" (i.e., abandon him) at the time of his suffering. See also 2 Cor 9:9.

dialyō διαλύω 1262

dialyō is a verb found only in Acts 5:36 with reference to the "scattering" of the followers of the false messiah, Theudas.

diaspeirō διασπείρω 1289

diaspeirō is a verb referring to the "scattering" of the early believers as a consequence of their persecution, found only in Acts 8:1, 4; 11:19.

diaspora διασπορά 1290

diaspora is the noun derived from ***diaspeirō*** (above), referring to the "scattering" of believers in the face of persecution in three contexts (John 7:35; Jas 1:1; 1 Pet 1:1).

SEND, SEND AWAY, SEND OUT

apostellō ἀποστέλλω 649

apostellō means "send," with a variety of nuances, and is found in approximately 130 contexts.

apostellō refers to "sending" people in the sense of assigning someone a mission or task (Matt 14:35; Mark 12:2ff.; Luke 14:17; Acts 10:8). In particular, it refers to Herod's royal decree to slaughter all male infants two years old and younger (Matt 2:16).

Jesus Christ also sends people — for example, he sends his disciples on an evangelistic mission (Matt 10:5, 16; Mark 6:7; Luke 9:2; 10:1ff.); and to preach in general (Mark 3:14). His angels are sent to uphold the authority of his kingdom and deliver his people from destruction (Matt 13:14; 24:31). In Luke 24:49, Jesus promises to send the Holy Spirit in accordance with the plan of the Father.

apostellō also refers to God sending Jesus Christ to live among humankind (Matt 10:40; Mark 9:37; Luke 4:18; John 3:17; 6:29; 17:3ff., 18ff.; 1 John 4:9ff.); and to God sending his prophets to his people (Matt 11:10; 23:34ff.; Mark 1:2; Luke 7:27; John 1:6; Rev 22:6). In particular, Acts 7:34ff. indicates that God sent Moses to deliver his people from captivity in Egypt. God also sends angels to comfort and protect believers (Heb 1:14), and to communicate his plan to his people — as in Luke 1:19, where Gabriel announces to Zechariah that his wife Elizabeth will bear a son, who would become John the Baptist, the forerunner and herald of Jesus Christ.

exapostellō ἐξαποστέλλω 1821

exapostellō is a variant form of ***apostellō*** (above). It occurs thirteen times and means "send away," "send out." It refers to people (Luke 1:53; 20:10ff.; Acts 7:12; 9:30; 11:22; 12:11; 17:14; 22:21); and to God "sending forth" his son, Jesus Christ into the world (Gal 4:4). Gal 4:6 affirms that God has sent his Spirit into our hearts.

synapostellō συναποστέλλω 4882

synapostellō is a rare verb, found only in 2 Cor 12:18 and meaning "to send with."

pempō πέμπω 3992

pempō is a synonym for ***apostellō*** (above) meaning "send" in most of its nearly eighty occurrences in a variety of contexts.

pempō refers to sending someone on an errand or mission (Matt 14:10; Acts 10:5, 32ff.; Phil 2:19ff.); to sending a message (Matt 11:2; Acts 19:31; 23:30); to sending letters to the seven churches of Asia (Rev 1:11); and to Jesus "sending" his disciples into the world (John 20:21).

In the sense of "expel" or "dismiss," Jesus "sends" a host of evil spirits into a herd of pigs (Mark 5:12).

pempō also refers to God "sending" in a number of contexts. For example, God sends prophets to his people (Luke 4:26) and sends his Son, Jesus Christ to earth to redeem his people (John 1:33; 5:23ff.; 6:38ff.; 12:44ff.; 13:16ff.; Rom 8:3. God also promises to send his Spirit after Jesus leaves the earth (John 14:26; 15:26; 16:7). And in 2 Thess 2:11, God is said to send judgment on unbelievers.

anapempō ἀναπέμπω 375

anapempō, a variant form of ***pempō*** (above), is found in five places and means "send," "send again," "send back." It refers to people in each case (Luke 23:7ff.; Phlm 12).

sympempō συμπέμπω 4842

sympempō is a rare variant of ***pempō*** (above) found only twice, in 2 Cor 8:18, 22. It means "send together with."

ekballō ἐκβάλλω 1544

ekballō is a verb found in around eighty contexts with the dominant meaning "cast out." In several contexts, however, ***ekballō*** means "send out," "send away." The sense of "sending people out" on a mission is noted in Matt 9:38; Luke 10:2; Jas 2:25. The sense of "send away" or "dismiss" is indicated in Mark 1:43; Acts 13:50.

▸ **79.** Throw, Send, Drive, Mix, Remove > THROW, THROW OUT, CAST, CAST OUT
▸ **79.** Throw, Send, Drive, Mix, Remove > DRIVE, DRIVE OUT

apolyō ἀπολύω 630

apolyō is a verb occurring approximately ninety times. It means "release," "put away," as well as associated senses, in most of these contexts. One of these related senses is "send away," referring to people being dismissed (Matt 14:15ff.; Mark 6:45; 8:3; Luke 9:12). Mark 6:36 speaks of people being sent away to buy food. In Luke 8:38, Jesus "expels" demons from those previously enslaved by the evil spirits.

▸ **25.** Family, Marriage, Adoption, Inheritance > DIVORCE
▸ **25.** Family, Marriage, Adoption, Inheritance > PUT AWAY
▸ **44.** Repentance, Forgiveness, Mercy, Redeem, Save > FORGIVE, FORGIVENESS, RELEASE
▸ **49.** Allow, Accept, Approve, Refuse > ALLOW
▸ **55.** Bondage, Captivity, Servitude > RELEASE

SEE ALSO

▸ **11.** Meteorology, Water > SEND RAIN ***brechō***
▸ **63.** Speak, Tell, Declare, Call > SEND FOR ***metapempō***

SEPARATE, DIVIDE

diamerizō διαμερίζω 1266

diamerizō is a verb meaning "divide" in the sense of "part."

The "parting" or "dividing" of Christ's garments by Roman soldiers at his crucifixion is recorded in Matt 27:35; Mark 15:24; Luke 23:34; John 19:24.

Luke 11:17; 12:52ff. affirm that a kingdom or house "divided" against itself, that is, experiencing internal dissension and strife, will collapse. See also Luke 11:18.

Luke 22:17 refers to the "dividing" or "sharing" of the Passover cup.

merismos μερισμός 3311

merismos is a rare noun, referring metaphorically to the powerful penetration and impact of the word of God in the life of the believer as a "dividing" of the soul and spirit.

▸ **70.** Give, Take, Seize, Touch > GIFT

aphorizō ἀφορίζω 873

aphorizō is a verb found in ten contexts, meaning "separate" or "divide."

"Separating" the righteous from the wicked, dividing them into two groups, is referred to in Matt 13:49; 25:32.

The idea of "setting apart" for gospel ministry is indicated in the usage of ***aphorizō***, meaning "separate" (Acts 13:2; Rom 1:1).

aphorizō also means "to separate," in the sense "withdraw from the company of" wicked people (2 Cor 6:17); and also from fellowship with Gentiles (Gal 2:12).

chōrizō χωρίζω 5563

chōrizō is a verb occurring thirteen times. It is synonymous with ***aphorizō*** (above) and means "separate" or "divide" in various contexts.

There are clear injunctions laid down in Matt 19:6; Mark 10:9; 1 Cor 7:10ff. for married couples not to separate, indicating that "divorce" is in view. The meaning "separate," in the sense of "part company," is indicated in Phlm 15.

Rom 8:35, 39 indicate that nothing can "separate" the believer from the love of Christ.

Christ, our great high priest, is declared to be "separate" (i.e., removed) from sinners in Heb 7:26.

SEE ALSO

▸ **27.** Community, Partnership, Unity, Discord > SEPARATE ***apodiorizō***

SHAKE OFF, SHAKE OUT

ektinassō ἐκτινάσσω 1621

ektinassō is a verb found four times meaning "shake off," "shake out." Matt 10:14; Mark 6:11; Acts 13:51 refer to "shaking (the dust) off" one's feet as a sign of contempt for those who refuse to extend hospitality to the servants of Christ. Acts 18:6 refers to the similar action of "shaking out" one's clothing as a sign of rejection of those Jewish citizens who refuse to respond to the message of the gospel of Christ.

apotinassō ἀποτινάσσω 660

apotinassō is a rare verb found only twice, meaning "shake off " in both instances. Luke 9:5 refers to "shaking (the dust) off (one's feet)" (see also ***ektinassō***, above). In Acts 28:5, ***apotinassō*** refers to Paul "shaking off " a viper from his arms.

SEE ALSO

- **85.** Movement, Position, State > SHAKE
saleuō, seiō

SPREAD OUT

strōnnymi στρώννυμι 4766
hypostrōnnymi ὑποστρώννυμι 5291

strōnnymi is a verb found in eight places, meaning "spread out" in Matt 21:8; Mark 11:8, in relation to people spreading their garments on the road to welcome Christ into Jerusalem as the coming messianic king. ***hypostrōnnymi*** has the same meaning in Luke 19:36.

SEE ALSO

- **43.** Prophecy, Preaching, Proclamation > SPREAD
dianemō
- **63.** Speak, Tell, Declare, Call > SPREAD
diaphēmizō

STRETCH OUT, STRETCH FORTH

ekteinō ἐκτείνω 1614

ekteinō is a verb found sixteen times meaning "stretch out" or "stretch forth" in most of these contexts.

ekteinō refers to Jesus Christ "stretching out" his hand to touch people as a means of effecting a miraculous cure for their affliction (Matt 8:3; Mark 1:41; Luke 5:13). See also Acts 4:30. It is also used as a gesture of identification in Matt 12:49. See also Mark 14:31; Acts 26:1.

In one instance, Jesus asks a man to stretch out his own, withered hand — which is subsequently cured (Matt 12:13; Mark 3:5; Luke 6:10).

TAKE AWAY, REMOVE

aphaireō ἀφαιρέω 851

aphaireō is a verb meaning "take away" in most of the ten contexts in which it is found.

Luke 1:25 mentions "taking away" or "removing" one's reproach. Luke 16:3 records the "removal" of a person's employment. In Luke 10:42, Mary (the sister of Lazarus) is told that her opportunity for service to Jesus will not be taken away. Rom 11:27 refers to God taking away the sins of his people. Heb 10:4 declares that the blood of bulls and goats can never by itself remove sin. See also Rev 22:19.

- **76.** Force, Harm, Oppress > CUT, CUT OFF

periaireō περιαιρέω 4014

periaireō is a verb occurring four times, meaning "take away" in each context. This happens to the veil of sin when a person turns to the Lord in faith (2 Cor 3:16). Heb 10:11 declares that sacrifices by themselves can never take away sin. See also Acts 27:20, 40.

napherō παραφέρω 3911

parapherō is found only in Mark 14:36; Luke 22:42, referring to Jesus' plea to his Father that his cup of suffering will be taken away.

- **79.** Throw, Send, Drive, Mix, Remove >
REMOVE, REMOVAL

SEE ALSO

- **35.** Clothing, Adornment, Textiles > TAKE OFF, STRIP
ekdyō
- **70.** Give, Take, Seize, Touch > TAKE, TAKE HOLD OF, TAKE UP, TAKE DOWN, TAKE AWAY, SNATCH
lambanō, paralambanō, analambanō, epilambanō, proslambanō, harpazō, apairō, kathaireō
- **85.** Movement, Position, State > TAKE WITH
symparalambanō

THROW, THROW OUT, CAST, CAST OUT

ballō βάλλω 906

The verb ***ballō*** is found over 120 times with the meaning "cast" or "throw" in a variety of contexts both literal and metaphorical.

The literal, general sense of "throw," "cast" is indicated in relation to various objects in Matt 3:10; 13:47; Mark 1:16; 11:23; Luke 3:9; John 21:6ff.; Rev 4:10. In particular, John 8:7, 59 speak of casting stones in the context of public execution. The action of "throwing" people down is indicated in Mark 9:22; 9:42; and "throwing oneself down" is noted in Matt 4:6. The sense of "throw away," "reject" is indicated in Matt 5:13; 13:48; 18:9; Luke 14:35. The judicial process of having people "thrown" into prison is indicated in Matt 5:25; 18:30; Luke 12:58; John 3:24; Acts 16:23ff.; Rev 2:10. The decision-making process of "casting lots" is indicated in Matt 27:35; Mark 15:24; Luke 23:34; John 19:24.

Where God is designated as the subject of ***ballō*** he is said to "throw" the wicked into the fire of eternal judgment in Matt 13:42, 50. Luke 12:49; Rev 8:5ff. affirm that God "throws" fire on the earth in the process of divine judgment.

In other contexts ***ballō*** is used metaphorically — indicating, for example, the phenomenon that perfect love "casts out" fear (1 John 4:18). In John's vision in Rev 12:9ff., the dragon and his angels are "thrown out" of heaven. Elsewhere, the satanic beasts are all "thrown into" the lake of burning sulfur (Rev 19:20; 20:10ff.), and into the bottomless pits in Rev 20:3.

- **80.** Related to Liquids > POUR, POUR OUT

rhiptō ῥίπτω 4496

rhiptō is a verb found eight times, meaning "throw" in most of these contexts.

Matt 27:5 describes the action of "throwing down" pieces of silver in the temple. A demon "throws down" its hopeless victim to the ground in Luke 4:35. Ship's tackle is "thrown into" the ocean in Acts 27:19; anchors are "cast out" in Acts 27:29. See also Luke 17:2.

apoballō ἀποβάλλω 577

apoballō is a rare verb describing the action of "throwing aside" one's cloak in Mark 10:50. Heb 10:35 warns believers not to "throw away" their confidence.

ekballō ἐκβάλλω 1544

ekballō is a verb found in around one hundred places with the underlying meanings "cast," "cast out" in a variety of contexts.

The exorcising or "casting out" of demons is indicated in Matt 7:22; 9:33ff.; 12:24ff.; Mark 1:34; 3:15ff.; 9:18ff.; Luke 9:40, 49; 11:14ff.

Being "cast into outer darkness," symbolizing eternal punishment, is indicated in Matt 8:12; 22:13; 25:30. The satanic ruler of the world is "cast out" by God in John 12:31. See also Acts 27:38.

People are "thrown out" of the temple in Matt 21:12; Mark 11:15; Luke 19:45; John 2:15. Other references to eviction of varying kinds include Matt 21:39; Mark 12:8; Luke 20:15; John 9:34ff.; Acts 7:58; Gal 4:30.

God's promise never to "cast out" those who come to Christ in the right spirit is noted in John 6:37.

- **79.** Throw, Send, Drive, Mix, Remove > DRIVE, DRIVE OUT
- **79.** Throw, Send, Drive, Mix, Remove > SEND, SEND AWAY, SEND OUT

emballō ἐμβάλλω 1685

emballō is a rare verb found only in Luke 12:5, citing God's power to "cast people into hell."

kataballō καταβάλλω 2598

kataballō is a rare verb with the passive sense of "being cast (or thrown) down" in the context of persecution in 2 Cor 4:9. The accuser of the saints is said to "be thrown down" in Rev 12:10.

epiriptō ἐπιρίπτω 1977

epiriptō is another rare verb, found only in 1 Pet 5:7 and meaning "to cast" all one's cares on the Lord.

SEE ALSO

- **21.** Die, Perish, Kill, Destroy > CAST DOWN ***katalyō, kathaireō***
- **29.** Boats, Fishing, Maritime Activity > CAST, THROW OVERBOARD ***aporiptō***

UNCOVER, REMOVE

apostegazō ἀποστεγάζω 648

apostegazō is a rare verb found only in Mark 2:4 with reference to "uncovering" or "removing" a roof.

SEE ALSO

- **85.** Movement, Position, State > UNCOVERED ***akatakalyptos***

WIPE OFF, WIPE AWAY, BLOT OUT

ekmassō ἐκμάσσω 1591

ekmassō is a verb meaning "wipe off, away." It occurs five times, referring to "wiping away" tears in Luke 7:38, 44, and also to "wiping" perfume from the feet of Christ in John 11:2; 12:3ff.

apomassomai ἀπομάσσομαι 631

apomassomai is a verb found only in Luke 10:11, referring to "wiping off" dust from one's feet.

exaleiphō ἐξαλείφω 1813

exaleiphō is a verb meaning "blot out" or "wipe away" in each of its five occurrences.

Acts 3:19 refers to God "blotting out" sin. Similarly, ***exaleiphō*** refers to Christ "blotting out" (i.e., canceling, writing off) the legal indictment against his people in Col 2:14. In Rev 3:5, Christ promises that he will never blot out from the Lamb's book of life those who persevere in faith until the end.

God is said to "wipe away" tears from the eyes of the saints in heaven in Rev 7:17; 21:4.

80. Related to Liquids

ANOINT

aleiphō ἀλείφω 218

aleiphō is a verb found nine times meaning "anoint." Its use in the NT is entirely non-ceremonial. "Anointing" is associated with personal ablutions during periods of fasting (Matt 6:17).

"Anointing with oil" is also indicated in the context of administering medicinal aid (Mark 6:13; Jas 5:14). The process of "anointing" in the context of embalming a body in preparation for burial is noted in Mark 16:1. In several places, Mary, the sister of Lazarus, is identified as the one who "anointed" the feet of Jesus with perfume, indicating a bathing or pouring action.

enchriō ἐγχρίω 1472

enchriō is found only in Rev 3:18, referring to "anointing" one's eyes by applying medicinal ointment to them.

epichriō ἐπιχρίω 2025

epichriō is a rare variant form of ***enchriō*** (above) denoting the action of "anointing" in applying moistened clay to the eyes. The term is found only in John 6:9, 11 with reference to Jesus' healing of a blind man.

myrizō μυρίζω 3462

myrizō is a verb occurring only in Mark 14:8. It refers to the action of the unnamed woman who "anointed" (i.e., poured expensive perfume onto) the head of Christ as an act of devotion. Jesus interpreted the act as a symbolic preparation of his body for burial.

SEE ALSO

- ▸ **38.** Covenant, Law, Rites, Roles > ANOINT, ANOINTING, CONSECRATE
  chriō, chrisma

DIP, IMMERSE

baptō βάπτω 911

baptō is a rare variant form of ***baptizō*** (below) found in only three contexts. It means to "dip" or "immerse," but without the ritual or theological significance of ***baptizō***. Luke 16:24 refers to the "dipping" of the finger in water, and John 13:26 denotes the "dipping" of bread into a dish. Rev 19:13 contains a metaphorical use of ***baptō*** in relation to a robe "dipped" in blood, worn by the Messiah-King going into battle.

embaptō ἐμβάπτω 1686

embaptō is a variant verb of ***baptō*** (above) found only three times. In each context, the action indicated is that of "dipping" one's hand into, or "dipping" bread into, a dish associated with eating a meal (Matt 26:23; Mark 4:20; John 13:26).

SEE ALSO

- ▸ **38.** Covenant, Law, Rites, Roles > BAPTISM, BAPTIST, BAPTIZE
  baptisma, baptismos, baptistēs, baptizō

DRAW

antleō ἀντλέω 501

antleō is a verb referring to the "drawing of water" in John 2:9; 4:7, 15; and to the miraculous "drawing" of wine from a jar that had been filled with water in John 2:8.

SEE ALSO

- ▸ **29.** Boats, Fishing, Maritime Activity > PULL, DRAW
  anabibazō
- ▸ **76.** Force, Harm, Oppress > DRAW
  spaō
- ▸ **79.** Throw, Send, Drive, Mix, Remove > DRAW, DRAG
  helkō, exelkō, syrō, anaspaō
- ▸ **86.** Movement Toward or Away From > COME, DRAW NEAR
  engizō

POUR, POUR OUT

ekcheō ἐκχέω 1632

ekcheō is found in nearly thirty contexts meaning "pour out" in about half of these, with two distinctive symbolic motifs.

ekcheō refers first of all to the outpouring of the Holy Spirit on his people, as a sign of the coming of the new covenant age (Acts 2:17ff., 33; 10:45). Secondly, the term indicates the "pouring out" of the judgment of God upon a wicked world (Rev 16:1ff.).

- ▸ **80.** Related to Liquids > SHED, SPILL

katacheō καταχέω 2708

katacheō occurs only in Matt 26:7; Mark 14:3, referring on both occasions to a repentant woman pouring ointment on the head of Jesus, thereby expressing her devotion to him.

ballō βάλλω 906

ballō is a common verb with the principal meaning "throw" or "cast," occurring nearly 130 times. On two occasions, however, it is translated "pour" — once with reference to a woman pouring ointment or perfume over Jesus (Matt 26:12); and once in regard to pouring water in a basin (John 13:5).

- ▸ **79.** Throw, Send, Drive, Mix, Remove > THROW, THROW OUT, CAST, CAST OUT

kerannymi κεράννυμι 2767

kerannymi is another rare verb meaning to "pour," "pour out," "mix" in a wholly symbolic sense. It occurs only in Rev 14:10; 18:6, with reference to the outpouring of God's wrath upon the wicked.

SEE ALSO

▸ **20.** Illness, Disease, Health, Healing > POUR
epicheō

SHED, SPILL

ekcheō ἐκχέω 1632

ekcheō is a verb found in nearly thirty contexts, meaning "to pour" in about half of these occurrences. In the remaining use of ***ekcheō***, the meaning "shed" is indicated.

Matt 23:35; Luke 11:50; Acts 22:20; Rom 3:15; Rev 16:6 refer to "shedding" the blood of human beings, in the sense of murder. Matt 26:28; Mark 14:24; Luke 22:20 refer to "shedding" the blood of Christ for the remission of sins. Mundane references to "spilling" (or shedding) liquids are found in Mark 2:22; Luke 5:37.

ekcheō is used metaphorically in Rom 5:5 with reference to the love of God being "shed abroad" in our hearts.

▸ **80.** Related to Liquids > POUR, POUR OUT

SEE ALSO

▸ **21.** Die, Perish, Kill, Destroy > SHED
haimatekchysia

WASH, BATHE, WASHING, WETTING

aponiptō ἀπονίπτω 633

aponiptō is found only in Matt 27:24, referring to Pontius Pilate's public washing of his hands in order to declare himself innocent of the blood of Christ, whom he handed over to be crucified.

brechō βρέχω 1026

brechō is a verb occurring eight times with the primary sense of "rain." However, in Luke 7:38, 44, ***brechō*** refers to a persistent woman "washing" or "wetting" the feet of Jesus with her tears.

▸ **11.** Meteorology, Water > RAIN

▸ **11.** Meteorology, Water > SEND RAIN

louō λούω 3068

louō is a verb found six times meaning "wash," or "bathe," in most of these contexts. Acts 9:37 refers to "washing" a corpse prior to burial; and "bathing" wounds is noted in Acts 16:33. In a metaphorical context, ***louō*** depicts bodies as "washed with pure water" in Heb 10:22, denoting their symbolic cleansing from sin.

apolouomai ἀπολούομαι 628

apolouomai is a rare variant of ***louō*** (above) referring to "washing away" sin in Acts 22:16; 1 Cor 6:11.

plynō πλύνω 4150

plynō is another rare verb denoting the action of "washing" in only two places. Luke 5:2 refers to "washing" fishing nets. In Rev 7:14, ***plynō*** refers metaphorically to "washing" the robes of the saints in heaven as a means of describing their purification.

baptismos βαπτισμός 909

baptismos is a noun denoting "washing" in all but one of its four occurrences. Mark 7:4, 8 refer to washing household utensils. Heb 9:10 refers to ceremonial "washings."

▸ **38.** Covenant, Law, Rites, Roles > BAPTISM, BAPTIST, BAPTIZE

SEE ALSO

▸ **20.** Illness, Disease, Health, Healing > WASH, WASHING
niptō, baptizō

▸ **39.** Clean, Pure, Holy > WASHING, CLEANSING
loutron

81. Forms, Groups, Patterns, Order

COMPARE, LIKEN

homoioō ὁμοιόω 3666

homoioō means "liken," "compare" throughout its fifteen occurrences.

The passive sense "be compared with" is evident in Matt 7:24, 26 in relation to the comparison between those who heed the words of Jesus and those who do not.

Matt 13:24; 18:23; 25:1; Mark 4:30; Luke 13:20 ask what the kingdom of heaven may be compared to. See also Matt 11:16; Luke 7:31.

CONFORM, CONFORMED TO, LIKE

symmorphizō συμμορφίζω 4833

symmorphizō is a rare verb with the meaning "to be conformed to," "become like," found only in Phil 3:10. It indicates Paul's desire to "become like" Christ by sharing in his suffering.

symmorphos σύμμορφος 4832

symmorphos is a rare adjectival form of ***symmorphizō*** (above) denoting that which is "conformed or likened to." Rom 8:29 speaks of believers whom God had predestined to be "conformed" to the image of his Son. Phil 3:21 refers to the believer's body at death becoming conformed to the body of Christ.

syschēmatizō συσχηματίζω 4964

syschēmatizō is a rare verb with the sense of "conform oneself to" found only in Rom 12:2, urging believers "not to be conformed" to ungodly passions.

COPY

hypodeigma ὑπόδειγμα 5262

hypodeigma is a noun denoting a "pattern," "example," or "copy" in the six occurrences of the term. Specifically, Heb 8:5; 9:25 both refer to the tabernacle and temple and their sacred furniture as "copies" of the heavenly realities which they symbolized.

▸ **81.** Forms, Groups, Patterns, Order > EXAMPLE, TYPE

DISTINCTION, DIFFERENCE

diastolē διαστολή 1293

diastolē is a noun found three times meaning "distinction" or "difference." Rom 3:22 affirms that there is no distinction between any who put their faith in Christ. Similarly, Rom 10:12 declares that there is no "distinction" in status between Jew and Gentile in their relationship with Christ. 1 Cor 14:7 mentions the "distinction" between music notes.

EXAMPLE, TYPE

deigma δεῖγμα 1164

deigma is a rare noun found only in Jude 7, referring to the cities of Sodom and Gomorrah as a solemn "example" of immorality and the object of divine judgment — a "lifestyle" to be scrupulously avoided.

deigmatizō δειγματίζω 1165

deigmatizō is a rare verb found only in Col 2:15, referring to Christ having destroyed the powers of darkness through his death and "having made a public example" of them through their destruction.

hypodeigma ὑπόδειγμα 5262

hypodeigma is a noun derived from ***deigmatizō*** (above) meaning "example" with several different nuances. It is found six times.

Christ's action of washing his disciples' feet is described as an "example," a pattern of behavior for his disciples to follow, in John 13:15. By way of a negative counterexample, 2 Pet 2:6 refers to the cities of Sodom and Gomorrah as a terrible "example" — a warning to those who followed the same example of ungodliness. A warning against falling into the same "pattern" of disobedience as demonstrated by the ancient Israelites in the wilderness is indicated in Heb 4:11. There, Heb 8:5; 9:23 both refer to the earthly tabernacle/temple as a "copy" of the heavenly sanctuary. Finally, Jas 5:10 refers to the prophets who served as an "example" to the people of God of suffering and patience.

▸ **81.** Forms, Groups, Patterns, Order > COPY

typos τύπος 5179

typos is a noun occurring sixteen times with the underlying literal meaning of a "print," in the sense of a mark on the body left by a wound. ***typos*** also exhibits an expanded metaphorical sense of "pattern," "figure," or "example." This term can also have the technical meaning "type."

The meaning "pattern" refers to that of the temple, duly prescribed by God, as noted in Acts 7:44; Heb 8:5. It is evident that the temple in Jerusalem constitutes a "typological" anticipation of Christ's eternal dwelling place in heaven alongside his Father. Rom 6:17 also refers to the apostolic "pattern" of teaching, embodied in the gospel.

The specific sense of "type" indicates a symbolic person, place, object, or event from the OT that prefigures or anticipates the person and work of the Messiah, Jesus Christ, in the NT. Adam is declared explicitly to be a "type" of Christ in Rom 5:14. While the term ***typos*** is rare in the NT with this specific meaning, the actual phenomenon of "typology" is everywhere present. The frequency of this phenomenon may be appreciated only when the full extent of the old covenant's anticipation of the person of the Messiah is understood.

typos is also translated "example" in 1 Cor 10:6, 11, referring to Israel's past sins, for which the people of God received due punishment from God. These "examples" serve as a warning for believers living in the present. Paul also calls upon his readers to imitate the "example" of the apostolic lifestyle (Phil 3:17; 2 Thess 3:9; 1 Tim 4:12; Titus 2:7).

▸ **81.** Forms, Groups, Patterns, Order > PATTERN, MODEL

hypotypōsis ὑποτύπωσις 5296

hypotypōsis is a variant form of ***typos*** (above) found only twice. It means "example" in 1 Tim 1:16 in relation to Christ setting a perfect example of patience to his followers. 2 Tim 1:13 contains Paul's exhortation to Timothy to follow the "example" or "pattern" of the sound words of the apostle's teaching.

hypogrammos ὑπογραμμός 5261

hypogrammos is a rare noun found only in 1 Pet 2:21, referring to Christ having left an "example" for his followers to keep.

FORM, SHAPE

morphē μορφή 3444

morphē is a rare noun found three times, meaning "form" in each case. Mark 16:12 records Jesus' appearance to two of his disciples in another "form" after his resurrection. This change of "form" relates to a noticeable difference in the body of Christ, transformed by his experience of resurrection. Phil 2:6 refers to Jesus being in the "form" of God, denoting the divine aspect of his dual nature. Then, Phil 2:7 declares that Jesus took upon himself the "form" of a servant — that is, he assumed a fully human nature, marking him out as a true man.

morphōsis μόρφωσις 3446

morphōsis is a rare variant of ***morphē*** (above) found only twice. The expression "form of knowledge" is found in Rom 2:20, designating the "embodiment" of knowledge as revealed in the law. 2 Tim 3:5 contains the apostolic warning against fellowship with godless men who hold merely to the "form" of religion but deny its power. This "form" denotes the "outward ceremony or ritual" of worship, without the accompanying heart devotion.

eidos εἶδος 1491

eidos is a noun found five times denoting "sight," "appearance," "form" with the underlying sense of "external appearance, or shape."

In Luke 3:22 the Holy Spirit is said to descend upon Jesus in the "form" (i.e., appearance, shape) of a dove. On the Mount of Transfiguration the "form" or "appearance" of Jesus' face is said to undergo a profound transformation, revealing a glimpse of his heavenly nature (Luke 9:29). John 5:37 affirms that no one has ever seen the "form" of God, referring to his "essence," his true spiritual "shape" (the reference here is entirely non-material). In 1 Thess 5:22 there is an exhortation to abstain from every "form" or "kind" of evil. See also 2 Cor 5:7.

▸ **45.** Faith, Belief, Trust, Promise > SIGHT

SEE ALSO

▸ **34.** Craftsmanship, Artisanship, Furniture, Implements > FORM, MOLD
morphoō, plassō, plasma

IMAGE, FIGURE, LIKENESS

eikōn εἰκών 1504

This term occurs around twenty times and has the predominant sense of "image," "figure," "likeness." ***eikōn***, however, refers not primarily to the false images of idolatry, but rather to images of people, as well as to heavenly realities including the person of Christ, in whose image believers have been created anew.

In a general, non-theological sense, ***eikōn*** designates the image of Caesar on Roman coins (Matt 22:20; Mark 12:16; Luke 20:24).

In relation to the phenomenon of idolatry, ***eikōn*** refers firstly to idolatrous images as the characteristic of pagan worship in Rom 1:23. Then, the term refers to the idolatrous image of the sea beast set up by the earth beast as the supreme object of worship for all people of the earth in Rev 13:14ff.; 14:9ff.; 16:2.

In contrast, ***eikōn*** is also found in reference to the image of Christ in Rom 8:29; 1 Cor 15:49; 2 Cor 3:18; Col 3:10. These texts make the point that the ultimate divine purpose for all believers is for them to be conformed to the "image" of Christ, to his person and character. Furthermore, Christ is declared to be the perfect image of God the Father in 2 Cor 4:4; Col 1:15. Human beings also portray the image and glory of God, as the supreme manifestation of divine creative activity (1 Cor 11:7).

In Heb 10:1, ***eikōn*** refers to the ritual law of temple worship as the mere image (or form) of the heavenly reality of good things to come in the new heavens and new earth.

charaktēr χαρακτήρ 5481

This term is found only in Heb 1:3, where it refers to the "express image" or "very stamp" of the nature found in Christ that reflects the essential glory of God.

IMITATE, IMITATOR, FOLLOW, FOLLOWER

mimētēs μιμητής 3402

mimētēs is a noun found seven times with the predominant meaning "follower" or "imitator" throughout.

Paul exhorts his readers to be "imitators" of him in 1 Cor 4:16; 11:1. See also 1 Thess 1:6; Phil 3:17; Heb 6:12. Eph 5:1 contains an exhortation to be an "imitator" of God. 1 Thess 2:14 calls the Thessalonian congregation to become "imitators" of the Judean churches in their suffering.

mimeomai μιμέομαι 3401

mimeomai is found four times, meaning "follow" or "imitate." Paul's direction to the Thessalonian congregation to imitate his way of life is found in 2 Thess 3:7, 9. The writer to the Hebrews calls upon his readers to imitate the faithful examples of their spiritual mentors in Heb 13:7. John instructs his readers not to imitate that which is evil in 3 John 11.

KIND

genos γένος 1085

genos is a noun with a fairly broad range of meaning emphasizing diversity of species, nationality, and other phenomena. ***genos*** occurs around twenty times. The translation "kind" is evident in eight of these contexts.

The meaning "kind" in the general sense of "diverse phenomena" is evident in Matt 17:21; Mark 9:29, where Jesus claims that this kind of demon can only be cast out through prayer and fasting. Various kinds of languages are mentioned in 1 Cor 12:10, 28; 14:10. With respect to nationality, Paul refers to people of his own kind, or his own race, in Gal 1:14; 2 Cor 11:26; Phil 3:5.

▸ **15.** Gender, Reproduction, Youth, Aging > CHILD, OFFSPRING

MARK, STAMP, BRAND

charagma χάραγμα 5480

charagma is a term denoting a physical "mark," "stamp," or "brand." It occurs nine times and is found on all but one occasion in the book of Revelation, where it refers to the "mark of the beast" (or antichrist), placed on the foreheads or hands of those who worshiped him (Rev 13:16ff.; 14:9ff.; 15:2; 16:2; 19:20; 20:4). See also Acts 17:29.

SEE ALSO

▸ **68.** Ability, Possibility, Effort, Succeed, Fail > GOAL, MARK
skopos

▸ **76.** Force, Harm, Oppress > SCAR, MARK
stigma

ORDER

taxis τάξις 5010

taxis is a noun that occurs in nine contexts. In all but one of these, it means "order."

In 1 Cor 14:40, ***taxis*** refers to "orderly" worship, or that which is carried out in accordance with a set of guiding principles. Paul insists here that worship in the Corinthian congregation be undertaken decently and "in order." Col 2:5 refers to the "orderly" character of the church at Colossae — that is, he commends them for their disciplined Christian lifestyle.

The remaining uses of ***taxis*** refer to the high priestly "order" of Melchizedek, the forerunner of the person of Christ in his ministry of intercession, patterned after the type or model of the ancient priest king of Salem (Gen 14:17ff.). These references are all found in the book of Hebrews (Heb 5:6, 10; 6:20; 7:11, 17, 21).

SEE ALSO

▸ **83.** Set, Put, Place, Prepare, Establish > ORDER, STRAIGHTEN
epidiorthoō

PART, PORTION, SECTION, PIECE, GROUP

meros μέρος 3313

meros is a noun occurring around forty times, with the general sense of "part" in most of these contexts, but with a variety of nuances.

meros refers to "parts" in the sense of geographic locations, sometimes translated as "districts." The term is used in a general sense in Acts 19:1; 20:2. In Eph 4:9, ***meros*** is used in the phrase "the lower 'parts' of the earth." Explicit references to various geographic "districts" are found, for example, in Matt 2:22 (Galilee); Matt 15:21 (Tyre); Matt 16:13 (Caesarea); Mark 8:10 (Dalmanutha); and Acts 2:10 (Libya).

meros means "part" in the sense of one's "fate" or "lot" in Rev 21:8, which describes the "fate" of the wicked in terms of destruction in the "lake of fire."

meros is also translated "part" in the sense of "party" or "group" in a political or theological sense. Acts 23:9 refers to the Pharisaic "party."

The word refers to a "portion" or "section" of the human body (Luke 11:36; Eph 4:16); to property (Acts 5:2); and to a city (Rev 16:19).

Matt 24:51; Luke 12:46 refer to one's "place" or "position." In John 13:8, Peter is threatened with having "no part" in Jesus.

In a more tangible context, ***meros*** is translated "piece" with regard to broiled fish consumed by the risen Christ in the presence of his disciples (Luke 24:42). John 19:23 refers to a "piece" of clothing.

meros is also used adverbially with the sense of "partially," "in part" (Rom 11:25; 1 Cor 11:18; 2 Cor 1:14; 2:5).

▸ **30.** Money, Business, Wealth, Poverty > CRAFT, TRADE, BUSINESS

PATTERN, MODEL

typos τύπος 5179

typos is a noun occurring sixteen times with the varying senses of "pattern," "type," "example." The meaning "pattern" is evident in two contexts. Acts 7:44; Heb 8:5 refer to the "pattern" of the tabernacle as revealed by God to Moses on Mount Sinai. Then, in Titus 2:7, ***typos*** refers to the "pattern" or "model" of good works that Paul desires Titus to demonstrate to his congregation.

▸ **81.** Forms, Groups, Patterns, Order > EXAMPLE, TYPE

STEP

ichnos ἴχνος 2487

ichnos denotes the phenomenon of "steps" in the context of "walking in the steps of . . ." or following or imitating one's example (Rom 4:12; 2 Cor 12:18; 1 Pet 2:21).

THING, MATTER

pragma πρᾶγμα 4229

pragma is a noun found eleven times with the underlying sense of "something accomplished or done," "an established fact." For the most part, it is translated "thing," "matter."

The sense of a "transaction" is indicated in Matt 18:19; Acts 5:4. Reference to "things" fulfilled by divine power is found in Luke 1:1. A "legal dispute or matter" is noted in 1 Cor 6:1 (see also 2 Cor 7:11). The "matter" of sexual purity is indicated in 1 Thess 4:6. With reference to God's utter truthfulness, ***pragma*** denotes two unchangeable "things" that make it impossible for God to lie (Heb 6:18). Heb 10:1 refers to spiritual "realities." See also Heb 11:1; Jas 3:16.

SEE ALSO

- ▸ **34.** Craftsmanship, Artisanship, Furniture, Implements > FORM, MOLD
  plasma
- ▸ **53.** Value, Worth > GOOD
  agathos

82. Change, Exchange, Transform

CHANGE, EXCHANGE

metathesis μετάθεσις 3331

metathesis is a rare noun denoting a "change" in the law in Heb 7:12.

▸ **79.** Throw, Send, Drive, Mix, Remove > REMOVE, REMOVAL

allassō ἀλλάσσω 236

allassō is a verb found six times with the meanings "change," "exchange." Acts 6:14 refers to "changing" the customs of the law. The perversity of "exchanging" the glory of God for the worship of idols is indicated in Rom 1:23. The experience of "being changed (i.e., transformed)" at the end of time in preparation for glory is described in 1 Cor 15:51, 52; Heb 1:12. See also Gal 4:20.

metatithēmi μετατίθημι 3346

The verb ***metatithēmi*** refers to the "changing" of the priesthood necessitating a corresponding change of the law as noted in Heb 7:12.

metaballō μεταβάλλω 3328

metaballō is a rare verb referring to "the changing" of one's mind, found only in Acts 28:6.

▸ **47.** Show, Persuade, Confidence, Doubt > UNCERTAIN, DOUBLE-MINDED

antallagma ἀντάλλαγμα 465

antallagma is a rare noun found only twice. Matt 16:26; Mark 8:37 both contain the poignant question posed by Christ "What shall a person give in exchange for their soul?"

metallassō μεταλλάσσω 3337

metallassō is a rare verb, found only twice in Rom 1:25, 26, referring first to the idolatrous action of men who had "exchanged" the truth of God for a lie in their idols; and secondly to the immorality of women who also had "exchanged" natural sexual relations for unnatural.

DISAPPEAR, VANISH

aphanismos ἀφανισμός 854

aphanismos is a noun found only in Heb 8:13, referring to the superseded Mosaic law covenant that will soon "disappear" (lit., that is ready for disappearing, or vanishing).

RESTORE

apokathistēmi ἀποκαθίστημι 600

apokathistēmi is a verb with the consistent meaning "to restore" in several distinctive contexts.

The meaning "restore" in the sense of "heal" or "cure," in relation to illness that yields to the divine power of Christ, is indicated in Matt 12:13; Mark 3:5; 8:25; Luke 6:10.

Another nuance of the term is that of "renew" or "transform," describing the ministry of John the Baptist, the new "Elijah," of whom it is said, "he will restore all things."

In Acts 1:6, the question is asked of the risen Christ as to whether he would restore (i.e., return) the kingdom to Israel.

Heb 13:19 expresses the writer's desire that he be "restored" (i.e., brought back) to his readers.

SEE ALSO

▸ **27.** Community, Partnership, Unity, Discord > RESTORE
katartizō

ROLL UP

helissō ἑλίσσω 1507

helissō is a verb found only in Rev 6:14, indicating the symbolic process of the heavens and earth vanishing like a scroll that is "rolled up."

SEE ALSO

▸ **21.** Die, Perish, Kill, Destroy > ROLL
apokyliō, proskyliō

TRANSFORM, TRANSFIGURE

metamorphoō μεταμορφόω 3339

metamorphoō is a verb found in four places meaning "to transform," "transfigure." In Matt 17:2; Mark 9:2, ***metamorphoō*** describes Christ's transfiguration (i.e., the transformation of his physical appearance) on the mountain, whereby his three disciples are granted a momentary glimpse of his heavenly glory.

metamorphoō also describes the transformation of the believer through the spiritual renewing of his mind (Rom 12:2); and into the likeness of Christ in glory (2 Cor 3:18).

TURN INTO

metastrephō μεταστρέφω 3344

metastrephō is a rare verb meaning "turn into," in the sense of "change into," in two contexts. Acts 2:20 speaks of the sun being turned into darkness before the coming of the Day of the Lord. Jas 4:9 contains the invocation that laughter be turned into mourning.

▸ **57.** Evil, Wickedness, Sin > PERVERSE, PERVERT

SEE ALSO

▸ **86.** Movement Toward or Away From > TURN, TURN AROUND, TURN TOWARD, TURN AWAY, TURN BACK
strephō, apostrephō, epistrephō, hypostrephō, anakamptō, diastrephō

UNCHANGEABLE

aparabatos ἀπαράβατος 531

aparabatos is a rare adjectival form found only in Heb 7:24, referring to the "unchangeable" high priestly ministry of the risen Christ that will remain forever the same.

UNFADING

amarantos ἀμάραντος 263

amarantos is a rare adjectival form found only twice. In 1 Pet 1:4 the believer's inheritance is described as "unfading," reserved in heaven with complete security. Similarly, 1 Pet 5:4 refers to the believer's "unfading" crown of glory.

SEE ALSO

▸ **21.** Die, Perish, Kill, Destroy > FADE AWAY
marainō

83. Set, Put, Place, Prepare, Establish

APPOINT, ORDAIN, ASSIGN

histēmi ἵστημι 2476

histēmi is a common verb with the principal meaning of "stand" in almost all of the nearly 160 occurrences of the term. In Acts 17:31, however, this term is translated "appoint" with reference to God "having appointed" a day in which he will judge the world.

- ▸ **70.** Give, Take, Seize, Touch > PRESENT
- ▸ **83.** Set, Put, Place, Prepare, Establish > ESTABLISH, FIX, GROUND, STRENGTHEN
- ▸ **83.** Set, Put, Place, Prepare, Establish > SET
- ▸ **85.** Movement, Position, State > STAND

kathistēmi καθίστημι 2525

kathistēmi is a verb found in about twenty places with the underlying senses of "placing someone in authority over" or "making someone ruler over," which leads to the primary translation of "appoint."

The appointment of a household manager is indicated in Matt 24:45ff.; 25:21ff.; Luke 12:42ff.; elders are appointed to church congregations as noted in Titus 1:5; deacons are likewise appointed to their tasks in Acts 6:3. Acts 7:10 refers to the appointment of Joseph as governor of Egypt. Heb 7:28; 8:3 make reference to men "being appointed" as high priests. See also Luke 12:14; Acts 7:35 for metaphorical usage of the term.

- ▸ **54.** Rule, Authority, Command, Obedience > RULE, RULER

tithēmi τίθημι 5087

tithēmi is a common verb found in nearly one hundred contexts with the dominant meanings "put," "set," plus related nuances. One of these nuances is that of "appoint" or "ordain." John 15:16 speaks of Christ "appointing" (i.e., setting aside) believers to bring forth spiritual fruit in their lives, demonstrating the indwelling power of God. 1 Thess 5:9 makes reference to God "appointing" or "ordaining" his people — not for wrath, but for salvation. Paul refers to his being "appointed" by God as an apostle and preacher of the gospel.

- ▸ **83.** Set, Put, Place, Prepare, Establish > PUT, PLACE, LAY
- ▸ **83.** Set, Put, Place, Prepare, Establish > SET

tassō τάσσω 5021

tassō is a verb found in eight places with the meanings "appoint," "ordain" in the sense of "set aside for a special purpose."

General reference to a soldier "set under authority" is found in Luke 7:8. The phenomenon of "being appointed, or ordained" to eternal life is noted in Acts 13:48. Governments are declared "to be appointed" by God in Rom 13:1. Acts 22:10; 28:23 make reference to "being set aside" for particular gospel service.

protassō προτάσσω 4384

protassō is a rare verb found in Acts 17:26 with reference to God "having ordained beforehand" the boundaries of human earthly kingdoms.

apokeimai ἀπόκειμαι 606

apokeimai is a verb expressing the meaning "to appoint" in Acts 9:27, where it is affirmed that people are "appointed once to die and then the judgment."

cheirotoneō χειροτονέω 5500

cheirotoneō is a rare verb found only twice, expressing the meaning "to appoint (to the office of elder)" in Acts 14:23; and also "assign (a particular ministry to)" in 2 Cor 8:19.

procheirizomai προχειρίζομαι 4400

procheirizomai is a rare middle verb, found only in Acts 22:14; 26:16, with reference to God "ordaining" or "appointing" Saul at the point of his conversion to gospel proclamation and ministry.

horizō ὁρίζω 3724

horizō is a verb found in eight places, with all but one referring to the sovereign divine action of "appointing," "determining" Jesus Christ as the Savior and Redeemer of the world, through his action of a sacrificial death on the cross (Luke 22:22; Acts 2:23; 10:42; 17:31). Christ is also described as one "appointed" by God to exercise judgment on the world. See also Rom 1:4. Heb 4:7 also makes reference to God "setting aside" (i.e., determining, appointing) a particular day for the final judgment.

- ▸ **48.** Will, Purpose, Decide, Advise > DETERMINE, PREDETERMINE, FOREORDAIN
- ▸ **63.** Speak, Tell, Declare, Call > DECLARE, DECLARATION

anadeiknymi ἀναδείκνυμι 322

anadeiknymi is a rare verb referring to the action of Jesus in "choosing" or "appointing" seventy of his followers to undertake an evangelistic mission to the towns of Judea (Luke 10:2). Acts 1:24 refers to God "choosing," "appointing" a replacement in the apostolic band for Judas Iscariot.

- ▸ **64.** Reveal, Explain, Hiddenness, Secrecy > SHOW, DISCLOSE, MANIFEST

poieō ποιέω 4160

poieō is a common verb found in nearly six hundred contexts with the predominant sense of "do," "make," plus a broad range of related meanings. In one context, ***poieō*** denotes God "having appointed" Christ as "the apostle and high priest" of his people (Heb 3:2).

- ▸ **40.** Holy Days, Feasts, Festivals > KEEP
- ▸ **84.** Do, Make, Accomplish, Occur > EXECUTE
- ▸ **84.** Do, Make, Accomplish, Occur > DO, MAKE, MAKER

ESTABLISH, FIX, GROUND, STRENGTHEN

stērizō στηρίζω 4741

stērizō is a verb found thirteen times with the primary senses of "establish," "strengthen."

The meaning "establish" in the context of "strengthening" one's faith is indicated in 1 Thess 3:2, 13; 2 Thess 3:3; 1 Pet 5:10.

In 2 Thess 2:17, ***stērizō*** is translated "establish" with the sense of "grounding" one's heart in good works. See also Jas 5:8. 2 Pet 1:12 depicts believers as "established" in the truth.

stereoō στερεόω 4732

stereoō is a variant form of ***stērizō*** (above) referring to churches being "established" or "strengthened" in their faith in Acts 16:5.

- ▸ **18.** Strength, Weakness, Capability > STRENGTH, STRONG, POWER, POWERFUL, MIGHT, MIGHTY

histēmi ἵστημι 2476

histēmi is a common verb found nearly 160 times with the predominant sense of "stand." In several instances, however, the meaning "establish" is also indicated.

Rom 10:3 refers to the Israelites seeking to "establish" their own righteousness apart from God's. The term specifically refers here to their futile attempt to "bring into being" or "create" that righteousness. Heb 10:9 speaks of Christ setting aside the sacrifices of the old covenant in order to "establish" the second, more perfect, sacrifice of his own. That is, he removed the sin of his people once and for all. 1 Thess 3:2 refers to the ministry of Timothy in "establishing" or "strengthening" his congregation in their faith.

- ▸ **70.** Give, Take, Seize, Touch > PRESENT
- ▸ **83.** Set, Put, Place, Prepare, Establish > APPOINT, ORDAIN, ASSIGN
- ▸ **83.** Set, Put, Place, Prepare, Establish > SET
- ▸ **85.** Movement, Position, State > STAND

bebaioō βεβαιόω 950

bebaioō is a verb found nine times with the sense of "confirm" in most of these contexts. The meaning "establish" is also found in the context of "strengthening" one's faith in Col 2:7. The "establishing" or "strengthening" of one's heart by grace is indicated in Heb 13:9.

themelioō θεμελιόω 2311

themelioō is a verb occurring six times, meaning "to ground" in the sense of "fix" or "establish" in Eph 3:17; Col 1:23. The former text speaks of believers being "grounded" in love for Christ; the latter refers to being "grounded" in the faith.

- ▸ **33.** Architecture > FOUNDATION, LAY A FOUNDATION

SEE ALSO

- ▸ **9.** Land, Geography, Topography > GROUND
  edaphos, chamai
- ▸ **21.** Die, Perish, Kill, Destroy > THROW TO THE GROUND
  edaphizō

ORDER, STRAIGHTEN

epidiorthoō ἐπιδιορθόω 1930

epidiorthoō occurs only in Titus 1:5 in relation to Paul's instruction to Titus to "set in order" or "straighten out" those matters left unfinished in the churches of Crete.

SEE ALSO

- ▸ **81.** Forms, Groups, Patterns, Order > ORDER
  taxis

PREPARE, MAKE READY

hetoimazō ἑτοιμάζω 2090

hetoimazō is the most common verb in the NT meaning "prepare," "make ready." The term occurs approximately forty times in a number of varying contexts.

General references to making preparation in mundane contexts are found in Matt 22:4; Luke 12:20, 47; 17:8; Acts 23:23; Phlm 22. In particular, Passover preparation is mentioned in Matt 26:17ff.; Mark 14:12ff.; Luke 22:8ff. Luke 23:56; 24:1 refer to preparing spices and perfumes for the burial of the body of Christ.

In a more explicit theological context, the mission of John the Baptist to "prepare" the way for the coming of the messianic king in the person of Jesus Christ is described in Matt 3:3; Mark 1:3; Luke 1:76; 3:4. The unique privilege of sitting at God's right hand is a prerogative prepared by God alone (Matt 20:23; Mark 10:40).

hetoimazō refers to preparations undertaken by God alone, including God preparing a people for himself (Luke 1:17); a kingdom for his people (Matt 25:34); and salvation for his people (Luke 2:31). John 14:2ff.; Heb 11:16 contain the promise that both Christ and God the Father are preparing a heavenly destiny for their people. 1 Cor 2:9 refers to the spiritual blessings prepared by God for those belonging to him. Conversely, Matt 25:41 affirms the terrible reality of the everlasting torment prepared by God for the wicked.

hetoimazō is also used metaphorically in several contexts. In Rev 8:6, angels prepare to blow the seven trumpets initiating divine judgment on a wicked world (see also Rev 9:15; 16:12). Rev 9:7 refers to demonic locusts preparing for battle. Rev 12:6 refers to the place prepared by God as a refuge to protect the woman and her messianic child-king from satanic attack. Rev 19:7; 21:2 depict the "bride" (i.e., the church) preparing to meet her "husband" (i.e., Christ, the Lamb of God).

proetoimazō προετοιμάζω 4282

proetoimazō only occurs in two places, meaning "prepare beforehand." Rom 9:23 speaks of the phenomenon of divine election, describing the "vessels of mercy" (i.e., his people) that he has prepared beforehand for glory. Eph 2:10 speaks of the good works presented by the people of God, works which God has "prepared beforehand." Both references indicate the saving purposes of God conceived in eternity, prior to the creation of the world.

kataskeuazō κατασκευάζω 2680

kataskeuazō is a verb occurring thirteen times, meaning "prepare" and "build." Most frequently, ***kataskeuazō*** refers to the task of "preparing" the way of the Lord, or the role of the herald announcing the coming of the Messiah (Matt 11:10; Mark 1:2; Luke 7:27). Luke 1:17 mentions a people "prepared" by God for his own glory.

▸ **33.** Architecture > BUILD, BUILDER, BUILDING

katartizō καταρτίζω 2675

katartizō is a verb found in only four places. It has the underlying sense of "making complete or perfect." It is with this sense that ***katartizō*** is used in Heb 10:5 to refer to God "having prepared a body" for his Son Jesus Christ in the context of his perfect submission to his Father's will.

▸ **27.** Community, Partnership, Unity, Discord > RESTORE

▸ **61.** Integrity, Innocence, Piety > PERFECT, PERFECTION, COMPLETE

SEE ALSO

▸ **40.** Holy Days, Feasts, Festivals > PREPARATION ***paraskeuē***

PUT, PLACE, LAY

tithēmi τίθημι 5087

tithēmi is a common verb meaning "put," "set," "lay (down)," as well as having several related nuances, throughout its nearly one hundred occurrences.

"Put," in the literal, mundane sense of "set (in place)," "place," or "lay," is indicated in relation to objects (Matt 5:15; Mark 4:21; Luke 8:16; John 19:19); and to the dead body of Christ in the tomb (Mark 16:6; Luke 23:53; John 11:34; 19:42; Acts 13:29). See also Acts 9:40; Rev 10:2.

More significantly, God "puts" or "places" his Spirit upon his servants (Matt 12:18). God is said to "place" his enemies under his feet (Matt 22:44; Mark 12:36; 1 Cor 15:25). Rom 9:33; 1 Pet 2:6 refer to God "laying" a stone in Zion, denoting the emergence of the future messianic ruler.

The "placing" or "setting down" of people in a variety of locations is noted for example, in connection with prison (Matt 14:3; Acts 5:18); eternal darkness (Matt 24:51); the market place (Mark 6:56); laying a foundation (1 Cor 3:10ff.); and bringing people to Jesus for healing (Luke 5:18). See also Acts 3:2.

"Laying" hands on people in the ritual of blessing is recorded in Mark 10:16. Bringing an offering and "placing" it at the feet of the apostles is noted in Acts 4:35ff.; 5:2.

The gesture of Christ "laying down" his life for his people is described in John 10:15ff.; the offer of his disciples to do the same is noted in John 13:37ff. The sublime nature of someone making such a sacrifice is described in John 15:13.

The prerogative of "being appointed" as a preacher of the gospel is indicated in 2 Tim 1:11. God's action in "appointing" his Son as the heir of all things is indicated in Heb 1:2.

▸ **83.** Set, Put, Place, Prepare, Establish > APPOINT, ORDAIN, ASSIGN

▸ **83.** Set, Put, Place, Prepare, Establish > SET

paratithēmi παρατίθημι 3908

paratithēmi is a variant form of ***tithēmi*** (above) found in nineteen places and meaning "to set," "place before."

The meaning "set before" is found in several places, denoting the "telling" of a parable in Matt 13:24, 31.

The action of "setting food before" people is indicated in Mark 6:41; 8:6ff.; Luke 9:16; 10:8; Acts 16:34; 1 Cor 10:27.

The meaning "to commit," "entrust" oneself to God, is indicated in 1 Pet 4:19.

▸ **83.** Set, Put, Place, Prepare, Establish > SET

epitithēmi ἐπιτίθημι 2007

epitithēmi is another variant of ***tithēmi*** (above) and means "to lay on," "put," "lay" throughout most of its nearly fifty occurrences.

The action of Christ "laying his hand on" those who would receive his healing is indicated in Matt 9:18; 19:13ff.; Mark 5:23; 8:23ff.; Luke 4:40; 13:13. See also John 9:15. In Acts 9:12, 17; 28:8, such healing is effected through human agency.

"Placing one's clothes on" a beast of burden is indicated in Matt 21:7. The "placing" of crowns on the head of Christ is noted in Matt 27:29; John 19:2. See also Luke 23:26.

The metaphorical sense of "placing" or "laying" burdens on people is found in Matt 23:4; Acts 15:10, 28.

"Laying one's hands" on those who are being set aside for ministry as an act of spiritual commissioning is noted in Acts 6:6; 13:3; 1 Tim 5:22. This is also indicated as a precursor to receiving the Holy Spirit in Acts 8:17.

Acts 28:3 also refers to "placing" or "laying down" objects.

▸ **7.** Quantity, Amount, Number, Size, Measure > ADD, INCREASE

peritithēmi περιτίθημι 4060

peritithēmi is yet another variant form of ***tithēmi*** (above) and has the underlying meaning "to set around," "put on" in all eight occurrences of the term.

The action of "setting a hedge around" a vineyard is indicated in Matt 21:33; Mark 12:1.

A scarlet robe is "placed" around Christ in Matt 27:28. A sponge filled with vinegar is "placed on" a stick and offered to Christ in Matt 27:48; Mark 15:36; John 19:29. Mark 15:17 refers to Roman soldiers "placing" a crown of thorns on Christ's head.

▸ **83.** Set, Put, Place, Prepare, Establish > SET

epiballō ἐπιβάλλω 1911

epiballō is a verb form found nineteen times with the primary meanings "to lay," "put."

The meaning "put" in the sense of "sew" is found in Matt 9:16; Luke 5:36, with reference to sewing a new piece of material onto an old one.

epiballō, used with the noun ***cheir***, is commonly translated "lay hands on," in the sense of "seize" or "arrest" someone (Matt 26:50; Mark 14:46; Luke 20:19; 21:12; John 7:30, 44; Acts 4:3; 5:18; 12:1; 21:27; 1 Cor 7:35).

Luke 9:62 refers to "putting" one's hand to the plow.

SEE ALSO

- ▸ **25.** Family, Marriage, Adoption, Inheritance > PUT AWAY
  apolyō
- ▸ **54.** Rule, Authority, Command, Obedience > PUT IN SUBJECTION
  hypotassō
- ▸ **79.** Throw, Send, Drive, Mix, Remove > PUT OFF, PUT AWAY, CAST ASIDE
  apotithēmi, apekdyomai

SEAL

sphragizō σφραγίζω 4972

sphragizō is a verb occurring about thirty times meaning "to seal," "set one's seal on," in a number of contexts.

The meaning "to seal" in the sense of "secure" or "lock up" is indicated in Matt 27:66, with reference to a stone over the entrance to Jesus' tomb. In Rev 20:3 it refers to Satan being prevented from deceiving the nations.

Elsewhere, the meaning "seal" means "to bind up," so as to prevent disclosure of divine revelation, as in Rev 10:4; 20:10. "Sealing" the people of God in Rev 7:3ff. functions as an ultimate measure of protection against divine judgment.

The expression "set one's seal on" is used in several contexts, all of them metaphorical. In John 3:33 this expression serves as a guarantee of truth for particular testimony, the validation of the truth of God. John 6:27 affirms that God sets his seal on Jesus Christ in order to validate his status as the Son of God. God is also said to "set the seal" of his Spirit on the hearts of believers in order to guarantee and preserve their status as belonging to him (2 Cor 1:22; Eph 1:13; 4:30).

sphragis σφραγίς 4973

sphragis is a noun derived from ***sphragizō*** (above) meaning "seal" or "signet ring" in all sixteen occurrences and in various contexts.

sphragis is used metaphorically to refer to a "seal" as a sign of a guarantee or validation of circumcision, described in Rom 4:11 as a "seal" of righteousness. In 1 Cor 9:2, the Corinthian congregation is designated as a "seal" of Paul's apostleship.

The phenomenon of "sealing" the people of God, identifying them as belonging to him, is indicated in 2 Tim 2:19. Rev 9:4 refers to the "seal" of God that protects the saints.

Rev 5:1ff.; 6:1ff.; 7:2; 8:1 refer to "seals" attached to a scroll. Each of these seals represents an aspect of God's universal judgment on wicked humankind.

katasphragizō κατασφραγίζω 2696

katasphragizō is a rare variant of the verb ***sphragizō*** (above) meaning "cover with a seal" and found only in Rev 5:1, in relation to the visionary scroll of John's revelation.

SET

tithēmi τίθημι 5087

tithēmi is a verb found in around one hundred places, meaning "set," "put," "place," "lay" in the majority of its usage in a variety of contexts.

The general sense of "put" or "set," in relation to placing objects in a certain place, is illustrated in Matt 5:15; Mark 4:21; Luke 8:16; John 13:4; Acts 4:37. In particular, Luke 23:53; John 19:42; Acts 13:29 refer to "placing" the body of Christ in a tomb; and John 11:34 refers similarly to the body of Lazarus. Rom 14:13 warns against putting a stumbling block in the way of a fellow believer.

tithēmi also refers to God "putting" or "setting" in a number of places. For example, he promises to put his Spirit on his anointed Servant (i.e., the Messiah) in Matt 12:18. "Laying" or "setting" a stone in Zion to make human beings stumble is a reference to God placing his Son, Jesus Christ, among human beings (Rom 9:33; 1 Pet 2:6ff.). "Setting" (i.e., appointing) various kinds of leaders in the church is indicated in 1 Cor 12:28; 1 Tim 1:12; 2 Tim 1:11, referring to their particular gifts for service. The "appointing" of Christ as the heir of all things is noted in Heb 1:2. 1 Cor 15:25 declares that God will "place" all of his enemies under his feet. See also Rev 10:2; 11:9.

- ▸ **83.** Set, Put, Place, Prepare, Establish > APPOINT, ORDAIN, ASSIGN
- ▸ **83.** Set, Put, Place, Prepare, Establish > PUT, PLACE, LAY

paratithēmi παρατίθημι 3908

paratithēmi is a variant form of ***tithēmi*** (above) occurring around twenty times and meaning "to set before" in about half of these contexts.

Christ is said to "set" parables before the people (Matt 13:24ff.). In Luke 23:46, he "places" (i.e., commends) his spirit into the hands of his Father.

paratithēmi also refers to "setting" food before people (Mark 6:41; 8:6ff.; Luke 9:16; Acts 16:34; 1 Cor 10:27).

- ▸ **83.** Set, Put, Place, Prepare, Establish > PUT, PLACE, LAY

peritithēmi περιτίθημι 4060

Another variant of ***tithēmi*** (above), ***peritithēmi*** is found six times meaning "to set (or put) around" in relation to various objects.

Matt 21:33; Mark 12:1 refer to "setting" a hedge around a vineyard. Roman soldiers place a crown of thorns on the head of Christ (Mark 15:17), and put a robe around him (Matt 27:28). Matt 27:48; Mark 15:36; John 19:29 refer to placing a sponge filled with vinegar on a reed for Christ on the cross.

- ▸ **83.** Set, Put, Place, Prepare, Establish > PUT, PLACE, LAY

histēmi ἵστημι 2476

histēmi is a common verb found in nearly 160 contexts with the dominant meaning "to stand." Occasionally, however, it means "set" or "place."

Christ is "set" (or placed) on the pinnacle of the temple by Satan in Matt 4:5; Luke 4:9. Sheep and goats are placed, metaphorically, at the right and left hand of God — referring to the righteous and the wicked, respectively (Matt 25:33).

More generally, ***histēmi*** refers to "setting up" false witnesses in Acts 6:13. Other references include those in Matt 18:2; Mark 9:36; Luke 9:47; John 8:3; Acts 4:7.

- ▸ **70.** Give, Take, Seize, Touch > PRESENT

- ▸ **83.** Set, Put, Place, Prepare, Establish > APPOINT, ORDAIN, ASSIGN
- ▸ **83.** Set, Put, Place, Prepare, Establish > ESTABLISH, FIX, GROUND, STRENGTHEN
- ▸ **85.** Movement, Position, State > STAND

keimai κεῖμαι 2749

keimai is a verb found nearly thirty times, usually with a passive sense — "to be laid," "be set up," "be appointed."

Matt 5:14 refers to city being set on a hill. Clothes are "laid aside" in Luke 24:12. Luke 2:34 affirms that Christ "is appointed" for the rise and fall of many in Israel. Phil 2:17 declares that Paul "is set" for the defense of the gospel.

- ▸ **85.** Movement, Position, State > LIE, LIE DOWN, RECLINE

prokeimai πρόκειμαι 4295

prokeimai is a variant form of ***keimai*** (above) found five times with the sense of "to be set," "placed before," "be set forth" in all but one of these contexts.

Hope is "set before" the believer in Heb 6:18. The race of life is also "set before" believers in Heb 12:1. Joy is "set before" Christ in Heb 12:2. In Jude 7, Sodom and Gomorrah are "set forth" as an example of divine punishment.

epibibazō ἐπιβιβάζω 1913

epibibazō is a verb found five times meaning "to set (or place) upon." It refers exclusively to helping people to mount and ride horses or donkeys (Luke 10:34; 19:35; Acts 23:24).

SEE ALSO

- ▸ **1.** Celestial Realm, Earthly Realm > SET
  dynō
- ▸ **51.** Knowledge, Wisdom, Remember, Forget > SET ONE'S MIND ON
  phroneō

84. Do, Make, Accomplish, Occur

CARRY OUT, COMPLETE, FULFILL, ACCOMPLISH

epiteleō ἐπιτελέω 2005

epiteleō is a verb found thirteen times meaning "perform," "bring to an end," "complete." The sense of human agents "completing" or "finishing" a task is indicated in Rom 15:28; 2 Cor 8:6, 11. In Phil 1:6, God is said to "bring his work of salvation to completion."

plēroō πληρόω 4137

plēroō is a verb found nearly one hundred times meaning "fulfill," "fill," "be full," as well as related nuances.

The phenomenon of "fulfilling" prophecy is indicated in a number of places with reference to the climactic realization of God's redemptive purposes in the person of Jesus Christ (e.g., Matt 1:22; 2:15ff.; Mark 1:15; 15:28; Luke 4:21; 24:44; John 13:18; 17:12ff.; Acts 3:18; 13:27). See also Jas 2:23.

In addition to fulfilling prophecy, ***plēroō*** also denotes the "fulfilling" of the requirements of the law, made possible solely through the sacrifice of Christ, enabling his people to live godly lives through the indwelling Holy Spirit (Rom 8:4).

The meaning "fulfill" with the sense of "complete" is indicated in Matt 3:15 in relation to Jesus' desire to "fulfill" all righteousness in his baptism. There are also mundane references to "fulfilling" or "completing" a task (Acts 12:25). Jesus' declared intention to "fulfill" the Law and the Prophets by bringing their purposes to completion is indicated in Matt 5:17.

The action of "fulfilling" the law in relation to believers obeying its terms is noted in Rom 13:8; Gal 5:14.

▸ **7.** Quantity, Amount, Number, Size, Measure > FILL, FILL UP, FULFILL, BE FULL, BE FILLED

ekplēroō ἐκπληρόω 1603

ekplēroō is a rare variant of ***plēroō*** (above). It is found only in Acts 13:33, referring to God "fulfilling" his covenant promises to raise up Jesus for the salvation of his people.

anaplēroō ἀναπληρόω 378

anaplēroō is another rare variant of ***plēroō*** (above). It means "fulfill" in Matt 13:14, where Jesus declares that the inability to understand the message of his parables is a direct consequence of the fulfillment of the prophecy recorded in Isa 6:9ff. Gal 6:2 contains Paul's injunction to "fulfill" the law of Christ by bearing one another's burdens.

▸ **7.** Quantity, Amount, Number, Size, Measure > FILL, FILL UP, FULFILL, BE FULL, BE FILLED

plērophoreō πληροφορέω 4135

plērophoreō is a verb found six times with a variety of meanings. Luke 1:1 refers to the things "most certainly believed." Rom 4:21; 14:5 both allude to the state of mind of "being completely or fully convinced." In 2 Tim 4:5, Paul's injunction to Timothy to "fulfill his ministry" means "discharging" or "carrying it out." In 2 Tim 4:17 ***plērophoreō*** is translated "to preach completely or fully" in relation to the gospel.

▸ **47.** Show, Persuade, Confidence, Doubt > PERSUADE, PERSUASION

plērōma πλήρωμα 4138

plērōma is a noun found seventeen times with the dominant meaning "fullness" throughout. However, in Mark 8:20 the term refers to love as "the fulfilling" of the law.

▸ **7.** Quantity, Amount, Number, Size, Measure > FULLNESS, FULFILLMENT

ekplērōsis ἐκπλήρωσις 1604

ekplērōsis is a rare noun found only in Acts 21:26 with reference to the "completion" or "accomplishing" of the days set aside for the performance of a vow.

teleō τελέω 5055

teleō is a verb found twenty-six times meaning "fulfill," "complete," "finish," "accomplish" for most of the usage. There is some overlap in meaning between these senses.

Luke 12:50 refers to the prospect of Christ's baptism "being accomplished, or completed." Luke 18:31 refers to Jesus' claim that everything prophesied about him as the Son of Man "will be fulfilled (i.e., accomplished)" in Jerusalem. Luke 22:37; John 19:28 contain similar claims. John 19:30 records Christ's last word on the cross, ***teleō***, translated "It is finished" and referring to the work of salvation given him by his Father to accomplish. Other references to the "fulfilling" of prophecy include those in Acts 13:29; Rev 10:7; 17:17.

The sense of "fulfilling (or keeping) the law" is indicated in Rom 2:27. See also Jas 2:8.

▸ **4.** Beginning, Continuing, Finishing, Postponing > FINISH, COMPLETE, FULFILL, BRING TO AN END, COME TO AN END

▸ **30.** Money, Business, Wealth, Poverty > PAY, RENDER

synteleō συντελέω 4931

synteleō is a variant form of ***teleō*** (above) found seven times with the predominant sense of "to finish" or "end." In Mark 13:4, however, the term denotes the "fulfilling" of the signs of the end times.

▸ **4.** Beginning, Continuing, Finishing, Postponing > END, BRING TO AN END

▸ **4.** Beginning, Continuing, Finishing, Postponing > FINISH, COMPLETE, FULFILL, BRING TO AN END, COME TO AN END

teleioō τελειόω 5048

teleioō is a verb with the synonymous meanings "to fulfill," "accomplish," "finish," "perfect," "complete" throughout most of its nearly twenty-five occurrences.

Jesus' determination to "fulfill" or "accomplish" the tasks given to him by God is indicated in John 4:34; 5:36; and the completion of that redemptive work is noted in John 17:4; 19:28.

- ▸ **4.** Beginning, Continuing, Finishing, Postponing > FINISH, COMPLETE, FULFILL, BRING TO AN END, COME TO AN END
- ▸ **61.** Integrity, Innocence, Piety > PERFECT, PERFECTION, COMPLETE

teleiōsis τελείωσις 5050

teleiōsis is a rare noun meaning "fulfillment" in relation to the word of the Lord spoken by the angel Gabriel to Mary, promising her that she would be the mother of the Messiah, the Christ child.

- ▸ **84.** Do, Make, Accomplish, Occur > PERFECTING

COME UPON

phthanō φθάνω 5348

phthanō is a verb found in nine contexts with the meaning "come upon," in the sense of "reach," "touch," or "make an impact on." Matt 12:28; Luke 11:20 speak of the kingdom of God "coming upon" unbelieving Pharisees. 1 Thess 2:16 refers to the wrath of God "coming upon" the Gentiles.

SEE ALSO

- ▸ **86.** Movement Toward or Away From > COME, DRAW NEAR ***erchomai, eperchomai, proserchomai, ginomai, hēkō***

CREATE, CREATION, CREATOR, CREATURE

ktizō κτίζω 2936

ktizō is a verb found in sixteen contexts with the predominant meaning "create."

References to God's creative activity with respect to the cosmos include Mark 13:19; Eph 3:9; Rev 4:11; 10:6. 1 Cor 11:9 specifically mentions God's creation of humankind. Creation effected in and through Christ is indicated in Col 1:16. See also 1 Tim 4:3. God is referred to as "Creator" in Rom 1:25; Col 3:10.

Believers are described symbolically as God's workmanship "created" in Jesus Christ for good works (Eph 2:10; 4:24).

Christ is said to have "created" in himself a new man by abolishing the effect of the law through his self-sacrifice (Eph 2:15).

ktisis κτίσις 2937

ktisis is a noun derived from ***ktizō*** (above). It is consistently translated "creation," "creature" throughout its nineteen occurrences.

General references to "creation" include Mark 10:6; 13:19; Rom 1:20; 8:39; 2 Pet 3:4. The despoiling of "creation" by the impact of sin, placing it in bondage, is noted in Rom 8:19ff. Included in this context also is the anticipated renewal of creation in the wake of the work of Christ.

"Creation" as the object and context of preaching the gospel is noted in Mark 16:15. References to "creatures" as the general product of God's creative power are found in Rom 1:25; Col 1:23; Heb 4:13.

Believers are described as a new "creation" in Christ in 2 Cor 5:17 (see also Gal 6:15). Christ is described as "the firstborn of all creation" in Col 1:15.

ktisma κτίσμα 2938

ktisma is a rare noun derived from ***ktizō*** (above) denoting a "creature" in a general sense in 1 Tim 4:4; Rev 5:13; 8:9. In Jas 1:18, believers are described as a kind of firstfruits of his creatures.

ktistēs κτίστης 2939

ktistēs is a rare noun found only in 1 Pet 4:19, denoting God as "Creator."

DEED, WORK

ergon ἔργον 2041

ergon is the predominant Greek term for "work(s)" or "deed(s)." It is found nearly two hundred times, in various contexts.

ergon refers generally to human "works" or "deeds" (Matt 23:5; Eph 2:9, 10; 2 Tim 1:9). 1 Cor 3:13ff. indicates that such "work" is to be judged by God. Jas 2:20ff. refers to "works" in relation to one's faith. ***ergon*** refers to good "deeds" (Matt 5:16; Acts 9:36; 2 Cor 9:8; 1 Tim 5:10; 2 Tim 3:17; Heb 10:24); evil "deeds" (Luke 11:48; 2 Pet 2:8; John 3:19ff.; Jude 15; Rev 16:11); and "deeds" subject to divine judgment (Rom 2:6; Eph 5:11; 1 Pet 1:17; Rev 2:2ff.; 3:1ff.; 20:12ff.; 22:12).

"Work" in the sense of formal employment is indicated in Mark 13:34; and in the context of gospel ministry in Acts 13:2; 14:26; 1 Cor 15:58; Eph 4:12; 1 Thess 5:13.

ergon is also used figuratively to denote "workmanship," referring to believers as the fruit of Paul's ministry (1 Cor 9:1). The term also denotes "the works of the law" in Rom 3:20, 28; 4:2ff.; 9:11, 32; 11:6; Gal 2:16; 3:2ff.

In relation to Christ, ***ergon*** indicates his miraculous signs (i.e., his works) (Matt 11:2; Luke 24:19; John 5:20; 7:3; Heb 3:9), and his "work" of redemption (Phil 3:20).

Rom 14:20 refers generally to the "work" of God in redemption. The "work" of redemption effected in and through the person of Christ, who is sent by God, is indicated in John 4:34; 5:36; 9:3ff.; 10:25ff.; 14:10ff.; 17:4. The divine "work" in the life of the believer that produces genuine righteousness is noted in Phil 1:6. Heb 1:10; 4:3 speak of the "work" of God's hands in creation.

ergon also refers to the "works" of the devil (1 John 3:8).

praxis πρᾶξις 4234

praxis is a noun occurring six times referring to "works," "deeds."

praxis refers to the "works" of human beings, subject to divine judgment (Matt 16:27; Luke 23:51; Acts 19:18), and to the "works" of the sinful nature (Rom 8:13; Col 3:9).

SEE ALSO

- ▸ **27.** Community, Partnership, Unity, Discord > WORK TOGETHER, FELLOW WORKER ***synergeō, synergos***

- ▸ **28.** Agriculture, Viticulture, Animal Husbandry > WORKING, TILLING
  geōrgeō
- ▸ **30.** Money, Business, Wealth, Poverty > GAIN, PROFIT
  ergasia

DO, MAKE, MAKER

dēmiourgos δημιουργός 1217

dēmiourgos is a rare noun found only in Heb 11:10, referring to God as the "maker" of the eternal city.

poieō ποιέω 4160

poieō occurs around six hundred times with the primary meanings "do," "make" in a variety of contexts.

When predicated of people, ***poieō*** refers to the action of "making" in a number of ways. With the sense of "build," "fashion," or "construct," ***poieō*** is found, for example, in Matt 17:4; Luke 9:33, where Peter offers to make shelters for the heavenly figures that appeared on the Mount of Transfiguration. ***poieō*** also refers to making clothes (Acts 9:39); and building a fire (John 18:18). The fashioning of idols is referred to in Acts 7:43; 19:24; Rev 13:14; and reference to the construction of the tabernacle is found in Acts 7:44; Heb 8:5. Food preparation is alluded to in Luke 5:29; 14:13.

Elsewhere, ***poieō*** means "make" with the underlying sense of "bringing about" a particular effect, or change, in the state of a person or object. For instance, Jesus declares to his disciples in Matt 4:19; Mark 1:7 that he will make them "fishers of men." In Matt 12:33 he also refers to making the fruit tree good or bad. In Matt 21:13; Luke 19:46; Mark 11:17; John 2:16, Jesus accuses a crowd of Jewish business people of making the temple a "den of thieves." Luke 6:9 refers to making friends, and Matt 23:15 to making a proselyte. In relation to miraculous healing, Acts 3:12 records the incident in which Peter and John make the lame man walk. There is an exhortation to "make straight the paths" of the coming messianic king in Matt 3:3; Mark 1:3; Luke 3:4 (Isa 40:3). In Rom 13:14, Paul exhorts his readers to make no concession to one's sinful nature.

Other general references to the action of "making" are found in Matt 5:36; Mark 3:12; 6:21; Rom 15:26; Jas 3:18; 1 Tim 2:1.

In relation to God "making," ***poieō*** is likewise found in numerous contexts. Matt 19:4; Mark 10:6 speak of God making (i.e., creating) humankind in the divine image, as male and female.

Related to this theme is the reference to God making all things new in Rev 21:5, and the creation of the new heavens and the new earth in Acts 4:24; 17:24; Heb 1:2; Rev 14:7. Heb 8:9 refers to God making a covenant with Israel. Rev 1:6; 5:10 mention God fashioning his chosen people into an eternal kingdom. In regard to his Son, God declares (through Peter) that he has made Jesus Lord (Acts 2:36). In 2 Cor 5:21, God is said to have made him who knew no sin to be sin on our behalf; and in Acts 2:36, Peter affirms that God has made Jesus Lord.

poieō is also predicated of Christ. In a number of places, Jesus is said to have made the deaf hear (Mark 7:37); made water into wine (John 4:46); made the blind see (Mark 8:25); and made a man whole (John 5:11, 15; 7:23).

In relation to other aspects of his ministry, Christ is described as the one who makes Jew and Gentile one, in a bond of peace (Eph 2:14, 15). Those Jews who opposed him at every stage of his career accused Jesus of "making himself equal with God," and thus wrongly charged him with blasphemy (John 5:18; 10:33; 19:7). Ironically, in reality, Jesus' own signs manifested his true divine nature — but unbelieving Jews would not, or could not, see it. See also John 2:15; 4:1; 9:6.

In addition, the satanic beast of Revelation is said to make war on the saints of God in Rev 11:7; 12:17; 19:19. In Rev 13:13, he makes fire come down from heaven.

- ▸ **40.** Holy Days, Feasts, Festivals > KEEP
- ▸ **83.** Set, Put, Place, Prepare, Establish > APPOINT, ORDAIN, ASSIGN
- ▸ **84.** Do, Make, Accomplish, Occur > EXECUTE

EXECUTE

poieō ποιέω 4160

poieō is a common verb found nearly six hundred times with the predominant meanings "do," "make," with a variety of related senses, including "to execute." John 5:27; Jude 15 mention the Son of God's divine authority to "execute (i.e., pass) judgment" on the wicked.

- ▸ **40.** Holy Days, Feasts, Festivals > KEEP
- ▸ **83.** Set, Put, Place, Prepare, Establish > APPOINT, ORDAIN, ASSIGN
- ▸ **84.** Do, Make, Accomplish, Occur > DO, MAKE, MAKER

EXPERIENCE, ENJOY

tynchanō τυγχάνω 5177

tynchanō is a verb occurring thirteen times with the predominant meaning "to obtain," "attain." The meaning "enjoy" is found only in Acts 24:2, referring to the Roman province of Judea "having enjoyed" (i.e., experienced) a long period of peace under the jurisdiction of Governor Felix.

- ▸ **69.** Have, Possess, Hold, Grasp, Bear, Carry > OBTAIN

SEE ALSO

- ▸ **50.** Love, Hate, Please, Be Pleased With > ENJOYMENT
  apolausis

HAPPEN, TAKE PLACE, COME TO PASS, ARISE

ginomai γίνομαι 1096

ginomai is a common verb (occurring over one thousand times) with quite generalized meanings such as "be," "become," "happen (i.e., come to pass)," "come," plus a number of other nuances.

In a few places, ***ginomai*** also expresses the sense of "rise" in the sense of "happen," "come to pass." It is used to denote the coming of persecution (Matt 13:21; Acts 11:19), a storm (Mark 4:37), flood (Luke 6:48), famine (Luke 5:14), civil unrest (Acts 19:23; 23:9), and a dispute (Acts 23:7ff.).

▸ **84.** Do, Make, Accomplish, Occur > USE

▸ **86.** Movement Toward or Away From > COME, DRAW NEAR

eiserchomai εἰσέρχομαι 1525

eiserchomai is a common verb with the predominant sense of "enter," "go in," "come in" for the large majority of its nearly two hundred occurrences. In Luke 9:46 the meaning "arise" is indicated, in relation to an argument among the disciples as to who is the greatest.

▸ **86.** Movement Toward or Away From > ENTER, ENTRANCE, ENTRY

symbainō συμβαίνω 4819

symbainō has an underlying literal sense of "go, come, or walk together," with the extended meaning to "happen," "come to pass." The term occurs eight times, with the sense of "happen" in six of these. Mark 10:32; Acts 3:10; 20:19; 1 Cor 10:11; 1 Pet 4:2 all contain ***symbainō*** with the idea of "happen to," "befall." In Luke 24:14 it means to "take place."

MEET, BEFALL

apantaō ἀπαντάω 528

apantaō is a verb meaning "meet," "go to meet." It occurs seven times.

With the general sense of "meet," in the context of coming face-to-face with someone, ***apantaō*** is found in Matt 28:9; Mark 5:2; 14:13; Luke 17:12; John 4:51; Acts 16:16. In Luke 14:31, ***apantaō*** means "meet" in the sense of a military confrontation between warring parties.

apantēsis ἀπάντησις 529

apantēsis is the noun derived from ***apantaō*** (above) and is found in four places. It conveys the sense of "meeting" in the context of a social gathering in the parable in Matt 25:1, 6, where wedding guests come out to meet the bridegroom. Acts 28:15 records a meeting between Paul and a group of Roman believers. In 1 Thess 4:17, Paul describes the blessed fate of those believers who are alive at the return of Christ, who will be caught up to meet him in the air.

hypantaō ὑπαντάω 5221

hypantaō is a variant form of ***apantaō*** (above) meaning "meet" in all five contexts in which it is found. The meeting of Jesus and his friend Martha (sister of Lazarus) is recorded in John 11:20, 30. John 12:18 speaks of the curiosity of the Jewish crowd wishing to meet Jesus as a result of his raising Lazarus from the dead. Matt 8:28; Luke 8:27 speak of the Gadarene demoniac confronting Jesus near the vicinity of the graveyard where he was living as an outcast.

hypantēsis ὑπάντησις 5222

hypantēsis is the noun derived from ***hypantaō*** (above) and is found only in John 12:13, where it refers to the Jerusalem population coming out to meet Jesus with palm tree branches, praising him as the coming King of Israel.

synantaō συναντάω 4876

synantaō is another variant form of ***apantaō*** (above) and is found in six contexts. This term is translated "meet" in the same general sense as the other terms (Luke 9:37; 22:10; Acts 10:25; Heb 7:1, 10). In Acts 20:22, ***synantaō*** is translated "to befall," referring to Paul's ignorance of what will happen to him when he arrives in Jerusalem.

synantēsis συνάντησις 4877

synantēsis is the noun derived from ***synantaō*** (above) and occurs only in Matt 8:34, where it refers to the population of Gadara coming out to meet Jesus, begging him to leave their region.

PERFECTING

teleiōsis τελείωσις 5050

teleiōsis is a noun occurring in two places and meaning "perfection." In Luke 1:45, ***teleiōsis*** refers to a "fulfillment" of divine prophecy, literally a "perfecting" of what was spoken from the Lord. Heb 7:11 refers to the impossibility of gaining spiritual or moral perfection through the ministry of the Levitical priesthood.

▸ **84.** Do, Make, Accomplish, Occur > CARRY OUT, COMPLETE, FULFILL, ACCOMPLISH

SEE ALSO

▸ **20.** Illness, Disease, Health, Healing > PERFECT HEALTH
holoklēria

▸ **61.** Integrity, Innocence, Piety > PERFECT, PERFECTION, COMPLETE
teleios, teleioō, katartizō, teleiotēs

▸ **88.** Qualities, Characteristics > ACCURATELY
akribēs

PRACTICE, COMMIT

prassō πράσσω 4238

prassō means "do," "commit" (i.e., practice) in its nearly forty occurrences.

References to "committing" practices that are an abomination to God are found in Rom 1:32; 2:2.

General references to "committing" sin are found in Acts 25:11, 25; 2 Cor 12:21.

TOIL

kopiaō κοπιάω 2872

kopiaō is a verb found in thirty contexts with the primary sense of "to toil," or grow weary through hard work.

Undertaking "labor" in general, without necessarily "growing weary," is noted in Eph 4:28; Phil 2:16. More commonly, people's "toiling" is expended in physical exertion, as indicated in Matt 11:28; Luke 5:5; John 4:6; 2 Tim 2:6. The idea of "toiling" is also evident in the context of the work of ministry (Acts 20:35; Rom 16:6, 12; 1 Cor 4:12; Gal 4:11; Col 1:29; 1 Thess 5:12; 1 Tim 4:10).

kopiaō is also used metaphorically in Matt 6:28; Luke 12:27, where the plants of the field are declared not to have engaged in wearying labor or toil.

SEE ALSO

- ▸ **20.** Illness, Disease, Health, Healing > WEARY
  kamnō
- ▸ **60.** Virtues > (NOT) GROW WEARY
  ekkakeō
- ▸ **75.** Suffering, Distress, Sadness > WEAR DOWN, WEAR OUT
  hypōpiazō

USE

chraomai χράομαι 5530

chraomai is a verb with the general meanings "use," "make use of," in half of the twelve contexts in which it occurs. 1 Cor 7:31 speaks of "making use of" the things of the world. Paul decides "not to make use of" his right to receive payment for his ministry (1 Cor 9:12, 15). In 2 Cor 3:10, the apostle hopes that he may "not have to make use of" severe disciplinary measures against the Corinthian congregation. 1 Tim 1:8 refers to "making proper use of" the law. Paul enjoins Timothy "to use (or take)" a little wine for his stomach ailments (1 Tim 5:23).

ginomai γίνομαι 1096

ginomai is a common verb with the primary meanings "to be, become," as well as associated senses, throughout its over one thousand occurrences. In 1 Thess 2:5, however, ***ginomai*** means "to use" in the context of Paul's denial that he "used" flattery in order to derive financial gain from his ministry.

- ▸ **84.** Do, Make, Accomplish, Occur > HAPPEN, TAKE PLACE, COME TO PASS, ARISE
- ▸ **86.** Movement Toward or Away From > COME, DRAW NEAR

WORK, LABOR, PRODUCE, BRING ABOUT, DEED

ergazomai ἐργάζομαι 2038

ergazomai is a verb found around forty times meaning "work," "labor."

With reference to human beings, the general sense of "engaging in manual labor" is indicated in Matt 21:28; Luke 13:14; John 6:27; Rom 4:4ff.; 1 Cor 4:12; Eph 4:28; 2 Thess 3:10ff. Similarly, ***ergazomai*** also refers to conducting business or trade (Matt 25:16; Rev 18:17). In addition, Matt 7:23 refers to "working (or doing) evil." 1 Cor 16:10; Col 3:23; 2 John 8; 3 John 5 refer to engaging in the work of gospel ministry.

ergazomai also denotes, in a nominal sense, the godly "deeds" of the believer (John 3:21).

ergazomai also indicates the work of God in the hearts of human beings, illuminating their hearts (John 5:17), and "performing" miraculous deeds (Acts 13:41). Similarly, in John 6:30; 9:4, Christ is said to "perform" a miraculous sign in order to fulfill the purposes of God.

- ▸ **30.** Money, Business, Wealth, Poverty > CRAFT, TRADE, BUSINESS

katergazomai κατεργάζομαι 2716

katergazomai is a verb found in about thirty contexts, a variant of ***ergazomai*** (above) meaning "to work," "produce," "accomplish."

Suffering and testing are said to "produce" or "bring about" endurance (Rom 5:3; 2 Cor 4:17; Jas 1:3). Conversely, sin is said to "bring about" or "produce" coveting that leads to death (Rom 7:8, 13). See also 2 Cor 7:10. In contrast, 2 Cor 7:11 affirms that godly sorrow "produces" a yearning for righteousness. The work of Christ in producing righteousness in the lives of believers is indicated in Rom 15:18. In Phil 2:12, the apostle exhorts believers "to work out" their salvation with fear and trembling.

energeō ἐνεργέω 1754

energeō is a verb found in around twenty contexts meaning "to work," "be at work" in a variety of contexts.

With reference to God, ***energeō*** refers to the divine power "at work" in the life of his people (Eph 3:20; Phil 2:13; Col 1:29). See also Matt 14:2; Mark 6:14; 1 Cor 12:11. God is also said to "work" miracles (Gal 3:5), as he "accomplishes" all things according to his will (Eph 1:11, 20). The word of God is also said to "be at work" in the life of the believer (1 Thess 2:13).

Sinful passions are said to "be aroused, produced" by the law in the life of the unbeliever (Rom 7:5). 2 Cor 4:12 affirms that death is "at work" in the human body, as is the spirit of Satan in unbelievers (Eph 2:2). Positively, faith is said to "work" in believers through love (Gal 5:6).

Gal 2:8 refers to believers "working" (i.e., engaging) in ministry with one another.

energeia ἐνέργεια 1753

energeia is a noun occurring eight times, denoting the superhuman "working" of either God or Satan. Satan's activity is noted in 2 Thess 2:9. God's power is evident in the life of the believer, as noted in Eph 1:19; 3:7; 4:16; Phil 3:21; Col 1:29; 2:12.

kopos κόπος 2873

kopos is a noun denoting "work," "labor" in the majority of its nineteen occurrences.

General references to "work," "labor" are found in John 4:38; 1 Cor 3:8; 11:23; 2 Thess 3:8. The "work" of ministry is noted in 1 Cor 15:58; 2 Cor 10:15; 1 Thess 1:3; Heb 6:10; Rev 14:13.

- ▸ **76.** Force, Harm, Oppress > TROUBLE, IRRITATE, BOTHER, ANNOY

SEE ALSO

- ▸ **27.** Community, Partnership, Unity, Discord > WORK TOGETHER, FELLOW WORKER
  synergeō, synergos
- ▸ **28.** Agriculture, Viticulture, Animal Husbandry > WORKING, TILLING
  geōrgeō
- ▸ **30.** Money, Business, Wealth, Poverty > GAIN, PROFIT
  ergasia

WORKER, WORKMAN, WORKMANSHIP

ergatēs ἐργάτης 2040

ergatēs is a noun denoting "laborer," "workman" throughout its sixteen occurrences.

General references to "laborer" include those in Matt 9:37ff.; 10:10; 20:1ff.; Luke 10:2ff.; 1 Tim 5:16; Jas 5:4. Acts 19:25; 2 Tim 2:15 specifically mention a "workman" (i.e., a skilled tradesman). The latter reference indicates one skilled in the knowledge of God's word. Conversely, ***ergatēs*** also denotes "workers of evil, iniquity" (Luke 13:27; 2 Cor 11:13; Phil 3:2).

poiēma ποίημα 4161

poiēma is a rare noun referring to believers as the product of God's "workmanship" (Eph 2:10).

SEE ALSO

- ▸ **27.** Community, Partnership, Unity, Discord > WORK TOGETHER, FELLOW WORKER
  synergeō, synergos
- ▸ **28.** Agriculture, Viticulture, Animal Husbandry > WORKING, TILLING
  geōrgeō
- ▸ **30.** Money, Business, Wealth, Poverty > GAIN, PROFIT
  ergasia

85. Movement, Position, State

ABSENCE, ABSENT

apousia ἀπουσία 666

apousia is a rare noun denoting personal, physical "absence" only in Phil 2:12.

apeimi ἄπειμι 548

apeimi is a verb with the consistent meaning "to be absent, away" in each of the seven occurrences of the term. The sense is that of physical, personal absence (1 Cor 5:3; 2 Cor 10:1, 11; 13:2, 10; Phil 1:27; Col 2:5).

ekdēmeō ἐκδημέω 1553

ekdēmeō is a verb found in three places, all expressing the metaphorical sense of "being absent" from the Lord, in that one is still "home" (i.e., alive) in one's body (1 Cor 5:6ff.).

ACCOMPANY

synepomai συνέπομαι 4902

synepomai is a rare verb, found only in Acts 20:4 and meaning "accompany" in the context of Paul traveling with his companions.

synerchomai συνέρχομαι 4905

synerchomai is a verb found in approximately thirty places with the primary meanings "come together," "go with." In several places, the meaning "accompany" is also evident in contexts where people are traveling together (John 11:33; Acts 1:21; 9:39; 10:23, 45; 15:38; 21:16). In particular, Acts 11:16 records the Spirit's command to Peter to "accompany" fellow believers to the home of Cornelius.

▸ **24.** Dwell, Live, Gather, Hospitality > ASSEMBLE, ASSEMBLY

propempō προπέμπω 4311

propempō is a verb found in nine places with the underlying meaning "to send on one's way," in the context of journeying or traveling. In Acts 20:38 the term carries the connotation of "accompany" (i.e., travel together with).

▸ **86.** Movement Toward or Away From > JOURNEY

BE PRESENT, COME

pareimi πάρειμι 3918

pareimi is an intransitive verb with the primary meanings "to be present," "come," in most of the twenty-three contexts in which it occurs.

The meaning "to be present" with reference to people in general, mundane contexts is indicated in Luke 13:1; 2 Cor 10:2, 11; 11:9; 13:2, 10; Gal 4:19. Acts 10:33 refers to a group of people being present in the sight of God. The setting here is the house of the Roman centurion, Cornelius. 1 Cor 5:3 speaks of Paul being absent in body, but "present" in spirit.

paraginomai παραγίνομαι 3854

paraginomai is an intransitive verb with the principal meaning "to come" in all but one of its nearly forty occurrences. In Acts 4:18 it is translated "to be present" with regard to the presence of the elders in the Jerusalem church who had come to meet with Paul and his missionary companions.

▸ **86.** Movement Toward or Away From > ARRIVE

sympareimi συμπάρειμι 4840

sympareimi is a verb found only in Acts 25:24, meaning "to be present."

SEE ALSO

▸ **3.** Periods of Time, Duration, Frequency, Speed > PRESENT
enistēmi

▸ **70.** Give, Take, Seize, Touch > PRESENT
paristēmi, histēmi

BEFORE, IN THE PRESENCE OF

enōpion ἐνώπιον 1799

enōpion is a preposition with the principal meaning "before," "in the presence of," "in the sight of." There is a significant amount of overlap between these meanings. ***enōpion*** occurs nearly one hundred times.

The meaning "before," in the sense of "in the presence of," is illustrated with respect to God in reference to the angel Gabriel standing in the presence of God (Luke 1:19); feasting in God's presence (Luke 13:26); the absence of boasting in the presence of God (1 Cor 1:29); and the torment of the beast in the presence of God (Rev 14:10).

The presence of individuals is indicated, for example, in Luke 14:10; 24:43; Acts 27:35; 1 Tim 5:20. Miracles performed by Jesus in the presence of his disciples are noted in John 20:30. Luke 15:10 affirms that angels in the presence of God rejoice over every sinner who repents.

prosōpon πρόσωπον 4383

prosōpon is a noun with the predominant sense of "face," "person," occurring in about eighty contexts. In five instances, however, ***prosōpon*** is used with prepositional force to mean "in the presence of." It refers to Pilate (Acts 3:13); and the Sanhedrin (Acts 5:41). Acts 3:19 speaks of refreshment gleaned from the presence of God; 2 Thess 1:9 refers to the wicked being thrust from the presence of God. Heb 9:24 describes Jesus appearing in heaven in the presence of God.

▸ **2.** Supernatural Beings/Forces, Spiritual Realm > PERSON, PRESENCE

▸ **16.** Body, Bodily Functions > FACE

parousia παρουσία 3952

parousia is a noun found in twenty-four contexts, meaning "appearing" or "coming" in most occurrences. In two contexts, however, the term is translated "presence," referring to the physical person of the apostle Paul (2 Cor 10:10; Phil 2:12).

▸ **86.** Movement Toward or Away From > COMING

katenōpion κατενώπιον 2714

katenōpion is a preposition, found in only five contexts with the principal meaning "before," "in the sight of," with reference to God. In Jude 24, however, it means "before his (glorious) presence."

CLOSE

kammyō καμμύω 2576

kammyō is a rare verb meaning "close, shut the eyes," found only in Matt 13:15; Acts 28:27.

ptyssō πτύσσω 4428

ptyssō is a rare verb found only in Luke 4:20 indicating the action of "closing" a book.

COVER, COVER UP

kalyptō καλύπτω 2572

kalyptō is a verb found eleven times meaning "cover," "hide."

A boat is said to be "swamped" (i.e., covered) by waves in Matt 8:24. The phenomenon of one's sins "being covered" is indicated in Jas 5:20; 1 Pet 4:8. 2 Cor 4:3 refers to the state of spiritual blindness inflicted on unbelievers whose minds "are veiled" (i.e., covered) by sin, impervious to the light of the gospel. See also Matt 10:26; Luke 8:16; 23:30.

▸ **64.** Reveal, Explain, Hiddenness, Secrecy > HIDE, CONCEAL, COVER

perikalyptō περικαλύπτω 4028

perikalyptō is a variant of ***kalyptō*** (above). It is found three times and means "to completely cover" or "cover up." The "covering up" of one's face is indicated in Mark 14:65. The ark of the covenant is described as "being covered" with gold in Heb 9:4. Luke 22:64 refers to the "blindfolding" of Christ.

▸ **85.** Movement, Position, State > OVERLAY

SEE ALSO

▸ **35.** Clothing, Adornment, Textiles > COVER, VEIL, CURTAIN, MANTLE
katakalyptō, peribolaion

▸ **44.** Repentance, Forgiveness, Mercy, Redeem, Save > COVER, FORGIVE
epikalyptō

▸ **64.** Reveal, Explain, Hiddenness, Secrecy > HIDE, CONCEAL, COVER
synkalyptō

FLY

petomai πέτομαι 4072

The verb ***petomai*** is found in five places and means "to fly" in each context, all of them metaphorical. Rev 4:7; 12:14 refer to a "flying" eagle, the latter text denoting the wings of an eagle bearing the mother of the messianic Christ child away from the clutches of the satanic dragon. Rev 8:13; 14:6 refer to "flying" angels. Rev 19:17 speaks of "flying" birds attacking the corpses of Satan's armies.

GO, WALK, GO BEFORE

poreuomai πορεύομαι 4198

poreuomai is a common verb with the mundane sense of "go," as well as some metaphorical usage, for most of its nearly 150 occurrences. The meaning "go," with the underlying sense of "walk," "make a journey (short or long)" is found, for example, in Matt 2:8ff.; 11:4ff.; Mark 16:12; Luke 1:39; 9:51ff.; John 8:1; Acts 5:20; 19:21; Rom 15:24ff.; 1 Cor 10:27; 1 Tim 1:3. See also 1 Pet 3:19.

The specific sense of "depart," "go away" (i.e., on an errand, or journey) is found in Matt 25:41; John 4:50; 8:11; Acts 5:41; 8:36ff. Of special note is Christ's intention to "leave" this world in order to facilitate the permanent coming of the Holy Spirit into the world (John 16:7, 28). See also Acts 1:10ff.; 1 Pet 3:22.

In particular, see Christ's command to his disciples to "go and make disciples of all nations," in the context of their lifelong mission (Matt 28:19; Mark 16:15). See also Acts 28:26.

The metaphorical sense of "walk" indicating a lifestyle of "living in obedience to God's commands" is evident in Luke 1:6. See Acts 14:16 for the meaning "to live according to one's own ways." The specifically negative sense of "living" contrary to God's ways is found in 1 Pet 4:3; 2 Pet 2:10; 3:3; Jude 16ff.

The exhortation and blessing "go in peace" is found in Luke 8:48; Acts 16:36.

▸ **86.** Movement Toward or Away From > JOURNEY

proagō προάγω 4254

proagō is a verb found in eighteen places with the primary meaning "go before."

Matt 2:9 describes the progress of the star from the east "going before" the magi to the place of Jesus' birth.

Mundane references to the physical spatial movement of "going before" are found in Matt 14:22; 21:9; 26:32; Mark 6:45; 10:32; 14:28; 16:7.

The temporal sense of "go before" is evident in Matt 21:31, referring to harlots and tax-collectors who will go into heaven before the hypocritical Pharisees.

▸ **86.** Movement Toward or Away From > BRING, BROUGHT

peripateō περιπατέω 4043

The verb ***peripateō*** occurs around one hundred times with the general, literal sense of "walk (about)," "go," "make one's way." It also means "to live," "conduct one's life" (for good or ill).

Literal references to "walking" include those in Matt 4:18; Mark 1:16; 6:48ff.; Luke 7:22; John 1:36; 10:23; Acts 3:6ff. Mark 12:38; Luke 20:46 refer to the Pharisees "walking about," "parading themselves." ***peripateō*** also refers metaphorically to the devil seeking out his victims (1 Pet 5:8).

peripateō is more frequently used in the figurative sense of "walk," indicating the conduct of one's lifestyle, orienting it towards a particular goal (Acts 21:21; 1 Cor 3:3). Examples include the phenomenon of "walking in the light," denoting a godly lifestyle (John 12:35; Eph 5:8; 1 John 1:7; Rev 21:24); and "walking in darkness," suggesting a sinful lifestyle (John 8:12; 11:10; 1 John 1:6; 2:11). See also 2 Cor 4:2. "Walking in accord with the flesh" also indicates a depraved lifestyle (Rom 8:4; 2 Cor 10:2; Eph 2:2; Col 3:7).

Other references to godly living include "walking in the Spirit" (Gal 5:16); "walking in newness of life in Christ" (Rom 6:4); and "walking worthy of the Lord" (Col 1:10). See also Rom 13:13; Eph 2:10; Col 4:5; 1 Thess 4:1; 2 John 6. "Walking by faith" is indicated in 2 Cor 5:7.

stoicheō στοιχέω 4748

stoicheō is a verb found five times, used exclusively in the figurative sense of "walk," or engaging in a particular way of life.

"Walking (i.e., living) in accordance with the law of God" is indicated in Acts 21:24; living in harmony with the implications of the new creation in Christ is noted in Gal 6:16 (see also Phil 3:16). Rom 4:12 exhorts the reader to follow the example of Abraham's faith (lit., "to walk in the footsteps of"). And Gal 5:25 commends "walking (i.e., living) in the spirit."

dierchomai διέρχομαι 1330

dierchomai is a verb occurring around fifty times with the general sense of "go," "pass," "walk through," or "travel," used both literally and figuratively.

General references to this activity are found in Luke 4:30; John 4:4; Acts 8:40; 13:6; 19:1. Specific examples of "traveling" are noted in Acts 11:19; 14:24; 15:41. Evil spirits are said to "pass or walk through" arid regions (Matt 12:43; Luke 11:24); and Israel's "passing through" the Re(e)d Sea is noted in 1 Cor 10:1.

dierchomai also refers to Christ "passing through" the heavens (Heb 4:14); and to the unlikely phenomenon of a camel "passing through the eye of a needle" (Matt 19:24; Mark 10:25).

Mark 4:35; Luke 8:12; 9:6 refer literally to "going, or walking across" a geographic location.

▸ **75.** Suffering, Distress, Sadness > PIERCE
▸ **85.** Movement, Position, State > PASS, PASS BY, PASS THROUGH, CROSS OVER
▸ **85.** Movement, Position, State > TRAVEL, TRAVELER

GROW, INCREASE

auxanō αὐξάνω 837

auxanō is a verb found about twenty times meaning "grow (up)," "increase," both literally and metaphorically, in a variety of contexts.

References to plants "growing," "increasing" (in size) are found in Matt 6:28; 13:32; Mark 4:8; Luke 12:27; 13:19.

The physical development (i.e., growth) of a child is indicated in Luke 1:80 (i.e., John the Baptist) and Luke 2:40 (Jesus).

The sense of "increase" in importance is indicated in relation to Jesus in John 3:30. In Acts 6:7; 12:24; 19:20 the meaning "increase" signifies a growth in impact or effect in relation to the preaching of God's word. This sense is applied to people in Acts 7:17, referring to the numerical expansion of the Israelites in Egypt. The "growth" or "expansion" of the early church is indicated in 1 Cor 3:6ff.

The metaphorical sense of "increase" is found in 2 Cor 9:10 in relation to people's righteousness; to faith in 2 Cor 10:15; and to knowledge in Col 1:10. The concept of the spiritual community of God's people "growing" into a holy temple in the Lord is indicated in Eph 2:21. See also Eph 4:15; Col 2:19; 1 Pet 2:2; 2 Pet 3:18 for similar contexts.

▸ **7.** Quantity, Amount, Number, Size, Measure > INCREASE, GROW

hyperauxanō ὑπεραυξάνω 5232

hyperauxanō is a rare variant of ***auxanō*** (above), found only in 2 Thess 1:3, with reference to the faith of the Thessalonian congregation "growing abundantly."

SEE ALSO

▸ **28.** Agriculture, Viticulture, Animal Husbandry > GROW, SPROUT, SPRING UP
synauxanō, anabainō, mēkynō

HANG

kremannymi κρεμάννυμι 2910

This is an uncommon verb occurring only seven times, meaning to "hang" in both a literal and metaphorical sense.

The meaning "hanged" in reference to execution is found in Luke 23:39, concerning the criminals who died with Jesus on the cross. In Acts 5:30; 10:39, ***kremannymi*** refers to Jesus himself. Gal 3:13 quotes the covenant sanction from the book of Deuteronomy: "Cursed is every one who is hung on a tree" (Deut 21:23). Matt 18:6 describes the "ideal" punishment for those who hinder little children from entering the kingdom of God — having a millstone hung around their neck and being cast into the sea.

Matt 22:40 contains the following affirmation from the teaching of Jesus: "On these two commandments hang all the law . . ." Here, ***kremannymi*** is used metaphorically to indicate "hang" in the sense of "derive significance from" or "depend on."

In Acts 28:4, ***kremannymi*** refers to the snake hanging from Paul's arm on the beach in Malta.

perikeimai περίκειμαι 4029

This term means "be hanged" in two of the five contexts in which it occurs (Mark 9:42; Luke 17:2). Both texts refer to the fate of those who actively turn people away from belief and trust in Christ (see ***kremannymi***, above).

▸ **85.** Movement, Position, State > SURROUND, ENCIRCLE

SEE ALSO

▸ **21.** Die, Perish, Kill, Destroy > HANG
apanchō

LIE, LIE DOWN, RECLINE

katakeimai κατάκειμαι 2621

katakeimai means "lie down," "recline." The former sense applies to those who are prostrate with illness or disability, the latter to those who are reclining at a meal table. ***katakeimai*** occurs eleven times.

Mark 1:30; 2:4; Luke 5:25; John 5:3, 6; Acts 9:33; 28:8 refer to those who are lying down, stricken with illness or infirmity. Mark 2:15; 14:3; Luke 5:29; 1 Cor 8:10 describe guests reclining at a meal.

▸ **85.** Movement, Position, State > SIT, SIT DOWN, SIT UP

keimai κεῖμαι 2749

keimai is found in fifteen contexts with the basic sense of "lie (down)" or "lay" that includes a variety of literal and metaphorical contexts with both an active and passive force.

General references to the action of lying down, or the position of lying down, are indicated, for example, in Matt 28:6; Luke 23:53, concerning the body of Christ lying in the tomb, dead. Luke 2:12, 16 describe the infant Jesus lying in a manger. Jesus' grave clothes are said to lie in the tomb in Luke 24:12; John 20:5ff. See also John 21:19.

Metaphorical usage of ***keimai*** is evident, first of all, in the context of divine judgment. With respect to the wickedness of Jewish society at the outset of Jesus' public ministry, John the Baptist indicates in Matt 3:10; Luke 3:9 that "the ax is laid at the root of the trees." In 2 Cor 3:15, Paul declares that a veil of spiritual darkness "lies" over the minds of unbelievers. 1 John 5:19 affirms that the world "lies" in the power of the evil one.

Secondly, in more neutral and positive contexts, 1 Cor 3:11 states that no other foundation is possible for gospel ministry other than that which is already laid, that of Jesus Christ himself. 1 Tim 1:9 states that the law has been laid down for the wicked. In Rev 21:16, the heavenly city is described as being laid out like a square. Finally, ***keimai*** refers in Matt 5:14 to a city set on a hill.

▸ **83.** Set, Put, Place, Prepare, Establish > SET

OPEN

anoigō ἀνοίγω 455

anoigō is the most common term in the NT meaning "to open." ***anoigō*** occurs about eighty times.

anoigō is used in a literal, mundane sense in Matt 2:11; 17:27; Luke 12:36; John 10:3; Acts 12:10. The resurrection of the woman Tabitha from the dead through the agency of the apostle Peter is accompanied by the reference to her "opening her eyes" (Acts 9:40). A metaphorical reference to opening the eyes of the blind is found in Acts 26:18 as part of the mission of the messianic Servant (quoted from Isa 42:7).

The expression "to open one's mouth" is found in a number of contexts. It is used in the description of Jesus' public teaching ministry (Matt 5:2; 13:5). Others are also said to open their mouths in order to speak — for example, Philip the evangelist (Acts 8:35); Peter (Acts 10:34); and Paul (Acts 8:14). In a citation from Isa 53:7, the messianic Servant's silence before his tormentors is noted in the phrase "he opened not his mouth." In Rev 13:6, the satanic sea beast is said to open his mouth in order to blaspheme.

Other significant uses of ***anoigō*** describe the action of "opening." In Rev 3:7, for example, it is used in an absolute sense to indicate the exercise of power and authority. Rev 3:20 contains the divine injunction "to open the door" of one's heart and life as a prelude to enjoying the intimate fellowship of the indwelling spirit of Christ. The divine challenge "to open the scroll" is recorded in Rev 5:2ff., and only the Lamb of God is capable of doing so. The "opening of the seals" of divine judgment is described in Rev 6:1ff.; 8:1. In Rev 9:2, the angelic "star" is given a key to open the bottomless pit of destruction.

anoigō is also used in the passive voice. The heavens are said to be opened by God, for example, in John 1:51; Acts 7:56; 10:11 in relation to divine revelation. In Rev 4:1; 19:11, John declares that he "saw heaven opened" as a prelude to further visionary revelation. Such a phenomenon is also recorded at the baptism of Jesus (Matt 3:16; Luke 3:21). The temple in heaven is said to be opened in Rev 11:19; 15:5; as are the books of judgment in Rev 20:12.

In the aftermath of Christ's crucifixion, graves are opened by the power of God (Matt 27:52). God likewise opens prison doors in order to bring about the miraculous release of various apostles (Acts 5:19; 16:26ff.). The healing of the blind was a significant element in the healing ministry of Jesus. Several texts declare that the eyes of the blind were opened (Matt 9:30; 20:33; John 9:10ff.; 10:21; 11:37). Saul also experienced such a healing at the time of his conversion (Acts 9:8). See also Luke 1:64.

Impersonal metaphorical uses of ***anoigō*** are found in a couple of places. The expression ". . . knock and it shall be opened to you" in Matt 7:7; Luke 11:9 conveys the truth that the knowledge of God and his way of salvation shall be made available to all those who seriously long for it. 1 Cor 16:9; 2 Cor 2:12 refer to a door (of opportunity) being opened for Paul.

anoigō is used adjectivally in Rom 3:13, referring to the throats of the wicked as "an open grave." Rev 3:8 speaks of an "open door of opportunity."

schizō σχίζω 4977

schizō is a verb with the principal sense of "tear" or "divide." It occurs ten times. In Mark 11:10, however, it refers to the heavens being "opened" at the baptism of Christ. The likely underlying meaning is that the heavens were spectacularly "torn apart."

▸ **27.** Community, Partnership, Unity, Discord > DIVIDE, DIVISIVE, DIVISION
▸ **35.** Clothing, Adornment, Textiles > TEAR

dianoigō διανοίγω 1272

dianoigō is a variant form of ***anoigō*** (above) meaning "to open" in both the active and passive voice. The term occurs eight times.

In Mark 7:34, 35, Jesus cures a deaf mute. He commands that the man's ears be opened, and the miraculous restoration immediately follows. Luke 2:23 refers to the sanctity of the firstborn male child, or the male "that opens the womb." Luke 24:31 records the enlightening of the two disciples of Christ on the road to Emmaus, who met the risen Lord but did not initially recognize him. The text records that "their eyes were opened" and they recognized him. Similarly, in Luke 24:45, the Lord "opened their minds" to understand the Scriptures. See also Luke 24:32; Acts 16:14. In Acts 17:3, ***dianoigō*** means "explain" with reference to Paul "opening" the Scriptures in order to demonstrate that Jesus was the Christ.

anaptyssō ἀναπτύσσω 380

anaptyssō is found only in Luke 4:17, where it refers literally to "unrolling" the scroll of Isaiah by Jesus, hence the translation "he opened the book."

OVERLAY

perikalyptō περικαλύπτω 4028

perikalyptō is found in only three places. This verb means "to cover" or "blindfold (one's face)" in two of these contexts. But in Heb 9:4 it refers to the ark of the covenant "overlaid" with gold.

▸ **85.** Movement, Position, State > COVER, COVER UP

PASS, PASS BY, PASS THROUGH, CROSS OVER

parerchomai παρέρχομαι 3928

parerchomai means to "pass," "pass away," "pass by" in around thirty contexts.

The principal meaning ***parerchomai*** is that of "pass away," with the underlying sense of "vanish" or "disappear." It is applied, for example, to the apocalyptic passing of the created heaven and earth at the end of time (Matt 5:18; 24:35; Luke 16:15; 21:33; 2 Pet 3:10; Rev 21:1). Such a passing is also attributed to the old covenant reign of the Mosaic law (2 Cor 5:17). Conversely, such a passing is denied in the case of the generation of Jesus' day, of whom it is said they "will not pass away" until the ministry of Christ is fulfilled on earth (Matt 24:34; Luke 21:32; Mark 13:30). Similarly, the teaching of Jesus will not pass away (Mark 13:31; Luke 21:33). See also Jas 1:10.

The meaning "pass by" in the sense of physical movement or passing is found in Matt 8:28; Mark 6:48; Luke 18:37; Acts 16:8. A significant use of ***parerchomai*** is found in Matt 26:39; Mark 14:38 with reference to Jesus' momentary prayer to let the "cup" of his suffering "pass him by."

Mundane references to the passing of time are found in Matt 14:15; 1 Pet 4:3.

dierchomai διέρχομαι 1330

dierchomai is a synonym for ***parerchomai*** (above) translated "to pass," "pass through," mostly with the underlying sense of "walk" or "go."

The literal sense of "pass through" in the context of traveling or walking is indicated in Matt 12:43; 19:24; Mark 4:35; Luke 17:11; 19:14; John 4:4; Acts 8:40; 14:24; 19:1. 1 Cor 10:11 mentions Israel passing through the Re(e)d Sea in their escape from the Egyptian army. In a spiritual context, Heb 4:14 refers to Jesus "passing through" the heavens and establishing his ministry as our great high priest.

There is one metaphorical use of ***dierchomai*** in Rom 5:12, which indicates that the disobedience of Adam has caused the "spread" (i.e., passing) of sin and death to all human beings.

▸ **75.** Suffering, Distress, Sadness > PIERCE
▸ **85.** Movement, Position, State > TRAVEL, TRAVELER
▸ **85.** Movement, Position, State > GO, WALK, GO BEFORE

diabainō διαβαίνω 1224

diabainō occurs only three times and is translated "pass through" in Heb 11:29 in relation to Israel crossing the Re(e)d Sea. It also means to "cross over" in the sense of "traveling, or going across to" in Luke 16:26; Acts 16:29.

diaperaō διαπεράω 1276

diaperaō is a verb that means "pass, or cross over" in the context of sailing a boat. This sense is found in five of the six occurrences of ***diaperaō*** (Matt 9:1; 14:34; Mark 5:21; 6:53; Acts 21:2). See also Luke 16:26.

paragō παράγω 3855

paragō means "pass on," "pass by," "pass away" in the ten places in which it occurs.

The literal sense of "pass by" is found in Matt 9:9; 20:30; Mark 2:14; 15:21; John 8:59; 9:1. The meaning "pass on" in the sense of "depart" is found in Matt 9:27. 1 Cor 7:3; 1 John 2:17 refer to the world "passing away" or "vanishing"; and in 1 John 2:8 the same thing is said of the darkness.

paraporeuomai παραπορεύομαι 3899

paraporeuomai occurs five times, meaning "pass through" in Mark 2:23; 9:30, and "pass by" in Matt 27:39; Mark 11:20.

antiparerchomai ἀντιπαρέρχομαι 492

antiparerchomai occurs only in Luke 10:31, 32, meaning "to pass by on the other side."

metabainō μεταβαίνω 3327

metabainō is a verb that occurs twelve times and has the primary sense of "leave" or "depart." However, it twice means "pass from," in the context of the promised transition from death to life (John 5:24; 1 John 3:14).

▸ **86.** Movement Toward or Away From > LEAVE, GO AWAY, LEAVE BEHIND, ABANDON

diodeuō διοδεύω 1353

diodeuō occurs only in Luke 8:1; Acts 17:1, meaning "pass through," "go through."

aperchomai ἀπέρχομαι 565

aperchomai is a much more common verb form, meaning "go," "depart" in the majority of the 120 occurrences of the term. However, Rev 21:4 refers to the former things "passing away," speaking of the demise of the created heaven and earth.

▸ **86.** Movement Toward or Away From > LEAVE, GO AWAY, LEAVE BEHIND, ABANDON

REMAIN, STAY, ABIDE, DWELL

menō μένω 3306

The verb ***menō*** is a common term meaning "abide," "dwell," "remain" in most of its 120 occurrences. There is a degree of overlap between these meanings. However, there are contexts where the sense of "remain" is distinct.

The meaning "remain" in the sense of "be preserved" is indicated hypothetically in the case of the city of Sodom in Matt 11:23; and also literally in regard to the earthly destiny of the disciple John (John 21:23).

The idea of remaining unmarried is found in 1 Cor 7:11 (see also 1 Cor 7:20, 24).

More commonly, ***menō*** is translated "remain" in the senses of "stay," "rest on," in several contexts. ***menō*** refers to staying in a house as a guest (Luke 10:7; 19:5; John 2:12; 4:40; Acts 9:43); or more generally, to staying in a particular place (John 8:31; 10:40). John 1:32 refers to the Spirit coming to permanently "rest on" the person of Christ. Paul's determination to "stay" with the Philippian congregation for the purposes of nurturing them is indicated in Phil 1:25. John 19:31 refers to the Mosaic legislation that forbids allowing bodies to remain on a cross of execution during the Sabbath day.

Where believers are concerned, their state of "remaining" in Christ, referring to their intimate relationship with him, is indicated in John 6:56; 1 John 2:24, 28; 3:6ff. Conversely, unbelievers are said to "remain" in darkness (John 12:46); and 2 Cor 3:14 affirms that the veil of unbelief remains over their understanding.

menō is also predicated of Christ and God. God's word is said to remain in the heart and life of the believer (1 John 2:24); as is God's love (1 John 3:17). In a negative context, the unbeliever is denied the presence of God's word in his heart (John 5:38). God himself is said to remain faithful (2 Tim 2:13); and John 12:35 declares that Christ remains forever.

The qualities of faith, hope, and love are said to remain, or endure (1 Cor 13:13). John 9:41 refers to guilt remaining.

▸ **4.** Beginning, Continuing, Finishing, Postponing > CONTINUE, REMAIN

▸ **4.** Beginning, Continuing, Finishing, Postponing > ENDURE, REMAIN

▸ **24.** Dwell, Live, Gather, Hospitality > ABIDE, STAY, REMAIN

▸ **24.** Dwell, Live, Gather, Hospitality > DWELL, DWELLING

perisseuō περισσεύω 4052

perisseuō is a verb found in approximately forty places with the predominant sense of "abound." It also has a number of additional nuances, including "to remain" in the sense of "be left over."

The meaning "remain" here is applied exclusively to the food left over after Jesus' miraculous provision of food for the multitude in Matt 14:20; 15:37; Luke 9:17; John 6:12ff.

▸ **7.** Quantity, Amount, Number, Size, Measure > ABOUND, INCREASE, EXCEED, OVERFLOW, ABUNDANCE

▸ **7.** Quantity, Amount, Number, Size, Measure > EXCEED, EXCEEDINGLY

▸ **7.** Quantity, Amount, Number, Size, Measure > INCREASE, GROW

▸ **23.** Food, Drink, Cooking > SPARE

perileipō περιλείπω 4035

perileipō is a verb found only twice, in 1 Thess 4:15, 17, referring to those who "remain" (i.e., who are still alive) at the time of Christ's return.

diamenō διαμένω 1265

diamenō is a variant form of ***menō*** (above) occurring five times and meaning "to remain" in the sense of "continue in the same state, or condition." Luke 1:22 refers to Zechariah the priest remaining in his mute condition. Jesus commends his disciples in Luke 22:28 for remaining with him in his trials. Gal 2:5 speaks of the importance of the truth of the gospel remaining with the Galatians. Heb 1:11 refers to God remaining unchangeable. 2 Pet 3:4 also speaks of the unchanging nature of the cosmos since the beginning of creation.

apoleipō ἀπολείπω 620

apoleipō is a verb translated "leave" or "remain" in the six occurrences of the term.

The meaning "remain" is used impersonally in Heb 4:6, 9 in the declaration: "There remains a Sabbath rest for the people of God." Heb 10:26 contains the negative affirmation that "there remains" no sacrifice for sin, once a person actively abandons his relationship with Christ.

▸ **86.** Movement Toward or Away From > LEAVE, GO AWAY, LEAVE BEHIND, ABANDON

loipos λοιπός 3062

loipos is a noun found approximately forty times, meaning "rest" in several of these contexts. The sense here is "that which remains," or "those that remain." Where people are concerned, ***loipos*** means "the rest" in the sense of "the remainder," "those who are left" (Matt 22:6; Mark

16:13; Luke 24:9; Acts 2:37; Rom 11:7; 1 Cor 7:12; Rev 12:17; 19:21).

Impersonal phenomena are also included in the usage of ***loipos***, meaning "the rest" or "(the) other things" (Luke 12:26; 1 Cor 11:34).

SEE ALSO

▸ **15.** Gender, Reproduction, Youth, Aging > REST
epiloipos

REMNANT

kataleimma κατάλειμμα 2640

kataleimma is a noun found only in Rom 9:27, referring to the "remnant" of Israel that alone will be saved.

leimma λεῖμμα 3005

leimma is a variant form of ***kataleimma*** (above) found only in Rom 11:27 with reference to a "remnant" of God's people chosen by grace.

REST

epanapauomai ἐπαναπαύομαι 1879

epanapauomai is another rare verb, occurring in only two places. Luke 10:6 speaks of peace resting upon a gracious host. Rom 2:17 warns against "resting" (i.e., relying) on the law for one's salvation.

episkēnoō ἐπισκηνόω 1981

episkēnoō is a verb found only in 2 Cor 12:9, where Paul speaks of the power of Christ "resting" upon him.

SEE ALSO

▸ **20.** Illness, Disease, Health, Healing > REST
anapauō, anapausis, katapausis, katapauō, anesis, sabbatismos, hēsychazō

RUN

trechō τρέχω 5143

trechō is a verb found in twenty contexts, meaning "to run" in most of these. It also has a number of derivative forms (see below).

The literal, physical action of running is indicated in Matt 27:48; 28:8; Mark 5:6; 15:36; Luke 15:20; 24:12; John 20:2ff.; 1 Cor 9:24ff.

The meaning "rush" is also indicated in Rev 9:9, referring to horses rushing headlong into battle.

trechō also has a figurative sense in Gal 2:2; 5:7; Phil 2:16; Heb 12:1, with reference to "running" the race. In these contexts, the metaphorical allusion is to the goal of maintaining one's faith in Christ throughout the whole course of life.

episyntrechō ἐπισυντρέχω 1998

episyntrechō occurs only in Mark 9:25 with the sense of "run together," referring to a crowd.

syntrechō συντρέχω 4936

syntrechō is found in only three places, meaning "to run together" in a literal sense in Mark 6:33; Acts 3:11. In 1 Pet 4:4, the term means "to join together" in the context of participating in a lifestyle — in this case a profligate one.

peritrechō περιτρέχω 4063

peritrechō is found only in Mark 6:55, meaning "to run through" a neighboring vicinity.

protrechō προτρέχω 4390

protrechō means "to outrun," "run ahead of," and is found only in Luke 19:4; John 20:4.

SEE ALSO

▸ **7.** Quantity, Amount, Number, Size, Measure > OVERFLOW, RUN OVER
hyperekchynnō

▸ **29.** Boats, Fishing, Maritime Activity > RUN UNDER, RUN AGROUND
hypotrechō, epikellō

▸ **86.** Movement Toward or Away From > RUN, RUN TOWARD, RUN DOWN
prostrechō, eistrechō, katatrechō, hormaō

SHAKE

saleuō σαλεύω 4531

saleuō is a verb meaning "shake" in a variety of contexts. It is found fifteen times.

Literal "shaking" involves the effect of the wind (Matt 11:7; Luke 7:24); rising floodwaters (Luke 6:48); an earthquake (Acts 16:26); and the Holy Spirit (Acts 4:31). See also Heb 12:26; Luke 6:38.

In metaphorical contexts, ***saleuō*** refers to the powers of heaven "being shaken" by the impact of the Day of the Lord (Matt 24:49; Mark 13:25; Luke 21:26). In Acts 2:25, ***saleuō*** is used negatively — David's confidence in God is said "not to be shaken," for he was protected by God from destruction.

▸ **27.** Community, Partnership, Unity, Discord > STIR UP

seiō σείω 4579

seiō is a verb found in five contexts meaning "shake," "quake" in all but one place.

seiō refers to an earthquake (Matt 27:51); to overturning nations (Heb 12:26); to the emotion of fear (Matt 28:4); and to the effect of strong wind (Rev 6:13).

▸ **9.** Land, Geography, Topography > QUAKE

SEE ALSO

▸ **79.** Throw, Send, Drive, Mix, Remove > SHAKE OFF, SHAKE OUT
ektinassō, apotinassō

SHUT

kleiō κλείω 2808

kleiō is a verb meaning "shut," "shut up" in most of its nineteen occurrences.

Literal references to shutting a door are found in Matt 6:6; 25:10; Luke 11:7; John 20:19ff.; Acts 5:23; 21:30.

The remaining uses of ***kleiō*** are metaphorical. Matt 23:13 refers to "shutting" the kingdom of God in people's faces. Rev 3:7ff. refers to "closing the entrance" to the kingdom of heaven by royal, messianic authority. Rev 20:3 refers to Satan's "confinement" in the bottomless abyss. Rev 21:25 affirms that the gates of the heavenly Jerusalem will never be shut. See also Luke 4:25; Rev 11:6.

apokleiō ἀποκλείω 608

apokleiō is a variant form of ***kleiō*** (above) found only in Luke 13:25 with reference to "shutting" the door.

SEE ALSO

▸ **32.** Law, Justice, Jurisprudence, Judgment > SHUT UP, CONFINE
katakleiō

SIT, SIT DOWN, SIT UP

kathēmai κάθημαι 2521

kathēmai is a verb found nearly ninety times with the underlying meaning "sit," as well as associated nuances.

The mundane sense of "sitting down" is evident in Matt 4:16; Mark 2:6; Luke 5:27; John 6:3; Acts 2:2; 8:28.

The risen Christ sits on (i.e., rides) a horse (Rev 19:11, 21) as the apocalyptic "rider on the white horse." Jesus rides on a donkey in fulfillment of OT prophecy (John 12:15; see Zech 9:9).

Other metaphorical uses of ***kathēmai*** include those in Matt 4:16; Luke 1:79, referring to people "sitting in darkness" (i.e., spiritual blindness). The "great harlot" Babylon is described in Rev 17:9 as "seated" on seven mountains. See also Rev 17:3, 15. The "Son of Man" is described as sitting on the clouds of heaven in Rev 14:14ff.

The privileged position of "sitting at the right hand of God" is referred to in Matt 22:44; 26:64; Mark 12:36; Luke 20:42; 22:69; Acts 2:34; Heb 1:13. God is portrayed as sitting on his throne in Matt 23:22; Mark 14:62; Rev 4:2ff.; 5:1, 13; 6:16; 7:10, 15; 19:4; 20:11; 21:5.

synkathēmai συγκάθημαι 4775

synkathēmai is a variant form of ***kathēmai*** (above) meaning "sit together with" in Mark 14:54; Acts 26:30.

kathizō καθίζω 2523

kathizō is a verb synonymous with ***kathēmai*** (above) occurring around fifty times and meaning "sit," "sit down" in most contexts.

Mundane references to sitting down include those in Matt 5:1; Luke 4:20; Acts 13:14; 1 Cor 10:7.

kathizō refers to "sitting on thrones" in various contexts — in relation to an earthly ruler (Acts 12:21); to the saints in glory (Luke 22:30; Rev 20:4); and to the Son of Man upon his throne (Matt 19:28). The privileged position of sitting at the right hand of the Son of Man in glory is noted in Matt 20:21ff.; 25:31; Mark 10:37ff. ***kathizō*** also refers to Christ sitting on his throne at the right hand of God (Mark 16:19; Heb 1:3; 10:12; Rev 3:21).

synkathizō συγκαθίζω 4776

synkathizō is a variant form of ***kathizō*** (above). It is found only twice and means "sit (down) together with" in a literal sense in Luke 22:55. Eph 2:6 mentions the believer's spiritual status of "sitting with Christ" in the heavenly places.

anakathizō ἀνακαθίζω 339

anakathizō is another variant of ***kathizō*** (above). It means "sit up" and is found only twice, in Luke 7:15; Acts 9:40.

parakathizō παρακαθίζω 3869

parakathizō is a rare variant of ***kathizō*** found only in Luke 10:39 with the sense of "sit down at, or beside."

anakeimai ἀνάκειμαι 345

anakeimai is a verb occurring fourteen times. It means "sit down" in the context of sharing a meal or banquet in the majority of these contexts (Matt 9:10; 26:7, 20; Mark 14:18; 16:18; Luke 7:37; 22:27; John 6:11; 13:28).

▸ **24.** Dwell, Live, Gather, Hospitality > RECLINE, SHARE A MEAL

katakeimai κατάκειμαι 2621

katakeimai is a variant of ***anakeimai*** (above). It is found in eleven places and means "lie (down)" in most of these. In four contexts, however, ***katakeimai*** indicates the sense of "sit down" (i.e., at a table for a meal) (Mark 2:15; 14:3; Luke 5:29; 1 Cor 8:10).

▸ **85.** Movement, Position, State > LIE, LIE DOWN, RECLINE

anaklinō ἀνακλίνω 347

anaklinō is a verb synonymous with the entries above, meaning "sit down" in the context of feasting in seven places (Matt 8:11; Mark 6:39; Luke 7:36; 9:15; 12:37; 13:29). See also Matt 14:19.

kathezomai καθέζομαι 2516

kathezomai is a verb with the sense of "sit down" (i.e., take one's seat), found in six places (Matt 26:55; Luke 2:46; John 4:6; 11:20; 20:12; Acts 6:15).

SEE ALSO

▸ **23.** Food, Drink, Cooking > SIT
synanakeimai, kataklinō, anapiptō

STAND

histēmi ἵστημι 2476

histēmi is the most common NT term meaning "to stand." It occurs in nearly 160 places in a variety of contexts with a number of nuances.

Mundane references to "standing" include those in Matt 2:6; Mark 1:5; Luke 7:38; John 1:26; Acts 1:11. See also Luke 1:11; Acts 7:33; Rev 12:4.

The meaning "stand" in the sense of "endure," "last," is indicated negatively in Matt 12:25; Mark 3:24ff.; Luke 11:18, where it is declared that a divided kingdom can never stand.

The process of "standing trial" is noted in Acts 26:6; and Rev 6:17 speaks of standing before the judgment of God. Rev 7:9ff. depicts the heavenly host of saints standing before the throne of God in worship.

With reference to the person of Christ, Acts 7:55ff. refers to him standing at the right hand of God (see also Rev 14:1). He is also said to stand at the door of the believer's heart in Rev 3:20.

The believer is exhorted to "stand" in the grace of God (i.e., live day by day in dependence on him) in Rom 5:2; 1 Pet 5:12. Similarly, 1 Cor 15:1 speaks of "standing" in the gospel. The believer is exhorted to "stand fast" in his faith (Rom 11:20; 2 Cor 1:24), and also to "stand against" (i.e., oppose) the trickery of the devil (Eph 6:11ff.).

In relation to the person of God, his foundation (i.e., his purposes in salvation) is said to stand firm (2 Tim 2:19).

▸ **70.** Give, Take, Seize, Touch > PRESENT
▸ **83.** Set, Put, Place, Prepare, Establish > APPOINT, ORDAIN, ASSIGN
▸ **83.** Set, Put, Place, Prepare, Establish > ESTABLISH, FIX, GROUND, STRENGTHEN
▸ **83.** Set, Put, Place, Prepare, Establish > SET

paristēmi παρίστημι 3936

paristēmi is a variant form of ***histēmi*** (above) occurring around forty-five times and meaning "stand," "stand by" in about one-third of these contexts.

Literal references to "standing by, or near" include those in Mark 14:47; Luke 19:24; John 18:22; Acts 1:10. Luke 1:19 refers to Gabriel "standing" in the presence of God. See also 2 Tim 4:17.

▸ **47.** Show, Persuade, Confidence, Doubt > SHOW
▸ **70.** Give, Take, Seize, Touch > PRESENT

ephistēmi ἐφίστημι 2186

ephistēmi is a verb occurring around twenty times, meaning "come (upon)," and "stand," "stand over." Luke 4:39 refers to "standing over" someone; and Luke 24:4; Acts 10:17; 22:13, 20; 23:11 refer to "standing by, or alongside."

synistēmi συνίστημι 4921

synistēmi is a verb meaning "to commend" in most of its sixteen occurrences. However, in Luke 9:32 it means "to stand alongside with."

periistēmi περιΐστημι 4026

periistēmi is a verb occurring four times, meaning "stand," "stand around" (John 11:42; Acts 25:7).

▸ **49.** Allow, Accept, Approve, Refuse > AVOID

stēkō στήκω 4739

stēkō is a verb found eight times meaning "stand fast," "stand by" throughout.

The position of "standing" in prayer is noted in Mark 11:25.

The metaphorical sense of "stand" is found in Rom 14:4 in relation to sustaining or maintaining one's office with integrity. In addition, 1 Cor 16:13; Gal 5:1; 2 Thess 2:15; Phil 4:1 encourage "standing firm" in one's faith. Phil 1:27 encourages "standing firm" in the unity of the Spirit.

SURROUND, ENCIRCLE

kykloō κυκλόω 2944

kykloō is a verb found five times meaning "surround," "encircle."

Luke 21:20 refers to the future "surrounding" of Jerusalem predicted by Christ. Heb 11:30 refers to the Israelites of old "encircling" Jericho. John 10:24; Acts 14:20 refer to "surrounding" people in general.

perikykloō περικυκλόω 4033

perikykloō is a rare variant of ***kykloō*** (above) found only in Luke 19:43 and referring to the enemies of God's people "surrounding" or "encircling" them.

perikeimai περίκειμαι 4029

perikeimai is a verb referring metaphorically in Heb 12:1 to God's people "being surrounded" by a host of faithful witnesses from the old covenant era.

▸ **85.** Movement, Position, State > HANG

TAKE WITH

symparalambanō συμπαραλαμβάνω 4838

This verb means "to take (along) with," as a companion, in all four occurrences (Acts 12:25; 15:37ff.; Gal 2:1).

SEE ALSO

▸ **35.** Clothing, Adornment, Textiles > TAKE OFF, STRIP
ekdyō

▸ **70.** Give, Take, Seize, Touch > TAKE, TAKE HOLD OF, TAKE UP, TAKE DOWN, TAKE AWAY, SNATCH
lambanō, paralambanō, analambanō, epilambanō, proslambanō, harpazō, apairō, kathaireō

▸ **79.** Throw, Send, Drive, Mix, Remove > TAKE AWAY, REMOVE
aphaireō, periaireō, parapherō

TRAVEL, TRAVELER

synekdēmos συνέκδημος 4898

synekdēmos is a rare noun found only in Acts 19:29; 2 Cor 8:19, with reference to "fellow travelers."

dierchomai διέρχομαι 1330

dierchomai is a verb with the primary sense of "pass through," "go through," occurring around fifty times. The meaning "travel through," "travel about" is found in Luke 5:15; 17:11; John 4:4; Acts 8:4; 9:32; 11:22; 19:1; 1 Cor 10:1; 16:5.

- ▸ **75.** Suffering, Distress, Sadness > PIERCE
- ▸ **85.** Movement, Position, State > PASS, PASS BY, PASS THROUGH, CROSS OVER
- ▸ **85.** Movement, Position, State > GO, WALK, GO BEFORE

apodēmeō ἀποδημέω 589

apodēmeō is a rare verb meaning "go, travel into a far country," found only in Matt 25:14.

- ▸ **9.** Land, Geography, Topography > COUNTRY, LAND
- ▸ **86.** Movement Toward or Away From > JOURNEY

UNCOVERED

akatakalyptos ἀκατακάλυπτος 177

akatakalyptos is an adjective found only in 1 Cor 11:5, 13, describing a woman's head as "uncovered" or "unveiled."

SEE ALSO

- ▸ **79.** Throw, Send, Drive, Mix, Remove > UNCOVER, REMOVE
  apostegazō

86. Movement Toward or Away From

APPROACH, DRAW NEAR, UNAPPROACHABLE

engizō ἐγγίζω 1448

The verb ***engizō*** occurs around forty times with the meanings "draw near," "approach" in the majority of these instances in a variety of contexts.

The act of "drawing near," "approaching" in a physical, geographic sense is indicated in relation to coming to Jerusalem in Matt 21:1; Mark 11:1; Luke 19:41. Other general references with this sense include Luke 7:12; 15:25; Acts 9:3. Other references to approaching people are found in Luke 12:33; 15:1; 18:40.

Elsewhere, ***engizō*** denotes the "approaching" of various times, seasons, and significant events (e.g., harvest; Matt 21:34); ceremonial festivals (Luke 22:1); the fulfillment of God's promise to Abraham (Acts 7:17); Christ's suffering and death (Luke 21:8); the final day of judgment (Luke 21:20; Rom 13:12; Heb 10:25; Jas 5:8 [regarding the return of Christ]; 1 Pet 4:7). In addition, reference to the imminent approach of the kingdom of God is indicated in Luke 10:9ff.

A general exhortation to "draw near to" God is found in Jas 4:8, with a promise that he will reciprocate. In Heb 7:19 the believer is guaranteed the right to approach God, on the basis of the person and work of Christ.

▸ **86.** Movement Toward or Away From > COME, DRAW NEAR

aprositos ἀπρόσιτος 676

aprositos is a rare adjectival form found only in 1 Tim 6:16. It refers to the light surrounding the being of God, which is "unapproachable."

ARRIVE

katantaō καταντάω 2658

katantaō is a verb found thirteen times meaning "arrive at," "come to" — designating a geographic location in most cases (Acts 16:1; 18:19ff.; 20:15; 21:7; 25:13; 26:7ff.; 27:12; 28:13). See also 1 Cor 10:11; 14:36 for "non-geographic" usage.

▸ **69.** Have, Possess, Hold, Grasp, Bear, Carry > ATTAIN, LAY HOLD OF

katapleō καταπλέω 2668

katapleō is a rare synonym of ***katantaō*** (above) found only in Luke 8:26 and also denoting "geographic arrival."

erchomai ἔρχομαι 2064

erchomai is another common verb with the primary sense of "come" in most of the nearly 650 occurrences of the term, along with various nuances. Occasionally, the meaning "come to," in the sense of "arrive at or in" a particular destination, is indicated (Matt 17:24; Mark 9:33; 10:46; Luke 2:51; John 12:1; Acts 13:13; 17:1; 20:14; 28:16).

▸ **86.** Movement Toward or Away From > COME, DRAW NEAR

paraginomai παραγίνομαι 3854

paraginomai is another synonymous term for the entries listed above. It occurs nearly forty times with the primary meaning "to come." However, in several places the term denotes the action of "arriving at" a particular location (Luke 11:6; Acts 9:26; 13:14; 14:27; 15:4; 1 Cor 16:3).

▸ **85.** Movement, Position, State > BE PRESENT, COME

BRING, BROUGHT

pherō φέρω 5342

The verb ***pherō*** means "to bring," along with related nuances, throughout its approximately sixty occurrences.

The meaning "bring" in the sense of "fetch" or "carry" — indicating movement toward the speaker — is noted generally in Matt 14:18; John 4:33; Acts 4:34. The phenomenon of "bringing glory" into the heavenly city is indicated in Rev 21:24ff. People are brought to Christ for healing in Mark 1:32; 9:17ff.; Luke 5:18.

The action of "bringing a charge or accusation against someone" is indicated in John 18:29; Acts 25:7; 2 Pet 2:11. Grain is said to "be brought forth" from good soil in Mark 4:8, as is fruit in John 12:24; 15:2ff.

▸ **29.** Boats, Fishing, Maritime Activity > DRIVE ALONG
▸ **69.** Have, Possess, Hold, Grasp, Bear, Carry > BEAR, CARRY
▸ **86.** Movement Toward or Away From > REACH, REACH OUT

katagō κατάγω 2609

katagō is another variant of the entries above, meaning "bring" in a variety of contexts, with several nuances.

The action of "bringing" ships to land, or putting in at a port, is indicated in Luke 5:11; Acts 27:3; 28:12. Acts 9:30; 22:30; 23:15, 28 describe "bringing (people) down" in the sense of "transport on a journey." Rom 10:6 refers to the attempt to "bring Christ down," to disparage or denigrate his authority and status.

proagō προάγω 4254

Although ***proagō*** usually means "go before," in three of its eighteen occurrences it signifies "to bring (someone) out, or before" and refers to Paul's appearances before several different audiences (Acts 12:6; 16:30; 25:26).

▸ **85.** Movement, Position, State > GO, WALK, GO BEFORE

prosagō προσάγω 4317

prosagō means to "bring, or lead to." In Luke 9:41 it describes how a boy is brought to Christ for healing; in Acts 16:20 it refers to Paul and Silas being arraigned before the Philippian magistrates. 1 Pet 3:18 denotes the action of Christ in "bringing" his people to God — reconciling them with him, through his death on the cross.

SEE ALSO

- ▸ **25.** Family, Marriage, Adoption, Inheritance > BRING UP, RAISE, NURTURE
  trephō, anatrephō, ektrephō
- ▸ **76.** Force, Harm, Oppress > BRING
  epagō

COME, DRAW NEAR

erchomai ἔρχομαι 2064

erchomai is a common verb meaning "come" in a variety of contexts throughout the approximately 650 occurrences of the term.

The "coming" of people is found in the context of traveling in Matt 2:2ff.; John 4:5ff.; Rom 15:22ff. Elsewhere, "coming" with a specific purpose is illustrated in relation to the Queen of Sheba's visit to Solomon (Luke 11:31); to people seeking healing from Christ (Mark 1:40; 2:3; Luke 8:47); and to those seeking baptism from John the Baptist (Luke 3:12). People come to Jesus to seek salvation (John 6:37); as well as spiritual nourishment (John 6:35; 7:37). John 3:21 speaks of those "coming" to the light of God for true spiritual illumination. John 6:44ff., 65 speak of God enabling people to "come" to him. There are blessings available for the one who "comes" in the name of the Lord.

A variety of contexts refer to the "coming" of various inanimate objects. ***erchomai*** describes the appearance of a star over the place where Christ was born in Matt 2:9. It also refers to the "coming" of faith in relation to the gospel in Gal 3:23ff.; to the arrival of the Day of the Lord (Acts 2:20); and similarly to the "coming" of the final judgment of the Lord (Matt 9:15; Mark 2:20; Luke 21:6; John 4:21ff.; 5:25). The "arrival" of the hour of Christ's suffering on the cross is noted in John 12:23; 17:1. The "coming" of a light to the world with reference to the incarnation of Christ is indicated in John 1:9, 29ff.; 3:19. The "coming" of the wrath of God is noted in Col 3:6; 1 Thess 1:10; Rev 6:17. God's voice is described as "coming out" of a cloud to commend his Son in Mark 9:7; John 12:28.

Christ's "coming" to earth in regard to his carrying out the divine plan of salvation is noted in a variety of contexts. He is said to come to earth in the Father's name (John 5:43).General references to his redemptive "coming" are found in Mark 1:7; 10:45; Luke 19:10; John 1:11; 4:25; 12:47; 16:28; 1 Tim 1:15. His "coming" to call sinners to repentance is noted in Matt 9:13; Mark 2:17; Luke 5:32. He "comes" to bring judgment on the earth as noted in Matt 10:34ff.; Luke 12:36ff.; John 7:27; 9:39. John 12:13ff. affirms Jesus' "coming" as the king of Israel. John 14:23 affirms that Christ and the Father "come" to believers in order to establish intimate relationships with them. Christ's "coming" in the flesh is understood as the revelation of himself as the true Messiah in 1 John 4:3; 2 John 7. Jesus' "coming" in his final glorious return to earth at the end of time is noted in Matt 16:27; Luke 21:27; Acts 1:11; 1 Cor 11:26; Rev 1:7.

In one or two places, the "coming" of Christ relates to his return to heaven on his ascension from earth. This is described as the "coming into his kingdom" in Matt 16:28; Mark 9:1.

Several places describe the "coming" of God's kingdom to earth (Matt 6:10; Luke 11:2; 22:18). Then, in John 16:8, Christ declares that the Holy Spirit "will come" to earth, sent by him on the authority of God the Father. This will take place, however, only after Jesus' return to his heavenly glory, for the purpose of convicting the world of sin.

▸ **86.** Movement Toward or Away From > ARRIVE

eperchomai ἐπέρχομαι 1904

eperchomai is a variant of ***erchomai*** (above) meaning "come," along with a number of related nuances.

The miraculous conception of Mary with the Christ child is described in terms of the Holy Spirit "coming upon" her in Luke 1:35. In addition, the baptism of the Holy Spirit is depicted in terms of the Spirit "coming upon" the disciples of Christ in Acts 1:8 (see also Acts 8:24). The meaning "overcome" in a physical sense is indicated in Luke 11:22. The "coming" of the Day of the Lord (the final judgment) is indicated in Luke 21:26, 35. See also Jas 5:1; Acts 13:40. The "coming ages" is another expression indicating the consummation of God's plan of salvation in Eph 2:7. "Come" in the mundane sense of "arrive" is indicated in Acts 14:19.

proserchomai προσέρχομαι 4334

proserchomai is another variant of ***erchomai*** (above) meaning "come," "draw near" in a variety of contexts throughout the nearly ninety occurrences of the term.

The literal mundane sense of "coming" in relation to people is illustrated in Matt 4:3; Mark 12:28; Luke 9:12; John 12:21; Acts 7:31.

There are a number of references to people "drawing near" to God's throne of grace in prayer (Heb 4:16; 7:25; 10:22; 11:6 [see also 1 Pet 2:4]). Heb 10:1 refers to worshipers "drawing near" to God through their sacrifices. Heb 12:22 speaks of the people of God "drawing near" to the heavenly Mount Zion.

Matt 28:2 mentions an angel "coming" from heaven in order to roll back the stone from Jesus' grave.

ginomai γίνομαι 1096

ginomai is a very common verb found over one thousand times meaning "be," "become," "happen," plus a variety of other related nuances. One of these nuances is "come."

The meaning "come" or "arrive" is evident in relation to evening in Matt 14:23; Mark 4:35; John 6:16; to morning in Matt 27:1; to a particular time of day (Mark 15:33; Luke 22:14); and also in the context of travel (Acts 9:3; 21:17).

A number of phenomena are described as emanating from God. The voice of God is said to "come" from a cloud for the purpose of commending his Son (Luke 9:35 [see ***erchomai***, above]). Acts 7:31 describes God's voice "coming" to Moses from out of the burning bush. See also Acts 10:13. Grace and truth are declared to "have come" through Jesus Christ in John 1:17.

ginomai also means "come upon" in several contexts. The Holy Spirit is said to "come upon" Jesus in Luke 3:22. Acts 2:43; 5:5ff. record fear "coming upon" people. The blessing of God is said to "have come upon" the Gentiles through Christ Jesus.

- ▸ **84.** Do, Make, Accomplish, Occur > HAPPEN, TAKE PLACE, COME TO PASS, ARISE
- ▸ **84.** Do, Make, Accomplish, Occur > USE

hēkō ἥκω 2240

hēkō is another synonym for the preceding entries meaning "come" throughout the nearly thirty occurrences of the term.

The mundane sense of "come," "arrive" is illustrated in the context of travel, as noted in Matt 8:11; Mark 8:3; Luke 13:29; John 4:47; Acts 28:23. The "coming" of the end of the world is indicated in Matt 24:14; as are the final days of this age in Luke 19:43. John 2:4 records the preordained "hour" (i.e., coming) of Christ's suffering.

The meaning "come upon" in the sense of "happen to" is indicated in Matt 23:36; Rev 18:8 in relation to the judgment of God "coming upon" unbelievers. 2 Pet 3:10 affirms that the Day of the Lord "will come" as a surprise.

The action of "coming" with a specific intention or purpose is noted in relation to people worshiping God in Rev 15:4; and to those coming to God seeking salvation in John 6:37. In relation to the person of Christ, Rev 2:25; 3:3 declare that he "will come" on the day of judgment. In several places Christ is described as "coming" from God in order to accomplish his Father's will (John 8:42; Rom 11:26; Heb 10:7ff.; 1 John 5:20).

engizō ἐγγίζω 1448

engizō is a verb found around forty times meaning "draw near," as well as associated nuances.

The action of "drawing near" to a physical location is indicated in Matt 21:1; Mark 11:1; Luke 7:12; 15:1; 18:35; 19:29, 41; Acts 9:3.

The meaning "approach," in the context of the coming harvest season, is indicated in Matt 21:34.

The meaning "be at hand" in the temporal sense of "draw near" in relation to a particular significant event, is indicated in Matt 26:45ff.; Mark 14:42; Luke 21:8; 22:1; Acts 7:17; Heb 10:25; Jas 5:8. This is particularly the case in relation to the coming of the kingdom of God (Mark 1:15; Luke 10:9ff.).

The process of "drawing near" to God through the person and work of Christ is indicated in Heb 7:19. See also Jas 4:8.

- ▸ **86.** Movement Toward or Away From > APPROACH, DRAW NEAR, UNAPPROACHABLE

SEE ALSO

- ▸ **29.** Boats, Fishing, Maritime Activity > PULL, DRAW
  anabibazō
- ▸ **76.** Force, Harm, Oppress > DRAW
  spaō
- ▸ **79.** Throw, Send, Drive, Mix, Remove > DRAW, DRAG
  helkō, exelkō, syrō, anaspaō
- ▸ **80.** Related to Liquids > DRAW
  antleō

COMING

parousia παρουσία 3952

The noun ***parousia*** denotes a "coming" in the primary sense of Christ's return at the end of the age. It is found twenty-four times (Matt 24:3; 1 Cor 15:23; 1 Thess 2:19; 2 Thess 2:1; Jas 5:7ff.; 2 Pet 1:16; 3:4; 1 John 2:28).

parousia also refers to the "coming of the lawless one" (i.e., the antichrist) in 2 Thess 2:9. Other mundane references to people "coming" include 1 Cor 16:17; 2 Cor 7:6ff.; Phil 1:26; 2 Thess 2:1, 8ff.

- ▸ **85.** Movement, Position, State > BEFORE, IN THE PRESENCE OF

eisodos εἴσοδος 1529

eisodos denotes the "coming" of Jesus in Acts 13:24.

- ▸ **86.** Movement Toward or Away From > ENTER, ENTRANCE, ENTRY

eleusis ἔλευσις 1660

eleusis is a rare noun, found only in Acts 7:52, referring to the "coming" of the righteous one — Christ the Messiah.

DEPART, DEPARTURE

analyō ἀναλύω 360

analyō is a rare verb with the meaning "depart" in Phil 1:23, where Paul expresses his desire to "depart" (i.e., to die) and be with the Lord.

analysis ἀνάλυσις 359

analysis is a rare noun derived from ***analyō*** (above). It is found only in 2 Tim 4:6, with reference to Paul's realization that the time for his "departure" (i.e., his execution) is near.

exodos ἔξοδος 1841

exodos is a noun found in three places referring metaphorically to Jesus' "departure" (i.e., his approaching death) in Luke 9:31, and likewise to Peter's demise in 2 Pet 2:15. Heb 11:22 refers to Israel's historical release or exodus (i.e., departure) from Egypt.

aphixis ἄφιξις 867

aphixis is a rare noun denoting a physical departure (i.e., leaving) in Acts 20:29.

ENTER, ENTRANCE, ENTRY

eiserchomai εἰσέρχομαι 1525

eiserchomai is a common verb with the predominant meanings "enter," "go, come in" throughout the nearly two hundred occurrences of the term.

Mundane references to "entering" various places include those in Matt 6:6; 24:38; Mark 1:21; 11:11; Luke 1:9; 7:44ff.; 10:5ff.; 24:3; John 18:28; 20:5ff.; Acts 1:13; 5:7ff.; 9:6; 10:25ff.;

23:16; 1 Cor 14:23ff.; Jas 2:2. The phenomenon of "entering the temple" in a visionary context is indicated in Rev 15:8.

Elsewhere, ***eiserchomai*** indicates the process of "entering" the kingdom of heaven (Matt 5:20; 7:13). In particular, "entering" into the heavenly kingdom is said to be dependent on doing God's will in Matt 7:21; on having one's name in the Lamb's book of life in Rev 21:27 (see also Rev 22:14); on adopting a childlike stance of faith in Matt 18:3; Mark 10:15; Luke 18:17; and it is likened to "entering" a banquet in Luke 14:23. Barriers to such an entry include an idolatrous attachment to wealth (Matt 19:23ff.; Mark 10:23ff.; Luke 18:25); and lack of repentance and faith in Jesus Christ (see also John 3:5, 14). "Entering" into eternal life is noted in Matt 18:8ff.; Mark 9:43ff. Jesus' exhortation to "enter" the kingdom of heaven by the narrow door of faith and repentance is found in Luke 13:24. Reference to Jesus as the gate of the sheepfold designates him as the sole entry point to salvation in John 10:9. Rom 11:25 mentions the full number of Gentiles "coming into" or "entering into" their salvation. The meaning "enter into" in the sense of "share in" is indicated in Matt 25:23.

The action of evil spirits "entering into" a herd of pigs is described in Mark 5:13. Other references to demons "entering into" people include Mark 9:25; Luke 8:30ff. In particular, Satan is said to "enter into" Judas Iscariot, enticing him to betray Christ in Luke 22:3; John 13:27.

The experience of three disciples "entering into" the theophanic cloud associated with Jesus' transfiguration is indicated in Luke 9:34.

Luke 24:26 mentions Christ "entering into" his glory after his resurrection. In significant related contexts Jesus is said to "have entered into" the inner sanctuary of the heavenly temple to both offer himself as a sacrifice and to mediate on behalf of his people before God as our great high priest (Heb 6:19ff.; 9:12, 24ff.). Metaphorical reference to savage wolves "entering into" the flock of God's people in Acts 20:29 emphasizes the ever-present danger of false teachers infiltrating the Christian community.

References to sin "entering" the world include Rom 5:12.

A highly significant group of texts describes the ancient Israelites' failure "to enter their rest," that is, the land of Canaan. Such a failure was precipitated by their lack of saving faith in God. A parallel warning is then issued to Christian believers, who are exhorted to maintain their faith in, and sole dependence on, Christ for their salvation, lest they too fail "to enter their rest," which in context clearly denotes eternal rest with God and Christ in heaven (Heb 3:11, 18, 19; 4:1ff., 10ff.).

The heavenly Christ is said to "enter into" fellowship with believers in Rev 3:20.

The breath of life is said to "enter into" martyred saints, thus bringing them back to life, in Rev 11:11.

▸ **84.** Do, Make, Accomplish, Occur >
HAPPEN, TAKE PLACE, COME TO PASS, ARISE

syneiserchomai συνεισέρχομαι 4897

syneiserchomai is a rare variant of ***eiserchomai*** (above) denoting the action of "entering" with other people. It is found in John 6:22 in connection with Jesus and his disciples on the Sea of Galilee. See also John 18:15.

pareiserchomai παρεισέρχομαι 3922

pareiserchomai is another rare variant of ***eiserchomai*** (above). It expresses the sense of "infiltrating" in relation to false teachers making inroads into Christian congregations in order to deceive them (Gal 2:4).

eisporeuomai εἰσπορεύομαι 1531

eisporeuomai is synonymous with ***eiserchomai*** (above) and means "enter," "go, come in" throughout the eighteen occurrences of the term.

The mundane sense of "entering" into various places and locations is indicated in Matt 15:17; Mark 1:21; 5:40; 6:56; 11:2; Luke 8:16; 11:33; 19:30; 22:10; Acts 3:2; 8:3; 28:30.

Elsewhere ***eisporeuomai*** refers to those things that "enter into" a person's body, such as food and drink (Mark 4:19; 7:15ff.).

In Luke 18:24 Christ laments how hard it is for a rich person to "enter" the kingdom of God.

anabainō ἀναβαίνω 305

anabainō is a verb with the predominant sense of "go, come up" for almost all of the nearly eighty occurrences of the term. However, in 1 Cor 2:9 ***anabainō*** refers to God's revelation to his people by his Spirit, which transcends the normal human senses. In particular, it is literally affirmed that "nothing has entered into the heart of human beings" to indicate the true reality of God's revelation prepared for them.

▸ **28.** Agriculture, Viticulture, Animal Husbandry >
GROW, SPROUT, SPRING UP

▸ **87.** Movement Upward or Downward >
ARISE, RISE UP, RAISE UP

epibainō ἐπιβαίνω 1910

epibainō is a rare verb found in only six places that means "enter," in the sense of "arrive in (a province)," in Acts 20:18; 25:1. In Acts 27:2 the term refers to "boarding (a boat)."

eiseimi εἴσειμι 1524

eiseimi is a rare verb found only four times with reference to people "entering" the temple in Acts 8:3; 21:6. Specifically, in Heb 9:6, ***eiseimi*** refers to the priests continually "entering" the temple precinct to conduct their ministry.

eisodos εἴσοδος 1529

eisodos is a rare noun found in five places and is variously translated as "coming," "visit," "welcome," and "entry." Heb 10:19 speaks of the believer's unique privilege in "gaining entry" into the very presence of God, that is, into the most holy place, through the sacrificial blood of Christ. 2 Pet 1:11 refers to the believer receiving a rich "welcome" (i.e., implying an entry) into the eternal kingdom of God.

▸ **86.** Movement Toward or Away From > COMING

SEE ALSO

- ▸ **29.** Boats, Fishing, Maritime Activity > BOARD, EMBARK
  embainō

GO AWAY, GET AWAY

hypagō ὑπάγω 5217

The verb ***hypagō*** means "go," "get away," as well as expressing related nuances, throughout its nearly eighty occurrences.

Mundane references to "go" in the sense of "go away," "leave" include those in Matt 5:24; 19:21; Mark 2:11; Luke 19:30; John 7:3. The coming and "going" of the wind is indicated in John 3:8.

Commands to "get away (from)" are found in Jesus' dismissal of Satan in the wilderness in Matt 4:10; Luke 11:8. See also Matt 16:23. Matt 8:32 describes Jesus exorcising a demon-possessed man.

The meaning "go" in the sense of "travel" is indicated in Matt 5:41; Mark 10:52; John 9:7. See also Rev 13:10; 16:1. Jesus commands his disciples to "go one's way" when he sends them on their mission in Luke 10:3. The benediction "go in peace" is found in Jas 2:16.

John 8:14, 21; 13:3, 33; 14:28; 16:5, 10, 17 describe Jesus "going" to his death and then to heaven back to his Father after resurrection. In stark contrast, the satanic beast is said to "go away" to eternal damnation in Rev 17:8, 11.

Moral confusion is indicated in 1 John 2:11, which speaks of people who walk in darkness and do not know where they "are going."

SEE ALSO

- ▸ **85.** Movement, Position, State > GO, WALK, GO BEFORE
  poreuomai, proagō

JOURNEY

hodos ὁδός 3598

hodos occurs around one hundred times and is commonly translated "way" in the sense of "road," "path," or "route." On five occasions, however, the term is translated "journey." In Matt 10:10; Mark 6:8; Luke 9:3; 11:6 the ordinary sense of travel is indicated. Luke 2:44; Acts 1:12 refer to a short journey of a day's travel.

- ▸ **9.** Land, Geography, Topography > WAY, PATH, ROAD

apodēmeō ἀποδημέω 589

apodēmeō is found on six occasions and signifies the action of traveling on a journey abroad. All occurrences are found in the parables of Jesus (Matt 21:33; 25:14, 15; Mark 1:21; Luke 15:13; 20:9).

- ▸ **9.** Land, Geography, Topography > COUNTRY, LAND
- ▸ **85.** Movement, Position, State > TRAVEL, TRAVELER

apodēmos ἀπόδημος 590

This is the noun derived from ***apodēmeō*** (above) and occurs only once, in Mark 13:34, again referring to a journey abroad.

hodoiporeō ὁδοιπορέω 3596

Occurring only once, ***hodoiporeō*** refers to a literal journey in Acts 10:9.

poreuomai πορεύομαι 4198

poreuomai is a common verb that normally means "go," "walk," or "come" in about 150 contexts. In one text, however, it indicates the specific action of taking a journey. Acts 9:3 speaks of Saul taking his fateful journey to Damascus, during which he was miraculously converted.

- ▸ **85.** Movement, Position, State > GO, WALK, GO BEFORE

diaporeuomai διαπορεύομαι 1279

diaporeuomai is a rare variant of ***poreuomai*** (above) and is found only five times, meaning "pass, go through" in all but one of these contexts. In Rom 15:24, a participial form of this verb refers to Paul's anticipated journey to Spain.

propempō προπέμπω 4311

This verb form occurs nine times and has the primary sense of "to send, or bring forward on a journey." The contexts are all literal, and all except one relate to the travels of the apostle Paul (Acts 15:3; 20:38; 21:5; Rom 15:24; 1 Cor 16:6, 11; 2 Cor 1:16; Titus 3:13; 3 John 6).

- ▸ **85.** Movement, Position, State > ACCOMPANY

LEAVE, GO AWAY, LEAVE BEHIND, ABANDON

aphistēmi ἀφίστημι 868

aphistēmi is a verb found fifteen times with the predominant sense of "depart from," "leave."

Literal references to physical departure or leaving are found in Luke 2:37; Acts 12:10; 15:38; 22:29.

In particular, the devil is said to leave Jesus after concluding in vain his efforts to tempt him to sin (Luke 4:13). In another context, Jesus anticipates the words of the Father to the unrighteous standing before him on the day of judgment. "Depart (i.e., leave, get away) from me, you workers of iniquity" (Luke 13:27).

In 2 Cor 12:8, Paul beseeches God for the mysterious thorn in the flesh "to leave" him. 1 Tim 4:1 mentions those who "abandon" the faith, and a warning against doing so is indicated in Heb 3:12. See also 2 Tim 2:19.

- ▸ **45.** Faith, Belief, Trust, Promise >
  FALL AWAY, APOSTATIZE, APOSTASY

aperchomai ἀπέρχομαι 565

aperchomai is a common verb found over 120 times with the predominant general senses of "go," "depart," "leave," as well as associated nuances.

Literal references to people "leaving," or going their way, include those in Matt 21:29; 27:5; Mark 5:20; Luke 1:23; 22:4; John 4:3; Acts 10:7; Jas 1:24.

Elsewhere, ***aperchomai*** refers to disease "leaving" a person (i.e., the experience of healing) (Mark 1:42; Luke 5:13).

- ▸ **85.** Movement, Position, State >
  PASS, PASS BY, PASS THROUGH, CROSS OVER

exerchomai ἐξέρχομαι 1831

exerchomai is another common verb form, a partial synonym for ***aphistēmi*** (above) found over two hundred times with the primary meanings "come out," "depart," "leave," as well as related senses throughout the occurrences of the term.

The literal meaning "leave," or go one's way, is evident, for example, in Matt 9:31; Luke 4:42; 9:4ff.; John 13:31; Acts 18:23; 20:1.

References to an evil spirit "coming out of" a man are found in Matt 12:43; 17:18; Mark 9:26; Luke 4:36; 8:29.

The meaning "get away from" is found in Luke 5:8 in the context of a command.

Luke 8:46 records Jesus' remark that power "had left" him.

metabainō μεταβαίνω 3327

metabainō is a verb found twelve times meaning "to leave" in most of these occurrences.

The meaning "leave" in the literal sense of "depart," "go one's way" is indicated in Matt 8:34; 11:1; 12:9; 15:29; John 7:3; Acts 18:7.

John 13:1 refers to Jesus' recognition that his time had come to "leave" this world, as he faced his inevitable crucifixion.

▸ **85.** Movement, Position, State >
PASS, PASS BY, PASS THROUGH, CROSS OVER

ekporeuomai ἐκπορεύομαι 1607

ekporeuomai is a verb found about thirty-five times meaning "proceed," "go out," as well as "leave" or "depart" in several contexts.

The literal sense of "leaving" is indicated in Mark 6:11; 10:46; 11:19.

exeimi ἔξειμι 1826

exeimi is a rare verb with the literal meaning "leave" or "depart" in Acts 13:42; 17:15; 20:7.

anachōreō ἀναχωρέω 402

anachōreō is a verb meaning "leave," in the sense of "set out on a journey," for most of its fourteen occurrences (Matt 2:12ff., 22; 14:13; John 6:15). See also Matt 9:24; 27:5.

apochōreō ἀποχωρέω 672

apochōreō is a rare variant of ***anachōreō*** (above). It is found only three times, meaning "leave," "go away," "depart." Matt 7:23 records the divine command to the wicked on the day of judgment: "Depart from me, you evildoers." Luke 9:39 refers to a demonic spirit "leaving" a person. Acts 13:13 refers to John Mark "leaving" the apostle Paul and returning to Jerusalem.

aphiēmi ἀφίημι 863

aphiēmi is a verb meaning "leave," with various related meanings, as well as "forgive," "persist," also with several nuances. The underlying sense of "leave," however, is predominant in the use of the term. ***aphiēmi*** occurs around 150 times and refers to the actions of both God and human beings.

Where people are concerned, ***aphiēmi*** indicates the action of leaving, in the sense of departure, in a number of general contexts (Matt 4:22; 18:22; John 4:3). In addition, the devil is said to leave Christ in Matt 4:11, after failing to succeed in tempting him. Then, in the context of healing, sickness is said to leave the afflicted in Matt 8:15; Mark 1:31; Luke 4:39.

The meaning "leave behind" is also evident in the use of ***aphiēmi***. Objects, for example, are in view in Matt 5:24; John 4:28. People constitute the object of this action in Matt 22:25; Mark 12:19ff.; 14:50; Luke 17:34. John 14:27 contains the promise of Jesus to leave his people peace after his return to glory. In a metaphorical context, the writer to the Hebrews exhorts his readers to leave behind elementary doctrines and strive for spiritual maturity in Heb 6:1.

The idea of abandonment is also quite frequent in the semantic range of ***aphiēmi***. The disciples of Christ are said to have left all to follow the Lord (Matt 19:27, 29; Mark 1:18; 10:28; Luke 5:11). In the context of divorce, Paul teaches that the believing wife should not abandon her unbelieving husband if he consents to live with her. Matt 26:56; Mark 14:50 refer to the followers of Jesus abandoning him at his arrest. Rom 1:27 speaks of people abandoning natural sexual relations with one another for unnatural ones. Jesus promises never to abandon his followers in John 14:18. The church at Ephesus is rebuked for abandoning their first love for Christ in Rev 2:4.

aphiēmi is also used passively in the sense of "be left" (or "remain") in the context of Jesus' prophecy of destruction regarding the temple. In Matt 24:2; Mark 3:2; Luke 21:6, he declares that a time will come when no stones of the temple shall be left standing on each other. A similar prophecy is made with respect to the walls of Jerusalem in Luke 19:44.

Regarding the actions of God, ***aphiēmi*** occurs in Acts 14:17, where it is said that God does not leave himself without a witness in the world. In Heb 2:8, the writer declares that God leaves nothing outside of his control.

▸ **44.** Repentance, Forgiveness, Mercy, Redeem, Save >
FORGIVE, FORGIVENESS, RELEASE

▸ **49.** Allow, Accept, Approve, Refuse > ALLOW

kataleipō καταλείπω 2641

kataleipō is found in about twenty-five places, meaning "leave," "leave behind," "abandon" in most of these contexts.

The action of "leaving behind" in a physical sense is found with regard to places (Matt 4:13; Heb 11:27); to one's flock (Luke 15:4); to people in general (Matt 16:4; Luke 10:40; Titus 1:5); to a deceased man leaving behind a wife but no children (Mark 12:19; Luke 20:31); and to leaving one's parents in order to marry (Matt 19:5; Mark 10:7; Eph 5:31).

kataleipō also refers to the action of leaving in the sense of "abandon." Luke 5:28 mentions Levi, who left everything to follow Christ. In Acts 2:31, it is declared that David was not abandoned to Hades. False teachers are condemned in 2 Pet 2:15 for having abandoned the way of truth.

enkataleipō ἐγκαταλείπω 1459

enkataleipō is found nine times, and on all but one occasion the term means "abandon."

The cry of Jesus Christ on the cross, "My God . . . why have you abandoned me?," signifies the consummate agony of his temporary separation from God (Matt 27:46; Mark 15:34). Acts 2:27 records the words of David, confident that God would not abandon his soul to Hades. Abandonment by one's friends is indicated in 2 Cor 4:9; 2 Tim 4:10, 16. The writer to the Hebrews warns his readers against "abandoning" their practice of meeting together regularly in Heb 10:25. The words of Jesus, promising never to abandon his followers, are recorded in Heb 13:5. The one exception to this usage is found in Rom 9:29, which cites Isa 1:9, reflecting on the fact that God had graciously "left" a sufficient number of descendants to ensure the continuity of the people of Israel.

apoleipō ἀπολείπω 620

apoleipō occurs six times and means "leave," "remain," with the former sense found only in 2 Tim 4:13, referring to Paul's cloak that he left behind in Troas, and in Jude 6, indicating the evil angels who had left their place in the heavenly realm.

▸ **85.** Movement, Position, State > REMAIN, STAY, ABIDE, DWELL

REACH, REACH OUT

pherō φέρω 5342

pherō is a verb occurring around sixty times with the predominant meanings "to bring (forth)," "bear" in the majority of its usage. Twice in John 20:27, however, the term is translated "reach out" (i.e., "stretch out") in the context of Jesus' invitation to the disciple Thomas to feel the scars in his hand and side with his own hands in order to satisfy himself that it was truly the same Jesus who had lived among them, died, and was now risen from the dead.

▸ **29.** Boats, Fishing, Maritime Activity > DRIVE ALONG
▸ **69.** Have, Possess, Hold, Grasp, Bear, Carry > BEAR, CARRY
▸ **86.** Movement Toward or Away From > BRING, BROUGHT

ephikneomai ἐφικνέομαι 2185

ephikneomai is a rare verb occurring only twice, in 2 Cor 10:13, 14. In the first of these texts, the sense of "reach" refers to an opportunity that Paul recognized as "extending" to the Corinthian congregation. In the second of these verses, ***ephikneomai*** expresses the idea of "reach" in the sense of "visit" or "come to."

RETURN, COME BACK

anakamptō ἀνακάμπτω 344

anakamptō is a verb meaning "return" in each of its four occurrences. Physical "return" to a geographic location is noted in Matt 2:12; Acts 18:21; Heb 11:15. Luke 10:6 refers metaphorically to a greeting of peace "returning" to the disciples in the face of inhospitable fellow countrymen.

▸ **86.** Movement Toward or Away From > TURN, TURN AROUND, TURN TOWARD, TURN AWAY, TURN BACK

hypostrephō ὑποστρέφω 5290

hypostrephō is a verb that occurs thirty-five times and is translated "return" in each of these, with all but one instance indicating a literal usage.

The literal sense of "return" or "go, come back" is found in Mark 14:40; Luke 1:56; 8:37ff.; 17:15ff.; Acts 8:25ff.; 14:21; Gal 1:17; Heb 7:1.

A metaphorical usage of ***hypostrephō*** is found in Acts 13:34, where it is affirmed that no corruption whatever "returns" to the resurrected body of Christ.

▸ **86.** Movement Toward or Away From > TURN, TURN AROUND, TURN TOWARD, TURN AWAY, TURN BACK

epistrephō ἐπιστρέφω 1994

epistrephō is a verb with the principal meaning "turn," as well as associated nuances. In several places, however, the meaning "return" is indicated.

The literal sense of "return" or "go, come back" is indicated in Matt 12:44; Luke 2:20; 17:31.

epistrephō refers metaphorically to "returning" in Matt 10:13, where a greeting of peace "returns" to the one who is not shown any hospitality by an inconsiderate prospective host.

In another literal, though highly significant, context, ***epistrephō*** indicates the "return" of a dead girl's spirit. Luke 8:55 records the resurrection of Jairus' daughter, which manifests the divine power of Christ.

▸ **86.** Movement Toward or Away From > TURN, TURN AROUND, TURN TOWARD, TURN AWAY, TURN BACK

anastrephō ἀναστρέφω 390

anastrephō occurs twelve times and means "return" in two of these contexts. The literal sense of "come back" is indicated in Acts 5:22. The other reference, found in Acts 15:16, is metaphorical. Here, God promises to return to his people and rebuild David's "fallen tent" (i.e., the ruined kingdoms of Israel and Judah) in an act of profound spiritual renewal (citing Amos 9:11, 12).

epanerchomai ἐπανέρχομαι 1880

epanerchomai occurs only twice, meaning "to return" in the sense of "come back" in Luke 10:35; 19:15.

RUN, RUN TOWARD, RUN DOWN

prostrechō προστρέχω 4370

prostrechō is a verb meaning "run towards, up to." It is found only in Mark 9:15; 10:17; Acts 8:30.

eistrechō εἰστρέχω 1532

eistrechō occurs only in Acts 12:14, meaning "to run" in a directional sense.

katatrechō κατατρέχω 2701

katatrechō means "to run down" (i.e., towards). It is found only in Acts 21:32.

hormaō ὁρμάω 3729

hormaō is a verb expressing the sense of "run, or rush violently (together)." It is found in five contexts. Matt 8:32; Mark 5:13; Luke 8:33 refer to a herd of pigs "rushing headlong" over a cliff to their death, drowning in the ocean. Acts 7:57; 19:29 refer to the violent rushing of a crowd.

SEE ALSO

- ▸ **7.** Quantity, Amount, Number, Size, Measure > OVERFLOW, RUN OVER ***hyperekchynnō***
- ▸ **29.** Boats, Fishing, Maritime Activity > RUN UNDER, RUN AGROUND ***hypotrechō, epikellō***
- ▸ **85.** Movement, Position, State > RUN ***trechō, episyntrechō, syntrechō, peritrechō, protrechō***

TURN, TURN AROUND, TURN TOWARD, TURN AWAY, TURN BACK

strephō στρέφω 4762

strephō is a verb meaning "turn," "turn around" in a variety of contexts.

Matt 5:39 refers to "turning" (i.e., offering) one's checks to one's tormentors.

The action of "turning toward (someone)" is noted in the context of speaking to others in Luke 7:44; 9:55; 10:23. See also Acts 7:42.

General references to the physical movement of "turning around" are found in Matt 16:23; Luke 7:9; John 1:38; 20:14ff. This is done in order to attack in Matt 7:6.

The meaning "turn into" is noted in the context of the miracle of water changing to blood in Rev 11:6.

strephō is also translated "turn" with reference to a change of heart resulting in a renewed attitude of devotion to God. Such an attitude is an indispensable prerequisite for entry into the kingdom of heaven (Matt 18:3). In a negative context, Acts 7:39 records the action of "turning one's heart away from God."

apostrephō ἀποστρέφω 654

apostrephō is a verb with the primary meaning "turn away" in each of its eleven occurrences. Matt 5:42 records the request not "to turn someone away" by refusing to lend him some money.

In other contexts, the translation "turn away" indicates the act of "rebelling against," "rejecting," or "refusing." In 2 Tim 1:15, Paul laments that virtually everyone has "deserted" him. Heb 12:25 warns of the danger of "rejecting" Christ. Titus 1:14 refers to those who "reject" the truth. See also 2 Tim 4:4.

Where God is the subject of this verb, he is said to "turn" people from their wickedness (Acts 3:26; Rom 11:26).

epistrephō ἐπιστρέφω 1994

epistrephō is a verb meaning "turn," "return" in a variety of contexts throughout its usage (approximately forty times).

The physical movement of "turning around" is noted in Matt 9:22; Mark 5:30; Luke 17:4; Acts 9:40; Rev 1:12.

Acts 14:15; 1 Thess 1:9 refer to "turning" from idolatry to worship the living God. Acts 26:18 speaks similarly of those who "turn" from darkness to light. More commonly, the phenomenon of conversion is denoted by the action of "turning" to God in repentance (Acts 3:19; 9:35; 26:20; 2 Cor 3:16). God himself is said to "turn" (i.e., bring) people to worship him (Luke 1:16ff.).

epistrephō also means "return" (i.e., come back) in general contexts such as Matt 24:18; Luke 2:20. Matt 10:13 specifically refers to peace "returning" to the home. Gal 4:9 contains a warning against "returning" to a life of enslavement under the law. See also 2 Pet 2:21ff. In contrast, 1 Pet 2:25 refers to the joy of "returning" to Christ, the chief shepherd of our souls.

- ▸ **86.** Movement Toward or Away From > RETURN, COME BACK

hypostrephō ὑποστρέφω 5290

hypostrephō is a verb found thirty-five times meaning "turn back," "return."

The general sense of "returning" to one's original point of departure is indicated in Mark 14:40; Luke 7:10; 8:37ff.; 24:9, 33; Acts 8:25; Heb 7:1.

The process of "returning home" is noted in Luke 1:56; 8:39; 11:24. The meaning "turn back" is used in the sense of "reverting" to an original condition. It is found only in Acts 13:34, referring to Christ as one who will never again "return (i.e., revert) to decay" after having risen from the dead.

- ▸ **86.** Movement Toward or Away From > RETURN, COME BACK

anakamptō ἀνακάμπτω 344

anakamptō is a rare verb found in four places meaning "return" or "come back." Three of these occurrences are in the context of a journey (Matt 2:12; Acts 18:21; Heb 11:15). The remaining text speaks of peace "returning" to the disciples on their missionary journey (Luke 10:6).

- ▸ **86.** Movement Toward or Away From > RETURN, COME BACK

diastrephō διαστρέφω 1294

diastrephō is a verb found seven times, meaning "to pervert" in most of these contexts. However, in Acts 13:8, it means "turn (away) from," referring to the sorcerer Elymas' attempt to "turn away" the Roman proconsul from the Christian faith.

- ▸ **57.** Evil, Wickedness, Sin > PERVERSE, PERVERT

SEE ALSO

- ▸ **82.** Change, Exchange, Transform > TURN INTO ***metastrephō***

WALK ON FOOT

pezeuō πεζεύω 3978

pezeuō is a rare verb meaning "to walk on foot," found only in Acts 20:13.

SEE ALSO

▸ **16.** Body, Bodily Functions > FOOT
pous

▸ **20.** Illness, Disease, Health, Healing > FOOT
basis

▸ **34.** Craftsmanship, Artisanship, Furniture, Implements > FOOTSTOOL
hypopodion

87. Movement Upward or Downward

ARISE, RISE UP, RAISE UP

anistēmi ἀνίστημι 450

anistēmi is a verb found over one hundred times with the primary sense of "arise," "rise (up)," "raise (up)" in a variety of contexts.

Commonly, ***anistēmi*** denotes the act of "rising," "arising" in the sense of "stand, get up." Mundane references include Matt 9:9; Mark 2:14; Luke 1:39; Acts 1:15; 9:6ff.; 1 Cor 10:7. The action of "standing up" as the result of a miraculous cure is noted in Acts 9:34; 14:10. See also Acts 13:16. The men of Nineveh are depicted as ones who "will rise up" in judgment against the unbelieving towns of Judea at the last "day" (Matt 12:41; Luke 11:32). Satan is also said to "rise up" in Mark 3:26. Christ himself is portrayed as "rising up" to rule the Gentiles in Rom 15:12; and also as a high priest after the order of Melchizedek (Heb 7:11, 15).

The phenomenon of resurrection frequently describes Christ, whose "rising from the dead" is both prophesied and recorded (Matt 17:9; 20:19; Mark 9:9ff.; 10:34; Luke 18:33; 24:7, 46; John 20:9; Acts 2:24ff.; 3:26; 13:33ff.; Rom 14:9). This experience is also predicated of others in Mark 12:25; Luke 9:8, 19; 16:31; John 11:23ff.; Eph 5:14; 1 Thess 4:16.

Elsewhere, ***anistēmi*** is translated "to raise up," for example in the context of "rearing" children in Matt 22:24. God is said to "raise up" his people to eternal life on the day of judgment (John 6:40ff.), and also raises up prophets for his service in Acts 7:37.

exanistēmi ἐξανίστημι 1817

exanistēmi is a rare variant form of ***anistēmi*** (above) found in only three places. In Mark 12:19; Luke 20:28, it refers to a man "raising up" children by the widow of his deceased brother in order to preserve the name of the family line in Israel (i.e., the custom of "levirate" marriage). In Acts 15:5 the meaning "rise up" is indicated in relation to the "emerging" of a Pharisaical sect.

egeirō ἐγείρω 1453

egeirō is a verb synonymous with ***anistēmi*** (above) occurring over 150 times with the senses of "rise," "arise," "raise (up)," and various nuances in different contexts.

The general, mundane sense of "rise," "stand, get up" is indicated in Matt 2:13; Mark 4:27; John 11:29; Rev 11:1. The action of "standing up" as a consequence of healing is noted in Matt 9:5ff.; Mark 2:9ff.; Luke 5:23ff.; John 5:8; Acts 3:6, 7. To "arise" in the sense of "come into public view," "to emerge," is indicated in Matt 11:11; 24:11, 24; Mark 13:22.

Where God is the subject of this verb, the predominant meaning is that of "raise up." The possibility of God "raising up" children from stones is indicated in Matt 3:9; Luke 3:8. Luke 1:69 affirms that God "has raised up" a "horn of salvation" for his people. Acts 13:22 records that God "raised up" David as king over Israel. There are a number of references indicating that God has power to raise the dead to life (Matt 10:8; 11:5; Acts 26:8; 1 Cor 15:12ff.; 2 Cor 1:9; 4:14). Christ in particular is the object of divine resurrecting power (Acts 3:15; 5:30; 13:30; Rom 4:24ff.; 8:11; 1 Cor 6:14; 15:12ff.; 2 Cor 5:15; Gal 1:1; Eph 1:20; Col 2:12; 1 Thess 1:10; 1 Pet 1:21).

People are said to "rise up" in judgment at the last day in Matt 12:42; Luke 11:31; and also in the context of armed conflict (Matt 24:7; Mark 13:8).

The action of "rising" from the dead is predicated of people, largely through the divine power demonstrated by Christ (Matt 14:2; 27:52; Mark 12:26; Luke 7:14ff.; 9:7; 20:37). More particularly, it is also commonly used with reference to Jesus Christ's own resurrection (Matt 16:21; 26:32; 27:63ff.; 28:6ff.; Mark 14:28; 16:6; Luke 9:22; John 21:14; 2 Tim 2:8). In John 2:19ff., this phenomenon is expressed in the metaphor of Jesus vowing "to raise the temple in three days" — referring to his own body.

diegeirō διεγείρω 1326

diegeirō is a variant form of ***egeirō*** (above) found in seven places with the primary sense of "awaken," "rouse from sleep" (Matt 1:24; Mark 4:38ff.; Luke 8:24; 2 Pet 1:13; 3:1). In John 6:18 it refers to the "rising" of the sea in a storm.

anabainō ἀναβαίνω 305

anabainō is a verb found in approximately eighty contexts, with the underlying meanings "go up," "come up," plus several related nuances. One of these nuances is "arise," indicated with respect to thoughts "rising" in the heart in Luke 24:38. The smoke of divine judgment "rising out" of the abyss is noted in Rev 9:2; 19:3. In Rev 13:1, 11, the two satanic beasts are depicted as "rising" out of the sea and the earth.

▸ **28.** Agriculture, Viticulture, Animal Husbandry > GROW, SPROUT, SPRING UP

▸ **86.** Movement Toward or Away From > ENTER, ENTRANCE, ENTRY

anatellō ἀνατέλλω 393

anatellō is a verb found in eleven places with primary reference to the "rising" of the sun.

Reference to God causing the sun to rise is found in Matt 5:45. Other references to the rising sun are indicated in Matt 13:6; Mark 4:6; 16:2; Jas 1:11.

Elsewhere, Luke 12:54 refers to a cloud "rising" in the west; and in 2 Pet 1:19 metaphorical reference is made to the morning star "rising" in the hearts of God's people.

exegeirō ἐξεγείρω 1825

exegeirō is a verb related to ***egeirō***, meaning "to raise up" in each of its three occurrences. Rom 9:17 twice refers to the action of God in raising up Pharaoh for the explicit purpose of manifesting his divine power in him. 1 Cor 6:14 indicates that God will likewise "raise us" up (i.e., from the dead), just as he raised Jesus from death.

SEE ALSO

▸ **22.** Life, Renewal, Immortality > RAISE
synegeirō

BOW, BOW DOWN

klinō κλίνω 2827

klinō is a verb found seven times with the meaning "bow," "bow down" in two of these contexts.

Luke 24:5 refers to the disciples "bowing down" in fear when first confronted by the angels announcing that Jesus had risen from the dead. John 19:30 depicts Christ as "bowing" his head at the point of death on the cross.

▸ **77.** Resist, Oppose, Fight, Rebel > ROUT, PUT TO FLIGHT

SEE ALSO

▸ **41.** Sacrifice, Offering, Worship, Praise > BOW, KNEEL
kamptō, gonypeteō

DESCEND, COME DOWN

katabainō καταβαίνω 2597

katabainō is a verb found about eighty times with the primary senses of "come down" and "descend," with some related nuances.

The literal sense of "descend" occurs in connection with the Spirit of God descending on Christ at his baptism in the form of a dove (Matt 3:16; Mark 1:10; Luke 3:22; John 1:32ff.). The "descending" of a road is noted in Acts 8:26.

Elsewhere, ***katabainō*** indicates the "coming down" of fire from heaven in Luke 9:54; Rev 13:13; 20:9. The "pouring down" of rain is noted in Matt 7:25ff.; and the "descent" of a windstorm in Luke 8:23. The sense of "come down" is also evident in the context of a person's movement or journey in Matt 8:1; Mark 3:22; Luke 6:17; John 2:12; Acts 7:15; 14:25. Angels "descending" from heaven are noted in Matt 28:2; John 1:51; 5:47; Rev 10:1; 18:1; 20:1. John 3:13 refers to the Son of Man "descending" from heaven, referring to his incarnation. In 1 Thess 4:16 Christ is likewise described as "descending" from heaven, but here it refers to his final return. God is also described as "coming down" to deliver his people from Egypt in Acts 7:34 (Exod 12, 13).

In metaphorical contexts, ***katabainō*** refers to the bread of God "coming down" from heaven, referring to Christ himself (John 6:33ff., 50ff.). The act of "descending" into the abyss of the dead is noted in Rom 10:7; Eph 4:9ff. A sheet of food "descending" from heaven in the vision of the apostle Peter is noted in Acts 10:11; 11:15. God's gifts are said to "come down" to human beings in Jas 1:17. Rev 3:12; 21:2, 10 refer to the new Jerusalem "coming down" from heaven. In a pagan context, gods are said to "come down" amongst human beings in Acts 14:11.

katerchomai κατέρχομαι 2718

The verb ***katerchomai*** expresses the meaning "come down," "descend" throughout the thirteen occurrences of the term.

The literal meaning of "come, go down" in the context of travel predominates (Luke 4:31; 9:37; Acts 8:5; 9:32; 12:19; 13:4; 18:5, 22; 21:10; 27:5). In Jas 3:15, there is a metaphorical usage of the term referring to earthly, unspiritual wisdom that "does not come down" from above.

SEE ALSO

▸ **25.** Family, Marriage, Adoption, Inheritance > DESCENT, ANCESTRY
agenealogētos, genealogeō

FALL, FALL DOWN, FALL UPON, FALL INTO

piptō πίπτω 4098

piptō is the most common verb meaning "fall," "fall down," and is found in approximately ninety places.

The meaning "fall down" in relation to the act of worshiping the Christ child is noted in Matt 2:11. The same action in connection with worshiping Satan is indicated in Matt 4:9 — a response that the devil failed to elicit from Christ in the wilderness. Matt 17:6 describes the disciples' veneration of Christ on the "Mount of Transfiguration." References to other people "falling down" to worship Christ include those in Mark 5:22; Luke 17:16. In 1 Cor 14:25; Rev 7:11; 19:4 the same action is performed to worship God. The action of "falling down" to worship the heavenly Christ is indicated in Rev 4:10; 5:8. Mundane references to "falling" are found in relation to rain (Matt 7:25ff.); birds (Matt 10:29; Mark 4:4ff.; Luke 8:5ff.; John 12:24); people stumbling (Matt 15:14; 17:15); and people begging for mercy (Matt 18:26ff.; Luke 5:12). See also Mark 9:20; Luke 6:49; John 11:32; Acts 9:4; 27:34; Rom 14:4; Heb 11:30.

Stars "falling" from heaven and mountains "falling" onto a desperate humanity as a sign of the dissolution of the cosmos at the end of time are described in Matt 24:29; Luke 23:30; Rev 6:16; 8:10; 11:16; 18:2. Satan is also described as "falling" in the context of his expulsion from heaven (Luke 10:18). Christ himself "fell" on his face in Gethsemane, praying that his Father might remove the threat of imminent crucifixion from him (Matt 26:39; Mark 14:35).

The metaphorical context of Luke 20:18 indicates that everyone who "falls" on the stone will be broken. The "stone" here refers to the Messiah, who will destroy those who reject him. The action of "falling" is equated with the act of "rejecting." See also Acts 15:16. The meaning "to fall" in the sense of "commit apostasy" is noted in Rom 11:11; Heb 4:11. The "fall" (i.e., eternal destruction) of Babylon is noted in Rev 14:8.

The fate of "falling" in battle is noted in Luke 21:24. The action of "falling down" dead is indicated in Acts 5:5, 10; 20:9; 1 Cor 10:8; Heb 3:17.

apopiptō ἀποπίπτω 634

apopiptō is one of the rare variants of the term ***piptō*** (above), found only in Acts 9:18 and referring to the scale-like substance that "fell" from the eyes of a blind man healed by Jesus.

ekpiptō ἐκπίπτω 1601

ekpiptō, a variant form of ***piptō*** (above), occurs in six places and also means "fall." Reference to stars "falling" from heaven as one of the signs of cosmic dissolution at the end of time is found in Matt 13:25. The effect of scorching heat on plants, resulting in the "dropping" of the flower, is noted in Jas 1:11; 1 Pet 1:24. Acts 12:7 describes chains "falling off" the hands of prisoners.

Gal 5:4 refers to those who "have fallen" from grace. See also Rev 2:5 for a similar context.

empiptō ἐμπίπτω 1706

empiptō is a verb found seven times meaning "fall among," "fall into."

Literal references to beasts "falling into" a pit are found in Matt 12:11; Luke 14:5; and to a man who "fell among" thieves in Luke 10:36. 1 Tim 3:6ff. warns believers against "falling into" satanic temptation.

Finally, Heb 10:31 declares that it is a terrible thing to "fall into" the hands of the living God.

epipiptō ἐπιπίπτω 1968

epipiptō means "fall upon," "fall," with several related nuances, throughout most of its thirteen occurrences.

The operation of the Holy Spirit who "fell" on those listening to the word of God resulted in their conversion in Acts 10:44; 11:15. See also Acts 8:15. The phenomenon of fear "falling upon" people is described in Luke 1:12; Acts 19:17.

The action of people "embracing" one another with the literal sense of "falling upon their neck" is indicated in Luke 15:20; Acts 20:10, 37. The phenomenon of "falling into" a trance is indicated in Acts 10:10. See also Rom 15:3.

katapiptō καταπίπτω 2667

katapiptō is a rare verb found only twice, meaning "fall down" in both places. In Acts 26:14 Paul relates how he and his companions "had fallen" to the ground in the wake of his revelation of Christ on the road to Damascus. In Acts 28:6, Paul's traveling companions expected him "to fall down" dead after being bitten by a poisonous snake.

prospiptō προσπίπτω 4363

prospiptō is a verb meaning "fall down before (someone)" throughout most of its eight occurrences.

Prostrating oneself in fear is an action noted in Mark 3:11; 5:33; Luke 8:28, 47; Acts 16:29. Mark 7:25 refers to a woman who fell down at Jesus' feet, imploring him to heal her daughter. Luke 5:8 refers to Peter acting this way in order to express sorrow at his own unbelief.

SEE ALSO

- ▸ **45.** Faith, Belief, Trust, Promise > FALL AWAY, APOSTATIZE, APOSTASY ***parapiptō, aphistēmi***
- ▸ **74.** Safety, Peace, Danger, Escape > FALL AMONG ***peripiptō***

KNEEL

gonypeteō γονυπετέω 1120

gonypeteō occurs only four times. On each occasion, it refers to people paying homage to Jesus. In Mark 10:17, a rich young man kneels before Jesus and asks what he must do to inherit eternal life. People fall on their knees, begging Jesus to bring healing — a man begs Jesus to heal his demon-possessed son in Matt 17:14; and a leper begs for healing in Mark 1:40. See also Matt 27:29.

▸ **41.** Sacrifice, Offering, Worship, Praise > BOW, KNEEL

LEAP

skirtaō σκιρτάω 4640

skirtaō occurs only three times, and on each occasion it means "leap for joy." In Luke 1:41, 44, ***skirtaō*** refers to Elizabeth's baby, John the Baptist, leaping in her womb. Luke 6:23 refers to the joy of true followers of Christ, who will leap for joy upon his return.

▸ **19.** Mind, Spirit, Emotions, Feelings, Desires > JOY, JOYFUL, REJOICE, GLADNESS

exallomai ἐξάλλομαι 1814

exallomai is found only in Acts 3:8, referring to the lame beggar who had been cured by Peter and John, and who immediately afterwards leapt up and walked into the temple.

hallomai ἅλλομαι 242

hallomai occurs three times, meaning "leap up" on two of these occasions. Acts 3:8; 14:10 refer to miraculous cures of crippled men, both of whom leapt to their feet immediately when they were healed. John 4:14 contains a related meaning for ***hallomai***, that of "spring up," referring to water as a symbol for the indwelling Spirit of Christ in the heart of a believer.

ephallomai ἐφάλλομαι 2177

ephallomai occurs only in Acts 19:16, referring to the evil spirit cast out of a man by seven Jewish exorcists (the sons of Sceva), who leapt upon those men and overpowered them.

LIFT UP

epairō ἐπαίρω 1869

epairō is translated "lift up" in a number of contexts, most of them in a literal sense. The term occurs around twenty times.

The sense of "lift up one's eyes" (i.e., "look") is indicated in Matt 17:8; Luke 6:20; 16:23; 18:13; John 4:35; 6:5; 17:1. To "lift one's voice" or "shout" is referred to in Luke 11:27; Acts 2:14; 14:11; 22:22. Luke 24:50 describes Jesus lifting up his hands to bless his disciples, and in 1 Tim 2:8 the action signifies an attitude of prayer. See also Luke 21:28. The rebellion or treachery of Judas against Christ is in view in John 13:28, where ***epairō*** is used in the expression "to lift one's heel against," symbolically describing that action of betrayal. Acts 1:9 refers to Jesus being "lifted up" into heaven before the very eyes of his followers.

STUMBLE

proskoptō προσκόπτω 4350

proskoptō is a verb expressing the sense of "stumble" in the majority of its eight occurrences.

A literal reference to stumbling is found in John 11:9ff.

In metaphorical contexts, ***proskoptō*** is translated "stumble" in relation to "falling" (in a spiritual sense) or failing to exercise faith. These consequences are evident in Rom 9:32; 1 Pet 2:8, with reference to those who "stumble over" the "stumbling stone," which is Christ. In Rom 14:21, ***proskoptō*** indicates the action of causing someone "to commit sin" (i.e., stumble).

▸ **78.** Act Upon, Push, Pull, Break, Cut > DASH, STRIKE

ptaiō πταίω 4417

ptaiō is a verb found in six places meaning "stumble." In Rom 11:11 it refers to the possibility — denied by Paul — of Israel "having lost all hope" of future salvation.

88. Qualities, Characteristics

ACCURATELY

akribōs ἀκριβῶς 199

akribōs is an adverb meaning "accurately" in Acts 18:25 in relation to Apollos' thorough knowledge of the Scriptures.

▸ **46.** Wait, Hope, Be Vigilant, Pay Attention To > DILIGENCE, DILIGENT, DILIGENTLY

akribēs ἀκριβής 197

akribēs is an adverb found only four times. In Acts 18:26 it refers to the ministry of Aquila and Priscilla, who explained the way of God "more accurately" to Apollos. See also Acts 23:15, 20; 24:22.

SEE ALSO

▸ **20.** Illness, Disease, Health, Healing > PERFECT HEALTH
holoklēria

▸ **61.** Integrity, Innocence, Piety > PERFECT, PERFECTION, COMPLETE
teleios, teleioō, katartizō, teleiotēs

▸ **84.** Do, Make, Accomplish, Occur > PERFECTING
teleiōsis

BEAUTIFUL

hōraios ὡραῖος 5611

hōraios is an adjectival form meaning "beautiful." It describes the "beautiful" appearance of whitewashed tombs (Matt 23:27) and constitutes the name "Beautiful," given to one of the gates of Jerusalem (Acts 3:2, 10). The feet of those who preach the gospel are described as "beautiful" in Rom 10:15 (Isa 52:7).

BITTER, BRACKISH, EMBITTER

pikros πικρός 4089

pikros is a rare adjective describing "bitter" or "brackish" water in Jas 3:11 and "bitter" jealousy in Jas 3:14.

pikrainō πικραίνω 4087

pikrainō is a verb found six times with the meaning "to embitter," "make bitter, sour." The sense of "embitter" is found in connection with an injunction to husbands not to embitter their wives (i.e., treat them harshly; Col 3:19). The meaning "make bitter" is found in relation to water made unfit for drinking (Rev 8:11). The term means to "turn (the stomach) sour" in Rev 10:10.

SEE ALSO

▸ **58.** Vices > BITTERNESS
pikria

▸ **75.** Suffering, Distress, Sadness > BITTERLY
pikrōs

COLD

psychos ψῦχος 5592

psychos is a rare noun found in three places, denoting in each case the sensation of "(being) cold" (John 18:18; Acts 28:2; 2 Cor 11:27).

psychros ψυχρός 5593

psychros is an adjective denoting "cold" in Matt 10:42; Rev 3:15, 16.

psychō ψύχω 5594

psychō is a rare verb found only in Matt 24:12 with the metaphorical sense "grow cold" in relation to human love for God.

CROOKED, CURVED

skolios σκολιός 4646

skolios is an adjectival form meaning "crooked," denoting a "curved" path in Luke 3:5. The term also means "crooked" in the sense of "morally perverse," referring to wicked people (Acts 2:40; Phil 2:15).

DRY, DRY UP, WITHER, WITHERED

xēros ξηρός 3584

xēros is an adjective found seven times referring to the "dry land" of the bed of the Re(e)d Sea over which the people of Israel crossed during their miraculous escape from Egypt.

xēros also refers to limbs that are "withered" (i.e., "dried up," rendered lame by disease) (Matt 12:10; Luke 6:6ff.). See also John 5:3.

xērainō ξηραίνω 3583

xērainō is a verb found in sixteen places meaning "wither," "dry up."

Matt 13:6; Mark 4:6; Luke 8:6; John 15:6; Jas 1:11; 1 Pet 1:24 all refer to grass or plants that "wither" or "dry out" in the heat. When Christ utters a curse against a fig tree in Matt 21:19ff.; Mark 11:20ff., the tree "withers" — a symbolic act of judgment against his people.

Elsewhere, ***xērainō*** indicates the "cessation" of a woman's chronic hemorrhage as the result of Christ's healing, literally the "drying up" of her blood flow (Mark 5:29). Rev 16:2 refers to the "drying up" of the Euphrates River in the visionary judgment of the "sixth bowl."

▸ **28.** Agriculture, Viticulture, Animal Husbandry > RIPE

SEE ALSO

▸ **11.** Meteorology, Water > DRY, WATERLESS
anydros

EQUAL

isos ἴσος 2470

isos is an adjective found in eight places, meaning "equal" in about half these occurrences.

The sense of equality of status in relation to wage earning is indicated in Matt 20:12. Christ's equality with his father in the sense of his standing, authority, and person is indicated in John 5:18; Phil 2:6. Equality of measurement is noted in Rev 21:16.

▸ **27.** Community, Partnership, Unity, Discord > DISAGREEMENT

SEE ALSO

▸ **60.** Virtues > EQUALITY, FAIRNESS
isotēs

FIRM, SOLID

stereos στερεός 4731

stereos is an adjective found in four places meaning "solid," "firm." 2 Tim 2:19 refers to the "foundation" of God's purposes being in his people's standing "firm." 1 Pet 5:9 also exhorts people to be "firm" in their faith.

FREELY

dōrean δωρεάν 1432

dōrean is an adverbial form found in nine places with the underlying sense of "freely," with several nuances.

The meaning "freely" in the sense of "without payment or costs" is indicated in Matt 10:8; 2 Cor 11:7; 2 Thess 3:8, with literal reference to monetary concerns. Rev 21:6; 22:17 use "freely" in a metaphorical sense to refer to God offering to all his people free access to the water of life in the heavenly city.

In order to emphasize the limitless generosity of God's grace, Rom 3:24 affirms that the people of God are justified "freely" by that grace — that is, as an unmerited gift.

▸ **53.** Value, Worth > VAIN, MAKE VAIN, MAKE VOID

SEE ALSO

▸ **55.** Bondage, Captivity, Servitude > FREE, FREEDOM, SET FREE, LIBERTY
eleutheros, eleutheroō, eleutheria, apeleutheros, dikaioō

GOOD, EXCELLENT, ADMIRABLE, WELL

agathos ἀγαθός 18

The dominant meaning of the adjective ***agathos*** is "good," in a broad sense. It is used both adjectivally and nominally, with a variety of nuances, throughout its nearly one hundred occurrences.

The nominal meaning "good" in the sense of "that which is morally upright," including people, is indicated in Matt 5:45; 12:35; John 5:29; Rom 2:10; 7:13, 18; 9:11; Eph 6:8. Elsewhere, "good" denotes "ultimate spiritual benefit" in Rom 8:28; 2 Cor 5:10; Heb 9:11; 10:1; and also "well-being" in relation to people in Rom 15:2; 1 Thess 5:15. The adjectival sense of "good," denoting that which is "of high quality" is found in Matt 7:11; Luke 1:53; 11:13; John 1:46; Gal 6:6; Jas 1:17. Such an attribute is predicated of the divine commandment in Rom 7:12.

Elsewhere, "good" indicates the sense of "healthy" in relation to non-personal phenomena — to a tree (Matt 7:18); soil (Luke 8:8); and conscience (1 Tim 1:5).

The adjectival sense of "virtuous" in relation to both deeds and people is indicated in Matt 19:17; 25:21ff.; Luke 6:45; John 7:12; Acts 9:36; Rom 5:7; 2 Cor 9:8; Eph 2:10; Titus 1:16. In particular, Christ is said to be "good" in Mark 10:17ff.; Luke 18:18, as is God in Mark 10:17ff.; Luke 18:19.

▸ **53.** Value, Worth > GOOD

kalos καλός 2570

kalos is an adjective found over one hundred times with the general meaning "good," as well as a variety of nuances.

The sense of "excellent," "choice," "of high quality" is indicated in Matt 3:10; 13:24ff.; Luke 3:9; John 2:10; 1 Tim 4:4; 2 Tim 2:3.

kalos denotes that which is "morally upright," primarily in relation to "good works" (Matt 5:16; Mark 7:27; John 10:32ff.; Rom 14:21; 1 Thess 5:21; 1 Tim 5:4, 25; Titus 3:8; Heb 10:24). The description "good" is applied to the law of God in this sense in Rom 7:16ff.; 1 Tim 1:8.

"Fertile" soil is indicated in Matt 13:23; Mark 4:8; Luke 8:15.

kalos is also used adverbially in the sense of "well," "better" in Matt 17:4; 18:8ff.; Mark 9:42ff.; 1 Cor 5:6; 1 Tim 3:13.

"Good" in the sense of "beautiful," "admirable" is evident in Matt 26:10; Mark 14:6; 1 Tim 3:1. Christ is referred to as the "good" shepherd in John 10:11ff., indicating his tender care for and love of his people.

kalos is used nominally in Heb 5:14; Jas 4:17 to denote "good" in contrast with "evil" in a moral sense.

Heb 13:18 refers to a "good" conscience (in the sense of "clear").

kalōs καλῶς 2573

kalōs is the adverbial form of ***kalos*** (above) and means "well" or "good" throughout most of its nearly forty occurrences.

The action of "doing good or well" in the sense of that which is "noble," "intrinsically valuable," is noted in Mark 7:37; Luke 6:27; 1 Cor 7:37ff.; Heb 13:18; 2 Pet 1:19.

kalōs means "well" in the sense of "accurately" in Matt 15:7; Mark 7:6; John 4:17; Acts 28:25.

kalōs means "well" in the sense of "skillfully" in Mark 12:28. See also Gal 5:7; 1 Tim 3:4. Speaking "well" of someone in the sense of commending them is indicated in Luke 6:26.

eu εὖ 2095

eu is an adverbial form occurring six times meaning "well" or "good" throughout. In most of these contexts ***eu*** denotes the commendation "Well done!" (Matt 25:21ff.; Luke 19:17). Mark 14:7; Acts 15:29 both indicate "doing good" in the sense of doing what is morally upright. The meaning "well" in the sense of "prosperous" is noted in Eph 6:3.

SEE ALSO

▸ **60.** Virtues > GOOD, GOODNESS, DO GOOD
agathōsynē, agathopoieō, agathoergeō, eupoiia, aretē

HARD, DIFFICULT, HARSH, SEVERE

sklēros σκληρός 4642

This adjective is found six times, and in five of these occurrences ***sklēros*** means "hard." With the sense of "harsh," "stern," "severe," ***sklēros*** is found in Matt 25:24, referring to a master, and in Jude 15 it indicates the nature of words coming from the mouths of the ungodly. ***sklēros*** occurs in John 6:60 meaning "difficult to understand," referring to the response of Jesus' disciples to his teaching concerning himself as the "bread of life." In Acts 9:5; 26:14, ***sklēros*** means simply "difficult," concerning Jesus' response to Saul during his conversion experience on the road to Damascus, when Jesus said to him: "It is hard for you to kick against the goads."

SEE ALSO

▸ **57.** Evil, Wickedness, Sin > HARDENING, HARDNESS, HARDHEARTEDNESS
sklērotēs, pōrōsis, pōroō, sklērynō

HEAVY, WEIGHTY, BURDENSOME

bareō βαρέω 916

bareō is found on six occasions with the sense of "be heavy," "weighed down," "be a burden." Referring to sleepiness (i.e., "heavy eyes"), the term is found in Matt 26:43; Mark 14:40; Luke 9:32. 2 Cor 1:8 tells of Paul being burdened with great trials and difficulties, as does 2 Cor 5:4, where the apostle is likewise "burdened" or "weighed down" with trouble and sorrow. 1 Tim 5:16 speaks of a responsibility that the church ought not to be burdened with — the support of widows where there are family members who would be capable of looking after them. The point here is that the support and care of such women who are truly destitute and alone should constitute the legitimate "burden" of the church.

barys βαρύς 926

barys is the adjectival form of ***bareō*** (above). This term occurs six times and means "heavy," "weighty," "burdensome." It is used metaphorically in all but one of these contexts.

Matt 23:4 condemns the Pharisees for binding heavy burdens on others without showing any compassion towards them. Similarly, Matt 23:23 accuses those same Jewish leaders of neglecting the "weighty" matters of the law, or those that are significant and of central importance. In 2 Cor 10:10 Paul records that many in the church thought that his letters lacked substance (i.e., were not "weighty"). Acts 25:7 refers to the serious (i.e., "weighty.") charges laid against Paul. And in 1 John 5:3, John affirms that God's laws are not burdensome (i.e., "weighty").

▸ **53.** Value, Worth > WEIGHT, WEIGHTY

SEE ALSO

▸ **75.** Suffering, Distress, Sadness > HEAVY
adēmoneō

INDESCRIBABLE, UNSPEAKABLE

anekdiēgētos ἀνεκδιήγητος 411

anekdiēgētos is an adjective found only in 2 Cor 9:15, describing the indescribable quality of God's gift of salvation.

arrētos ἄρρητος 731

arrētos is another rare adjectival form, found only in 2 Cor 12:4, describing Paul's heavenly vision as a phenomenon that is "unspeakable," "incapable of verbal description."

aneklalētos ἀνεκλάλητος 412

aneklalētos is an adjective referring to the believer's "unspeakable" (i.e., indescribable) joy in knowing Christ (1 Pet 1:8).

NARROW

stenos στενός 4728

stenos is an adjective with the sense of "narrow," found in only three places and referring metaphorically to the "narrow gate" that leads to the heavenly kingdom, as opposed to the "wide gate" that leads to destruction (Matt 7:13, 14; Luke 13:24).

NATURAL, NATURE, KIND, PHYSICAL

physikos φυσικός 5446

physikos is an adjective that occurs in only three places, meaning "natural," "born of instinct." Rom 1:26, 27 refer to the sin of homosexuality, where men and women give up "natural" sexual relations for one another and transfer them to members of their own sex — inclinations explicitly forbidden by God. In 2 Pet 2:12, false teachers are likened among other things to irrational animals, "born of instinct" to be caught and destroyed.

physis φύσις 5449

physis is a noun occurring fourteen times, meaning "nature" or "kind" in several different contexts.

In the first instance, ***physis*** conveys the idea of "nature," meaning that which is created by God. Gal 2:15, for example, refers to those who are Jewish "by nature," as opposed to people born as Gentiles. Rom 1:26 refers to the unnatural desires of homosexuality as "contrary to nature."

Similarly, "nature" may refer to that which is in accord with a natural order, without explicit reference to the divine origin of the phenomenon. For instance, Rom 2:14

refers to Gentiles who do things required by the law "by nature," even though they do not have the law of Moses. The physical or "natural" condition of "uncircumcision" is indicated in Rom 2:27. The custom of Paul's day dictated that long hair on a man was a shameful thing, something that was contrary to "nature" (1 Cor 1:14). Idolatry, in Gal 4:8, is depicted as a bondage to beings that were "by nature" no gods. Eph 2:3 declares that all human beings are "by nature" children of wrath, under the judgment of God.

physis also has the adjectival sense of "natural," or that which occurs in the physical world. In Rom 11:21, 24, the expression "natural branches" refers metaphorically to the people of Israel. In a related context, Rom 11:24 refers symbolically to "wild olive branches," designating the Gentiles as those branches that are literally "wild by nature."

physis also indicates the sense of "nature" in relation to the person of God. 2 Pet 1:4 speaks of sharing in the "divine nature," which is the ultimate goal of all believers.

physis refers in Jas 3:7 to "all kinds of animals (etc.)," where "kind" conveys the sense of "species."

psychikos ψυχικός 5591

psychikos is an adjective that is found in only five contexts, meaning "natural" with the underlying neutral sense of that which is purely physical, or the negative connotation of that which is devoid of true spirituality in a godly sense.

The neutral sense of ***psychikos*** is indicated in 1 Cor 15:44, 46, with reference to the human body before the resurrection as a purely "physical" or "natural" entity. 1 Cor 2:14, however, refers to the "natural" person as one who is unspiritual, unreceptive to the gifts of the spirit of God. Similarly, Jas 3:15; Jude 19 refer to the unspiritual as those who are impervious to spiritual realities.

SEE ALSO

▸ **58.** Vices > HEARTLESS, MERCILESS, RUTHLESS
astorgos

ONLY, ALONE

monos μόνος 3441

monos is an adjectival form occurring about fifty times with the meaning "alone," as well as the adverbial sense of "alone," "only." There is, however, some degree of overlap between these two meanings.

The meaning "alone" in an adverbial sense is indicated in relation to people in Matt 18:15; Mark 9:8; Luke 24:18; Gal 6:4; 1 Thess 3:1; Heb 9:7. Jesus is described as being alone in Matt 14:23; John 6:15; 8:9. Matt 4:4; Luke 4:4 both contain the affirmation that human beings do not live by bread alone. See also Luke 24:12; John 12:24.

References with the general adverbial sense of "only" are found in Matt 12:4; 17:8; Luke 6:4; 1 Cor 9:6. The command to serve God "only" (or "alone") is noted in Matt 4:10; Luke 4:8. Luke 5:21 affirms that "only" God (or God alone) can forgive sin. God's knowledge of the day of judgment is also unique (i.e., only he knows; Matt 24:36).

monos is also used with the adjectival sense of "only" or "sole" with reference to the person of God as divine (John 5:44; 17:3; Rom 16:27; 1 Tim 1:17; 6:15ff.; Jude 4, 25; Rev 15:4). See also Col 4:11.

monon μόνον 3440

monon is a variant adverbial form of ***monos*** (above) found in nearly seventy contexts, with the consistent sense of "only."

Usage of this term in relation to people is evident in Matt 5:47; Luke 8:50; John 11:52; Acts 8:16 and also concerning Jews in particular (Rom 3:29; 9:24).

More frequently, ***monon*** is used in the context of non-personal phenomena, including the expression "not only . . . but also." The sense of "only" is found in particular association with commands or instruction in Matt 8:8; circumcision in Rom 4:12; Gal 6:12; the mercy of God in 1 Thess 1:5; the gospel in 1 Thess 2:8; the baptism of John in Acts 18:25. Jas 2:24 makes the significant declaration that people are justified by works with faith, indicating in context that faith without the evidence of accompanying good works is invalid.

Other general references to ***monon*** include Matt 21:19; Acts 27:10; Rom 8:23; 1 Cor 15:19; 2 Tim 2:20; Heb 12:26; 1 John 2:2.

QUIET, CALM

katastellō καταστέλλω 2687

katastellō is a verb found in only two contexts. In Acts 19:35 it refers to "quieting" or "calming" a crowd; and in Acts 19:36 it means "to be quiet" or "be calm."

SEE ALSO

▸ **60.** Virtues > PEACE, PEACEFUL, QUIET
hēsychazō, ēremos, hēsychios

SHARP

oxys ὀξύς 3691

oxys is an adjective with the primary meaning "sharp." It occurs only in the book of Revelation and refers to a sword (Rev 1:16; 2:12; 19:15) and a sickle (Rev 2:14ff.).

▸ **21.** Die, Perish, Kill, Destroy > SWIFT

tomos τομός 5114

tomos is an adjective found only in Heb 4:12, used metaphorically to describe the word of God as "sharper" than any two-edged sword.

apotomōs ἀποτόμως 664

apotomōs is a noun found in only two places, meaning "sharpness" in the sense of "severity," referring to a disposition or mood (2 Cor 13:10; Titus 1:13).

STRAIGHT

euthys εὐθύς 2117

euthys is an adjective found in sixteen places, meaning "straight" in the sense of "free from obstacle" in Matt 3:3; Mark 1:3; Luke 3:4, 5, referring to the preparation of a straight path for the coming Messiah. The sense of "right" or "morally upright" is indicated in Acts 8:21; 13:10; 2 Pet 2:15.

euthynō εὐθύνω 2116

euthynō is an adverbial form translated verbally as "to make straight" (i.e., remove obstacles, level out) in John 1:23, citing the prophecy of the coming Messiah in Isa 40:1ff.

orthos ὀρθός 3717

orthos is an adjective found twice, meaning "straight" in the sense of "(standing) physically upright" (Acts 14:10), and "morally upright" (Heb 12:13).

UNCERTAIN, INDISTINCT, UNMARKED

adēlos ἄδηλος 82
adēlotēs ἀδηλότης 83

These two rare terms indicate "that which is uncertain." ***adēlos*** is an adjective referring to the "uncertain" or "indistinct" sound of a bugle (1 Cor 14:8); and to graves that are "unmarked" (i.e., uncertain in their location) (Luke 11:44). ***adēlotēs*** is a noun used adjectivally in 1 Tim 6:17 to refer to "uncertain" riches.

UNSTABLE

akatastatos ἀκατάστατος 182

akatastatos is an adjective found only in Jas 1:8 denoting the "unstable" nature of the double-minded person, who doubts the goodness of God.

astēriktos ἀστήρικτος 793

astēriktos is an adjectival form found in 2 Pet 2:14, 16. It is used nominally to refer to "unstable persons" who are immature and indecisive in their faith, easily led astray.

WONDERFUL

thaumasios θαυμάσιος 2297

thaumasios is an adjectival form meaning "wonderful" in the sense of "amazing," "marvelous." It is found only in Matt 21:15, referring to the deeds of Christ.

thaumastos θαυμαστός 2298

thaumastos is an adjectival form synonymous with ***thaumasios*** (above). It is found only in Matt 21:42 in relation to the "wonderful" (i.e., marvelous) work of salvation wrought by God in Christ.

Index of English Words

Index of Greek Words